July 22–26, 2013
Indianapolis, Indiana, USA

Association for Computing Machinery

Advancing Computing as a Science & Profession

JCDL'13

Proceedings of the 13th ACM/IEEE-CS
Joint Conference on Digital Libraries

Sponsored by:

ACM SIGIR and ACM SIGWEB

Technical Supporters:

IEEE, IEEE Computer Society, and TCDL

Supported by:

Indiana University, The iSchool at Illinois, Indiana University at Bloomington, University of Pittsburgh, EBSCO Publishing, Purdue University, University of Illinois at Urbana-Champaign, Digital Library Federation, CIRSS, University of North Carolina, NSF, iSchool @ UBC, and Coalition of Networked Information

Association for
Computing Machinery

Advancing Computing as a Science & Profession

The Association for Computing Machinery
2 Penn Plaza, Suite 701
New York, New York 10121-0701

ISBN: 978-1-4503-2077-1 (Digital)

ISBN: 978-1-4503-2518-9 (Print)

Additional copies may be ordered prepaid from:

ACM Order Department
PO Box 30777
New York, NY 10087-0777, USA

Phone: 1-800-342-6626 (USA and Canada)
+1-212-626-0500 (Global)
Fax: +1-212-944-1318
E-mail: acmhelp@acm.org
Hours of Operation: 8:30 am – 4:30 pm ET

Printed in the USA

JCDL 2013 Conference Co-Chairs' Welcome

On behalf of Indiana University and the University of Illinois, we want to welcome you to the 2013 ACM/IEEE Joint Conference on Digital Libraries. Our institutions are delighted to co-host this major international forum for those working in the field of digital libraries. It is the first time that we have had joint iSchool and library participation to co-host the event from two major state universities

We also welcome you to our wonderful Midwestern urban venue, Indianapolis, Indiana. That Indianapolis sits at the crossroads of America inspired, in part, this year's conference theme, *Digital Libraries at the Crossroads*. The conference will be held at the JW Marriott located in the heart of Indianapolis – only a short walk to some of the best shopping in the U.S., cafes and coffee shops, over 200 nearby restaurants, nightlife, museums, and the beautiful urban White River State Park. We have no doubt that each of you will enjoy the venue and convenience of our location as well as the warm hospitality of the Circle City.

The Organizing Committee has been working all year to assemble a program that is rich and varied in depth and coverage of topics. Our program starts with a full day of tutorials along with our Doctoral Consortium (sponsored by the National Science Foundation and the University of British Columbia). The next two and half days are replete with conference paper sessions, keynotes, and panels. The conference wraps up and we offer a set of workshops that span over a two-day period. We are particularly excited by the addition of a new unconference event: We are proud to be hosting the first ever CURATEcamp: Digital Libraries. This special session is held in conjunction with JCDL and is sponsored by the Digital Library Foundation (DLF), the Center for Informatics Research in Science and Scholarship of the Graduate School of Library and Information Science at the University of Illinois, and the School of Information and Library Science, University of North Carolina, Chapel Hill.

In addition to an excellent technical program organized by the Program Committee, you will enjoy many opportunities for informal networking on Tuesday evening at our annual Banquet. This conference highpoint will be held in the nearby Indiana State Museum that will have several special exhibits featured. Do not miss our other social highlight, the Poster & Demonstrations Reception on Wednesday evening, where both the Vannevar Bush JCDL 2013 Best Paper Award and the Best Student Paper Award will be announced.

We have secured an excellent group of keynote speakers for this year's event. Clifford Lynch, Executive Director of the Coalition for Networked Information, Jill Cousins, Executive Director of the Europeana Foundation and David DeRoure, Director of the interdisciplinary Oxford e-Research Centre at the University of Oxford will be our featured keynote speakers. The themes they expect to address are focused on our conference theme of *Digital Libraries at the Crossroads*. Additionally, we will have our keynote speakers featured during one of our panel discussions in order for them to provide more perspective on current trends in digital libraries.

Finally, we would like to express our sincere thanks to the JCDL Local Organizing Committee and our many volunteers from Indiana University and the University of Illinois, our generous sponsors, and the JCDL Program Committee chairs (Tim Cole, Rob Sanderson, and Frank Shipman) for their dedicated hard work and incredible support. Last but not least, we would also like to thank the active participants of JCDL (researchers and practitioners), who make this one of the best academic conferences year after year.

Welcome to JCDL 2013 – We hope you have a rewarding and enjoyable experience in our Midwestern crossroads.

J. Stephen Downie
JCDL 2013 Conference Co-Chair
University of Illinois at Urbana-Champaign

Robert H. McDonald
JCDL 2013 Conference Co-Chair
Indiana University-Bloomington

Program Chairs' Welcome

Welcome to the *13th ACM/IEEE Joint Conference on Digital Libraries – JCDL 2013*. It has been our pleasure to work with the Program Committee and with our colleagues on the Organizing Committee to build a program for this year's conference consistent with *JCDL*'s long-standing reputation for high quality. *JCDL* remains the premier international forum for exploring research, practice, and social issues in digital libraries. The Program Committee has selected a diverse array of papers, panels, posters and demonstrations that illustrate both the breadth and depth of ongoing digital library scholarship. Some themes explored in this year's 13 sessions of full and short papers are familiar from *JCDL*s of the recent past (e.g., Digital Preservation, Metadata, Name Entity Extraction) and some themes are new this year, reflecting emerging and shifting foci of interest (e.g., Information Ranking, Information Clustering, Specialist DLs, Historical DLs).

Presentations of the papers included in this proceedings volume will be complemented by 36 posters and 10 demonstrations showcasing a broad range of innovative research and practical digital library applications. The extended abstracts for these Posters and Demonstrations are also included in this proceeding volume. This year's Poster & Demonstration Reception on the second evening of the main conference (Wednesday) will be preceded the ever-popular 'Minute-Madness' session. As in past years, reception attendees will vote to determine the winner of the *Best Poster Award*. Additionally this year, the *Vannevar Bush Best Paper Award* and the *Best Student Paper Award* will be presented at the Poster Reception. This year's program also includes three panel sessions. Wednesday's panel, chaired by Dan Cohen (Digital Public Library of America), will feature *JCDL 2013* keynote speakers Jill Cousins, Cliff Lynch and David De Roure. Distinguished panels also have been assembled to discuss *Managing Big Data and Big Metadata: Contributions from Digital Libraries* (Tuesday) and to tackle the issues surrounding *Volume, Variety, and Velocity: Big Data Collection and Curation in Cultural Heritage Repositories* (Thursday).

Of course the essential pre-requisite for a conference of this quality and breadth is high quality submissions that span the full range of digital library scholarship. Again this year *JCDL* received a wealth of quality submissions. Each paper was read and rated by 3 reviewers. Each paper was then read by 2 additional meta-reviewers who reconciled first level reviews and formulated a recommendation for the Program Committee as a whole. During a day and a half in-person meeting in Chicago, the Program Committee made final selections. For this year's conference 28 of 95 full paper submissions (29%) and 22 of 72 short paper submissions (31%) were accepted. We wish to recognize the accomplishment of accepted paper authors and to acknowledge the many others who submitted strong paper proposals. An additional 13 papers submitted, a mix of both full and short, were converted to and accepted as Posters or Demonstrations on the advice of the Program Committee. Finally, we wish to thank Program Committee members for again meeting the challenge of reviewing a large number of papers both quickly and well; this conference would not be possible without their dedication and generous contribution of effort.

We hope that this year's conference and your time in Indianapolis provides you the opportunity to make the acquaintance of new colleagues, renew friendship with colleagues from past conferences, and share ideas with DL researchers and practitioners from around the world.

Timothy W. Cole
JCDL 2013 Program Co-Chair
University of Illinois at UC
USA

Robert Sanderson
JCDL 2013 Program Co-Chair
Los Alamos National Laboratory
USA

Frank Shipman
JCDL 2013 Program Co-Chair
Texas A&M University
USA

Table of Contents

Session 5: Evaluation

Session 6: Information Clustering

Session 7: Specialists DLs

Session 8: Name Extraction

Session 9: Metadata

Session 10: Web Replication

Session 11: Data

Session 12: Historical DLs

Session 13: Preservation II

Posters

Demonstrations

JCDL 2013 Conference Organization

General Chairs: J. Stephen Downie *(University of Illinois at Urbana-Champaign, USA)*
Robert H. McDonald *(Indiana University Bloomington, USA)*

Program Chairs: Timothy W. Cole *(University of Illinois at Urbana-Champaign, USA)*
Robert Sanderson *(Los Alamos National Laboratory, USA)*
Frank Shipman *(Texas A&M University, USA)*

Panels Chairs: David Bainbridge *(University of Waikato, New Zealand)*
George Buchanan *(City University London, UK)*

Poster & Demonstration Chairs: Stacy Kowalczyk *(Dominican University, USA)*
Jerome McDonough *(University of Illinois at Urbana-Champaign, USA)*
Mark Newton *(Columbia University, USA)*

Doctoral Consortium Chairs: Sally Jo Cunningham *(University of Waikato, New Zealand)*
Edie Rasmussen *(University of British Columbia, Canada)*

Workshop Chairs: Miles Efron *(University of Illinois at Urbana-Champaign, USA)*
Geneva Henry *(Rice University / George Washington University, USA)*
Unmil Karadkar *(The University of Texas at Austin, USA)*

Tutorial Chairs: Jon W. Dunn *(Indiana University Bloomington, USA)*
William H. Mischo *(University of Illinois at Urbana-Champaign, USA)*
Cassidy R. Sugimoto *(Indiana University Bloomington, USA)*

Continuity Advisor: Michael Nelson *(Old Dominion University, USA)*

Publicity Chairs: Heather Coates *(Indiana University-Purdue University Indianapolis, USA)*
Rachel Frick *(Digital Library Federation / Council on Library and Information Resources, USA)*

Webmasters: Courtney Greene *(Indiana University Bloomington, USA)*
James Little *(University of Illinois at Urbana-Champaign, USA)*

Publications Chairs: Mary Schlembach *(University of Illinois at Urbana-Champaign, USA)*
Xiaozhong Liu *(Indiana University Bloomington, USA)*

Local Organizing Chairs: Michelle Marquart *(Conference and Institutes, University of Illinois, USA)*
Maeve Reilly *(University of Illinois at Urbana-Champaign, USA)*
Megan Finn Senseney *(University of Illinois at Urbana-Champaign, USA)*

Student Volunteers Chairs: Xiao Hu *(University of Hong Kong, Hong Kong)*
Xiaozhong Liu *(Indiana University Bloomington, USA)*

Treasurer & Registration: University of Illinois Conference Services *(USA)*

Steering Committee:
Ed Fox *(Virginia Polytechnic Institute and State University, USA)*
Edie Rasmussen *(University of British Columbia, Canada)*
David Hicks *(Aalborg University, Esbjerg, Denmark)*
Richard Furuta *(Texas A&M University, USA)*
Sally Jo Cunningham *(University of Waikato, New Zealand)*
Ronald Larsen *(University of Pittsburgh, USA)*
Michael Nelson *(Old Dominion University, USA)*
Ingeborg Sølvberg *(Norwegian University of Science & Technology, Norway)*
Shigeo Sugimato *(University of Tsukuba, Japan)*

Senior Program Committee:
Maristella Agosti *(University of Padua, Italy)*
David Bainbridge *(University of Waikato, New Zealand)*
Jose Borbinha *(IST / INESC-ID, Portugal)*
Christine Borgman *(University of California Los Angeles, USA)*
George Buchanan *(City University London, UK)*
Mike Christel *(Carnegie Mellon University, USA)*
Sally Jo Cunningham *(University of Waikato, New Zealand)*
Jon W. Dunn *(Indiana University Bloomington, USA)*
Edward Fox *(Virginia Tech, USA)*
Luis Francisco-Revilla *(The University of Texas at Austin, USA)*
Richard Furuta *(Texas A&M University, USA)*
C. Lee Giles *(Pennsylvania State University, USA)*
Gene Golovchinsky *(FX Palo Alto Laboratory, USA)*
Marcos Andre Goncalves *(Federal University of Minas Gerais, Brazil)*
Geneva Henry *(Rice University / George Washington University, USA)*
Jane Hunter *(The University of Queensland, Australia)*
Min-Yen Kan *(National University of Singapore, Singapore)*
Carl Lagoze *(University of Michigan, USA)*
Ray Larson *(University of California Berkeley, USA)*
Cathy Marshall *(Microsoft Research, Silicon Valley, USA)*
Jerome McDonough *(University of Illinois at Urbana-Champaign, USA)*
Michael Nelson *(Old Dominion University, USA)*
Edie Rasmussen *(University of British Columbia, Canada)*
Tamara Sumner *(University of Colorado Boulder, USA)*
Herbert Van de Sompel *(Los Alamos National Laboratory, USA)*

Program Committee:
Stephen Abrams *(California Digital Library, USA)*
Piotr Adamczyk *(University of Illinois at Urbana-Champaign, USA)*
Robert B. Allen *(Victoria University of Wellington, New Zealand)*
Smiljana Antonijevic *(Pennsylvania State University, USA)*
Andrew Ashton *(Brown University, USA)*

Program Committee (continued):

David Bainbridge *(University of Waikato, New Zealand)*
Steven Bethard *(University of Colorado Boulder, USA)*
Christian Bizer *(University of Mannheim, Germany)*
Charles Blair *(University of Chicago, USA)*
Paul Bogen *(Oak Ridge National Laboratory, USA)*
Johan Bollen *(Indiana University Bloomington, USA)*
Paul Bracke *(Purdue University, USA)*
Hennie Brugman *(Meertens Instituut, Netherlands)*
Jason Casden *(North Carolina State University, USA)*
Lillian Cassel *(Villanova University, USA)*
James Caverlee *(Texas A&M University, USA)*
Youngok Choi *(Catholic University of America, USA)*
Tom Cramer *(Stanford University, USA)*
Lois Delcambre *(Portland State University, USA)*
Ying Ding *(Indiana University Bloomington, USA)*
Michael Durbin *(University of Virginia, USA)*
Miles Efron *(University of Illinois at Urbana-Champaign, USA)*
Ricky Erway *(OCLC, USA)*
Nicola Ferro *(University of Padova, Italy)*
Randall Dean Floyd *(Indiana University Bloomington, USA)*
Schubert Foo *(Nanyang Technological University, Singapore)*
Muriel Foulonneau *(CRP Henri Tudor, Luxembourg)*
Peter Fox *(Rensselaer Polytechnic Institute, USA)*
Rachel Frick *(Digital Library Federation / Council on Library and Information Resources, USA)*
Stéphane Gançarski *(Laboratoire d'Informatique de Paris 6, France)*
Stefan Gradmann *(KU Leuven, Belgium)*
Tom Habing *(University of Illinois at Urbana-Champaign, USA)*
Myung-Ja Han *(University of Illinois at Urbana-Champaign, USA)*
Bradley Hemminger *(University of North Carolina at Chapel Hill, USA)*
Patricia Hswe *(Pennsylvania State University, USA)*
Xiao Hu *(University of Hong Kong, Hong Kong)*
Jimmy Huang *(York University, Canada)*
Antoine Isaac *(Europeana & VU University Amsterdam, Netherlands)*
Adam Jatowt *(Kyoto University, Japan)*
Unmil Karadkar *(The University of Texas at Austin, USA)*
Michelle Kazmer *(Florida State University, USA)*
Michael Khoo *(Drexel University, USA)*
Martin Klein *(Los Alamos National Laboratory, USA)*
Rick Kopak *(University of British Columbia, Canada)*
Stacy Kowalczyk *(Dominican University, USA)*
Ron Larsen *(University of Pittsburgh, USA)*
Dongwon Lee *(Pennsylvania State University, USA)*

Additional reviewers:

Scott Ainsworth
Ahmed Alsum
Catherine Blake
Justin Brunelle
Cornelia Caragea
Miao Chen
Yinlin Chen
James Creel
Soheil Danesh
Ogheneovo Dibie
Anne Doucet
Kai Eckert
Katrina Fenlon
Giorgos Giannopoulos
Chun Guo
Shu Huang
Xiaomo Liu
Bruno Martins
Dana McKay
Amber Mckenzie
Louis Nguyen
Chaoqun Ni
Heiko Paulheim
Zeynep Pehlivan
Magnus Pfeffer
Myriam Ben Saad
Hany Salaheldeen
Andrés Sanoja
Xin Shuai
Gianmaria Silvello
Linda C. Smith
MD. Arafat Sultan
Giannis Tsakonas
Theresa Velden
Erjia Yan
Dayu Yuan
Guo Zhang

JCDL 2013 Sponsors & Supporters

Sponsors:

SIGIR
Special Interest Group
on Information Retrieval

sig web

Technical Supporters:

IEEE

IEEE COMPUTER SOCIETY

TCDL

acm

Conference Co-hosts:

INDIANA UNIVERSITY

ILLINOIS

Silver Supporters:

PERVASIVE TECHNOLOGY INSTITUTE
INDIANA UNIVERSITY

GRADUATE SCHOOL OF LIBRARY AND INFORMATION SCIENCE
The iSchool at Illinois

LIBRARIES
INDIANA UNIVERSITY
Bloomington

UNIVERSITY OF PITTSBURGH
VERITAS 1787 VIRTUS

Bronze Supporters:

EBSCO PUBLISHING

PURDUE UNIVERSITY LIBRARIES

ILLINOIS
UNIVERSITY OF ILLINOIS AT URBANA-CHAMPAIGN
UNIVERSITY LIBRARY

CurateCamp Supporters:

DLF DIGITAL LIBRARY FEDERATION

CIRSS

UNC SCHOOL OF INFORMATION AND LIBRARY SCIENCE

Doctoral Consortium Supporters:

NSF

iSchool@UBC
SCHOOL OF LIBRARY, ARCHIVAL & INFORMATION STUDIES

Cooperating Organizations:

cni
Coalition for Networked Information

Identification of Useful User Comments in Social Media: A Case Study on Flickr Commons

Elaheh Momeni
University of Vienna
Währinger Strasse 29, A-1090 Vienna
momeni@cs.univie.ac.at

Ke Tao
Delft University of Technology
Mekelweg 4, 2628 CD, Delft
k.tao@tudelft.nl

Bernhard Haslhofer
Cornell University
Ithaca, NY 14850
bh392@cornell.edu

Geert-Jan Houben
Delft University of Technology
Mekelweg 4, 2628 CD, Delft
g.j.p.m.houben@tudelft.nl

ABSTRACT

Cultural institutions are increasingly opening up their repositories and contribute digital objects to social media platforms such as Flickr. In return they often receive user comments containing information that could be incorporated in their catalog records. Since judging the usefulness of a large number of user comments is a labor-intensive task, our aim is to provide automated support for filtering potentially useful social media comments on digital objects. In this paper, we discuss the notion of *usefulness* in the context of social media comments and compare it from end-users as well as expert-users perspectives. Then we present a machine-learning approach to automatically classify comments according to their usefulness. Our approach makes use of syntactic and semantic comment features and also considers user context. We present the results of an experiment we did on user comments received in six different Flickr Commons collections. They show that a few relatively straightforward features can be used to infer useful comments with up to 89% accuracy.

Categories and Subject Descriptors

H.3.m [**Information Storage and Retrieval**]: Miscellaneous

Keywords

User-generated Comment, Social Media, Usefulness Prediction, Flickr Commons

1. INTRODUCTION

Cultural institutions are increasingly contributing content to social media platforms to increase awareness and use of their collections. The Library of Congress, for instance, has published more than 18,000 photos organized in 24 sets on Flickr Commons[1]. The British Library maintains several Facebook pages exposing digitized images, manuscripts, and other digital resources. Many of these platforms support annotation features, ranging from simple Like-button clicks to user-contributed full-text comments.

Comments can add supplemental information to existing digital resources, which might be interesting for other users. They may also contain factual information, such as names and places depicted on a photo, which is not available in existing metadata records. Such information can be gathered by institutions to improve descriptive metadata records and consequently to support efficient information retrieval and digital resource management [18, 10].

However, not all user-generated comments are useful for institutions and users. Users have different backgrounds, levels of expertise, and different intentions when contributing comments. As a result, the quality of user-generated comments varies from useful to useless and can even be abusive or off-topic. The two examples below, both taken from Flickr, illustrate the different nature of useful comments. The first one is useful and the second one is non-useful (labeled in our study [2]):

- (useful) "James Beauchamp Champ Clark (1850 - 1921) Speaker of the House (1911 - 1919), Missouri Senator. This picture may be from the Democratic Convention of 1912, where Clark was initially considered a frontrunner for the Presidential nomination. By the end, though, the nomination went to Woodrow Wilson."[3].
- (non-useful) "My great grandfather was an engineer at that time. I'd love to get a list of the names in that photo."[4]

Moderation by means of a dedicated human curator or forum administrator to identify useful comments is costly and time consuming and often not feasible given the potentially

JCDL'13, July 22–26, 2013, Indianapolis, Indiana, USA.

[1]Library of Congress Flickr Pilot Project Report Summary `http://www.loc.gov/rr/print/flickr_report_final_summary.pdf`

[2]It is worth mentioning that comments which in our study are inferred as "non-useful" might be useful for other context and the term "useful" is a term that we use in our study.

[3]`http://www.flickr.com/photos/library_of_congress/2163461798/#comment72157603858091482`

[4]`http://www.flickr.com/photos/library_of_congress/2536790306/#comment72157629444651496`

high number of comments and typically small number of staff members in cultural institutions. Therefore, we believe that automated approaches are needed that can segregate useful comments from non-useful ones.

Approaches to automatically estimate the usefulness of user-generated content (tags, tweets, and product reviews, etc) are gaining increasing attention [1, 17, 19]. However, each type of free-text user-generated content (e.g., product reviews, tweets, etc) has different characteristics compared to free-text comments and, furthermore, definitions and usage of useful user-generated content vary in different application scenarios. Some scenarios tend to prefer objective and informative content due to the promise of additional, potentially interesting information, while others see more value in the combination of subjective and objective content.

For the purposes of our current research, we are interested in identifying the possible characteristics of useful social media comments. The notion of usefulness is in itself very subjective and is largely determined by how different institutions apply it in specific scenarios. Therefore, in this paper, first we discuss the notion of *usefulness* with regard to comments that provide additional descriptive information of media objects from two perspectives – from users as well as experts perspectives. Then we show that comments which are useful for users are also useful for experts. To this end, the central contributions of this paper can be summarized as follows:

- *Identification of the characteristics of useful comments:* We gather a dataset of image comments from Flickr Commons[5] and collect users' and experts' usefulness judgments (by using a crowd-sourcing approach) to identify the usefulness of gathered comments. Then we identify technical features that can be derived from textual content and the author's context and characterize the usefulness of a comment.
- *Providing an automated method for identifying potentially useful comments.* We apply the technical features in a series of experiments to build a classifier that can automatically identify the usefulness of comments. Furthermore, we investigate to what extent certain topics of media objects play a role with regard to usefulness classification.

Our findings reveal that a few relatively straightforward features can be used to infer the usefulness of comments. However, an analysis of the important features among different topic areas (place, person, and event) of media objects indicates that when inferring the usefulness of comments the influence of features varies slightly according to the topic areas of media objects. The major differences appear among the psychological content characteristics. Therefore, if prior to inferring usefulness we are able to determine the topic area of a media object, this helps to classify useful comments with higher accuracy. Thus, for a more accurate classification of useful comments, a model should be trained that takes into account the topic area of media objects.

[5]"The key goals of The Commons on Flickr are to firstly show users hidden treasures in the world's public photography archives, and secondly to show how users' input and knowledge can help make these collections even richer. Users are invited to help describe the photographs you discover in The Commons on Flickr, either by adding tags or leaving comments." `www.flickr.com/commons`

We believe the comments which are useful for users and experts have potentially valuable information which may improve the retrieval and management applications. However, this is beyond the scope of this paper.

This paper is organized as follows: In Section 2 we discuss the notion of usefulness and identify possible characteristics of useful social media comments by analyzing related work on assessing and modeling the quality of user-generated content. Section 3 provides an overview of different technical features to characterize the comment. Section 4 describes our data acquisition process to collect usefulness judgments and presents a series of usefulness classification experiments and evaluation of the derived features. Finally, we discuss and conclude our work in Section 5.

2. USEFUL SOCIAL MEDIA COMMENTS

The Oxford dictionary describes *usefulness* as "*a quality or fact of being able to be used for a particular or in several ways*". Thus, any characterization of usefulness depends on the institutional context and the application scenario. We found that the notion of usefulness has previously been discussed in two main research contexts: *assessing the quality of user-generated tags* and *assessing and ranking of user-generated free-text content.*

2.1 Assessing user-generated tags

Several works in the area of tagging and folksonomy research discuss the assessment of user-generated tags or the selection of tags that allow people to better describe their content. Sigurbjoernsson and van Zwol [19] propose approaches for the selection of useful tags by computing tags and URL co-occurrence patterns. They find that the tag frequency distribution follows a perfect power law, and they indicate that the mid section of this distribution contains the most interesting candidates for tag recommendation. Weinberger et al [22] define a measure of tag ambiguity, based on a weighted Kullback-Leibler (KL) divergence of tag distributions. Hall and Zarro [9] compare the abstracting and indexing practices of a semi-expert community (metadata creators for the digital library, ipl2) and the social tags generated by Delicious.com users for the same corpus of materials and show these two groups still remain dissimilar to provide description.

However, useful tags also provide descriptive information for objects despite the fact that user-generated comments have different characteristics from user-generated tags. User-generated comments are longer and have an informal structure and users can converse, express their subjective opinions and emotions, and describe informative useful information about a media resource.

2.2 Assessing user-generated free-text content

Assessing the quality of user-generated free-text information is critical in other domains such as question answering platforms, micro-blogging services (e.g.,Twitter), or product reviews.

Agichtein et al. [1] introduce a general graph-based classification framework for combining features from different sources of information in order to assess high-quality questions and answers in CQA (Community Question and Answer). Liu et al. [16] propose a method for predicting information seeker satisfaction in CQA and develop a variety of content, structure, and community-focused features

Features Groups	Ref	Short Description
Text statistics and syntactic features	[1, 4, 14, 6, 7, 17, 5]	Aggregate statistics extracted from the text such as length, readability, #token, etc
Semantic and topical features	[6, 7, 21, 22, 19, 13, 4, 15]	The semantics of a comment and its semantic similarity or diversity to other comments, such as subjectivity tone and topical conformity to other comments.
User and social features	[17, 16, 21, 4, 6, 1]	Different characteristics of users and their social context, #uploaded object, and #contact

Table 1: Abstract overview of features used in related work for characterizing user-generated content

for this task. Harper et al. [11] propose an algorithm that reliably categorizes questions as informational or conversational. Castillo et al. [4] propose automatic methods for assessing the quality and credibility of a given set of tweets, first by analyzing postings related to trending topics, and then by classifying them as credible or non-credible. Diakopoulos et al. [6] develop methods for filtering and assessing the variety of sources found through social media by journalists. They take a human centered design approach for developing a system, which is informed by journalistic practices and knowledge of information production in events. Becker et al. [2] presented relevant Twitter content selection approaches and show that the centroid (as a centrality-based approach) emerged as the preferred way to select relevant tweets.

Furthermore, predicting the helpfulness of a product review (e.g., how many people have considered a particular product review helpful) is one of the related problems. Several approaches demonstrate that a few relatively straightforward features can be used to predict with high accuracy, whether a review will be deemed helpful or not. These features are length of the review [14, 7], mixture of subjective and objective information [7], readability such as checking the number of spelling errors [7], and conformity (a review is evaluated as more helpful when its star rating is closer to the consensus star rating for the product) [14, 5]. Moreover, Lu et al [17] illustrate how the social features of reviewers can help the assessment process.

2.3 Taxonomy of Useful Social Media Comments

A preliminary exploration of these assessment and ranking techniques demonstrates that some relatively straightforward features and strategies, derived from content and context of comments, can be used to characterize with high accuracy whether a user-generated content (tags, Q&A postings, tweets, and product reviews) is helpful, relevant, high quality, or credible. In Table 1 we categorize these features and strategies into three feature groups.

In this paper, we define a comment as useful, if it provides additional descriptive information of media objects. More precisely, this paper focuses on understanding the characteristics of useful comments from users as well as experts perspectives and furthermore on the development of automated mechanisms for classifying useful and non-useful comments. We evaluated to what extent users' and experts' perspective of usefulness match. In systems with numerous users and comments automated mechanisms for classifying useful and non-useful comments can support curators and system managers in selecting potentially useful comments and saving time and costs.

3. FEATURES ENGINEERING

With regard to available approaches and features for similar problems, explored in Section 2, we believe that there are some observable features in social media platforms themselves, that are useful to assess the usefulness of comments.

We provide an overview of the different features to characterize each comment in our feature collection. We select influential features from related work. These features are aligned with our assumptions of characteristics of useful comments. These include some features specific to the Flickr platform, but most of them are quite generic and can also be applied to other platforms. Our feature set is listed in Table 2. According to our study, in Section 2 we group potentially important features into three different groups:

Text Statistics and Syntactic Features (TS) This group captures surface-level identification of the usefulness and includes the following features:

- *Punctuation Mark*, counts the number of punctuation marks. We assume that comments, which contain a higher number of punctuation marks are less likely to be useful.
- *Text Statistics*, measures aggregate statistics extracted from the text such as number of words (#WC), number of verbs, number of adverbs, and the average length of sentences (WPS). We collect statistics based on the POS tags to create features such as percentages of verbs, adverbs, etc. We use the LingPipe toolkit[6] to obtain the relative POS taggers. We assume that comments containing a higher number of words are likely to be useful [14, 7].
- *Linkage Variety*, counts the number of unique hyperlinks in a comment. We assume that the more links are contained in the comment, the more likely it is to be useful [4].
- *Informativeness*, measures the novelty of terms, t, of a comment, c, compared to other comments on the same object, calculated using:

  $$\Sigma_{t \in c} tfidf(t, c)$$

  We assume that comments with higher informativeness score are more informative and, therefore, they are likely to be useful [21].
- *Readability*, measures how difficult the comment is to parse by using the Gunning fog index [8]. We assume that comments with a higher readability score are likely to be useful, because they are easier to parse for humans.

Semantic and Topical Features (ST) The semantics of a comment may increase or decrease the likelihood of a

[6]`http://alias-i.com/lingpipe/`

Feature	Short Description
Text Statistics and Syntactic Features (TS)	
Punctuation Mark	#punctuation marks
Text Statistics	#WC, #Verbs, #Adverb, average length of sentences (WPS)
Linkage Variety	#Hyperlinks in a comment
Informativeness	novelty of terms of a comment compared to other comments on the same objects
Readability	how difficult it is to parse the comment
Semantic and Topical Features (ST)	
Sentiment Polarity	positive and negative sentiment of content
Subjectivity Tone	the subjectivity or objectivity tone
Name Entities	#Name Entities
NE Types Variety	#distinct types of Name Entities that are mentioned in a comment
Psychological content characteristics	psychological dimensions of the content of a comment: Swear, Sadness, Anger, Family, Friends, Humans, Anxiety, Health, Sexuality, Home, Religion, Relativity, Leisure, Insight, Certainty, Tentativeness, Self-reference scores
Topical Conformity	the distance between the topics of a comment and the topics belonging to other comments on the same object
User Topic Entropy	the topical focus of the user via the entropy of topic distributions of the user
User and Social Features (US)	
User Linkage Behavior	#Hyperlinks posted by the user
User Conversational Behavior	#conversational comments posted by the user
User Activity	#Comment, #UploadedObject, #FavoriteObject scores
User Social Relation	#Contact, Prestige scores

Table 2: Overview of Features

comment being useful regardless of its text structure. Furthermore, this group includes standard topical model features, that measure the topical concentration of the author of a comment and topical distance of a comment compared to other comments on an object. This group includes the following features:

- *Named Entities*, counts number of named entities (NE) that are mentioned in a comment. We assume that the more named entities are mentioned in a comment, the more aspects of the object are covered. In this group, for NE related features we used GATE toolkit[7].

- *NE Types Variety*, counts distinct types of named entities (such as person, place, date, etc) that are mentioned in a comment. We assume that the more the types of entities are mentioned in a comment, the more aspects of the object are introduced. Therefore, the greater the diversity of concepts mentioned in a comment is, the more likely it is to be useful.

- *Subjectivity Tone*, the subjectivity or objectivity tone of a comment may impact the usefulness of the comment. We used Subjectivity Lexicon [23] to calculate subjectivity. We assume the subjectivity or objectivity tone may have influence on the usefulness of the comments [7].

- *Psychological content characteristics*, identifies psychological dimensions: leisure, anger, family, friends, humans, anxiety, sadness, sexuality, home, religion, relativity, affective process, and self-reference scores. We used LIWC [20] for analyzing psychological characteristics of the content of comments. LIWC identifies psychological dimensions in the text of comments such as self-reference scores (usage of "I"), anger score (e.g. hate, loathe, etc).

- *Topical Conformity*, measures the distance between the topics of a comment and the topics belonging to other comments on the same object. An LDA model (Latent Dirichlet Allocation [3]), was trained to handle features that depend on topic models. To train the LDA model we aggregated all the comments on photos in our database into an artificial photo document to infer topic distribution and chose the following hyper-parameters: $\alpha = 50/T$, $\beta = 0.01$ and T = 1,000. Then, we used the Jensen-Shannon (JS) divergence to measure the topic distribution distance of all comments on an object (A) compared to the comment's topic distribution (C).

$$D_{JS} = \frac{1}{2}(D_{KL}(C \parallel A) + (D_{KL}(A \parallel C)$$

and KL divergence is calculated as:

$$D_{KL}(C \parallel A) = \Sigma C(i) log \frac{C(i)}{A(i)}$$

We assume that very high or very low topical conformity has an impact on predicting usefulness of the comment [22, 21].

- *User Topic Entropy*, measures the topical focus of an author via the entropy of topic distributions of a user, inferred via the comments she authored. To handle this feature we also trained an LDA model [3]. To train the LDA model we aggregated all the comments authored by one user in our database into an artificial user document to infer topic distribution by users and we chose the following hyper-parameters: $\alpha = 50/T$, $\beta = 0.01$ and T = 1,000. Then, we measured the distance topic distribution of each user. We define entropy of topic distribution of all comments authored by an author, a_i as:

$$H(a_i) = -\Sigma_{j=1}^{n} p(t_{i,j}) \log p(t_{i,j})$$

Where t is a topic and n is #topics. We assume the topical focus of users has influence on the usefulness of their comments.

- *Sentiment Polarity*, measures the sentiment polarity of a comment as:

$$SenPolarity = \#(PosTerm) + \#(NegTerm)$$

Based on [7, 4], we assume the sentiment polarity may have influence in the usefulness of the comments.

User and Social Features (US) Different characteristics of users and their social context may increase or decrease the likelihood of their comments being useful. Due to limitations of access to this information, we apply a lightweight characterization of authors and their social contexts. This group includes the following features:

[7]http://gate.ac.uk

- *User Linkage Behavior*, counts the number of unique hyperlinks posted by a user. A high linkage balance indicates that linkage is part of the commenting behavior of a user. We assume that the comments by users that use other resources as references are more likely to be useful.

- *User Conversational Behavior*, counts comments which contain a @reply. We assume that users who write comments to converse with other users are less likely to write useful comments.

- *User Activity*, measures different activities completed by a user, such as: number of comments (counts the number of comments authored by the user), number of uploaded objects (counts the number of media objects uploaded by the user), and number of favorite objects (counts the number of media objects selected as favorite by the user). Based on [6, 4], we assume that the users' activities influence the usefulness of their comments.

- *User Social Relation*, counts the number of contacts of the user and measures Prestige score (measures the number of the Flickr Commons members in the contact list of the user). We assume that users with a higher number of social interactions are more likely to write useful comments [17].

4. EXPERIMENTS

In this section we describe how we collect usefulness judgments for characterizing useful comments and then we report the results of different machine learning methods for training an inference method that attempts to automatically infer if a comment is useful or not. Furthermore, we evaluate the quality of the features for inferring the usefulness of a given topic.

4.1 Data Acquisition

First, we build a dataset from real world comments harvested from Flickr Commons. Second, we extract those comments that have attracted a response by experts of cultural institutes. Third, we use a crowd sourcing approach, set up a user study, and request people to state if they consider that a certain set of comments could be useful for them. In order to compare how users' perspectives of usefulness is similar to experts' perspectives we compare characteristics of useful user-judged and expert-judged comments.

Dataset: We compile our dataset from real world comments harvested from Flickr Commons. We crawl 32,132 comments written on 11,130 photos on Flickr Commons. The photos are selected from six different institutes. From each institute we select the photo-sets with the highest number of comments on their photos. Each of these photo-sets corresponds to what we call a topic. All topics - according to the titles of the selected photo sets - are selected with three broader topical focuses: events (e.g., Irish civil war, News in 1910, World War 1, etc), places (e.g., old New York, old Edinburgh, ruins in the Middle East, etc), and persons (e.g., Neil Armstrong,etc). Finally, in our dataset we have three sets of comments on three topics: place, person, and event. In one of the Library of congress photo sets (News in 1910), we recognize that it contains many photos about persons. Therefore, we separate photos which show only a photo of a person from other photos, which belonged to topics related to event, according to their titles. Furthermore, for training a classifier and analyzing users' features, we crawl all profile information of all users who wrote comments. Table 3 shows the summary statistics of the dataset.

Photoset	Topic	Comments	Objects	Users
Library of Congress	Person, Event	27,603	9,029	4.343
Brooklyn Museum	Place	2,178	251	1,687
National Library of Ireland	Event, Person	1,740	135	470
New York Public Library	Place	251	98	151
National Gallery of Scotland	Place	257	32	201
NASA Collections	Person	103	28	82
All		**32,132**	**11,130**	**6,934**

Table 3: Summary statistics of dataset

Collecting Expert Judgements for Defining Usefulness: With regard to comments written on photos of the Library of Congress (LOC), we recognize some of these comments are commented upon by the LOC experts[8]. In order to ensure that these comments are useful for LOC we asked LOC staff members what causes them to comment back. They confirmed that commenting back is one indicator of a useful comment: "all Flickr comments are being read by LOC staff. The vast majority of comments are useful, but we only have the resources to comment back when we verify that a suggested change was on target, so that the Flickr users will know that their information is making a difference.". Based on these observations, first we crawled all comments written by LOC staff and containing terms such as "thanks", "thank you", etc. Second, in order to find related comments to these comments, we used the crowd sourcing approach and we asked coders to assist us in defining relevant comments. We used CrowdFlower.com which is a crowd-sourcing platform, showing each coder a comment written by LOC staff and links to the related Flickr photo and asking them to find all relevant comments to LOC experts' comments. In total we gathered amounted to 2,068 comments, which we presume to be considered as useful by experts. It is worth mentioning that LOC experts have not explicitly classified comments as useful and non-useful. This means that comments which in our study are inferred as "non-useful" might be useful for other context and the term "useful" is a term that we use in our study.

Collecting User Judgements for Defining Usefulness: In order to understand the characteristics of useful comments from user's perspective and to collect non-useful comments for training a classifier, we randomly selected 3,500 comments and crowd sourced to collect user usefulness judgments by using CrowdFlower.com. We asked coders to assist us in identifying useful comments. We showed each coder a comment and links to the related Flickr photo and asked them to answer four questions:

1. Text-box question, "How many Web links does the comment contain?"

2. Option-choice question, "Does the comment contain Web links?"

3. Text-box question, "Select 1 to 4 main keywords used in the comment."

[8]Those user accounts which have the pattern "Name (LOC P&P)" and use the Library of Congress logo

4. Option-choice question, "Compared to the description provided by the uploader of the photo, is this comment useful for you to learn more about the content of the photo?"

In order to ensure the quality of the work by coders, for each comment we asked each coder to answer 3 objective questions, which can be computed automatically (questions 1 to 3) and one question (question 4) with regards to the usefulness of the comment. The first two questions are semantically the same but asked in two different ways. Inconsistency in answering the first two questions gave us the chance to exclude randomly selected answers. With regard to the third question we ask coders to enter text, which gives greater possibility to validate non-serious contributions. Therefore, inconsistency in selecting relevant keywords gave us the chance to exclude non-serious selected answers. Finally, the coders contributed to our task by answering the fourth question and the main question. For each comment we collected 3 independent judgments.

As result of this study, 1,345 of 3,500 comments (38.42%) received majority agreement on being useful. In order to examine the user agreement, we compute the level of the (inter-rater) agreement between coders based on Fleiss' Kappa for each comment. The mean Kappa score for all comments is above the score of 86%, indicating almost perfect agreement for the usefulness inference between coders.

Characteristics of Expert-judged vs User-judged Useful, and Non-Useful Comments In order to prepare a training-set for developing a usefulness classifier, first, we selected 1,000 user-judged useful comments with high agreements on being useful and 1,000 comments with high agreements on being non-useful from our labeled data. Furthermore, in order to compare characteristics of user-judged with expert-judged useful comments we randomly selected 1000 expert-judged useful comments.

Second, we assess the mean values and standard deviations of each feature, which shown in Table 4. As expected, the average semantic and topical-based scores for comments which are judged as useful is different from those for non-useful comments. The *Sentiment Polarity* and *Subjectivity Tone* scores for comments which are judged as non-useful are much higher than those for useful comments. A comparison of the NE-dependent semantic features reveals that useful comments generally contain more entities (2-3 entities) than non-useful comments (0-1 entity). The *NE Type Variety* (only person, organization, location, and date are considered) is higher for the useful comments than for the non-useful comments. Among the psychological characteristics of the content, the average *Insight*, *Friends*, *Health & Body*, *Religion*, *Swear* and *Sexual* scores for comments, which are judged as useful, are different from those for non-useful comments. With regard to user and social features, the user *Linkage Behavior* and *Prestige* scores for comments, which are judged as non-useful are much higher than for those for useful comments. For features related to the text statistics and syntactic we observe that regardless of whether the comments are useful or not, the ratios of comments with higher text statistic scores are almost the same. For example, it seems that the presence of punctuation marks is not necessarily an indicator of usefulness. However, the presence of hyperlinks (*Linkage* score) and the number of words per sentence (WPS) are potentially good indicators.

Third, we assess the mean values and standard deviations of each feature for expert-judged comments. Table 5 shows these values in comparison with user-judged useful comments in detail. This table shows the mean and standard deviations of almost all features from both datasets are in the same range. This result suggests that characteristics of user-judged comments are very similar to characteristics of expert-judged useful comments and therefore the non-useful comments (labeled in our study) can be assumed to be non-useful from both perspectives.

Features	Mean-U	STD-U	Mean-N	STD-N
Text Statistics and Syntactic Features (TL)				
Informativeness	14.50	21.91	05.02	06.37
Readibility	06.05	04.07	05.70	03.54
#Punctuation Marks	77.76	131.4	77.10	214.7
#WC	41.70	49.41	09.32	12.52
#WPS	15.63	10.99	06.36	06.50
#Verb	09.06	08.61	09.05	11.38
#Adverb	02.91	04.81	05.10	10.30
Linkage Variety	01.72	01.82	0.521	05.92
Semantic and Topical Features (ST)				
#Name Entities	03.62	05.33	0.466	0.956
NE Types Variety	01.39	01.07	00.36	00.58
Topical Conformity	01.34	01.67	01.07	01.10
Sentiment Polarity	01.62	03.75	29.26	32.77
Subjectivity Tone	0.151	0.160	0.910	0.750
Sadness	0.190	0.880	0.160	0.940
Insight	0.150	01.56	0.096	0.810
Anger	0.369	01.74	0.197	01.80
Family	0.460	01.63	0.126	01.40
Friends	0.060	0.950	0.130	02.98
Humans	0.590	01.93	0.840	03.64
Health & Body	0.790	02.41	01.93	07.02
Sexual	0.065	1.086	0.970	05.10
Religion	0.409	02.86	0.103	01.21
Leisure	01.30	02.99	0.460	02.51
Swear	0.058	0.087	0.198	0.682
Home	0.450	01.74	0.180	01.35
Relativity	12.86	09.18	06.14	09.87
Certainty	0.616	1.980	1.290	6.750
Tentative	01.79	03.65	01.21	03.98
Self-reference	01.02	2.587	02.27	05.42
User Topic Entropy	04.74	01.67	04.34	02.69
User and Social Features (US)				
User Linkage Behavior	758.0	1225	09.93	88.44
User Conversational Behavior	0.480	02.35	19.20	33.65
#UploadedObject	20250	3869	1390	3134
#FavoriteObject	243.5	220.5	269.1	219.5
#Contact	179.1	261.7	204.6	283.6
Prestige score	04.96	09.61	01.62	4.274

Table 4: The comparison of the mean and standard deviation values of each feature between useful (U) and non-useful (N) comments. The underlined values point out considerable differences between useful (U) and non-useful (N) comments

4.2 Experimental Setup

First, we selected 1,000 useful comments with high agreements with regard to their usefulness and 1,000 comments with high agreements with regard to their non-usefulness from our labeled data. This amounted to a total of 2,000 comments for the training-set. Second, we evaluate the performance of four classifier algorithms for inferring the usefulness of comments: Logistic Regression, SVM, Naive Bayes and the decision-tree classifier J48. For analyzing the influence of the different sets of features on their performance, each classifier was set with all combinations of feature sets and they were evaluated against each other, using four measures: precision, recall, F1-measure (the harmonic mean between precision and recall) and area under the Receiver Operator Curve (ROC).

Results of Classification Evaluations Table 6 shows the performance of different sets of features and classification methods for predicting the usefulness of comments. It demonstrates the effectiveness of using semantic and user features for inferring useful comments. Training a classification model using semantic and user feature shows improved performance compared to the same models trained using

Features	Mean-U	STD-U	Mean-E	STD-E
Text Statistics and Syntactic Features (TL)				
Informativeness	14.50	21.91	15.36	25.47
Readibility	06.05	04.07	06.78	04.31
#Punctuation Marks	77.76	131.4	185.9	219.0
#WC	41.70	49.41	48.60	62.59
#WPS	15.63	10.99	17.53	12.82
#Verb	09.06	08.61	07.60	07.47
#Adverb	02.91	04.81	01.59	03.08
Linkage Variety	01.72	01.82	03.87	03.76
Semantic and Topical Features (ST)				
#Name Entities	03.62	05.33	06.93	08.50
NE Types Variety	01.39	01.07	01.83	01.01
Topical Conformity	01.34	01.67	01.56	01.19
Sentiment Polarity	01.62	03.75	01.78	03.49
Subjectivity Tone	0.151	0.160	0.105	0.078
Sadness	0.190	0.880	0.143	0.659
Insight	0.150	01.56	0.965	02.33
Anger	0.369	01.74	0.336	01.09
Family	0.460	01.63	0.538	01.64
Friends	0.060	0.950	0.055	0.541
Humans	0.590	01.93	0.596	01.74
Health & Body	0.790	02.41	0.234	01.14
Sexual	0.065	1.086	0.035	0.310
Religion	0.409	02.86	0.303	01.56
Leisure	01.30	02.99	01.18	02.84
Swear	0.058	0.087	0.014	0.272
Home	0.450	01.74	0.225	0.923
Relativity	12.86	09.18	11.61	09.58
Certainty	0.616	1.980	0.425	2.217
Tentative	01.79	03.65	01.13	02.58
Self-reference	01.02	2.587	00.61	1.931
User Topic Entropy	04.74	01.67	04.75	01.34
User and Social Features (US)				
User Linkage Behavior	758.0	1225	771.0	1378
User Conversational Behavior	0.480	02.35	0.520	02.35
#UploadedObject	20250	3869	30250	7869
#FavoriteObject	243.5	220.5	298.4	247.5
#Contact	179.1	261.7	184.0	192.0
Prestige score	04.96	09.61	04.74	09.64

Table 5: The comparison of the mean and standard deviation values of each feature between user-judged (U) and expert-judged (E) useful comments.

Feature-Sets	Classifier	Precision	Recall	F1	ROC
TL	LR	0.76	0.75	0.75	0.85
	SVM	0.75	0.74	0.74	074
	NB	0.74	0.71	0.71	0.77
	J48	0.79	0.79	0.79	0.84
ST	LR	0.83	0.82	0.82	0.91
	SVM	0.84	0.82	0.82	0.82
	NB	0.81	0.80	0.79	0.89
	J48	0.83	0.82	0.81	0.88
US	LR	0.71	0.69	0.69	0.80
	SVM	0.71	0.66	0.65	0.67
	NB	0.71	0.66	0.65	0.80
	J48	0.78	0.78	0.78	0.86
TL + ST	LR	0.85	0.85	0.85	0.89
	SVM	0.83	0.82	0.82	0.82
	NB	0.79	0.79	0.79	0.88
	J48	0.83	0.82	0.82	0.82
ST+ US	LR	0.85	0.85	0.85	0.93
	SVM	0.85	0.85	0.85	0.85
	NB	0.84	0.83	0.83	0.92
	J48	0.85	0.85	0.85	0.90
TL+ US	LR	0.83	0.83	0.83	0.90
	SVM	0.82	0.81	0.81	0.81
	NB	0.80	0.77	0.77	0.86
	J48	0.84	0.84	0.84	0.87
ALL	**LR**	0,88	0.90	**0.89**	**0.95**
	SVM	0.85	0.83	0.85	0.89
	NB	0.80	0.891	0.85	0.92
	J48	0.88	0.88	0.88	0.89

Table 6: Classification results of useful comments from non-useful comments using four classifier algorithms: Logistic Regression (LR), SVM, Naive Bayes (NB) and the decision-tree (J48) with all features-sets combinations

text-related features. By combining all the features we are able to achieve an F1 score of 0.89, coupled with high precision and recall when using the Logistic Regression classifier.

J48 classifier performs similarly, while SVM and Naive Bayes perform with lower accuracy. This demonstrates the poor precision and recall levels when using text features only. In such a case, each model fails to provide the same performance compared to when the semantic and user features are used.

Influence of Features on Usefulness Inference So far we have only analyzed the use of features grouped together. We now evaluate the quality of each individual feature for classifying useful comments.

In order to detect how the features were associated with the usefulness of comments, the coefficients of the Logistic Regression model were inspected from the selected best performing model (using all sets of features). A positive coefficient denotes a higher probability that the feature better correlates with usefulness. Table 7 shows detailed coefficient ranks. In addition to interpreting the statistically significant coefficients, we also ranked the features of the best performing feature group by using the Information Gain Ratio (IGR) as a ranking criterion. Table 7 shows the 20 top-ranked features, which are dominated by semantic features. Figure 1 shows the contributions by each of the top-10 features to classify usefulness in the training set, where the affective process (such as *Subjectivity Tone* and *Sentiment Polarity*) and Name Entities- related features of the comments seem to correlate strongly with inferring useful comments.

More precisely, coefficient ranks show that comments that expressing emotional and affective processes of the author (higher *Subjectivity Tone*, *Sentiment Polarity*, *Anger*, and *Sadness*) scores have a negative impact on the usefulness inference model) are more likely to be inferred as non-useful. Comments with offensive language (*Swear* score has a negative impact on the usefulness inference model) are more likely to be inferred as non-useful. Nevertheless, comments which have higher *Name Entities*, *NE Type Variety* and *Linkage* scores contain potentially interesting information and are likely to be inferred as useful. With regard to user features the *User Linkage Behavior* is a good indicator showing that users may diligently cite references for the information they provide. This increases reliability when inferring usefulness for such comments. Interestingly, a higher *User Topical Entropy* has a negative impact on the usefulness inference. Users with a higher entropy have a lower topical focus and therefore might write comments with less focus on the specific topic. Therefore, their comments are likely to be inferred as non-useful. A higher score of *Self-reference* and a higher *Conversational Behavior* score also have a negative impact. This suggests that users, who mostly use systems to converse and describe their personal experiences do not write useful comments. A higher *Contact* score does not have a negative impact. However, a *Prestige* score has a positive impact. This indicates that having influential contacts in the contact list is more important than having a higher number of contacts.

A high readability score does not have an important impact on usefulness inference. This is the case for many useful comments and is due to the fact that comments which are longer and contain more complex words are less readable based on the Gunning fog score [8]. The usage of insight terms (such as "think", "know", "consider") shows a positive correlation with usefulness. Furthermore, the usage of certainty terms (such as "always", "never" etc) has a negative impact on the model. This might be due to the fact that users who are assertive and express certainty tend to be seen as more subjective and less analytical. In contrast, the usage of tentative terms (such as "maybe", "perhaps", "guess", etc) shows that authors do not make any claims as to the cor-

Rank	Features	Coefficient
1	ST-Subjectivity Tone	-3.828
2	ST-Sentiment Polarity	-1.157
3	ST-NE Types Variety	0.550
4	US-User Linkage Behavior	0.025
5	ST-#Name Entities	0.211
6	ST-Self-reference	-0.148
7	TS-WPS	0.031
8	ST-User Topic Entropy	-0.049
9	ST-Insight	0.049
10	ST-Swear	-0.045
11	TS-Linkage	0.173
12	US-User Conversational	-0.023
13	ST-Certainty	-0.032
14	TS-Future Verb	-0.043
15	TS-Impersonal-pronoun	0.025
16	US-Prestige score	0.060
17	ST-Religion	0.089
18	ST-Sadness	-0.075
19	ST-Family	0.016
20	ST-Relativity	-0.006

Table 7: Top-20 features and their coefficient, derived from Logistic Regression model. Ranks are based on IGR ranking

rectness or certainty of their comments and such comments are likely to be inferred as useful.

In order to observe the effects of iteratively increasing features, and the impact on classification performance, our next experiment explored the effects of training a classification model using only the top-ranked features. We selected the Logistic Regression classifier for training - based on its optimum performance during the model selection phase - and trained the classifier using the training split from each dataset. Figure 2 shows the results from our experiments, where at lower levels of ranked features we observe similar levels of performance. As we included more features within our classification model, we observe improvements in F1 scores. As we include the lower-ranked features, our plots show only a minor increase in performance.

The results of this analysis show that a few relatively straightforward features can be used to characterize and infer the usefulness of comments. It is interesting to note that many text features, while being positively aligned with usefulness inference, do not belong to the most important features. However, Semantic and Topical features play important roles.

Influence of Topics on Usefulness Inference In all reported results so far, we have considered the entire set of topics. Therefore, we investigate to what extent certain topic characteristics play a role with regard to usefulness inference and to what extent those differences lead to a change in the inference models.

From our training data we creat three different test-sets of comments related to each area of topics (person, place, and event) and then, for each set we predicted the usefulness of comments using two models: first, the usefulness classification model, which was trained with regard to the area of topic, second, a general usefulness classification model for all topics (the model, that does not take into consideration the topic of media objects). Furthermore, we perform three Pearson's Chi-squared tests between the two predicted results for each topic from different models. Our findings from Table 8 show that, despite the F1 and ROC measures for both prediction results are slightly different for all topics, the p-value means are evidence ($p < 0.01$) for topics related to person and place, that the two predicted samples come from different distributions. These results suggest, if prior to inferring usefulness we are able to determine the topic area

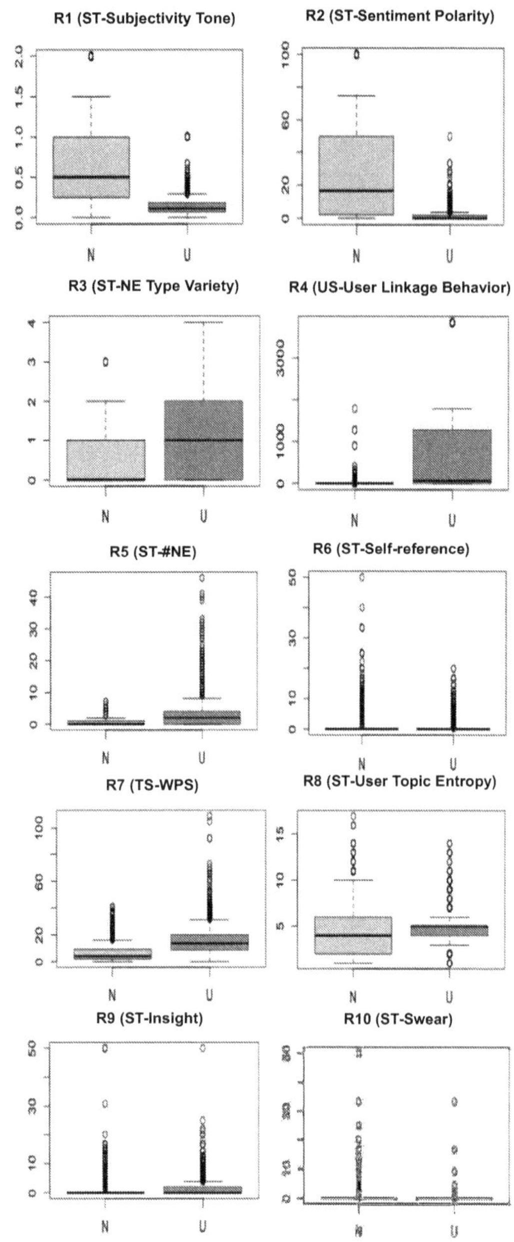

Figure 1: Box plots for the top 10 features according to IGR and Coefficient ranking. Yellow boxes (class N, left) represent non-useful comments, green boxes (class U, right) represent useful comments

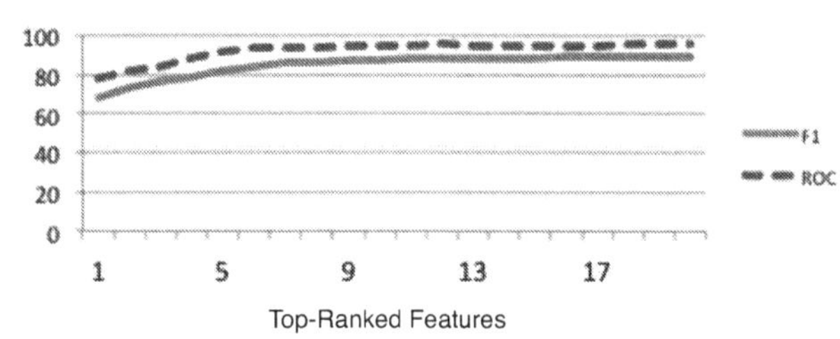

Figure 2: Performance results of classification using top-20 features

Model	Person		Place		Event	
	All	Person	All	Place	All	Event
F1	0.82	0.89*	0.73	0.87*	0.93	0.94
ROC	0.93	0.97	0.93	0.97	0.96	0.96

Table 8: Evaluation results of classification models for different topics. All is the model, which does not take into consideration the topic of media objects. The star next to the F1 means that there is evidence ($p < 0.01$) that the two predicted samples come from different distributions.

of a media object, this helps to classify useful comments with higher accuracy.

We investigate the difference between the models derived for each of the topics. Table 9, shows detailed coefficient ranks for different models. An analysis of the most important features among different areas of topics (place, person, and event) shows some differences. More precisely, coefficient ranks show that comments related to the topics person and event express the users' emotional and affective processes, which are more likely to be inferred as non-useful. An analysis of the *Subjectivity Tone* in different topics shows that the *Subjectivity Tone* for person-related topics is also higher than for other topics. An analysis of the *Swear* score among different topics shows that the *Swear* score for comments related to person is the most negative one. For comments on event, the *Swear* score is more negative than for topics related to place. This concurs with our observation that users express more emotion and may use more offensive language when writing comments about topics related to persons and events. Such comments are more likely to be inferred as non-useful.

A topic related to an event is often also related to a person, a place, or both. Therefore, the coefficient ranks are influenced by the two other topics. For example, the *Relativity* score which includes physical place and motion has a positive impact on places and events, while it has a negative impact on topics related to persons. It is interesting to note that for topics related to place, *Relativity* scores have a positive impact on the model. *Friend* and *Family* scores have a negative impact on the model. This might be because that people describe different physical phenomena and motion processes on this topic, which may be seen as useful information by other users. Instead, giving information about friends and family is non-useful for other users. With regard to topics related to person, *Family, Health & Body* scores have a positive impact on the model. This might be because that people describe more about various health and body aspects of a person on these topics. Furthermore, they describe the background of family members of the target person. This information may be useful information for other people.

Our results indicate that, for a more accurate classification of useful comments, a classification model should take into account the topic of media objects.

5. DISCUSSION

We conducted an analysis of user-generated comments on media objects of different museums and libraries to shed some light on the characteristics of useful comments and to identify the important key features of comments for inferring usefulness. We analyzed three different sets of features: text statistics and syntactic, semantic and topical, and user and social.

Rank	Features	Place	Person	Event
1	ST-Subjectivity Tone	-4.271	-6.228	-3.406
2	ST-Sentiment Polarity	-0.157	-0.223	-0.647
3	ST-NE Types Variety	-0.138	0.113	0.776
4	US-User Linkage Behavior	0.046	0.003	0.002
5	ST-#Name Entities	0.203	0.109	0.201
6	ST-Self-refrence	-0.161	-0.136	-0.177
7	TS-WPS	0.055	0.029	0.016
8	ST-User Topic Entropy	-0.112	-0.302	-0.059
9	ST-Insight	-0.124	0.081	0.064
10	ST-Swear	-0.005	-90.42	-3.363
11	TS-Linkage	0.084	3.028	0.610
12	US-User Conversational	-0.086	-0.086	-0.066
13	ST-Certainty	0.110	0.042	-0.054
14	TS-Future Verb	-0.071	-0.027	-0.027
15	TS-Impersonal-pronoun	-0.052	-0.040	-0.042
16	US-Prestige score	0.162	0.005	0.070
17	ST-Religion	-0.361	0.322	0.089
18	ST-Sadness	-0.110	-0.403	-0.038
19	ST-Family	-0.196	1.111	-0.004
20	ST-Relativity	0.163	-0.160	0.029

Table 9: Coefficient for features of models derived for different topics with regard to usefulness inference

Our experimental findings show that Semantic and Topical features play important roles for inferring the usefulness of comments. This suggests that comments which contain a higher number of references, a higher number of Name Entities, a lower self-reference and affective process (lower sentiment polarity, lower subjectivity tone, swear score, etc) are more likely to be inferred as useful. Therefore, we suggest that a commenting system should give and motivate users to define references [12]. This adds unambiguous users-verified concept references to social media comments, which in turn has a positive impact on the usefulness of comments.

An analysis of features related to users suggests that by leveraging users' previous activities we may be able to increase the probability for inferring the usefulness of a comment. Therefore, we suggest that by designing a commenting service, designers should take this into account when designing users' profile pages.

An analysis of the important features among different topics (place, person, and event) indicates that when inferring the usefulness of comments, the influence of features varies slightly according to the topic areas of media objects. Users express more emotion and may use more offensive language when writing comments about topics related to persons and events. Such comments are more likely to be inferred as non-useful. For topics related to place, people describe more physical phenomena and motion processes on this topic, which may be seen as useful information by other users. On the other hand, giving information about family is non-useful for other users. In contrast, for topics related to person, users describe more about the background of family members, their health, and physical characteristics of the person. This information may be useful information for other people. Therefore, if prior to inferring usefulness we are able to determine the topic area of a media object, this helps to classify useful comments with higher accuracy.

We believe that our results may also apply to other social media platforms. However, we believe the influence of features may vary according to the commenting cultures of platforms. Therefore, in future work, we will further explore the impacts of features on other platforms. We will also explore, different aspects of topics of media objects (such as temporal, polarization, etc), which might have influence on building better classification models.

6. ACKNOWLEDGMENTS

This work was supported in part by a Marie Curie International Outgoing Fellowship within the 7th European Community Framework Program (PIOF-GA-2009-252206). We also thank members of the Library of Congress and especially Helena Zinkham for their insightful comments and advice on the result of the LOC project on Flickr Commons.

7. REFERENCES

[1] E. Agichtein, C. Castillo, D. Donato, A. Gionis, G. Mishne, E. Agichtein, C. Castillo, D. Donato, A. Gionis, and G. Mishne. Finding high-quality content in social media with an application to community-based question answering. In *Proceedings of WSDM*, 2008.

[2] H. Becker, D. Iter, M. Naaman, and L. Gravano. Identifying content for planned events across social media sites. In *Proceedings of the fifth ACM international conference on Web search and data mining*, WSDM '12. ACM, 2012.

[3] D. Blei, A. Ng, and M. Jordan. Latent dirichlet allocation. *the Journal of machine Learning res*, 2003.

[4] C. Castillo, M. Mendoza, and B. Poblete. Information credibility on twitter. In *the 20th international conference*, WWW, 2011.

[5] C. Danescu-Niculescu-Mizil, G. Kossinets, J. Kleinberg, and L. Lee. How opinions are received by online communities: a case study on amazon.com helpfulness votes. In *Proceedings of the 18th international conference on World wide web*, WWW '09, 2009.

[6] N. Diakopoulos, M. De Choudhury, and M. Naaman. Finding and assessing social media information sources in the context of journalism. In *Proceedings of the 2012 ACM annual conference on Human Factors in Computing Systems*, CHI '12. ACM, 2012.

[7] A. Ghose and P. G. Ipeirotis. Designing novel review ranking systems: predicting the usefulness and impact of reviews. In *ICEC '07: Proceedings of the ninth international conference on Electronic commerce*, 2007.

[8] R. Gunning. *The Technique of Clear Writing.* McGraw-Hill, New York, 1952.

[9] C. E. Hall and M. A. Zarro. What do you call it?: a comparison of library-created and user-created tags. In *Proceedings of the 11th annual international ACM/IEEE joint conference on Digital libraries*, JCDL '11. ACM, 2011.

[10] H. Halpin, V. Robu, and H. Shepherd. The complex dynamics of collaborative tagging. In *Proceedings of the 16th international conference on World Wide Web*, WWW '07, 2007.

[11] F. M. Harper, D. Moy, and J. A. Konstan. Facts or friends?: distinguishing informational and conversational questions in social q&a sites. In *Proceedings of the SIGCHI Conference on Human Factors in Computing Systems.* ACM, 2009.

[12] B. Haslhofer, W. Robitza, C. Lagoze, and F. Guimbretiere. Semantic tagging on historical maps. In *ACM Web Science 2013*, Paris, France, May 2013. ACM.

[13] Y. Kammerer, R. Nairn, P. Pirolli, and E. H. Chi. Signpost from the masses: learning effects in an exploratory social tag search browser. In *Proceedings of the SIGCHI Conference on Human Factors in Computing Systems*, CHI '09, pages 625–634, New York, NY, USA, 2009. ACM.

[14] S.-M. Kim, P. Pantel, T. Chklovski, and M. Pennacchiotti. Automatically assessing review helpfulness. In *Proceedings of the 2006 Conference on Empirical Methods in Natural Language Processing*, EMNLP '06, 2006.

[15] J. Liu, Y. Cao, C. Y. Lin, Y. Huang, and M. Zhou. Low-Quality Product Review Detection in Opinion Summarization. In *Proceedings of the 2007 Joint Conference on Empirical Methods in Natural Language Processing and Computational Natural Language Learning (EMNLP-CoNLL)*, 2007.

[16] Y. Liu, J. Bian, and E. Agichtein. Predicting information seeker satisfaction in community question answering. In *Proceedings of the 31st annual international ACM SIGIR conference on Research and development in information retrieval.* ACM, 2008.

[17] Y. Lu, P. Tsaparas, A. Ntoulas, and L. Polanyi. Exploiting social context for review quality prediction. In *Proceedings of the 19th international conference on World wide web*, WWW '10, 2010.

[18] K. Seki, H. Qin, and K. Uehara. Impact and prospect of social bookmarks for bibliographic information retrieval. In *Proceedings of the 10th annual joint conference on Digital libraries*, JCDL '10, 2010.

[19] B. Sigurbjörnsson and R. van Zwol. Flickr tag recommendation based on collective knowledge. In *Proceedings of the 17th international conference on World Wide Web*, WWW '08. ACM, 2008.

[20] Y. R. Tausczik and J. W. Pennebaker. The psychological meaning of words: Liwc and computerized text analysis methods. 2010.

[21] C. Wagner, M. Rowe, M. Strohmaier, and H. Alani. What catches your attention? an empirical study of attention patterns in community forums. In *ICWSM*, 2012.

[22] K. Q. Weinberger, M. Slaney, and R. Van Zwol. Resolving tag ambiguity. In *Proceedings of the 16th ACM international conference on Multimedia*, MM '08. ACM, 2008.

[23] T. Wilson, J. Wiebe, and P. Hoffmann. Recognizing contextual polarity in phrase-level sentiment analysis. In *Proceedings of the conference on Human Language Technology and Empirical Methods in Natural Language Processing*, HLT '05, pages 347–354, Stroudsburg, PA, USA, 2005. Association for Computational Linguistics.

WikiMirs: A Mathematical Information Retrieval System for Wikipedia

Xuan Hu, Liangcai Gao*, Xiaoyan Lin, Zhi Tang
Institute of Computer Science & Technology, Peking University, Beijing, China
{xuan.hu, glc, linxiaoyan, tangzhi}@pku.edu.cn

Xiaofan Lin
A9.com
Palo Alto, CA, USA
xiaofanl@a9.com

Josef B. Baker
School of Computer Science, University of Birmingham
Birmingham, UK
J.Baker@cs.bham.ac.uk

ABSTRACT

Mathematical formulae in structural formats such as MathML and LaTeX are becoming increasingly available. Moreover, repositories and websites, including ArXiv and Wikipedia, and growing numbers of digital libraries use these structural formats to present mathematical formulae. This presents an important new and challenging area of research, namely Mathematical Information Retrieval (MIR). In this paper, we propose WikiMirs, a tool to facilitate mathematical formula retrieval in Wikipedia. WikiMirs is aimed at searching for similar mathematical formulae based upon both textual and spatial similarities, using a new indexing and matching model developed for layout structures. A hierarchical generalization technique is proposed to generate sub-trees from presentation trees of mathematical formulae, and similarity is calculated based upon matching at different levels of these trees. Experimental results show that WikiMirs can efficiently support sub-structure matching and similarity matching of mathematical formulae. Moreover, WikiMirs obtains both higher accuracy and better ranked results over Wikipedia in comparison to Wikipedia Search and Egomath. We conclude that WikiMirs provides a new, alternative, and hopefully better service for users to search mathematical expressions within Wikipedia.

Categories and Subject Descriptors

H.3.3 [**Information Systems**]: Information Search and Retrieval

Keywords

Mathematical Information Retrieval, Mathematical Resource Management, Structure Matching

*Liangcai Gao is the corresponding author.

1. INTRODUCTION

Mathematical formulae are commonly used to present essential ideas and concepts formally in many areas, including mathematics, physics and computer science. Nowadays, due to the increased compatibility of web-browsers in rendering formats like MathML and LaTeX along with improved tools for creating them in documents, more and more mathematical resources are produced, presented and distributed in structural formats. As a result, a growing number of these resources are available in information systems including mathematical knowledge management systems, academic digital libraries and digital education systems. In order to make these resources searchable and accessible, Mathematical Information Retrieval (MIR) is required for various reasons: *1)* In mathematical knowledge management systems (e.g., ArXiv, Wolfram), tremendous amount of work on classifying math contents has to be done manually to make resources searchable. Due to the current explosive growth in the area, manual classification is no longer suitable and MIR techniques are needed to achieve effective searching; *2)* In academic digital libraries, math expressions are commonly used to present the essential ideas of research work and a math-aware search engine would provide researchers a brand-new way of finding related works based on the most valuable components of publications; *3)* A growing number of education resources (books, lecture notes and exercises, etc) are being digitalised. Since students initially have limited background knowledge, it is difficult for them to find related mathematical contents in their learning materials with existing search engines. MIR techniques would be beneficial for them to find the needed information effectively via retrieving the math contents directly.

Because mathematical formulae are highly structured and domain specific, conventional search engines, which mainly focus on plain text retrieval, can hardly meet the needs. Although MIR has been discussed for nearly a decade [19], at present there exist few search engines that can provide satisfactory public information retrieval service. The challenges in constructing a MIR system can be mainly attributed to normalization, indexing, matching, query interface, and relevance feedback [19]. The performance of a MIR system is primarily determined by the first three challenges, which will be discussed in detail as follows.

Normalization: In MIR system, the purpose of normalization is to find the equivalent mathematical formulae with different presentations. Different from word stemming and thesaurus operation in text retrieval techniques, normalization should overcome variation in the spatial layout or semantic presentation of the same formula. Since the equivalent transformations of a formula are very flexible in both spatial layout and semantic presentation, normalization becomes rather complicated. For instance, formulae can have the same structure but different variable or constant names (e.g., $a+b$ vs. $x+y$). Formulae can also have equivalent semantic transformation (e.g., $k*(x+y)$ vs. $k*x+k*y$). Objects of normalization can range from identities of variables or constants to semantic calculation equivalence (e.g., order of operands).

Indexing and matching: Since mathematical formulae are naturally expressed in a tree-structure, matches of formulae are supposed to support matching in both text contents and structures. In order to calculate the structural similarities of formulae, attributes of tree structures are commonly considered, such as sub-trees and levels. For example, formulae containing the same main structure with different sub-trees (e.g., $a+b\times y$ vs. $x+y$), and formulae containing different main structure with the same sub-trees (e.g., $a+b\times y$ vs. $b\times y$). Therefore, to support such matching, the structural attributes of formulae need to be extracted and indexed. Indexing all sub-expressions keeps all the structural information of a formula, but the corresponding index space increases explosively. Therefore, it becomes difficult to strike a balance between having sufficient indexing and keeping a reasonably sized index space. Moreover, how to calculate the similarity score according to the attributes of structures remains an open problem, because the motivations of different users of the MIR systems vary according to their background and specific tasks [21].

In this paper, WikiMirs is proposed to facilitate mathematical formula retrieval in Wikipedia. And the system is publicly available[1]. In order to support mathematical formula retrieval considering similarities of both text contents and spatial structures, we propose a presentation tree parser to parse formula structures from a layout presentation markup, such as LaTeX. Moreover, a hierarchical generalization technique is proposed to generate fine-grained sub-trees (index terms) from the presentation tree. Furthermore, the similarity score of formulae is calculated based on both text matching and structure matching at different levels.

It is worth noting that, by now WikiMirs is unable to retrieve formulae which are semantically equivalent to the queried formulae (e.g., $\sqrt{x}$ and $x^{\frac{1}{2}}$), due to the following reasons: Firstly, the conversion of semantic equivalent math expressions requires high level domain specific knowledge, which are difficult to be processed by machine for the moment. The semantics of math expressions themselves can be quite ambiguous. Even people cannot understand them directly without sufficient context (e.g., "*ab*" can be understood as a variable "*ab*" or an expression, "*a*" multiplies "*b*"). Therefore, we intend to utilise the presentation layout of formulae rather than semantics in MIR in this paper. Secondly, a large amount of layout presentations can be converted into semantic presentations directly, e.g., displayed fraction expressions. In this sense, we believe that the layout presentation of formulae can greatly facilitate MIR. As a result, WikiMirs can provide better MIR service than the traditional search engines or text-based MIR systems through making full use of both the text and structure information in the layout presentations of formulae.

[1]`http://www.icst.pku.edu.cn/cpdp/wikimirs/`

2. RELATED WORK

MIR has attracted much attention from researchers in the past decade, and several related systems or methods on this task have been reported [21]. We compare the existing MIR systems in Table 1 and illustrate the related research on the following three basic aspects of MIR, namely formula presentation, indexing and ranking.

2.1 Formula Presentation

The most well-known markup formats for mathematical formulae are MathML[8], LaTeX and OpenMath[7]. MathML provides two representation forms for formulae, namely Presentation and Content MathML. Presentation MathML is designed to mark up the spatial layout of formula in order to present math contents accurately on screen, whereas Content MathML intends to mark up the semantic meanings of formula. Similarly, OpenMath is proposed to represent mathematical objects with their semantics. LaTeX is designed to be used by authors to create documents with high presentation quality and similarly to Presentation MathML, only the geometric layouts of formulae are coded. Obviously, Content MathML and OpenMath are the ideal representations to support semantic MIR because of the embedded semantics. However, existing mathematical resources are often written in Presentation MathML or LaTeX due to the ease of authoring and high quality rendering when used with display engines such as MathJax [6]. Moreover, LaTeX has been widely used by authors and editors since 1980s. Therefore, although mathematical retrieval techniques using Content MathML or OpenMath [3] can better support semantic retrieval, it is difficult to apply them to existing repositories of mathematical information. In other words, in order to design a practical MIR system, the focus must be on the intrinsic similarity of formulae using their layouts, which has not been well studied by now.

2.2 Indexing

According to the index model, the existing techniques can be generally classified into two categories, namely text-based or tree-based, as classified in Table 1.

The main idea of text-based MIR technique [1, 12, 13, 2, 14, 5] is to convert mathematical formula markups into plain text strings and then tokenize the strings linearly into terms, so that they can be indexed and ranked using existing information retrieval tools like Lucene. Because mathematical formulae are highly symbolic and structured, the transformation from structural formulae into plain text strings mainly focuses on how to encode structures in text strings and normalize different presentations of formulae. Miller et al. convert all non-alphanumeric symbols in LaTeX into alphanumeric symbols and normalize the order of operands into a canonical form [1, 12]. A similar method is proposed by Misutka et al. [2, 14] with improvement via normalization of variables and constants. In these methods, structures of formulae are lost. Aimed at matching formula

Table 1: **Comparison of Mathematical Information Retrieval Systems**

Systems	Presentation	Normalization	Matching	Ranking	Corpus	Available
Text-based indexing						
DLMF[1, 12]	LaTeX	Order†	Exact	*tf-idf*	DLMF	Y
Mathdex[13]	Presentation MathML	Variables	Similar	*tf-idf* with weights	arXiv; Wikipedia	N
EgoMath[2, 14]	Presentation MathML	Variables and constants	Exact	*tf-idf*	Wikipedia	Y
LaTeXSearch[5]	LaTeX	Unknown	Similar	Edit distance	Springer	Y
Tree-based indexing						
MathWebSearch[3, 11]	Content MathML	/	Similar	/	Connexions; Wolfram	Y
MIaS[4, 18]	Presentation MathML	Order; variables and constants	Similar	*tf-idf* with weights	arXMLiv	Y
[17]	LaTeX	Order and variables	Similar	Similarity of matched sets	arXiv	N
Other						
[15]	Content MathML	Variables	Similar	Similarity of feature sets	Constructed dataset	N
[16]	LaTeX	/	Similar	*tf-idf* with learned weights	Math Overflow	N

† "Order" denotes the order of operands.

structures in the text-based retrieval model, Miner et al. [13] index n gram terms which are sub-structures with no more than n successive tags. However, n is only set to five in their system, meaning only sub-structures with a few nodes are indexed. Therefore, high level structure matching of expressions with complex structures cannot be considered. LaTeXSearch [5] is a related commercial text-based system, but its scheme is not reported publicly.

In tree-based methods, attributes of formula tree structures (e.g., sub-expressions [4, 18] or paths [10]) are extracted as index terms. Sojka et al. [4, 18] index all sub-structures of formulae. This method can guarantee high recall rate, but it may cause explosive growth of index space in real-world applications. To solve this problem, Kohlhase et al. [3, 11] apply a substitution tree indexing technique to index sub-structures of semantic formula presentation. A substitution tree represents the structure of all the indexed first-order logic terms. Exact or similar matches can be found by backtracking all nodes of the substitution tree using different strategies. Similarly, Schellenberg et al. [17] employ the substitution tree indexing technique to index layout presentation of formulae.

Besides text-based and tree-based methods, there are some other indexing approaches. Asperti et al. [9] present a meta-data based method, in which math notations are presented by a logic-independent meta-data model, so as to serve a large database. Based on Formal Concept Analysis, Nguyen et al. [15] extract math features for each formula and index them via constructing a mathematical concept lattice of these features.

2.3 Ranking

Ranking is always highly related to indexing because the similarity score calculation has to depend on the indexed contents. Most text-based methods use *tf-idf* to calculate similarities of formulae, which usually only consider the number of terms. Miner et al. [13] introduce weights for terms according to their levels, lengths and complexities. However, as only limited structure information of formulae is indexed in text-based models, the structure matching score is difficult to calculate properly. Some tree-based methods also use the modified *tf-idf* to calculate the matching scores of sub-structures. Using *tf-idf*, Sojka et al. [4, 18] introduce weights to discriminate sub-structure matches in different levels based on the assumption that structures in higher level are more important than those at lower levels.

Besides *tf-idf*, some methods evaluate the similarities of formulae according to the similarity of feature sets. Nguyen et al. [15] index formulae in the mathematical concept lattice structure based on similarities of feature sets of each formula. To search for a formula, the query is inserted into the mathematical concept lattice and similar formulae are ranked according to their distances from the query. In the literature [17], each formula can be presented by a set of sub-expressions with their attributes (e.g., contents, neighbours, etc) presented in 5-tuples. Retrieved formulae are ranked according to the set similarity between formulae. Zanibbi et al. [20] employ content-based image retrieval technique to search formulae in document images. Since this method calculates the similarity score based on visual features of formulae, its performance is sensitive to typesetting styles of formulae.

3. OVERVIEW

The workflow of the proposed system, WikiMirs, is illustrated in Figure 1, which includes four main modules, namely preprocessor, tokenizer, indexer and ranker. The index is constructed offline as described by solid lines in Figure 1. Firstly, the off-line Wikipedia corpus is downloaded as the source dataset of our system, then internal LaTeX markups of mathematical formulae are extracted by the preprocessor. Next, indexing terms are extracted by the tokenizer, where formulae representations are first normalized to support equivalent formula search; then, sub-structures, as well as fuzzy sub-substructures, are

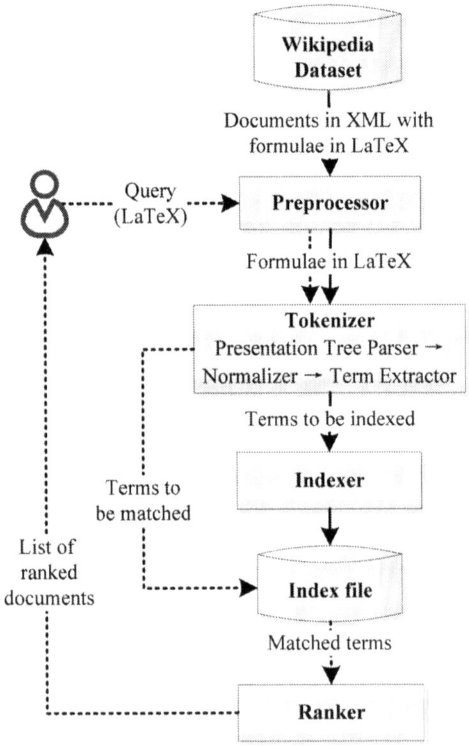

Figure 1: Workflow of WikiMirs (Dotted lines denote online query flows and solid lines denote offline index flows).

extracted hierarchically. Finally, attributes of these terms are calculated and stored in inverted index files by the indexer.

When a user searches a formula online as described by dotted lines in Figure 1, the query will be first preprocessed into the internal LaTeX markup. Then, query terms are generated by the tokenizer following a similar process set in indexing above. Next, these terms are passed into the ranker to find relevant formulae and calculate the corresponding similarity score. Lastly, a list of documents are ranked according to the similarity scores of relevant formulae and returned to the user. In the following sections, we detail the four modules of WikiMirs, the preprocessor, tokenizer, indexer and ranker.

4. PREPROCESSOR

The Wikipedia database[2] presents web pages in a single XML file in which mathematical formulae are presented via LaTeX markup tagged by "$" and "$". The database is downloaded and then parsed by the preprocessor to extract LaTeX markup of formulae by identifying the tags.

After the LaTeX markup of formulae is extracted, normalization is carried out. This has to be completed as in LaTeX authors can use many different commands and user-defined macros to create formulae that are visually and semantically identical. As documents in Wikipedia are edited by many contributors from all around the world, it is inevitable to introduce various styles and commands of LaTeX into the dataset. For instance, spaces with different widths can be produced using different commands (e.g., "\qquad", "\quad", "\;", "\," etc). To overcome the impacts of typesetting differences, four rules are adopted to normalize the LaTeX markup: *1)* Line breaks inside encoding are filtered; *2)* Spaces before and after encoding are filtered; *3)* Successive multiple spaces are converted into a single space; *4)* Different presentations of space commands are removed.

[2] `http://en.wikipedia.org/wiki/Wikipedia:Database_download`

5. TOKENIZER

5.1 Conventions

In order to propose a more reasonable index scheme, we first analyse the common conventions used in reading or understanding the structures of mathematical formulae before introducing our tokenizer and indexer.

Firstly, because structures of mathematical formulae are naturally hierarchical, they are conventionally read or understood in a hierarchical way. An assumption commonly used in previous work [13, 4, 18] is that higher level structures are more important than those at lower levels. This is because the top level usually determines the category or the skeleton of the formula, whereas the lower level nodes usually store variables or constants whose contents do not matter to the meaning of the structure. Although this convention is true when understanding a single formula, it seems unfeasible when comparing two formulae, because the same sub-structure may be present in both at different levels, thus it is hard to decide which level should be considered in calculating the importance of the match. To decide whether two formulae are similar or not, a more practical way is to compare how many contents they share at the corresponding level. In other words, the closer the levels of the matched sub-expressions are, the more they should contribute to the overall similarity score. For instance, when comparing $a^2+b^2=c^2$ with the following three expressions: $\frac{1}{a^2+b^2}=1$, $a^2+b^2=1$ and a^2+b^2, there is only one matched sub-expression, a^2+b^2. When calculating the score of this match, a higher score should be assigned to $a^2+b^2=1$ in which a^2+b^2 is in the same level with the query formula, whereas $\frac{1}{a^2+b^2}=1$ and a^2+b^2 should be assigned lower scores since the matched a^2+b^2 are in different levels compared with the query expression. According to this convention, in Section 7, a specific measurement will be proposed to calculate the similarity of term levels.

Secondly, when reading mathematical formulae with complicated structures, generalization is commonly used to simplify the formula. More specifically, most of the formulae can be viewed as expressions containing an operator with a list of operands. Generalizing the content of operands as a variable or alias is commonly applied to simplify complex structure into concise expression. For example, the expression $\frac{\sqrt{a+b}}{(c+d)^2}$ can be recognized step by step from $\frac{\sqrt{*}}{*^2}$ to $\frac{*}{*}$. Similarly, when comparing two mathematical formulae, generalized forms of expressions are commonly used to evaluate how similar two formulae appear. However, generalized forms of formulae are rarely used in existing MIR methods. In Section 5.4, a method is proposed to extract generalized sub-structures of formulae, so as to be served in finding relevant formulae.

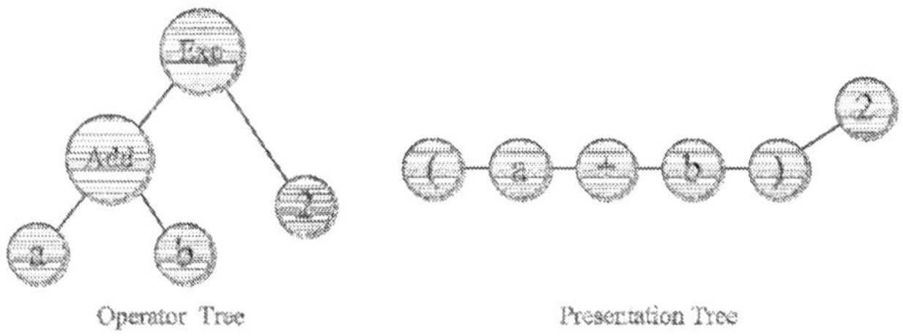

Figure 2: Operator tree and presentation tree of $(a+b)^2$ [19].

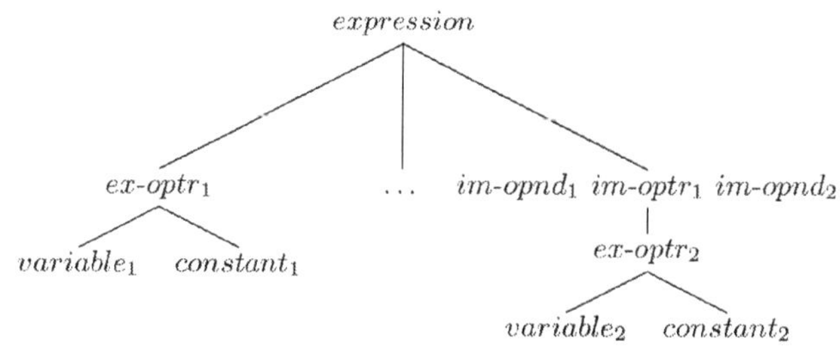

Figure 3: Presentation tree template.

5.2 Presentation Tree Parser

The presentation tree parser aims at parsing LaTeX markup into an internal presentation tree, which is an intermediate format and is processed by downstream components, namely the normalizer and term extractor.

5.2.1 Presentation Tree

Different from an operator tree which is well-known for presenting the semantic meaning of formula directly, a presentation tree describes the spatial layout of formulae. In the presentation tree, spatial relations (e.g., horizontal, subscript, superscript, etc) are utilized to describe the geometric layouts of symbols in a formula. The presentation tree is also named as a Symbol Layout Tree in some literature [19]. Comparison of the operator tree and the presentation tree of a sample expression is given in Figure 2.

In this paper, the presentation tree of formula is presented according to the LaTeX markup. This definition can also be applied to Presentation MathML or other formula presentation formats with little modification. Basically, there are two ways to present a formula using LaTeX markup: *1)* Typically, expressions are presented by predefined operators (e.g., "\frac", "\sqrt", etc) with their operands explicitly encoded inside a pair of tags, "{}". In this paper, operators, which present their operands explicitly, are named as *explicit operator* and referred to as *ex-optr* hereafter. Their operands are referred to as *ex-opnd*. *2)* Other expressions composed of binary operators (e.g., "+", "÷") or delimiters (e.g., "(", ")") are presented linearly with their operands implicitly encoded. Each operand and each operator are placed linearly from left to right without any tag denoting operands. We call operators which present their operands implicitly as *implicit operators* and refer them as *im-optr* hereafter. Their operands are referred to as *im-opnd*. These two types of operators can be easily distinguished through checking the pair of tags, "{}" in the LaTeX markups.

According to the two types of operators defined, two templates are defined as follows to describe the expressions in LaTeX. Expressions with *ex-optr* can be parsed using Template 1 and expressions with *im-optr* can be parsed using Template 2. The mathematical formulae presented in LaTeX can be parsed by these templates or the combination of them via checking up the types of operators encountered from left to right in its LaTeX markup. Each operand (*ex-opnd* or *im-opnd*) can be a sub-expression, a variable or a constant. It should be noted that custom commands defined in user-defined macros are now processed in the same way with the pre-defined commands in LaTeX. The general presentation tree template is shown in Figure 3.

Template 1:

$$ex\text{-}optr\ \{ex\text{-}opnd_1\}\{ex\text{-}opnd_2\}\ldots\{ex\text{-}opnd_n\}$$

Template 2:

$$im\text{-}opnd_1\ im\text{-}optr_1\ im\text{-}opnd_2\ im\text{-}optr_2\ \ldots\ im\text{-}optr_n\ im\text{-}opnd_{n+1}$$

5.2.2 Tree Construction

After parsing LaTeX markups of formulae using the above templates, they can be further built into presentation trees. Firstly, if an expression conforms to Template 1, the *ex-optr* is taken as a node and its operands inside "{}" tags become its children. Otherwise, the expression should conform to Template 2. In this case, there may exist more than one *im-optrs* and the priorities of these *im-optrs* are unknown without semantic analysis. Thus, it can not be decided which *im-optr* should be the node of the current level. Therefore, when the expression conforms to Template 2, the whole expression itself will be considered as a node and will not grow as one operator node with several operand children. Secondly, the operands in Template 1 and Template 2 are taken as individual expressions and parsed recursively following the above process. It is worth noting that the expression conforming to Template 2 will have children only if at least one of its operands conforms to Template 1. The tree building process continues until no more children nodes can be added into the existing tree.

An example of the presentation tree of a specific formula (see Figure 4(a)) is shown in Figure 4(c) whose LaTeX markup is described in Figure 4(b).

5.3 Normalizer

The role of the normalizer is to normalize the variables, constants and order of operands. Challenges of employing the normalizer towards LaTeX markup include: *1)* Different from MathML, in which identifying variables and constants is quite straightforward, since variables and constants are usually tagged explicitly with special tags (e.g., "ci"), in LaTeX there exist no explicit commands to denote them. *2)* Similar to Presentation MathML, LaTeX markups do not contain semantic information of formulae, so it is difficult to decide the priorities of operators without additional semantic analysis. As a result, equivalent transformation of the operand order cannot be carried out, either.

Given that, techniques on semantic understanding of mathematical formulae have not been well studied, and this paper does not leverage semantic analysis to overcome the aforementioned problems. Alternately, we propose a normalizer for variables and constants based on the

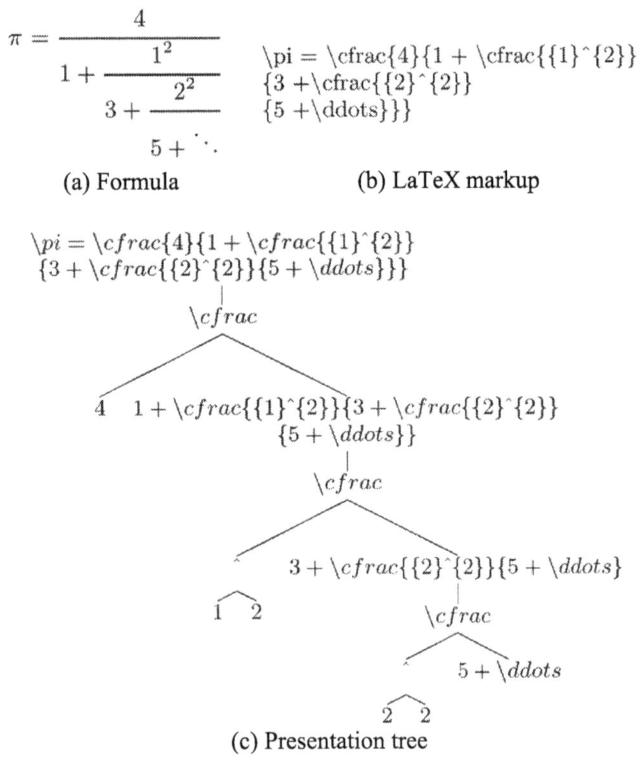

Figure 4: An example of presentation tree.

presentation tree parsed in the previous stage as explained in Section 5.2. Given a presentation tree, all leaf nodes are examined by the normalizer. If a leaf node does not confirm to Template 2, it should be identified as a variable or a constant. In this case, a unified alias will replace the content of this leaf node. If a leaf node confirms to Template 2, the ordinary presentation will be kept.

5.4 Term Extractor

As aforementioned, formulae in LaTeX are parsed into the presentation tree and then normalized. Based on the normalized presentation tree, fine-grained terms are extracted using a hierarchical generalization technique. In this way, matches in different levels, as well as matches between generalized expressions, can be taken into consideration for the similarity score calculation.

The term extractor will generate two categories of terms, namely *original terms* and *generalized terms*. The *original terms* are generated directly from the original sub-expressions of the formulae. The *generalized terms* are generated from the fuzzy sub-expressions. The *generalized terms* is proposed to describe the sketch of the expression.

For each term, three attributes are extracted and recorded in a triple, namely $\{content, level, is\_fuzzy\}$. The content of the term is recorded in the *content* field. The level of the term in the formula presentation tree is stored in the *level* field. is_fuzzy field denotes whether the term is a *generalized term* or not.

The term generation algorithm is illustrated in Algorithm 1. The presentation tree is traversed using depth-first search. For each expression (exp) in a different level (lev), terms are recursively generated. The original term is generated as shown in line 2 of Algorithm 1. The original LaTeX markup ($LaTeX\_markup(exp)$) of the expression is extracted as the *content*. The generalized term is extracted as shown in line 5. The content of this term is generated using Algorithm 2 to be detailed later. After the *original term* and *generalized term* are extracted, operands of the expression are traversed. If the $operand_i$ is a sub-expression rather than a variable or constant, the term generation algorithm will be recursively called with $operand_i$ and $lev + 1$ as inputs.

Algorithm 1 Term generation

```
1: procedure TERM_OF_EXPRESSION(exp, lev)
2:     term_set ← (LaTeX_markup(exp), lev, false)
3:                                   ▷ Extract original term
4:     if GEN_LATEX_MARKUP(exp) is not "" then
5:         term_set ← (GEN_LATEX_MARKUP(exp), lev, true)
6:     end if
7:                                   ▷ Extract generalized term
8:     for operand_i := each operand in exp do
9:         if operand_i is not a variable or constant then
10:            TERM_OF_EXPRESSION(operand_i, lev + 1)
11:        end if
12:    end for
13: end procedure
```

In order to record the rough outline of an expression without the details of its sub-expressions, Algorithm 2 is proposed. The main idea is to reserve the structure of the top level of the expression and neglect the contents of its sub-expressions. As described in Algorithm 2, to generate the generalized LaTeX markup of an expression (exp), the operands are traversed. If the operand is a sub-expression rather than a variable or constant, all the operands of this sub-expression should be removed and replace by "{}". In this way, a generalized term is created to record the dominating structure of the expression.

Algorithm 2 Generalized LaTeX markup generation

```
procedure GEN_LATEX_MARKUP(exp)
    is_exist ← false
    gen_str ← ""
    for operand_i := each operand in exp do
        if operand_i is not a variable or constant then
            replace all operands of operand_i with "{}";
            gen_str ← gen_str ^ operand_i
            is_exist ← true
        else
            gen_str ← gen_str ^ operand_i
        end if
    end for
    if is_exist then return gen_str
    else return ""
    end if
end procedure
```

Taking the expression in Figure 4 as an example, the terms generated are illustrated in Table 2.

6. INDEXER

To run queries more efficiently we employ the inverted index data structure, which is commonly used in text-based

Table 2: Terms of Expression in Figure 4

Terms: Content[†]	Level[‡]	Fuzzy	Expression
\pi=\cfrac{C}{1+ \cfrac{{C}^{C}}{3+ \cfrac{{C}^{C}}{5+ \ddots}}}	1	false	$\pi = \cfrac{4}{1+\cfrac{1^2}{3+\cfrac{2^2}{5+\ddots}}}$
\pi=\cfrac{}{}	1	true	$\pi = \frac{*}{*}$
1+\cfrac{{C}^{C}} {3+\cfrac{{C}^{C}} {5+\ddots}}	2	false	$1+\cfrac{1^2}{3+\cfrac{2^2}{5+\ddots}}$
1+\cfrac{}{}	2	true	$1+\frac{*}{*}$
{C}^{C}	3	false	1^2
3+\cfrac{{C}^{C}} {5+\ddots}	3	false	$3+\cfrac{2^2}{5+\ddots}$
3+\cfrac{}{}	3	true	$3+\frac{*}{*}$
{C}^{C}	4	false	2^2
5+\ddots	4	false	$5+\ddots$

† "C" denotes the normalized alias of constant.
‡ Level of root is defined as 1.

Table 3: Data Structure of the Inverted Index File

Term	iff	$formula_1$	...	$formula_j$
t_1	$iff(t_1)$	$tf(t_1, formula_1)$ $tl(t_1, formula_1)$	...	$tf(t_1, formula_j)$ $tl(t_1, formula_j)$
...	...	...	...	...
t_i	$iff(t_i)$	$tf(t_i, formula_1)$ $tl(t_i, formula_1)$	...	$tf(t_i, formula_j)$ $tl(t_i, formula_j)$

search engine, to index formula terms. For each term, a list of formulae which contain this term is recorded. A formula (f) "contains" a term (t) denotes that the *content* field of one of the terms extracted from f is exactly the same with that of t. The structure of the inverted index file is presented in Table 3. Term level $tl(t_i, formula_j)$ denotes level of t_i in $formula_j$. However, since there may be several occurrences of t_i in $formula_j$ and their term levels may also be different, $tl(t_i, formula_j)$ is defined as a 64-bit integer in which the k-th bit denotes whether t_i appears in the k-th level of the formula. Similar to the traditional text-based information retrieval model, for each term (t_i), $iff(t_i)$ is employed to describe the inverted formula frequency of t_i as defined in Equation 1:

$$iff(t_i) = \log \frac{Number\ of\ formulae}{1 + Number\ of\ formulae\ containing\ t_i}. \tag{1}$$

$tf(t_i, formula_j)$ describes the frequency of t_i occurring in $formula_j$ as defined in Equation 2:

$$tf(t_i, formula_j) = \frac{Number\ of\ t_i\ in\ formula_j}{Number\ of\ terms\ in\ formula_j}. \tag{2}$$

As previously stated, the tokenizer extracts two types of terms, *original terms* and *generalized terms*. In the indexer, *original terms* and *generalized terms* are indexed in two inverted index files separately according to the *is_fuzzy* field of terms. This is because separated index files can support flexible query demands efficiently. If an exact query is requested, only the index file of the *original terms* should be looked up, since the matches in the index file of *generalized terms* will not contribute to the overall similarity score calculation and the time of checking the generalized terms can be saved.

7. RANKER

When users search a formula via entering the LaTeX markup of the formula, WikiMirs first preprocesses the query into normalized LaTeX markups as described in Section 4. Then, the query is tokenized into terms by the tokenizer as introduced in Section 5. After the terms are generated, they are used to look up all the matched terms in the inverted index file. For each term t generated from the query Q, a similarity score is calculated as defined in Equation 3:

$$score(Q, F) = \sum_{t \in Q} tf(t, F) \times iff(t) \times W_{lev}(t, Q, F) \times W_{gen}(t), \tag{3}$$

$iff(t)$ and $tf(t, F)$ are defined in Equation 1 and Equation 2 respectively. The similarity score between the query and a formula is calculated by summing up the similarity score of each matched term. A weight of level, $W_{lev}(t, Q, F)$, is introduced to evaluate the distance of the matched terms on different levels, as defined in Equation 4:

$$W_{lev}(t, Q, F) = \frac{1}{1 + \min_i\{|level(t, Q) - level_i(t, F)|\}}. \tag{4}$$

In this equation, $tf(t, F)$ is stored in the index file and $tf(t, Q)$ is obtained by the tokenizer. It is worth noting that there may be several occurrences of the term t in the formula F and they might be at different levels of the formula F. Therefore, different level distances may be obtained through calculating distances between the query term level ($level(t, Q)$) and each matched term level ($level_i(t, F)$). In our system, a minimum among these level distances is taken as the level distance between the query term t and the formula F. In order to ensure that the exactly matched terms would always get higher similarity score than those who are only approximately matched, the weight of generalization, $W_{gen}(t)$, is also defined in Equation 5:

$$W_{gen}(t) = \begin{cases} 1 & \text{if } t \text{ is not generalized} \\ 0.5 & \text{if } t \text{ is generalized} \end{cases}. \tag{5}$$

8. EXPERIMENTAL RESULTS

In this section, the query efficiency of the proposed system, WikiMirs, is evaluated. In addition, we compare the accuracy of WikiMirs with two existing search engines; Wikipedia Search and Egomath [2].

8.1 Dataset

The dataset used in WikiMirs is the Wikipedia dataset. The version being used is the 2012-10-01 dump with a size of approximately 8.7 GB compressed and 30 GB uncompressed. This dataset contains approximately 13 millions web pages and 495,958 mathematical formulae. Compared with other mathematical document corpuses (e.g., ArXiv), which are relative more domain-specific or academic, Wikipedia is widely used by users with different background. Because there is no benchmark dataset for evaluation in MIR research community, it is difficult to compare performances of MIR systems. However, since Wikipedia is a publicly available dataset and some reported work [14] does use it, performance evaluation can be done through using the same Wikipedia dataset.

8.2 Query Efficiency

To evaluate the query efficiency of our proposed method, growth trends of the index file size and the query time with increasing amount of indexed formulae are evaluated. Table 4 depicts the sizes of index files with increasing amount of indexed formulae. It can be seen that as the number of indexed formulae grows at ten times scale, the size of index file increases steadily. Table 5 illustrates the query times with increasing amount of indexed formulae. The minimum, maximum and average query time over ten test queries are tested with an increasing number of indexed formulae. On average, the query time is less than 1 second when the index size is less than 420 MB. The steady trend of the index file size and query time growing with the number of indexed formulae implies that the WikiMirs has good scalability for real-world realistic applications with a much larger dataset.

Table 4: Sizes of Index Files with an Increasing Number of Indexed Formulae

Number of formulae	1,000	10,000	100,000	495,958
Size (MB)	0.26	1.83	21.41	419.55

Table 5: Query Times with an Increasing Number of Indexed Formulae

Number of formulae	1,000	10,000	100,000	495,958
Min (ms)	0.48	0.48	0.51	1.1
Max (ms)	58.04	115.34	922.42	1431.41
Average (ms)	9.76	31.56	222.57	510.65

8.3 Accuracy

To evaluate the accuracy of the results found by WikiMirs, experiments are carried out to compare WikiMirs with Wikipedia Search and Egomath. In addition, it is worthy to note that the traditional search engines perform rather poorly in searching formulae on Wikipedia according to our testing. In fact, so poorly that it seems meaningless to compare with Google and Bing. Therefore, we choose to compare the proposed system with Wikipedia Search and Egomath rather than those traditional search engines. Wikipedia Search is a search engine built in Wikipedia, and it can be used to locate content on Wikipedia based on plain text retrieval techniques. Egomath is a text-based math search engine on Wikipedia. To compare their accuracies, we first analyse the retrieval results of several sample queries, then compare the *Precision* and *Discounted Cumulative Gain* (*DCG*) of their top-k retrieval results.

8.3.1 Case Study

In this section, specific expressions are selected from different categories as sample queries to test in Wikipedia Search, Egomath and WikiMirs. Table 6 shows six sample queries with their retrieved expressions, ordered by their similarity scores with the queries.

Taking the first query ($\frac{x^2-1}{x^2+1} - \frac{2ix}{x^2+1}$) as an example, Wikipedia Search finds relevant formulae according to distinguishable terms in the query (e.g., "\frac" or "x^2"), so formulae with these terms are ranked first. High frequencies of the particular terms (e.g., "\frac") will cause irrelevant results to rank highly, such as the fourth and fifth formulae. In contrast to Wikipedia Search, which obtains high recall but low accuracy, Egomath returns only one result for this query. A portion of this retrieved formula is exactly matched with the query. WikiMirs finds the exactly matched expression followed by a list of partially matched expressions which share similar sub-structures with the query formula.

Let us look at the the fourth query ($\sum_{i=0}^{\infty} a_i X^i$). Wikipedia Search ranks the results according to frequency of particular terms in the query (e.g., "\sum" and "x^"). Egomath returns no result mainly because of its exact matching policy. WikiMirs finds the expressions with similar structures with the query and ranks them according to structure similarities. The upper bounds of "$\sum$" in these expressions are "n" rather than "∞", but this difference should not matter in the structure matching. Owing to the generalization technique presented in our tokenizer, this difference is ignored properly and therefore fuzzy matched formulae are found.

8.3.2 Performance of the Top-k Results

Figure 5 shows the performance of Wikipedia Search, Egomath and WikiMirs based on 20 test queries. To evaluate the performance results, average *Precision* and *Discounted Cumulative Gain* (*DCG*) are calculated respectively, based on the top 5, 10 and 20 retrieved expressions over all queries. *Precision* is a set-based evaluation metric which is used to evaluate the accuracy of retrieved results without considering the difference of positions of results in the ranked list. In order to take the order of results into consideration, *DCG* is introduced. Using a graded relevance scale of the formula in the ranked list, *DCG* measures the relevant score of a formula based on its position in the result list. In other words, more contribution is made if a relevant formula is ranked higher in the result list, otherwise less contribution is made.

For each test query, the top k results are retrieved and then labelled manually by subjects to denote whether the retrieved formula is relevant to the query or not. For each query, a list of labels of the top-k results are obtained. Here, the list is named rel in which the i-th element (rel_i) denotes whether the i-th retrieved formula is relevant to the query ($rel_i = 1$) or not ($rel_i = 0$). Based on the list rel, P of the top-k retrieved results can be calculated using Equation 6:

$$P_k = \sum_{i=1}^{k} \frac{rel_i}{k}. \quad (6)$$

DCG of the top-k retrieved results can be calculated using Equation 7:

$$DCG_k = \sum_{i=1}^{k} \frac{2^{rel_i} - 1}{\log_2(i+1)}. \quad (7)$$

It is shown from Figure 5 that WikiMirs outperforms Wikipedia Search and Egomath in P_5, P_{10} and P_{20} by more

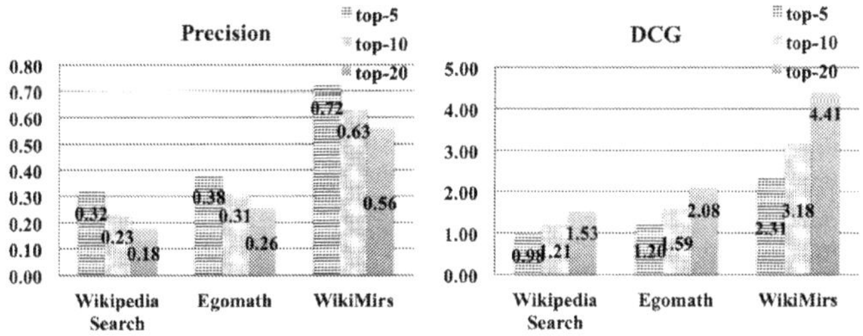

Figure 5: Comparison of Precision & DCG of the top-5, top-10 and top-20 results.

than 30%. It is also seen that DCG_5, DCG_{10} and DCG_{20} of WikiMirs are about twice higher than those of Egomath and Wikipedia Search, showing that WikiMirs ranks the relevant results more properly. Many irrelevant formulae are found and ranked highly by Wikipedia Search because it retrieves results according to textual contents solely. In Egomath, although some features of math formulae are considered, due to the exact matching technique adopted, limited amount of results are found and sometimes only less than 5 results are returned. This is the main reason causing low precision and DCG in Egomath.

9. CONCLUSIONS

In this paper, we propose WikiMirs, a tool to facilitate searching mathematical formulae, which consists of four major components, preprocessor, tokenizer, indexer, and ranker. In order to support both the textual and structural matching of formulae, we propose a tokenizer to produce fine-grained sub-structures of mathematical formulae, extracted using a hierarchical generalization technique from the presentation tree. The ranker calculates the similarity between formulae using both text matching and structure matching at different tree levels. Experimental results show that WikiMirs has both satisfactory query efficiency and good scalability. Experiments on accuracy have been carried out from several different perspectives. They show that WikiMirs retrieves more accurate results and ranks formulae better in Wikipedia compared to two existing search engines, Wikipedia Search and Egomath. In order to facilitate the wide adoption of MIR in real-world digital libraries, it is important to study the gap between the performance of MIR and the user's expectations. Therefore, we plan to conduct a survey of user requirements of the digital libraries. Moreover, utilising the contexts and semantics of mathematical formulae, as well as the metadata of the documents to improve the performance of mathematical information retrieval is another meaningful research direction.

10. ACKNOWLEDGMENTS

This work is supported by the National Natural Science Foundation of China (No.61202232) and National Key Technology R&D Program of China (No.2012BAH40F01). We also thank the anonymous reviewers for their valuable comments.

11. REFERENCES

[1] http://dlmf.nist.gov/.

[2] http://egomath.projekty.ms.mff.cuni.cz/.

[3] http://search.mathweb.org/.

[4] https://mir.fi.muni.cz/mias/.

[5] http://www.latexsearch.com/.

[6] http://www.mathjax.org/.

[7] http://www.openmath.org/.

[8] http://www.w3.org/math/.

[9] A. Asperti, F. Guidi, C. Coen, E. Tassi, and S. Zacchiroli. A content based mathematical search engine: Whelp. *Types for Proofs and Programs*, pages 17–32, 2006.

[10] Y. Hijikata, H. Hashimoto, and S. Nishida. Search mathematical formulas by mathematical formulas. *Human Interface and the Management of Information. Designing Information Environments*, pages 404–411, 2009.

[11] M. Kohlhase and I. Sucan. A search engine for mathematical formulae. In *Artificial Intelligence and Symbolic Computation*, pages 241–253. Springer, 2006.

[12] B. Miller and A. Youssef. Technical aspects of the digital library of mathematical functions. *Annals of Mathematics and Artificial Intelligence*, 38(1):121–136, 2003.

[13] R. Miner and R. Munavalli. An approach to mathematical search through query formulation and data normalization. *Towards Mechanized Mathematical Assistants*, pages 342–355, 2007.

[14] J. Mišutka and L. Galamboš. Extending full text search engine for mathematical content. *Towards Digital Mathematics Library. Birmingham, United Kingdom, July 27th, 2008*, pages 55–67, 2008.

[15] T. Nguyen, S. Hui, and K. Chang. A lattice-based approach for mathematical search using formal concept analysis. *Expert Systems with Applications*, 2011.

[16] T. T. Nguyen, K. Chang, and S. C. Hui. A math-aware search engine for math question answering system. In X. wen Chen, G. Lebanon, H. Wang, and M. J. Zaki, editors, *CIKM*, pages 724–733. ACM, 2012.

[17] T. Schellenberg, B. Yuan, and R. Zanibbi. Layout based substitution tree indexing and retrieval for mathematical expressions. In *Proceedings of SPIE*, volume 8297, page 82970I, 2012.

[18] P. Sojka and M. Líška. Indexing and searching mathematics in digital libraries. *Intelligent Computer Mathematics*, pages 228–243, 2011.

[19] R. Zanibbi and D. Blostein. Recognition and retrieval of mathematical expressions. *International Journal on Document Analysis and Recognition*, pages 1–27, 2012.

[20] R. Zanibbi and B. Yuan. Keyword and image-based retrieval of mathematical expressions. In *IS&T/SPIE Electronic Imaging*, pages 78740I–78740I. International Society for Optics and Photonics, 2011.

[21] J. Zhao, M.-Y. Kan, and Y. L. Theng. Math information retrieval: user requirements and prototype implementation. In *Proceedings of the 8th ACM/IEEE-CS joint conference on Digital libraries*, pages 187–196. ACM, 2008.

Table 6: Comparison of the Top-5 Retrieval Results of the Sample Queries

Queries	Systems	Top-5 results
$\frac{x^2-1}{x^2+1}-\frac{2ix}{x^2+1}$ (Sub-structure match)	Wikipedia Search	1) $\frac{x^2+1}{(x+2)(x-1)\left(x^2+x+1\right)}$; 2) x^n-1; 3) $\frac{d}{dx}arctanx=\frac{1}{x^2+1}$; 4) $E_{KL}=\frac{1}{2}\left(\frac{U_K}{X_L}+\frac{U_L}{X_K}+\frac{U_M}{X_K}\frac{U_M}{X_L}\right)$; 5) $B_{16}\left(x\right)=x^{16}-8x^{15}+20x^{14}-\frac{182}{3}x^{12}+\frac{572}{3}x^{10}-429x^8+\frac{1820}{3}x^6-\frac{1382}{3}x^4+140x^2-\frac{3617}{510}$
	Egomath	1) $g\left(x\right)=\frac{x^2-1}{x^2+1}-\frac{2ix}{x^2+1}$; No more results.
	WikiMirs	1) $g(x)=\frac{x^2-1}{x^2+1}-\frac{2ix}{x^2+1}$; 2) x^2+1; 3) $Imf\left(f\left(x\right)\right)=\frac{2x}{x^2+2}$; 4) $\frac{1}{x^2+1}$; 5) $\left(\arctan\left(x\right)\right)'=\frac{1}{x^2+1}$
$\frac{\tan\frac{A-B}{2}}{\tan\frac{A+B}{2}}$ (Sub-structure match)	Wikipedia Search	1) $\tan\frac{\alpha}{2}\tan\frac{\beta}{2}+\tan\frac{\beta}{2}\tan\frac{\gamma}{2}+\tan\frac{\gamma}{2}\tan\frac{\alpha}{2}=1$; 2) $\frac{a-b}{a+b}=\frac{\tan[\frac{1}{2}(\alpha-\beta)]}{\tan[\frac{1}{2}(\alpha+\beta)]}$; 3) $\frac{a-b}{a+b}=\frac{\tan[\frac{1}{2}(\alpha-\beta)]}{\tan[\frac{1}{2}(\alpha+\beta)]}$; 4) $\frac{\tan\frac{A-B}{2}}{\tan\frac{A+B}{2}}=\frac{a-b}{a+b}\frac{\tan\frac{A-C}{2}}{\tan\frac{A+C}{2}}=\frac{a-c}{a+c}\frac{\tan\frac{B-C}{2}}{\tan\frac{B+C}{2}}=\frac{b-c}{b+c}$; 5) $\frac{\frac{d[D]}{dt}}{\frac{d[C]}{dt}}=\frac{k_2K[A]}{k_1[A]}=\frac{k_2K}{k_1}$
	Egomath	No result.
	WikiMirs	1) $\frac{\tan\frac{A-B}{2}}{\tan\frac{A+B}{2}}=\frac{a-b}{a+b}\frac{\tan\frac{A-C}{2}}{\tan\frac{A+C}{2}}=\frac{a-c}{a+c}\frac{\tan\frac{B-C}{2}}{\tan\frac{B+C}{2}}=\frac{b-c}{b+c}$; 2) $A-B$; 3) $A+B$; 4) $\frac{1}{AB}=\frac{1}{A-B}\left(\frac{1}{B}-\frac{1}{A}\right)=\frac{1}{A-B}\int_B^A\frac{1}{z^2}dz$; 5) $\left(0.9\left(\frac{A+B}{2}+\frac{A-B}{2}\sin\left(4\right)\pi f_pt\right)+0.1\sin\left(2\right)\pi f_pt\right)\times 75kHz$
$\sqrt{2+\sqrt{2+\sqrt{2}}}$ (Sub-structure match)	Wikipedia Search	1) $\sin(84\frac{3}{8}^\circ)=\frac{1}{2}\sqrt{2+\sqrt{2+\sqrt{2+\sqrt{2}}}}$; 2) $x=\sqrt{2+\sqrt{2+\sqrt{2+\sqrt{2+\cdots}}}}$; 3) $\frac{\sqrt{2}}{2}\cdot\frac{\sqrt{2+\sqrt{2}}}{2}\cdot\frac{\sqrt{2+\sqrt{2+\sqrt{2}}}}{2}\cdot\cdots=\frac{2}{\pi}$; 4) $\pi=2\times\frac{2}{\sqrt{2}}\times\frac{2}{\sqrt{2+\sqrt{2}}}\times\frac{2}{\sqrt{2+\sqrt{2+\sqrt{2}}}}\times\frac{2}{\sqrt{2+\sqrt{2+\sqrt{2+\sqrt{2}}}}}\times\cdots$; 5) $2+\sqrt{2}+\sqrt{6}$
	Egomath	1) $\pi=2\times\frac{2}{\sqrt{2}}\times\frac{2}{\sqrt{2+\sqrt{2}}}\times\frac{2}{\sqrt{2+\sqrt{2+\sqrt{2}}}}\times\frac{2}{\sqrt{2+\sqrt{2+\sqrt{2+\sqrt{2}}}}}\times\ldots$; 2) $\frac{2}{\pi}=\frac{\sqrt{2}}{2}.\frac{\sqrt{2+\sqrt{2}}}{2}.\frac{\sqrt{2+\sqrt{2+\sqrt{2}}}}{2}\ldots$; No more results.
	WikiMirs	1) $\sin(78\frac{3}{4}^\circ)=\frac{1}{2}\sqrt{2+\sqrt{2+\sqrt{2}}}$; 2) $\sin(84\frac{3}{8}^\circ)=\frac{1}{2}\sqrt{2+\sqrt{2+\sqrt{2+\sqrt{2}}}}$; 3) $\pi=2\times\frac{2}{\sqrt{2}}\times\frac{2}{\sqrt{2+\sqrt{2}}}\times\frac{2}{\sqrt{2+\sqrt{2+\sqrt{2}}}}\times\frac{2}{\sqrt{2+\sqrt{2+\sqrt{2+\sqrt{2}}}}}\times\cdots$; 4) $\frac{2}{\pi}=\frac{\sqrt{2}}{2}\cdot\frac{\sqrt{2+\sqrt{2}}}{2}\cdot\frac{\sqrt{2+\sqrt{2+\sqrt{2}}}}{2}\cdots$; 5) $2+\sqrt{2}$
$\sum_{i=0}^{\infty}a_iX^i$ (Fuzzy match)	Wikipedia Search	1) $\int x^m\exp\left(ix^n\right)dx=\int\sum_{l=0}^{\infty}\frac{i^lx^{m+nl}}{l!}dx=\sum_{l=0}^{\infty}\frac{i^l}{(m+nl+1)}\frac{x^{m+nl+1}}{l!}$; 2) $\frac{1}{(1-x)^2}=\sum_{n=1}^{\infty}nx^{n-1}$; 3) $e_1=\sum_i x_i$; 4) $\sum_{i=1}^n w_i{x_i}^p{}^{\frac{1}{p}}\leq\sum_{i=1}^{n}w_i{x_i}^q{}^{\frac{1}{q}}$; 5) $\frac{1}{NT}\int_{NT}\left[\sum_{n=-\infty}^{\infty}x[n]\cdot\delta(t-nT)\right]e^{-i2\pi\frac{k}{NT}t}dt$
	Egomath	No result.
	WikiMirs	1) $\left(\sum_{i=0}^n a_iX^i\right)+\left(\sum_{i=0}^n b_iX^i\right)=\sum_{i=0}^n\left(a_i+b_i\right)X^i$; 2) $\left(\sum_{i=0}^n a_iX^i\right)+\left(\sum_{i=0}^n b_iX^i\right)=\sum_{i=0}^n\left(a_i+b_i\right)X^i$; 3) $f\left(x\right)=\sum_{i=0}^n a_ix^i;g\left(x\right)=\sum_{i=0}^m b_ix^i$; 4) $i=0$; 5) $\ldots=\sum_{i=0}^N\left(N\right)_iA^{-i}-\sum_{i=0}^N\left(N-1\right)_iA^{-i}$
$\log\frac{z}{(1-z)^2}$ (Sub-structure match & Fuzzy match)	Wikipedia Search	1) $\arcsin\left(z\right)=-i\log\left(iz+\sqrt{1-z^2}\right)$; 2) $\Gamma\left(z\right)\Gamma\left(z+\frac{1}{2}\right)=2^{1-2z}\sqrt{\pi}\Gamma\left(2z\right)$; 3) ${}_2F_1(a,1-a;c;z)=\Gamma(c)z^{\frac{1-c}{2}}(1-z)^{\frac{c-1}{2}}P_{-a}^{1-c}(1-2z)$; 4) $\mathrm{Li}_{-1}\left(z\right)=\sum_{k=1}^{\infty}kz^k=\frac{z}{(1-z)^2}$; 5) $\frac{1}{1-z}\sum\left(k-1\right)\frac{z^k}{k}=\frac{z}{(1-z)^2}-\frac{1}{1-z}\log\left(\frac{1}{1-z}\right)$
	Egomath	No result.
	WikiMirs	1) $\frac{1}{2}\exp\left(\frac{1}{2}\log\left(\frac{1}{(1-z)^2}\right)\right)+\frac{1}{2}\exp\left(\frac{1}{2}\log\left(1+z\right)^2\right)$; 2) $=\frac{a^2}{1-z}+\frac{az}{(1-z)^2}+\frac{az}{(1-z)^2}+\frac{z}{(1-z)^2}+\frac{2z^2}{(1-z)^3}=\frac{a^2}{1-z}+\frac{(2a+1)z}{(1-z)^2}+\frac{2z^2}{(1-z)^3}$; 3) $\mathrm{Li}_{-1}\left(z\right)=\sum_{k=1}^{\infty}kz^k=\frac{z}{(1-z)^2}$; 4) $\log\left(\frac{1}{\lvert z\rvert}\right)$; 5) $=\frac{a^2}{1-z}+\frac{(2a+1)z}{(1-z)^2}+\frac{2z^2}{(1-z)^3}$
$\sum_{n=0}\frac{f^{(n)}(a)}{n!}(x-a)^n$ (Sub-structure match & Fuzzy match)	Wikipedia Search	1) $N(x)=\sum_{n=0}^{\infty}H(x-E_n)$; 2) $\sum_{n=0}^{\infty}\frac{f^{(n)}(a)}{n!}(x-a)^n$; 3) $\left(\sum_{n=0}^{\infty}a_nx^n\right)\left(\sum_{n=0}^{\infty}b_nx^n\right)=\sum_{i=0}^{\infty}\sum_{j=0}^{\infty}a_ib_jx^{i+j}=\sum_{n=0}^{\infty}\left(\sum_{i=0}^n a_ib_{n-i}\right)x^n=\sum_{n=0}^{\infty}c_nx^n$; 4) $r_6(n)=\frac{\pi^3n^2}{2}\left(\frac{c_1(n)}{1}-\frac{c_4(n)}{8}-\frac{c_3(n)}{27}-\frac{c_8(n)}{64}+\frac{c_5(n)}{125}-\frac{c_{12}(n)}{216}-\frac{c_7(n)}{343}-\frac{c_{16}(n)}{512}+\ldots\right)$; 5) $T_f(z)=\sum_{k=0}^{\infty}\frac{(z-c)^k}{2\pi i}\int_\gamma\frac{f(w)}{(w-c)^{k+1}}dw=\frac{1}{2\pi i}\int_\gamma\frac{f(w)}{w-c}\sum_{k=0}^{\infty}\left(\frac{z-c}{w-c}\right)^kdw=\frac{1}{2\pi i}\int_\gamma\frac{f(w)}{w-c}\left(\frac{1}{1-\frac{z-c}{w-c}}\right)dw=\frac{1}{2\pi i}\int_\gamma\frac{f(w)}{w-z}dw=f(z)$
	Egomath	No result.
	WikiMirs	1) $\sum_{n=0}^{\infty}\frac{f^{(n)}(a)}{n!}(x-a)^n$; 2) $\left(\sum_{n=0}^{\infty}a_nX^n\right)\left(\sum_{n=0}^{\infty}b_nX^n\right)=\sum_{n=0}^{\infty}c_nX^n$; 3) $\left(\sum_{n=0}^{\infty}2^nx_n,\sum_{n=0}^{\infty}2^ny_n\right)\leftrightarrow\sum_{n=0}^{\infty}2^{2n}x_n+\sum_{n=0}^{\infty}2^{2n+1}y_n$; 4) $u=\sum_{n=0}^{\infty}f_i^{(n)}u_n=\sum_{n=0}^{\infty}e_i^{(n)}v_n$; 5) $n=0$

Interacting with and through a Digital Library Collection: Commenting behavior in Flickr's The Commons

Sally Jo Cunningham
University of Waikato
New Zealand
sallyjo@cs.waikato.ac.nz

Malika Mahoui
Polis Center, IUPUI
1200 Waterway Blvd,
Indianapolis, IN 46202

ABSTRACT
There is growing interest by digital collection providers to engage collection users in interacting with the collection (e.g. by tagging or annotating collection contents) and with the collection organizers and other users (e.g. to form loose 'communities' associated with the collection). At present, little has been documented as to the uptake of these mechanisms in specific collections, or the range of behaviors that emerge as users bend existing facilities to their own needs. This paper is one step in that direction: it describes the social information behaviors exhibited in a cultural heritage photography collection in The Commons on Flickr, and suggests implications for digital library design in response to these behaviors.

Categories and Subject Descriptors
H.3.7 [**Digital Libraries**]: User issues

General Terms
Design, Human Factors

Keywords
Social Commenting, Public Photography Collection

1. INTRODUCTION & PREVIOUS WORK
Social tagging provides a tremendous opportunity for collection providers to better support the search/browsing of images, whereby users - not necessarily librarians, voluntarily tag resources they have accessed. Initial users' tagging activity was all grouped under one category, namely "tagging" to differentiate it from the expert generated metadata. However as the annotator community continues to grow, a new need emerges to differentiate between the types of tags (i.e. annotations) provided by users. Flick is among the pioneers in making this feature available for users. Three types of annotations are available: tags, notes, and comments. In this paper we focus on an examination of notes and comments, as these annotation types are less well studied than tags (eg, [1], [2], [4], [8]).

Specifically, we examine note and comment behavior in a collection of historic photographs housed in Flickr's The Commons. We are not the first to analyze activity in The Commons. Vaughn [7] includes an overview user annotation behavior as reported by institutions contributing to The Commons. Stvilia and Jorgensen [4] examined tagging and commenting over the Library of Congress Flickr photostream. That work primarily focused on tags quality; it examined over 28,000 tags posted to 7,192 photos, but the sample of comments was limited to 257, over 20 photos. Further, the convenience sampling of comments aimed to include mainly comments likely to include potential metadata. In contrast, this present study focuses primarily on user-provided notes and comments rather than tags, and examines a larger set of comments (2022) and notes (586), with a view to exploring the full range of user behavior as exhibited in those user annotations of the photos.

2. DATA AND METHODS
The photostream from the National Media Museum or NMM (physically located in West Yorkshire, the UK) was selected for the analysis, based on its size (462 photos; small enough to be manageable but large enough to include a reasonable variety in the set of responses). The NMM was an early adopter of The Commons, joining in 2008. The collection focuses on 19th century and early 20th century photography, and includes both professional and amateur photos over a broad range of topics.

The NMM's offerings on The Commons are professionally curated into related groups, with each group accompanied by contextual commentary. Individual photographs are presented with basic metadata where known (i.e., photographer, date, location, identification of people/places/activities depicted in the photo), a brief descriptive title (e.g. "Baby show", "Lord and Lady Curzon on an elephant"), and an initial set of tags. Users are encouraged to submit additional tags, which are then considered by curators for inclusion in the photo's tag set.

Users can also interact with the collection by: favorite-ing a photo; including this photo in a personally curated gallery based on The Commons; adding a comment to the comment stream for the photograph, or adding a brief textual note directly to the photo itself, together with a bounding box indicating the portion of the photo being described.

The Flickr API (www.flickr.com/services/api/) was used to extract the following metadata for each of the 462 photographs in the NMM photostream: image id; photo page URL; number of views; number of comments, text for each comment, and user-id of each comment creator; number of notes, text for each note, and user-id of note creator; number of user-created galleries that the photo is included in; number of tags, and tag text. This snapshot of use was created in January 2012. The number of times that each photo was favorite-ed could not be reliably extracted via the Flickr API, and so was added manually.

Comments and notes frequently reflect the poster's opinion of the document, either explicitly through sentiment-bearing words (e.g. "lovely", "hate") or more subtly (e.g., through the use of emoticons and modified spelling and punctuation for emphasis). Sentiment analysis techniques seek to provide a quantitative measure of whether the opinion expressed in a document reflects a generally positive or negative attitude towards its subject.

Table 1. Summary of user interactions with the NMM photostream

Interaction type	Count of photos with interaction	Total no. of interactions for all photos	Minimum	Maximum	Mean	Median	Std dev
Views	420	2,595,417	6	14,0495	6,155.75	11,553	135,417
Favorites	350	27,782	0	2,370	66.15	7.5	174.96
Tags	414	4,595	1	48	11.1	7.5	8.69
Comments	219	4,199	1	500	19.17	5	46.22
Galleries	165	972	1	46	5.89	4	7.1
Notes	116	586	1	32	5.05	3	5.51

For this present paper, we use the SentiStrength software [5] (http://sentistrength.wlv.ac.uk) to analyze note and comment text. SentiStrength is tailored to brief documents, and has been tested and validated over corpora broadly similar in length to the notes and comments posted to the NMM photographs (e.g., MySpace [5] posts). Accuracy in categorization compares favorably to that obtained by other machine learning methods and approaches that of manual classification for negative sentiment (though it is slightly less accurate in classifying positive sentiment) [5].

We also conducted a content analysis of all 586 of the Notes and roughly half of the Comments (2022). Initial potential codes were drawn from previous literature analyzing tags in commercial and social media sites [8] and of Flickr and The Commons ([1] [4] [7]); additional categories emerged from an iterative coding of first the Notes and then the Comments. One researcher conducted the initial coding. The second researcher examined the coding for a sample of 200 Comments; agreement was reached on the categories and coding for this sample, indicating >90% reliability.

3. ANALYSIS

In this section we describe quantitative analysis (frequency counts, sentiment analysis) over the full set of notes and comments from the NMM The Commons collection. For the qualitative analysis (Sections 4.3 – 4.5) the data set was reduced to a more manageable size by including all 586 notes, and roughly half of the comments (2022). In total, of the 219 photographs in the NMM collection that included at least one note or comment, 190 photos had their notes, their comments, or both notes and comments analyzed.

3.1 Overview of Datasets

Table 2 summarizes the counts of tags, gallery inclusion, notes, inclusion, 'favorites', notes, and comments across all photos in the NMM collection. The relative frequencies of each type of interaction can likely be explainable by the ease of executing the action and its similarity to facilities in other common systems: a photo must be viewed before any other action can be taken; 'favorite-ing' takes a single mouse click and is common on social media sites; tagging is a common activity for images that was popularized by the host site, Flickr, and tags are also seeded by the NMM; comments are usually longer than tags and require more effort than adding a favorite; galleries take more effort still, as they involve creating a sub-collection of photos; and finally the notes facility is less common in other websites and the availability of the notes creation functionality is less visible to users.

Table 2. Summary of text in notes and comments

	Total words	Avg words	Total chars	Avg chars
Notes (586)	4,052	6.91	22,357	38.15
Comments (2022)	32,517	16.07	332,361	164.29

Users must create an id and log in, in order to add comments and notes—and so a unique userid is attached to each user posting. For the NMM photostream, 180 unique posters contributed the 586 analyzed notes, and 1488 unique posters contributed the 2022 analyzed comments.

3.2 Sentiment Analysis

The SentiStrength software [50] was used to analyze the text of the notes. As the standard version of SentiStrength is tuned to process English text, non-English comments (primarily Chinese and Spanish) were removed, and URLs and mark-up symbols were removed—a total of 5. The remaining 581 notes were analyzed using the default SentiStrength settings; sentiment values for each comment are calculated on a range of 1 (slightly positive) to 5 (strongly positive) and -1 (slightly negative) to -5 (strongly negative). Comments were culled of spam postings, leaving a total of 1967 comments for sentiment analysis.

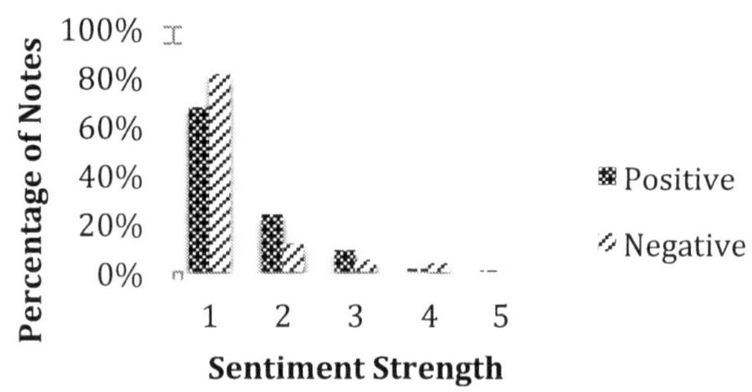

Figure 1a. Sentiment strength for 581 notes.

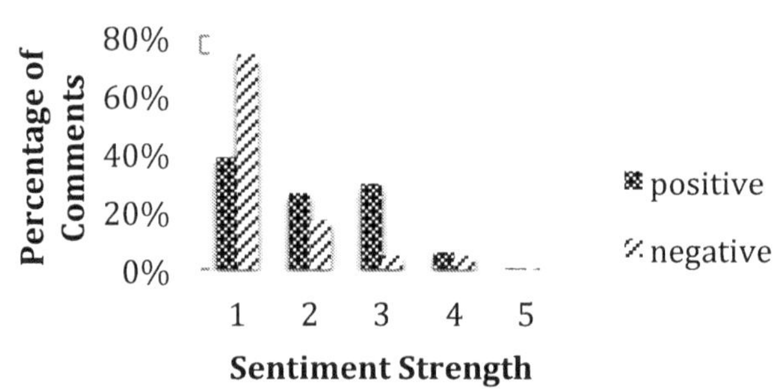

Figure 1b. Sentiment analysis for 1968 comments

Note text tends to be neutral, though slightly skewed to the positive: the mean strength of positivity is 1.44 while the mean strength on the corresponding negativity scale is -1.31. From Figure 1 we see that strong sentiment is rare, but when it occurs, it is usually positive.

Comments text shows a more pronounced positive tendency: the mean strength of positivity is 2.03 and the mean strength on the negativity scale is -1.41.

3.3 Behavior categories

Table 3 presents the broad categories of posting categories that emerged in the analysis of the NMM collection Notes and Comments. We see that the lengthier Comments lend themselves to a greater variety of behaviors.

Table 3. Categorization of notes and comments

	Notes (586 total)		Comments (2022 total)	
Category	Count	%	Count	%
Opinion	123	21%	1138	56.3%
Question	79	13.5%	70	3.5%
Assertion	144	24.5%	292	14.3%
Performance	198	33.8%	198	9.8%
Self-presentation	28	4.8%	344	17%
Response to other posters	39	6.7%	80	4%
Reference to NMM	—	—	85	4.2%
Action taken with photo	—	—	31	1.5%
Spam	—	—	353	17.4%
Un-interpretable	40	6.8%	67	3.3%

Opinion statements present the poster's personal viewpoint on some aspect of the photograph (this category is further analyzed in Section 3.4), where *Assertions* present more objectively grounded statements (further analyzed in Section 3.5). With *Questions* and *Responses to other posters*, posters engaged each other in (sometimes extended) conversations. Questions ranged from the highly specific (*Anyone else see a faint ring here?*) to broad queries encompassing the entire photo (*WTF!?*).

Performance and *Self-presentation* posts are also socially directed, though in these cases the focus shifts at least partially to the poster. Both categories are drawn from an earlier analysis of social tagging [8]. With *Performance* posts, the poster is almost literally putting on a show: expressing a sarcastic, witty, joking, or otherwise extreme reaction to the photograph (for example, annotating a photo of infants with *We represent, the Lolipop kids, the Lolipop kids, the Lolipop kids*). These posts often assume that the readers can interpret the pop- or sub-cultural references (in this case, to the 1939 movie version of *The Wizard of Oz*). *Self-presentation* is closely associated with *Performance*, but here the emphasis is on the poster and her engagement with the photograph (eg, *i deserve to have this picture*). We also note that both *Performance* and *Self-presentation* frequently also entail a positive or negative *Opinion* (and so a post may also be coded to *Opinion*).

References to the NMM are found only in the Comments. These are uniformly positive and primarily express appreciation for the availability of the photostream (*thanks for sharing them*). Their absence from the Notes can likely be ascribed to the briefer nature of the notes (these *References* most commonly appear at the end of a longer comment).

Spam queries are just that—off-topic messages frequently attempting to direct the reader to a commercial site or irrelevant Flickr photostream—though the cleverer spammers also include a positive *Opinion* about the photograph. *Un-interpretable* posts are generally either too brief (*whoa*) to be categorized or otherwise were not understandable by the researchers (*kgjdudnviniumidheiwsgzibynihilgi*)—though we recognize that some posts may have fallen into this category through a failure to recognize cultural references posts intended as *Performance*.

The descriptions of *Actions taken with the photo* provide an intriguing glimpse of what some users of The Commons do with photographs beyond viewing them. These users may 'Photoshop' the images to, for example, add color to the black and white photos or to create more amusing or attractive images. Users also describing incorporating them into personal Flickrstreams or other photo displays (beyond their use in Flickr Galleries) and adding photos to Wikipedia pages.

3.4 Characterizing Opinion statements

Table 4 presents a further breakdown of the subject of the Opinions expressed in the NMM collection Notes and Comments. As would be expected from the sentiment analysis (Section 3.2), opinions directed at the *Image as whole* were largely positive (*amazing!, beautiful shot*)—though as stated in Section 4.3, this response is skewed by *Spam* posts including a brief positive statement. Note that as a single Comment or Note could include more than one Opinion, the percentages do not total 100%

The Notes mechanism for attaching to a post directly to a bounding box on the photograph itself makes that form of posting more natural for entering statements or questions specific to a particular *Person, Animal or object* in the photograph. A surprising proportion of Notes were directed at the *Image as a whole*—and these posts tended to be problematic, either to interpret or to view. If the bounding box encompassed a small part of the photo then its reference could be ambiguous; on the other hand if the bounding box encompassed all or most of the photo then it often obscured other Notes, sometimes completely (though they could still be extracted via the Flickr API).

Opinions on an abstract aspect of the images, such as *Photographic techniques* employed, are more naturally presented through the Comments mechanism. Unexpectedly, the *Mood or emotion* inspired in the viewer occurs proportionally slightly more frequently in the Notes—though in the Notes these posts most often refer to emotion inspired by the element in the bounding box, where the Comments refer to the emotion inspired by the photograph as a whole (*sad,hope..woried..all in one single shot*).

Table 3. Breakdown of subject of Opinion statements (from 123 notes, 1138 comments)

	Notes		Comments	
Opinion subject	Count	%	Count	%
Photographer	1	0.8%	14	1.2%
Activity	3	2.4%	53	4.7%
Mood or emotion	13	10.6%	170	14.9%
Animal or object	29	23.6%	38	3.3%
Image as a whole	37	30.1%	784	68.9%
Person	41	33.3%	67	5.9%
Activity			53	4.7%
Photographic technique/staging			95	8.3%

3.5 Characterizing assertions

The bulk of the assertions for both Notes and Comments consist of statements presenting *Factual statements about the subjects* of the photo, *Identifying an object* appearing in the photo, or explaining or giving background on *a Photographic technique or the staging* of the photo (81.3% of Assertions in Notes, 90.1% in Comments). These categories appear promising as sources of user-supplied metadata, perhaps first subject to quality control from curators [4] [7]. Posts asserting *Agreement or Disagreement with another poster* are often corroborating or refuting a statement in one of the former categories; so while these posts are relatively rare, they may prove valuable as evidence for whether or not to accept metadata suggested by previous posts. Similarly, posts explaining the false *Resemblance of an object in the photo* to something else may be useful in rejecting metadata suggestions, or perhaps in adding metadata to clarify the identity of people/objects in the photographs where that may be uncertain.

Table 5. Breakdown of Assertion category (from 144 Notes, 323 comments)

	Notes		Comments	
Assertion type	Count	%	Count	%
(Dis)Agreement with another poster	3	2.1%	10	3.1%
Fact / metadata for subject(s)	21	14.6%	124	38.4%
Resemblance to something else	24	16.7%	19	5.9%
Photographic technique or staging of photo	37	25.7%	97	30%
Identification of object in photo	59	41%	70	21.7%
			31	9.6%

4. Communities characteristics

To better understand the characteristics of each users' contributing community, namely tags' contributors (TC), notes' contributors (NC), and comments' (CC), we studied the overlapping between these three types of users' communities. We used the Positive Specific Agreement (PSA) [5] measure to compute the overlapping. PSA is a measure of the degree of overlap between two sets. The PSA value ranges from 0 to 1, where the value "1" is an indication of maximum overlapping between two sets.

More specifically, given an image in NMM collection, and two sets of contributors C1 and C2 from (TC, NC, CC) associated to the image: $\text{PSA}(C1, C2) = \frac{2a}{2a+b+c}$

where "a" is the number of common annotators in both C1 and C2 and "b" and "c" correspond to the number of distinct annotators in C1 and C2 respectively. Both C1 and C2 need to be not empty sets to be considered in the computation. Given any two types of annotators from (TC, NC, CC), the overlapping between them is determined by the average overlapping computed over all images in the study. We also extended the PSA measure to compute the users' overlapping between the 3 communities. The results of the analysis (Table 6) show very little overlap between the user communities. In the few instances where the overlap was relatively high, it corresponded to only one person contributing to the image by creating a short note and then an extended comment about the same topic.

Table 6. Overlap between user communities

TC & NC	TC & CC	CC & NC	TC & NC & CC
2%	6%	5%	0%

5. Conclusions

This study supports the conclusions of earlier research (eg, [4] [7]) that user annotations such as notes and comments may be useful in suggesting additional factual metadata for collection documents. Our more detailed analysis of the comment and note texts also uncovers other potential categories of metadata: specifically, the general mood or emotion of an image and the potential sources of confusion in a photo (that is, the objects that resemble something else).

We also uncover evidence that users wish to interact with other users—sometimes purposefully by asking and answering 'serious' questions about a photograph, but often playfully (as seen in the Performance and Self-expression posts). These sorts of interactions are less useful to collection curators but obviously enjoyed and appreciated by users; it may be time to, as [3] suggests, "give digital libraries a social life" by augmenting the (often minimal or non-existent) facilities for this sort of interaction in digital library systems.

Automated techniques such as Sentiment Analysis allow the curator to gauge the users' reactions to individual documents, sub-collections, and the collection as a whole. Strong reactions—either positive or negative—could be useful in guiding further collection development, by identifying 'hot' or 'cold' elements.

Analysis of community overlap indicates that there are few users who post with both the Notes and the Comments. This provides supporting evidence for our initial hypothesis that the different affordances of the two posting mechanisms would inspire different behaviors in posting. It would be interesting to incorporate a similar choice of annotation mechanisms in other existing digital libraries, to observe the emergent user behaviors in those domains.

6. REFERENCES

[1] Angus, E., and Tehlwall, M. 2010. Motivations for image publishing and tagging on Flickr. *14th International Conference on Electronic Publishing*, 189-204.

[2] Golder, S.A. and B.A. Huberman. 2006. *Usage patterns of collaborative tagging systems.* J. Inf. Sci., 32(2), 198-208.

[3] Marshall, C., and Bly, S. 2004. Sharing encountered information: digital libraries get a social life." *Digital Libraries, 2004. Proceedings of the 2004 Joint ACM/IEEE Conference on.* IEEE, 218-227.

[4] Stvilia, B., and Jorgensen, C. 2010. Member activities and quality of tags in a collection of historical photographs in Flickr. *Journal of the American Society for Information Science and Technology*, 61(12), 2477-2489.

[5] Thelwall, M., Buckley, K., Paltoglou, G., Cai, D, and Kappas, A. 2010. Sentiment strength detection in short informal text. *Journal of the American Society for Information Science and Technology,* 61(12), 2544-2558.

[6] Hripcsak, G., Rothschild, A.S. 2005. Agreement, the F-Measure, and Reliability in Information Retrieval. *Journal of the American Medical Informatics Association,* 12(3): 296-298.

[7] Vaughan, Jason. 2010. Insights into the Commons on Flickr. *portal: Libraries and the Academy* 10.2, 185-214.

[8] Zollers, A. 2007. Emerging motivations for tagging: Expression, performance, and activism. *Workshop on Tagging and Metadata for Social Information Organization*, held at the 16th International World Wide Web Conference.

A Comparative Study of Academic and Wikipedia Ranking

Xin Shuai
School of Informatics and Computing
Indiana University
Bloomington
IN, USA
xshuai@indiana.edu

Zhuoren Jiang
College of Transportation Management
Dalian Maritime University
Dalian, China
jzr1986@hotmail.com

Xiaozhong Liu
School of Library and Information Science
Indiana University
Bloomington
IN, USA
liu237@indiana.edu

Johan Bollen
School of Informatics and Computing
Indiana University
Bloomington
IN, USA
jbollen@indiana.edu

ABSTRACT

In addition to its broad popularity Wikipedia is also widely used for scholarly purposes. Many Wikipedia pages pertain to academic papers, scholars and topics providing a rich ecology for scholarly uses. Scholarly references and mentions on Wikipedia may thus shape the "societal impact" of a certain scholarly communication item, but it is not clear whether they shape actual "academic impact". In this paper we compare the impact of papers, scholars, and topics according to two different measures, namely scholarly citations and Wikipedia mentions. Our results show that academic and Wikipedia impact are positively correlated. Papers, authors, and topics that are mentioned on Wikipedia have higher academic impact than those are not mentioned. Our findings validate the hypothesis that Wikipedia can help assess the impact of scholarly publications and underpin relevance indicators for scholarly retrieval or recommendation systems.

Categories and Subject Descriptors

H.3.7 [**Information Storage and Retrieval**]: Digital Libraries

Keywords

Wikipedia; Scholar Impact; Citation Analysis

1. INTRODUCTION

Science Citation Index established by Garfield [2] makes citation statistics a gold standard for the assessment of scholarly impact. Citation data is held to be a valid and reliable indicator of scholarly impact because it represents an explicit and objective acknowledgement of influence by expert authors. Yet, the Web 2.0 is revolutionizing scholarly practices. A growing number of scholars discuss and share the research literature on Twitter and Facebook [6], organize it in social reference managers like Mendeley, and review it in blogs [5]. The increasing role of social media in scholarship requires new ways to assess impact beyond traditional approaches on the basis of citation data. Wikipedia, as a collaboratively edited, multilingual, and free Internet encyclopedia, has become an important source for the creation, distribution, and acquisition of scientific knowledge. Kittur et al. shows that over 25% of pre-2008 articles in Wikipedia are related to natural or social sciences [3].

Wikipedia editors frequently reference scholarly entities, such as papers, scholars, and topics. We refer to such mentions as "Wikipedia citation", implying that their value or influence has been explicitly recognized by the Wikipedia community. Unlike "academic citations" that represent the explicit recognition of expert scholars, the authority of a "Wikipedia citation" is uncertain and will need to be examined further.

Several studies have compared "academic citations" with "Wikipedia citations". Nielsen [8] showed that citations in Wikipedia correlate well with statistics from the Journal Citation Reports. Evans and Krauthammer [1] investigated this relationship at the journal article level and found that PubMed journal articles that are mentioned in Wikipedia have significantly higher academic citation counts than an equivalent random article subset. Although these findings show that Wikipedia citations are an indicator of academic impact, their results are limited to journals or articles published in the same journal.

Here we extend this line of work to larger-scale data and across a broader research area for a more diverse set of scholarly entities. This paper makes an effort to quantitatively compare the rankings of articles, authors, and topics selected from ACM Digital Library publication data on the basis of their academic citations and Wikipedia citations. Our major findings include:

- Academic and Wikipedia rankings exhibit a positive correlation across all types of scholarly entities.
- Papers, authors, and topics that are mentioned on Wikipedia have a higher average academic impact than those that are not mentioned.
- Wikipedia mentions are biased towards high-impact scholars who publish many papers.
- Wikipedia mentions are biased towards trending topics that occur in many articles.

2. RELATED WORK

Studying the influence of social web on the scholarly community opens a new direction for scientometrics. Priem et al. propose scientometrics 2.0 [4] and Altmetrics [5] to measure scholarly impact from social media data. Xin et al. [6] compare different types of online responses to newly submitted preprint publications, namely article downloads, Twitter mentions and citations. Nielsen [8], Evans and Krauthammer [1] correlate journal citations to Wikipedia and academia. Our study extends this work by comparing the rankings of three different scholarly entities, i.e. papers, authors, and keywords, from a large-scale dataset in the field of Computing between scholarly sources and Wikipedia.

3. PROBLEM DEFINITION

The framework of our study is shown in Figure 1. P is a set of scientific papers, A is a set of authors, K is a set of keywords (topics) and W is a set of Wikipedia articles. $X = P \cup A \cup K$ is a set of heterogeneous scholarly entities.

[Academic Citation] AC includes paper citation $AC_p = \{(p_i, p_j)|p_i \ cites \ p_j, p_i, p_j \in P\}$, author citation $AC_a = \{(a_i, a_j)|a_i \ cites \ a_j, a_i, a_j \in A\}$ and keyword citation $AC_k = \{(k_i, k_j)|k_i \ cites \ k_j, k_i, k_j \in K\}$

[Wikipedia Citation] $WC = \{(w_i, x_i)|w_i \ mentions \ x_i, w_i \in W, x_i \in X\}$ represents the acknowledgement of the scholarly entity x_i from Wikipedia article w_i

[Paper Citation Network] $G_p = \{P, A, K, AC_p\}$ is a directed and unweighted heterogeneous network.

[Author Citation Network] $G_a = \{A, AC_p, F_a\}$ is a directed and weighted network derived from G_p, where F_a is a weight function that maps each edge (a_i, a_j) to an positive integer $f(a_i, a_j) \in \mathbb{N}^+$ that corresponds to the number of citations passing from a_i to a_j.

[Keyword Citation Network] $G_k = \{K, AC_k, F_k\}$ is a directed and weighted network derived from G_p, where F_k is a weight function that maps each edge (k_i, k_j) to a positive integer $f(k_i, k_j) \in \mathbb{N}^+$ that corresponds to the number of citations passing from k_i to k_j

[Wikipedia Interlinking Network] $G_w = \{W, E\}$ is a directed and unweighted network composed of Wikipedia articles and their internal links, where $(w_i, w_j) \in E$ indicates that w_i contains a hypertext linking to w_j.

[Ranking Function] $R(X, \Theta)$ maps $X = \{x_i\}$ into a sorted permutation X^* where $\Theta(x_i) \geq \Theta(x_j)$.

[Academic Ranking] $AR(X, \Theta)$ ranks X based on statistics calculated from ACM database, where $\Theta(x_i)$ can be Θ_{af} (the frequency of x_i), Θ_{ac} (the citation of x_i in G_x), or Θ_{ap} (the Pagerank of x_i in G_x).

[Wikipedia Ranking] $WR(X, \Theta)$ ranks X based on statistics calculated from Wikipedia, where $\Theta(x_i) = \sum_{w_j} S(w_j)$ satisfying that $(w_j, x_i) \in WC$. Especially, $S(w_j)$ is a score attached to each Wikipedia article, which can be constantly equal to one, or the total count of edits of w_j, or the Pagerank score of w_j in G_w. Therefore, we have three types of Θ for WR: Θ_{w1}, Θ_{we} and Θ_{wp}.

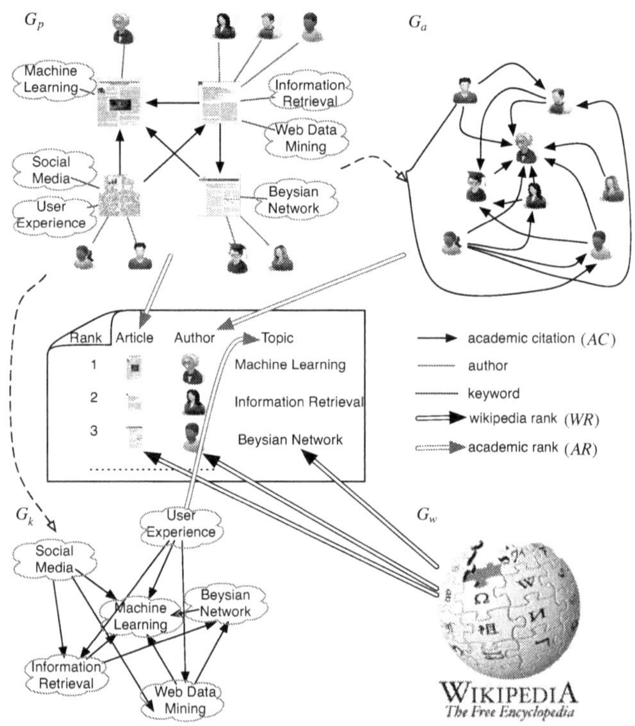

Figure 1: Academic ranking and Wikipedia ranking

The main goal of this study is to examine the relationship between $AR(X, \Theta)$ and $WR(X, \Theta)$. Specifically, we investigate three questions:

- What's the correlation between $AR(X)$ and $WR(X)$?
- How do different types of Θ affect above correlation?
- Are those scholarly entities mentioned in Wikipedia ranked higher in $AR(X)$ than those not mentioned?

4. METHODS

Two types of data sources, i.e. the ACM database and Wikipedia data, are involved in our study. Our analysis consists of three steps. First, we select a set of papers, authors, and keywords from the ACM database. Second, we build a Wikipedia search index and query it for these set papers, authors, and keywords. Third, we rank all papers, authors, and keywords based on $AR(X, \Theta)$ and $WR(X, \Theta)$, and compare the resulting rankings.

4.1 ACM data selection

The ACM database stores over 200K papers published in computer science journals and conferences, from 1980 to 2010. Most papers contain three types of metadata: a title, author, and keywords field. Each type of metadata needs careful filtering before we search for them in Wikipedia, since short queries (title, author names, keywords) may lead to false positives. We therefore decide to remove titles, authors, and keywords from our ACM database that match the properties in Table 1.

metadata	removed type
title	less than three non-stop words e.g. "On the Level", "Behavioral synthesis"
author	less than six tokens or one-letter first name e.g. "C. Richard" or "Li Li"
keyword	single word or occurs only once in database e.g. "program", i.e. "system initiated dialogue"

Table 1: Criteria to remove titles, authors, and keywords from our ACM database.

Once P, A, and K are selected, we construct G_p, G_a and G_k, based on which $AR(X, \Theta_{af})$, $AR(X, \Theta_{ac})$ and $AR(X, \Theta_{ap})$ are obtained.

4.2 Wikipedia search

The export data of the English version of Wikipedia is publicly available in XML format[1]. We use a Perl script *WikiPrep*[2] to parse this data and remove all discussion and talk pages, leaving only article pages. We further remove category, file, disambiguation, and redirect pages to make sure that each article page is about an explicit concept.

Since the to-be-ranked sets of papers, authors, and keywords come from the ACM database, the Wikipedia articles that are used to build the search index should match the topics of the ACM repository. Our preliminary tests showed that including Wikipedia articles that do not match ACM fields in the process of searching will enormously reduce the retrieval precision. Therefore, we adopt a two-step Wikipedia index building process on the assumption that the set of keywords K selected from ACM database are representative topics in computer science. First, all Wikipedia article pages are indexed using Lucene[3]. Second, we run a full-text search in the complete Wikipedia index for every keyword from K. In the retrieval results, only those Wikipedia articles containing at least two keywords are selected to construct G_w and build a computing-exclusive index named Wiki$_{cs}$. For each node in G_w, we compute the PageRank score and query its historical edit frequency using WikiMedia API[4]. Finally, we search P, A and K in Wiki$_{cs}$ and generate $WR(X, \Theta_{w1})$, $WR(X, \Theta_{we})$ and $WR(X, \Theta_{wp})$.

4.3 Evaluation measures

When X is searched in Wiki$_{cs}$, only a subset of X is found in Wikipedia and denoted as X_{wiki}. The complement of this subset X is denoted X_{nowiki}. We propose two measures to perform two types of ranking comparisons: (1) the ranking of X_{wiki} in ACM and Wikipedia , (2) the ranking of X_{wiki} and X_{nowiki} in ACM.

First, we use Spearman's rank correlation coefficient [7] to measure the quantitative relation between $AR(X, \Theta)$ and $WR(X, \Theta)$:

$$\rho = \frac{\sum_i (I_{x_i} - \bar{I_{x_i}})(I_{y_i} - \bar{I_{y_i}})}{\sqrt{\sum_i (I_{x_i} - \bar{I_{x_i}})^2 (I_{y_i} - \bar{I_{y_i}})^2}}, x_i, y_i \in X_{\text{wiki}} \quad (1)$$

where I_{x_i} and I_{y_i} are the index of x_i and y_i in X^* ranked by $AR(X, \Theta)$ and $WR(X, \Theta)$, respectively, and

$$\bar{I_{x_i}} = \frac{\sum_{x_i \in X_{\text{wiki}}} I_{x_i}}{|X_{\text{wiki}}|}, \bar{I_{y_i}} = \frac{\sum_{y_i \in X_{\text{wiki}}} I_{y_i}}{|X_{\text{wiki}}|} \quad (2)$$

Next, we define a Normalized Average Ranking (NAR) to measure the average ranking positions of a subset of entities in the whole ranking list.

$$\text{NAR}(X_{\text{sub}}) = \frac{\bar{I_{x_i}}}{\max(I_{x_j})}, x_i \in X_{\text{sub}}, x_j \in X, X_{\text{sub}} \subseteq X \quad (3)$$

where, X_{sub} can be either X_{wiki} or X_{nowiki}, and $\max(I_{x_j})$ is the maximum ranking index in X

5. RESULTS AND DISCUSSION

We obtain 122,350 papers, 163,172 authors[5] and 35,518 keywords from the ACM database. In addition, we select 357,345 Wikipedia articles from the Sep 2, 2012 Wikipedia dump, and build the search index Wiki$_{cs}$. After querying all selected papers, authors, and keywords in Wiki$_{cs}$[6], we find 3836 papers, 17564 authors and 20891 keywords that are mentioned on Wikipedia. We can see that only a very small portion of papers (0.03) and authors (0.1) but more than half of keywords occur in Wikipedia.

The statistics of G_p, G_a, G_k and G_w are shown in Table 2.

measure	G_p	G_a	G_k	G_w
num of nodes	122,350	163,172	35,518	357,345
num of edges	395,152	2,877,723	1,746,734	17,947,480
density	2.64-e^5	0.0001	0.0014	0.0001
clustering	0.1326	0.2754	0.4784	0.2903

Table 2: Descriptive statistics of paper, author, keywords, and Wikipedia citation networks.

The Spearman rank correlations between $AR(X)$ and $WR(X)$ using different Θ, i.e. Θ_{af}, Θ_{ap} and Θ_{ac}, for $AR(X, \Theta)$ and Θ_{w1}, Θ_{wp} and Θ_{we} for $WR(X, \Theta)$) are shown in Table 3.

The overall scholarly ranking and Wikipedia ranking are positively correlated. The p-values for all correlations are less than 0.001, hence we can reject the null-hypothesis that the two variables are not correlated. However, none of correlation coefficients are greater than 0.5, indicating significant differences between the scholarly community and the community of Wikipedia editors in recognizing the impact or importance of scholarly entities.

We note several interesting results. First, the inclusion of Wikipedia article weight does not improve the ranking correlation. Wikipedia ranking using Θ_{w1} consistently shows

[1]http://dumps.wikimedia.org/enwiki/
[2]http://www.cs.technion.ac.il/ gabr/resources/code/wikiprep/
[3]http://lucene.apache.org/
[4]http://www.mediawiki.org/wiki/API:Query

[5]We do not consider name ambiguity here and leave it for future work
[6]Titles and keywords use exact match, and authors use fuzzy match

	$WR(X, \Theta_{w1})$	$WR(X, \Theta_{wp})$	$WR(X, \Theta_{we})$
Paper			
$AR(P, \Theta_{ap})$	**0.1716**	0.1342	0.0913
$AR(P, \Theta_{ac})$	0.1652	0.1316	0.0863
Author			
$AR(A, \Theta_{af})$	0.2159	0.1319	0.0635
$AR(A, \Theta_{ap})$	**0.2521**	0.1753	0.0882
$AR(A, \Theta_{ac})$	0.2422	0.1684	0.0811
Keyword			
$AR(K, \Theta_{af})$	**0.4638**	0.3818	0.3478
$AR(K, \Theta_{ap})$	0.3235	0.2646	0.2340
$AR(K, \Theta_{ac})$	0.3311	0.2714	0.2437

Table 3: The Spearman rank-order correlation between scholarly ranking and Wikipedia ranking using different ranking criteria. The academic ranking is based on frequency of occurrence (Θ_{af}), citation PageRank (Θ_{ap}), and citation frequency (cited) (Θ_{ac}). The Wikipedia ranking takes into account Wikipedia page weight, including one (Θ_{w1}), editing frequency (Θ_{we}) and inter-linking PageRank (Θ_{wp}).

better correlation with the academic ranking than Θ_{wp} and Θ_{we}. It seems that "Authority" of Wikpedia page cannot provide information to better weight the importance of scholarly outcomes[7]. Second, Wikipedia pages tend to cite scholars of high scholarly reputation more than those who are "merely" productive. Θ_{af} tends to rank productive authors higher while Θ_{ap} and Θ_{ac} tend to rank the most cited authors higher. Ranking with Θ_{ap} shows higher correlation with Wikipedia ranking than Θ_{af} and Θ_{ac}, implying that reputable authors who published influential works are more favored by Wikipedia community than those that are new and productive. Third, Wikipedia tends to mention trending research topics more than classical or traditional topics. The situation of keyword ranking is different than author ranking, i.e. frequently occurring keywords are more likely to be mentioned in Wikipedia than most cited keywords ("classical" topics). It implies that Wikipedia editors prefer to discuss trending scientific topics when they create new, or edit existing Wikipedia pages.

	$AR(*, \Theta_{af})$	$AR(*, \Theta_{ap})$	$AR(*, \Theta_{ac})$
Paper			
P_{wiki}	N/A	0.3912	0.3316
P_{nowiki}	N/A	0.7576	0.7063
Author			
A_{wiki}	0.5307	0.4808	0.4362
A_{nowiki}	0.8185	0.7731	0.7290
Keyword			
K_{wiki}	0.3274	0.5369	0.5034
K_{nowiki}	0.5068	0.7125	0.6731

Table 4: The average academic ranking comparison between Wikipedia mentioned (X_{wiki}) and non-mentioned (X_{nowiki}) scholarly entities

Table 4 shows the differences in academic ranking between scholarly entities that are mentioned and those that are not mentioned in Wikipedia. It is apparent that papers, authors, and keywords that are mentioned on Wikipedia are ranked higher in the scholarly community than those are not mentioned. We use t-test to examine the differences and all corresponding p-values (consistently smaller than 0.001) confirm the statistical significance. It indicates that Wikipedia is a good social filtering system that recommends high impact papers, authors, and topics to the public.

[7]It is also possible that we did not find the correct way to measure Wikipedia article importance.

6. CONCLUSIONS

This paper compares the scholarly ranking and Wikipedia ranking of a set of selected papers, authors, and keywords (topics), from the field of Computer science. We run a full-text search of those papers, authors, and keywords in Wikipedia, and separate the sets into two subsets: X_{wiki} denotes the set of papers, authors, and keywords that are mentioned in Wikipedia, while X_{nowiki} represents the set that are not mentioned. First, we compute the Spearman rank-order correlation coefficient between scholarly and Wikipedia rankings of X_{wiki} using different ranking methods. We find that the two rankings are statistically significantly correlated and that the Wikipedia community favors reputable authors and trending topics. Second, we compare the average ranking of X_{wiki} and X_{nowiki} and found the former had much higher values than the latter. This implies that Wikipedia does serve as a collaborative social filtering system which is able to favor "classical" papers, authors, and topics, and recommend them to the general public.

7. ACKNOWLEDGMENTS

One of the authors Xin Shuai thanks the National Science Foundation for its support of his work under grant SBE #0914939

8. REFERENCES

[1] P. Evans and M. Krauthammer. Exploring the use of social media to measure journal article impact. *AMIA Symposium*, 2011(January):374–81, 2011.

[2] E. Garfield and R. K. Merton. Citation indexing-its theory and application in science, technology, and humanities. *garfield.library.upenn.edu*, Jan. 1979.

[3] A. Kittur, E. H. Chi, and B. Suh. What's in wikipedia?: mapping topics and conflict using socially annotated category structure. CHI '09, pages 1509–1512, New York, NY, USA, 2009. ACM.

[4] J. Priem and B. H. Hemminger. Scientometrics 2.0: New metrics of scholarly impact on the social web. *First Monday; Volume 15, Number 7 - 5 July 2010*, 2010.

[5] J. Priem, H. A. Piwowar, and B. M. Hemminger. Altmetrics in the wild: Using social media to explore scholarly impact. *ArXiv e-prints*, Mar. 2012.

[6] X. Shuai, A. Pepe, and J. Bollen. How the Scientific Community Reacts to Newly Submitted Preprints: Article Downloads, Twitter Mentions, and Citations. *PloS ONE*, 11(7), 2012.

[7] C. Spearman. The proof and measurement of association between two things. *The American journal of psychology*, 100(3-4):441–471, 1987.

[8] F. Ąrup Nielsen. Scientific citations in wikipedia. *First Monday*, 12(8), 2007.

A Distributed Archival Network for Process-Oriented Autonomic Long-Term Digital Preservation

Ivan Subotic Lukas Rosenthaler
Digital Humanities Lab
University of Basel
Switzerland
{ivan.subotic|lukas.rosenthaler}@unibas.ch

Heiko Schuldt
Databases and Information Systems
University of Basel
Switzerland
heiko.schuldt@unibas.ch

ABSTRACT

The reliable and consistent long-term preservation of digital content and metadata is becoming increasingly important – even though the storage media used are potentially subject to failures, or the data formats may become obsolete over time. A common approach is to replicate data across several sites to increase their availability. Nevertheless, network, software, or hardware failures as well as the evolution of data formats have to be coped with in a timely and, ideally, an autonomous way, without intervention of an administrator. In this paper we present DISTARNET, a distributed, autonomous long-term digital preservation system. Essentially, DISTARNET exploits dedicated processes to ensure the integrity and consistency of data with a given replication degree. At the data level, DISTARNET supports complex data objects, the management of collections, annotations, and arbitrary links between digital objects. At process level, dynamic replication management, consistency checking, and automated recovery of the archived digital objects is provided utilizing autonomic behavior governed by preservation policies without any centralized component. We present the concepts and implementation of the distributed DISTARNET preservation approach. Most importantly, we provide details of the qualitative and quantitative evaluation of the DISTARNET system. The former addresses the effectiveness of the internal preservation processes while the latter evaluates DISTARNET's performance regarding the overall archiving storage capacity and scalability.

Categories and Subject Descriptors: H.3 [Information Storage and Retrieval]: Digital Libraries

Keywords: Long-Term Preservation; Autonomic System

1. INTRODUCTION

Digital data, either digitized or born-digital, are increasingly gaining importance in our everyday and professional lives. As a consequence, a large spectrum of applications require that data are preserved over long periods of time.

An essential requirement of a digital preservation system is that the information carried by the initially stored digital object remains accessible and usable.

Metadata is the key to providing long-term digital preservation. The Open Archival Information System (OAIS) Reference Model [1, 2] categorizes metadata that need to be preserved and managed together with the original bitstream into the following categories: representation information, reference information, context information, fixity information, and provenance information. There is also additional metadata that is created during the preservation process when a digital object evolves (e.g., annotations, links between information objects, collection/subcollection information). We will use the term *Information Object* to denote the digital data, including its associated metadata.

In short, digital long-term preservation combines policies, strategies, and actions for preserving information objects, despite potential changes of the formats in which objects are stored or changes of the underlying hardware environment.

Digital preservation comes with a set of requirements, independent of the domain in which it is applied and the type of data to be preserved:

Replication and Distribution. A secure environment for long-term storage needs to store more then one copy of each archived object at different locations. Thus, we need some form of a distributed and replicated storage environment.

Fault Tolerance and Failure Management. The failure of one or more components in a distributed preservation system should not endanger the whole system, and only have isolated effects. Failure or disaster resulting in destruction or corruption of some of the stored information objects should not result in a complete loss of the archived data. Automated replication mechanisms should maintain a minimum number of geographically dispersed replicas. Any data loss event should trigger automated recovery activities that re-establish the minimum number of replicas.

Management of Complex Information Objects, i.e., objects that are comprised of or are part of other information objects. The complexity stems from the requirement of preserving additional supporting information besides the bitstream of the archived data object (e.g., representation, reference, context, fixity, provenance, and other information). The challenge lies in the automated management of such complex objects in a distributed setting. Preserving the integrity of complex objects is a twofold problem. First, the integrity of the referential information needs to be maintained and second, the integrity of the objects themselves has to be guaranteed. Any loss of integrity needs to automatically launch activities to restore the integrity of the information object. If the information object cannot be repaired solely by the information it carries itself, other remote replicas need to be used. Integrity is also an important challenge in the context of synchronization of information objects that are changing during the preservation process (e.g., annotations, links between information objects, collection/subcollection information). A system needs to make sure that such changes do not break the integrity of the information objects.

Scalability. The growing production of digital data that need to be archived requires a scalable distributed preservation system, i.e., a system that scales both with an increasing number of users and collection sizes.

Openness and Extensibility by providing clearly separated and publicly available interfaces to enable easy extensions to existing components and the possibility of adding new components to cope with new, unforeseen challenges (e.g., novel data formats).

Resource Discovery and Load Balancing. The discovery of newly available resources, together with the monitoring and management of existing resources should be handled efficiently. When selecting replica locations, aspects like the nodes' load shall be considered as well.

Curation. For an effective use of data, tasks like data format migration should be executed immediately.

Authentication, Authorization, and Auditing. Access to resources should be secured to ensure only known users are able to perform allowed operations. Ownership of data has to be enforced, i.e., no access should be possible if foreign data (e.g., of a cooperating organization) is hosted on the local node for redundancy reasons.

In this paper, we introduce DISTARNET (DISTributed ARchival NETwork), a distributed, autonomous long-term digital preservation system that jointly addresses all these requirements. Automated processes are first-class citizens in DISTARNET as they implement the necessary preservation functionality for dynamic replication, consistency checks, and recovery of the archived digital objects. Based on these processes, the system features an autonomic behavior, governed by preservation policies. From an architectural point of view, it follows a fully distributed approach, without any centralized component [14].

In order to show the broad applicability of DISTARNET, consider the following scenarios:

i.) A Multinational Pharmaceutical Corporation aims at implementing a new digital archiving solution which is compliant to the company's preservation policy. In addition to the standard requirements for digital preservation (integrity, authenticity, etc.), this policy imposes that data have to be redundantly stored at least three different locations, with added constraints regarding minimum distance between locations and – for some types of data – also the country or state in which the data are allowed to be stored. The company operates several data centers worldwide; DISTARNET will be deployed on nodes at several data centers. These nodes connect to each other and exchange information on the available storage resources. As soon as data get ingested at either of the nodes, DISTARNET autonomously searches for suitable nodes inside the company's DISTARNET network and initiates the creation of replicas. DISTARNET periodically checks the integrity of the archived data and synchronizes changes (e.g., propagates new annotations that have been made). All this is handled automatically, without the need of manual intervention. In case of failures (e.g., nodes become unavailable or data are corrupted due to hardware and/or software failure), the built-in monitoring functionality of DISTARNET will detect the problem and automatically initiate countermeasures by instantiating workflow processes that create additional replicas at other suitable nodes adhering to the specified policies.

ii.) The National Museum of History & Native Art in a small European country aims at implementing a new archiving system for preserving the country's cultural heritage. This new system should comprise redundant off-site replicas, although the museum itself has only one site available that can be used to deploy such a system. However, there is a collaboration agreement between the national museums of different countries that include access to the other institutions' computation and storage resources for deploying replicas, together with the enforcement of access restrictions on these shared data (pretty much like in a virtual organization known in the context of Grid computing). As before, the issues of data integrity, authenticity, chain of custody, and trustworthiness need to be addressed. Each museum deploys a DISTARNET node. When data are ingested, they will be handled according to the policies specified by their owner and will automatically be distributed across the storage resources of different museums. Again, DISTARNET will periodically instantiate maintenance processes and launch recovery processes whenever necessary. In case of error (e.g., corrupted or lost replicas, etc.), the system will autonomously initiate countermeasures without the need of external intervention. When corresponding policies are defined, DISTARNET will even automatically trigger processes to migrate the archived content while still providing concurrent access.

The main contribution of this paper is twofold: first, we introduce in detail the novel concepts of the DISTARNET approach to long-term digital preservation, with particular focus on the system's self-* properties. Second, we present the DISTARNET implementation and we report in detail on the thorough qualitative and quantitative evaluations that have been done. Essentially, these evaluations show the feasibility of the system as it has proven to scale to very large volumes of data to be preserved, even in case of very conservative assumptions regarding failures, frequencies of processes for dynamic replication, consistency checks, automated recovery, and format migration.

The remainder of this paper is organized as follows. In Section 2, we introduce the concepts of DISTARNET and Section 3 describes the implementation of the system. We report on the evaluation of DISTARNET in Section 4. Section 5 discusses related work and Section 6 concludes.

2. A DISTRIBUTED ARCHIVAL SYSTEM

The challenges summarized before can only be met by a distributed archival system, although distribution imposes additional failures that need to be handled. In what follows, we describe the distributed system model, all failure classes, and the concepts employed for managing these failures.

2.1 Distributed Archival Network

The system model specifies a fully distributed system consisting of collaborating sites; the preservation system is deployed on nodes at these sites. To provide security regarding

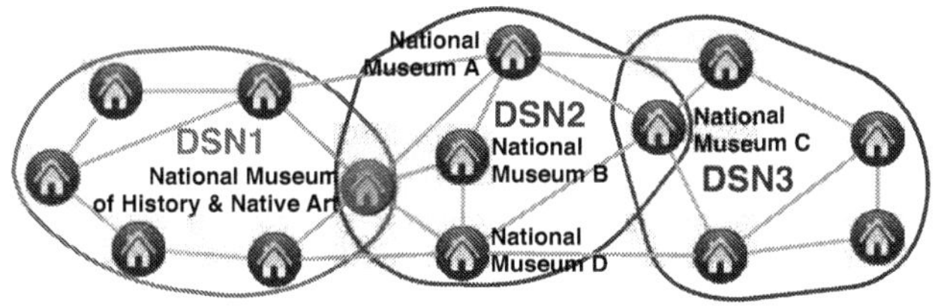

Figure 1: Distributed Archival Network

content access, we organize the sites together into Virtual Organizations (VO), much like in Grid computing. In a VO, each participating institution is able to define their access policies for the archived content. Moreover, we structure the network inside the VO in a self-organizing fashion, like in Peer-to-Peer (P2P) networks. This P2P-structured VO constitutes a *DISTARNET Sub-Network (DSN)*. We refer to the complete network of nodes that consists of multiple sub-networks, where each node runs the DISTARNET software, as the *DISTARNET Network*. The example in Figure 1 shows one DISTARNET Network consisting of multiple independent DSNs. A node can be part of one or more DSNs (e.g., the National Museum of History & Native Art is part of DSN1 and DSN2). The resources are partitioned and can only be accessed by sites within the same DSN.

Due to the P2P and VO nature of a DSN, the resulting distributed system is free of any single point of failure and provides, at the same time, a high degree of scalability (both in terms of numbers of nodes and users, and volume of content to be archived), availability (through replication), and access security (through VOs).

2.2 DISTARNET Processes

The goal of DISTARNET is to provide dynamic replication, automated consistency checks, and recovery of the archived digital objects in an autonomic way. This is done by means of dedicated predefined processes which are governed by preservation policies and which lead to certain *self-** properties (see Table 1) briefly described in the following. For more information on the functionality of each of these processes, please refer to [16]. All these processes are inherently distributed, i.e., they span several nodes of the system. In addition, based on the overall architectural paradigm of DISTARNET, also the orchestration of these processes is done in a decentralized way, without any centralized component.

Self-Configuration.

In DISTARNET, self-configuration refers to the ability of the system to automatically detect changes in the network. Events such as nodes joining or leaving are being constantly monitored, and taken into account. Involved are the *Node Joining Process*, the *Periodic Neighbor-Node Checking Process*, and the *Automated Dynamic Replication Process*.

Self-Healing.

Due to the continuous monitoring of nodes, content, and processes, the DISTARNET system detects abnormal situations that may harm its proper functioning and it is able to automatically recover by means of predefined processes. DISTARNET is designed as a fault-tolerant system with detection and recovery mechanisms for failures at the infrastructure, content, or node engine level. The main processes are the *Periodic Integrity Checking Process*, the *DAO Repairing Process*, the *Node Lost Process*, the *Reliable Copying Process*, and the *Data-Format Migration Process*.

Table 1: Self-* DISTARNET Processes

Self-Configuration
– Node Joining Process (NJP)
– Periodic Neighbor-Node Checking Process (PNCP)
– Automated Dynamic Replication Process (ADRP)
Self-Healing
– Periodic Integrity Checking Process (PICP)
– DAO Repairing Process (DRP)
– Node Lost Process (NLP)
– Reliable Copying Process (RCP)
– Data Format Migration Process (DFMP)
Self-Optimization
– Resource Discovery
– State Dissemination Process (SDP)
– Parameter Optimization

Self-Optimization.

The DISTARNET system must know its environment, especially the available resources, so as to track their changes over time. This information is provided by the *State Dissemination Process* and it is used to autonomously manage and maintain resource allocation through the *Automated Dynamic Replication Process* (e.g., to find suitable nodes where data can be replicated to, automatic policy-based geographical distribution of data, etc.), and other processes needed for the operation of DISTARNET.

2.3 Failure Classification

The faults that need to be coped with during the lifetime of a preservation system and that are addressed by the aforementioned self-* DISTARNET processes can be divided into three classes. The *Distributed Infrastructure class* contains all failures that endanger the distributed nature of the proposed solution. The *Content class* comprises all faults that can lead to the loss of the archived data. Finally, the *Node Engine class* subsumes all the faults that can happen during the execution of the processes running on a node.

Distributed Infrastructure Faults.

Node Loss. Through general failures like power outage, hardware crashes, etc., or through a disastrous event like a flood or fire, a node can get compromised to the point that it is not properly working anymore — i.e., a node is lost. Such loss is detected through the PNCP. When a node does not respond within a predefined time span, its status is set to Lost Node and the Node Lost Event is triggered. The DISTARNET system then automatically reacts and initiates countermeasures in the form of the Node Lost Process (NLP), by reevaluating the DAOs affected by the disappeared node by the ADRP, and if needed create new replicas so that redundancy and availability requirements defined in the Preservation Policy are upheld again. Also, a higher replication degree can be implemented for nodes deemed unreliable. Through predefined responsibility chains (an ordered list of the next responsible node in case of Node Loss), a new responsible node will be selected for the continued management of the now orphaned DAOs, and initiate the ADRP for these DAOs. This new responsible node should have information stored in the Replica Location Repository as this information is shared with all members of the DSN.

Node Dependability. Intermittent or periodic connection loss is detected by the PNCP which logs all successful and unsuccessful communication attempts. The latter will have the consequence that the dependability of a node is downgraded, which in itself is a measure used by the ADRP in the selection of remote storage nodes.

Content Faults.

DAO Corruption. Through localized hardware problems, e.g., disk crash, through improper handling of the data, or through malicious acts, the integrity of a DAO can be compromised. Periodic integrity checks are done by the PICP, and if integrity is breached, it automatically triggers countermeasures like finding healthy replicas in the DSN, and by using the RCP to get remote healthy copies, and use them to repair the corrupted DAOs, to rectify the problem.

DAO Representation Unreadable. This failure is caused by the obsolescence of data formats, which may make the representation of a DAO to be unreadable. To prevent such cases, the data formats of the archived data objects are constantly monitored and warnings are issued if a given data format is becoming obsolete as defined in the Preservation Policy. The DFMP can be initiated to migrate the obsolete data formats by following a predefined migration path.

Node Engine Faults.

This class addresses faults that can emerge during the execution of the DISTARNET processes, during their interaction with the different parts of the system, or the interaction of any part of the system with another. As the handling of failures belonging to this class is strongly dependent on the actual implementation of the overall system, we will discuss it in greater depth in Section 3.

3. THE DISTARNET SYSTEM

3.1 DISTARNET Layers and Modules

The DISTARNET architecture (Figure 2), is based on a network of equal nodes that form a fully distributed system.

Node Layers.

The *Data Layer* encompasses the DAO Triple Store, the DAO File Store, and the Data Objects Catalog. This layer is used for the storage of DISTARNET Archival Objects (DAOs), the DISTARNET-specific realization of the Information Object (IO). An IO encompasses the archived digital objects (e.g., image, audio/video, text document, etc.), corresponding metadata (e.g., annotations), relations between other information objects (e.g., links, sub-/collections), and properties (e.g., access rights, availability requirements, etc.).

The *Content and Network Management Layer* includes the complete digital preservation functionality as well as data repositories needed for running the system. The digital preservation logic consists of the DISTARNET processes and basic-services used during the execution of these processes. The design of this layer allows a reliable and fault-tolerant execution of the processes and archival management of DAOs in a distributed setting. This layer also contains the different repositories, like the distributed Replica Location Repository (RLR) where the locations of all replicas are stored, the distributed Node Information Repository (NIR) where information such as location, country, free/used space, etc. of nodes in the network are stored, the Copy Job Repository (CJR) used for storing information about pending remote replica creation jobs, and the Migration Job Repository (MJR) used for storing information regarding data migration jobs. The RLR and the NIR are built and updated with information gathered about other nodes through the State Dissemination Process which runs periodically on every node in a DSN.

The *User Interaction Layer* provides all external interactions (user and administrative) with the system. This layer basically represents the user interface that the users exploit for working with the system.

DISTARNET Modules.

The three layers are broken down into independent functional modules (see Figure 2) which communicate with each other via messages. The reason behind this modularization is threefold. Firstly, the separation of concerns: building blocks shall have a clear separation of functionality and, at the same time, a minimum overlap and dependencies, so that they can function independently of each other as much as possible. Secondly, to ease the maintenance of the system, this modular design provides the ability to independently exchange and/or extend the functionality of each module with different implementations in the future. The only restriction imposed on alternative implementations is the correct processing of the predefined messages and the external effects, but they are otherwise free from any restrictions regarding the internal implementation. Thirdly, the modularization provides additional possibilities on the implementation side, for fault-tolerant behavior on the node level.

The three DISTARNET node layers are subdivided into six functional modules. The User Interaction Layer is composed of the User Interaction Module. The Content & Network Management Layer is divided into four modules which are the Digital Preservation Logic Module, the Repositories Module, the Services Module, and the Network Module. Finally, the Data Layer is contained in the DAO Storage Module.

To allow for maximum flexibility in the structure inside each module, they are further divided into submodules. On top of all submodules, there is a so-called Module Manager, which functions as an access point to all communication with the module. Hence, the structure inside each module can be changed without having to perform any additional changes outside of the module.

3.2 DISTARNET Module Implementation

The implementation of the DISTARNET system, in particular the implementation of the individual modules is based on the Akka Framework[1] which follows the Actor Model and allows to create an event-based distributed system.

All interactions between modules are based on messages. Every module has a dedicated Actor functioning as the entry point for intermodule communication. In addition, a ded-

[1] `http://akka.io`

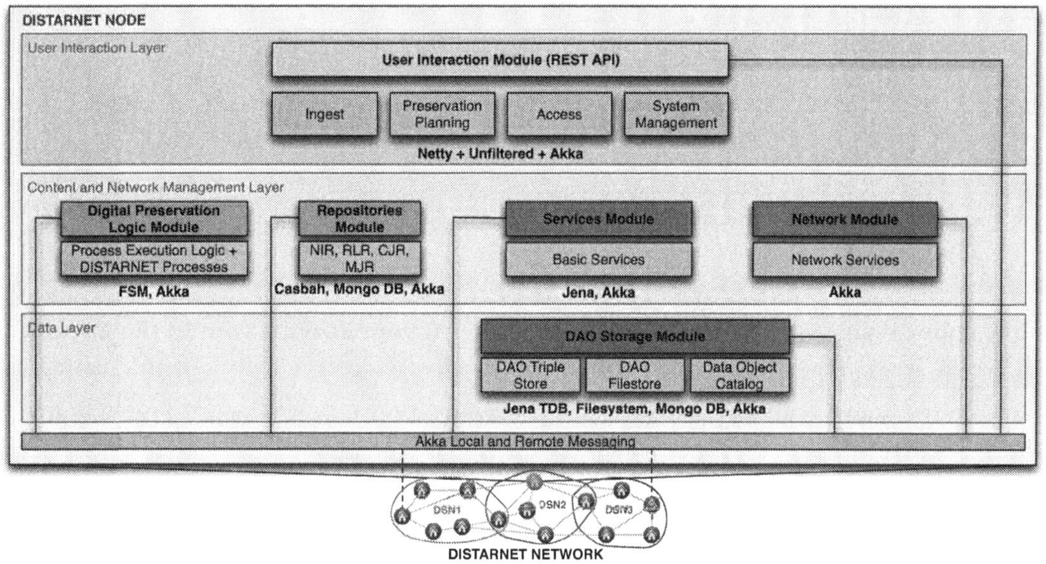

Figure 2: DISTARNET System Architecture

icated Actor has been implemented for each functionality inside the modules.

Node Actor System.

The modular Actor-based design has the following advantages: First, with regard to the long-term use of the system, it provides flexibility and independence regarding the implementation as it allows exchanging and/or extending modules individually. Second, regarding node engine fault-tolerance (Node Engine Fault Class), such a modular design paired with a message-based communication between the modules, allows full decoupling of the modules. A supervisor strategy additionally provides finer-grained fault tolerance.

Each Actor representing a module is supervised by a System Level Supervisor, which allows to isolate the failure by allowing only parts of the system to be restarted if needed. Furthermore, all communication inside a module is also done via messaging, and each module Actor takes on the role of a supervisor for the Actors created underneath. This allows the restarting of the different Actors providing the module's functionality in case of failure.

This architecture defines a distributed system of service providers. Service executions are mutually isolated so that the failure of one service execution does neither affect the services of co-located services, nor of the complete node.

User Interaction Module.

The User Interaction Module is implemented as an HTTP Server providing a RESTful API. This API allows to interact with and controls the deployed DISTARNET system node. For the implementation of the HTTP server, Netty[2] is used in combination with Unfiltered[3]. The REST functionality if provided through the implementation of the routes with Unfiltered, which respond to the different HTTP request received by the Netty server. The main functionality is provided as an interface between the HTTP requests, and the DISTARNET modules, by translating the requests into messages which are then sent to Actors in the different module, and serving the response back to the requester.

Digital Preservation Logic Module.

The Digital Preservation Logic Module is implemented as a series of Actors organized in an Actor hierarchy. The Process Execution Logic (PEL) Manager is the root of this hierarchy. The PEL Manager controls the execution of the DISTARNET processes. Each process is implemented as a distinct Actor and is instantiated by the PEL Manager either in a timer-based or request-based way.

DISTARNET Process Execution. All DISTARNET processes are implemented as Finite State Machines (FSM). Each state in the machine corresponds to one task in the process. The PELManager initiates a process when triggered, by creating and starting a Process Instance (PI). During the execution of a PI, an External Monitor (EM) receives a message on every state transition, which allows to persist the current state of a running process instance in the System Information Repository (SIR).

DISTARNET Process Implementation. The DISTARNET processes are implemented on the basis of the Akka FSM library. Each task in a process is implemented as a state. When all messages are exchanged, and a task is finished (e.g., send a message to execute service and receive service execution result), the FSM transitions to the next state.

All DISTARNET processes deliberately do not use synchronous calls, to avoid blocking behavior.

Repositories Module.

The Repositories Module hosts all repositories for the storage of information needed by the system. The Repositories-Manager manages the Node Information Repository (NIR), the Replica Location Repository (RLR), the Copy Job Repository (CJR), the Migration Job Repository (MJR), and the System Information Repository (SIR) used to store the current state of a running process instance. The repositories

[2]`http://netty.io`

[3]`http://unfiltered.databinder.net`

are also implemented as Actors and store their corresponding information in separate MongoDB[4] collections.

Services Module.

The ServicesManager Actor routes any incoming request to the corresponding Actor implementation of the invoked service instance. All Actor instances are instantiated and monitored by the ServicesManager when the node is started.

Network Module.

The Network Module contains the NetworkManager which is responsible for routing messages to remote nodes. It implements a simple name to full address resolver, where messages internally addressed with DSN name and node name, are looked up in the DSN member registry, and forwarded accordingly. In our implementation, the DSN member registry is a simple list loaded when the node is started, which contains the full addresses of every node in the DSN.

DAO Storage Module.

The Storage Module implements the DAO Triple Store, the DAO File-Store, and the Data Objects Catalog. The StorageManager instantiates and monitors every Actor at node startup. The TripleStore Actor uses the Jena API to manage and store the DISTARNET Archival Objects (DAOs) which are represented as RDF graphs, in the Jena TDB triple store. The Filestore Actor mirrors the data stored in the triple store by storing them in RDF-XML representation on the filesystem. Finally, the DAO Object Catalog Actor, stores the bitstream data of the DAOs to the filesystem, and uses the Casbah API to communicate with a MongoDB instance, which is used to store the index of the managed objects in the catalog.

4. EVALUATION

The main focus of the evaluation is on the DISTARNET processes and their ability to cope with infrastructure and content faults, as described in Section 2.3.

The evaluation is structured as follows. First, we do a qualitative evaluation of the system, for which we use four test scenarios that involve the main processes running in the DISTARNET system. These scenarios cover single infrastructure and content faults, data format migration tasks, and a combination of all three.

Second, we conduct a quantitative evaluation, by using measurements of the execution times of a series of processes in combination with approximations, and through extrapolation provide an overall performance of the system.

Cooperating Image Archives Scenario.

Both the qualitative and the quantitative evaluation of DISTARNET use a scenario with a network of four cooperating Image Archives. In this scenario, every Image Archive deploys one node running the DISTARNET system software and uses the other nodes in the network for the storage of remote replicas. This setup is motivated by the second scenario described in Section 1 (co-operating museums).

The scenario represents an Image Archive, where each Image DAO is comprised of three representations, i.e., Dublin core metadata, JPEG, and TIFF. The JPEG and TIFF representations have additionally references to randomly generated bitstream data. The DAOs are grouped together into collections, where one collection is comprised of 100 Image DAOs. Additionally, the collection also contains 100 Annotation DAOs. In summary, one collection thus contains 100 Image DAOs and 100 Annotation DAOs. We use synthetically generated data, consisting of one such collection, as our base data for the qualitative and quantitative evaluations. Different scaling factors considered during the evaluation allow to consider collection sizes which are a multiple of this base set-up. Figure 3 depicts an overview of the data structure used for the evaluation.

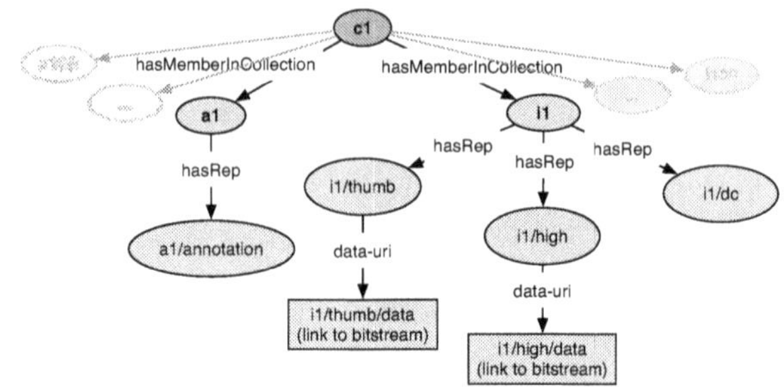

Figure 3: Structure of the Evaluation Data

4.1 Qualitative System Evaluation

During the qualitative system evaluation, we exposed the described network of Image Archives to a series of test scenarios which are characterized by failure situations that have to be handled automatically. In (1) we simulate the destruction of one node, in (2) we simulate the corruption of archived content, in (3) we simulate data format migration, and in (4) we combine all three together.

Evaluation Environment.

The test scenarios are implemented as a collection of multi-JVM test cases.The setup allows to run a predefined number of DISTARNET nodes, and create a DISTARNET network on the same physical hardware while still running each node in its own JVM. The different test cases are used to send messages in an orderly fashion to the nodes running in the DISTARNET network and by doing so initiate certain effects, e.g., kill nodes, corrupt content, etc. They are followed by tests evaluating the reactions of the individual nodes, e.g., additional replicas generation, content repair, etc.

The execution of the test cases is synchronized between all nodes, which allows to control their execution order throughout the network, and also allows to query the state of each node at key points in time during the execution of a test.

Running these tests in a multi-JVM environment, has shown to have a negative impact on the speed of the execution, as the system resources are divided between multiple threads of execution. Thus, this kind of execution can not be used for quantitative evaluation, as it would distort the results. However, for the purpose of the qualitative evaluation it can be used as long as the number of the running nodes is restricted, and each node has enough resources to provide a correct execution, The evaluation is performed on an Apple MacPro with 2 x 3 GHz Dual-Core Intel Xeon CPUs, with 24 GB RAM, and a dedicated 2 TB SATA disk drive. As we need to run at most four nodes during this qualitative eval-

[4]http://www.mongodb.org/

uation, the four cores provided by our hardware are enough to ensure a correct execution during the evaluation.

Initial Network State.

Before running each test scenario, we bring the network of Image Archive nodes to the same initial state which consists of four nodes (each representing an archive) being started. Each node is ingested with its own collection of DAOs consisting of 100 Image DAOs and 100 Annotation DAOs, as described earlier. All four nodes belong to the same DSN. The nodes are named NODE01 – NODE04. Each node creates for each DAO ingested on this node, two additional replicas on the next two nodes, e.g., NODE01 on NODE02 and NODE03, NODE02 on NODE03 and NODE04, etc.

This initialization represents the state of the DISTARNET network after all nodes have been ingested with the objects that need to be archived and after all replicas have been created and distributed across the archival network.

Test Scenario 1: Node Destruction.

In the first test scenario, we simulate that one of the nodes in the DISTARNET network of Image Archives has permanently gone off-line (e.g., destructed through an earthquake, flood, etc.). Hence, this case falls into the distributed infrastructure failure class discussed earlier.

This scenario represents an extreme situation. Nevertheless, its occurrence needs to be countered promptly as this event endangers all the DAOs throughout the network, whose replicas were stored on the now destructed node, as the redundancy prescribed by the preservation policies is not upheld anymore. The system needs to employ measures to bring the DISTARNET network back to a stable state providing the same redundancy of the stored content as it was before the occurrence of the node destruction.

To successfully pass this test scenario, the archive network needs to provide the following behavioral sequence: (1) After a node in the network is killed, the other nodes in the network must detect, through the Periodic Neighbor-Node Checking Process (PNCP), that a node is lost, (2) the next node in the responsibility chain must take over the responsibility for the DAOs ingested on the lost node, and (3) the node taking the responsibility must initiate the creation of additional replicas in the network, to compensate for the lost replicas stored on the missing node.

Test Scenario 2: Content Corruption.

We now simulate the corruption of parts of the archived content, which falls into the content faults class.

This is a likely event, that will occur at a higher rate than the previously discussed scenario involving node destruction, especially in larger archives, as the number of hard disk failures, for instance, rises with the number of deployed drives. When this event occurs, it needs to be dealt with immediately as any subsequent content corruption on say other nodes can lead in the worst case to a complete loss of the archived content, if as a result of content corruption all the replicas of the same DAO become unusable.

The DISTARNET network under test will need to present the following behavior: (1) the Periodic Integrity Checking Process (PICP) should check all local DAOs and find corrupted content on the node on which the corruption has happened, and (2) the node will then initiate the repairing of the corrupted DAOs by getting fresh copies of the missing content from other nodes in the network.

Test Scenario 3: Data Format Obsolescence.

In this scenario, we address the problem of data format obsolescence where the interpretability of some of the DAOs in the DISTARNET network is threatened by an obsolete data format. To counter this threat, we need to perform a data format migration task. This test scenario falls into the content faults class.

As DISTARNET provides a long-term preservation solution, the task of data format migration is very likely to happen in the future of every archive. As time goes by, the requirement of interpretability of the archived content will raise the need for data format migration as data formats become inevitably obsolete. As such, we need to provide the means to allow controlled changes to the archived content, and subsequently consistently propagate these changes throughout the network to all the remote replicas.

To successfully pass this test scenario, our network of Image Archives must provide the following behavior: (1) Execute migration job, (2) the additional representation created in the course of the migration job execution must be appended to the DAO for which the data format migration is performed, (3) the DAO's checksums (graph and bitstream) need to be updated, and (4) the updated DAO (graph and bitstream) will need to be sent out to all remote nodes where the old version is stored.

Test Scenario 4: Multi-Failure.

This scenario jointly considers a combination of infrastructure failure, content corruption, and data format migration. Hence, this scenario represents the worst case, which should not be very common. Nevertheless, if such situation occurs, DISTARNET has to be able to correctly deal with it. As in all the other previous scenarios, the goal is to finally reach a DISTARNET network of Image Archives in which remaining nodes reside in a stable and consistent state.

To successfully pass this test, the system needs to provide the following behavioral sequence: (1) PNCP on all nodes should detect that NODE01 is lost and NODE02 takes over the responsibility by creating additional replicas, (2) PICP on NODE02 should detect DAO corruption and initiate DRP, and (3) migration job executed on NODE03.

Qualitative Evaluation Results.

For each of the four scenarios, the system passes the execution of all the defined test cases without any errors. This error free execution leads us to the conclusion that the core functionality provided by the implementation of the DISTARNET System is effective and is working correctly.

4.2 Quantitative System Evaluation

The quantitative system evaluation is based on a combination of practical measurements in combination with analytical approximations. We measure the execution time of different processes running on one node, with the deployed DISTARNET prototype as used in the qualitative evaluation. We then combine this measure with approximations for inter-node transfer times, to attain a comprehensive measure, that represents a good approximation of a running DISTARNET network at very large scale. Additionally, we extend these results with additional extrapolated data points.

Table 2: Evaluation Results Overview

Scaling Factor	1	10	100	1'000	10'000	100'000	1'000'000
Image DAOs	100	1 K	10 K	100 K	1 M	10 M	100 M
Archive Size	10 GB	100 GB	1 TB	10 TB	100 TB	1 PB	10 PB
Duration w. 100 Mb/s	129.415 s	0.36 h	3.59 h	35.95 h	15 d	150 d	1'495 d
Duration w. 1 Gb/s	50.894 s	0.14 h	1.41 h	14.14 h	6 d	59 d	589 d

The goal is to provide approximations regarding the quantitative performance of the system, i.e., how many TB of data can be managed on one node under the constraint that the main DISTARNET processes need to finish running within 24 h. As this 24 h constraint represents a very conservative restriction, we also discuss more practical and relaxed alternatives, and how they affect the overall result.

Test Data.

The data used is the same as described previously. For an easier discussion, we assume that the overall size of an Image DAO is 100 MB (i.e., just the size of the TIFF bitstream, neglecting the Dublin core, and JPEG representations), and neglect the size of the Annotation DAO. Taking this data collection as the base for our evaluation, i.e., scaling factor $F = 1$, we can derive through extrapolation the overall data collection size for each scaling factor we use in the evaluation. As an example, for a scaling factor $F = 100$, we thus have 100 collections with each containing 100 Image DAOs and 100 Annotation DAOs. As we only count the Image DAOs with 100 MB each, we totally have 10'000 Image DAOs with an approximated overall size of 1 TB.

Evaluation Procedure.

For the evaluation we time the duration a DISTARNET node needs to execute the process mix with a data scaling factor $F = 1$, and then under a linear scaling assumption extrapolate the theoretical system performance for the different scaling factors.

Process Mix. First, we run the PICP over the Image Archive which suffers from a 10 % data loss rate (i.e, 10 % of the TIFF images have been deleted beforehand). The PICP will detect the data loss, and start the DRP to repair the data by using the RCP to recover from fresh copies. In the second step, the DFMP will run for one DAO, converting a TIFF representation to JPEG2000. Is uses the RCP to send the updated DAO with the newly created representation to two remote nodes. Essentially, we very conservatively assume that this process mix has to be executed within 24 h. Hence, the evaluation aims at emulating one day in the lifetime of a digital archive. This set-up, which aims at showing the scalability characteristics of the system, is deliberately very challenging, to have a clear indicator on the size of the archive that can be handled in practice (i.e., with a typically much less challenging load to be handled).

Inter-Node Transfer Times. To attain a good approximation of a running DISTARNET network, we use approximations of the inter-node network transfer times to be added to the times previously measured, to compensate for time needed for network traffic. Using approximated values gives us one more parameter whose influence can be analyzed, and provides us with additional data points for the discussion. For the approximation of the inter-node transfer times, we use two network bandwidth assumptions. The first representing a 100 Mb/s network, with a theoretical transfer capability of 12.5 MB/s, where it theoretically takes 8 seconds to transfer 100 MB of data. The second representing a 1 Gb/s network between the nodes, with a theoretical capability of 125 MB/s, where it theoretically takes 0.8 s to transfer 100 MB of data, over the wire.

Quantitative Evaluation Results.

Table 2 shows the evaluation results for the different scaling factors (timed and extrapolated), network bandwidths, and additionally also the overall archive sizes with the corresponding number of Image DAOs. The color reflects the adherence to the 24 h constraint imposed for the maximum overall run-time of the processes, where green lies under and red over the 24 h mark. An analysis of the scalability characteristics of DISTARNET's triple store-based metadata management under a mix of read-only and update requests is given in [15]. According to the metadata management benchmark we have developed, the overall archive size that can be managed with DISTARNET's metadata management (not taking into account the actual operation on the content) are in the range between 1 PB and 10 PB. In comparison, this evaluation also considers bitstream data and the additional time needed for checksum calculation, network transfer, and data format migration. As a result, we see that the estimated overall archive size that can be managed on one node, is at around 10 TB.

However, it has to be noted that the 24 h constraint is a very conservative assumption. For a productive running system, we can relax this assumption, if for example the DISTARNET node uses a RAID storage system, providing higher data storage reliability and thus lessening the need for frequent integrity checking. In the case with the higher network bandwidth, we could achieve archive sizes of up to 100 TB, if we allow the processes to run for almost a whole week, or even 1 PB if we give the node 2 months for the running of the processes (note that the process mix also includes format conversion processes which have to be supported in an archive, but not very frequently).

Figure 4 shows the evaluation results for scaling factor $F = 1$ and the two network bandwidths. It also shows to what extent the different processes in the process mix contribute to the overall execution time. Actually, the PICP/DRP/RCP mix (1) is responsible for 95 % of the duration. Looking further at (1), we see that in the case of the slower network, the main time is consumed by the RCP part of the mix (64.76 %). When looking at (1) in the case of the faster network, then the situation is reversed. The main time contribution stems from the checksum calculation including a small amount of process execution overhead. If we now look at the DFMP/RCP mix (2), then we will see a similar picture. In the case of the slower network, the main contribution comes from the network transfer in RCP with approx. 2/3, whereas the TIFF to J2P conversion use

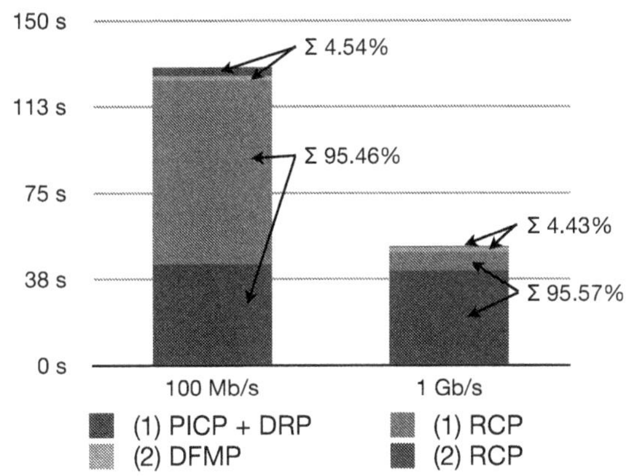

Figure 4: Results with Scaling Factor $F = 1$

approx. 1/3 of the time. Here, the picture also reverses as before, when looking at the faster network scenario.

To further increase the performance of the archive, we would need to decrease the processing time needed for checksum calculation in (1) and also of the TIFF to J2P conversion in (2). With more powerful hardware (e.g., with multiple cores, high performance disk arrays) leading to faster processing by a factor of 10, this would roughly cut the overall processing time by 30 % in the case of the slower network connection, and by 75 % for the faster network connection. Looking at Table 2, this would provide a shift to the "right" for the case with the lower bandwidth, and almost a shift for the faster network.

If we additionally relax the 24 h constraint in conjunction with the rise in processing power, then the 1 PB archive size can be handled with overall processing times of around two weeks. To shift further to the right side of the performance table, we would then again need to increase the network bandwidth. One (initially possibly rather surprising) inexpensive option to further increase "network bandwidth" between sites could be simply to ship hard-drives by courier – which may however indeed be more efficient when dealing with very large volumes of data compared to the on-line transfer over the wire.

In summary, even when using commodity hardware with current technology, we estimate that one DISTARNET node can effectively manage around 10 TB of archived data under the 24 h constraint. Under a more relaxed constrained of 2 weeks, and using high performance hardware, we estimate that the system can effectively manage around 1 PB of archived data.

5. RELATED WORK

Long-term digital preservation projects can be subdivided in two classes. The first one encompasses preservation-aware digital repositories integrating with other systems to provide support for preserving their content; the second category includes digital archive, which are systems with a focus on functionality for digital preservation.

Preservation-Aware Digital Repositories.

Fedora Commons[5] and DSpace [17], both open source digital repositories for managing (complex) digital objects, have merged into DuraSpace[6], which is creating DuraCloud[7]. DuraCloud provides both storage and access services, including content replication and monitoring services that can span multiple cloud storage providers. DuraCloud and DISTARNET share some concepts as both provide processes that implement long-term preservation functionality. The main difference lies in the location of the preservation services which, in the case of DuraCloud, are completely situated in the cloud, outside of direct control of the content owners, while in the case DISTARNET, they are situated locally on the premises of each cooperating site in the network.

SHERPA DP [7] describes a preservation framework that distinguishes between institutional repositories acting as content providers and external service providers with expert knowledge in long-term preservation. In the SHERPA DP architecture the preservation services are provided centrally, and shared between different institutional repositories.

Digital Archives.

LOCKSS (Lots Of Copies Keep Stuff Safe) [11] provides digital preservation through replication in a peer-to-peer network, and can be used to build open or closed networks. This project shares the common idea with DISTARNET for a cooperating network, and using shared resources to provide preservation services.

Cheshire 3 [18] integrates a data Grid, digital repositories, and text/data mining. Similarly to DISTARNET, it jointly addresses complex objects organized in collections/subcollections and long-term preservation services, by employing distributed technology for large-scale support.

kopal[8] is a long-term archiving solution for electronic publications. The main difference between kopal and DISTARNET lies in the architecture of both systems as the former is built as a centralized system, not allowing to collaboratively share resources with related institutions.

The emphasis of the long-term preservation service-based framework CASPAR [6] is the preservation of representation information, the preservability of the infrastructure itself, and the validation of the proposed concepts. While DISTARNET provides a data model which supports the preservation of representation information with each object, the CASPAR approach additionally defines a complete infrastructure for creating, registering, storing, and preserving extensive representation metadata.

The PLANETS system [5], built on a service-oriented architecture, provides a suite of software tools and services to support the preservation and long-term access to digital content. The main components are Plato [4], the Testbed and the Interoperability Framework. Plato provides preservation planing services, helping the user to identify the best course of action. The Testbed can then be used to test selected actions. The interoperability framework provides standard services such as authorization, authentication, orchestration, data and metadata management. Additionally, it allows the integration of third-party services (e.g., emulation services).

SHAMAN[9] uses iRODS [9], an integrated rule-oriented data Grid as implementation technology. iRODS provides transparent support for local and remote storage and even

[5] `http://fedora-commons.org`

[6] `http://duraspace.org`

[7] `http://www.duracloud.org`

[8] `http://kopal.langzeitarchivierung.de`

[9] `http://shaman-ip.eu/shaman/`

allows to additionally leverage the Cloud [19] for storage purposes. It provides a distributed preservation-policy and workflow-driven preservation environment, with a strong focus on preservation of context, discoverability of the content, and risk management through geographically dispersed replication support. In contrast to DISTARNET, SHAMAN is a framework from which individual solutions can be developed. For example, a preservation solution could be implemented with SHAMAN, in which the DISTARNET concepts and processes are implemented as workflows.

Hoppla [13] is an archiving solution that combines back-up and fully automated migration services for data collections in environments with limited expertise. By employing data format identification and characterization tools, and through externally defined rules, the system provides file format migration services that will ensure long-term readability and usability of the digital objects.

6. CONCLUSIONS AND FUTURE WORK

In this paper, we have presented DISTARNET which allows geographically dispersed organizations to collaboratively build a fully distributed, Internet-based fault-tolerant long-term preservation system. Through process-based autonomic behavior featuring self-configuration, self-healing, and self-optimization capabilities governed by preservation policies, DISTARNET provides dynamic replication, automated consistency checking, and recovery of the archived digital objects. By developing a highly flexible data model and the specification of sophisticated management processes, it also supports complex data objects, user generated annotations, collections, and arbitrary links between objects. The quantitative evaluation of DISTARNET, even though based on very conservative assumptions on failures, frequency of processes and format migrations, has shown that the collection sizes that can be effectively managed area in the are of hundreds of TBs, up to 1 PB.

Future work will address two directions. First, the current development in the digital library community is going towards Semantic Digital Libraries [8]. This development should also be followed in the digital preservation community leading to research in the direction of Semantic Digital Archives (SDA). We understand SDAs as a further development of current ideas for a Digital Preservation System, combined with Semantic Web technologies, with the goal to allow not only access to the archive on the basis of archival metadata, but also according to the connections the archived objects have with internally or externally defined concepts. The data model implementation of DISTARNET is based on RDF, thus providing a good basis. For the realization it is planned to use DISTARNET as the archival layer for SALSAH [12], a virtual research environment providing the access layer. Moreover, context is identified as a critical aspect of preservation metadata in digital preservation [3] (e.g., metadata on the objects' origins, composition, and purpose). A particular challenge that will be addressed by DISTARNET is the evolution of preservation contexts over time. Second, also the preservation of processes [10] will be addressed. At present, DISTARNET preserves static objects, or in the best case, static representations of dynamic objects. In future work, we plan to add support for preserving the whole execution chain of processes, i.e., not only the resulting digital objects are preserved, but also the sequence of actions by which they have been created.

7. REFERENCES

[1] Reference Model for an Open Archival Information System (OAIS) – Blue Book. CCSDS, January 2002.

[2] Reference Model for an Open Archival Information System (OAIS) – Pink Book. *Draft.* CCSDS, 2009.

[3] J. E. Beaudoin. Context and Its Role in the Digital Preservation of Cultural Objects. *D-Lib Magazine*, 18(11/12), 2012.

[4] C. Becker, H. Kulovits, A. Rauber, and H. Hofman. Plato: a Service-Oriented Decision Support System for Preservation Planning. *In: Proc. JCDL'08*, June 2008.

[5] A. Farquhar and H. Hockx-Yu. Planets: Integrated Services for Digital Preservation. *The International Journal of Digital Curation*, 2(2):88–99, 2007.

[6] D. Giaretta. The CASPAR Approach to Digital Preservation. *International Journal of Digital Curation*, 2(1):112–121, 2007.

[7] G. Knight. SHERPA DP: Establishing an OAIS-Compliant Preservation Environment for Institutional Repositories. *Digital Repositories: Interoperability and Common Services*, 2005.

[8] S. R. Kruk and B. McDaniel, editors. *Semantic Digital Libraries.* Springer, 2009.

[9] A. Rajasekar, R. Moore, C.-Y. Hou, C. A. Lee, R. Marciano, A. de Torcy, M. Wan, W. Schroeder, S.-Y. Chen, L. Gilbert, P. Tooby, and B. Zhu. *iRODS Primer: Integrated Rule-Oriented Data System.* 2010.

[10] A. Rauber. Digital Preservation in Data-Driven Science: On the Importance of Process Capture, Preservation and Validation. *SDA'12*, Sept. 2012.

[11] V. Reich and D. Rosenthal. Lockss (Lots of Copies Keep Stuff Safe). *New Review of Academic Librarianship*, 6:155–161, 2000.

[12] L. Rosenthaler. Virtual Research Environments – A new approach for dealing with digitized sources in research in Arts and Humanities. *Humanities and Computing*, August 2011, Lausanne.

[13] S. Strodl, P. Petrov, M. Greifeneder, and A. Rauber. Automating logical preservation for small institutions with Hoppla. *Proc. ECDL'10*, pages 124–135, 2010.

[14] I. Subotic, H. Schuldt, and L. Rosenthaler. The DISTARNET Approach to Reliable Autonomic Long-Term Digital Preservation. *Proc. DASFAA'11*, Springer LNCS, Vol. 6588, pp. 93–103, 2011.

[15] I. Subotic, L. Rosenthaler, and H. Schuldt. A Benchmark for RDF-based Metadata Management in Distributed Long-Term Digital Preservation. *Proc. DESWeb'12*, April 2012.

[16] I. Subotic. A Distributed Archival Network for Process-Oriented Autonomic Long-Term Digital Preservation. PhD Thesis, University of Basel, 2013.

[17] R. Tansley, M. Bass, D. Stuve, and M. Branschofsky. The DSpace Institutional Digital Repository System: Current Functionality. *JCDL'03*, pages 87–97, 2003.

[18] P. Watry. Cheshire 3 Framework White Paper: Implementing Support for Digital Repositories in a Data Grid Environment. In: *Proc. MSST'05*, 2005.

[19] P. Wittek and S. Darányi. Digital Preservation in Grids and Clouds: A Middleware Approach. *Journal of Grid Computing*, 10(1):133–149, Mar. 2012.

Evaluating Sliding and Sticky Target Policies by Measuring Temporal Drift in Acyclic Walks Through a Web Archive

Scott G. Ainsworth
Old Dominion University
Norfolk, VA, USA
sainswor@cs.odu.edu

Michael L. Nelson
Old Dominion University
Norfolk, VA, USA
mln@cs.odu.edu

ABSTRACT

When a user views an archived page using the archive's user interface (UI), the user selects a datetime to view from a list. The archived web page, if available, is then displayed. From this display, the web archive UI attempts to simulate the web browsing experience by smoothly transitioning between archived pages. During this process, the target datetime changes with each link followed; drifting away from the datetime originally selected. When browsing sparsely-archived pages, this nearly-silent drift can be many years in just a few clicks. We conducted 200,000 acyclic walks of archived pages, following up to 50 links per walk, comparing the results of two target datetime policies. The Sliding Target policy allows the target datetime to change as it does in archive UIs such as the Internet Archive's Wayback Machine. The Sticky Target policy, represented by the Memento API, keeps the target datetime the same throughout the walk. We found that the Sliding Target policy drift increases with the number of walk steps, number of domains visited, and choice (number of links available). However, the Sticky Target policy controls temporal drift, holding it to less than 30 days on average regardless of walk length or number of domains visited. The Sticky Target policy shows some increase as choice increases, but this may be caused by other factors. We conclude that based on walk length, the Sticky Target policy generally produces at least 30 days less drift than the Sliding Target policy.

Categories and Subject Descriptors

H.3.7 [**Information Storage and Retrieval**]: Digital Libraries

Keywords

Digital Preservation, HTTP, Resource Versioning, Temporal Applications, Web Architecture, Web Archiving

1. INTRODUCTION

To browse archived pages from a web archive such as the Internet Archive [19], the user begins with the selection of a URI followed by selection of a Memento-Datetime (the datetime the resource was archived). Following these selections, the user is able to browse the archive's collection of mementos (archived copies) by clicking links on displayed pages; a process similar to browsing the live Web. However, with each click, the target datetime (the datetime requested by the user) is changed to the Memento-Datetime of the displayed page. Although this constant change is visible in the web browser address bar and the archive's user interface (UI), the change is easy to overlook because the change happens without explicit user interaction.

The screen shots in the top row of Figure 1 illustrates a clear case of this phenomenon. Archives of the Old Dominion University Computer Science and College of Sciences home pages are shown. The process begins by entering `http://www.cs.odu.edu` in the Internet Archive's archive browser, The Wayback Machine. The user is then presented with a list of archive datetimes, from which May 14, 2005 01:36:08 GMT is selected. The user views the Computer Science home page [Figure 1(a)]. The page URI is `http://web.archive.org/web/20050514013608/http://www.cs.odu.edu/`; note that the datetime encoded[1] in the URI matches the date selected. When the user clicks the *College of Sciences* link, the page is displayed [Figure 1(b)]. However, the encoded datetime changed to 20050422001752, a drift of 22 days. This datetime also becomes the new target datetime. When the user clicks the *Computer Science* link, the result is a different version than first displayed, as shown in Figure 1(c).

On the other hand, using a Memento-enabled browser, such as Firefox with the MementoFox add-on [20], maintains a consistent target datetime as the user follows links. The bottom row of Figure 1 shows the results. Using the API, each visit to the Computer Science home page returns the same version [Figures 1(d) and 1(f)]. The rough statistics in Table 1 show the potential improvement that can be achieved using the Memento API.

The simple example above raises many questions. How much drift do users experience when browsing archives using user interfaces such as the Wayback Machine? If the Memento API is used instead, how much drift is experienced? Which method is better and by how much? What factors contribute, positively or negatively, to the amount of drift? In particular, does the number of links available

[1] Date and time formatted YYYYMMDDHHMMSS

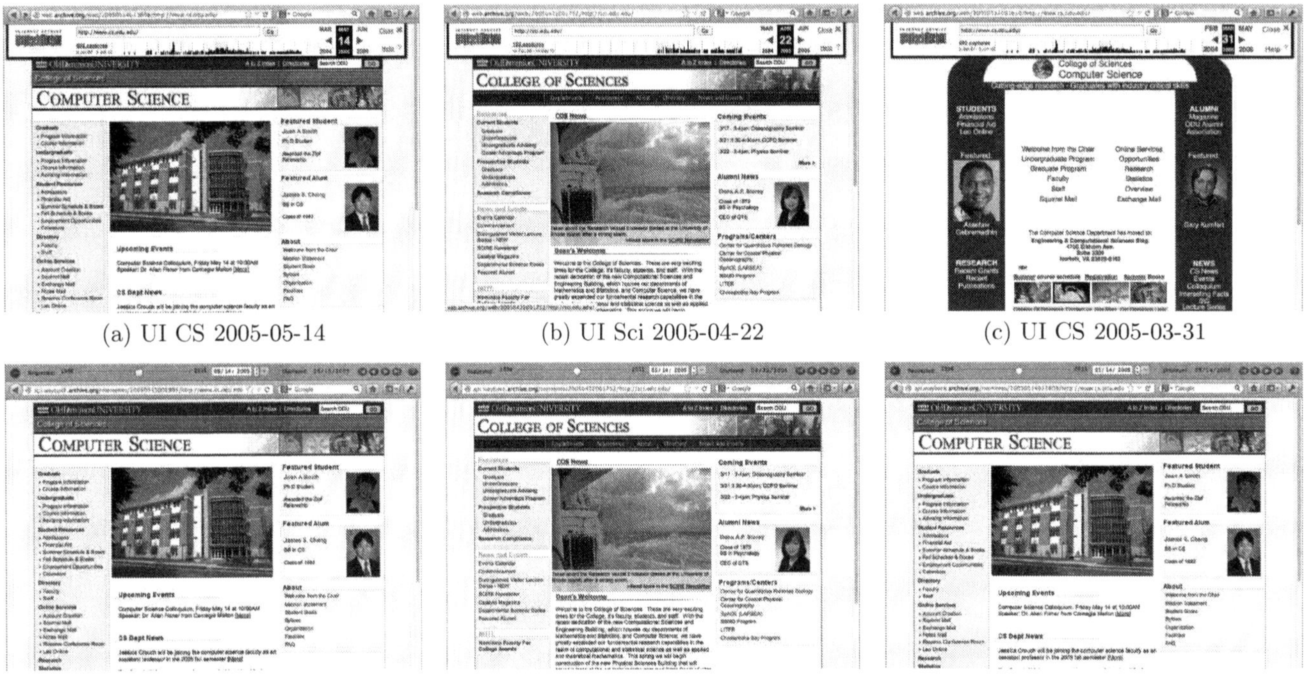

(a) UI CS 2005-05-14 (b) UI Sci 2005-04-22 (c) UI CS 2005-03-31

(d) API CS 2005-05-14 (e) API Sci 2005-04-22 (f) API CS 2005-05-14

Figure 1: Impact of Drift on Archive Browsing

Table 1: Temporal Drift Example

	Wayback Machine UI		Memento API	
Page	Datetime	Drift	Datetime	Drift
CS Home	2005-05-14	–	2005-05-14	–
Sci Home	2005-04-22	22 days	2005-04-22	22 days
CS Home	2005-03-31	44 days	2005-05-14	0 days
Mean		33 days		11 days

(choice), number of domains visited, or the number of links followed (walk length) contribute to drift?

2. RELATED WORK

Although the need for web archiving has been understood since nearly the dawn of the Web [8], these efforts have been for the most part independent in motivation, requirements, and scope. The Internet Archive, the first archive to attempt global scope, came into existence in 1995 [15]. Since then, many other archives have come into existence. Some of these use software developed by the Internet Archive and have similar capture behavior and user interfaces; however, other archives such as WebCite [12] have significantly different capture behaviors.

Large-scale web archiving requires resolution of issues and approaches on several axes. Although somewhat out of date, Masanès [16] is an excellent introduction. Masanès covers a broad range of web archiving topics. Of significance to this research are the technical aspects of acquisition, organization and storage, and quality and completeness. A major area not addressed by Masanès is access to archives, in particular the lack of standards or conventions for accessing archived resources. Van de Sompel et al. [26] addressed this lack with Memento.

2.1 Acquisition

Acquisition is the technical means of bringing content into an archive. Client-side archiving essentially emulates web users following links, obtaining content using the HTTP protocol. The Heritrix [18] crawler and the mirroring capability of *wget*[2] are examples of client-side archiving. A significant issue with client-side archiving is that only those parts of the Web exposed as linked resources are captured. Transactional archiving is specifically designed to overcome this limitation. Transactional archiving [7, 11, 13] inserts the capture process between the user and the data source, for example an Apache web server filter, which requires the cooperation of the server operator. Unique request-response pairs are archived, including requests for resources that are not linked. Server-side archiving makes a direct copy of the content from the server, bypassing HTTP altogether. Although conceptually simple, access to the resulting server-side archive can be difficult, requiring different URIs and navigational structures than the original. Many systems, e.g. content management systems and wikis, perform server-side archiving by design.

2.2 Organization and Storage

Once acquired content must be stored. Masanès [16] describes three organization and storage methods that are commonly used. Local archives store content in the local file system, transforming the content just enough to allow off-line browsing. Links must be modified to reference either locally-stored archived resources or the live web. Strict adherence to the original content is generally impractical and size is limited by local storage capacity and speed. Thus, local archives are most suitable for small-scale archiving. A

[2]`http://www.gnu.org/software/wget/`

common method of creating local archives is *wget* mirroring. Web-served archives, like the IA, commonly store content in WARC (Web ARChive) container files, which allows the original content and URIs to be stored unmodified. This also overcomes many limitations imposed by file systems. Content is provided to users over HTTP. Web-served archiving is highly scalable and suitable for large-scale archiving. Non-web archives generally transform web content into other forms. For example, Adobe Acrobat has the ability to download web content and produce a corresponding PDF. This type of archiving is generally best suited for resources, such as digitized books, originally created independently from the Web. Of the three types of organization and storage methods, only web-served archives are relevant to this study.

2.3 Access

An area of web archives that remained unresolved until recently was lack of methods or a standard API for time-based access to archived resources. Each archive provides a user interface (UI) to access the archive's resources. (Many archive's use the Internet Archive's Wayback Machine [24] and therefore share similar UIs.) In general, UI access to archives starts with a user-selected URI and datetime, after which the archive allows the user to simply click links to browse the collection. UI archive access is addressed in greater detail in Section 3.1.

Van de Sompel et al. addressed the lack of a standard API with Memento [25, 26], an HTTP-based framework that bridges web archives with current resources. It provides a standard API for identifying and dereferencing archived resources through datetime negotiation. In Memento, each original resource, URI-R, has zero or more archived representations, URI-M_i, that encapsulate the URI-R's state at times t_i. Using the Memento API, clients are able to request URI-M_i for a specified URI-R by datetime. Memento is now an IETF Internet Draft [25]. Memento archive access is addressed in greater detail in Section 3.2.

2.4 Quality and Completeness

In general, quality is functionally defined as fitting a particular use and objectively defined as meeting measurable characteristics. This examination of web archive content is concerned with the latter. For web archives, most quality issues stem from the difficulties inherent in obtaining content using HTTP [16]. Content is not always available when crawled, leaving gaps in the coverage. Web sites change faster than crawls can acquire their content, which leads to temporal incoherence. Ben Saad et al. [6] note that quality and completeness require different methods and measures *a priori* or *a posterior*, that is during acquisition or during post-archival access respectively.

2.4.1 Completeness (Coverage)

When crawling to acquire content, the tradeoffs required and conditions encountered lead to incomplete content or coverage. A web archive may not have the resources to acquire and store all content discovered. Associated compromises include acquiring only high priority content and crawling content less often. The content to be acquired may not be available at crawl time due to server downtime or network disruption. The combination of compromises and resource unavailability create undesired, undocumented gaps in the archive.

Although much has been written on the technical, social, legal, and political issues of web archiving; little detailed research has been conducted on the archive coverage provided by the existing archives. Day [9] surveyed a large number of archives as part of investigating the methods and issues associated with archiving. Day however does not address coverage. Thelwall touches on coverage when he addresses international bias in the Internet Archive [23], but does not directly address how much of the Web is covered. McCown and Nelson address coverage [17], but their research is limited to search engine caches. Ben Saad et al. [5, 4] address qualitative completeness through change detection to identify and archive important changes (rather than simply archiving every change). This research primarily addresses *a priori* completeness. *A posteriori* web archive coverage is addressed by Ainsworth et al. [1]. Leveraging the Memento API and pilot infrastructure, Ainsworth et al. [1] obtained results showing that 35–90% of publicly-accessible URIs have at least one publicly-accessible archived copy, 17–49% have two to five copies, 1–8% have six to ten copies, and 8–63% at least ten copies. The number of URI copies varies as a function of time, but only 14.6–31.3% of URIs are archived more than once per month. The research also shows that coverage is dependent on social popularity.

2.4.2 Temporal Coherence

When crawling to acquire content, tradeoffs are required. Crawling consumes server resources, thus crawls must be polite, e.g. paced to avoid adversely impacting the server. The web archive may not have the bandwidth needed to crawl quickly. These and other constraints increase crawl duration, which in turn increases the likelihood of temporal incoherence.

Spaniol et al. [21] note that crawls may span hours or days, increasing the risk of temporal incoherence, especially for large sites, and introduces a model for identifying coherent sections of archives, which provides a measure of quality. Spaniol et al. also present a crawling strategy which helps minimize incoherence in web site captures. In a separate paper, Spaniol et al. [22] also develop crawl and site coherence visualizations. Spaniol's work, while presenting an *a posteriori* measure, concerns the quality of entire crawls.

Denev et al. present the SHARC framework [10], which introduces a stochastic notion of *sharpness*. Sites changes are modeled as Poisson processes with page-specific change rates. Change rates can differ by MIME type and depths within the site. This model allows reasoning on the expected sharpness of an acquisition crawl. From this they propose four algorithms for site crawling. Denev's work focuses on *a priori* quality of entire crawls and does not address the quality of existing archives and crawls.

Ben Saad et al. [6] address both *a priori* and *a posteriori* quality. Like Denev et al. [10], the *a priori* solution is designed to optimize the crawling process for archival quality. The *a posteriori* solution uses information collected by the *a priori* solution to direct the user to the most coherent archived versions.

All of the above research shares a common thread: evaluation and control of completeness and temporal coherence during the crawl with the goal of improving the archiving process. In contrast, our research takes a detailed look at the quality and use of existing archives.

3. BROWSING AND DRIFT

Fundamentally, drift is the difference between the target datetime originally required and the Memento-Datetime returned by an archive. Drift can be forward or backward in time; in this study only the amount of drift is relevant. This paper examines two target datetime policies:

- **Sliding Target**: the target datetime changes as the user browses. The Memento-Datetime of the current page becomes the new target datetime.
- **Sticky Target**: the target datetime is set once at the beginning of the browsing session.

3.1 Sliding Target (The Wayback Machine)

Browsing using the Internet Archive's Wayback Machine User Interface (UI) employs the *Sliding Target* datetime policy. This policy has the potential to introduce permanent drift at every step. Here is the browsing process in detail:

1. **Select URI-R**. Navigate to `http://www.archive.org` and enter a URI-R. Clicking the *Take Me Back* button displays a calendar of the most recent year for which the URI-R is archived. The 2005 calendar for the ODU Computer Science home is shown in Figure 2.

2. **Select Memento-Datetime**. Dates covered by blue circles have mementos for the URI-R. Larger circles indicate multiple mementos for the same date. Hovering over a circle pops up a box that allows mementos to be selected. When a memento is selected, its Memento-Datetime becomes the target datetime and the corresponding memento it is displayed (as was previously shown in Figure 1). Drift is introduced when the selected memento redirects to another memento that has a different Memento-Datetime than originally selected.

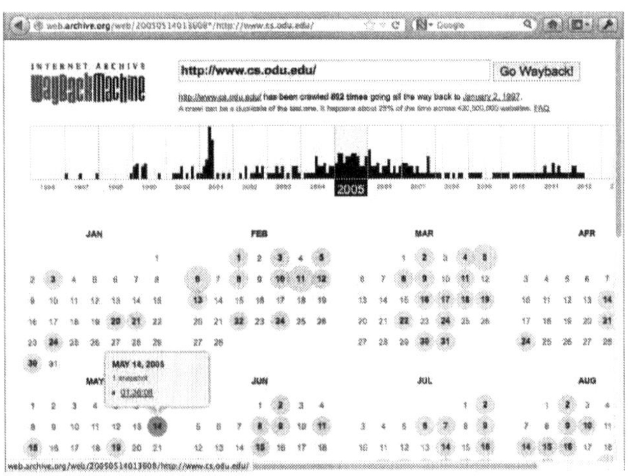

Figure 2: Wayback Machine Calendar

3. **Browse additional URI-Rs**. To simulate browsing the Web within the context of the archive, links are rewritten to reference the archive instead of the original URI and to embedded the Memento-Datetime of the displayed memento. Each link followed uses the embedded datetime as the new target datetime (the selection from step 2 is forgotten), which introduces drift. Additionally, it is unlikely that the selected URI-R was archived at the new target datetime; therefore, one or more additional redirects, each introducing drift, will be required before the best memento is displayed.

Browsing using the *Sliding Target* policy introduces two kinds of drift: *Memento drift* by redirection to the actual memento and *Target drift* by changing the target datetime.

3.2 Sticky Target (Memento API)

Browsing the Internet Archive using the Memento API uses the Sticky Target policy. The Sticky Target policy also introduces drift; however, the drift is constrained because the target datetime is maintained. Here is the browsing process using Firefox and the MementoFox add-on:

1. **Select URI-R**. Open Firefox and enable MementoFox. Move the requested datetime slider to the desired target datetime. All URI-Rs entered in the address bar or followed through clicking a link, are now dereferenced using the Memento API and redirected to the *best* URI-M, which is the URI-M with Memento-Datetime closest to the target datetime. Figure 3 shows the ODU Computer Science home for 2005-05-15T00:28:03Z as dereferenced by MementoFox. Drift is introduced when the target datetime redirects to a memento with a Memento-Datetime that is not the target datetime.

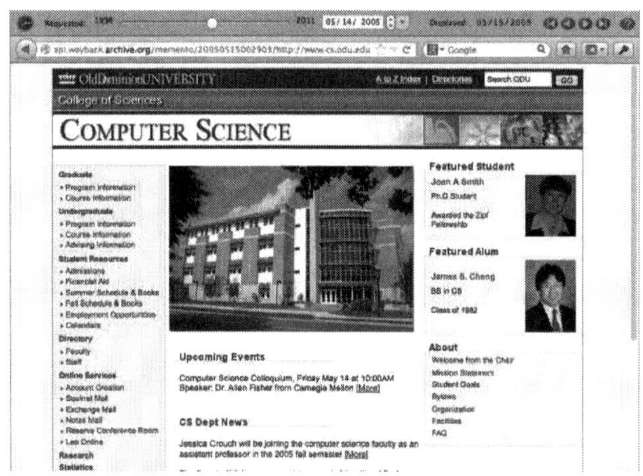

Figure 3: Memento API and MementoFox

2. **Browse additional URI-Rs**. Each subsequent link clicked uses the target datetime selected by the slider. Drift continues to be introduced by redirects as in step 1; however, using MementoFox and the Memento API allows the target datetime to remain the same for every request.

Thus, browsing using the Memento API introduces only memento drift and does not introduce target drift.

4. EXPERIMENT

4.1 Samples

Building on our previous coverage work, we use the same four URI sample sets (DMOZ, Delicious, Bitly, and Search

Engines) as in [1]. Each sample contains 1,000 randomly-selected URIs for 4,000 URI total. URI random selection details can be found in [2].

Table 2: Archival Rates

Sample	2013	2011
DMOZ	95.2%	79%
Delicious	91.9%	68%
Bitly	23.5%	16%
Search Engine	26.4%	19%
Aggregate	59.4%	46%

Table 2 shows the percentage of URI-Rs in the sample that were found to be archived during the experiment. There are several notable differences from our 2011 results [27]. The DMOZ and Delicious samples are archived at a considerably higher rate; the Bitly and Search Engine samples rate are only slightly higher. We attribute this to the increased archive availability provided by the Internet Archive over the past two years [14].

4.2 Procedure

The examination of temporal drift was accomplished in January 2013. To ensure adequate number of successful walks, 200,000 walks were attempted. Each walk was accomplished in three phases:

- Obtain the initial memento,
- Follow links, and
- Calculate drift and statistics.

Each walk iterates through the process of selecting URI-Rs and downloading mementos until either 50 steps are successful or an error is encountered. The details of each walk step are captured, including steps that encounter errors. The last step will contain the stop reason, unless the walk completed 50 successful steps (in which case there is no stop reason). The vast majority of walks encounter an error before reaching step 50. The length of a walk is the number of successful steps. For example, a walk that stops on walk step 6 (i.e. step 6 encounters an error), is length 5 because the first 5 steps were successful. Table 3 defines the symbols used in the procedure description.

To ensure repeatability, a set of 200,000 random numbers (one per walk) were generated. These random numbers were used as both the walk identifier and as the seed to initialize the walk's random number generator. The experiment was run under Apple OS X 10.8.2 using Python 2.7.2 (the version included with OS X). The built-in Python random number generator, `random.Random`, was used. Resources were downloaded using *curl*, which is much more robust than the Python libraries.

Phase I. First Walk Step

Phase I selects a walk's first URI-R, downloads the corresponding timemap, and downloads the first API and UI mementos. Phase I accomplishes the first step of a walk.

1. Randomly select R_1 from the 4,000 sample URIs.
2. Retrieve the timemap for R_1 from the Internet Archive using the Memento API.

Table 3: Definitions

Term	Definition
W	An acyclic walk.
w	An acyclic walk index.
i	A walk step index.
t	The target datetime. t_i is the target for walk step i.
R	A URI-R. R_i is the R selected for walk step i.
M	A URI-M.
M^a	A Memento API URI-M. M_i^a is the M^a for walk step i.
M^w	A Wayback Machine UI URI-M. M_i^w is the M^w for walk step i.
L	The set of link URI-Rs in a memento (dereferenced URI-M).
$\mathcal{T}(M)$	The Memento-Datetime of M.
$\mathcal{L}(M)$	The set of link Rs in the memento identified by M.
$\Delta(M)$	The drift of M relative to the corresponding t. $\Delta(M_i) = \|t_i - \mathcal{T}(M_i)\|$
δ^a	Memento API memento drift. $\delta_i^a = \Delta(M_i^a)$.
δ^w	Wayback Machine UI memento drift. $\delta_i^w = \Delta(M_i^w)$.

3. Randomly select a URI-M, M_1, from the timemap. M_1 yields this step's target datetime, $t_1 = \mathcal{T}(M_1)$.
4. Dereference M_1^a using t_1 from the IA Memento API. HTTP redirects may occur during dereferencing, yielding $M_1^{a\prime}$ as the final dereferenced URI-M. Note that $M_1^{a\prime} = M_1^a$ may not hold. It follows that $\mathcal{T}(M_1^{a\prime}) = t_1$ also may not hold. This is the *Sticky Target* policy.
5. Calculate the corresponding M_1^w and dereference it. As in step 4, HTTP redirects may occur during dereferencing, yielding $M_1^{w\prime}$ as the final dereferenced URI-M. In addition, the Wayback Machine returns *soft* redirects. These responses have HTTP status 200 but contain embedded JavaScript redirects; these are detected and followed. Note that $M_1^{w\prime} = M_1^w$ may not hold. It follows that $\mathcal{T}(M_1^{w\prime}) = t_1$ also may not hold. This is the *Sliding Target* policy.

Phase II. Additional Walk Steps

Phase II accomplishes a walk's second and subsequent steps. It selects a link common to the API and UI mementos from the previous walk step and downloads the corresponding timemap and mementos. If there are no common links, the walk stops. In the following, i is the current walk step.

6. Extract the sets of link URI-Rs, $L^a = \mathcal{L}(M_{i-1}^a)$ and $L^w = \mathcal{L}(M_{i-1}^w)$, from the previous walk step's mementos. Denote the set of URI-Rs used in previous walk steps is L^p. Then, the set of common, usable URI-Rs for this walk step is $L_i^u = (L^a \cap L^w) - L^p$. Randomly select R_i from L_i^u.
7. Download the timemap for R_i from the IA Memento API.
8. Select the *best* URI-M, M_i^a, from the timemap. M_i^a is the URI-M that minimizes $|t_1 - \mathcal{T}(M)|$, e.g. the URI-M nearest the initial target datetime.

9. Dereference M_i^a using t_1 from the IA's Memento API. As in step 4, HTTP redirects may occur during dereferencing, yielding $M_i^{a\prime}$. $M_i^{a\prime} = M_i^a$ and $\mathcal{T}(M_i^{a\prime}) = t_1$ may not hold. This is the *Sticky Target* policy.

10. Calculate M_i^w using $t_i = \mathcal{T}(M_{i-1}^{u\prime})$, as the target datetime. Dereference M_i^w. As in step 5, HTTP redirects and *soft* redirects may occur, yielding $M_1^{w\prime}$ as final. Again, $M_i^{w\prime} = M_i^w$ and $\mathcal{T}(M_i^{w\prime}) = t_i$ may not hold.

11. Repeat Phase II until L_i^u is empty, an error occurs, or 50 walk steps have been completed successfully.

Phase III. Drift Calculations

Phase III calculates drift and statistics, ignoring duplicate walks. Duplicate walks occurs for a number of reasons. A common reason is failure on the first walk step because R_1 has never been archived. A limited number of links or mementos is another reason.

12. Calculate API drift, $\delta_i^a = \Delta(M_i^{a\prime})$, for each successful walk step. Calculate the API drift mean, median, and standard deviation for the entire walk.

13. Calculate Wayback Machine drift, $\delta_i^w = \Delta(M_i^{w\prime})$, for each successful walk step. Calculate the Wayback Machine drift mean, median, and standard deviation for the entire walk.

4.3 Results

The 200,000 acyclic walks attempted resulted in 53,926 unique walks, of which 48,685 had at least 1 successful step. Overall there were 240,439 successful steps, with an average of 3.85 successful steps per walk. Table 4 summarizes walks and steps by sample.

Table 4: Walks and Steps

	DMOZ	S.Eng.	Delicious	Bitly	Total
Steps	64,661	26,047	124,020	25,711	240,439
Succ. Steps	48,445	20,177	98,560	20,189	187,371
w/δ^u > 1yr	1,761	1,212	3,028	700	6,701
w/δ^u > 5yr	75	13	16	7	111
Unique Walks	16,221	5,873	25,482	5,524	53,100
Succ. Walks	15,009	4,604	24,451	4,621	48,685
Pct. Succ.	92.5%	78.4%	96.0%	83.7%	91.7%
Mean Succ. Steps/Walk	3.2	4.4	4.0	4.4	3.8

4.3.1 Walk Length and Stop Causes

Figure 4 shows the distribution of successful walks by length. (Note that *Occurrences* is a log scale.) Table 5 shows the details behind Figure 4, broken out by sample. Walks greater than 25 in length are summarized in groups of 5. The number of steps decreases exponentially as walk length increases. Less than 1% of walks progress past step 21. For DMOZ, less than 1% progress step past 19; Search Engine, step 23; Delicious, step 23; and Bitly, step 24.

Table 6 summarizes the reasons walks stop before reaching step 50, split by timemap and memento. Because the selection processes for the first and subsequent mementos differ, separate statistics are shown. The stop causes are dominated by 403s, 404s, 503s, and *No Common Links*. The 403s are generally an archived 403; the original URI-R returned a 403 when accessed for archiving. The timemap 404s indicate that the URI-R is not archived. Memento 404s can have two meanings: either the original URI-R returned a 404 when it was accessed for archiving or the memento has been redacted, i.e. removed from public access. The 503s most likely indicate a transient condition such as an unavailable archive server, thus there is a chance that on repetition the resource will be found. Resources that returned 503s were retried a single time one week after the first 503 was received. Less than 1% succeed on the second try. *Download failed* indicates that *curl* was unable to download the resource; like the 503s, these were retried once. *Not HTML* indicates that the downloaded resource was not HTML and therefore not checked for links. *No common links* indicates that although both Memento API and Wayback Machine UI mementos were found, content divergence due to drift caused the two mementos to have no common links.

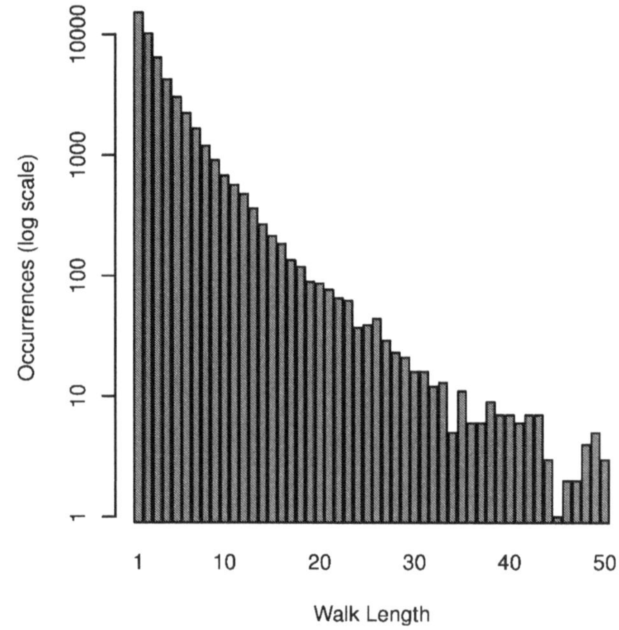

Figure 4: Occurrences by Walk Length

4.3.2 Drift

Figure 5 illustrates the distribution of Wayback Machine mementos by drift (δ^w). The horizontal axis is the walk step number. The vertical axis is the drift in years from the walk step's target datetime. Color indicates memento density on an exponential axis. As expected, density is highest for early steps and tapers off with as walk length increases. Density is also highest at low drift values and many mementos appear to have very high drift. However, only 11,093 (4.6%) exceed 1 year and only 172 (0.07%) exceed 5 years (Table 4). It is also interesting that the first step shows drift (as high as 6.5 years). The first target datetime is selected from a timemap, which sets the expectation that a memento for the datetime exists. However, redirects (4.2 steps 4, 5, 9, and 11), from the URI-M in the timemap to the final URI-M cause drift—even on the first walk step.

Figure 6 illustrates the distribution of Memento API mementos by drift (δ^a), which at first glance appears very sim-

Table 5: Occurrences by Length

Walk Length	DMOZ	Search Engine	Delicious	Bitly	Total
1	5,355	1,239	7,193	1,289	15,076
2	3,571	924	4,857	817	10,169
3	1,891	598	3,311	623	6,423
4	1,212	381	2,228	415	4,236
5	791	315	1,588	314	3,008
6	583	232	1,168	259	2,242
7	417	178	877	186	1,658
8	258	153	651	136	1,198
9	187	111	498	108	904
10	144	79	377	79	679
11	114	71	306	74	565
12	99	51	279	48	477
13	72	44	200	46	362
14	54	32	144	35	265
15	39	30	119	26	214
16	33	26	108	20	187
17	20	23	76	18	137
18	24	14	68	12	118
19	19	12	46	12	89
20	14	10	47	15	86
21	20	11	36	9	76
22	7	13	28	16	64
23	11	11	33	7	62
24	7	4	22	4	37
25	8	3	25	3	39
26–30	27	18	68	20	133
31–35	7	7	30	14	58
36–40	6	3	23	3	35
41–45	6	2	14	2	24
46–50	6	3	6	1	16
Totals	15,002	4,598	24,426	4,611	48,637

Table 6: Stop Causes

Stop Cause	First Step Count	First Step Percent	Other Steps Count	Other Steps Percent
Timemaps				
HTTP 403	74	1.7%	4,803	9.1%
HTTP 404	1,327	30.1%	15,850	29.9%
HTTP 503	0	0.0%	43	0.1%
Other	2	0.0%	180	0.3%
Mementos				
HTTP 403	52	1.2%	476	0.9%
HTTP 404	215	4.9%	3,633	6.8%
HTTP 503	1,957	44.4%	10,535	19.9%
Download failed	154	3.5%	589	1.1%
Not HTML	514	11.7%	2,856	5.4%
No Common Links		0.0%	12,957	24.4%
Other	117	2.7%	1,128	2.1%
Totals	**4,412**		**53,050**	

ilar to Figure 5. Closer examination reveals that many mementos have lower drift when using the Memento API. Figure 7 shows the mean drift by step (solid circles) and standard deviation (hollow circles) for both the Memento API (green) and Wayback Machine URI (blue). The Memento API, which uses the Sticky Target policy, results in 40–50 days less mean drift than the Sliding Target policy. This delta appears to decrease above step 40, but there are only 40 walks (0.0082%) that achieve this many steps (see Table 5), so the decrease is not significant.

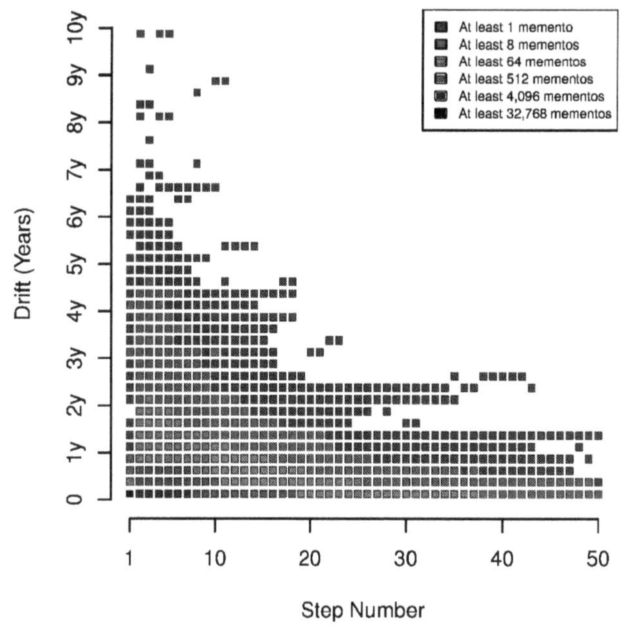

Figure 5: UI Drift by Step

Even below step 40, mean as a useful indicator of central tendency is in doubt. As Figure 7 shows, the standard deviation significantly exceeds the mean, particularly at low step numbers. This indicates that median may be a better indicator of the central tendency. Note the horizontal line of squares at 1.25 years in Figures 5 and 6. Investigation revealed that well-archived, self-contained sites contribute more long walks than groups of loosely-linked sites. For example, left column of every `http://www.101celebrities.com` page includes nearly 1,000 links to pages within the site; it is a primary contributor to the horizontal line. The number of domains in a walk and their impact on the walk are discussed in 4.3.4. The median is shown in Figure 8. The median shows lower average drift than the mean because it is less impacted by the outliers. For this data, we believe median is the better measure of central tendency and will use median from here forward.

4.3.3 Choice

Every walk step has a limited number of links to choose from. Given a starting URI-R and Memento-Datetime, it is possible to represent all possible walks as a tree (4.2 step 6 disallows revisits). Choice is the number of children common to both the Memento API and Wayback Machine mementos. Figure 9 shows the median drift by choice for the Memento API and Wayback Machine UI. Clearly as choice increases, drift also increases.

4.3.4 Number of Domains

Through casual observations, we began to suspect that the number of domains accessed in a walk also impacted drift. Figure 10 graphs the relationship between the number of domains and drift. The number of domains has a significant correlation with drift, but only for the Sliding Policy.

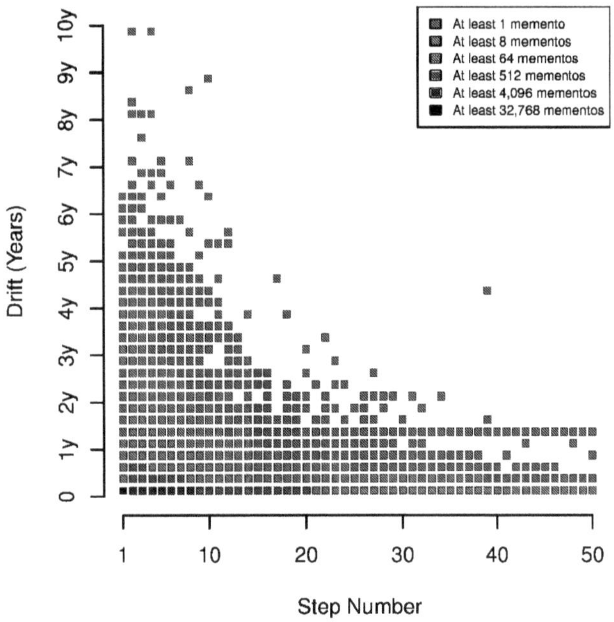

Figure 6: API Drift by Step

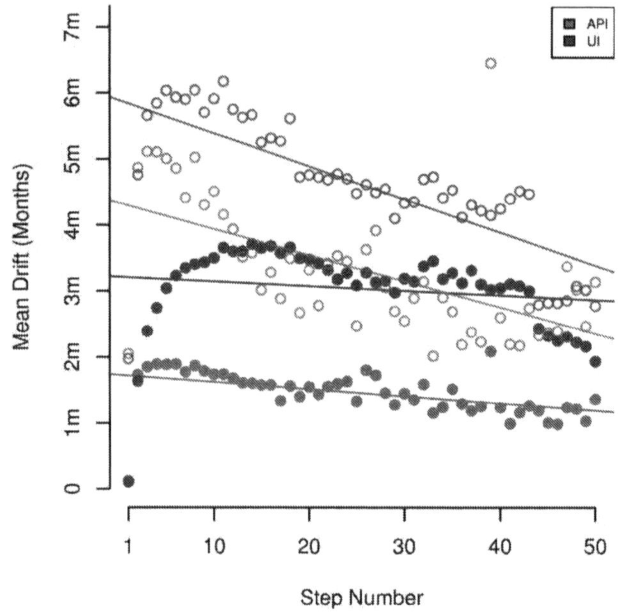

Figure 7: Standard Deviation Drift by Step

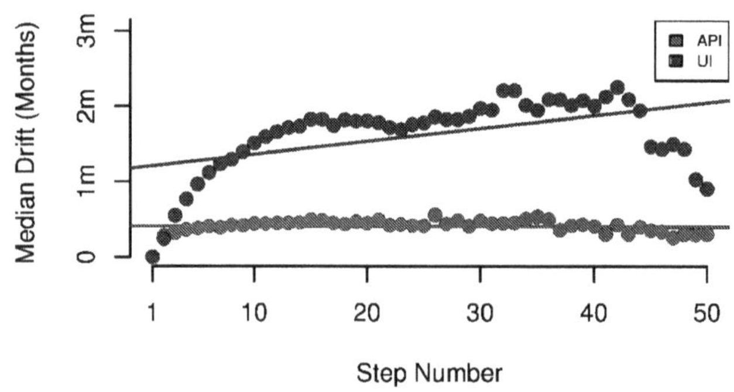

Figure 8: Median Drift by Step

4.3.5 Sample Differences

In our 2011 research [1], we found that archival rates varied from 16%–79% (see Table 2) depending on the sample from which the URI-R originated. This led to exploration of possible differences between acyclic walks based on sample. We found there is not a significant drift difference based on sample source.

4.3.6 Relaxed Shared URI Requirement

An average walk length of 3.2 steps seems short. Anecdotally, the authors' experience has been much longer walks when browsing the Internet Archive. Much of this difference is likely due to the random rather than human browsing approach [3], but questions arose about requiring common URI-Rs at every walk step (4.2 step 6). The experiment was run again using the same sample URI-Rs and random numbers while relaxing the requirement. When a common URI-R was not available, two different URI-Rs were selected. The results are summarized in Table 7. Compared with Table 4, there is little change. The number of steps and successful steps increased about 5% each. The number of unique and successful walks only increased by about 2.5% and the average number of successful steps per walk increased by only 2.3%. Figure 11 shows the median drift by step after relaxing the shared URI requirement; it is very similar to Figure 8. API drift is essentially the same and UI drift slightly reduced. Even though relaxing the shared URI requirement reduces comparability between the two policies, the results also show that the Sticky Target policy controls temporal drift and that drift grows under the the Sliding Target policy.

5. FUTURE WORK

We see several avenues of future work for this line of research. The experiments conducted so far have focused on randomly-generated walks through a single archive. Alnoamany et al. [3] have looked at real-world walk patterns through analysis of the Internet Archive's web server logs. Using these patterns to guide walks will provide more realistic link streams and result in temporal drift data more in line with actual user experience. There are also domains that users tend to avoid, such as link farms, SEO, and spam sites. Detecting and avoiding them, as a user would, will also move the data toward real-world user experience. We also suspect that long walk drift is heavily influenced by clusters of closely-related domains and domains that primarily self-reference. Applying an appropriate measure of clustering or similarity may shed some light on this topic.

Preliminary research has shown that the amount of drift can vary based on the starting date. Repeating this study with a focus on the earliest and latest archived versions available will bear out (or disprove) our preliminary evidence. Closely related to choosing the earliest or latest versions is starting with a variety of fixed datetimes. In this case, we hypothesize increased first step drift for early dates followed by drift settling out after a few steps.

Recently, additional archives (e.g. the UK Web Archive) have implemented native Memento support and the Wayback Machine UI. It will be interesting to see if other archives

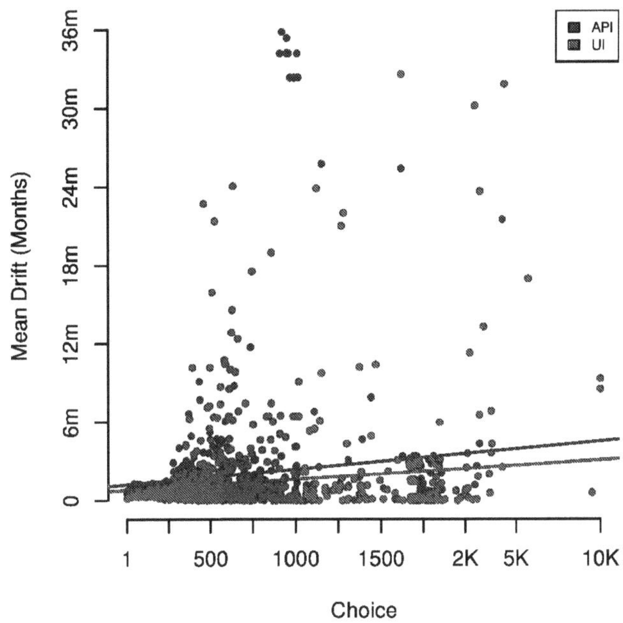

Figure 9: Median Drift by Choice

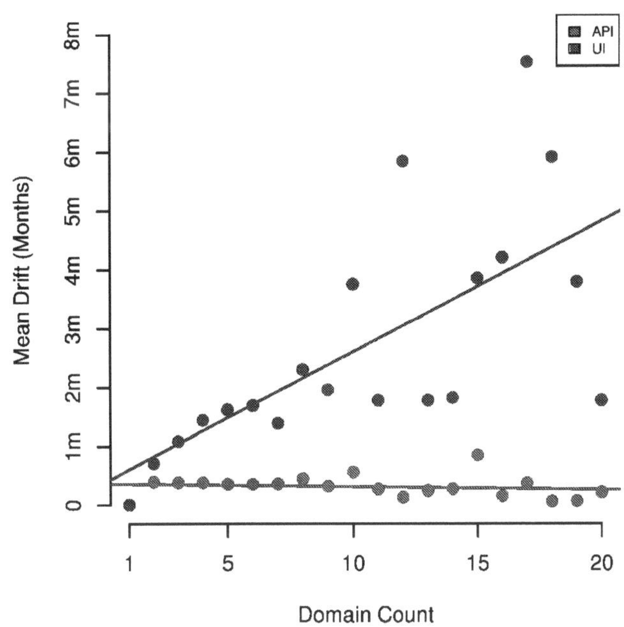

Figure 10: Median Drift by Number of Domains

have temporal drift similar to the Internet Archive's. Finally, the Memento architecture provides for aggregators, which are servers that combine the timemaps from multiple archives into a single, unified timemap. The aggregators will make it possible to study drift across multiple archives.

6. CONCLUSION

We studied the temporal drift that occurs when browsing web archives under two different policies: Sliding Target and Sticky Target. Acyclic walks through the Internet archived were conducted using the Memento API, which

Table 7: Change in Walks and Steps w/Relaxed Shared URI Requirement

	Strict	Relaxed	Change
Steps	240,439	251,439	+4.6%
Succ. Steps	187,371	196,999	+5.1%
w/δ^u > 1yr	6,701	6,344	-5.3%
w/δ^u > 5yr	111	118	+6.3%
Unique Walks	53,100	54,474	+2.6%
Succ. Walks	48,685	50,043	+2.8%
Pct Succ.	91.7%	91.9%	+0.2%
Successful Steps/Walk	3.2	3.9	+2.3%

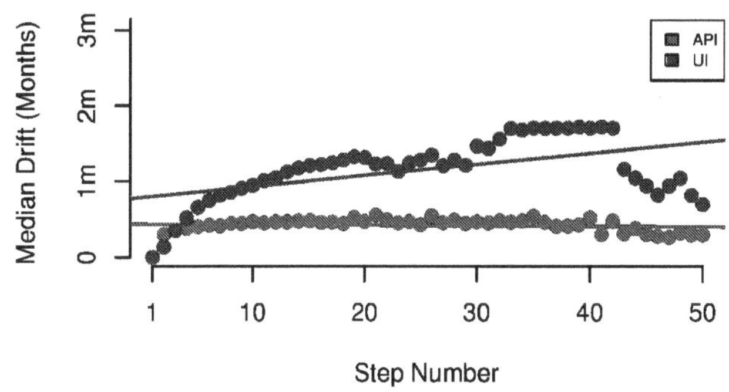

Figure 11: Median Drift by Step (Relaxed URI Requirement)

uses the Sticky Target policy, and the Wayback Machine UI, which employs the Sliding policy. Measurements of drift were taken on three axis: number of steps (Table 8), choice (Table 9), and number of domains (Table 10). All three showed a showed a positive correlation with increased temporal drift for the Sliding Target policy. For the Sticky Target policy, drift by step and drift by domain count showed no correlation. Drift by choice showed low correlation for both policies; however, median drift for the Sticky Target was still lower overall. The Sticky Target policy clearly achieves lower temporal drift. Based on walk length, the Sticky Target policy generally produces at least 30 days less drift than the Sliding Target policy.

7. ACKNOWLEDGMENTS

This work supported in part by the NSF (IIS 1009392) and the Library of Congress. We are grateful to the Internet Archive for their continued support of Memento access to their archive. Memento is a joint project between the Los Alamos National Laboratory Research Library and Old Dominion University.

8. REFERENCES

[1] S. G. Ainsworth, A. Alsum, H. SalahEldeen, M. C. Weigle, and M. L. Nelson. How much of the Web is archived? In *Proceedings of the 11th Annual International ACM/IEEE Joint Conference on Digital libraries*, JCDL '11, pages 133–136, June 2011.

[2] S. G. Ainsworth, A. Alsum, H. SalahEldeen, M. C. Weigle, and M. L. Nelson. How much of the Web is archived? Technical Report arXiv:1212.6177, Old Dominion University, December 2012.

[3] Y. AlNoamany, M. C. Weigle, and M. L. Nelson. Access patterns for robots and humans in web archives. In *Proceedings of the 13th Annual International ACM/IEEE Joint Conference on Digital libraries*, JCDL'13, July 2013.

[4] M. Ben Saad and S. Gançarski. Archiving the Web using page changes patterns: a case study. In *Proceedings of the 11th annual international ACM/IEEE joint conference on Digital libraries*, JCDL '11, pages 113–122, 2011.

[5] M. Ben Saad and S. Gançarski. Improving the quality of web archives through the importance of changes. In *Proceedings of the 22nd international conference on Database and expert systems applications - Volume Part I*, DEXA'11, pages 394–409, 2011.

[6] M. Ben Saad, Z. Pehlivan, and S. Gançarski. Coherence-oriented crawling and navigation using patterns for web archives. In *Proceedings of the 15th international conference on Theory and practice of digital libraries: research and advanced technology for digital libraries*, TPDL'11, pages 421–433, 2011.

[7] J. F. Brunelle and M. L. Nelson. Evaluating the sitestory transactional web archive with the apachebench tool. Technical Report arXiv:1209.1811, Old Dominion University, September 2012.

[8] C. Casey. The Cyberarchive: a look at the storage and preservation of web sites. *College & Research Libraries*, 59, 1998.

[9] M. Day. Preserving the fabric of our lives: A survey of web preservation initiatives. In *Proceedings of the 7th European Conference on Research and Advanced Technology for Digital Libraries (ECDL 2005)*, pages 461–472, 2003.

[10] D. Denev, A. Mazeika, M. Spaniol, and G. Weikum. SHARC: Framework for quality-conscious web archiving. volume 2, pages 586–597, August 2009.

[11] C. E. Dyreson, H.-l. Lin, and Y. Wang. Managing versions of web documents in a transaction-time web server. In *Proceedings of the 13th international conference on World Wide Web*, WWW '04, 2004.

[12] G. Eysenbach and M. Trudel. Going, going, still there: Using the WebCite service to permanently archive cited web pages. *Journal of Medical Internet Research*, 7(5), 2005.

[13] K. Fitch. Web site archiving: an approach to recording every materially different response produced by a website. In *9th Australasian World Wide Web Conference, Sanctuary Cove, Queensland, Australia,*, pages 5–9, 2003.

[14] B. Kahle. Wayback machine: Now with 240,000,000,000 URLs. `http://blog.archive.org/2013/01/09/updated-wayback/`, January 2013.

[15] M. Kimpton and J. Ubois. Year-by-year: from an archive of the Internet to an archive on the Internet. In J. Masanès, editor, *Web Archiving*, chapter 9, pages 201–212. 2006.

[16] J. Masanès. Web archiving: issues and methods. In J. Masanès, editor, *Web Archving*, chapter 1, pages 1–53. 2006.

[17] F. McCown and M. L. Nelson. Characterization of search engine caches. In *Proceedings of IS&T Archiving 2007*, pages 48–52, May 2007.

[18] G. Mohr, M. Stack, I. Rnitovic, D. Avery, and M. Kimpton. Introduction to Heritrix, an archival quality web crawler. In *4th International Web Archiving Workshop, Bath, UK*, September 2004.

[19] K. C. Negulescu. Web archiving @ the Internet Archive. `http://www.digitalpreservation.gov/news/events/ndiipp_meetings/ndiipp10/docs/July21/session09/NDIIPP072110FinalIA.ppt`, 2010.

[20] R. Sanderson, H. Shankar, S. Ainsworth, F. McCown, and S. Adams. Implementing time travel for the Web. *Code{4}Lib Journal*, (13), 2011.

[21] M. Spaniol, D. Denev, A. Mazeika, G. Weikum, and P. Senellart. Data quality in web archiving. In *Proceedings of the 3rd Workshop on Information Credibility on the Web*, WICOW '09, pages 19–26, 2009.

[22] M. Spaniol, A. Mazeika, D. Denev, and G. Weikum. "Catch me if you can": Visual analysis of coherence defects in web archiving. In *The 9 th International Web Archiving Workshop (IWAW 2009) Corfu, Greece, September/October, 2009 Workshop Proceedings*, pages 27–37, 2009.

[23] M. Thelwall and L. Vaughan. A fair history of the Web? examining country balance in the Internet Archive. *Library & Information Science Research*, 26(2), 2004.

[24] B. Tofel. 'Wayback' for accessing web archives. In *Proceedings of the 7th International Web Archiving Workshop (IWAW07)*, 2007.

[25] H. Van de Sompel, M. Nelson, and R. Sanderson. HTTP framework for time-based access to resource states — Memento, November 2010. `http://datatracker.ietf.org/doc/draft-vandesompel-memento/`.

[26] H. Van de Sompel, M. L. Nelson, R. Sanderson, L. L. Balakireva, S. Ainsworth, and H. Shankar. Memento: Time travel for the Web. Technical Report arXiv:0911.1112, 2009.

[27] M. C. Weigle. How much of the web is archived? `http://ws-dl.blogspot.com/2011/06/2011-06-23-how-much-of-web-is-archived.html`, June 2011.

Medusa at the University of Illinois at Urbana-Champaign: A Digital Preservation Service Based on PREMIS

Kyle Rimkus
University of Illinois at Urbana-Champaign
44 Library
Urbana, IL 61801
(+1) (217) 300-3842
rimkus@illinois.edu

Thomas Habing
University of Illinois at Urbana-Champaign
155 Grainger Engineering Library
Urbana, IL 61801
(+1) (217) 244-4425
thabing@illinois.edu

ABSTRACT

The Medusa digital preservation service at the University of Illinois at Urbana-Champaign provides a storage environment for digital content selected for long-term retention by content managers and producers affiliated with the Library in order to ensure its enduring access and use. This paper reports on Medusa development, with emphasis on the research processes that informed key decisions related to its design, the central role of PREMIS metadata in its architecture, and future directions of integrating PREMIS management into a Fedora repository architecture. In so doing, it describes a strategy of digital preservation content management that draws strength from the creation and management of comprehensive PREMIS preservation metadata records.

Categories and Subject Descriptors

H.3.7 [Digital Libraries]: Systems issues

Keywords

Digital Preservation, Medusa, PREMIS

1. Digital Preservation Research at UIUC

1.1 National Digital Information Infrastructure Preservation Program (NDIIPP) Grants

In 2004, digital preservation was still a young library practice. The Open Archival Information System specification was relatively new, having been finalized in 2002 [1], while the working group to establish Preservation Metadata: Implementation Strategies, or PREMIS, had been formed in 2003 [5]. With such developments catalyzing interest and a sense of urgency in the library community, the National Digital Information Infrastructure and Preservation Program, or NDIIPP [9] arose in the United States to support efforts to develop the tools and methodologies necessary to initiate and sustain digital preservation activities in libraries and other historical memory institutions across the country.

JCDL '13, July 22–26, 2013, Indianapolis, Indiana, USA.

The University of Illinois at Urbana-Champaign received two rounds of NDIIPP funding from 2004-2007 and 2007-2010, respectively. These grants, undertaken in partnership with the Graduate School of Library and Information Science, the National Center for Supercomputer Applications, OCLC Inc., peer institutions, and several state libraries throughout the United States, were known together as the ECHO DEPository or "ECHODep" [6], and featured research on web archiving tools, repository software interoperability, the semantics of preservation metadata, and tools for file evaluation and assessment. In particular, grant activities related to the development of the Hub and Spoke, or "HandS" suite of tools for repository interoperability [8] established a broad knowledge-base of digital preservation concepts, technologies, and standards among institutional library faculty and staff. Lessons learned from this project went on to inform current digital preservation repository development, so they bear some further explanation.

1.2 Hub and Spoke, or HandS Framework Tool Suite

Repository research in the first phase of ECHODep focused on evaluating the interoperability characteristics of five platforms then available to digital library practitioners: the open source DSpace, Fedora, Greenstone, and ePrints platforms, as well as the hosted OCLC Digital Archive service. Taking it as a given that the packaging and transfer of digital content and its associated metadata from one repository platform to another has become an inevitable event in the lifecycles of contemporary digital materials, and that this poses definite digital preservation risks, the research team undertook a variety of experiments moving sets of digital objects from one platform to another, thereby gaining knowledge of the metadata and file packaging profiles for ingest and export native to each respective system.

These activities continued in Phase Two with the development of a suite of tools for moving content between repository platforms. Given the name of "Hub and Spoke" or "HandS," the Illinois team developed an open-source, Java-based tool with a graphical user interface for packaging data as it moved from a central "hub" to any number of "spokes," or ingest destinations. This approach was taken to mitigate the implicit inefficiency of Phase One's method:

"To reduce the complexity of interoperability, the Hub and Spoke uses a common packaging format for interchange of digital resources between different repositories. Digital packages coming from a repository are transformed into this common format before any further processing, and digital packages are transformed from the common format into the native repository format when being placed into a repository. The idea is to reduce an N^2 problem into a 2N problem…" [4].

The hub through which all transfers of content passed, however, was not a repository itself, but a Metadata Encoding and Transmission Standard, or METS file that grew every time an object made the trip from one spoke repository to another, by retaining all original and crosswalked metadata files produced during transfers and organizing them into a structured XML document. This approach was distinguished by several key factors:

1. the reliance on PREMIS for digital preservation metadata;
2. the reliance on MODS for descriptive metadata;
3. the packaging of PREMIS, MODS, and other associated metadata and file information in METS wrappers, to describe relationships between files and significant events in their respective lifecycles; and
4. the implicit assertion that digital object packages designed to serve a long-term preservation need ought to be repository-independent.

Three METS profiles that embody this approach were registered with the Library of Congress [12]. This work also contributed to the publication of *Guidelines for using PREMIS with METS for exchange* [3], and went on to define in large part the approach taken to building Medusa, with one important exception. Namely, Medusa's developers decided to implement their service without METS in favor of a purely PREMIS-centric model for managing digital preservation metadata. This will be discussed in some detail following a broad overview of Medusa.

2. Digital Preservation Services at UIUC

2.1 The Need

By 2010, the Library still had much in common with the problems investigated by ECHODep's Hub and Spoke research – that is, it was (and remains) an organization with a variety of content producers and systems for managing and delivering content to patrons. As of October, 2012, a preliminary assessment conducted by the Library's Preservation Unit identified at least eight platforms in the library for managing access to locally produced digital library content, including ContentDM, DSpace, ARTStor, the Internet Archive, the HathiTrust Digital Library, Archon, and Olive ActivePaper.

In addition, the master files created for the access systems listed above were not all being stewarded in a single, unified storage environment. While the majority of them existed on file servers managed by the Library's Information Technology group, a significant number of them could be found on optical media in an off-site storage facility, on hard drives on staff members' shelves, or on file servers leased from external companies (a full analysis of the preservation needs of these collections prior to Medusa ingest is being prepared for future publication). Given these circumstances, significant motivation has existed for several years within the Library to introduce a more reliable infrastructure for the long-term preservation of locally managed digital content.

After six years of research into the theory and practice of digital preservation, the University of Illinois Library nevertheless found itself without a full-fledged service to ensure enduring access to its own digital collections. It relied on several external preservation services for specific formats of digital collections, and has, in the intervening years, introduced others. Taken together, these include the HathiTrust for digitized books, the Web Archiving Service for web content, and the LOCKSS Alliance and Portico for subscription electronic journals. Medusa fills a special need not addressed by these external services. Namely, its collections consist of unique digital content that the University of Illinois Library has the need, authority, and responsibility to store, manage, and preserve locally. This includes but is not limited to text, image, audio, and video preservation master files created for Library units by its digital reformatting operations, as well as electronic records acquired by its repositories of special collections.

2.2 Medusa is Born

At the heart of Medusa is a Collection Registry written in Ruby on Rails (public collection entries may be viewed at https://medusa.library.illinois.edu/). This web application allows preservation managers to survey digital collections outside of the repository, assess their potential risk factors, and ingest them into a secure preservation storage environment. The Open Archival Information System (OAIS) reference model, as well as the complementary Trustworthy Digital Repository certification framework, have both strongly informed Medusa's infrastructure. Its designated community of users consists primarily of managers of digital content to which the University of Illinois Library allows access. This includes curators of archival and special collections, subject specialists, and managers of repositories of scholarly content, as well as internal units that produce and manage digital files.

3. PREMIS in Medusa

3.1 The PREMIS Philosophy

The philosophy underpinning Medusa is that all of its objects are self-describing. Medusa objects and the events that occur to them throughout their respective lifecycles are represented entirely by PREMIS records. By virtue of their rigorously maintained metadata, Medusa digital objects are therefore able to stand on their own independently of their underlying repository software and hardware.

To achieve this, every digital asset stewarded in Medusa – whether a content or metadata file – is assigned a unique ID and an associated PREMIS file. In contrast, for example, to the common repository practice of storing digital content files on a file server and metadata in a database, the "self-contained object" approach favors managing objects in their native formats using a common storage layer. Risk increases when the constituent parts of digital objects are split up across a variety of systems subject to their own specific threats, a problem that Medusa's architects seek to avoid.

For similar reasons, Medusa's technical team has also decided to forego METS. While many practitioners deploy PREMIS within METS wrappers [2][13], leveraging METS's richness in expressing relationships between files with PREMIS's affordances in file and representation-level preservation metadata, others have pointed out significant challenges in bundling PREMIS in METS, due to the lack of shared and agreed-upon practices for managing the complexity of hierarchical item and metadata records, as well as redundancies between the two schemas [7].

With respect to tag overlap, metadata managers who implement PREMIS in METS must choose whether to place file information such as file type and file size, among other things, in METS tags,

PREMIS tags, or duplicate them in both. The overlap in available tags is so significant, in fact, that one could argue that the only thing that significantly differentiates METS from PREMIS is the lone required METS tag-set called the "structMap," which provides a structural map of METS packages and describes the relationships between the metadata and bit-streams they contain.

Furthermore, expressing complex relationships in consistently valid METS XML is challenging. The nesting of multiple XML files within a single METS wrapper requires complex validation procedures, the maintenance and debugging of which cause bottlenecks in production workflows, not to mention significant overhead in programming reliable METS tools tailored to local needs.

In other words, there's a lot to keep track of when utilizing METS as the centerpiece of a digital preservation system. PREMIS, on the other hand, offers a flatter data structure which nevertheless enables similarly rich and complex modeling of relationships between digital objects. Namely, its "relationship" tag, by allowing a "relationshipType" and a "relationshipSubType" to refine it, presents the ability to link any one object to any other object with elegant simplicity. What one ends up with, in effect, is the ability to define any imaginable relationship between any single entity and any number of others. Similar flexibility is also enabled, via the same mechanism, to defining Events, Agents, and Rights specific to assets in one's digital preservation environment. (For a closer look at PREMIS controlled vocabularies in Medusa, visit the Medusa wiki at https://wiki.cites.uiuc.edu/wiki/display/LibraryDigitalPreservation/PREMIS+Controlled+Vocabularies). Inspired by current trends in linked data and its underlying concepts, the Medusa implementation team has committed itself to utilizing the PREMIS "relationship" tag to define structured relationships between objects and their constituent parts, and sees it as preferable to the strictly hierarchical METS alternative.

3.2 PREMIS Implementation

Two simplified figures illustrate how Medusa uses PREMIS to model the relationships within a digital object. Figure 1 displays a PREMIS collection-level "representation" record with a root-level MODS metadata record describing the collection itself, as well as a Rights statement and Event metadata testifying to the circumstances of the collection's instantiation in Medusa, in this case its ingest by the "Agent" Tom Habing. Figure 2 shows a related object, namely, an Archival Information Package that belongs to the same collection. This object's PREMIS metadata shows that the object consists of the front and back of a digitized postcard with both archival JPEG2000 and access JPEG image files available for both, and a MODS XML descriptive metadata record. The object is also linked to data declaring its Rights information. The archival images link to an Event detailing their ingest, or capture, into Medusa.

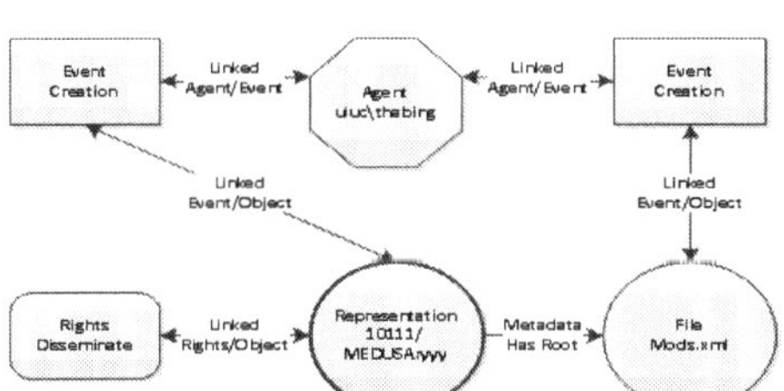

Figure 1. PREMIS Model for a Collection Described by a Single MODS File

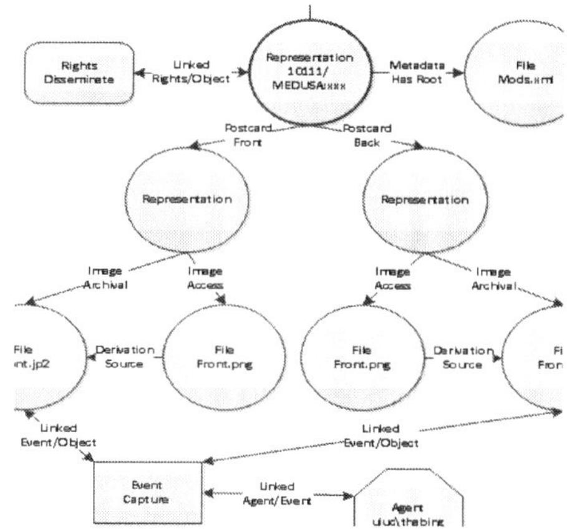

Figure 2. Simplified PREMIS Model Representing the Front and Back a Digitized Postcard

4. Fedora Implemenation

Considerable work has also gone into how best to map Medusa's PREMIS-based object models into a broader Fedora architecture for its object-level preservation store. The approach under consideration is often referred to in Fedora circles as the 'atomistic' model, in which each Fedora object contains no more than a single datastream (not including the standard datastreams such as "DC" or "RELS_EXT"). In this model, each PREMIS entity will reside in a single Fedora object; for example, each PREMIS Agent will be modeled as a Fedora object containing a PREMIS Agent XML file as its only datastream. Likewise, each PREMIS Event will be modeled as a Fedora object containing a single PREMIS Event XML datastream. PREMIS Representation Objects are modeled similarly. The only exceptions to this are PREMIS File Objects. File Objects contain two datastreams, the PREMIS File Object XML file and the actual content file itself. Figure 3 is a simple illustration of this. The boxes are Fedora objects with their PIDs shown at the top and their datastreams shown below. The RELS_EXT relationship between objects are shown with arrows. Note that the relationships between PREMIS objects are converted into RELS_EXT predicates in of the form *relationshipType.subType* in a custom namespace.

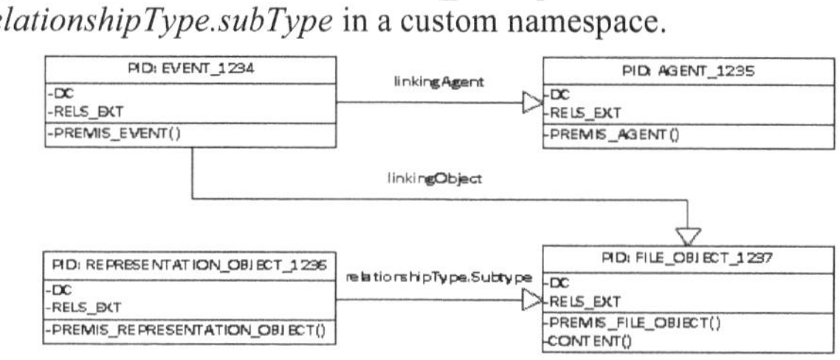

Figure 3. PREMIS Event linked to Agent as Fedora objects

To avoid redundantly encoding the same data in multiple places, all relationships between PREMIS entities will be encoded using Fedora RELS_EXT relationships. PREMIS-based submission packages (SIPs) into the repository may use PREMIS linking mechanisms, but as part of the ingest process these relationships will be encoded in RELS_EXT streams and removed from the corresponding PREMIS entities. Conversely, the repository will provide archival information packages (AIPs) where these relations are represented using PREMIS linkages derived from their respective Fedora RELS_EXT, in keeping with the guiding principle of repository-independent file packages.

The directionality of RELS_EXT relationships is driven by the desire to minimize the frequency of modifications to any individual object over time. For example, it is anticipated that objects may accumulate many events throughout the course of their existence in Medusa. When an event occurs to a repository object, a new PREMIS Event record will be created as a Fedora object. This event will have a RELS_EXT link back to its associated object, but the RELS_EXT for the object itself will not be modified to point to all of its events. However, all events associated with a given objects can still be discovered by querying the repository's underlying RDF triple store.

5. Current Status

As of April 2013, the Medusa development team has implemented a functioning collection registry, bit-level ingest feature, and an object-level PREMIS packager. All project code is available in a Github repository at https://github.com/medusa-project. Development is ongoing, following an agile methodology with representatives of the Library's Preservation Unit providing user specifications to programmers who work in weekly sprints to add and enhance features. Although much administrative information is limited to authenticated system users, interested researchers and library practitioners may view unrestricted collection registry records as https://medusa.library.illinois.edu/. In addition, the project team maintains repository policies and specifications in a regularly updated wiki at https://wiki.cites.uiuc.edu/wiki/display/LibraryDigitalPreservation/Medusa+Digital+Preservation+Service.

Currently, Medusa managers are drafting Submission, Archival, and Dissemination Information Package specifications with content producers to inform the next steps of object-level content management in Medusa. One important looming decision is that of broader repository architecture. While all progress to date has been made developing local code to meet preservation managers' immediate needs, the Library's Software Development Group is, as mentioned above, planning next steps to include a Fedora digital object management layer. More specifically, the Medusa development team is considering the Hydra application stack of Fedora, SOLR, Blacklight, and Ruby on Rails [10][11] as a viable framework for broader repository services. Hydra, so named because of its flexibility to support multiple "heads," or customizable services on top of a single Fedora repository, is seen as a potential long-term solution to the challenge described throughout this paper – that is, the proliferation of access repository services at Illinois without a central hub in which to exercise institutional control over the life-cycle of digital library objects.

6. Conclusion

In conclusion, the establishment of a digital preservation service at the University of Illinois at Urbana-Champaign Library is firmly rooted in lessons learned from six years of NDIIPP grant research from 2004-2010. This research underscored the importance to reliable digital preservation management of PREMIS metadata and the practice of packaging digital objects in a repository-independent manner. This philosophy has carried over to the intellectual and technical modeling of Medusa, the Library's developing digital preservation service. Medusa relies heavily on a comprehensive implementation of PREMIS. It currently consists of a web-accessible collection registry that allows preservation managers to, among other things, ingest packages of files into a long-term storage environment. Medusa development is ongoing, with the goal of providing a model for fully integrating PREMIS metadata into the life cycle of digital content stewarded for long-term access at the University of Illinois at Urbana-Champaign Library.

7. REFERENCES

[1] Consultative Committee for Space Data Systems, "Reference Model for an Open Archival Information System (OAIS)." CCSDS Secretariat, Jan-2002.

[2] R. S. Guenther, "Battle of the Buzzwords," *D-Lib Magazine*, vol. 14, no. 7/8, Jul. 2008.

[3] R. S. Guenther, R. Wolfe, O. Brandt, M. Enders, T. G. Habing, F. Lazzarino, C. Redding, and J. Riley, "Guidelines for using PREMIS with METS for exchange," Library of Congress, Washington, DC.

[4] T. Habing, J. Eke, M. A. Cordial, W. Ingram, and R. Manaster, "Developments in digital preservation at the University of Illinois: The Hub and Spoke architecture for supporting repository interoperability and emerging preservation standards," *Library Trends*, vol. 57, no. 3, pp. 556–579, 2009.

[5] PREMIS Editorial Committee, "PREMIS Data Dictionary for Preservation Metadata: version 2.2," Jul. 2012.

[6] J. Unsworth and et al, "ECHO DEPository Technical Architecture Phase 1 Final Report: Report of project activities from Fall 2004 through 2007," University of Illinois at Urbana-Champaign in partnership with OCLC, Dec. 2008.

[7] S. Vermaaten, "A Checklist and a Case for Documenting PREMIS-METS Decisions in a METS Profile," *D-Lib Magazine*, vol. 16, no. 9/10, Sep. 2010.

[8] "UIUC Echodep Hub and Spoke Documentation." [Online]. Available: http://dli.grainger.uiuc.edu/echodep/hands/index.html. [Accessed: 25-Sep-2012].

[9] "Digital Preservation (Library of Congress)." [Online]. Available: http://www.digitalpreservation.gov/index.php. [Accessed: 25-Sep-2012].

[10] "Medusa - Hydra - DuraSpace Wiki." [Online]. Available: https://wiki.duraspace.org/display/hydra/Medusa. [Accessed: 13-Nov-2012].

[11] "The Hydra Project - Hydra - DuraSpace Wiki." [Online]. Available: https://wiki.duraspace.org/display/hydra/The+Hydra+Project. [Accessed: 13-Nov-2012].

[12] "ECHO Dep Generic METS Profile for Preservation and Digital Repository Interoperability, ECHO Dep METS Profile for Web Site Captures, and ECHO Dep METS Profile for Master METS Documents." [Online]. Available: http://www.loc.gov/standards/mets/profiles/00000016.html. [Accessed: 17-Jan-2013].

[13] "PREMIS in METS Toolbox." [Online]. Available: http://pim.fcla.edu/. [Accessed: 31-Jan-2013].

First Steps in Archiving the Mobile Web: Automated Discovery of Mobile Websites

Richard Schneider
Harding University
Computer Science Dept
Searcy, Arkansas, USA 72149
rschneid@harding.edu

Frank McCown
Harding University
Computer Science Dept
Searcy, Arkansas, USA 72149
fmccown@harding.edu

ABSTRACT

Smartphones and tablets are increasingly used to access the Web, and many websites now provide alternative sites tailored specifically for these mobile devices. Web archivists are in need of tools to aid in archiving this equally ephemeral Mobile Web. We present Findmobile, a tool for automating the discovery of mobile websites. We tested our tool in an experiment examining 10K popular websites and found that the most frequently used technique used by popular websites to direct mobile users to mobile sites was by automated client and server-side redirection. We found that nearly half of mobile web pages differ dramatically from their stationary web counterparts and that the most popular websites are those most likely to have mobile-specific pages.

Categories and Subject Descriptors

H.3.7 [**Information Storage and Retrieval**]: Digital Libraries – *Collection.*

General Terms

Design, Experimentation, Measurement.

Keywords

Mobile web, web crawling, web archiving.

1. INTRODUCTION

Individuals are increasingly using mobile devices like smartphones and tablets to access the Web. A recent report shows that 69% of respondents have used mobile devices to access the Web in the past 12 months [11], and StatCounter shows an upward trend in mobile web surfing with 14% of all web traffic in 2013 coming from mobile devices [17]. Due to the smaller screen size and limited bandwidth of mobile devices, many websites provide web pages designed specifically for these devices. These *mobile pages* make up the Mobile Web. Search engines like Google have recently started crawling the Mobile Web in order to provide better search results for mobile device users [9].

Web archivists are also turning their attention to the Mobile Web. Mobile pages are often significantly different than their stationary counterparts, containing smaller images, constrained text, fewer links, and interfaces designed for finger input. To preserve the Mobile Web for posterity, web archivists need tools to identify mobile web pages, crawl them, and present them to users.

We present a tool called Findmobile which automates the discovery of mobile pages. We share an experiment using Findmobile to examine the top 10K websites ranked by Alexa. We determined the most popular methods websites commonly use to expose their mobile sites, compared the content of mobile pages of these sites with their stationary-page counterparts, and found a clear correlation between a website's Alexa rank and its use of mobile web pages. We hope our efforts will kick-start the efforts of web archivists who are interested in preserving the Mobile Web for future generations.

2. BACKGROUND & RELATED WORK

National libraries, archives, and other memory organizations have worked for more than a decade to archive the Web. However, fundamental changes in web technology have created numerous problems for web archivists, including the growth of the Mobile Web. David Rosenthal summarized a recent workshop at the IIPC General Assembly 2012 which focused on problems of preserving the "future" Web:

> "But the clear message from the workshop is that the old goal of preserving *the* user experience of the Web is no longer possible. The best we can aim for is to preserve *a* user experience, and even that may in many cases be out of reach [15]."

Despite its many challenges, it is important that archivists preserve some semblance of the growing cultural artifact that is the Mobile Web.

In the pre-smartphone era, web pages designed for mobile devices (what we call *mobile pages*) were created with a variety of markup languages like C-HTML, WML, and XHTML-MP [18]. But as smartphones armed with higher bandwidth, more powerful processors and web browsers have been widely adopted in recent years, mobile websites have begun using the same markup languages used by the *stationary* (or traditional) *web*, namely XHTML and HTML5.

Today's smartphones and tablets have web browsers that are nearly as functional as desktop browsers, but they still suffer from latency issues, limited screen size and memory, and slower JavaScript engines which make viewing the stationary web problematic at times [19]. Usability experts also suggest altering the website experience for smaller mobile devices [11]. This is sometimes done by creating pages with completely different content or by using methods like responsive web design [10] which use media queries to format the page to best fit the targeted device's screen size.

Mobile pages are commonly served to mobile devices by examining the web browser's User-Agent in an HTTP request. Some websites will serve different content using the same URL to mobile user agents. Figure 1 illustrates how `cnn.com` will serve a very dense web page to a Chrome browser running on a desktop machine, but it will serve a smaller and easier-to-navigate mobile page to the iPod's web browser. Other websites will redirect mobile browsers to different URLs that serve mobile pages. For example, a request to `http://yahoo.com/` on a mobile device will redirect the browser to `http://m.yahoo.com/`.

Figure 1. http://www.cnn.com/ on a desktop browser (back) and iPod browser (front)

Search engines have recently taken an interest in identifying mobile pages. Google reported in 2011 that they are crawling the Mobile Web using a variety of user agents from feature phones and smartphones in order to optimize the search experience for mobile users [9]. Yahoo! obtained a patent for identifying mobile pages using a number of methods including content and link analysis [14]. Our method for identifying mobile pages takes a somewhat simplified approach, focusing on URL analysis and content analysis with pages obtained using different user agents.

So far there has been little attention given to archiving the Mobile Web in the literature. Previous studies on the Mobile Web have examined the link structure of the Mobile Web [8], finding significant differences when compared to the stationary web's link structure. A pre-smartphone era study [18] characterized mobile pages in terms of characteristics like markup languages, page sizes, and image content. Other studies (e.g., [4][12][16]) examine usability issues of the Mobile Web. To the best of our knowledge, this is the first work that addresses the Mobile Web from a web archiving perspective.

3. FINDMOBILE TOOL

In order to help web archivists discover mobile websites, we created the Findmobile tool to automatically discover mobile pages for a website. The tool can be used by a web crawler like Heritrix to discover websites that have a mobile site in order to perform a crawl using a mobile user agent. Findmobile is initially fed a set of seed URLs that point to the root pages of websites. It uses three processors (useragent, urldiff, and mediaqueries) which use different methods to determine if a website is serving up mobile web pages or just standard web pages.

3.1 useragent

This processor initially makes two HTTP requests using user agents representing two of the most popular desktop and mobile browsers: Chrome for the desktop and Safari on the iPhone. We will refer to Chrome's user agent as *stationary* and Safari's as *mobile*. We realize that some websites may handle other user agents differently, but to reduce the total number of requests issued, we use just these two. PhantomJS [13], a headless WebKit browser stack, is used to make the HTTP requests. PhantomJS downloads all the resources making up the page (images, CSS, JavaScript, etc.) and executes any JavaScript. This is important because many websites use JavaScript to transform the page's structure, to download style sheets, or to redirect mobile web browsers to mobile pages. PhantomJS will also follow any 3xx HTTP redirects. Unfortunately, a known bug in PhantomJS stops some client-side redirects from working properly.

If the server or client redirects the mobile agent to a URL that is different than the URL the stationary agent is directed to, we assume the server is redirecting the browser to a mobile page. This page may not be significantly different than the page retrieved via the stationary agent, but we assume the behavior indicates the *intension* of the website to serve something different to mobile agents. If no redirect occurs, the web server might serve different style sheets to mobile user agents. So if no redirect is detected, the URLs for the web pages' style sheets are examined. If they are identical, the processor then examines the tag structure of the two pages since the structures are likely to vary significantly between regular web pages and mobile pages. The processor performs a tag frequency distribution analysis (TFDA) which computes a numerical score indicating the magnitude of the difference; a value of 0 indicates the structures are identical [3]. When non-zero values are calculated, it could be because the website was caught changing its content as some sites frequently do. Therefore the processor will make seven more requests using the stationary user agent in order to calculate additional TFDA scores. The tool can be configured to determine that a mobile page is detected for values over a particular threshold. In our experiments (next section), we occasionally detected extremely low TFDA values because websites would make very small and seemingly insignificant changes, like introducing a single <div> tag, when requested with a mobile user agent.

3.2 urldiff

If the useragent processor was unable to discover a mobile page for a given website, the urldiff processor will attempt to discover other URLs that a website might be using for their mobile page. This processor uses the redirects discovered by the useragent processor to infer what the mobile page's URL might be. The algorithm used to infer mobile URLs uses the Diff, Match and Patch library [6]. Here are some examples of URLs that were created by urldiff when given `www.example.com`:

```
http://m.www.example.com/
http://www.example.com/m/
http://mobile.example.com/
http://www.example.com/?m=1
http://www.example.com/mobile/
```

After applying the transformation rules to the list of URLs, the processor requests the inferred URLs to see if valid pages are returned and uses the same technique as the useragent processor to confirm that a mobile page was detected. Because this method often results in soft 404s [2], redirection to the site's home page or a search page, the processor uses Ben Hoyt's soft 404 detection script [7] to detect soft 404s. The script is not foolproof, and it sometimes produces false positives.

3.3 mediaqueries

This processor handles any URLs that passed through the previous two processors without detecting a mobile page. It looks specifically for CSS media queries which target mobile devices via their small screen size to indicate that the web page is targeted to a mobile device. A web page using media queries presents itself different on a small screen instead of a large one, but the HTML, CSS, etc. is identical. Therefore a web archive would not need to archive anything in addition to the stationary web page, but it might want to provide emulators for showing users how the page would render on a mobile device.

4. EXPERIMENT

We devised an experiment to test the Findmobile tool on well-known websites. We obtained a list of Alexa's top ranked 1,000,000 websites [1]. These are websites that Alexa Toolbar users frequently access and are therefore a good representation of popular websites. From this list we created two data sets: a random selection of 10K URLs (RAND) and the top 10K URLs (TOP). We fed the URLs from RAND and TOP into Findmobile in July 2012 and recorded *if* Findmobile found a mobile page and *how* it was able to make that determination. The experiment was performed again a few weeks later, and the findings differed little, so we present only the results from the first run here.

As mentioned in Section 3.1, Findmobile initially makes two HTTP requests for each URL, one with a stationary user agent (Chrome desktop) and one with a mobile agent (Safari/iPhone). When the experiment was executed, requests made by Findmobile that produced responses with error codes (4xx, 5xx, etc.), timed-out, or were garbled for either of the HTTP requests were ignored. So of the 10K URLs in the RAND data set, 9,342 of them produced a valid HTTP response for both requests, and 8,970 of the TOP URLs produced valid responses for both requests.

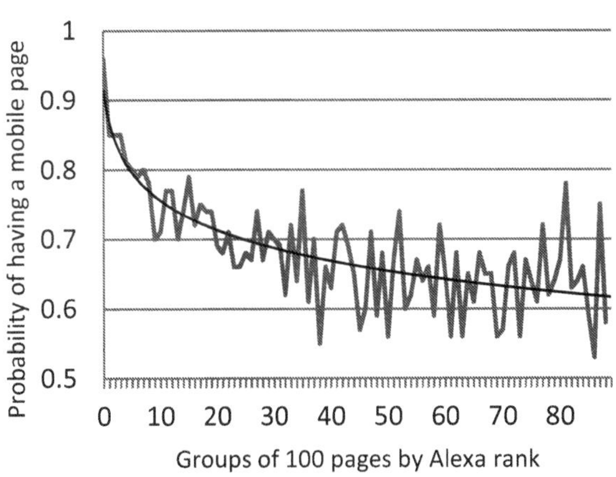

Figure 2. Relationship between Alexa rank and probability of having a mobile page

Findmobile found 50.2% of the 9,342 RAND sites produced a mobile page, and 68.5% of the TOP sites did. Since TOP has websites with higher Alexa popularity, this finding suggests that more popular sites are more likely to have mobile pages. To determine if there was a relationship between a website's Alexa rank and the likelihood of it having a mobile site, we grouped websites from TOP by Alexa rank in bins of 100 and then plotted the probability of each bin having a mobile site. The result, shown in Figure 2, shows a clear relationship between Alexa rank and the probability of having a mobile website. The top 100 sites have more than a 95% chance of having mobile pages, whereas the least popular sites in TOP have little better than a 60% chance of having a mobile site. It is perhaps not surprising that more popular websites have greater resources to produce mobile web pages.

Returning to the mobile page URLs that were discovered by Findmobile, we recorded *how* these mobile pages were discovered for both data sets and show the results in Table 1. Each of the methods in Table 1 is defined as follows:

- **Redirection** – the client or server redirected the browser to a new URL that contained the mobile page. For TOP sites, this was one of the most popular methods used.
- **Style Sheets** – the server responded with a mobile page that requested style sheets that were different from the stationary page. This was usually because the mobile page differed structurally from the stationary page (just like cnn.com in Figure 1). This technique accounted for many of the discovered mobile pages in RAND and TOP.
- **Adaption** – the server responded with a mobile page at the same URL that was requested by the stationary agent, and both the mobile and stationary pages used the same style sheets, but the pages were *structurally different*. The small numbers in this category in RAND and TOP are because most of the time when the structure differed, so did the style sheets (accounted for in the previous category).
- **URL Guessing** – the requests with the mobile and stationary agents returned identical content, so the mobile page was discovered by guessing its URL by the urldiff processor. Some false positives due to soft 404s likely inflated this category some, but many of the sites included links to these mobile pages from their stationary pages.
- **Media Queries** – the requests with the mobile and stationary agents returned identical content, but the mediaqueries processor discovered media queries were transforming the page for the mobile device. This technique was used very infrequently in both RAND and TOP.

Table 1. How mobile pages were discovered by Findmobile

Method	*RAND*	TOP
Redirection	15.9%	34.8%
Style Sheets	32.3%	25.1%
Adaptation	9.0%	11.7%
URL Guessing	38.2%	24.6%
Media Queries	4.6%	3.8%

If a mobile page was discovered, we wanted to know *how different* it was from its stationary web counterpart. Our analysis focused on the textual content of the web pages. In other words, we wanted to know if the pages said the same thing or something very different. The images, style sheets, and other resources were likely also different, but we limited our analysis to textual content and left further analysis to future work.

To measure the textual content differences, we calculated the Jaccard similarity coefficient between the stationary web page and mobile web page in both the TOP and RAND data sets. The results showed a bimodal distribution in both sets with a large number of pages having nearly identical content (values close to 1) and a large number having very little in common (values close to 0). Figure 3 shows a histogram of the TOP (mean=0.457, median=0.281), and RAND (mean=0.522, median=0.459) data sets. TOP, which had far more mobile pages than RAND, had a larger percent of dissimilar pages than did RAND. Perhaps this is because more popular sites have more resources to dedicate to creating a unique, tailored mobile site.

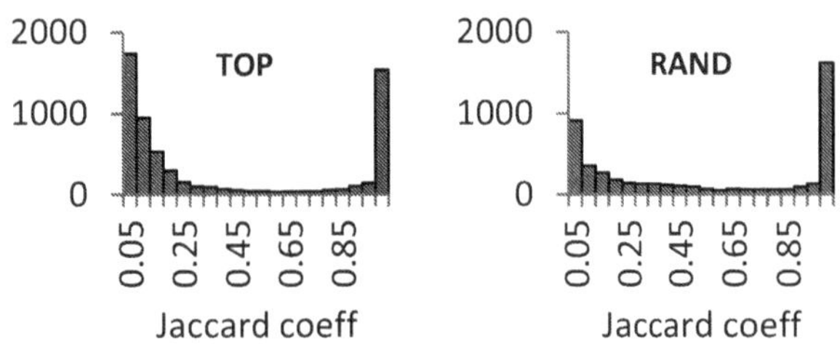

Figure 3. Distribution of TOP and RAND Jaccard coeff comparing the rendered text from stat. & mobile pages

When we manually examined a selection of the pages that fell in the two modes, we discovered pages where only the formatting differed on one extreme and pages that were entirely different on the other. For example, at the date of writing, the desktop version of MIT's web site (http://www.mit.edu/) is very different from the mobile version (http://m.mit.edu/), while the mobile version of Facebook (http://m.facebook.com/) has most of the same textual content as the desktop version (http://www.facebook.com/).

5. FUTURE WORK AND CONCLUSIONS

In this paper we have described our Findmobile tool which could aid web archivists with the task of archiving the Mobile Web. Through experimentation, we have demonstrated 1) how the tool discovered the proportion of techniques websites typically employ to direct mobile users to their mobile pages, 2) that popular websites are more likely to have mobile pages, and 3) that the textual content of a web page and its mobile page counterpart is half the time nearly identical and half the time widely divergent. These findings give archivists an idea of what to expect when charged with the task of archiving a website's mobile presence. It also suggests more work is needed to determine if archivists should invest more resources into archiving widely divergent web content or if mobile content that is almost identical to its stationary counterpart can be safely ignored.

There is much work to be done in scoping just those pages that make up the Mobile Web. Many sites have mobile-only pages that link to non-mobile pages, blurring the line between Mobile Web vs. Stationary Web, but Findmobile could be modified to help a crawler target mobile-only pages. Also, mobile pages are often tailored to users based on their location and other factors which leave plenty of work for archivists.

Our tool has been made available to the public, and we solicit feedback [5]. There is a need for more thorough evaluation of the methods used to discover mobile pages as some of the assumptions we made in detecting mobile pages do not always hold. We have started developing a new tool called IDmobile to augment Findmobile. It uses neural network classifiers to examine a web page's content and determine if it is designed specifically for a mobile device. Early tests show it as 80-90% accuracy detecting mobile pages in a limited domain.

6. ACKNOWLEDGMENTS

We would like to thank Adam Miller at the Internet Archive for his assistance in devising the Findmobile tool and feedback on our work. This research was supported by the National Science Foundation (IIS 1008492).

7. REFERENCES

[1] Alexa's top 1,000,000 websites. http://s3.amazonaws.com/alexa-static/top-1m.csv.zip

[2] Bar-Yossef, Z., Broder, A. Z., Kumar, R., Tomkins, A. 2004. Sic transit gloria telae: towards an understanding of the web's decay. In *Proceedings of the 13th international conference on World Wide Web*. ACM, New York, NY, USA, 328-337.

[3] Cruz, I. F., Borisov, Sl., Marks, M. A., Webb, T. R. 1998. Measuring structural similarity among web documents: preliminary results. *Electronic Publishing, Artistic Imaging, and Digital Typography, Lecture Notes in Computer Science*, 1375, 513-524.

[4] Cui, Y., Roto, V. 2008. How people use the web on mobile devices. In *Proceedings of the 17th international conference on World Wide Web* (WWW '08). ACM, New York, NY, USA, 905-914.

[5] Findmobile, http://www.harding.edu/fmccown/research/findmobile/

[6] Fraser, N. Diff, Match and Patch Library. http://code.google.com/p/google-diff-match-patch/

[7] Hoyt, B. 2008. Link rot, soft 404s, and DecentURL. http://blog.brush.co.nz/2008/01/soft404s/

[8] Jindal, A., Crutchfield, C., Goel, S., Kolluri, R., Jain, R. 2008. The mobile web is structurally different. *IEEE INFOCOM 2008 - IEEE Conf. on Computer Communications Workshops*. (Apr. 2008), 1-6.

[9] Kato, Y. 2011. Introducing smartphone Googlebot-Mobile. http://googlewebmastercentral.blogspot.com/2011/12/introducing-smartphone-googlebot-mobile.html

[10] Marcotte, E. 2010. Responsive web design. *A List Apart Magazine* (online - May 25, 2010). http://www.alistapart.com/articles/responsive-web-design/

[11] Mobile Web Watch 2012, Accenture, http://www.accenture.com/SiteCollectionDocuments/PDF/Accenture-Mobile-Web-Watch-Internet-Usage-Survey-2012.pdf

[12] Nielsen, J. Mobile Site vs. Full Site. Jakob Nielsen's Alert Box (Apr. 10, 2012). http://www.nngroup.com/articles/mobile-site-vs-full-site/

[13] PhantomJS, http://phantomjs.org/

[14] Rao, S., Prabhakar, B., Seth, S., Murugesan, S., Gupta, A. 2011. US Patent No. 8041703.

[15] Rosenthal, D. 2012. DSHR's Blog. http://blog.dshr.org/2012/05/harvesting-and-preserving-future-web.html

[16] Schmiedl, G., Seidl, M., Temper, K. 2009. Mobile phone web browsing: a study on usage and usability of the mobile web. In *Proceedings of the 11th International Conference on Human-Computer Interaction with Mobile Devices and Services* (MobileHCI '09). ACM, New York, NY, Article 70.

[17] StatCounter Global Statistics, Mobile vs. Desktop for 2013, http://gs.statcounter.com/#mobile_vs_desktop-ww-monthly-201205-201304

[18] Timmins, P. J., McCormick, S., Agu, E., Wills, C. E. 2006. Characteristics of mobile web content. In 2006 1st IEEE Workshop on Hot Topics in Web Systems and Technologies (Nov. 2006). 1-10.

[19] Zakas, N. C. 2013. The evolution of web development for mobile devices. *Queue*. 11, 2 (Feb. 2013).

Vertical Selection in the Information Domain of Children

Sergio Duarte Torres, Djoerd Hiemstra and Theo Huibers
University of Twente
The Netherlands
duartes,hiemstra,huibers@cs.utwente.nl

ABSTRACT

In this paper we explore the vertical selection methods in aggregated search in the specific domain of topics for children between 7 and 12 years old. A test collection consisting of 25 verticals, 3.8K queries and relevant assessments for a large sample of these queries mapping relevant verticals to queries was built. We gather relevant assessment by envisaging two aggregated search systems: one in which the Web vertical is always displayed and in which each vertical is assessed independently from the web vertical. We show that both approaches lead to a different set of relevant verticals and that the former is prone to bias of visually oriented verticals. In the second part of this paper we estimate the size of the verticals for the target domain. We show that employing the global size and domain specific size estimation of the verticals lead to significant improvements when using state-of-the art methods of vertical selection. We also introduce a novel vertical and query representation based on tags from social media and we show that its use lead to significant performance gains.

Categories and Subject Descriptors

H.3.3 [**Information Storage and Retrieval**]: Information Search and Retrieval

Keywords

vertical selection, aggregated search, children, social media, evaluation

1. INTRODUCTION

In aggregated search, content is retrieved from different search services in the web and the content retrieved is integrated in a meaningful and consistent way. These search services are often referred as verticals, which are defined as domain specific collections, (*e.g.* entertainment, shopping, news) or collections from specialized types or genres (*e.g.* videos, images, songs). Generally, aggregated search systems are assumed to have complete access to the verticals, which implies having access to the query logs and to detailed statistical descriptors of the verticals.

In this work, we envisage a search system that integrates heterogeneous content from verticals, which are not fully accessible for the system (third party verticals). The system we envisage is intended to integrate content of different genres as it is done in aggregated search. In particular, we are interested in verticals that contain high quality information for children from 7 to 12 years old. In this system parents, teachers and other specialist on children care are allowed to add resources for children. For instance, they could add a vertical dedicated to coloring pages: `http://ivyjoy.com/colouring/search.html`, which only returns sheets of paper to be colored and that are suitable for children, or a vertical dedicated to search only videos: `http://www.youtube.com`, in this case the vertical provide content for all kind of public segments. We believe that an aggregated search system is a better solution for searching in the web content for children than simply crawling and indexing websites, or listing suitable content (*e.g.* `http://www.kids.yahoo.com`) because *(i)* it is more scalable, *(ii)* we can leverage and exploit the knowledge of parents and other experts by using hundreds of services suggested by them. Nonetheless, we believe a similar system would be also highly beneficial in other domains (*e.g.* business, health, sports) and other demographical segments (*e.g.* seniors, teenagers).

Under this scenario, once a query is submitted, the system has to decide first which are the most relevant verticals for the query. This problem has been characterized as a multi-class classification problem [3, 26] in which the objective is to predict the set of relevant verticals (or single vertical in [2]) from a set of predefined verticals that are accessible by the system. This problem is referred as vertical selection and it has been widely studied [2, 26, 15].

Our problem differs from those addressed in previous studies in that: *(i)* the vertical selection is carried out under the restriction of targeting a specific information domain (*e.g.* content for children); *(ii)* these users search for domain specific content in a set of verticals that may not be completely suitable for them, thus some verticals may provide only suitable content (*e.g.* coloring pages) but others may or may not contain suitable content for their information needs (*e.g.* youtube) since it contains content for all type of public and *(iii)* a test collection for this domain has not been built until this work and the process of gathering assessments is not straight forward given the nature of the targeted users.

JCDL'13, July 22–26, 2013, Indianapolis, Indiana, USA.
Copyright 2013 ACM 978-1-4503-2077-1/13/07 ...$15.00.

The contributions of this paper are summarized as follow: *(1)* We provide a novel test collection for the problem of vertical selection in the domain of content for children. We describe its construction in sections 2 and 3. Given the novelty of the collection we describe two methodologies to gather relevant assessments using crowd sourcing: first assuming that the Web vertical is always displayed (which is the case in state-of-the-art aggregated search interfaces) [2] and the second methodology easing this restriction. We found that the two methodologies lead to a different set of relevant verticals and we show under which conditions this difference can be mitigated. We also observed that the first methodology is more prone to visual verticals preference bias, which has consequences in the design of the content aggregation algorithm and aggregated interfaces (Section 4).

(2) We estimate the children suitability of verticals by estimating the amount of child-friendly content and we compare them against the estimation of general content. We propose a simple approach to combine both estimations (children and non children vertical sizes) and we show that their used in *ReDDe* [19], a state-of-the-art vertical selection method, lead to significant improvements. We found that this method also outperform other state of the art methods such as *Clarity* (sections 5 and 6). *(3)* We present a novel method of vertical selection for domain specific scenarios based on a vertical representation using tags from social media and language models. Concretely, verticals are represented based on tags describing the urls from a sample of each vertical and a language model on these tags is employed to rank the relevancy of the verticals given a query. As far as we know social media has not been employed before as a source of evidence in the problem of vertical selection (sections 6.1 and 6.2).

2. COLLECTION CONSTRUCTION

The collection built consists of a carefully chosen set of queries and verticals. A set of vertical results was also retrieved for each (*query,vertical*) pair and relevant assessments mapping a set of relevant verticals to each query were gathered. Using this annotation schema, we can test and compare any pair of vertical selection methods. In the following sections we described in detail the methodology carried out to build the collection and we justify our decisions in the design of the collection.

2.1 Query set selection

The query set was extracted from the AOL query log [16]. We extracted queries landing on domains listed in the *Kids and Teens* directory. Given that only domains are displayed in the AOL log we carefully extracted those entries in which the exact domain is listed in the Dmoz directory (*i.e.* exact matching). An analogous procedure has been suggested for this information domain in [23, 7] and the Dmoz directory has been used in previous research in information retrieval for children [8, 10].

We leave out navigational queries by filtering out query-click pairs in which the domain is mentioned in the query. For instance, the query *sesame street* is filter out if it lands on the domain *www.sesamestreet.org*. We also filter out query containing tokens such as *.com www.*, *http* and *.org*. The Levenshtein distance between the query and domain mentioned in the url was also employed to filter out queries that misspell a domain (*e.g.* pbkids). Concretely, the queries

Query	Dmoz Category
1950's television shows	News
science fair projects ideas	School - Time/Science
barometric pressure	School - Time/Science
bingo song copyright	Arts/Music
rabbit ears	Sports - Hobbies/Crafts
secret code game	Games/Word_Play

Table 1: Example of queries and their Dmoz category

were selected from search sessions satisfying either of the following restrictions:

1. There is at least one click event after submitting the query which lands in a domain listed in Dmoz and the duration of the click event is of at least 60 seconds
2. There is a click on the Dmoz domain is the last event of the session

The first restriction is employed to capture only the cases for which the click event has a long duration, that is, if users spend more than 1 minute on a web result is a strong indication that the result clicked is relevant for the query [13]. The second condition is also employed because previous query log studies have shown that the last click of the session can be often associated to successful searches [6]. We extracted a set of 3.8K queries by using both restrictions. Table 3 provides examples of the queries extracted and the Dmoz *Kids and Teens* category in which they belong.

2.2 Selection of verticals

The list of verticals selected is shown in Table 2. The verticals were manually selected to cover the information needs found in the query set and the distribution of topics targeted by children between 7 to 12 years old in the Web [9]. We found that several genre verticals need to be split into fine-grained information services to fit the topic interests of children. For instance in our system the vertical *games* may refer to the *video games* or to the *online gaming* vertical. Similarly the genre *images* may refer to *coloring pages*, *printable worksheets* or the standard *pictures* vertical. In previous literature, these services are wrapped under a single vertical (either images or games respectively) [3]. This fine-representation of verticals is highly convenient for young users because it increases the accessibility to rich media and this niche of users have been found to struggle identifying and searching information in non-web verticals [11]. Dedicated verticals offering content for children may be found in the Internet (*e.g.* video-games, stories, health), however some of the verticals displayed in Table 2 were constructed artificially by modifying the search parameters of general web services. For instance, the vertical *coloring pages* is constructed by using the *line-drawing* parameter of the Google Image search service. For the case of the *printable worksheets*, we employed the *line-drawing* parameter of the Google Image service and we modified the user's query by expanding it with the terms *worksheets*.

3. DATA CHARACTERISTICS

We describe the collection based on the number of queries covered per vertical and the distribution of the numbers of

Vertical	Websites
web	google.com
games online	onlineflashgames.com
games	gamespot.com
images	google.com/imghp
coloring pages	google.com/imghp (line drawing option)
worksheets	google.com/imghp (query + worksheets)
books	books.google.com
question/answers	worldoftales.com
stories	worldoftales.com
shopping	amazon/toys
music	allmusic.com
videos	youtube.com
movies	rottentomatoes.com
enciclopedia	wikipedia.com
reference	dictionary.kids.net.au
how-to	www.instructables.org
school aid	livescience.com
	howstuffworks.com
	dsc.discovery.com
school activities	sciencekids.co.nz
	enchantedlearning.com
	howtosmile.org
lyrics	lyricsdrive.com
health	kidshealth.org

Table 2: List of verticals and their urls

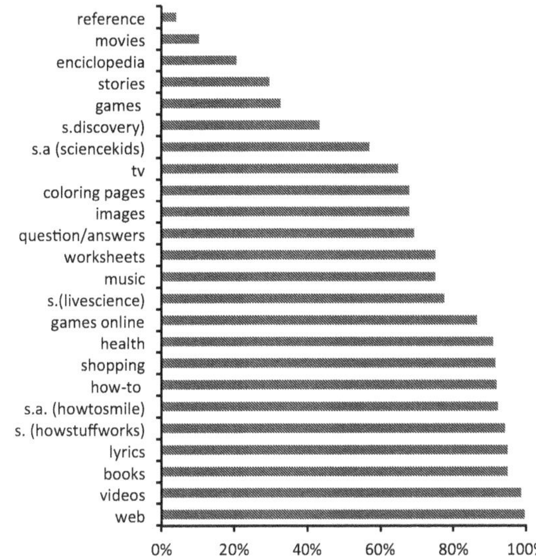

Figure 1: Queries covered by each vertical

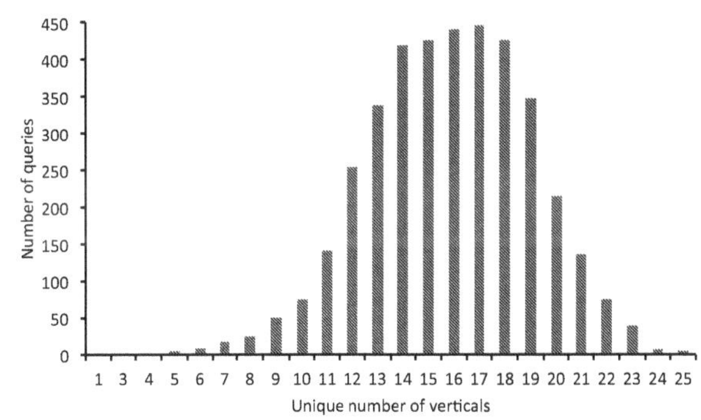

Figure 2: Distribution of unique verticals per query

verticals covering a query. Figure 1 depicts the vertical coverage, which refers to the proportion of queries covered by each vertical. A vertical is said to cover a query if it returns at least one result when the query is submitted. From this figure, we observe that large verticals such as *web* and *videos* tend to cover most of the queries in the dataset. Note that even relatively small verticals such as *how-to* or *stories* have high query coverage, which suggest that the verticals chosen are appropriate for the information needs targeted by the chosen queries. Nonetheless, we observed that the verticals *movies* and *reference*, which are widely used in previous vertical selection studies, cover less than 25% of the queries in our data set. This result may indicate that these verticals are less suitable for the audience we are interested in. Figure 2 shows the number of queries in the collection that are covered by a specific number of verticals. For instance from this figure we can observe that there are no queries in the collection that are covered by exactly two or three distinct verticals. Similarly around 75 queries are covered by exactly 10 verticals. Interestingly we observed almost a normal distribution in which most of the queries are covered between 10 and 21 verticals (84% of the queries). On average, queries from the entire collection are covered by 16.8 verticals. This result shows that the problem of vertical selection in the domain of children topics is not straight forward since each query has on overage a set of 16 verticals from which to choose relevant verticals.

4. GATHERING VERTICAL RELEVANCE ASSESSMENTS

We gather assessments by employing the crowd-sourcing engine Crowdflower [1] and a sample of 90 queries from the set of queries described previously. This sample was chosen to be representative of all the possible topics in the collection (based on the Dmoz categories of the queries). We carried out two experimental protocols for gathering the assessments. In the first protocol assessors were asked to chose between two set of vertical results: the results of the target vertical against the results returned by the web vertical (*i.e.* Google Web), each result set was displayed in a column next to each other in the survey page. Concretely, the top 4 results of each vertical were shown in each column and the order in which the columns appear was randomized. Nonetheless, the ranking of the results of each vertical was preserved. Adult assessors were able to choose *the most relevant set of results for the query (given that the content has to be suitable for users between 7 to 12)* between the two columns. The special option *none of the sets are relevant and suitable for children* was also given. This option was provided to avoid false positives since with this option users are not forced to chose a vertical when both sets are inadequate. The motivation of comparing each vertical against the web vertical is that in modern search engines the web results are always displayed and the results from other verticals are only displayed when the vertical results *add value* to the current web results, that is, when their results are preferred over the standard web results [1]. The main drawback

[1] http://crowdflower.com/

of this protocol is that we are unable to identify the cases in which the results from the web verticals are unsuitable for the query.

In the second protocol, we asked assessors to judge vertical results independently. This protocol is motivated by the fact that in an information system for children we may not always want to present the results from the *Web* vertical since the user may be requiring a different type of content (*e.g.* coloring pages, videos) or because the results from the web vertical are not suitable for children given query. For this reason we asked users to assess each set of vertical results independently using a scale-graded system of 5 points, from *bad* to *excellent* in terms of relevance to the query and appropriateness for children in the targeted age range. An advantage of this method arises in the possibility of evaluating directly the quality of the web vertical results when the information needs are targeted at young users. We can also rank the verticals based on the graded score assigned.

For both protocols, adult users were asked to make the judgments. We consider it reasonable to assume that adults can easily discern between content oriented for adults and children and thus that they are able to judge the results in the context of the domain. We also provide the queries to the assessors without a close description. The motivation for this was to let the assessors identify all the possible content that can be relevant for children given a query. To ensure the quality of the assessments a set of 120 golden judgments was created by the authors of this paper for each experimental protocol. These gold judgments were employed to avoid spammers by: *(i)* forcing the users of *CrowdFlower* to complete a training session in which they are shown only *units* (survey page) from the gold judgement set. They are allowed to start the task if they answer correctly at least 6 of these units; *(ii)* during the task the gold units are mixed with the units under evaluation, users answering incorrectly more than 8% of the gold units shown to them during the survey are ignored. Only users from the United States were allowed to carry out the survey to ensure language proficiency and domain knowledge (the queries were extracted from the US market). Each unit work was paid with 0.01 dollar cents and each unit was evaluated by at least 3 assessors. In the following paragraphs, we describe the assessments gathered and we compare the results obtained by both experimental protocols.

4.1 Distribution of relevant verticals

A gold test set was created by mapping each query in the sample to a set of relevant verticals by using the assessments collected in *Crowdflower*. For the first protocol (*i.e.* paired assessments), we map a query to a vertical if at least a certain percentage of annotators select the vertical as relevant for the query. The threshold 60% and 80% were used in the results reported. As a point of reference 60% means that more of half of the assessors agreed on classifying the target vertical as relevant while 80% means that most of the assessors agreed.

For all the thresholds we observed in Figure 3 a long tail distribution in which visual-oriented verticals are preferred, that is *YouTube*, *Google Images*, *Coloring pages* and *Worksheets* are the most frequent verticals assessed as relevant. This result may be due to the bias generated by visual content in the paired assessments. We believe that the exposition of visual content is more appealing to the user when they are asked to make an assessment against text based results. This hypothesis is also supported by the fact that the best performing verticals at higher threshold values are the image oriented verticals (*Google Images* and *Worksheets*). The bias towards visual oriented verticals has also been reported before in the literature [4, 20]. Anecdotally we also observed that children oriented educational websites (*e.g.* science for kids, instructables) were more frequently chosen as relevant than *Wikipedia*, which is a relatively trusted source. All the other verticals (*e.g.* music, lyrics, games) were less frequent and were located in the bottom of the long tail distribution.

For the second experiment protocol a vertical is said to be relevant if the averaged score assigned by all the assessors to a (*query*, *vertical*) pair is greater that a given threshold. Figure 4 shows the distribution obtained when using the values 3.0 and 4.0 as threshold (recall we used a graded system from 1 to 5 to judge each result set).

Additionally, we also employed as thresholds the averaged score obtained by the *Google Web* vertical (on a query basis) and the maximum score between the *Google Web* vertical averaged core and 3.0 respectively. The last two thresholds were employed in order to make a fair comparison between the relevant verticals obtained with the two experimental protocols. Recall that in the first experimental protocol we compare each set of vertical results against the *Google Web* vertical, for this reason we employed the Web vertical score as threshold for the experiments.

In Figure 4 we observed similar distributions for the thresholds 3.0 and 4.0, although all the frequencies in the latter are lower as a consequence of the higher threshold value. Some of the verticals in the long tail also rank differently (e.g. *Amazon*, *KidsHealth*, *Tv*). Nonetheless, the most frequent verticals are the same when using both thresholds: *Google Web*, *Google Images*, *YouTube* and *Yahoo! Answers*. For the thresholds *google-score* and *max(google-score,3.0)* we observed large differences in the distribution in respect to the first two thresholds employed. Even though the top 2 most frequent relevant verticals are the same (*Google Web* and *Google Images*. Verticals such as *Youtube*, *Yahoo! Answers* and *Google Books* are not prominent as it was the case before. In general terms all the other verticals were assigned as relevant with less frequency. This result suggests that the score obtained by the *web vertical* is often higher that the score assigned to the other verticals given that the frequency of the relevant verticals are significantly trimmed when using *Google Web*'s score as threshold. It is important to mention that even though this is the case, in about 10% of the queries, *Google Web* is not chosen as relevant (when using as reference 3.0 and 4.0 as thresholds).

An important observation of the previous results is that in the second experimental protocol we did not observed the visual content bias observed with the first experimental protocol, as it was shown with all the thresholds. These results suggest that the second methodology can also simulate the first when using the *web vertical* score as threshold while avoiding the bias generated when comparing text results against visual content.

4.2 Inter-assessor agreement

We analyzed the inter-assessor agreement for both experimental protocols to quantify the quality of the assessments under different relevant thresholds and to identify the rel-

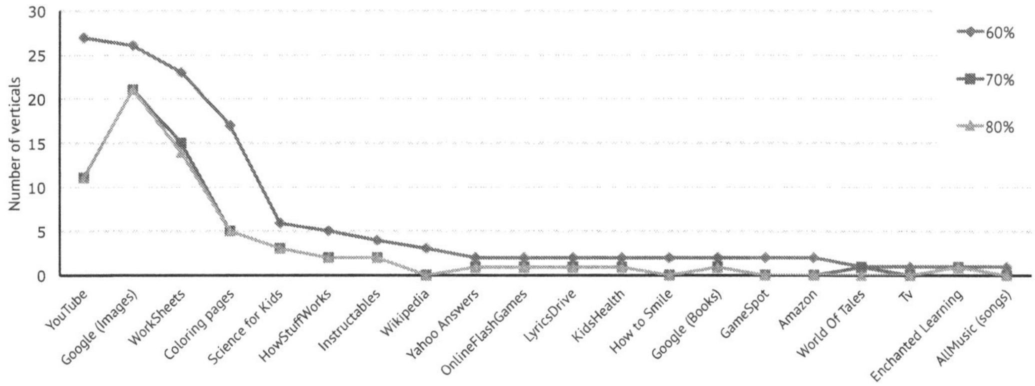

Figure 3: Frequency distribution of verticals for the first experimental protocol

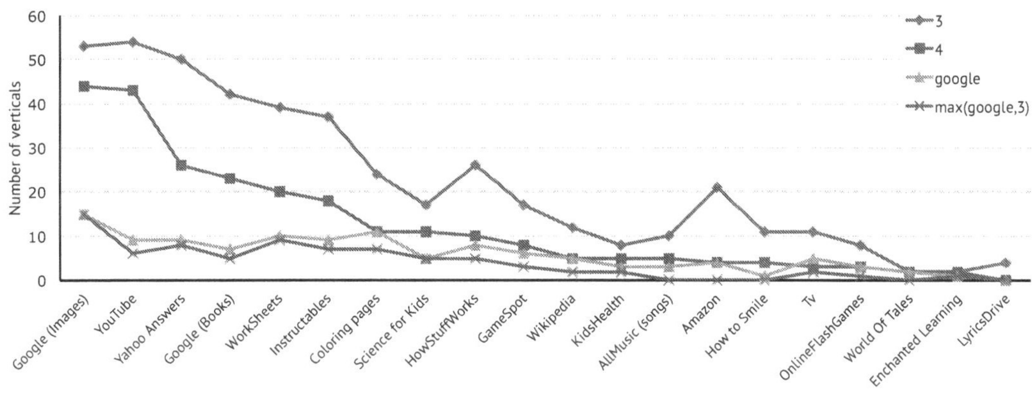

Figure 4: Frequency distribution of verticals for the second experimental protocol

Inter-agreement metric	Score
average pairwise percent agreement	82.86%
fleiss' kappa	0.683
FK agreement	0.828
average pairwise cohen's kappa	0.682
krippendorff's alpha	0.683

Table 3: Inter-agreement scores found for the task

evant threshold values that maximize assessor agreement. The motivation is to use these thresholds in our experiments of vertical selection. We are also interested in investigating the threshold for which both protocols lead to a similar set of relevant verticals. For the first experimental protocol, the survey consisted of a sample of 90 queries which lead to 3360 decisions (comparisons between the web vertical and each one of the other verticals) and each pair was evaluated on average by three assessors. Table 3 shows the inter-assessor scores obtained for the experiment. We list the most common metrics employed in IR and natural language processing. All the metrics show a substantial agreement between assessors. This result indicates that the task was consistently interpreted by the assessors and that assessors agreed in discerning content that is suitable for children in the age range specified.

For the second experiment protocol we measured the inter-assessor agreement by establishing that each pair *query, vertical* is assessed by n assessors (*e.g.* 3 coders) and the assessment is binary (relevant or non-relevant) based on the threshold defined in the previous section: 3, 4, web vertical score and *max(web vertical, 3.0)*. Note that this encoding is slightly different to the one employed in the first experimental protocol, in which we had three possible values: (relevant, non relevant (*web vertical* is preferred) and none of the two sets are relevant. Figure 5 shows the inter-assessor agreement using the Krippendorff's alpha score. We only report these results since the averaged Fleiss' kappa agreement obtained was almost identical to the Krippendorff's alpha scores. We found that at lower threshold values the inter-assessor agreement in higher, which is expected since lower threshold values represent a larger score interval to discern between relevant and non-relevant. It was observed that the lowest agreement is obtained when using the *web vertical* score as threshold. In general terms, the inter-assessor agreement was slightly lower that in the first experimental protocol.

Additionally we compared the agreement between the lists of relevant vertical collected using both experimental protocols. The agreement was also measured using the Krippendorff's alpha score. In this case, we have two coders (the results of each experimental protocol) and the coding is binary: relevant or not relevant. We compute the score for all the possible threshold combinations of the two methods. Recall that in the first protocol the threshold refers to the percentage of users assessing a vertical as relevant while in the second protocol the threshold refers to the graded score (between 1 and 5) and the cut-off is performed by considering non-relevant the pairs for which the averaged score of

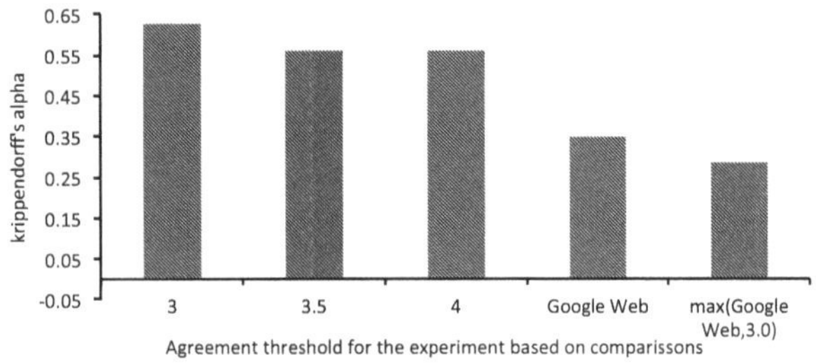

Figure 5: Inter-assessor agreement for the second experiment protocol for several thresholds

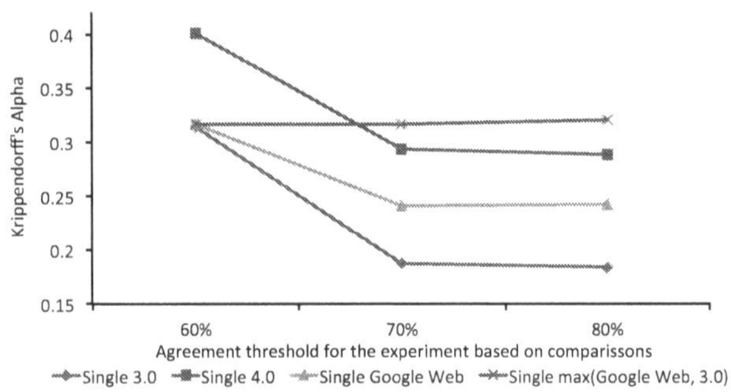

Figure 6: Agreement between the two experiment protocols

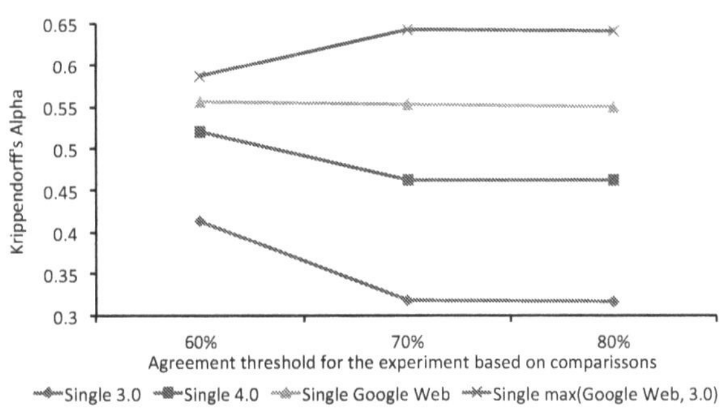

Figure 7: Agreement between the two experiment protocols (Including Google Web)

all the assessors fall below the threshold defined. It is important to mention that we estimated the agreement scores under two scenarios: with and without considering the *web vertical*. We made the distinction because this vertical is not assessed directly in the first protocol since it assumes that the results from verticals are relevant only if they add value to the results provided by the *web vertical*. Nonetheless, we artificially created an assessment for this vertical by setting it as relevant if for a given query it is preferred by all the assessors at least in one of the paired comparisons. Figure 6 and Figure 7 shows the results obtained using these two modalities (*i.e.* with and without the *web vertical*) respectively. For the former the maximum agreement score obtained was 0.41 using as threshold 4.0 for the second protocol and 60% for the first protocol. Scores between 0.4 and 0.6 are considered moderate agreement [5, 17]. Nonetheless we observed that the score values were more stable when we set the second protocol threshold as *max(web vertical, 3.0)*. This result is interesting because it suggest that by using the *web vertical* score we can simulate, at some extend, the vertical set obtained by the first protocol, having the advantage of avoiding the visual bias identified. In Figure 7, we observed larger agreement scores (maximum of 0.632). Similarly, higher values of agreement are obtained consistently when using the score of the Google Web vertical.

On overall, the previous results suggest that both approaches lead to relatively high inter-assessor agreement. However, the first protocol provides more consistent results since the inter-assessor agreement is higher. It is important to mention that the second protocol is not prone to visual bias and provide a wider set of relevant verticals per query, which is useful in the construction of exploratory information systems. In addition, we found that for the second protocol that the threshold *60%* lead to the highest assessor-agreement, thus we will employed this threshold for our experiments (Section 6.2).

5. VERTICAL SIZE ESTIMATION

The corpus size estimation is highly important to understand verticals' characteristics and quality. The size estimation of a corpus is also a key feature in the selection of search engines in federated search and distributed search [22, 25]. In our scenario, the estimation of the vertical size is crucial since this statistic is needed in the best performing resource selection methods such as *ReDDe*. Recall that the system for children we envisage has only access to the verticals through limited query interfaces in which is only possible to submit a query to receive a limited number of results. Under this non-cooperative environment, the search engines do not provide collection summaries from which global statistics about the vocabularies of the collection can be inferred, for this reason they need to be estimated from vertical samples. We will show how these estimations are used in vertical selection in Section 6.

Si and Callan [19] proposed the use of the *capture-recapture* method through query-based sampling to estimate the size of the collections for the problem of resource selection in non-cooperative environments. The capture-recapture method has been used traditionally in the Ecology field for the estimation of the population size of species. It works as follow: a predefined number of animals are captured, marked and then released. After a certain amount of time, a second sample of animals is captured in the same area and the new sample is inspected to estimate the intersection between the two samples. The population is estimated using the sizes of the two samples and their intersection using the following expression:

$$s' = \frac{|sample_A| * |sample_B|}{|sample_A \cap sample_B|} \tag{1}$$

In search engines this process is carried out using query-based sampling: A set of queries is sent to the target search engine and the documents returned by the search engines are collected. This process is repeated and the estimation is based on the size of the number of documents collected in the two samples.

Shokouhi et al. [18] explores the problem of resource selection in non-cooperative environments and propose a query-based sampling *QBS* method based on the capture-recapture method [19] referred as *multiple capture-recapture*. They showed with a large set of heterogeneous collections that their method outperforms previous approaches using search engines in non-cooperative environments. We employed their method to estimate the sizes of the verticals chosen for our collection. In their method, the *capture-recapture* process is repeated T times using samples of size m and the estimation is carried out by counting the size of the intersection of each pair of samples. Concretely the estimation is performed with the following expression:

$$s' = \frac{T(T-1)k^2}{2D} \tag{2}$$

where T is the size chosen for each sample, k is the number of samples and D is the accumulated number of duplicates found in the intersection within each pair. In our approach, we are not only interested in estimating the size of the collection but also in the size of the content available for the target domain in each vertical. We employed the *multiple capture-recapture method* and a random samples of queries from the query set of our collection to estimate the size of the content of interest for children in each vertical . Recall that these queries were chosen to be representative of the topics of interest for children, as it was described in 2.1.

We carried out an analogous process to estimate the size of the verticals of content that is not oriented to children. For this purpose we employed a set queries known to be submitted to extract information in other domains (*i.e.* non for children). For this set we employed the same methodology described in section 2.1 but instead of using the *Kids and Teens* seed urls we employed the global categories of Dmoz which are not present in the categories for children. In this fashion, we obtained size estimations for each vertical of content that is oriented for children and non-children. The results of the estimates are shown in Table 4. These values were obtained by using a set of 2K queries. We set the parameters T and k to 50 and 25 respectively. The sample was constructed by choosing randomly 5 queries from the set of 2K queries (with replacement) and collecting the top 10 results for each query. Similar parameter values have been used in previous studies [18]. It is important to mention that the set of 90 queries employed to gather user assessments were not employed in the samples generated for the size estimation process to avoid bias in the evaluation of vertical selection methods.

Consistently, we observed large ratios between the estimations using the *grown up* and *kids* queries with verticals known to be large and targeting all kind of public. For instance, the ratios for the verticals *web*, *question/answers*, and *images* were 34.0, 1.6 and 13.0 respectively. Inverse ratio trends were observed when considering verticals focused on children topics, such as the gaming and educational verticals.

The ratio found for the verticals *games online* and *education (livescience)* were 0.6 and 0.4 respectively. These results are interesting for resource selection because the ratio gives us an estimation of the likelihood to find content for children in the vertical. In the following section, we will explore the use of this ratio along with the vertical size estimation in the problem of vertical selection.

Vertical	Kids	Grown ups
web	803,297	27,377,757
games online	51,235	31,282
games	79,910	36,965
images	4,749,306	63,878,640
coloring pages	776,072	1,258,471
worksheets	931,287	1,006,777
books	963,956	30,115,533
question/answers	8,613,190	14,553,214
stories	3,928	3,478
shopping	562,308	22,485,899
music	121,920	540,501
videos	728,842	177,227
movies	61,443	131,131
encyclopedia	61,186	409,160
how-to	172,481	114,445
school(livescience)	11,666	5,308
school(howstuffworks)	3,267	3,674
school(discovery)	18,241	23,117
s. activities (sciencekids)	4,851	3,597
s. activities (howtosmile)	3,267	11,027
lyrics	455,305	161,271
health	7,185	2,939
tv	13,390	310,538

Table 4: Vertical size estimations using the set of *kids* and *grown up* queries

6. RESOURCE SELECTION METHODS IN IR FOR CHILDREN

We employed two well-known vertical selection methods: *ReDDe* and *Clarity*. The former has been shown as one of the most effective methods for resource selection in federated search in cooperative and non-cooperative environments [19]. More recently, this method was adapted for state-of-the-art aggregated search systems [2] and it was proven to be one the most discriminative sources of evidence in vertical selection. It is important to mention that models built on query logs have been shown to provide higher performance than *Redde* [2, 3]. However query logs are inaccessible in the settings of the aggregated search system we are interested in since the verticals belong to third parties, contrary to the case of the aggregated search considered in [2]. For this reason, we employed in this work *ReDDe*, which is defined in equation 3.

$$ReDDe_q(V_i) = |V_i| \sum_{d \in R} I(d \in S_i^*) p(q|M_d) p(d|S_i^*) \tag{3}$$

where $p(d|S_i^*) = \frac{1}{|S_i^*|}$, $|V_i|$ is the size of the vertical, S_i^* is the set of sampled vertical documents and $p(q|M_d)$ is the query likelihood score of the document d. The score is estimated from an index combining the document samples of all the verticals. In this work we index the documents using the Terrier search engine[2] and score them using the Hiemstra's Language Model [14].

The second baseline employed is *Clarity*, which was originally used as a measure of retrieval effectiveness. *Clarity* is

[2] http://terrier.org

defined in the following way:

$$Clarity_q(C) = \sum_{w \in V}^{|V|} p(w|M_q) log \left(\frac{p(w|M_q)}{p(w|M_c)} \right) \quad (4)$$

where $P(w|M_q)$ is defined as:

$$p(w|M_q) = \frac{1}{z} \sum_{d \in R} p(w|M_d) p(q|M_d) \quad (5)$$

where $p(w|M_c)$ is the probability of w which is estimated using the collection language model and $p(w|M_c)$ is the query likelihood score of the document and it is estimated using a index of the documents of the target collection only: $p(q|M_d)$. The variable z is defined as $\sum_{d \in R} p(q|M_d)$. The documents are also scored using language model with linear interpolation smoothing [14]. For *ReDDe* and *Clarity* the top 100 documents where employed to calculate the document scores.

We also redefine *ReDDe* to exploit the size estimations obtained with the children and non-children queries. The intuition is to use the ratio between these two size estimations to boost those verticals that contain more content available for children since these verticals have a higher likelihood of providing content that is suitable for them. Equation 6 shows the new definition:

$$ReDDe'_q(V_i) = \frac{|V_i^{kids}|}{|V_i^{adults}|} \sum_{d \in R} I(d \in S_i^*) p(q|M_d) \quad (6)$$

where $|V_i^{kids}|$ and $|V_i^{adults}|$ are the size estimations obtained using the two set of queries. We will show in the next section that this definition lead to better performance when using our test collection.

6.1 Representing verticals through social media

Nowadays, social media is widely used to describe and share web resources in the Internet. We believe that the descriptions provided by these thousands of users can be beneficial for the problem of vertical selection, particularly on specialized domain environments.

In this work, we utilize bookmarks from the social website *Delicious*[3] in which users can share bookmarks of their favorites websites by providing a list of describing tags. For instance, tags describing the domain *www.howtosmile.org* (such as *science, math, lessons*) can be used to emphasize this vertical if we are able to infer that the tags are related to the intent of the query (*e.g.* which is the case for the query *school science fair*).

For this purpose we create a tag representation of the query and the vertical. A language model is employed to assign a retrieval score to the verticals. For both representations we used the Delicious crawl collection built in [24], which contains around 130 million bookmarks.

The query is represented as a bag of tags using the top *10* results of an index containing the documents in the Dmoz *kids and teens* section. The intuition is that the tags describing the top results from this index are a fair representation of the intent that the query has in the domain of information for children. Similarly, a vertical is represented as a bag of tags associated to the urls from the sample of documents extracted from the target vertical. It is important to mention that we associate each url to a set of tags by *(i)* finding the url in the collection provided in [24], and by *(ii)* extracting tags from the title and snippet of the results by using the vocabulary of tags. The latter strategy was used given the low coverage of the collection for the small verticals.

Based on this vertical representation we rank the verticals for a query using a language model: $p(V|Q)$, which is defined in the following fashion:

$$p(V_i|Q) = \frac{p(Q|V_i)p(V_i)}{p(Q)} \propto p(t) \prod_{j=1}^{|Q|} p(q_j|V_i) \quad (7)$$

$$p(q_j|V_i) = \frac{cf(q_j, V_i) + \mu \, p(q_j)}{|V_i| + \mu} \quad (8)$$

where $p(q_j)$ is the prior probability of q_j and μ is the Dirichtlet smoothing parameter. These probabilities are estimated using MLE on the artificially documents of tags created for each vertical and query.

We combine this probability score with the *ReDDe* score defined in Equation 3. For this purpose, we normalize *ReDDe* scores across verticals for each query and we weighting in the following manner:

$$LMReDDe_q(V_i) = p(V_j|Q) * ReDDe_q(V_i)^* \quad (9)$$

where $ReDDe_q(V_i)^* = ReDDe_q(V_i) / \sum_{k=1}^{|V|} ReDDe_q(V_k)$. An analogous definition was applied to *ReDDe-R* expressed in Equation 6.

6.2 Experimental Results and Discussion

We compared the performance of *ReDDe-R* (Equation 6), the social media language model (Equation 7), *LMReDDe* and *LMReDDe-R* (Equation 9) against the state-of-the-art methods*ReDDe* and *Clarity*. For our experiments, we employed the 90 queries annotated with human assessments using both protocols: paired comparisons and single vertical assessments, which will be referred in our results as protocol *A* and *B* respectively. We employed as threshold values 60% and 3.0 to define a relevant vertical in the experimental protocols *A* and *B* respectively. For the language model we set experimentally the parameter μ to 2500. It is important to mention that other threshold values lead to consistent results, nonetheless due to space restrictions we only reported results with the values mentioned.

Figures 8 and 9 shows the precision and recall curves obtained for all the methods using the gold set obtained through the experimental protocol *A*. We found that *Clarity* is consistently outperformed by all the other methods and that the best performing methods are the ones based on *ReDDe*. We also observed that our three *ReDDe* variations outperformed both baselines being *LMReDDe* the best performing method for protocol *A* and *LMReDDe-R* for protocol *B*.

We noted that the *web* verticals is generally the first ranked vertical by most of the methods and that several queries in out test collection were only associated to this *web vertical*. Concretely, we found that from the 90 queries of the test set, 27 queries were associated only to the *web vertical*. For this reason, we decided to repeat our experiments ignoring this vertical from the collection. We believe that by ignoring this vertical we will have a clearer picture of the performance of the methods, especially on smaller verticals.

[3]`http://delicious.com`

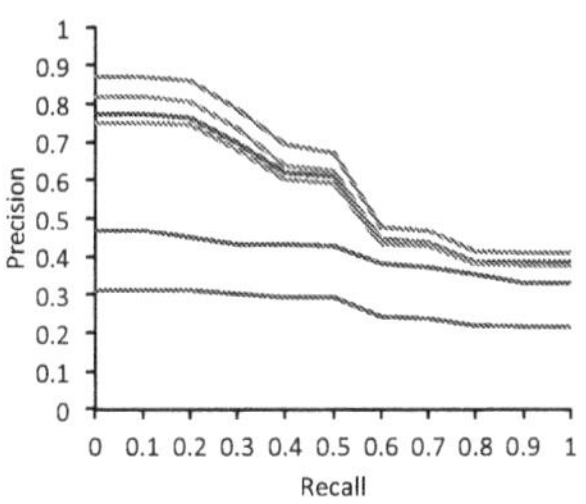

Figure 8: Protocol A (with *web vertical*)

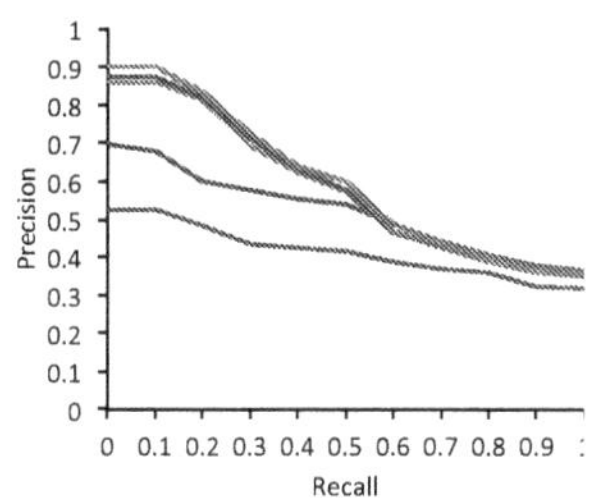

Figure 9: Protocol B (with *web vertical*)

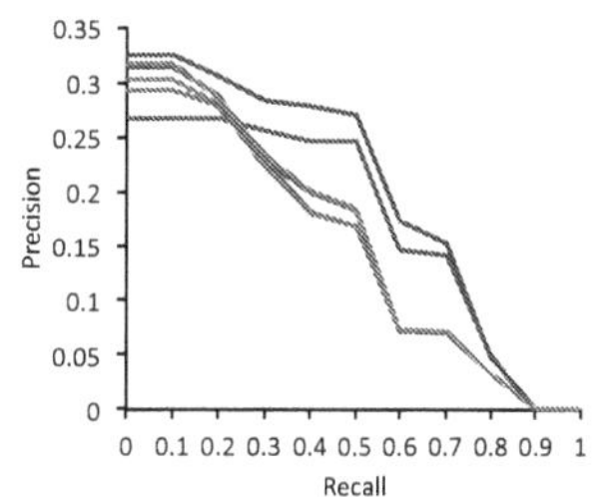

Figure 10: Protocol A (without *web vertical*)

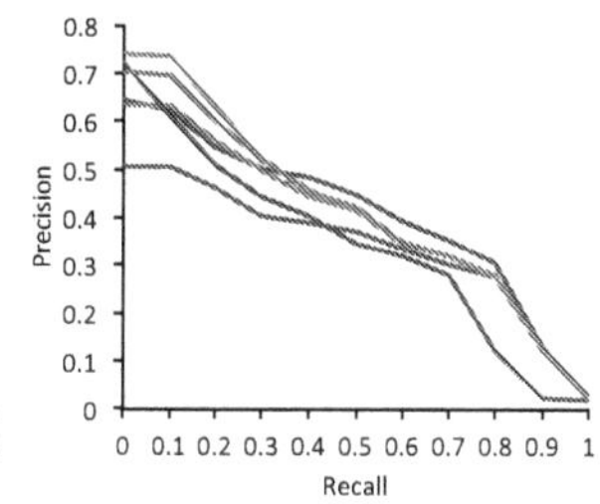

Figure 11: Protocol B (without *web vertical*)

Protocol	Web vertical	Clarity	LM	ReDDe	ReDDe-R	LMRedde	LMReDDe-R
A	Yes	0.242	0.375	0.527	0.548	**0.606**	0.564
	No	0.150	**0.179**	0.137	0.146	0.137	0.149
B	Yes	0.305	**0.588**	0.552	0.556	0.573	0.564
	No	0.287	0.377	0.360	0.382	0.382	**0.393**

Table 5: MAP results

Figure 10 and 11 shows the precision-recall curves obtained by ignoring the effect of the *web vertical*. As it was the case before, *clarity* was outperformed by all the other methods. However we observed that *LM* outperform all the other methods using protocol *A*, similarly with *LMReDDe-R* for protocol *B*. We believe this result is interesting because it shows the potential of using social media for vertical representation. Recall this metric makes only used of social media tags to rank the verticals while all the other methods make uses of the entire content of the sampled documents.

Table 5 shows the MAP values obtained by all the methods with the two test sets and with and without the *web vertical*. The results are in line with the performance observed in the precision-recall curves. We verify the statistical significance of our results by comparing each pair of methods using the paired t-test for the equality of means with unequal variance. A statistical significance was acknowledged if the probability of the two means being equal (*e.g.* null hypothesis) is smaller than 5%. We found that all the differences were statistical significant except for the pairs: *ReDDe* - *LMReDDe* (using protocol A without the web vertical), *ReDDe-R* - *LMReDDe* (with *B* without the web vertical) and *ReDDe-R* - *LMReDDe-R* (with *A* and without the web vertical).

As a final remark, we observed that the models can behave differently according the test set. For example, the *LM* method seems to provide more gain for the test set created with the first protocol. We believe that further research is required to provide more robust mechanism to combine the scores of the different methods and to understand the scenarios in which each methods is more beneficial.

7. RELATED WORK

7.1 Aggregated Search

In [2, 3] is proposed a machine learning approach to combine the scores of several resource selection methods. *ReDDe*, which was initially proposed for federated search and databases[19], is adapted for large-scale aggregated search systems. Our work differs from theirs in that: *(i)* we are interested on domain specific areas (*e.g.* content for children); *(ii)* our methods are applied on public available resources instead of proprietary environments (absent of query logs); *(ii)* we relax the restriction of having only one relevant vertical per query since we observed that even though the number of relevant verticals is small, the average is far greater than 1 (around 3.5); *(iv)* a collection is provided to the research community. We hope this will motivate the further study of vertical selection in the domain of children.

In [2] vertical relevance assessments are gathered by asking trained annotators to find the most suitable vertical for the query. In [1] aggregated search interfaces are assessed using paired comparisons. This methodology was used in IR initially in [21]. In this work, we employed the paired comparison methodology to gather assessments and we show that these may lead to preferences towards visual oriented verticals. We proposed an alternative methodology that does not suffer of this bias.

7.2 IR for children

Duarte et al. [23, 7] presented a methodology to extract queries focused on retrieving information for children using public data. Their motivation is to carried out a query log analysis to compare the behavior of children and grown ups. In [9], the authors contrast their first results against the results obtained with a set of queries actually submitted by children. They found consistent results in terms of topic trends and topic distribution in both data sets. For this reasons we used their work as a starting point to build our collection. Our work differs in that we are interested in the evaluation of vertical selection methods. Our collection builds on top of this query set by adding a set of verticals, their documents and vertical relevance assessments. In [12] is proposed a variation of page rank to promote websites appropriate for children. Eickhoff et al. [10] proposed a learner to classify web pages in appropriate and non-appropriate for children. In [8] is proposed a biased random walk to recommend queries for children. All these studies employed the Dmoz *kids and teens* directory, which is also employed by us. However, these studies focus only on the web vertical while our work involves a large set of verticals of heterogeneous genres, and our interest is on choosing the best collection for children instead of filtering content or re-ranking solely on the web vertical.

8. CONCLUSIONS AND FUTURE WORK

We presented a detailed description of a simple methodology to build a collection for the problem of vertical selection in the domain of content for children. We contrast two methodologies to gather relevant assessments using *CrowdFlower*. We proved that the two methods lead to a different set of relevant verticals and that the former is prone to visual bias. We show that the different sets obtained by these methods can also lead to differences in the performance of vertical selection methods. We believe that the choice of either methodology is highly dependent of the targeted aggregated search system. For instance if the web vertical is always displayed it may be more beneficial to employ the paired comparison method since it has higher inter-assessor agreement. Nonetheless, further refinements are needed given the visual bias obtained by this method. We found that tags from social media are an effective resource for the problem of vertical selection given that for several experiment settings was the best performing feature. Similarly, the ratio between the sizes estimations (*i.e.* children and grown ups) lead to a significant performance gain.

There are several directions for future work. We would like to verify that grown ups judgments correlate with the judgments of children in the targeted age group. We showed a simple language model to rank verticals using tags from social media. However, more sophisticated methods to exploit these resources are worth to explored (*e.g.* random walk, semantic latent models). We also consider worth verifying the applicability of the methods proposed in this paper in other information domains. (*e.g.* teenagers, elderly)

9. ACKNOWLEDGEMENTS

This research was partially funded by the European Community's Seventh Framework Programme FP7/2007-2013 under grant agreement no. 231507.

10. REFERENCES

[1] J. Arguello, F. Diaz, J. Callan, and B. Carterette. A methodology for evaluating aggregated search results. In *Proceedings of the 33rd European conference on Advances in information retrieval*, ECIR'11, pages 141–152, Berlin, Heidelberg, 2011. Springer-Verlag.

[2] J. Arguello, F. Diaz, J. Callan, and J.-F. Crespo. Sources of evidence for vertical selection. In *SIGIR '09*, pages 315–322, New York, NY, USA, 2009. ACM.

[3] J. Arguello, F. Diaz, and J.-F. Paiement. Vertical selection in the presence of unlabeled verticals. In *SIGIR*, pages 691–698, 2010.

[4] J. Arguello, W.-C. Wu, D. Kelly, and A. Edwards. Task complexity, vertical display and user interaction in aggregated search. SIGIR '12, pages 435–444, New York, NY, USA, 2012. ACM.

[5] A. Bermingham and A. F. Smeaton. A study of inter-annotator agreement for opinion retrieval. SIGIR '09, pages 784–785, New York, NY, USA, 2009. ACM.

[6] D. Downey, S. Dumais, D. Liebling, and E. Horvitz. Understanding the relationship between searchers' queries and information goals. CIKM '08, pages 449–458, New York, NY, USA, 2008. ACM.

[7] S. Duarte, D. Hiemstra, and P. Serdyukov. An analysis of queries intended to search information for children. In *IIiX 2010*.

[8] S. Duarte Torres, D. Hiemstra, I. Weber, and P. Serdyukov. Query recommendation for children. CIKM '12, pages 2010–2014, New York, NY, USA, 2012. ACM.

[9] S. Duarte Torres and I. Weber. What and how children search on the web. CIKM '11, pages 393–402, New York, NY, USA, 2011. ACM.

[10] C. Eickhoff, P. Serdyukov, and A. P. de Vries. A combined topical/non-topical approach to identifying web sites for children. WSDM '11, pages 505–514, New York, NY, USA, 2011. ACM.

[11] E. Foss, A. Druin, R. Brewer, P. Lo, L. Sanchez, E. Golub, and H. Hutchinson. Children's search roles at home: Implications for designers, researchers, educators, and parents. *JASIST*, 63(3):558–573, 2012.

[12] K. Gyllstrom and M.-F. Moens. Wisdom of the ages: toward delivering the children's web with the link-based agerank algorithm. In *CIKM*, pages 159–168, 2010.

[13] A. Hassan, R. Jones, and K. L. Klinkner. Beyond dcg: user behavior as a predictor of a successful search. In *Proceedings of the third ACM international conference on Web search and data mining*, WSDM '10, pages 221–230, New York, NY, USA, 2010. ACM.

[14] D. Hiemstra. Term-specific smoothing for the language modeling approach to information retrieval: the importance of a query term. In *SIGIR*, pages 35–41, 2002.

[15] Ilad Shokouhi and L. Si. Federated search. In *FNTIR*, 2011.

[16] G. Pass, A. Chowdhury, and C. Torgeson. A picture of search. In *Proceedings of the 1st international conference on Scalable information systems*, InfoScale '06, New York, NY, USA, 2006. ACM.

[17] P. Schaer. Better than their reputation? on the reliability of relevance assessments with students. In *CLEF*, pages 124–135, 2012.

[18] M. Shokouhi, J. Zobel, F. Scholer, and S. M. M. Tahaghoghi. Capturing collection size for distributed non-cooperative retrieval. SIGIR '06, pages 316–323, New York, NY, USA, 2006. ACM.

[19] L. Si and J. Callan. Relevant document distribution estimation method for resource selection. SIGIR '03, pages 298–305, New York, NY, USA, 2003. ACM.

[20] S. Sushmita, H. Joho, and M. Lalmas. A task-based evaluation of an aggregated search interface. In *SPIRE*, pages 322–333, 2009.

[21] P. Thomas and D. Hawking. Evaluation by comparing result sets in context. CIKM '06, pages 94–101, New York, NY, USA, 2006. ACM.

[22] P. Thomas and D. Hawking. Evaluating sampling methods for uncooperative collections. SIGIR '07, pages 503–510, New York, NY, USA, 2007. ACM.

[23] S. D. Torres, D. Hiemstra, and P. Serdyukov. Query log analysis in the context of information retrieval for children. In *SIGIR*, pages 847–848, 2010.

[24] R. Wetzker, C. Zimmermann, and C. Bauckhage. Analyzing social bookmarking systems: A del.icio.us cookbook. In *MSoDa*, pages 26–30, 2008.

[25] J. Xu, S. Wu, and X. Li. Estimating collection size with logistic regression. SIGIR '07, pages 789–790, New York, NY, USA, 2007. ACM.

[26] K. Zhou, R. Cummins, M. Lalmas, and J. Jose. Evaluating large-scale distributed vertical search. LSDS-IR '11, pages 9–14, New York, NY, USA, 2011. ACM.

Automatic Extraction of Core Learning Goals and Generation of Pedagogical Sequences Through a Collection of Digital Library Resources

Ifeyinwa Okoye
Institute of Cognitive Science
Department of Computer Science
University of Colorado at Boulder
okoye@colorado.edu

Tamara Sumner
Institute of Cognitive Science
Department of Computer Science
University of Colorado at Boulder
sumner@colorado.edu

Steven Bethard
Institute of Cognitive Science
Department of Computer Science
University of Colorado at Boulder
steven.bethard@colorado.edu

ABSTRACT

A key challenge facing educational technology researchers is how to provide structure and guidance when learners use unstructured and open tools such as digital libraries for their own learning. This work attempts to use computational methods to identify that structure in a domain independent way and support learners as they navigate and interpret the information they find. This article highlights a computational methodology for generating a pedagogical sequence through core learning goals extracted from a collection of resources which in this case, are resources from the Digital Library for Earth System Education (DLESE). This article describes how we use the technique of multi-document summarization to extract the core learning goals from the digital library resources and how we create a supervised classifier that performs a pair-wise classification of the core learning goals; the judgments from these classifications are used to automatically generate pedagogical sequences. Results show that we can extract good core learning goals and make pair-wise classifications that are up to 76% similar to the pair-wise classifications generated from pedagogical sequences created by two science education experts. Thus we can dynamically generate pedagogically meaningful learning paths through digital library resources.

Categories and Subject Descriptors

H.1.2 [**Information Systems**]: Models and Principles—*User/Machine Systems*; I.2.7 [**Computing Methodologies**]: Artificial Intelligence—*Natural Language Processing*; L.3.6 [**Science and Technology of Learning**]: Methodology/Tools/Technology—*Technology Enhanced Learning*

Keywords

pedagogical sequence; core learning goal; digital libraries; machine learning; learning trajectory; learning pathway

1. INTRODUCTION

Nowadays, many people get their information from online sources such as search engines, portals for dedicated topics and social networks which provide free and ubiquitous access to information. However with free and ubiquitous access to information, comes the potential problem of information overload and learner disorientation [6]. One way learning systems can mitigate these cognitive problems is by providing a pedagogical sequence [25]. A pedagogical sequence is a learning trajectory or route taken by a learner through a range of learning goals in order to achieve understanding of a topic. According to conceptual change learning theory [22], a good pedagogical sequence is important because the order in which knowledge is learned can be crucial, in that if the basic building knowledge blocks are incorrect, it can lead to misconceptions in assimilation of higher order knowledge later. For example, if you have unremedied problems with addition and subtraction, you will probably have problems when doing algebra and with unremedied problems in algebra you can expect problems with calculus. Table 1 shows some learning goals about seasons generated by the Center for Curriculum Materials in Science [24]. The seasons learning goals released by the Center states that learning goal 1 should be understood before learning goal 2, learning goal 2 and 3 can be learned in any order and should be, before attempting to understand learning goal 4. So two suggested pedagogical sequences through the learning goals in Table 1 are $1 \to 2 \to 3 \to 4$ and $1 \to 3 \to 2 \to 4$.

In this article, we use machine learning and natural language processing approaches to create two computational models, one that extracts core learning goals from a collection of digital library resources and another that puts the core learning goals into a pedagogically meaningful sequence. The pedagogical sequences we generate are adaptive sequences and can be generated on the fly given a collection of digital resources as opposed to textbooks or school curricula whose pedagogical sequences are static and take a lot of money and time to create. The resources we are working with are digital library resources from the Digital Library for Earth System Education (DLESE). There are several use cases for pedagogical sequences. They can be used to drive the presentation of content in an adaptive educational hypermedia environment. That is, given a pedagogical sequence *ab* of core learning goals *a* and *b*, an adaptive educational hypermedia system can rearrange the order in which documents are presented to the user such that a document that contains information about core learning goal *a*, the first learning goal the user should learn about, is presented first or

#	Core learning goals about seasons
(1)	Light and other electromagnetic waves can warm objects. How much an object's temperature increases depends on how intense the light striking its surface is, how long it shines on the object, and how much of the light is absorbed.
(2)	The temperature of a location on the surface of the earth depends upon the number of hours of sunlight and the intensity of that sunlight.
(3)	The axis of the Earth's rotation is tilted relative to the plane of the Earth's yearly orbit around the sun. As the Earth orbits the sun, the axis remains pointed the same place in space.
(4)	The seasonal variations in temperature at different places on the surface of the Earth are explained by the differential heating of the Earth's surface as it rotates on an axis that is tilted relative to the plane of the Earth's orbit around the sun.

Table 1: Core learning Goals about Seasons

made more discoverable than a document which contains information about core learning goal *b*, which the user should learn after understanding core learning goal *a*.

A meta analysis of the use of personalized feedback has shown it can induce an average effect size of up to 0.79 [13]. This means that initial knowledge levels being equal, an average person that received personalized feedback would score higher in a test than about 79% of a control group that didn't receive personalized feedback. Pedagogical sequences can be used to guide personalized feedback in a learning environment when we have access to aspects of users knowledge states, such as misconceptions as shown in Figure 1. For example given a learner with two misconceptions (1 and 2) that can be mapped to two core learning goals *b* and *a* respectively in a pedagogical sequence *ab*, we can surmise that the student should work on misconception 2 first, before tackling misconception 1. Both the extraction of core learning goals and the generation of pedagogical sequence can help provide effective feedback to learners and support learners understanding of science concepts. According to the effective feedback model proposed by Hattie [13], feedback has to answer 3 questions; 1: *Where am I going?*, 2: *How am I going?* and 3: *Where to next?*, in order for it to be effective in reducing the gap between what the learner understands and what the learner needs to understand. Extracting core learning goals answers *Where am I going?* by producing what the learner needs to learn, Sequencing the learning goals answers *How am I going?* by showing in what order the core learning goals should be learned while prioritizing the misconceptions using the pedagogical sequence as a feature, answers *Where to next?*. In addition, the pedagogical sequences can provide structure and guidance when learners use unstructured and open tools such as digital libraries for their own learning.

There are two research questions guiding the research reported in this article:

1. *(RQ1) How well can different multi-document summarization methods identify the core learning goals in a collection of documents?* US schools have been criticized for not emphasizing the big ideas in science. Subsequently, there has been a push to target big ideas in depth rather than a long list of ideas in a superficial manner so as to promote robust understanding and produce citizens that are capable of reasoning correctly about scientific phenomena in the time constraints of the classroom [23, 9]. Hence in order to guide a learner towards an efficient path of understanding, it is imperative that learning systems work towards identifying significant learning goals and not just assume that the student needs to see and learn every concept in a resource. So the question here is, given a collection of documents (chapters in a textbook or online resources), can we determine a good method for identifying the main ideas/ core learning goals in this collection?

2. *(RQ2) How well can machine learning classifiers model the pedagogical sequence of core learning goals produced by science education experts?* Some concepts serve as building blocks for other concepts, and thus it is essential to learn the basic concepts before moving on to other concepts that depend on them (i.e the learning trajectory or sequence of acquisition of knowledge is important in promoting science understanding) [23, 19, 9]. For example, students must first understand the concept of the revolution of the Earth around the sun and the concept of the tilt of the Earth before they can understand the concept of seasons in the northern and southern hemisphere. There may exist several different but reasonable pedagogical sequences given a set of core learning goals. We focus on generating a single sequence to provide students with a meaningful learning path through the core learning goals. The sequence of core learning goals that results from this research will serve as input for a later module that prioritizes students misconceptions as shown in Figure 1.

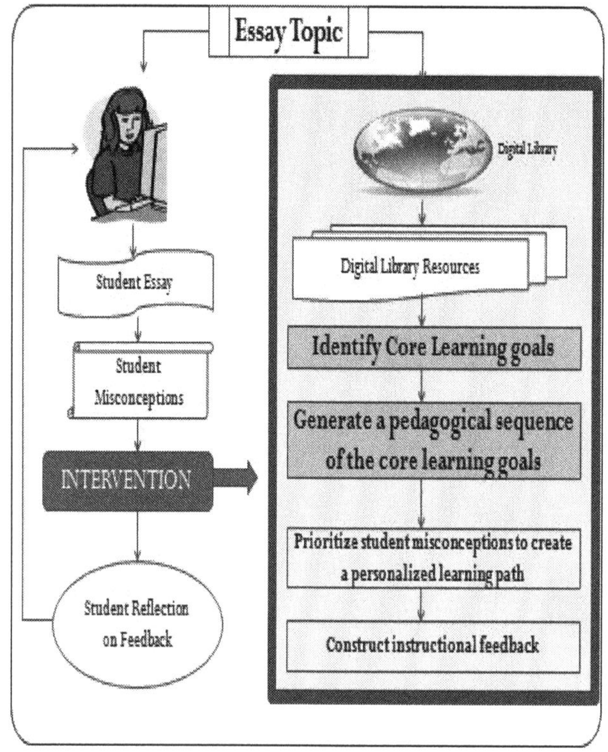

Figure 1: Use case for pedagogical sequence

A key challenge facing educational technology researchers is how to provide structure and guidance when learners use unstructured and open tools for their own learning. This research attempts to identify that structure in a domain independent way and support the learner as they navigate and interpret the information they find.

Connections to Prior Work

Pedagogical sequencing also known as learning trajectory and learning pathway is an active research area in the field of technology enhanced education. Prior work have focused on using the learner's knowledge state [18, 14, 1, 15], modeled through an overlap of the domain ontology [18] or testing responses of individual learners [14] to generate a personalized pedagogical sequence. Acampora et al. [1] exploit ontological representations of the learner's knowledge state and uses memetic optimization algorithm to generate a pedagogical sequence while Huang et al. [15] uses case-based reasoning on computer-adaptive tests to generate the learner knowledge model and a genetic-based algorithm to create a personalized pedagogical sequence. However, the initial cost to build systems that generate such pedagogical sequences is huge because they depend on ontologies or test questions, which take a lot of human effort to build thus making these systems less able to scale to other domains. Even when provided with a free ontology, these systems' reliance on learner knowledge is still a bottleneck because there are circumstances in which the learner knowledge will not be available but in which the system still should generate a pedagogical sequence for the learner. Pedagogical sequencing in formal intelligent tutoring systems such as IT-TUTOR *katuk2010finding* is usually done manually by curriculum sequencing experts.

"Adaptive Hypermedia systems build a model of the goals, preferences and knowledge of each individual user, and use this model throughout the interaction with the user, in order to adapt to the needs of that user" [4]. Adaptive Hypermedia learning environments such as INSPIRE [17] and AHA [7] are a solution to the problem of sequencing in an informal environment when the learner knowledge is not readily available. While the benefits of such systems such as increased speed of learning [5] and improved content understanding [3] have been documented, the drawback to such systems are that they depend on the resources being hyperlinked. They are not particularly effective in the scenario in which the user wants to sequence resources in different formats (pdf, html, plaintext) that are hyperlinked. Collaborative filtering can be used in such a scenario (i.e monitor how users traverse through the collection of resources and suggest the most common paths to similar users). However, this technique is deluged with the cold start problem. It requires a lot of users to use the system in similar ways, they have to access the same type of materials and resources before it can present similar users with an emergent pedagogical sequence. But to get lots of users to use the system, the system has to provide some value to them right away. In addition, the most trodden path might not be an ideal learning path. So we need a different technique for generating pedagogical sequences for a learning system where users are in control of the location and format of resources and where the learner knowledge is not readily available.

2. COMPUTATIONAL METHODOLOGY

We use the technique of multi-document summarization to extract the learning goals and the technique of supervised classification to train a machine learning classifier. The judgments from the classification are used to generate the pedagogical sequences. The scientific topic for this study is Plate tectonics.

2.1 Extraction of Core Learning Goals via Multi-document Summarization

Multi-document summarization is a technique for generating a summary from a collection of documents. We use a multi-document summarization tool for Earth Science called COGENT [8], which is built on MEAD [20], a general purpose multi-document summarizer. Previous research has shown that COGENT is capable of adequately extracting important and non-overlapping earth science sentences from a collection of digital library resources[8]. COGENT has been used to build a plate tectonics domain knowledge base which contains the plate tectonics knowledge that a middle or high school student should know [2]. In addition, COGENT has been shown to scale relatively well to other topics within Earth Science such as weather and climate [16]. In this study, we compare two different approaches for identifying core learning goals from a collection of documents; Extraction-Rate and Ranking-Score. These two methods were selected because they are important variables to be considered when optimizing multi-document summarization techniques for different domains. In this study, learning goals are sentences.

2.2 Generation of Pedagogical Sequence via Supervised Classification

We compare and contrast three different machine learning models for generating a pedagogical sequence. To break this down into a tractable task, we cast this as a pair-wise ordering problem so rather than focusing on trying to automatically generate entire pedagogical sequences, we are focusing on developing a model capable of identifying when one learning goal precedes another. The output of the trained models will be evaluated on science education experts pair-wise orderings of learning goals. To generate a pedagogical sequence from the resulting pair-wise judgments, first, we construct a precedence table from the pair-wise judgments and then generate a pedagogical sequence from the precedence table. Table 2 is an example of a precedence table that contains four sentence labels which have been pair-wise classified. The pair-wise classification model from which this precedence table was generated, produced the following pairwise classifications; $C < A$, $A < B$, $C < B$, and $C < D$. Three pedagogical sequences that can be generated from this table are: (1) $C \to A \to D \to B$, (2) $C \to D \to A \to B$ and (3) $C \to A \to B \to D$.

Concept	Preceded by
A	C
B	A , C
C	
D	C

Table 2: Example of a Precedence table

3. AUTOMATIC EXTRACTION OF CORE LEARNING GOALS

The purpose of this study is to compare two methods for extracting core learning goals from a collection of documents. The core learning goals of a scientific topic are the major facts or information about the topic that a learner is expected to know, in order for the learner to adequately understand the topic. Table 1 shows some of the core learning goals for the topic of seasons. The material for this study was twenty digital library resources related to plate tectonics selected from the Digital Library for Earth System Education (DLESE) [1] by an earth science expert. The twenty resources were chosen for containing most, if not all the information a middle or high school student should know about plate tectonics.

[1]http://www.dlese.org

The second set of material is a set of domain sentences, which were extracted from the twenty DLESE resources using COGENT at an extraction rate of 5%. Five percent was chosen for this task because a study has shown that given twenty DLESE resources on plate tectonics and asked to manually build a plate tectonics domain competency map, which would contain the important information that middle and high school students should know about plate tectonics, several earth science experts jointly built a knowledge base that contained 5% of all the sentences in the twenty resources [2]. This extraction yielded 97 sentences which we call the *domain sentences*. These 97 sentences can be considered as learning goals for the twenty resources. The task of the two algorithms we are comparing, is to determine which of these 97 sentences can be considered *core learning goals*. For both algorithms, we use an Earth Science multi-document summarizer called COGENT [8].

3.1 Methodology

The measures we use to assess core learning goals are coverage and coreness. Our measure of coverage is based on how well the resulting set of identified learning goals correspond to the twelve American Association for the Advancement of science (AAAS) benchmark learning goals for plate tectonics. These twelve AAAS benchmarks for plate tectonics, six for middle and six for high school, represent the core knowledge of plate tectonics that students who have graduated from middle or high school are expected to have if they are to achieve the AAAS Adult science literacy goals. We use the AAAS benchmarks because it is an international standard and is independent of the requirements of any curriculum. Our measure for coreness is how well the learning goals identified by the two algorithms correspond to coreness rating of human science education experts.

3.1.1 Producing the human expert evaluation set

We worked with two science education experts to create the evaluation set. The two science education experts were asked to annotate the 97 domain sentences on two dimensions: coverage and coreness to AAAS benchmark learning goals for plate tectonics. Coverage refers to similarity to the 12 AAAS benchmark learning goals for plate tectonics. The experts assigned each domain sentence to the AAAS benchmark learning goal, to which the sentence was most related (coverage). They also assigned a coreness rating of 1 to 4 to each sentence, with 4 being the most core. In general, we consider sentences with a coreness value of 3 as being good but those with a coreness value of 1 or 2 as being poor. Coreness refers to how similar the domain sentence is to the AAAS benchmark learning goal that it was assigned to during the coverage annotation. This resulted in a coverage and coreness rating for the domain sentences. A human-identified (gold standard) set of core learning goals was created by pulling together all the domain sentences which had a rating of 4 into a set. This yielded learning goal data 1 *(LGD1)*, a set of 29 core learning goals which at least one science education expert had rated as having a coreness of 4.

3.1.2 Algorithm 1 : Extraction-Rate

The Extraction-Rate algorithm uses COGENT [8] to extract core learning goals from the twenty DLESE resources by reducing the percentage of sentences extracted by COGENT. We chose to use an extraction rate of 1% in order to produce a similar number of sentences to those produced by the human identification. This Extraction Rate algorithm resulted in 32 sentences, which we call learning goal data 2 *(LGD2)*. The poor core learning goals (coreness value of 1 or 2) generated by this algorithm are shown in Table 3. The intuition to use the Extraction-Rate algorithm which reduces the extraction rate in COGENT to identify core learning goals came from a study which showed that as the extraction rate of sentences for the topic of plate tectonics was decreased from 5% to 0.5%, with a 0.5 point decrease each time, the average coreness of the extracted sentences increased steadily [10].

#	**Sentences with a coreness of 1 or 2**
1	Shaping the Ocean Floor at the Mid-Ocean Ridges
2	Some scientists, such as David James of the Carnegie Institution of Washington, believe that the continents are anchored into the mantle by deep keels of rock that extend hundred of miles below the surface, and the continental crust and mantle therefore move in concert).
3	Structure of the Earth History of plate tectonics Plates Plate boundaries Forces in the Earth Faults Hypercard Resources
4	As the plate dives into the mantle – the layer of hot, flexible rock on which the plates glide – it gradually is heated.

Table 3: Poor learning goals produced by Extraction-Rate Algorithm

3.1.3 Algorithm 2 : Ranking-Score

We use the Ranking-Score algorithm to identify core learning goals from the set of domain sentences. Ranking is a technique used in information retrieval for identifying the most relevant resources. COGENT has a built-in ranker, which it uses during the last stage of the multi-document summarization process, to decide which sentences in a collection of documents to extract to create a summary. In the Ranking-Score algorithm, we use the COGENT rankings to generate a third set of core learning goals which we call learning goal data 3 *(LGD3)*. Learning goal data 3 *(LGD3)* are the top ranked 29 sentences in the domain sentences. The bad core learning goals (coreness value of 1 or 2) generated by this algorithm are shown in Table 4. Essentially, this algorithm can be taken to be the baseline.

3.2 Results

We evaluate the core learning goals generated from both algorithms and the human-identified set for coverage of and coreness to the AAAS benchmark learning goals for plate tectonics. We use the human experts' annotations of coverage and coreness to score the output of the Extraction-Rate and Ranking-Score algorithms. Only a few of the domain sentences were doubly annotated. So if both human experts said a core learning goal in a learning goal data set covered two different AAAS benchmarks, we assumed both benchmarks were covered by the learning goal data set. For coreness, we assumed the higher of both experts' rating. So if one expert assigned a core learning goal a coreness value of 4 and another assigned the same learning goal a coreness value of 2, we assumed the coreness for that learning goal was 4.

Table 5, Table 6 and Figure 2 show the results. In Table 5, PT-BMK, refers to the AAAS plate tectonics-benchmark. MS1 refers to middle school 1 and HS1 refers to high school 1. Thus PT-BMK-HS1, refers to the first AAAS high school plate tectonics benchmark learning goal while PT-BMK-MS3 refers to the third AAAS middle school plate tectonics benchmark learning goal. The Extraction-Rate algorithm outperforms the Ranking-Score algorithms on both coverage and coreness. Table 5 shows that the Extraction-Rate algorithm generated core learning goals that covered more of the AAAS benchmark learning goals (75%) than the core learn-

#	Sentences with a coreness of 1 or 2
1	The diagrams below show the break-up of the supercontinent Pangaea (meaning "all lands" in Greek), which figured prominently in the theory of continental drift – the forerunner to the theory of plate tectonics
2	Until the 1700s, most Europeans thought that a Biblical Flood played a major role in shaping the Earth's surface.
3	Other mismatches of geology and climate included distinctive fossil ferns (Glossopteris) discovered in now-polar regions, and the occurrence of glacial deposits in present-day arid Africa, such as the Vaal River valley of South Africa.
4	But at the time Wegener introduced his theory, the scientific community firmly believed the continents and oceans to be permanent features on the Earth's surface.
5	The mantle, which contains more iron, magnesium, and calcium than the crust, is hotter and denser because temperature and pressure inside the Earth increase with depth.
6	This submerged mountain range, which extends from the Arctic Ocean to beyond the southern tip of Africa, is but one segment of the global mid-ocean ridge system that encircles the Earth.
7	In 1983, this evidence, in addition to the earlier recorded history of earthquake activity, led the USGS to predict that there was a 95 percent chance of a 6.0 earthquake striking Parkfield before 1993.
8	Figures 10k-1 and 10k-2 show the location of some of the major mountain systems found on the Earth's surface.
9	In an ocean-continent convergence, the collision of ocean and continental plates causes the accretion of marine sedimentary deposits to the edge of the continent.
10	How Volcanoes Work - Earth's Internal Heat, Energy, and Interior Structure
11	Increased compaction resulted in the conversion of gravitational energy into heat energy, much like a bicycle pump heats up due to the compression of air inside it.
12	The very lightest volatile materials (derived from comets) were easily melted or vaporized, rising beyond the earth's rocky surface to form the early oceans and the atmosphere.
13	With a thickness of about 100 km, the lithosphere is composed of an upper layer of crust (7 km thick under the oceans, and 35 km thick under the continents) and a lower, denser layer of the earth's upper mantle.
14	The lithosphere is underlain by the asthenosphere, a hot, mobile layer of partially molten rock lying within the earth's upper mantle.
15	Plate Tectonics - Earth Like a Puzzle - Children learn about plate tectonics, earthquakes, and volcanoes at this site in Scripps Institution of Oceanography
16	The Earth's longest mountain chain isn't the Andes in South America, or the Himalayas in Asia, or even North America's Rockies.

Table 4: Poor learning goals produced by Ranking-Score Algorithm

ing goals generated from the Ranking-Score algorithm (58%). As expected, LGD1, the human-identified set, had the best coverage (83%). The Extraction-Rate and Ranking-Score algorithms had 5 core learning goals in common. As Figure 2 shows, the Extraction-rate algorithm identified more core learning goals than the Ranking-Score algorithm. Table 6 shows that the average coreness of the sentences gotten from the Extraction-Rate algorithm was 3.25, while the Ranking-Score sentences had an average coreness of 2.41.

#	AAAS plate tectonics learning goal	LGD1 Human Identified	LGD2 Extraction Rate algorithm	LGD3 Ranking Score algorithm
(1)	PT-BMK-MS1	YES	YES	YES
(2)	PT-BMK-MS2	YES	YES	YES
(3)	PT-BMK-MS3	YES	NO	YES
(4)	PT-BMK-MS4	NO	NO	YES
(5)	PT-BMK-MS5	YES	YES	NO
(6)	PT-BMK-MS6	NO	NO	NO
(7)	PT-BMK-HS1	YES	YES	YES
(8)	PT-BMK-HS2	YES	YES	YES
(9)	PT-BMK-HS3	YES	YES	YES
(10)	PT-BMK-HS4	YES	YES	NO
(11)	PT-BMK-HS5	YES	YES	NO
(12)	PT-BMK-HS6	YES	YES	NO
		83% (10/12)	75% (9/12)	58% (7/12)

Table 5: Coverage Results for Extracting Core Learning Goals

Coreness Rating	LGD1 Human Identified	LGD2 Extraction Rate algorithm	LGD3 Ranking Score algorithm
1	0	3	9
2	0	1	7
3	0	13	5
4	29	15	8
AVERAGE	4.00	3.25	2.41

Table 6: Average Coreness for Learning Goal Data Sets

4. AUTOMATIC GENERATION OF PEDAGOGICAL SEQUENCES

The purpose of this study is to establish a computational technique for generating a pedagogical sequence from the core learning goals of a collection of documents. This study uses two sets of materials. The first set of materials is the core learning goals identified using the Extraction-Rate algorithm (LGD2). We chose to use LGD2 because it is the best set of core learning goals that we can generate algorithmically. The second set of materials are the pedagogical sequences produced by science education experts using LGD2. We collected 5 pedagogical sequences from 2 experts. As described later, each of these pedagogical sequences was then converted into judgments between pairs of core learning goals. These pair-wise judgments are used for both training and evaluating the machine learning models.

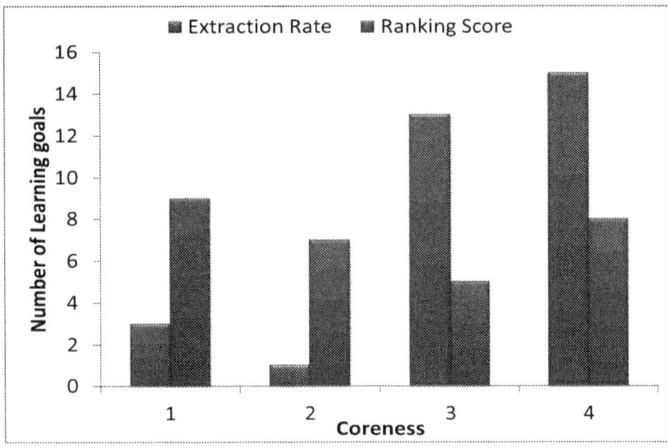

Figure 2: Distribution of coreness in Extraction-Rate and Ranking-Score

4.1 Methodology

The methodology process for this study is shown in figure 3. We trained three machine learning classifier models, Maxent and 2 support vector machine models, SMO and LibSVM in order to compare and contrast their performance on experts' pedagogical sequences. We trained the models using a 10-fold cross validation on the data set where both experts agreed on the classification. We used the default settings for the three classifiers in WEKA [12].

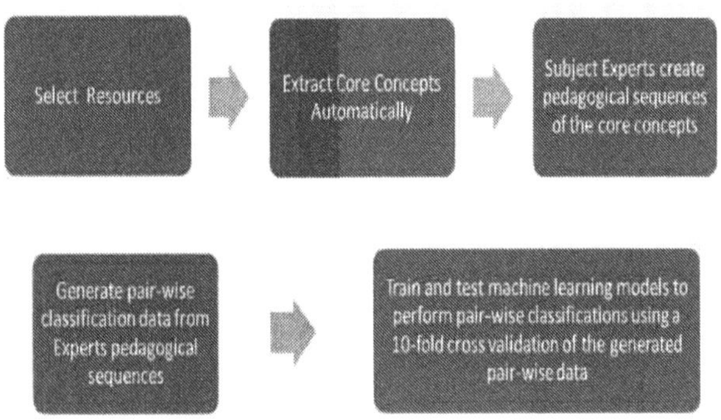

Figure 3: Methodology process

4.1.1 Producing the human expert evaluation set

The human expert evaluation set for this study is the second set of materials, the pair-wise orderings generated from experts' sequencing of LGD2. We asked two science education experts to come up with pedagogical sequences each for LGD2 but constrained the task. We requested that the first sequence follow an *evidence or research based* pedagogical sequence while the second sequence follow a *traditional or lecture-based* pedagogical sequence. An *evidence or research based* pedagogical sequence is a pedagogy where students are encouraged to use the scientific method to learn about a phenomena, i.e they gather information by observing the phenomena, forming a hypothesis, performing experiment, collecting and analyzing data and then interpreting the data and drawing conclusions that hopefully align with the current understanding about the phenomena. A teacher that uses this pedagogical sequence acts as a *guide on the side*. A *traditional or lecture-based* pedagogical sequence, on the other hand, is the pedagogy where teachers are simply trying to pass on the correct information to students rather than letting the students discover the information themselves. In a classroom environment, a teacher using this pedagogical sequence would be seen as the classical *sage on stage*.

#	**Learning goals with a coreness of 4**
1	The scraping of one plate on another generates powerful earthquakes; the heating of the plate within the depths of the mantle releases fluids which melt the rock over it, producing blobs of molten rock, or magma, that surface as volcanoes.
2	Though hidden beneath the ocean surface, the global mid-ocean ridge system is the most prominent topographic feature on the surface of our planet.
3	The Earth's surface is covered by a series of crustal plates.
4	According to the plate tectonic model, the surface of the Earth consists of a series of relatively thin, but rigid, plates which are in constant motion.
5	The surface layer of each plate is composed of oceanic crust, continental crust or a combination of both.
6	The Earth's internal heat source provides the energy for our dynamic planet, supplying it with the driving force for plate-tectonic motion, and for on-going catastrophic events such as earthquakes and volcanic eruptions.
7	Plate boundaries are found at the edge of the lithospheric plates and are of three types, convergent, divergent and conservative.

Table 7: Sample Good learning goals produced by Extraction-Rate Algorithm

Given the learning goals in Table 7 which are part of LGD2, An evidence pedagogy could sequence the learning goals by emphasizing discovery in this way:

- Evidence that something was going on about plate motion: 2
- There are plates: 3
- Plate movement: 4
- Plate Boundaries: 7
- What makes the plates and layers of the Earth: 5
- Results of plate motion and interactions: 1
- Sources of energy: 6

while a traditional approach would sequence the learning goals without emphasizing discovery, just stating the facts in this way:

- Sources of Energy: 6
- What makes the plate and layers of the Earth: 5
- There are plates: 3
- Evidence for plate tectonics: 2
- Plate movement: 4
- Plate Boundaries: 7
- Results of plate motion and interactions: 1

Both science education experts agreed that 2 of the 32 learning goals in LGD2, #1 and #3 in Table 3, were not learning goals, therefore they excluded them when generating pedagogical sequences from LGD2. Table 8 shows the pedagogical sequences generated by two science education experts. The first expert came up with one pedagogical sequence for evidence based (Expert1 Evidence) and two pedagogical sequences for traditional (Expert1 Traditional1 and Expert1 Traditional2) while the second expert came up with one each (Expert2 Evidence and Expert2 Traditional), so we had five pedagogical sequences for 30 of the 32 sentences in LGD2.

Level	Expert1 Traditional1	Expert1 Traditional2	Expert2 Traditional	Expert1 Evidence	Expert2 Evidence
(1)	27, 9, 16	27, 9, 16	9,27	1	4
(2)	3	3	5, 14	9, 27	9, 27
(3)	29	29	15	16	5, 14
(4)	5, 15	5, 15	21	5, 15	15, 21, 12
(5)	14	14	12	14	16
(6)	21, 12	21, 12	16	12, 21	22
(7)	28	28	22	28	1
(8)	17, 18, 19	17, 18, 19	1	4	6
(9)	22	22	6	13, 23	17
(10)	6	6	17, 18, 19	8	19
(11)	2, 20	4	4	25	18
(12)	10, 32	13, 23	25	17, 18, 19	25
(13)	30	8	8	24	8
(14)	11, 31	25	31	11, 31	31
(15)	4	2, 20	2	10, 32	2
(16)	13, 23	10, 32	20	30	20
(17)	8	30	3	2, 20	3
(18)	25	11, 31	29	22	29
(19)	24	24	28	6	28
(20)	1	1	10	29	10
(21)			30	3	30
(22)			32		32
(23)			24		24
(24)			13		13
(25)			23		23
(26)			11		11

Table 8: Human Experts Pedagogical sequencing of LGD2

The science education experts produced a partial ordering of the learning goals. As shown in Table 8, although there are 30 sentences to be sequenced in LGD2, both experts produced only 21 and 26 levels of ordering respectively for the evidence based pedagogical sequences and 20 and 26 levels of ordering respectively for the traditional based pedagogical sequences, with more than one learning goal occupying a level. If two learning goals are on the same level, it means that they do not have any precedence relationship between themselves and can be learned in any order. From these partial orderings, we generated a pair-wise ordering of all the sentences in the learning goal set and assigned each pair to a class ($C1 < C2$) or ($C1 >= C2$). For example as shown in Table 8, Expert1 for the evidence based pedagogy (column 5, row 1 and 2), assigned sentence 1 to level 1 and sentences 9 and 27 to level 2. The pair-wise orderings 1-9 and 1-27 will be assigned to class ($C1 < C2$) i.e sentence 1 should be learned before sentences 9 and 27. The pair-wise ordering 9-27, 9-1 and 27-1 will be assigned to class ($C1 >= C2$) because the partial ordering does not indicate that 9 and 27 should be learned in any specific order, and the partial ordering says they should be learned after sentence 1.

Type	Instances	(C1<C2)	(C1>=C2)
Evidence	589 (65.0%)	49.5%	50.5%
Traditional	613 (70.5%)	49.5%	50.5%

Table 9: Distribution of agreement pair-wise pedagogical sequence data

Table 9 describes the second set of materials, which we will use as the training and testing data for our pedagogical sequence model. The *Type* column shows which pedagogical sequence data set we are dealing with, Evidence or Traditional, the sentences are the same for both pedagogies and are 30 of the 32 LGD2 but the pedagogical sequencing are different. The *Instances* column is the number of instances that were generated by pairing the core learning goals and then pulling together the instances with which both experts agreed on the class label. For a pair of learning goals *a* and *b*, we pair them both ways to generate two instance ab and ba. Because getting the correct class label for one ordering, *ab*, helps with predicting the class label of the second ordering, *ba*, when dividing the data set for training and testing, we ensure that both *ab* and *ba* are both contained together in either the training or the testing data set. The total number of pair-wise orderings we can generate from 30 core learning goals are 870.

As can be seen from Table 9, for the Evidence pedagogy, the experts agreed on the class labels for 65% (589) of the 870 and for Traditional pedagogy, 70.5% (613). For the Traditional pedagogy, there were three sequences, 2 from the first expert and 1 from the second expert. We are using only the pairs for which all three sequences agree, even though 2 sequences were produced by 1 expert. Furthermore, although all core learning goals are paired with all other core learning goals, because the experts produce partial orderings, the number of agreements for each type of ordering may not be the same. Consider sentences 2 and 20 as assigned to levels by Expert1 in Traditional2 (column 3, row 15) and Expert2 in Traditional (column 4, rows 15 and 16) in Table 8. For the pair 20-2, they agree on the relation $C1 >= C2$, but disagree on the relation $C1 < C2$ for the pair 2-20. As a result, the class $C1 >= C2$ is slightly larger than the $C1 < C2$ class as can be seen in Table 9.

4.1.2 *Training models using 10-fold cross validation*

We used 10-fold cross validation on the second set of materials, the agreed pair-wise orderings from the science education experts, to train the three models. Cross-validation is a standard technique used in machine learning for training a model and estimating its' accuracy, especially when there isn't enough data to have dedicated training and evaluation sets. In K-fold cross validation, the data set is split into mutually exclusive subsets of approximately equal size for training and testing. The model is then trained with K-1 parts and evaluated on 1 part K times, using the K possible combinations. The result is the average of the values produced by evaluating the model K times. We used this method because we have a limited supply of subject-expert sequenced core learning goal data.

Tanaka-ishii et al. [21] used local and global word count features only to build a pair-wise classifier for sorting texts by readability that had an accuracy of 90% for sorting English text in which the text vectors were concatenated into a pair. Our task is similar to the Tanaka-ishii task as we are also building a pair-wise classifier for sorting texts so we use the same local and word count features. In addition, we used word counts because we felt there might be information contained within words that makes it obvious that one sentence should precede another. For example, a sentence containing the phrase *Plate boundaries* might suggest that it should be learned before one containing *Earth quakes*, since in order to understand the current scientific reasoning about earth quakes, you need to understand plates and plate boundaries.

So as a first pass on this task, we decided to use word count features only and concatenate the vectors. First, we extracted all the unique words in a similar corpus (same topic but different documents), removed stop words (such as *the*, *a* and *and*), and ended up with 1702 words. Then, we indexed the English Gigaword, a background corpus that reflects how often we can expect to use each word in a normal day to day context and got the word count in Gigaword for each of the corresponding 1702 words. From these we generated two main features;

- **local word count** - the number of times the word appeared in this sentence
- **global word count** - the log of the ratio between the number of times the word occurred in the sentence and the number of times it occurred in the background corpus, Gigaword [11].

In addition, we included the COGENT ranking feature, which is 1 if in a pair-wise ordering *ab* of learning goals *a* and *b*, the first learning goal, (a) was extracted by COGENT before the second learning goal (b) and 0 otherwise. So for each core learning goal (sentence), we calculated 3404 features and a vector in the classifier had 6809 features since we concatenated two sentences into one vector by placing them side by side and then added the cogent ranking feature.

4.2 Results

For evaluating our models, we had two baselines. The first baseline is the majority class. This is the easiest classifier to build. The classifier just looks at the training data and calculates the most frequent class. In this case, it would be $(C1 >= C2)$. Then for all the data in the test set, the classifier says they belong to class $(C1 >= C2)$. The second baseline, cogent rankings, was the order in which COGENT outputs the learning goals. So given a pair of learning goals, 2 and 20, that were the second and twentieth sentences output by COGENT, this classifier assigns the pairing 2-20 to class $(C1 < C2)$ and the pairing 20-2 to class $(C1 >= C2)$. As Table 4.2 shows, using the majority baseline classifier resulted in an accuracy of 50.5% for both the Evidence and Traditional pedagogy. While using the cogent rankings baseline classifier resulted in an accuracy of 62% for the Evidence pedagogy and 57% for the Traditional pedagogy. The two support vector classifiers, SMO and LibSVM perform better than both baselines for the two pedagogies using the default SVM parameters. However, Maxent with its default parameters performs consistently better than both baselines and the other two models. So going forward, we will be using Maxent to build pedagogical sequence models.

Id	Majority baseline	COGENT rankings	SMO	Lib SVM	Maxent
Evidence	50.5	62.0	76.3	74.9	76.9
Traditional	50.5	57.0	60.6	59.0	60.6

Table 10: Accuracy results on pair-wise classification

5. DISCUSSION

The results in section 3.2 shows that we can identify learning goals with a high coreness rating from a collection of resources by using the technique of multi-document summarization. However, there is room for improvement because ideally, all our core learning goals would have a coreness of 4, which is not the case with the computationally extracted LGD2 and LGD3. As can be seen from Table 4, there were lots of learning goals generated by the Ranking-Score (Baseline) algorithm that had a low coreness value. Clearly we can do much better because we know the sentences with high coreness values exist in the domain sentences that the Ranking-Score algorithm is working from. We are exploring using other pre-existing rankers and building one ourselves for use in the Ranking-Score algorithm since the built-in ranker in COGENT does not seem to generate sentences with a high coreness rating at the top of the pile. Another method we are exploring for increasing the coreness values of the extracted sentences for both algorithms is by post-processing the generated data. We will look for words like *figure*, *map*, *table* or *pictures* and remove those sentences containing these words from our data set since sentences containing these words most likely refer to items that are not extracted by the multi-document Summarizer, COGENT, which only extracts text. This would take care of #1, #8 in Table 4. We could also remove sentences that are not complete sentences. This would take care of #10 and #15 in Table 4 and #3 in Table 3.

With respect to coverage of the AAAS learning goals on plate tectonics, the Extraction-Rate algorithm covered 75% of the 12 AAAS learning goals, performing better than the Ranking-Score algorithm which only covered 58%. The human-identified core learning goals covered only 83% of the AAAS learning goals. Since we were using well trained science education experts, we can conclude that these were the only AAAS learning goals covered by the DLESE resources used in the study. Hence in this situation, 83% is the best we could hope to do for coverage. And so the 75% and 58% coverage results for Extraction-Rate and Ranking-Score algorithm respectively, are actually 90% and 69% of the best we can do.

In section 4, we trained Maxent, SVM and LibSVM models using only local and global word counts. Maxent outperformed the SVM models and the two baselines on the traditional and evidence pair-wise data sets with an accuracy score of 76.9% for the Evidence data set and 60.6% for the traditional data set. We are exploring three ways of improving the classifications. First, we are exploring other features such as percentage of domain specific words contained in a sentence, the intuition being that sentences with less domain words are probably setting the stage for a learner to use the domain words and so should precede a sentence with more domain words. Second, we are examining how to select and combine the most discriminating features. And third, we are analyzing different parameter combinations for the classifiers.

Hence given a collection of digital library resources, our computational models can dynamically generate a pedagogically meaningful path through the resources by extracting core learning goals from the digital library resources and creating a pedagogical sequence through the core learning goals. A learner can then assimilate the learning goals in the suggested sequence in more detail by exploring the digital library resource from which each particular core learning goal sentence was extracted.

One drawback in how we evaluate our pedagogical sequence model is that we are using science education experts to do the evaluation, with the intuition being that science education experts will come up with the most generally ideal pedagogical sequence for learners. However, what is ideal to science education experts might not be ideal to learners especially in an informal learning environment. We should evaluate our pedagogical sequence model on real learners to see if and how the pedagogical sequences we generate correlate with learner outcomes. This is one of the research paths that we are currently pursuing. In addition, during such a study, we can contrast the impact of both types of pedagogy (traditional or evidence-based) on students learning. Currently, we are applying our methodology for generating pedagogical sequences to a similar but different topic of *seasons* in order to evaluate its' scalability.

6. CONCLUSION

We have shown that given digital library resources on plate tectonics written for middle and high school students, our system can generate plate tectonics learning goals that are similar to and cover most of the plate tectonics learning goals set forth by the American Association for the Advancement of Science for middle and high school students. We have also shown that our pedagogical sequence model can make pair-wise classifications that are up to 76% similar to the pair-wise classifications generated from science education experts' pedagogical sequences.

Consequently, we have shown that the task of generating a pedagogical sequence through a collection of digital library resources can be modeled as a two-part process of first, using the technique of multi-document summarization to extract core learning goals in the form of sentences from the resources and then using supervised classification to generate a pedagogical sequence through the core learning goals.

The dynamically generated pedagogical sequences can provide structure and guidance to digital library users by giving them a pedagogically-meaningful learning sequence through which they can explore related documents they retrieve from a digital library. Furthermore, the dynamically generated pedagogical sequences can support the task of providing personalized feedback to students on what digital library resources they need to explore in order to satisfy a competency requirement or remedy a knowledge deficiency.

7. ACKNOWLEDGEMENTS

This article is based in part upon work supported by the National Science Foundation under Grant Number REAL/SMET-0835393. Any opinions, findings, and conclusions or recommendations expressed in this material are those of the author(s) and do not necessarily reflect the views of the National Science Foundation.

8. REFERENCES

[1] G. Acampora, M. Gaeta, V. Loia, P. Ritrovato, and S. Salerno. Optimizing learning path selection through memetic algorithms. In *Neural Networks, 2008. IJCNN 2008.(IEEE World Congress on Computational Intelligence). IEEE International Joint Conference on*, pages 3869–3875. IEEE, 2008.

[2] Faisal Ahmad, Sebastian de la Chica, Kirsten Butcher, Tamara Sumner, and James H. Martin. Towards automatic conceptual personalization tools. In *Proceedings of the 7th ACM/IEEE-CS joint conference on Digital libraries*, JCDL '07, pages 452–461, New York, NY, USA, 2007. ACM.

[3] C. Boyle and A.O. Encarnacion. Metadoc: an adaptive hypertext reading system. *User Modeling and User-Adapted Interaction*, 4(1):1–19, 1994.

[4] P. Brusilovsky. Adaptive hypermedia. *User modeling and user-adapted interaction*, 11(1):87–110, 2001.

[5] P. Brusilovsky and L. Pesin. Adaptive navigation support in educational hypermedia: An evaluation of the isis-tutor. *Journal of Computing and Information Technology*, 6(1):27–38, 1998.

[6] C.M. Chen. Intelligent web-based learning system with personalized learning path guidance. *Computers & Education*, 51(2):787–814, 2008.

[7] P. De Bra, D. Smits, and N. Stash. Creating and delivering adaptive courses with aha! *Innovative Approaches for Learning and Knowledge Sharing*, pages 21–33, 2006.

[8] S. de la Chica, F. Ahmad, J.H. Martin, and T. Sumner. Pedagogically useful extractive summaries for science education. In *Proceedings of the 22nd International Conference on Computational Linguistics-Volume 1*, pages 177–184. Association for Computational Linguistics, 2008.

[9] R. Duschl, S. Maeng, and A. Sezen. Learning progressions and teaching sequences: a review and analysis. *Studies in Science Education*, 47(2):123–182, 2011.

[10] James Foster, Arafat Sultan, Holly Devaul, Ifeyinwa Okoye, and Tamara Sumner. Identifying core concepts in educational resources. In *Proceedings of the12th ACM/IEEE-CS joint conference on Digital libraries*, JCDL '12, New York, NY, USA, 2012. ACM.

[11] David Graff. English Gigaword. *Linguistic Data Consortium*, 2002.

[12] M. Hall, E. Frank, G. Holmes, B. Pfahringer, P. Reutemann, and I.H. Witten. The weka data mining software: an update. *ACM SIGKDD Explorations Newsletter*, 11(1):10–18, 2009.

[13] J. Hattie and H. Timperley. The power of feedback. *Review of educational research*, 77(1):81–112, 2007.

[14] C.M. Hong, C.M. Chen, M.H. Chang, and S.C. Chen. Intelligent web-based tutoring system with personalized learning path guidance. In *Advanced Learning Technologies, 2007. ICALT 2007. Seventh IEEE International Conference on*, pages 512–516. IEEE, 2007.

[15] M.J. Huang, H.S. Huang, and M.Y. Chen. Constructing a personalized e-learning system based on genetic algorithm and case-based reasoning approach. *Expert Systems with Applications*, 33(3):551–564, 2007.

[16] I. Okoye, K. Maull, and T. Sumner. Algorithms for robust knowledge extraction in learning environments. In *Intelligent Tutoring Systems*, pages 245–247. Springer, 2010.

[17] K.A. Papanikolaou, M. Grigoriadou, H. Kornilakis, and G.D. Magoulas. Personalizing the interaction in a web-based educational hypermedia system: the case of inspire. *User Modeling and User-Adapted Interaction*, 13(3):213–267, 2003.

[18] R. Pirrone, G. Pilato, R. Rizzo, and G. Russo. Learning path generation by domain ontology transformation. *AI* IA 2005: Advances in Artificial Intelligence*, pages 359–369, 2005.

[19] Julia Plummer and Lori Agan. Reasoning about the seasons: middle school students' use of evidence in explanations. In *Proceedings of the 9th International Conference of the Learning Sciences - Volume 2*, ICLS '10, pages 464–465. International Society of the Learning Sciences, 2010.

[20] Dragomir Radev, Timothy Allison, Sasha Blair-Goldensohn, John Blitzer, Arda Çelebi, Stanko Dimitrov, Elliott Drabek, Ali Hakim, Wai Lam, Danyu Liu, Jahna Otterbacher, Hong Qi, Horacio Saggion, Simone Teufel, Michael Topper, Adam Winkel, and Zhu Zhang. MEAD - a platform for multidocument multilingual text summarization. In *LREC 2004*, Lisbon, Portugal, May 2004.

[21] K. Tanaka-Ishii, S. Tezuka, and H. Terada. Sorting texts by readability. *Computational Linguistics*, 36(2):203–227, 2010.

[22] S. Vosniadou. *International handbook of research on conceptual change*. Taylor & Francis, 2008.

[23] S. Vosniadou, C. Ioannides, A. Dimitrakopoulou, and E. Papademetriou. Designing learning environments to promote conceptual change in science. *Learning and instruction*, 11(4-5):381–419, 2001.

[24] T. Willard, J.E. Roseman, and L.P. Plenary. Progression of understanding of the reasons for seasons. *Knowledge Sharing Institute of the Center for Curriculum Materials in Science, Washington, DC*, 2007.

[25] Juan Yang, Hongtao Liu, and Zhixing Huang. Smap: To generate the personalized learning paths for different learning style learners. In Xiaopeng Zhang, Shaochun Zhong, Zhigeng Pan, Kevin Wong, and Ruwei Yun, editors, *Entertainment for Education. Digital Techniques and Systems*, volume 6249 of *Lecture Notes in Computer Science*, pages 13–22. Springer Berlin / Heidelberg, 2010.

Building a Search Engine for Computer Science Course Syllabi

Nakul Rathod, Lillian N. Cassel
Department of Computing Sciences
Villanova University
Villanova PA 19085
+1 610 519 7341
nakulrathod@gmail.com, lillian.cassel@villanova.edu

ABSTRACT
Syllabi are rich educational resources. However, finding Computer Science syllabi on a generic search engine does not work well. Towards our goal of building a syllabus collection we have trained various Machine Learning classifiers to recognize Computer Science syllabi from other web pages and the discipline that they represent (AI or SE for instance) among other things. We have crawled 50 Computer Science departments in the US and gathered 100,000 candidate pages. Our best classifiers are more than 90% accurate at identifying syllabi from real-world data. The syllabus repository we created is live for public use [1] and contains more than 3000 syllabi that our classifiers filtered out from the crawl data. We present an analysis of the various feature selection methods and classifiers used.

Categories and Subject Descriptors
H.3.3 [Information Search and Retrieval]: Information filtering. H.3.7 [**Digital Libraries**]:Collection. I.5.2 [**Design Methodology**]: Feature evaluation and selection, Classifier design and evaluation

Keywords
Digital Libraries, Collections, Machine Learning, Text Mining, Web Mining, Web Crawling, Classification, Feature Selection.

1. INTRODUCTION
Syllabi have always played a central role in guiding the learning process in institutions of higher education. At their most basic level, they are a contract between the instructor and the learners about the learning objectives, topics and assessment policies. However, they also contain the most current high-quality learning resources in the form of readings, textbooks, presentations and assignments. Many educators make their syllabi freely available on the web in the hopes that others will find these materials useful. Interested learners can use syllabi to keep abreast of the new developments or learn about new topics. Professors planning their courses can get an idea of what others are teaching. Also, Computer Science is a very rapidly evolving field. That makes easy access to Computer Science syllabi even more important.

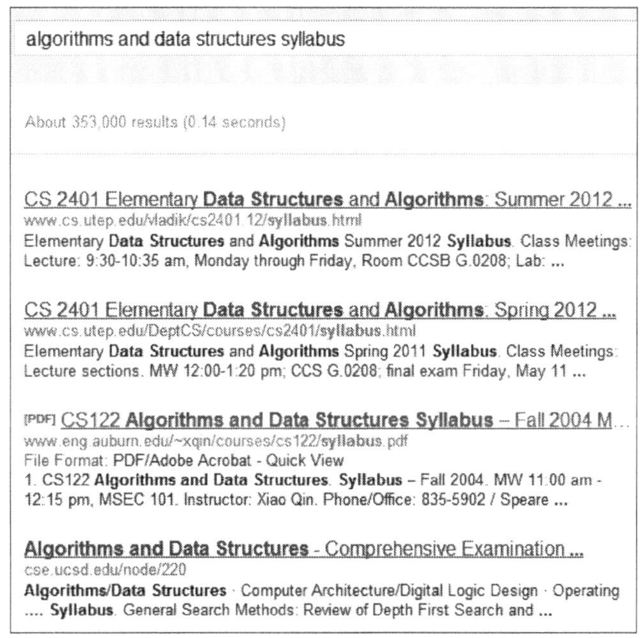

Figure 1. Searching for 'algorithms and data structures syllabus' on Google

However, generic search results for Computer Science syllabi fail to meet the need [2]. Figure 1 shows the first four results when searching for the most widely taken CS course—'algorithms and data structures' on Google with no user account logged in. The first two results are duplicates, the third result is 8 years old, and the fourth is not a course syllabus. When searching for syllabi on a generic search engine the best case scenario is that the first handful of links returns the most popular syllabi and the rest of them are not very relevant. Also, it is very difficult to search for syllabi on a per-subject basis or restrict the search to just syllabi if one is looking for something specific—like how many syllabi use a certain text book for instance.

With the emergence of efforts like Stanford led Coursera [3], MIT's MITx [4] and Sebastian Thrun's Udacity [5], which teach Computer Science courses for free over the internet, figuring out what exactly is taught in various courses is going to be even more important. Projects like Ensemble [6] provide faculty with access to a wide variety of resources. We believe a syllabus is a key resource in promoting learning and collaboration. We use machine learning to identify syllabi here for two reasons. First, a syllabus is not strictly defined and various syllabi vary widely in content. So our algorithms must have the ability to adapt and learn. Second, we are dealing with web-scale data and need highly automated algorithms that can quickly look at hundreds of thousands of pages and make intelligent decisions about them.

This paper describes how we went about creating our computer science course repository [Figure 2]: We first hand-tagged 536 syllabi as well as their component pages (schedule pages, assignment pages, etc), and the discipline that they belong to. We then crawled 6 levels deep starting from the homepages of 50 CS departments in the US and collected 100,000 candidate pages. We then used various machine learning classifiers with a number of feature-sets to identify syllabi from the crawl data. Finally, we created a public repository that has convenient faceted search features [1]. These allow one to filter the search results by syllabus disciplines, schools and syllabus components (syllabus pages, associated schedule pages, assignments pages, etc).

Figure 2. Project Overview

2. DATA COLLECTION

We needed two kinds of data-sets to build our repository. First, a hand-tagged sample of training examples on which we could test various feature sets and machine learning classifiers. Second, real world data from the web so that we can run our classifiers on it, filter out the syllabi and build our repository with it.

2.1 Collecting Training Examples

To enable better search, we not only wanted to classify whether a document was a syllabus, but also the discipline, school and syllabus component (whether it was a syllabus introduction page, schedule page, assignment page, etc) it belonged to [Figure 3]. We needed to collect training examples for each of these except the school, which we could infer easily from the url.

To collect our training examples, we first chose 10 major disciplines of CS (Artificial Intelligence, Algorithms and Data Structures, Databases, Human-Computer Interaction, Mathematics of CS, Computer Networks, Programming Languages, Software Engineering, Computer Security) and then the major focus areas that made up these disciplines. So, for instance, the discipline 'Computer Systems' would contain these focus areas: Operating Systems, File Systems, UNIX and C Programming, Assembly, etc and 'Mathematics of CS' would contain Discrete Structures, Analysis of Algorithms, Theory of Computation, Logic, etc. Each discipline had about 5 focus areas and for each of these focus areas we collected ~10 syllabi using Google searches of the form '<focus area> syllabi'. This meant that for each of our 10 disciplines we had about 50 syllabi. Overall we tagged 561 syllabi.

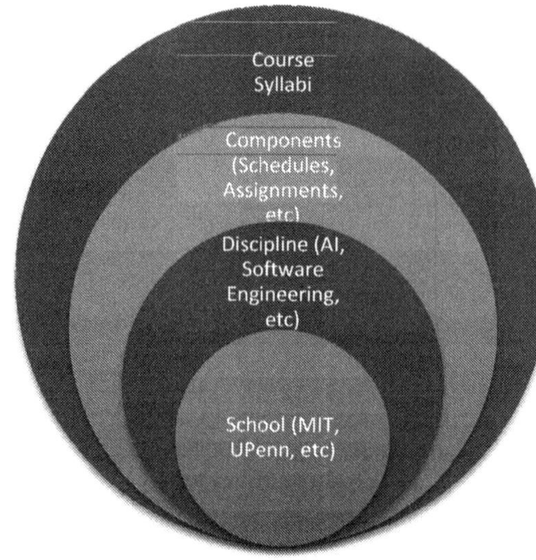

Figure 3. The tags applied to each syllabus correspond to the various training corpora tagged

2.1.1 *Syllabus or Not*

The most important task was to identify a computer science course syllabus from other web pages. To make a representative training set of real world data we collected Professor's Pages, Syllabi, and Other Pages from Computer Science departments [Figure 4]. We collected Professor's Pages as most syllabi are linked to from the teaching professor's own page and it would be very helpful to identify it. The Syllabi consisted of Complete Syllabi, Distributed Syllabi and Root Pages. Complete Syllabi were the ones for which the entire syllabus was on one web page. Distributed syllabi were spread out over a number of pages. The Root page is the root of a syllabus—the one that contains course introduction and links to other syllabus pages (like schedule, etc). The Other pages consisted of syllabi from non-CS areas as well as web pages found in CS departments like news, research interests of faculty, etc. However, we did not use Syllabi of other areas (Liberal Arts and Science syllabi) as we restricted our crawler to just CS departments and it was not likely that non-CS syllabi would be posted on CS department websites.

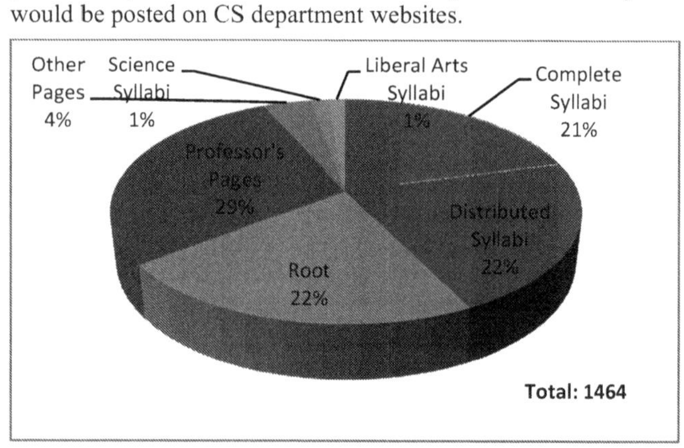

Figure 4. Distribution of training examples for identifying syllabi from other web pages

2.1.2 *Syllabus Components*

For each of the 561 syllabi we also tagged their various component pages [Figure 5]. Components are the usual pages that are included with a syllabi: Schedule pages, links to resources (readings, slides), Assignments, Tests, etc.

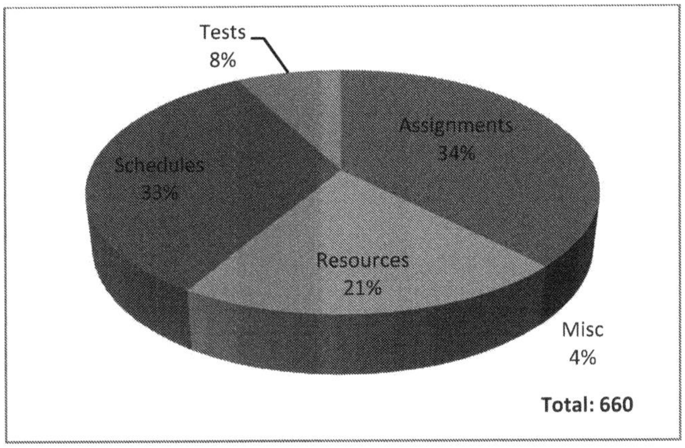

Figure 5. Distribution of training examples for identifying syllabus components

2.1.3 Syllabus Disciplines

We also tagged each syllabus with the discipline that it belonged to [Figure 6]. Figure 7 shows our three training corpora combined to give us a single view of the data.

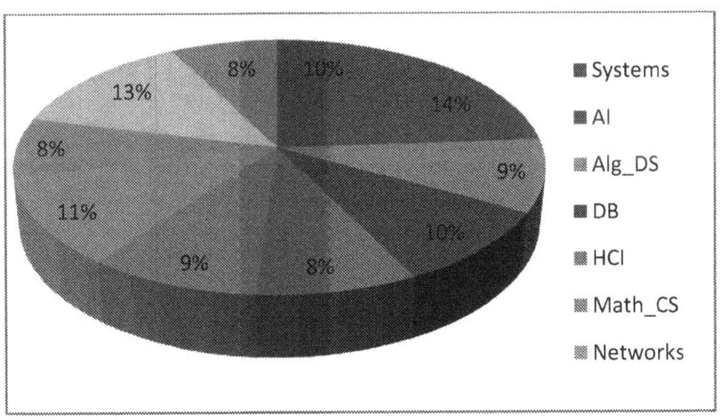

Figure 6. Distribution of training examples for identifying syllabus disciplines

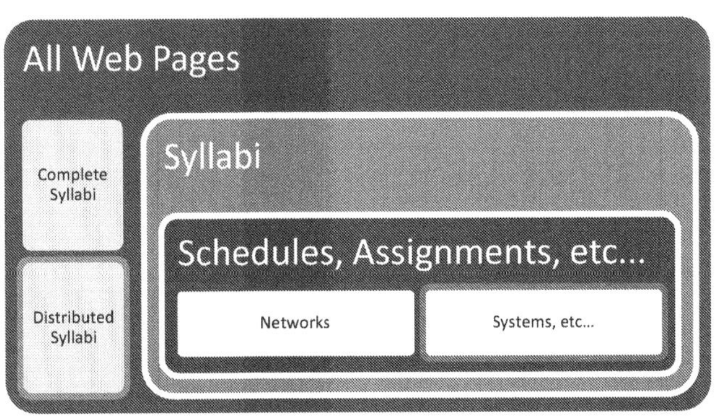

Figure 7. All three corpora collected

2.2 Crawling the Web

To gather our candidate pages, we needed a reasonable number of CS Departments to crawl for our first attempt. So rather than having to decide which departments to crawl, we selected the top 50 CS departments as ranked by US News and World Ranking Survey hoping it would give us a reasonable representation of all CS departments. We also limited our crawl to 6 levels deep within those departments. Finally, we limited ourselves to html documents and did not look at PDFs, docs, etc. This allowed us to perform a meaningful experiment in a reasonable amount of time with limited resources.

Our crawler processed ~300,000 urls and found that ~100,000 of them were html documents. This sharp decline was because we did not retrieve images (each of which has a valid url and there are many embedded in any single page), css pages, java script pages, PDFs, docs, etc. Out of those 100,000 pages we could only process 88,003 pages as there were still some binary files that had crept in, and there were broken links where syllabi had been taken offline by the time we got around to processing them.

3. FEATURE SELECTION

3.1 Custom feature sets

In line with our previous work on the topic [7] (which involved trying these feature sets on a significantly smaller data set and no web crawling and repository building), we identified 15 typical topics like overview, schedule, evaluation, etc. that occurred in a typical syllabus along with the various ways (or synonyms) in which one could refer to them by brainstorming and using other work done on the topic [8] [9]. So, for instance, the Evaluation component can be called evaluation, grading or assessment; the Professor component can be called professor, instructor, lecturer or Dr, etc. In the end, we identified 72 total synonyms that fell into 15 typical topics [Figure 8].

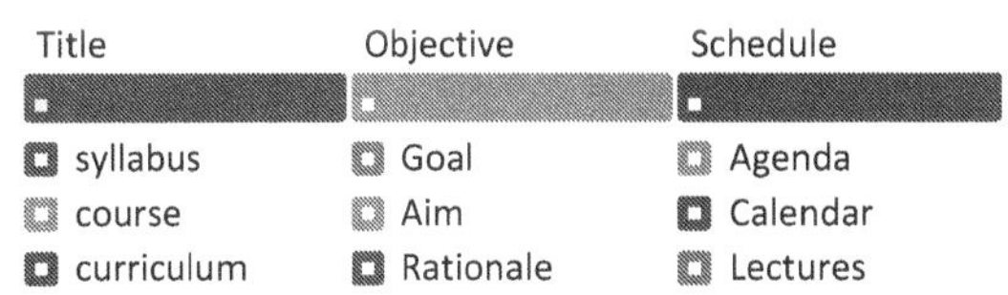

Figure 8. Partial list showing 3 of the topics and some of their synonyms

We then constructed four different feature sets:

1. topic_bool (fifteen 1s and 0s): whether a topic occurred in a syllabus by way of presence of any of its identified synonyms.
2. topic_count (fifteen integers): the number of times each topic occurred in a syllabus by way of presence of its identified synonyms.
3. word_bool (Seventy-two 1s and 0s): whether any of the pre-identified synonyms themselves appeared in a web page. This did not force a word to identify a topic like in the previous two cases.
4. word_count (Seventy-two integers): the number of times each word occurred in a syllabus by itself

We created the 15 topics from the 72 different words, rather than just testing the words by themselves (like in word_bool), because in Machine Learning it is preferred to have fewer attributes that capture the tendency of the data over many variables that do the same individually. However, we still included word_bool feature-set because we did not know if each of the words in a topic was as good as the other at distinguishing syllabi. So, for instance, if one of the words is very noisy, it could throw-off the whole topic and render it useless; but that would not happen in the word_bool feature-set. In conclusion, we knew that collectively the 72 words we identified would do a good job of identifying syllabi, but we did not know how well they would stand up individually by themselves or as individual topics, so we experimented with both.

3.2 Bag of words

We also used a standard Text Mining feature set, bag-of-words, in addition to the above mentioned three feature sets. Bag of words is just a list of all words in all the documents and performs very closely to custom feature-sets in general text classification tasks. However, the problem with bag of words is that it gives us so many more features than our classifiers can handle effectively. A general rule in statistics, and just a general rule, is that one should have about 30 times more training examples than feature sets to use any machine learning algorithm effectively. So we trimmed down our bag of words by getting rid of stop words and using the more aggressive Lancaster stemming algorithm in Python's NLTK to stem down words to their roots [10]. So, for instance, intelligence and intelligent would stem down to 'intellig'. Even then, we ended up with seven times more features than training examples [Figure 9].

Syllabi (Total Unique roots: 34,330)

- Top 10 (ranked by IG): assign, grad, syllab, exam, fin, instruct, due, homework, prerequisit, requir

Discipline (Total Unique roots: 18, 583)

- Top 10 (ranked by IG): network, intellig, cryptograph, databas, protocol, norvig, query, sql sec, russel

Components (Total Unique roots: 16,625)

- Top 10 (ranked by IG): due, introduc, break, exam, review, fin, assign, top, week, schedule

Figure 9. Bag of words for each of the three classification tasks

This is the infamous 'curse of dimensionality' that is often used in a biological computation context and plagues text mining also. The problem is that we have so many features and no easy way to identify which ones are the best at distinguishing between the classes. There are univariate measures like Information Gain (IG) that measure exactly this, but the problem is that they cannot measure how a number of features together affect a class. So for instance, if a disease was common in young males and older females, IG could not grasp this. Secondly, because we have so many more features than training examples, it is inevitable that a few features would be randomly related and any selection we perform will capture this random tendency of our training examples. To get around the latter problem, we manually tested the features (see next section) to select the best ones.

Dimensionality reduction is an active area of research and there are no effective techniques yet. Although techniques like principal component analysis allow one to capture the attributes' relevance, one still needs significantly more examples than features for it to work. An efficient algorithm would lead to breakthroughs in fields as varied as detecting cancer and identifying possible extra-terrestrial radio communication from all the cosmic noise. However, Yang et al. [11] in their study of selection methods for text categorization found that IG along with Mutual Information performed as good as anything we currently have for selecting features, so we used the top-100 features as ranked by IG from the many thousands we had in our bag of words feature set. Figure 9 shows the top-10 word roots as ranked by IG for each of the three corpora.

3.3 Feature Testing

The machine learning classifiers can only perform as well as the feature sets that they were fed. Here we illustrate how well the features work.

3.1.1 Syllabus or Not?

Figure 10 and Figure 11 show a comparison between the topic_bool and the word_bool feature sets. On the x-axis are the top 5 words as scored by IG and on the y-axis are two values: 1 on top and 0 on the bottom. Each document is represented as a line flowing through the graph from left to right. If a document does *not* have most of the words it would keep to the bottom of the graph like most 'Other pages' (blue) do.

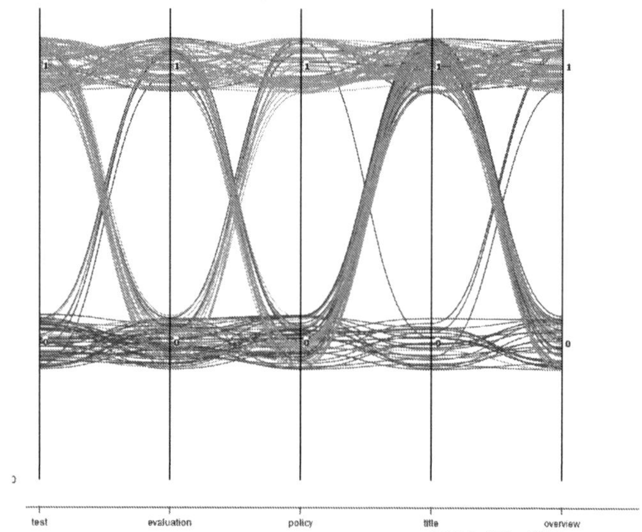

Figure 10. topic_bool feature set

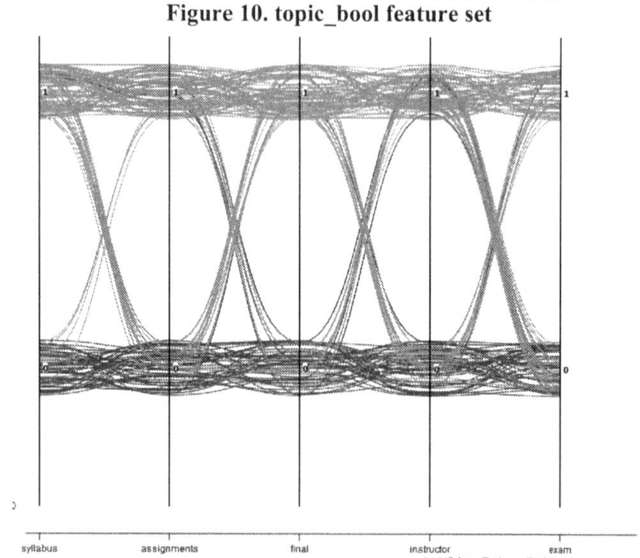

Figure 11. word_bool feature set

Notice how word_bool (Figure 11) is a better feature set than topic_bool (Figure 10) because Figure 11 is better able to contain the Other Pages (blue) to the bottom of the graph than Figure 10.

3.1.2 Syllabus Components

As discussed in the previous section, even though univariate measures like IG are the best we have, there is no guarantee that random correlations will not creep into our bag of words feature sets. To prevent this, and optimize the top features selected by IG, we manually tested them. Figure 12 shows an illustration distinguishing between Schedule Pages and Assignment Pages using just two word roots 'break' and 'introduc'.

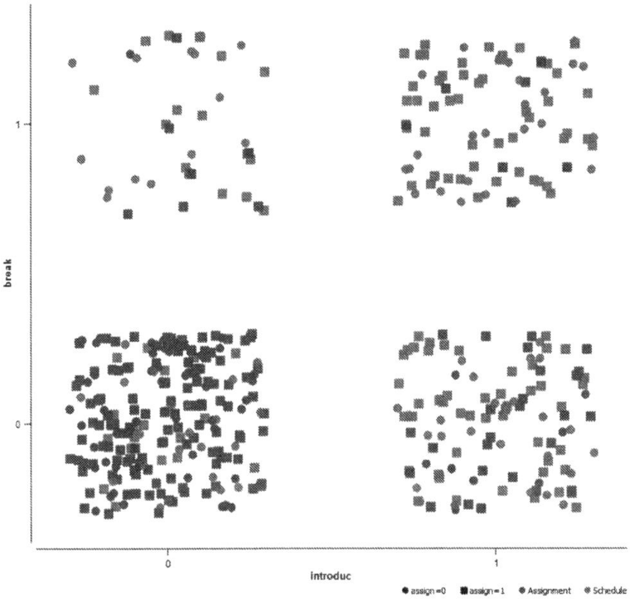

Figure 12. Distinguishing between Assignments and Schedules

In Fig 12 notice how having either or both of the roots 'break' or 'introduc' makes a document far more likely to be a Schedule page (red). It makes sense that most schedule pages mention introductions and something about breaks (fall break, midterm break, thanksgiving break, etc) whereas assignments pages do not contain such information. We can get an even better selection by using more than two features.

3.1.3 Syllabus Disciplines

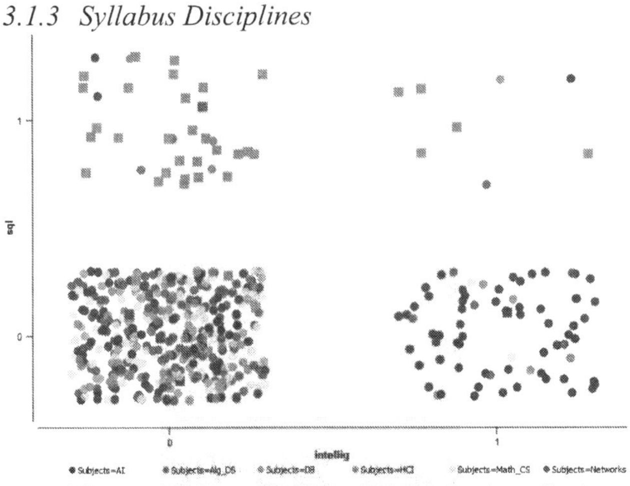

Figure 13. Distinguishing between AI or DB Syllabi

After identifying the syllabus itself, the next most important task is to identify the discipline of the syllabus. A repository with thousands of syllabi without any way to restrict one's search to a specific discipline would not be very useful.

Figure 13 shows that we can use the roots 'sql' and 'intellig' to filter out AI (blue) and DB (green) syllabi from the rest. Now if we look for a third feature 'query' within the DB syllabi (ie square green), we can obtain an even better selection of DB syllabi.

Figure 14 shows a how to distinguish AI syllabi from yet another discipline—networks.. The root 'databas' splits the diagram into two sections, larger left and narrower right in the proportion of documents that fall into each group. Further, the root 'network' splits the graph into top and bottom parts. Our area of interest is top-left marked by the orange-brackets. We can split this further by root 'intellig'. Notice that we have mostly networks (pink) syllabi on the left and mostly AI syllabi (blue) on the right.

Just looking for the root 'network' did not help us distinguish between AI and Networks syllabi as many AI syllabi talk about neural networks. So, we looked for the root 'intellig'. This illustrates why feature selection is a manual process.

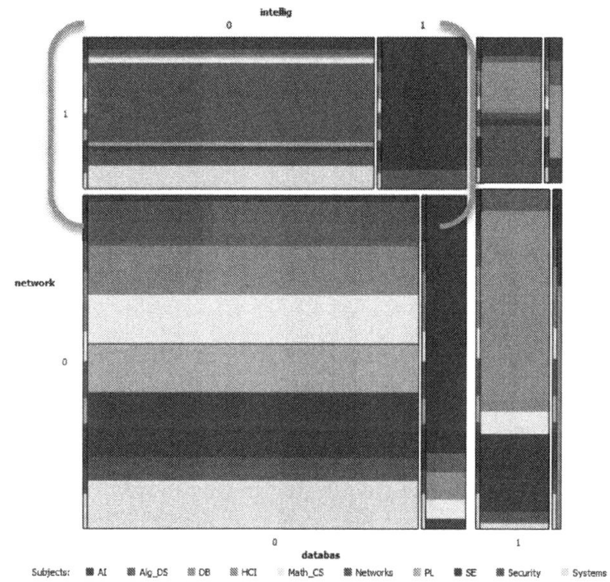

Figure 14. Distinguishing between Networks and AI syllabi

In Figure 13 and 14, we separated AI syllabi from DB and Networks syllabi respectively. Figure 15 shows that by using 10 root words on 10 different axes, we can distinguish between all three of them quite well. A document is placed near the end of an axis if it contains that root word. If it contains the root words marked by two or more axes, it is placed in between all of them..

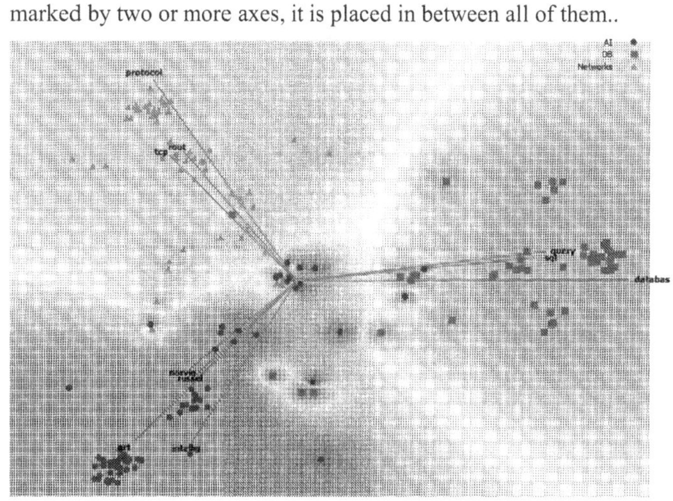

Figure 15. Distinguishing between AI, DB or Networks Syllabi

4. BUILDING CLASSIFIERS

For identifying syllabi we used all the four feature sets to build Decision Trees (DT) [12], Naive-Bayes Classifiers (NB) [13] and Support Vector Machines (SVM) [14]. We also used Multi-Layer Feed-Forward Neural Networks [15] in our previous study [7] and found no significant performance gain over SVM to warrant the additional processing power required. Additionally, for distinguishing between syllabus disciplines and components, in addition to the above three classifiers we also used two clustering algorithms: K-nearest neighbor and Random Forests.

For the DT, we split the nodes based on IG in line with previously mentioned research that has found it best for text categorization tasks [11]. We also stopped splitting into nodes when there were just two examples left. For the NB Classifiers we assumed prior class probabilities based on relative frequency which was calculated as the ratio of number of examples belonging to a certain class to the total number of examples in the training set. This ratio was pretty close to 1:1 for the syllabus discipline corpora. For our SVM, we always used a linear kernel to keep the classifier simple and consistent across different feature sets. This allowed us to see which feature sets were performing the best.

Figure 16 shows a Decision Tree for classifying the syllabus components. Even though it is restricted to three levels for illustration purposes, it manages to catch a lot of Schedule and Assignment pages cleanly. Our real DT has hundreds of levels.

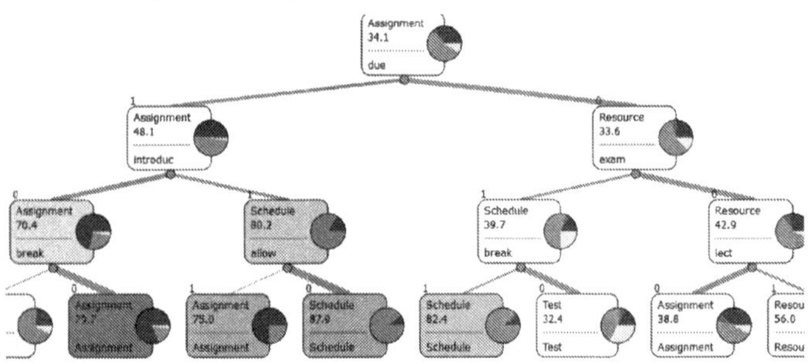

Figure 16. Decision Tree for Syllabus Components

Figure 17 shows a nomogram for a Naïve Bayes Classifier (NB). NB and DT differ from SVMs because their 'reasoning' is easy to observe. This allows one to optimize and over-rule the decisions they make. Fig 17 shows the NB classifying a single document. The blue dots represent whether the document contains a certain feature. One simply totals up the score on top for each of the features and looks at the corresponding probability at the bottom.

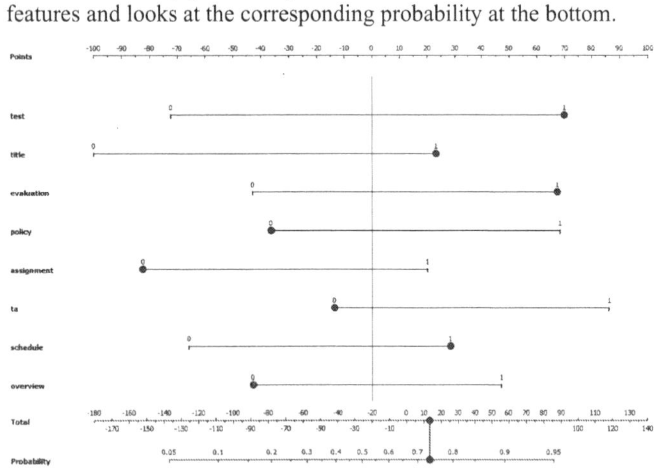

Figure 17. NB: This document is 72% likely to be a syllabus

This diagram is very powerful because it shows exactly how much each feature weighs. The features with longer horizontal lines have more influence in determining the outcome. So we can see that having the test feature (first one) is more important than having the overview (last one) feature. Also, having the test feature weighs more positively (line extends further to the right), than having the title feature (second one). However, the title feature weighs more negatively (line extends further to the left than the one on top). It is easy to make sure that this makes intuitive sense. In terms of whether we think a document is a syllabus, if it does not mention tests it should indeed mean less than it not having a syllabus title.

Figure 18 shows the results of K-nearest neighbor clustering (KNN). Clustering is different from the other algorithms we looked at because it is totally unsupervised ie the algorithm is not trained with any training examples. As such, one cannot control the clusters it will end up with except how one defines the distance between documents. We defined document distance based on the number of similar words they contain. Therefore it is reassuring to see that the clusters for the most part match up with the 10 disciplines that we chose. This shows that our categorization scheme is not arbitrary but captures well the common words that appear in the syllabi of each discipline.

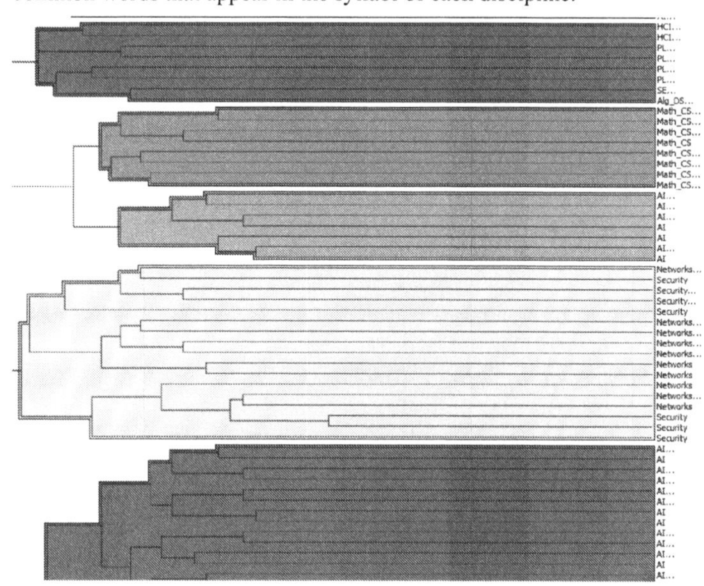

Figure 18. Clustering the Syllabus Disciplines

5. SYLLABUS REPOSITORY

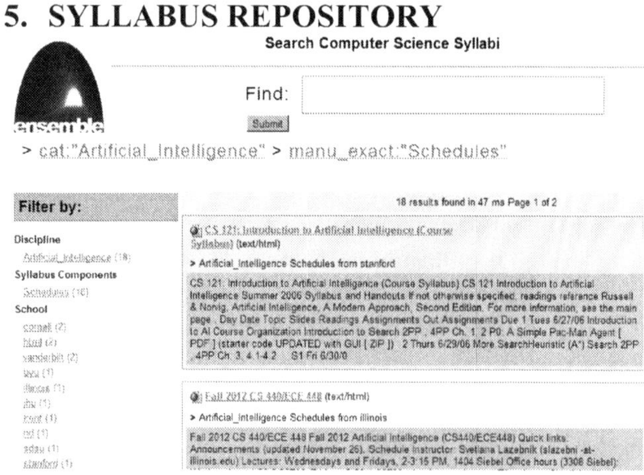

Figure 19. Our Syllabus repository allows effortless browsing

With all our classifiers trained, we ran them on our crawl data of 88,003 pages and collected 2946 syllabi. Having a specialized syllabus repository allows us to do so much more than a regular search engine. So, for instance, if one is planning to teach an AI course, one can look at all the schedules that follow Professor Norvig's Seminal AI Text Book with just two clicks [Figure 19]. It is just as easy to look for all the syllabi that talk about a hot upcoming technology like Scala and then drill down by the school that the course is offered at. Searches like these are not possible on a generic search engine.

6. RESULTS

To test how well the various feature sets and classifiers were doing we split the training examples into two sets randomly: a training set containing 70% of the examples and a test set containing the remaining 30%. We then measured their accuracy and repeated this process 10 times and averaged the results.

Testing the classifiers on the unseen 30% training set allows us to test how well the classifiers generalize on unseen data rather than test just how well they learn to fit the data presented to them. Training them with 10 random training samples allows us to average out the effects of each training sample.

For both the tasks where we constructed the word_bool feature set, it performed better than any other data set. These two tasks were when we distinguished syllabi from other web pages [Table 1] and when we distinguished between various syllabus components (Schedule Page, Assignment Page, etc) [Table 2]. When distinguishing syllabi from other web pages, all the feature sets, including the bag of words feature set, performed very similarly. When distinguishing between syllabus components, the word_bool feature set out-performed the others, but bag of words and the other feature sets performed similarly. So we can say that the 15 topics that we divided our syllabus synonyms into (topic_bool, topic_count), did not work better than using the synonyms separately (word_bool, word_count). This means that some of the synonyms are very noisy and are throwing off the entire topic that they belong to, whereas the word feature sets do not suffer from the same problem. As each word is measured independently in the word feature sets, each of them weighs in differently in determining the final outcome and noisy ones can be easily discarded by the classifier.

Table 1. Distinguishing Syllabi from Professor's Pages and Other Pages

Classification Accuracy (%)						
	topic_bool	topic_count	word_bool	word_count	BOW	AVG
NB	85	80	90	86	88	86
CT	85	54	89	83	87	80
SVM	88	88	91	89	88	89
AVG	86	74	90	86	88	

We can also say that counting the number of features (topic_count and word_count) does not give us an advantage over just looking for whether they are present (topic_bool and word_bool). The only cases where counting the features would be useful is in the case where there were lists of courses or workshops being misclassified as a single syllabus by the other feature sets. However, most machine learning algorithms only work on discrete data and counting adds another layer of complexity where the continuous data has to be discretized. The performance penalty of this added complexity is greater than the advantage gained by not misclassifying lists of syllabi as a single syllabus.

Table 2. Distinguishing Syllabi Schedule Pages from Other Component Pages (Assignments, Tests, Resources)

Classification Accuracy (%)						
	topic_bool	topic_count	word_bool	word_count	BOW	AVG
NB	71	72	82	75	68	74
CT	70	67	77	75	63	70
SVM	71	75	82	81	75	77
AVG	71	71	81	77	69	

As for the Machine Learning algorithms, SVM performed the best in all three cases [Table 1, Table 2, Table 3] and NB either tied with it in performance or finished a close second. The additional clustering algorithms we used (Random Forest, KNN) when classifying syllabi into their discipline area [Table 3], did not perform better than SVMs or even NB. In this case, the only feature set which performed reasonably was bag of words. Predictably, one cannot distinguish between syllabi belonging to different disciplines by using our four custom feature sets which were designed to identify a generic syllabus.

Table 3. Distinguishing between 10 Syllabus Disciplines

By Discipline (Accuracy %)	
Classifier	bow_top_100
NB	83
CT	62
SVM	88
Random Forest	73
KNN	78
Average	77

7. EVALUATION

Even though classification accuracy, which is the measure of performance we have been using until now, gives us a great intuitive sense of performance and allows fast comparisons of lots of feature sets and classifiers, it has its flaws. First of all, not all classification mistakes are equal. A classifier misclassifying an 'other page' (negative example) as syllabus (positive example) may not be a big deal. But if we miss any syllabi, it may matter more—or vice-versa depending on whether comprehensiveness takes precedence over specificity. Similarly, in a medical context, a classifier missing some sick patients may be potentially lethal. It is more forgivable if it selects some healthy patients for additional testing. However, any classifier can be 100% accurate if it says that all web pages are syllabi or that all patients are sick. It will indeed capture all the positive examples, but such a system will not be very useful. Our repository will not be different from a generic search engine, and forcing every patient to undergo additional testing is cost ineffective and may subject them to additional testing risks. So we used additional measures to zero in on the performance of classifiers.

Sensitivity is the probability that a positive example (syllabus) is classified as positive and specificity is the probability that a negative example (other web page) is classified as negative. There is always a trade-off between sensitivity and specificity. One can control this trade-off by adjusting the classification threshold.

A ROC curve [Figure 20] plots sensitivity over the inverse of specificity to show graphically how the classifiers are doing. A perfect classifier would shoot straight up and then across the top of the graph. A classifier that just made random guesses would follow the black diagonal line shown in Figure 20. In the Figure, one can see that the SVM (red) follows the 'perfect classifier' better than NB or CT

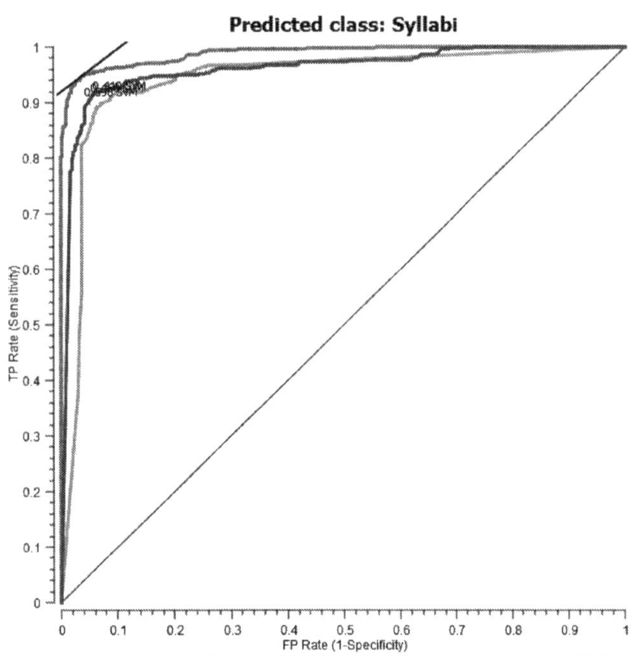

Figure 20. ROC Curve showing the performance of SVM (red), NB (blue), and CT (green) when identifying Syllabi with the word_bool feature set

Fig 20 also shows the sensitivity vs specificity trade-off. One can have perfect sensitivity for zero specificity. For any other point on the graph one can improve sensitivity by lowering the specificity and vice-versa. However, one cannot change the area under the curve this way. So Area Under Curve (AUC) measures something innate about the classifier and allows us to represent the performance of a classifier by a single convenient number [Table 4]. A 0.5 AUC would mean the classifier follows the diagonal line and it is no better than one making random guesses. A 0.7 classifier is acceptable performance, and anything in the 0.90s is considered excellent performance. Most of the classifiers we used had AUC in 0.90s and none performed worse than 0.80.
Based on the results discussed we chose to use SVM for all three classification tasks.

8. REAL WORLD ADAPTATIONS

When we ran the trained classifier on the 88,003 pages that we had retrieved from crawling CS departments, we found that it was over-zealous in classifying syllabi. It was collecting syllabi alright, but it was also getting us lists of courses and syllabus components. The 'lists of courses' problems we foresaw but the 'syllabus components' problem missed our attention. Syllabus components are technically a part of any course syllabus (like Assignment Pages or Schedule Pages), but they are not the root of a syllabus. The root is the page most commonly understood as a syllabus: It is the page that introduces the course and contains links to all the other components.

Fortunately, we already had another corpus of 660 syllabus components that we had hand-tagged for distinguishing *between* the individual components. So we trained our classifier to avoid the syllabus components along with other pages and professor's pages when identifying syllabi. This had a performance penalty and our performance dropped by 2%. This is because our classifier was now making much finer distinctions between syllabus root and syllabus components. We also switched to using NB for identifying syllabi as even though SVM had better Classification Accuracy (CA), NB had a higher AUC [Table 4]. This meant that even though the SVM was slightly better at capturing all the syllabi, NB was better at avoiding all the other pages.

Table 4. Classifier Performance with additional training when identifying syllabi with word_bool feature set

Advanced Performance Measures				
	CA	Sens	Spec	AUC
NB	87	85	88	92
CT	89	86	92	89
SVM	89	86	92	88

We then ran the NB classifier on the 88,000 page crawl data and captured 3852 pages (or 4.5% of all CS department pages crawled) that were classified as syllabi. We then went through each one of them to see how well our classifier did in a real-world setting. Table 5 breaks down the mistakes that our classifier made by the type of page it was.

Table 5. Identifying Syllabi from the Crawl Data

Type	Count	Percent
true_syllabus	2946	76.48
syllabus_components	451	11.71
syllabus_lists	80	2.08
other_pages	138	3.58
program_MS_BS_info	130	3.37
research_info	78	2.02
Professor's Pages	29	0.75
TOTALS	3852	100

On real world data our classifying accuracy dropped by 11% from 87% to 76%. If one is a little more generous and counts the syllabus components and syllabus lists [first three bolded entries in Table 5] as syllabi, then the classifier was correct 90% of the time.

We attribute the performance drop to the fact that our original data set only had 4% of other pages, so no matter how much we learned to recognize syllabi, we did not have enough other pages for the classifier to learn to avoid. To illustrate this further, as we had lots of Professor's Pages to train the classifier against, only 0.75% of its mistakes involved those. Also, our classifier still caught syllabus component pages because our feature sets are just words that we look for in each page. So as long as any of the syllabus components (schedule pages, assignment pages, etc) contain back links to all the other components with the words that we are looking for in the anchor text, they will be classified as syllabi.

In the future, we would like to improve our feature sets by incorporating back links as features. We would also like to analyze more than one web page to determine whether it's a syllabus. We used text-only features here because we wanted our classifiers to work on syllabi that occur in any format: html, PDFs, DOCs, etc. Also, our classifiers perform with very high accuracy (95%) for syllabi that are complete syllabi, ie syllabi that are contained in a single web page. This means that they would be just as effective (95% accuracy) at identifying syllabi that occur in PDF or DOC formats. The major performance drop happens when we start dealing with distributed syllabi, which are syllabi spread over multiple pages, and avoiding syllabus component pages.

Now that we know the kind of pages that our classifier misclassified, we can plug those specific holes by training against the misclassified pages. We have already done that and our classification accuracy is up to 88%. However, even though we hope that this improvement generalizes to real world data as we used real world training examples, we cannot know this for sure until we perform another deeper, more comprehensive crawl and can test on data our revised classifier has not seen yet.

Lastly, even with the 76% accuracy, the classifier was enormously helpful in cutting down the time it took to build our repository. It took one of us just a little under three hours to manually verify all of the classifier's predictions on real world data. This data consisted of 3852 (4.5%) pages identified as syllabi out of the 88,003 pages (which came out of the 300,000 urls analyzed) collected by crawling. Compared to having to look at all the pages/urls this is a big improvement.

9. RELATED WORK

Educators have realized that there is valuable content locked away in syllabi and a few projects have tried to make this content more available. MIT's OpenCourseWare [16] effort manually collects MIT syllabi in a central repository. However, this approach does not scale well and is very human-intensive. Syllabus Finder [17] tried to solve this problem by performing sophisticated regex searches on Google's cache. However, Syllabus Finder has been completely non-functional since 2002 when Google deprecated its SOAP Search API. Matsunga et al. [8] and Yu et al. [9] developed thesaurus based approaches which inspired ours to identify syllabi from other web pages. Yu et al. [9] also used contextual and content features in addition to the thesaurus based structural features and identified partial syllabi as well.

None of the efforts, though, have gone so far as to distinguish between the subject areas (like AI or SE) and syllabus component pages (like Assignment Pages, Schedule Pages, etc), or even identifying professor's pages where most syllabi are linked to in the first place. A few researchers have also directly attacked the problem of lack of standardization among syllabi that gives rise to this whole problem in the first place. Both the SylVia project [18] and Tungare et al. [19] have developed extensive ontologies to help instructors tag the various resources they use to make their syllabus. Both these projects have also developed syllabus annotation, creation and viewing tools to encourage adopting standard formats for syllabus representation.

These tools have been around for some time now and face the problem of getting adopted by enough people to be useful. In light of this, genre-classification approach like ours [7] and others [8] [9] will be more efficient at capturing resources locked away inside syllabi. Genre classification is being actively researched and has been used for all kinds for purposes including recognizing home pages from other web pages [20].

10. CONCLUSION

In conclusion, using the 72 synonyms we identified individually (word_bool) rather than grouping them into 15 topics (topic_bool) works best when trying to identify syllabi. Also, bag of words performs very closely (just 3 % drop) to our custom developed feature set. Also, NB performs just as well as SVMs in many cases, and it is more appropriate to use it even if it has a slight performance drop over SVMs. As the workings of a NB classifier are easy to understand, it is easy to tweak and maintain. On the other hand, SVM quickly becomes a black-box as the number of features increase.

We attribute the performance drop, when identifying syllabi from 90% in the training stages to 76% in real world use, to not having enough 'other' web pages in the original data set and to only using text features (ie not using any html markup as features).

11. FUTURE WORK

We would like to build a focused crawler that intelligently gathers syllabi by doing two things. First, we can use our classifier's ability to detect professor's pages to improve performance. As syllabi are most often linked at most three levels deep from professor's pages, this is a strong positive signal for the classifier. Second, we can use our classifier's ability to detect syllabus components like assignments pages, lecture schedules, etc to intelligently gather syllabi that are spread out over different pages. Even though a course syllabus usually consists of multiple web pages, logically it is one document and including it as one document in the repository enables better search. We would also like to identify historical versions of the same course using url-matching and document similarity measures, and include them under 'previous versions' rather than separate syllabi. This will allow us to better retrieve unique syllabi when a user searches our repository. For classifying syllabi into discipline areas, we would like to do multi-class classification to better capture the inter-disciplinary nature of courses like computational biology, analyzing social networks, etc.

Our goal with the project is to create a repository of computer science course syllabi that is comprehensive and enables efficient search. Towards that goal, we have bootstrapped our repository with 3049 syllabi collected entirely from the web using Text Mining techniques. This repository is live for public use [1]. To make swift progress towards comprehensiveness, we would like to provide an interface for educators to submit their syllabi directly as well as develop custom scrapers that work with certain popular backends—SunGuard for instance, to scrap institutional repositories of Syllabi. This would prove very valuable where there is a state mandated requirement to maintain all syllabi like in the state of Texas. Lastly, we would like to run a more comprehensive crawl than we did here to collect more candidate pages. As the techniques we developed work fairly well on real-world data, filtering syllabi pages from a full web-scale crawl seems plausible.

12. ACKNOWLEDGMENTS

This material is based upon work supported by the National Science Foundation under Grant No. 0840713 and Villanova Undergraduate Research Program 2012. We would like to thank Indu Bhargavi Guduri and Pranay Kumar Muthineni for helping us collect our training examples.

We would also like to acknowledge the work of developers that release quality open source software that make work like this possible. In particular: we use Nutch as our crawler [21], Orange [22] and Python NLTK [10] for our machine leraning needs and Solr for our indexing needs [23].

13. REFERENCES

[1] Ensemble Syllabus Repository, http://syllabus.sdakak.com

[2] Baeza-Yates, R., Ribeiro-Neto, B. Modern Information Retrieval. Addison Wesley (1999).

[3] Coursera: Education Everywhere, https://www.coursera.org/

[4] MITX: MIT's new online learning initiative, http://mitx.mit.edu/

[5] Udacity: Free online university classes for everyone, http://www.udacity.com/

[6] Ensemble Computing Portal, http://www.computingportal.org/

[7] Rathod, N., Cassel, L. Machine Learning in Building a Collection of Computer Science Course Syllabi. In Theory and Practice of Digital Libraries, 7489, pp. 357-362. http://dx.doi.org/10.1007/978-3-642-33290-6_38 (2012).

[8] Matsunaga, Y., Yamada, S. A web syllabus crawler and its efficiency evaluation. In Proceedings of ISEE (2002).

[9] Yu, X., Tungare, M., Fan W., Yuan, Y., Pérez-Quiñones M., Fox, E., Cameron W., Cassel L. Automatic Syllabus Classification using Support Vector Machines. In Handbook of Research on Text and Web Mining Technologies. Information Science Reference (2008).

[10] Bird, S., Klein, E., Loper, E. Natural Language Processing with Python. O'Reilly Media (2009).

[11] Yang, Y., Pedersen, J.O. A Comparative Study on Feature Selection in Text Categorization. In Proceedings of the 14 th International Conference on Machine Learning, pp. 412--420 (1997).

[12] Quinlan, J.R. Induction of decision trees. Machine Learning. 1-1, 81--106 (1986).

[13] Kim, S., Han, K., Rim, H., Myaeng, S. Some effective techniques for naive bayes text classification. In IEEE Transactions on Knowledge and Data Engineering 18 (2006).

[14] Joachims, T. Text Categorization with Support Vector Machines: Learning with many re-levant Features. In Proceedings of the European Conference on Machine Learning (1998).

[15] Anderson C. Learning and problem solving with multilayer connectionist systems. Technical Report, University of Massachusetts (1986).

[16] MIT Open Course Ware: Free Online Course Materials, http://ocw.mit.edu/index.htm.

[17] Syllabus Finder, http://chnm.gmu.edu/syllabus-finder/syllabi/.

[18] SylViA: The Syllabus Viewer Application, http://groups.sims.berkeley.edu/sylvia/.

[19] Tungare, M., Yu X., Cameron W., Teng G., Pérez-Quiñones M., Fox E., Fan W., Cassel L. Towards a syllabus repository for computer science courses. In Proceedings of the 38th Technical Symposium on Computer Science Education (SIGCSE) (2007).

[20] Kennedy, A., Shepherd, M. Automatic Identification of Home Pages on the Web. In Proceedings of the 38th Hawaii International Conference on System Sciences (2005).

[21] Khare, Rohit, et al. "Nutch: A flexible and scalable open-source web search engine." *Oregon State University* (2004).

[22] Demsar, J., Zupan, B. Orange: Data Mining Fruitful and Fun. University of Ljubljana.

[23] Smiley, D. Solr 1.4 Enterprise Search Server. Packet Publishing. (2009)

Ranking Experts using Author-Document-Topic graphs

Sujatha Das G.
Computer Science and Engineering
The Pennsylvania State University
University Park, PA 16802 USA
gsdas@cse.psu.edu

Prasenjit Mitra, C. Lee Giles
Information Sciences and Technology
Computer Science and Engineering
The Pennsylvania State University
University Park, PA 16802 USA
{pmitra,giles}@ist.psu.edu

ABSTRACT

Expert search or recommendation involves the retrieval of people (experts) in response to a query and on occasion, a given set of constraints. In this paper, we address expert recommendation in academic domains that are different from web and intranet environments studied in TREC. We propose and study graph-based models for expertise retrieval with the objective of enabling search using either a topic (e.g. "Information Extraction") or a name (e.g. "Bruce Croft"). We show that graph-based ranking schemes despite being "generic" perform on par with expert ranking models specific to topic-based and name-based querying.

Categories and Subject Descriptors

H.3.3 [**Information Search and Retrieval**]: Retrieval Models

Keywords

PageRank, Author-Document-Topic graphs, Expert Search, Similar Expert Finding

1. MOTIVATION

Entity search and retrieval where the goal is to retrieve "objects" (such as cars, books, people) in response to user queries is an emerging research interest in the Information Retrieval community. In particular, expert finding where the goal is to rank people with expertise (experts) in response to a topic query was well-studied in the TREC community[1]. Similarly, the list completion tracks in TREC and INEX[2] competitions address similar entity finding or exemplar-based search for the general domain. In these setups, the evidence for expertise is derived based on webpages or documents on a intranet. Documents in the academic domain are different from webpages in terms of their type (e.g. homepages, publications), structure (e.g. abstract, sections), associated metadata (e.g. venue, authors) and connections (e.g. citations). In this paper, we focus on expert (researcher/author) search in academic domains in response to both topic queries (e.g. "Information Retrieval") and name queries (e.g. "Bruce Croft").

In academic domains, an expert search system that allows queries based on topics and expert names has several potential applications. Consider the following use-cases: The program chair of a conference is desirous of selecting a panel of researchers for the "Information Retrieval" track. A potential list of PC members can be obtained by firing an appropriate topic query to an expert search system. On the other hand, consider a student applying to graduate schools who is interested in working with researchers like "Bruce Croft".

In this paper, we refer to the use case, where the input is a "topic" as *expert finding* or *topic-based search* whereas *similar expert finding* or *name-based search* is used to refer to cases when an example expert name is specified as the input. For the example in the previous paragraph, "Bruce Croft" might be associated with several other expertise areas apart from "Information Retrieval". Thus the results of these two queries need not be the same. Our focus in this paper is to explore models that are **generic** in that they allow ranking of experts in response to both topic and name queries. This is different from previous research where different models are studied for handling the two query scenarios.

Contributions and Organization: We study two graph-based models for ranking experts in response to topic-based and name-based queries. The first model is an extension of PageRank for graphs having multiple edge-types and was proposed by us previously for expert finding [9]. We show that the PageRank-based model can be used effectively for ranking experts in response to name queries as well as topic queries by constructing an appropriate query-specific graph in each case (Figure 2). The second set of scoring models is based on modeling the underlying corpus using a weighted, undirected, tripartite graph representing the Authors, Documents and Topics in the corpus (Figure 1). In contrast with the PageRank-based models that score nodes depending on their **structural connections** with other nodes in the graph, the ADT models, are designed to capture the **content-based similarity** between nodes via edges to the "topic" nodes in the graph. Indeed, nodes in ADT graphs are scored with respect to each other based on the association strengths of paths connecting them.

We study the performance of our proposed ranking models and baselines on two datasets. The first dataset is based on

[1] http://trec.nist.gov
[2] https://inex.mmci.uni-saarland.de/about.html

JCDL'13, July 22–26, 2013, Indianapolis, Indiana, USA.
Copyright 2013 ACM 978-1-4503-2077-1/13/07 ...$15.00.

ArnetMiner[3] and CiteSeer[4] and represents the retrieval environments of academic domains we seek to model where as the second dataset, the UvT collection from Tilburg university[5] provides a sparse retrieval environment [3]. Our experimental results indicate that despite being "generic" enough to handle both the querying scenarios, graph-based models rank experts on par with other query-specific models.

Section 1 described the problem addressed in this paper along with a summary of contributions. Previous research that is closely related to our problems is presented in Section 2. Details of our ranking models and a description of the baselines used in comparison experiments are described in Section 3. Section 4 provides descriptions of our datasets, experimental setup and evaluation. Finally, we conclude in Section 5 with some directions for future work.

2. RELATED WORK

The participants of the Enterprise track of TREC studied expert finding in context of enterprise data on the W3C collection. Balog, et al. proposed probabilistic models for expertise profiling and expert finding in context of sparse data environments such as webpages pertaining to research institutes and universities where the documents are more structured and relatively noise-free [2, 3].

Relevance propagation models on author-document graphs were studied by Serdyukov, et al. [25], whereas topic models were used for the same task by several researchers [12, 13, 26]. For bibliographic data, Deng, et al. showed that complicated topic models only provide slight benefits compared to probablistic models with appropriate priors [12]. Simpler voting models and vector-space representations were also studied for the expert finding task [11, 21]. In view of their simplicity and competitive performance we choose the probabilistic models proposed by Deng, et al. for bibliographic domains as the baseline method for the expert finding task in our experiments.

The list-completion tasks in TREC and INEX address the similar-entity finding task in the general domain. The proceedings of these competitions discuss various approaches for handling this task. In contrast to our problem, the input queries in these systems include a query topic description with examples of entities. The participating systems need to extract the relation between the example entities and the topic description and propose entities that hold a similar relation with the topic description, as part of the answer. For academic domains, "similar expert finding" is slightly simpler in that the objective is to find researchers that are similar to a queried researcher.

Preliminary models for "similar expert finding" were previously studied by Balog and Rijke [5] and Das, et al [10]. Balog and Rijke studied similar expert finding on the TREC data using the relations a candidate expert has with other experts, documents and terms. Hofmann, et al. considered the contextual factors such as organizational setup and combined them with content-based retrieval scores to find similar experts within an organization [17]. Das, et al. studied the same problem for academic domains and proposed several models for computing researcher profiles and similarity between researchers using these profiles.

[3]http://arnetminer.org

[4]http://citeseerx.ist.psu.edu

[5]http://ilk.uvt.nl/uvt-expert-collection

Chen, et al. presented CollabSeer that uses the structure of the co-author network to predict research collaborators in academic environments [8]. Xu, et al. use a two-layer network model that combines co-author network and researcher-concept network for making researcher recommendations [28]. Our approach targets the prediction of researchers with similar expertise profiles based on content they generate and not necessarily "co-authors". Thus while co-authorship provides evidence of similarity, we wish to design models that are capable of exploiting other sources of evidence, such as content similarity, citation behavior and so on. As an additional goal, we seek models that support both name-based and topic-based querying.

3. RANKING MODELS

Most recent works in text and document analysis adopt the view of a document as a mixture of a small number of topics. Indeed, models like Latent Dirichlet Allocation (LDA) and probabilistic latent semantic analysis (pLSA) target the extraction of abstract concepts or topics given a collection of documents [18, 6]. These models also enable the expression of a document in the corpus in terms of its topic proportion vector that corresponds to a low-dimensional representation of the document. Given a set of documents, authored by an expert, generative distribution on topics and terms can be estimated for that expert. LDA was effectively used to model scientific documents and their authors previously [13, 23].

Although modeling of authors in terms of their topic distribution is intuitive, previous work that used author similarity based on their topical profiles did not yield good performance for similar expert finding [10]. For expert retrieval in response to topic queries, LDA-style models were shown to only yield marginal benefits over simpler probabilistic counterparts [12]. *Are there alternate ways to compute similarity between authors while retaining the topical aspect of document representation?* We seek to address this question via the ADT representation (next section). We start by expressing documents in terms of their topics using content modeling tools like LDA. Next, the author-document and document-topic associations are represented via edges in a graph and paths within this graph are used to measure similarity between any pair of nodes in the graph.

3.1 The ADT tripartite graph

Let T represent the set of topics[6] associated with a document collection, D. Intuitively, an expert on a topic, $t \in T$ would have authored documents related to t and other closely-related topics. Similarly, if an author, a has expertise on a topic $t \in T$, authors similar to a could be expected to write about t and topics related to t. The associations between documents and their authors and documents and their topics can be represented by a weighted tri-partite graph as follows: Let $G = (V, E)$ represent such a graph where the vertex set, $V = A \cup D \cup T$ is the union of author, A, document, D and topic nodes, T. Edges between A and D reflect the authorship relation between documents and au-

[6]Note: In this paper, we use the term 'topic' in two senses. The first is in the context of the ADT graph and refers to the topics or concepts as extracted by tools such as LDA We also use the term in the sense of topic-queries (such as "information extraction") in context of expert finding.

thors whereas edges between D and T reflect the topical association of documents.

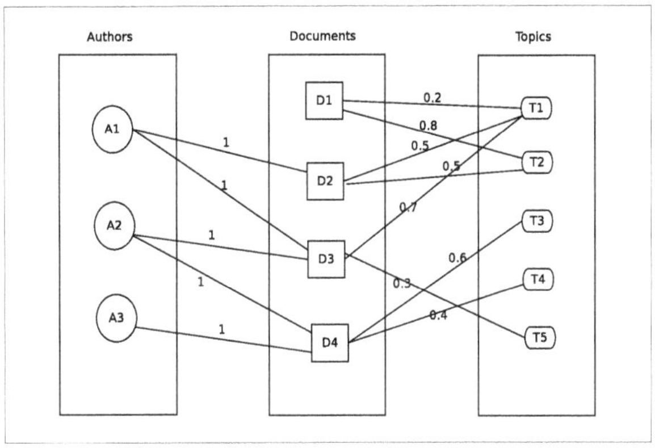

Figure 1: An example Author-Document-Topic (ADT) graph

Weights assigned to the edges in ADT capture the association strength between two nodes. For instance, in our experiments, we assign a uniform weight of 1 to all edges between author and document nodes whereas edges between document and topic nodes are assigned weights in correspondence with the proportion of that topic in the document (a positive real number). Document modeling tools such PLSI and LDA can be used for estimating these topic proportions. An example ADT graph is shown in Figure 1.

We now describe how the ADT is constructed for a given query. Consider for example, a given document node, d. First, the weighted links between this document node and its associated topic nodes are added using the proportions obtained from LDA(or PLSI). Next, other document nodes related to these topics are added to the graph along with the related edges. Finally, the known author links between the document and author layers are added to obtain a document-specific graph. If a set of documents is given as input instead of a single document (for example, documents retrieved in response to a topic query), we proceed, as in the case of a single document, by incrementally building the subgraph related to each document in the set to obtain the final graph. Instead, if for a name-query, an author node, a, is specified as input we first retrieve the documents associated with a and then follow the same procedure as with that of a set of documents.

Several well-known measures exist for comparing two nodes in weighted graphs (particularly for directed graphs). For instance, if the edge weights represent distances between nodes, one can compute proximity between two nodes in terms of the shortest path between them. In the field of network analysis, researchers have studied measures for computing vertex similarity and importance scores. A recent comparison of network similarity measures for various recommendation tasks was studied by Boldi, et al [7]. In particular, vertex similarity measures in co-authorship networks were evaluated for collaborator recommendation by Chen, et al [8].

In our preliminary experiments, we found that network centrality measures such as degree centrality, PageRank and betweenness of nodes in the ADT graph are not useful for expert ranking tasks. This is not surprising since in general centrality measures capture a node's impact with respect to the overall graph structure. These measures are not very meaningful in context of the ADT graph due to its undirected nature and the heterogenity of the underlying nodes. Moreover, our focus is on estimating a node's similarity with reference to the query nodes rather than its influence at a macroscopic level. To capture this aspect, we propose measuring the similarity between two nodes in a graph in terms of strength of paths between the nodes. Let p be a path betwen nodes a and d comprising of edges such that $p = e_1 e_2 \dots e_n$. Let

$$\mathbf{sweight(p)} = \sum_i weight(e_i)$$

$$\mathbf{pweight(p)} = \prod_i weight(e_i)$$

Let $P(a, d)$ be the set of all paths between nodes a and d. We studied the following schemes for computing similarity between a and d:

1. **MaxPath** The similarity between two nodes is given by the path between them having the maximum association strength. If we assign weights to edges using a transformation function that assigns weights to edges that are inversely proportional to association strengths, this scheme picks the path having the shortest distance between the nodes.

$$score(a, d) = \max_{p \in P(a,d)} \mathbf{sweight(p)}$$

2. **SumPaths** Consider a document that is related to two topics. An author who is associated with both the topics should be assigned credit for both the topics. The SumPaths scoring method seeks to capture this intuition by aggregating scores of all paths between two nodes in the ADT graph.

$$score(a, d) = \sum_{p \in P(a,d)} \mathbf{sweight(p)}$$

3. **ProductPaths** This scoring method is similar to SumPaths but we use a multiplicative scheme for aggregating edge association into a path association.

$$score(a, d) = \sum_{p \in P(a,d)} \mathbf{pweight(p)}$$

For a running example, suppose we would like to score the node $A1$ with respect to $D1$ in Figure 1. Assume the topic proportions for the documents are given as:

$$D1 = \{0.2, 0.8, 0, 0, 0\}, D2 = \{0.5, 0.5, 0, 0, 0\}$$

$$D3 = \{0.7, 0, 0, 0, 0.3\}, D4 = \{0, 0, 0.4, 0, 0.6\}$$

There are three paths between $D1$ and $A1$, viz.

$$\{(D1, T1), (T1, D2), (D2, A1)\}$$

$$\{(D1, T2), (T2, D2), (D2, A1)\}$$

$$\{(D1, T1), (T1, D3), (D3, A1)\}$$

With the **sweight** function, these paths have weights, 1.7, 2.3 and 2.1 respectively where as with the **pweight** function, the paths are assigned scores, 0.1, 0.4 and 0.14 respectively. Therefore, the score of $A1$ w.r.t. $D1$ is 2.3 with MaxPath, 6.1 with SumPaths and 0.64 with ProductPaths.

Notice that our scoring schemes are agnostic to the choice of nodes in the sense that all nodes are treated equally and given a node of any type, other types of nodes are assigned scores purely based on the association strengths as captured by the scoring schemes described above. This aspect is a virtue of graph-based models where query objects and the objects to be scored are both nodes and the assigned scores are simply due to some property of the underlying graph (e.g. paths, degree of nodes). Although PageRank-style measures are not meaningful for ADT graphs as we mentioned previously, we can exploit importance-based measures by constructing the underlying graph differently. An extension of PageRank using query-dependent graphs with multiple edge types was previously studied by us for scoring author nodes in response to topic queries [9]. We now show that this model can also be used for similar expert finding by constructing an appropriate query-specific graph.

3.2 PageRank on typed graphs

Objects in digital libraries have nodes corresponding to different objects such as authors, papers, venues and homepages. Similarly, edges in such graphs can represent authorship association, citation links, publication-venue links and so on. First, we briefly summarize our PageRank-based model for finding experts in response to topic-based queries before discussing name-based search.

Let $G = (V, E)$ represent a directed graph where V is the set of nodes and the edges in E have types assigned to them ($t \in T$). We use distinct transition matrices ($\mathbf{P}_t$) to capture edges corresponding to each edge type, t. Each matrix is constructed to be aperiodic and irreducible such that the aggregate transition matrix obtained by a linear combination of individual transition matrices is also irreducible and aperiodic.

$$\mathbf{P} = \sum_t w_t \mathbf{P}_t \text{ where } \sum_t w_t = 1 \text{ and } \forall w_t, 0 \le w_t \le 1$$

By Ergodic theorem, the matrix $\mathbf{P}$ has a unique stationary (or limiting) distribution over the nodes of V and this can be obtained by computing the principal eigen vector of the transpose of $\mathbf{P}$ (for example, using the power method [24, 14]).

The PageRank vector captures the behavior of a random surfer on the underlying graph where the final score for a node represents the probability that the surfer visits that node in the limit or as time tends to infinity. In effect, this value captures the "importance" of a node in the underlying graph based on its edge connections with the other nodes. In our extended model, we start with a query-dependent graph that has edges of different types. At every node, n, the surfer chooses at random (with probability, w_t) an edge-type, t, after which she proceeds to select one of outgoing edges of type, t, uniformly at random. The mixing coefficients, w_ts are indicative of the importance of each edge-type and can be set by domain knowledge or cross-validation.

For Expert Finding in response to topic queries, the graph on which the above model is run is ensured to be topic query dependent by using the following process: The topic query is used to retrieve the top matching documents via a search engine. This set of documents is used as an initial set of nodes, from which the remaining graph is built via expansion. For instance, the set of author nodes corresponding to the retrieved documents are added via author-document links. Other document nodes can also be added, for instance via the citation edges. We refer the reader to our previous paper for further details and experiments that show that this model performs on par with the probabilistic models for expert finding [9]. Although, this model is an extension to the original PageRank algorithm, in this paper, we use the terms **PageRank** or **PR** to refer to this extended model.

The PageRank model just described has an obvious extension that enables us to score other author nodes in response to a query-author node: We construct the query-specific graph for applying PageRank as follows. The documents associated with the queried author, a, are first retrieved to form the initial set of documents. This document set is expanded by adding other documents (via citation edges or neighbors based on content similarity). Note that this expansion step is crucial to ensure we do not only capture "co-authors". However, once an initial document set is obtained, the process is similar to that of the topic-based search case. For example, consider the graph in Figure 2 and let $A3$ correspond to the query node. The documents, $D2$ and $D3$ are retrieved via their direct association with $A3$ whereas $D4$, $A2$ and $A4$ correspond to the nodes added via our expansion process. The shaded nodes comprise the query-dependent graph used for computing PageRank scores.

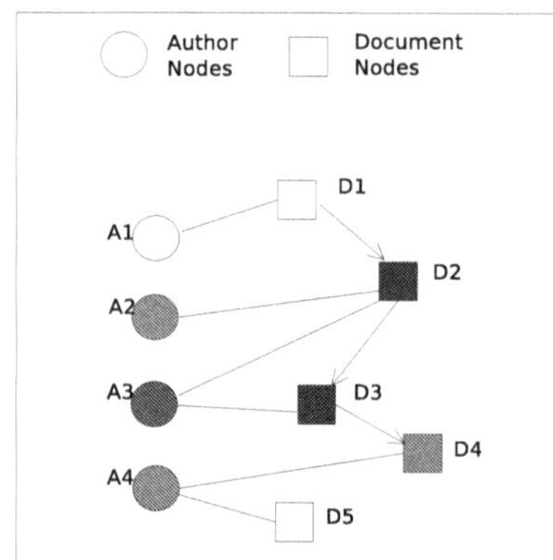

Figure 2: An example author-document graph to illustrate the PageRank-based model

There is an important difference between the ADT graph models when compared with the PageRank-based models. Due to the types of nodes and semantic meaning behind edges between nodes, similarity of nodes in the ADT models pertains to similarity based on the **topical profiles** whereas the PageRank scores capture importance based on **structural connections** in the graph. For example, an author who has written documents that are linked from other relevant documents via citation edges would be scored better in the PageRank scoring models whereas this aspect is not captured in the ADT model.

3.3 Baselines

We briefly summarize some models previously proposed for topic-based expert finding and similar expert finding.

1. **Expert Finding**: Balog, et al. [2, 3] use the estimates of $p(ca|q)$ where q is the query and ca is a candidate

for ranking experts. $p(ca|q) = \frac{p(ca,q)}{p(q)}$ and $p(ca,q)$ is defined as

$$p(ca,q) = \sum_{d \in D} p(d)p(ca,q|d) = \sum_{d \in D} p(d)p(q|d)p(ca|d,q) \quad (1)$$

D is the set of documents related to the query that a candidate ca is associated with. Assuming ca is conditionally independent of q given a document one can write $p(ca|d,q) = p(ca|d)$ and treating $p(d)$ and $p(q)$ as uniform:

$$p(ca|q) \propto \sum_{d \in D} p(q|d)p(ca|d)$$

$p(ca|d)$ is defined as $\frac{a(d,ca)}{\sum_{c' \in C} a(d,c')}$ where C is the set of all candidates and $a(d,ca)$ is the association between document d and candidate ca. The $p(q|d)$ scores for a document are estimated using language modeling.

Deng, et al. extended the probabilistic model proposed by Balog, et al. for bibliographic data [12]. The $p(ca|d)$ values were defined as $\frac{1}{n_d}$ or 0 depending on whether ca is the author of d and n_d is the number of authors for d. The prior probability, $p(d)$, was defined in terms of the number of citations that the document has. For example, $p(d) \propto ln(e + c_d)$ where c_d is the citation number for d. This probabilistic model forms a competitive baseline and complicated author-topic models were shown to obtain only marginal improvements for topic-based expert finding in bibliographic data [12].

2. **Similar Expert Finding** Adaptations of expert finding techniques were studied for similar expert finding by Balog, et al. [5] and Das, et al. [10]. In both these works, the authors in the collection are represented via their profiles constructed using the documents associated with them. Experts are recommended based on the profile similarity between two authors. We implemented these methods and chose the best performing of them as baselines (Section 4). We found that simple similarity based on TFIDF vector representation of the author profiles out-performed more complicated techniques. We briefly describe the best performing models here.

   (a) **Okapi BM25**: Given an author for whom similar experts are to be recommended, the TFIDF vector of the author is treated as a term query and the profiles of the remaining authors in the dataset are scored using the Okapi BM25 ranking function given by:

$$\sum_{w \in s_1} IDF(w) * \frac{tf(w,s_2) * (k_1 + 1)}{tf(w,s_2) + k_1 * (1 - b + b.\frac{|D|}{avgdl}}$$

   In the above formula, $IDF(w)$ refers to the inverse document frequency of the word, a measure of rareness of the word computed as:

$$IDF(w) = log\frac{N - N(w) + 0.5}{N(w) + 0.5}.$$

   N is the total number of profiles in the collection, $N(w)$, the number of profiles containing w and $tf(w,s_2)$, the number of times, the term w appears in the profile of e_2. The parameter k_1 is typically set to a value between $[1.2, 2]$ whereas b is typically set to 0.75 in this formula in absence of other information. Additional details on this formula and parameter settings can be found in Jones, et al. [19].

   (b) **Trace-based Similarity**: The author profiles are represented in terms of normalized TFIDF vectors of dimensionality and using the **Relevance Model** [15] studied by He, et al. the the similarity between two profiles, q and d is computed using the formula: $Rel(q,d) = (q.d)^2$.

4. EXPERIMENTS

To the best of our knowledge, no standard datasets exist for evaluating the similar expert finding task in the academic domain. However, sets of topic queries and lists of experts (traditionally referred to as qrels in TREC) for each topic are available for evaluating topic-based expert finding from ArnetMiner and Tilburg university.

4.1 Datasets

1. The ArnetMiner (**AM**) dataset provides topic+experts lists previously used by Tang, et al [27] and Deng, et al. [12] for studying topic-based expert finding in academic domains. We mapped these researcher names to the author names in CiteSeer using exact string matching. To obtain a suitable corpus for modeling the researchers, we collected a subset of document abstracts from CiteSeer by matching venues of documents with the keywords from venue names listed on Wikipedia[7]. The topic queries were used to select a subset of suitable venues in this list. We only considered authors having at least three papers in the CiteSeer collection and documents related to these authors are obtained to form the corpus.

2. The **UvT** collection was made available via the Webwijs system developed at Tilburg University. This collection contains information on UvT employees who are involved in research or teaching along with their homepages, research profiles, publications and course pages. The list of topics+experts available with this collection was used to study expert finding and profiling tasks in sparse environments by Balog, et al [3, 4]. We only considered pages in this collection that are in English.

Both the AM and the UvT datasets have 'topic' queries and manually-identified lists of authors with expertise for each topic. For evaluating similar expert finding, we need the list of experts that are similar to a given expert. We created test datasets for this purpose as follows: for a given topic query, from the set of experts listed with the query, we randomly choose one of the experts as the "name query". The other experts in the set comprise the similar researchers (or the 'gold' list) for this query. Due to the manner of construction, our 'gold' lists are in fact conditioned on the topic. Despite this dependence, we think that this dataset can be used for comparing the relative performance across ranking models. We restrict ourselves to topics that have at least five experts

[7]http://en.wikipedia.org/wiki/List_of_computer_science_conferences

Name	Description	Corpus Size	Total Authors	Queries	QRels Size
AM	ArnetMiner/CiteSeer	103838	27108	13	901
UvT	The UvT Collection	19127	1168	203	1751

Table 1: Summary of datasets used

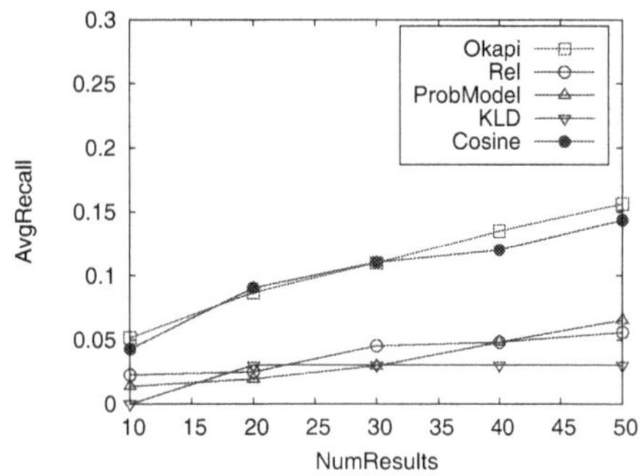

Figure 3: Comparison of baselines for Name-based search (AM)

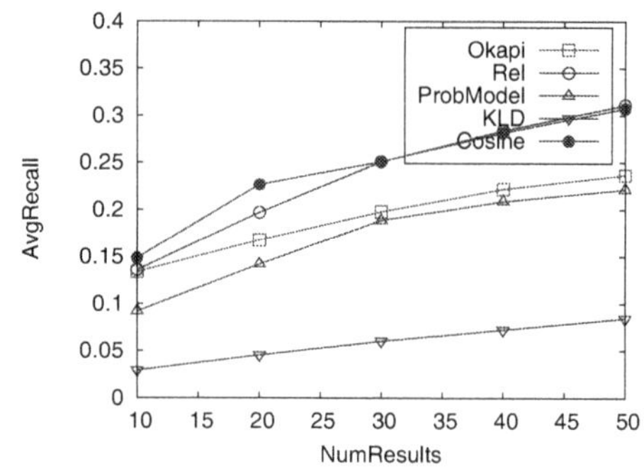

Figure 4: Comparison of baselines for Name-based search (UvT)

listed with them while forming our test set. A summary description of the datasets thus obtained is given in Table 1.

From Table 1, it can be noticed that the AM and UvT datasets correspond to rather different operating environments. The number of documents and authors and documents per author is higher in the CiteSeer/ArnetMiner although known expert-qrels are less in number. Documents in CiteSeer represent research publications and have citation links between them. In contrast, the UvT collection is sparse in that the documents mostly comprise webpages (homepages, research descriptions etc.). The number of documents per expert is limited and very few experts have more than ten documents associated with them (Table 2).

NumDocs->	1	3	5	10	20
AM/CSX	n/a	8153	2994	717	167
UvT	384	65	40	22	5

Table 2: Each entry represents the number of authors having a given number of documents associated with them. For example, the number of authors in UvT having only one document is 384

For ADT models the underlying document collection is represented in terms of topics. The "number of topics" comprises a tunable parameter for most document modeling tools like pLSA or LDA. This number is typically chosen to maximize the "likelihood" or "perplexity" of a held-out set of documents in the corpus [16]. However Azzopardi et al. showed that low perplexity representations do not necessarily result in high precision/recall for retrieval problems [1]. For this reason, we tune the "number of topics" parameter separately for each task on each dataset by using a *held-out* set of queries. In each dataset, 20% of the queries (randomly-selected) comprise the held-out set whereas the other 80% of the queries are used for evaluation and comparisons across models (Tables 5 and 6).

We present sample topic-terms for both the CiteSeer and UvT document collections in Tables 3 and 4 respectively. These topics clearly highlight the difference in the two document collections. The CiteSeer collection corresponds to documents in Computer Science and related areas and consequently the identified topics are closely related in the area. In contrast, the document collection in UvT pertains to a broader set of topics. We contend that the retrieval performance is typically better on the UvT collection since it is easier to discriminate between expertise areas corresponding to the authors.

4.2 Evaluation Setup and Metrics

The document collections in both datasets were indexed using the search engine, Indri[8]. Indri uses language modeling techniques for ranking documents in response to topic queries. We evaluate the performance of our models at different number of retrieved results ($k = 10, 20, 30, 40, 50$). In our expert finding experiments, we set the size of document set retrieved in response to the topic queries to 100 per query. The document-topic associations were obtained by running the LDA (Latent Dirichlet Allocation) implementation provided as part of Mallet[9].

We measure the performance of our proposed and baseline models using the recall, mean average precision (MAP), mean reciprocal rank (MRR) measures [22]. Let R_q represent the set of known experts for a given test query, q. If S represents the set of recommendations made by the expert retrieval system for q, we compute recall and precision for q as:

$$Recall = \frac{|S \cap R_q|}{|R_q|}$$

$$Precision = \frac{|S \cap R_q|}{|S|}$$

Average precision (AvgP) refers to the average precision with S after each relevant document is retrieved whereas MAP (mean average precision) aggregates the average precision value over all the queries (Q) to to provide a single

[8]http://www.lemurproject.org/indri/

[9]http://mallet.cs.umass.edu/

305	distribution probability random distributions show number size model independent expected uniform rate average
409	knowledge learning domain reasoning system case problem acquisition machine task expert solving base process learn
448	model models bayesian probability gaussian mixture distribution estimation likelihood maximum parameters probabilistic
302	management distributed applications system systems service application support requirements dynamic services computing
414	query queries database data databases relational processing optimization evaluation join sql efficient execution support
66	mobile devices computing wireless location users device environment user access environments services network ubiquitous
408	computational complexity based algorithm paper proposed efficient algorithms cost techniques efficiency advantage reduced
109	learning training classification data supervised labeled set approach labels learn examples class task unlabeled unsupervised
439	mining data discovery patterns association rules knowledge databases database rule frequent discover large discovering
342	semantic ontology web ontologies knowledge abstract domain semantics concepts rdf language describe resources metadata

Table 3: Sample Topics from the CiteSeer corpus

99	estimation statistics probability regression model statistical distribution estimators methods multivariate variables
98	lines prior summary top half reflects implication patterns trends greater numbers wide variety continued portion
90	index cluster clusters space target ranking coming multi group collected clustering included mixed retrieved entry
89	mind important made sense relation make arguments common consists remarks full case interpretation existence view
87	markets industrial journal firms organization competition economics collusion oligopoly consistency letters market
86	ethics law moral ethical social legal morality politics human society theory state philosophy ideals political care
83	republic europe poland czech hungary eastern state german west east central russia french case government ten
78	asia regions areas india africa rural agricultural urban historical america agriculture spread southern cities
72	criminal crime law justice police european investigation court victims prosecution enforcement victim crimes drug
71	face brain related expressions facial cognitive emotion affective emotional expression neuroscience emotions perception

Table 4: Sample Topics from the UvT collection

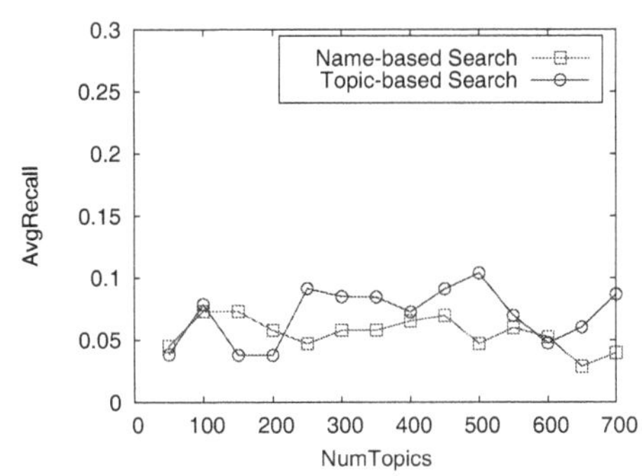

Figure 5: ADT performance variation with number of topics (AM)

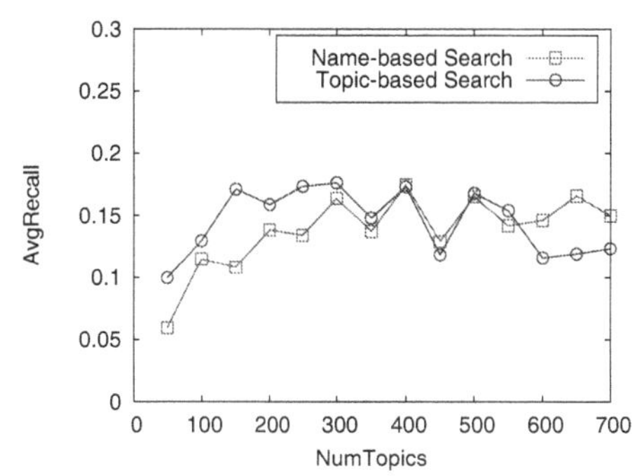

Figure 6: ADT performance variation with number of topics (UvT)

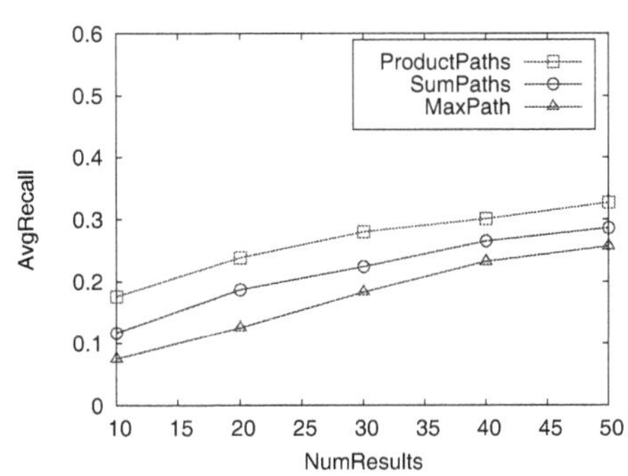

Figure 7: ADT methods for Topic-based search (UvT)

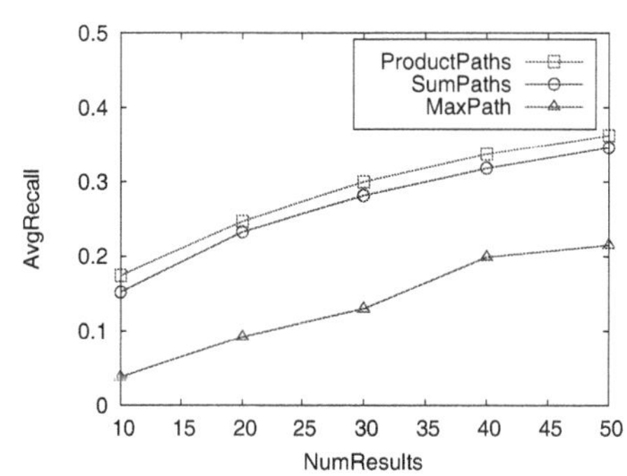

Figure 8: ADT methods for Name-based search (UvT)

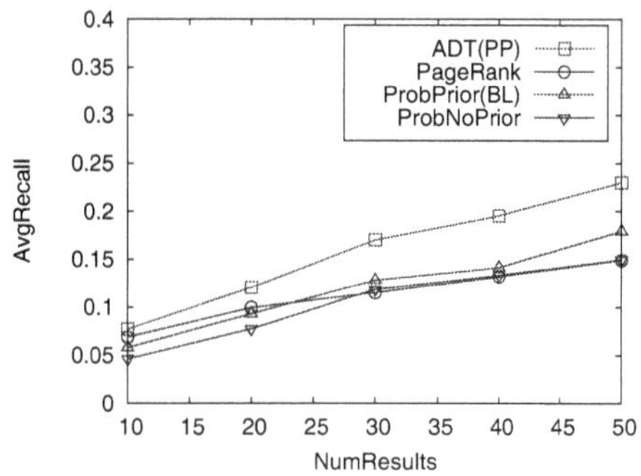

Figure 9: Recall@K for Topic-based search(AM)

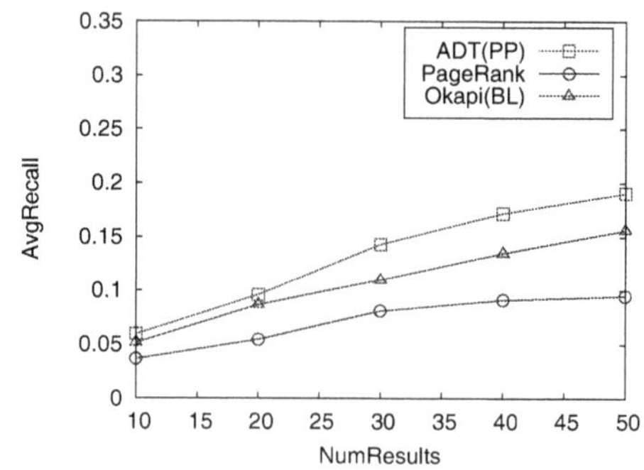

Figure 10: Recall@K for Name-based search(AM)

measure for precision as:

$$MAP = \frac{\sum_{q=1}^{Q} AvgP(q)}{|Q|}$$

The mean reciprocal rank, in contrast, values the rank at which the first correct answer is found for every query in Q and is computed using the following formula:

$$MRR = \frac{1}{|Q|} \sum_{q=1}^{Q} \frac{1}{rank(q)}$$

In the above formula, $rank(q)$ refers to the rank of the first relevant expert found for a query, q. Queries for which no relevant experts are found are considered to contribute 0 to the formula. When only the top-k predictions in S are considered for computing these measures, we append @k while referring to them (e.g. Recall@10). We argue that for expert finding, recall is a more meaningful measure since it captures the number of correct experts in the gold lists that are retrieved by a method. Therefore, we use recall as the criterion for choosing the number of topics or the appropriate baselines to compare with.

4.3 Results and Observations

The performance of ADT models on the held-out queries for different number of topics is shown in Figures 5 and 6. As can be seen in these figures, "number of topics" for modeling the documents in the corpus forms a crucial parameter that affects the performance of the ADT models. Moreover, the best setting for number of topics is task-dependent. We found $numTopics = 400$ works well for both the tasks on the UvT dataset whereas for the AM dataset, $numTopics = 450, 500$ are the best settings for name-based and topic-based search respectively.

Our next set of experiments compares the different scoring schemes proposed for ADT models in Section 3 on the AM dataset for both topic-based search and name-based search (Figures 11 and 12). The SumPaths and ProductPaths clearly out-perform the MaxPath scheme that assigns scores based on the best-path connecting two nodes. For our tasks, it appears important to accumulate the scores along various paths between a given set of nodes, a feature captured by both SumPaths and ProductPaths scoring schemes. For comparison with other models, we choose ProductPaths since it is slightly better than SumPaths on the held-out queries. Similar behavior is observed on the UvT dataset in Figures 7 and 8.

Next, we compare our proposed models (ADT and PR) with the state-of-the-art baselines for these tasks. Figures 9 and 10 show the recall of the models for different number of retrieved results for the ArnetMiner dataset whereas figures 13 and 14 show similar plots for the UvT dataset. As can be seen in these figures, graph-based models (PageRank or ADT) typically outperform or perform on-par with the problem-specific baseline models in terms of recall on both the datasets. The other retrieval measures are summarized in Tables 5 and 6. For the UvT collection, simpler TFIDF-based methods seem to be better at ranking the results (as captured by MRR, for instance). We used the default setting of assigning edge-type weights (w_ts) equally in our PageRank models. The citation edges were used to expand the document set in case of name-based search in the ArnetMiner dataset whereas content-similarity (top-100 neighbors) was used to expand the set for the UvT collection (Section 3.2).

Our experiments highlight results that indicate that unified models can be designed for handling both the querying scenarios in expert search without compromising on the retrieval performance. The probablistic model was chosen as baseline for topic-based search based on its competitive performance shown in previous work [12, 9]. For name-based search, since existing work on this problem is still preliminary, we evaluated all applicable models previously proposed for this problem [5, 10] on our datasets and choose the best performing models as baselines (Figures 3 and 4).

Finally, for the sake of illustration, we provide anecdotal examples in Tables 7 and 8. These lists of top-10 recommendations were retrieved using the ADT model with the ProductPaths scoring scheme. We chose popular subject areas in Computer Science as "topic queries" and known experts in these fields as "name queries". While not all entries are perfect we found upon manual examination that most recommended authors typically publish in conferences in the related subject areas (as listed on DBLP[10]). The entries which do not seem relevant to the specified query are highlighted in italics in these tables.

5. SUMMARY AND FUTURE WORK

In this paper, we presented graph-based models for enabling expert search in response to name and topic queries. Our ADT models ranks experts based on content-similarity captured via document-topic edges. In contrast, our PageRank-

[10] http://www.informatik.uni-trier.de/~ley/db/

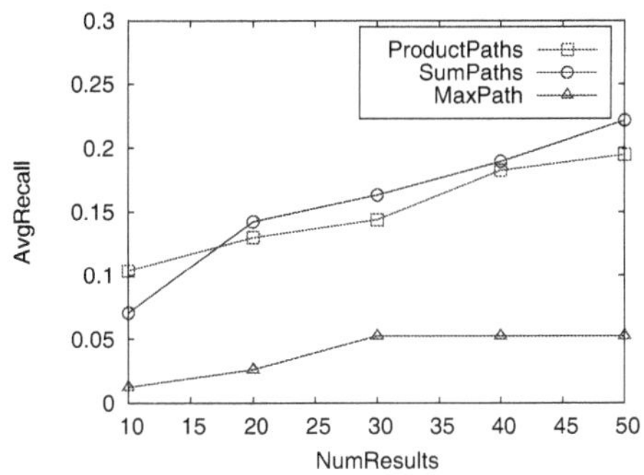

Figure 11: ADT methods for Topic-based search (AM)

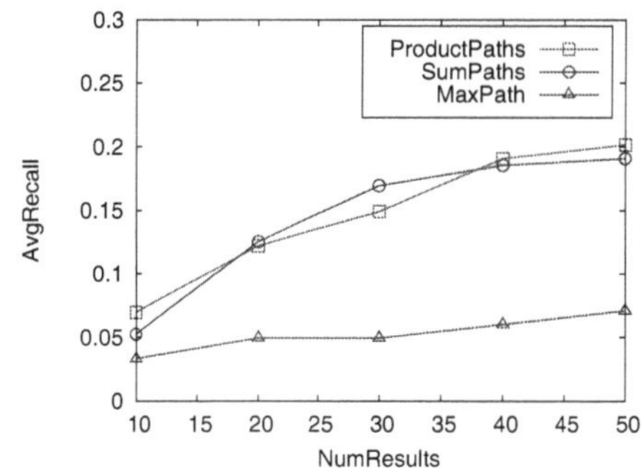

Figure 12: ADT methods for Name-based search (AM)

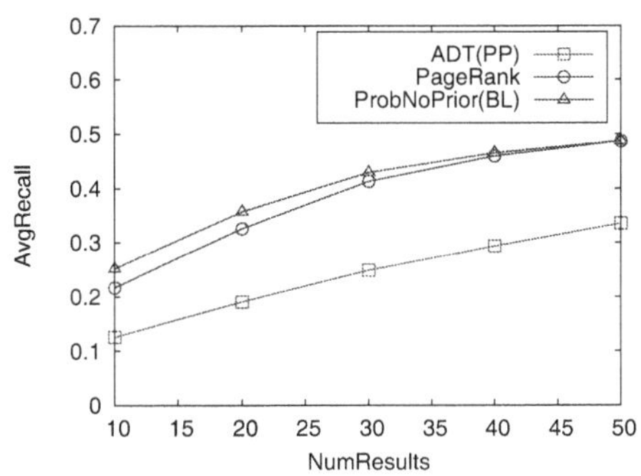

Figure 13: Recall@K for Topic-based search(UvT)

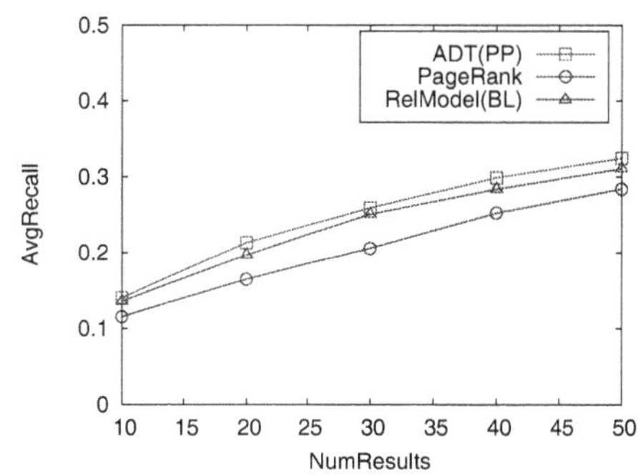

Figure 14: Recall@K for Name-based search(UvT)

ArnetMiner			
	BL(Okapi)	PR	ADT
Prec@10	0.2699	0.2100	**0.3200**
MRR@10	**0.5792**	0.3211	0.4493
MAP@10	0.1614	0.1115	**0.1999**
Prec@50	0.1720	0.1436	**0.2000**
MRR@50	**0.5908**	0.3277	0.4523
MAP@50	0.0793	0.0437	**0.1008**
UvT			
	BL(Rel)	PR	ADT
Prec@10	**0.1242**	0.1029	0.1191
MRR@10	**0.3190**	0.2673	0.2627
MAP@10	**0.0914**	0.0623	0.0875
Prec@50	0.0565	0.0529	**0.0619**
MRR@50	**0.3268**	0.2784	0.2759
MAP@50	**0.1070**	0.0729	0.1003

Table 5: Comparison Summary: Name-based Search

ArnetMiner			
	BL(Prob)	PR	ADT
Prec@10	0.3300	0.3400	**0.4300**
MRR@10	0.5009	0.6350	**0.8433**
MAP@10	0.1844	0.2097	**0.3397**
Prec@50	0.1980	0.1680	**0.2900**
MRR@50	0.5009	0.635	**0.8433**
MAP@50	0.0987	0.0851	**0.1986**
UvT			
	BL(Prob)	PR	ADT
Prec@10	**0.2158**	0.1856	0.1088
MRR@10	**0.5145**	0.4304	0.3021
MAP@10	**0.1506**	0.1245	0.0759
Prec@50	0.1245	**0.1246**	0.0598
MRR@50	**0.5201**	0.4393	0.3167
MAP@50	**0.1793**	0.1558	0.0943

Table 6: Comparison Summary: Topic-based Search

Natural Language Processing	**Machine Learning**	**Information Retrieval**	**Semantic Web**
Hermann Ney	Raymond J. Mooney	W. Bruce Croft	Ian Horrocks
Aravind K. Joshi	Vasant Honavar	Douglas W. Oard	Dieter Fensel
Raymond J. Mooney	Manuela Veloso	*Hermann Ney*	Enrico Motta
Bonnie J. Dorr	Jude Shavlik	Jamie Callan	Amit Sheth
Alex Waibel	David B. Leake	Hector Garcia-molina	Steffen Staab
Martha Palmer	Peter A. Flach	Justin Zobel	Frank Van Harmelen
Kathleen Mckeown	Pat Langley	C. Lee Giles	Stefan Decker
Udo Hahn	Yoram Singer	*Shih-fu Chang*	Rudi Studer
Alon Lavie	Ryszard S. Michalski	*Alex Waibel*	*Wolfgang Nejdl*
Bonnie Webber	Johannes Furnkranz	Jaap Kamps	*Tim Finin*

Table 7: Top-10 recommendations made by ADT models for example topic queries

Christopher D. Manning	Tom M. Mitchell	W. Bruce Croft	James Hendler
Aravind K. Joshi	Raymond J. Mooney	Douglas W. Oard	Ian Horrocks
Martha Palmer	Sebastian Thrun	Jamie Callan	Dieter Fensel
Raymond J. Mooney	Peter Stone	Justin Zobel	Amit Sheth
Timothy Baldwin	Jude Shavlik	Norbert Fuhr	Frank Van Harmelen
Bonnie J. Dorr	Vasant Honavar	Maarten De Rijke	*Wolfgang Nejdl*
John A. Carroll	Andrew Mccallum	Jaap Kamps	Enrico Motta
Ted Briscoe	Andrew G. Barto	Hector Garcia-molina	Steffen Staab
Mark Johnson	Richard S. Sutton	*Rong Jin*	*Geoffrey Fox*
Fernando Pereira	Manuela Veloso	Mounia Lalmas	Stefan Decker
Walter Daelemans	Pat Langley	*Ophir Frieder*	*Carole Goble*

Table 8: Top-10 recommendations made by ADT models for example name queries

based models rank experts using the structural connections between authors and documents and within documents. We showed via experiments that our graph-based models are capable of providing a unifed framework for ranking experts in response to both name and topic queries. In addition, we showed that these models demonstrate retrieval performance on-par with problem-specific models. Since the two proposed models are based on different types of graphs and capture different aspects of ranking (structure vs. content), a future direction to explore is the combination of model to obtain the best from both.

We are also looking to extend our expert retrieval models for panel recommendation. In contrast with topic or name-based search, recommending panels of experts imposes several problem-specific constraints. For instance, we may wish to ensure diversity in the list of experts with respect to affiliations. Metadata information available with authors (e.g. from CiteSeer or author homepages) can be used for this purpose. Similarly, personal preferences of authors with respect to each other may need to be accounted for during panel recommendation [20].

6. ACKNOWLEDGMENTS

This material is based upon work supported by the National Science Foundation.

7. REFERENCES

[1] L. Azzopardi, M. Girolami, and K. van Risjbergen. Investigating the relationship between language model perplexity and ir precision-recall measures. In *SIGIR*, 2003.

[2] K. Balog, L. Azzopardi, and M. de Rijke. Formal models for expert finding in enterprise corpora. In *SIGIR*, 2006.

[3] K. Balog, T. Bogers, L. Azzopardi, M. de Rijke, and A. van den Bosch. Broad expertise retrieval in sparse data environments. In *SIGIR*, 2007.

[4] K. Balog and M. de Rijke. Determining expert profiles (with an application to expert finding). In *IJCAI*, 2007.

[5] K. Balog and M. de Rijke. Finding similar experts. In *SIGIR*, 2007.

[6] D. M. Blei, A. Y. Ng, and M. I. Jordan. Latent dirichlet allocation. *J. Mach. Learn. Res.*, 2003.

[7] P. Boldi, M. Rosa, and S. Vigna. Robustness of social networks: comparative results based on distance distributions. In *Social informatics*, 2011.

[8] H.-H. Chen, L. Gou, X. Zhang, and C. L. Giles. Collabseer: a search engine for collaboration discovery. In *JCDL*, 2011.

[9] S. Das, P. Mitra, and C. L. Giles. Ranking authors in digital libraries. In *JCDL*, 2011.

[10] S. Das, P. Mitra, and C. L. Giles. Similar researcher search in academic environments. In *JCDL*, 2012.

[11] G. Demartini, J. Gaugaz, and W. Nejdl. A vector space model for ranking entities and its application to expert search. In *ECIR*, 2009.

[12] H. Deng, I. King, and M. R. Lyu. Formal models for expert finding on dblp bibliography data. In *ICDM*, 2008.

[13] T. L. Griffiths and M. Steyvers. Finding scientific topics. *Proceedings of the National Academy of Sciences*, 2004.

[14] T. Haveliwala, S. K. Kamvar, D. Klein, C. Manning, and G. G. Golub. Computing pagerank using power extrapolation. In *Stanford University Technical Report*, 2003.

[15] Q. He, J. Pei, D. Kifer, P. Mitra, and C. L. Giles. Context-aware citation recommendation. In *WWW*, 2010.

[16] G. Heinrich. Parameter estimation for text analysis. Technical report, 2004.

[17] K. Hofmann, K. Balog, T. Bogers, and M. de Rijke. Contextual factors for finding similar experts. *JASIST*, 2010.

[18] T. Hofmann. Probabilistic latent semantic indexing. In *SIGIR*, 1999.

[19] K. S. Jones, S. Walker, and S. E. Robertson. A probabilistic model of information retrieval: development and comparative experiments. *Inf. Process. Manage.*, 2000.

[20] T. Lappas, K. Liu, and E. Terzi. Finding a team of experts in social networks. In *KDD*, 2009.

[21] C. Macdonald and I. Ounis. Voting for candidates: adapting data fusion techniques for an expert search task. In *CIKM*, 2006.

[22] C. D. Manning, P. Raghavan, and H. SchÃijtze. *Introduction to Information Retrieval.* Cambridge University Press, 2008.

[23] M. Rosen-Zvi, T. Griffiths, M. Steyvers, and P. Smyth. The author-topic model for authors and documents. In *Uncertainty in artificial intelligence*, 2004.

[24] S. M. Ross. *Introduction to Probability Models, Ninth Edition.* Academic Press, Inc., 2006.

[25] P. Serdyukov, H. Rode, and D. Hiemstra. Modeling multi-step relevance propagation for expert finding. In *CIKM*, 2008.

[26] J. Tang, R. Jin, and J. Zhang. A topic modeling approach and its integration into the random walk framework for academic search. In *ICDM*, 2008.

[27] J. Tang, J. Zhang, L. Yao, J. Li, L. Zhang, and Z. Su. Arnetminer: extraction and mining of academic social networks. In *KDD*, 2008.

[28] Y. Xu, J. Hao, R. Y. Lau, J. Ma, W. Xu, and D. Zhao. A personalized researcher recommendation approach in academic contexts: Combining social networks and semantic concepts analysis. In *PACIS*, 2010.

Aggregating Productivity Indices for Ranking Researchers across Multiple Areas

Harlley Lima, Thiago H. P. Silva, Mirella M. Moro,
Rodrygo L. T. Santos, Wagner Meira Jr., Alberto H. F. Laender
Universidade Federal de Minas Gerais
Belo Horizonte, Brazil
{harlley,thps,mirella,rodrygo,meira,laender}@dcc.ufmg.br

ABSTRACT

The impact of scientific research has traditionally been quantified using productivity indices such as the well-known h-index. On the other hand, different research fields—in fact, even different research areas within a single field—may have very different publishing patterns, which may not be well described by a single, global index. In this paper, we argue that productivity indices should account for the singularities of the publication patterns of different research areas, in order to produce an unbiased assessment of the impact of scientific research. Inspired by ranking aggregation approaches in distributed information retrieval, we propose a novel approach for ranking researchers across multiple research areas. Our approach is generic and produces cross-area versions of any global productivity index, such as the volume of publications, citation count and even the h-index. Our thorough evaluation considering multiple areas within the broad field of Computer Science shows that our cross-area indices outperform their global counterparts when assessed against the official ranking produced by CNPq, the Brazilian National Research Council for Scientific and Technological Development. As a result, this paper contributes a valuable mechanism to support the decisions of funding bodies and research agencies, for example, in any research assessment effort.

Categories and Subject Descriptors

H.4 [**Information Systems Applications**]: Miscellaneous

Keywords

Research performance; Bibliometric indicators; Ranking aggregation; Cross-disciplinarity

1. INTRODUCTION

Evaluating a group of researchers is a permanent problem within research and academic institutions, laboratories and funding agencies. Usually, this process involves forming highly qualified committees that must meet, define evaluation criteria and perform the evaluation. Moreover, it is very costly in terms of time, because evaluating numerous researchers (their curricula and publications) is not a simple process.

The decision of which researchers should be at the top (for hiring, promoting, funding, or distributing grants, scholarships, awards and so on) is typically based on criteria such as number of publications, impact of publications, number of undergraduate and graduate students under supervision, number of advised MSc and PhD theses, and participation in committees (conferences, journal editorial boards, technical committees, etc). Clearly, the effectiveness of the resulting ranking depends on how each criterion is assessed and the period of time covered in the assessment [1, 23]. Although a researcher's performance cannot be measured solely by bibliometric indices, such indices have become widely used to measure the productivity of researchers. Examples include the number of citations, h-index [16], g-index [11] and citation z-score [22]. Likewise, most academic search platforms (such as ArnetMiner,[1] Google Scholar[2] and Microsoft Academic Search[3]) use some of such indices to rank researchers. However, a common limitation of global bibliometric indices

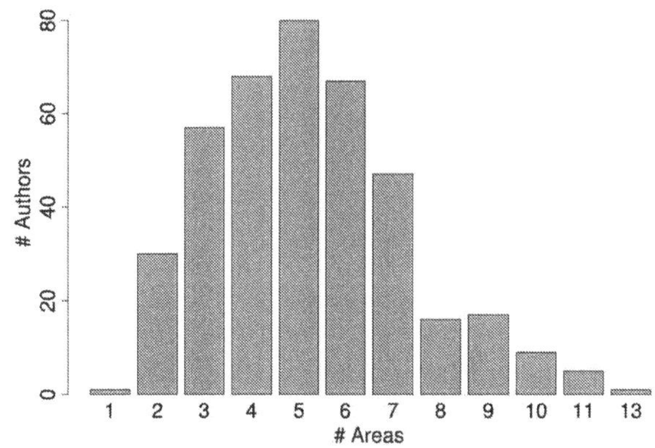

Figure 1: Distribution of Brazilian CS researchers per number of active areas. A researcher is deemed active in an area if at least 10% of the researcher's publications have been classified in the area.

[1]http://arnetminer.org/
[2]http://scholar.google.com/
[3]http://academic.research.microsoft.com/

is that they do not account for the dynamics of different areas when assessing a researcher's performance.

Ranking researchers without regarding the specificity of different areas is arguably unfair and potentially error-prone. For instance, consider the area of Human-Computer Interaction within the broad field of Computer Science (CS) [2]. Experimental evaluation in this area usually takes more time than in other CS areas when arranging and assessing users' feedback is necessary. On the other hand, CS areas such as Databases and Computer Graphics do not usually face the same problem because their experimental evaluations depend on assessing the outcome of an automatic process, such as a query evaluation or a graphics rendering engine. Likewise, researchers from some areas may have fewer publications than others, but with a potentially higher impact in their community. To aggravate the problem, many researchers publish in more than one area. To illustrate this observation, Figure 1 shows the distribution of Brazilian CS researchers per number of areas where they have at least 10% of their publications.[4] The figure shows a normal distribution with an average of 5 active areas per researcher. Most notably, almost all researchers are active in more than one area, with a few being active in up to 13 areas.

In order to improve the assessment of academic research, we introduce a novel approach for ranking researchers across multiple—and potentially distinct—research areas within an academic field. In particular, our approach estimates the performance of a researcher in each area relatively to the performance of other researchers in the same area, so as to ensure that the specificity of each area is accounted for accordingly. The researcher's relative performance in multiple areas is then aggregated into a unified ranking, by projecting the performance in each individual area to the corresponding performance in the researcher's base area, i.e., the area in which the researcher has most of her academic production. Our approach is generic and can be used to leverage different criteria for ranking researchers across areas. In particular, to demonstrate the feasibility of our approach, we devise cross-area rankings based on three different criteria: publication volume, number of citations and h-index. Our thorough evaluation considering multiple areas of researchers shows that our cross-area indices outperform their global counterparts when assessed against an official ranking produced by CNPq[5], the Brazilian National Research Council for Scientific and Technological Development.

The contributions of this paper are three-fold:

1. We demonstrate the limitation of a one-size-fits-all approach for ranking researchers across multiple areas, using the Brazilian CS community as a case study;

2. We introduce a novel ranking aggregation approach to rank researchers across multiple areas, which respects the idiosyncrasies of different areas;

3. We thoroughly evaluate the proposed approach applied to three well-known productivity indices: publication volume, citation count and h-index.

In the remainder of this paper, Section 2 provides background on related approaches to assess academic research. Section 3 introduces our novel approach for ranking researchers across multiple areas. In turn, Sections 4 and 5 describe the experimental methodology and the results of the evaluation of our approach, respectively. Lastly, Section 6 discusses our conclusions and directions for future research.

2. RELATED WORK

A classic problem in science consists in ranking scientists from distinct academic fields, such as mathematics, physics, and CS [5, 23, 24]. For instance, Podlubny [24] proposed an equivalence table for citations in different academic fields based upon the continued observation of the citation rates in these fields. After normalization, this table established, for instance, that one citation in mathematics corresponded roughly to 5 citations in engineering, 19 in physics, and 78 in the biomedical field, among others. However, the ad hoc nature of this study requires a periodical correction of the equivalence table over time, which is further aggravated by the unstable evolution of individual fields. Likewise, Radicchi et al. [25] performed an empirical analysis of the distribution of citations for publication among research fields. They proposed a relative indicator $c_f = c/c_o$, where c is the publication citation number and c_o is the average number of citations per article for the scientific field, which rescaled the distributions of citation for publication in different scientific fields upon the same curve when c_f is applied. Later, Bornmann and Daniel [4] explored the advantages of such indicator for the area of chemistry.

Claro and Costa [9] proposed the x-index as a cross-field bibliometric indicator in order to compare researchers from distinct scientific fields. The proposed index considers the top authors in each field (based upon the publication volume) as a reference set for the field. The productivity of the remaining authors in each field is then computed relatively to the field's reference set, so as to enable a cross-field comparison. A limitation of this approach is that the reference authors may be actually outliers, since publication volume is not necessarily an indicator of publication quality.

Another bibliometric indicator that tries to reduce the possible discrepancies between scientific fields is the crown index [28]. In particular, this index builds upon the observation that the average number of citations per publication varies across fields [21, 24]. To exploit this observation, the crown index normalizes a researcher's citation count by the expected number of citations in each field. Lundberg [22] extended this idea by normalizing the citation count at the publication (as opposed to the researcher) level. An additional extension used a logarithm-based normalization and assigned a weight to each publication according to a skewed distribution of citations over publications.

Freire and Figueiredo [14] proposed a productivity index to rank individuals within a target group (as opposed to ranking all individuals) in a collaboration network using solely the relationships among these individuals. In particular, the importance assigned to a specific individual by this index was proportional to the intensity of his or her collaboration with other individuals outside the target group. In the same work, the authors also considered a variation of their index to rank entire groups of individuals and applied it to rank graduate programs in the CS field.

In online rankings, such as the ones provided by Microsoft Academic Search and ArnetMiner, the top authors are classified according to their h-index by default. The h-index of a

[4]More details about the dataset used to generate the statistics in Figure 1 will be given later in Section 4.

[5]http://www.cnpq.br

researcher is defined as the largest number h for which the researcher has h publications with at least h citations each [16]. The main disadvantage of solely applying the h-index is that it favors researchers with long academic careers [6]. This index is also insensitive to authors with many papers with few or no citations, and those with few papers but many citations. In order to overcome these limitations, the h-index has also been adapted and combined with other indices to produce improved researcher rankings [11, 13, 16, 23]. In this vein, Bollen et al. [3] conducted an evaluation of different rankings by using 39 impact indicators and concluded that the concept of scientific impact is multi-dimensional and cannot be measured by using only one indicator.

Regarding cross-area ranking, according to Glänzel and Schubert [15] and Oliveira et al. [23], the performance of a researcher may significantly vary depending on his or her areas of activity. Furthermore, the impact factor of a journal[6] in basic and fundamental areas usually receive higher values than in specialized or applied areas [2]. In other words, bibliometric indicators provide a relative comparison that needs to be adapted or combined with other indicators as well as with additional information to cover the singularities of the desired classification. Despite some recent efforts to provide indices to enable the comparison of researchers across distinct fields [9, 15, 28], to best of our knowledge, our proposed approach is the first attempt to produce an aggregated ranking of researchers based upon their performance across distinct areas within the same field.

3. RANKING RESEARCHERS ACROSS MULTIPLE RESEARCH AREAS

Assessing the impact of scientific research is a challenging task, which has led to several productivity indices in the past, as discussed in the previous section. Nonetheless, the majority of these indices disregards the specificity of different research areas and assesses researchers based on global statistics, such as each researcher's publication volume and citation count. As these statistics may vary substantially across different areas, such indices may be unsuitable in a cross-area research evaluation effort. To illustrate this observation, Table 1 summarizes the distribution of publication volume and citations for researchers in the 23 CS areas represented in the dataset used in our evaluation, as described later in Section 4.1.

As observed from Table 1, different research areas have different publishing targets, with some focusing on conferences more than journals, and others doing the other way around. More importantly, researchers in different areas show clearly distinct publishing patterns, with the average volume and number of citations per researcher varying greatly within each area and across multiple areas. In order to provide an unbiased assessment of a researcher's productivity across multiple research areas, we argue that a productivity index should possess the following properties:

- *Plurality.* The productivity of a researcher should be assessed in all areas in which the researcher has published.
- *Diversity.* The profile of each research area should be considered when assessing a researcher's productivity.
- *Equality.* All research areas should be regarded as equally important and deserving of scientific merit.

To overcome the limitation of existing productivity indices and address the above requirements, we introduce a novel approach for ranking researchers across multiple research areas, by aggregating evidence of each researcher's productivity in each individual area. Inspired by ranking aggregation approaches in distributed information retrieval [7], our approach is generic and can be used to leverage any existing productivity index (e.g., publication volume and citation count, and even the well-known h-index) as evidence for ranking researchers across areas. In particular, our approach aims to produce a global ranking of researchers in a given field by tracking the position of each researcher in the rankings produced for the various research areas within that field. By doing so, we recognize the *plurality* of a researcher's publishing pattern, as previously demonstrated in Figure 1.

To formalize our approach, let s_i^a be the score assigned to researcher i with respect to a given research area a. This score is calculated adding up the contribution of each of the researcher's publications to the area a. To this end, we assume that each publication can be classified into multiple areas, based upon, e.g., the areas of interest of the venue where the publication appeared. Under this assumption, score s_i^a is defined as:

$$s_i^a = \sum_{j=1}^{n_i} \mathbf{1}_j^a \frac{s_{i,j}}{m_{i,j}}, \tag{1}$$

where n_i is researcher i's total number of publications, $\mathbf{1}_j^a$ is an indicator function (which is 1 if the researcher's j-th publication covers the area a and 0 otherwise), $s_{i,j}$ is the score conferred by this publication to researcher i,[7] and $m_{i,j}$ is the total number of areas covered by this publication. The latter quantity acts as a normalization factor, so as to ensure that the score $s_{i,j}$ is not accounted for more than once when aggregating the researcher's scores across multiple areas.

Given the aforementioned discrepancies between areas, as illustrated in Table 1, the area scores produced for a researcher may not be comparable across areas. In order to ensure that the *diversity* of areas is respected, we propose to use the percentile rank p_i^a of researcher i in each area a instead of the researcher's raw area score s_i^a. As a result, we consider the position of the researcher relatively to other researchers in the area. To formalize this intuition, we estimate the percentile rank p_i^a as:

$$p_i^a = \frac{l_i^a + 0.5e_i^a}{N^a}, \tag{2}$$

where N^a is the total number of active researchers in area a, l_i^a and e_i^a are the number of such researchers with a score lower than or equal to that of researcher i, respectively. The latter quantity ensures that tied researcher scores are accounted for appropriately [17].

Lastly, we must ensure that the *equality* between areas is respected. To this end, we introduce a novel ranking aggregation approach, which enforces an equal treatment between areas. In particular, our approach equates the percentile rank attained by a researcher in a particular area to

[6] http://thomsonreuters.com/products_services/science/free/essays/impact_factor/

[7] For a volume-based score, we have $s_{i,j} = 1, \forall j \in [1, n_i]$; for a citation-based score, $s_{i,j}$ is the total number of citations of researcher i's j-th publication.

the same percentile rank in other areas. Formally, let b_i denote the base area of researcher i, i.e., the area in which the researcher has the highest percentile rank p_i^a, according to:

$$b_i = \arg\max_{a \in A} p_i^a, \quad (3)$$

where A represents the set of all areas under consideration within a field. In order to aggregate the scores attained by a researcher across multiple areas, we first project the percentile rank attained by the researcher in each of her areas of activity onto her base area. As a result, we can further reward the researcher with the base area score corresponding to her percentile ranks in multiple areas. For example, a researcher with a percentile rank 90 in Databases and 30 in Computer Graphics should be rewarded with the scores corresponding to the 90 and 30 percentiles in Databases, assuming that this is the researcher's base area. Formally, the aggregated, cross-area score s_i of researcher i in light of all areas $a \in A$ in a field of interest is given by:

$$s_i = \sum_{a \in A} \frac{f_b(p_{i,a})}{f_b(1.0)}, \quad (4)$$

where the projection function $f_b(p_{i,a})$ maps the percentile rank $p_{i,a}$ attained by researcher i in area a to the score corresponding to this percentile in the researcher's base area b, and $f_b(1.0)$ returns the maximum score in b among all researchers in this area. This normalization step eliminates any bias towards researchers with a prolific base area (e.g., an area with a profile of high publication volume and citations), further enforcing the equality between areas.

4. EXPERIMENTAL METHODOLOGY

This section discusses the methodology underlying the experiments described in Section 5 for the evaluation of our proposed approach to rank researchers across areas. In particular, we aim to answer the following research questions:

Q1. Can we improve existing productivity indices with our cross-area ranking approach?

Q2. Can we effectively combine global and cross-area indices for an improved ranking?

Q3. Which other factors may impact our cross-area ranking approach?

In the remainder of this section, Section 4.1 describes the dataset used to support our investigation.The baseline indices derived from this dataset are discussed in Section 4.2. Lastly, Section 4.3 discusses the procedure for evaluating these baselines as well as our proposed ranking approach.

4.1 Publication Dataset

High-quality bibliometric indices typically depend on a high-quality dataset of publications. Digital libraries, such as DBLP and IEEE Xplore provide information about the authors, title, venue, and year of a publication. However, they do not provide the citation count of each publication or the h-index of each author. Then, online research-oriented search engines (such as Google Scholar, ArnetMiner and Microsoft Academic Search) do provide h-index and other bibliometric indices but their organization by author is cumbersome. Specifically, the publications of each author are not properly grouped due to name ambiguity: the same author may appear with distinct names (synonyms), or distinct authors may have similar names (polysems) [12], thus causing split and mixed citations [20]. Furthermore, the collection indexed by such search engines may comprise everything that a person has ever authored, including non-scientific pieces, technical reports and web pages.

Therefore, we need to build a dataset with the following features: it includes only qualified publications which appeared in conference proceedings and journals; it correctly groups publications and its authors; it provides citation figures (which allows to calculate the h-index for each author); it allows to identify the area (or areas) of each publication. To do so, the next sections explain: the original data source used as base for this complex dataset (Section 4.1.1), its expansion to include journal articles (Section 4.1.2), how it was disambiguated (Section 4.1.3), and how its publications were classified into areas (Section 4.1.4).

4.1.1 Data Source for Conference Publications

We got an initial dataset from the SHINE (Simple H-INdex Estimator) project[8], which collected conference publications based on a list of venues provided by the Brazilian Computer Society's (SBC) Special Interest Groups. Each SBC SIG provided the list of conferences that cover its topics of interest. The dataset then aggregates one set of conferences for each CS area. Specifically, the SHINE dataset contains more than 800,000 publications from approximately 1,800 conferences, covering 23 CS areas, and 7.5 millions of citations, as collected in the beginning of 2011. We notice that each conference may have been suggested by more than one SIG.Table 1 shows the coverage for each of the 23 CS areas, in which the average for all areas is 88%. For 19 of those areas, SHINE covers more than 80% of the conferences from the reference list (suggested by SBC SIGs). For 13 areas, the coverage is above 90%, and for only one area the coverage is smaller than 70%.

4.1.2 Adding Journal Publications

The SHINE dataset covers only publications from conferences. In order to get publications from journals, we first obtained the list of all CS journals ranked by Qualis[9]. Specifically, Qualis is an initiative of CAPES (the Brazilian Ministry of Education agency in charge of evaluating all graduate programs in Brazil, among other goals) for rating publication venues. In order to get the complete article references, we merged the list of journal titles with the DBLP XML dataset by using the International Standard Serial Number (ISSN) or, in the absence of ISSN, the journal title. With this effort, the original SHINE dataset was expanded with 271,000 articles from 188 journals.

4.1.3 Author Name Disambiguation

Having all bibliographic data of conference papers and journal articles into one dataset, the next step is to identify the researchers and group their publications accordingly. In this step, we had to deal with the ambiguity among the author names existing in the dataset. Hence, we have applied a state-of-art Heuristic-Based Hierarchical Method for name disambiguation [10]. This method works based on the

[8]`http://shine.icomp.ufam.edu.br`
[9]`http://qualis.capes.gov.br`

Table 1: **Number of covered conferences and journals and summary statistics (average, standard deviation, and median) of the distributions of publication volume and citations for researchers in 23 CS areas.**

Research Area	#Conf.	#Jour.	Volume			Citations		
			Avg.	SD.	Med.	Avg.	SD.	Med.
Algorithms and Theory	354	188	10.65	9.97	8	95.98	151.95	41
Artificial Intelligence	264	163	9.82	13.24	5	72.56	119.90	26
Collaboration Systems	10	14	8.25	16.02	2	49.00	101.16	6
Computational Biology	25	28	2.55	2.53	2	14.73	19.17	7
Computer Graphics and Image Processing	108	105	9.95	10.97	5	58.34	115.63	13
Computer Networks and Distributed Systems	297	161	13.46	18.77	6	84.95	177.22	29
Computer Science Education	35	37	3.25	5.04	1	10.49	23.45	1
Databases	184	127	8.55	13.99	4	73.30	182.51	12
Fault Tolerant Systems	32	7	2.45	3.02	1	23.35	54.80	5
Formalism	49	68	2.67	4.13	1	17.51	32.93	4
Game and Entertainment	17	6	2.37	3.06	1	13.97	56.92	0
Geoinformatics	14	11	4.59	7.92	2	20.95	42.42	2
Hardware, Architecture and Embedded Systems	124	112	5.61	12.36	2	34.93	122.71	5
Health Informatics	25	67	3.56	5.83	2	13.70	34.21	3
Human-Computer Interaction	21	31	2.71	3.19	1	17.48	26.15	6
Information Systems	487	188	22.02	19.15	17	160.01	230.76	75.5
Music Computing	15	6	2.59	3.28	2	4.21	8.21	0
Natural Language Processing	59	43	4.26	4.41	2	37.80	95.34	7
Neural Networks	84	82	7.83	12.10	4	40.52	77.37	14
Programming Languages	56	23	3.81	4.46	2	47.23	104.88	8
Robotics	56	63	3.24	3.80	2	29.71	70.27	4
Security	100	98	10.05	12.81	4	31.61	142.57	3
Software Engineering	95	42	7.72	12.71	3	57.98	144.89	13

similarity of the usual citation information such as work and venue titles, and considers the coauthorship network as well.

4.1.4 *Classification into Areas*

The final step is to classify each publication according to one (or more) CS area. Given that the conference papers were already classified (as given by the SBC SIGs), all journal articles had also to be classified into the same 23 areas. To do so, we applied the LAC (Lazy Associative Classifier) algorithm [27], which uses associative rules to classify items. As one journal article could potentially be associated to more than one area, we have employed the multi-label classification version of the LAC algorithm [26].

Specifically, we used the already classified conference papers as the training set. Then, we used the journal articles as the test set. The classification explored title and venue as main features. LAC estimates the probability of each instance being classified in each class. Therefore, we have specified a minimum threshold to select the areas of each article. This threshold was tuned so that the distribution in the test set matched that of the training set. As a result: the average number of articles in each area is 24,424; the maximum number of articles is in *Algorithms and Theory* with 172,799; and the minimum in *Music Computing* with only 7 articles. This number also follows the ratio from Table 1.

4.2 Ranking Baselines

Having the dataset, our next step is to define which indexes (or metrics) we will compare our approach against. We have chosen the same ones from academic social platforms (such as ArnetMiner, Microsoft Academic Search and Google Scholar): volume of publications, citation count and h-index. In volume of publications, the researchers are sorted in descending order of the total of their publications. In citation count, the researchers are sorted in descending order of the sum of all citations received by its publications. In h-index, the researchers are sorted in descending order of their h-Index [16].

4.3 Evaluation Procedure

In the following, Section 4.3.1 defines the ground-truth used in our evaluation, whereas Section 4.3.2 describes the evaluation metric used to report our experimental results.

4.3.1 *Evaluation Ground-Truth*

The first step in this experimental setup is defining the ground truth to which our result will be compared. Since there is no world wide ranking for computer scientists, we have decided to use a real ranking for Brazilians only. Specifically, each year, CNPq distributes research fellowships for researchers from all fields. To do so, CNPq bases its decisions on reports from special committees created for each field, where each committee is responsible for evaluating all researchers who have applied for such a fellowship in that field. The fellowships are awarded in two categories. The first category comprises 4 subcategories (1A, 1B, 1C, 1D) and each of those includes a research grant. The second category (2) is the entrance one and does not include a grant. Currently 14,713 researchers from 48 different fields have such scholarships. For Computer Science, there are 406 researchers distributed over the categories as illustrated in Figure 2. Note that 32% out of the 406 researchers are attributed to category 1, and 68% to category 2.

Even though CNPq considers much more than publications in its evaluation (e.g., a research project proposal and international insertion), the CS committee emphasizes that a qualified set of publications is a fundamental requirement for success[10]. Also, given that such a rank is produced by specialized committees, it seems reasonable to consider their resulting rank as a ground truth in our experimental evaluation. To do so, we evaluated all publications of researchers

[10]`http://memoria.cnpq.br/cas/ca-cc.htm`

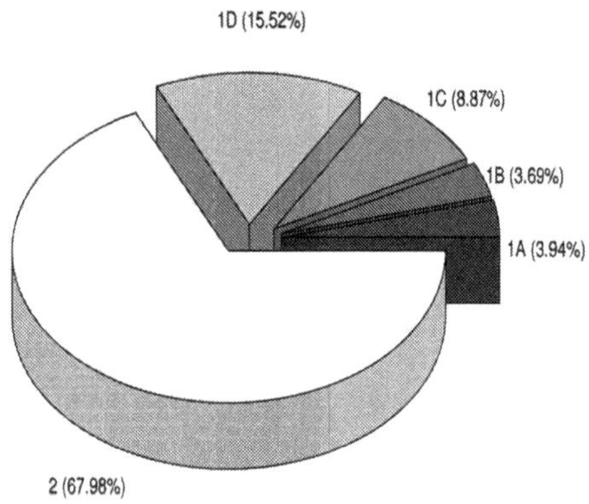

Figure 2: Distribution of CS researchers according to the ground-truth assessment provided by CNPq.

classified by CNPq in categories 1 or 2 in 2011, and disregarded all further publications from our base dataset.

4.3.2 Evaluation Metric

In order to evaluate our ranking approach as well as the baselines described in Section 4.2 in light of the ground-truth defined in Section 4.3.1, we use the discounted cumulative gain (DCG) metric [19]. This metric has been widely used to evaluate ranking approaches in several information retrieval tasks, most notably web search [8]. In particular, DCG adopts a non-binary notion of relevance, by assessing a given ranking based upon a graded scale, from less relevant to more relevant. In addition, this metric applies a log-based discount factor to model the fact that relevant items ranked high are preferred over the lower ranked ones [18]. Formally, the DCG at a rank position k can be defined as:

$$\text{DCG@}k = \sum_{i=1}^{k} \frac{2^{g_i} - 1}{\log_2(i+1)}, \quad (5)$$

where g_i denotes the non-binary relevance grade associated with the item ranked at the i-th position. For our particular case, we define a graded relevance scale based upon each researcher's classification according to CNPq, as defined in Section 4.3.1. Specifically, we map the CNPq categories 1A, 1B, 1C, 1D and 2 to the relevance labels 5, 4, 3, 2 and 1, respectively. Finally, to bind the reported effectiveness within the interval [0,1], we use the normalized version of DCG, denoted nDCG, which is obtained by dividing the DCG@k value given by Equation (5) by the best obtainable value at the same rank cutoff k. In our experiments, we report the effectiveness of the different approaches across multiple k values, from 5 to 100, with steps of 5.

5. EXPERIMENTAL EVALUATION

In this section, we address the research questions stated in Section 4 in order to validate our proposed approach for ranking researchers across multiple scientific areas. In particular, Section 5.1 addresses research question Q1, by instantiating our ranking approach to produce cross-area versions of popular productivity indices. Section 5.2 addresses Q2, by assessing the impact of publication volume and citations as features for producing an effective ranking of researchers. Lastly, Section 5.3 addresses Q3, by performing a failure analysis of our produced rankings.

5.1 Single-Index Ranking

In order to address research question Q1, on the effectiveness of our proposed cross-area ranking approach, we contrast it to one of the most widely used productivity indices nowadays, namely, the h-index [16]. As discussed in Section 2, the h-index can be seen as a combination of the publication volume and the number of citations attained by a researcher. To obtain a cross-area version of the h-index, here called the *ca*-index ("ca" for cross-area), we propagate the global h-index from a researcher to each of his or her publications, and from each publication to the areas covered by the publication, according to Equation (1).

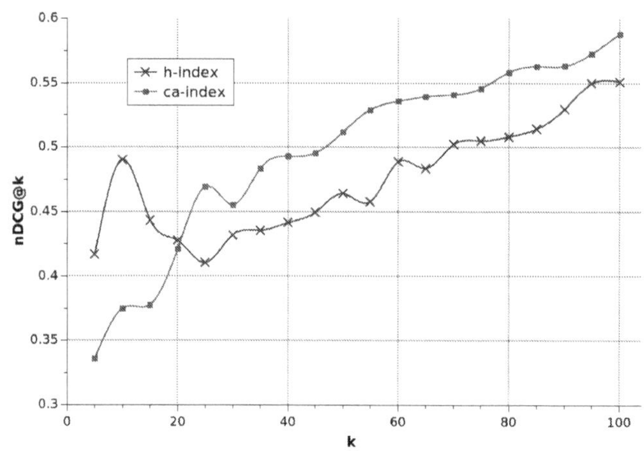

Figure 3: Comparison between researcher rankings based on the standard h-index and our ca-index.

Figure 3 compares the ranking produced by our ca-index against that produced by the original h-index, in terms of their attained nDCG@k, for a rank cutoff k varying from 5 to 100. From the figure, we first observe that our ca-index consistently outperforms the standard h-index for almost the entire range of k. The exception is for $k \leq 20$, in which case the standard h-index is the best performing. Upon further analysis, we noted that the observed difference in these top ranks is due to the presence of relevant researchers with a high specialization in only a few areas. Indeed, as shown in Figure 4, the cross-area normalization performed by ca-index reduces the dispersion of scores among the researchers classified by CNPq in each of the five considered relevance levels. Such a normalization may smooth out the performance of individual researchers, eventually missing over-specialized outliers. On the other hand, it allows for a clearer characterization of the researchers within each level, and for a better distinction between researchers across different levels, as denoted by the strictly descending median score from level 1A towards level 2 in Figure 4(b).

To further investigate the reasons behind the improvements observed in Figures 3 and 4, we analyze the impact of our cross-area ranking approach separately on the two sources of evidence underlying the h-index: publication volume and citations. Figures 5 and 6 show the results of these analyses, contrasting publication volume and citations against their counterpart cross-area indices, ca-volume and ca-citation, respectively. From Figure 5, we first observe that the estimation of publication volume is massively improved by our cross-area ranking approach. Indeed, ca-

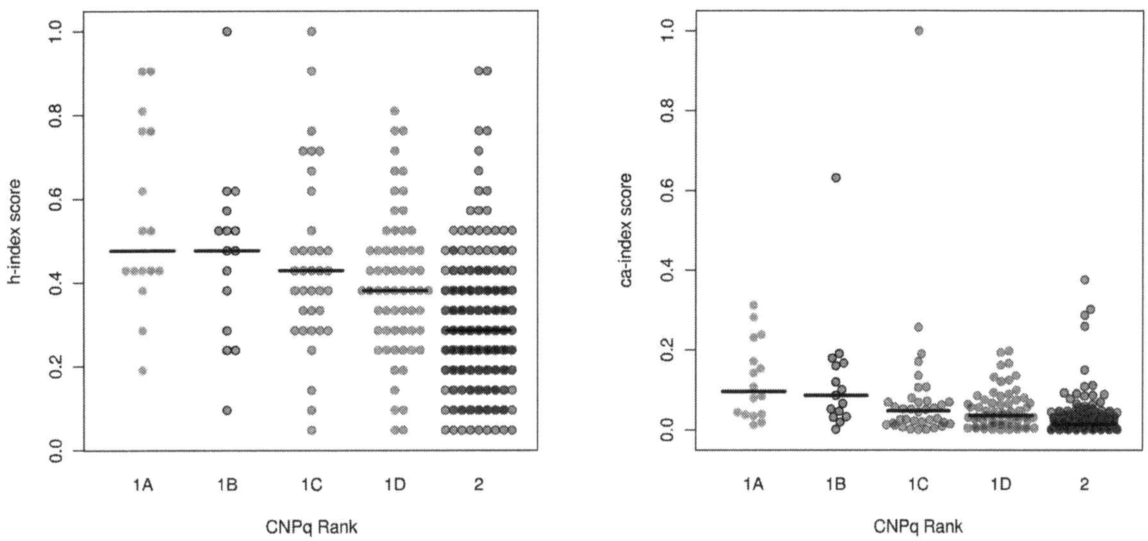

(a) h-index score distribution

(b) ca-index score distribution

Figure 4: Distribution of (a) h-index and (b) ca-index scores across the five considered relevance levels.

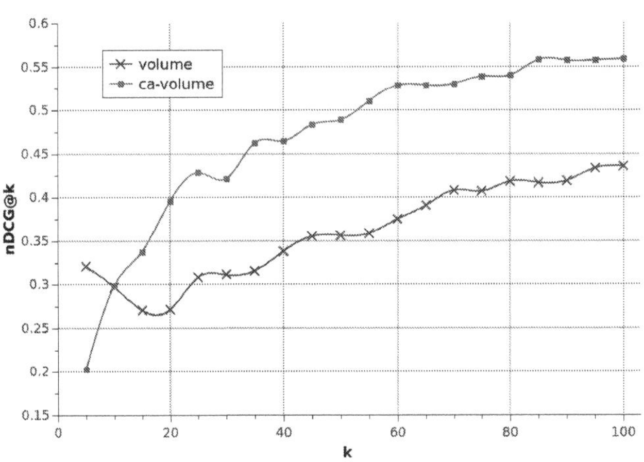

Figure 5: Comparison between researcher rankings based on publication volume and our ca-volume.

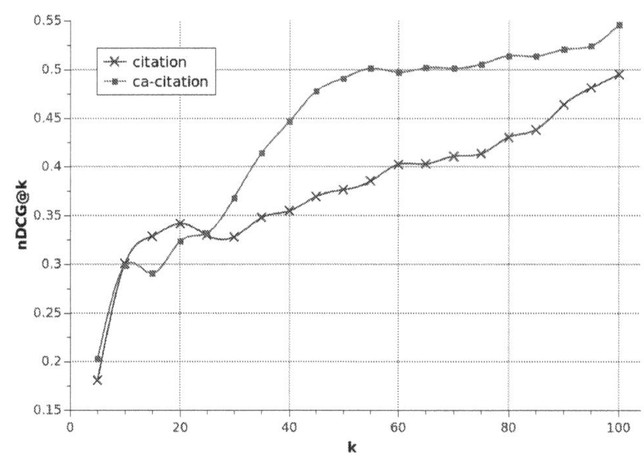

Figure 6: Comparison between researcher rankings based on citation count volume and our ca-citation.

volume outperforms the standard publication volume index by a large margin from the ranking cutoff 10 onward. A similar trend is observed for ca-citation compared to the standard citation count in Figure 6, albeit with slightly less pronounced improvements compared to those observed in Figure 5.

Lastly, to further demonstrate the improvements brought by our approach for better estimating both publication volume and citation count, Figure 7 shows the dispersion of the scores produced using these two indices, prior to and after the application of our cross-area normalization. From the figure, we can observe that our approach acts as a correction for the distortion caused by simply counting volume and citations without regards to the specificity of different areas. Indeed, both ca-volume (Figure 7(b)) and ca-citation (Figure 7(d)) show a strictly descending median score from the highest rank (1A) to the lowest (2), while their global counterparts (i.e., volume in Figure 7(a) and citation in Figure 7(c)) fail to correctly align the two most distinguished categories, namely, 1A and 1B.

Overall, the results in this section answer research question Q1, by demonstrating the effectiveness of our approach for ranking researchers across multiple areas of a scientific field. Indeed, as shown in this section, our approach improves upon standard productivity indices based on publication volume and citation count, as well as upon their combination, as embodied by the well-known h-index.

5.2 Multi-Index Ranking

The results in the previous section attest the effectiveness of our cross-area ranking approach in contrast to standard productivity indices. On the other hand, the relatively higher performance attained by these global indices at early ranks suggests that they provide complementary evidence to that exploited by our approach. To investigate whether this is the case, in this section, we address research question

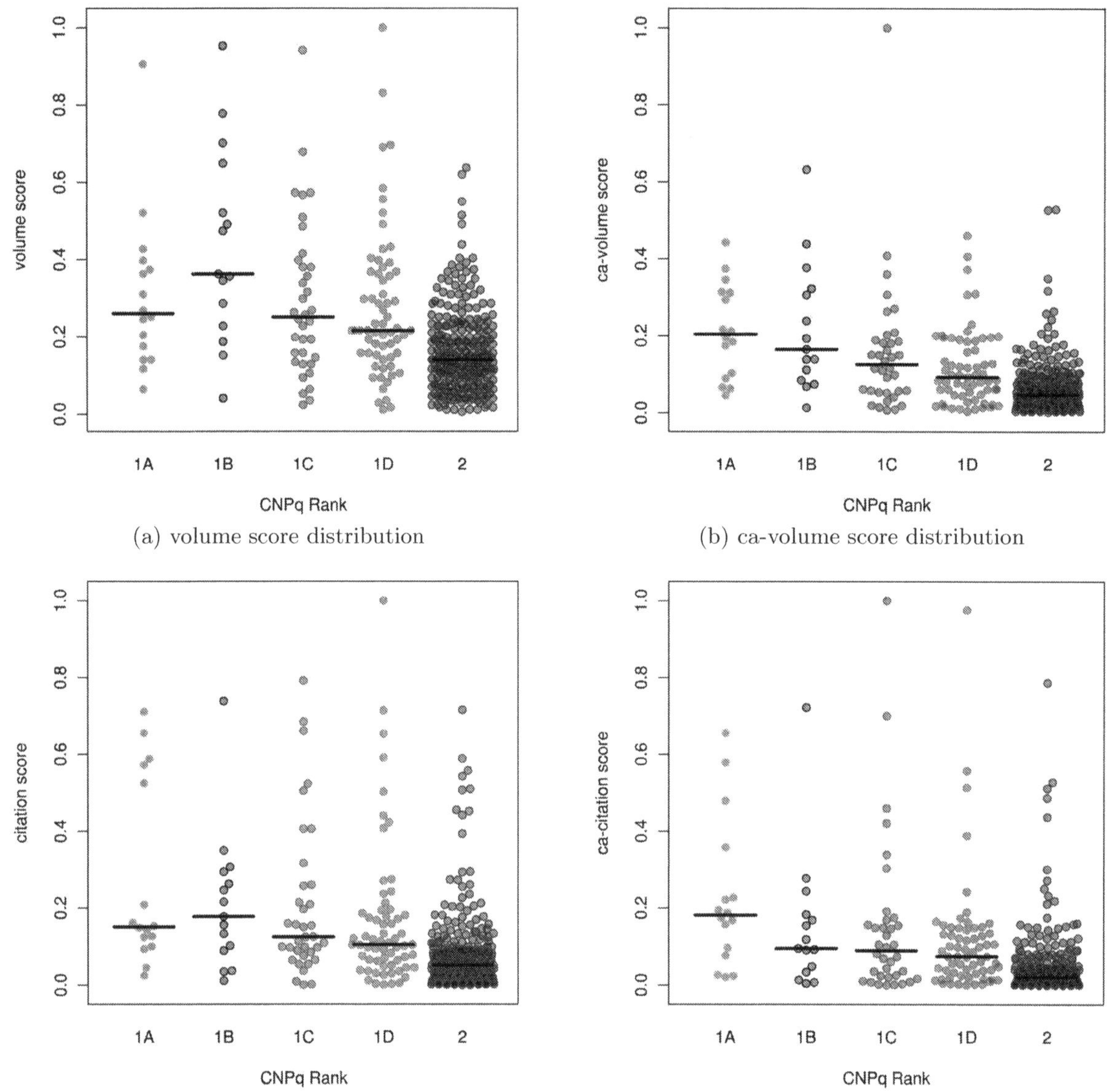

(a) volume score distribution

(b) ca-volume score distribution

(c) citation score distribution

(d) ca-citation score distribution

Figure 7: Distribution of (a) volume, (b) ca-volume, (c) citation, and (d) ca-citation scores across the five considered relevance levels.

Q2, by assessing the potential for combining the standard h-index with our novel ca-index. To this end, we linearly combine these two indices, giving equal weights to both in the final combination. We leave the automatic identification of optimal weights from the available data as future work.

Figure 8 shows the results of this experiment. In particular, the figure shows curves corresponding to h-index, ca-index, and their combination. From the figure, we observe that the combination h-index+ca-index performs at least as effectively as ca-index (the top performing of the two individual indices) in terms of nDCG for almost all considered ranking cutoffs. This observation answers research question Q2, by demonstrating that there is scope for further improving our ca-index, particularly at higher ranks, by combining it with other indices, such as the global h-index.

5.3 Failure Analysis

This section further analyses our ca-index ranking results in light of the ground-truth classification of Brazilian CS researchers provided by CNPq. It specifically addresses research question Q3, on which other factors may impact our index results. It also discusses how our ranking may be used for spotting researchers that may be shortlisted for promotion or demotion (of course, subject to further analysis).

In order to aid this comparison, Table 2 presents a confusion matrix, organizing the universe of researchers under consideration according to their classification by CNPq and by our ca-index approach.[11] In particular, each cell c_{ij} in

[11]The classification by ca-index is performed by splitting the score distribution produced by ca-index into five categories with the same sizes as the corresponding categories in the ground-truth produced by CNPq, as depicted in Figure 2.

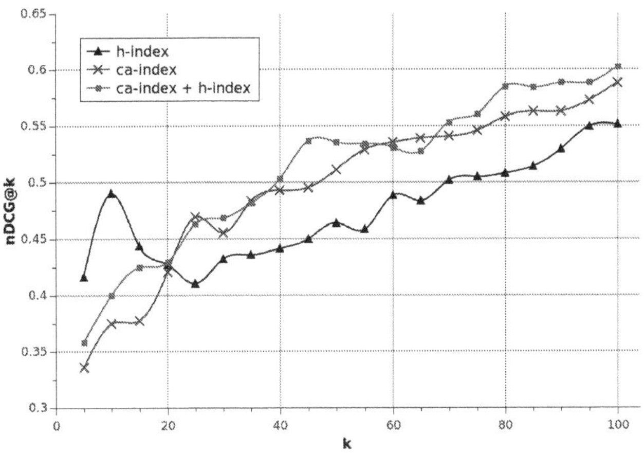

Figure 8: Comparison between researcher rankings based on the standard h-index, our ca-index, and their linear combination.

Table 2 presents the percentage of researchers classified by CNPq in the i-th category and by our ca-index in the j-th category. Note that percent figures are computed with respect to *all* considered researchers, as opposed to only those in a particular category. In other words, row 1A shows how ca-index has ranked the researchers that are currently on CNPq category 1A. For example, ca-index has classified 0.75% of CNPq researchers 1A as 1B (as shown by the first row, second column), and so on.

CNPq \ ca-index	1A	1B	1C	1D	2
1A	1.01	0.75	0.75	0.5	1.01
1B	0.75	0.75	0.5	1.51	0.25
1C	0.75	0.75	1.76	3.02	2.76
1D	1.01	1.01	1.76	3.52	8.54
2	0.5	0.5	4.27	7.04	55.03

Table 2: Confusion matrix for the rankings induced by ca-index (columns) and the CNPq classification (rows). The highlighted cells show informative discrepancies between the classification of category 1 and category 2 researchers. Percent figures are computed with respect to *all* considered researchers.

The percentage of researchers correctly classified (according to CNPq) is presented in the main diagonal (for a total or 62%). If all researchers were perfectly ranked, the main diagonal would add up to 100%, whereas the remaining cells would be 0. Overall, the values in the main diagonal are relatively high, particularly for the classification of researchers in category 2. The observed discrepancies can be explained mainly because CNPq uses other sources of evidence to rank researchers, such as their number of graduate students, contribution to innovation, research group leadership, and participation in international committees.

A similar analysis can be conducted by grouping together all researchers in the subcategories 1A-1D into a broad category 1. The major difference between CNPq categories 1 and 2 is that researchers in the former get an extra grant (besides a regular scholarship stipend). Therefore, a classification of researchers in either of these two categories can be useful for CNPq for two main reasons: to decide which researchers should receive a scholarship and which should also receive a grant. Note that the distinction between category 1 and category 2 researchers is also the most time consuming one, as most researchers fall into the latter category. In this binary classification scenario, our approach produces a correct classification for 75% of all considered researchers (20% in category 1 and 55% in category 2).

Another interesting way of interpreting the results in Table 2 is by considering that this table summarizes the distribution of scholarships related to the researchers' production. Therefore, these results may aid the decision making process by pointing out researchers that could be potentially promoted or demoted. Specifically, all researchers above the main diagonal could be further considered for a demotion, whereas those below the main diagonal could be further considered for a promotion. For example, the highlighted row at the bottom of the table represents researchers ranked by ca-index in category 1 that currently have a category 2 scholarship. Those could be further analyzed and face a "promotion" to category 1. Likewise, the highlighted column on the right represents researchers ranked in category 2 that are currently in CNPq category 1. These researchers could also be further analyzed and face a "demotion" to category 2.

Normally, such decisions should not be automatically made, because it is also important to understand why such discrepancies (for more or less) appear in Table 2. For example, the researchers at row 1A column 2 (CNPq 1A ranked by ca-index as 2) may be those who have stronger contributions other than publications. On the other hand, the researchers at row 2 column 1A (CNPq 2 ranked by ca-index as 1A) may be those who have many publications but weaker overall profiles (for example, they may not have formed PhD students yet).

6. CONCLUDING REMARKS

In this work, we have addressed the problem of ranking researchers by their scientific production. Motivated by defining a fair ranking process, our ranking is tuned to work across different research areas, a feature that distinguishes it from other previous work. To do so, our ca-index focuses on the principles of plurality, diversity, and equality of research areas. Then, it builds upon individual ranks for each area by aggregating them into one cross-area ranking.

Moreover, each year, specialized committees must evaluate hundreds of researchers for dozens of scholarships, job positions, grants, and so on. Applying ca-index quickly provides an insight on the overall production of the researchers, with the extra benefit of being tailored to work across areas. Furthermore, as illustrated by the CNPq case study, ca-index does indeed point out outliers that are worth further analysis for demotions and promotions.

Our approach was also further evaluated and compared to widely used indices such as the h-index. Our experimental evaluation has shown that ca-index outperforms the h-index when considering a comparison against our ground truth. The results for a multi-index ranking have also shown the potential for combining ca-index to other commonly used indices. As future work, we plan to expand even further our approach by considering other indicators from the researchers' profiles (including years since they have been awarded their PhD and their number of supervised students, for example). Finally, we aim to apply the ca-index to other fields, with different characteristics.

7. ACKNOWLEDGMENTS

The authors would like to thank Thiago C. M. Salles and Itamar S. V. Hata for their invaluable help with the disambiguation and classification of the SHINE dataset, as well as the team behind the SHINE project, notably Altigran S. da Silva. The authors would also like to acknowledge their individual grants from the CNPq and FAPEMIG agencies.

References

[1] B. M. Althouse, J. D. West, C. T. Bergstrom, and T. Bergstrom. Differences in impact factor across fields and over time. *JASIST*, 60(1):27–34, 2009.

[2] S. D. J. Barbosa and C. S. de Souza. INTERACTING WITH PUBLIC POLICY: Are HCI researchers an endangered species in Brazil? *ACM Interactions Magazine*, 18(3):69–71, 2011.

[3] J. Bollen, H. V. de Sompel, A. A. Hagberg, and R. Chute. A principal component analysis of 39 scientific impact measures. *CoRR*, abs/0902.2183, 2009.

[4] L. Bornmann and H.-D. Daniel. Universality of Citation Distributions - A Validation of Radicchi et al.'s Relative Indicator cf = c/c0 at the Micro Level Using Data From Chemistry. *JASIST*, 60(8):1664–1670, 2009.

[5] L. Bornmann, R. Mutz, and H.-D. Daniel. Are there better indices for evaluation purposes than the *h* index? A comparison of nine different variants of the *h* index using data from biomedicine. *JASIST*, 59(5):830–837, 2008.

[6] Q. L. Burrell. Hirsch's index: A stochastic model. *J. Informetrics*, 1(1):16–25, 2007.

[7] J. Callan. Distributed information retrieval. In W. B. Croft, editor, *Advances in Information Retrieval*, chapter 5, pages 127–150. Kluwer Academic Publishers, 2000.

[8] C. L. A. Clarke, N. Craswell, and I. Soboroff. Overview of the TREC 2009 Web track. In *Procs. of TREC*, Gaithersburg, MD, USA, 2009.

[9] J. Claro and C. A. V. Costa. A made-to-measure indicator for cross-disciplinary bibliometric ranking of researchers performance. *Scientometrics*, 86(1):113–123, 2011.

[10] R. G. Cota, A. A. Ferreira, C. Nascimento, M. A. Gonçalves, and A. H. F. Laender. An unsupervised heuristic-based hierarchical method for name disambiguation in bibliographic citations. *JASIST*, 61(9):1853–1870, 2010.

[11] L. Egghe. Theory and practise of the *g*-index. *Scientometrics*, 69(1):131–152, 2006.

[12] A. A. Ferreira, M. A. Gonçalves, and A. H. F. Laender. A brief Survey of Automatic Methods for Author Name Disambiguation. *SIGMOD Record*, 41(2):15–26, 2012.

[13] F. Franceschini and D. A. Maisano. Proposals for evaluating the *regularity* of a scientist's research output. *Scientometrics*, 88(1):279–295, 2011.

[14] V. P. Freire and D. R. Figueiredo. Ranking in collaboration networks using a group based metric. *J. Braz. Comp. Soc.*, 17(4):255–266, 2011.

[15] W. Glänzel and A. Schubert. A new classification scheme of science fields and subfields designed for scientometric evaluation purposes. *Scientometrics*, 56(3):357–367, 2003.

[16] J. E. Hirsch. An index to quantify an individual's scientific research output. *PNAS*, 102(46):16569–16572, 2005.

[17] R. J. Hyndman and Y. Fan. Sample quantiles in statistical packages. *The American Statistician*, 50:361–365, 1996.

[18] B. J. Jansen, A. Spink, and T. Saracevic. Real life, real users, and real needs: A study and analysis of user queries on the Web. *Inf. Process. Manage.*, 36(2):207–227, 2000.

[19] K. Järvelin and J. Kekäläinen. Cumulated gain-based evaluation of IR techniques. *ACM Trans. Inf. Syst.*, 20(4):422–446, 2002.

[20] D. Lee, J. Kang, P. Mitra, C. L. Giles, and B.-W. On. Are your citations clean? *Commun. ACM*, 50(12):33–38, 2007.

[21] L. Leydesdorff. Alternatives to the journal impact factor: I3 and the top-10% (or top-25%?) of the most-highly cited papers. *Scientometrics*, 92(2):355–365, 2012.

[22] J. Lundberg. Lifting the crown - citation z-score. *J. Informetrics*, 1(2):145–154, 2007.

[23] E. A. Oliveira, E. A. Colosimo, D. R. Martelli, I. G. Quirino, M. C. Oliveira, L. S. Lima, A. C. Simões E Silva, and H. Martelli-Júnior. Comparison of Brazilian researchers in clinical medicine: are criteria for ranking well-adjusted? *Scientometrics*, 90(2):429–443, 2012.

[24] I. Podlubny. Comparison of scientific impact expressed by the number of citations in different fields of science. *Scientometrics*, 64(1):95–99, 2005.

[25] F. Radicchi, S. Fortunato, and C. Castellano. Universality of citation distributions: Toward an objective measure of scientific impact. *PNAS*, 105:17268–17272, 2008.

[26] A. Veloso, W. Meira, Jr., M. Gonçalves, and M. Zaki. Multi-label lazy associative classification. In *Procs. of ECML/PKDD*, pages 605–612, 2007.

[27] A. Veloso, W. Meira Jr., and M. J. Zaki. Lazy associative classification. In *Procs. of ICDM*, pages 645–654, Washington, DC, USA, 2006.

[28] L. Waltman, N. J. van Eck, T. N. van Leeuwen, M. S. Visser, and A. F. J. van Raan. Towards a new crown indicator: Some theoretical considerations. *CoRR*, abs/1003.2167, 2010.

IFME: Information Filtering by Multiple Examples with Under-Sampling in a Digital Library Environment

Mingzhu Zhu, Chao Xu, Yi-Fang Brook Wu
Information Systems Department
New Jersey Institute of Technology
Newark, NJ 07102, USA
{mz59, cx26, wu}@njit.edu

ABSTRACT
With the amount of digitalized documents increasing exponentially, it is more difficult for users to keep up to date with the knowledge in their domain. In this paper, we present a framework named IFME (Information Filtering by Multiple Examples) in a digital library environment to help users identify the literature related to their interests by leveraging the Positive Unlabeled learning (PU learning). Using a few relevant documents provided by a user and considering the documents in an online database as unlabeled data (called U), it ranks the documents in U using a PU learning algorithm. From the experimental results, we found that while the approach performed well when a large set of relevant feedback documents were available, it performed relatively poor when the relevant feedback documents were few. We improved IFME by combining PU learning with under-sampling to tune the performance. Using Mean Average Precision (MAP), our experimental results indicated that with under-sampling, the performance improved significantly even when the size of P was small. We believe the PU learning based IFME framework brings insights to develop more effective digital library systems.

Categories and Subject Descriptors
H.3.3 [**Information Search and Retrieval**]: Information Retrieval

General Terms
Algorithms, Experimentation

Keywords
Information Retrieval, Positive Unlabeled Learning, Text Classification, Search by Multiple Examples, Relevance Feedback

1. INTRODUCTION
Most researchers keep themselves up to date with the literature by using keyword-based information retrieval (IR) and digital library systems such as Google Scholar, ACM digital libraries, PubMed, etc. However, it is difficult to use keyword-based search to get all the relevant literature on an idea, or a research topic, because most of the knowledge in the modern era is a combination of concepts, topics, methods, and ideas.

Traditionally, handcrafted controlled vocabularies are used for improving the efficiency and comprehensiveness of information retrieval, but their effectiveness is largely depending on the quality of the controlled vocabularies. Besides, extensive human input and oversight are needed to create and maintain them.

Theoretically, a search task can be accomplished by using a keyword-based search engine. However, depending on the complexity of the information need, the information seeking process might require a few iterations of searching and browsing of the search results. In this paper, we aim to improve the information seeking process with machine learning approaches.

If a user has a long-term information need, it should be relatively easy for him/her to select relevant documents from search results or provide relevant documents gathered from previous searches. Under that assumption, we propose a framework named Information Filtering by Multiple Examples, which is denoted as IFME here, to assist users to explore relevant articles from a digital library. In this framework, users can express their information needs using a set of relevant documents. Then the documents in the digital library will be ranked based on the relevant documents provided by the user. It is not ideal to extract keywords from user provided examples to form a long query, as the modern keyword-based search systems are not capable at providing good results for long queries. We apply PU learning [1] to solve the ranking problem in the IFME framework by treating the documents in the digital library as unlabeled data, and the relevant documents from the user as the positive data P, then a PU learning model is trained to rank the unlabeled data.

There are many approaches of using unlabeled data to improve the performance of the supervised learning algorithms. The specific approach of using a small size of labeled set and a large size of unlabeled set is called semi-supervised learning, where positive, negative examples and unlabeled data are needed. As a special case of semi-supervised learning, the Positive Unlabeled Learning (PU learning) works on only a positive set P and an unlabeled set U, which is perfectly suited for the digital library environment where there is a large collection of documents in the database and users can easily provide/identify some relevant documents as examples for the system to learn from.

The PU learning method we incorporate in our framework is proposed in [2], but our focus is not to build a classifier for generalization. Instead, we follow a transductive learning paradigm aiming at ranking the positive examples in the unlabeled data as high as possible to help users identify more documents similar to the provided examples. In this paper, the method is denoted as Tranducitve Positive Unlabled Learning (TPULearning). It simply assumes the unlabeled data U as negative to train a traditional classifier (i.e. SVM) with the positive examples P. The classifier is in turn applied on the same unlabeled data to make predictions on the probability that an instance in U is positive. Then the unlabeled data is ranked based on the predicted probability values.

JCDL '13, July 22–26, 2013, Indianapolis, Indiana, USA.

One problem of the TPULearning is that when the size of P (denoted as |P|) is small, the performance is poor. It is very common in search engine or digital library environment where users provide very few relevant feedback documents. We propose a novel method, called USTPULearning, which combines under-sampling with the TPULearning method to improve its performance. The main goals of this research are:

1) Proposing a PU learning based IFME framework in a digital library environment;

2) Proposing a novel method that combines under-sampling and the TPULearning to significantly improve the performance of the original TPULearning method.

The rest of the paper is organized as follows: in section 2 we describe the related work in PU learning; in section 3, we present the research framework; in section 4 we illustrate the experimental framework. We conclude the paper with a summary of the research in section 5.

2. RELATED WORK

There are many techniques for learning with unlabeled data. Nigam et al. [5] use a small set of labeled instances and a large set of unlabeled instances to build a classifier. When both positive and unlabeled data are available, the positive training data can be used to estimate the positive class' conditional probability, p(x|+), and the unlabeled data can be used to estimate p(x). With the prior p(+), which is known or can be estimated using data from other sources, the negative class' conditional probability can be obtained as follows:

$$p(x \mid -)=(p(x)-p(+)p(x \mid +))/(1-p(+))$$

Denis et al. adopt the conditional probability p(x|-) to perform text classification with Naïve Bayes methods [6]. Liu et al. adopt an Expectation Maximization (EM) algorithm and naïve Bayesian classification method to separate positive and negative instances [8]. Yu et al. propose a mapping-convergence algorithm for PU learning. There are two stages in their algorithm: mapping stage and convergence stage. In the mapping stage, they perform initial approximation of reliable negative instances (denoted as RN). In the convergence stage, they iteratively run an internal classifier that maximizes margins to progressively achieve the true boundary of the positive class in the feature space [9].

Most PU learning algorithms belong to such a two-stage strategy category. The inherent problem of this strategy is that the newly trained classifier, which is based on RN, may have a similar decision boundary to the classifier that is trained based on the original labeled data, as RN are usually far from the decision boundary. Another problem of this approach is that the negative instances usually are from different sources. Some researchers suggest that negative instances from diverse sources may be harmful to the performance of supervised learning algorithms [10].

Another direction of using PU learning is identifying positive examples from unlabeled data directly. Elkan et al. describe an iterative relabeling algorithm, which assumes that the unlabeled instances are negative to learn a traditional classifier iteratively. The authors show that their algorithm works well in identifying biomedical documents related to proteins [2]. In the IFME framework, we choose this direction.

Zhang et al [13] also use multiple examples to express user's information needs. They consider the problem of QBME (Query-By-Multiple-Examples) from the perspective of PU learning in two scenarios: online queries and offline queries. For the online queries, they propose a one-class SVM learning from the query set; for offline queries, they propose to learn a SVM learning from the query set as well as the entire corpus. Our research is different from [13] in that we follow an iterative re-ranking approach of TPULearning and adopt under-sampling to improve each run of the approach.

3. THE FRAMEWORK

In this section, we describe the proposed framework (shown in Figure 1). The iterative document re-ranking using PU learning is the core of the framework.

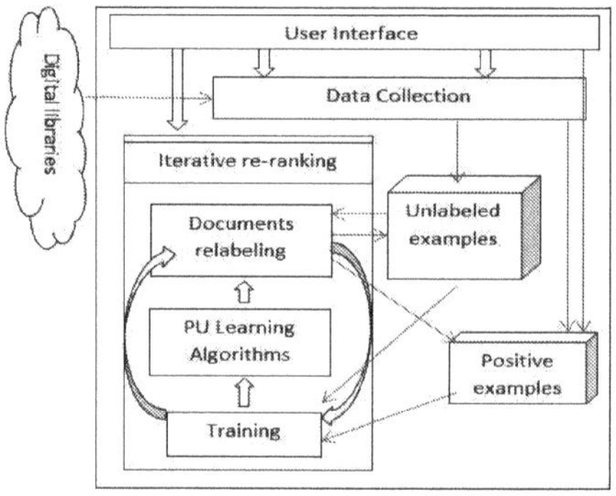

Figure 1. PU learning based IFME framework.

Through the interface, a user can initialize the scope of the text collection to form the searching space. This is helpful for the users who are only interested in the articles contained some specific keywords, or published in some specific journals. In default, all of the documents in the digital library form the searching space.

After the initialization, the user can provide relevant feedback documents to express their information needs. The feedback documents can be the documents in the system similar to the binder function in ACM digital library, or documents that are from other sources such as the documents in the user's local computer. These feedback documents form the positive data P and the rest of the documents in the searching space form the unlabeled data U. After the system conducts feature selection, all the documents are transferred into vectors. Then a standard PU learning model is trained from P and U. The model is then applied on U to rank the documents based on the probability values that the documents in U are predicted as being positive.

The ranked list will be returned to the user for screening. After more positive examples are identified, a re-ranking procedure will be conducted iteratively. In this paper, we focus on the first run of the document ranking process. The other iterative runs of the document ranking process are the same as the first run, except with more positive examples as inputs. As more positive documents are identified, it is expected that performance of the re-ranking will improve after each run.

Following the PU learning algorithm (called TPULearning) [2], we simply assume the unlabeled data as negative instances, and train a supervised learning model (i.e. SVM), which is applied on the unlabeled data to predict the likelihood that the instances in U are positive. The main difference between our approach and the method in [2] is that we apply it in the transductive scenario, while theirs is conducted in the inductive scenario. In addition, we want to explore whether such a method is applicable in the IFME setting, which is quite different from the experimental case conducted in inductive learning.

In a digital library environment, it is often the case that the provided relevant feedback documents from a user are much fewer than the documents in the searching space. So the data for training the PU leaning model is imbalanced: the positive examples are much fewer than the unlabeled data. An efficient strategy for dealing with class imbalance is under-sampling [7]. We propose a novel method that combines under-sampling with TPULearning. Specifically, we sample K percent of the unlabeled data N times during the same procedure of the TPULearning, and the final rank of an instance in U is the average rank of them in the N runs. The pseudo code for the proposed method is listed as follows:

Input: positive set $P=\{X_1,X_2,\ldots,X_{|P|}\}$, and

unlabeled set $U=\{X_1,X_2,\ldots X_{|U|}\}$.

For i=1 to N

1. Under-Sampling: Randomly sample a subset SU_i from U.
2. Feature selection on P and SU_i.
3. Learning a Classifier Ci using P and SU_i;
4. Prediction: R_i=Rank (SU_i, C_i).

End for

For i=1 to U

R_i= Combine(Rank(X_i), i=1 to N).

End for

Output: a rank list for U based on R_i

"Rank (SU_i, C_i)" uses the classifier C_i to predict data SUi, which will be ranked based on the probability that an instance is predicted as being positive. The basic idea of the proposed method is that by under-sampling a small set from U, the size of P and SU_i is more equal, thus the training set is more balanced. The final ranking for each of the instances in U is combined using all the information from each of the prediction from the classifier trained on P and SUi. Here, we simply calculate the new rank for an instance in U using the weighted mean rank of X_i from each of the under-sampling stage. Let R_{ik} denote the rank of X_i in the k_{th} run of the under-sampling stage, and let P_{ik} denote the corresponding probability value of X_i being predicted as positive. The final rank for X_i is calculated using the following formula:

$$R_i = \frac{\sum_{k=1}^{k=N} R_{ik} \times P_{ik} \times S_k}{\sum_{k=1}^{k=N} P_{ik} \times S_k}$$

where S_k=1, if X_i is selected in the k_{th} run of the under-sampling, otherwise S_k=0.

4. EXPERIMENTS AND RESUTLS

4.1 Datasets

We conducted experiments using the Reuters-21578 dataset, which is a commonly used benchmark news article collection in text classification. Each article has topic labels such as "acq", "crude" and "money-fx". Some stories belong to multiple topics. We only used stories that belonged to a unique topic in the experiments. We chose categories where the number of documents exceeded 250 to make up our datasets. There were 6 topics satisfying such a requirement; altogether there were 7,272 documents. For each of the 6 topics, the documents belonged to it were considered as positive data, and other documents formed the negative data. Altogether, we had 6 positive, and 6 negative pools respectively, which were used to generate different datasets for the experiments.

In real word applications of information retrieval, the unlabeled dataset is usually much bigger than the positive example set that represents a user's information need. So, in our experiments, we randomly generated unbalanced class distributions to simulate the real search scenarios.

4.2 Feature Selection and Learning Algorithm

We used Stanford core NLP [11] for stop words removal, stemming and lemmatization. The CHI method [1] was adopted for feature selection. The top K features that had highest CHI scores were selected. The optimal K was 1,000 for our dataset. After feature selection, each document was preprocessed and transferred into a vector and we used tf-idf to calculate the feature value for the document vectors. Mean Average Precision (MAP) [12] was adopted to evaluate the performance of the method. Lib-SVM [7] was used as the supervised learner for the experiments. The Radial Basis Function (RBF) kernel was selected, as in a preliminary informal experiments, it performed as well as or better than other standard kernels. In the preliminary informal experiments, we conducted grid search on C and γ using a five-fold cross-validation. Different pairs of (C, γ) values were tried, the optimal pair was C=1, and γ =0.005.

4.3 Experimental Design

Each run of an experiment was conducted using the following procedure. The positive and negative example pools were formed as described in 4.1. From the positive pool, we randomly sampled a subset of |P| examples to form the positive training data, and the same was done on |PU| examples to form the unlabeled training data, with the constraint that there was no overlap between P and PU. Then we randomly sampled a subset of |NU| examples from the negative pool for the unlabeled training data. Then an SVM classifier was trained on the training data (P+U), and it was in turn applied on U to predict the probability that a document in it was positive. The documents in U were ranked based on the probability values, and an MAP score was calculated for the rank. The final MAP score for each run of the experiment was calculated using the mean MAP for all the selected topics. For each dataset, we carried out 10 runs for an experiment, and the final MAP score was calculated by averaging over the MAP scores from the 10 runs.

4.4 Experimental Results

We present the results of the performance comparison between the under-sampling based method (USTPULearning) and the original TPULearning method. In all experiments, the under-sampling method was carried out 100 times (e.g. N=100). In each run of the sampling, 20% of the documents in U were randomly sampled to form the training data.

We changed P with different combinations of PU and NU to conduct the experiments (Figure 2 and Figure 3). We actually tried many other combinations of PU and NU, but the results were similar and thus are not included here. Observations include:

1) When more positive examples were provided, the performance of the TPULearning increased;

2) The under-sampling based method increased the performance of TPULearning significantly;

3) Given the same size of P, with the increase of the proportion of PU in U, the performance of the two methods gradually decreased.

4) When the size of P was large, say |P|>80, the performance of the under-sampling method appeared to become stable with the increase of |P|. However, the performance of the original method appeared to increase consistently with the increase of |P|.

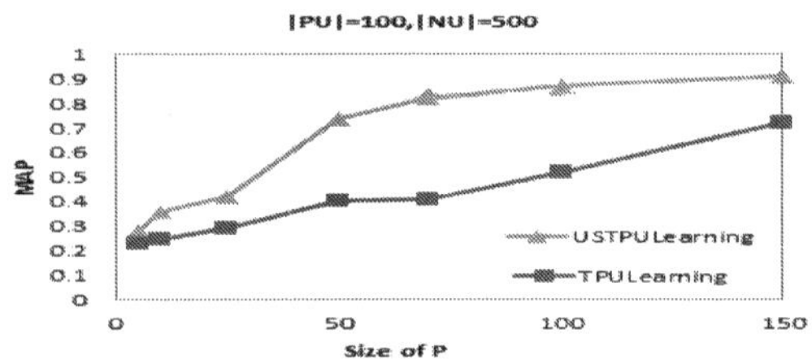

Figure 2. Performance comparison for the two methods under different numbers of |P|, when |PU|=100, |NU|=500.

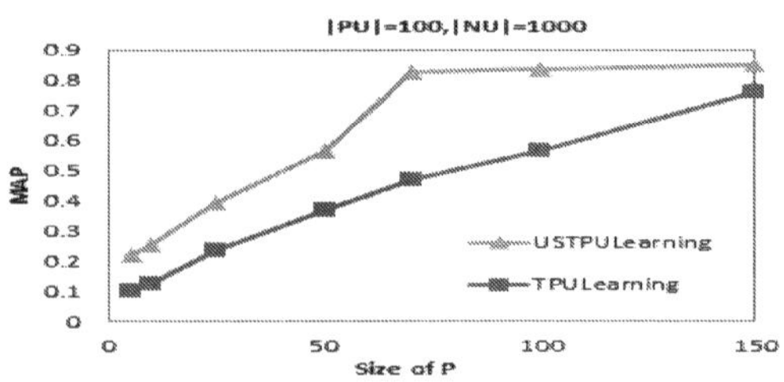

Figure 3. Performance comparison for the two methods under different numbers of |P|, when |PU|=100, |NU|=1000.

5. DISCUSSION

In this paper, we propose an information filtering framework in the digital library environment, and adopt PU learning for ranking. By treating the documents in the digital library as unlabeled data, and the relevant feedback documents from a user as positive data, a PU learning model is trained to predict the likelihood that the documents in U are positive. Then the likelihood values are used for ranking documents in the unlabeled data.

Our experiments show that TPULearning is very promising, when |P| is large. This suggests that when a large set of positive examples are available, the TPULearning method can be used to identify more relevant documents.

However, in an online search environment, it is often the case that |P| is usually very small. When |P| is small, the performance of the TPULearning method is poor. There are two possible reasons. First, when the number of features is large, the performance tends to decrease, as most features are from the unlabeled data. Second, when |P| is small, the dataset becomes seriously imbalanced. In this case, the probability of a true positive instance in U predicted as being positive is as low as or even lower than that of the true negative instance in U. We then incorporated under-sampling method which reduced the imbalance by sampling a small set from U in each run, thus improving the performance of the method. Experiments show that the performance was improved by as much as 40% when |P| is around 70 (Figure 2).

We believe that such a PU learning based approach augmented with under-sampling is highly desirable in a digital library environment for users who have information needs which are persistent, interdisciplinary and highly specialized.

One issue of this framework is that digital libraries usually have huge amounts of documents which indicate a large |U| and a possible efficiency concern. In future, distributed computing methodologies can be adopted to do the random sampling in a parallel manner.

6. REFERENCES

[1] B. Liu. Web Data Mining: Exploring Hyperlinks, Contents and Usage Data. *Springer*, 2006.

[2] K. Noto, M. Saier, C. Elkan. Learning to find relevant biological articles without negative training examples. In *Proceedings of 21st Australasian Joint Conference on Artificial Intelligence*, pages 202-213, 2008.

[3] B. Liu, W. S. Lee, P. S. Yu, X. Li. Partially supervised classification of text documents. In *Proceedings of the Nineteenth International Conference on Machine Learning*, pages 387–394, San Francisco, CA, USA, 2002.Morgan Kaufmann Publishers Inc.

[4] Y. Altun, D. McAllester, M. Belkin. Maximum margin semi-supervised learning for structured variables. In *Proceedings of Neural Information Proccessing Systems*, 2005.

[5] K. Nigam, A. McCallum, S. Thrun, T. Mitchell. Learning to classify text from labeled and unlabeled documents. In *Proceedings of the Fifteenth National Conference on Artificial Intelligence*, pages 792-799, 1998.

[6] F. Denis, R. Gilleron, M. Tommasi. Text classification from positive and unlabeled examples. In *Proceedings of the 9th International Conference on Information Processing and Management of Uncertainty in Knowledge-Based Systems*, pages 1927-1934, 2002.

[7] C.-C. Chang, C.-J. Lin. LIBSVM: a library for support vector machines. *ACM Transactions on Intelligent Systems and Technology*, 2(3): 1-27, 201.

[8] B. Liu, W. Lee, P. Yu, X. Li. Partially supervised classification of text documents. In *Proceedings of the Nineteenth International Conference on Machine Learning*, pages 387-394, 2002.

[9] H. Yu, J. Han, K. C. Chang. PEBL: Web page classification without negative examples. *IEEE-Transactions on Knowledge and Data Engineering*. 16(1): 70-81, 2004.

[10] X. Li, B. Liu, S. Ng. Negative Training Data can be Harmful to Text Classification. In *Proceedings of the 2010 Conference on Empirical Methods in Natural Language Processing*, pages 218–228, 2010.

[11] Stanford University. Stanford Core NLP Software. http://nlp.stanford.edu/software/corenlp.shtml, 2012.

[12] E. Agichtein, E. Brill, S. Dumais. Improving web search ranking by incorporating user behavior information. In *Proceedings of the 29th annual international ACM SIGIR conference on Research and development in information retrieval*, pages 19-26, 2006.

[13] D. Zhang, W.S. Lee. Query-By-Multiple-Examples using Support Vector Machines. *Journal of Digital Information Management*. 7(4): 202-210, 2009.

Can't See the Forest for the Trees? A Citation Recommendation System

Cornelia Caragea[1], Adrian Silvescu[2], Prasenjit Mitra[3], C. Lee Giles[3]
[1]Department of Computer Science and Engineering, University of North Texas
[2]Naviance, Inc., Washington DC
[3]School of Information Sciences and Technology, The Pennsylvania State University
ccaragea@unt.edu, silvescu@gmail.com, pmitra@ist.psu.edu, giles@ist.psu.edu

ABSTRACT

Scientists continue to find challenges in the ever increasing amount of information that has been produced on a world wide scale, during the last decades. When writing a paper, an author searches for the most relevant citations that started or were the foundation of a particular topic, which would very likely explain the thinking or algorithms that are employed. The search is usually done using specific keywords submitted to literature search engines such as Google Scholar and CiteSeer. However, finding relevant citations is distinctive from producing articles that are only topically similar to an author's proposal. In this paper, we address the problem of citation recommendation using a singular value decomposition approach. The models are trained and evaluated on the Citeseer digital library. The results of our experiments show that the proposed approach achieves significant success when compared with collaborative filtering methods on the citation recommendation task.

Categories and Subject Descriptors

H.3.3 [**Information Storage and Retrieval**]: Information Search and Retrieval

Keywords

citation recommendation; information filtering; collaborative filtering; singular value decomposition.

1. INTRODUCTION

As science advances, scientists around the world continue to produce a large number of research articles. These articles provide the technological basis for worldwide collection, sharing, and dissemination of scientific discoveries. Unfortunately, our ability to manually process and filter this huge amount of information lags far behind the number of research articles available today.

Research ideas are generally developed based on high quality citations. The search for such citations is usually done using specific *keywords* submitted to literature search engines such as Google Scholar [5] and CiteSeer [4]. However, text-based search engines return poor results when there is vocabulary mismatch between a query and the relevant documents. Moreover, finding relevant citations is distinctive from retrieving articles that are only topically similar to an author's proposal. For example, Teufel et al. [16] showed that citations can be of various types, and provided an annotation scheme for the citation function that consists of twelve different categories. Among these categories, some citations are topically similar, others are used as survey articles to provide background information to the reader, while yet others contain tools/algorithms/data that are adapted or modified in the new proposal [16].

What is a good strategy to uncover both topically-related and, at the same time, distant, but highly-relevant citations for a particular query, while filtering out irrelevant information, given today's very large collections of published articles? McNee et al. [10] studied the applicability of collaborative filtering (CF) to recommend citations for papers. However, CF algorithms have several limitations such as data sparsity and scalability [12]. In the citation recommendation task, the underlying citation graph tends to be noisy and sparse (potentially due to errors in citing, missing citations, or space limitation imposed by submission guidelines).

Against this background, in this work, we address the problem of citation recommendation using singular value decomposition (SVD) [3] on the adjacency matrix associated with the citation graph to construct a latent "semantic" space, where citing and cited papers, that are highly correlated, are placed closed to each other. The idea behind SVD is to project the original high-dimensional data into a lower-dimensional space, in which patterns in the data can be more easily identified. We exploit information available in CiteSeer to train and evaluate our models. The assumption is that, when writing a paper, an author has some background knowledge about the topic he writes about and that an initial set of citations (i.e., a "basket" of citations) is provided as input to the system. The system retrieves other relevant works that the author might have missed (works that *should* be cited or the author *should be aware of*).

Contributions. We present an application of SVD to build a reliable citation recommendation system and to address the limitations of memory-based CF algorithms. The results of our experiments show that the SVD-like recommender systems achieve significant success when compared with CF approaches on a subset of the CiteSeer citation graph, a newly constructed data set, made available online from the first author homepage.

JCDL'13, July 22–26, 2013, Indianapolis, Indiana, USA.

2. RELATED WORK

A variety of approaches to citation recommendation (detailed below) have been recently proposed in the literature.

Collaborative filtering. Using the adjacency matrix associated with a citation network, McNee et al. [10] tested the ability of CF to recommend appropriate additional citations for a target paper, given an initial set of citations (i.e., a "basket" of citations). The analogy with the conventional CF is that citing papers correspond to users and citations correspond to items. Tested in both online and offline settings, CF resulted in high-quality recommendation lists [10].

Citation ranking using content and graph-based information. Strohman et al. [14] presented a graph-based approach in order to generate a references list for a query paper (i.e., a paper with no citation information). The assumption is that the query paper has several pages in length that are written on a specific topic. The approach exploits both the textual similarity and the citation information between the papers in a collection. Bethard and Jurafsky [1] enriched the set of features used in [14] in the same framework, with the exception that the query paper consists only of the abstract.

Topic models-based link prediction. Nallapati et al. [11] extended topic models [2] to discover clusters of topical words as well as clusters of "topical citations", while exploiting the information flow from the citing to the cited documents.

Context-aware citation recommendation. Tang and Zhang [15] considered a topic-based approach to context-aware citation recommendation and proposed to match citation contexts with recommended papers, using Restricted Boltzmann Machines [13]. The context-aware approach to citation recommendation is defined as follows: given a query paper, for each citation placeholder, the task is to recommend a set of citations based on the context of the placeholder, also known as the *citation context* (i.e., a window of n words around the placeholder). Rather than generating a global references list for a query paper, local references lists are generated for each placeholder, based on the keywords in the citation contexts.

He et al. [6] proposed non-parametric probabilistic models to citation recommendation for placeholders in query manuscripts, which measure the context-based relevance between a citation context and a candidate citation for ranking a candidate set. Kataria et al. [8] extended the approach of Nallapati et al. [11] to jointly model content and citations by explicitly incorporating citation context information into the model. Lu et al. [9] and Huang et al. [7] proposed to use translation models to address the differences in vocabularies between the content of papers and the citation contexts, and show improvement in performance over the context-aware relevance model [6].

In contrast to the approaches reviewed above, we address citation recommendation using SVD. Rather than providing as input to the recommender system several pages of text, with no citation information, our system requires the user to input an initial set of citations (i.e., some background information about a research area). In formulation, our work is most similar to the work by McNee et al. [10]. For this reason, we compare SVD with collaborative filtering [10] only.

3. RECOMMENDER ALGORITHMS

Before reviewing the recommender algorithms compared in this study, we introduce some notations used in the paper.

Notations: Let $\mathcal{G} = (\mathcal{V}, \mathcal{E})$ denote a directed citation graph, where the vertices p_i in $\mathcal{V}$, $i = 1, \cdots, |\mathcal{V}|$ represent papers, and the edges $[p_i \to p_j]$ in $\mathcal{E}$ represent the citations between papers. Let $C = \{c_{ij}\}$ denote the adjacency matrix associated with $\mathcal{G}$, such that $c_{ij} = 1$ if there is an edge from p_i to p_j, and $c_{ij} = 0$, otherwise. Note that the matrix C, also referred to as the *link matrix*, is asymmetric.

Similar to McNee et al. [10], we distinguish between *citing* and *cited* papers. Specifically, we define a *citing paper* (denoted by p) as a paper for which we have access to its content and the reference list, and a *cited paper* (or a *citation*, denoted by q) as a paper that occurs in the references list of at least one citing paper in the corpus, and for which we have access to its content (title and/or abstract), but may or may not have access to its references list. Because standard CF algorithms require the transformation of a dataset into a matrix of ratings, i.e., the columns of the matrix represent "items", the rows represent "users", and the entries in the matrix represent users' ratings of particular items, we adopted the matrix representation introduced by McNee et al. [10]. That is, the "users" from standard CF are replaced by *citing papers* (i.e., the matrix rows), and the "items" are replaced by *cited papers* (i.e., the matrix columns). Each citing paper would then "vote" for (or rate) the cited papers in its references list, and in contrast to standard CF, citing papers do not add more "votes" over time, after a citing paper is entered into the system. We denote by $\mathcal{P}$ the set of citing papers, and by $\mathcal{Q}$ the set of cited papers (or citations).

3.1 User-Based Collaborative Filtering

The user-based collaborative filtering algorithm first compares citing papers in $\mathcal{P}$ (rows) to determine a neighborhood $\mathcal{N}$ of the most similar n papers to the target paper (i.e., the size of $\mathcal{N}$ is n). The algorithm then computes a score for each citation in $\mathcal{Q}$ by counting the number of occurrences of the citation in the neighborhood $\mathcal{N}$, with each occurrence weighted by the similarity of the neighbor to the target paper. Finally, the algorithm recommends the top N citations with the highest scores. That is, for the jth citation in $\mathcal{Q}$:

$$score_j = \sum_{i \in \mathcal{N}} c_{ij} \cdot w_i, \tag{1}$$

where w_i represents the cosine similarity of neighbor i with the target paper, and c_{ij} is the "vote" of neighbor i on the citation j. We call this method user-based simple-weighted-sum recommendation, denoted by CF User (SWS). We also experimented with a naïve user-based approach where the summation in Eq. 1 is not weighted by the neighbors similarities. That is, for the jth citation in $\mathcal{Q}$:

$$score_j = \sum_{i \in \mathcal{N}} c_{ij}. \tag{2}$$

We call this method user-based most-frequent-item recommendation, denoted by CF User (F).

3.2 Item-Based Collaborative Filtering

The item-based collaborative filtering compares citations in $\mathcal{Q}$ (columns) to determine a neighborhood $\mathcal{N}$ of the most similar citations to each *known* citation (i.e., each citation in the "basket") of a target citing paper. Specifically, for a target citing paper p, a candidate set of citations is first identified by taking the union of the n most similar papers (denoted by $\mathcal{N}(j)$) for each known citation j of p, and excluding any of the known citations of p (i.e., $\mathcal{N} = \cup_j \mathcal{N}(j)$).

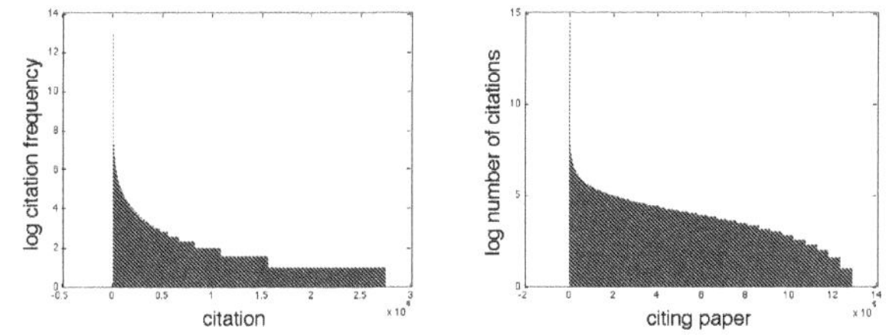

Figure 1: The CiteSeer citation graph information: (a) Frequency of citations, shown on a logarithmic scale; (b) Number of citations per citing paper.

For each citation c in the candidate set, the algorithms computes its similarity to the citations j in p, as the sum of similarities between all citations $j \in p$ and c, given only the n most similar papers of j. The algorithm recommends the top N citations from the candidate set with the highest scores. That is, for the c citation in the candidate set:

$$score_c = \sum_{j \in p} w_{jc}, \quad (3)$$

where $w_{jc} = 0$ if $c \notin \mathcal{N}(j)$ and w_{jc} is the cosine similarity between j and c, otherwise.

3.3 Regularized Singular Value Decomposition

SVD is a popular technique for identifying latent semantic factors, where association patterns in the data can be more easily identified, compared with the original space [3]. In our setting, using SVD, both citing and cited papers are mapped into a joint k-dimensional latent factor space, and the citing-cited correlations are modeled as inner products in this space. That is, each paper is represented as a vector in $\mathbf{R}^k$. Let $\mathbf{q}_i \in \mathbf{R}^k$ and $\mathbf{p}_u \in \mathbf{R}^k$ denote the vectors associated with the cited paper q_i and the citing paper p_u, respectively. The inner product $\mathbf{q}_i^T \mathbf{p}_u$ reflects the correlation between p_u and q_i, and approximates the "vote" of p_u on q_i, i.e.,

$$\hat{c_{ui}} = \mathbf{q}_i^T \mathbf{p}_u. \quad (4)$$

To avoid overfitting, we adopted a regularized formulation of SVD [17]. Regularized SVD learns the factor vectors by minimizing the regularized squared error on the training set (i.e., the link matrix C, or the matrix of "votes"):

$$\min \sum_{(u,i)} (c_{ui} - \mathbf{q}_i^T \mathbf{p}_u)^2 + \lambda(||\mathbf{q}_i||^2 + ||\mathbf{p}_u||^2), \quad (5)$$

where (u, i) denote pairs of citing-cited papers with non-zero entries in C. In experiments, we used *stochastic gradient descent* to minimize Eq. 5. The algorithm iterates through all "votes" in the training, predicts c_{ui}, and computes the error between the actual and predicted "votes". That is,

$$err_{ui} = c_{ui} - \mathbf{q}_i^T \mathbf{p}_u. \quad (6)$$

The parameters are then updated, using the following updating rules:

$$\mathbf{q}_i \leftarrow \mathbf{q}_i + \alpha \cdot (err_{ui} \cdot \mathbf{p}_u - \lambda \cdot \mathbf{q}_i) \quad (7)$$
$$\mathbf{p}_u \leftarrow \mathbf{p}_u + \alpha \cdot (err_{ui} \cdot \mathbf{q}_i - \lambda \cdot \mathbf{p}_u) \quad (8)$$

We use regularized SVD to get predictions on individual "votes" and return top N recommendations for citing papers.

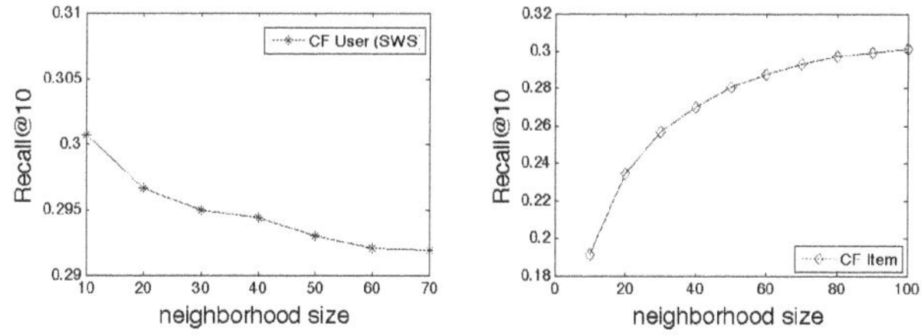

Figure 2: Neighborhood size estimation for: (a) CF User (SWS) and (b) CF Item.

4. EXPERIMENTS AND RESULTS

Here, we describe our compiled CiteSeer data set [4] used in our experiments, and present the results of the comparison of SVD with the collaborative filtering approaches.

4.1 Dataset

The citation recommendation data set used in our experiments is compiled from the CiteSeer citation graph and the metadata available for each paper indexed in CiteSeer [4], as of December 2011. As already mentioned, we define a *citing paper* as a paper for which we have access to its content and the reference list, and a *cited paper* or a *citation* as a paper that occurs in the reference list of at least one citing paper in the corpus, and for which we have access to its content, but may or may not have access to its reference list. In the CiteSeer citegraph, there are $1,345,249$ unique citing papers and $9,150,279$ unique citations. The total number of links in the graph, i.e., [citing paper $\rightarrow$ citation], is $25,526,384$.

Figure 1(a) shows the frequency of citations in CiteSeer (on a logarithmic scale). As can be seen, the citations in CiteSeer typically follow a Zipf distribution, i.e., only a few citations are cited by very many citing papers, whereas the majority of them are cited rarely. Figure 1(b) shows the number of citations per citing paper, i.e., the size of the reference list. As shown, very few citing papers have a large number of citations, whereas for most of the citing papers the number of citations ranges between 8 and 32. From the citation graph and the available metadata, we constructed a smaller data set as follows: we filtered out papers that do not have title and abstract, as well as papers that are cited by other papers in the corpus less than 10 times and more than 100 times. In addition, we filtered out papers that cite less than 15 or more than 50 other papers. In the resulting citegraph, there are $81,508$ unique cited papers, $16,394$ unique citing papers, and $341,191$ links.

4.2 Experimental Design

Our experiments are designed to explore the following question: How does SVD compare with CF on the citation recommendation task for the returned top N citation recommendation lists?

To answer this question, we split the data set into training and test sets by randomly selecting one non-zero entry from each citing paper, to be part of the test set, whereas the remaining non-zero entries are considered part of the training set (i.e., the "basket items" for each citing paper). Thus, we sampled $16,394$ non-zero entries from the $s = 16,394$ citing papers and used them to test the models. Furthermore, in a similar manner, we sampled $16,394$ non-zero entries from

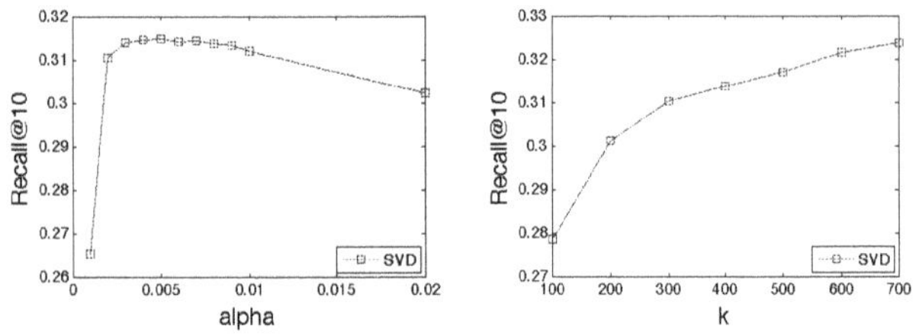

Figure 3: The estimation of: (a) the learning parameter α, and (b) the dimension of the latent space k.

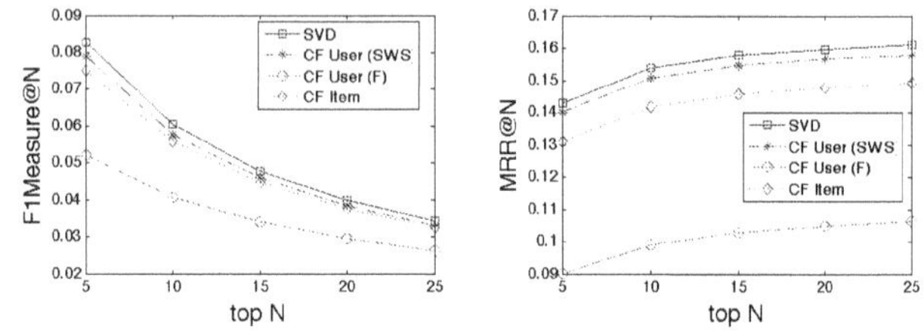

Figure 4: Comparison of SVD with CF, in terms of F1 Measure, and MRR, for various values of N.

the training set to be part of a validation set, which was used to estimate model parameters (detailed below).

In our experiments, all four algorithms return a list of top N recommendations for each citing paper. If a hidden citation (in the test set) is part of the top N recommendation list returned by an algorithm, the algorithm was considered accurate for the citing paper. We repeated each experiment 5 times to ensure the results are not sensitive to a particular train-test split. The results are averaged across the five runs.

Performance Measures. We used Recall, F1 Measure and the Mean Reciprocal Rank (MRR). The higher these measures are, the more accurate the results returned.

Parameter Tuning. To select a set of "good" parameters, i.e., a set of parameters that result in high-accuracy models, we trained the models on the training set (from which we removed the entries in the validation set), and selected the parameters on the validation set, as follows: we fixed N to 10 (i.e., the size of the recommendation list made by any algorithm). For user- and item-based CF, we chose the neighborhood size n that resulted in the highest recall on the validation set (see Figure 2). The selected values for n are: $n = 10$ for both CF User (SWS) and (F), and $n = 100$ for CF Item models (data not shown for CF User (F)).

For SVD, we fixed $N = 10$, and chose the learning rate α, the regularization factor λ, and the dimension of the latent space k that resulted in the highest recall on the validation set (see Figure 3). These values are: $\alpha = 0.005$, $\lambda = 0.001$, $k = 600$ (data not shown for the estimation of λ).

4.3 Results

Figure 4 show the results of the comparison of SVD with CF, i.e., user-based simple-weighted-sum, CF User (SWS), user-based most-frequent-item, CF User (F), and item-based, CF Item, in terms of F1 Measure, and MRR, for various values of N of the size of the top N recommendation lists, with N ranging from 5 to 25 in steps of 5. As can be seen in the figure, SVD outperforms the CF models in terms of both performance measure reported, for all values of N. This suggests that the citation graph data contain patterns of association of citations that SVD is able to find in the latent low-dimensional factor space.

Furthermore, the fact that SVD outperforms CF in terms of MRR, for all values of N, suggests that the original citations (in the references list of a citing paper) are higher ranked in the top N recommendation lists returned by SVD, compared to the lists returned by CF.

Again, as can be seen in Figure 4, the performance of CF User (F), is much worse than that of CF User (SWS) (as expected). On the other hand, the performance of item-based, CF Item, is similar to that of CF User (SWS), in terms of F1 Measure for all values of N, but is worse than that of CF User (SWS) in terms of MRR, suggesting that the original citations are ranked higher in the top N recommendation lists by CF User (SWS), compared with CF Item.

5. CONCLUSION

In this paper, we studied the applicability of SVD to citation recommendation and found that SVD-based recommender systems perform better compared to standard CF in a recommendation experiment. We also introduced a new citation graph data set, compiled from the CiteSeer digital library [4], that consists of multiple types of information such as textual information, author and venue information, citation context information, in addition to the citation graph data, which is made available to the research community.

In future, because SVD allows for easy incorporation of additional information, we plan to integrate other types of information (e.g., textual information, author, venue) into our models. The compiled data set facilitates further experimentation with more complex models that are able to exploit such information. It would also be interesting to see how other recommendation algorithms perform on the compiled CiteSeer data set, and design new ones for this task.

6. REFERENCES

[1] S. Bethard and D. Jurafsky. Who should i cite? learning literature search models from citation behavior. In *Proceedings of the 19th ACM international conference on Information and knowledge management, CIKM '10*, 2010.

[2] D. M. Blei, A. Y. Ng, and M. I. Jordan. Latent dirichlet allocation. *Journal of Machine Learning Research*, 3:993–1022, 2003.

[3] S. Deerwester, S. T. Dumais, G. W. Furnas, T. K. Landauer, and R. Harshman. Indexing by latent semantic analysis. *Journal of the American Society for Information Science*, 41(6):391–407, 1990.

[4] C. L. Giles, K. Bollacker, and S. Lawrence. Citeseer: An automatic citation indexing system. In *Digital Libraries '98*, pages 89–98, 1998.

[5] Google. Google scholar. In *http://scholar.google.com*.

[6] Q. He, J. Pei, D. Kifer, P. Mitra, and C. L. Giles. Context-aware citation recommendation. In *Proceedings of the 19th international conference on World Wide Web '10*, pages 421–430, 2010.

[7] W. Huang, S. Kataria, C. Caragea, P. Mitra, C. L. Giles, and L. Rokach. Recommending citations: Translating papers into references. In *Proceedings of the 21st ACM CIKM '12*, 2012.

[8] S. Kataria, P. Mitra, and S. Bhatia. Utilizing context in generative bayesian models for linked corpus. In *Proceeding of AAAI*, 2010.

[9] Y. Lu, J. He, D. Shan, and H. Yan. Recommending citations with translation model. In *Proceedings of CIKM '11*, pages 2017–2020, 2011.

[10] S. M. McNee, I. Albert, D. Cosley, P. Gopalkrishnan, S. K. Lam, A. M. Rashid, J. A. Konstan, and J. Riedl. On the recommending of citations for research papers. In *Proceedings of the 2002 ACM conference on Computer supported cooperative work '02*, pages 116–125, 2002.

[11] R. M. Nallapati, A. Ahmed, E. P. Xing, and W. W. Cohen. Joint latent topic models for text and citations. In *Proc. of KDD*, pages 542–550, 2008.

[12] B. Sarwar, G. Karypis, J. Konstan, and J. Riedl. Application of dimensionality reduction in recommender system a case study. In *WebKDD-2000 Workshop*, 2000.

[13] P. Smolensky. Parallel distributed processing: explorations in the microstructure of cognition. volume 1, pages 194–281. 1986.

[14] T. Strohman, W. B. Croft, and D. Jensen. Recommending citations for academic papers. IR 466, 2006.

[15] J. Tang and J. Zhang. A discriminative approach to topic-based citation recommendation. In *Proceedings of the 13th PAKDD '09*, pages 572–579, 2009.

[16] S. Teufel, A. Siddharthan, and D. Tidhar. Automatic classification of citation function. In *Proceedings of EMNLP-06*, 2006.

[17] B. Webb. Netflix update: Try this at home. In *http://sifter.org/~simon/journal/20061211.html*, 2006.

Comparative Appraisal: Systematic Assessment of Expressive Qualities

Melanie Feinberg
School of Information
The University of Texas at Austin
Austin, TX USA
feinberg@ischool.utexas.edu

ABSTRACT

Clifford Lynch describes the value of digital libraries as adding interpretive layers to collections of cultural heritage materials. However, standard forms of evaluation, which focus on the degree to which a system solves problems, are insufficient assessments of the expressive qualities that distinguish such interpretive content. This paper describes a form of comparative, structured appraisal that supplements the existing repertoire of assessment techniques. Comparative appraisal uses a situationally defined set of procedures to be followed by multiple assessors in examining a group of artifacts. While this approach aims for a goal of systematic comparison based on selected dimensions, it is grounded in the recognition that expressive qualities are not conventionally measurable and that absolute agreement between assessors is neither possible nor desirable. The conceptual basis for this comparative method is drawn from the literature of writing assessment.

Categories and Subject Descriptors

H.5.m. Information interfaces and presentation (e.g., HCI): Miscellaneous

General Terms

Design

Keywords

Evaluation; criticism; assessment

1. INTRODUCTION

In 2002, Clifford Lynch suggested that the "aggregation of materials in a digital library can be greater than the sum of its parts" [21]. For Lynch, a digital library does not just make "raw material" (which Lynch calls "collections") available; a digital library adds "layers of interpretation" that weave together items perhaps held by multiple institutions, enacting a coherent, purposeful perspective upon the assembled contents. Lynch contends that this synthetic, expressive activity might form the substrate onto which intellectual communities would coalesce around digital libraries.

JCDL'13, July 22–26, 2013, Indianapolis, Indiana, USA.
Copyright © ACM 978-1-4503-2077-1/13/07...$15.00.

In 2011, as social media tools began to proliferate, Marty and Kazmer considered the efforts of cultural heritage institutions to focus social media toward the co-construction of knowledge with their user communities [22]. While Lynch was referring to the interpretive digital library as catalyst for a scholarly community, and Marty and Kazmer were imagining a wider public audience, the broader vision is similar: the deployment of collection materials as expressive elements to structure an array of interpretive possibilities. Tools like Storyspace, which facilitates the development of narratives that join museum objects in interpretively illuminating ways, are emerging to support the realization of such ideas [30].

In commenting about potential difficulties regarding the sustainability of such interpretive layers for digital libraries, Lynch pinpoints a complex problem for these initiatives: how to determine when an interpretation is interesting, when it requires updating, and when it has perhaps become outmoded or no longer viable. The question of what makes an interpretive element interesting, or provocative, or thoughtful, among myriad potential expressive qualities, and relatedly what makes one such element more or less interesting (or provocative, or thoughtful, or any such quality) than another, is not easily answered. While standard evaluative techniques such as user surveys and usability tests are undeniably helpful in determining how and to what extent digital libraries address user information needs, they are less appropriate when considering questions like "How does each set of metadata elements explore the subtleties of cultural interplay in these art objects?" or "How strongly does the unique perspective of the author appear in these user-contributed personal collections?" While user opinions can certainly be generated to comment upon such areas, it is difficult to use these opinions for systematic comparison along defined dimensions, because user opinions may all differ in how they define a unique authorial voice, or any other expressive quality. Additionally, qualities such as cultural interplay and authorial voice are not measurable in conventional ways, unlike performance metrics and similarly quantifiable characteristics, such as precision and recall or task completion times.

In this paper, I describe a form of comparative, structured appraisal, focused on expressive qualities, that supplements the existing repertoire of assessment techniques. The approach that I describe resembles experimental evaluation in using a standard set of procedures to be followed by multiple assessors in examining a group of artifacts. However, this approach is also grounded in the recognition that expressive qualities are not conventionally measurable and that absolute agreement between assessors is neither possible nor desirable. Accordingly, the mode of appraisal that I propose is situationally defined for particular contexts. This paper provides an example of such an appraisal as developed for a particular project.

The conceptual basis for this comparative method comes from the literature of writing assessment. Instructors and researchers in the field of composition and rhetoric have long struggled with the task of providing fair, accurate assessments of student writing proficiency while acknowledging that the characteristics of good writing are difficult to define precisely, impossible to measure quantitatively, and reliant upon an indeterminate range of contextual factors [5, 26]. Additionally, while writing assessments follow similar principles in their design, they must flexibly account for different pedagogical goals, instructional situations, and particular values in terms of what constitutes writing skill.

In the next section, I summarize the motivating scenario that provoked my investigation into comparative appraisal and present several additional use cases. Next, I situate comparative appraisal in the context of other forms of assessment for both information systems and human-computer interaction. Following this extended project rationale, I describe how writing assessment provides a conceptual grounding for developing a project-specific comparative appraisal procedure. Finally, I summarize the comparative appraisal developed for the motivating scenario and its implementation in two related studies.

This paper's contribution lies in presenting the goals, justification, and utility of this form of assessment as demonstrated through a case study, and not in the particular approach used in the motivating scenario. The argument presented here is meant to inform the fashioning of project-specific appraisal methods that are tailored to their contexts.

2. PROJECT RATIONALE: MOTIVATING SCENARIO AND ADDITIONAL USE CASES

The need for comparative appraisal arose in an interdisciplinary project that sought to translate the insight of humanistic criticism to the realm of digital library design. An initial study used a humanities-based approach to explore what makes personal digital collections (shared sets of resources such as Pinterest boards and YouTube playlists) interesting as forms of creative expression [9]. This foundational work proposed a set of three more specific expressive qualities that personal collections might exhibit: an original purpose, an authorial voice, and emotional intimacy. A subsequent study involved a lab experiment to see whether exposure to collections that embodied all three of these qualities would affect the process or product of collection design [10]. Working within an easy-to-use digital video library environment, the Open Video Digital Library Toolkit, participants created personal collections using a library of source material focused around a particular theme [14]. After creating initial collections, participants interacted with example expressive collections, created by the researchers to enact all three qualities under investigation. Participants compared their designs to the examples. Then participants created a second collection using another source library.

This protocol required a way to systematically compare participant collections to the examples and to each other, to determine if interacting with the examples had an effect on subsequent designs (see Figure 1). To accomplish this goal, we had to determine how, and to what extent, a collection demonstrated the expressive qualities of original purpose, authorial voice, and emotional intimacy. We needed to establish whether participant collections showed, for example, a stronger voice after exposure to the expressive examples, or whether this exposure had no clear effect.

2.1 Additional use scenarios

Additional use cases appear in design-focused research that attempts to identify and exploit particular expressive qualities. For example, in the City of Lit digital library described by Hsieh and colleagues, undergraduate literature students contribute to a collection focused on Iowa City authors and locations. Initial evaluations of the system focused on students' perceptions of usability and on the system's utility for their own learning [15]. A comparative appraisal of students' contributions, perhaps focused around qualities such as comprehensiveness and local color, would provide another stream of information to support continued system development.

Another scenario involves systematic assessment of design alternatives designed to enact certain qualities. In an example from HCI design research, Petrelli and colleagues proposed a set of four ideas to exhibit "playfulness and engagement across generations" in the context of Christmas celebrations [28]. While these designs were discussed by focus groups, a comparative appraisal could additionally interrogate the degree to which the selected qualities appear in each prototype, as well as identifying factors that contribute to the generation of each quality. The information generated from such a comparative appraisal could help select prototypes for continued development and also help researchers refine their ideas of the interactive qualities being enacted.

A third use scenario involves the design of authoring environments for users to develop collections or other artifacts that highlight expressive qualities. Storyspace, created by Wolff and colleagues, enables museum curators to assemble museum database records that combine to tell a coherent story [30].

Storyspace uses a sophisticated ontology that can propose alternate narrative structures for a particular object group. A structured comparison of such alternatives generated for particular collections would provide another means of assessment for the Storyspace ontology, in addition to the planned elicitation of feedback from curators using the prototype system. As another example, Likarish and Winet describe a collaboratively authored Twitter novel created as part of a public art project [19]. The completed novel exhibited a polyphonic voice, which made it seem incoherent, and the novel also lacked interaction between the characters. Likarish and Winet propose writing tools to facilitate increased consistency of voice and increased character interaction in collaborative fiction. A comparative appraisal to assess the products created with such tools would help to characterize the tools' effects.

3. PROJECT RATIONALE: LIMITATIONS OF CURRENT ASSESSMENT TECHNIQUES

In this section, I describe how existing approaches to assessment do not adequately address the needs of the motivating scenario and accompanying use cases. First, I consider traditional means of evaluation focused around solving user problems, and then I examine alternative means of assessment developed by design-oriented human-computer interaction research.

3.1 Traditional evaluation: measuring effectiveness and efficiency in solving identified problems

Surveying the state of the art in digital library evaluation, Fuhr and colleagues define a three-part model that incorporates

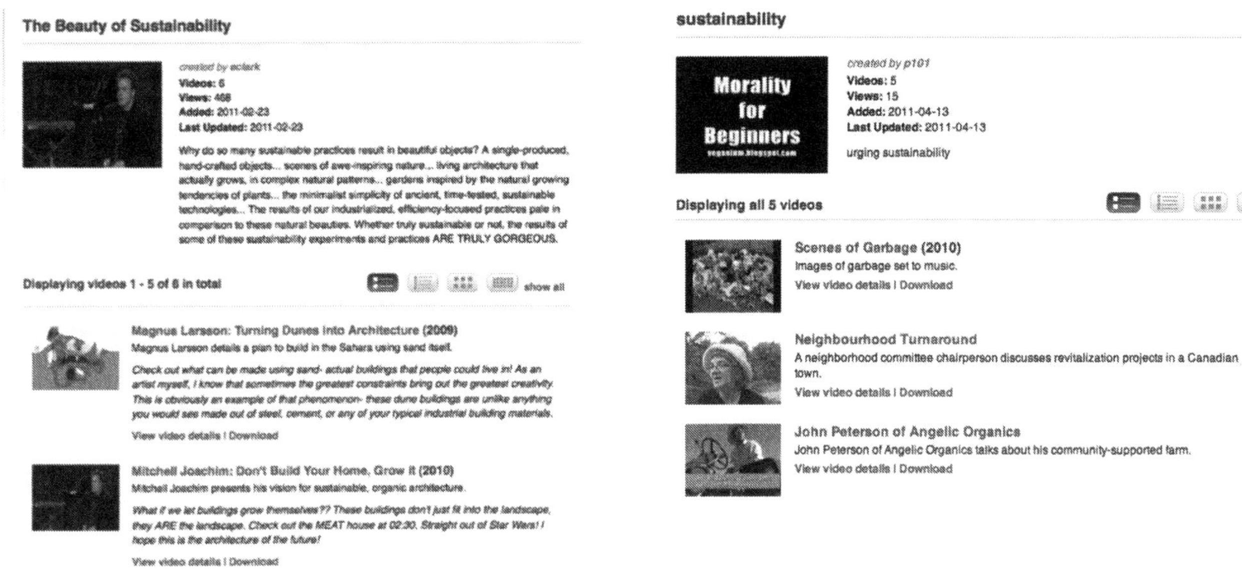

Figure 1: In the motivating scenario, we needed to compare qualities such as original purpose between personal digital collections like these. The left-hand collection snippet is an example created by researchers; the collection snippet on the right was created by a study participant. (The title and text paragraph that precede the video list are collection-specific annotations. In the video list, the plain text comes from the system and is not created by the collection author; the italic text is a collection-specific annotation.)

usability, usefulness, and performance [11]. Performance evaluation focuses on measurement of system properties, such as precision and recall for resource retrieval, usage rates for individual resources, quality of multimedia playback, and so on. Usability involves the ease, speed, and satisfaction with which users can perform tasks, and usefulness describes the extent to which the library's content is appropriate for users' information needs.

The evaluation model developed by Fuhr and colleagues, which relates system, content, and user elements, adopts a standard problem-solving orientation, in which a digital library's purpose is oriented around facilitating an identified goal, typically that of satisfying information needs. Although the composition of such models may vary, they tend to maintain this problem-solving focus. Khoo and MacDonald's evaluation model, for example, incorporates broader organizational components to consider the goals of the sponsoring institution and how those goals are facilitated [17]. While this model includes additional elements, its object remains the degree to which a digital library solves identified problems, or produces established outcomes (for example, does item metadata make it easier and faster for users to find what they are looking for?).

A task-based focus for evaluation is of course valuable and necessary. The fulfillment of identified user needs through digital library services, and the accomplishment of other institutional goals (such as increasing a user base) is undeniably crucial, and such models support this form of assessment. However, interpretive elements and the expressive qualities associated with them don't fit neatly into models oriented around problems and solutions, or information needs and the satisfaction of those needs. A metadata element set that enacts relationships to reveal cultural interplay between museum objects achieves its interest partly from illuminating the materials in unanticipated ways, in addition to supporting existing, recognized information needs. Similarly, a personal digital collection of diverting novels for long airplane trips that gains its character from a unique, engaging authorial voice might solve no identified problems but still represent a compelling interpretive layer that enriches a digital library experience. Expressive qualities such as cultural interplay and authorial voice speak to the transformative potential of digital library design as an intellectual or aesthetic experience, rather than support for existing tasks. It makes sense to ask users how a system supports the resolution of their information needs, because users are experts in their own needs. It is less clear that user surveys or interviews could inform confident judgments of expressive qualities, without instructing users about what those qualities are and how they might manifest in the digital library. (This doesn't mean than the effects of these qualities wouldn't be perceived by users, just that users might not have the vocabulary or expertise to productively articulate such effects for purposes of comparison and appraisal.)

3.2 Alternate modes of assessment from HCI research

Design-oriented HCI research has begun to explore the interactive artifact as a cultural form. Such research highlights the qualities of interaction as generator of aesthetic experience, and the software artifact as a means of shaping that experience [1, 23]. For example, the Prayer Companion was created to enrich the spiritual activities of cloistered nuns by unobtrusively displaying brief informative messages, including notifications of current events, via a small custom device [12]. The Prayer Companion was not designed to solve a problem but to contribute an interpretively flexible extension of the nuns' prayer experience.

In HCI, various alternatives to experimental evaluation have been proposed to support principled assessment of such expressive interactive artifacts. One alternative has focused on incorporating reflective elements into the design process itself, as a resource for the evolution of ideas and prototypes. These reflective approaches interrogate in-progress designs through the exploitation of expert judgment that resides within a skilled design community, sometimes in conjunction with the reflections of potential users [13, 29].

Another mode of assessment has looked to the humanities. Humanistic criticism produces illuminating interpretations of creative works by employing intricate theoretical frameworks in conjunction with close readings of selected examples [1, 2]. In HCI, research inspired by humanistic criticism has introduced particular theoretical orientations to the field, such as feminism and critical theory, and has proposed how such frameworks can help interpret existing artifacts and generate new ones [3, 4]. Complementary work has developed critical vocabularies specific to the HCI context [20].

Design reflections and humanistic criticism typically focus on unique qualities of the examples they analyze, producing interpretations that reveal previously unarticulated properties. For example, a critical reading of the maeve database pinpoints the integration of content and navigation as a distinctive element of the interactive experience [2]. In our case, however, the needs of the motivating scenario required the comparison of expressive qualities in a more systematic way, along consistent dimensions. And yet the identification of expressive qualities does involve interpretive judgment, which in turn relies on a certain level of knowledge and skill in the assessor. This judgment goes beyond user preferences that emerge via crowdsourced ratings [as in, for example, 18]. In short, we needed to develop a new means of assessment, in which informed judgment is deployed in a controlled, systematic way across multiple exemplars.

4. LESSONS FROM WRITING ASSESSMENT

To develop such an appraisal procedure for the motivating scenario, I turned to writing assessment, which wrestles with similar situations: how to assign composition students to an appropriate course level, for example, when students may approach the writing of sample essays using different but equally acceptable strategies, and where the notion of acceptability itself may be difficult to define.

To be clear, writing assessment is not criticism. Criticism is a form of research inquiry in itself, and it relies upon skilled interpretive expertise in conjunction with a grounding in appropriate literature. Such criticism has traditionally been intended to produce new scholarly knowledge, not to provide a basis for discriminating between potential designs as part of an ongoing project. The science-based constructs of reliability and validity are meaningless in the critical context: the goal of criticism is to illuminate new conceptual space, not to prove or disprove hypotheses.

In contrast, writing assessment is a pragmatic activity focused on making decisions; it is not itself research. An assessor in a university's writing program, for example, might determine whether a student's portfolio should pass the university writing requirement. While assessors are trained to identify criteria employed in a particular assessment, and while they typically have knowledge and expertise in writing, they need not be scholars.

Writing assessments must be consistent enough across multiple raters to ensure confidence in decisions such as passing or failing. Accordingly, reliability and validity have been employed in this domain. However, their meaning and the nature of their relevance has been debated for this context. Indeed, the literature of writing assessment has been characterized as a progressive conflict between reliability and validity [5, 7, 26]. These debates inform my own approach to comparative appraisal.

While indirect quantitative testing methods, such as multiple-choice examinations of grammar mechanics, might be statistically reliable, writing teachers have long contended that such methods do not achieve face validity as a determination of writing ability; a student can master the rules of grammar and yet not be able to write proficiently or persuasively [7]. However, experts judge writing samples differently, as famously demonstrated in a study conducted by the Educational Testing Service (ETS) in 1961 [8]. 300 writing samples written by college students were sent to 53 experts in a variety of fields, who rated the samples and commented upon strengths and weaknesses. Agreement was dismal: 94 percent of the essays received at least seven different grades out of nine possibilities. From this set of varied assessments, the ETS researchers analyzed rater comments to derive five broad areas that captured most criteria variously employed by the raters: Ideas, form, flavor (style), mechanics, and wording [8]. To decrease variability of the sort described in the ETS report, writing assessment researchers developed holistic scoring methods based on standardized rubrics that formalize a small set of generalized criteria such as those isolated in the ETS study, supported by rater training sessions in which applying the rubric consistently is emphasized [16]. In the U.S., such methods have been widely adopted for both national (such as Advanced Placement exams) and institutional testing purposes [5, 7, 26].

However, while the formalization of assessment criteria via standardized rubrics increased rating consistency, concerns about test validity continued. Moss notes that reliability decreases when assessors examine portfolios of student work, instead of single test essays, because portfolio samples are created under different circumstances, unlike test essays that respond to a single prompt [24]. Surely, Moss contends, the evidence provided through the "complex, authentic tasks" represented in a portfolio is more indicative of writing ability than a context-stripped essay from a test. In their courses, instructors teach how to compose appropriate written material for different contexts, because they believe, as a core value, that good writing responds to a situation. Yet assessment protocols have devalued this skilled expertise in favor of techniques that can be implemented widely and consistently. Accordingly, Moss asserts that focusing on reliability in writing assessment can impede validity, suggesting that disagreement between raters might be an opportunity for productive dialogue regarding assessment criteria and implementation—in other words, a means through which the ultimate validity of the assessment instrument can be solidified [24].

Various researchers have extended this argument, emphasizing the pedagogical poverty of context-independent assessment criteria and the need to judge writing according to local values (e.g., according to the instructional philosophy of a particular composition department). Accordingly, the assessment process, including development and implementation of localized procedures, becomes a means to articulate those values for a particular instructional community [16, 5]. While some proposals for localized assessment argue for getting rid of rubrics entirely, contending that they thwart the recognition of imaginative solutions to writing problems, others retain the structure of rubrics in a more flexible, context-specific manner [6]. But the point of the rubric becomes less to assign points or grades consistently and more to structure a principled conversation about good writing, either between multiple assessors or between assessors and students.

Parkes proposes that reliability of such localized assessment procedures be formulated as a type of argument [27]. For each assessment situation, the most applicable values associated with reliability (dependability, accuracy, and so on) are selected as appropriate for the assessment purpose, along with a proposed level of reliability for the situation (accuracy may need to be high if an assessment is a graduation requirement, but lower if the assessment is used for class placement). The assessment designer musters evidence to demonstrate that the procedure adheres to the defined reliability construct [27].

To summarize, in developing a comparative appraisal procedure to respond to situations such as that represented in the motivating scenario, the literature of writing assessment suggests that:

- The criteria being assessed should be grounded in project-specific goals and values.
- A systematic procedure and set of assessment criteria can direct assessors' attention consistently on the artifacts being examined; however, the aim should center on consistent focus, rather than consistent ratings (that is, disagreement can be as informative as agreement).
- Reliability and validity must be confronted; their meaning cannot be assumed, but neither can their potential relevance be dismissed. Instead, the designer of a comparative appraisal formulates an argument that defines validity and reliability appropriately for the situation and that provides evidence to support the proposed definitions.

One might note a certain level of similarity between a writing assessment that examines certain characteristics of a work according to criteria and procedures made systematic via a rubric and the popular usability inspection method of heuristic evaluation, as initially defined by Nielsen and Molich [25]. In heuristic evaluation, a small group of usability evaluators reviews an interface for problems, as identified according to an agreed-upon list of usability principles. From a procedural perspective, heuristic evaluation does resemble the localized expression of writing assessment that I have described here: a set of trained assessors examines an artifact according to identified criteria. However, heuristic evaluation operates under a problem-solving orientation similar to most traditional software evaluation modes. In heuristic evaluation, assessors are specifically looking for "problems" as defined according to generally applicable principles (that is, that would be considered problems in all software systems). The goals and values of heuristic evaluation are universal, not local, and the review is focused on problems to be fixed, not on characterizing the extent to which criteria manifest and the (perhaps unanticipated) effects thus generated. Moreover, the assessors in heuristic evaluation are expected to agree; while multiple assessors are used to ensure that more problems are identified, the sense is that individual assessors merely miss some issues, instead of having principled agreements about what constitutes an issue. Finally, the procedure of a heuristic evaluation is not adapted based on situationally specific needs for reliability and validity. Accordingly, the comparative appraisal method developed for the motivating scenario, described in the next section, differs from heuristic evaluation in all three of these ways: its criteria are based upon locally determined goals and values, the assessors are not expected to agree, and its procedures align with situationally determined requirements for reliability and validity.

5. EXAMPLE COMPARATIVE APPRAISAL PROCEDURE FOR MOTIVATING SCENARIO

This section presents a comparative appraisal procedure that responds to the motivating scenario. I begin by describing the values addressed through the appraisal and its ultimate goals. I then summarize procedure components and provide an argument to demonstrate the procedure's reliability and validity for the situation of its use. While this example appraisal procedure is deeply enmeshed in the motivating scenario and cannot be merely exported to other research contexts, its goals, justification, and subsequent implementation can serve to inform the development of similar protocols, for use cases such as those described earlier in the paper.

5.1 Appraisal goals and values

In the localized approach to writing assessment, evaluative criteria are generated based on the values of the immediate instructional community as to what constitutes good writing. For the motivating scenario, criteria were generated based on the proposed values examined in the research project: the three expressive qualities defined in [9] and the overall expressiveness potentially enabled through the synthesis of those characteristics. While this may seem like an obvious decision, the larger point is that *any* comparative appraisal relies for its conceptual basis upon project-specific criteria. Moreover, the assessor's evidence for determining the relative presence of appraisal criteria is based in the mechanisms of expression appropriate to the specific artifact at hand. For the motivating scenario, mechanisms include the selection, description, and arrangement of items in a personal digital collection.

Localized modes of writing assessment also emphasize the rubric as procedural infrastructure to systematically focus an assessor's attention in particular ways, and accordingly downplay the rubric as a means of generating reliably consistent scores between assessors. Similarly, in the appraisal procedure developed for the motivating scenario, the presence of a certain number or type of these mechanisms does not mandate a particular judgment. The goal is to consistently direct the attention of each assessor in similar way, and not to create a formalized scale that ensures consistent ratings across multiple assessors. The ultimate assessments are open to the possibility of principled interpretive differences and yet are still comparable across defined dimensions. Additionally, the artifacts being appraised are not being "graded" or described as holistically good or bad. The appraisal only compares perceived differences in the strength in which the particular characteristics of interest appear.

5.2 Procedure components

For the motivating scenario, the artifact being assessed is the personal digital collection (see Figure 1 for examples). For each collection, assessors perform the same tasks for each of the three expressive qualities identified in [9]: an original purpose, authorial voice, and emotional intimacy. These tasks involve describing how the quality is exhibited through the collection, rating the strength of the quality, and describing how each mechanism through which expression is generated—selection, description, and arrangement of resources—contributes to the manifestation of the quality. A worksheet documents each task and provides for standardized recording.

For each collection, assessors performed the following tasks for each of the three expressive qualities (purpose, voice, and emotion):

1. Describe, in free text, the way that the quality is enacted through the collection.
2. On a scale of 1–10, rate the strength of that quality in the collection.
3. According to a brief coding scheme (less than ten categories) developed through preliminary review of the collections to be assessed, record all the instances in which selection of resources contributed to the manifestation of the quality.
4. Using another brief coding scheme, record all instances in which the description of resources through labels or annotations contributed to the manifestation of the quality.
5. Describe, in free text, contributions that the arrangement of resources (such as the order of items) makes to the manifestation of the quality. (This mechanism does not employ coding categories because there was less regularity in its employment across collections.)
6. Describe, in free text, any contribution resulting from the integration of three expressive mechanisms—selection, description, and arrangement—to the manifestation of the quality.

After assessing the manifestation of each expressive quality according to these defined tasks, the assessor provided an overall expressiveness rating on a scale of 1 to 10, along with a brief explanation of that rating. (Overall expressiveness is not a simple average of the three expressive qualities, providing for the sum to be either more or less than the parts.)

Prior to beginning the appraisal, assessors discussed a draft worksheet to promote shared understanding of appraisal elements: expressive qualities under examination, mechanisms that work to produce the qualities, codes for various forms of selection and description, and so on. After revision of the worksheet, each assessor conducted several preliminary appraisals, which were then discussed to resolve discrepancies in how assessors understood appraisal elements (and not to force agreement on specific explanations or ratings). As the appraisal continued, regular discussions were held, and individual assessors prepared for these by writing memos in which they explored their rationale for rating collections differently. After completing preliminary appraisals of all collections, assessors internally harmonized their ratings, making adjustments as necessary to ensure that their own idea of what constituted a 3 or an 8 was consistent over the set of items to assess, even as their evidence for each rating might differ for each collection.

5.3 Reliability and validity argument for comparative appraisal procedure

In the literature of writing assessment, researchers identified problems with validity when students were asked to produce assessment materials that were not congruent with what instructors valued as good writing [16, 24]. For example, writing instructors might believe that good writing requires revision, and yet students would write under timed test conditions for assessment.

The comparative appraisal procedure as created for the motivating scenario avoids these problems and achieves construct validity. First, the study participants produced precisely the same materials, personal digital collections, as those examined in the first study, [9], that identified the expressive qualities. Additionally, the example and participant collections were produced in the same manner, using the same materials. Second, the characteristics of interest are directly examined in the appraisal procedure, not via indirect substitutes. The procedure looks at each expressive quality separately and provides three complementary means of registering that characteristic's presence in the collection being assessed: through a holistic numerical rating, through a holistic text explanation, and as specifically manifested through each of the three expressive mechanisms appropriate for collections: selection, description, and arrangement. Identification of selection and description contributions to each quality is systematized with defined coding categories. This three-stage process enabled us to see if a quality's manifestation is due to some previously unidentified mechanism in addition to selection, description, and arrangement: if the quality's strength is given a high rating, and yet neither selection, description, nor arrangement contributes to the presentation of that characteristic, then we have learned that the theoretical construct underlying the study is insufficient to explain the observed phenomena. Similarly, the overall expressiveness rating and explanation are separate from the assessments of the three identified expressive qualities. If collections are consistently rated more highly or poorly than the ratings for their particular qualities, then we may be able to identify additional contributors to expressiveness, or to determine that some of the previously identified qualities are more or less important than others.

In terms of a reliability argument as articulated by Parkes, the purpose of the comparative appraisal procedure is to sort the collections, both participant and example, into relatively rough ranges that represent different levels of expressiveness [27]. The goal is to merely confirm a difference between, say, an 8 and a 2, and not to draw conclusions about the difference between a 4 and a 5. Additionally, the appraisal procedure is not intended to *explain* the differences between ranges (that is, how a collection in the 8–10 range is different from a collection in the 1–3 range) or to illuminate the unique qualities of each collection in the manner of criticism, although the appraisal procedure does provide a means for identifying complementary close readings that might produce such explanations. Accordingly, the primary value enacted through this comparative appraisal procedure is consistency within the assessments contributed by a particular assessor. It is important that each rater be confident that, say, all of the 2s for overall expressiveness and for each individual characteristic are equivalent, although each 2 might be placed in that category for different reasons, and that the relative distance between a 2 and a 6, for example, is clear in the assessor's mind. Accordingly, a secondary value is coherence of explanation in each assessor's rationale for making appraisal decisions. Another secondary value is consensus between assessors on the meanings of the constituent concepts of the appraisal and on the goals of the procedure itself. The overall tolerance required for any particular appraisal is relatively low across assessors, because we are interested only in sorting into ranges, and this sorting is not designed to be an explanation of anything in itself, but only the means through which both trends and discrepancies can be characterized and explained via other means (such as close readings).

Utility of the appraisal findings does not depend on agreement across assessors for particular judgments. While relative agreement regarding placement into ranges may provide useful information, discrepancies across assessors also provide useful information. As evidence for reliability, several elements contribute to the primary value of consistency within raters. For each appraisal, an assessor provides multiple forms of judgment: numerical ratings, explanations of these ratings, and systematic identification of elements that contribute to the production of each quality (either by codes or free text). These multiple forms of judgment constitute internal checks on the assessor, ensuring a well-developed rationale for each appraisal. Moreover, the final harmonization process ensures that shifts in how judgments are applied over the length of the appraisal procedure are identified and adjustments made. The value of coherence is achieved through the writing of text explanations to supplement other forms of judgment, and through the discussions conducted throughout the process. While these discussions are not meant to persuade any assessor to change a reasoned opinion, they do require assessors to express their rationale cogently in language that others can understand, which can sometimes reveal flaws in one's initial interpretive logic. The value of consensus is also produced through discussions, in particular the initial norming sessions where the appraisal worksheet is debated, and where preliminary assessments are shared and questioned to increase mutual understanding of the constituent concepts and goals.

In sum, this section demonstrates how the comparative appraisal procedure developed for the motivating scenario achieves validity and presents a case through which a limited form of reliability is claimed to be necessary. In providing an example of such an argument, this section shows the process through which similar arguments might be made for any such appraisal, as developed for different project situations.

6. IMPLEMENTATION OF COMPARATIVE APPRAISAL IN TWO STUDIES

The comparative appraisal method developed for the motivating scenario was used in both [10] and in a subsequent experiment. It has proved successful as a key component of our data analysis, as it facilitates systematic comparison of the expressive artifacts created in our study while remaining sensitive to the complex, subtle nature of the qualities being investigated.

6.1 Initial implementation of comparative appraisal: the utility of assessor agreement

After the laboratory sessions for [10] were completed, it was apparent that the participant collections used many fewer descriptive elements (titles and annotations) than the expressive examples did. Accordingly, we assigned three assessors for the example collections, where greater complexity seemed more likely to lead to potential difference of opinions, and two for each participant collection. We also decided to focus on the more complex examples in the initial norming sessions where preliminary appraisals were discussed. As described in the previous section, while it was not important to achieve agreement between assessors, it was important for the logic used by a single assessor to be consistent within and across appraisals. This was initially confusing to some assessors; it was crucial to emphasize that there was no pressure to change assessments, only to justify them.

Additionally, it was necessary to clarify that the appraisal procedure was not meant as a vehicle to perform an abbreviated mode of criticism, that is, to explain the unique properties of a collection in an original and comprehensive way. For example, while an assessor might have had a personal reaction against a brash authorial persona expressed through a particular collection, an exploration of that reaction would not align with the goals of the appraisal; the appraisal only examined the strength and manner in which an authorial voice was presented, not the effect of that characteristic on the assessor. An appropriate appraisal in this case might claim that the use of capital letters, short phrases, and evocative wording choices in annotations produced a strong authorial voice. However, a remark that the assessor found this authorial personal distasteful would not be germane to the appraisal's goals.

Ultimately, in this study, disagreement between the assessors for each artifact was minimal. The appraisal found a large difference between participant and example collections, before and after the experimental intervention. In short, participant collections demonstrated expressive qualities much less strongly than the examples, and interacting with the examples did not have a clear effect.

With confidence in this assessment, we were then able to focus on isolating, via the close reading of both individual collections and participant interview comments, reasons for these differences. It is important to emphasize that while the comparative appraisal was a vital element in our data analysis, it did not in itself explain differences between participant and example collections. However, the findings from the appraisal enabled us to focus our subsequent efforts and construct such explanations. Briefly, our finding was that participants, despite understanding that their collections created for the study were meant for a public audience, and not for personal information management, were nonetheless building collections based on a personal information management orientation, instead of creating the collections as public expression. A significant manifestation of this personal information management approach was that participant collections used very few annotations and titles, in contrast to the example collections. While this difference in descriptive metadata was immediately apparent to us, a cogent explanation emerged only following the appraisal process and subsequent closer examination of certain collections in conjunction with interview commentary.

6.2 Second implementation of comparative appraisal: the utility of assessor disagreement

In a follow-up experiment (the findings are not yet published), we attempted to reorient participants to a mode of creative expression, instead of personal information management, by creating a test condition that explicitly separated out the mechanisms of selecting, arranging, and describing resources as distinct tasks. To keep the experiment focused on task structure, we used a physical environment instead of a digital one: participants created their collections with notecards and bulletin boards, instead of a digital library environment (see Figure 2 for an example).

In this experiment, the participant collections were much more complex (both for the test condition and the control, which did not include separate subtasks) than the previous study. Accordingly, three assessors performed appraisals on all participant collections as well as all example collections. It was especially helpful for assessors to write internal memos that made explicit rationale for

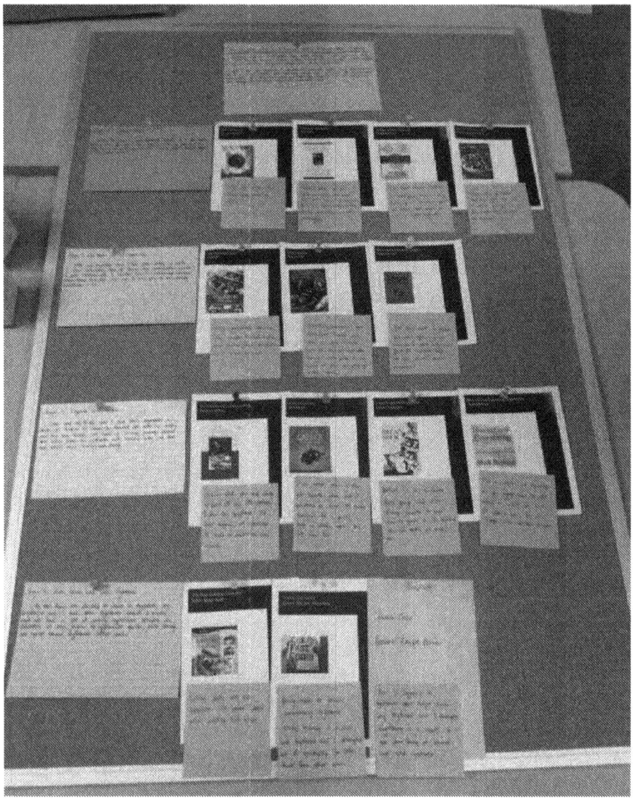

Figure 2: Participant collection from the second experiment. The white slips represent cookbooks selected for the collection; the colored notes are participant annotations.

high, low, and middle ratings. For example, one assessor wrote a memo that identified the role of cohesion, particularly regarding the characteristic of original purpose, in her judgments. This assessor realized that she consistently found collections where all the items adhered to a clearly defined purpose to be more expressive overall, and that she found digressive annotations distracting.

In this second study, findings from the appraisals showed two things. First, the participant collections as a group were much more expressive than the first study, although not quite as expressive, in terms of general ranges, as the examples. Second, there was no clear difference between the two test conditions, using a structured task to create the collections, or using an unstructured task.

As with the first experiment, the appraisal findings were necessary but not sufficient. They demonstrated differences (and lack of difference) between groups, but did not provide explanations. Despite the much greater diversity of collection expressiveness in the second study, differences in numerical ratings between assessors were modest: 1 to 2 points overall between all three assessors for the vast majority of cases. In four collections (out of 24 total), there was a discrepancy of 3 points in overall expressiveness (and none larger than 3). These discrepancies, however, were extremely productive in gaining insight from the data. In examining assessors' rationale for the divergent appraisals, it became clear that cohesion, as identified in one assessor's memo, was an important factor for all assessors but sometimes in different ways. For the first assessor, cohesion of purpose was always the most important. For the two other assessors, a fractured sort of cohesion was sometimes acceptable, as when digressive annotations for collection items contributed to the quality of authorial voice at the expense of purpose. This identification of cohesion as a primary contributor to appraisal then turned our attention to the means through which cohesion was enabled, which led us to focus on the contributions of the study's material conditions (the use of physical items) as a means of framing the collection as a creative work. The framing process became the focus of this study's findings.

7. Conclusion

Our experiences illustrate both the utility and limitation of comparative appraisal: its findings provide a solid basis for comparison, but they do not in themselves explain observed differences. However, the systematic procedure and focused attention of the appraisal, as well as assessment findings, can suggest a path toward constructing such explanations.

In summary, comparative appraisal is not a lightweight version of humanities-style criticism, nor is it a less strict means of traditional evaluation, and it is not meant to replace either. It performs a separate, useful function, just as writing assessment does: to develop criteria and associated processes to systematically sort and relate alternatives. Given the interpretive richness of the materials under consideration, any comparative appraisal must be explicitly devised to accommodate the particularities of the research or practice situation: the goals of the appraisal, the values that inform it, and the artifacts being appraised will need to be taken into account when determining what to assess, the form in which assessments should be conveyed, and the appropriate evidence to support assessment. While the localized approach advocated here is not simple, it is nonetheless tractable, and it achieves a necessary and useful balance between existing assessment modalities.

8. ACKNOWLEDGMENTS

This work was partially funded by the John P. Commons Teaching Fellowship and the Alumni Fellowship from the School of Information at the University of Texas at Austin. Many thanks to Gary Geisler, Eryn Whitworth, Ramona Broussard, Emily Clark, Eliot Scott, and Rachel Appel, my collaborators in the motivating studies. Thanks as well to Ciaran Trace for helpful comments on an earlier draft.

9. REFERENCES

[1] J. Bardzell. Interaction criticism: an introduction to the practice. *Interacting with Computers* 23, 604–621, 2011.

[2] J. Bardzell, J. Bolter, and J. Lowgren. Interaction criticism: three readings of an interaction design, and what they get us. *Interactions,* 32–37, 2010.

[3] S. Bardzell. Feminist HCI: Taking stock and outlining an agenda for design. *Proceedings of ACM CHI 2010,* 1301–1310, 2010.

[4] S. Bardzell, et al. Critical design and critical theory: the challenge of designing for provocation. *Proceedings of ACM DIS 2012,* 288–297, 2012.

[5] B. Broad. *What we really value: beyond rubrics in teaching and writing assessment.* Logan, UT: Utah State University Press, 2003.

[6] B. Broad. Introduction. *Organic writing assessment: dynamic criteria mapping in action.* Logan, UT: Utah State University Press, 2009.

[7] D. Charney. The validity of using holistic scoring to evaluate writing: a critical overview. *Research in the Teaching of English* 18(1): 65–81, 1984.

[8] B. Diederich, J. French, and S. Carlton. Factors in judgments of writing ability. Princeton, NJ: ETS report number RB-61-16, 1961.

[9] M. Feinberg. Personal expressive bibliography in the public space of cultural heritage institutions. *Library Trends* 59(4): 588–606, 2011.

[10] M. Feinberg, G. Geisler, E. Whitworth, and E. Clark. Understanding personal digital collections: an interdisciplinary exploration. *Proceedings of ACM DIS,* 200–209, 2012.

[11] N. Fuhr, et al. Evaluation of digital libraries. *Int'l Journal of Digital Libraries* 8: 21-38, 2007.

[12] B. Gaver, et al. The Prayer Companion: openness and specificity, materiality and spirituality. *Proceedings of ACM CHI 2010,* 2055–2064, 2010.

[13] B. Gaver. Cultural commentators: Non-native interpretations as resources for polyphonic assessment. *International Journal of Human-Computer Studies* 65: 292–305, 2007.

[14] G. Geisler. Open Video Digital Library Toolkit software. Documented at http://www.open-video-toolkit.org/

[15] H. Hsieh, et al. The "City of Lit" digital library: a case study of interdisciplinary research and collaboration. *Proceedings of JCDL 2012,* 203-212, 2012.

[16] B. Huot. Toward a new theory of writing assessment. *College Composition and Communication* 47(4): 549–566, 1996.

[17] M. Khoo and C. MacDonald. An organizational model for digital library evaluation. *Proceedings of TPDL 2011,* 329-340, 2011.

[18] B. Lee, et al. Designing with interactive example galleries. *Proceedings of ACM CHI 2010,* 2257–2266, 2010.

[19] P. Likarish and J. Winet. Exquisite corpse 2.0: qualitative analysis of a community-based fiction project. *Proceedings of ACM DIS 2012,* 564-567, 2012.

[20] J. Lowgren and E. Stolterman. *Thoughtful interaction design.* Cambridge, MA: MIT Press, 2004.

[21] C. Lynch. Digital collections, digital libraries, and the digitization of cultural heritage material. *First Monday* 7(5): 2002. (Available at: http://firstmonday.org/htbin/cgiwrap/bin/ojs/index.php/fm/article/view/949/870)

[22] P. Marty and M. Kazmer. Introduction to understanding users. *Library Trends* 59(4): 563–567, 2011.

[23] J. McCarthy and P. Wright. *Technology as experience.* Cambridge, MA: MIT Press, 2004.

[24] P. Moss. Can there be validity without reliability? *Educational Researcher* 23(2): 5–12, 1994.

[25] J. Nielsen and R. Molich. Heuristic evaluation of user interfaces. *Proceedings of ACM CHI 1990,* 249-256, 1990.

[26] P. O'Neill, C. Moore, and B. Huot. *Guide to college writing assessment.* Logan, UT: Utah State University Press, 2009.

[27] J. Parkes. Reliability as argument. *Educational Measurement: Issues and Practice,* Winter 2007.

[28] D. Petrelli, et al. Digital Christmas: an exploration of festive technology. *Proceedings of ACM DIS 2012,* 348-357, 2012.

[29] P. Sengers, et al. Reflective design. *Proceedings of AARHUS 2005,*49-58, 2005.

[30] A. Wolff, et al. Storyspace: a story-driven approach for creating museum narratives. *Proceedings Hypertext 2012,* 89-98, 2012.

Charting the Digital Library Evaluation Domain with a Semantically Enhanced Mining Methodology

Eleni Afiontzi
Department of Informatics, Athens University of Economics & Business, Athens, Greece
afiontzhe@aueb.gr

Giannis Kazadeis
Department of Informatics, Athens University of Economics & Business, Athens, Greece
kazadehsi@aueb.gr

Leonidas Papachristopoulos
Department of Archives and Library Science, Ionian University, Corfu, Greece
l11papa@ionio.gr

Michalis Sfakakis
Department of Archives & Library Science, Ionian University, Corfu, Greece
sfakakis@ionio.gr

Giannis Tsakonas
Department of Archives & Library Science, Ionian University, Corfu, Greece
gtsak@ionio.gr

Christos Papatheodorou
Department of Archives & Library Science, Ionian University, Corfu, Greece
papatheodor@ionio.gr

ABSTRACT
The digital library evaluation field has an evolving nature and it is characterized by a noteworthy proclivity to enfold various methodological orientations. Given the fact that the scientific literature in the specific domain is vast, researchers require tools that will exhibit either commonly acceptable practices, or areas for further investigation. In this paper, a data mining methodology is proposed to identify prominent patterns in the evaluation of digital libraries. Using Machine Learning techniques, all papers presented in the ECDL and JCDL conferences between the years 2001 and 2011 were categorized as relevant or non-relevant to the DL evaluation domain. Then, the relevant papers were semantically annotated according to the Digital Library Evaluation Ontology (DiLEO) vocabulary. The produced set of annotations was clustered to evaluation patterns for the most frequently used tools, methods and goals of the domain. Our findings highlight the expressive nature of DiLEO, place emphasis on semantic annotation as a necessary step in handling domain-centric corpora and underline the potential of the proposed methodology in the profiling of evaluation activities.

Categories and Subject Descriptors
H.3 [**Information Storage and Retrieval**]: H.3.7 Digital Libraries

Keywords
Digital library evaluation; ontologies; semantic annotation; data mining; research trends.

1. INTRODUCTION
Digital Library (DL) evaluation experimenting is "a complex and challenging proposition, theoretically and pragmatically" [1] that requires thoughtful planning and precise decisions. Deep knowledge of the research gaps, as well as awareness of the benefits and drawbacks of specific experimental methods can be acquired with comprehensive exploration and understanding of the literature. But with the constantly growing literature, researchers experience difficulties in finding specific information that will help them propel their work. The growth of scientific literature coincides with important developments in web content management and the proliferation of sophisticated tools, which emerge as an important aid in the researchers' endeavor. These tools can play a catalytic role in the untangling of conceptually complex and disperse fields, such as DLs and their evaluation, while at the same time they can semantically represent these fields in a way that alleviates heterogeneity. Each scientific field of the DLs contributes to the heterogeneity of the domain in terms of research paradigms, approaches, methods and tools. For instance, several studies can be conducted for the same DL or DL system, but they can differ in terms of goals, means or metrics. These ambiguities are often misrepresented in the scientific literature, especially in the conference literature, where several restrictions apply, and prohibit the communication of critical information in a coherent manner.

The goal of this paper is to propose a methodology for discovering meaningful evaluation patterns (profiles) in the DL literature. Such patterns recommend evaluation activities for particular DL settings. We decompose this goal to the following research questions and investigate them by exploiting data mining techniques:

1. How to select the corpus of studies focusing on DL evaluation from a collection on DL literature? We investigate this sub-goal applying supervised learning techniques.
2. How to semantically annotate the corpus of the studies on DL evaluation? To accomplish this sub-goal we exploit the Digital Library Evaluation Ontology (DiLEO) [2] and describe an annotation process based on supervised learning.
3. Can we define a solid method for the formulation of meaningful profiles of evaluation initiatives? For this purpose we utilize unsupervised learning techniques to group and organize common evaluation practices. On the outcome of this process, we propose three metrics to characterize the derived groups and generate the evaluation patterns.

To investigate the applicability of the proposed methodology we validate it on the papers presented in the ACM/IEEE Joint Conference on Digital Libraries (JCDL) and the European Conference on Digital Libraries (ECDL, now known as the

International Conference on Theory and Practice of Digital Libraries) in the period 2001 to 2011. The exploitation of data mining to qualify evaluation concepts within studies could assist the classification of future evaluation initiatives to coherent groups according to their characteristics. Furthermore, researchers could "zoom and pan" on the domain and select the study profile that interests them, such as to discover goals that can be further explored. Our attempt emphasizes on the bidirectional relationship between annotations and text classification as an efficient way of handling capacious corpora. The present study is structured as follows: section 2 gives the background of our study and section 3 gives the research setting emphasizing on the corpus formulation and its semantic annotation. Section 4 presents the findings of the DL evaluation patterns discovery procedure, which are discussed in section 5, and section 6 concludes and outlines the future steps.

2. BACKGROUND

The abundance of information is a crucial problem for all researchers. In 2003, early before the breakthrough of semantic technologies, a report of a NSF workshop mentioned that one of the central research directions of DLs would be to "Reduce Data to Actionable Information" and that "Key to the effective use of ever-growing information is reducing the human overhead required to obtain from digital libraries and the Web more generally, while retaining the valuable contents..." [3]. While the report refers to web content, the same truth applies in scientific literature too, which is now entirely digitally born and up to a point self managed. Researchers have employed several methods to manage the literature and search into it for relevant information. Structured methods of literature reviewing and coding, such as content analysis or systematic reviews, are important tools to this end. Christie and Fleische [4] have used content analysis techniques to categorize evaluation studies presented in prominent evaluation focused journals, according to their design features and data collection methods. Recently, Kelly and Sugimoto [5] used a systematic review protocol to uncover research design details in the field of Interactive Information Retrieval in a time span of forty years. These are significant tools that assist researchers to acquire useful overviews of each field, yet their effect is limited as they only portray specific views of its evolution and cannot be easily reused. Furthermore, what is needed is to add-value to the outcomes of the processes by contextualizing information and giving meaning by associating to other information aspects. Attwood et al. [6] mention that "For information to be usable, it must be stored and organized in ways that allow us to access it, to analyze it, to annotate it and *to relate it* to other information; only then can we begin to understand what it means; only with the acquisition of meaning do we acquire knowledge" (emphasis ours). The advance of semantic technologies has enabled well known and established initiatives, such as the Cochrane Collaboration, to explore the transformation of existing corpora (in this case reviews) to machine-readable formats. Biolchini et al. [7] introduced the Scientific Research Ontology for Software Engineering, which is an ontology adhering to systematic review protocols for the structured representation of research data in the field of software engineering.

Furthermore, researchers can take advantage of the developments in the nanopublications area and semantically integrate and disseminate snippets of information, which is so far rigidly 'stored' in the literature. A nanopublication is a citable unit containing a set of annotated statements that capture knowledge in the form of Resource Description Framework (RDF) triples, representing three concepts (a subject, a predicate and an object) [8]. These statements are scientific assertions organized on domain semantics, such as ontologies (according to [9] "should be treated as the smallest building blocks of them"), and at the same time are receptive to provenance declarations and citation. Other semantic enabling constructs, such as the OAI-ORE model [10], have been used to represent relationships among research entities and present common scientific workflows.

Soldatova and King [11] used the EXPO ontology to express domain independent research processes and they claimed that a formal description of experimental designs "...will make scientific knowledge more explicit, help detect errors, promote the interchange and reliability of experimental methods and conclusions, and remove redundancies in domain-specific ontologies". Recently, Brahaj, Razum and Schwichtenberg [12] described the transformation process of the Core of Scientific Metadata Model metadata schema into the Core of Scientific Metadata Ontology in order to facilitate the re-usability of research data that are acquired during laboratory experiments. Soo et al. [13] showcased that retrieval metrics can be improved through semantically processed texts. Indeed, semantic annotation is important for the enrichment of a corpus and its transformation to machine-readable formats.

This paper proposes a methodology for the automatic discovery of research patterns in the domain of DL evaluation. To reach this aim we exploit a domain ontology, DiLEO [2], to semantically annotate the scientific literature and structure research patterns from the generated corpus of annotations. DiLEO has been used as an analytical tool of semantic annotations in [14, 15], however the need to progress to the stage of automated semantic annotation process and then to annotations clustering in an efficient mode is imperative, for reasons of effective management of large corpora. Furthermore the present study extends the results of [16] and compares clustering algorithms in an effort to organize common evaluation practices to a dynamic thematic map. The exploitation of such a methodology in an evolving literature could improve the discovery of relevant studies in a reusable, contextualized and semantically enhanced way, so that tasks for DL evaluation planning can be performed in a convenient way.

3. RESEARCH SETTING

The investigation of the research questions is obtained by a data mining methodology which consists of the following stages:

- the first stage aims to formulate a corpus by selecting the DL evaluation related studies from the collection of the DL literature with the use of a trained classifier.
- the second stage concerns the annotation of the corpus on the basis of the DiLEO ontology. The results of the annotation fed a multi-label classification mechanism so that any new corpora can be automatically semantically annotated.
- the third stage regards the clustering of the annotations' corpus to identify meaningful evaluation patterns.

3.1 Corpus

A crucial step of the process was to select the most appropriate classifier for the papers referring to DL evaluation. To train the classifier, the studies of the ACM/IEEE Joint Conference on Digital Libraries and the European Conference on Digital Libraries during the period 2001-2011 were separated into two categories: papers mentioning DL evaluation processes (positive) and papers that were irrelevant to DL evaluation studies (negative). The data set consisted of the full and short papers of the two conferences, as well as the studies that reported posters, totally 1,824 documents.

3.1.1 Training and Pre-processing

For the training phase of classification two researchers worked independently and in parallel to categorize the papers, while a third researcher was responsible for the troubleshooting and the supervision of the procedure. A triple of descriptive fields, namely the papers' (i) title, (ii) abstract and (iii) author keywords, which were all common in both conferences, was the criteria for this categorization. Rater's agreement calculation resulted in 78% for ECDL and 82.96% for JCDL, while the inter-rater agreement calculation on Cohen's Kappa [17] was found at moderate level for both conferences (κ=0.508 for ECDL and κ=0.458 for JCDL). Each disagreement was resolved by another researcher who provided a third opinion, while additional discussions were conducted if the ambiguity for a paper's inclusion persisted.

Finally, from the 1,824 papers, a corpus of 224 positive (relevant to DL evaluation) and 1,600 negative (non relevant) papers was formed, retaining a distribution of 12% positive and 88% negative. More specifically, 97 (43%) positive papers were presented at the JCDL, while 127 (57%) at ECDL, as well as 1,063 (66%) negative papers were presented at JCDL, while 537 (34%) where presented at ECDL.[1] It is worth mentioning that the highly imbalanced proportion between the positive and the negative classes in the data set has influence on the performance of the learning system during the classification model generation.

Since the distribution of positive/negative papers was found to be skewed we adopted re-sampling techniques [18]. The approaches applied to the data were under-sampling, a method that eliminates examples from the majority class (the negative class in our case), as well as over-sampling, a technique that balances the data set by replicating positive examples from the minority class [18, 19]. In particular, the Tomek Links [20] was used as the under-sampling method. Two training examples E_i and E_j belonging to different classes form a Tomek Link, if there is not an example E_l, such that $d(E_i, E_l) < d(E_i, E_j)$ or $d(E_j, E_l) < d(E_i, E_j)$, where $d(E_i, E_j)$ is the distance between the elements E_i and E_j. As an over-sampling technique we used random over-sampling, which randomly copies to the data set minority class examples, in our case the positive examples.

The full text of the 1,824 pdf documents was extracted to plain text. Words were converted to lowercase, while formatting elements, emails and numbers not measuring evaluation quantities (e.g. section numbers) were eliminated. However, all numbers referring to measures were normalized to a common pattern. The words of each paper were represented using the 'bag-of-words' approach.

3.1.2 Classification algorithm

Naïve Bayes algorithm was selected for the categorization of the documents, despite its simplicity and the fact that its conditional independence assumption rarely holds in real-world problems. Naïve Bayes text classifiers tend to perform well, even to small data sets [21], while they are optimal for certain problem classes with highly dependent features [22].

In the Naïve Bayes approach, the class c which has the maximum value of the conditional probability $P(c|d)$ is assigned to a given document d. Assuming feature independence, the $P(c|d)$ is estimated as the product of the prior probability $P(c)$ of the class c times the conditional probabilities $P(w|c)$ of observing word w given class c, for all words w in d. Our training method consists of relative-frequency estimation of $P(c)$ and $P(w|c)$ using add-one smoothing.

3.1.3 Corpus Definition

The data set of the 1,824 documents was randomly split into two sets, the development set, which consisted of the 75% of the data and the test set, which consisted of the remaining 25% of the data. In both development and test data sets the proportion of the positive and negative classes was preserved. The parameters of the classification algorithms were tuned using a ten-fold cross-validation method on the development set, in which the set was divided randomly into ten equal sets and the classifier used a 9/10 portion as training set and the rest 1/10 as test set for each of the ten different training and evaluation steps. The proportion of the positive and the negative classes was also preserved in every step of the ten-fold validation process.

For the evaluation and comparison of the Naïve Bayes performance the measures *Accuracy*, *True Positive Rate* (*tp rate*) and *False Positive Rate* (*fp rate*) were used. However due to the unbalanced data *Accuracy* cannot be considered a precise measure [18]. Therefore *tp rate* and *fp rate* can provide us more realistic results. *tp rate* measures the proportion of the positive correctly classified documents over the total positives, while the *fp rate* measures the proportion of the negative incorrectly classified documents over the total negatives. It is worth mentioning that *tp rate* and *fp rate* are independent of the class distribution.

Each row of Table 1 presents the performance of the Naïve Bayes algorithm to the development and test data sets using alternative re-sampling methods. The second row corresponds to the unbalanced data set produced by the elimination of the negative papers using the Tomek Links method. The third row refers to the balanced data set produced by applying Tomek Links to the negative papers for under-sampling, with the combination of random over-sampling for the positive papers. The last two rows are balanced data sets using, either random under-sampling, or over-sampling. All the values in the columns that correspond to the development set are averages from the ten-fold cross validation procedure. From this procedure we selected the median classifier, which was applied to the test set and the respective results appear to the test data set columns.

Table 1. Performance results of document classification

Data sets	Development			Test		
Measures	*Accuracy*	*tp rate*	*fp rate*	*Accuracy*	*tp rate*	*fp rate*
Original	0.82	0.33	0.12	0.87	0.39	0.07
Tomek Links	0.8	0.52	0.16	0.84	0.65	0.13
Tomek Links & random over-sampling	0.87	0.95	0.19	0.84	0.68	0.14
Random under-sampling	0.67	0.81	0.47	0.64	0.77	0.38
Random over-sampling	0.89	0.91	0.13	0.86	0.45	0.08

An accepted classifier has to balance the highest *tp rate* with the minimum *fp rate*. In our case the highest *tp rate* corresponds to the selection of the highest number of the papers that was relevant to DL evaluation and the minimum *fp rate* corresponds to the mistaken selection of non-relevant papers. Even though random

[1] Dataset available at http://www.ionio.gr/labs/dbis/jcdl-addendum.html

sampling methods perform well and can be easily implemented, they can either increase the possibility of over fitting, or discard potentially useful data for the classifier [18]. As shown in Table 1, the random sampling methods do not provide balanced results between *tp* and *fp rates*. They provide either high *tp* and also high *fp rates*, or low *tp* and low *fp rates*. Using Tomek Links as the under-sampling method and balancing the class distribution by applying random over-sampling, we achieved the best balance between the *tp rate* (68%) and the *fp rate* (14%) that can be considered acceptable for the classifier on the test-set.

3.2 Semantic Annotation

3.2.1 DiLEO as annotation schema

The semantic annotation of the literature requires a highly structured schema that could contextualize the information by linking any related bits together. Therefore, the use of DiLEO, an ontology developed for the DL evaluation domain, was opted, as it constitutes an instrument for the unified conceptual management of the domain of DL evaluation. DiLEO addresses the need for "a conceptual model which contains a certain formality that can meaningfully correlate evaluation data and cover the wide spectrum of the respective initiatives." [2] DiLEO is divided in two layers (Figure 1), namely the strategic and the procedural.

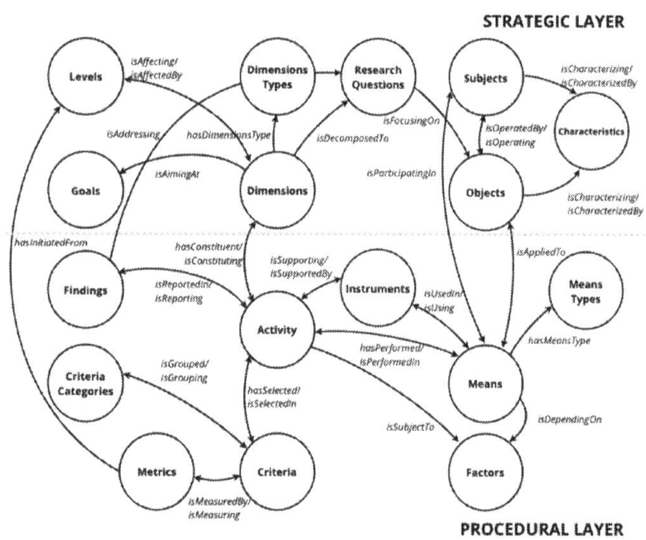

Figure 1. The ontology's two-tiered organization

The strategic layer is a host of classes that outline high-level concepts of the evaluation, such as *Goals*, *Dimensions*, *Dimensions Type*, *Research Questions*, *Levels*, evaluation *Objects* and *Subjects*. In each evaluation study there is a *Goal* that is defined by the subclasses *describe*, *document* and *design*. Similarly, the class of *Dimensions* outlines the scope of an evaluation, which can be one or more of the subclasses *effectiveness*, *performance measurement*, *service quality*, *outcome assessment* and *technical excellence*. The stage in which an evaluation is taking place characterizes the *Dimension Type* and comprises the subclasses *summative*, *formative* and *iterative*. Every *Research Question* provides a detailed view of the aim of the study and is related with the entire research design, as well as with the expected *Findings*. The *Levels* class denotes the aspects of a DL which are affected by the evaluation and includes the subclasses *content level*, *engineering level*, *processing level*, *interface level*, *individual level*, *institutional level* and *social level*.

An *Object* in an evaluation process is the entity under focus and is sub-divided to the subclasses *product* and *operation*. Similarly a *Subject* is an actor in typical DL tasks and is divided to the subclasses *human agent* and *machine agent*. Both *Subject* and *Object* have *Characteristics*, which are giving them qualitative and quantitative features.

The second layer, the procedural, hosts a set of classes that specify in detail the practical aspects of an evaluation. The *Activity* class includes the operations that are performed by the evaluators in several stages and comprises the subclasses *record*, *measure*, *compare*, *analyze*, *interpret*, *report* and *recommend*. The performance of the aforementioned activities is subject to several limiting or amplifying conditions, which constitute the *Factors* class comprising the subclasses *time*, *cost*, *infrastructure* and *personnel*. During their activities, the evaluators utilize several methods that define the class *Means* and its subclasses *logging studies*, *laboratory studies*, *field studies*, *survey studies expert studies*, *comparison studies*. Furthermore, the performance of *Means* presupposes the usage of research *Instruments*; the subclasses of this class are *devices*, *narrative items*, *research artifacts*, *scales*, *software* and *statistics*. Consequently, these instruments are used according to some *Criteria*, which control the evaluation processes and consist of the subclasses standards, toolkit and specific aim criteria. *Criteria* are grouped in broader logical units, the *Criteria Categories*, which represent areas of research interest. *Metrics* are these constructs that help evaluators capture the state of a system or outline subject opinions and preferences, and to indicate any gaps between this state and the expected or ideal one. The *Metrics* subclasses are *user originated*, *content originated* and *system originated*. Finally, the class of *Findings* is a receiver for the main study findings which can be cross-checked with the research questions.

All DiLEO classes are related through a set of properties, which define the extent and the quality of the relationship in terms of particular constraints. These properties are catalytic in the support of precise reasoning. The ontology instances generate a knowledge base upon which a researcher can query and extract knowledge on evaluation initiatives.

3.2.2 Supervised Annotation

Since the semantic annotation could be considered a multi-label classification process, we exploited classification algorithms to automatically annotate our corpus. The training of the classification algorithms was based on the identification of the 54 DiLEO subclasses on the corpus of the 224 papers derived by the process described in section 3.1. A critical step preceding the training phase was the affirmation both of the domain knowledge and the familiarity with the ontology to produce a qualitative result. To actualize the specific goal, the annotators followed the process in [23], which is established on repetitive training and discussion to create solid guidelines. After the familiarization with the corpus and the structure of the ontology, an initial meeting was held to present thoroughly the latter and resolve any inquiries. A stage followed, where annotators applied the ontology on a random set of papers to point out special cases, which needed clarification. Iterative meetings led to the formation of guidelines, which were followed strictly at the core annotation process.

The full text of each of the papers in the corpus was semantically annotated manually by an ontology expert and two domain experts with the goal to identify instances of the DiLEO subclasses. The ontology expert worked independently in order to support the decision of the team in case of conflict and the other two cooperated in order to create a single annotated corpus. Each sentence of each paper of the corpus was investigated in order to find if it identifies a DiLEO instance. To assess the correctness of annotation and to produce unanimous results, random crosschecks were performed during that phase and any disagreements were resolved through discussion.

For the annotation procedure the semantic annotation tool GoNTogle [24] was used and an RDFS knowledge base was generated. GoNTogle is built on top of Lucene and uses the weighted k-NN classifier allowing either manual or automated ontology-based annotation. Given a sentence of a DL paper, GoNTogle estimates a score for each class/subclass, calculating the presence of this class in the k nearest (in text similarity terms) neighbors (annotated sentences). Finally, a ranked list of the suggested classes/subclasses and their score ranging from 0 to 1 is presented to the user. The user may choose none, one or more of suggested classes/subclasses to conclude the annotation process. Totally 2,672 annotations were manually generated. Several sentences were not annotated as DiLEO class instances, while some others carry instances of more than one class.

3.2.3 *Classification of Annotations*

The RDFS statements were exported from the database of GoNTogle and were processed to construct a new data set. Stopwords, symbols and numbers were removed; words were converted to lowercase and word frequencies were calculated to be used by certain algorithms. Again, experiments were conducted both with un-stemmed (4,880 features in total) and stemmed (3,257 features) words using the Lovins Stemmer. The ontology classes were represented by 54 additional binary features; if an annotated sentence, represented by a vector, belonged to a class then the respective feature had the value of 1, otherwise it was represented by 0. The machine learning framework Meka [25] was used for multi-label classification, which expands Weka's functionalities by providing support for development, execution and evaluation of multi-label classifiers.

Multi-label classification methods can be categorized into two different groups: (i) problem transformation methods and (ii) algorithm adaptation methods. The first group contains methods that are algorithm independent. They transform the multi-label classification task into one or more binary classification, regression or ranking tasks. In our experiments we tested three problem transformation methods: (i) binary relevance (BR), which considers the prediction of each label as an independent binary classification task, (ii) label power-set (LP), where each different set of labels in a multi-label training set becomes a different class in a new binary classification task and (iii) RAkEL, which uses random k-label sets for LP instead of the full label set. For each of these methods we ran four commonly used algorithms, namely:

- Naïve Bayes (NB), which estimates the probability of each class for a document based on Bayes theorem.
- Multinomial Naïve Bayes (MNB), which is a specialized version of Naïve Bayes. It explicitly models the word counts and adjusts the underlying calculations, whereas simple Naïve Bayes models a document as a binary vector.
- k-Nearest-Neighbors (k-NN). Given a test point, a predefined similarity metric is used to find the k most similar points from the train set. The instance is classified by a majority vote of its k neighbors.
- Support Vector Machines (SVM). The SVM problem is to find the decision surface that maximizes the margin between the data points of the two classes.

The algorithm adaptation group contains methods that extend specific learning algorithms to handle multi-label data directly. From this group we tested the multi-label k-nearest neighbor (MLkNN) algorithm [26].

The evaluation of multi-label classification methods requires different measures than those used in the case of single-label data. The following evaluation measures were used [26]:

- Hamming Loss, which evaluates how many times an instance-label pair is misclassified and is defined as follows:

$$\text{Hamming Loss} = \frac{1}{\mathrm{N} * \mathrm{L}} * \sum_{i=1}^{\mathrm{N}} \left| Y_i \Delta \hat{Y}_i \right|$$

  where N is the number of instances, L the number of labels, Y_i and $\hat{Y}_i$ the correct and predicted values of a label set and Δ stands for the logical operator XOR. Lower Hamming Loss values, indicate better classification.
- A multi-label measure of accuracy was used, which does not take into account the true negative (TN) predictions and is calculated as:

$$Accuracy = \frac{1}{N} * \sum_{i=1}^{N} \frac{\left| Y_i \cap \hat{Y}_i \right|}{\left| Y_i \cup \hat{Y}_i \right|}$$

- One-error, which evaluates how many times the top-ranked label is not in the set of proper labels of the instance:

Table 2. Performance comparison of multi-label classification algorithms

Method	Binary Relevance								Label Powersets								RAkEL								ML-kNN	
	NB		MNB		k-NN (k=9)		SVM		NB		MNB		k-NN (k=9)		SVM		NB		MNB		k-NN (k=9)		SVM			
stem	*no*	*yes*	*no*	*yes*	*no*	*yes*	*no*	*yes*	*no*	*yes*	*no*	*yes*	*no*	*yes*	*no*	*yes*	*no*	*yes*	*no*	*yes*	*no*	*yes*	*no*	*yes*	*no*	*yes*
Hamming Loss	0.02	0.02	0.03	0.02	0.03	0.02	0.01	0.01	0.01	0.01	0.02	0.02	0.03	0.02	0.01	0.01	0.02	0.02	0.02	0.02	0.02	0.02	0.01	0.01	0.02	0.02
Accuracy	0.41	0.45	0.28	0.29	0.22	0.36	0.53	0.58	0.55	0.58	0.47	0.45	0.28	0.35	0.62	0.63	0.46	0.49	0.29	0.24	0.03	0.07	0.56	0.59	0.31	0.42
One-Error	0.33	0.29	0.31	0.35	0.65	0.50	0.39	0.35	0.36	0.33	0.46	0.48	0.65	0.57	0.29	0.27	0.46	0.44	0.63	0.68	0.91	0.87	0.35	0.31	0.52	0.44
F_1 macro	0.34	0.37	0.19	0.22	0.18	0.26	0.42	0.47	0.34	0.36	0.22	0.21	0.14	0.21	0.41	0.44	0.36	0.38	0.21	0.20	0.04	0.05	0.43	0.48	0.25	0.32

$$One-Error=\frac{1}{N}*\sum_{i=1}^{N}\delta(\arg\min r_i(\lambda))_{\lambda\in L}$$

where $r_i(\lambda)$ denotes the rank predicted by a method for a label λ and

$$\delta(\lambda)=1\ if\ \lambda\notin Y_i,0\ otherwise$$

- F1 measure was calculated using macro-averaging:

$$F_{1macro}=\frac{2*(\frac{1}{L}*\sum_{\lambda=1}^{L}Precision_\lambda)*(\frac{1}{L}*\sum_{\lambda=1}^{L}Recall_\lambda)}{(\frac{1}{L}*\sum_{\lambda=1}^{L}Precision_\lambda)+(\frac{1}{L}*\sum_{\lambda=1}^{L}Recall_\lambda)}$$

To evaluate the accuracy of the multi-label classification algorithms the data set was divided into three sections. The first part, including approximately 60% of the annotations (1,600), is defined as the training set, while 510 annotations (approximately 20%) were used as the development set for tuning the parameters of the problem. The remaining annotations (20%) formed the test set. The performance results for each of the four multi-label classification methods are presented in Table 2.

It was observed that stemming improves the classification performance of all different algorithms and methods. Concerning the multi-label methods, label power-set achieves the best performance for all algorithms. As far as the classification algorithms are concerned, SVM outperforms the other algorithms given the specific dataset and labels. The derived results are encouraging since they are in accordance with the performance results from experiments held on large-scale text corpora [25].

Table 3. GoNTogle performance tests

Threshold >	*0.16*	*0.18*	*0.2*
Hamming Loss	0.0199	0.0182	0.0176
Accuracy	0.5	0.4926	0.4607
One-Error	0.29	0.29	0.29
F_1 macro	0.415	0.3932	0.3665

The performance tests were repeated using GoNTogle. The system can be adjusted by setting a score threshold above which a class is assigned to a new instance. Our experiments ran for three thresholds: 0.16, 0.18 and 0.20 and the evaluation results are presented in Table 3. The threshold value of 0.18 provides better (lower) results in terms of Hamming Loss and has almost identical values of Accuracy and F1 measure as threshold 0.16. On the other hand, value 0.20, while achieving slightly better results in Hamming Loss, is at great disadvantage at Accuracy and F1 measure. One-Error is not affected by the threshold selection. Therefore, a 0.18 threshold is recommended for this dataset in GoNTogle. Overall, GoNTogle achieves good results in comparison to the tested multi-label classification algorithms, considering that the appropriate threshold is chosen.

3.3 Pattern Discovery

The first stage of the discovery of DL evaluation patterns was to aggregate the annotations of each paper from the GoNTogle knowledge base. 53 out of the 54 selected subclasses of DiLEO were found in the annotations; hence these subclasses were used as features of the documents to be clustered (the subclass *machine agents* did not appear in the annotations). Thus the derived data set consists of 224 vectors of 53 features, representing the assigned annotations from the DiLEO vocabulary to the document corpus. More specifically, the annotated documents are defined as vectors A_m=(f_1, f_2, ..., f_n), where A_m, m=1, ..., 224 denotes an annotated document representation and f_n, n=1, ..., 53 denotes a feature representing a DiLEO subclass.

During our experimentation we opted for two different methods of clustering algorithms. The first method is the K-Means algorithm, well-known for partitioning M data points to K clusters, and the Agglomerative Hierarchical Clustering, which seeks to build an hierarchy of clusters by applying a 'bottom up' approach [27]. Moreover, the algorithms were applied to the vectors using different weighting schemata and similarity measures.

In order to select the number of clusters K, the K-means algorithm was applied for values of K between 1 and 53 and the results of the objective (cost or error) function were recorded. After plotting the objective function results against the number of the clusters K, the rate of decrease peaked at the values between 9 and 13 for K. Thereafter, we examined the clustering resulted from the values of K equal to 11, 12 and 14. The clustering that resulted in 11 clusters outperforms the other clustering processes, for both algorithms according to the evaluation procedure that follows. Moreover, given that the K-means is highly dependent on the initialization of centroids, it was run 200 times using different randomly initialized centroids. Then the clustering with the lowest cost was selected.

For the hierarchical clustering algorithm, the *agnes* function (Agglomerative Nesting) of the *Clustering* package of the R software was used [27, 28]. Cosine similarity was used as the similarity measure between the vectors, while for the inter-cluster distance during the bottom up process of the clustering Lance-Williams formula [29] was selected.

Two alternative formulations were tested for the annotation vectors A_m assigning different types of values to the features. In the first formulation the features were binary, therefore the feature f_i had the value of one if the respective to f_i subclass was assigned to the document m, or zero otherwise. In the second formulation, the value of the feature f_i was determined according to a variation of the *tf-idf* weighting schema. To formulate this representation it should be pointed out that each of the 53 DiLEO subclasses is assigned at most once to a document. Therefore, the feature frequency ff_i of the feature f_i in all vectors was equal to one when the respective subclass was annotated to the respective document, or zero otherwise. Thereafter, given that the ff_i value corresponds to the *tf* part of the weighting schema, the feature f_i in the vector A_j is calculated according to the following variation of the *tf-idf* schema:

$$idf_i=\log\left(\frac{M}{1+df_i}\right), tf-idf_{i,j}=ff_{i,j}*idf_i$$

where M is the number of documents, df_i is the document frequency of the feature f_i and idf_i expresses the inverse document frequency of the feature f_i.

The most significant features of each cluster model the DL evaluation patterns. To enable their discovery by characterizing each cluster with respect to the terms of DiLEO, we used the *frequency increase* measure (henceforth FI), which calculates the increase of the frequency of a feature f_i in the cluster k, ($cf_{i,k}$) compared to its document frequency df_i in the whole data set. The frequency increase of the feature f_i in the cluster k, $FI_{i,k}$, is defined as the difference between the squares of the two frequency measures as specified by the following formula, where C_k is the number of documents in the cluster k:

$$FI_{i,k} = \left(\frac{cf_{i,k}}{C_k}\right)^2 - \left(\frac{df_i}{M}\right)^2$$

Intuitively, a representative feature of a cluster should be used to annotate a large number of documents in the cluster; hence its frequency in the cluster will increase. In contrast, for a non representative feature the values of FI measure will be low and probably negative. A feature is defined as representative for a cluster if $FI_{i,k} > \alpha$, where α is the required extent of frequency increase. If $\alpha > 0$ then the frequency of the feature within a cluster is greater than the frequency of that feature in the initial dataset. If the FI value of a feature in a cluster becomes negative or lower than α then the feature will be filtered out from the representative features of that cluster, even if this feature has been assigned to several documents. As α increases, the number of the representative features in the clusters decreases and clusters become more distinct, generating clear evaluation profiles. The question that arises is how to determine objectively the value of the threshold parameter α, so that to define a set of features that characterizes a cluster.

In order to estimate the impact of the threshold parameter α, two indicators are defined: Coverage and Dissimilarity Mean. Hence, the selected value of the threshold α is the value that maximizes both Coverage and Dissimilarity Mean measures.

Coverage is defined as the proportion of the features participating in the clusters, for a particular FI value, to the total number of features used for annotation and is specified by the formula:

$$Coverage = \frac{\left|\bigcup_{k=1}^{K}\{f_i : FI_{i,k} \geq a\}\right|}{N}$$

Dissimilarity Mean expresses the average distinctiveness of the clusters and is defined in terms of the dissimilarity $d_{i,j}$ between all possible pairs of the clusters. Specifically, the dissimilarity $d_{i,j}$ between two clusters i and j, the mean of dissimilarity $DMean_i$ of a cluster i and the Dissimilarity Mean are specified by the following formulas respectively:

$$d_{i,j} = 1 - \frac{|\{f_n : (FI_{n,i} \geq \alpha) \wedge (FI_{n,j} \geq \alpha)\}|}{|\{f_n : (FI_{n,i} \geq \alpha) \vee (FI_{n,j} \geq \alpha)\}|}$$

$$DMean_i = \frac{1}{K-1}\sum_{j=1}^{K} d_{i,j}, \quad i \neq j$$

$$DissimilarityMean = \frac{1}{K}\sum_{k=1}^{K} DMean_k$$

F1-measure is the harmonic mean of Coverage and Dissimilarity Mean and expresses an acceptable balance between them. It is specified as follows:

$$F1 - measure = 2 * \frac{Coverage * DissimilarityMean}{Coverage + DissimilarityMean}$$

The highest value of the F1-measure determines the desired value of the threshold parameter α.

Concluding, given the document annotations based on the DiLEO ontology, the workflow for discovering patterns of evaluation practices consists of the following steps: (i) representation of the annotated documents by two alternative vector models, the binary and the weighted *tf-idf*, (ii) clustering of the vector representations of the annotations by applying the two clustering algorithms, (iii) assessment of the features of each cluster using the frequency increase metric, (iv) selection of the threshold α that maximizes the F1-measure between the Coverage and Dissimilarity Mean indicators, and (v) identification of the evaluation patterns based on the representative features of the clusters.

4. DL EVALUATION PATTERNS

In general K-Means outperforms the hierarchical clustering algorithm, especially when the *tf-idf* weighted schema is used. The curves of Coverage, Dissimilarity Mean and F1-measure with respect to the parameter α -as it ranges from 0 to 1 with a step of 0.05- are shown in Figures 2-4. The curves correspond to the performance of the K-Means algorithm when applied to both binary and *tf-idf* representations of the annotated documents and the performance of the hierarchical algorithm when applied only to the *tf-idf* representation of the documents. For the majority of threshold α values, K-Means indicates better results for Coverage (Figure 2) and F1-measure (Figure 4). For the Dissimilarity (Figure 3) hierarchical algorithm indicates better results, while all algorithms converge to 1 when $\alpha > 0.7$.

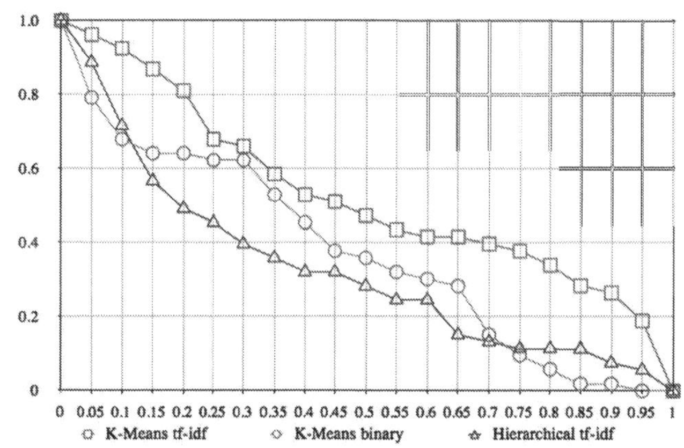

Figure 2. Coverage using different values for α

Regarding the two document representation approaches (binary and *tf-idf*) it can be observed from Figure 4 that the best score for F1-measure is 0.85. For both K-Means and hierarchical algorithms, the *tf-idf* representation indicates this score at different threshold values, 0.1 and 0.05 respectively. On the other hand, the best score for the binary representation is 0.78, when α=0.05.

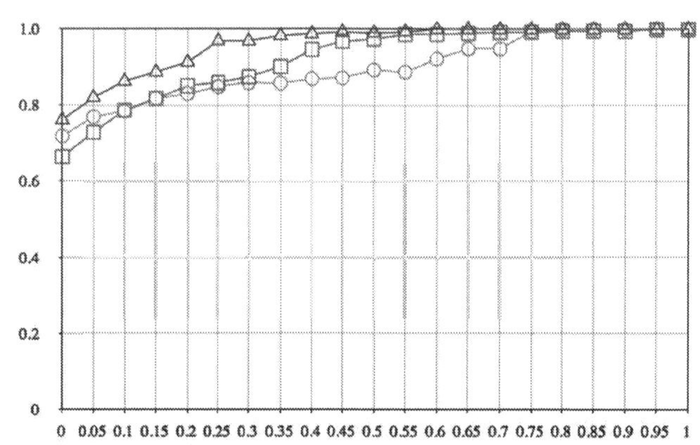

Figure 3. Dissimilarity Mean using different values of α

Concerning the binary representation, the features are eliminated from the first step of α and the distinctiveness of the clusters reaches its maximum value when $\alpha > 0.75$. Hence, we could conclude that the *tf-idf* weighting schema provides more precise results.

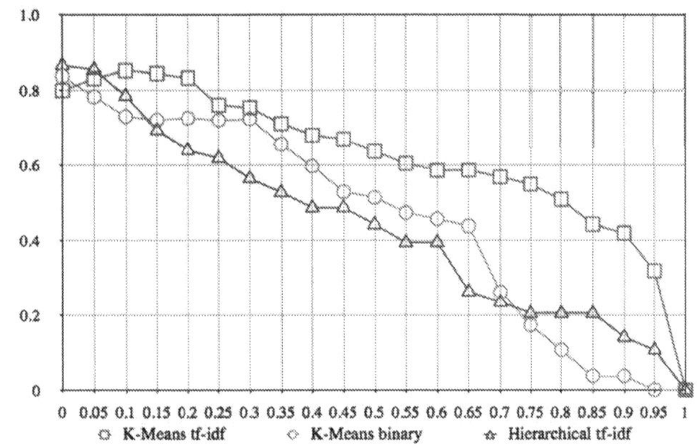

Figure 4. F1-measure scores

Table 4. Indicative DL evaluation patterns

Cluster	K-Means	Hierarchical
1	field studies: 0.99, record: 0.57, human agents: 0.53, survey studies: 0.47, devices: 0.38, analyze: 0.37, design: 0.36, software: 0.33, report: 0.25	interpret: 0.50, measure: 0.34, logging studies: 0.23, describe: 0.19, human agents: 0.15, narrative items: 0.13, survey studies: 0.12, statistics: 0.12, service quality: 0.05
2	performance: 0.31, compare: 0.22, measure: 0.21, research artifacts: 0.19, statistics: 0.16	metrics: 0.99, statistics: 0.53, measure: 0.33, research artifacts: 0.22, laboratory studies: 0.16, service quality: 0.13, compare: 0.11
3	social_ level: 0.99, design: 0.52, survey studies: 0.49, analyze: 0.37, report: 0.29, operation: 0.24, recommend: 0.22, devices: 0.22, technical excellence: 0.21, human agents: 0.15, outcomes assessment: 0.10	human agents: 0.61, survey studies: 0.36, record: 0.33, effectiveness: 0.35, laboratory studies: 0.31, quantitative: 0.18, interface level: 0.17, compare: 0.18, describe: 0.12
4	summative: 0.99, technical excellence: 0.96, discipline: 0.94, software: 0.92, report: 0.84, design: 0.83, survey studies: 0.8, effectiveness: 0.78, count: 0.77, human agents: 0.71, laboratory studies: 0.67	performance: 0.63, compare: 0.62, research artifacts: 0.45, measure: 0.33, laboratory studies: 0.23, statistics: 0.10
5	interpret: 0.99, age: 0.97, discipline: 0.94, research questions:0.93, software: 0.92, profession: 0.91, describe: 0.86, survey studies: 0.8, count: 0.77, human agents: 0.71, statistics: 0.53, measure: 0.52	record: 0.73, devices: 0.64, human agents: 0.53, survey studies: 0.39, field studies: 0.24, report: 0.25, narrative items: 0.21, design: 0.18, software: 0.13

Based on these observations, Table 4 presents the most indicative patterns generated by the two algorithms when applied on the *tf-idf* representation of our data set and which derived eleven clusters. Each pattern consists of the representative features in each cluster that identifies subsets of DiLEO subclasses and form ontology paths.

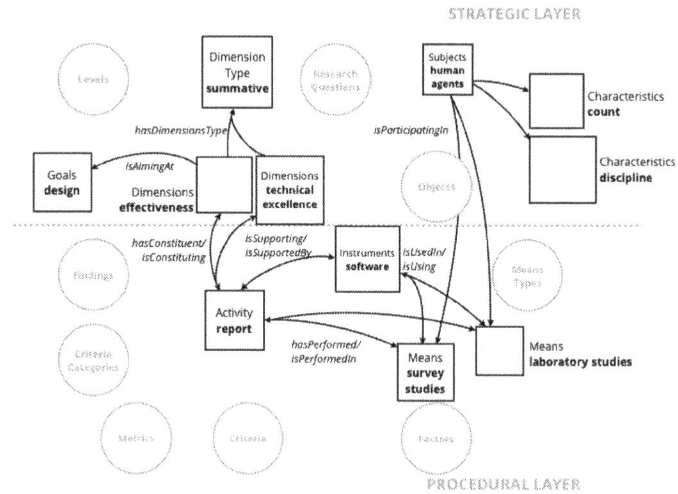

Figure 5. Pattern created by the K-Means algorithm

Two indicative patterns are presented in Figure 5 and 6. The circular shapes represent classes, the squares represent subclasses and the size of the feature signals the frequency increase. Figure 5 presents the pattern derived by the Cluster 4 of the K-Means clustering. The pattern highlights that the studies which aim at the improvement of the DLs design focus on the combination of effectiveness and technical excellence. This practice comes as a summative procedure and requires experimentation in laboratory environment, which is combined with surveys and requires some sort of software during its processes.

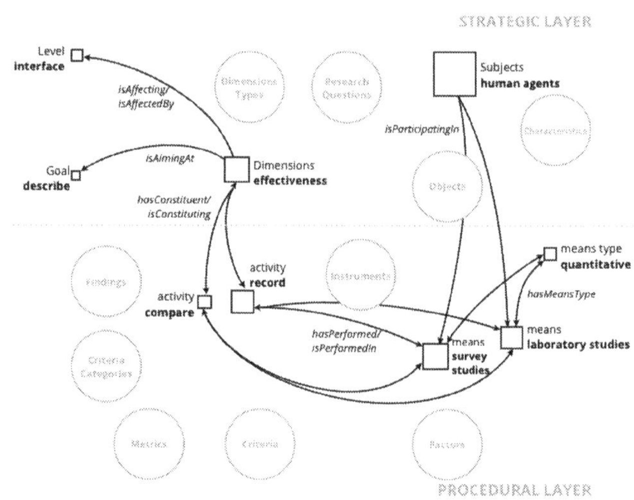

Figure 6. Pattern created by the hierarchical algorithm

Figure 6 presents the pattern resulted by Cluster 3 of the hierarchical clustering algorithm. This pattern implies that the description of the effectiveness of the DL interface could be obtained by recording and comparing users (*human agents*), in quantitative studies such as laboratory studies or surveys.

Moreover, the pattern of Cluster 1 derived by K-Means showcases the use of field studies and survey studies for the purpose of improving the DL design. The evaluators typically use devices and software for recording users (*human agents*), as well as for the analysis and the reporting of findings. Other patterns seem to reflect specific practices, like in the case of Cluster 5 of K-Means. This pattern mainly reflects connections in the lower layer of the ontology, with the use of software and statistics taking place in *survey studies* and *laboratory studies* for measurement and interpretation. The features in the upper layer of the ontology are mainly separated with the exception of *human agents* and their characteristics.

It should be noted that some patterns are similar in both clusters. For example, the patterns in Cluster 2 of K-Means and in Cluster 4 of the hierarchical algorithm are almost identical; they both state that the performance evaluation requires measurement and comparison activities. The hierarchical algorithm complements the pattern by underlying that such evaluations are usually held in laboratory settings. This is a significant pattern, quite frequently observed in the studies presented in both conferences.

5. DISCUSSION

In general, both algorithms generate informative patterns, which can assist the exploration of DL evaluation trends. The patterns reflect and - up to a point - confirm the anecdotally evident research practices of DL researchers. Similarly to a map, they can provide the prevailing and the alternative routes one can follow to reach to a destination, taking into account several practical parameters that might not know. By exploring the previous profiles, they can weight all the available options.

The patterns generated by K-Means are longer, covering more DiLEO subclasses, while the FI values are higher than those of the hierarchical algorithm's patterns. For instance the pattern derived from Cluster 3 highlights an ignored evaluation approach that – although not usually applied in the literature – is present in practice. The pattern shows that outcome assessment focuses on the social impact of a DL and is mainly investigated through survey studies. Another interesting pattern, which due to space limits does not appear in Table 4, reveals that expert studies are used in summative evaluations, aiming to improve the design of a DL by exploring its effectiveness and technical excellence.

The hierarchical clustering algorithm is also revealing important patterns that exist in the literature. For instance, the pattern in Cluster 1 relates logging studies with the service quality dimension. Moreover, Cluster 2 confirms the approach in which the evaluation of service quality requires mainly measurement activities and consequently implies the utilization of metrics.

Several classes appear frequently in the patterns. For instance, the subclass *effectiveness* of *Dimension* is met in five out of eleven clusters derived by K-Means. The subclass *design* of *Goal* appears the same number of times, whereas the subclass *document* appears only twice. The subclass *human agents* appears in eight out of the eleven clusters, implying that a significant part of the papers of both the conferences deal with human-based evaluations. Furthermore, given the absence of the subclasses *content level*, *engineering level*, *processing level* and *product*, one can infer that the DL evaluation research is mainly user-oriented. This result is confirmed by the observation that the subclasses *record* (of the *Activity* class) and *survey studies* (of the class *Means*) appear eight times in the K-Means clusters. These results extend the findings in [15], where the research in two conferences was found to be governed by system-wise foci.

It should be noted that the experimentation with other clustering parameters, such as the number of clusters, revealed some shorter in length patterns, which could be considered significant tips or checklist items for the design of DL evaluation studies. For instance a pattern comprised by Means/comparison_studies – *has_selected*– Criteria suggests that a comparative study should be based on pre-determined comparison criteria. Furthermore, several technical excellence studies focus on the evaluation of the interfaces of a DL; hence the derived path is Dimensions/technical_excellence –*isAffecting*– interface_level. Additionally it is observed that the study of log files usually is the main means for performing effectiveness or service quality studies. Therefore, the implied ontology paths could be either Dimensions/effectiveness –*hasConstituent*– Activity/compare – *isPerformedIn*– Means/logging_studies or Dimensions/ service_quality –*hasConstituent*– Activity/analyze – *isPerformedIn*– Means/logging_studies. Finally, another interesting piece of information coming from shorter paths is that service quality evaluations typically use field studies when their type is considered as qualitative and survey studies when their type is considered quantitative. Sometimes service quality experiments use also expert studies.

6. CONCLUSIONS

In this paper we proposed a data-mining assisted methodology for the exploration of the DL evaluation literature. We combined several methods, such as document classification to identify relevant papers in a large corpus of documents and semantic annotation processes to mark up important concepts. The output of these techniques contributed to the formation of eleven coherent clusters via two key algorithms that were further interpreted with the assistance of the DiLEO schema. This is a semantically enhanced interpretation process that can reflect the knowledge of the domain, and also help the design of future evaluation projects by highlighting not obvious patterns, though there exist in the literature.

During the formation of the methodology we performed benchmarking tests that qualified specific components (methods and algorithms) to effectively automate the exploration of large parts of the literature and the discovery of meaningful research patterns. We argue that researchers from other domains, for which formal conceptualization have been developed, can apply the methodology to explore capacious corpora and discover scientific trends. For instance the proposed methodology could be applied on the generic domain of the digital libraries for which a variety of formal conceptualizations exist enabling the semantic annotation of the literature volumes.

Future work includes the development of methods for the specification of patterns between different venues and their comparison. While in this study we give an overview of the practices in two important DL conferences, it is argued that the comparison of each one's practices can further contextualize the analysis of the domain. Additionally, we intend to exploit the capabilities of the specific annotated corpus in the introduction of nanopublications in the digital library evaluation field. Nanopublications would be a useful advisory tool for determining the appropriate methodology path to be followed by the evaluators.

7. REFERENCES

[1] Saracevic, T. 2009. The framework for digital library evaluation. In *Evaluation of digital libraries: an insight to useful applications and methods*. Chandos, Oxford.

[2] Tsakonas, G. and Papatheodorou, C. 2011. An ontological representation of the digital library evaluation domain. *JASIST*, 62, 8, 1577-1593.

[3] *Knowledge lost in information: Report of the NSF Workshop on Research Directions for Digital Libraries, 2003.* Retrieved from http://www.sis.pitt.edu/~dlwkshop/report.pdf

[4] Christie, C.A. and Fleischer, D.N. 2010. Insight into evaluation practice: a content analysis of designs and methods used in evaluation studies published in North American evaluation-focused journals. *American Journal of Evaluation*, 31, 3, 326–346.

[5] Kelly, D. and Sugimoto, C. 2013. A systematic review of Interactive Information Retrieval evaluation studies, 1967-2006. *JASIST*, 64, 1, 745–770.

[6] Attwood, T.K., Kell, D.B., McDermott, P., Marsh, J., Pettifer, S.R. and Thorne, D. 2009. Calling international rescue: knowledge lost in literature and data landslide! *The Biochemical journal*, 424, pt 3, 317–333.

[7] Biolchini, D.A.C.J., Mian, P.G., Candida, A.N.C., Conte, T.U. and Travassos, G.H. 2007. Scientific research ontology to support systematic review in software engineering. *Advanced Engineering Informatics*, 21, 21, 133–151.

[8] Groth, P., Gibson, A. and Velterop, J. 2010. The anatomy of a nanopublication. *Information Services & Use*, 3, 51–56.

[9] Mons, B., Haagen, H.V., Chichester, C., Hoen, P.B., Dunnen, J.T.D., Ommen, G.V., Mulligen, E.V., Singh, B., Hooft, R., Roos, M., Hammond, J., Kiesel, B., Giardine, B., Velterop, J., Groth, P. and Schultes, E. 2011. The value of data. *Nature Genetics*, 43, 281–283.

[10] Pepe, A., Mayernik, M. and Borgman, C.L. 2010. From artifacts to aggregations: modeling scientific life cycles on the Semantic Web. *JASIST*, 61, 3, 567–582.

[11] Soldatova, L.N. and King, R.D. 2006. An ontology of scientific experiments. *Journal of the Royal Society, Interface*, 3, 11, 795–803.

[12] Brahaj, A., Razum, M. and Schwichtenberg, F. 2012. Ontological formalization of scientific experiments based on Core Scientific Metadata Model. In *Proceedings of TPDL 2012*. Springer, Berlin, pp. 273–279.

[13] Soo, W. Von, Yang, Y.S., Chen, L.S. and Fu, T.Y. 2004. Ontology acquisition and semantic retrieval from semantic annotated Chinese poetry. In *Proceedings of the 4th ACM/IEEE-CS Joint Conference on Digital Libraries*. New York, ACM, pp. 345.

[14] Tsakonas, G., Mitrelis, A., Papachristopoulos, L. and Papatheodorou, C. 2012. An exploration of the research trends in the digital library evaluation domain. In *Proceedings of the 12th ACM/IEEE-CS Joint Conference on Digital Libraries*. New York, ACM, pp. 347-348.

[15] Tsakonas, G., Mitrelis, A., Papachristopoulos, L. and Papatheodorou, C. 2013. An exploration of the digital library evaluation literature based on an ontological representation. *JASIST* (in press).

[16] Mitrelis, A., Papachristopoulos, L., Sfakakis, M., Tsakonas, G. and Papatheodorou, C. 2012. Mining digital library evaluation patterns using a domain ontology. In *8th International Workshop on Ontology Content.* Springer, Berlin, pp. 464–473.

[17] Cohen, J. 1960. A coefficient of agreement for nominal scales. *Educational and Psychological Measurement*, 20, 1, 37-46.

[18] Batista, G.E.A.P.A., Prati, R.C. and Monard, M.C. 2004. A study of the behavior of several methods for balancing machine learning training data. *ACM SIGKDD Explorations*, 6, 1, 20-29.

[19] KrishnaVeni, C.V. and Sobha Rani, T. 2011. *On the classification of imbalanced datasets*. *IJCST*, 2, sp. 1, 145-148.

[20] Tomek, I. 1976. Two modifications of CNN. *IEEE Transactions on Systems Man & Communications* SMC 6, 1, 769-772.

[21] Lewis, D. 1998. Naïve (Bayes) at forty: the independence assumption in information retrieval. In *Proceedings of the 10th European Conference on Machine Learning*. Berlin, Springer, pp. 4-15.

[22] Domingos, P. and Pazzani, M. 1997. On the optimality of the simple Bayesian classifier under zero-one loss. *Machine Learning*, 29, 2-3, 103-130.

[23] Roberts, A., Gaizauskas, R., Hepple, M., Davis, N., Demetriou, G., Guo, Y., Kola, J., Roberts, I., Setzer, A., Tapuria, A. and Wheeldin, B. 2007. The CLEF corpus: semantic annotation of clinical text. In *AMIA Annual Symposium Proceedings*, pp. 625-629.

[24] Giannopoulos, G. Bikakis, N., Dalamagas, T. and Sellis, T. 2010. GoNTogle: a tool for semantic annotation and search. In *Proceedings of the 7th international conference on The Semantic Web: research and Applications - Volume II*. Berlin, Springer, pp. 376-380.

[25] Read, J. 2012. *Tutorial Meka 1.0: a multilabel / multitarget Extension to WEKA*. Retrieved from http://freefr.dl.sourceforge.net/project/meka/meka-1.2/Tutorial.pdf

[26] Tsoumakas, G., Katakis, I. and Vlahavas, I. 2010. Mining multi-label data. In *Data Mining and Knowledge Discovery Handbook - Part 6*. Springer, Berlin, pp. 667-685.

[27] Kaufman, L. and Rousseeuw, P.J. 1990. *Finding groups in data: an introduction to Cluster Analysis*. Wiley, New York.

[28] *R: A Language and Environment for Statistical Computing*. R Foundation for Statistical Computing, Vienna. Retrieved from http://www.R-project.org.

[29] Lance, G.N. and Williams, W.T. 1967. A general theory of classifactory sorting strategies: I. Hierarchical systems. *The Computer Journal*, 9, 4, 373-380.

Mendeley Group as a New Source of Interdisciplinarity Study: How Do Disciplines Interact on Mendeley?

Jiepu Jiang
School of Information Sciences,
University of Pittsburgh
jiepu.jiang@gmail.com

Chaoqun Ni
School of Informatics and Computing,
Indiana University Bloomington
chni@indiana.edu

Daqing He, Wei Jeng
School of Information Sciences,
University of Pittsburgh
{dah44, wej9}@pitt.edu

ABSTRACT
In this paper, we studied interdisciplinary structures by looking into how online academic groups of different disciplines share members and followers. Results based on Mendeley online groups show clear interdisciplinary structures, indicating Mendeley online groups as a promising data source and a new perspective of disciplinarity and interdisciplinarity studies.

Categories and Subject Descriptors
H.2.8 [**Database Applications**]: Scientific Databases.

General Terms
Measurement, Verification.

Keywords
Interdisciplinarity, disciplinarity, Mendeley, group, altmetrics.

1. INTRODUCTION
Disciplinarity is usually conceptualized based on the social elements of a discipline. For example, Price et al. regarded grouping of scholars as invisible college [10] and Valenza defined a discipline as a "recognized community of researchers" [12]. However, the bibliometrics community often empirically characterizes disciplinarity through the cognitive connections of entities in academic publishing (e.g. authors, venues, keywords) based on bibliographic data, e.g. [9]. Such approach has long been criticized, mainly due to the slow response of publication data and the limited representativeness of academic publishing on the ubiquitous scholarly activities [7, 11].

Seeking alternative and complementary evidence of scholarly communication has been a long quest. Studies of usage bibliometrics [7] and altmetrics [11] all more or less agree on this objective. Particularly, the trending approach altmetrics features the utilization of social web data complementing the bibliographic publication data. However, existing altmetrics studies are mostly evaluative studies [1, 11]. Only a few scholars studied using social web data on relational bibliometrics [5, 6] and none from the aspects of disciplinarity and interdisciplinarity.

In this paper, we study interdisciplinarity based on Mendeley online groups. As "social grouping of scholars", the members and followers of a group may characterize disciplinary profiles of the group. Intuitively, the more similar two groups in their members and/or followers, the more connected the underlying communities and disciplines of the two groups. Thus, we can build networks of Mendeley groups based on their sharing of group members and followers, with the expectation of looking into the interaction of the groups as well as their disciplines. The rest of the paper introduces our approach and preliminary findings.

2. DATA AND METHODS

2.1 Data
Mendeley[1] is a reference management website as well as an online academic community. In Mendeley, users can not only organize references, but also maintain their profile pages and develop connections with other users. Besides, users can create online groups and join or follow others' groups. Each group can have a message wall and reference repository shared among all the members and followers. However, only group members can contribute to the group repository. Joining a group requires group owners' permission, whereas following does not.

Mendeley website provided a directory[2] of open groups. We followed the directory and collected members and followers of each group in April 2012. Then, we aggregated all the members and followers and crawled for their profile pages, including user's real name, affiliation, position, etc. Note that only users who were members or followers of the open groups were collected. In total, we collected information about 34,838 open groups, 54,703 unique members and 12,268 followers (61,257 unique users).

Mendeley lists 25 disciplines. Each group was assigned by the group owner to at least one but no more than three disciplines. We simply labeled each group by the primary discipline assigned by the group owner. Further, we characterized each discipline by the groups with the discipline label and studied the interaction among disciplines by looking into the connection among groups.

2.2 Methods
A previous study venue-author-coupling (VAC) [8] enlightened our approach. In VAC, Ni et al. [8] considered venues (e.g. journals and conferences) as communities of authors for formal scientific discourse and assumed that the overlap of authors may disclose disciplinary structure. They built journal VAC networks for analysis, in which each node was a venue and the connection of two nodes was measured by the number of shared authors.

In light of VAC, we used group-member-coupling and group-follower-coupling to study the interdisciplinary structure of the 25 Mendeley disciplines. As discussed in Section 3.1, the majority of Mendeley group users are scholars. Therefore, Mendeley online groups, as collections of these users (scholars), may help indicate disciplinary and interdisciplinary structures from a perspective of informal scholarly communication and activities.

Similar to the VAC network in [8], we built group-member-coupling and group-follower-coupling networks, where each node is a Mendeley group and the strength of connection between two

[1] http://www.mendeley.com
[2] http://www.mendeley.com/groups/

nodes (groups) was measured by the number of common members or followers. We colored nodes by discipline in Mendeley and pictured the interaction among disciplines by the interaction of the disciplines' groups. We calculated group centrality measures to analyze the centrality of each discipline in the networks.

3. RESULT ANALYSIS

3.1 Mendeley Group Members & Followers

A fundamental issue regarding the validity of our approach is the identity of Mendeley group users and their roles in scholarly communication. If these users did not participate in scholarly communication, their behaviors can hardly indicate disciplinarity or inter-disciplinarity. Therefore, we analyzed the composition of group users by the position information in their profiles.

13.37% of the members and 27.09% of the followers provided detailed position information. We categorized the top 100 most frequent positions (positions beyond the top 100 were categorized as "other positions"). Table 1 shows the results. The largest four categories suggested that the users were very likely in academia, including: research scientists, doctoral student, faculty, and post-doctoral researchers. 87.63% of the members and 84.58% of the followers who provided detailed position information were categorized into these four types. The rest of the users were very likely consumers of academic resources, such as other types of students, librarians, and industrial employees.

As the proportion of members and followers who provided detailed position information varied greatly (13.37% vs. 27.09%), it is very likely that group members and followers have intrinsic differences. Due to the limited user information we obtained, we could not fully answer their differences. However, we did found that group followers had a higher proportion of junior scholars (e.g. doctoral student) and consumers of academic information (e.g. other students), whereas group members had a higher proportion of senior scholars (e.g. faculties and research scientists).

To conclude, results confirm that both members and followers of Mendeley groups comprise mostly scholars.

Table 1. Categories of Mendeley group members & followers.

Category	Examples in Mendeley	% of members	% of followers
Research scientists	"researcher fellow", "research associate", "research scientist"	28.77%	25.83%
Doctoral student	"PhD student", "doctoral student"	26.72%	28.69%
Faculty	"assistant professor", "lecturer"	24.11%	21.83%
Postdoc	"postdoc", "postdoctoral fellow"	8.03%	8.23%
Other students	"master student", "student"	6.36%	9.14%
Industrial employee	"software engineer", "consultant", "project manager"	2.79%	2.97%
Librarian	"librarian"	2.27%	1.54%
Other positions		0.94%	1.77%

3.2 Mendeley Groups

Though we verified the identity of Mendeley group users, it remains unclear to which end Mendeley groups were created and why scholars join or follow these groups. As there are no existing studies on this issue, we followed Jeng et al. [3]'s study and identified possible motivations from group descriptions.

Table 2 lists three identified motivations of using Mendeley groups and some example groups in Mendeley. Collaboration and sharing are two "official" motivations of using Mendeley groups. As noted in Mendeley's instruction page of creating a new group[3], groups are used "to collaborate with other researchers in your field, share research papers, and change the world". Besides, Mendeley group features, such as group message wall and repository, do support collaboration and sharing among scholars. Since online groups accumulate scholars of similar interests, they also offer scholars with spaces and opportunities of networking.

Group owners and members may have all the three identified motivations, whereas the motivation of group followers may only be getting shared with group resources due to the limited priorities of followers to participate in group activities. Though group users' actual activities may vary, the listed ones should to some extent explain why groups were created and why people join or follow groups. All the three motivations are related to scholarly activities with disciplinary characteristics, which to some extent support the validity of using group-member/follower-coupling for disciplinary and interdisciplinary studies. Here we leave the actual motivations for future studies and simply adopt these plausible motivations.

Table 2. Possible motivations of group users.

Motivation	Users	Example Group & Description
collaboration	owner, member	Bioimaging@KAIST[4]: "This is collaborative research group at KAIST focusing on biophotonics and biomedical imaging."
sharing	owner, member, follower	Machine Learning Basics[5]: "collection of papers describing basic algorithms and topics in machine learning ..."
networking	owner, member	Onomastics Switzerland[6]: "A communication platform for onomastic science in Switzerland. Use this Mendeley group to stay connected with other scientists of this topic ..."

3.3 Mendeley Disciplines

Conventional bibliometrics studies rely on the categorization of academic database as discipline labels, e.g. the Web of Science categories. In comparison, the 25 disciplines are defined by Mendeley and the discipline of each group is assigned by its owners. Table 3 displays the number of groups, unique group members and unique group followers for Mendeley disciplines.

The number of unique group members indicates the size of a discipline in terms of how many scholars participate in the online collaboration, sharing, and networking of the discipline. From this angle, "Computer & Information Science" is the largest discipline in Mendeley, followed by "Biological Science" and "Medicine". The 25 disciplines vary greatly in their size.

The number of groups to some extent indicates the activeness of a discipline in Mendeley. The more active a discipline, the more likely that groups of the discipline will be created. From this aspect, the three largest disciplines are also the three most active ones in Mendeley. Some of the 25 disciplines are comparatively very active in terms of their relatively small size, such as "Psychology", "Economics" and "Earth Sciences". In comparison, disciplines such as "Management Science / Operations Research", "Mathematics", "Humanities", and "Philosophy" are relatively inactive in Mendeley.

The number of unique followers may indicate the influence of a discipline's knowledge to Mendeley users, as the followers of a group are very likely those who are interested in consuming the knowledge in the group's repository. The three largest Mendeley disciplines are still overwhelming in terms of unique followers. We found that some disciplines did not attract sufficient number of followers for its size, such as such as "Engineering", "Physics" and "Chemistry". In contrast, "Humanities", "Philosophy" and

[3] http://www.mendeley.com/groups/create/

[4] http://www.mendeley.com/groups/1787671/bioimaging-kaist/

[5] http://www.mendeley.com/groups/509181/machine-learning-basics/

[6] http://www.mendeley.com/groups/1005661/onomastics-switzerland/

"Linguistics", although small in size, did attract comparatively lots of followers in Mendeley.

As it is difficult to match the 25 Mendeley disciplines with other widely-used classification schemes of academic databases such as Web of Science and Library of Congress, it is unclear how do sizes of disciplines shown in Mendeley compare with those shown in publication data. However, previous studies did report that large communities existed in disciplines close to "Biological Sciences" and "Medicine" presented here [2]. The overwhelming size of "Computer & Information Science" may benefit from the high adoption of online social communities in this discipline.

Table 3. Size of discipline in terms of the number of groups, unique group members, and unique group followers.

Discipline	groups		unique members		unique followers	
	#	rank	#	rank	#	rank
Com Inf Sci	5,392	2	11,692	1	3,932	1
Biological Sci	6,181	1	8,660	2	1,828	2
Medicine	3,764	3	6,354	3	1,744	3
Engineering	2,410	4	5,007	4	892	10
Education	1,655	6	3,620	5	1,010	7
Management Sci	702	16	2,942	8	982	8
Physics	1,253	11	2,571	9	454	16
Chemistry	1,353	8	2,398	10	436	17
Mathematics	420	18	2,338	12	903	9
Humanities	664	17	2,333	13	1,012	6
Psychology	1,291	9	2,270	14	610	11
Philosophy	231	22	1,416	17	578	12
Economics	825	13	1,372	18	323	20
Earth Sciences	798	14	1,328	19	282	21
Linguistics	339	21	815	20	464	15

3.4 Group-member-coupling Network

We built a group-member-coupling network using the approach introduced in Section 2. In our dataset, the number of members in each group follows a power law distribution: 89.82% of the groups had less than 5 members, accounting for 45.53% of the group members; 54.47% of the group members participated in 10.18% of the groups. Therefore, we considered the 10.18% (3,541) groups with 5 or more members as the most active groups in Mendeley. We further removed 621 isolated groups which did not share members with other groups and built the group-member-coupling network based on the rest 2,920 groups.

Figure 1 (left) shows the degree of groups in the group-member-coupling network for each discipline. Figure 2 (left) and Figure 3 (left) show the group-member-coupling network visualized using Pajek with Kamada-Kawai (free) layout and circular (partition) layout. The size of a node was set proportional to its degree and the width of an edge proportional to the number of shared members between two nodes being connected.

Results disclose interdisciplinary structures of the 25 disciplines in terms of the collaboration, sharing, and networking of scholars in Mendeley. As the largest three disciplines, "Computer & Information Science", "Biological Science" and "Medicine" groups are most visible in Figure 2 (left) and Figure 3 (left). According to Figure 3 (left), lots of connections exist between "Computer & Information Science" and "Biological Science", probably due to the increasing adoption of information techniques in some subfields of biology, such as bio-informatics. As shown in Figure 3 (left), disciplines such as "Mathematics" and "Management Science / Operations Research", although relatively small in size, have many strong connections with other disciplines.

Figure (3) left shows that both "Computer & Information Science" and "Biological Science" have many connections with other disciplines. However, "Computer & Information Science" are connected to almost every active discipline, whereas connections to "Biological Science" mainly come from "Computer & Information Science", "Chemistry", "Medicine", and "Mathematics". According to Figure 1 (left), it seems the many highly active groups (the outliers in Figure 1 (left)) in "Computer & Information Science" and "Biological Science" that contribute to the overall activeness of the two disciplines. The median of the degree values for groups of the two disciplines are not observably higher than that of all groups in Mendeley.

Among the top 10 pairs of groups by the number of shared group members, 6 pairs are between-discipline pairs, i.e. groups in each pair are from two different disciplines. This to some extent indicates active multi-disciplinary scholarly interactions in Mendeley and a high degree of interdisciplinarity.

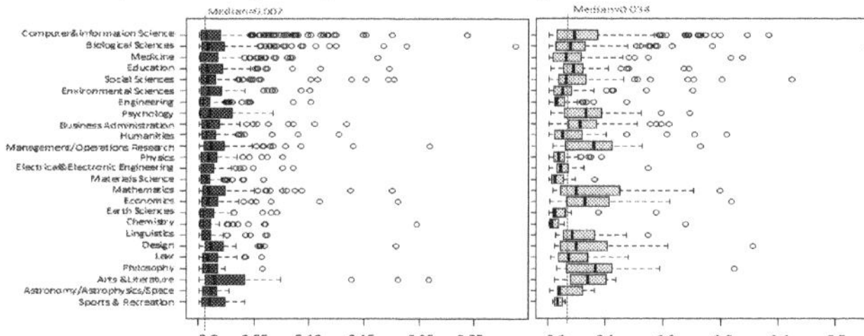

Figure 1. Degree of groups in the group-member-coupling network (left) and group-follower-coupling network (right).

3.5 Group-follower-coupling Network

We built a group-follower-coupling network for comparison. As discussed in Section 3.2, followers are shared with the references in group repositories. Therefore, the number of shared followers suggests to which extent the two groups' repositories can attract the same group of scholars, indicating the level of integration of the knowledge from the two groups and their disciplines.

Since the number of followers in each group also follows a power law distribution, we built the group-follower-coupling network based on 1,287 groups with 5 or more followers (isolated groups were removed). Figure 1 (right) shows the degree values of groups. Figure 2 (right) and Figure 3 (right) show the network with Kamada-Kawai (free) layout and circular (partition) layout.

Compared with the group-member-coupling network in Figure 3 (left), Figure 3 (right) shows that the connections among several disciplines are apparently stronger in the group-follower-coupling network, such as: "Biological Sciences" and "Medicine", "Computer & Information Science" and "Social Science", "Education" and "Humanities", "Design" and "Computer & Information Science". This indicates that these pairs of disciplines are usually adopted by scholars as common knowledge base, whereas the explicit interaction of scholars between these pairs of disciplines (in terms of collaboration, sharing, and networking in Mendeley) is comparatively inactive.

Similarly, we found that the connections of several disciplines in the group-follower-coupling network are weaker than those in the group-member-coupling network, such as: "Management Science / Operations Research" and "Business Administration", "Management Science / Operations Research" and "Computer & Information Science", and "Chemistry" and "Biological Science". This indicate that, although scholars of these disciplines interact a lot in Mendeley, knowledge of these disciplines are only limitedly integrated as scholars' knowledge base.

Among the top 10 pairs of groups by the number of shared group followers, 4 pairs are between-discipline pairs, indicating the integration of multi-disciplinary knowledge is very common among scholars in Mendeley.

4. CONCLUSION AND FUTURE WORKS

This paper studied how groups and disciplines in Mendeley interact with each other by looking into the proposed group-member-coupling network and group-follower-coupling network. The former indicates explicit interactions among online groups in terms of scholars' collaboration, sharing, and networking, while the latter shows comparatively implicit connections, i.e. the level of integration of the knowledge between groups. The two networks disclose interdisciplinary structure of online scholarly groups in Mendeley.

However, our current study suffers from the following major limitations, which are left for future works:

(1) As discussed in Section 3.1 and 3.2, it remains unclear who Mendeley users are and why they create, join, and follow groups in Mendeley. Studies on their population and motivations can help clarify results indicated from the proposed two networks.

(2) In our study, we simply adopted the discipline labels defined by Mendeley, which makes it difficult to compare our results with those based on bibliographic data (such as a VAC network). This also makes it difficult to analyze the expected differences between formal and informal scholarly communications.

(3) As Jiang et al. [4] found that social web data in CiteULike are highly biased to certain disciplines, it is very likely that users and groups in Mendeley also have disciplinary bias. It is not clear how such biasness (if any) affect our approach and results.

Despite these limitations, our study shows that online groups in academic social community as a promising data source and a new perspective for disciplinary and interdisciplinary studies. Besides, our study also complements existing altmetrics studies that highly focus on evaluative purpose.

5. REFERENCES

[1] Bar-Ilan, J. et al. 2012. Beyond citations: Scholars' visibility on the social. arXiv:1205.5611

[2] Börner K, Klavans R, Patek M, Zoss AM, Biberstine JR, et al. 2012. Design and Update of a Classification System: The UCSD Map of Science. PLoS ONE 7(7): e39464.

[3] Jeng, W., He, D., Jiang, J. and Zhang, Y. 2012. Groups in Mendeley: Owners' descriptions and group outcomes. In Proceedings of the 2012 ASIS&T annual meeting.

[4] Jiang, J., Ni, C., He, D. 2012. Altmetrics and social reference: merely fads? Presented in Metrics 2012, a workshop of ASIS&T 75th annual meeting.

[5] Jiang, J., He, D., and Ni, C. 2011. Social reference: aggregating online usage of scientific literature in CiteULike for clustering academic resources. In Proceedings of the 11th annual international ACM/IEEE joint conference on Digital libraries (JCDL '11).

[6] Kraker, P. et al. 2012. Harnessing User Library Statistics for Research Evaluation and Knowledge Domain Visualization. In Proceedings of the 21st International Conference Companion on World Wide Web (WWW '12 Companion).

[7] Kurtz, MJ et al. 2011. Usage Bibliometrics. Annual Review of Information Science and Technology. 44, 1, 3–64.

[8] Ni, C., Sugimoto, C. R. and Jiang, J. 2013. Venue-author-coupling: A measure for identifying disciplines through author communities. Journal of the American Society for Information Science and Technology. 64, 2, 265–279.

[9] Porter, A. and Rafols, I. 2009. Is science becoming more interdisciplinary? Measuring and mapping six research fields over time. Scientometrics. 81, 3, 719–745.

[10] Price, D.J. and Beaver, D.D. 1966. Collaboration in an invisible college. American Psychologist. 21, 11, 1011–1018.

[11] Priem, J. et al. 2012. Altmetrics in the wild: Using social media to explore scholarly impact. arXiv:1203.4745

[12] Valenza, R. 2009. Literature, Language, and the Rise of the Intellectual Disciplines in Britain, 1680–1820. Cambridge University Press.

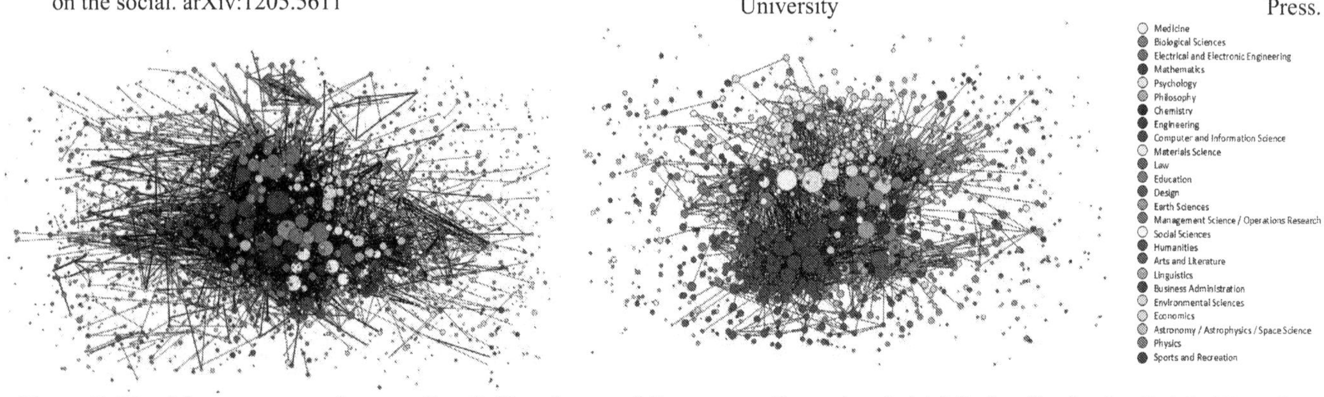

Figure 2. Mendeley group-member-coupling (left) and group-follower-coupling network (right) visualized using Pajek (Kamada-Kawai (free) layout). Edges with values less than 5 were removed for clearer outlooks of the graphs.

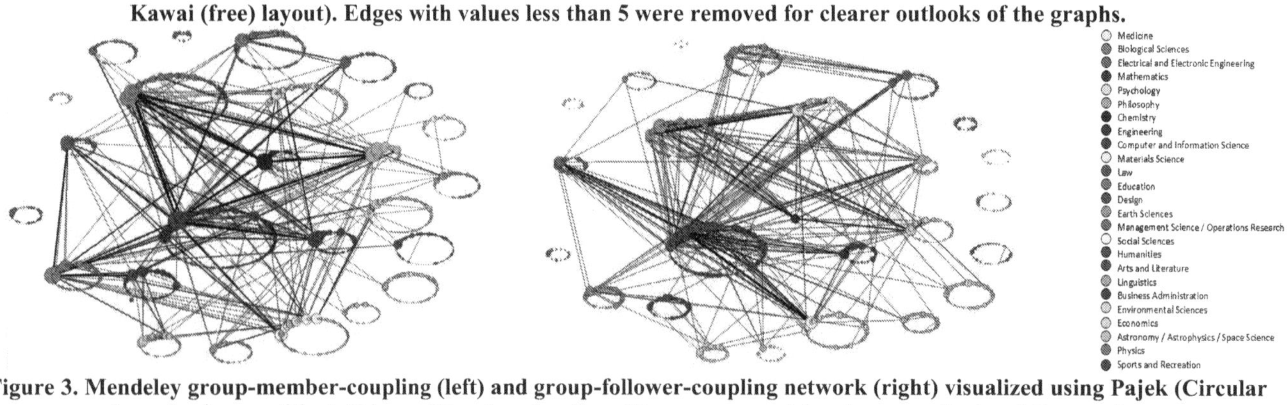

Figure 3. Mendeley group-member-coupling (left) and group-follower-coupling network (right) visualized using Pajek (Circular layout using partition). Edges with values less than 10 were removed for clearer outlooks of the graphs.

Following Bibliometric Footprints: The ACM Digital Library and the Evolution of Computer Science

Shion Guha[1], Stephanie Steinhardt[2], Syed Ishtiaque Ahmed[1]
[1]Department of Information Science
[2]Department of Communication
Cornell University, Ithaca, NY 14850
Email: {sg648, sbg94, sa738}@cornell.edu

Carl Lagoze
School of Information
University of Michigan
Ann Arbor, MI 48109
Email: clagoze@umich.edu

ABSTRACT

Using bibliometric methods, this exploratory work shows evidence of transitions in the field of computer science since the emergence of HCI as a distinct sub-discipline. We mined the ACM Digital Library in order to expose relationships between sub-disciplines in computer science, focusing in particular on the transformational nature of the SIG Computer-Human Interaction (CHI) in relation to other SIGs. Our results suggest shifts in the field due to broader social, economic and political changes in computing research and are intended as a prolegomena to further investigations.

Categories and Subject Descriptors

K2. History of: Theory.

Keywords

scientometrics; CHI; digital libraries

1. INTRODUCTION

In a recent article, Jon Kleinberg articulates that the past decade has seen a major transition within the field of computer science as a result of drivers like the internet and social networking [12]. This is a trend that is shaped by technical factors (e.g., increasing ubiquity of mobile devices) and by the growing socially embedded nature of computing that has developed with the pervasive internet and popular social media applications. As computing is increasingly entwined with our lives, the discipline of computer science has incorporated human factors into it.

In our research we quantitatively analyze and examine the Association of Computing Machinery (ACM) Digital Library (DL) to uncover evidence of this transition. The ACM is the "world's largest educational and scientific computing society" [1] and the ACM DL contains "every article ever published by ACM and bibliographic citations from major publishers in computing." [2] Almost all the articles in the ACM DL are affiliated with Special Interest Groups (SIG), each of which roughly corresponds to a subfield of the computer science discipline. The coverage and partitioning of this digital library therefore provides an excellent data source for an analysis of the shape of the discipline.

We analyzed all ACM SIG publications over time, their relative proportion to total publication output in the digital library, and their citation linkages to publications in other SIGs to mine evidence of the activity level of each subfield and the collaborations among them. The ACM's SIG in Computer-Human Interaction (SIGCHI) served as our lens. SIGCHI describes itself as "the world's largest association of professionals who work in the research and practice of computer-human interaction"[3] defined as an interdisciplinary group "composed of computer scientists, software engineers, psychologists, interaction designers, graphic designers, sociologists and anthropologists." [3] In addition to this qualitative reasoning, SIGCHI also has the largest number of publications of any SIG (27,964) with a very high growth rate in recent years (4.7%).

Our data shows an emergence of CHI as a top SIG coincident with the materialization of the Internet as a public resource, further emphasized in trends leveraging its massive amounts of online data and phenomena such as social media. We suggest that this emergence corresponds to a transition of computer science from traditional topics such as algorithms and complexity theory through an increasingly interdisciplinary flavor integrating designers, social scientists and artists.

The exploratory study detailed within this note is an important precursor toward understanding emerging forms of scientific work. The quantitative field-wide analysis leveraging the digital library provides a gateway to uniquely address issues of social and technical concern, such as developing theories to support interdisciplinary scientific collaboration, or defining relationships between funding and publication output.

2. BACKGROUND

Much research has explored paradigm shifts in science and computing, emphasizing the connection between government and trends in computer science. For example, the U.S. National Research Council Committee on Innovations in Computing and Communications published a report entitled "Funding a Revolution" [13] detailing the role of the federal government in the rise of major trends in computer science such as relational databases, the development of the internet, theoretical computer science, artificial intelligence, and virtual reality.

Further research explores the embedding of the computer and networking as part of daily social interaction. Scholars use field introspection for evaluating conference practices and field directions, organizational policies and structure, and for using this knowledge to think critically about the field's successes and failures in current structures. In particular, the CHI community has recently seen an increased attention to bibliometric methods as a self-reflection tool for understanding trends within the sub-discipline. Bibliometric is used as an approach that defines "What is CHI?" [5] and "How can HCI be evaluated?" [4]. Previous analyses of the ACM SIGCHI have been completed through a series of approaches: clustering CHI publications into thematic categories [11, 14, 17]; geographical analysis of the distribution of authors in one year at the CHI conference [6]; or authorship propensities within its sub-communities [10]. Barkhuus [4] sought to define the changes in evaluation methods published in the CHI conference to date and ground these approaches in historical trends of the subject of CHI papers: from a focus on the technical elite user and scientific technologies, to global widely-accessible internet tools and the layman user.

Shi et. al. [16] performed a comprehensive analysis of the ACM Digital Library and JSTOR to find that recent citation trends in computer science are biased towards interdisciplinary research and bridging different groups. We extend these inferences and investigate temporal citation patterns of sub-groups within computer science.

3. THE PRESENT STUDY

We performed a bibliometric analysis of all publications since SIGCHI's inception in order to reveal evidence of the evolution of the computer science field.

3.1. Data Processing and Analysis

We extracted metadata records from the ACM Digital Library that includes information on all of the conference proceedings through 2012. We used Digital Object Identifier (DOI) as the primary key to differentiate between two publications. We used Python's BeautifulSoup library to parse the XML metadata files; and then we made a number of manual adjustments to cope with any inconsistencies in the data (any auto-entry errors, non-standard characters, duplications, missing information etc.). We extracted citations from the metadata of each publication. For this iteration of the research, citations external to ACM were included in our analysis.

We then classified the publications in different SIGs by mining the Series ID of each of the conference proceedings. Each of the ACM conference proceedings falls under a series, and each series belongs to one or more SIGs. Because some conferences contained multiple series IDs in which multiple SIGs laid claim to them, our resulting sets of publications were not mutually exclusive by SIG. After preparing the dataset, we performed a statistical analysis on the intra- and inter-SIG citations. Intra-SIG is the average percentage of citations in a single publication of that SIG that refer to a publication internal to the SIG (intra-SIG). The inter-SIG citations refer to publications outside of its sub-discipline: SIG-to-CHI is the average percentage of citations in a single publication, which refers to SIGCHI; CHI-to-SIG is the average number of citations within a single publication of SIGCHI to that SIG.

3.2. Results

We focus our statistical analysis on average growth rates (Fig. 1) of citations per publication by year to distinguish evolving patterns and to compare these growth rates.

3.2.1 CHI-to-SIGs

When considering citations in CHI publication to other SIGs, we note some interesting differences.

A particularly salient relationship is found between SIGGRAPH (Computer Graphics and Interactive Techniques) and CHI. The inter-SIG citation rate between SIGGRAPH and CHI has been growing linearly ($R^2=0.998$, $p<0.001$, GR= 0.036) indicating a constant, strong, temporal relationship.

Conversely, SIGSOFT (Software Engineering) and CHI had a weak relationship in the early 1980s, but have since exhibited quadratic growth ($R^2=0.966$, $p<0.001$, GR= 0.021) indicating a strengthened relationship in the last 15 years. Towards the other extreme, SIGWEB (Hypertext and the Web) had no citation relationship with SIGCHI until the year 1997, despite that SIGWEB was born prior to CHI in 1987. At this point, there is an exponential growth pattern in citations between SIGWEB and CHI ($R^2=0.974$, $p<0.001$, GR= 0.12). SIGKDD (Knowledge Discovery and Data) holds an increasingly strengthened relationship with CHI since its inception in 1999, exhibiting a quadratic growth rate ($R^2=0.997$, $p<0.001$, GR= 0.092).

3.2.2 SIGs-to-CHI

On the other hand, CHI has also shown influence within the citation patterns of other SIGs. SIGIR (Information Retrieval) and SIGMOD (Management of Data) hold distinctly strong relationships in the SIG-to-CHI direction.

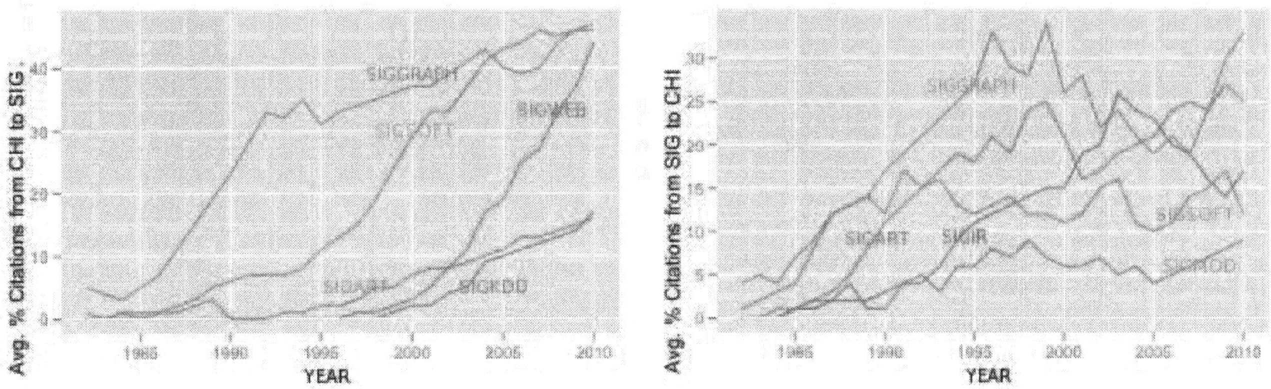

Figure 1: Top 5 SIG-to-CHI and CHI-to-SIG citation percentages per article from 1983 to 2010

These are not particularly strong in the direction of CHI and citing outward. Both groups exhibit linear relationships with CHI (SIGIR: R2=0.918, $p<0.001$, SIGMOD: GR= 0.021; R2=0.953, $p<0.001$, GR= 0.018) indicating a mild but constant amount of influence from CHI over the years. Perhaps somewhat unsurprisingly, SIGGRAPH citations show a reciprocal linear relationship with CHI (R2=0.993, $p<0.001$, GR= 0.042). There is also a constant linear growth exhibited by SIGART (Artificial Intelligence) citing CHI (R^2=0.977, $p<0.001$, GR= 0.034), suggesting a moderately strong influence from CHI over the years.

3.2.3 An Aggregative & Egocentric Vision of CHI

Aggregating citation patterns throughout CHI's lifespan and normalizing by raw publication count, developed an egocentric representation of the citation relationships between CHI and other SIGS. We refer to this calculation as ACP (Average Number of Citations per Publication). CHI and SIGGRAPH hold a very strong reciprocal relationship, as seen in their closeness within the CHI-centric model in Figure 2. Not only did SIGMOD and SIGIR's intertwining with SIGCHI grow over time as evidenced by Figure 1, but these two groups also represent the next most-cited SIGs by CHI after SIGGRAPH (1.73 ACP, 10%; SIGIR 1.68, 10%). While SIGOPS (0.14 ACP, 1%) and SIGWEB (3.2 ACP, 19%) represent the furthest nodes from CHI in Figure 2, we limited this visualization to only 10 total nodes, selected by largest average percentage of citations from CHI per publication.

SIGGRAPH (12.87 ACP, 54%), SIGART (12.64 ACP, 79%) and CHI (16.76 ACP, 51%) exhibit similarly dense self-citation patterns. In contrast, publications within SIGWEB on average exhibit a very weak self-citation percentage (1.28 ACP, 79%)

4. DISCUSSION

Our results show the patterns of evolution of the field of computer science during the 29 years of SIGCHI's existence, largely through positive citation relationships between SIGCHI and other SIGs. Not only has there been a movement within CHI, but also a shift in the focus of all SIGs as seen by citations into CHI by core computer science sub-disciplines which is presented in Figure 1.

We believe this is evidence of at least three significant paradigm changes in the field of computer science since its inception in the post-World War II period. First, in the 1980s there was a shift from a focus on algorithms toward use cases, and the introduction of human factors into the field of computer science. From this, the field of HCI was built as the interface between computer science and social science and bloomed as an interdisciplinary sub-discipline of computer science, which recognizes the importance of the human in technology development. Barkhuus [4] outlines the trends in early HCI work as being concerned with the technical elite: how technical users use command

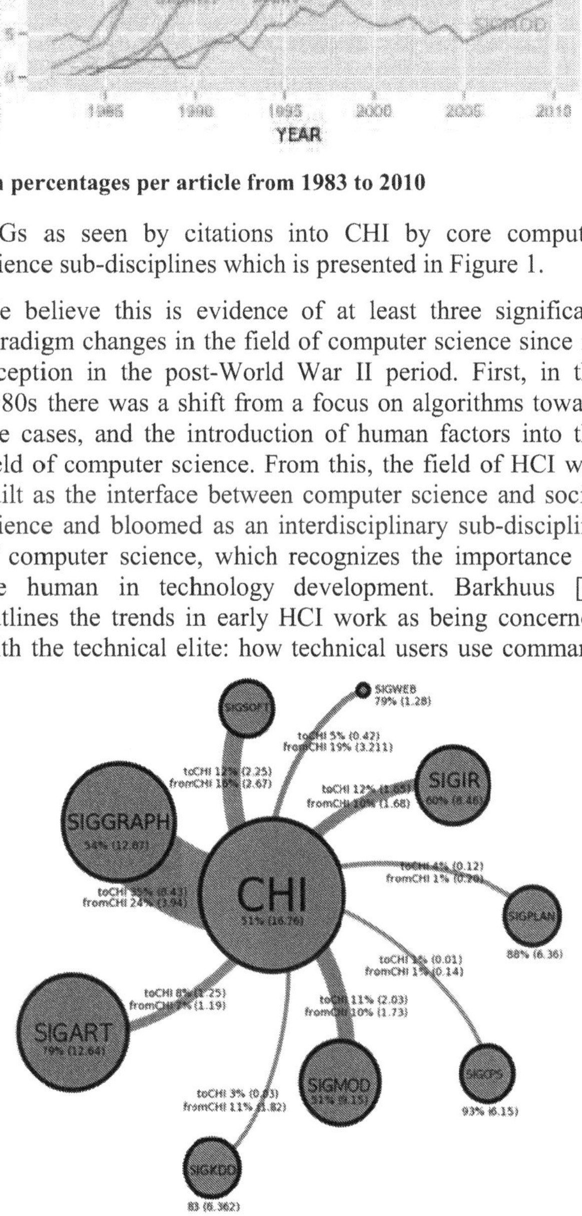

Figure 2: An aggregative snapshot of ACM SIGCHI's lifespan of and nine (9) SIGs with largest percentage of CHI citations per publication normalized by the total number of publications: node size is the average percentage of in-SIG citations, edge is the average percentage of SIG-to-CHI citations and edge length is 1 /average percentage of CHI-to-SIG citations.

lines [8], use their tacit programming knowledge [15] and handle an interface [9].

During the first decade of its existence, CHI reached its highest level of self-citation, indicating the emergence of HCI as a new thread of computer science with a distinct identity from the algorithm-focused research. At the time of CHI's origins, SIGGRAPH produced the largest output of any SIG in the ACM.

The second paradigm shift in computer science occurred in the late 1990s when the internet and personal computer redefined the end-user from the technical elite and brought with it studies of how the layman interacts with new technologies [4, 7]. As a result of the increased necessity to understand how to build new technologies for public consumption, the graphical user interface (GUI) also received increased attention during this time. Our data suggests that it was here when HCI research shifted from the command line toward a closer integration of SIGGRAPH concerns (interaction, design and information) and solidified a reciprocally strong intertwining between the two sub-disciplines. This period also coincides with the CHI's large publication output, surpassing in raw numbers such "core" computer science sub-disciplines as programming languages, operating systems, software development.

In the early 2000s, we see what appears to be another shift in the field of computer science, as social media integrated even more closely the relationship between technology and the everyday user. During this period, the interchange between CHI and SIGKDD intensified, as large-scale data mining of online social systems became one of the foundations of HCI research.

5. CONCLUSIONS AND FUTURE WORK

Major implications from this work are two-fold. First, we have quantitatively shown the complex, temporal citation relationships between different sub-areas of computer science with a slant towards human-computer interaction. Second, we have sought to ensconce these relationships in a broader, historical context to show the evolution of computer science over the last few decades from being algorithm-driven to being driven by human data. The analysis presented here describes high-level trends that could be identified through our data set. To the best of our knowledge, our exploratory work is the first to show this evidence using bibliometric reasoning. Future work intends to address more acute shifts with less obvious relation to the dialog and rhetoric surrounding computer science.

We hope to spark interest in the politics that shape computer science, such as relationships of funding agencies to these paradigm shifts in field focus; the roles of universities, industry and government in moving forward computing; and potential future directions for the field and sub-disciplines. In the future, we intend to probe deeper into the citation relationships between other disciplines (sociology, communication, psychology) and computer science and the trichotomous relationship between funding, productivity and impact in computer science.

6. ACKNOWLEDGMENTS

We wish to thank the ACM Digital Library for providing their corpus to us for our research.

7. REFERENCES

[1] ACM. 2013. http://www.acm.org/

[2] ACM Digital Library. 2013. https://dl.acm.org/

[3] ACM Special Interest Groups. 2013. https://dl.acm.org/sigs.cfm?CFID=273142187&CFTOKEN=24062479

[4] Barkhuus, L and Rode, J. 2007. From Mice to Men - 24 Years of Evaluation in CHI. In Proc. CHI'07. DOI=10.1145/1240624.2180963

[5] Bartneck, C and Hu, J. 2009. Scientometric analysis of the CHI proceedings. In Proc. CHI'09, pg. 699-708.

[6] Diakopulous, N. Geographical distribution of CHI authors. http://www.cc.gatech.edu/~nad/Projects/CHIViz

[7] Grier, D.A. 2007. When Computers Were Human. Princeton University Press.

[8] Haggett, A, McFadden, J and Newsted, P. 1981. Naive user behavior in a restricted interactive command environment. SIGSOC Bull. 13, 2-3, 139-.

[9] Hammond, N, Jørgensen, A, MacLean, A, Barnard, P and Long, J. 1983. Design practice and interface usability: Evidence from interviews with designers. In Proc. CHI'83, 40-44.

[10] Horn, D, Finholt, T, Birnholtz, J, Motwani, D and Jayaraman, S. 2004. Six degrees of jonathan grudin: a social network analysis of the evolution and impact of CSCW research. In Proc. CSCW'04, 582-591.

[11] Kaye, J. 2009. Some statistical analyses of CHI. In Proc. CHI EA'09, 2585-2594.

[12] Kleinberg, J. 2011. The Human Texture of Information. Is the Internet Changing the Way You Think? Eds. Brockman, J. Harper Perennial.

[13] Nat. Res. Council Com. on Inn. in Comp. and Comm.1999. Funding a Revolution: Government Support for Computing Research. Nat. Academy Press.

[14] Newman, W. 1994. A preliminary analysis of the products of HCI research, using pro forma abstracts. In Proc. CHI'94, 278-284.

[15] Soloway, E, Ehrlich, K & Bonar, J. 1982. Tapping into tacit programming knowledge. In Proc. CHI'82, 52-57.

[16] Shi, X, Leskovec, J and McFarland, D. 2010. Citing for high impact. In Proc. JCDL'10, 49-58.

[17] Wulff, W and Mahling, D. 1990. An assessment of HCI: issues and implications. SIGCHI Bull. 22, 1 (June 1990), 80-87.

Information-theoretic Term Weighting Schemes for Document Clustering

Weimao Ke
Lab for Information Network & Computing Studies
College of Information Science and Technology
Drexel University, Philadelphia, PA 19104, U.S.A.
wk@drexel.edu

ABSTRACT

We propose a new theory to quantify information in probability distributions and derive a new document representation model for text clustering. By extending Shannon entropy to accommodate a non-linear relation between information and uncertainty, the proposed Least Information theory (LIT) provides insight into how terms can be weighted based on their probability distributions in documents vs. in the collection. We derive two basic quantities in the document clustering context: 1) LI Binary (LIB) which quantifies information due to the observation of a term's (binary) occurrence in a document; and 2) LI Frequency (LIF) which measures information for the observation of a randomly picked term from the document. Both quantities are computed given term distributions in the document collection as prior knowledge and can be used separately or combined to represent documents for text clustering. Experiments on four benchmark text collections demonstrate strong performances of the proposed methods compared to classic TF*IDF. Particularly, the LIB*LIF weighting scheme, which combines LIB and LIF, consistently outperforms TF*IDF in terms of multiple evaluation metrics. The least information measure has a potentially broad range of applications beyond text clustering.

Categories and Subject Descriptors

H.3.1 [**Information storage and retrieval**]: Content Analysis and Indexing; H.3.3 [**Information storage and retrieval**]: Information Search and Retrieval—*Clustering*

General Terms

Theory, Algorithms, Performance, Experimentation

Keywords

term weighting, information measure, semantic information, document representation, text clustering

1. INTRODUCTION

Clustering, or unsupervised classification, is the process of bringing like entities together [12]. Text clustering is focused on partitioning unstructured text documents and underlies many applications for information organization and knowledge management [6]. Document clustering also supports important processes in text mining and information retrieval [21, 33].

In text clustering research, TF*IDF has been extensively used for term weighting and document representation [21, 34]. While term frequency (TF) indicates the degree of a document's association with a term, inverse document frequency (IDF) is the manifestation of a term's specificity, key to determine the term's value toward weighting and relevance ranking [15]. While many clustering algorithms have been developed, TF*IDF and its variations remain the *de facto* standard for term weighting in text clustering [33, 21, 34, 14]. Given strong empirical performances of classic TF*IDF, limited research has focused on innovation of term weighting schemes.

Information and probability theories have provided important guidance on the development of classic techniques such as probabilistic and language modeling [27]. Information-theoretic measures such as mutual information and Kullback-Leibler (KL) divergence[1] have also been used for various processes including feature selection and matching [18, 33].

The probabilistic retrieval framework provides an important theoretical ground to IDF weights [26]. IDF in the form of $-\ln \frac{n_i}{N}$, where n_i is the number of documents containing term i among N total number of documents, resembles the entropy formula in Shannon's information theory. Several works have attempted to justify IDF from an information-theoretic view. IDF can be viewed as Kullback-Leibler (KL) information (*relative entropy*) between term probability distributions in a document and in the collection [1].

From an information-centric view, this research aims to develop a new model for term weighting and document representation. By quantifying the amount of information required to explain probability distribution changes, the proposed *least information* theory (LIT) establishes a new basic information quantity and provides insight into how terms can be weighted based on their probability distributions in documents vs. in the collection. We derive two basic quanti-

[1]The literature has used a variety of names in reference to *KL divergence*. While Kullback preferred *discrimination information* for the principle of minimum discrimination information (MDI) [17], the literature has often referred to it as divergence information or relative entropy.

ties, namely LI Binary (LIB) and LI Frequency (LIF), which can be used separately or combined to represent documents. We conduct experiments on several benchmark collections for text clustering to demonstrate the proposed methods' effectiveness compared to TF*IDF. The major contribution here is more than another term weighting scheme that is empirically competitive. More important is the new *least information* (LIT) measure that can be used to attack many other problems related to quantifying semantic amounts of information.

2. PROPOSED THEORY

In this section, we propose a new theory to quantify meaning of information via extension of Shannon's entropy equation. We start with a discussions on issues of existing information measures, what to expect about the desired information quantity, and introduce the *least information* theory (LIT) in which expected characteristics are observed.

2.1 Information Measures and Problems

Shannon entropy measures uncertainty as a property of a probability distribution whereas the amount of (missing) information is a function of linear uncertainty reduction [29]. The underlying assumption for this entropy-information relation is that information (always) reduces uncertainty. The amount of information is determined by a specified probability distribution regardless of the ultimate outcome [5].

In reality, however, there are many situations in which information does not necessarily reduce uncertainty – uncertainty may increase or decrease due to new information. In addition, the amount of information depends not only on the overall uncertainty change but also on how individual probabilities vary. For example, an unlikely event being the ultimate outcome requires more explanation (information) than in the case of a very likely event happening.

Different amounts of information are needed to explain different (and perhaps opposite) outcomes. We reason that, while uncertainty is a property of a specified probability distribution, the amount of information required to explain an outcome and more generally to explain a change in the probability distribution is interpretation/meaning-dependent and is more complex than a linear function of uncertainty.

Indeed, using Shannon's entropy measure to quantify the amount of *meaningful* information (with proper interpretation) is beyond the scope of classic information theory. The original purpose of Shannon's theory was for engineering communication systems where the "*meaning* of information was considered irrelevant" [29, p. 379]. As Rapoport (1953) put it, it is about technical problems that can be treated independently of the semantic content of messages [25].

Digital libraries technologies such as those related to information organization and retrieval deal with issues of semantics and relevance, beyond pure engineering problems. Measuring *semantic quantities* of information requires innovation on the theory, better clarification of the relationship between information and entropy, and justification of this relationship.

While related quantities such as KL information (*relative entropy*) offer alternatives to the simplified entropy reduction view of information, some characteristics of *relative entropy* do not meet our expectations about such a measure. Specifically, the asymmetry of the KL function due to the assumption about a benchmark distribution in the evaluation disqualifies it as a metric [8].

In addition, *relative entropies* over the course of continuous probability changes in one direction do not add up to the overall amount. Finally and very important, extreme probability changes (e.g., when an event changes from being very unlikely to almost certainty) lead to infinite KL information, which is a particularly undesirable property for term weighting. We address these issues in the proprosed *least information theory* (LIT) below.

2.2 Least Information Theory (LIT)

In this section, we present the *least information* theory (LIT) to quantify meaning (semantics) in probability distribution changes. Here we shall clarify on the definition of *meaning* by reusing D. M. MacKay's terms, in which the meaning of information is defined as a "selective function on a range of the recipient's states of conditional readiness for goal-directed activity." [23, p.24] Meaning is a relationship between information and the recipient rather than a property alone. Information is not restricted to the amount in message transmission but is subject to interpretation [11]. Introduction of information results in changes of readiness states or belief (as in probabilities). In this view, meaning can (at least in part) be quantified by what varies in the beliefs or estimated probabilities of inferences.

Let X be prior (initially specified) probabilities for a set of exhaustive and mutually exclusive inferences: $X = [x_1, x_2, .., x_n]$, where x_i is the prior probability of the ith inference on a given hypothesis. Let Y denote posterior (changed) probabilities after certain information is known: $Y = [y_1, y_2, .., y_n]$, where y_i is the *informed* probability of the ith inference. Uncertainties/entropies of the two distributions can be computed by Shannon entropy:

$$H(X) = -k \sum_{i=1}^{n} x_i \ln x_i \quad (1)$$

$$H(Y) = -k \sum_{i=1}^{n} y_i \ln y_i \quad (2)$$

The amount of information obtained from X to Y, in Shannon's treatment, can be measured via the reduction of entropy:

$$\Delta H = H(X) - H(Y) \quad (3)$$

The inferences are exclusive and involve different meanings. When probabilities X to Y are not identical, the two distributions are semantically different and it is obvious that some amount of information is responsible for the variance. We can examine the amount of information associated with individual inferences via the measurement of uncertainty change. With Equation 3, however, it is easy to show that when there are changes in the probabilities, there may be increases, decreases, or no change in the overall uncertainty. We observe that even when there is no change in the entropy, there is still an amount of information responsible for any variance in the probability distribution. To use the overall (system-wide) uncertainty for the measurement of information ignores semantic relevance of changes in individual inferences.

Here our new *least information* model departs from the classic measure of information as reduction of uncertainty (entropy). First, we reason that any change in the uncertainty of an inference, either an increase or decrease, requires a relevant amount of information that is responsible for it. The overall information needed to explain changes in all inference probabilities is the sum of individual pieces of information associated with each inference.

Second, for an individual inference i, the probability may vary in one of the two semantic directions, i.e., to increase or to decrease the likelihood. In either case, there is always a (positive) amount of information responsible for that variance. If we assume inferences are semantically independent[2], the absolute values of these independent pieces of information add linearly to the overall amount of information.

In addition, it is reasonable for such an information quantity to meet the condition that continuous, smaller changes in one direction add incrementally to a bigger change in the same direction. That is, pieces of information responsible for small, continuous changes of an inference probability in the same direction should add up to the amount of information for the overall change. For example, if the ith inference's probability increases from x_i to y_i and then to z_i, the (least) amount of information required for the change from x_i to y_i and the amount from y_i to z_i should add up to the overall (least) information required for the change from x_i to z_i.

We define dH_i as the amount of entropy change due to a tiny change dp_i of probability p_i:

$$dH_i = -\ln p_i dp_i \tag{4}$$

In the configuration view of entropy, this microscopic variance of entropy due to a small change in an inference's probability is the change of the weighted (p_i) number of configurations ($\ln \frac{1}{p_i}$) [10, 5]. In other words, it is the change in the number of configurations ($\ln \frac{1}{p_i}$) due to a varied probability weight (p_i).

Every tiny change in the probabilities requires some explanation (information). Aggregating (integrating) the small changes of uncertainty leads to the amount of information required for a macro-level change. A macroscopic uncertainty change due to a significant probability shift of an inference is the sum (integration) of continuous microscopic changes in the variance range. Therefore, we define the least amount of information I_i required to explain the probability change of the ith inference as the integration (aggregation) of all tiny absolute (positive) changes of entropy dH_i:

$$\begin{aligned} I_i &= \left|\int_{x_i}^{y_i} dH_i\right| \\ &= \left|\int_{x_i}^{y_i} -\ln p_i dp_i\right| \\ &= \left|p_i(1-\ln p_i)\right|_{x_i}^{y_i} && (5) \\ &= \left|y_i(1-\ln y_i) - x_i(1-\ln x_i)\right| && (6) \end{aligned}$$

[2]Inference probabilities are never perfectly independent of one another given the degree of freedom. But to simplify the discussion and formulation, we use the independence assumption.

where x_i is the initial probability of the ith inference and y_i the posterior probability of the same inference. We define *informative entropy* g_i as a function of an inference's probability:

$$g_i = p_i(1-\ln p_i) \tag{7}$$

The equation for *least information* I_i for the ith inference in Equation 6 can be rewritten as:

$$I_i = \left|g(y_i) - g(x_i)\right| \tag{8}$$

The total *Least Information* I is the sum of partial least information for every inference:

$$\begin{aligned} I &= \sum_{i=1}^{n} I_i \\ &= \sum_{i=1}^{n} \left|g(y_i) - g(x_i)\right| \\ &= \sum_{i=1}^{n} \left|y_i(1-\ln y_i) - x_i(1-\ln x_i)\right| && (9) \end{aligned}$$

where n is the number of inferences, x_i is the initially specified probability of the ith inference, and y_i the revised probability of the ith inference.

2.3 Important Model Characteristics

It is worth noting that Equation 9 is to measure the *least amount* of information required to explain a probability distribution change for a set of inferences. Here is why we include the word *least* in the nomenclature. Given that information may alter a probability distribution in various semantic directions and change the uncertainty in both positive and negative directions, the actual amount of information leading to such a change may consist of multiple pieces of information acting in different directions.

Without an exhaustive analysis of the process, the actual amount of information cannot be deduced solely from an investigation of probability distributions. It is only reasonable to quantify the *least information* needed for that change – that is, the sum of all needed amounts of information at the very least, every tiny piece of which contributes in the same direction of a change. In addition, this model does not consider the process of removing information, which, in effect, is equivalent to adding another piece of information that has perfectly opposite semantics[3] in the same amount.

Based on Equation 9, several important characteristics of *least information* can be observed. Figure 1 compares the *least information* measure with entropy reduction and relative entropy in a two-exclusive-inference case. We summarize some of these characteristics below.

- Absolute information and symmetry: The amount of *least information* required for a probability change from X to Y is the same as that from Y to X, though their semantic meanings are different.

[3]The term *opposite* does not indicate true vs. false information. Opposite information semantics are essentially to increase vs. to decrease the probability of an inference, e.g., good news vs. bad news about a candidate that may influence the outcome of an election.

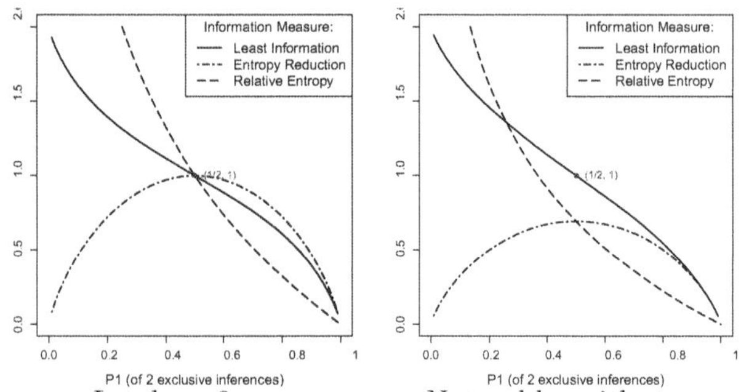

Log base 2 Natural logarithm

Figure 1: Least Information vs. Entropy: Reducing two exclusive uncertain inferences to certainty. X denotes P_1 which is the probability for 1st inference of 2 mutually exclusive. Y denotes the amount of information (I) in terms of each measure. The 1st inference is assumed to be the ultimate outcome in the figure. The asymmetry of *least information* in the plot is a manifestation of its dependence on the outcome. Compare to Fig. 7 in Shannon (1948).

- Addition of continuous change: Amounts of *least information* for small, continuous probability changes in the same semantic directions add linearly to the amount of *least information* responsible for the overall change. In short, $I(X \to Z) = I(X \to Y) + I(Y \to Z)$, if and only if $X \to Y$ and $Y \to Z$ are in the same semantic direction.
- Unit Information: In the special case when there are two equally possible inferences, the amount of *least information* needed to explain an outcome (certainty) is one: $I(p_1 = p_2 = \frac{1}{2} \to p_1 = 1) = 1$, regardless of the log base in the equation (see data point $(\frac{1}{2}, 1)$ in Figure 1).
- In the special case of reducing uncertain inferences to certainty (with the ultimate case):
  - With equally likely inferences, when there are more choices, the least information needed to explain an outcome is larger.
  - The less likely the outcome, the larger the amount of *least information* needed to explain it.
- Zero least information: The amount of *least information* is zero if and only if there is no change in the probability distribution (identical distributions).

2.4 Least Information for Term Weighting

Now we apply the proposed *least information* theory to term weighting and document representation. A text document can be viewed as a set of terms with probabilities (estimated by frequencies) of occurrence. We conjecture that the larger amount *least information* is needed to explain a term's probability in a document (vs. in the collection), the more heavily the term should be weighted to represent the document [2]. Hence, we transform the question of document representation to weighting terms according to their amounts of *least information* in documents.

In this study, we propose two specific weighting methods, one based on a binary representation of term occurrence (0 vs. 1) and the other based on term frequencies. These two methods will be used separately and combined in fusion methods as well. We use maximum likelihood estimates (MLE) to get term probabilities based on observed data [24].

2.4.1 LI Binary (LIB) Model

In the binary model, a term either occurs or does not occur in a document. If we randomly pick a document from the collection, the chance that a term t_i appears in the document can be estimated by the ratio between the number of documents containing the term n_i (i.e., document frequency) and the total number of documents N using MLE. Let $p(t_i|C) = n_i/N$ denote the probability of term t_i occurring in a randomly picked document in collection C; $p(\bar{t_i}|C)$ is the probability that the term does not appear:

$$p(\bar{t_i}|C) = 1 - p(t_i|C) = 1 - n_i/N$$

When a specific document d is observed, it becomes certain whether a term occurs in the document or not. Hence the term probability given a specific document $p(t_i|d)$ is either 1 or 0. Given the definition of g_i in Equation 7, the least amount of information in term t_i from observing document d can be computed by:

$$\begin{aligned} I(t_i, d) \quad = \quad & \Big|g(t_i|d) - g(t_i|C)\Big| \\ & + \Big|g(\bar{t_i}|d) - g(\bar{t_i}|C)\Big| \end{aligned} \qquad (10)$$

The above equation gives the amount of information a term conveys in a document regardless of its semantic direction. When a query term t_i does not appear in document d, the least information associated with the term should be treated as *negative* because it makes the document less relevant to the term. Hence, the ranking function should not only consider the amount of information but also the *sign* (positive vs. negative) of the quantity. Hence, LI Binary (LIB) can be computed by:

$$\begin{aligned} LIB_2(t_i, d) \quad = \quad & g(t_i|d) - g(t_i|C) \\ & - g(\bar{t_i}|d) + g(\bar{t_i}|C) \end{aligned} \qquad (11)$$

For term weighting, we are more interested in the likelihood of a term appearing in a document. Keeping only quantities related to t_i (and removing those associated with $\bar{t_i}$), we simplify the LIB equation to:

$$LIB(t_i, d) \quad = \quad g(t_i|d) - g(t_i|C) \qquad (12)$$

$$\quad = \quad g(t_i|d) - \frac{n_i}{N}\Big(1 - \ln\frac{n_i}{N}\Big) \qquad (13)$$

The quantity depends on the observation of term t_i in the document: $g(t_i|d)$ is 1 when t_i appears in document d and 0 if otherwise, according to Equation 7. That is:

$$LIB(t_i, d) = \begin{cases} 1 - \frac{n_i}{N}\Big(1 - \ln\frac{n_i}{N}\Big) & t_i \in d \\ -\frac{n_i}{N}\Big(1 - \ln\frac{n_i}{N}\Big) & t_i \notin d \end{cases} \qquad (14)$$

where n_i is the document frequency of term t_i and N is the total number of documents. The larger the LIB, the more information the term contributes to the document and should be weighted more heavily in the document representation. LIB is similar in spirit to IDF and its value represents the discriminative power of the term when it appears in a document.

2.4.2 LI Frequency (LIF) Model

In the LI Frequency (LIF) model, we use term frequencies to model *least information*. Treating a document collection C as a meta-document, the probability of a term randomly picked from the collection being a specific term t_i can be estimated by: $p(t_i|C) = F_i/L$, where F_i is the total number of occurrences of term t_i in collection C and L the overall length of C (i.e., the sum of all document lengths).

When a specific document d is observed, the probability of picking term t_i from this document can be estimated by: $p(t_i|d) = tf_{i,d}/L_d$, where $tf_{i,d}$ is the number of times term t_i occurs in document d and L_d is the length of the document. Again, for each term t_i, there are two exclusive inferences, namely the randomly picked term being the specific term (t_i) or not ($\bar{t_i}$). To quantify a term's LIF weight, we measure *least information* that explains the change from the term's probability distribution in the collection to its distribution in the document in question:

$$\begin{aligned} LIF_2(t_i, d) &= g(t_i|d) - g(t_i|C) \\ &\quad + g(\bar{t_i}|C) - g(\bar{t_i}|d) \qquad (15) \end{aligned}$$

We focus on the quantities $g(t_i|d)$ and $g(t_i|C)$ to estimate *least information* of each term when a specific document is observed. Without quantities $g(\bar{t_i}|C)$ and $g(\bar{t_i}|d)$, the LIF equation is simplified to:

$$\begin{aligned} LIF(t_i, d) &= g(t_i|d) - g(t_i|C) \qquad (16) \\ &= \frac{tf_{i,d}}{L_d}(1 - \ln \frac{tf_{i,d}}{L_d}) \\ &\quad - \frac{F_i}{L}(1 - \ln \frac{F_i}{L}) \qquad (17) \end{aligned}$$

where $tf_{i,d}$ is term frequency of term t_i in document d and L_d is the document length. F_i is collection frequency of term t_i (the sum of term frequencies in all documents) whereas L is the overall length of all documents. In a sense, LIF can be seen as a new approach to modeling term frequencies with document length and collection frequency normalization. In this study, we use raw term frequencies with MLE to estimate probabilities and do not use any smoothing techniques to fine tune the estimates.

2.4.3 Fusion of LIB & LIF

While LIB uses binary term occurrence to estimate least information a document carries in the term, LIF measures the amount of least information based on term frequency. The two are related quantities with different focuses. As discussed, the LIB quantity is similar in spirit to IDF (inverse document frequency) whereas LIF can be seen as a means to normalize TF (term frequency).

In light of TF*IDF, we reason that combining the two will potentiate each quantity's strength for term weighting. Hence we propose three fusion methods to combine the two quantities by addition and multiplication:

1. LIB+LIF: To weight a term, we simply add LIB and LIF together by treating them as two separate pieces of information.
2. LIB*LIF: In this fusion method, we follow the idea of TF*IDF by multiplying LIB and LIF quantities for each term. Because a *least information* quantity falls in the range of $[-1, 1]$ and can be a negative value, we normalize LIB and LIF values to $[0, 2]$ by adding 1 to each before multiplication.
3. LIB*TF: This method multiplies the LIB quantity by a document length normalized TF (term frequency), similar to the above LIB*LIF method.

These fusion methods allow us to examine potential strengths and weaknesses of the proposed *least information* term weights for clustering. We study LIB and LIF as well as the above fusion methods in experiments. And given the extensive use of TF*IDF in text clustering research, we use it for comparison in the study.

3. EXPERIMENTAL SETUP

3.1 Data Collections

Several benchmark collections were used in the study to evaluate the effectiveness of proposed term weighting methods for text clustering. Some of these collections, including the WebKB 4 universities data, the 20 Newsgroups collection, and the RCV1 Reuters corpus, had been widely used for text clustering and classification research. The New York Times annotated corpus was a relatively new development and had not been extensively adopted for clustering experiments.

- WebKB 4 Universities Data (WebKB): This data set contains 8,282 web pages collected in 1997 from computer science departments of various universities, which were manually categorized into seven categories such as student, faculty, and department. This was developed by the WebKB project at CMU [9].
- 20 Newsgroups (20News): The collection contains 20,000 messages from 20 news groups (categories) [19]. The messages were randomly picked to distribute evenly among the categories. We used a revised version which retained 18,828 messages after duplicate removal. We used all 20 categories as gold standard labels.
- Reuters Corpus Volume 1 (RCV1-v2): The RCV1 collection contains 804,414 newswire stories made available by Reuters. RCV1-v2 is a corrected version of the original collection, in which documents were manually assigned to a hierarchy of 103 categories [20]. There are four top-level categories (under the hierarchical root), which we used as labels for evaluation.
- New York Times Annotated Corpus (NYTimes): The NYTimes corpus contains more than 1.8 million articles in New York Times from 1987 - 2007 [28]. The corpus is very rich in human annotation such as summaries and subject descriptors. For each year, we identified articles assigned to one and only one *taxonomic classifier* and used the third-level categories under *top/news/* (e.g., *top/news/science* and *top/news/business*)

as labels. After several categories such as *corrections* were removed, the final data set contained 179,175 documents in 15 categories.

3.2 System Settings

We developed an experimental clustering system based on the Weka data mining framework [32]. We implemented various document representation methods including the proposed term weighting schemes and TF*IDF based on a Weka vectorization filter. Existing implementations in the framework for k-means clustering [3] and hierarchical agglomerative clustering (HAC) were reused in experiments [35]. We tokenized documents into single words, removed stop-words, and normalized terms using an iterated Lovins stemmer [22]. A number of most frequent words were selected as features (DF thresholding); 1,000 features were used in main experiments. We varied the number of features in experiments to study the influence of feature selection. All documents were normalized to unit vectors.

In k-means clustering, we used the euclidean distance and set the maximum number of iterations to 200. We conducted 30 runs of k-means for each experimental setting, in which clustering was performed on a random sample of 2,000 documents. The HAC clustering used *complete link* and angle distance (based on an arc cosine function). For each experimental setting, HAC was performed on a random sample of 1,000 documents for 20 runs. We set the number of desired clusters to the number of classes/labels in each data collection.

3.3 Evaluation Metrics

Using categorical labels available in data as the gold standard, we evaluated clustering results based on several classic metrics, namely, *purity*, *rand index*, *precision*, *recall*, and F_1. By assigning each cluster to the most frequent class (label) in it, we can compute *purity* by:

$$purity(C, L) = \frac{1}{N} \sum_i \max_j |c_i \cap l_j| \quad (18)$$

where N is the total number of documents. C is the set of clusters and c_i is the ith cluster. L is the set of labels (classes) where l_j is the jth label.

Computing the other metrics such as *rand index* is by viewing document clustering as a series of decision making [24]. Given the following table which summarizes the numbers of correctly and incorrectly clustered document pairs:

Table 1: Decision table of clustering

System⇒ Labels⇓	**Same Cluster**	**Diff Clusters**
Same Class	*TP*: True Positive	*FN*: False Negative
Diff Classes	*FP*: False Positive	*TN*: True Negative

Rand Index measures the ratio of correct decisions and is computed by:

$$RI = \frac{TP + TN}{TP + FP + FN + TN} \quad (19)$$

Likewise, precision, recall, and F_1 can by computed by:

$$P = TP/(TP + FP) \quad (20)$$
$$R = TP/(TP + FN) \quad (21)$$
$$F_1 = 2 * P * R/(P + R) \quad (22)$$

Whereas *rand index* measures clustering accuracy by taking into account both true positive and true negative, classic IR evaluation metrics such as precision and recall emphasize the ability to find relevant answers/pairs (true positive). Purity and precision are similar in that they both focus on the internal accuracy within each cluster. Recall, on the other hand, addresses the effectiveness of having as many relevant document pairs as possible in one cluster. With these various metrics, we were able to examine strengths and weaknesses of the proposed methods in multiple perspectives.

4. RESULTS

In each set of experiments presented here, best scores in each metric are highlighted in **bold** whereas *italic* values are those better than TF*IDF baseline scores. A significant better result according to t-test at 0.05 is shown with an asterisk (*). We first present results using k-means clustering with various weighting schemes and with 1,000 features in sections 4.1 - 4.4. Analysis of the impact of feature selection on clustering effectiveness in section 4.5 will show overall best results were obtained with 1,000 features in WebKB, 20News, and RCV1 collections. We discuss hierarchical agglomerative clustering (HAC) results in section 4.6.

4.1 WebKB 4 Universities Data

Table 2 shows k-means clustering results on the WebKB 4 Universities data set. The proposed methods LIB, LIB+LIF, and LIB*LIF all outperformed TF*IDF in terms of purity, rand index, and precision. LIF and LIB*TF, which have an emphasis on term frequency, achieved significantly better recall scores.

Table 2: WebKB with k-means clustering

Method	Purity	RIndex	Prec.	Recall	F_1
TF*IDF	0.504	0.655	0.343	0.245	0.283
LIB	*0.520**	**0.686***	**0.383***	0.215	0.275
LIF	0.455	0.600	0.282	*0.277**	0.276
LIB*TF	0.459	0.571	0.273	**0.323***	**0.292**
LIB+LIF	*0.517**	*0.680**	*0.377**	0.214	0.272
LIB*LIF	**0.524***	*0.681**	*0.376**	0.208	0.268

4.2 20 Newsgroups Data

K-means clustering with the 20 Newsgroups data, as shown in Table 3, presents a slightly different picture. While best scores were achieved among the proposed methods, LIF appeared to have produced most of the best scores, with purity, precision, and F_1 scores significantly higher than those of TF*IDF. Overall, k-means was not very effective in terms of within-cluster accuracy (purity and precision).

4.3 RCV1 Reuters Corpus

K-means clustering experiments on the RCV1 corpus showed a pattern quite similar to WebKB results. As shown in

Table 3: 20 Newsgroup with k-means clustering

Method	Purity	RIndex	Prec.	Recall	F_1
TF*IDF	0.229	0.771	0.0973	0.350	0.145
LIB	_0.241_	**0.832**	_0.111∗_	0.286	_0.154_
LIF	**0.269∗**	_0.816_	**0.117∗**	_0.372_	**0.173∗**
LIB*TF	0.174	0.631	0.0757	**0.489∗**	0.126
LIB+LIF	_0.231_	0.732	_0.106_	_0.408_	_0.155_
LIB*LIF	0.214	_0.793_	0.0957	0.309	0.137

Table 4, the proposed methods outperformed TF*IDF in terms of multiple metrics. Compared to TF*IDF, LIB*LIF, LIB+LIF, and LIB performed significantly better in purity, rand index, and precision whereas LIF and LIB*TF achieved significantly better scores in recall.

Table 4: RCV1 with k-means clustering

Method	Purity	RIndex	Prec.	Recall	F_1
TF*IDF	0.699	0.678	0.511	0.576	0.531
LIB	_0.733∗_	_0.711∗_	_0.543_	0.538	_0.539_
LIF	_0.719_	_0.699_	_0.546_	_0.663∗_	**0.588∗**
LIB*TF	0.650	0.637	0.468	**0.670∗**	_0.542_
LIB+LIF	_0.725_	_0.711∗_	_0.544_	0.554	_0.547_
LIB*LIF	**0.741∗**	**0.713∗**	**0.549∗**	0.531	_0.539_

4.4 New York Times Collection

With the NY Times corpus, LIB*LIF continued to dominate best scores and performed significantly better than TF*IDF in terms of purity, rand index, and precision (Table 5). This is very consistent with WebKB and RCV1 results. While LIB and LIB+LIF did well in terms of rand index, LIF and LIB*TF were competitive in recall.

Table 5: NYTimes with k-means Clustering

Method	Purity	RIndex	Prec.	Recall	F_1
TF*IDF	0.825	0.632	0.683	0.383	0.456
LIB	0.819	_0.634_	_0.691_	_0.399∗_	_0.469_
LIF	0.807	0.627	0.662	_0.433∗_	**0.481∗**
LIB*TF	0.813	0.622	0.672	**0.435∗**	_0.473∗_
LIB+LIF	_0.829_	_0.640_	_0.700_	_0.405∗_	_0.476∗_
LIB*LIF	**0.837∗**	**0.647∗**	**0.719∗**	_0.391_	_0.472∗_

Overall, LIB*LIF had a strong performance across the data collections. Methods with the LIB quantity, especially LIB, LIB+LIF, and LIB*LIF, were effective when the evaluation emphasis was on within-cluster (internal) accuracy, e.g., in terms of purity and precision. Similar to IDF, LIB was designed to weight terms according to their *discriminative* powers or *specificity* in terms of Sparck Jones [15]. Hence, it helped improve precision-oriented effectiveness. The other methods such as LIF and LIB*TF emphasize *term frequency* in each document and, with the ability to associate one document to another by assigning term weights in a *less discriminative* manner, were able to achieve better recalls.

4.5 Impact of Feature Selection

Now we look at the impact of feature selection on the effectiveness of document representation for clustering. In this work, we selected features based on their frequencies in the collection (DF thresholding), which was computationally simple and had been found in several studies to be a very effective feature selection technique for clustering and categorization [21, 33, 34]. We varied the number of features N_f in each set of experiments, for which the top N_f most frequent terms were kept for document representation. We performed this experimental analysis on three collections, namely, WebKB, 20Newsgroup, and RCV1.

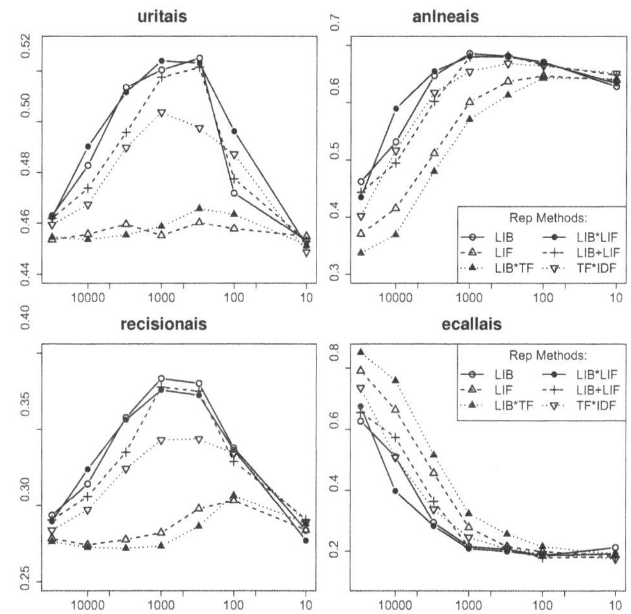

Figure 2: WebKB: Impact of feature selection. X denotes # of features and is log-transformed. Y is the metric score.

Figure 2 shows the influence of the number of selected features on clustering effectiveness with the WebKB data. Note that the X axis is logarithmic and the number of features N_f decreases from left to right. Recall appears to decrease when N_f decreases because less common features lead to ineffective identification of related documents (smaller *true positive*) and a larger number of false negative (larger *false negative*).

In terms of purity, rand index, and precision, there exists an inflection point around $N_f = 1000$, where optimal clustering results were achieved. With a large feature space (e.g., with 30,000 features for WebKB), unrelated documents were likely to be grouped together because of irrelevant common terms, leading to a large number of false positive (hence lower precision). Some degree of feature removal reduced the amount of *noise* in the feature space and improved clustering effectiveness. It was shown in research that using various feature selection methods to eliminate up to 90% of term features resulted in either no loss or improvement of clustering and categorization accuracy [21, 33]. Further feature reduction from the inflection point degraded clustering performance when there were insufficient features for accurate document representation. As shown in Figures 3 and

4, similar patterns about the influence of feature selection were found with 20Newsgroup and RCV1 data.

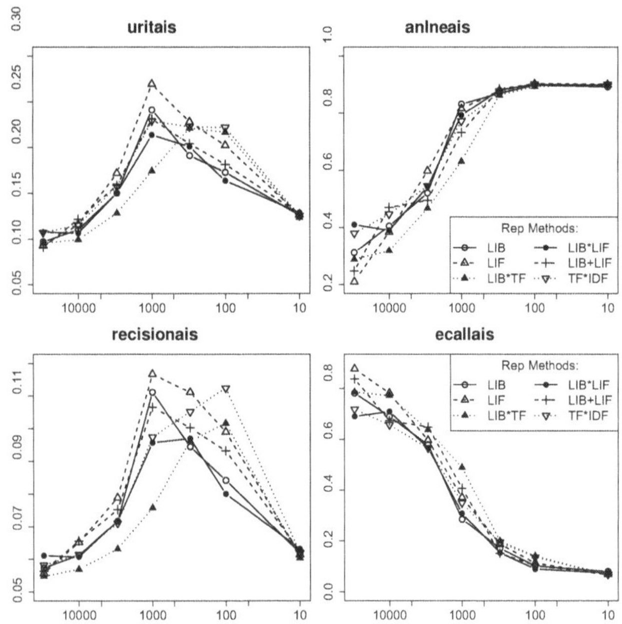

Figure 3: 20Newsgroup: Impact of feature selection

Interestingly, dramatically reducing the number of features from the inflection point only degraded *rand index* to a certain degree. We suspect that with an extremely small number of features to represent a large, diverse collection, clustering did not perform effectively. Having a good *rand index* score with only 10 features, for example in Figure 3 on the 20 Newsgroups data, is against our intuition about the situation. This raises questions about the effectiveness of *rand index* in evaluating clustering results and the circumstances under which *true negative* should or should not be considered.

4.6 HAC Clustering Results

The main experiments above were conducted using k-means clustering. In this section we present results from hierarchical agglomerative clustering (HAC) using complete link and an arc cosine distance function. From Tables 6, 7, 8, and 9, we have found results consistent with those from k-means clustering.

Table 6: WebKB with hierarchical clustering

Method	Purity	RIndex	Prec.	Recall	F_1
TF*IDF	0.459	0.623	0.283	0.235	0.253
LIB	*0.464*	*0.628*	*0.295*	0.233	*0.259*
LIF	0.453	0.484	0.239	**0.391**∗	**0.296**∗
LIB*TF	0.452	0.623	0.275	0.223	0.244
LIB+LIF	*0.473*∗	**0.641**	**0.308**∗	0.228	*0.261*
LIB*LIF	**0.485**∗	*0.633*	*0.301*∗	0.226	*0.257*

With WebKB and 20 Newsgroups data (shown in Tables 6 and 7), for example, LIB+LIF and LIB*LIF continued to perform competitively in terms of within-cluster accuracy metrics such as purity and precision. LIF achieved better recall and F_1 than TF*IDF did on WebKB (Table 6).

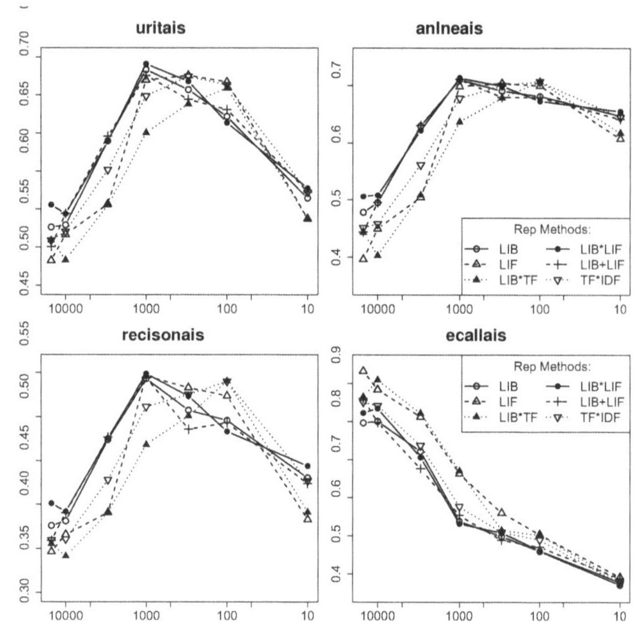

Figure 4: RCV1: Impact of feature selection

Table 7: 20 Newsgroup with hierarchical clustering

Method	Purity	RIndex	Prec.	Recall	F_1
TF*IDF	0.192	0.584	0.0582	0.475	0.103
LIB	0.183	*0.614*	0.0575	0.429	0.101
LIF	**0.240**∗	*0.891*∗	*0.0987*∗	0.142	*0.116*∗
LIB*TF	0.172	0.568	0.0567	**0.483**	0.101
LIB+LIF	*0.232*∗	*0.886*∗	**0.0988**∗	0.154	**0.120**∗
LIB*LIF	*0.224*∗	**0.892**∗	*0.096*∗	0.134	*0.111*∗

Table 8: RCV1 with hierarchical clustering

Method	Purity	RIndex	Prec.	Recall	F_1
TF*IDF	0.448	0.357	0.312	0.865	0.458
LIB	*0.477*∗	*0.384*∗	*0.324*∗	0.864	**0.470**∗
LIF	**0.542**∗	**0.622**∗	**0.398**∗	0.391	0.392
LIB*TF	*0.464*∗	*0.370*	*0.319*∗	**0.875**	*0.467*∗
LIB+LIF	*0.489*∗	*0.399*∗	*0.325*∗	0.829	*0.466*
LIB*LIF	*0.492*∗	*0.399*∗	*0.322*∗	0.804	*0.458*

With 20 Newsgroups, RCV1, and NYTimes data, LIF consistently outperformed TF*IDF in multiple metrics (see Tables 7, 8, and 9). With the RCV1 corpus, all proposed methods produced significantly higher scores in purity, rand index, and precision than TF*IDF did.

5. DISCUSSION AND RELATED WORK

In the various experiments presented here, the proposed term weighting methods based on *least information* modeling performed very strongly compared to TF*IDF. In all experiments on the four benchmark collections, top perfor-

cumulative gain (nDCG). We also show that our approach can outperform state-of-the-art scholarly paper recommendation systems.

2. RELATED WORK

As the field of recommendation systems is large, we focus our literature review on systems for scholarly paper recommendation. In addition, as finding potential papers can be viewed as a type of link discovery, we also briefly review two types of work, citation link prediction and content link detection.

2.1 Scholarly Paper Recommendation

With respect to scholarly paper recommendation, McNee *et al.* [10] proposed an approach to recommending citations. Their approach applied collaborative filtering (CF) to social networks to create a graph formed by the citations between research papers. This data can be mapped into a framework of CF and used to overcome the cold-start problem. Expanding this approach, Torres *et al.* [18] proposed a method for recommending research papers by combining CF and content-based filtering (CBF). However, a single final ranking obtainable by merging the output from both CF and CBF is purposefully not done, as the authors claim that pure recommendation algorithms are not designed to receive input from another recommendation algorithm. Gori and Pucci [3] devised a PageRank-based method for recommending research papers. But in their approach, a user must prepare an initial set of relevant articles to obtain better recommendations, and the damping factor *d* that affects the score of PageRank is not optimized. Yang *et al.* [23] presented a scholarly paper recommendation system using a ranking-oriented CF. Although their system overcomes the cold-start problem by utilizing implicit behaviors extracted from a user's access logs, the predefined settings for parameters used to select effective data are not justified nor investigated in detail. In recent work, Nascimento *et al.* [13] developed a scholarly paper recommendation system, in which they use the title to construct user profiles, and the title and abstract to generate feature vectors of candidate papers to recommend. However, we feel that such a small span of text does not effectively represent a user's interest and candidate papers.

Scholarly paper recommendation studies are also emerging in data mining. Wang and Blei [20] proposed collaborative topic regression model which combines ideas from CF and content analysis based on probabilistic topic modeling. They used the abstract and title of the paper to model a user and characterize candidate papers to recommend, which occasionally results in irrelevant recommendations, similar to [13]. El-Arini and Guestrin [2] proposed a method for discovering a small set of scholarly papers that are relevant to a query yet diversified. They defined "influence" to capture the transfer of ideas as individual concepts among papers in the query. Their approach then returns papers related to these concepts. However, users need to prepare trusted papers in advance to discover relevant and diverse papers.

2.2 Link Discovery

Citation Link Prediction. Researchers can benefit from a citation recommendation system because searching for the right paper to cite is a laborious task. Strohman *et al.* [17] experimented with a citation recommendation system where the relevance between two documents is measured by a linear combination of text features and citation graph features. They concluded that similarity between bibliographies of documents and Katz distance [9] are the most important features. He *et al.* [5] developed a citation recommendation system based on a non-parametric probabilistic model. Their system requires a user to prepare query manuscript without a bibliography that indicates locations where citations are needed, resulting in additional burden for the user. In their subsequent work, they solved this problem by automatically analyzing the query manuscript to suggest locations where citations are needed [4].

Content Link Detection. Content link detection aims to discover similar content across different input and make such links explicit. In Wikipedia link detection, Milne and Witten [12] created explanatory links to all documents using supervised machine learning. They observed that decision tree generator gives better results than other learning techniques. West *et al.* [21] addressed the same task using unsupervised learning through principal component analysis. Following these studies, Kaptein *et al.* [8] proposed finding links from Wikipedia pages to external Web pages by using a language modeling approach. In story link detection, Nomoto [14] proposed a two-tier model of similarity, at both the document and collection levels. His similarity model adapted the idea of relevance feedback to link detection, where stories are measured for similarity not merely based on the document, but on a collection of relevant documents. Finally, by combining two algorithms proposed in [12] and [21], West *et al.* [22] created a hybrid algorithm that suggests topics to authors of text documents.

3. PROPOSED METHOD

Our work tackles the core problem of matching users to candidate papers. Unlike existing scholarly paper recommendation systems which focused on user profile construction [3, 16, 13], our work leverages the scholarly papers more effectively, through the modeling of potential citation papers and their fragments, and enhancing the citation network with automatically identified potential citation papers. Unlike citation link prediction, we apply collaborative filtering to discover potential citation papers that help model target papers to recommend. And unlike previous work in content link detection which mainly focused on finding an effective learning framework, we focus on how to best use the scholarly corpora available to us.

3.1 Baseline System [16]

Our method starts with our former scholarly paper recommendation system [16], and as such it is instructive to first describe our system and its basis. It consists of three steps:

Step 1: Construct a user profile $\boldsymbol{P}_{user}$ from a researcher's list of published papers;

Step 2: Compute feature vectors $\boldsymbol{F}^{p_j}$ $(j = 1, \cdots, t)$ for each of the papers in its scholarly paper knowledge base;

Step 3: Compute the cosine similarity $Sim(\boldsymbol{P}_{user}, \boldsymbol{F}^{p_j})$ between $\boldsymbol{P}_{user}$ and $\boldsymbol{F}^{p_j}$ $(j = 1, \cdots, t)$, and recommend papers with high similarity to the target user.

A candidate paper to recommend (p) is represented as a feature vector $\boldsymbol{f}^p$. We employ TF and TF-IDF schemes in Steps 1 and 2, respectively. Both $\boldsymbol{P}_{user}$ and $\boldsymbol{F}^{p_j}$ are constructed as the combination of $\boldsymbol{f}^p$ as defined by Equation (1). As such, our method views both user profiles and candidate papers to recommend as vectors of terms with specific, per-term tuned weights. As CBF relies on the item's content to provide its recommendations, it is important to represent an item's contents faithfully. A key innovative step in [16] is to model a target paper of interest based on not merely its own textual content but also an appropriately weighted inclusion of the text from its context as defined by the neighborhood of scholarly works it referenced, as well as those works that cite it (see Figure 1 (a)). In this past work, we found that when the text of such

Table 9: NYTimes with hierarchical Clustering

Method	Purity	RIndex	Prec.	Recall	F_1
TF*IDF	0.840	0.709	0.785	0.511	0.586
LIB	*0.840*	0.693	0.777	0.489	0.564
LIF	**0.867***	**0.741***	**0.845***	0.501	*0.616**
LIB*TF	0.839	0.699	*0.788*	0.483	0.567
LIB+LIF	*0.844*	0.700	*0.787*	0.490	0.570
LIB*LIF	0.839	*0.728**	0.780	**0.544***	**0.617***

mance scores were achieved among the proposed methods. Whereas LIF well supported *recall*, LIB*LIF was overall the best method in the experiments and consistently outperformed TF*IDF by a significant margin, particularly in terms of purity, precision, and rand index. Although detailed results varied, the general observations from k-means clustering and hierarchical clustering were consistent.

Experiments showed that methods with the LIB quantity were more effective in terms of within-cluster accuracy (e.g., precision and purity). By emphasizing the discriminative power (specificity) of a term, LIB reduces weights of terms commonly shared by unrelated documents, leading to fewer of these documents being grouped together (smaller *false positive* and higher precision). LIF, on the other hand, helped to boost recall with the integration of term frequency. The different strengths of LIB and LIF indicate that they can be combined or used separately to serve various clustering purposes.

An additional interesting finding in this study is the inflection point in the clustering performance vs. # features plots. In various data and experimental settings, optimal clustering performance was achieved with 1000 features (selected by DF thresholding). Increasing or decreasing the number of features from the inflection point degraded clustering effectiveness in terms of purity, rand index, and precision. While similar patterns were observed in text clustering and categorization research, further investigation is needed to understand factors related to this phenomenon.

5.1 Related Models

The LIB*LIF scheme is similar in spirit to TF*IDF. By modeling (binary) term occurrences in a document vs. in any random document from the collection, LIB integrates the document frequency (DF) component in the quantity. LIF, on the other hand, models term frequency/probability distributions and can be seen as a new approach to TF normalization. Despite the similarity, our experiments showed LIB*LIF, based on the new *least information* formulation, were more effective than TF*IDF for document representation in the text clustering context. Least information modeling can be applied to other important processes such as information retrieval ranking, for which TF*IDF and its BM25 variation have produced strong empirical results.

Several works have attempted to justify clasic IDF from an information-theoretic view but have not established a direct, concrete connection [26]. Further development of notions around information-theoretic entropy led to findings such as *maximum entropy* and *minimum (mutual) information* principles, providing important guidance to inferential statistics for retrieval and evaluation [13, 31, 16, 4].

It has been shown that a term's IDF is the mutual information between the term and the document collection [30]. Mutual information is an application of *relative entropy* (KL divergence) that quantifies the difference between the joint probabilities and product probabilities of two random variables [8]. In the light of language modeling, IDF is equivalent to Kullback-Leibler (KL) divergence (relative entropy) between term probability distribution in a document and in the entire collection [1, 18].

KL divergence (relative entropy) measures discrimination information between two probability distributions by quantifying the entropy change in an asymmetric manner [18]. The asymmetry of KL divergence is due to the fact that it works in a directed manner to quantify bits needed to code samples of one distribution based on another. The proposed least information theory (LIT) offers a symmetric function and can be used as a distance measure. In addition, whereas KL is infinite given extreme probabilities (e.g., for rare terms), the amount of least information is bounded by the number of inferences.

5.2 Novelty and Significance

The least information theory is a new extension of Shannon entropy based on integration of micro uncertainty changes over a shifted probability distribution. LIB and LIF represent our initial attempt to apply LIT in modeling document representation for text clustering, which offers promising baseline results. The presented models may be further improved, for example, by integrating various randomness models and probability estimators such as those in [2]. LIT provides a new information quantity with which more sophisticated models can be proposed. Its implications will be beyond text clustering.

While the LIB and LIF models bear some resemblance to existing approaches such as divergence from randomness in [2] and information-based models in [7], the LIT formulation is fundamentally different. It is true that the common idea is to weight terms by measuring information they contribute, relative to signals in the collection/randomness. The key lies in how information is measured. LIT quantifies variances in $p(1 - \ln p)$, where p denotes the probability of an inference (e.g., that a term appears). Although this can be related to classic quantities such as $-\ln p$ (IDF-related), $-p \ln p$ (entropy-related), and $p \ln p/q$ (KL-related) commonly used in the literature, least information is not an arbitrary combination of existing quantities but a derivation based on close examination of expected characteristics. To our knowledge, no existing information theory or models share the major characteristics (see section 2.3) of the presented least information quantity (in equation 9).

6. CONCLUSION

We presented the *least information* theory (LIT), which quantifies information in varied probability distributions. We observed several important characteristics of the proposed information quantity. Two basic quantities were derived from the theory for term weighting and document representation, which we used separately and combined in fusion methods for document clustering.

Research was conducted to evaluate the effectiveness of proposed methods compared to TF*IDF, which had been extensively used in text clustering research. Experiments on several benchmark collections showed very strong performances of LIT-based term weighting schemes. In most experiments, the proposed methods, especially LIB*LIF fusion, significantly outperformed TF*IDF in terms of several evaluation metrics.

While we have demonstrated superior effectiveness of the proposed methods, the main contribution is not about improvement over TF*IDF. Of greater significance is the new approach to information measurement and term weighting based on the *least information* theory (LIT), which enables a different way of thinking and provides a new information measure for modeling various information processes.

Acknowledgment

This research is partially supported by IMLS grant #LG-06-11-0332-11. We thank Xiaoli Song and anonymous JCDL'13 reviewers for constructive comments.

7. REFERENCES

[1] A. Aizawa. The feature quantity: an information theoretic perspective of TFIDF-like measures. In *SIGIR'00*, pages 104–111, 2000.

[2] G. Amati and C. J. van Rijsbergen. Probabilistic models of information retrieval based on measuring the divergence from randomness. *ACM Transactions on Information Systems*, 20(4):357–389, October 2002.

[3] D. Arthur and S. Vassilvitskii. k-means++: the advantages of carefull seeding. In *SIAM'07*, pages 1027–1035, 2007.

[4] J. A. Aslam, E. Yilmaz, and V. Pavlu. The maximum entropy method for analyzing retrieval measures. In *SIGIR'05*, pages 27–34, 2005.

[5] R. Baierlein. *Atoms and Information Theory: An Introduction to Statistical Mechanics.* W.H. Freeman and Company, 1971.

[6] M. W. Berry. *Survey of text mining: clustering, classification, and retrieval.* Springer, 2004.

[7] S. Clinchant and E. Gaussier. Information-based models for Ad Hoc IR. In *SIGIR'11*, pages 234–241, 2011.

[8] T. M. Cover and J. A. Thomas. *Entropy, Relative Entropy and Mutual Information*, pages 12–49. John Wiley & Sons, 1991.

[9] M. Craven, D. DiPasquo, D. Freitag, A. McCallum, T. Mitchell, K. Nigam, and S. Slattery. Learning to extract symbolic knowledge from the World Wide Web. In *AAAI'98*, pages 509–516, 1998.

[10] J. D. Fast. *Entropy: the Significance of the Concept of Entropy and Its Applications in Science and Technology.* McGraw-Hill, 1962.

[11] C. Fox. *Information and misinformation: an investigation of the notions of information, misinformation, informing, and misinforming.* Contributions in librarianship and information science. Greenwood Press, 1983.

[12] A. K. Jain, M. N. Murty, and P. J. Flynn. Data clustering: a review. *ACM Comput. Surv.*, 31(3):264–323, Sept. 1999.

[13] E. T. Jaynes. Information theory and statistical mechanics. ii. *Phys. Rev.*, 108:171–190, Oct 1957.

[14] X. Ji and W. Xu. Document clustering with prior knowledge. In *SIGIR'06*, pages 405–412, 1996.

[15] K. S. Jones. A statistical interpretation of term specificity and its application in retrieval. *Journal of Documentation*, 60:493–502, 2004.

[16] P. B. Kantor and J. J. Lee. The maximum entropy principle in information retrieval. In *SIGIR'86*, pages 269–274, 1986.

[17] S. Kullback. Letters to the editor: The Kullback-Leibler distance. *The American Statistician*, 41(4):338–341, Nov 1987.

[18] S. Kullback and R. A. Leibler. On information and sufficiency. *Annals of Mathematical Statistics*, 22:79–86, 1951.

[19] K. Lang. Newsweeder: Learning to filter netnews. In *Proceedings of the Twelfth International Conference on Machine Learning*, pages 331–339, 1995.

[20] D. D. Lewis, Y. Yang, T. G. Rose, and F. Li. RCV1: A new benchmark collection for text categorization research. *J. Mach. Learn. Res.*, 5:361–397, 2004.

[21] T. Liu, S. Liu, Z. Cheng, and W.-Y. Ma. An evaluation on feature selection for text clustering. In *ICML'03*, 2003.

[22] J. B. Lovins. Development of a stemming algorithm. *Mechanical Translation and Computational Linguistics*, 11:22–31, 1968.

[23] D. M. MacKay. *Information, Mechanism and Meaning.* The M.I.T. Press, 1969.

[24] C. D. Manning, P. Raghavan, and H. Schütze. *Introduction to Information Retrieval.* Cambridge University Press, 2008.

[25] A. Rapoport. What is information? *ETC: a review of general semantics*, 10(4):5–12, 1953.

[26] S. Robertson. Understanding inverse document frequency: on theoretical arguments for IDF. *Journal of Documentation*, 60:503–520, 2004.

[27] S. Robertson and H. Zaragoza. The probabilistic relevance framework: BM25 and beyond. *Foundations and Trends® in Information Retrieva*, 3(4):333–389, 2009.

[28] E. Sandhaus. The New York Times annotated corpus. Linguistic Data Consortium, 2008.

[29] C. E. Shannon. A mathematical theory of communication. *Bell System Technical Journal*, 27:379–423 and 623–656, July and October 1948.

[30] M. Siegler and M. Witbrock. Improving the suitability of imperfect transcriptions for information retrieval from spoken documents. In *ICASSP'99*, pages 505–508. IEEE Press, 1999.

[31] F. Snickars and J. W. Weibull. A minimum information principle: Theory and practice. *Regional Science and Urban Economics*, 7(1):137–168, 1977.

[32] I. H. Witten and E. Frank. *Data Mining: Practical machine learning tools and techniques.* Morgan Kaufmann, San Francisco, 2nd edition, 2005.

[33] Y. Yang and J. O. Pedersen. A comparative study on feature selection in text categorization. In *ICML'97*, pages 412–420, 1997.

[34] D. Zhang, J. Wang, and L. Si. Document clustering with universum. In *SIGIR'11*, pages 873–882, 2011.

[35] Y. Zhao and G. Karypis. Evaluation of hierarchical clustering algorithms for document datasets. In *CIKM'02*, pages 515–524, 2002.

Exploiting Potential Citation Papers in Scholarly Paper Recommendation

Kazunari Sugiyama
National University of Singapore
Computing 1, 13 Computing Drive,
Singapore 117417
sugiyama@comp.nus.edu.sg

Min-Yen Kan[1,2]
[1]National University of Singapore
[2]NUS Interactive and Digital Media Institute
Computing 1, 13 Computing Drive,
Singapore 117417
kanmy@comp.nus.edu.sg

ABSTRACT

To help generate relevant suggestions for researchers, recommendation systems have started to leverage the latent interests in the publication profiles of the researchers themselves. While using such a publication citation network has been shown to enhance performance, the network is often sparse, making recommendation difficult. To alleviate this sparsity, we identify "potential citation papers" through the use of collaborative filtering. Also, as different logical sections of a paper have different significance, as a secondary contribution, we investigate which sections of papers can be leveraged to represent papers effectively.

On a scholarly paper recommendation dataset, we show that recommendation accuracy significantly outperforms state-of-the-art recommendation baselines as measured by nDCG and MRR, when we discover potential citation papers using imputed similarities via collaborative filtering and represent candidate papers using both the full text and assigning more weight to the conclusion sections.

Categories and Subject Descriptors

H.3.3 [**Information Search and Retrieval**]: Information filtering, Search process; H.3.7 [**Digital Libraries**]: Systems issues, User issues

General Terms

Algorithms, Experimentation, Performance

Keywords

Digital library, Information retrieval, Recommendation, Citation analysis, Collaborative filtering

1. INTRODUCTION

Newly discovered knowledge is now largely captured in digital form and archived throughout the world. Archival materials are also being digitized and are increasingly becoming more accessible online. The modern researcher has unprecedented level of access to the sum total of human knowledge. While certainly advantageous, this creates a problem of over abundance, commonly known as "information overload": where researchers find an overwhelming number of matches to their search queries, but for which the majority are largely irrelevant to their latent information needs.

Work in recommendation systems is one promising approach to address the information overload. In digital library studies, this approach has been employed to obtain and refine search results to satisfy each user's information needs [10, 18, 3, 23, 13]. However, these approaches do not fully leverage the user's context, largely relying on the idea of session-as-context. This legacy is ported from research in Web search, where session click-through data are used to form the context. To address this problem, in our previous work we observed that the scholarly context allows us to leverage the role of the searcher-as-author [16]. We modeled a searcher's context in the form of a profile by capturing previous research interests embodied in their past publications, and showed elevated success at scholarly paper recommendation. Our approach in [16] also took advantage of the explicit citation network of publications a a source of knowledge to improve recommendation accuracy. Th contents of papers that cite an author's papers as well as the contents of the works referenced in the papers provide supplementar evidence used in modeling the author's research interests.

In this paper, we propose two extensions of [16] that further min additional signals from the full text and citation network – usin (1) potentially cited papers and (2) their fragments. Citation paper are papers that explicitly cite previous work and often contain summary of its salient points. Such citation papers may be viewe as an endorsement of the cited paper, and they may help model th target paper more accurately. In addition, fragments are parts of paper such as abstract, introduction, conclusion, and so on.

Authors of papers also may not cite certain relevant papers i their publications, either purposefully (*e.g.*, to save space) or n (*e.g.*, were unaware of the specific relevant work). If we enhanc the citation network with such potentially citable papers (hereafte *pc*), we hypothesize that we can model the target papers to recon mend more accurately to achieve better recommendation perfo mance. In our work, we apply collaborative filtering (CF) to fir such potential citation papers. While CF is often used to recon mend items to users directly, we apply CF to discover potential c tation papers that help in representing target papers to recommen

Through a series of experiments on a scholarly paper recomme dation dataset, we show that proper modeling of potential citatic papers – as well as properly representing papers with both their fu text and assigning more weight to the conclusion – improve re ommendation accuracy significantly ($p < 0.05$ or better) as judg by both mean reciprocal rank (MRR) and normalized discount

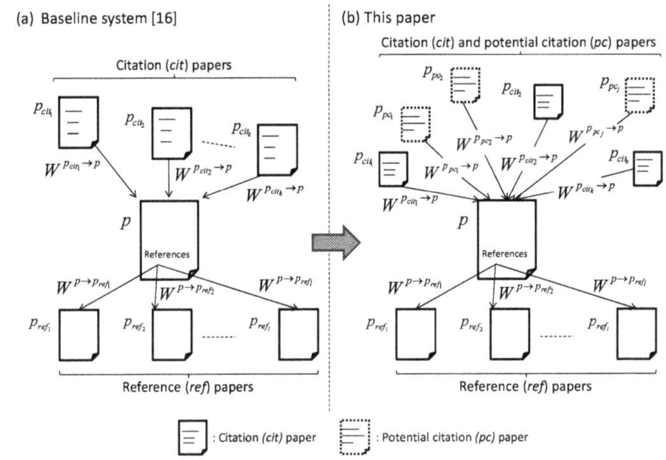

Figure 1: Comparison of paper representations between our former work [16] and the current paper (notations simplified from [16]). Our work in this paper leverages additional potential citation papers to enrich the description of a target paper.

contextual papers is added to the original target paper weighted by cosine similarity to the target paper, recommendation accuracy is improved the most among other alternatives explored.

In the current paper, we further enhance Step 2 above, by both **enlarging** what is meant by context through the discovery of potential citation papers, as well as **refining** its use in specific, well-linked parts of the contextual documents through the specific modeling of potential citation papers and their fragments (Figure 1(b)).

To facilitate our discussion later, we show the formula for Step 2 defined in [16] to compute the feature vector for each paper p:

$$\boldsymbol{F}^p = \boldsymbol{f}^p + \sum_{x=1}^{k} W^{p_{cit_x} \to p} \boldsymbol{f}^{p_{cit_x}} + \sum_{y=1}^{l} W^{p \to p_{ref_y}} \boldsymbol{f}^{p_{ref_y}}, \quad (1)$$

where p_{cit_x} $(x = 1, \cdots, k)$ and p_{ref_y} $(y = 1, \cdots, l)$ denote papers that cite p and papers that p refers to, respectively. In addition, $W^{p_{cit_x} \to p}$ and $W^{p \to p_{ref_y}}$ are weights for the citation papers and weights for the reference papers, respectively. We can define these weights in a more general form as follows: Let $W^{u \to v}$ be the coefficient used to compute the weight for between target v and its source u. In addition, let $\boldsymbol{f}^u$ and $\boldsymbol{f}^v$ be the feature vectors of the source u and target v papers, respectively. Then cosine similarity $sim(\boldsymbol{f}^u, \boldsymbol{f}^v)$ between the two vectors is used as $W^{u \to v}$.

Generally speaking, a target paper's feature vector comprises of three parts: words from its own body, words from papers that cite it, and words from papers that it refers to (first, second and third terms in Equation (1), respectively).

3.2 Leveraging Potential Citation Papers

While a rich source of information, a citation network is subject to certain limitations that blunt its effectiveness in modeling target papers. We note that the citation network is constantly expanding; with every new publication, new citation links are added to older work. In studies depending solely on the citation network, cutting-edge work is marginalized as they do not have any citations yet; this is a kind of "cold-start problem" in scholarly recommendation systems that is analogous to the same problem in recommendation systems in general.

Also, because references and citations in a paper are static and never change, newer relevant papers to older ones have the "responsibility" of creating a citation link between them. The static nature of the citation network exacerbates missing and noisy citations.

Finally, the citation network is an artifact of the physical scholarly paper. In many cases, listing all relevant work would be infeasible, as the reference list may grow too long. Many venues have space limitations (including this one), to help encourage authors to use their editorial powers to choose the most relevant references to include. However, this can also cause authors to prune potentially citable references from their bibliographies. Especially, when authors save the space, the surplus may be used to expand the description of their own approaches or experiments.

The above factors led us to believe that the observable, explicit citation network – while certainly of high-quality – is just "the tip of the iceberg"; where *iceberg* refers to the implicit set of relevant works for a target paper. We term papers in this implicit set *potential citation* (*pc*) papers. If we can predict these implicitly relevant papers, we obtain more content for representing a scholarly paper, which in turn, will improve recommendation performance.

In our approach, we discover such potential citation papers by applying collaborative filtering (CF). CF is usually used to recommend items directly to users. However, we employ it indirectly, by using it to discover potential citation papers, which are then used to represent papers to recommend. This discovery process is needed to better represent papers, which in turn enhances recommendation accuracy. Importantly, our use of CF operates on the paper-citation matrix, and is markedly different from its traditional one-step use in the user-item matrix; in contrast, we employ the citation network twice: both in directly represent target papers through citations and references as well as in finding potential citation papers. The details of our approach also break down into discovery of potential citation papers ((A1) using CF and (A2) imputation-based CF) and (B) feature vector construction for target papers using the discovered potential citation papers.

(A1) Discovery of Potential Citation (pc) Papers with CF

We apply the neighborhood-based algorithm [6] in CF for use in discovering potential citation papers, by substituting papers for users and items for citations. At a high level, we can think of papers as actors that can recommend citations to each other, where CF lets papers that are more similar to a target paper (from a citation perspective) recommend citations with more weight. The algorithm has the following steps analogous to neighborhood-based CF:

A1.1: Weight all papers with respect to similarity to a target paper. As with the original CF algorithm, paper similarity is measured using the Pearson correlation coefficient between their citation vectors.

A1.2: Select n papers that have the highest similarity with the target paper. These papers form the *neighborhood* for the target.

A1.3: Compute a prediction from a weighted combination of the neighbor's values using a suitable similarity score.

In Step A1.1, the similarity between target paper p_{tgt} and other citation papers p_{cit_u} $(u = 1, \cdots, N)$, denoted as $S_{tgt,u}$ is computed using the Pearson correlation coefficient:

$$S_{tgt,u} = \frac{\sum_{i=1}^{N}(r_{tgt,i} - \bar{r}_{tgt}) \times (r_{cit_u,i} - \bar{r}_{cit_u})}{\sqrt{\sum_{i=1}^{N}(r_{tgt,i} - \bar{r}_{tgt})^2 \times \sum_{i=1}^{N}(r_{cit_u,i} - \bar{r}_{cit_u})^2}}, \quad (2)$$

where $r_{tgt,i}$ is the score given to citation paper p_{cit_i} by paper p_{tgt}, and $\bar{r}_{tgt}$ is the mean score given by paper p_{tgt}, and N is the total number of papers in the dataset.

In Step A1.2, a subset of appropriate papers is chosen based on their similarity to the target paper and a weighted aggregate of

(a) Binary [*pc*-BIN]

	p_{cit_1}	p_{cit_2}	......	p_{cit_i}	......	p_{cit_N}
p_1		1		1		1
p_2	1			1		1
⋮						
p_{tgt}		1				1
⋮						
p_N	1	1		1		

(b) Similarity [*pc*-SIM]

	p_{cit_1}	p_{cit_2}	......	p_{cit_i}	......	p_{cit_N}
p_1		0.212		0.735		0.687
p_2	0.212			0.328		0.436
⋮						
p_{tgt}		0.581				0.330
⋮						
p_N	0.687	0.436		0.525		

p_{tgt} : Target paper p_{cit_i}: Paper that prediction is computed

Figure 2: Paper-citation matrix for our adapted collaborative filtering using (a) binary [pc-BIN] and (b) similarity [pc-SIM] weighting.

their ratings is used to generate predictions for the target paper in Step A1.3.

In Step A1.3, predictions are computed as the weighted average of deviations from the neighbor's mean, shown in Equation (3):

$$p_{tgt,i} = \bar{r}_{tgt} + \frac{\sum_{u=1}^{n}(r_{u,i} - \bar{r}_u) \times S_{tgt,u}}{\sum_{u=1}^{n} S_{tgt,u}}, \quad (3)$$

where $p_{tgt,i}$ is the prediction for a target paper p_{tgt} for a citation paper p_{cit_i}. n is the number of papers in the neighborhood.

We explored two possible methods for calculating $S_{tgt,u}$ and $p_{tgt,i}$ above; a binary notion of citation (Figure 2 (a)) as well as a fine-grained similarity version of citation (Figure 2 (b)).

The binary scheme is illustrated in Figure 2 (a), which shows a paper-citation matrix with binary incidence values [pc-**BIN**]. Entries with a '1' indicate citations by the paper identified by the column to the target paper identified by the row (*e.g.*, paper p_{tgt} is only cited in papers p_{cit_2} and p_{cit_N}).

It is generally agreed that citations have different functions. A key reference that acts as the foundation for the current work is likely more of a positive endorsement than a citation within a list of examples of applications of a particular model. We choose to use cosine similarity between papers as a simple means to model endorsement strength. Figure 2 (b) shows a corresponding paper-citation matrix with similarity values [pc-**SIM**]. For example, in Figure 2 (b), the similarity between the target paper p_{tgt} and p_{cit_2}, and the target paper p_{tgt} and p_{cit_N} is 0.581 and 0.330, respectively.

To be clear, in both models, multiple citations to the same target paper within a paper are not represented.

(A2) Discovery of Potential Citation (pc) Papers with Imputation-based CF

In Figure 2, the matrices are sparse because each paper can only make a limited number of citations (see Section 4 about how sparse our dataset is). This affects the process of finding relevant potential papers. However, when the corpus of publications is large, we can utilize the fact that there are many other similar papers that potentially could have been cited but were not.

To leverage this opportunity and address sparseness, we employ imputation (hereafter, [pc-**IMP**]) as we can directly compute similarity between papers and citation papers, unlike the case of the user-item matrix based CF which requires manual ratings. This is a variant of [pc-SIM] and consists of three steps:

A2.1: Impute similarities between all papers, recording them into an intermediate imputed paper-citation matrix (Figure 3).

A2.2: For the target paper, find the n most similar papers from the "(a) original matrix" in Figure 3:

- Weight all papers with respect to similarity to the target paper (*e.g.*, p_1). This similarity between papers is measured using the Pearson correlation coefficient between the papers' citation vectors,
- Select n papers that have the highest similarity with the target paper. These papers form the *n-neighborhood* for the target paper. In the left of Figure 4, p_2, p_4, and p_5 are determined to be the 3-neighborhood for p_1.

A2.3: Compute a prediction from a weighted combination of the neighbor's similarity (Figure 4, right). We use Figure 3's "(b) intermediate imputed matrix" for the n-neighborhood.

(a) Original matrix

	p_{cit_1}	p_{cit_2}	p_{cit_3}	p_{cit_4}	p_{cit_5}
p_1		0.233			0.628
p_2	0.233		0.147		
p_3		0.147		0.265	
p_4			0.265		
p_5	0.628				

(b) Intermediate imputed matrix

	p_{cit_1}	p_{cit_2}	p_{cit_3}	p_{cit_4}	p_{cit_5}
p_1	1.000	0.233	**0.723**	**0.538**	0.628
p_2	0.233	1.000	0.147	**0.476**	**0.156**
p_3	**0.723**	0.147	1.000	0.265	**0.521**
p_4	**0.538**	**0.476**	0.265	1.000	**0.268**
p_5	0.628	**0.156**	**0.521**	**0.268**	1.000

Imputation

Figure 3: Similarity imputation: (a) original matrix and (b) intermediate imputed matrix (imputed values are bolded).

[Target paper p_1 and corresponding imputed similarities of neighborhood (p_2, p_4, and p_5) from "(b) imputed matrix" in Figure 3]

	p_{cit_1}	p_{cit_2}	p_{cit_3}	p_{cit_4}	p_{cit_5}
p_1	1.000	0.233	?	?	0.628
p_2	0.233	1.000	0.147	**0.476**	**0.156**
⋮	⋮	⋮	⋮	⋮	⋮
p_4	**0.538**	**0.476**	0.265	1.000	**0.268**
p_5	0.628	**0.156**	**0.521**	**0.268**	1.000

Prediction of similarity for target paper p_1

	p_{cit_1}	p_{cit_2}	p_{cit_3}	p_{cit_4}	p_{cit_5}
p_1	1.000	0.233	**0.682**	**0.453**	0.628

Figure 4: Predictions computed for the target paper p_1 using corresponding neighbors, p_2, p_4, and p_5 with similarities from the intermediate imputed matrix.

(B) Feature Vector Construction for Target Papers

With the discovery and weightage of our discovered potential papers, we can now build the feature vector for target papers. Let $\boldsymbol{F}^p$ be the feature vector for a paper to recommend p. We then define $\boldsymbol{F}^p$ as follows:

$$\begin{aligned} \boldsymbol{F}^p = \boldsymbol{f}^p \quad &+ \sum_{x=1}^{j} W^{p_{pc_x} \to p} \boldsymbol{f}^{p_{pc_x}} \\ &+ \sum_{y=1}^{k} W^{p_{cit_y} \to p} \boldsymbol{f}^{p_{cit_y}} \\ &+ \sum_{z=1}^{l} W^{p \to p_{ref_z}} \boldsymbol{f}^{p_{ref_z}}, \end{aligned} \quad (4)$$

where p_{pc_x} $(x = 1, \cdots, j)$, p_{cit_y} $(y = 1, \cdots, k)$, and p_{ref_z} $(z = 1, \cdots, l)$ denote potential citation papers, papers that cite p, and papers that p refers to, respectively. We employ cosine similarity weight for $W^{p_{pc_x} \to p}$, $W^{p_{cit_y} \to p}$, and $W^{p \to p_{ref_z}}$ as it was found effective in our previous work [16].

3.3 Leveraging Fragments in Potential Citation Papers

In the above, we have artificially enriched the citation network to combat sparsity. We now also consider refining and improving the quality of information in the existing citation network. As scholars, we often acknowledge the importance of others' previous work by citation, an explicit reference to previous work which is accompanied by a bibliographic reference to help others locate and trace the prior work. The in-text citation often clearly and succinctly describes a key point of the target paper of import to the current paper, as illustrated below:

Resnik (1999) addressed the issue of language identification for finding Web pages in the languages of interest.

Citation sentences have been used to build summaries of target papers [11, 15] as well as for supporting scientific literature search [1]. However, to the best of our knowledge, they have not been used as an evidence source for recommendation.

Since citation sentences often present a clear representation of a target paper, we hypothesize that careful weighting of citation sentences improves recommendation accuracy. On the other hand, citation sentences are very small text fragments in citation papers. Larger text fragments of the (potential) citation papers may be more useful than using just single citation sentences. Thus, we also experiment with other larger fragments of the source paper: its abstract, introduction, and conclusion sections. We also examine the impact of using other short texts as evidence: keywords (1 to 10 words with the highest TF-IDF score), in place of citation sentences to model candidate papers to recommend.

We note that Mei and Zhai [11] proposed generating summaries using a paper and its citation context (hereafter, [CC]), rather than just using the bare citation sentence. Their approach fixed the citation context to two sentences before and after the citing sentence. For these reasons, we also explore varying the context, the number of sentences before and after the citing sentence, N_{cs} ($1 \leq N_{cs} \leq 3$).

Given these possible (potential) citation paper fragments, we tried the following two different schemes to weight the fragments' words in constructing the target candidate paper's feature vector $\boldsymbol{F}^p$.

1. [frg-SIM]: Fragments with cosine similarity weighting. In this approach, we add an additional vector obtained from the fragment in the actual or potential citation paper. This approach effectively allows the tunable weights to assign customized weights to the words that appear in the associated fragments, modifying the feature vector $\boldsymbol{F}^p$ to:

$$\begin{aligned}\boldsymbol{F}^p = & \sum_{x=1}^{j} W_{(frg)}^{p_{pc_x}\rightarrow p}\, \boldsymbol{f}_{(frg)}^{p_{pc_x}} + \sum_{y=1}^{k} W_{(frg)}^{p_{city}\rightarrow p}\, \boldsymbol{f}_{(frg)}^{p_{city}} \\ & + \boldsymbol{f}^p + \sum_{x=1}^{j} W^{p_{pc_x}\rightarrow p}\, \boldsymbol{f}^{p_{pc_x}} \\ & + \sum_{y=1}^{k} W^{p_{city}\rightarrow p}\, \boldsymbol{f}^{p_{city}} \\ & + \sum_{z=1}^{l} W^{p\rightarrow p_{refz}}\, \boldsymbol{f}^{p_{refz}}, \qquad (5)\end{aligned}$$

where the first row are two added terms to Equation (4) that account for evidence from the fragments in potential and explicit citation papers, respectively. As in previous sections, we use cosine similarity as the weighting scheme for both coefficients.

2. [frg-TW]: [frg-SIM] with tunable weight. In this variation, we further augment the feature vector obtained from a fragment with tunable constant weight α ($0 \leq \alpha \leq 1$), which changes the feature vector calculation to:

$$\begin{aligned}\boldsymbol{F}^p = & \;\alpha \left(\sum_{x=1}^{j} W_{(frg)}^{p_{pc_x}\rightarrow p}\, \boldsymbol{f}_{(frg)}^{p_{pc_x}} + \sum_{y=1}^{k} W_{(frg)}^{p_{city}\rightarrow p}\, \boldsymbol{f}_{(frg)}^{p_{city}}\right) \\ & + (1-\alpha)\left(\boldsymbol{f}^p + \sum_{x=1}^{j} W^{p_{pc_x}\rightarrow p}\, \boldsymbol{f}^{p_{pc_x}} \right. \\ & + \sum_{y=1}^{k} W^{p_{city}\rightarrow p}\, \boldsymbol{f}^{p_{city}} \\ & \left. + \sum_{z=1}^{l} W^{p\rightarrow p_{refz}}\, \boldsymbol{f}^{p_{refz}}\right), \qquad (6)\end{aligned}$$

where α represents the balance between the contribution from the full text and the fragments, and allows our model a bit more expressiveness by finding optimal parameters.

To be clear, in both the [frg-SIM] and [frg-TW] methods, only contribution of terms in a fragment is changed; *i.e.*, Equations (5) and (6) only differ from Equation (4) in the first row, dealing with the contribution of the fragments.

4. EXPERIMENTS

We use the publication lists of 50 researchers who have been engaged in various fields in computer science such as databases, embedded systems, graphics, information retrieval, networks, operating systems, programming languages, software engineering, security, user interface. The researchers also have publication lists in DBLP[1]. As DBLP lists many important venues in computer science, we assume here that a researcher's DBLP list is representative of their main interests.

We construct the user profile for each researcher using their respective publication list in DBLP. All of 50 researchers' names are no ambiguity in the list.

The candidate papers to recommend is constructed from proceedings in the ACM Digital Library[2] (ACM DL). Among them, we collected 100,351 papers published in English, in conferences, symposiums, and workshops held more than three times. We also manually collected citation and reference papers for each paper. In collecting citation and reference papers, we used information on the "Cited By" tab attached in each paper in ACM DL, and those in the references section of each paper. Then, we construct feature vectors for these papers as described in Section 3. Stop words[3] were eliminated from each user's publication list and from the candidate papers to recommend. Stemming was performed using the Porter Stemmer[4]. We manually compiled the gold-standard results, by asking each researcher to mark papers relevant to their recent research interest. We divided these datasets into a training set (for parameter tuning) and a test set (for evaluation). Table 1 shows some statistics about our experimental data. In the paper-citation matrix in Figure 2, only 17.2% of all cells are filled, demonstrating that the paper-citation matrix for our dataset is sparse. Our dataset is publicly available[5].

4.1 Evaluation Measure

As in standard information retrieval (IR), top ranked documents are the most important, since users often scan just the first ranks. As such, we adopt ranked IR evaluation measures, specifically: (1)

[1] http://www.informatik.uni-trier.de/~ley/db/

[2] http://dl.acm.org/

[3] ftp://ftp.cs.cornell.edu/pub/smart/english.stop

[4] http://www.tartarus.org/~martin/PorterStemmer/

[5] http://www.comp.nus.edu.sg/~sugiyama/SchPaperRecData.html

Table 1: Some statistics on our scholarly paper dataset.

(a) Reseachers

	Training set	Test set
Number of researchers	25	25
Average number of DBLP papers	10.4	9.6
Average number of relevant papers in our dataset	76.3	74.5
Average number of citation papers	15.3 (max. 169)	14.4 (max. 145)
Average number of reference papers	15.8 (max. 47)	14.2 (max. 58)

(b) Candidate papers to recommend

	Training set	Test set
Number of papers	50,176	50,175
Average number of citation papers	19.4 (max. 175)	16.5 (max. 158)
Average number of reference papers	15.7 (max. 45)	15.4 (max. 53)

normalized discounted cumulative gain (nDCG) [7], and (2) mean reciprocal rank (MRR) [19].

(1) Normalized Discounted Cumulative Gain (nDCG). NDCG is well suited to evaluation of recommendation system, as it rewards relevant items in the top ranked results more heavily than those ranked lower. For a given user profile $\boldsymbol{P}_{user_i}$, the ranked results are examined top-down, where nDCG is computed as:

$$nDCG_i = Z_i \sum_{j=1}^{R} \frac{2^{r(j)} - 1}{log(1+j)},$$

where Z_i is a normalization constant calculated so that a perfect ordering would obtain nDCG of 1; and each $r(j)$ is an integer relevance level (for our case, $r(j) = 1$ and $r(j) = 0$ for relevant and irrelevant recommendations, respectively) of result returned at the rank j ($j = 1, \cdots, R$). Then, $nDCG_i$ is averaged over all our target researchers. As a typical recommendation system will just recommend a few items, we are only concerned about whether the top ranked results are relevant or not. Therefore, in this work, we use $nDCG@R$ ($R = \{5, 10\}$) for evaluation where R is the number of top-R papers recommended by our proposed approaches.

(2) Mean Reciprocal Rank (MRR). MRR indicates where in the ranking the first relevant item is returned by the system, averaged over all researchers. This measure provides insight in the ability of the system to return a relevant paper at the top of the ranking. Let r_i be the rank of the highest ranking relevant paper for a target researcher i, then MRR is just the reciprocal rank, averaged over all target researchers, N_{tr}:

$$MRR = \frac{1}{N_{tr}} \sum_{i=1}^{N_{tr}} \frac{1}{r_i}.$$

4.2 Experimental Results

We first optimize our method's parameters using the training set, and then show experimental results after applying the optimal parameters to the test set. Since there are a few parameters to tune in our approach, we divide the tuning into two halves, where the first half (Phase 1) determines optimal parameters to discover potential citation papers, used in the two independent phases in the second half (Phases 2A and 2B) to leverage fragments.

For simplicity, we only show the best results obtained by using optimal tunable weight α in [*pc*-BIN] as the improvement compared with the baseline system (see Section 3.1) is marginal and we observe the same trends as [*pc*-SIM] and [*pc*-IMP]. In addition, in [CC] and "keywords," we only show the best result, namely, $N_{cs} = 1$ and 5 keywords, respectively. The remaining parameters ("Weight SIM," Th, γ, and d) that are inherited from the previous framework, are optimized here, following the methodology in [16].

We also compare our proposed approach with state-of-the-art scholarly paper recommendation systems [13, 20]. We apply their optimal settings to our experiments. For our implementation of [13], we construct user profile using the title, and construct the feature vector of candidate papers to recommend using the title and abstract, both of which are generated by bigram frequency. In [20], we apply their "in-matrix prediction" to predict the score of paper-citation matrix in Figure 2 to discover potential citation papers, as their experimental setting is similar to ours. Note that collaborative filtering is *indirectly used* to discover potential citation papers and expand citation network – our method's use of collaborative filtering is not a direct application, and thus we cannot compare our content-based filtering with collaborative filtering to recommend papers (*i.e.*, we do not have user ratings for papers).

Table 2: Tuning to address paper-citation matrix sparsity: Recommendation accuracy in [TUNE:*pc*] when modeling candidate papers using (potential) citation papers under [*pc*-BIN].

pc-BIN	nDCG@5	nDCG@10	MRR
$n = 2, N_{pc} = 5$	0.541	0.506	0.765
$\boldsymbol{n = 4, N_{pc} = 5}$	**0.547**	**0.514**	**0.768**
$n = 8, N_{pc} = 5$	0.530	0.500	0.758
$n = 10, N_{pc} = 5$	0.525	0.496	0.755
Baseline [16] (Weight "SIM," $Th = 0.4, \gamma = 0.23, d = 3$)	0.519	0.486	0.748

Phase 1 – Parameter tuning to discover potential citation papers [TUNE:*pc*]. We first optimize parameters for finding the potential citation papers, namely the number of neighborhood n and the number of potential citation papers N_{pc}. We optimize these parameters by using [*pc*-BIN], [*pc*-SIM], and [*pc*-IMP] approaches as described in Section 3.2. Table 2, Figure 5 (a) to (c), and Figure 5 (d) to (f) show experimental results obtained by using [*pc*-BIN], [*pc*-SIM], and [*pc*-IMP], respectively.

From Table 2 and Figure 5, we observe that the optimal parameters that give the best recommendation accuracy are ($n = 4$, $N_{pc} = 5$) in [*pc*-BIN] and [*pc*-SIM], and ($n = 4$, $N_{pc} = 6$) in [*pc*-IMP]. These n and N_{pc} values are held constant in Phase 2.

Phase 2A – Tuning fragments in frg-SIM [TUNE:frg-SIM]. After obtaining the optimized parameters n and N_{pc} to find potential citation papers, we further explore which fragments in the citation and potential citation papers give the best recommendation accuracy using Equation (5). Table 3 shows the results.

Phase 2B – Tuning α and fragments in frg-TW [TUNE:frg-TW]. In the other second phase experiment, we optimize the weight for α in Equation (6), and fragments in citation and potential citation papers that give the best recommendation accuracy. Table 4 (a) and Figure 6, Table 4 (b) and Figure 7 show recommendation accuracy obtained by using "only fragments" and "both full text and fragments" in citation and potential citation papers, respectively.

Finally, after applying the optimized parameters on the test set, we arrive at the final test recommendation accuracies. These results are shown in Table 5 and discussed in full later.

4.3 Discussion

In the experiment in [TUNE:*pc*], according to Figure 5, when the number of neighbors n is too small ($n = 2, 3$) or too large ($n \geq 10$), we obtain poor predictions which result in selecting irrelevant potential citation papers. On the other hand, when the number of neighbors n is 4, our method can select relevant potential citation papers (N_{pc}), resulting in higher recommendation accuracy. We also observe that N_{pc} remains stable – 5 in [*pc*-BIN] (Table 2) and [*pc*-SIM] (Figure 5 (a) to (c)), and 6 in [*pc*-IMP] (Figure 5 (d) to (f)). This indicates that [*pc*-IMP] finds potential citation papers more effectively than [*pc*-BIN] and [*pc*-SIM]. We believe that its

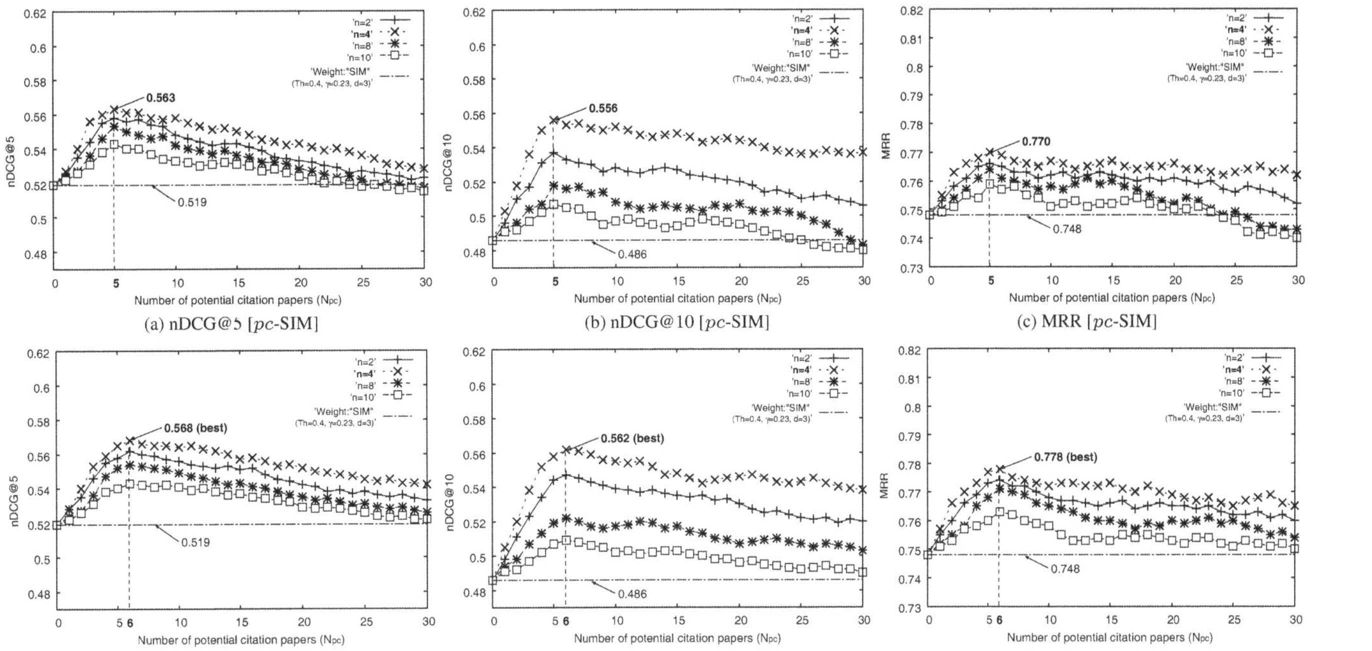

(a) nDCG@5 [*pc*-SIM] (b) nDCG@10 [*pc*-SIM] (c) MRR [*pc*-SIM]

(d) nDCG@5 [*pc*-IMP] (e) nDCG@10 [*pc*-IMP] (f) MRR [*pc*-IMP]

Figure 5: Tuning to address paper-citation matrix sparsity: Recommendation accuracy [TUNE:*pc*] when using a variable number of citation and potential citation papers in [*pc*-SIM] ((a) to (c)) and [*pc*-IMP] ((d) to (f)).

effectiveness is due to its use of the additional n-neighborhood of context papers used to impute the missing values for a target paper.

According to the experimental results in [TUNE:frg-SIM] (Table 3), we obtain the best recommendation accuracy ("Full text + Conclusion": nDCG@5 of 0.574, nDCG@10 of 0.570, MRR of 0.789) in [*pc*-IMP]. We again observe that [*pc*-IMP] generally gives better results compared with [*pc*-BIN] and [*pc*-SIM]. Across the board, we see that fragments by themselves perform less well; but that they have a meaningful positive effect if used in conjunction with the full text. The length of the individual fragments may be an important consideration; as keywords and citation sentences are generally quite short. The conclusion may also serve as a factual summary of a paper, not needing to include introductory or motivating material common in abstracts and introduction fragments.

Table 4, Figures 6 and 7 show experimental results in [TUNE:frg-TW]. In this approach, we obtain the best recommendation accuracy ("α = 0.4, Full text + Conclusion": nDCG@5 of 0.577, nDCG@10 of 0.580, MRR of 0.790) when we employ [*pc*-IMP] (see Figure 7 (d) to (f)). When we employ "only fragments," according to Table 4 (a) and Figure 6, we observe that "Conclusion" gives better results than other fragments. Other fragments also yield better results when appropriately tuned. For example, "citation context (CC $(N_{cs} = 1)$)" in nDCG@5 gives the recommendation accuracy of 0.533, 0.546, and 0.552 at $\alpha = 0.9$ in [*pc*-BIN] (Table 4 (a)), [*pc*-SIM] (Figure 6 (a)), and [*pc*-IMP] (Figure 6 (d)), respectively. The same trends are also observed in nDCG@10 (Figure 6 (b) and (e)) and MRR (Figure 6 (c) and (f)). However, recommendation accuracy obtained by fragments, "Abstract," "Introduction," "Citation Context (CC)," and "5 keywords" generally underperform "Conclusion." The same trend is also observed with nDCG@10 (Figure 6 (b) and (e)) and MRR (Figure 6 (c) and (f)).

On the other hand, when we employ "both full text and fragments" (Table 4 (b) and Figure 7), the recommendation accuracy generally outperforms that obtained using "only fragments." For example, "Full text + Conclusion" in nDCG@5 gives the best recommendation accuracy of 0.559, 0.573, and 0.577 at $\alpha = 0.4$ in [*pc*-BIN] (Table 4 (b)), [*pc*-SIM] (Figure 7 (a)), and [*pc*-IMP] (Figure 7 (d)), respectively. As well as experimental results obtained using "only fragments" described above, other fragments do not give the better recommendation accuracy.

According to Table 4, and Figures 6 and 7, we observe the followings about the value of α: From Table 4, we observe that the value of α that gives the best recommendation accuracy is different between the approach that uses "(a) only the fragment" ($\alpha = [0.7 - 0.9]$) and the approach that uses "(b) both full text and fragments" ($\alpha = [0.4 - 0.6]$). This indicates that in order to characterize candidate papers better, fragments (which contain relatively less text) need to be given larger weight compared to when they are used in conjuction with the full text. Interestingly, in Figures 6 and 7, we see the same trends graphically, but further observe that fixing a particular α value leads to different fragments being more important: in Figure 7, an α value of 0.6 yields "Citation Contexts (CC)" as most useful, 0.5 yields the "Abstract" as being most useful and 0.4 yields the "Conclusion" as best. This indicates that the tunable weight α is an important factor to set if optimal results are desired. We do note that the "Conclusion" fragment's performance is noticeably better and hence more stable than other fragments' performance levels, so we recommend this setting.

Table 5 shows recommendation accuracy obtained by applying optimal parameters and fragments to the test set. In the test set, we observe the same trends as in training: [*pc*-IMP] outperforms both [*pc*-BIN] and [*pc*-SIM]. In particular, [*pc*-IMP] (n = 4, N_{pc} = 6) with [frg-TW] (α = 0.4, "Full text + Conclusion") gives the best recommendation accuracy, similar to the best results in the training settings. This shows that our dataset keeps a useful balance between the training and test sets.

Furthermore, we observe that our baseline system [16] outperforms others ([13] and [20]) and our approach proposed in this paper ([*pc*-IMP] + [frg-TW]) gives the best recommendation accuracy. As described in Section 2.1, in [13], user profiles are con-

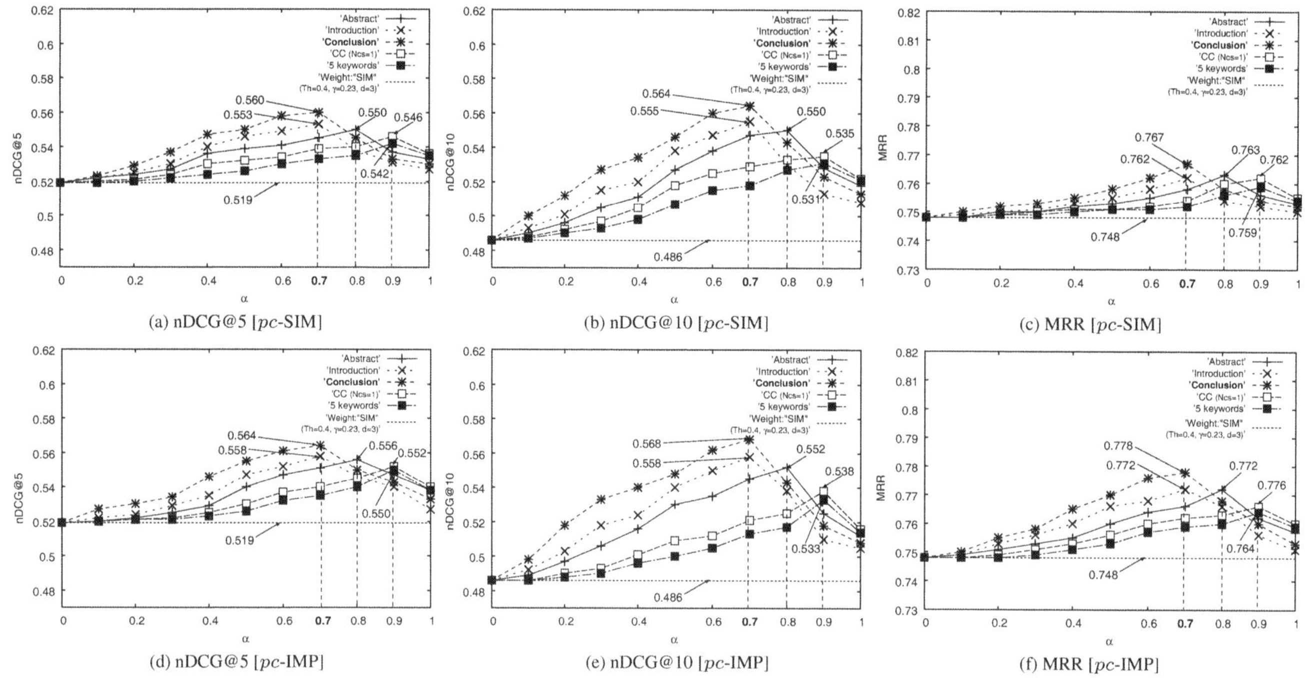

Figure 6: Tuning (potential) citation papers' text weight: Recommendation accuracy in [TUNE:frg-TW] obtained by modeling candidate papers using "*only fragments*" in (potential) citation papers discovered by [pc-SIM] ((a) to (c)) and [pc-IMP] ((d) to (f)).

structed from title, and feature vectors of candidate papers are generated from title and abstract, resulting in poor recommendation accuracy. This indicates that better representation of users and papers cannot be achieved by using short fragments such as title and abstract only. As described in Section 4.2, in [20], user-paper matrix with binary value, which is similar to Figure 2 (a), is applied to predict missing values to discover potential citation papers. These missing values are computed based on a probabilistic topic model generated from words in the abstract and title. These fragments are too short and uninformative, resulting in discovery of ineffective potential citation papers and irrelevant recommendation of scholarly papers. In light of these observations, we believe that our approach that uses full text and effective fragment (conclusion) in potential citation papers with appropriate tuning contributes to characterize candidate papers to recommend much better, resulting in much more relevant scholarly paper recommendation.

Microscopic Analyses. Diving into individual results, we observed that one of the researchers who works on computer graphics, received relevant recommendations in our optimized system, where the first relevant recommendation was at the first rank. In the baseline system, he could not obtain any relevant recommendation in the top-10 results, and the first relevant result was ranked 63rd. Another researcher, who works on mobile computing, also was provided a relevant recommendation in the first rank, while his most relevant recommendation is ranked 52nd using the baseline.

Inspecting the topics of the papers identified as potential citations also helps to further understand the reach of our algorithm. We observed that our approach discovers relevant potential citation papers to characterize candidate papers to recommend. For example, when the topic of candidate paper to recommend is "access control of business documents based on role mining," often cited by security papers, our approach identifies papers about data mining in databases and papers about information theory related to security as potential citation papers. In another example, given the candidate paper topic of "real world gesture analysis," often cited in human-computer interaction, our imputation approach discovers potential citation papers whose topics are biomechanics, computer-based music conducting systems, and machine learning. These examples indicate how our approach can characterize papers better than the baseline. This is then reflected in more relevant recommendations and higher accuracy.

Limitations. We also observed that if the topic of the target paper is interdisciplinary, our proposed approach may perform erratically. Further analysis shows that the imputation approach discovers "skewed" potential citation papers. In one instance, where the topic of candidate paper was "understanding mobile user's behavior patterns" that is equally embodied by mobile technology, user search behavior and clustering, our approach discovers potential citation papers that only addressed mobile technology. Examining further, we found that this skewed discovery of potential citation papers was caused by the fact that the selected n-neighborhood of papers consists almost exclusively of the mobile technology topic. Therefore, we need to develop a method for selecting a balanced neighborhood relevant to the target paper in future work, akin to work on addressing data skew in other fields.

Finally, our approach is statistically significant compared with the baseline system [16], improving recommendation accuracy by almost 10% when measured by nDCG@10 ($p < 0.01$), and by over 4% when measured by MRR ($p < 0.05$). We believe that our proposed approach is effective in characterizing candidate papers to recommend to obtain much higher recommendation accuracy.

5. CONCLUSION

We have explored two significant approaches to improve the state-of-the-art in scholarly paper recommendation. In particular, we examine (1) how to alleviate data sparsity using collaborative filtering to find potential citation papers, and (2) how to refine the use of citing papers in characterizing a target candidate paper using fragments in the citation and potential citation papers.

Our results show that, in discovery of potential citation papers,

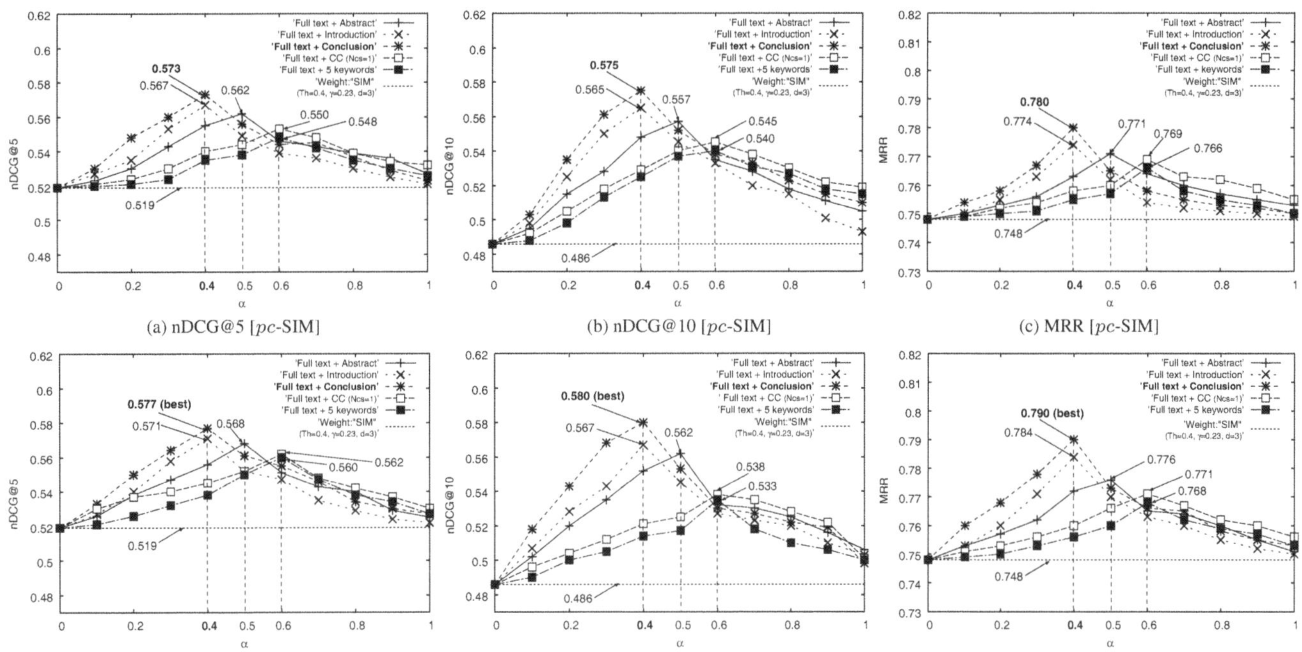

(a) nDCG@5 [*pc*-SIM] (b) nDCG@10 [*pc*-SIM] (c) MRR [*pc*-SIM]

(d) nDCG@5 [*pc*-IMP] (e) nDCG@10 [*pc*-IMP] (f) MRR [*pc*-IMP]

Figure 7: Tuning (potential) citation papers' text weight: Recommendation accuracy in [TUNE:*frg*-TW] obtained by modeling candidate papers using "*both full text and fragments*" in (potential) citation papers discovered by [*pc*-SIM] ((a) to (c)) and [*pc*-IMP] ((d) to (f)).

imputation-based CF is more effective than CF with binary or similarity values. Additionally, the potential citation paper approach, when appropriately tuned, can improve recommendation accuracy significantly. Especially, when we characterize candidate papers to recommend using "full text and conclusion" in both citation and potential citation papers, we achieve the best accuracy and outperform state-of-the-art scholarly paper recommendation systems.

We believe that our approach can be applied more generally. The notion of enriching a network with potential items can be applied to any network that feature asymmetric directional links, such as social networks, patent documents and email dialogues. The notion of using potential citation papers can be applied wherever textual evidence is associated with the links, such as in patent documents and customer testimonials.

To discover much more relevant potential citation papers, in future work, we plan to develop a method for selecting balanced neighborhood for interdisciplinary target papers in collaborative filtering. Moreover, small-sized text fragments in papers might be better characterized by modifying the classical term weighting schemes appropriately. Our future work direction also aims to produce such a novel term weighting scheme suitable for short text.

6. REFERENCES

[1] S. Bethard and D. Jurafsky. Who Should I Cite? Learning Literature Search Models from Citation Behavior. In *Proc. of the 19th International Conference on Information and Knowledge Management (CIKM'10)*, pages 609–618, 2010.

[2] K. El-Arini and C. Guestrin. Beyond Keyword Search: Discovering Relevant Scientific Literature. In *Proc. of the 17th ACM SIGKDD International Conference on Knowledge Discovery and Data Mining (KDD'11)*, pages 439–447, 2011.

[3] M. Gori and A. Pucci. Research Paper Recommender Systems: A Random-Walk Based Approach. In *Proc. of the 2006 IEEE/WIC/ACM International Conference on Web Intelligence (WI 2006)*, pages 778–781, 2006.

[4] Q. He, D. Kifer, J. Pei, P. Mitra, and C. L. Giles. Citation Recommendation without Author Supervision. In *Proc. of the 4th International Conference on Web Search and Data Mining (WSDM'11)*, pages 15–24, 2011.

[5] Q. He, J. Pei, D. Kifer, P. Mitra, and C. L. Giles. Context-aware Citation Recommendation. In *Proc. of the 19th International World Wide Web Conference (WWW2010)*, pages 421–430, 2010.

[6] J. Herlocker, J. Konstan, A. Borchers, and J. Riedl. An Algorithmic Framework for Performing Collaborative Filtering. In *Proc. of the 22nd Annual International ACM SIGIR Conference on Research and Development in Information Retrieval (SIGIR '99)*, pages 230–237, 1999.

[7] K. Järvelin and J. Kekäläinen. IR Evaluation Methods for Retrieving Highly Relevant Documents. In *Proc. of the 22nd Annual International ACM SIGIR Conference on Research and Development in Information Retrieval (SIGIR 2000)*, pages 41–48, 2000.

[8] R. Kaptein, P. Serdyukov, and J. Kamps. Linking Wikipedia to the Web. In *Proc. of the 33rd Annual International ACM SIGIR Conference on Research and Development in Information Retrieval (SIGIR'10)*, pages 839–840, 2010.

[9] L. Katz. A New Status Index Derived from Sociometric Analysis. *Psychometrika*, 18(1):39–43, 1953.

[10] S. M. McNee, I. Albert, D. Cosley, S. L. P. Gopalkrishnan, A. M. Rashid, J. S. Konstan, and J. Riedl. Predicting User Interests from Contextual Information. In *Proc. of the 2002 ACM Conference on Computer Supported Cooperative Work (CSCW '02)*, pages 116–125, 2002.

[11] Q. Mei and C. Zhai. Generating Impact-Based Summaries for Scientific Literature. In *Proc. of the 46th Annual Meeting of the Association for Computational Linguistics : Human Language Technologies (ACL-08: HLT)*, pages 816–824, 2008.

Table 3: Recommendation accuracy (nDCG@5, nDCG@10, and MRR) in [TUNE:frg-SIM] obtained by fragments in potential citation papers. The parameters n and N_{pc} are optimized ones in [pc-BIN], [pc-SIM], and [pc-IMP].

pc-BIN ($n = 4$, $N_{pc} = 5$)	nDCG@5	nDCG@10	MRR
Abstract	0.520	0.468	0.746
Introduction	0.522	0.472	0.745
Conclusion	0.525	0.476	0.748
CC ($N_{cs} = 1$)	0.518	0.471	0.738
5 keywords	0.514	0.466	0.727
Full text	0.547	0.514	0.768
Full text + Abstract	0.551	0.518	0.771
Full text + Introduction	0.554	0.523	0.772
Full text + Conclusion	**0.558**	**0.528**	**0.773**
Full text + CC ($N_{cs} = 1$)	0.552	0.524	0.771
Full text + 5 keywords	0.550	0.521	0.772

pc-SIM ($n = 4$, $N_{pc} = 5$)	nDCG@5	nDCG@10	MRR
Abstract	0.524	0.476	0.747
Introduction	0.527	0.483	0.745
Conclusion	0.531	0.488	0.758
CC ($N_{cs} = 1$)	0.522	0.473	0.740
5 keywords	0.518	0.469	0.733
Full text	0.563	0.556	0.770
Full text + Abstract	0.560	0.556	0.772
Full text + Introduction	0.565	0.562	0.773
Full text + Conclusion	**0.569**	**0.566**	**0.776**
Full text + CC ($N_{cs} = 1$)	0.560	0.555	0.772
Full text + 5 keywords	0.559	0.554	0.773

pc-IMP ($n = 4$, $N_{pc} = 6$)	nDCG@5	nDCG@10	MRR
Abstract	0.535	0.498	0.757
Introduction	0.538	0.507	0.755
Conclusion	0.543	0.514	0.762
CC ($N_{cs} = 1$)	0.535	0.510	0.754
5 keywords	0.532	0.505	0.745
Full text	0.568	0.562	0.778
Full text + Abstract	0.570	0.565	0.788
Full text + Introduction	0.569	0.563	0.787
Full text + Conclusion	**0.574**	**0.570**	**0.789**
Full text + CC ($N_{cs} = 1$)	0.569	0.564	0.788
Full text + 5 keywords	0.568	0.563	0.787

Table 4: Tuning results: Recommendation accuracy in [TUNE:frg-TW] obtained by modeling candidate papers to recommend using "(a) *only fragments*" and "(b) *both full text and fragments*" in citation and potential citation papers discovered by [pc-BIN].

(a) Only fragments

pc-BIN ($n = 4$, $N_{pc} = 5$)	nDCG@5	nDCG@10	MRR
Abstract ($\alpha = 0.8$)	0.537	0.515	0.760
Introduction ($\alpha = 0.7$)	0.539	0.518	0.761
Conclusion ($\alpha = 0.7$)	**0.546**	**0.525**	**0.764**
CC ($N_{cs} = 1$)($\alpha = 0.9$)	0.533	0.509	0.758
5 keywords ($\alpha = 0.9$)	0.529	0.506	0.756
Baseline system [16] (Weight "SIM," $Th = 0.4, \gamma = 0.23, d = 3$)	0.519	0.486	0.748

(b) Both full text and fragments

pc-BIN ($n = 4$, $N_{pc} = 5$)	nDCG@5	nDCG@10	MRR
Full text + Abstract ($\alpha = 0.5$)	0.548	0.520	0.768
Full text + Introduction ($\alpha = 0.4$)	0.552	0.525	0.772
Full text + Conclusion ($\alpha = 0.4$)	**0.559**	**0.533**	**0.778**
Full text + CC ($N_{cs} = 1$)($\alpha = 0.6$)	0.543	0.517	0.766
Full text + 5 keywords ($\alpha = 0.6$)	0.540	0.514	0.764
Baseline [16] (Weight "SIM," $Th = 0.4, \gamma = 0.23, d = 3$)	0.519	0.486	0.748

Table 5: Recommendation accuracy obtained by applying optimal parameters and fragments to the test set. "" and "*" denote the difference between the best results in the baseline system [16] (underlined scores) and the each result in this paper is significant for $p < 0.01$ and $p < 0.05$, respectively.**

	nDCG@5	nDCG@10	MRR
pc-BIN ($n = 4$, $N_{pc} = 5$)			
frg-SIM (Full text + Conclusion)	0.556*	0.535*	0.766*
frg-TW ($\alpha = 0.4$, Full text + Conclusion)	0.561*	0.540*	0.773*
pc-SIM ($n = 4$, $N_{pc} = 5$)			
frg-SIM (Full text + Conclusion)	0.566*	0.563**	0.770*
frg-TW ($\alpha = 0.4$, Full text + Conclusion)	0.572**	0.570**	0.781*
***pc*-IMP** ($n = 4$, $N_{pc} = 6$)			
frg-SIM (Full text + Conclusion)	0.572**	0.568**	0.787*
***frg*-TW** ($\alpha = 0.4$, Full text + Conclusion)	**0.579****	**0.577****	**0.793***
Baseline system [16] (Weight "SIM," $Th = 0.4, \gamma = 0.23, d = 3$)	<u>0.525</u>	<u>0.479</u>	<u>0.751</u>
Nascimento *et al.* [13] ("Frequency of bi-gram" obtained from title and abstract)	0.336	0.308	0.438
Wang and Blei [20] ("In-matrix prediction" in collaborative topic regression)	0.393	0.371	0.495

[12] D. Milne and I. H. Witten. Learning to Link Wikipedia. In *Proc. of the 17th International Conference on Information and Knowledge Management (CIKM'08)*, pages 509–518, 2008.

[13] C. Nascimento, A. H. F. Laender, A. S. da Silva, and M. A. Gonçalves. A Source Independent Framework for Research Paper Recommendation. In *Proc. of the 11th ACM/IEEE Joint Conference on Digital Libraries (JCDL 2011)*, pages 297–306, 2011.

[14] T. Nomoto. Two-Tier Similarity Model for Story Link Detection. In *Proc. of the 19th International Conference on Information and Knowledge Management (CIKM'10)*, pages 789–798, 2010.

[15] V. Qazvinian and D. R. Radev. Scientific Paper Summarization Using Citation Summary Networks. In *Proc. of the 22nd International Conference on Computational Linguistics (Coling'08)*, pages 689–696, 2008.

[16] K. Sugiyama and M.-Y. Kan. Scholarly Paper Recommendation via User's Recent Research Interests. In *Proc. of the 10th ACM/IEEE Joint Conference on Digital Libraries (JCDL '10)*, pages 29–38, 2010.

[17] T. Strohman and W. B. Croft and D. Jensen. Recommending Citations for Academic Papers. In *Proc. of the 30th Annual International ACM SIGIR Conference on Research and Development in Information Retrieval (SIGIR 2007)*, pages 705–706, 2007.

[18] R. Torres, S. M. McNee, M. Abel, J. A. Konstan, and J. Riedl. Enhancing Digital Libraries with TechLens. In *Proc. of the 4th ACM/IEEE Joint Conference on Digital Libraries (JCDL 2004)*, pages 228–236, 2004.

[19] E. M. Voorhees. The TREC-8 Question Answering Track Report. In *Proc. of the 8th Text REtrieval Conference (TREC-8)*, pages 77–82, 1999.

[20] C. Wang and D. M. Blei. Collaborative Topic Modeling for Recommending Scientific Articles. In *Proc. of the 17th ACM SIGKDD International Conference on Knowledge Discovery and Data Mining (KDD'11)*, pages 448–456, 2011.

[21] R. West, D. Precup, and J. Pineau. Completing Wikipedia's Hyperlink Structure through Dimensionality Reduction. In *Proc. of the 18th International Conference on Information and Knowledge Management (CIKM'09)*, pages 1097–1106, 2009.

[22] R. West, D. Precup, and J. Pineau. Automatically Suggesting Topics for Augmenting Text Documents. In *Proc. of the 19th International Conference on Information and Knowledge Management (CIKM'10)*, pages 929–938, 2010.

[23] D. Yang, B. Wei, J. Wu, Y. Zhang, and L. Zhang. CARES: A Ranking-Oriented CADAL Recommender System. In *Proc. of the 9th ACM/IEEE Joint Conference on Digital Libraries (JCDL 2009)*, pages 203–211, 2009.

Addressing Diverse Corpora With Cluster-Based Term Weighting

Peter Organisciak
Graduate School of Library and Information Science
University of Illinois at Urbana-Champaign
501 E. Daniel Street, MC-493
Champaign, IL, USA
organis2@illinois.edu

ABSTRACT

Highly heterogeneous collections present difficulties to term weighting models that are informed by corpus-level frequencies. Collections which span multiple languages or large time periods do not provide realistic statistics on which words are interesting to a system. This paper presents a case where diverse corpora can frustrate term weighting and proposes a modification that weighs documents according to their class or cluster within the collection. In cases of diverse corpora, the proposed modification better represents the intuitions behind corpus-level document frequencies.

Categories and Subject Descriptors

H.3.3 [**Information Search and Retrieval**]: Retrieval models

Keywords

term weighting; diverse corpora

1. INTRODUCTION

Term weighting in the style of TF-IDF has been shown to be very effective in information retrieval. However, in the case of *diverse corpora*, corpus-based term weighting violates the intuitions underlying the measure and can give poor results. This paper describes the problem of retrieval over a highly heterogeneous corpora, and demonstrates a modification utilizing class-based document frequencies.

2. CONTEXT

Term weighting has been an important concept in information science since the mid-19th century[1]. By the late seventies, models were being formalized with term weighting in the style of TF-IDF [6], based on earlier work on term frequency and inverse document frequency [9, 8].

The intuition behind Inverse Document Frequency (IDF) is that terms which occur frequently in a collection of texts are uninteresting because they do not offer much intuition about what any particular document is about. IDF allows a term's importance to be weighted downward as it occurs in more documents within the collection. This is a generally robust way of ensuring that terms like *the* and *and* do not hold too much algorithmic power in representing a document.

Term Frequency (TF) is combined with IDF to give a sense of how much of the term's occurrences occur in the specific document. Where IDF is a constant over all occurrences of a word, TF is document-specific. If a term appears 100 times in the collection, 99 times in *doc*1 and once in *doc*2, TF makes sure that the term is considered a much more important part of *doc*1 than of *doc*2.

Combined, the TF-IDF style of term weighting encourages rare words that occur often in a document, while downplaying words that are very common in the full collection.

3. PROBLEM

Diverse corpora present a challenge to TF-IDF -like term weighting. Since IDF is derived from the language of a corpus, a corpus with greatly heterogeneous language use would violate the intuitions behind TF-IDF.

Numerous types of hotereogenous corpora conflict with the intuitions of corpus informed term weighting. For example, if a corpus has a mix of languages, such as French/English commonly found in Canadian collections, it is no longer sensible to inform term weight based partially on information from a completely different language. Similarly, making inferences in corpora that span long periods of time is difficult because both the style of speech and the vocabulary of a language evolves with time. Collections that span decades or even centuries, such as JSTOR or HathiTrust, can aggravate the diverse corpora problem.

As an illustrative example, we can see words like *eskimo* and *mohammadan*, which fell out of favour in the English language very rapidly (replaced by *inuit* and *muslim*, respectively). A user researching early occurrences of *inuit* would be disadvantaged if its high frequency modern usage was informing documents from the time period in which they are interested in. The intuition behind TF-IDF no longer holds in the context of such historic documents – a common word is not uninteresting if it was uncommon in the context of when its document was written.

While different languages and time periods are apparent areas of the diverse corpora problem, the issue is possible in many forms of heterogeneous collections. For example, a web retrieval engine might be expected to deal with docu-

JCDL'13, July 22–26, 2013, Indianapolis, Indiana, USA.

Table 1: IDF in French + English Google Books collection compared to a French-only corpus

	French + English	French-only
pays	0.9907	0.5525
des	0.6923	0.05911
our	0.9613	1.2652

	doc1	doc2	doc3	query
sim.full	0.7264748	0.9485864	0.8681502	1
sim.french	0.4010961	0.9990927	0.9963987	1

Table 3: Document scores of *pays des ours* when informed by a full collection and a French-only collection.

ments about hard science and teenage gossip concurrently. Similarly, microblogging platforms entail colloquial discussion among highly disparate groups.

The problems of diverse corpora are all problems of differing language use. Treating the terms of diverse classes of documents as if they were generated from the same corpus language model loses discriminatory power. When there are identifiable groups in the data, IDF has difficulty telling whether a term is very common in a single part of the corpus, or rarer but uniformly distributed among all documents.

3.1 Example Problem

A French user searching for *pays des ours* (Bear country) in a multilingual corpus would have difficulty finding survival tips. Intuitively, the most discriminating word in the query is "bear" (ours) and the least is "of" (des). However, IDF in a multilingual corpus does not reflect this intuition. With document occurrence data from the Google Books French 1-grams and English 1-grams corpus[5], IDF scores were calculated as:

$$IDF = \log \frac{N}{df_{t,\cdot}} \qquad (1)$$

Table 1 shows the term IDFs for the Google Books corpus – excluding additional languages for simplicity – compared to a corpus that only contained the French documents from the collection. The full corpus distorts the intuitive discriminatory value of each word – *des*, one of the most common French words, is raised from a nearly null weight, while *ours* loses considerable weight.

Table 2 shows three example documents, with term frequencies for the query term. *Doc*1 is a non-relevant "List of Countries of the World", while *Doc*2 and *Doc*3 are relevant documents on safety in bear country.

With a simple implementation of the Vector Space Model as described in [7] and documents represented by occurrances of the query terms, the cosine similarity between sample documents is shown in Table 3. Terms are weighted with TF-IDF with no term normalization.

Using the interlingual corpus in this example gives an inappropriately high similarity to the non-relevant document, while punishing the two relevant documents.

4. CLUSTER DOCUMENT FREQUENCY

The problem that diverse corpora presents to the generally robust body of TF-IDF term weighting approaches is that IDF is independent from document-level context when collection-level information is too general. To improve its performance in these problem areas, this paper proposes keeping the same underlying mechanism but introducing a class variable $c \in C$, changing the scope of $IDF_t, \cdot$, to IDF_t, c. For simplicity, we will refer to this approach as *ICDF* (*Inverse cluster/class document frequency*). This approach is agnostic to whether grouping is a classification or clustering problem; both are demonstrated below.

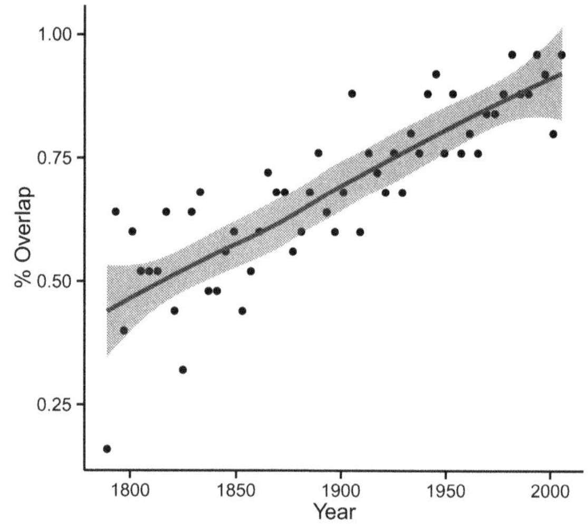

Figure 1: Overlap in the 25 most interesting inaugural words determined by TF-IDF and by TF-ICDF

ICDF assumes that if uninteresting terms are truly uniform across the corpus, then they will likewise be visible in subsets of data. By grouping a large collection into a conservative number of clusters, uniform corpus language will resemble IDF. However, schisms in the language, such as those through multilingual or historical separations, will be better represented and terms within those areas will be judged in context.

In the remainder of this paper, ICDF is explored in the context of the problem of diverse corpora.

4.1 Category-dependent IDF

Representation and retrieval of historical texts is a classification problem. Documents have a known class – year – which is correlated to changes in language (as will be discussed shortly).

To test traction of ICDF over historical texts, the Google Books n-grams data [5] was used as a stand-in for per-year corpus frequencies. A mechanism for finding the most interesting words in presidential inaugural speeches was created, using both the n-gram-informed ICDF and the corpus-wide IDF. Here, classes are defined by year, $c \in \{1789...2005\}$, and $ICDF$ is calculated from the term-volume frequencies of the Google Books project. For a fair comparison, IDF was also informed by this corpus.

$$tficdf = tf_{t,d,c} * \log \frac{N}{idf_{t,c}} \qquad (2)$$

A comparison of the most interesting terms according to the respective models suggests that the intuition about lan-

Table 2: Example documents and word counts for *pays des ours*

Document	n(t=pays)	n(t=des)	n(t=ours)
Liste des pays du monde | Cet article recense les pays du monde, quel que soit leur statut : reconnus par l'ONU, par plusieurs autres pays ou auto-proclamés.	3	1	0
Safety in Bear Country | sécurité au pays des ours fournit des informations pour aider à réduire les blessures infligées aux humains et les dégâts matériels causés par les grizzlys.	1	2	1
Sécurité au pays des grizzlis et des ours noirs | Les parcs et les lieux historiques nationaux présentent aux visiteurs des paysages particuliers au Canada. Ces parcs et lieux sont plus que des ...	1	3	1

guage change over time is correct. The top terms overlap greatly in recent decades, but diverge going back in time (Figure 1). For computation purposes, the corpus from the most recent year was used as the constant IDF against which other years were compared. If the full corpus were calculated, IDF would bias toward the best represented years in the corpus (early 1880s, mid-1990s).

The diminishing overlap going back in time suggests that TF-IDF is distracted by uninteresting words that are simply novel to the modern day. For example, TF-IDF finds *meliorate* to be Adams's most discriminating term, which is simply a verb meaning *to improve*. Table 4 compares speeches where TF-ICDF diverges most from TF-IDF.

This implementation could be improved. For example, rather than classes being calculated for each year, 5-year classes might reflect the language of the time better and smooth outliers in the dataset. Still, it shows traction in the class-based approach to term weight.

4.2 Cluster-dependent IDF

Often, heterogeneous corpora do not have clear classes separating the individual language groups within them. Thus, we performed an exploratory evaluation based using inferred clusters for ICDF. A tentative clustering evaluation was done on the French-English Europarl multilingual corpus[2]. Representing documents as term frequency vectors, *k-means* was used to cluster 1000 chapters of proceedings. TF-ICDF was calculated per cluster while TF-IDF on the full corpus, both approaches using sublinear TF scaling (i.e. WF, [4]). Since clusters should be conservative, the data was separated into two clusters. Table 5 compares top TF-IDF and TF-ICDF terms. Even with the sublinear TF, common words still problematize the full-corpus IDF.

Clustering a two-language corpus into two clusters is a synthetically simple problem, but shows how our problem of diverse corpora corrupting TF-IDF is possible. Performing a similar experiment on a corpus of four languages showed similar results, but more drastically. IDF on the four-language corpus no longer performs its function.

Applying this approach to highly diverse English-only documents is worth exploring.

4.3 Implementation and Issues

ICDF introduces some difficulties. Now that IDF is dependent on a class, it is no longer a constant for all words. Since IDF uses observed data, the class-specific constants are not computationally problematic and can be precalculated. However, the class-dependence presents challenges to comparisons across classes. The IDF used here is proportional to the class/corpus size (i.e. $\frac{N}{IDF}$ is the inverse *proportion*

Chapter	Top WF-IDF Words	Top WF-ICDF
English-250	the parties funding completely european conference for is that in and of to - party mrs political between report their	parties funding completely the conference - party projects citizenship flags entrance gill proportion rooms, enabling accountable justification
English-300	the allowances emission and of to chechnya chechnya greenhouse emissions gas russian will energy this i for is that in	allowances emission chechnya greenhouse emissions gas russian energy the eur and of to frattini commendable less separatist gases ossetia
English-350	the hyland human of to answers labelling fisheries would will be this i for is that in and approach certainly	hyland labelling answers fisheries human the approach of to certainly something ,Äì would vary examine justified awaited us witnesses violator foresee
English-400	oil of the renewable income prices price has energy we for is that in and to high help increase become	oil renewable income prices price energy high of the help increase become commissioner overturned resource picture admixture mr karlsson reserves consequence

Table 5: Top words in multilingual documents using ICDF with hard-clusters.

1789 WASHINGTON Overlap=0.16		1797 ADAMS Overlap=0.40		1821 MONROE Overlap 0.44		1825 ADAMS Overlap 0.32	
TF-ICDF	TF-IDF	TF-ICDF	TF-IDF	TF-ICDF	TF-IDF	TF-ICDF	TF-IDF
impressions	impregnably	legislatures	meliorate	defense	defrayed	defense	dissensions
assure	despondence	endeavor	helvetic	reelection	fortifications	fulfillment	unexaggerated
despondence	unpracticed	defense	confederacies	buccaneering	burthen	accountability	waketh
mislead	palliated	suffrage	colorable	excises	ceded	woodsmen	imbittered
consecrate	auspiciously	equaled	unessential	reciprocated	floridas	expenditures	concernment
asylum	misdirect	neighbors	engraven	preeminently	amity	defenses	afte
designates	inquietude	signally	batavian	sabine	buccaneering	unexaggerated	floridas
presides	indispensably	discouragement	venality	harbors	sabine	rancor	confederacies
station	actuate	destinies	disquisitions	extenuating	excises	waketh	transcendently
myself	providential	disquisitions	legislatures	ratifications	pretensions	uprooted	jealousies

Table 4: Top words in speeches with the greatest divergence between IDF and ICDF.

of documents which contain the document), somewhat addressing the concern.

Utilizing a cluster-based document frequency measure can disrupt the expectation of the system implementing it. In some cases, it is concievable that users of information retrieval systems may desire the uncorrect term weights regardless of the flaws. For example, even though *countrymen* was not a novel term in 1837, a user querying it may specifically intend to bias their search toward that time period.

It remains to be seen how an IDCF term weighting model would function in an information retrieval system. In cases of non-problematic corpora, it resembles basic IDF closely. However, it is likely that the added complexity of the approach will require parameter tuning. While this paper opted for conservative cluster counts when performing unsupervised clusting, increasing the cluster size too largely could negate the benefits of IDF. The extent of damage from too many clusters remains to be seen.

One way to keep ICDF from being overzealously applied is through a mixture of cluster-dependent and solely collection-level document frequencies. This could smooth over quirks of the individual classes while still offering improvements for collection diversity. Doing so would be conceptually similar to the language modeling approach that was effective in [3].

5. OTHER APPROACHES

TF-IDF is a straightforward representation of the intuition that a document's frequently used rare terms are important markers of a documents aboutness. More sophisticated approaches bring additional robustness by virtue of less reliance on the IDF intuition. Probabilistic methods such as Okapi BM25[10] still rank on IDF-like intuitions, but often use smoothing to reduce reliance on observed data.

6. CONCLUSION

Despite its general effectiveness, term weighting in the style of TF-IDF can run into problems both in practice and in assumptions when used on diverse corpora. This paper described an approach that, while introducing complexity to the solution, shows improvements in cases of heterogeneity while functioning similar to TF-IDF in collections with uniform language distribution. In presenting this approach, we showed a use of Google's n-gram dataset for determining class-specific collection statistics according to both year and language. In the absence of such information, however, unsupervised hard clustering with a very conservative number of clusters gave promising results.

7. REFERENCES

[1] D. Harman. The history of IDF and its influences on IR and other fields. In J. I. Tait, editor, *Charting a New Course: Natural Language Processing and Information Retrieval*, number 16 in The Kluwer International Series on Information Retrieval, pages 69–79. Springer Netherlands, Jan. 2005.

[2] P. Koehn. Europarl: A parallel corpus for statistical machine translation. In *MT summit*, volume 5, 2005.

[3] X. Liu and W. B. Croft. Cluster-based retrieval using language models. In *Proceedings of the 27th annual international ACM SIGIR conference on Research and development in information retrieval*, SIGIR '04, pages 186–193, New York, NY, USA, 2004. ACM.

[4] C. D. Manning, P. Raghavan, and H. Schütze. *Introduction to Information Retrieval.* Cambridge University Press, Sept. 2008.

[5] J.-B. Michel, Y. K. Shen, A. P. Aiden, A. Veres, M. K. Gray, J. P. Pickett, D. Hoiberg, D. Clancy, P. Norvig, J. Orwant, S. Pinker, M. A. Nowak, and E. L. Aiden. Quantitative analysis of culture using millions of digitized books. *Science*, 331(6014):176–182, Jan. 2011.

[6] S. E. Robertson and K. Spärck Jones. Relevance weighting of search terms. *Journal of the American Society for Information Science*, 27(3):129–146, 1976.

[7] G. Salton, A. Wong, and C. S. Yang. A vector space model for automatic indexing. *Commun. ACM*, 18(11):613–620, Nov. 1975.

[8] G. Salton and C. S. Yang. On the specification of term values in automatic indexing. 1973.

[9] K. Spärck Jones. A statistical interpretation of term specificity and its application in retrieval. *Journal of Documentation*, 28(1):11–21, Dec. 1972.

[10] K. Spärck Jones, S. Walker, and S. E. Robertson. A probabilistic model of information retrieval: development and comparative experiments. *Inf. Process. Manage.*, 36(6):779–808, Nov. 2000.

Interactive Search Result Clustering: A Study of User Behavior and Retrieval Effectiveness

Xuemei Gong, Weimao Ke
Lab for Info Network & Computing Studies
College of Information Science and Technology
The iSchool at Drexel, Drexel University
3141 Chest St, Philadelphia, PA 19104
xg45@drexel.edu, wk@drexel.edu

Yan Zhang, Ramona Broussard
School of Information
University of Texas at Austin
1616 Guadalupe Street, Austin, TX 78701
yanz@ischool.utexas.edu,
lindley.broussard@gmail.com

ABSTRACT

Scatter/Gather is a document browsing and information retrieval method based on document clustering. It is designed to facilitate user articulation of information needs through iterative clustering and interactive browsing. This paper reports on a study that investigated the effectiveness of Scatter/Gather browsing for information retrieval. We conducted a within-subject user study of 24 college students to investigate the utility of a Scatter/Gather system, to examine its strengths and weaknesses, and to receive feedback from users on the system. Results show that the clustering-based Scatter/Gather method was more difficult to use than the classic information retrieval systems in terms of user perception. However, clustering helped the subjects accomplish the tasks more efficiently. Scatter/Gather clustering was particularly useful in helping users finish tasks that they were less familiar with and allowed them to search with fewer words. Scatter/Gather tended to be more useful when it was more difficult for the user to do query specification for an information need. Topic familiarity and specificity had significant influences on user perceived retrieval effectiveness. The influences appeared to be greater with the Scatter/Gather system compared to a classic search system. Topic familiarity also had significant influences on query formulation.

Categories and Subject Descriptors

H.3.1 [**Information storage and retrieval**]: Content Analysis and Indexing; H.3.3 [**Information storage and retrieval**]: Information Search and Retrieval—*Clustering*

General Terms

Algorithms, Performance, Experimentation

Keywords

Text clustering, Search result presentation, Scatter/Gather, User interface, Exploratory search, Interaction, Relevance

1. INTRODUCTION

With classic information retrieval systems such as web search engines, users are served by ranking algorithms that produce ordered lists of documents based on search queries. It is often assumed that users know what they need as well as how to articulate those information needs. Sometimes, however, people either do not know what they need, or do not know how to articulate their needs. Alternative information retrieval techniques are needed to help users specify what is desired and to identify novel and diverse information that facilitates investigation and enriches understanding/knowledge.

Scatter/Gather is a document browsing and information retrieval method based on text clustering [2]. A Scatter/Gather system provides the user topical clusters of documents, in which documents are related (similar) to each other. The user can select one or more clusters in terms of information needs/interests. Documents in the selected clusters will be then gathered and clustered again to produce a new set of topical groups to the user. A more focused data subset can be obtained through Scatter/Gather iterations. It is potentially useful for information access with non-specific goals, for which query specification is often difficult.

This research aims to study Scatter/Gather effectiveness in general web search tasks and understand the impact of Scatter/Gather browsing iterations on the user's retrieval interactions and potential influences of user and task characteristics on information seeking behaviors.

2. RELATED WORK

Document clustering has been adopted to support interactive browsing and searching. The cluster hypothesis states that "closely associated documents tend to be relevant to the same requests" [10]. Based on document clustering, the Scatter/Gather paradigm was proposed to facilitate user articulation of information needs through iterative clustering, selection, and navigation [2]. In each Scatter/Gather iteration, the system presents a set of clusters (main topics) and summaries to the user based on the information space being explored. The user can select one or more clusters he or she is interested in and recluster the subset. After each step, a more focused data subset can be reached, with a better-defined (implicit) query. The system and the user can thus achieve a better mutual understanding about what is needed and together identify relevant information. Clustering can also help the user explore the inherent associations among documents and topics in the information collection being served, potentially enabling exploratory learning [5]. Research studied the effects of Scatter/Gather on incidental learning of topic structure, and found that it can induce a more coherent conceptual image of a text collection and a richer vocabulary for constructing search queries [9].

Various search tasks have been studied to understand user's information needs and behaviors. A search task is not only about a user' information need [1] but also about the activity performed to satisfy the need [3]. Therefore, particular task attributes, such as its specificity and the user's familiarity with it, should be taken into consideration when studying user behaviors and system design. In terms of search objectives/purposes, research has identified multiple categories including known-item tasks and exploratory tasks [8]. In known-item tasks searchers find specific information while exploratory tasks often require searchers to collect relevant information and assure adequate coverage of the search area.

Scatter/Gather is useful in exploratory sense-making activities that occur when a user encounters a large unknown document collection, and should be integrated with the other kinds of retrieval techniques [9]. In a recent user study, users found Scatter/Gather helpful in some search situations but not in others [6]. In particular, topic specificity and familiarity appeared to affect the user's perception of Scatter/Gather effectiveness in exploratory searches.

3. RESEARCH QUESTIONS

In this study, we are interested in the following specific research questions:

1. Is Scatter/Gather browsing more effective in helping subjects complete web search tasks than a classic information retrieval system (based solely on ranking)?
2. What are the factors affecting user perceived effectiveness of systems and query formulation? Does Scatter/Gather help the users formulate search queries?
3. What is the impact of topic familiarity and topic specificity on Scatter/Gather effectiveness?
4. What does the evidence of user behavior show about user perception of document relevance?

4. METHODOLOGY

We conducted a within-subject user study of 24 undergraduate students at Drexel University to study related research questions, to examine the strengths and weaknesses of a Scatter/Gather system, and to receive feedback from users to improve the system.

4.1 Systems

Two systems were developed for this study: 1) a hybrid Scatter/Gather system that clustered search results and performed Scatter/Gather iterations thereafter, and 2) a classic web search system that returned search results in the classic, sequential order.

We developed the Scatter/Gather system based on the Bing Search API[1] and the Weka machine learning and data mining package [4]. The systems called the Bing Search API to retrieve top 200 results for each user query. The Scatter/Gather system then tokenized the documents, removed stop-words, and performed vectorization using the TF*IDF weighting scheme. The top 1000 frequent words were kept as features for document vector representations (DF thresholding). We reused a k-means implementation in Weka for clustering or identification of topical groups (7 clusters by default) in the data. The top 10 keywords were identified based on their tf*idf weights within each cluster.

The classic web search system also integrated Bing search API but directly presented search results to the user in a list with no clustering, as a typical popular search engine would do.

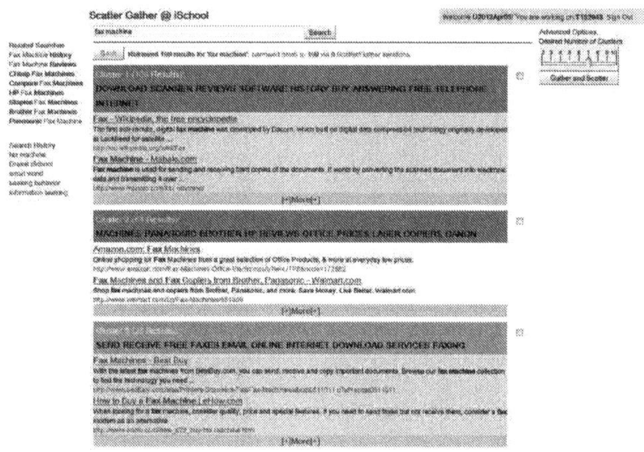

Figure 1: Scatter/Gather browser interface

Figure 1 is a screen shot of the Scatter/Gather interface. In the first iteration, seven clusters are identified and presented to the user. A cluster description shows the number of member pages assigned to the cluster and top 10 key words generated from these results. An advanced option panel in the upper right corner enables the users to select the desired number of clusters that will be shown in the next iteration, ranging from 2 to 10.

4.2 Tasks

Four tasks with different levels of query topic specificity were chosen, including two known-item tasks and two exploratory tasks. Three tasks were from TREC 2005 HARD track whereas an additional exploratory task was created based on a well-discussed search scenario [11]. The selected topics included tropical storms, price fixing, overseas tobacco sales (exploratory), and travel planning (exploratory).

4.3 Procedure

The methodology employed for this study is a within-subject study of 24 subjects. The investigators and subjects met one-on-one in a usability lab. Each subject was asked to complete a demographic questionnaire and then watch a 5-minute video tutorial. Following the tutorial, the subject was allowed some time to try out and get familiar with the systems. Then the subject was given up to 15 minutes to search on each task. Two tasks were performed on the classic search system and the other two on the Scatter/Gather system, with the order rotated among subjects to eliminate potential learning effects. The order, in which systems were used and search tasks were conducted, was arranged using a Graeco-Latin square rotation [7]. After each task, the subject was asked to evaluate the system using a

[1]Bing - developer: `http://www.bing.com/developers/`

post-task questionnaire about familiarity with topics of the tasks, overall satisfaction with the systems and results received. Finally, the subject filled out an exit questionnaire to provide feedback on the Scatter/Gather system and research. The systems kept track of activity information such as user clickthroughs and viewing time. Subjects evaluated the relevance and usefulness of each document they viewed during searches, which were also recorded.

5. RESULTS

5.1 Effectiveness of Systems

Although Scatter/Gather offers functionality for iterative clustering and browsing, not all subjects took advantage of that feature because of its novelty. We analyzed the number of levels (iterations) subjects went through to retrieve information with Scatter/Gather. Among subjects who used Scatter/Gather system, 15 subjects narrowed down their search results via clustering iterations, while the other subjects used the Scatter/Gather system in the same way as they used the classic system.

For subjects who only used basic functions, there were roughly the same numbers of subjects who preferred Scatter/Gather vs. classic system in terms of helpfulness (S/G 3 vs. classic system (CS) 3) and overall preference (S/G 3 vs. CS 4). Nonetheless, more subjects considered that the classic system was easier to use because of familiarity with the interface (S/G 3 vs. CS 6). Some subjects struggled with the notion of "cluster" and tended to avoid related functionality. For subjects who used the Scatter/Gather iterations, more than twice as many reported Scatter/Gather to be more helpful than the classic system (S/G 10 vs. CS 4). There were twice as many subjects who chose classic system as those who chose Scatter/Gather in terms of ease of use (S/G 5 vs. CS 10). As for the overall preference, the numbers were roughly the same (S/G 8 vs. CS 7). According to subjects' responses to open-ended questions in the exit questionnaire, the main reason for some subjects preferring the Scatter/Gather system was that the results were well organized and the clusters provided specific answers.

Now we compare the two systems based on data acquired from post-task questionnaires. According to the mean values of subjects' evaluations of each system in terms of each question, it was more difficult for the subjects to get started on a search and do the search with Scatter/Gather system. But Scatter/Gather was more useful in helping them accomplish the tasks. Subjects made less effort to complete the tasks with Scatter/Gather system, and learned more during the searching.

As for the queries, subjects used fewer queries to search with Scatter/Gather, and each query contained fewer words. This supports the statement that Scatter/Gather can facilitate the user's query formulation. As Scatter/Gather can cluster documents and provide keywords for each cluster, users can get more information about the topics and the sub-topics by entering fewer general words, learn from the keywords and find appropriate queries after fewer steps of adjusting queries, reducing the number of queries and the number of words in each query.

5.2 Task Type

Scatter/Gather is considered to be useful for information access with non-specific goals, and has been found to be helpful under related circumstances. We analyzed users' feedback on Scatter/Gather to investigate its effectiveness in different kinds of tasks. By comparing the mean values of evaluations for the questions in post-questionnaires between known-item tasks and exploratory tasks, which were completed with Scatter/Gather, it was found that those two known-item tasks are relatively more specific and easier to complete for subjects than the exploratory tasks. Subjects appeared to be more familiar with them, make less effort to complete them, and use more queries to search. However, no significant differences were found about the effects of these two types of tasks on Scatter/Gather effectiveness.

Significant differences in terms of the above factors were found among the individual tasks. According to the results of an LSD test on the tasks conducted on Scatter/Gather and by the subjects who took advantages of Scatter/Gather function, task 3 was significantly different from the other tasks in terms of easy start, easy search, satisfaction and words in query. Task 3 was more difficult than the other three – subjects made more effort to finish it and used more words in each query. In terms of usefulness, Scatter/Gather was more useful for task 1 than task 3. It was also found that subjects were less familiar with the task 2, and used fewer queries to search. Interestingly, they tended to use more queries in searches when they were familiar with the task, and used more words to formulate the queries when conducting a tough task. Scatter/Gather was useful in helping users finish tasks they were less familiar with and allowed them to use fewer words to search, consistent with the observation that Scatter/Gather is potentially useful when query specification is difficult.

5.3 Contributing Factors

We analyze factors that have influences on the Scatter/Gather effectiveness. Using linear regression, we analyzed the impacts of task, system, familiarity with the task, specificity of the task and previous knowledge on the following outcome: the effort to finish the task, usefulness of the system, time spent to finish the task, the pages opened and the number of queries.

Previous knowledge and familiarity with the task had positive influence on the usefulness of the system and the number of pages opened at the 0.1 significance level respectively. Subjects felt that the system was more useful when they had more previous knowledge about the task. When the subjects were more familiar with the task, they would open more pages to find the answer and use more queries. Specificity of the task produced negative effects on the time spent at the 0.1 level, indicating that when the task is more specific, subjects spent more time to finish it. As for the individual tasks, task 2, 3 and 4 had negative influence on the number of queries at the 0.01, 0.1 and 0.05 levels respectively, while only task 3 had positive effects on the effort at the 0.1 level. Subjects used fewer queries in task 2 than those in task 3 and task 4, and made more efforts to finish task 3 than others. Familiarity with the tasks significantly affected their perception about the usefulness of the system.

5.4 Topic Familiarity and Specif city

In earlier discussions, we reasoned that Scatter/Gather and the classic system may support different types of search tasks. Scatter/Gather likely works better in exploratory topics. Hence the impact of task-related variables on perceived retrieval effectiveness in the study was likely different across the two systems. Hence, we performed interaction analyses of the system variable and task-related variables to examine potential influences.

Relying on linear regression, we analyzed the impacts of topic familiarity, system (binary variable), and their interaction on user perception of system effectiveness in the post-task questionnaire. The user's familiarity with a search topic positively and significantly influenced perceived system effectiveness in terms of most questions in the post-task.

The system variable also had a positive influence in some aspects. For example, the classic search engine was significantly easier to start with and to perform searches, as compared to Scatter/Gather. Topic familiarity has a greater impact on perceived effectiveness in the Scatter/Gather system than in the classic search system.

We conducted a similar analysis of the impacts of topic specificity, system (binary variable), and their interaction. According to the result, topic specificity had significant influences on the user's perceived Scatter/Gather system's ease of use and the perception about whether there was sufficient time to conduct searches. User perception of specificity had a significant influence on satisfaction at the 0.1 level. However, the interaction with the system variable did not result in significant influences.

5.5 User Evidence and Relevance

We analyzed clickthrough data and users' relevance judgment to identify potential associations. On average, subjects spent 57 seconds viewing a page after the link was clicked. Perceived usefulness and relevance are highly correlated (Pearson 0.864) – users tended to regard a useful page as a relevant one as well. Viewing time (relative viewing time[2]) also had positive correlations with both relevance and usefulness.

According to the results of linear regression analysis with relevance and usefulness as independent variables and with viewing time or relative viewing time as dependent variable, usefulness had positive influence on viewing time and relative viewing time at the 0.05 level. It indicates that the usefulness of a page plays an important role in affecting users searching behaviors, including viewing time and relative viewing time.

6. CONCLUSION

Based on data collected from a user study, we discussed user's perceptions of Scatter/Gather system vs. a classic search interface, analyzed the influences of task-related variables on perceived system effectiveness, and examined correlations among relevance-related variables in user logs.

Overall, subjects were divided in terms of their preferences toward Scatter/Gather. The classic search interface appealed to those who viewed Scatter/Gather as a more complex system; others felt that Scatter/Gather was more useful to interact with because its new way of results presentation/organization. Scatter/Gather was more helpful in supporting the subjects to accomplish the search tasks, but not as easy as the classic to use because of the design of interface. Subjects learned more during the searching and used fewer queries to search, and each query contains fewer words in the Scatter/Gather approach.

There were significant differences in the numbers of queries for the different tasks and at different levels of familiarity. The user's familiarity with the tasks also played an important role in query formulation. Scatter/Gather was found to be useful in helping users finish tasks they were less familiar with and allowing them to use fewer words to search – it was potentially useful when query specification was difficult.

Topic familiarity and specificity had significant influences on user perceived retrieval effectiveness. Perceived relevance and usefulness were highly correlated. Users tended to regard a useful page as a relevant one as well. Perceived usefulness of a page affected users' searching behaviors manifested in viewing time and relative viewing time.

Further research is needed to examine a wider variety of task types, and to investigate the effects of more task-related features on the effectiveness of Scatter/Gather and user information seeking behaviors.

[2]Relative viewing time is the time a user spent on a specific page normalized by the user's average viewing time.

7. REFERENCES

[1] N. J. Belkin, R. N. Oddy, and H. M. Brooks. Ask for information retrieval: Part i. background and theory. *Journal of Documentation*, 38(2):61–71, 1982.

[2] D. R. Cutting, D. R. Karger, J. O. Pedersen, and J. W. Tukey. Scatter/gather: A cluster-based approach to browsing large document collections. In *SIGIR '92*, pages 318–329. ACM Press, New York, 1992.

[3] J. A. T. Hackos and J. Redish. *User and task analysis for interface design*. Wiley computer publishing. Wiley, New York, 1998.

[4] M. Hall, E. Frank, G. Holmes, B. Pfahringer, P. Reutemann, and I. H. Witten. The weka data mining software: an update. *SIGKDD Explorations Newsletter*, 11(1):10–18, 2009.

[5] M. A. Hearst and J. O. Pedersen. Reexamining the cluster hypothesis: Scatter/gather on retrieval results. In *SIGIR '96*, pages 76–84. ACM Press, New York, 1996.

[6] W. Ke, C. R. Sugimoto, and J. Mostafa. Dynamicity vs. effectiveness: Studying online clustering for scatter/gather. In *SIGIR '09*, pages 19–26. ACM Press, Boston, 2009.

[7] D. Kelly. *Methods for Evaluating Interactive Information Retrieval Systems with Users*. Now Publishers Inc., Boston, MA, 2009.

[8] C. T. Meadow, B. R. Boyce, D. H. Kraft, and C. Barry. *Text Information Retrieval Systems*. Academic Press, London, UK, third edition, 2007.

[9] P. Pirolli, P. Schank, M. Hearst, and C. Diehl. Scatter/gather browsing communicates the topic structure of a very large text collection. In *CHI '96*, pages 213–220, New York, NY, USA, 1996. ACM.

[10] C. J. van Rijsbergen. *Information Retrieval*. Butterworths, London, second edition, 1979.

[11] R. W. White, G. Marchionini, and G. Muresan. Evaluating exploratory search systems: Introduction to special topic issue of information processing and management. *Information Processing & Management*, 44(2):433–436, 2008.

Tipple: Location-Triggered Mobile Access to a Digital Library for Audio Books

Annika Hinze
University of Waikato,
Hamilton, New Zealand
hinze@cs.waikato.ac.nz

David Bainbridge
University of Waikato,
Hamilton, New Zealand
davidb@cs.waikato.ac.nz

ABSTRACT

This paper explores the role of audio as a means to access books in a digital library while being at the location referred to in the books. The books are sourced from the digital library and can either be accompanied by pre-recorded audio or synthesized using text-to-speech. The paper details the functional requirements, design and implementation of *Tipple*. The concept was extensively tested in three field studies.

Categories and Subject Descriptors

H.3.7 [Dissemination]: Digital Libraries

Author Keywords

Design, Experimentation, Human Factors

1. Introduction

Physical spaces are (mostly invisibly) inhabited by literary figures: Joyce's Mr Bloom walks through Dublin, Tremain's Harriet goes shopping in Christchurch. Sometimes their presence is marked by physical references, such as quotations on the pavement (O'Connell Street in Dublin) or commemorative plaques on houses. Book lovers can go on 'literary tours' to follow their heroes' footsteps.

Electronic navigation and geographic positioning is increasingly common as travel support— many new mobile apps on smart phones offer location-aware information. We explore here the use of audio and text-to-speech functions to make digital books available (that is, 'audible') in their appropriate location context. In this paper, we describe our work in developing this idea from conception to realization in *Tipple*, which in turn draws upon research into alerting services as well as digital libraries [7].

As a scenario, imagine a visitor to Christchurch, New Zealand. Installed on their phone is *Tipple* loaded with a profile of their interests, which includes the English author Rose Tremain. Walking from ChristChurch Cathedral towards Latimer Square, their phone makes a "chirp chirp" noise alerting them to an area of interest nearby—Worcester Street—a location where Harriet Blackstone, the protagonist of Tremain's book "The Colour" buys a book before heading out into the New Zealand bush. Using the map displayed on screen, our visitor decides to divert to this location. Once there they select the opening chapter of "The Colour", one of several chapters listed on their phone as being set at this location, and start listening to it as it is read aloud through their headphones.

In this paper, we describe our work in developing *Tipple* and an exploration of its use. We start with a summary of the nine functional requirements that were established to meet the aims of the work. In this there is a strong focus on audio, as this medium is well suited to a mobile environment. We then review related work. As there are no other systems providing audio access to digital libraries, we studied audio use in travel guide systems. We also include overviews of TIP and Greenstone, the two systems that the work builds upon. In Sect. 4 the overall design and details of the implementation are presented. Sects. 5 and 6 describe the setup and results of our field study, in which participants visited the Hamilton Gardens using *Tipple*. Section 7 reports on two studies executed with sequential books. Section 8 discusses the insights gained from our field study in comparison to related results and projects.

2. Functional Requirements

A functional requirements analysis was undertaken to establish the characteristics of the desired software. Digital books include both audio books via MP3 files and books in text form loaded from the digital library (DL).

(R1) Playing Chapter-based Books (MP3). Chapter-based books typically follow a narrative and should be available for reading in chronological order. The service should also let the user know about the order and location of other chapters in the book.

(R2) Playing Reference Books (MP3). Reference books are collections of articles; only parts of the book may be related to the user's current position and profile. Users should receive selective information sourced from this material relating to their current location and be able to choose whether or not to play them.

(R3) Text-to-Speech. Books from the digital library need to be read to a user. Books are loaded based on a user's current location and their profile information. When the texts are loaded from the digital library, Text-to-Speech software needs to convert the text to voice.

(R4) Text-to-speech and Text Display. In addition to having the text read out, a user may want to follow the textual form. They should be given the option to read the text, listen to the spoken text, or to do both at the same time.

	chapter-based	reference	text2speech	text2speech & display	audio for this book	audio books control	anti-overlap	interaction audio-control	user preferences
	R1	R2	R3	R4	R5	R6	R7	R8	R9
Access Sight	-	+	+	+	-	-	+	+-	-
Augmented audio reality system	-	+	-	-	-	-	+	+	-
Tour Guide for Travellers	-	-	-	-	-	+	o		-
GUIDE	-	-	-	-	-	-	o	+	+
Automated Tour Guide	-	+	-	-	-	+	+	-	-

(+ meets the requirement, +- somewhat meets the requirement, - does not meet the requirement, o requirement does not apply)

Figure 1. Evaluation results for analysis of related work

(R5) Audio for this Book. Additional MP3 files may be available and are independent of the text. When accessing a chapter in the digital library, the corresponding audio of this chapter should be loaded and played from the database if available. Hyperlinks should connect MP3 books and those from the digital library so that a user can switch between the two modes.

(R6) Audio Books Control. The system should alert the user (e.g., by a sound) to let them know that a book (chapter) is available to be played/displayed at a location. A user dialogue window should give the user the option to play the book and also indicate other relevant chapters or items that are available.

As Digital Libraries are being transported onto mobile devices [3] it became clear that displaying library content requires adjustments to accommodate the limitations of screen size and limited input options. Furthermore, the context of the usage situations is dominated by multi-tasking and distracted attention [21]. We therefore identified general requirements that need to be fulfilled to support easy reception of audio content.

(R7) Anti-Overlap. When a new object presents itself or the user wants a book to be read, the user should be able to choose whether to interrupt any current audio.

(R8) Interaction Audio Control. This feature is similar to standard audio players using play lists and play control functions. It gives the user control over the audio play-back. Users can use the play list to insert and delete audio from the queue.

(R9) User Preferences. Users should be able to set their preferences, e.g., for repeat-gap and anti-overlap. The repeat-gap is used to identify the time between each loop of an audio alert. The anti-overlap parameter allows the user to select whether they want the alerts for multiple sites to be mixed together, or played one by one, and if they are to interrupt book readings.

This list of requirements is used for both, comparison of related work and as a guideline for the implementation.

3. Related Work

We first describe the two systems this research builds upon: TIP and Greenstone. Then we discuss related approaches and studies. As there are no comparable studies for location-based audio books in digital libraries we evaluated mobile guide systems that use audio support (see Table 1) and audio books in digital libraries. A general discussion and comparison of our study results to related studies on audio presentation for mobile users is included in the discussion (Section 6).

Tourist Guide System TIP.

The mobile Tourist Information Provider (TIP) combines an event notification service and a location-based service to alert its users to attractions in the vicinity [19]. TIP was selected as basis for *Tipple* as it provides the location-awareness part of the project. The information in TIP is tailored to the user's context: their personal interests (as defined in a profile) and their current and past location (as measured by GPS). Users will not receive the same information twice, except when they explicitly ask for it. To achieve the capabilities envisioned in the introduction, we designed *Tipple* based on some existing components of TIP.

Digital Library: Greenstone.

The open source Greenstone software was chosen for the digital library component for this project [4]. It can organize many types of electronic documents such as text, HTML, pictures, music, and audio or video. Of particular significance to this project is Greenstone's ability to configure the structure of information, such as links to documents and sections within documents. We use the digital library as a document server accessed via the TIP system. This differs from the normal pattern of usage in Greenstone, where it is the user who formulates and initiates the query. Greenstone itself was only minimally modified in this project; we relied mainly on an extension of the Greenstone/TIP bridge (see Section 4).

Travel Guides.

The tourist system Access Sight [23] is designed for both sighted and blind users, using 'hearcons' to indicate points of interest. Different groups are used for different types of objects, and text-to-speech identifies places of interest. The spoken text is not based on chapters, however, so the application does not need Audio Books Control. Anti-overlap is used to let blind people decide when to hear the audio information.

The Augmented Audio Reality System [17] provides basic mechanisms for navigation and orientation with a digitally recorded voice. The system does not use text-to-speech. It is not based on chapters, nor does it support Audio Books Control. The sound radius and volume level used are increased for those artefacts that relate to the current interest of the user. The system does not give explicit control of audio, rather this is inferred from their motion (e.g., stopped, or walking quickly). For instance, to minimize overlap of audio, the number of audio items played is controlled by their walking speed.

The Tour Guide for Travellers [6] delivered multimedia information to a user's palmtop computer. When a user is close to a place of interest they will be alerted by an audio *hearcon*. They are asked whether they want to visit the signalled place (similar to Audio Books Control). This system does not use text-to-speech or digital recording.

The GUIDE system [8] indicated new points of interest by a notice sound and display. It provides two options for anti-overlap: when a display overwrite occurs the user can simply press a back button; alternatively the system can be configured to retain the current information but alert the user that new information is available. While the information presented by the GUIDE is text/graphics, the interactions for 'pushing' new information to the user and the anti-overlap measures are similar to our project.

The Automated Tour Guide [5] is a museum guide system that can play descriptions of museum artefacts. The audio is triggered by walking close to the artefacts, and will stop by walking away. The audio is not based on a user's interest, however. An infrared transmitter placed in the ceiling provides accurate position information so only the audio for the nearest artefact is played thus avoiding any overlap. The anti-overlap mechanism has no explicit interaction with the user. The additional information is similar to Audio Books Control, which means users play it when they need it. In this system, users carry their own audio source, which contain a digital record, so that the descriptions can be heard according to the user's time schedule. This system does not use text-to-speech and digital record so it does not support the requirements related to Books via MP3, Books via a digital library, and most of the interactions.

Digital Library Systems.

A number of digital library projects have employed components that are also used in our work, such as text-to-speech synthesis, interactive map visualizations, and access from mobile devices. Since these projects focussed on different issues, and use a different mixture of these components, we restrict ourselves to a brief overview of the differences and similarities. As with Access Sight, a primary use of text-to-speech technology in DL systems has been to provide capabilities for print-disabled users such as the visually impaired [2,24,25]. While the "hands-free" aspect is of relevance to this work, our requirements are not so strict. For example, Near Field Communication (NFC), to simplify user certification [1], is not required. Indeed, as we are exploring the inter-relationship between text and audio it is necessary in our design to allow tactile interaction with the user interface in addition to hands-free.

A gazetteer to link the text in the digital library with geographical information is at the heart of most map-based DL systems, e.g., [10,27], together with interfaces designed for access from a desktop PC or laptop in mind, as our empirical testing demonstrates. Our work investigates how users access such geo-spatially enhanced DL content from a GPS-enabled mobile device. The findings reported below, therefore, are directly applicable to such projects.

Some projects take a more mobile-centric DL view [13,15,25]. Here the emphasis is very much on access through mobile phones (as with our project), but with more emphasis on content creation and/or enrichment (significantly different to our project). In the case of the projects in India and South Africa [13,25], the target user groups were strong in oral tradition but low in literacy rates, which is not the case with our project.

4. 4 DESIGN and Implementation

The design of *Tipple* is based on the functional requirements analysis reported in Section 2. *Tipple* builds on and extends concepts from both TIP and Greenstone. We first briefly describe the components of TIP that we extended to achieve this. Then we describe the implementation of *Tipple*.

Design considerations

We previously used the Greenstone/TIP bridge [18] to provide location-based access to a digital library. This service uses the TIP user's location and profile to create a query, which is then sent to the digital library to search for possible documents. Greenstone documents are prepared in advance (when the digital library is formed), for location-based search using a place name recognition package that adds location mark-up to the documents. For *Tipple*, we needed to provide audio information to the user even though the books in the digital library may not be available with pre-recorded audio. For those cases, a text-to-speech function was added.

Access to the books uses the chapter-level metaphor for narrative books (order of chapters predefined) and an article metaphor for reference books (independent of ordering). For audio-books we required a Greenstone location-search at chapter level and changed the indexing in Greenstone to operate at the chapter level. The system selects audio books that are relevant to the user's location. Their relevance is determined at a chapter level: if any chapter of a book is related to a given location, the book will be selected. All relevant audio books will be listed for the user, with high-lighted chapters referring to the current location. The user can choose to listen to the audio content or to view the Greenstone text. We also offer the option to play these chapters by travel route sequence.

Implementation details

Figure 2 provides a schematic overview of the software architecture for *Tipple*, which was informed by two previous prototypes (*references removed*). The main division in the software is between the interactive application that runs on the phone and the geo-tagged documents that reside in a digital library. Communication between the two is via HTTP, with the *Tipple* application being the initiator in the exchange, and the services of the DL software accessed through a Servlet. More specifically, the digital library component is built using Greenstone 3 [11] using a Solr derived Search Service to support numeric and location based searching in addition to the regular metadata and full text retrieval.

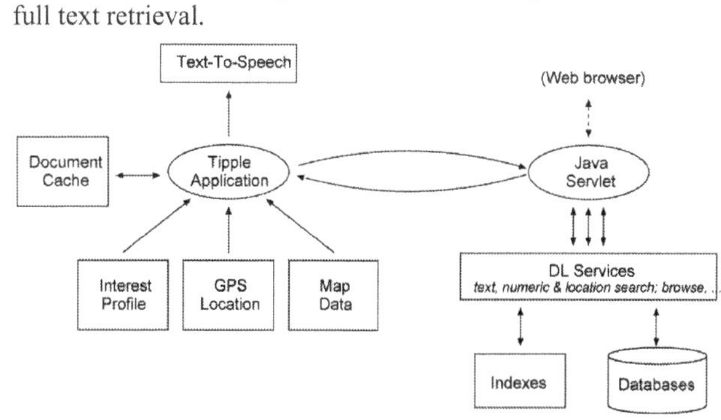

Figure 2. Components of the Audio Book Service within TIP and Greenstone

Developing the software this way has the fringe benefit that the same collated tourist information is available to "virtual" travelers too, who can access the information from their current location (wherever that might be) through their web browser (say, from a desktop PC when based at home) using the standard search and browse access methods provided by the DL. Moreover, Greenstone 3 has been ported to run, self-contained, on mobile smart phones such as the iPhone [3] and more recently Android devices. This makes it possible to run a completely self-sufficient version of the tourist information system on the phone. Indeed this was needed in the version we evaluated (Section 5 and 6) as the location used (the city's public gardens) has little or no cell phone coverage. Even when the DL component is installed on the phone in this fashion, communication is still carried over HTTP (localhost) as this simplifies the software design.

A significant difference of note in this design, over our previous ones, is the pattern of communication between the application and the DL. Given that HTTP is client-side initiated, much of the complexity of these designs was taken up dealing with ways that the server could asynchronously "push" data to the client (a kind of reverse-AJAX technique), requiring the use of components such as a socket server running on the client's device. In this implementation we introduced a document cache on the client side so we could provide for all our event-triggered needs solely with traditional client-side initiated requests (i.e., solely with client-side "pull" operations).

Instead of waiting for the server to notify the client the moment the user's GPS location matches a specific location—as we did before, requiring everyone's GPS location to be continually sent to it—the client is responsible for monitoring where the user is *and* what potential places of interest might be nearby. It does this by retrieving, through the DL search service, the set of documents that fall within a catchment area centered on the user's current GPS location. These documents are then stored in the Document Cache, and accessed locally as needed when the user moves around. The new approach does mean that a *Tipple* application typically goes through periods where it places a high demand on the server to deliver content, followed by quiet spells; however, overall we have found that (because the client is no longer trying to provide real-time information to the user sourced from a remote server) this new configuration delivers a more responsive experience to the user.

For the map component of *Tipple* we used the open source library MapsForge (*code.google.com/p/mapsforge/*) that offers a GoogleMap's inspired API that works with Open Street Map (OSM). In our version we chose to implement this as static files on the phone (again motivated by our requirement that the entire application work without network connectivity). Prior to installation an OSM Protocol-buffer Binary Format (PBF) file for the area the subject will be travelling in is prepared using a desktop computer, and subsequently transferred onto the phone as part of the installation procedure. MapsForge also provides support for retrieving and displaying map information live from the OSM web server; the required changes would be a straightforward procedure. This would shift our design from a traditional client-server approach to one that is more of a "mash-up" in spirit.

Android phones come equipped with a Text-to-Speech API, and so there was not much implementation work involved in getting *Tipple* to speak out loud the textual information it has about a location. One complication specific to our pilot study was that, while the information provided about the gardens was predominantly in English, there were also a significant number of Māori words intermingled. The pronunciation of these words by the TTS system was less than ideal. Even though the TTS API is tied in with Android's support for locales, there was not a version for Māori available, and indeed even if there was it is not entirely obvious how this could be utilized in the mixed language environment we had. We therefore chose to augment our implementation with a dictionary lookup method that mapped Māori words to phonetically expressed versions. Text displayed on the phone's screen was presented "as is", however any text sent to the TTS API first had any occurrences of words in our bespoke dictionary changed to its phonetic version.

System walkthrough.

Figure 3 shows four screen shots of the audio book service application. Fig 3 (a) and (b), on an iPhone, demonstrate chapter-based books taken from an example of listening to the works of Jane Austen whilst walking around the city centre of Bath, England. Fig 3 (c) and (d), on an Android phone, are taken from an example of travelling around the Hamilton Public Gardens, New Zealand, of which more details can be found in our user study (see Section 6).

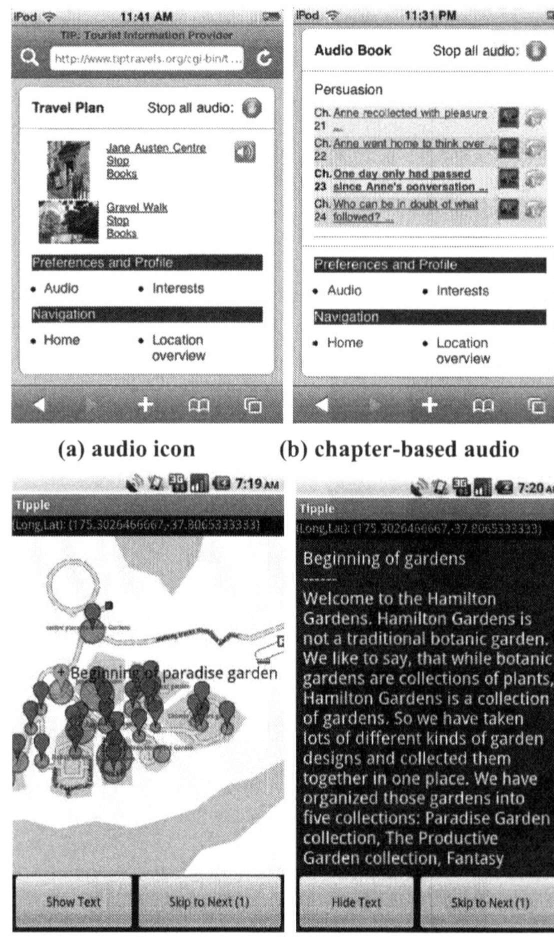

(a) audio icon **(b) chapter-based audio**

(c) audio at location **(d) text at location**

Figure 3. The role of audio in TIP

Fig 3(a) is a screenshot of the audio icons service. Fig 3(b) shows the audio books service, chapter view of Persuasion. In Figure 3(c)—which captures the user's tour after their first initial minutes when using the Audio-Only mode—the user has passed through the first location (chirp chirp) on the map but chosen not to play the audio commentary just yet, and progressed to the second location (where a second "chirp chirp" rings out). This is the point the snapshot has been taken. From here the user can start listening to the first location (Play) which will automatically continue on to play the audio for the second location (with a 'bing' to separate the two audio descriptions). Alternatively they can skip to the next location in the queue (press Skip to Next button once). From there they can start the audio for the second location (Play) or press the "Skip" button for a second time (now labelled "End") to clear the queue of locations.

Text only mode, shown in Figure 3(d), is similar to the Audio mode, except the Play button is replaced with a Show/Hide text button, for displaying—superimposed over the map—a text rendition of the commentary. The figure captures the same moment of the visitor's tour as before. Despite the name of this mode, audio alerts are still played (as well as a vibration alert) to notify the user of a new location. Having heard the second "chirp chirp" sound the user has elected to press the Show text button in this case to read about the first location they visited. The same choices to view the next location's commentary or clear the queue are also available in this mode using the skip button. There is also a mixed text-and-audio mode, which is not shown here.

5. User Study Methodology

We conducted a first user study using a book about the Hamilton Gardens, the text of which was semantically enriched with location data. This user study tested the viability of the concept and the usability of the interaction design as implemented. One of the difficulties of studying location-based audio books is the need to provide users with sufficient example data. We decided to first explore the use of a location guide book, as no suitable works of fiction were available for the Waikato region. Two follow-up studies using works of fiction are reported in Section 7.

Setup Data

We used a customized book for the Hamilton Gardens (*www.hamiltongardens.co.nz*) that was created by extending an existing work with information gained from a transcribed guided tour. Explicit references to relative locations were avoided (e.g., "to the left"). The data was prepared in book form and split into separate chapters based on the different gardens in the Paradise Garden collection. Each of the chapters was manually analysed for location information, and location mark-up was inserted using GPS coordinates as the centre of a circular area.

No electronic map was readily available to be used for the study. All available online maps provided satellite views that were either not available at the desired resolution or (if available) too complex to be used (with many trees, flower beds and lawns that were hard to distinguish). None of the available raster maps distinguished any features for the gardens. This made it necessary to create a raster map with sufficient resolution so that it could be used in the study. Figure 4 shows the electronic map that was created for this study using Open Street Map (*www.openstreetmap.com*).

The participants were invited to visit the Hamilton Gardens. After a brief introduction and a general questionnaire, they were given an android phone with the *Tipple* software pre-installed. For the Hamilton Gardens location, only one book was made available during the study. Participants were then encouraged to visit the Paradise Gardens deciding their own route and timing. The gardens provide a number of options for which route to take; the book did not make any references to particular routes. No groups participated. The researchers met the participants at the exit of the gardens for a follow-up interview. No particular tasks were set for the visit. The motivation was to simulate a 'normal' visit to the gardens without any unnecessary interference.

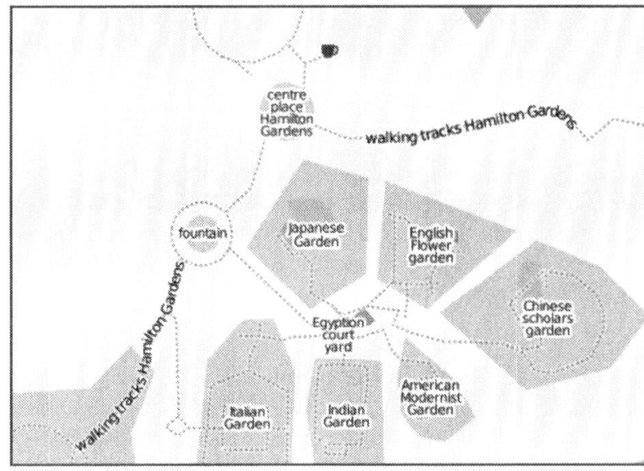

Figure 4. Paradise Gardens

Questions

The following question areas were explored in the questionnaire and the follow-up interview:

- General questions about the participant and their usage of books and audio books
- Usability and affordability of the Hamilton Gardens audio guide
- Usage analysis of the Hamilton Gardens audio guide

A summary of the participants' answers and a discussion of our analysis are presented in the next two sections.

6. Study results

We now present the results of the introductory questionnaire, system usage, and the follow-up interviews.

Participant Background

The 16 participants who took part were students at the Computer Science Department (14 participants aged 20 to 35, two aged 35 to 50; three female and 13 male). Most of the study participants had previously visited the Gardens (only six had visited rarely or never), which allowed us to compare visits with and without the audio book system.

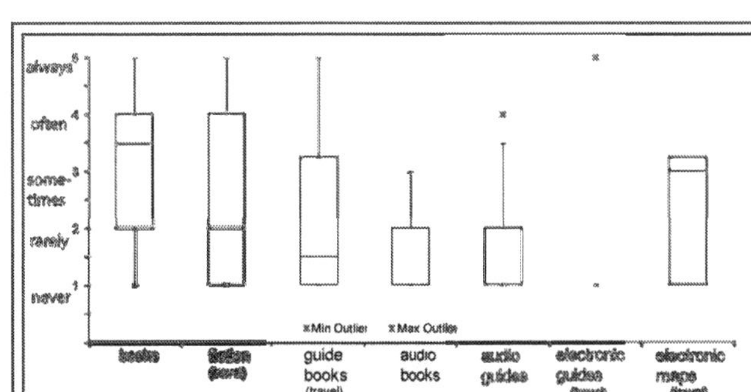

Figure 5. Use of (audio) books

Figure 5 gives an overview of the participants' familiarity with and use of books and audio books (presented as a boxplot) using a five-point Likert scale. Participants fall into two groups: most of them read books often or always (50%, 8 of 16), 6 read rarely or never, two read sometimes. The majority would not take works of fiction on travels (median of 'rarely'), even fewer would take travel guides (median at 1.5; mode is 'never'). Audio books, audio guides and electronic guides are almost completely unused.

Several participants use mobile electronic maps on their phone (10 of 16 'sometimes' or more often); one of them typically uses digital photographs of maps to save bandwidth. The reason most often cited for low usage of electronic information is the cost of internet connections.

Audio-books at Hamilton Gardens

Fig. 6 shows the overall length of time participants spent using the service. 12 of the 16 participants were given the audio service (blue/light gray), with a control group of four participants the text-based display (red/dark gray).

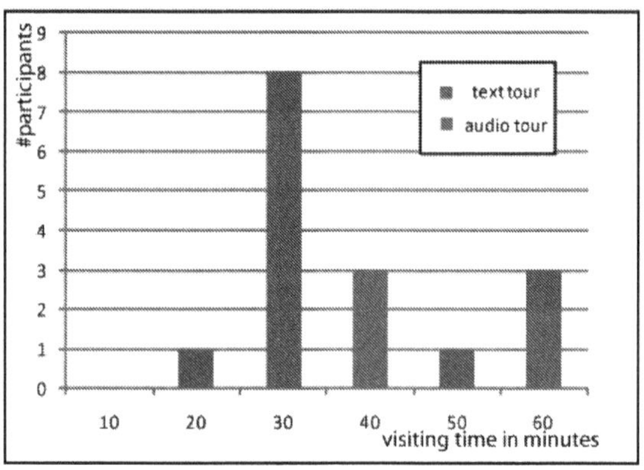

Figure 6. Usage Times

No relationship could be found between each participant's preference for books and the time spent using the service; however there was evidence that lack of familiarity with the general location led to impatience. For the two shortest visits in our trial—20 mins (P9, text) and 25 mins (P5, audio)—neither participant had been to the gardens before. Both found it difficult to relate the audio/text to their surroundings; P5 never stopped to listen to the audio, and P9 expected the book text to be matched by physical signs in each garden. It seemed that these two participants found the audio book concept difficult and had expected something more akin to an audio travel guide.

Figures 7, 8, and 9 summarize the participants' feedback about the usability of the system.

Figure 7 shows the participants' feedback about the navigation (summarized from a number of open questions in the interview with the participants). Most participants (10 of 16) were satisfied with the localisation (map and location identifiers). Problems identified were the need to look at the map for navigation (P3) and the lack of feedback about direction of movement (P5). Participants who were satisfied with the map also observed that additional explicit information about the direction of their current movements would have helped. They suggested the use of additional indications, such as arrows.

Figure 8 shows a summary of the participant feedback about the information access interactions. The audio icon (chirp) signalling the availability of text and audio information was generally described as being helpful. Two participants confused it with their phone ringtone and found repetitive signals annoying (the active areas in the gardens were relatively close to each other). The majority of participants (15 of 16) understood and enjoyed the book content. Suggestions for improvements were to create smaller items with an option to continue instead of offering all available information for each location at once.

All four readers of the digital text were satisfied with the interaction (see Figure 9); 8 of the 11 participants with audio were satisfied, with one not answering. Both P1 and P11 observed that the text-to-speech audio became boring after some time, as it is rather monotonous.

Figure 10 (next page) summarises the presentation preferences of the participants for our study. All audio participants preferred the audio presentation over text; none of them asked for text representation. The reason most often given was the advantage of being able to look at the surroundings and not having to read from a small screen. As a possible additional use of text, they mentioned the advantage of skimming and quick decision making.

Two participants using the text display preferred text over audio; P13 felt it would have 'looked crazy' if they had been walking around with an audio guide and they preferred the option of quick skimming. P14 was a non-native speaker and preferred to read the text in their own time.

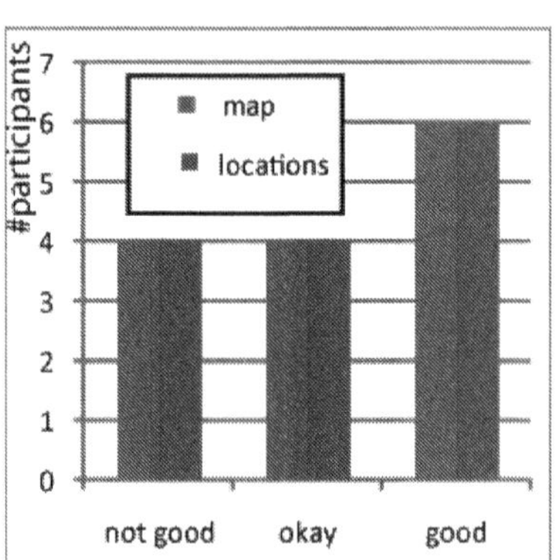

Figure 7.

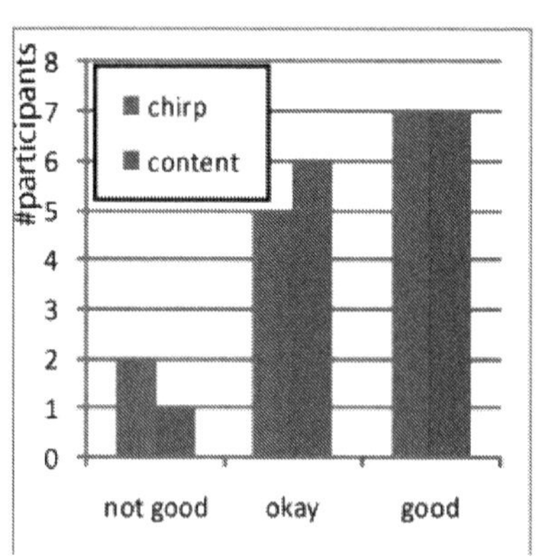

Figure 8. Information

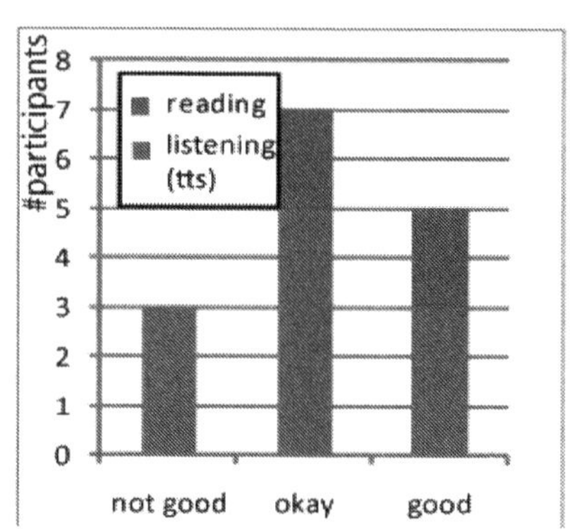

Figure 9. Presentation

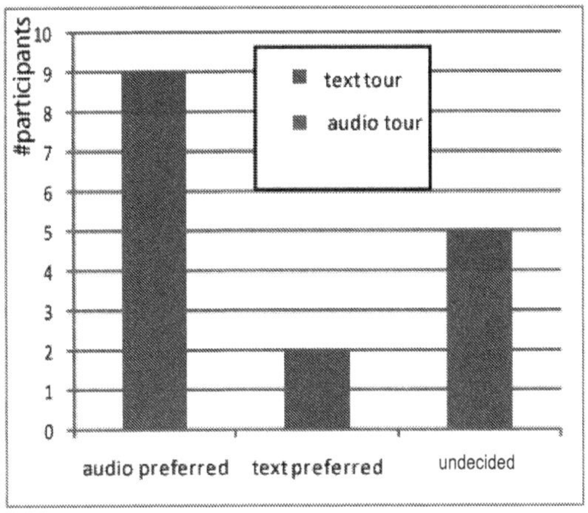

Figure 10. Presentation Preferences

Figure 11 shows the suggestions made by participants for further information: layered information refers to breaking the text into smaller units, open text refers to a DL-like search functionality. Participants liked the idea of displaying further information (text or photographs) of other locations mentioned in the text, which a link/bridge to a digital library service would be well placed to support.

Additionally, they suggested the use of photographs to identify any artefacts the text mentions. In short, participants felt that increasing the exposure of the underlying DL services in the mobile application would enrich its functionality in line with users' expectations.

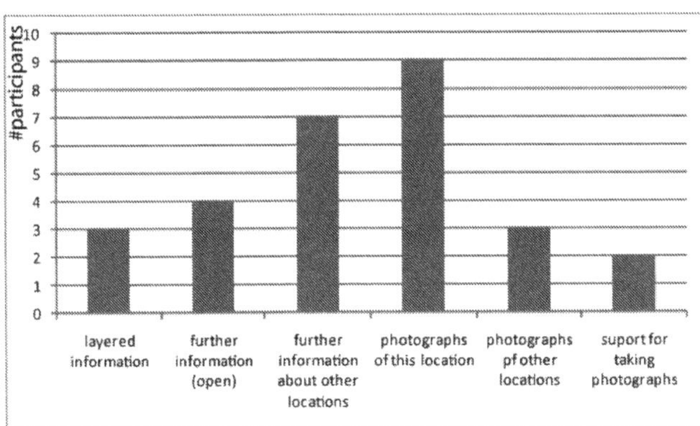

Figure 11. Additional Information Options

7. Two User studies using works of fiction

In addition to the Hamilton Gardens study that tested viability and usability of the software, we executed two studies in which participants used *Tipple* for location-based access to works of fiction.

Stations at the Gardens

The Stations at the Gardens is a yearly arts event that uses a well-known story separated into 14 Chapters (=stations). Each part of the story is illustrated by pieces of art that are installed in the Paradise Gardens in Hamilton every evening for one week. We used *Tipple* to make location-based audio recordings of the story available to visitors of the event. As the event happened during the evenings, any alternative paper-based text distribution suffered poor readability.

The software was installed on 11 Android phones belonging to visitors to the event. It was also available from the event's website and in an audio-only version for other phones. Additionally we distributed *Tipple*-installed phones to selected visitors. We observed and briefly interviewed eight participants between 8pm and 10pm on several evenings, another eight filled in a short questionnaire. The results data are therefore of somewhat mixed quality, due to the event character of the study.

Visiting times using *Tipple* lasted between 30 and 60min for 14 participants (average 40min); two phones had low battery power (visiting curtailed after 10 & 20min).

Six of the 8 participants using the questionnaire were satisfied with the audio sound. The audio was generally described as being "helpful" and "interesting". One participant said "It was exciting to hear [the story] when looking at [the artists'] works." A problem was created by the close proximity of some stations (leading to the wrong chapter being offered). The majority of participants played and read the audio in order. One participant preferred to play the chapters by selecting them from the map as they "would not have to be close to the location but [are] still able to read the story." Other participants also suggested that the audio not be queued by locations visited (latest one always played first) but to allow audio to be played in their own time independent of location.

Eight users tried both audio and text during the study; eight used audio only. The majority of audio participants (7 of 8) preferred the audio presentation (one preferred text). Five of the participants who tried both options preferred audio, two the text, while for one participant no data is available. Two participants who preferred text were non-native speakers who wanted to read the text in their own time. One participant with preference for audio said that it was "not comfortable to read in the dark and on a small screen." Some participants felt the chirping noise the system made to alert them to another chapter was disturbing in quiet areas (when used without ear phones). Participants suggested integration into social networking services to record their own photographs (six participants) or receive more information (four participants).

Overall we received positive feedback from the participants but technical issues and the experience of *Tipple* users "in the wild" made the experience somewhat haphazard.

Poetry on the Pavement

Poetry on the Pavement is an event in Auckland City. Throughout the city, a selection of poems was placed on the pavement, which together tell the story of Auckland. Each poem was treated as a separate chapter. Learning from the experiences of the Stations event, for the Poetry on Pavement study, we did not distribute the software to participants' phones but used pre-installed *Tipple* phones. The study had 20 participants, 15 invited in-situ from the public on Auckland's streets and five participants with computer science backgrounds.

We observe that the use of digital content in this group is quite different to the one participating in the Hamilton Gardens: 18 of 20 participants used digital maps while travelling, 9 used audio guides in museums, 9 read novels while travelling and 8 used electronic travel applications.

We received positive feedback about the system features such as showing book chapter locations, chapter number, and travel path (showing connections between chapters on the map). Several participants mentioned particularly that they enjoyed the location-trigged system, the presentation of chapter order, and the clear design of the travel paths. They observed that the chapter order becomes very clear through the use of the travel path on the map. One participant suggested that the travel path should stand out more on the map.

Nineteen of 20 participants were satisfied with the overall experience of *Tipple*. They observed that the chirping alert is occasionally intrusive during travel. The advantage of also being able to read the chapters in their own time was explicitly mentioned. Participants recommended additional features such as support for taking several pictures in one location and provision of further book-related information. They also suggested closer integration with social networking services such as *twitter* or *facebook*.

8. DISCUSSION

We first compare our findings from the three studies to those of earlier studies. It needs to be stressed again that no directly comparable study has been previously executed. The available studies are mainly for audio output in tourist guide systems or navigation systems. Spoken audio in digital libraries has so far only been considered for desktop-based system, e.g., for reading learning tools or for text-to-speech for easy access (e.g., systems for visually impaired or dyslexic people [16,2,28]).

Studies of related work

User studies have never systematically explored large numbers of audio guides. Related work in HCI has typically focused on technological innovation (such as context-awareness). Available studies predominantly focus on system design and evaluation. The general need for field trials in particular is still under discussion as they are difficult to conduct and time consuming [22]. However, we believe that mobile and adaptive systems that explore new interaction pathways provide richer results in field studies and cannot be adequately tested in a lab-based study.

Most studies on audio guides in museums focus on (re) evaluation of the user requirements (e.g., [29,30]). Audio museum guides follow similar design strategies to travel guides. Because they are restricted to enclosed spaces, they typically need different means to identify locations or exhibition items. Audio information is more easily distributed (dedicated hardware available in the museum) and is typically pre-recorded. These characteristics do not hold for a system like *Tipple* – a digital library that is accessed while being at the location referred to in the book.

Sharing audio books

All our study participants used *Tipple* alone. However, in an informal pilot to our first study, two participants went together and expressed the desire to listen to the audio book together. This would constitute a new DL access pattern as users do not typically search and read documents in digital libraries in groups. Audio interaction and collaboration between users has been evaluated by Aoki at al. [1], who developed an electronic guide book that allowed museum visitors to explicitly share audio information (pre-recorded and spoken). They found that most couples used shared audio as a conversational resource. Evjemo et al. [12] also report that nearly 40% of their study participants explicitly asked for the opportunity to share audio content in a museum and this included nearly 90% of those who usually had company when visiting museums. Most of our participants reported that they typically went travelling with friends or family. However, none asked for an opportunity to share the information, which may be due to the participants being on their own during our studies.

Directions and object identification

Some participants wished to receive information not only about their location but also about the direction of their movements. Additionally, several participants reported difficulties in identifying items that were mentioned in the book in their immediate surroundings. Combined audio and directional signage were previously evaluated [9] (note that our system does not provide audio directions). That study found that a map with photographs or directional arrows and photographs allows users to find their way more quickly than when using the map alone. We believe that audio messages in addition to audio book readings would lead to confusion as our participants already complained about the spoken feedback provided (when a sight was previously visited). Directing users to items based on sound (similar to [20]) may be worth exploring as alternative.

Previous evaluation of audio tourism guides used short pre-recorded audio (ca. 30 sec) [12]. In contrast, audio from our DL books is typically longer and relies on text-to-speech. They observed that participants in their studies preferred audio over video and more extensive use of still images was requested. This is similar to our study, where participants asked for additional photographs to identify and relate to the objects mentioned in the book. This request finds a direct parallel in their study, where approximately 60% of the participants reported that it was occasionally difficult to link the information given to the surrounding buildings.

Interaction model with the book

It is typically observed that a visual user interfaces takes attention away from the physical surroundings, whilst listening to audio clips seem to balance the attention much better [1]. Nevertheless, we had four participants overall who preferred to read text and a number of participants were undecided. A strong reason for this preference was the self-paced access (easier understanding for non-native speakers, faster skimming for proficient readers).

Tourism system versus digital library

We have repeatedly pointed out that previous systems evaluated belong to the category of tourism or museum guides. Digital libraries have been implemented typically as desktop-based applications and only recently in mobile applications [3]. We did not find any studies for audio books in digital libraries. We here briefly discuss the differences between the two approaches to highlight that even though studies in tourism guides allow some comparison with our study they are still clearly limited. The differences between guide systems and audio books are matters of recording, length, purpose, and the need for pre-processing.

Tourist audio guides typically provide relatively short snippets of pre-recorded audio ([12] describes 3min as a particularly long recording). An exception was AccesSights [23] with text-to-speech for guiding visually impaired users. In contrast, book chapters or even parts of book chapters easily span more than several minutes. Readings that are only a few seconds would be almost unheard of in audio books. Typically guides are purpose-built for a particular location whereas audio readings of books are usually not intended for automatic reading on location. One of the consequences is the necessary pre-processing, which is inherent in building a guide system but constitutes an additional step for books. Locations need to be identified and attached to (parts of) book chapters. Automatic location mark-up of text is still an open research issue.

Two participants in the Hamilton Gardens had difficulties interacting with the system as they expected it to more clearly refer to significant locations and give routing guidance. We believe that their interaction model was that of a tourist guide and not an audio book. This aspect needs further exploration. This problem did not occur for either of the two studies on fiction/sequential books. We believe that participants in those cases formed mental models that were more strongly influenced by the book concept.

Language issues

Several participants noted the limited quality of the text-to-speech function. They reported that listening to the very monotonous voice becomes "boring" and thus hard to follow. The researchers observed an additional issue when developing the chapters referring to the Māori garden (beyond the SW corner, Figure 5). No text-to-speech implementation is available for Māori, moreover, the spoken text was to be delivered in English and a mixing of languages is not supported. As a work-around we had to duplicate each chapter that contained Māori names: one for displaying the text and one in which all Māori words were transcribed into phonetic English. Culturally this is not a viable option nor is it manageable for larger bodies of text.

9. CONCLUSION

In this paper, we presented work on an audio-based tourist information system that sources a large portion of its information from geo-tagged documents contained in a digital library and optionally structured as chapters. Having established the functional requirements and reviewed related work, we detailed our system's design and implementation followed by a user study that investigated the roles text and audio play in delivering location-aware information to the user. Emphasis was placed on the role of audio as this is a less well understood area. Our field study is the first one of its kind, exploring the use of audio books on location. Finally, there is no particular reason to limit the scope to works of literature. Subjects like religion, geography or history would work equally well.

REFERENCES

1. Aioki, P., Grinter R.E., Hurst A., Szymanski M., Thornton J. and Woodruff, A. Sotto Voce: Exploring the Interplay of Conversation and Mobile Audio Spaces, *CHI'02*, 431-438, 2001
2. Bae, K.-J., Jeong, Y.-S., Shim, W.-S. and Kwak, S.-J.. The ubiquitous library for the blind and physically handicapped. *IFLA Journal*, 33(3):210–219, 2007.
3. Bainbridge, D., Jones, S., McIntosh, S., Jones, M. and Witten I. Running Greenstone on an ipod. *JCDL'08*, 419–419, 2008.
4. Bainbridge, D, and Witten, I. H. Greenstone digital library software: current research. *JCDL'04*, 416–416, 2004.
5. Bederson, B. Audio augmented reality: a prototype automated tour guide. *CHI '95*, 210–211, 1995.
6. Bellotti, F., Berta, R., De Gloria, A. and Margarone, M. Implementing tour guides for travelers *Hum. Factor. Ergon. Manuf.*, 15(4):461–476, 2005.
7. Buchanan, G. and Hinze, A. A generic alerting service for digital libraries. *JCDL'05*, 131–140, 2005.
8. Cheverst, K., Mitchell, K. and Davies, N. The role of adaptive hypermedia in a context-aware tourist guide. *CACM*, 45(5):47–51, 2002.
9. Chittaro, L. and Burigat, S. Augmenting audio messages with visual directions in mobile guides: an evaluation of three approaches. *MobileHCI*, 107-114, 2005.
10. Christel, M., Olligschlaeger, A.M. and Huang, C. Interactive maps for a digital video library. *IEEE MultiMedia*, 7:60–67, January 2000.
11. Don, K., Bainbridge, D. and Witten, I. H. The design of Greenstone 3: An agent based dynamic digital library, Greenstone manual, available online, 2002.
12. Evjemo, B., Akselsen S. and Schormann, A. User acceptance of digital tourist guides lessons learnt from two field studies. *HCI*, 746-755, 2005
13. Frohlich, D., Rachovides, et al. StoryBank: Mobile digital storytelling in a development context. *CHI*, 1761–1770, 2009.
14. Gao, X. A service for audio icon and audio books in the mobile tourist information system (TIP) via the greenstone digital library. Master's thesis, University of Waikato, 2007.
15. Goh, D., Sepoetro, L., Qi, M., Ramakhrisnan, R., Theng, Y.-L., Puspitasari, F. and Lim, E.-P. Mobile tagging and accessibility information sharing using a geospatial digital library. *ICADL*, 287–296, 2007.
16. Golub, K. Digital libraries and the blind and visually impaired, *CARNet Users Conference*, 25-27, 2002
17. Hatala, M., Kalantari, L., Wakkary, R. and Newby, K. Ontology and rule based retrieval of sound objects in augmented audio reality system for museum visitors. *SAC*, 1045–1050, 2004.
18. Hinze, A., Gao, X. and Bainbridge, D. The TIP/Greenstone bridge: A service for mobile location-based access to digital libraries. ECDL'06, 99–110, 2006.
19. Hinze, A., Voisard, A. and Buchanan, G. TIP: Personalizing information delivery in a tourist information system. *Journal of Information Technology and Tourism*, 11(4), 2009.
20. Holland, S., Morse, David R. and Gedenryd, Henrik. AudioGPS: Spatial Audio Navigation with a Minimal Attention Interface. *PUC*. 6, 4 253-259, 2002
21. Jones, M. and Marsden, G. *Mobile Interaction Design*, John Wiley & Sons, 2005
22. Kjeldskov, J., Skov, M.B., Als, B.S. and Høegh, R.T. Is it worth the hassle? Value of evaluating the usability of context-aware mobile systems in the field. *MobileHCI* 61–73, 2004
23. Klante, K., Krosche, J. and Boll, S. AccesSights - a multimodal location-aware mobile tourist IS *ICCHP'04*, 2004.
24. Kwak, S.-J. and Bae, K.-J. Ubiquitous library usability test for the improvement of information access for the blind. *The Electronic Library*, 27(4):623–639, 2009.
25. Marsden, G., Ladiera, I., Reitmaier, T., Bidwell, N. J. and Blake, E. Digital storytelling in Africa. *International Journal of Computing*, 9(3):257–265, 2010.
26. Pavani, A. *Making ETDs Accessible to the Visually Impaired and the Blind: a Project Under Way*. PhD thesis, The Robert Gordon University, 2010.
27. Smith A. and Crane, G. Disambiguating geographic names in a historical digital library. *ECDL*, 127–136, 2001
28. Prahallad, K. and Black, A. A text to speech interface for Universal Digital Library, *Journal of Zhejiang University SCIENCE*, vol.6A, no.11, 1229-1234, 2005
29. Petrelli, D. and Not, E. User-Centred Design of Flexible Hypermedia for a Mobile Guide. *User Modeling and User-Adapted Interaction* 15, 3-4, 303-338, 2005
30. Zimmermann, A., Lorenz, A. and Specht, M. User Modeling in Adaptive Audio-Augmented Museum Environments. *User Modeling*, 403-407, 2003.

Redeye: A Digital Library for Forensic Document Triage

Paul Logasa Bogen II, Amber McKenzie, Rob Gillen
Computational Data Analytics Group
Oak Ridge National Laboratory
Oak Ridge, TN
redev@ornl.gov

ABSTRACT

Forensic document analysis has become an important aspect of investigation of many different kinds of crimes from money laundering to fraud and from cybercrime to smuggling. The current workflow for analysts includes powerful tools, such as Palantir and Analyst's Notebook, for moving from evidence to actionable intelligence and tools for finding documents among the millions of files on a hard disk, such as Forensic Toolkit (FTK). Analysts often leave the process of sorting through collections of seized documents to filter out noise from actual evidence to highly labor-intensive manual efforts. This paper presents the Redeye Analysis Workbench, a tool to help analysts move from manual sorting of a collection of documents to performing intelligent document triage over a digital library. We will discuss the tools and techniques we build upon in addition to an in-depth discussion of our tool and how it addresses two major use cases we observed analysts performing. Finally, we also include a new layout algorithm for radial graphs that is used to visualize clusters of documents in our system.

Categories and Subject Descriptors

H.3.7 [Digital Libraries]: Collection, Systems issues. I.7.5 [Document Capture]: Document analysis.

Keywords

Redeye, Document Triage, Forensic Science

1. INTRODUCTION

In late 2011, a team of analysts at a federal law enforcement agency were facing a problem: How do you manage the deluge of documents generated by an executed search warrant in a manner that can help the analysts make sense of the information, given that the bulk of documents obtained are most likely noise? This is essentially a classic digital libraries problem of ingesting, processing, and storing documents in a manner that enables easy retrieval of documents by users. With this insight into the problem, we began work on a tool, the Redeye Analysis Workbench, which could bridge the gap in forensic tools between forensic data recovery tools, such as FTK, and case preparation tools, such as Analyst's Notebook.

The remainder of this paper is divided into seven parts. First, we will talk about the background and predecessor systems that Redeye is built from and the challenges that necessitated a new tool. This will be followed by a discussion of related work on document suggestion, document clustering, document triage, and collection management. Third, we will discuss the design of Redeye in detail followed by discussion of the problem of forensic digital libraries and document triage. Finally, we will present our conclusions and areas of future work.

JCDL'13, July 22–26, 2013, Indianapolis, Indiana, USA.

2. BACKGROUND

Previously, the ICR has produced three general-purpose tools – Piranha, Raptor and Distribute The Highest Selected Textual Recommendation (DTHSTR) – for filtering a collection of documents down to relevant ones. Our work on the Redeye Analysis Workbench is largely inspired by adapting and packaging these tools in concert with existing open source text and forensic tools into a single workbench for forensic science document triage tasks. This section will briefly discuss each of these tools.

2.1 Piranha

Piranha was motivated by the need to address the challenges most people face when sifting through a large amount of data for accurate and relevant information [1]. The approach the ICR team took to address this was to create software that can quickly filter, relate, and show documents and relationships based on textual similarity to them.

The result of this work is the ICR's software agent approach to text analysis using a large number of agents distributed over very large computer clusters. This approach combined with the ICR's corpus-based term weighting scheme (TF-ICF) [2] allows Piranha to achieve high performance requirements faced with large data sets.

Piranha provides two primary functions: finding similar documents and document sampling. Finding similar documents allows a user to select a document of interest and then quickly find other documents that are a close match to it. For example, you may have an e-mail message of interest and want to find other similar e-mails in your collection; Piranha provides a visualization based on textual similarity that allows quick determination of those similar documents. Second, document sampling takes advantage of the common themes and topics often found over a coherent set of documents. Since a set of documents will usually contain common themes or topics, we can quickly identify a smaller number of representative documents from the set and return those documents to the analyst for review.

2.2 Raptor and DTHSTR

The other predecessor systems to the Redeye Analysis Workbench are Raptor and DTHSTR. They are knowledge-sharing tools that leverages the DTHSTR techniques in semi-supervised machine learning and unsupervised text analytics to enhance and motivate sharing [3]. They accomplish this by providing an increased benefit of sharing personal documents through helping a user retrieve relevant documents from the collection. This is accomplished by using information provided by the user to build a profile of what they are interested in, which is then used to match documents from the repository.

3. RELATED WORK

Beyond the prior systems the Redeye Analysis Workbench has descended from, there is a variety of work that we have drawn from for inspiration and direction. In general these works fall in to two categories: document triage and digital forensics.

3.1 Document Triage

Document triage was originally coined by Bae *et al.'s* 2005 work on the subject [4]. In this work, the authors drew on their prior work in an area known as information triage. While information triage focused on the sorting and assessing of information in documents [5], document triage focuses on the evaluation of "the merit and disposition" of the document itself [4]. This transition from supporting work on the information level to the entire document level was motivated by results found in Shipman *et al.*'s 2004 study on personal collections in spatial hypertext where the authors noticed that users were often not just organizing information inside the VKB spatial hypertext tool, but they were often organizing documents themselves [6]. This has led to further work that seeks to automatically organize documents in a spatial hypertext system based on the inferred interests and the characteristics of the documents with which users interact [7].

While document triage was born out of work on spatial hypertext, the concept of evaluating merit and disposition to aid in sorting and assessing of documents is not limited to this area. Buchanan and Owen approached the problem of skim reading as a document triage problem [8] by identifying relevant information in the document and giving it a more pronounced presentation in a page's thumbnail. Similarly document triage has also been applied to evaluating work on both large displays [4] and small displays [9].

Recently, Gary Cantrell *et al.* have taken the concept of document triage and brought it into the realm of digital forensics [10]. While prior work had mainly focused on the interfaces for document triage [7] and processes of organizing documents [11], Cantrell *et al.* primarily focuses on modeling the entire triage process formally [10]. Their formal model includes seven stages.

First is planning and readiness which is focused on training of forensic staff in tools and techniques. The second is the live forensics phase which encompasses making available information from a target machine whether that is on an encrypted disk, in volatile memory or just hidden in some obscure folder in the file system, and includes work on hardware write-lockers as well as software tools we will discuss in the next section. The third phase is the computer profile. This is the phase the authors identify as being poorly supported. In this phase, files are actually copied off and information about the imaged machine is stored. At this point, Cantrell *et al.* suggest a triage should occur to reduce the number of noise documents that go on to later stages. The fourth stage is the crime potential phase, in which the analyst applies their domain knowledge on a case to build a story from the data. Next, this story is presented in the fifth phase. This presentation then is used to further analyze the information in stage six, the triage examination phase. Finally, the seventh stage is the preservation stage, where evidence is formally collected along with analysis in a manner that ensures the chain of evidence is maintained.

While tools currently exist for many of these stages, which will be discussed in the following section, the computer profile and crime potential phases are lacking dedicated tools. At these stages we see an opportunity for document triage with a focus on helping an analyst make sense out of documents they have already processed through the first two stages.

3.2 Analysis Tools and Digital Forensics

Because detailing the breadth of analysis and digital forensics applications is out of the scope of this paper, we will focus on two of the more common technologies available – Palantir and Analyst's Notebook – and also look at the area of digital archiving in which digital forensics tools are being implemented.

Arguably one of the frontrunners in digital forensics applications is the Palantir platform, targeted at enabling analysts to discover relevant information within large, heterogeneous data sets [12]. Palantir comprises three parts: a data platform, an application platform and a computer platform. The data platform is geared toward ingesting both structured and unstructured data for use during the analysis process. The application platform is designed to incorporate a number of data analysis and visualization tools with an API that allows developers to create their own applications or tools within Palantir. Implementing a MapReduce framework, the Palantir Compute Platform facilitates running Palantir applications using HPC clusters to ensure that the computationally-heavy text analysis can be accomplished without lengthy lag times. The focus of the Palantir architecture is openness and flexibility, allowing the design and development of custom applications using the provided framework, but lacks sufficient support at the data ingestion stage for adapting unstructured data for optimal utilization during analysis.

One of the more widely used platforms among Department of Defense organizations, IBM's Analyst's Notebook highlights four aspects of its platform: data acquisition, data modeling, analytic capabilities and communication of complex data [13]. Analyst's Notebook's flexible data acquisition capabilities involve drag and drop functionality, volume structured data importing, and integration with other IBM analytical products [14]. The built-in flexible data model minimizes constraints on the representation of complex relational data in order to facilitate analysis and visualization.

These applications and platforms suffer from the same limitation in that they all assume that the input data is all relevant and useful. This relies on the analyst to expend the effort needed to determine which data to input or else risk inundating the system with superfluous data that the analysts have no interest in examining.

Taking a different approach, a separate body of research has aimed at utilizing techniques and applications from digital forensics for improving digital media archival ingest and preservation workflows. J. John targets the use of existing technologies in his approach to the capture, preservation and access of personal digital archives [15]. Computer forensics applications are one of three categories of applications that he investigates, due to the area's overlapping requirements of evidence preservation and analysis repeatability. He notes that no single forensics product meets all the requirements of a forensic analyst resulting in the number of competing products available. He also notes two limitations of computer forensics

technologies: (1) the limited applicability of these applications to legacy or obsolete systems and media and (2) the inability for these technologies to recreate the initial state and layout of the data.

4. USE CASES

As shown in our related work, there is a gap in the workflow of forensic document analysts between their document recovery and cataloging tools and their analysis tools. Currently this gap is filled with extensive manpower that manually filters the uninteresting from interesting documents for further analysis. This is where document triage work has the potential to improve the workflow of analysts. This section will discuss two use cases we observed and how a document triage system improves that workflow.

4.1 Actor Search

In the sponsor's previous workflow, a major portion of an analyst's time was spent manually searching through documents for information about entities and actors. This information could be geographical data, names, or contact information. This information was then collated to identify aliases and assemble profiles of the actors involved in the case. The process as it previously stood is described with the following narrative:

Julius and Dan are analysts working for a federal law enforcement agency. They are currently working on a case with suspected money laundering aspects. In order to pursue this case, the agency has obtained a warrant and conducted a search of the homes and offices of a suspected money launderer. This search yielded tens of thousands of documents both scanned from paper originals and retrieved using FTK from hard disk images taken during the search. These documents are then indexed into a database that allows users to browse through the files one at a time. Julius and Dan divide the set of documents between them and then begin to look through each one. If Microsoft Office or other pre-installed software cannot open a document, the file is passed by. If a document is not in English, they determine based on appearance if it is important enough to send to a translator. Scanned documents are simple TIF files in which the text cannot be searched once opened. As relevant material is found, the locations of the original files on the disk image are kept track of so the files can later be copied into a folder for import into Analyst's Notebook where further analysis can then occur.

As the narrative shows, the analyst's job was fraught with manual tasks that could be automated. By contrast, the following narrative shows the workflow we imagined when using Redeye.

Julius and Dan have now moved to using Redeye as a document triage tool. When documents are acquired under a warrant, the Redeye Ingestion tool is directed to their location and begins to process the documents. Instead of splitting the documents amongst themselves and looking at all of them, Julius and Dan now interact with the collection via search looking by relevant names, places, or other keywords. Relevant documents are saved in a sub-collection that can later be exported with one click and are ready for import into Analyst's Notebook. Scanned documents are also now searchable due to the integration of Optical Character Recognition in the ingestion pipeline. If foreign language documents are found, the system provides a rough machine translation that informs the analysts if they should send it to a linguist. Tasks that took Julius and Dan longer than a year can now be accomplished in weeks or days. Comments can now be stored on documents allowing Julius and Dan to easily see each other's insights when documents are re-examined.

Using Redeye, the analyst's work has become markedly more efficient and interactions between analysts occur with greater frequency. In general, Redeye has altered the nature of their work from sifting through documents to searching for entities. Analysts are now free to ask more questions and revisit documents. Additionally, since searching can be performed across cases, they can build links between cases – something that was difficult-to-impossible previously.

4.2 Term Matching

The second observed activity in the prior workflow was spent on term matching. The term matching task involves manually scanning through documents looking for relevant keywords from a list of terms. Unlike searching, the goal is not to find one, all or none but to find documents that match several critical phrases. This process is used to filter the potentially relevant documents out. This process can be imagined with the following narrative:

Julius and Dan are provided a several page list of important terms for the case at hand from a forensic accountant. The list includes terms that may indicate money laundering divided by categories as well as names, organizations, and locations of interest. None of the terms by themselves are indicative nor is the full, multi-page list of terms likely to be found in a single document. Instead Julius and Dan browse through documents looking for documents that contain several of the phrases. The location of these documents is recorded and later the documents are copied off to a folder for further analysis in Analyst's Notebook. Due to the inherent poorly defined nature of the human task of determining what a sufficient number of terms is, the process is not easily reproducible nor is it comprehensive as it relies on the Julius and Dan not overlooking particular documents or missing terms in a document.

Much like the previous search case, the term matching case is fraught with automatable processes. The use case we envisioned for automating this process draws from the prior work on Raptor.

Julius and Dan are provided a list of key terms in categories from a forensic accountant; however instead of manually looking through documents for these terms, Julius and Dan divide the list by category and load their term sets into the Redeye Analysis Workbench. After several minutes of waiting, the Workbench produces a set of result lists each corresponding to a category of terms. The documents in the set are ordered according to the similarity of the document to the terms in the category it matched against.

By providing these analytical tools to help filter down a large noisy set of documents to a more manageable size, we enable analysts to more quickly triage documents in to sets that are relevant to the case and that are not. Thus, we believe that we have helped bridge the gap between the document acquisition phase and the evidence-reporting phase.

5. SYSTEM DESIGN

Redeye is a combination of three major components: an ingestion pipeline, an Apache SOLR repository [16], and an Eclipse RCP-based [16] user tool. Each component will be covered in this section.

5.1 Ingestion

Each case processed presents different needs and interests. This leads to a design wherein the ingestion process is broken up into a series of steps that can be arranged via a pipeline to match the specific requirements of each case. This pipeline is loosely coupled and backed by a temporary state management store implemented using MongoDB [17]. The objectives of the ingestion process are to extract all of the relevant metadata from files as well as perform pre-processing to aid in performance during the analysis stages. Once this process is complete, the analysis tools do not need to interact with the original files other than to display them if requested.

Some examples of the pipeline steps include: tree building, text extraction, entity extraction, metadata extraction, duplicate file consolidation, compressed file extraction, machine translation, tokenization, and population into SOLR. With the exception of tree building, which is a recursive crawl of the raw data that builds the initial tree structure in the state management store, the majority of the stages can be ordered, included/excluded, re-run, etc. as desired. The pipeline is exposed via a simple graphical user interface that serves as a harness by which the analyst can control which stages are run, in what order, and how many times.

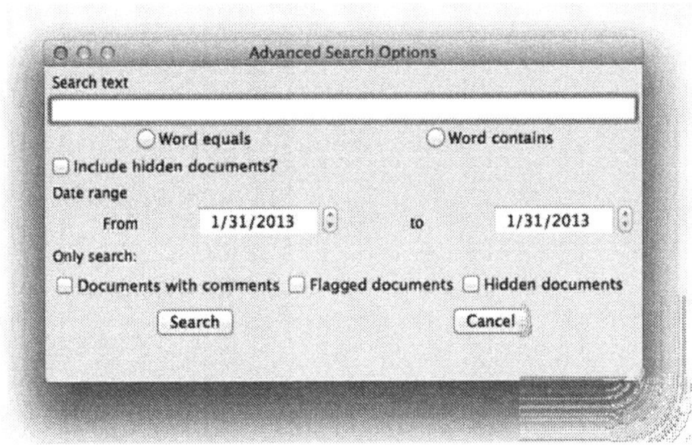

While most of the stages mentioned are self-explanatory, the text extraction stage warrants some additional detail. Previous "home grown" iterations of the toolset utilized either custom text extraction techniques or a combination of open source text extraction libraries such as Apache's POI project [18]. While these approaches had some success, our results were disappointing when faced with the variety of the datasets our sponsor needed to process. Eventually, we elected to utilize the Microsoft IFilter plugin system that is part of the Windows Desktop Search platform [19]. The IFilter system provides a single API to interface with a wide range of file formats, providing a simple way to create format agnostic text and metadata extraction tools. While the experience has not been free of problems, the number of documents that fail extraction has dropped significantly (failure rates average less than 2% of supported files as compared to 30% with our prior infrastructure). Additionally, the number of file types from which we are able to extract text is far greater than our previous tool sets.

5.2 Repository

Apache SOLR, a full text search server built on the Apache Lucene search engine [20], is used as a repository and index for ingested data. This collection of data is then made available for searching from within the workbench.

SOLR provides a myriad of possible options and customizations to produce a full-fledged search application. For the Redeye Workbench, extracted textual content and metadata is indexed for each ingested document and made available to be searched by the user. SOLR also maintains information on comments made by analysts and whether documents are flagged or hidden. SOLR's facetted search capabilities are employed to allow the user to make more detailed searches on select portions of the collection. Another SOLR feature, integrated within the workbench, is the terms component, which provides a list of the top terms within the data set along with their frequency. The terms component is utilized to implement the autosuggest feature that takes the characters typed into the search bar and provides a drop down box with suggested completions. Through SOLR's multicore option, the data set is broken up into different cores. This allows us to scale SOLR horizontally as the collection of documents grows. An empty core with a merged schema solves the problem of searching across a number of cores with different properties.

5.3 Workbench

The workbench represents the user interface for analysts in Redeye. It is built in the Eclipse RCP framework [16] around three major tasks. Each task is supported with a perspective containing one or more views. The three tasks as mentioned in section four are search, advisor, and analysis. Search and Advisor each have a single view, while analysis has three views: List View, Graph Visualization, and Detail View. Each of the three analysis views represents an alternative way of looking at relevant documents identified in the search and advisor perspectives.

5.3.1 General Features

Throughout the various views in the Redeye Analysis Workbench, there are a number of common panes that can be seen in the screenshots. These include the Data Sets view, Scratch Pad, and the console view. Data Sets is the staging ground between the pre-triage search stage and the main triage stage. Data sets contain a list of each set of documents for further examination. These sets can be generated from either the search view or the advisor view. The scratch pad is a place for the analyst to organize the results of interest to be exported out of the Redeye tool for import into an analysis tool like Analyst's Toolkit. Finally, the console view provides a detailed look in to the background processes of the system and provides status updates for long-running processes. Additionally debugging information for reporting errors to the development team are also displayed in the console view.

5.3.2 Search View

The initial view a user interacts with allows a traditional search of the data. The search interface can be seen in Figure 1. The view represents an initial pre-triage stage where an analyst can select which documents are relevant for further analysis using the summary of the document. Searches can be as simple as a list of optional terms or complex with Boolean logic and constraints on fields to search.

We also support filtering of results based on facets. These facets are drawn from a variety of metadata associated with documents such as file type and document collection.

In addition to the standard search interface, we also provide an advanced search dialog that allows additional complex querying to be performed simply. Options in the advanced search dialog include searching by date range, searching for hidden documents, either exclusively or inclusively, with unhidden results, and searching for documents that are flagged or have comments attached to them. A screenshot showing the use of the advanced search dialog can be seen in Figure 2.

Once documents are retrieved, we support two different mechanisms for saving them to a document set. First a user can select the save button which either saves all checked documents or prompts the user for a number of documents to save in order of the documents relevance to the search query. Alternatively, documents can be dragged to either the scratch pad or the data sets view

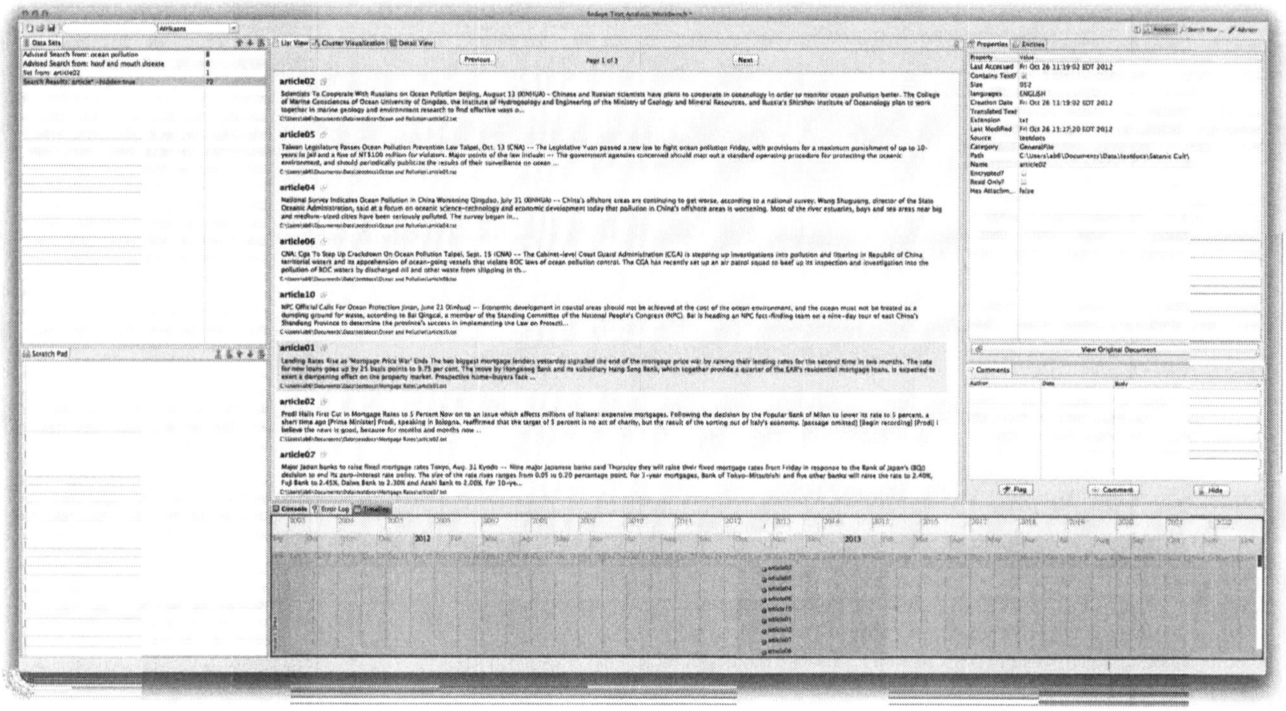

5.3.3 Advisor View

In addition to the search view, the Redeye tool also provides the advisor view. The advisor view (Figure 3) is the implementation of the Raptor and the DTHSTR techniques as mentioned in our prior work.

The advisor view provides a large text entry box that can be populated by the user through direct entry, copy and pasting from another application or by loading a text file already on the user's machine. The user can then control the number of documents returned per set with a slider from 1 to the number of coarse-selected documents. This number of coarse selected documents is adjustable in the system properties but is considered an advanced feature that most users would not normally use.

Finally the user can push the build result sets button and the system begins processing the term list and comparing the terms to documents in the SOLR repository. The process, which the advisor performs, is described as follows: first, the input is split on empty lines to form sets of category documents. The first line in each category becomes the title of the category and the remaining lines become individual terms. Using a predefined threshold the terms to be searched are evaluated on their discriminatory value and are either kept or trimmed from the search. Using these trimmed terms, the solr repository is searched for all documents that match one or more terms. The results are ranked by textual similarity to the search terms and the top documents up to a certain number – the coarse selection number set in the system preferences – are kept. Second, for each document retrieved by the coarse filter, the TF-ICF weighted term vector is compared to the TF-ICF weight term vector of the category using a standard cosine similarity metric. This provides a ranking of documents that is cut off after a certain number of documents – the fine selection number set by the slider. Each of the resulting document sets are then saved to data sets for further analysis in the system.

5.3.4 List View

Once pre-triage filtering has been conducted either using the search or the advisor views, the user can then switch to the list view. The list view, as shown in Figure 4, consists of five major components: the list, properties, entities, comments, and the timeline.

The list shows the main information about documents in the selected document set. In order to simplify the information presented the list is paginated into sets of a user specified size. Each document shown has a title, a number of status indicators, a snippet from the content of the document and the path to the original document. The status indicators help show various information about the document. These indicators are whether the original document is available, if the document has been flagged as important, if there are any comments about the document and, if hidden documents are set to be shown, if the document has been hidden.

Once a document is selected a number of views are populated with information about that document. The first of them is the properties view. The properties view shows metadata extracted about the file itself such as when it was created, if it has text, and if it was encrypted. If the file is an email, properties from the email header are displayed in addition to properties about the file itself. These include subject, sender, recipient, and date sent.

The entities view, in contrast to the properties view, shows metadata about the document instead of the file. This is currently restricted to entities extracted during ingestion using a number of regular expressions. Entities include phone numbers, and email addresses among others.

The last view is the timeline view. The timeline view is a customized instance of the SIMILE JavaScript timeline inside an embedded web browser [21]. The timeline is hosted via an embedded instance of the Jetty web server. Additionally two J2EE web services provide both the JSON dataset to populate

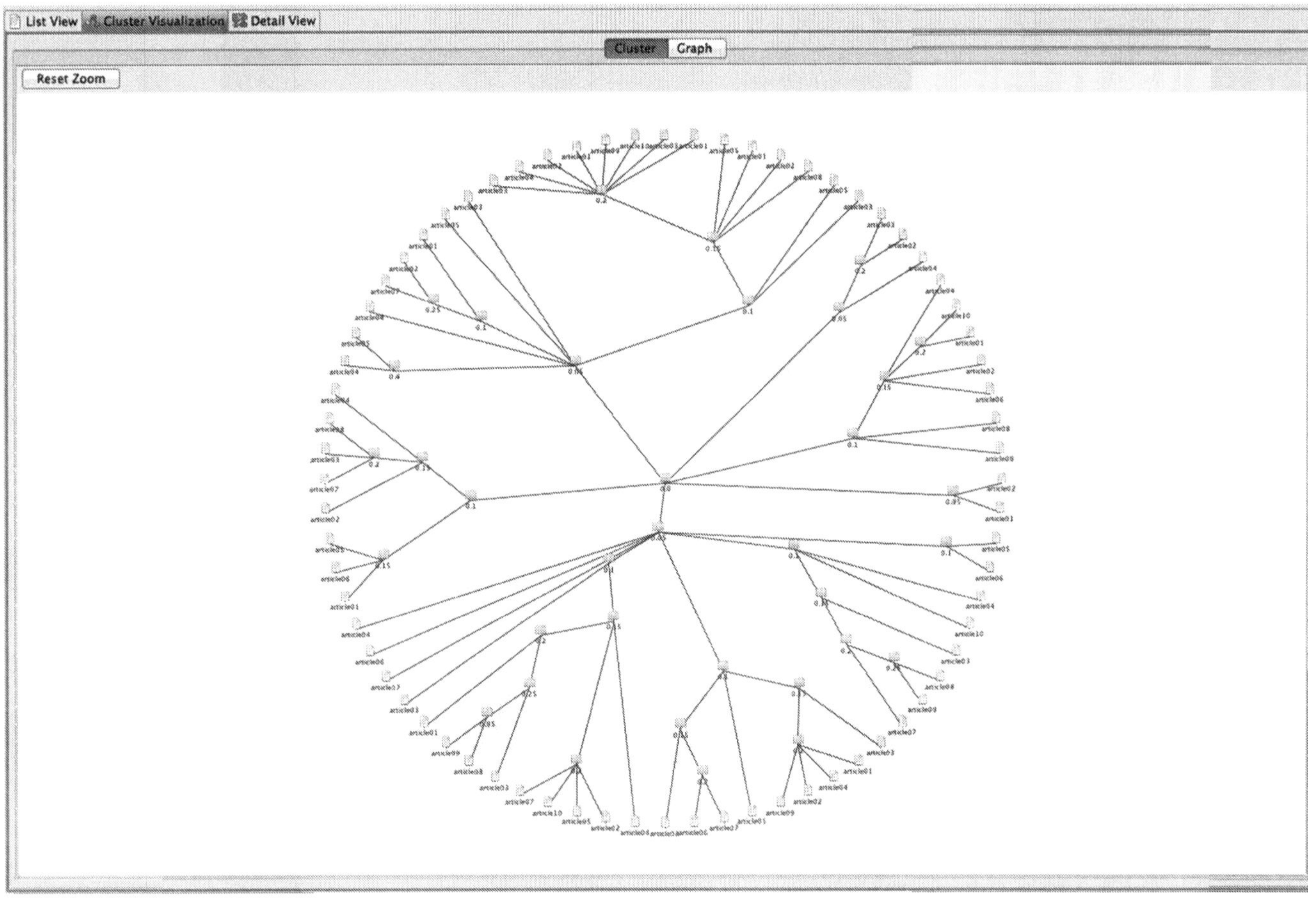

the timeline and a callback feature to feed information about document selection from the timeline back into the Redeye Workbench.

In addition to this view of the data, we also provide two additional views. One for viewing clusters of documents, and another for delving into the terms and entities in detail. Next we will discuss the cluster visualization and then the detail view.

5.3.5 Cluster Visualization

One of the major features of one of the predecessor tools of the Redeye Workbench, Piranha, is a hierarchical clustering of pages best on top terms and phrases with-in the document [1]. This was presented as a radial graph. This same technique has been adapted into Redeye along with a new implementation of the cluster visualization. Unlike the visualization in Piranha, the Redeye tool allows smooth zooming and panning without pauses between actions. This allows a more natural investigation of the graph [22]. Analysts, as part of their training, must verify the importance of every document to a case. Traditionally this meant wading individually through millions of documents for a few relevant ones. The cluster visualization allows the analyst to still look at each one but in a more intelligent manner. Instead of looking at each document in depth, they can first look at the clusters to triage which sets of documents are more likely to contain pertinent information. This enables the analyst to not only prioritize their search for relevant information, but allows them a means, by viewing the top terms of a document or a cluster, to more rapidly perform an exhaustive search as the top terms help inform the analyst of how extensive they need to review documents in a cluster. An example of this view can be seen in Figure 5.

We have devised a novel graph layout algorithm around the desired properties of the graph. The properties we wish to guarantee are all documents nodes are on the same radius of the graph and that the root of the tree is located in the center. Additionally we sought to minimize label overlap and edge length without relying on a dynamic layout algorithm, such as force atlas [23]. Our solution is to flip the problem of laying out a graph upside down and layout the leaves first and then walk up the tree. This differs from other layouts that start from the root and work their way down to the leaves [24].

In order to perform this, we first need to know the leaves in order of their height. This is performed by first walking the tree using a post-order traversal and storing each node in to a stack.

After this is complete, we iterated through the stack setting the height of each node to either zero or the maximum height of the node's children plus one. These height labeled nodes are placed on to another stack that is then iterated through to calculate the angle of the node on its level.

If a node has no children, the angle of the node is equal to the following:

$$\theta = \frac{2\pi}{n} i - \pi \frac{h}{2H}$$

where n is the number of leaf nodes, i is the count of leaf nodes already laid out, h is the height of the current node, and H is the maximum height of all nodes. If a node does have children, the angle is equal to the average angle of its children.

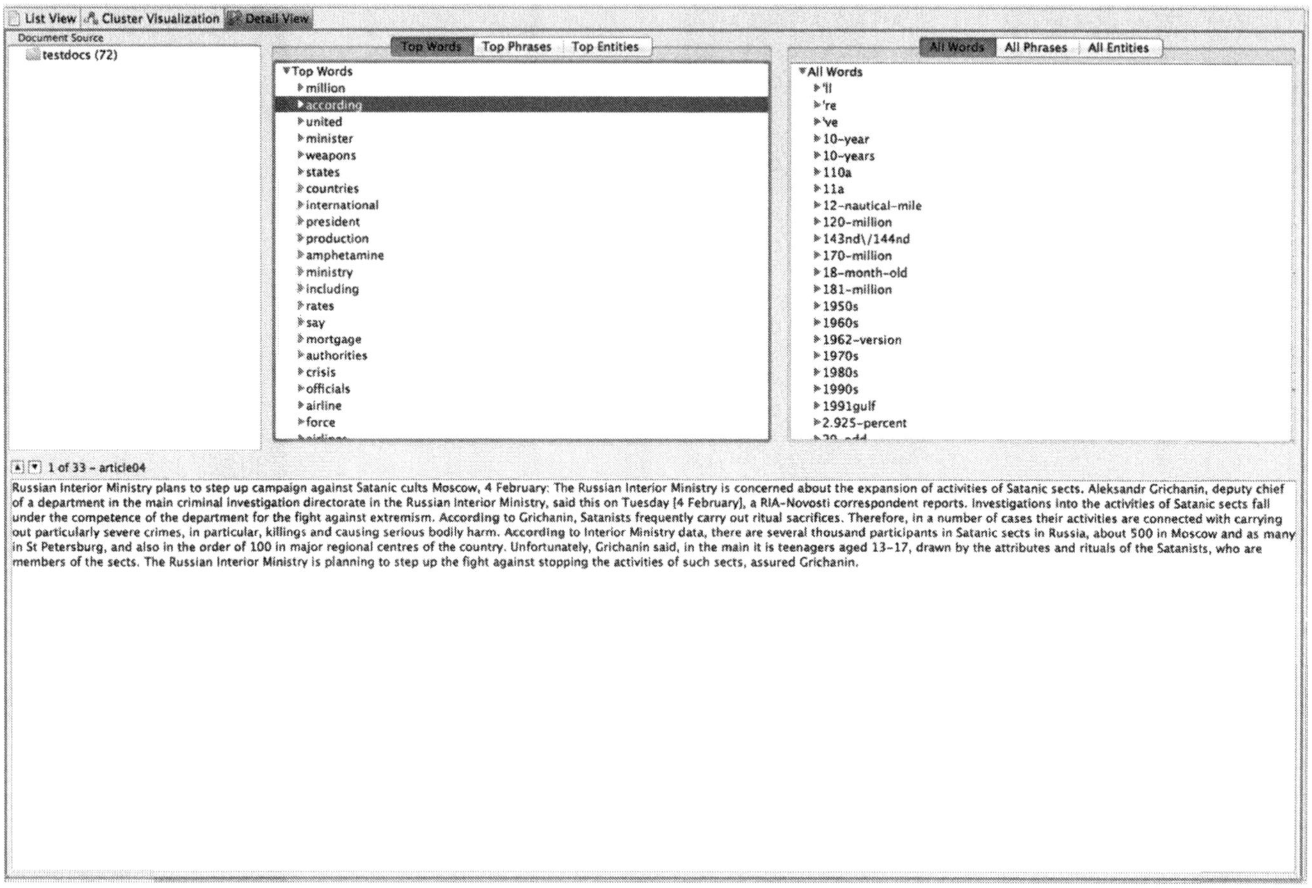

Finally, we calculate a radius for each node in the graph. The formula of the radius is the following:

$$r = \frac{d}{H} \mathrm{B}(\alpha, \beta, h)$$

where d is the maximum distance in pixels that a node can be from the center of the graph, $\mathrm{B}(\alpha, \beta, h)$ is the beta value at h with tuning parameters α and β [25]. We have experimentally determined satisfactory values of $\alpha = 1$ and $\beta = 2$.

Once we have obtained a (r, θ) value for each node, we use standard trigonometric formulas to convert to an (x, y) position in the window.

Interactions with the graph view are fully integrated into the workbench. Selected documents are highlighted in red and mousing over a node changes the selection. Double clicking on a node opens the original document in an external viewer.

5.3.6 Detail View

The final view in the Redeye Analysis Workbench is the detail view. This view flips the notion of documents with terms upside down and instead presents terms, phrases, and entities with the documents that contain them. This view, like the cluster visualization, was inherited in part from Piranha [1]. The view in Redeye has been refined and focused to present only information the analysts deemed useful upon evaluating Piranha for their needs.

The view consists of four main areas: document source, "Top" tabs, "All" tabs, and the document display. The document source contains a list of the various collections the current document set has documents from. This allows the detail view to be restricted to results from a particular collection.

The "Top" and "All" tabs are similar in that they consist of three tabs, each of which is dedicated to words, phrases, or entities. The primary difference between the two is that "Top" only displays the top 50 of each in order of importance in the collection measured by a TF-ICF weighted term count while "All" displays every word/phrase/entity in alphanumeric order.

The document display is populated based on the current selection in the two tab groups. By selecting a term/phrase/entity, all documents of that contain that term/phrase/entity can be browsed using the up and down arrows above the document display. If a single document is selected, as Figure 6 shows, then just that single document is available in the document display. Lastly, the term/phrase/entity that the document is being viewed as part of is highlighted in the document to allow the analyst to quickly find the context in which the term is contained.

6. CONCLUSIONS

The gap in the forensic pipeline between file collection and the analysis of actionable intelligence provides a challenge in terms of manpower, time to completion and completeness of analysis. In order to bridge this gap, we identified two primary use cases that are currently fully manual operations – actor searching and term matching – and designed the Redeye Analysis Workbench to automate the analyst's time-consuming tasks. Our solution has been deployed to our sponsor and is currently being used in active investigations. The response to our tool has been highly positive and we are currently evaluating further use cases in which we would be able to extend Redeye to help reduce the demands of document pre-processing on the analyst. We are currently considering four possible areas of future work.

Our sponsor has indicated a strong interest in semi-automatic generation of social network graphs from documents. This area of work would extend on existing work on social network extraction to help provide a visual and analyst-updatable representation of the graph of actors involved in an investigation.

Another area is in the area of alias resolution. With the kinds of cases the sponsor deals in, individuals may be using several alternate names, companies may have various shell names, and both use more than one email address, phone number or mailing address. By analyzing clues in documents, the analysts currently resolve several virtual identities in-to one physical identity or organization. Providing tools and techniques to speed the process could provide a significant speed up in the analysis of documents involved in a case.

Furthermore, there may be value in investigating visualization of the document collection in bulk. This kind of visualization could help analysts rapidly narrow down documents of interest or potentially allow them to spot abnormal documents in a collection that may contain important facts about a case.

Finally, we'd like to apply more advanced named entity extraction techniques to help identify actors, locations, addresses and other important pieces of information contained in documents. Due to the changing domain of cases and the often highly technical nature of the domains, traditional corpus-based named entity recognition (NER) techniques may not prove adequate to provide sufficiently high levels of performance on multiple cases. Instead, we are looking in to developing novel semi-supervised and unsupervised techniques of NER in order to address these concerns in dealing with technical cross-domain collections for NER.

In conclusion, we have identified a need for support in forensic document analysis, examined an existing workflow in use by a law enforcement agency and singled out two use cases where computer support could improve their workflow, and designed a digital-library-inspired tool for managing their document collections. We have shown that a digital libraries approach to forensic document analysis meets the analysts' need and provided a direction for further work in this area.

7. ACKNOWLEDGEMENTS

This document was prepared by Oak Ridge National Laboratory, P.O. Box 2008, Oak Ridge, Tennessee 37831-6285; managed by UT-Battelle, LLC, for the US Department of Energy under contract number DE-AC05-00OR22725.

This manuscript has been authored by UT-Battelle, LLC, under contract DE-AC05-00OR22725 with the U.S. Department of Energy. The United States Government retains and the publisher, by accepting the article for publication, acknowledges that the United States Government retains a non-exclusive, paid-up, irrevocable, world-wide license to publish or reproduce the published form of this manuscript, or allow others to do so, for United States Government purposes.

8. REFERENCES

[1] J. W. Reed, T. E. Potok, and R. M. Patton, "A multi-agent system for distributed cluster analysis," in *Proceedings of Third International Workshop on Software Engineering for Large-Scale Multi-Agent Systems (SELMAS'04) Workshop in conjunction with the 26th International Conference on Software Engineering Edinburgh, Scotland, UK: IEE*, 2004, pp. 152-5.

[2] J. W. Reed, Y. Jiao, T. E. Potok, B. A. Klump, M. T. Elmore, and A. R. Hurson, "TF-ICF: A new term weighting scheme for clustering dynamic data streams," in *Machine Learning and Applications, 2006. ICMLA'06. 5th International Conference on*, 2006, pp. 258-263.

[3] R. M. Patton, W. McNair, C. T. Symons, J. N. Treadwell, and T. E. Potok, "A Text Analysis Approach to Motivate Knowledge Sharing via Microsoft SharePoint," in *System Science (HICSS), 2012 45th Hawaii International Conference on*, 2012, pp. 3670-3678.

[4] S. Bae, R. Badi, K. Meintanis, J. Moore, A. Zacchi, H. Hsieh, C. Marshall, and F. Shipman, "Effects of display configurations on document triage," *Human-Computer Interaction-INTERACT 2005,* pp. 130-143, 2005.

[5] C. C. Marshall and F. M. Shipman III, "Spatial hypertext and the practice of information triage," in *Proceedings of the eighth ACM conference on Hypertext*, 1997, pp. 124-133.

[6] F. M. Shipman, H. Hsieh, J. M. Moore, and A. Zacchi, "Supporting personal collections across digital libraries in spatial hypertext," in *Proceedings of the 4th ACM/IEEE-CS joint conference on Digital libraries*, 2004, pp. 358-367.

[7] S. Bae, D. H. Kim, K. Meintanis, J. M. Moore, A. Zacchi, F. Shipman, H. Hsieh, and C. C. Marshall, "Supporting document triage via annotation-based multi-application visualizations," in *Proceedings of the 10th annual joint conference on Digital libraries*, 2010, pp. 177-186.

[8] G. Buchanan and T. Owen, "Improving skim reading for document triage," in *Proceedings of the second international symposium on Information interaction in context*, 2008, pp. 83-88.

[9] F. Loizides and G. R. Buchanan, "Performing document triage on small screen devices. part 1: structured documents," in *Proceedings of the third symposium on Information interaction in context*, 2010, pp. 341-346.

[10] G. Cantrell, D. Dampier, Y. S. Dandass, N. Niu, and C. Bogen, "Research toward a Partially-Automated, and Crime Specific Digital Triage Process Model," *Computer and Information Science,* vol. 5, p. p29, 2012.

[11] G. Buchanan, "Rapid document navigation for information triage support," in *Proceedings of the 7th ACM/IEEE-CS joint conference on Digital libraries*, 2007, pp. 503-503.

[12] J. Payne, J. Solomon, R. Sankar, and B. McGrew, "Grand challenge award: Interactive visual analytics palantir: The future of analysis," in *Visual Analytics Science and Technology, 2008. VAST '08. IEEE Symposium on*, 2008, pp. 201-202.

[13] IBM Corporation. (2012). *IBM i2 Analyst's Notebook datasheet.* Available: http://public.dhe.ibm.com/common/ssi/ecm/en/zzd03127usen/ZZD03127USEN.PDF

[14] i2 Limited, "i2 Analyst's Notebook 8: product overview.," i2 Limited 2009.

[15] J. L. John, "Adapting existing technologies for digitally archiving personal lives," *iPRES 2008,* p. 48, 2008.

[16] D. Rubel, "The heart of eclipse," *Queue,* vol. 4, pp. 36-44, 2006.

[17] 10gen Incorporated. (2013). *mongoDB*. Available: http://www.mongodb.org/

[18] Apache Software Foundation. (2012). *Apache POI - the Java API for Microsoft Documents.* Available: http://poi.apache.org

[19] Microsoft Corporation. (2012). *IFilter interface.* Available: http://msdn.microsoft.com/en-us/library/ms691105(v=vs.85).aspx

[20] Apache Software Foundation. (2012). *Apache Solr.* Available: http://lucene.apache.org/solr/

[21] Massachusetts Institute of Technology. (2009). *SIMILE Widgets Timeline*. Available: http://www.simile-widgets.org/timeline/

[22] I. Herman, G. Melançon, and M. S. Marshall, "Graph visualization and navigation in information visualization: A survey," *Visualization and Computer Graphics, IEEE Transactions on,* vol. 6, pp. 24-43, 2000.

[23] M. Bastian, S. Heymann, and M. Jacomy, *Gephi: An Open Source Software for Exploring and Manipulating Networks*, 2009.

[24] G. M. Draper, Y. Livnat, and R. F. Riesenfeld, "A survey of radial methods for information visualization," *Visualization and Computer Graphics, IEEE Transactions on,* vol. 15, pp. 759-776, 2009.

[25] K. Pearson, "Mathematical Contributions to the Theory of Evolution. XIX. Second Supplement to a Memoir on Skew Variation," *Philosophical Transactions of the Royal Society of London. Series A, Containing Papers of a Mathematical or Physical Character,* vol. 216, pp. 429-457, January 1, 1916 1916.

Local Histories in Global Digital Libraries: Identifying Demand and Evaluating Coverage

Katrina Fenlon
Graduate School of Library and Information Science
University of Illinois at Urbana-Champaign
501 E. Daniel St.
Champaign, IL 61820
Kfenlon2@illinois.edu

Virgil E. Varvel Jr.
Graduate School of Library and Information Science
University of Illinois at Urbana-Champaign
501 E. Daniel St.
Champaign, IL 61820
Vvarvel@illinois.edu

ABSTRACT
Digital collections of primary source materials have potential to change how citizen historians and scholars research and engage with local history. The problem at the heart of this study is how to evaluate local history coverage, particularly among large-scale, distributed collections and aggregations. As part of an effort to holistically evaluate one such national aggregation, the Institute of Museum and Library Services (IMLS) Digital Collections and Content (DCC), we conducted a national survey of reference service providers at academic and public libraries throughout the United States. In this paper, we report the results of this survey that appear relevant to local history and collection evaluation, and consider the implications for scalable evaluation of local history coverage in massive, aggregative digital libraries.

Categories and Subject Descriptors
H.3.7 [**Information Storage and Retrieval**]: Digital Libraries – *collection, user issues, dissemination.*

Keywords
Local history, collections, metadata, aggregations, evaluation

1. INTRODUCTION
Digital collections of primary source materials have potential to change how citizen historians and scholars research and engage with local history [14]. State libraries and national aggregations have rushed to realize this potential, by bringing together and exposing previously isolated, local collections on the Web.

Intensive digitization programs have targeted local, special collections at public libraries. State libraries have cooperated to build state- or region-centric databases. National and international aggregations, including the Digital Public Library of America (DPLA, http://dp.la/) and Europeana (http://europeanalocal.eu/), seek to capitalize on these efforts by integrating local historical materials from different places with one another. How successful these efforts are, from varying perspectives, is unclear. How can we evaluate the success of such collections in order to guide future digital library development?

The problem at the heart of this study is how to evaluate local history coverage, particularly among large-scale, distributed collections and aggregations. As part of an effort to holistically evaluate one such national aggregation, the IMLS DCC (http://imlsdcc.grainger.illinois.edu/), we conducted a national survey of reference service providers at academic and public libraries throughout the United States. In this paper, we report select results of this survey that are relevant to local history and collection evaluation. The full survey results are in a forthcoming report [2]. In brief, regardless of whether their library was small or large, public or academic, respondents to our survey expressed great zeal for local history above all other topics, for improved local history coverage, and for improved geographic browsing facilities.

In our discussion of survey results, we consider how to begin meeting local history demand through curatorial approaches to collection and aggregation development. We suggest that curatorial development to meet a specific demand, like that evident for local history, must be guided by collection evaluations. We describe challenges to evaluating and leveraging local history, which present ripe opportunities for future research.

2. BACKGROUND
2.1 Local History and Users
Local history is known to be popular among library users in both public and academic settings, as it occupies "a borderland between knowledge that is personal...and knowledge that is generalizable and therefore worthy of scientific attention" [14]. It has therefore engendered much attention in the collection development literature, especially for public libraries [12,13]. Recent work explores infrastructures for local history and digital collection development [7,14,17]. However, the literature is weaker on specific development and evaluation methods for digital libraries or aggregations of collections. While the general public, from students to citizen historians to genealogists, are presumed to be the primary audience for local history, scholarly historians have an increasingly recognized stake in the discoverability and accessibility of digital heritage materials. Historians are known to use websites of repositories and other electronic means to locate primary materials for research [15], and scholars have been shown to gather together digitized primary sources into thematic research collections for intensive study [9]. It has been demonstrated that contextual information about objects and how they are organized is imperative to scholarly

navigation and interpretation of digital primary sources [3]. As a result, there is an increasing emphasis on the curation of digital primary sources for scholarly use [4].

How scholarly practice engages local history collections is not well understood. A collection may function both as a local history resource and, depending on its content, as a resource for broader, un-localized interest. The local function of any given collection, as opposed to its more general research utility, is not always well defined or leveraged in practice (in description, search, browse, or interactive facilities). This problem is compounded when resources are pulled out of their local contexts, which happens when distributed collections are aggregated into Europeana, DPLA, or DCC. Libraries tend to focus on "global approaches to digital collection building by producing expansive gateways for all their user communities" [9]. How do we continue the work of making local collections globally discoverable and accessible, without sacrificing the local context of collections, or compromising the strength of collections *as* local history resources? Methods and tools for the evaluation and exploitation of digital local history collections, especially in the context of massive aggregations, are yet rare (for one counterexample, see [10].)

In addition to results of our survey, which offer new evidence on the value of local history to public and academic library users, this paper gives an exploratory analysis of the challenges of assessing not only geographic, but local history coverage in cultural heritage metadata. We aim, with this paper, to lay the groundwork for future research on evaluating and exploiting local history in large-scale aggregations.

3. DCC SURVEY

The Institute of Museum and Library Services (IMLS) Digital Collections and Content (DCC) is among the largest cultural heritage digital libraries in the U.S., aggregating more than 1,500 collections and 1 million items from a diverse range of institutions in 44 states. DCC maintains a co-searchable registry of heritage collections and repository of item-level metadata, which together have served as both a unique public resource and a test bed for research into metadata interoperability, topic modeling and other advanced techniques for improving subject access to digital libraries, interface design, and collection evaluation.

3.1 Survey Method

In 2011/12, the DCC project conducted a survey to evaluate the DCC aggregation from the perspective of reference service providers at public and academic libraries. This study asked fifteen questions designed to help determine (1) the primary user groups for DCC and topics of interest; (2) how DCC compares to similar digital resources, in terms of both scope of coverage of history and perceived quality; (3) the effectiveness of collection metadata; and (4) suggested improvements to the resource.

The research used two reference frames: public and academic libraries. To reduce internal bias, this data collection purposefully excluded institutions from the sample that have contributed content to the IMLS DCC aggregation. We randomly sampled within each of these two frames. One reference service provider was targeted to represent each institution.

In total, 1,274 academic libraries and 1,192 public libraries were sampled from a total population of 3,689 academic (according to most recent NCES Academic Libraries Survey [11]) and 8,870 public libraries (according to combined IMLS and CIRSS listing [16]). The survey data was collected using Limesurvey open-source web survey software. As usual in this domain, the response rate was low despite multiple rounds of follow-up and sample expansion. 420 responses were used in the final analysis: 168 academic and 252 public library respondents. Cutoffs for the categories of small, medium, and large for public libraries were standardized by the American Library Association's Definition of Levels for Organizational Membership. Categories for academic libraries were derived from the National Center for Education Statistics' Academic Library Statistics reference. Medium libraries comprised approximately 30% and 23% of academic and public library respondents, respectively. Large libraries comprised approximately 20% and 26% of academic and public library respondents, respectively.

Method and survey results are fully elaborated in a technical report for the Institute of Museum and Library Services [2]. This paper focuses on the implications of a few questions that asked about users' topical interests and needs in local history from the resource and general collection evaluation.

3.2 Survey Results Relevant to Local History

Responses to the question, "Please list 5 – 10 examples of historical topics of interest to your users", were particularly relevant to understanding user requirements for local history representation in digital libraries. This question garnered 408 responses comprising more than 2,100 distinct topical terms or phrases. Academic respondents were fewer but offered a greater diversity of topics (see Table 1). Approximately 50% of each of public and academic respondents represented small libraries.

The diverse spread of responses – from ancient history to surprising assertions like, "businesses looking for historical photos as decoration (seriously)" – made manual coding into anything more than general, umbrella topics infeasible. Coding was iterative, and grounded by patterns in responses; therefore codes exhibited some semantic overlap. For example, the subject "Civil War" is ontologically within "Military history". However, each counted independently as the coding aimed to align as closely as possible with expressed topics. The distributions of codes for both public and academic libraries turned out to be long tailed, as expected.

Table 1. Comparative quantitative summary

Library Type	States Represented	Total Responses	Distinct topics	Codes assigned
Academic	48	160	710	166
Public	47	248	1,008	155

The top historical subject cited by both public and academic libraries was local history. See the distribution of top 5 topics in Figures 1 and 2. Local history accounted for 31% of public library topics and 13.5% of academic library topics. For academic libraries, responses coded as local history were in the vein of, "History of specific industries of the region", "History of the peoples settling in surrounding areas", and "Regional special collections". For public libraries, responses included, "Citizens who have gone on to make a difference in our country", "What was life like here when my ancestor was alive?", and "When was this county formed?".

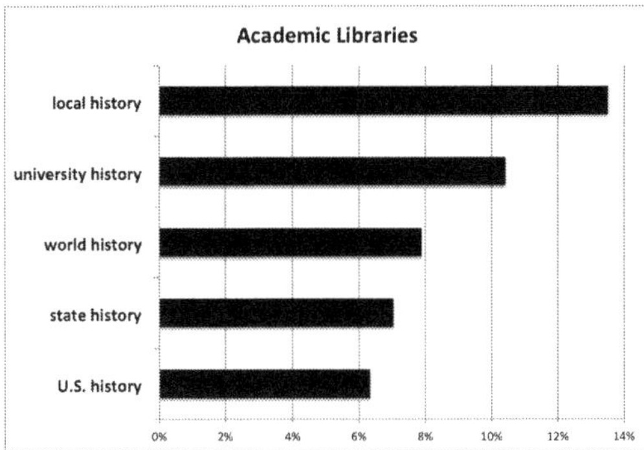

Figure 1. Code occurrences, Academic snapshot, n = 710

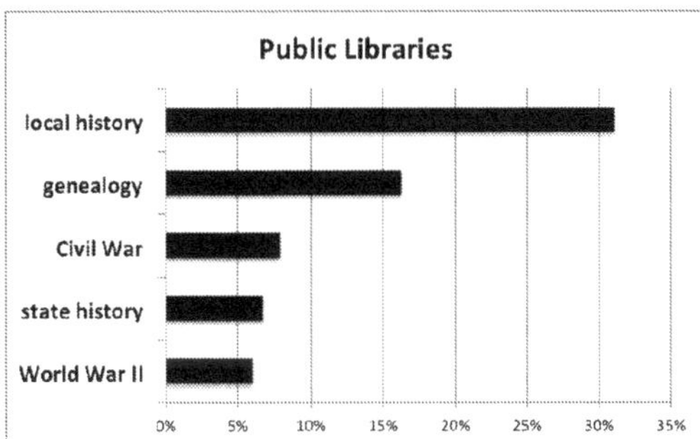

Figure 2. Code occurrences, Public snapshot, n = 1574

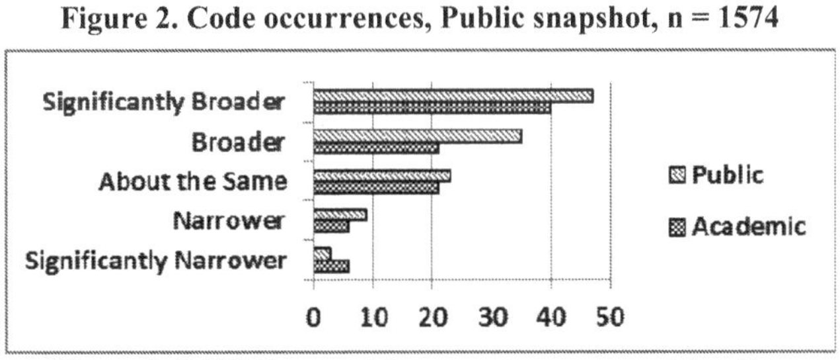

Figure 3. DCC Geographic coverage compared to other digital history resources

These already dramatic figures grow when clusters of topics are considered. Topics closely related to local history – namely state history, local architecture, and cemeteries – all fall into the top ten public library responses. When combined with local history terms, this family of codes accounts for approximately 45% of all public library responses. Responses were well distributed among states; 89% of represented states expressed interest in local history. A comparable cluster – with the addition of University history as a localized topic – accounts for 35% of academic library responses with 67% of responding states included. For both academic and public libraries, regardless of size and apparently location, local history is by far the most cited topic of historical interest to library users. Local history and its offshoots together account for between one third and one half of both academic and public library topics of interest, as reported by reference librarians.

Corroborating our results from the question of topics of interest were results of, "What kind of materials could be added to make [the resource] more valuable to you and your service community?" While the number of responses was too slim to claim generality, it is striking that nearly 50% of responses to this question (or 12% of total respondents) suggested the addition of local history materials. When asked how well the browsing categories match the interest of users, respondents, both academic and public, suggested topical and regional browsing would be useful. In addition, in response to another question about how to improve interface and functionality, respondents called for improved geographic browsing functionality, for clickable maps, narrower geographic categories for browsing (especially cities), and tools that reveal the relationships between items, e.g., "For instance, a church building postcard for Moline, Illinois is linked to church buildings, postcards, Moline, Illinois, and the church's denomination". Significantly, both academic and public library respondents considered overall geographic coverage of DCC to be broader than other digital history resources, as shown in Figure 3.

4. EVALUATING LOCAL HISTORY

The survey produced unprecedented qualitative evidence of library users' overriding interest in local history. Our results suggest that, when feasible, the addition of content and facilities for local history exploration have the greatest potential to add value to a cultural heritage digital library, whether intended for public or academic audiences.

Evaluating the success of a library in serving local history research, in order to set priorities for strategic development, will depend on evaluations of local history coverage. Such evaluations could also help enrich metadata and build refined browsing mechanisms (e.g., with geocoding and more precise mapping).

To curate collections or aggregations as local history resources for public or scholarly use, administrators must understand the topical, geographic, and temporal coverage of collections and the aggregation as a whole. These analyses can be laborious, but emerging, automatic evaluation techniques offer some help. Hillmann (2008) describes metadata quality problems endemic to aggregation and reviews attempts to systematize scalable evaluation techniques. However, Hillmann's techniques are quality-centric, while we seek to add descriptive evaluation for higher-order, curatorial work. How do we help administrators perform the kinds of evaluation necessary to curating cultural heritage collections at scale? The concept of curation for digital collections needs further elaboration ([10] offers some guidance). Besides activities focused on metadata quality, curation in an aggregation context will rely on strategic, policy-driven collection development, based in turn on analyses of the topical landscape of aggregations, topical density of constituent collections, collection interconnectedness, diversity, and small/large collection complementarity.

Evaluation techniques specific to geographic information largely arise from Geographic Knowledge Discovery (GKD) and data mining. Data quality evaluation and visualization techniques – often geared at improving search or browse [1,7] – are both prominent in the GKD literature, but are usually applied to structured geospatial information designed to support scientific inquiry [4]. These techniques have limited application to unstructured or semi-structured text in cultural heritage metadata records.

In response to the survey results obtained, which offer new evidence on the value of local history to public and academic library users, we are conducting an exploratory analysis of the challenges of assessing local history coverage, which subsume the challenges of GKD and metadata quality evaluation. Future work aims to help aggregators serve the local history needs of users. Specifically, we will confront the following challenges to evaluating local history in large aggregations of cultural metadata:

A minority of metadata records contains readily identifiable spatial information. For example, at DPLA's launch in April 2013, only one fifth of its 2.5 million items appeared to have codifiable geographic information in dedicated metadata fields, so that they could be made accessible through a browsing map and menu. Location information is often embedded in free-text descriptions or subject terms, which impede extraction. In addition, records may contain multiple instances of spatial information. The difficulties of location disambiguation are notorious, besides which libraries employ multiple geographic naming conventions. How can administrators get a read on the scope of coverage, if only a small fraction of records contain readily accessible geographic information?

Descriptions of spatial coverage vary wildly in granularity, and browsing facilities and maps struggle to comprehend the variety. Assuming spatial information can be automatically gleaned from records, the resulting mass of data is difficult to interpret. Common visualization techniques, while critically important, often fail to represent the full range of geographic information in cultural heritage records. For example, DPLA employs a cutting-edge interactive map on which items are grouped by location; the larger the group, the more visible the items become on the map. Groups with fewer items only appear at higher levels of zoom. Local results, therefore, can effectively disappear, becoming invisible without cumbersome zooming and dragging. In addition, while records variously name regions and counties and landmarks, only city and state information tends to be pinpointed on maps. The metadata most useful for local historical inquiry may obscure items in the results of search and data visualizations. Critical mass, in principle, determines the discoverability of local items by browsing and maps. But most places rarely obtain a critical mass of items within an aggregation.

Breadth of geographic coverage alone does not determine a collection's usefulness for local history research. To describe a collection as being *about* local history is to imply that it achieves contextual mass [8] centered on the theme of locality. This is a much stronger statement than saying a collection has many items from one place. It implies that a collection has been curated to facilitate research on the subject of local history. We need improved understanding of other factors that contribute to an aggregation's local history utility, such as the range of types of materials available, how items and collections complement or contextualize one another, and temporal coverage.

5. CONCLUSION

Local history holds proven interest for academic and public library users, yet remains problematic in digital cultural heritage aggregations. Evaluations of local history are impeded not only by the difficulties of wrangling geographic information in heterogeneous descriptions, but by persistent gaps in our understanding of collection curation for digital libraries. In future work, we will address conceptual and technical challenges of exploiting local history in large-scale aggregations of geographically distributed collections.

6. ACKNOWLEDGEMENTS

IMLS supported this research. The authors wish to acknowledge PI Carole Palmer, along with Jacob Jett and Megan Senseney for their contributions to experimental design and implementation.

7. REFERENCES

[1] Baziz, M., Etcheverry, P., Marquesuzaa, C., & Sallaberry, C. (2008). Accessing heritage documents according to space criteria within digital libraries. *Journal of Digital Information Management*, 6(1).

[2] DCC. (2013). *Report on the Institute of Museum and Library Services Opening History Evaluation Survey*. K. Fenlon, V. Varvel, C. Palmer (Eds.). CIRSS Report DCC1301. (Forthcoming)

[3] Duff, W. M., & Johnson, C. A. (2002). Accidentally found on purpose: Information-seeking behaviors of historians in archives. *Library Quarterly*, 72(4), 472–496.

[4] Flanders, J., & Muñoz, T. (n.d.). An Introduction to Humanities Data Curation. In *DH Curation: A Community Resource Guide to Data Curation for the Digital Humanities*. Champaign, IL. Retrieved from http://guide.dhcuration.org/intro/

[5] Gervais, M., Bedard, Y., Levesque, M., Bernier, E., & Devillers, R. (n.d.). Data quality issues and geographic knowledge discovery. In *H. J. Miller & J. Han (Eds.), Geographic Data Mining and Knowledge Discovery*. 2009: CRC Press.

[6] Hillmann, D. (2008). Metadata Quality: From Evaluation to Augmentation. *Cataloging & Classification Quarterly*, 46(1).

[7] Lenstra, N. (2010). The history and future of local history infrastructure: Open access and commodification of local history in the United States and the Anglosphere. Presented at the 5th International Conference on Cooperation and Promotion of Information Resources in Science and Technology: Information Sharing in U-Era, Beijing, China. Retrieved from http://hdl.handle.net/2142/17434

[8] Palacio, D., Cabanac, G., Sallaberry, C., & Hubert, G. (2010). On the evaluation of Geographic Information Retrieval systems. *International Journal on Digital Libraries*, 11(2), 91–109. doi:10.1007/s00799-011-0070-z

[9] Palmer, C. (2004). Thematic Research Collections. In *A Companion to Digital Humanities*. Blackwell Publishing.

[10] Palmer, C. L., Zavalina, O., & Fenlon, K. (2010). Beyond size and search: Building contextual mass in digital aggregations for scholarly use. In *Proceedings of the ASIS&T Annual Meeting*. Pittsburgh, PA.

[11] Phan, T. Hardesty, L., & Sheckells, C. (2011, December). *Academic Libraries: 2010*. Report NCES 2012-365. US Department of Education, Washington, DC: National Center for Education Statistics.

[12] Phillips, F. (1995). *Local History Collections in Libraries*. Libraries Unlimited.

[13] Reference and User Services Association. (2006). RUSA guidelines for establishing local history collections. ALA. Retrieved from http://www.ala.org/rusa/resources/guidelines/

[14] Reid, P. H., & Macafee, C. (2007). The philosophy of local studies in the interactive age. Journal of Librarianship & Information Science, 39(3).

[15] Tibbo, H. (2003). Primarily history in America: How U.S. historians search for primary materials at the dawn of the digital age. The American Archivist, 66(1), 9–50.

[16] Varvel, V., & Hughes, K. (Eds.). (2011). *Public Library Data Service Statistical Report 2011*. Chicago, IL: American Library Association.

[17] Weessies, K. W. (2012). Local history maps in full text resources. Journal of Map and Geography Libraries, 8, 230–241. doi:10.1080/15420353.2012.700300

Instrument Distribution and Music Notation Search for Enhancing Bibliographic Music Score Retrieval

Laurent Pugin
Swiss RISM Office
Hallwylstrasse 15 / CH-3000 Bern
laurent.pugin@rism-ch.org

Rodolfo Zitellini
Swiss RISM Office
Hallwylstrasse 15 / CH-3000 Bern
rodolfo.zitellini@rism-ch.org

ABSTRACT

Because of the unique characteristics of music scores, searching bibliographical music collections using traditional library systems can be a challenge. In this paper, we present two specific search functionalities added to the Swiss RISM database and describe how they improve the user experience. The first is a search functionality for instrument and vocal part distribution that leverages coded information available in the MarcXML records of the database. It enables scores for precise ensemble distribution to be retrieved. The second is a search functionality of music notation excerpts transcribed from the beginning of the pieces, known as music incipits. The incipit search is achieved using a well-known music information retrieval (MIR) tool, Themefinder. A novelty of our implementation is that it can operate at three different levels (pitch, duration and metric), singularly or combined, and that it is performed through a specifically-developed intuitive graphical interface for note input and parameter selection. The two additions illustrate why it is important to take into consideration the particularities of music scores when designing a search system and how MIR tools can be beneficially integrated into existing heterogeneous bibliographic score collections.

Categories and Subject Descriptors

H.3.7 [**Information Storage and Retrieval**]: Digital Libraries—*User issues*; J.5 [**Computer Applications**]: Arts and HumanitiesMusic

Keywords

Music information retrieval, Music instruments, User interfaces

1. INTRODUCTION

Searching a bibliographic music score collection using a traditional library system is a challenging task. Multiple versions of the same work can exist, or a score can contain only a part of a work, an aria from a larger work for example. With large databases, having a tailored system becomes necessary. The particularities of music scores, however, make conceiving such systems complicated [6].

One particularity of music scores is that they are intended for a specific instrumentation. Although instrumentation is only one of their particularities, it is known to be a very important one for end-users. Musicians especially often search for scores with an instrument or voice distribution matching their particular ensemble. But searching for instrument or voice distribution is generally problematic. Typically, a singer searching scores for bass voice with "basso" will obtain a result list including also all the scores of the Baroque area because of the "basso continuo", very common in this repertoire. In practice, it often discourages the users from utilizing the resources that are available.

Our bibliographic music score database contains musical incipits of the pieces. Music incipits are short music notation excerpts transcribed from the beginning of the scores. They are useful for identifying anonymous works, in particular for sacred music where works often have no title but the text incipit of the sacred text. At the Répertoire International des Sources Musicales (RISM), the largest bibliographic database of music sources, incipits have been introduced for the Series A/II in 1984 [2]. They are encoded in Plain and Easy (PAE), an ASCII code developed specifically for music bibliography. With traditional library system, music incipits in PAE can be searched using standard string matching operations. However, this will retrieve only the exact matches encoded in exactly the same way. It also requires the user to know the PAE code, which is of course a considerable obstacle.

In this paper, we present how the search capabilities of the Swiss RISM database were improved by enhancing search by instrument and voice distribution and search by music incipits. In the following sections, we review related work and existing projects and then describe the database infrastructure. Finally, we present and discuss the search functionalities introduced. Remarks on future work conclude the paper.

JCDL'13, July 22–26, 2013, Indianapolis, Indiana, USA.

2. RELATED SYSTEMS

2.1 Instrument and vocal parts distribution

Standard practices for cataloging instrumentation of music scores are well documented [4]. To our knowledge, searching scores by instrumentation, on the other hand, has not been covered by dedicated studies. Looking at existing databases and their limitations, however, can be very informative.

Even in systems where there is a dedicated search for instruments, extraneous results will often be returned because the abbreviations used for instrumentation can appear elsewhere in the database. The Bach Cantata Website[1] illustrates this problem. Searching for duets for soprano and alto using the recommended query "“”+S +A –T –B" will indeed retrieve some duets but also pieces with other distribution such as a movement with soprano solo from a mass in A major. This is because the +S matches the voice soprano, but the +A also matches the tonality of the mass, A major.

In the case of the IMSLP,[2] an interesting alternative to searching is available, namely browsing by instrumentation and genre. So-called genres are grouped into four categories, namely “Keyboard”, “Chamber-Instrumental”, “Orchestral” and “Vocal”. Most genres can be browsed by subgenre. For example, the “For voices with solo instruments” genre contains 386 subgenres such as “For 4 voices, lute”. While this approach is certainly valuable, it is definitely not optimal for the users due to the very large number of genres and subgenres. A searching option in the instrumentation and genre is available, but the results retrieved seem rather unsatisfactory. Searching for “bass” returned 746 genres, including “double bass”, “guitar bass”, or “bassoon”, which we could not exclude by changing the search query.

The Bach Digital database[3] provides an example with a more structured search functionality for music instruments in the expert search for works. Instrument or vocal parts can be selected in hierarchical drop-down lists. The main problem is that selecting ensembles might be difficult since every single instrument needs to be selected. Exclusions are not possible.

2.2 Music incipits

Incipit searching, a symbolic music similarity problem, has been a topic of interest for decades [3]. It has also been a field widely covered by the MIR community, and in 2005 and 2006 RISM incipits were used for the symbolic similarity MIREX task [1]. Numerous approaches have been proposed, such as editing distance of string-based representations, n-grams methods, or geometric representation comparisons [7].

Musipedia[4] is a good example of a production system offering incipit searching. Melodic, contour-based and rhythm-based searches are possible. The contour-based search is based on Parsons codes. The melodic and rhythm-based searches use the Earth Mover's Distance algorithm. Several input methods are offered (music keyboard, piano roll, query by humming). However, the scope of the database is vast, and because every entry can be edited by anybody, it contains many musical genres from classical to pop music, which poses the risk of comparison problems between dissimilar repertoires.

A well-known project is the Themefinder database.[5] It includes classical themes, folksong themes and Renaissance incipits. It uses regular expressions on different representations of the melodies for finding matches. The search in the Themefinder database can be performed by pitch, interval, scale degree, gross contour and refined contour. The query is entered in text fields following the syntax of each search type. Rhythmic search is not available in the current implementation of the web interface.

More recently, search by melody has been introduced on IMSLP through Peachnote [9]. Since it operates on full-text but uncorrected data produced by optical music recognition software applications, the comparison with search on human encoded incipit is not really relevant.

In the RISM database for Series A/II,[6] incipit searching has been available since 2011. The database contains over a million incipits. The query is performed simply by entering note pitches (A, B, C, etc.) in a normal text field. Transposition is taken into account, but not accidentals, and the notes are searched at the beginning of the incipits only. Rhythmic search is not possible.

3. THE SWISS RISM DATABASE

The Swiss RISM database consists of MarcXML bibliographic records of heterogeneous manuscript or printed scores from the 17th to the 20th century. Each score is described by one or more MarcXML records. It currently contains about 67,000 records. The instrumentation is catalogued in the $m MarcXML subfield for ‘medium of performance’ of the X30 ‘uniform titles’ fields following standard practices for music. In MarcXML, instrumentation can also be coded in the field 048. However, because the list of instrument codes provided for this field is too restricted for the RISM project, this field was not used. Detailed instrumentation is instead given in local field with several subfields.

Five subfields are used to code vocal and instrument distributions following a system well-known by musicians and used for describing orchestral material. The coded vocal parts (choir and solo) subfield uses 4 digits, one for each voice. For example, 2011 stands for two sopranos, no alto, one tenor and one bass. For strings, the digits represent the number of voices for violin 1, violin 2, viola, cello, and double bass. For example, 11211 stands for a string ensemble with two viola parts. For woodwinds the voices are flute, oboe, clarinet and bassoon, and finally for brass, horn, trumpet and trombone. For the other subfields (plucked, percussion, keyboard, basso continuo instruments), a list of abbreviations is used.

Most of the titles in the database have at least one incipit of an instrumental part and of a vocal part. The incipits are coded in PAE in the 031 MarcXML field. The PAE code represents a transcription of the graphical music notation, with explicit pitch. It means that a distinction is made between different enharmonic spellings, which make it more precise than the widely used MIDI code where differentiating a C-♯ from D-♭ is not possible. In total, our database contains 86,934 incipits for a total of 1,232,137 notes, which means an average incipit length of 14 notes.

[1]<http://www.bach-cantatas.com>

[2]<http://www.imslp.org>

[3]<http://www.bach-digital.de>

[4]<http://www.musipedia.org>

[5]<http://www.themefinder.org>

[6]<http://opac.rism.info>

4. ENHANCED SEARCH CAPABILITIES

4.1 Distribution search

A specific distribution search option that leverages the encoded instrumentation available in the MarcXML was added to our database.[7] For the coded subfields, the search field is a drop-down list with all the code combinations available in the data, and the number of scores for each them. For example, the user can search for a vocal distribution 2011, seeing directly that 134 scores match it. For the other subfields, the search field is a simple input text field. For each field, the list of abbreviations used in the database is given in an inline help. Any of the subfields can be excluded from the search. It makes it possible to search, for example, for scores with a specific vocal part distribution together with strings and woodwinds but with no brass. The search can also be combined with any other metadata field available in the database (composer, title, liturgical feast, etc.).

Measuring the improvement of this approach is not straightforward. We nevertheless did compare the results we get with and without the new search option for typical problematic queries, such as searching for solo bass (voice). We compared the results when searching with "basso" and "solo" with the normal text-based search and when selecting solo voice (0001) with the new search option. As shown on Table 1, the normal text-based search produces not only a significant number of false positives but also of false negatives. If we try to exclude the basso continuo in the text-based search by adding "-org", we have a high number of false negatives – all these are scores that do actually have basso solo but were quite likely ignored by excluding most of the sacred music and Baroque repertoire.

We also noticed that the new search is also more effective when searching for combined distributions. A normal search for "alto", "basso" and "solo" retrieves 626 scores, but the enhanced search shows there are actually only 54 scores for this pair (0101). Conversely, a normal search for "soprano", "alto" and "solo" retrieves only 86 scores out of 920 scores. Finding unusual distributions is also much easier. For example, duos for viola and double bass are easily found with the string distribution 00101. It appears only 6 times in our database, but a normal search for "vla" and "vlne" retrieves 1,146 scores because these instruments are so commonly used. The exclusion option also reveals itself to be quite powerful. A search for scores with 2 horns and 2 trumpets (220) retrieves 1,721 scores. By excluding choir voices, it drops to 744, and by excluding strings it falls to 14 scores.

4.2 Incipit search

Evaluating melodic similarity systems has been a MIREX task for several years, including for incipit similarity specifically. Choosing an algorithm for a production system, however, is not straightforward. The performance of an algorithm will highly depend on the dataset, and it is expected to change from one music repertoire to another. For example, an algorithm that performs well on baroque vocal music will not necessary perform identically well on nineteenth century instrumental music. Evaluating algorithms to such a level of detail is problematic and, to our knowledge, has never been done. Also, what approach to use for evaluation remains a debatable question, especially when using ground-truth data [8].

	Text	New	FP	FN
basso solo	1,191	644	668	121
basso solo -org	404	644	191	431

Table 1: Comparison of the results with a normal text search and the new enhanced search method. The new search method retrieves the exact number of scores (644), whereas the normal text search produces false positives (FP) and false negatives (FN).

For our implementation, we selected Themefinder, a well-known incipit search engine. With this tool an evaluation as performed in MIREX is not possible because the algorithm does not emit any similarity score. However, it offers a great flexibility in how search parameters can be adjusted and how the level of fuzziness can be controlled, which makes it an excellent choice for our heterogeneous dataset.

What seemed to us very important was to provide the user with a flexible interface to the engine. This is particularly important because music similarity is a multi-faceted question, and querying by incipit often requires the parameters to be adjusted several times before the user obtains results relevant to him. It is crucial in our implementation because our interface integrates rhythm and metric search features of the engine that make searching more complex. All these features are not available in the current Themefinder database.

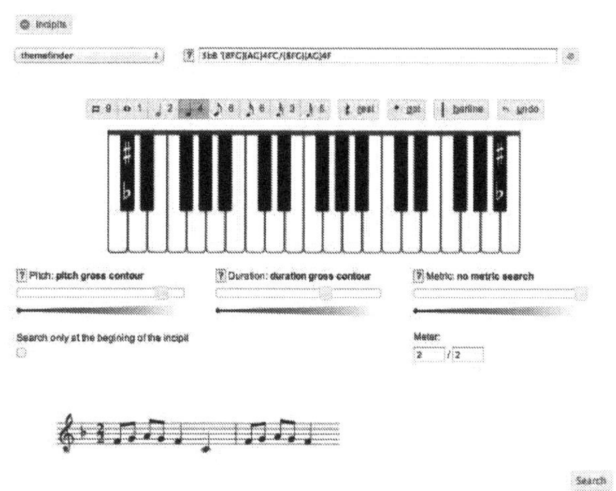

Figure 1: The search interface to the Themefinder. Notes can be entered with the music keyboard and the search parameters can be changed with sliders.

A virtual keyboard is provided to enter the notes. It means that the user does not need to know PAE to make a query. The note duration is selected from a toolbar. The fourteen search features provided by Themefinder are grouped into three categories: pitch, rhythm, and metric. In the interface, each category is a slider, where the user can select the degree of fuzziness. The pitch search has seven levels of fuzziness, the rhythm search three and the metric search five. The three search types can be combined freely. Other controls include anchoring the search to the beginning of the incipit and restricting the results by time signature. The music notation of the query is visualized in the interface.

[7] <http://www.rism-ch.org>, "Advanced search"

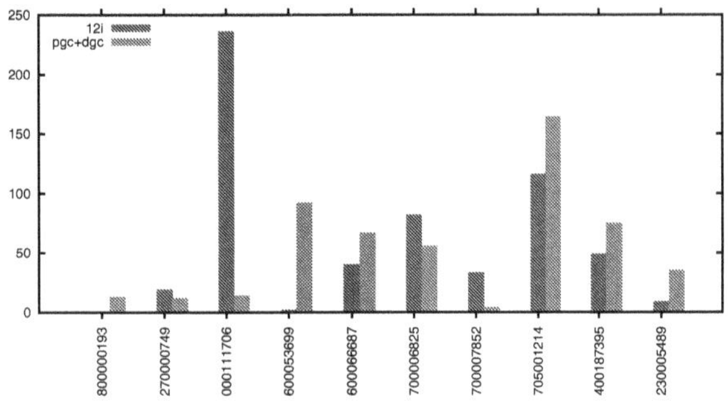

Figure 2: Number of matches for 12i and pgc+dgc searches with five notes on 10 MIREX incipits. The ratio of number of matches between the two search parameters can vary significantly.

When submitted, the query is converted on the fly into a search input suitable for Themefinder. Of course, depending on the search type used, only some features of the input melody might be used. For example, if a rhythm-only search is performed, all the pitch information of the PAE will be discarded. From the user's point of view, the advantage is that all queries function in the same way because the actual Themefinder query is generated from the PAE. In this way, the search functionalities of Themefinder are accessed in a simple and intuitive manner. The user does not need to know or learn the Themefinder syntax, and can also change the search parameter for his query without having to retype it with the syntax of the other parameter.

A way of evaluating Themefinder's performance is to compare the number of matches depending on the query length and search parameters used. When querying our dataset with eleven test incipits from the MIREX 2005 symbolic similarity task, we obtained very similar results as in [5]. According to the number of results retrieved, the best parameters are either a search only on pitch with a low level of fuzziness (twelve-tone interval = 12i), or with a higher level of fuzziness but by combining pitch and rhythm (pitch gross contour joined with duration gross contour = pgc+dgc). It is interesting to notice, however, that even if on average the two searches (12i and pgc+dgc) tend to perform similarly, the ratio of number of matches between the two search parameters can vary significantly from one query to another as shown in Figure 2.

Looking at the number of matches is only quantitative and does not provide any qualitative information as to how the engine performs. Furthermore, choosing a fix target of 10 matches is arbitrary and debatable. For this reason, we compared how 12i and pgc+dgc performed by looking at the incipits that actually match. Statistically, it is noteworthy that on the MIREX data, nearly half the queries had no intersection between 12i and pgc+dgc with a search with five notes. It means that the two parameters returned completely different incipits. Overall, the average intersection percentage (the number of common incipits over the total number of distinct incipits retrieved) was about 3%. This confirms that determining what is the most appropriate search parameter depends greatly on the type of results desired.

5. CONCLUSION AND FUTURE WORK

In this paper, we presented two enhancements added to an existing bibliographic music score database. While instrument distribution is often unsatisfactory when searching for specific ensemble, our approach, making the most of data in MarcXML, appears to be a valid method for offering refined results and ameliorating the potential of the system. The integration of Themefinder in our system is an emblematic example of how MIR research can be beneficial to music library systems. Our system also integrates the new duration and metric capabilities of the Themefinder search engine. The evaluation of the MIREX data, even if limited, shows significant differences in types of similarity, even for search parameters that return on average the same number of results. It confirms the need for a simple interface for making the query, in which the user can easily and intuitively adapt the search parameters to his needs without having to retype it.

Our future work will include the collection of user data to evaluate which are the preferred search parameters. It will help us make the otherwise difficult selection of the default parameters for the incipit search. Other music similarity algorithms will also be integrated into the system and compared. We believe that offering appropriate search capabilities for music instrumentation and for music incipits is a way of encouraging musicians to use existing resources such as our bibliographic music score database. Ultimately, it may stimulate them to discover unknown scores they can eventually perform in concert and thus contribute to some extent to the revival of a cultural heritage.

6. REFERENCES

[1] J. Downie et al. The music information retrieval evaluation exchange: Some observations and insights. In *Advances in Music Information Retrieval*, pages 93–115. Springer Berlin Heidelberg, 2010.

[2] H. Heckmann. Das Répertoire International des Sources Musicales (RISM) in Geschichte und Gegenwart. *Fontes Artis Musicae*, 57(2):140–147, 2010.

[3] W. Hewlett and E. Selfridge-Field, editors. *Melodic similarity: Concepts, procedures, and applications.* The MIT Press, Cambridge MA, 1998.

[4] M. Koth. *Uniform Titles for Music.* The Scarecrow Press, Lanham MD, 2008.

[5] C. Sapp, Y. Liu, and E. Selfridge-Field. Search-effectiveness measures for symbolic music queries in very large databases. In *Proceedings of the 5th ISMIR Conference*, pages 266–73, 2004.

[6] R. Scherle and D. Byrd. The anatomy of a bibliographic search system for music. In *Proceedings of the 5th ISMIR Conference*, pages 489–496.

[7] R. Typke, F. Wiering, and R. Veltkamp. A survey of music information retrieval systems. In *Proceedings of the 6th ISMIR Conference*, pages 153–160, 2005.

[8] J. Urbano, M. Marrero, D. Martín, and J. Lloréns. Improving the generation of ground truths based on partially ordered lists. In *Proceedings of the 11th ISMIR Conference*, pages 285–290, 2010.

[9] V. Viro. Peachnote: Music score search and analysis platform. In *Proceedings of the 12th ISMIR Conference*, pages 359–362, 2011.

A Search Engine Approach to Estimating Temporal Changes in Gender Orientation of First Names

Brittany N. Smith[1], Mamta Singh[2], and Vetle I. Torvik[3]
Graduate School of Library and Information Science
University of Illinois at Urbana-Champaign
Champaign, IL 61820, USA
[1]bnsmith3@illinois.edu, [2]mamta2.singh@gmail.com, [3]vtorvik@illinois.edu

ABSTRACT
This paper presents an approach for predicting the gender orientation of any given first name over time based on a set of search engine queries with the name prefixed by masculine and feminine *markers* (e.g., "Uncle Taylor"). We hypothesize that these markers can capture the great majority of variability in gender orientation, including temporal changes. To test this hypothesis, we train a logistic regression model, with time-varying marker weights, using marker counts from Bing.com to predict male/female counts for 85,406 names in US Social Security Administration (SSA) data during 1880-2008. The model misclassifies 2.25% of the people in the SSA dataset (slightly worse than the 1.74% pure error rate) and provides accurate predictions for names beyond the SSA. The misclassification rate is higher in recent years (due to increasing name diversity), for general English words (e.g., Will), for names from certain countries (e.g., China), and for rare names. However, the model tends to err on the side of caution by predicting neutral/unknown rather than false positive. As hypothesized, the markers also capture temporal patterns of androgyny. For example, *Daughter* is a stronger female predictor for recent years while *Grandfather* is a stronger male predictor around the turn of the 20th century. The model has been implemented as a web-tool called Genni (available via http://abel.lis.illinois.edu/) that displays the predicted proportion of females vs. males over time for any given name. This should be a valuable resource for those who utilize names in order to discern gender on a large scale, e.g., to study the roles of gender and diversity in scholarly work based on digital libraries and bibliographic databases where the authors' names are listed.

Categories and Subject Descriptors
I.5.1 [**Pattern Recognition**]: Models - *Statistical*; H.3.1 [**Information Storage and Retrieval**]: Content Analysis and Indexing – *Linguistic processing.*

General Terms
Algorithms, Measurement, Experimentation.

Keywords
Gender, androgyny, data mining, temporal prediction, bibliometrics, search engine, textual markers, semantic orientation

1. INTRODUCTION
Does Taylor refer to a boy or a girl? Answering that type of question can be quite difficult when only given a first name and no other contextual clues. For common, gender-specific names like Michael or Mary humans can answer that question with a high degree of confidence but how can we make a machine coupled with easily accessible digital resources answer that question? Even humans have difficulty with rare or unfamiliar names (e.g., Kuulei or Aagot) because of personal biases such as the number of people that they personally know that happen to be male or female with that name or a similar name. The answer to the question may also vary depending on when the question is posed partly because many androgynous names are increasingly given to girls over time [16]. For example, Taylor was given to more boys than girls prior to 1985, but today, Taylor most often refers to a girl, at least in the USA. In instances like this, can machines do better?

Table 1. Temporal gender markers selected from common first name prefixes in the Google n-gram dataset [31].

	Feminine markers	Masculine markers
1	Mrs	Mr
2	Mother	Father
3	Grandmother	Grandfather
4	Wife	Husband
5	Daughter	Son
6	Aunt	Uncle
7	Sister	Brother
8	Girl	Boy
9	He married	She married

Our motivation stems from analyzing the roles of gender and diversity in the publication and collaboration strategies of authors in large-scale digital libraries and bibliographic databases. This requires an automatic process for confidently assigning gender to each instance of an author name at a certain time point. In this paper, we test the accuracy of a temporal gender prediction model based solely on search engine results as predictors. The model is trained using US Social Security Administration (SSA) data, which includes the frequency with which a name is given to males and females over time. Search result counts are collected from Bing.com queries consisting of temporal and gender-specific markers (see Table 1 for a complete list) concatenated with the name under consideration. Using multiple markers should not only help make predictions less sensitive to noisy search engine query results but should also help capture more nuanced changes in individual names over time. Relying solely on web searches as predictors has several advantages: web searching is easy to automate and thus scales well, the data is public and not domain or genre specific (i.e., it covers personal pages, industry sites, news, social media, blogs, genealogy documents, etc. not just one of these), nor is the data region specific (i.e., not just English names).

It should be noted that a last name can also be useful for gender attribution in some cultures (e.g., Slavic last names ending in -ova or Icelandic names ending in -dottir are given to females). We chose not to train the model using last names because this phenomenon is much less common globally and is rare in the USA specifically. However, one can still use the trained model to make predictions using a last name (or a combination of first and last name) as input.

2. RELATED WORK

Our approach builds on several different areas of work including work that has looked at the manual assignment of gender using names, the automated assignment of gender, and work on semantic orientation.

2.1 Manual Gender Assignment

Several recent studies have looked at gender differences in disparate areas of academia and industry. Though some studies used data from large centers, e.g., the National Center for Education Statistics [12], which one would assume has rather accurate and complete data including individuals' gender, other studies used more imprecise methods to discern gender. These methods included using publications and the author's first name to guess the gender, searching for author information online, or by looking at pronoun usage in biographical notes and/or author bylines, e.g., [6, 21, 22]. While this essentially manual process yields fairly accurate information, it takes a great deal of time to cultivate the data, and if no supporting data can be found to help ascertain gender, sometimes names are simply excluded from the analysis.

2.2 Automated Gender Assignment

In addition to manual assignment, some models have been created to infer gender using automated means. Otterbacher [18] explored the contribution of style, content, and metadata from movie reviews in inferring the gender of movie reviewers on the Internet Movie Database site. Cucerzan and Yarowsky [9] used nouns with known attributed genders to create a bootstrapping process that determines the grammatical gender of other nouns in five different languages, and Bergsma, Lin, and Goebel [4] created a model that uses contextual, morphological, and categorical gender features to classify nouns in documents. The Never-Ending Language Learner developed by Carlson et al. [7] also uses information about noun phrases and other language and text patterns to guess gender in cases where appropriate. We too utilize markers to help infer gender, but we use the help of a search engine.

In two recent papers, Zheleva and Getoor [33] and Tang et al. [23] use user profile data from social network sites like Facebook in order to infer information about individuals including gender. Zheleva and Getoor [33] create eight different models that use varying amounts of an individual's profile data and at times even the individual's friends' data in order to approximate things like gender and political view. Our models use less information and information that is publicly available to achieve a similar goal.

Though Tang et al. [23] also utilize social network data, data from Facebook, they take an approach similar to ours in that they use publicly available data and words therein (e.g., relationship status and who the person is "interested in" or "looking for") to build models that attempt to discern an individual's gender. Our models differ in that we use less personal, easily attainable data by using general search engine results augmented simply by common gender-specific words and phrases. Our models are also different in that we can look at the way that the name was assigned to people of different genders over time while Tang et al. [23] only evaluate the present usage of names.

In addition to the aforementioned models, there are some websites that provide information on the gender of names, and perhaps not surprisingly, they are mostly proposed as sites to help with the naming of children. Two such tools include NameVoyager [30] and its accompanying site Baby Name Wizard [3] and Baby Name Guesser [2]. NameVoyager is a tool that was initially built to display SSA data from 1900 to 2001 in a way that promotes discovery and reflection. It has since grown to include more recent and detailed information. Baby Name Guesser is a tool that uses Google information to calculate name statistics and includes a gender predictor [2]. It is not made public how Google information is used, but it is perhaps the most similar to our strategy.

2.3 Semantic Orientation

Using known characteristics of some words to determine the orientation of others is not a new idea. The idea of semantic orientation is discussed by Turney and Littman [27] who infer the orientation of a word from its statistical association with other words. Efron [11] used the work of Turney and Littman [27] to build a model that uses cocitation information to estimate the political orientation of web documents. Though we do not use pointwise mutual information or latent semantic analysis measures, the idea of using one word with a known association to infer the association of another is what we utilize when creating Bing API web search queries to predict gender for given names.

3. TRAINING A GENDER PREDICTION MODEL

This section describes how we built a prediction model using US SSA data on gender counts as the target and results of web search queries submitted to the Bing API [5] as predictors.

3.1 Data

The US SSA provides data consisting of the frequency of names and gender on Social Security card applications for each year going back to 1880. To protect privacy, names are only included in the yearly SSA data if the name was given to at least 5 people during that year [20]. From those sets, we included only names that appeared during the 1880 to 2008 time span. This left 85,406 distinct names, which varied greatly in popularity with some names assigned to individuals only 5 times during that time span, e.g., Zaccariah and Ahmeer, to names given to over 5,000,000 individuals, e.g., James and John.

For each name in the dataset, 258 dimensions of SSA data was recorded: 1) the number of females for each of the 129 years during the 1880 to 2008 time span (e.g., there are 2,514 females with the name Alicia in 2004 and 2,333 in 2005) and 2) the number of males for each of the 129 years during the 1880 to 2008 time span. Also, for each name, the results of 72 Bing API web searches were recorded as follows: the estimated total number web pages that contain the phrase made up of the name prefixed by one of 18 markers (see Table 1), for each of 4 different Bing offset parameters (0, 10, 100, and 1000). Note that Bing gives different estimates depending on the offset setting. Table 2 illustrates this effect for the name Genni where, for example, the phrase "Mother Genni" resulted in 38, 7, 7, and 7 results for each of these respective offsets. Query variability is due to the way the Bing API is designed to take into account certain factors like query popularity and the set of results requested (i.e., asking for the 11-20 results to be returned as opposed to requesting the first ten results) [1]. By recording results from different Bing offsets, this parameter setting can be optimized for the predictive model. Using 18 markers also helps deal with query variability. Weights are distributed across the markers which helps reduce the potential effect due to noise in any one marker count. Each search was formulated to ensure that no query correction occurred and the exact phrase was found excepting punctuation marks. For example, +"Mother Jean," will include "mother. Jean" but not "mother of Jean."

Table 2. Marker counts for the name "Genni".

Offset	0	10	100	1000
Mrs vs. Mr	88 vs 27	88 vs 5	16 vs 5	16 vs 5
Mother vs. Father	38 vs 5	7 vs 1	7 vs 1	7 vs 1
Grandmother vs. Grandfather	5 vs 0	1 vs 0	1 vs 0	1 vs 0
Wife vs. Husband	94 vs 11	94 vs 1	16 vs 1	16 vs 1
Daughter vs. Son	44 vs 33	8 vs 3	8 vs 3	8 vs 3
Aunt vs. Uncle	116 vs 0	116 vs 0	17 vs 0	17 vs 0
Sister vs. Brother	44 vs 5	8 vs 1	8 vs 1	8 vs 1
Girl vs. Boy	66 vs 11	66 vs 2	12 vs 2	12 vs 2
He married vs. She married	0 vs 0	0 vs 0	0 vs 0	0 vs 0

3.2 Logistic Regression Modeling

Given a name characterized by an 18-dimensional vector of marker values *x*, the purpose of the model is to estimate the proportion of individuals that are female for the given *x* and *year*: $p(Female|x; year)$. The *i*-th element of the vector x_i represents a gender predictor and is encoded by transformed Bing® results for each of the following markers: x_1 = Mrs, x_2 = Mr, x_3 = Mother, x_4= Father, x_5 = Grandmother, x_6 = Grandfather, x_7 = Wife, x_8 = Husband, x_9 = Daughter, x_{10} = Son, x_{11} = Aunt, x_{12} = Uncle, x_{13}= Sister, x_{14} = Brother, x_{15} = Girl, x_{16} = Boy, x_{17} = He married, x_{18} = She married. Each marker value was defined by a simple transformation of the corresponding Bing count as follows:

$$x_i = adjust(\log(bing\_count + \delta))$$

A δ correction was applied to avoid undefined values for the natural log, and two different values $\delta \in (1,5)$ were tested for their effect on the predictions. When plotting the results of the transformation, we noticed fixed artificial gaps, presumably due to Bing's estimation procedure (see Figure 1 for an example). The gaps identified for each offset value were as follows: gap = 2.7-3.6 for 0 offset; gap = 1-1.8 and 2.7-3.6 for 10 offset; gap = 2-2.8 and 3.6-4.05 for 100 offset; no gaps for 1000 offset. The *adjust()* function creates a continuous distribution by collapsing the gaps as follows: subtract the gap size for points above the gap and shift the points inside the gap to the lower bound.

A weighted combination of the transformed attribute values, using a logistic regression model, is used to estimate the probability. Temporal changes in the weights assigned to the markers were captured in two different ways. The "full" model creates a quadratic fit for each marker weight across the entire 129 years, while a "sliding-window" model fits separate linear models to each 9-year window across the 129 years. The "sliding-window" model should capture more local changes over time, while the "full" model smoothes out the local changes and only captures global trends over time. The logistic regression models can be expressed in the following generic form:

$$logit(p) = \sum_{i=0}^{18}(\alpha_i + \beta_i y + \gamma_i y^2)x_i$$
$$+ \sum_{i=1}^{18}(\alpha_{i+18} + \beta_{i+18} y + \gamma_{i+18} y^2)(x_i = 0)$$
$$+ \sum_{i=1}^{18}(\alpha_{i+36} + \beta_{i+36} y + \gamma_{i+36} y^2)(0 < x_i \leq c)$$

Each x_i refers to a transformed attribute value and each $\alpha_i + \beta_i y + \gamma_i y^2$ corresponds to the weight assigned to that attribute for a given year = $y \in (1880, 1881, \cdots, 2008)$ for the "full" model. Note that we define $x_0 = 1$ to capture the intercepts. The "sliding-window" model excludes the quadratic year terms (i.e., $\gamma_i = 0$). Two sets of indicator attributes capture effects due to low counts: whether x_i is 0 or not, and whether x_i is a small positive value $\leq c$. The values for c were set empirically: $c = 5$ for offset = 0, and 1 for all other offsets. The "full" model is trained on all observed names across all 129 years whereas the "sliding-window" models consist of a series of submodels each of which is trained using observations for a given year +/- a window of 4 years: $y \in (1880-1888, 1889-1897, \cdots, 2000-2008)$. The reason for fitting the less restrictive "sliding-window" model is to test whether the "full" model captures the full extent of temporal change in weights. Overall, the models were trained with a combination of different parameter settings: $\delta \in (1,5)$, $offset \in (0,10,100,1000)$, and with and without the indicator attributes. This gives sixteen "full" models and the sixteen "sliding-window" models from which to select.

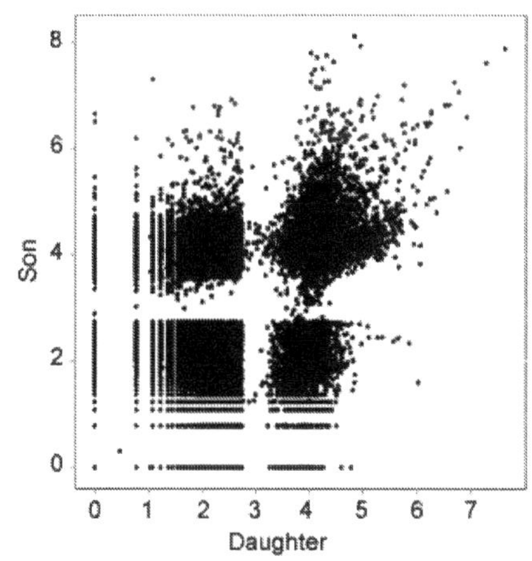

Figure 1. Bing result counts (δ = 1, offset = 0) for all names in the SSA dataset. Note the sharp separation of points reflecting Bing's step-estimation for values above a fixed cut-off.

4. RESULTS AND DISCUSSION

4.1 Overall misclassification rates and model selection

Figure 2 shows the proportion of individuals in the SSA dataset misclassified by some of the models over time and compared against the pure (within name*year and within name; labeled SSA w/year and SSA w/o year, respectively) error rates under two different classification scenarios. The first scenario requires classification of all individuals as either male or female (i.e., probability > 50% implies female, otherwise male) which yields higher error rates than the second scenario which permits unknown or neutral classifications (where 10% < probability < 90%) that are excluded from error calculations. The second scenario captures errors on highly confident predictions only.

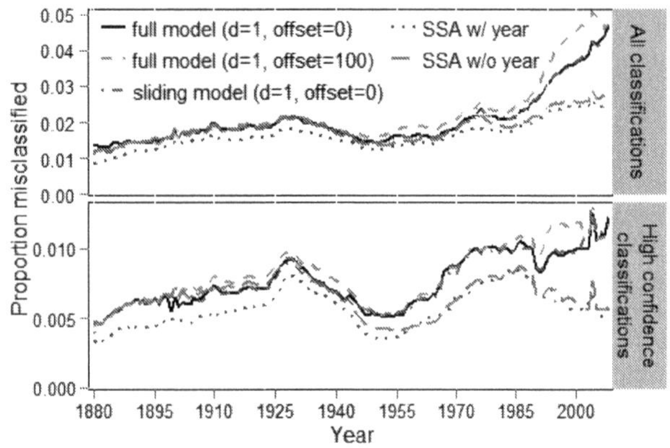

Figure 2. The proportion of individuals in the SSA dataset misclassified over time under two different scenarios: *All classifications* (female if p > 0.5; male otherwise) and *High confidence classifications* only (female if p > 0.9, male if p < 0.1, unknown otherwise). *SSA w/ year* corresponds to the pure (within name*year) error and represents a lower bound for any model. *SSA w/o year* refers to within-name error; and its difference with *SSA w/year* reflects total error due to time.

The models with the indicators produced more consistent and lower error rates than the models without indicators (not shown), and there were no effective differences in error curves between $\delta = 5$ vs. $\delta = 1$ (not shown). The error curves for the "full" and "sliding-window" models are very similar, which implies that the sliding-window approach to capture local time variations does not contribute to the overall performance. The offset matters though. The "full" model with offset of 0 performs better than all other offsets ("full" model with offset 100 is shown in Figure 2), particularly in more recent years. Out of the thirty-two models, the indicator "full" and the indicator "sliding-window" model with offset of 0 and $\delta = 1$ were selected, and the remainder of the paper will utilize either one or both of these models. They will be referred to as the "full" and "sliding" model, respectively.

The "full" model misclassifies 2.25% of the people in the SSA dataset, which is slightly higher than the 1.74% pure (within name*year) error rate; when excluding low confidence predictions the model has an SSA misclassification rate of 0.82% vs. 0.59% pure error. Figure 2 shows that the misclassification rates range from 1% to 4.5% over the entire 129 years, while the high confidence rates range from 0.5% to 1%. Overall the misclassification rates and pure errors rates tend to increase over time, likely due to increasing diversity of names and the fact that more names are being given to individuals of both genders than in the past. The downturn during ~1930-1950 probably reflects, in part, lower immigration rates during the Depression and World War II.

It should also be noted that the SSA data is not 100% reliable as a gold standard for two reasons. First, the SSA data is likely to contain human recording errors e.g., from the transcription of newly minted parents hand-written notes on paper forms. It would not be surprising if this occurred at a rate of ~1%, e.g., for older records, but is more likely to occur at a scale 0.1%. Second, the model predictions are based on mentions of the Bing-indexed names across the world-wide web and these mentions represent a sample of a population that is much broader than the one captured in the SSA dataset. As a result, the model can provide better worldwide estimates than the SSA data, e.g., for names like Andrea which is dominated by females in the US but dominated by males in Italy. We will further discuss this effect in subsequent sections.

4.2 Characterizing the model

Figure 3a shows the weights of the phrase markers (and their indicator attributes in Figures 3b and 3c) as they change over time in the two selected models. Overall, the "full" model weights change smoothly over time capturing general trends, while the "sliding" model captures short term changes as shown by fluctuations and occasional spikes. This is because the "full" model takes into account data from all 129 years using a quadratic approximation while the "sliding" model is based on separate linear approximations for each possible 9-year window.

The marker weights vary in systematic and meaningful ways, both in direction and absolute values. For example, *He married* and *She married* were the most heavily weighted positive (i.e., female) and negative (i.e., male) markers, respectively, during the earliest years but have gradually lost about 50% of their weights during the time period covered. Married references often point to genealogy and family tree descriptions going back 100 or more years. The weights for *Grandmother* and *Grandfather* are much smaller but follow a similar pattern, except that they switch direction (*Grandmother* becomes male; *Grandfather* becomes female) in the 1930s. *Daughter* and *Son* (and *Girl* and *Boy*) follow a similar pattern, except time-reversed, while *Sister* and *Brother* peak in the middle of the time period, as does *Wife* and *Husband.* It makes perfect sense that mentions of grandparents, the "oldest" markers, peak at the earliest time, while children, the "youngest" markers, peak today, and other family members peak in between.

Interestingly, the gender-opposite paired curves tend to vertically mirror one another, except for *Father* and *Mother*. We expected this mirroring to occur across the zero-line with the feminine indicator being positive and the masculine indicator being negative. Many of the pairings followed this pattern but some did not. *Boy*, for example, has a positive weight until the late 1960s.

It is not clear why this is the case but it should not matter much. It is important to note that the model takes into account all markers simultaneously, and the anomalous weights make up a fraction of the total weight. Also, some of the well-behaved markers, *He married* and *She married* and *Aunt* and *Uncle* for example, also tended to result in lower, more accurate Bing counts than the other phrase markers such as *Boy* and *Girl*. As these counts reach thousands or more, Bing starts returning approximations instead of actual result counts, which was the case with most of the queries initiated using the more popular phrase markers like *Mr* and *Father*. It may be the case that these approximations and the large numbers themselves affected the weight sizes and direction.

The weights associated with the zero and low count indicators show similar patterns across the paired phrase markers (Figures 3b and 3c). The indicators were used to relax the continuity of the models near the zero and small Bing counts. We expect the weights to have opposite signs from the transformed Bing result count weights. If a *Daughter* query returns few or no results, we would expect the name to be more likely masculine, which is why in Figure 3b and Figure 3c we mostly see that the masculine indicators have positive weights and the feminine indicators have negative weights in all cases except the *He married* and *She married* pairing. This probably just reflects the fact that they were, by far, the most likely to return zero or low counts.

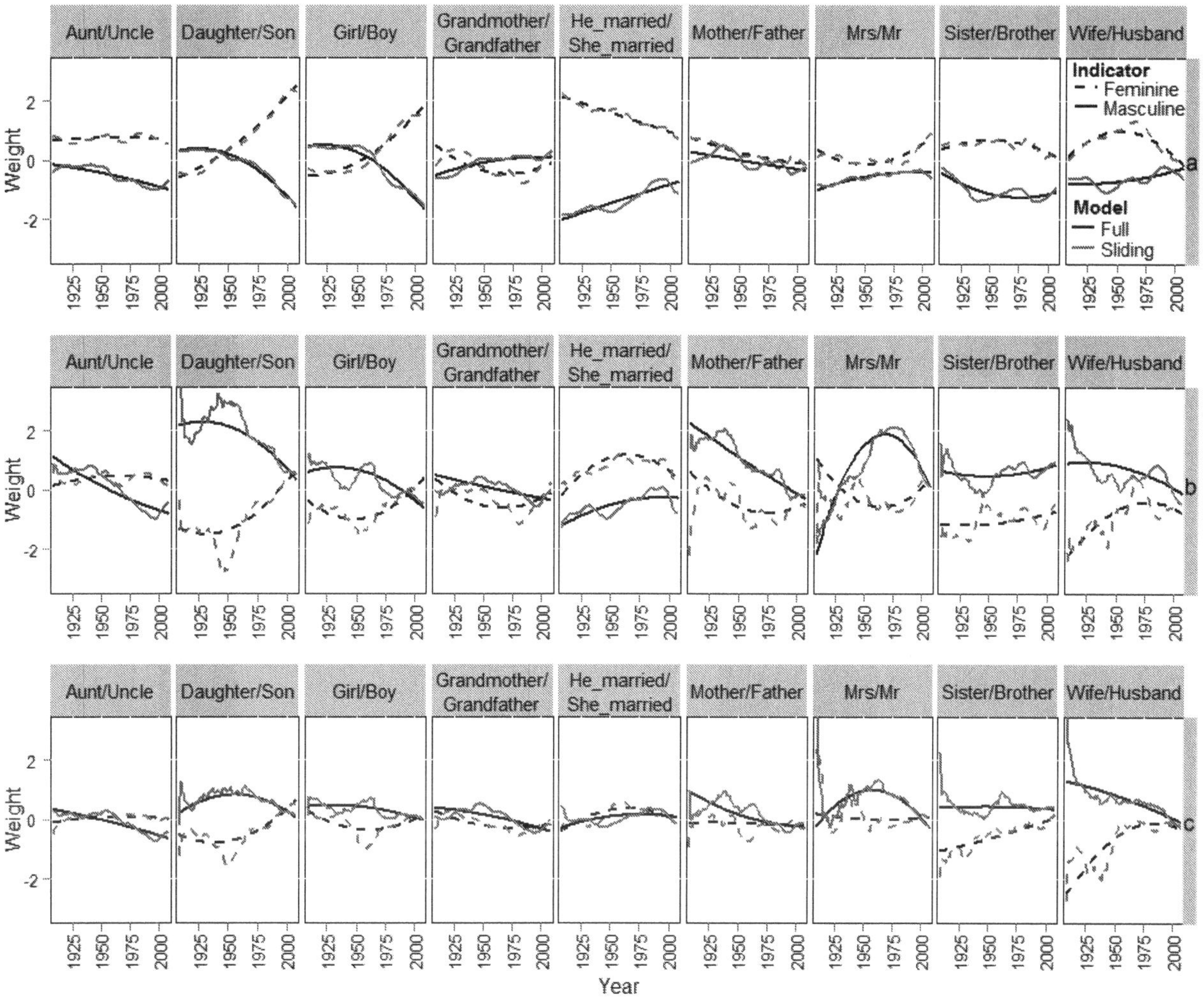

Figure 3. Time-varying weights of the markers: a) transformed Bing counts, b) zero count indicators, c) low count indicators.

4.3 Model performance on select names

We first tested cases where the models are expected to perform well: four popular male names (William, Andrew, Thomas, and Joseph) and four popular female names (Katherine, Julia, Mary, and Catherine). As shown in Figure 4, the predictions vary little and follow the "true" SSA proportions. Also, note that the "sliding" model mimics some name-specific SSA spikes a bit too closely, which suggests that it is over-trained. Keep in mind that the error rates are very low, at a scale that is probably approaching the human clerical error rate.

Second, the models were tested on cases where we expect noisy predictions: ten androgynous names (Alex, Dana, Jackie, Jessie, Jordan, Leslie, Marion, Pat, Terry, and Willie). As Figure 5 shows, these names either switch genders over time (as with Leslie, Dana, and to some extent Willie), remain consistently androgynous (as with Pat), or they change moderately but remain largely attributed to one gender (as with Alex, Jackie, Jessie, Jordan, Marion, and Terry). Overall the models do surprisingly well in identifying these as androgynous names and capturing the direction of gender-orientation changes over time. As expected, the models smooth out highly non-linear changes such as the step-like pattern observed for Leslie. Note also that some predictions differ significantly from the SSA, partly reflecting the global nature of the model (vs. the US-centric SSA data). Both of these effects are beneficial for generalization purposes.

Third, we used a set of author names on computational linguistics papers labeled as male or female using a combination of database lookup and manual annotations[29]. Within this set, the full model (female probability averaged over the years 1955, 1965, and 1975) agreed with 91.9% of 2,755 female labels, and 95.6% of 6,862 male labels. The model strongly disagreed (female prob. < 0.05) with 16 of their female labels (Deryle, Gerik, Helmar, Steffan, Craige, Chikara, Ransom, Chul, Muath, Stephane, Ryosuke, Yuya, Elvan; some occurred multiple times) most of which actually refer to males. The model strongly disagreed (female prob. > 0.95) with 18 of their male labels (Itziar, Sina, Raymonde, Einav, Vivi, Xiaohong, Michele, Sanja, Korin, Ales, and Dorry; some occurred multiple times) several of which actually refer to females.

4.4 Sources of errors

The models are trained on popular US names and will therefore tend to agree when the SSA indicates that a name is strongly female or male. However, there are numerous cases when the models differ from the SSA data. This is partly due to the fact that the predictive markers are based on a global resource (the web as captured by Bing). As Figure 5 shows, the model predictions systematically differ from the SSA proportions for Marion, which is largely given to females in France and other parts of Europe but is given to both males and females in the US. Andrea, Michele, Ira, Jan, and Joan are other examples that have different gender-orientations in the US vs. other places in the world. To study these types of variations systematically, we created nine different subsets of names. Figure 6 shows the overall proportion misclassified for each set using the 50% cutoff. Below we discuss these sets and the sources of errors therein.

4.4.1 Non-US Names

We first compiled a list of common non-US first names with a high co-occurrence rate with non-US affiliations (relative to US co-occurrence) in PubMed. The model performs surprisingly well for these names (see grey dashed line in Figure 6a). The error rates are lower than for all SSA names (solid black line) but worse than for common US names (red dashed line). Even though these names are more popular in other countries, many are also present in the US e.g., Isabella and Zoe. Tightly gendered names in some non-US countries (e.g., due to national naming laws) is likely to lead to greatly skewed Bing results with high counts for masculine markers and low to no counts for feminine markers or vice versa.

Second, we assess model performance on subsets of names that are common in countries with recent immigration to US: 300 popular Mexican names [17] and 620 Asian names [19], including but not limited to Chinese, Japanese, Indian, Korean, and Vietnamese names. Figure 6a shows the misclassification rates using SSA numbers as ground truth. Some spikes in the Asian names and Mexican names reflect individual names: Jo (1931), Kim (1954), and Jaime (1976). Jaime's spike in 1976 represents a drastic increase in females named Jaime, and coincides with the introduction of the popular US TV series Bionic Woman and the lead character Jaime Sommers. Jo and Kim are popular diminutives in the US. Setting aside these three names gives us a better perspective of the collective effect of Asian and Mexican names. Error rates for Mexican names are about the same as error rates averaged across all SSA names, while Asian names have higher error rates, particularly since ~1970 and onwards. There are four major reasons for higher error rates amongst names in this group: 1) they are typically short names; 2) transliterations from the original language into English is many-to-many (e.g., the gender-specific aspects of Asian characters or symbols are lost in translation to ASCII); 3) they are typically more androgynous than English names; and 4) they are often used as both first and last names. So, searching for +"Brother Kaoru", for example, may yield results where Kaoru is one's surname and not one's first name.

In some countries, names are often made up of compound combinations of male, female, and androgynous names such as Jose Maria (male in Spain) vs. Jose (male) and Maria (female). The model tends to do well in these cases, as long as the names are relatively common.

4.4.2 Surnames, famous people, and common words

Carlson and Cooper are examples of surnames that are also used as first names, and they are both typically given to males (see Figure 7). As discussed earlier, androgynous names are typically given to more females over time, yet the model predictions indicate that Cooper defies this trend by moving from being somewhat feminine to almost completely masculine in recent years. Carlson, on the other hand, does trend towards becoming more feminine as time progresses. Generally, surnames will give high counts for both the *Mr* and *Mrs* markers which forces the predictions towards neutral.

Unlike names that serve as both first names and surnames, one would expect the names of famous people to be predicted strongly feminine or masculine. Paris (the city and the famous socialite Paris Hilton), Theresa (Mother Theresa), and Guadalupe (the Virgin of Guadalupe, the Roman Catholic icon of the Virgin Mary) are three such names. Both Guadalupe and Theresa are both strongly feminine, as expected, while Paris ends up feminine after climbing there steadily over almost 60 years (see Figure 7). This might be another case where a single famous person has shifted a global trend (also see previous discussion of Jaime).

Given a recent trend to choose nontraditional names for babies, we were also curious how well the model performs for names that are also common English words (including the markers themselves). These names were downloaded from a British baby name website [32] to which we added seven colors in the SSA dataset. As Figure 6b shows, misclassification rates are high for word names, particularly in recent years because of an increase in name creativity. Figure 8 shows predictions of four word names typically attributed to males (i.e., Cash, Given, Hero, and Will) and four word names typically attributed to females (i.e., April, Lily, May, and Summer). While April, Lily, and Summer are given to a greater proportion of females over time, May becomes more masculine over time. The male names, with the exception of Given, remain mostly attributed to males throughout the entire period. Verb names like May and Will are expected to be problematic because many of the markers are nouns, and so search queries become commonly used noun-verb phrases. As with surnames, the resulting word-name predictions tend to err towards neutral rather than false positive male or female.

The name Given is an interesting example in this set of names. As expected, the model predicts more feminine over time but the change occurred earlier than expected (in the 1950s). This is due to the way search engines process punctuations when indexing documents, and how specific phrasing is used across domains. For example, most results from the queries *He married Given* and *She married Given* without punctuation were from obituaries, newspapers, alumni newsletters, genealogical records, and the like. Results from *He married Given* with punctuation interspersed, however, were common in dating advice sites, such as: "but I doubt he's married, given the information..." and "...admitted he's never been tested before he married. Given this information about both our pasts..." The marker *He married* is feminine-oriented in the model. So, despite the baby name site suggesting Given is a masculine name, the model moves towards female prediction because these dating advice sites amplify the *He married* marker relative to the *She married* marker. These findings do not necessarily imply that one should attempt to exclude these types of search results generally, nor is it to say that the *He married* and *She married* markers should not be utilized. This does illustrate, however, that some common words may create unanticipated phrasing that might yield a strong signal in the wrong direction.

Figure 9 shows the predictions for colors used as names in the SSA dataset. The predictions indicate that colors were used only for boys 100 years ago. Since then, Blue, Brown, Green, Orange, and Red remained male, while Pink, White, and Cyan follow the pattern noted by Lieberson, Dumais, and Baumann [16] and become increasingly feminine over time. Some of these colors are strongly attributed to a certain gender in the US. For example, blue is attributed to males while pink is attributed to females [13, 15]. The predictions made by the model in recent years reflect this trend. It is also interesting to see how Pink in particular starts as masculine and becomes feminine around the 1950s as this is also when the gender stereotyping of the color changed. Pink was considered more of a boy's color and blue more of a girl's color until around the 1950s [13].

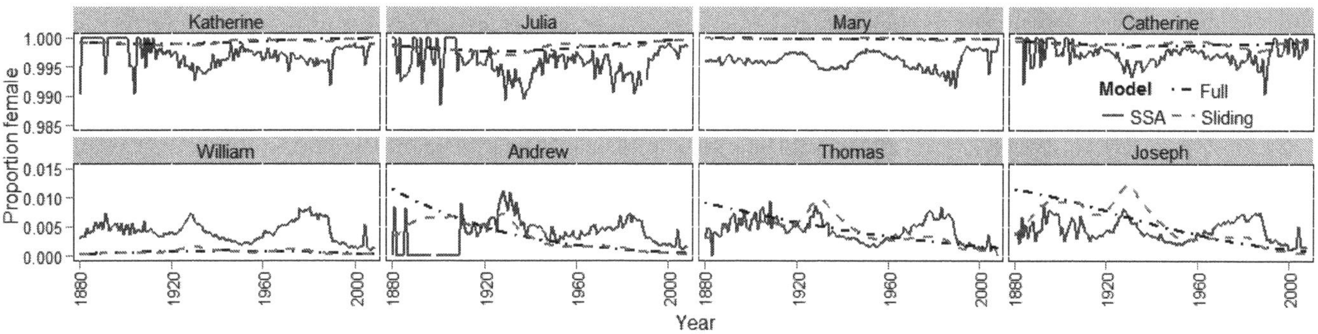

Figure 4. Predictions vs. SSA proportions for popular names given predominantly to either females or males over time.

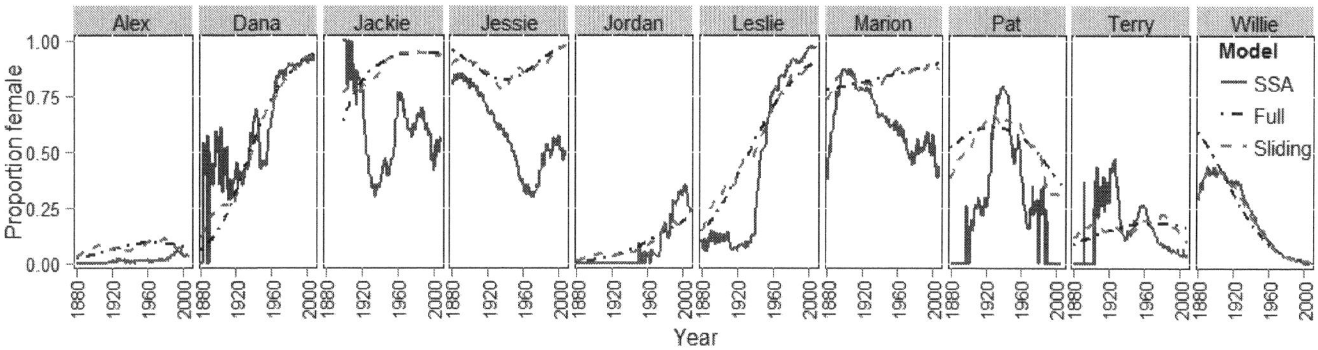

Figure 5. Predictions vs. SSA proportions for names given to both males and females at varying rates over time.

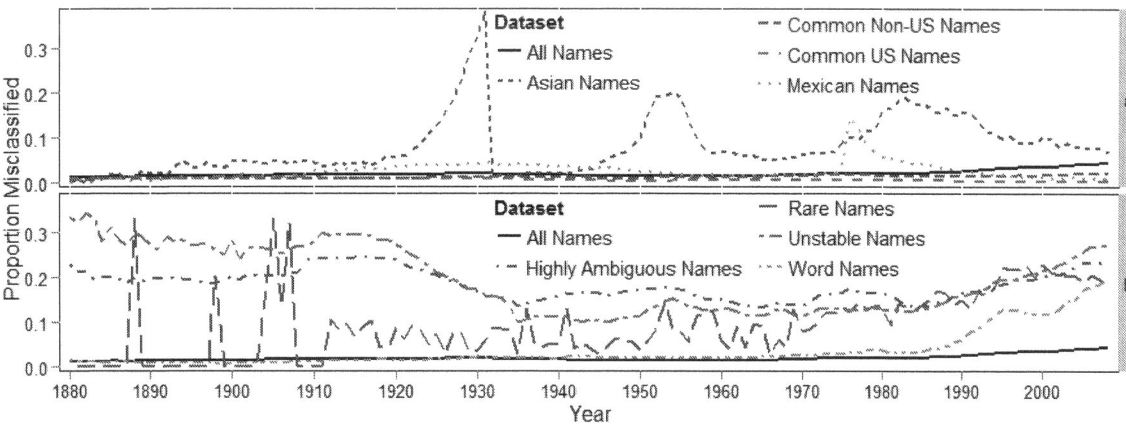

Figure 6. The proportion of people in the SSA dataset misclassified by the "full" model for different categories of names. a) *Asian names* [19]; *Common Non-US Names* correlated with non-US country affiliation in PubMed; *Common US names* with at least 500,000 individuals in the SSA dataset; *Mexican names* [17]. b) *Highly ambiguous names* have roughly equal males vs. females for any given year in the SSA dataset; *Rare names* given to < 11 people in the SSA dataset; *Unstable names* exclusively male at one point but changed to exclusively female (or vice versa); and *Word names* [32]. Some misclassification spikes in the Asian names and Mexican names reflect individual names: Jo (1931), Kim (1954), and Jaime (1976).

Two of the other colors, Brown and Green, are also popular surnames. As noted earlier, some of the prediction curves may be affected in unexpected ways simply because of the format of the search queries used to make the predictions. However, in this case, Brown and Green are names that one would expect to be more associated with males, and that is supported by the predictions generated by the model.

4.4.3 Rare names

The model performs worse with rare names (Figure 6b), here defined as names given to ten or fewer people in the SSA dataset. This is primarily because the Bing query counts tend to be low for all the phrase markers, although the low count indicator variables in the model help somewhat in these instances. Interestingly, many of the rare names are spelling variants of traditional, popular names (e.g., Ashlii, Ashliy, Ashlae, Ashlely vs. Ashley).

4.5 Robustness of model to potential changes in search engine coverage and estimation

A concern with using search engines is that their coverage, query processing, and count estimation change over time. To simulate how these changes might affect the model, we gathered Google search result counts for a sample of 2,645 names using the same search methods as with Bing. The set of names was sampled due to Google API limitations. One can think of this as a worst-case scenario simulation of Bing changes because the queries were submitted to Google at least a year before that of Bing data collection (i.e., reflects a temporal change of the web itself), and Google counts represent different web crawling methods, indexing, and count estimation. Figure 10 shows that using Google counts in the Bing optimized model introduces surprisingly little noise. Misclassifications go from ~1% to ~2% with some periodic variations. This suggests that the model is quite robust to changes in search engine coverage, query processing, and estimation over time.

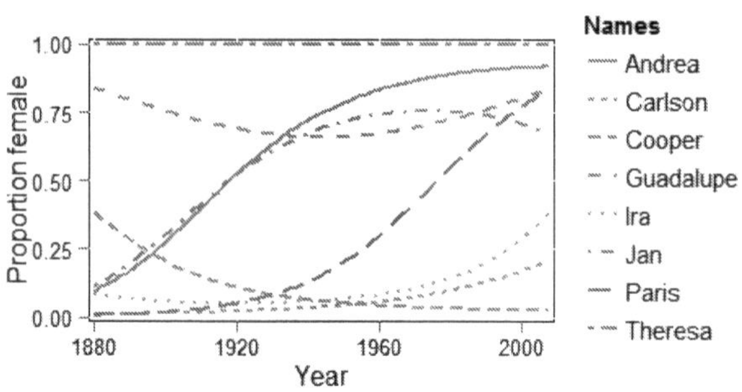

Figure 7. Predictions for some names with "atypical" patterns.

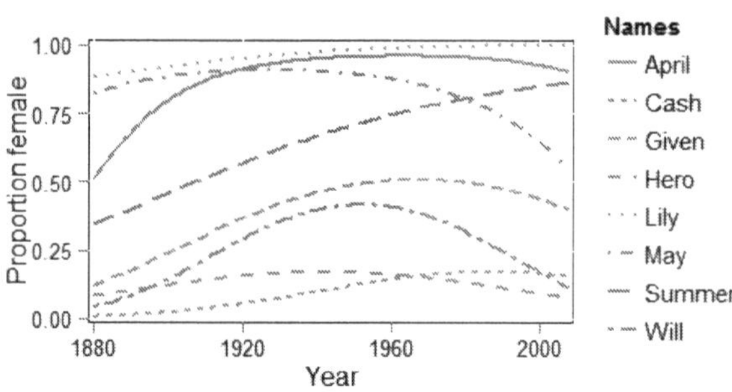

Figure 8. Predictions for names that are also common words.

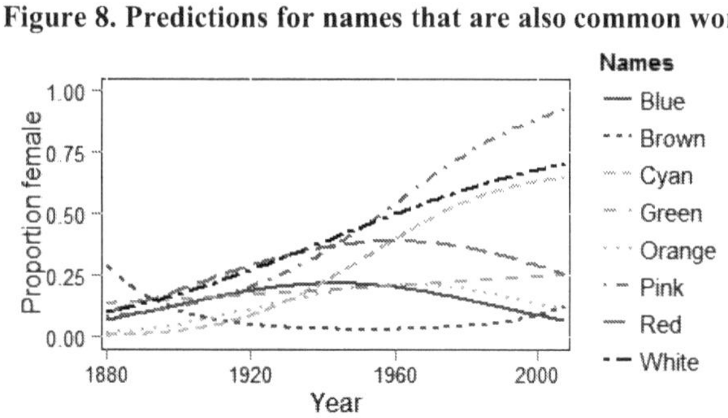

Figure 9. Predictions for names that are also colors.

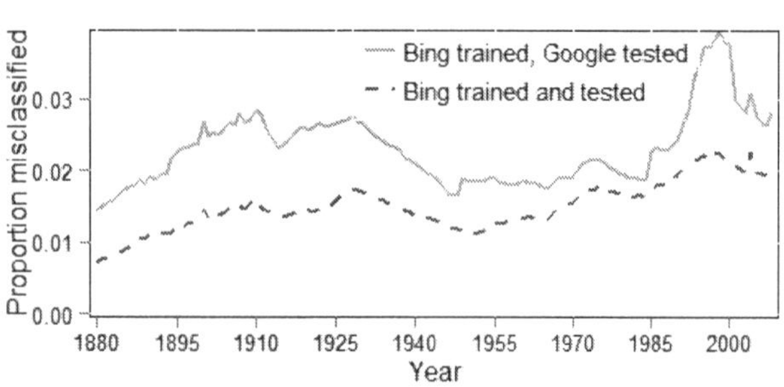

Figure 10. Potential degradation of model predictions due to changes in search engine coverage and count estimation as reflected by using Google counts in a Bing trained model.

4.6 Naming patterns over time

The statistical model allows one to study naming patterns over time so that periods of name popularity for individuals of specific genders and general trending patterns can be noted. For example, Figure 4, shows that Katherine, Julia, Mary, and Catherine have been strongly associated with females during the entire time period covered by the SSA dataset. However, Figure 5 shows that Dana and Leslie switched from being mostly male to mostly female. Several additional names in Figure 5 further illustrate the observation made by Lieberson, Dumais, and Baumann [16] that names considered androgynous are increasingly given to females over time. Willie exhibits the opposite trend. Pat, as well, seems to be becoming more associated with males. This may be because Pat is both a popular nickname for females (Patricia) and males (Patrick). As Patricia has decreased in popularity and Patrick has increased, the prediction curve for Pat is drawn towards that of Patrick and becomes more masculine over time. Alex is another example in this vein. Alex is a common nickname for both names associated with males, e.g., Alexander, and females, e.g., Alexandra, Alexa, and Alexandria. However, its formal use is most often associated with males. The model predict a majority of male but less so than the SSA data. In other words, even though the model was trained using formal given names (on SSA applications), we see that the model captures both the formal and informal (nickname) uses of each name (on the web).

4.7 Gender patterns over time in bibliographic databases

With a model in place we turn to illustrating its use in characterizing the temporal changes in gender for a selection of readily available bibliographic databases covering books, articles, patents, and grants: Harvard University Library, University of Illinois library, PubMed (biomedical articles), DBLP (computer science articles), patents from the United States Patent and Trademark Office (USPTO), and grants from the US Department of Health and Human Services (HHS), primarily NIH. For each of the bibliographic datasets we only considered records with a publication date from 1800 to 2010 that had at least one author (or inventor, or principal investigator) name and only assigned the gender to the first listed author (or inventor, or investigator). Gender was assigned if the model produced high confidence classification and these classification were consistent over time (female if $p > 0.9$, male if $p < 0.1$ for all of the years 1955, 1965, 1975; unknown otherwise), and the name was already in the Genni database. Each dataset contains millions of records: Harvard Library Bibliographic Dataset [14]: ~8 million records, 1800-2010; University of Illinois Library (provided by library staff): ~3 million records, 1800-2009; PubMed (leased for free from the NLM): 18+ million records, 1865-2010. Note that PubMed started consistently recording first names only in 2002, so we used a disambiguated dataset of authors [24, 25] to assign a first name to older records that were matched with complete records. DBLP [10]: ~1.7 million records from major computer science journals and conference proceedings, 1936-2010. NIH Exporter CRISP legacy grant data [8]: ~2 million records, 1970-2009. USPTO patents distribution by Google [28]: ~4 million records, 1976-2010.

Figure 11 shows two plots reflecting trends over time. The top plot shows the proportion of records that were assigned with high confidence within each dataset, and the bottom plot shows the proportion of high confidence classifications that were female. Note that the spikes in these curves often reflect low counts. For example, the 1878 spike in PubMed (and the 1940 spike in DBLP) in the bottom plot represents only 5 people.

Two major driving forces can explain the patterns for these curves: indexing practices and human behavior, both of which may exhibit gender bias. We expect the top plot to primarily reflect indexing practice, and the bottom plot to primarily reflect human behavior, more specifically participation bias. For example, NIH and USPTO have consistently indexed nearly all of the records with first names over time, while DBLP and the two libraries have been consistent over time but at a lower rate. PubMed first started recording first names in 2002, and even though disambiguation helps assign gender to some older records, we see a dramatic increase over time. The recent downward trend in DBLP, USPTO, and PubMed is not due to indexing practice but rather an increasing presence of non-US names for which the model predicts neutral. In analyzing these gender trends, we are confident in the statistics for the datasets that are "complete" in the sense that USPTO covers all US patents, and CRISP covers all extramural NIH grants. The other datasets reflect selective inclusion driven and constrained by a variety of factors. For example, PubMed (and DBLP) probably aim at covering the most important publication venues in biomedicine (and computer science, respectively), whereas the libraries cater to their (local) patrons. All are constrained by limited resources. One might wonder how much of the selective inclusion reflects gender bias, beyond the general participation bias in these specific domains (biomedicine and computer science).

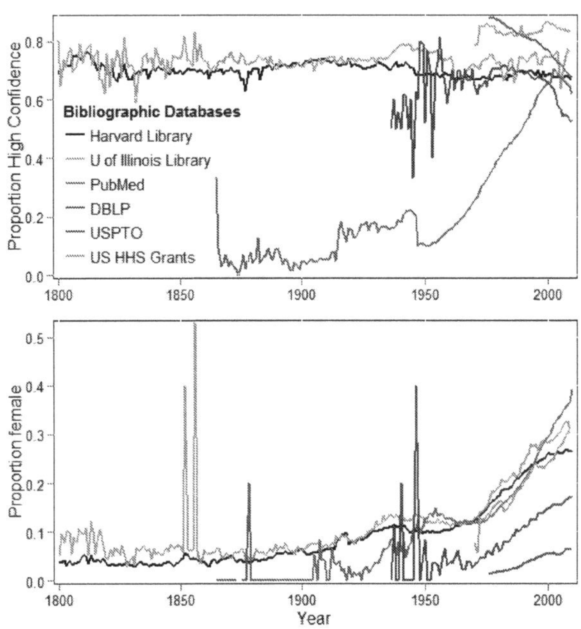

Figure 11. Gender classifications in bibliographic databases.

In terms of participation, all domains reflect a bias towards male. USPTO clearly has the lowest female participation (7% peak), followed by DBLP (17% peak), Harvard Library (27% peak), NIH grants (31% peak), Illinois Library (31% peak), and PubMed (39% peak). Female participation has consistently increased in all datasets since 1970, although the growth varies: USPTO has slow growth, DBLP moderate growth, and the remaining datasets have fast growth. If the trends continue, PubMed will reach the magical 50% female in ~10-20 years, DBLP in ~100 years, and USPTO in ~300 years. These are obviously very rough estimates that rest on a suite of assumptions that probably will not hold in the future. For example, a) Harvard library already appears to have stagnated about 10 years ago; b) females on NIH grants and PubMed followed each other closely from the 1970s to the mid-1990s when NIH suffered a setback and has been trying to catch up ever since. These global patterns hint at potential in-depth studies addressing confounding factors. For example, among younger authors in PubMed, today's proportion female is probably closer to 50%.

5. CONCLUSIONS AND FUTURE WORK

Discerning the gender orientation of a first name given no other information can be a difficult task. Our approach performs surprisingly well despite its simplicity. It misclassifies 2.25% of the people in the SSA dataset, which is just slightly higher than the 1.74% pure error rate, and it utilizes simple web searches that are highly scalable and its predictions are based on public data covering names beyond the SSA dataset.

Very rare names are the most challenging for our approach because of limited search engine coverage. Performance would improve if the search engine could: 1) provide higher recall by covering more of the surface web, if not the deep web, 2) provide higher precision by permitting exact phrase searching (to avoid cases where punctuation occurs between words in a phrase), and 3) provide better estimates of result counts. Other groups of names have high rates of misclassification as well. For names that are intrinsically ambiguous (or made so by many-to-many transliteration from the original language into English), no model can do better without contextual clues surrounding the mention of the name. Other names like Andrea and Ira are globally androgynous but not so locally because of different naming conventions across countries and cultures. A natural extension of our work is to assess the promise of additional markers (for gender, time, geography/language) and relaxing the strict phrase searching for predicting the culture or geographic origin of names, either alone or in conjunction with gender. One could also combine our approach with name features extracted directly from the name and use other sources for training data such as Wikipedia or Facebook (as demonstrated by Treeratpituk and Giles [26] and Tang et al. [23]). Other sources of training data and new attributes could also help improve predictions for diminutive names or nicknames such as Alex which serves as a nickname for a female while it is also a formal given name for a male. Future work could also study more in-depth some of the (unexpected) temporal patterns revealed by our model.

Nevertheless, the present model permits accurate and automatic assignment of gender to names beyond the public SSA dataset. The model has been implemented as a web-tool called Genni (available via http://abel.lis.illinois.edu/) that displays the predicted proportion of females vs. males over time for any given name. This should be a valuable resource for those who utilize names in order to discern gender on a large scale, e.g., to study the roles of gender and diversity in scholarly work based on digital libraries and bibliographic databases where the authors' names are listed.

6. ACKNOWLEDGMENTS

Funding for this study was provided in part by NSF Science of Science and Innovation Policy (SciSIP) program award 0965341.

7. REFERENCES

[1] API Basics: 2011. *http://www.bing.com/developers/s/APIBasics.html*. Accessed: 2012-05-21.

[2] Baby Name Guesser - analysis of first names, first names statistics, popular boy and girl names, male names, female names: *http://www.gpeters.com/names/baby-names.php*. Accessed: 2011-05-03.

[3] Baby Names: 2011. *http://www.babynamewizard.com/*. Accessed: 2011-05-03.

[4] Bergsma, S. et al. 2009. Glen, Glenda or Glendale: unsupervised and semi-supervised learning of English noun gender. *Proceedings of the Thirteenth Conference on Computational Natural Language Learning* (Boulder, Colorado, 2009), 120–128.

[5] Bing API, Version 2: *http://msdn.microsoft.com/en-us/library/dd251056.aspx*. Accessed: 2013-04-04.

[6] Breuning, M. and Sanders, K. 2007. Gender and Journal Authorship in Eight Prestigious Political Science Journals. *PS: Political Science & Politics*. 40, 02 (Apr. 2007), 347.

[7] Carlson, A. et al. 2010. Toward an Architecture for Never-Ending Language Learning. *Proceedings of the AAAI-10 24th AAAI Conference on Artificial Intelligence* (2010).

[8] CRISP LEGACY DATA: 2010. *http://exporter.nih.gov/crisp_catalog.aspx*. Accessed: 2013-04-10.

[9] Cucerzan, S. and Yarowsky, D. 2003. Minimally supervised induction of grammatical gender. *Proceedings of the 2003 Conference of the North American Chapter of the Association for Computational Linguistics on Human Language Technology - Volume 1* (Edmonton, Canada, 2003), 40–47.

[10] DBLP FAQ: What is the meaning of "DBLP"?: 2013. *http://www.informatik.uni-trier.de/~ley/db/about/faqdblp.html*. Accessed: 2013-04-04.

[11] Efron, M. 2004. The liberal media and right-wing conspiracies: using cocitation information to estimate political orientation in web documents. *Proceedings of the 13th ACM international conference on Information and knowledge management* (Washington D.C., USA, 2004), 390–398.

[12] England, P. et al. 2007. Why Are Some Academic Fields Tipping Toward Female? The Sex Composition of U.S. Fields of Doctoral Degree Receipt, 1971–2002. *Sociology of Education*. 80, 1 (2007), 23–42.

[13] Frassanito, P. and Pettorini, B. 2008. Pink and blue: the color of gender. *Child's Nervous System*. 24, 8 (2008), 881–882.

[14] Harvard Library Bibliographic Dataset | Open Metadata: 2012. *http://openmetadata.lib.harvard.edu/bibdata*. Accessed: 2013-04-04.

[15] Karniol, R. 2011. The Color of Children's Gender Stereotypes. *Sex Roles*. 65, 1 (2011), 119–132.

[16] Lieberson, S. et al. 2000. The Instability of Androgynous Names: The Symbolic Maintenance of Gender Boundaries. *The American Journal of Sociology*. 105, 5 (Mar. 2000), 1249–1287.

[17] Mexican Babies Name List: *http://www.top-100-baby-names-search.com/mexican-babies-name.html*. Accessed: 2013-04-04.

[18] Otterbacher, J. 2010. Inferring gender of movie reviewers: exploiting writing style, content and metadata. *Proceedings of the 19th ACM international conference on Information and knowledge management* (Toronto, ON, Canada, 2010), 369–378.

[19] Popular Asian Names: *http://www.top-100-baby-names-search.com/popular-asian-names.html*. Accessed: 2013-04-04.

[20] Popular Baby Names: 2010. *http://www.ssa.gov/oact/babynames/*. Accessed: 2011-02-17.

[21] Reece-Evans, L. 2010. Gender and Citation in Two LIS E-Journals: A Bibliometric Analysis of LIBRES and Information Research. *Library & Information Science Research Electronic Journal*. 20, 1 (Mar. 2010), 1–18.

[22] Sassen, C. 2009. Gender and authorship in The Indexer, 1958-2007. *Indexer*.

[23] Tang, C. et al. 2011. What's in a name: a study of names, gender inference, and gender behavior in facebook. *Proceedings of the 16th international conference on Database systems for advanced applications* (Hong Kong, China, 2011), 344–356.

[24] Torvik, V.I. et al. 2005. A probabilistic similarity metric for Medline records: A model for author name disambiguation: Research Articles. *Journal of the American Society for Information Science and Technology*. 56, 2 (Jan. 2005), 140–158.

[25] Torvik, V.I. and Smalheiser, N.R. 2009. Author name disambiguation in MEDLINE. *ACM Transactions on Knowledge Discovery from Data (TKDD)*. 3, 3 (Jul. 2009), 11:1–11:29.

[26] Treeratpituk, P. and Giles, C.L. 2012. Name-Ethnicity Classification and Ethnicity-Sensitive Name Matching. *Proceedings of the 26th AAAI Conference on Artificial Intelligence* (2012), 1141–1147.

[27] Turney, P.D. and Littman, M.L. 2003. Measuring praise and criticism: Inference of semantic orientation from association. *ACM Trans. Inf. Syst.* 21, 4 (2003), 315–346.

[28] USPTO Bulk Downloads: Patent Grant Bibliographic Data: *http://www.google.com/googlebooks/uspto-patents-grants-biblio.html*. Accessed: 2013-04-29.

[29] Vogel, A. and Jurafsky, D. 2012. "He Said, She Said: Gender in the ACL Anthology. *ACL 2012 Special Workshop: Rediscovering 50 Years of Discoveries* (2012).

[30] Wattenberg, M. 2005. Baby Names, Visualization, and Social Data Analysis. *Proceedings of the Proceedings of the 2005 IEEE Symposium on Information Visualization* (2005), 1.

[31] Web 1T 5-gram Version 1: 2006. *http://www.ldc.upenn.edu/Catalog/CatalogEntry.jsp?catalogId=LDC2006T13*. Accessed: 2013-04-04.

[32] Word Names: which words are being used for Brit Babies?: 2011. *http://britishbabynames.typepad.com/blog/2011/05/word-names-which-words-are-being-used-for-brit-babies.html*. Accessed: 2013-04-04.

[33] Zheleva, E. and Getoor, L. 2009. To join or not to join: the illusion of privacy in social networks with mixed public and private user profiles. *Proceedings of the 18th international conference on World wide web* (Madrid, Spain, 2009), 531–540.

A Relevance Feedback Approach for the Author Name Disambiguation Problem

Thiago A. Godoi, Ricardo da S. Torres, and Ariadne M. B. R. Carvalho
Institute of Computing
University of Campinas
{thiago.godoi,rtorres, ariadne}@ic.unicamp.br

Marcos André Gonçalves
Dept. of Computer Science
Federal University of Minas Gerais
mgoncalv@dcc.ufmg.br

Anderson A. Ferreira
Dept. of Computer Science
Federal University of Ouro Preto
ferreira@iceb.ufop.br

Weiguo Fan and Edward A. Fox
Dept. of Computer Science
Virginia Tech
{wfan,fox}@vt.edu

ABSTRACT

This paper presents a new name disambiguation method that exploits user feedback on ambiguous references across iterations. An unsupervised step is used to define pure training samples, and a hybrid supervised step is employed to learn a classification model for assigning references to authors. Our classification scheme combines the Optimum-Path Forest (OPF) classifier with complex reference similarity functions generated by a Genetic Programming framework. Experiments demonstrate that the proposed method yields better results than state-of-the-art disambiguation methods on two traditional datasets.

Categories and Subject Descriptors

H.3.3 [**Information Search and Retrieval**]: Information Retrieval; I.5.2 [**Pattern Recognition**]: Classifier design and evaluation

General Terms

Algorithms, Experimentation

Keywords

Name Disambiguation, Relevance Feedback, Genetic Programming, Optimum-Path Forest Classifier

1. INTRODUCTION

Scholarly digital libraries (DLs) such as DBLP[1], Citeseer[2], BDBComp[3], and MEDLINE[4] are fundamental tools for the advance of science and technology. However, one fundamental issue which concerns all of them is the *quality* of their data, which affects not only data but also the effectiveness of the services provided. Among the many potential data quality problems faced by these DLs, the *author name ambiguity* problem is one of the hardest to solve. This problem occurs when a same author publishes under similar but distinct names (synonyms) or distinct authors share the same name or close variations of this name (homonyms).

The task of disambiguating author names may be formulated as follows. Consider a collection of *citation records*, each of which has a list of *attributes*. That list necessarily includes author names, work title, and publication venue title. Each attribute associates a specific value with a citation. An attribute may be composed of several *elements*. In case of the attribute "author names", an element corresponds to the name of a single unique author. Each author name element is a *reference* to an author. The objective of the disambiguation task is to produce a disambiguation function that is used to partition the set of references to authors, so that each partition block contains ideally all the references to a same author and no references to other authors.

We assume that each reference to an author extracted from a citation record contains at least the following attributes: author name, coauthor names, work title, and publication venue title. To disambiguate the bibliographic citations of a digital library (DL), first we split the set of references to authors into groups of references called *ambiguous groups*. In each ambiguous group, the author name values are similar. The ambiguous groups may be obtained by using blocking methods [1] which address scalability issues, avoiding the need for comparisons among all references.

A large number of methods have been proposed in the literature to deal with the author name ambiguity problem [2]. However, there is still room for substantial improvement,

[1]`http://www.informatik.uni-trier.de/~ley/db/` (as of Jan. 2013).
[2]`http://citeseerx.ist.psu.edu/index` (as of Jan. 2013).
[3]`http://www.lbd.dcc.ufmg.br/bdbcomp/` (as of Jan. 2013).
[4]`http://www.ncbi.nlm.nih.gov/pubmed/` (as of Jan. 2013).

JCDL'13, July 22–26, 2013, Indianapolis, Indiana, USA.

mainly in the case where only the minimum amount of information exists in the citations, i.e, each citation contains only author and coauthor names, work title, and publication venue title. Moreover, the best methods in the literature are usually supervised, requiring very costly training data.

In this paper we propose a novel disambiguation method which only requires a small manual intervention from the DL administrator. Indeed, the feedback provided by the administrator is given only in a few iterations, applied to the most ambiguous cases. The method detects these cases by exploiting a combination of automatically generated similarity functions. These functions are discovered using genetic programming (GP) and a state-of-the-art classifier (optimum-path forest (OPF) [3,4]). The classifier uses these similarity functions to decide whether or not citations belong to a same author. As we shall see in our experiments, our proposed method reduces drastically the amount of manual intervention. Furthermore, it outperforms some state-of-the-art disambiguation methods, including one that also exploits some feedback from the user.

The rest of this article is organized as follows. Section 2 discusses related work. Section 3 describes our proposed approach. Section 4 presents the results of our experimental evaluation. Finally, Section 5 presents our conclusions and offers possible directions for future work.

2. RELATED WORK

This section presents an overview of related work on author name disambiguation methods and relevance feedback.

2.1 Author Name Disambiguation Methods

Most of the automatic name disambiguation methods proposed in the literature adopt solutions that may be classified according to the main type of approach they exploit. In [2], the authors classify these approaches as performing either *author grouping* or *author assignment*.

Author grouping methods try to group the references to the same author using some type of similarity among reference attributes [5–20]. These methods attempt to group references to a same author using some clustering technique along with a similarity function. The similarity function is applied to the attributes of the references (or group of references) in order to decide whether to place references in a same group or not, using the clustering technique. This similarity function may be predefined (based on existing ones and depending on the type of the attribute) [5, 8, 11, 12, 17, 20], learned using a supervised machine learning technique [6, 9, 15, 16, 21], or extracted from the relationships among authors and coauthors, usually represented as a graph [7, 19, 22].

Author assignment methods aim at directly assigning the references to their respective authors [18, 23–28]. These methods use either a supervised classification technique [18, 23, 27, 28], or a model-based clustering technique [24–26]. They infer models that represent the authors (for instance, the probabilities of an author publishing an article with other (co-)authors, in a given publication venue and using a list of specific terms in the work title).

2.2 Relevance Feedback

Relevance Feedback (RF) has been used mainly in search tasks in Information Retrieval [29]. In such tasks, the results obtained from a given search are evaluated as relevant or not by the user who issued the query. This information is given as feedback to the system which modifies the original query with terms belonging to the indicated documents. The new modified query is then used to retrieve new documents and this process continues until the user is satisfied or gives up.

Some types of user feedback in author name disambiguation tasks were proposed in [28,30,31]. Wang et al. [30] proposed ADANA (Active Name Disambiguation) that works in an interactive mode. It asks the user for corrections, instead of passively waiting for user inputs. For this, it chooses a few potentially erroneous disambiguated results, after a disambiguation process has been run. The active selection aims at minimizing the number of interactions needed to maximize effectiveness. Notice that in order to obtain good results, the authors make use of a lot of additional information, such as affiliation, bibliographic references etc., that is usually not available in most cases. We, on the other hand, focus only on the minimum amount of information in a citation (i.e., author and coauthor names, publication, and venue title).

Li et al. [31] proposed the use of a Perceptron as a classifier. They incorporated the user feedback of a scientific cooperation network as features and constraints, in order to improve the disambiguation performance. Initially, they use only features extracted from the publication and from the Web, such as homepage. After the first disambiguation, the users look for possible problems. The feedback features and constraints are then used by a classification system, jointly with the other features, to revise the classification model. That work differs from ours because it also uses other attributes beyond those commonly found in all publications. Moreover, it attempts to solve only the homonym problem and does not suggest possible errors (e.g., ambiguous references) to guide user feedback.

Ferreira et al. [28] extended a self-training author name disambiguator [18, 27] by incorporating user feedback. It works in two steps. In step 1, the references are grouped in clusters using the coauthorship graph. Some of these clusters are automatically selected and their references are used as initial training examples in the next step. The remaining references will compose the test set. Step 2 uses an associative classifier that is capable of detecting new authors. This classifier works in two phases. In the first phase, it selects a percentage of the most doubtful predictions and asks the administrator to assign them to the correct authors (user feedback). In the second phase, the doubtful predictions whose labels were defined by the user are inserted into the training set and the authors of the references in the test set are predicted. Our method instead works iteratively, i.e., users may provide feedback on ambiguous references across several iterations. Furthermore, we propose to learn reference similarity functions that are employed in the assignment of references to authors by the OPF classifier. The state-of-the-art methods described in [18,28] are used as baselines in our evaluation protocol.

Relevance feedback (RF) approaches have been proposed based on the OPF classifier [32–34]. Those initiatives, however, focus on content-based image retrieval [32,33] and classification [34] tasks. In the approaches presented in [32,34], GP is also used to determine edge weights in OPF graphs. Those RF methods, however, adopt a binary classification model in which each image is classified as either relevant or non-relevant. In our case, we have a multiple-class problem, because references may be assigned to different authors. Multi-classification is intrinsically a much more complex problem. First, the definition of suitable training sets, in terms of coverage and size, is much harder. Furthermore, many classifiers that are successful in binary classification problems fail when used or extended for dealing with multiple classes. In practical situations, the common strategy employed is costly, as it relies on the combination of multiple binary classifiers.

3. PROPOSED METHOD

The proposed disambiguation approach exploits some of the strategies used by both author grouping and author assignment methods. For instance, we use a machine learning framework to learn reference similarity functions and a supervised classification system to assign references to authors. The novelty here relies on the machine learning methods employed to implement each strategy and on the combination of those strategies with learning samples defined through user feedback. We use genetic programming (GP) for learning reference similarity functions and the Optimum-Path Forest (OPF) classifier for labeling references. The combination of OPF and GP has been very effective in relevance feedback approaches [32], yielding better results than methods based on using only GP-based similarity functions.

The disambiguation method consists in partitioning a set of references to authors $R = \{r_1, r_2, \ldots, r_m\}$ into a set $S = \{s_1, s_2, \ldots, s_n\}$, so that each partition block s_i has all the references to the same author.

We present an interactive approach for the name disambiguation problem. Our strategy relies on the use of a relevance feedback scheme, which enables the correct assignment of ambiguous references to their corresponding authors. We propose a two-step approach to perform this partition, as illustrated in Figure 1. The first step is unsupervised and has as objective of the automatic creation of training examples to be used in the following step (module labeled with A in Figure 1). The second step follows a relevance feedback scheme, and is supervised and interactive (dashed box B). Users interact with the disambiguation system providing feedback on ambiguous references (arrow labeled with D). The disambiguation system, in turn, trains a classifier based on user's feedback and the training examples obtained in the first step. The system then uses the generated classification model to relate each input reference to an author. The training and classification phases are performed in module C. This second step is executed iteratively until a stopping criterion is reached (e.g., a pre-defined number of iterations). The following subsections present both steps in more detail.

3.1 Unsupervised Step

This step is inspired by the method proposed in [18, 28] to automatically generate "pure" clusters of references to be used as a training set. Two references within the same cluster should be very similar to each other while dissimilar to references in other clusters. A cluster is *pure* if it contains mostly (ideally only) references to the same author.

Ferreira et al. [18, 28] proposed the use of coauthorship graphs to create pure clusters: two references belong to the same cluster if they have at least one co-author in common. It is based on the observation that two authors with ambiguous names very rarely will have two different co-authors who also have ambiguous names. That strategy, however, may

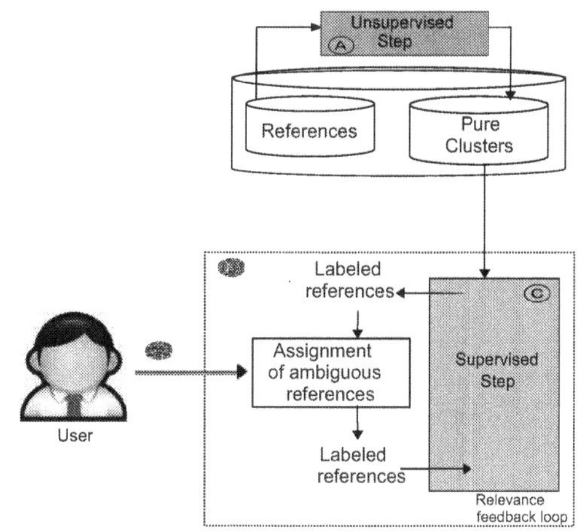

Figure 1: Proposed two-step name disambiguation method.

lead to fragmented clusters, i.e., distinct references to the same author may be placed into different clusters. The authors proposed a strategy based on both the size of clusters and their similarities to discard fragmented clusters [18, 28] to compose the training data for the next step of the method.

3.2 Supervised Step

Figure 2 summarizes the supervised step. The elements of this figure are described in this section. Initially, the disambiguation system learns appropriate similarity functions based on (I) the pure clusters produced by the unsupervised step described before (arrow 1 in Figure 2), and (II) the user feedback (arrow 6), i.e., cluster assignments of ambiguous references. A classifier then uses these similarity functions to determine the authorship of the remaining ambiguous references (arrow 5).

The process of learning similarity functions is implemented using a Genetic Programming (GP) framework (module II in Figure 2). GP is an evolutionary mechanism widely used in optimization problems. Solutions of a target problem are represented as individuals of a population that evolve along generations by means of genetic operations (e.g., crossover, mutation, and reproduction). That process continues until a stopping criterion is reached. At the end, the best solutions (individuals) are selected. In our problem, an individual encodes a reference similarity function, which can be used to compute the similarity between two references (arrow 4). We chose GP for several reasons, including (i) high effectiveness in previous studies on similarity function discovery [35–41], and (ii) ability to find near-optimal solutions in large search spaces.

In order to use the disambiguation system in practical situations, we have to employ a fast and robust learning approach. We adopt the Optimum-Path Forest (OPF) classifier [3, 4] (module I), a graph-based technique, which has some advantages with respect to the traditional classifiers: (i) it is parameter-free, (ii) it does not assume any *a priori* separability of objects in the feature space, and (iii) it handles natively multiclass classification. OPF models the classification task as a graph partition problem. The graph is partitioned into optimal discrete regions called Optimum-Path Trees (OPTs), which are rooted at some representative class objects (prototypes). The optimality criterion is given by the path-cost function, which guides the competition process among the prototypes. In our interactive disambiguation system, each OPF class represents a cluster of references to a same author. The similarity score defined by GP individuals weights the arc linking two references.

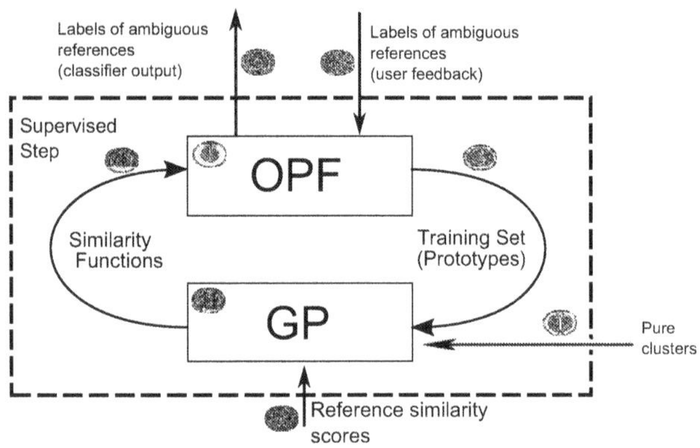

Figure 2: Supervised step of the disambiguation system.

3.2.1 *Discovery of the Reference Similarity Function based on GP*

We propose the use of GP to discover appropriate reference similarity functions. A GP individual is represented as a binary tree. Every internal node of the tree is an operator and every leaf node, known as *terminal*, represents either a variable or a constant. An example of a GP individual is presented in Figure 3. In this example, an individual combines the values of three distinct features (d_1, d_2, and d_3) – the similarity value or distance (e.g., cosine similarity) between two references r_1 and r_2 – into a single score value ($d(r_1, r_2)$). This individual corresponds to the function: $f(d_1(r_1,r_2), d_2(r_1,r_2), d_3(r_1,r_2)) = \frac{d_1(r_1,r_2) \times d_2(r_1,r_2)}{d_3(r_1,r_2)} - \sqrt{d_1(r_1,r_2) + d_2(r_1,r_2)}$.

The higher the score $d(r_1, r_2)$, the higher the probability of references r_1 and r_2 belonging to the same author.

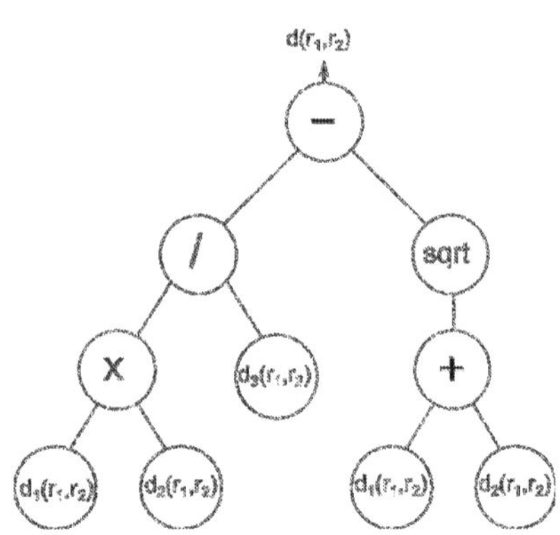

Figure 3: Example of GP individual

Using this representation model, an initial population of individuals is created in a random fashion. Once an initial population is generated, the evolutionary process starts. The first step is to assess the quality of the solution produced by each individual. For that, a fitness function is used to assign a fitness score to each individual. Next, individuals associated with the highest fitness values are selected to construct the subsequent generation. After that, a new population is created by applying to each of those individuals genetic transformation operations, such as *reproduction*, *crossover*, and *mutation*.

The reproduction operator selects the best individuals and copies them to the next generation. The crossover operator combines the genetic material of two parents by swapping a subtree of one parent with a part of the other. The mutation operator selects a point at random in the tree of an individual and replaces the existing subtree at that point with a new randomly generated subtree.

In this paper, we adopt the GP framework proposed in [38] for combining reference similarity functions. The overall framework is presented in Algorithm 1. Starting with a set of training data containing labeled references, GP first operates on a large population of random combination functions. These combination functions are then evaluated. If the stopping criterion is not met, genetic transformations are executed in order to create and evaluate the next generation iteratively. Finally, after a predefined number of generations, the individual with the highest fitness value is selected.

Algorithm 1 GP Framework

```
Generate an initial population of random similarity trees
while number of generations ≤ N_gen do
    Calculate the fitness of each similarity tree
    Record the top N_top similarity trees
    for all the N_top individuals do
        Create the new population, using the operations of
        reproduction, crossover, and mutation
    end for
end while
Apply the best similarity tree (i.e., the best tree of the
last generation) on a set of testing data
```

The input of the GP framework is a set of reference clusters. This input is converted into a list of pairs of references, considering all possible combinations. A GP individual is used to compute the similarity between two references and this score is used to rank all pairs. A good individual should assign a high similarity score to references that belong to the same author. Suppose that references r_1 and r_2 belong to the same author, say a_1, while references r_3 and r_4 belong to authors a_2 and a_3, respectively. Let F be a function that receives a pair of references (r_i, r_j) as input and returns 1, if r_i and r_j belong to the same cluster (e.g., $F((r_1, r_2)) = 1$) and 0, otherwise (e.g., $F((r_1, r_3)) = 0$). Table 1 presents an example of ranking of reference pairs according to a GP individual and their respective F function values.

The fitness of an individual is computed as a function of the quality of the ranking of reference pairs. An ideal ranking would have all pairs whose F function returns 1 at the first positions. In that case, the accuracy is maximum, i.e., there is a position in the rank that separates all pairs that belong to a same author ($F = 1$) from the others. In other cases, the position that maximizes the accuracy can be determined (e.g., the second position in the ranked list in our example).

Table 1: Individual Fitness

Pairs of references	GP similarity score	F output
(r_2, r_3)	0.92	0
(r_1, r_2)	0.89	1
(r_1, r_3)	0.76	0
(r_3, r_4)	0.69	0
(r_2, r_4)	0.65	0
(r_1, r_4)	0.45	0

The fitness is defined as the number of pairs correctly classified divided by the number of pairs. In our example, the fitness is equal to $5/6 = 0.83$ (where 5 is the number of pairs above the double line that has $F_{output} = 1$ plus the number of pairs below the double line that has $F_{output} = 0$, and 6 is the total number of pairs).

3.2.2 *Classification of ambiguous references using the OPF classifier*

We use a classification system based on the optimum-path forest (OPF) classifier [3,4] to assign new references to appropriate authors.

Algorithm 2 outlines the OPF training process. The first step refers to the creation of a graph-based representation of training samples. Let T be a training set defined in terms of the pure clusters of references, i.e., each cluster contains references to a same author. The set T includes clusters defined in the unsupervised step of the disambiguation algorithm and also references labeled by users along feedback iterations.

Let $G = (T, E)$ be a weighted complete graph, where the set of vertices of G is the set T of references and E is the set of edges. The arcs (r_i, r_j) linking references r_i and r_j are weighted by $d(r_i, r_j)$, a function inversely proportional to the similarity of r_i and r_j. The weight $d(r_i, r_j)$ is defined by a GP individual (see Section 3.2.1) that combines reference similarity scores based on the author names, work title, and publication title of references r_i and r_j. Figure 4(a) illustrates a training set with 11 references divided into three clusters (three authors). No edges of the complete graph are shown (for improved visibility).

In the next step, a set S of class representantives (prototypes) is obtained by computing a minimum spanning tree (MST) [42] in the complete graph. Let $\lambda(r_i)$ be a function that returns the class label of a reference r_i (e.g., author name). For each arc (r_i, r_j) in the MST, if $\lambda(r_i) \neq \lambda(r_j)$ then r_i and r_j are selected as prototypes and added to the set S. Figure 4(b) illustrates the definition of prototypes.

Algorithm 2 OPF Classifier: Training Phase

1: Generate the complete graph $G = (V, E)$ using the training set T
2: Compute the prototype set $S \subseteq V$ using the MST
3: Split the graph into trees (whose roots are the prototypes) by computing the optimum-path forest

For every node $r_i \in T$, we wish to compute a minimum-cost path with terminus r_i and origin in S. The idea is to obtain an optimum partition of T such that the different classes represented by the prototypes in S will compete with each other. The use of prototypes, therefore, avoids misclassification caused by an optimum path coming from a different class. Every training node $r_i \in T$ will be assigned to the class of its most strongly connected prototype. This partition is computed as an optimum-path forest P, an acyclic graph which stores all optimum paths in a predecessor map P. More precisely, for each node $r_i \in T \setminus S$, $P(r_i)$ denotes its predecessor node in the optimum path from S, whereas $P(r_i) = \text{nil}$ for each node $r_i \in S$. Figure 4(c) illustrates the optimum-path forest generated from the prototypes defined in Figure 4(b).

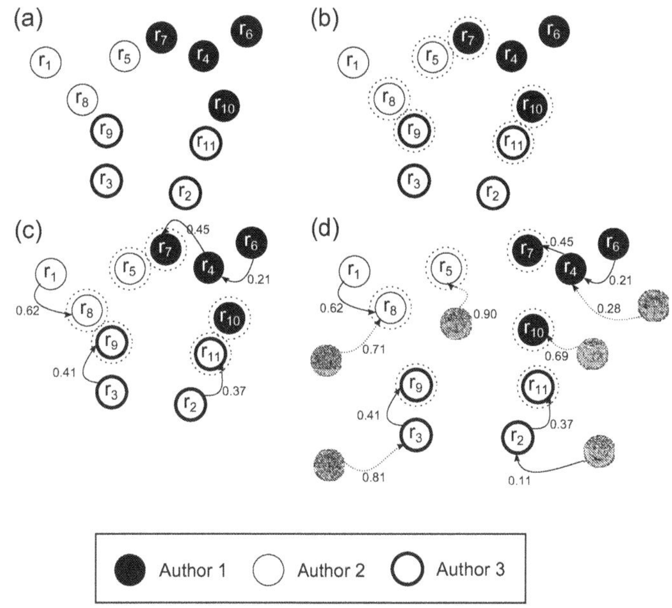

Figure 4: (a) Example of a training set in a graph with three classes represented by black nodes, white nodes, and white nodes delimited by heavy circles, (b) prototypes (bounded by dashed cycles) obtained from the MST, (c) optimum-path forest generated from the prototypes, (d) classification of reference r_{12} through its predecessor node r_2 in the optimum-path forest.

Algorithm 3 outlines the OPF classification phase. Let $D = \{C_1, C_2, \ldots, C_k\}$ be a set of k clusters whose references need to be labeled. In the classification phase, for every $r_i \in C_j$ $(C_j \in D)$, the optimum path with terminus r_i can be easily identified by finding which training node $r\star \in T$ provides the minimum-cost path from r_i to any node in S. Node $r\star$ is the predecessor $P(r_i)$ in the optimum path with terminus r_i. The reference r_i is then classified as $\lambda(r\star)$. Figure 4(d) illustrates the classification phase. In this example, the shortest path from r_{12} to any node in S is $r_{12} \rightarrow r_2 \rightarrow r_{11}$, where the path cost is 0.48, then reference r_{12} is assigned to the same class as r_2, its predecessor in this path.

3.2.3 *Identification of novel authors*

Some instances of the training set do not cover all the possible authors in the ambiguous groups. In order to handle this problem in the classification phase of our approach, we define a cost threshold τ to guide the creation of new clusters. For each reference r_i, we denote by $d_\star(r_i)$ the optimum-path cost from r_i to a prototype $r_\star$. If $d_\star(r_i) \geq \tau$, then a new cluster is created to represent a new author, and reference r_i is assigned to this new cluster.

Algorithm 3 OPF Classifier: Classification Phase

1: **for** each $C_j \in D$ **do**
2: **for** each $r_i \in C_j$ **do**
3: Compute the shortest path from r_i to each prototype in S
4: Add r_i to the tree whose root (prototype $r_s \in S$) is connected to r_i by the shortest path
5: Add r_i to the same cluster containing r_s
6: **end for**
7: **end for**

3.2.4 *Selection of instances for feedback*

Our strategy for selecting the most informative cases for the user interaction is to get a fixed number of references which are the closest to the threshold τ. The goal is to choose a new and reliable sample to be used as a training set in the next iteration, maximizing the learning potential.

4. EXPERIMENTS AND RESULTS

This section presents the experiments performed in order to evaluate the proposed disambiguation method.

4.1 Experimental Setup

This section presents the experimental setup.

4.1.1 *Collections*

For evaluation purposes, we use two collections derived from the DBLP Computer Science Bibliography (DBLP).

DBLP

The first collection derived from DBLP, hereafter referred to as DBLP, sums up 4,287 references associated with 220 distinct authors, which means an average of approximately 20 references per author. Small variations of this collection have been used in several other works [5,14,18,23,24,28,43]. Its original version was created by Han et al. [23] by manually labeling the references. For this, they used the author's publication home page, affiliation name, e-mail, and coauthor names in a complete name format, and also sent emails to some authors to confirm their authorship. They eliminated the references for which they had insufficient information to identify the correct author. Han et al. [23] also replaced the abbreviated publication venue titles by their complete version obtained from DBLP. We used 11 ambiguous groups extracted by Han et al. [23] with some corrections[5].

KISTI

The second collection derived from DBLP, hereafter referred to as KISTI, was built by the Korea Institute of Science and Technology Information [44] for English homonym author name disambiguation. The top 1000 most frequent author names from late-2007 DBLP citation records were obtained jointly with their citation records. Afterwards, for each author name in each citation record, a reference was built. To disambiguate this collection, the authors submitted a query composed of the surname of the author and the work title of each reference to the Google search engine, aiming at finding personal publication pages. The first 20 web pages retrieved for each query were manually checked to identify the correct personal publication page for each authorship record. This identified page was then used to disambiguate the record. This collection has 37,613 citation records, 881 groups of same-name persons and 6,921 authors[6]. Due to the very large number of experiments and comparisons we perform, in our evaluation we use the top 40 most frequent ambiguous groups, i.e., the groups with the largest number of ambiguous authors. These groups are potentially the most difficult ones to disambiguate. In this subset, there are 7,841 citation records, 40 groups of same-name persons and 1,132 authors, with an average of 28.3 different ambiguous authors per group (with a maximum of 59).

4.1.2 *Baselines*

We used as baseline the method proposed by Ferreira et al. [28], referred to as SANDRef. This technique is the state-of-the-art solution for the author name disambiguation problem using relevance feedback. SANDRef yields better results than other methods based on SVM [6], or Naïve Bayes (NB) [23], also used as baselines. We also include the method SAND [18] as baseline. SAND is similar to SANDRef, but does not consider any feedback information.

4.1.3 *Evaluation metrics*

To evaluate the effectiveness of our approach on author name disambiguation, we used the K metric and pairwise F1 measure. They have been used before to assess the quality of name disambiguation methods [28,43]. These metrics allow us to have a numerical score representing the quality of the generated clusters and compare it with the values that were obtained by the other methods at the experiments realized by their authors.

K Metric

The K metric [45] implements a trade-off between the average cluster purity (ACP) and the average author purity (AAP). Given an ambiguous group, ACP evaluates the purity of the empirical clusters with respect to the theoretical clusters for this ambiguous group. Thus, if the empirical clusters are pure (i.e., they contain only references associated with the same author), the corresponding ACP value will be 1. ACP is defined as

$$\text{ACP} = \frac{1}{N}\sum_{i=1}^{e}\sum_{j=1}^{t}\frac{n_{ij}^2}{n_i}, \tag{1}$$

where N is the total number of references in the ambiguous group, t is the number of theoretical clusters in the ambiguous group, e is the number of empirical clusters for this ambiguous group, n_i is the total number of references in the empirical cluster i, and n_{ij} is the total number of references in the empirical cluster i which are also in the theoretical cluster j.

For a given ambiguous group, AAP evaluates the fragmentation of the empirical clusters with respect to the theoretical clusters. If the empirical clusters are not fragmented, the corresponding AAP value will be 1. AAP is defined as

$$\text{AAP} = \frac{1}{N}\sum_{j=1}^{t}\sum_{i=1}^{e}\frac{n_{ij}^2}{n_j}, \tag{2}$$

[5]Available at `http://www.lbd.dcc.ufmg.br/lbd/collections/disambiguation` (as of Jan. 2013).

[6]Available at `http://www.kisti.re.kr` (as of Jan. 2013).

where n_j is the total number of references in the theoretical cluster j.

The K metric is defined as the geometric mean between ACP and AAP values:

$$K = \sqrt{\text{ACP} \times \text{AAP}}. \quad (3)$$

It evaluates the purity and cohesion of the empirical clusters extracted by each method.

Pairwise F1

Pairwise F1 (pF1) is the F1 metric [46] calculated using pairwise precision and pairwise recall. Pairwise precision (pP) is calculated as $pP=\frac{a}{a+c}$, where a is the number of pairs of references in an empirical cluster that are (correctly) associated with the same author, and c is the number of pairs of references in an empirical cluster not corresponding to the same author. Pairwise recall (pR) is calculated as $pR=\frac{a}{a+b}$, where b is the number of pairs of references associated with the same author that are not in the same empirical cluster. The F1-metric is defined as

$$p\text{F1} = 2 \times \frac{pP \times pR}{pP + pR}. \quad (4)$$

4.1.4 Disambiguation method parameters

Table 2 presents the values, defined empirically, used for different GP parameters. We have not identified much variation in our results with different configurations. Our future work considers the use of a factorial design to evaluate the impact of different parameters [47].

Table 2: Values for GP parameters.

GP parameter	Value
Initial population method	randomly generated
Initial population size	200
Maximum individual height	6
Number of generations	10
Operators	×, ÷, +, cos(), exp()

GP individuals combine reference similarity scores defined in terms of only the work and publication titles. These scores were obtained by computing the Cosine Similarity, Jaccard Similarity, Jaro Winkler, and Levenshtein distance on those reference fields.

Our best results were observed for $\tau = 0.82$. This score was obtained by performing experiments with *pure* clusters defined in the unsupervised step of our method.

4.1.5 Experimental Protocol

For comparison purposes, we use the same experimental protocol employed in [28]. We use a random selection of 50% of each ambiguous group (test set). The remaining part of the collection was used for training by the SVM [6] and NB [23] baselines, since these are supervised baselines that require training. Each experiment was executed 10 times and the average scores of each method applied to the test set were computed with a confidence interval of 95%.

We simulate the presence of ideal users providing feedback, a typical strategy used to evaluate relevance feedback systems [32–34]. In our case, ideal users always assign ambiguous references to the correct author at each iteration.

4.2 Results

Figures 5 and 6 present the K and $F1$ measures for evaluated methods in the DBLP collection. In these figures, SAND and SANDRef are baselines (see Section 4.1.2). GOPF stands for the GP-OPF proposed disambiguation method with *no* user feedback. GOPFRef-3 and GOPFRef-5 refer to the proposed disambiguation method with relevance feedback considering, respectively, 3 and 5 labeled references at each iteration per ambiguous group.

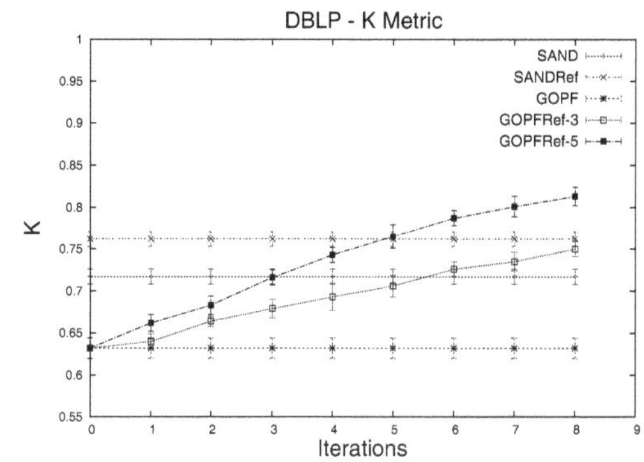

Figure 5: K scores for evaluated disambiguation methods in the DBLP dataset.

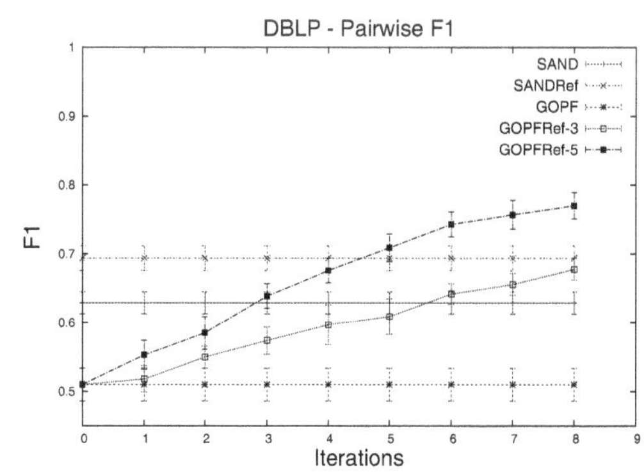

Figure 6: F1 scores for evaluated disambiguation methods in the DBLP dataset

As can be observed, as the number of iterations increases, the proposed disambiguation method yields better results. We also notice that the more references labeled at each iteration, the better the results. In fact, from the sixth iteration on, GOPFRef-5 is statistically better ($p{-}value < 0.05$) than all baselines. Note also that GOPFRef-5 is already statistically tied with SANDRef, the best baseline, at the fourth iteration. At this point, however, only 20 references per ambiguous group (4 iterations × 5 references per iteration) were labeled in the GOPFRef-5 method.

Figures 7 and 8 present the K and $F1$ measures for the evaluated methods in the KISTI collection. The results are similar to those observed for the DBLP dataset. Note, however, that for this dataset, with only 3 iterations (15 labeled references per ambiguous group), GOPFRef-5 is statistically better ($p - value < 0.05$) than all baselines according to the K metric. For the F1 measure, GOPFRef-5 is tied with SANDRef at the third iteration, but is better from the fourth on.

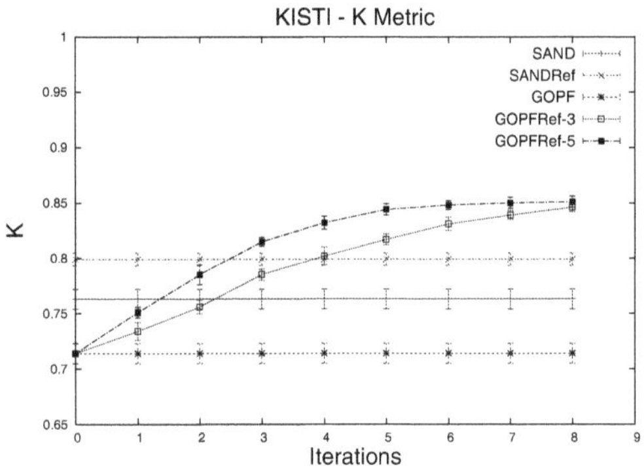

Figure 7: K scores for evaluated disambiguation methods in the KISTI dataset.

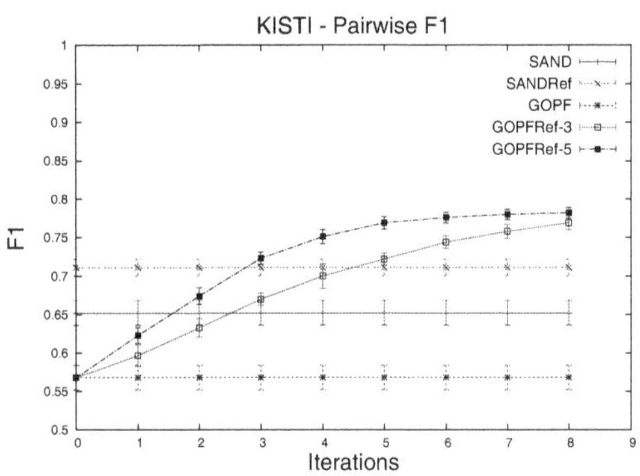

Figure 8: F1 scores for evaluated disambiguation methods in the KISTI dataset.

Table 3: Comparison of proposed methods with baselines in the DBLP and KISTI datasets (best results in bold).

Collection	Method	K	F1
DBLP	SAND	0.717 (0.013)	0.629 (0.022)
	SANDRef	0.762 (0.013)	0.694 (0.025)
	SVM	0.799 (0.008)	0.721 (0.010)
	NB	0.736 (0.009)	0.647 (0.012)
	GOPFRef-3	0.750 (0.009)	0.678 (0.016)
	GOPFRef-5	**0.813 (0.011)**	**0.770 (0.019)**
KISTI	SAND	0.763 (0.012)	0.652 (0.022)
	SANDRef	0.799 (0.008)	0.711 (0.016)
	SVM	0.761(0.007)	0.576 (0.006)
	NB	0.745 (0.004)	0.601 (0.006)
	GOPFRef-3	0.846 (0.004)	0.769 (0.009)
	GOPFRef-5	**0.851 (0.005)**	**0.782 (0.007)**

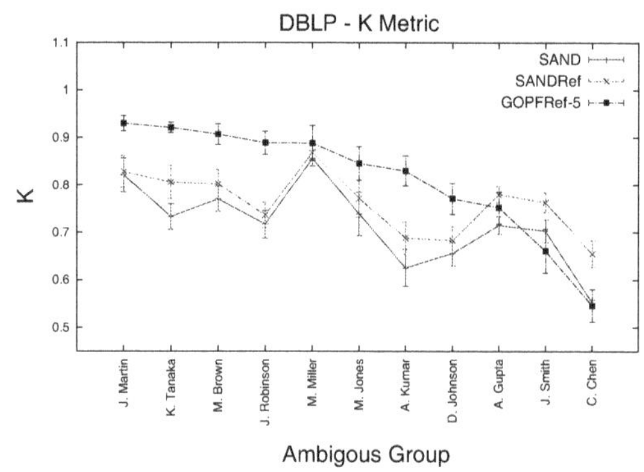

Figure 9: K scores for evaluated methods for each ambiguous group in the DBLP dataset.

Table 3 summarizes the average results (with standard deviation) of the proposed methods and all baselines in the DBLP and KISTI datasets. In this table, we also report the results of two supervised methods based on SVM [6] and Naïve Bayes (NB) [23], trained with 50% of each dataset. The results of the proposed methods consider the execution of 8 iterations. As can be observed, the best results are observed for GOPFRef-5 in both datasets.

We also conducted comparisons considering the average performance results of evaluated methods for each ambiguous group. Figure 9 presents the results concerning the K metric on the DBLP dataset. Similar results were observed for the KISTI dataset and F1 measure. GOPRef-5 refers to the result considering 8 relevance feedback iterations.

We can notice that GOPRef-5 outperforms or ties with all baselines for 9 out of 11 ambiguous group. The worse results were observed for the most ambiguous groups (e.g., J. Smith and C. Chen). In fact, we believe that if more references are labeled at each iteration, instead of only 5, the disambiguation results would be better. Therefore, we also conducted experiments to evaluate the impact of the number of labeled references at each iteration in the most ambiguous groups. Figure 10 shows the K metric results for the ambiguous group related to the author C. Chen in the DBLP dataset. Similar results were observed for other ambiguous groups. As can be observed, the best results are produced when more references are labeled at each iteration. GOPFRef-20, which considers 20 labeled references per iteration, yields the best results from the sixth iteration on, with a statistical tie with SANDRef at the fourth and fifth iteration.

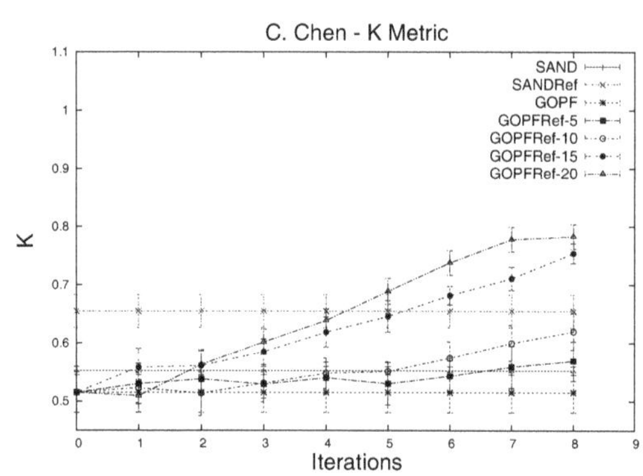

Figure 10: K scores for evaluated methods for the ambiguous group related to author C. Chen.

5. CONCLUSIONS

In this paper, we presented a novel disambiguation method that takes advantage of user feedback to define classification models to assign references to authors. Users (e.g., DL administrators) provide feedback by labeling ambiguous references. The proposed system uses that information along with *pure* training samples defined by an unsupervised approach, in a hybrid classification scheme. Our classification approach combines a genetic programming (GP) framework, which is used to define suitable reference similarity functions, with the Optimum-Path Forest (OPF) classifier, a graph-based approach that uses GP-based edge weights to assign input references to the correct authors.

We conducted a set of experiments aiming to evaluate the proposed disambiguation system in comparison with state-of-the-art methods on two well-known datasets. Obtained results demonstrate the effectiveness of the proposed method. In a few iterations and with a low number of labeled references per iteration, the proposed disambiguation method outperforms all baselines.

Future work considers the evaluation of the proposed method by real users in real-world DL collections. We also plan to include, in the GP framework, other reference similarity functions based on different metadata fields.

Acknowledgements

The authors are grateful to CAPES, FAPESP, FAPEMIG, CNPq and Santander for their support.

6. REFERENCES

[1] Byung-Won On, Dongwon Lee, Jaewoo Kang, and Prasenjit Mitra. Comparative study of name disambiguation problem using a scalable blocking-based framework. In *Proceedings of the 5th ACM/IEEE Joint Conference on Digital Libraries*, pages 344–353, Denver, CO, USA, 2005.

[2] Anderson A. Ferreira, Marcos Andre Gonçalves, and Alberto H. F. Laender. A brief survey of automatic methods for author name disambiguation. *SIGMOD Record*, 41(2):15–26, 2012.

[3] J. P. Papa, A. X. Falcão, and C. T. N. Suzuki. Supervised pattern classification based on optimum-path forest. *International Journal of Imaging Systems and Technology*, 19(2):120–131, 2009.

[4] J. P. Papa, A. X. Falcão, V. H. C. Albuquerque, and J. M. R. S. Tavares. Efficient supervised optimum-path forest classification for large datasets. *Pattern Recognition*, 45(1):512–520, 2012.

[5] Hui Han, Hongyuan Zha, and C. Lee Giles. Name disambiguation in author citations using a k-way spectral clustering method. In *Proceedings of the 5th ACM/IEEE Joint Conference on Digital Libraries*, pages 334–343, Denver, CO, USA, 2005.

[6] Jian Huang, Seyda Ertekin, and C. Lee Giles. Efficient name disambiguation for large-scale databases. In *Proceedings of the European Conference on Principles and Practice of Knowledge Discovery in Databases*, pages 536–544, Berlin, Germany, 2006.

[7] Byung-Won On, Ergin Elmacioglu, Dongwon Lee, Jaewoo Kang, and Jian Pei. Improving grouped-entity resolution using quasi-cliques. In *Proceedings of the 6th IEEE International Conference on Data Mining*, pages 1008–015, 2006.

[8] Indrajit Bhattacharya and Lise Getoor. Collective entity resolution in relational data. *ACM Transactions on Knowledge Discovery from Data*, 1(1), 2007.

[9] Aron Culotta, Pallika Kanani, Robert Hall, Michael Wick, and Andrew McCallum. Author disambiguation using error-driven machine learning with a ranking loss function. In *Proceedings of the International Workshop on Information Integration on the Web*, Vancouver, Canada, 2007.

[10] In-Su Kang, Seung-Hoon Na, Seungwoo Lee, Hanmin Jung, Pyung Kim, Won-Kyung Sung, and Jong-Hyeok Lee. On co-authorship for author disambiguation. *Information Processing & Management*, 45(1):84–97, 2009.

[11] Byung-Won On and Dongwon Lee. Scalable name disambiguation using multi-level graph partition. In *Proceedings of the 7th SIAM International Conference on Data Mining*, pages 575–580, Minneapolis, Minnesota, USA, 2007.

[12] José M. Soler. Separating the articles of authors with the same name. *Scientometrics*, 72(2):281–290, 2007.

[13] Yang Song, Jian Huang, Isaac G. Councill, Jia Li, and C. Lee Giles. Efficient topic-based unsupervised name disambiguation. In *Proceedings of the 7th ACM/IEEE Joint Conference on Digital Libraries*, pages 342–351, Vancouver, BC, Canada, 2007.

[14] Denilson Alves Pereira, Berthier A. Ribeiro-Neto, Nivio Ziviani, Alberto H. F. Laender, Marcos André Gonçalves, and Anderson A. Ferreira. Using web information for author name disambiguation. In *Proceedings of the 2009 ACM/IEEE Joint Conference on Digital Libraries*, pages 49–58, 2009.

[15] Vetle I. Torvik and Neil R. Smalheiser. Author name disambiguation in medline. *ACM Transactions on Knowledge Discovery from Data*, 3(3):1–29, 2009.

[16] Pucktada Treeratpituk and C. Lee Giles. Disambiguating authors in academic publications using random forests. In *Proceedings of the 2009 ACM/IEEE Joint Conference on Digital Libraries*, pages 39–48, Austin, TX, USA, 2009.

[17] Ricardo G. Cota, Anderson Almeida Ferreira, Marcos André Gonçalves, Alberto H. F. Laender, and Cristiano Nascimento. An unsupervised heuristic-based hierarchical method for name disambiguation in bibliographic citations. *Journal of the American Society for Information Science and Technology*, 61(9):1853–1870, 2010.

[18] A.A. Ferreira, A. Veloso, M.A. Gonçalves, and A.H.F. Laender. Effective self-training author name disambiguation in scholarly digital libraries. In *Proceedings of the 10th annual joint conference on Digital libraries*, pages 39–48. ACM, 2010.

[19] Xiaoming Fan, Jianyong Wang, Xu Pu, Lizhu Zhou, and Bing Lv. On graph-based name disambiguation. *ACM Journal of Data and Information Quality*, 2:10:1–10:23, February 2011.

[20] Ana Paula Carvalho, Anderson A. Ferreira, Alberto H. F. Laender, and Marcos André Gonçalves. Incremental unsupervised name disambiguation in cleaned digital libraries. *Journal of Information and Data Management*, 2(3):289–304, 2011.

[21] Michael Levin, Stefan Krawzyk, Steven Bethard, and Dan Jurafsky. Citation-based bootstrapping for large-scale author disambiguation. *Journal of the American Society for Information Science and Technology*, 63(5):1030–1047, 2012.

[22] Felipe H. Levin and Carlos A. Heuser. Evaluating the use of social networks in author name disambiguation

in digital libraries. *Journal of Information and Data Management*, 1(2):183–197, 2010.

[23] Hui Han, C. Lee Giles, Hongyuan Zha, Cheng Li, and Kostas Tsioutsiouliklis. Two supervised learning approaches for name disambiguation in author citations. In *Proceedings of the 4th ACM/IEEE-CS Joint Conference on Digital Libraries*, pages 296–305, Tuscon, USA, 2004.

[24] Hui Han, Wei Xu, Hongyuan Zha, and C. Lee Giles. A hierarchical naive Bayes mixture model for name disambiguation in author citations. In *Proceedings of the 2005 ACM Symposium on Applied Computing*, pages 1065–1069, Santa Fe, New Mexico, USA, 2005.

[25] Indrajit Bhattacharya and Lise Getoor. A latent dirichlet model for unsupervised entity resolution. In *Proceedings of the Sixth SIAM International Conference on Data Mining*, Bethesda, MD, USA, 2006.

[26] Jie Tang, Auvis C. M. Fong, Bo Wang, and Jing Zhang. A unified probabilistic framework for name disambiguation in digital library. *IEEE Transactions on Knowledge and Data Engineering*, 24(6):975–987, 2012.

[27] Adriano Veloso, Anderson A. Ferreira, Marcos A. Gonçalves, Alberto H.F. Laender, and Wagner Meira Jr. Cost-effective on-demand associative author name disambiguation. *Information Processing & Management*, 48(4):680 – 697, 2012.

[28] A.A. Ferreira, T.M. Machado, and M.A. Gonçalves. Improving author name disambiguation with user relevance feedback. *Journal of Information and Data Management*, 3(3):332, 2012.

[29] Ricardo Baeza-Yates and Berthier Ribeiro-Neto. *Modern Information Retrieval*. Addison-Wesley Publishing Company, 2nd edition, 2008.

[30] X. Wang, J. Tang, H. Cheng, and P.S. Yu. Adana: Active name disambiguation. In *Proceedings of the 11th International Conference on Data Mining*, pages 794–803, Vancouver,Canada, 2011.

[31] Yuhua Li, Aiming Wen, Quan Lin, Ruixuan Li, and Zhengding Lu. Incorporating user feedback into name disambiguation of scientific cooperation network. In *Proceedings of the 12th international conference on Web-age information management*, WAIM'11, pages 454–466, 2011.

[32] A.T. da Silva, J.A. dos Santos, A.X. Falcão, R.S. Torres, and L.P. Magalhães. Incorporating multiple distance spaces in optimum-path forest classification to improve feedback-based learning. *Computer Vision and Image Understanding*, 116(4):510–523, 2012.

[33] A.T. da Silva, AX Falcão, and L.P. Magalhães. A new cbir approach based on relevance feedback and optimum-path forest classification. *Journal of WSCG*, 18(1-3):73–80, 2010.

[34] Jefersson Alex dos Santos, André Tavares da Silva, Ricardo da Silva Torres, Alexandre X. Falcão, Léo Pini Magalhães, and Rubens A. C. Lamparelli. Interactive classification of remote sensing images by using optimum-path forest and genetic programming. In *14th International Conference on Computer Analysis of Images and Patterns (CAIP)*, pages 300–307, 2011.

[35] R. Calumby, R. da S. Torres, and M. A. Gonçalves. Multimodal retrieval with relevance feedback based on genetic programming. *Multimedia Tools and Applications*, pages 1–29, 2012.

[36] F. S. P. Andrade, J. Almeida, H. Pedrini, and R. da S. Torres. Fusion of local and global descriptors for content-based image and video retrieval. In *Iberoamerican Congress on Pattern Recognition*, pages 845–853, 2012.

[37] F. F. Faria, A. Veloso, H. M. Almeida, E. Valle, R. da S. Torres, M. A. Gonçalves, and W. Meira Jr. Learning to rank for content-based image retrieval. In *ACM MIR*, pages 285–294, 2010.

[38] R. da S. Torres, A. X. Falcão, M. A. Gonçalves, J. P. Papa, B. Zhang, W. Fan, and E. A. Fox. A genetic programming framework for content-based image retrieval. *Pattern Recognition*, 42(2):283–292, 2009.

[39] C. D. Ferreira, J. A. Santos, R. da S. Torres, M. A. Gonçalves, R. C. Rezende, and W. Fan. Relevance feedback based on genetic programming for image retrieval. *Pattern Recognition Letters*, 32(1):27–37, 2011.

[40] Weiguo Fan, Praveen Pathak, and Mi Zhou. Genetic-based approaches in ranking function discovery and optimization in information retrieval - a framework. *Decision Support Systems*, 47(4):398–407, 2009.

[41] H. M. de Almeida, M. A. Gonçalves, M. Cristo, and P. P. Calado. A combined component approach for finding collection-adapted ranking functions based on genetic programming. In *ACM SIGIR*, pages 399–406, 2007.

[42] T.H. Cormen, C.E. Leiserson, R.L. Rivest, and C. Stein. *Introduction to algorithms*. MIT press, 2001.

[43] A.A. Ferreira, R. Silva, M.A. Gonçalves, A. Veloso, and A.H.F. Laender. Active associative sampling for author name disambiguation. In *Proceedings of the 12th ACM/IEEE-CS joint conference on Digital Libraries*, pages 175–184. ACM, 2012.

[44] In-Su Kang, Pyung Kim, Seungwoo Lee, Hanmin Jung, and Beom-Jong You. Construction of a large-scale test set for author disambiguation. *Information Processing and Management*, 47(3):452–465, May 2011.

[45] Itshak Lapidot. Self-Organizing-Maps with BIC for Speaker Clustering. Technical report, IDIAP Research Institute, Martigny, Switzerland, 2002.

[46] C. J. Van Rijsbergen. *Information Retrieval, 2nd edition*. Butterworths, London, 1979.

[47] Robert Feldt and Peter Nordin. Using factorial experiments to evaluate the effect of genetic programming parameters. In *EuroGP*, pages 271–282, 2000.

Extracting and Matching Authors and Affiliations in Scholarly Documents

Huy Hoang Nhat Do[1,2] Muthu Kumar Chandrasekaran[2] Philip S. Cho[2]
Min–Yen Kan[1,3*†]
[1]Department of Computer Science, School of Computing
[2]Asia Research Institute
[3]NUS Interactive and Digital Media Institute
National University of Singapore
{a0079636,a0092669,aripcss,dcskmy}@nus.edu.sg

ABSTRACT

We introduce *Enlil*, an information extraction system that discovers the institutional affiliations of authors in scholarly papers. Enlil consists of two steps: one that first identifies authors and affiliations using a conditional random field; and a second support vector machine that connects authors to their affiliations. We benchmark Enlil in three separate experiments drawn from three different sources: the ACL Anthology, the ACM Digital Library, and a set of cross-disciplinary scientific journal articles acquired by querying Google Scholar. Against a state-of-the-art production baseline, Enlil reports a statistically significant improvement in F_1 of nearly 10% ($p \ll 0.01$). In the case of multidisciplinary articles from Google Scholar, Enlil is benchmarked over both clean input ($F_1 > 90\%$) and automatically-acquired input ($F_1 > 80\%$).

We have deployed Enlil in a case study involving Asian genomics research publication patterns to understand how government sponsored collaborative links evolve. Enlil has enabled our team to construct and validate new metrics to quantify the facilitation of research as opposed to direct publication.

Categories and Subject Descriptors

H.3.7 [**Information Storage and Retrieval**]: Digital Libraries

General Terms

Algorithms, Experimentation

Keywords

Metadata Extraction, Logical Structure Discovery, Conditional Random Fields, Support Vector Machine, Rich Document Features

*This work was supported in part by the National University of Singapore - Global Asia Institute Research Grant [AC-2010-1-004] and the Fetzer Franklin Trust project on Culture and Cognition.
†Contact Author.

JCDL'13, July 22–26, 2013, Indianapolis, Indiana, USA.

1. INTRODUCTION

Quantifying scholars' performance is a difficult problem. While there are many instruments to use to argue one's scientific prowess, it is generally accepted that others' use of a scholar's publications represents key evidence. Measuring "use" is none the easier, but has often been interpreted in terms of citation count or aggregate citation metrics such as *h-index* [15], *g-index* [9], or more recently, *ħ-index* [16].

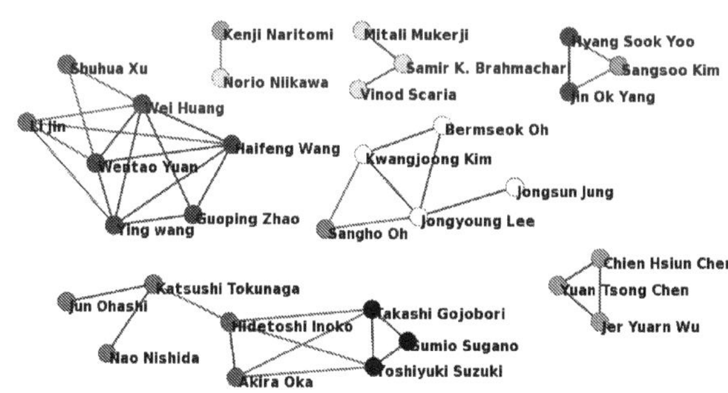

Figure 1: An example of a co-author network coded with institutional affiliations. Like-colored nodes indicate identical affiliations and edges represent publications. Blue edges indicate coauthorship among authors in the same institution; red, across institutions.

While benchmarking individual scholars is important to their promotion and tenure, higher-level (i.e., aggregate) bibliometrics and scientometrics are perhaps even more important. For example, a researcher may publish little, but play a significant role over time by forging critical connections among others to facilitate research. We have recently addressed this issue and developed research facilitation or RF-metrics [6] for individuals and groups. Measuring the performance of whole academic units, institutions or countries is important for department heads and deans, and also a key knowledge management issue for the policymakers and funding agencies that support their research work.

The institutional affiliations[1] of authors of scholarly papers is an important piece of metadata for enabling such publication data aggregation. Research works in social sciences, scientometrics, bibliometrics and knowledge management such as [24] also use publi-

[1]We use "affiliations" and "institutions" interchangeably, although an *affiliation* properly refers to just the correspondence between an author and his institution.

cations records and associated metadata. The correct identification of author's affiliations is crucial for research works such as [26] that study the impact of location, geography on emergent behavior. In the current scholarly publication practice, this data is manually entered by publishers or authors, and thus a valuable asset to publishers. Commercial services such as Thompson Reuters' Web of Science, Elsevier's Scopus and Google Scholar sometimes provide inaccurate mappings between the different authors and their institutional affiliations, incomplete listings of affiliations for publications with many authors, or do not provide the authors' affiliation at all. Also, access to such metadata can be prohibitively expensive, restricting research and benchmarking exercises that rely on this metadata to well-provisioned institutions[2].

However, thanks to the triad of open access, self-archiving and institutional repositories, scholarly publications themselves are now easier to obtain from web sources. Armed with an automated system that extracts authors from digital copies and associates them with their affiliations, the public can now perform their own bibliographic research, case studies and comparative benchmarking.

As a case in point, Figure 1 shows the actual co-authorship network of a large set of authors involved in the Pan-Asian SNP Consortium from 2004, where edges represent jointly published works. This international consortium was sponsored by various national government funding bodies. In our umbrella project, we are interested to know whether such funding resulted in sustained collaborative links, after the sponsored funding finished. With a system that can reliably extract author and affiliation information, construction of such networks becomes easy and the subsequent knowledge management and analyses of such networks becomes possible.

We report on *Enlil*, a system that performs this task in a two-step process: first, the extraction of author and institutions from scholarly documents via supervised sequence labeling; and second, the matching of authors to their institutions via relation classification. The key contributions of this paper are: 1) describing the features used by our system and their efficacy on the problem, 2) performance that significantly outperforms the current state-of-the-art, 3) detailed analysis of the major error classes of our system and the difficulties in author and affiliation extraction and matching, and 4) a discussion of the knowledge management which Enlil enables.

2. RELATED WORK

Extracting authors, institutions and correlating them relates to the domain of automated document processing, of which the general problem of document structure analysis has been an active research area since the 1960's. Many of these works focus on the scholarly record, and more recently at those encoded in rich text formats, such as Portable Document Format (PDF). Klink *et al.* [18] and Kim *et al.* [17] introduce methods that use both the textual and the layout features of a document to discover its structure, however, these systems rely on hand-tuned rule sets and templates. Such methods are brittle and may fail when presented with documents that follow new or different publishing styles. Gao *et al.* [12] recently described SEB, a framework to detect the hierarchy and reading order of a document using weighted bipartite graphs but its fixed rules are again not flexible enough to capture document metadata in practical scenarios.

A common method to address the fragility of handcrafted rule-based systems is to employ statistical learning methods that automatically construct the model from annotated data. This approach removes the need for experts to construct the rule base. It also enables adaptability, as when new annotated data arrives, the learned model can be regenerated to fit the new distribution of examples. While general information retrieval now uses statistical learning techniques at its core, current research in document analysis has started to use statistical learning only recently. For the problem of general document structure inference, Belaid *et al.* [2] has employed neural networks, while the SectLabel system [22] adopted a Conditional Random Field (CRF) as their learning approach. We build our work upon SectLabel, as its broad categories and adequate overall performance provide a good base for improvement.

Other research has tried to apply more fine-grained methods on smaller parts of the document to discover various types of relationship between different entities. Systems by both Gao *et al.* [12] and Lopez *et al.* [21] correlate figures to their captions, enabling better document figure retrieval.

With respect to scholarly document metadata, Cortez *et al.* [7], Councill *el al.* [8], aim to recover the citation network by recognizing and parsing the reference strings that appear in scholarly documents' reference section, using a knowledge-based approach and a CRF model, respectively. Chen *et al.* [4] integrated both knowledge-based and data driven approaches into a single architecture for the same problem. The BibAll system [10] integrates several existing systems such as ParsCit while also utilizing new digital library services including Google Scholar to provide a complete extraction of all the fields in a citation string. The CEBBIP system by Gao *et al.* [11] also demonstrated that a CRF works for the same problem for written Chinese. While all do identify and delimit author names in reference strings present in a paper's bibliography, they do not perform the recognition, delimitation and extraction of author names on the title page (i.e., they do not identify the authors of the document itself, but the authors of the documents which the document cites).

Our work here continues the automation process where previous work has left off. In particular, we focus our attention on the title page of a scholarly work, delimiting the document's authors and their institutions and building their correspondence. We observe that good performance on such extractions from title pages often requires knowledge of the spatial layout and font information in addition to the text itself. This is in contrast to author processing in reference strings in the bibliography that largely depends only on lexical information.

Most closely related to our work is work by the CiteSeer team at Penn State. Initial work by Han *et al.* [14] uses a Support Vector Machine (SVM) to extract document metadata. The work is comprehensive but limited by two important factors. First, only the textual features of the document header are used, which leads to issues in chunk identification in names that are delimited only by whitespace. Second, as the dataset contains only computer science research papers, its performance outside of this domain is unknown. Later work in SeerSuite [25] includes exactly our problem scope in this work as one component: SVM Header Parser. This system is closest to Enlil in terms of functionality: accepting PDF input and extracting and matching authors with affiliations. As such, we use SVM Header Parser as a comparative baseline in our system's evaluation. Our results show the improvement of our system over SVM Header Parser in both cross-domain and computer science datasets.

3. SYSTEM OVERVIEW

Our author and affiliation extraction and matching system, Enlil[3], comprises of two steps run in serial – an extraction step and a

[2]Thompson Reuters' Web of Science and Elsevier's Scopus can each cost between 10K to 100K USD per year [20].

[3]Enlil is the name of the air god in the Sumerian myth of the Huluppu tree, the World Tree that connects heaven and earth.

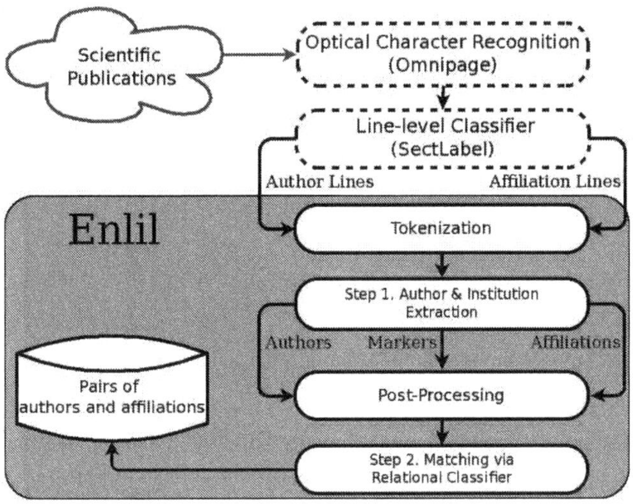

Figure 2: Enlil's system architecture. The rounded rectangle indicates the system modules detailed in this paper; modules outlined by dashes indicate preprocessing steps.

matching step. Figure 2 shows the overview of Enlil's modules and their interaction. The first step is modeled as sequence labeling tasks that use a CRF as the supervised learning model, while an SVM is used in the second step for relational classification. A significant preprocessing pipeline provides our system with the necessary textual and spatial input needed to complete our processing, which we detail first.

OCR. Portable Document Format (PDF), while now an open standard and the most common method for disseminating published scholarly work, composes the rendered or printed page in several different ways. While PDFs can be semantically rich, complete with document logical structure (e.g., indicating which text are headers, page numbers, titles), they can also lack the basic textual content shown in the image of the pages rendered – especially when scanned without an accompanying character recognition step. To produce a pipeline for author–affiliation matching that works under all such circumstances, we choose to treat (pages of) PDF documents as images, and use a commercial off-the-shelf optical character recognition software, Nuance OmniPage[4] to canonicalize any input PDF into a standard format. We use OmniPage to output an XML version of the document that provides both the textual and spatial information (i.e., the X- and Y-coordinates) for each word that appears on each page.

We then run SectLabel [22], an open-source module that takes this type of input, to assign one of 23 semantic classes to each line of text, including *Author* and *Affiliation*. Note that SectLabel does not further process individual lines to delimit authors or institutions. Enlil collects all reported author and affiliation lines as its input for processing, discarding the rest of the input document, as they are irrelevant to our problem. At this point, the system has the required input for starting – two sets of lines of text marked as either Author or Affiliation.

Tokenization. While individual lines of text classified as authors or institutions are the input to Enlil, there still remains significant processing needed to delimit the author and institutions correctly. Lines marked as *Authors* may contain multiple author names, markers that signify a correspondence between authors and footnotes or affiliations (hereafter called "markers"). Lines marked by the SectLabel preprocessor as *Affiliation* may also contain phone numbers

[4]Versions 16 and 17.

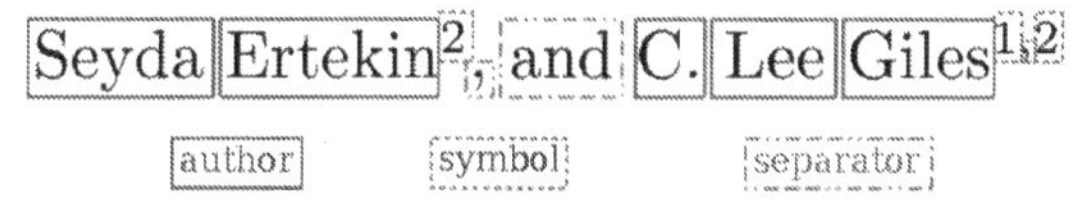

Figure 3: An example of name splitting.

or email addresses. Enlil's first step is to correctly tokenize and delimit the author and institutional information in the input. Tokenization is needed as author, marker and author-separating tokens are commonly concatenated into a single printed token without internal spacing, as shown in Figure 3. To perform this tokenization, we apply a short list of rules, starting with delimiting tokens by spaces. In addition to the use of spaces, we also use the change in formatting between characters (e.g., change to superscript or subscript) or the presence of punctuation marks to force the tokenizer to break the token into smaller components. For example, in the *Author* line, the signifier "$Seyda\ Ertekin^2,$" can be split into four tokens "$Seyda$", "$Ertekin$", "2" and ", ".

3.1 Author and Institution Extraction

Once tokens are identified, we use supervised sequence labeling to assign each of the tokens in both author or affiliation input lines to one of three classes: *name*, *symbol*, and *separator*. These classes correspond to an author or institution token, a correspondence marker, and any separating token, respectively.

We use a linear Conditional Random Field (CRF) [19] to tackle each of these two problems, as it has been shown to work well on related sequence labeling tasks, such as reference string parsing, as well as part-of-speech tagging. We use the freely-available CRF++ implementation[5], which permits us to design feature classes that describe the traits of hidden nodes, as well as the relationships between them. We use the same feature sets for both of the problems of labeling author lines as well as affiliation lines, but use different training data. Two CRF models are learned from labeled training data sets (described later) – one for author line labeling and one for affiliation line labeling.

Enlil has two logically separate sets of feature classes that it uses for this extraction step. The first set of features are *content* features – ones related to the textual content of the tokens. However, we have found that relying solely on punctuations and token identity features that can be found in raw text fails to demarcate author and affiliation sections well. This is due to the fact that many publication formats depend on the visual layout of a title page for this task. A human reading the formatted rich text can easily detect different logical units by their font sizes or positions. For this reason, Enlil also utilizes a second set of features based on the text *layout* – these features capture font size or spatial position. We will see that this second set of features is especially important and it significantly improves performance (Section 4).

Our system only uses binary-valued features. Note that all but the first layout feature depends on rich text input that is provided by our OCR / line classification preprocessing pipeline. We list the feature classes used by the CRF for both author and affiliation line token labeling, listing the content features first.

— **Token Identity** (*content*): We encode separate features for each token in three different forms: 1) as-is, 2) lowercased, and 3) lowercased, stripped of punctuation. For this feature and the following n-gram feature, the feature sets are the binary presence or absence of the token.
— **N-gram prefix/suffix** (*content*): The first as well as the last 1-4 characters of the token in lowercase format.

[5]`http://crfpp.sourceforge.net/`

Table 1: **Gazetteers used by Enlil and their sources.**

	Dictionary Type	# of Entries
Person	First name (Male)[a]	3,901
	First name (Female)[a]	4,955
	Last name[b]	88,799
	Last name (Romanized Chinese)	286
Location	Countries and cities[c]	50,000

[a] ftp://ftp.funet.fi/pub/doc/dictionaries/DanKlein/
[b] http://www.census.gov/genealogy/names/
[c] http://world-gazetteer.com

— **Length** (*content*): The length of the token is also an important feature, as separators and markers are often fixed in length. Enlil counts the total number of characters in the token and turns on only ("1") of the following features: *1Char*, *2Char*, *3Char*, or *4+Char*.
— **Punctuation** (*content*): Any punctuation present in the token is detected and categorized into one of three groups: *continuingPunctuation* (e.g. commas, semicolons), *stopPunctuation* (e.g. periods), *others* (e.g. apostrophe), or *noPunctuation*. The first two groups usually serve as separators that demarcate authors' names, while the third can serve as a part of a name (e.g. "O'Reilly").
— **Number** (*content*): We identify numbers present in the token using simple regular expressions, assigning the numeric sequence to one of four mutually-exclusive categories – *1Digit*, *2Digit*, *3Digit* or *4+Digit*; otherwise, the feature gets the value *noDigit*. The number feature helps to distinguish numeric markers, and parts of addresses present in affiliations.
— **Gazetteers** (*content*): We incorporate several gazetteers of common tokens in place and people names into our system. Each token is checked for its presence on each of the gazetteers. Table 1 details the source and demographics of each.
— **First word in line** (*layout*): We check if the token is the first word in an input line, as an author name is usually short and contained within a single line, so the first word in a line may mark the start of a new author.
— **Source Section** (*layout*): Rich text formats (as provided by the OCR XML output format) propagate high-level document structures such as paragraphs and columns. We use this information to decide whether different tokens are in the same section. Two tokens cannot belong to the same logical unit if they are in two different sections of the text, which may occur when reading inputs line by line. Figure 4 shows an example of three lines of text logically containing six separate lines, due to the two-column format.
— **Orthographic case** (*layout*): We assign the token one of the following values: *Initialcaps*, *MixedCaps*, *ALLCAPS*, or *others*.
— **Sub–Superscript** (*layout*): Tokens have one of these two features turned on if it is a subscript or a superscript. This feature is especially useful for detecting affiliation correspondence markers, such as in Figure 3.
— **Font format** (*layout*): We use three features – *Bold*, *italic*, and *underline* – to indicate the tokens' respective format.
— **Font size** (*layout*): Different logical portions of the document may be rendered in different font sizes. Author names are usually in the same font size or in a larger font than affiliations and rarely smaller. This feature captures the regularities in size. However, as different documents may use different sizes, it is the relative difference between the base font size in a document and the target token that we encode using this feature class. The values for our feature are *small*, *normal*, and *large*.
— **Format change** (*layout*): This is a differential feature which is conditioned on two consecutive labels in the CRF model. It captures the change of layout format when moving from one token to the next. This feature encodes whether two consecutive tokens have the same format. Here, "format" is defined as the combination of "*Font format*", "*Sub–superscript*", and "*Font size*" features. The "*Format change*" is assigned the value "*fbegin*" if any of these three component features changes its value from the previous token to the current; otherwise, it is assigned the value "*fcontinue*".

Post-Processing then constructs author and institution names from the labeled tokens. As author names may occur in various format, such as "*S. Ertekin*" or "*Ertekin, S.*", each name is converted to its normalized form "*S Ertekin*" using regular expressions to detect locations of any separator characters, and transposing the internal results as needed. We define the normalized form to be the first initial, any middle initial, followed by last name (e.g., "S Ertekin"). This form is used when Enlil is evaluated under *relaxed* match conditions (See Section 4.1).

We then group consecutive tokens with the same class together to form a list of author names and a list of affiliations together with their markers. In Figure 3, Enlil generates "$Seyda\ Ertekin$" as the author name and "2" as the correspondence marker. As we use the change in formatting between characters in the tokenization step, consecutive tokens in the same word need to be concatenated differently. One common example is when an author name is written using small capitals, such as "ERTEKIN", there are two tokens "*E*" and "*RTEKIN*". In such cases, we need to ensure that no extra space is inserted between them to form the correct name.

In the previous steps, Enlil does not make use of the actual distance between tokens in rich text formats where larger spaces usually serve as implicit separators. For example, in Figure 4, the second affiliation line contains two occurrences of the string "*National University of Singapore*", separated only by a large gap with no explicit separator, hence, appending them together leads to an incorrect result. In post-processing, we measure the actual distance between consecutive words and check for tab characters if present. When a larger than usual space appears inside a string, it is split. This processes the authors and affiliations in Figure 4 correctly. Identifying the complete list of authors and affiliations ends the first step.

3.2 Author Matching via Relational Classifier

The second step then matches affiliations to authors, also using a supervised classification model. While quadratic in complexity ($O(nm)$, where n is the number of authors, and m the number of institutions), in practice this process is efficient as the total number of authors and affiliations is usually small. However, exceptions do occur in certain consortium papers common in fields such as High-Energy Physics, where hundreds of authors and tens of institutions are common.

While it is easy to decide the correct affiliations using simple heuristic rules with accompanying affiliation markers for the majority of cases, there are complications that we observed that led us to use a more sophisticated supervised learning approach. This is because the format of scholarly documents is diverse and many formats do not contain markers. Moreover, the input extraction process is not error-free and a learning system can deal better with noise than absolute, heuristic rules. Hence, our system also takes the distance between a candidate author and a candidate institution as evidence to improve accuracy. One limitation of this approach is that the spatial distance is only available in rich text formats. Fortunately, our processing pipeline provides this evidence source.

For humans, the relationship between an author and an institution is often easily detected using simple observations. First, these names are usually clearly separated from the other parts of the document, and are at a close proximity to each other. Second, there are

Figure 4: An example of names in different columns in a rich text format document.

usually markers that indicate the connection between them. We use two sets of features that can capture this evidence: the markers provided by the previous module and the distances between the author and the affiliation. There are two distance features in our system: *Euclidean distance* and *Logical distance*. The *Euclidean distance* between two strings is measured by calculating the difference in the $x - y$ coordinates of the strings' center (as measured by their bounding box). The *logical distance* measures the difference in the document logical addresses of the strings' line. Each line can be assigned a unique logical address comprising of four components: its page, column, paragraph, and line index. For example, two lines are in the same paragraph if their page, column, and paragraph indices are equal. The logical distance can be computed in Enlil from the input XML that is provided by Omnipage, which structures its OCR output into such hierarchical text units.

Note that because we generate features for all possible pairs of authors and institutions, our matching problem is not an exclusive (hard) matching task: an author may have more than one affiliation and an institution may serve for more than one author's affiliation. A common scenario is when several authors have the same marker, thus, belonging to the same institution. In Enlil, we allow both author and institution to be associated with multiple markers, although we observe that it is rare for an institution to have more than one marker.

We use a standard SVM with a Gaussian kernel as the learning paradigm for this pointwise classification step, implemented using LibSVM [3], with the below binary features:

— **Signal symbol:** This feature is turned on when a candidate author and institution are both marked by an identical marker. All markers are stored in plain text with no additional format information as correspondence markers of an author and an affiliation may have different formatting. An author and an affiliation can also be associated with more than one marker. For example, an author "*C. Lee Giles*" in Figure 3 will be associated with two markers "*1*" and "2" that follow immediately after it. This one-to-many relationship helps finding the correct affiliations if there are more than one.
— **Logical distance:** This feature class is a collection of three features indicating whether the two strings are in the same *page*, *column*, and *paragraph*. We observe that the affiliated institution is usually in the same structure as the author.
— **Euclidean distance:** OmniPage assigns the x-y coordinates in pixels of the bounding box of every word in the document. Enlil uses these values to compute the coordinates of every author and affiliation strings. We then compute the distance between an author and all possible affiliations along the x- and y-axis and use the Euclidean distance to find the nearest affiliation, as the correct affiliation is often the nearest, as exemplified in Figure 4. To further favor author names that appear before a potential affiliation, we penalize affilations that appear before the author name by a factor of 2. If an affiliation is computed to be the nearest, value of the feature is *yes*, otherwise, the value is *no*. This feature is useful when there is no correspondence marker, as is typical in some publication styles (e.g., ACM proceedings).

4. EVALUATION

In evaluating Enlil, we have the following questions we want to answer:

Q1. How effective is Enlil at recovering exact author and institution strings from scholarly papers, when compared with a suitable baseline? Is Enlil also effective at matching authors to institutions to form correct affiliations?

Q2. Does performance vary when the documents come from different domains?

Q3. What type of errors does Enlil typically make and what sources cause them? How does performance vary when it is provided with real-world or clean input?

Q4. What impact do the different features have on author–affiliation matching performance?

We first describe the datasets used in our evaluation, experimental results and finish with a detailed analysis.

4.1 Datasets

We evaluate Enlil on three different datasets to illustrate both evaluation in depth (volume) and in breadth (variety): For volume, we used articles from the the ACM Digital Library, and a larger corpus from the Association for Computational Linguistics' (ACL) Anthology. For variety, we collected a set of cross-disciplinary scientific journal articles by querying Google Scholar.

The first two datasets are from specific technical domains. We sampled computer science papers and their metadata from the ACM Portal, representing 2,243 documents and 6,625 authors[6]. The metadata from the ACM contains a list of all authors and their affiliations, making it a useful gold standard for author extraction. However, it does not list the exact number of institutions shown as appearing in the actual PDF file. For example, it is common for two authors in a paper to be associated with the same institution. In this case there might be a single institution string for both authors, or two duplicated ones (one for each author, as in Figure 4). Hence, the ACM metadata does not represent a complete gold standard for institution extraction, and hence we omit institution extraction evaluation on this dataset.

The ACL Anthology Corpus is the largest of our datasets, containing 23,533 documents[7]. However, there is no ground truth so we need to manually extract and label the data. In evaluating Enlil's results on this dataset, we randomly selected 100 papers from this source, sampling mostly from its conference proceedings. Papers from the same conference usually use an identical conference template, so we made an assumption (discussed later) that the result would be indicative of Enlil's performance over the whole ACL Anthology Corpus. In addition, the processing time grows linearly with the number of articles and Enlil takes about 42 seconds on average to process one document in this corpus (cost is mostly based on the prerequisite OCR).

As Enlil aims to process scientific publications in general – primarily journal articles and conference proceedings – we must also test breadth-wise, on documents drawn from diverse sources. Enlil needs to perform well for both humanities and general sciences to support its downstream use cases, so we deemed the breadth-wise evaluation the most critical. To achieve this, we manually constructed and labeled a corpus of 800 documents from various scholarly journals across four large branches of science, as shown

[6]We sampled Portal by retrieving all results returned by Google Scholar for the query "site:dl.acm.org".

[7]`http://www.aclweb.org/anthology`, visited on May 22th, 2013

in Table 2. Documents were chosen from different fields and from different journals and publishers to ensure a wide variety of formats, indicative of the input we expect Enlil will need to handle when processing both science and humanities publications. Documents were also sampled uniformly – we drew each fourth of the corpus from four different major branches of science, extending the uniform sampling into the individual component fields. All documents were downloaded from our institution's library subscription or from freely-available Web sources. Documents were all uniformly in PDF and processed by our preprocessing pipeline to obtain the input content and layout information. We created the gold standard by manually performing both steps in the process: 1) extracting the authors and institutions from each document in the corpus, and 2) then matching author and institution pairs together to form affiliations. The dataset used in our experiments (minus the copyrighted PDFs) – including the gold standard are publicly available[8].

We trained a single pair of CRF (linear CRF with the window size of 2) and SVM (standard SVM with a Gaussian kernel) models for all of the results reported in the subsequent experiments. A small training dataset was separately (non-overlapping with the testing sets) compiled from articles from the same three sources. We used a total of 390 instances of author and institution extractions for the CRF model and 1,969 instances of author-affiliation matching for the SVM model. All the training data was annotated by the first author.

Within a document, we deem an author's name to be his unique identity. However, an author can have both his full name as well as a shortened version within the same paper (this occurs, for example, in Springer's proceedings template) and in such cases, we have chosen to retain the short name – as the full name can easily be converted to its short form for evaluation, described later. To maintain consistency in annotation we apply the following rules. First, titles (e.g., *PhD* or *MSc*) are removed if present; second, email addresses and phone numbers are discarded, but any physical address information in an affiliation is retained as part of the affiliation. Finally, the author and affiliation strings should be preserved in their original form if not otherwise affected (e.g. *National University of Singapore* is retained over its abbreviated form *NUS*, when both forms are present). Diacritics are also allowed to be represented by ASCII close equivalents (e.g., *université* for *universite*).

While our preprocessing pipeline affords rich text format input, it is not perfect; the output from the preprocessing is not always clean and contributes significant amount of noise. In analyzing the page image to produce the textual and spatial features the commercial OCR package occasionally misrecognizes content. In our observation, this problem occurred most frequently with characters with diacritics (as shown in Figure 5), as the commercial OCR package we used is tuned for English input. The SectLabel preprocessing runs after OCR, to infer the document logical structure and assign lines to their semantic categories. However, some lines may be incorrectly identified or missed, as shown in Figure 6.

As the preprocessing is a significant source of error, we also wish to benchmark Enlil on both clean input data and real input data. To enable such analyses, we selected a subset of 160 articles from the cross-disciplinary corpus which produce correct OCR and Sectlabel results. We use this smaller collection (dubbed the *Clean* dataset from Google Scholar) to assess Enlil's performance without cascading errors that come from preprocessing, whereas the original 800 document collection (dubbed *Full*) is used to approximate Enlil's expected, real-world performance.

[8]http://wing.comp.nus.edu.sg/downloads/enlilCollection/

Table 2: Demographics on our cross-disciplinary dataset. The dataset comprises of 800 documents, manifesting 2,217 instances of author and 1,821 instances of institution names.

Branch	Field	Number of Journals / Documents	Number of Authors / Affiliations
Applied	Aerospace	2 / 20	879 / 507
	Agricultural	2 / 20	
	Biomedical	2 / 20	
	Dentistry	2 / 20	
	Forestry	2 / 20	
	Mechanical	2 / 20	
	Medical	2 / 20	
	Mining	2 / 20	
	Nursing	2 / 20	
	Robotics	2 / 20	
Formal	Computer	5 / 50	519 / 388
	Logic	5 / 50	
	Mathematics	5 / 50	
	Statistics	5 / 50	
Natural	Astronomy	4 / 40	813 / 516
	Biology	4 / 40	
	Chemistry	4 / 40	
	Ecology	4 / 40	
	Physics	4 / 40	
Social	Anthropology	4 / 40	470 / 410
	Criminology	4 / 40	
	Economics	4 / 40	
	History	4 / 40	
	Psychology	4 / 40	

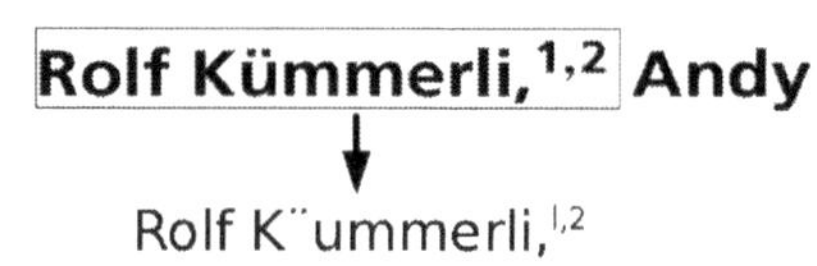

Figure 5: An example of incorrect character recognition from preprocessing by OmniPage. The umlaut (¨) is separated from its base *u* and the affiliation marker number *1* ("one") is misrecognized as the character l ("ell").

4.2 Experimental Results

We report extraction results using two schemes: exact match and relaxed match. *Exact* match judges an extraction as correct only when the author or affiliation name matches the ground truth with canonicalization – i.e., after minor, automatable rules, such as removing multiple spaces, trimming, lowercasing, and removing unnecessary punctuation, are applied. *Relaxed* match relaxes the exact match, by allowing small name variations (e.g., short name and full name, with or without middle initials). Figure 6 shows an example of author names in their short forms that can be matched with their full forms in relaxed mode. We do this by using the Jaro-Winkler string metric to compare the ground truth against the extracted output. We use a similarity threshold of 0.95 for author names and 0.85 for affiliation names. We chose a lower threshold for affiliation names, as observation showed that they are usually much longer and contain more variation as compared to author names. To be precise, relaxed matching performance will always be equal or greater to exact matching performance.

We use SVM Header Parser from SeerSuite [25] as the baseline in our experiments. As mentioned, this tool focuses only on the computer and information science domains and related areas. To be expected, it does not work well with our cross-disciplinary collection and significantly underperforms Enlil in three of our cross-disciplinary datasets while performing equivalently only on the corpus of documents from the *Formal* domain.

We first review the results of the evaluation, examining each dataset in turn, to answer our evaluation Q1. We answer Q2–4 in the discussion immediately following.

Q1 (Performance vs. Baseline) – ACM Corpus. The evaluation results of the ACM Corpus show large improvements of Enlil over the current state-of-the-art SVM Header Parser in both author extraction and affiliation matching (Table 3). In relaxed mode, F_1 scores increase by 9.9% and 9.7% in these two experiments, respectively. When comparing two systems, both Enlil and SVM Header Parser can process PDF documents. However, SVM Header Parser only focuses on the textual content, while Enlil also accounts for the document's spatial layout and font information. Because of this loss of fidelity in its input representation, SVM Header Parser encounters some issues that do not occur in Enlil; for example, chunk identification in space-separated names, as illustrated by Figure 4.

ACL Anthology. Both the ACM Corpus and the ACL Anthology contain computer science research papers in well-defined templates so we had expected their evaluation results to be very similar. However, Table 3 shows that the affiliation matching performance of both systems drop noticeably in the ACL Anthology corpus. We believe two reasons are responsible for the drop. First, as we only sample a small number of documents from the ACL Anthology, failing to match authors and affiliations correctly in some documents greatly affect F_1. In order to get a better approximation, we need to build the gold standard for a larger number of documents; however, this task requires manual annotation, effort that we preferentially allocated to the cross-disciplinary dataset. Second, a number of the ACL Anthology articles are older records (dating from the 1970s and 80s, before digital desktop publishing), published with different layout formats. This is in contrast to the ACM Corpus whose papers are largely contemporary. These legacy documents are an important factor that reduces the performance of both Enlil and SVM Header Parser.

Cross Disciplinary Corpus. Table 4 shows the affiliation matching performance with the cross disciplinary corpus. Detailed, per-task performance for Enlil is detailed in Tables 5 and 6. Generally we can see that performance in terms of F_1 measure for both tasks is in the upper 80s for both tasks when the full automated pipeline is used. Extraction performance betters matching performance slightly as correct matching is preconditioned on correct extraction. In addition, invalid correspondence markers affect the matching result even though the extraction might be correct. Although the extraction of affiliation is much harder than author extraction due to its complex structure – for example some may use *Department, School, Address*, while others use *Institute* – name canonicalization is beyond the scope of the current work. Thus, there is little difference in performance between author and affiliation extraction in Enlil.

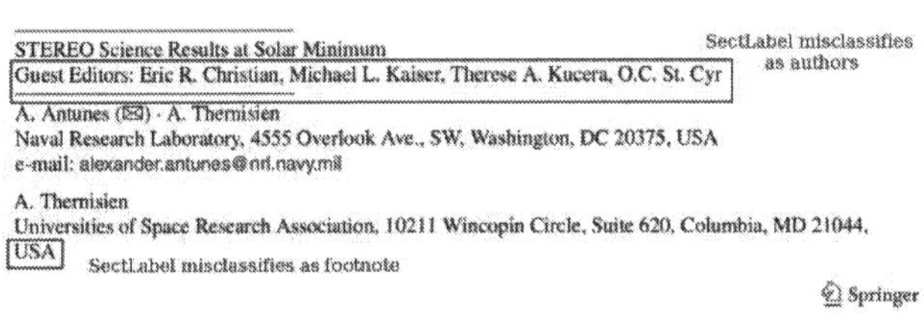

Figure 6: Examples of incorrect classifications by the second stage of preprocessing by Sectlabel, in which an *Editor* line is misclassified as *Author*, and a part of an institution is misclassified as *Footnote*.

Q2 (Domain Sensitivity). To answer the second question, we analyse the evaluation results of Enlil on different domains in Table 4. In general, the performance drops noticeably in the *Nature* and *Social* subsets. This indicates that the current models of Enlil fail to recognize some paper formats in these categories. This is a common problem of systems employing statistical learning methods when encountering new types of input data. We try to alleviate this by collecting training data from many major publishers, such as Elsevier or Springer. Their articles not only have well-defined structure and conform to a limited number of templates but also cover multiple scientific disciplines. The result is that Enlil can handle cross-disciplinary papers better than SVM Header Parser. In SVM Header Parser, there are large gaps between the *Formal* and other subsets. In our experiments, it always achieves the best performance in the *Formal* subset because its training data contained mostly computing-related papers which are most similar to this subset (Table 2). The t–test result in Table 4 supports this finding, showing significant differences between Enlil and SVM Header Parser in *Applied*, *Nature*, and *Social* datasets ($p < 0.01$).

Q3 (Clean vs. Noisy). We observe that cascading errors from OmniPage and SectLabel do significantly affect performance. When we remove these errors in the *Clean* dataset (Table 4), the average performance increases significantly ($p \ll 0.01$) with gain of 10.3% for exact match and 9.7% under the relaxed match scheme. These values indicate that there is significant difference in Enlil's performance when the dataset is clean than when it is not, and that proper clean input is important to ensure optimum performance. As in many other cases, the main difficulty comes from the fact that such tools also need to deal with a variety of input forms from various disciplines.

In particular, the effects of three minor types of error are alleviated when our system is in *relaxed* mode: 1) incorrect character recognition caused by OCR, 2) missing words in affiliations extracted by the SectLabel line classifier, and 3) occurrences of mixed use of both full and short names in a document. In Table 4, the average difference between two matching modes in *Full* dataset (3.4%) is slightly larger than this number in the *Clean* dataset (2.5%), because the first two errors are removed in the second dataset and only the third type remains (interleaved full/short names). This kind of mixture deserves special care as it affects our system in two ways: First, when the full name and the short name of the same author are stored as different entities, it reduces the system's precision. This is ignored in *relaxed* mode where all names are converted to a standard form, first initial, middle initial, and last name. However, the second effect, caused by the different positions of the full name and the short name within the document, still remain. Our system uses various types of distances between the author's name and the affiliation as features, and the correct affiliation is likely to be the nearest one. So, an author may be associated with incorrect affiliations because the nearest ones are usually not the same with respect to the locations of his full name and short name.

With respect to clean input, we would like to highlight two other systematic errors that are intrinsic to Enlil. First, when lines contain author or affiliation data but co-occur with other metadata (e.g., authors or email addresses concatenated with institution names), Enlil's extraction CRF may fail to correctly identify the data and discard the noise. Although we try to remove redundant parts of a line in pre-processing using regular expressions, this does not filter

Table 3: Performance comparison between Enlil and SVM Header Parser (SHP) on the ACM and ACL datasets. Double asterisks (**) indicates that F_1 performance was significantly better than SHP ($p < 0.01$).

Experiment	Corpus	Mode	Enlil			SVM Header Parser		
			Precision	Recall	F_1	Precision	Recall	F_1
Author Name Extraction	ACM	Exact	95.7	93.5	94.6**	84.1	73.5	78.4
		Relaxed	97.9	95.5	96.7**	93.2	81.3	86.8
	ACL	Exact	93.4	90.1	91.8**	84.8	72.7	78.3
		Relaxed	94.7	91.3	92.9**	92.2	79.1	85.1
Affiliation matching	ACM	Exact	89.6	88.2	88.9**	78.8	68.8	73.5
		Relaxed	91.4	89.9	90.6**	87.0	75.7	80.9
	ACL	Exact	84.5	82.8	83.6**	74.2	62.9	68.1
		Relaxed	85.7	84.0	84.8**	79.3	67.2	72.7

Table 4: Enlil's affiliation matching comparison between Enlil and SHP on the cross-domain full and clean datasets. Exact match results shown, with relaxed matching results shown in parentheses. Significant improvement in Enlil between the full and clean datasets denoted by "*" ($p < 0.05$) and "" ($p < 0.01$). "†" indicates significance ($p < 0.01$) of Enlil's performance over SHP.**

Dataset	Branch	Enlil			SVM Header Parser		
		Precision	Recall	F_1	Precision	Recall	F_1
Full	Applied	86.3 (89.7)	89.7 (90.9)	87.9 (90.3)†	38.1 (46.3)	7.99 (9.63)	13.2 (15.9)
	Formal	87.8 (90.1)	87.9 (89.5)	87.9 (89.8)†	57.6 (62.6)	41.1 (44.5)	47.9 (52.0)
	Natural	80.1 (80.7)	81.2 (81.8)	80.7 (81.3)†	55.7 (56.7)	28.3 (28.8)	37.5 (38.2)
	Social	70.4 (81.4)	83.4 (92.7)	76.3 (86.7)†	37.4 (44.9)	26.7 (32.1)	31.2 (37.4)
	Average	81.6 (85.5)	85.6 (88.7)	83.6 (87.0)†	47.2 (52.6)	26.0 (28.8)	32.5 (35.9)
Clean	Applied	95.9 (96.8)	98.1	97.0 (97.4)**†	41.3 (44.4)	12.1 (13.1)	18.8 (20.2)
	Formal	95.6 (95.6)	97.3	96.4 (96.4)**†	63.9 (68.6)	51.9 (55.7)	57.3 (61.5)
	Natural	95.4 (96.7)	96.7 (97.4)	96.1 (97.0)**†	47.1 (50.6)	26.5 (28.5)	33.9 (36.5)
	Social	80.4 (92.3)	90.9 (97.0)	85.3 (94.6)*†	38.7 (44.0)	29.3 (33.3)	33.3 (37.9)
	Average	92.0 (95.4)	95.9 (97.5)	93.9 (96.4)**†	47.8 (51.9)	29.9 (32.6)	35.8 (38.8)

Table 5: Author extraction comparison between the cross-domain full and clean dataset. Exact match results shown, with relaxed results in parentheses when different. Significant improvement denoted by "*" ($p < 0.05$) and "" ($p < 0.01$).**

Dataset	Branch	Precision	Recall	F_1
Full	Applied	81.9 (85.7)	95.9 (96.4)	88.3 (90.7)
	Formal	89.5 (94.1)	94.0 (94.6)	91.7 (94.3)
	Natural	85.5 (86.4)	94.6 (95.1)	89.8 (90.5)
	Social	73.8 (85.3)	95.3 (97.4)	83.2 (90.9)
	Average	82.7 (87.9)	95.0 (95.9)	88.4 (91.6)
Clean	Applied	97.5 (99.5)	100.0	98.8 (99.7)**
	Formal	96.4	100.0	98.1 **
	Natural	94.8 (96.7)	99.3	97.0 (97.9)**
	Social	80.5 (93.1)	100.0	89.2 (96.4)*
	Average	92.3 (96.4)	99.8	95.8 (98.0)**

Table 6: Institution name extraction comparison between the cross-domain full and clean dataset, using exact match. Relaxed results are identical. Significant improvement denoted by "*" ($p < 0.05$) and "" ($p < 0.01$).**

Dataset	Branch	Precision	Recall	F_1
Full	Applied	88.2	95.7	91.8
	Formal	90.6	89.7	90.2
	Natural	87.8	87.9	87.9
	Social	80.9	93.2	86.6
	Average	86.8	91.7	89.2
Clean	Applied	96.1	99.0	97.5**
	Formal	98.7	97.4	98.1*
	Natural	96.7	98.9	97.8**
	Social	87.8	95.2	91.3
	Average	94.8	97.6	96.2**

all of the noise. To address this, the CRF also needs to be trained to handle noisy input. As our current feature set caters only to characterize names, separators and markers, further work needs to encode features dedicated to marking such noise. A second error happens when the relationship between an author and his affiliations is expressed in the prose content, rather than relying on visual or spatial effects or stylistic conventions. Figure 7 shows an example of such error. Solving this problem requires understanding its content, beyond the scope of the current work.

Table 7: Effect of different feature sets – (Log)ical distance, (Euc)lidean distance and (Sig)nal symbol – on the *Full* and *Clean* dataset. Exact match results shown, with relaxed matching results shown in parentheses when different. "" show significant differences from the 'All' feature set ($p < 0.01$).**

Data-set	Branch	Features			
		Log+Euc**	Sig+Log**	Sig+Euc	All
Full	Applied	49.4 (51.2)	82.4 (83.6)	86.9 (89.2)	87.9 (90.3)
	Formal	73.1 (74.9)	68.0 (68.1)	87.9 (89.8)	87.9 (89.8)
	Natural	48.8 (58.9)	73.9 (74.3)	79.3 (79.6)	80.7 (81.3)
	Social	58.7 (68.9)	66.7 (68.4)	75.3 (85.5)	76.3 (86.7)
	Average	57.5 (63.5)	72.8 (73.6)	82.4 (86.0)	83.6 (87.0)
Clean	Applied	57.2 (58.5)	85.9 (86.4)	96.8 (97.2)	97.0 (97.4)
	Formal	78.7	71.6	96.4	96.4
	Natural	58.0 (58.9)	85.4	95.4 (96.4)	96.1 (97.0)
	Social	65.1 (73.3)	67.4 (69.8)	83.6 (92.2)	85.3 (94.6)
	Average	64.8 (67.4)	77.6 (78.3)	93.0 (95.6)	93.9 (96.4)

Q4 (Effectiveness of different features). As our contribution is primarily with using logical structure, we focus our discussion on the effectiveness of the layout features proposed for use in the author–affiliation matching task. In Enlil, we use a set of three features – *signal symbol*, *logical distance* and *Euclidean distance* – in the SVM model. We compare their effects in Table 7 by carrying out feature ablation testing.

It is clear that the *signal symbol* is the most important feature in both *exact* mode and *relaxed* mode. On average, the removal of this feature causes significant drop ($p < 0.01$) in Enlil's performance –

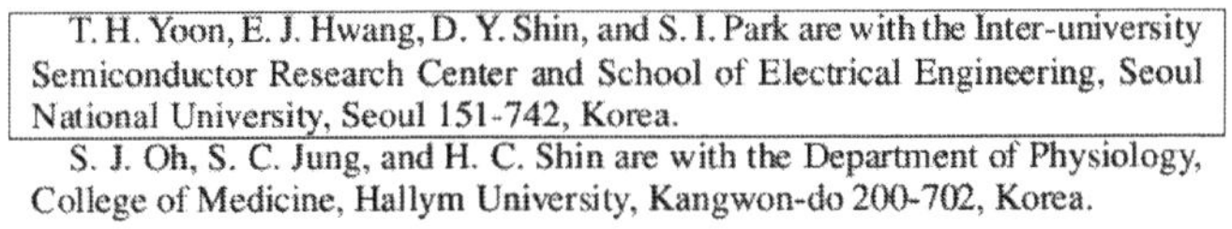
T. H. Yoon, E. J. Hwang, D. Y. Shin, and S. I. Park are with the Inter-university Semiconductor Research Center and School of Electrical Engineering, Seoul National University, Seoul 151-742, Korea.
S. J. Oh, S. C. Jung, and H. C. Shin are with the Department of Physiology, College of Medicine, Hallym University, Kangwon-do 200-702, Korea.

Figure 7: A complex scenario when Enlil fails.

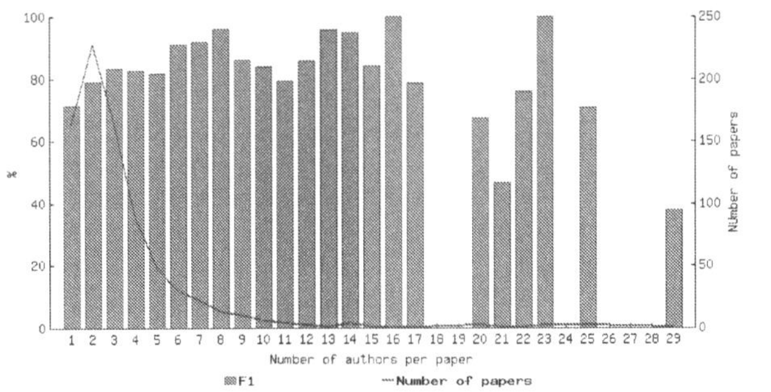

Figure 8: Enlil's exact match performance on the *Full* dataset, broken down by number of authors per paper. The dark line shows the number of papers represented by it (for e.g., in the leftmost cluster the F_1 score of .72 is the averaged performance of Enlil on 163 singly-authored papers).

26.1% in *exact* mode and 23.5% in *relaxed* mode – compared with the full feature set. These differences reflect the common use of correspondence markers in scholarly documents.

The second most important feature is the *Euclidean distance* between authors and affiliations. Its effect is less than that of *signal symbol* but still important. Enlil's performance decreases by 10.8% ($p < 0.01$) and 13.4% ($p < 0.01$) on average in *exact* and *relaxed* modes respectively. In some specific domains, such as *Formal* and *Social*, the effect of *Euclidean distance* may even outweigh the importance of *signal symbol*. We conjecture that in domains where the number of authors per publication is small, affiliations can be juxtaposed with authors' name. In such cases, correspondence markers are unnecessary and can be dismissed, which reduces the effect of *signal symbol* feature. The average numbers of authors per publication from *Social* and *Formal* domain are 2.35 and 2.60 respectively, which are smaller than the value of *Applied* domain (4.40) and *Natural* domain (4.07). This evidence strengthens our conclusion.

Logical distance is the feature which has the least significant ($p > 0.05$) effect on performance. In all cases, the performance gain of this feature is very small (from 1.0% to 1.2%). It is interesting to note that this feature is the only feature that can be obtained reliably from raw text – the other two are only available in rich text formats that encode layout information. This result implies that raw text input (provided by text extraction software *e.g. PDFBox*) will likely be problematic for any solution looking to perform author–affiliation matching.

Given that one of ten authors/institutions are incorrectly extracted and one in fifteen affiliations are incorrectly matched by Enlil, is this performance sufficient to support downstream analytics? We think the answer is yes. Extraction and matching failures happen in specific papers, and as such, errors are not uniformly distributed. Documents that do not follow regular conventions (e.g., Figure 7) will generate low-confidence results, and should be easy to detect. We note that problems also occur more frequently on scholarly documents with many authors and institutions (Figure 8), as these demonstrate more exceptions than documents with few authors.

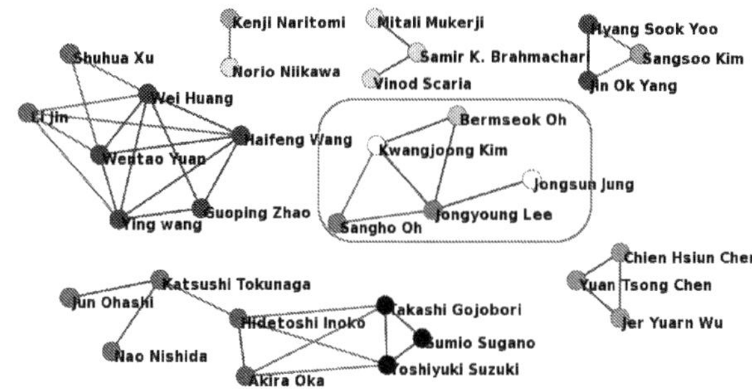

Figure 9: The same co-author network as in Figure 1 where the affiliation data is provided automatically by Enlil, compiled from freely-available publications. The circled group indicates a discrepancy in comparison to the ground truth in Figure 1.

5. APPLICATIONS

Enlil has proven immediately useful in several scholarly analyses. Our umbrella project (from which Enlil's development was funded) aimed to define Asia via natural scholarly collaboration patterns rather than by geopolitical boundaries. By associating scholars to their institutions and countries via Enlil, we have developed novel metrics that discover nascent collaboration trends, and uncover institutions/countries that facilitate collaborations between other researchers (rather than direct publications) [6]. Cho *et al.* [5] used Enlil's author-affiliation output to aggregate the micro-patterns of collaboration among authors to macro-patterns of collaboration among Asian countries. As an example, Figure 9 shows the same network as the manually constructed version in Figure 1, but the latter uses data automatically acquired by Enlil. In this example, Enlil fails to process a publication of authors in a single marked group. Hence, all of them are assumed to have different affiliations. The rest of the network remains almost the same with only minor changes between closely related authors.

We also have created a public website[9] that allows students and laymen to perform their own scholarly network analyses through a simple four-step serial workflow. In the website, Enlil is a primary component on the backend pipeline processing. Users first input some seed authors of interest. They are then presented with a set of results harvested from Google Scholar, with which they can refine and visualize the resultant co-authorship network. The site allows the visualization of the network over time, showing how collaborations and network/citation metrics evolve. Previous scientometric work (e.g., [1]) has largely been the province of experts working with clean and costly data sources (such as Thomson Reuters' Web of Science). Our work in integrating Enlil into such a web-based frontend shows that such knowledge management tasks can now be relatively cost-free and taken back by citizen science.

We are currently using Enlil for tracking the migration of research networks. Based on publication co-authors and institutions, a researcher's changing institutional affiliations and collaborative network can be traced over time. This information can be used to construct large-scale patterns in the migration of research networks to elucidate the shifting centers of intellectual labor (Luukkonen *et al.* [23], Glanzel *et al.* [13]). Such information is vital for policy makers, economists, and social scientists to gauge how well investments into research capital and Big Science facilities have translated into the production of innovation hubs.

[9] `http://www.huluppu.net/`

6. CONCLUSIONS

We have studied the extraction of author-affiliation relationship in scholarly documents and introduced *Enlil*, a complete system for matching authors and affiliations from publications in PDF format. Our system employs both sequence and pointwise machine learning models (CRF and SVM) to outperform the previous state-of-the-art in author/affiliation extraction and matching. The features in our system are also carefully selected and analyzed to make better use of the layout information in rich text documents.

Our evaluation over three datasets assessed Enlil's performance in breadth as well as depth. For computer science articles, Enlil significantly outperforms prior work by almost 10% in F measure. Enlil's performance gain widens when tested with articles representing a variety of domains. Analysis shows that Enlil's combined representation of both spatial and logical document structure significantly aids its performance, validating work [22] arguing in favor of rich document representations for document analysis input.

Enlil is but one component of a digital library and knowledge managment solution for scholarly publications. We have used Enlil in our various scientometric projects of which we have highlighted the PASNP case study. It has shown its value in creating network analyses in a simple and less costly manner than previous work that required clean, publisher-provisioned metadata and expert knowledge.

7. REFERENCES

[1] D. Aumüller and E. Rahm. Affiliation analysis of database publications. *SIGMOD Record*, 40(1), 2011.

[2] A. Belaïd and Y. Rangoni. Structure extraction in printed documents using neural approaches, 2006.

[3] C.-C. Chang and C.-J. Lin. LIBSVM: A library for support vector machines. *ACM Transactions on Intelligent Systems and Technology*, 2:27:1–27:27, 2011. Software available at http://www.csie.ntu.edu.tw/∼cjlin/libsvm.

[4] C.-C. Chen, K.-H. Yang, C.-L. Chen, and J.-M. Ho. Bibpro: A citation parser based on sequence alignment. *Knowledge and Data Engineering, IEEE Transactions on*, 24(2):236–250, 2012.

[5] P. S. Cho, N. Bullock, and D. Ali. The bioinformatic basis of pan-asianism. *East Asian Science, Technology, and Society*, 7(2), 2013.

[6] P. S. Cho, H. H. N. Do, M. K. Chandrasekaran, and M.-Y. Kan. Identifying research facilitators in an emerging asian research area: A case study of the pan-asian snp consortium. *Scientometrics*, 2013 Forthcoming.

[7] E. Cortez, A. S. da Silva, M. A. Goncalves, F. Mesquita, and E. S. de Moura. FLUX-CIM: flexible unsupervised extraction of citation meta-data. In *Proceedings of the ACM/IEEE-CS Joint conference on Digital libraries*, 2007.

[8] I. G. Councill, C. L. Giles, and M.-Y. Kan. ParsCit: An open-source CRF reference string parsing package. In *LREC*, May 2008.

[9] L. Egghe. Theory and practise of the g-index. *Scientometrics*, 69(1):131–152, 2006.

[10] L. Gao, X. Qi, Z. Tang, X. Lin, and Y. Liu. Web-based citation parsing, correction and augmentation. In *Proceedings of the 12th ACM/IEEE-CS joint conference on Digital Libraries*, pages 295–304. ACM, 2012.

[11] L. Gao, Z. Tang, and X. Lin. Cebbip: A parser of bibliographic information in chinese electronic books. In *Proceedings of the 9th ACM/IEEE-CS joint conference on Digital libraries*, 2009.

[12] L. Gao, Z. Tang, X. Lin, Y. Liu, R. Qiu, and Y. Wang. Structure extraction from PDF-based book documents. In *Proceedings of the 11th ACM/IEEE-CS Joint conference on Digital libraries*, 2011.

[13] W. Glanzel, K. Debackere, and M. Meyer. 'triad' or 'tetrad'? on global changes in a dynamic world. *Scientometrics*, 74(1):71–88, 2008.

[14] H. Han, C. L. Giles, E. Manavoglu, H. Zha, Z. Zhang, and E. A. Fox. Automatic document metadata extraction using support vector machines. In *In JCDL '03: Proceedings of the 3rd ACM/IEEE-CS Joint Conference on Digital Libraries*, pages 37–48, 2003.

[15] J. E. Hirsch. An index to quantify an individual's scientific research output. In *Proceedings of the National Academy of Sciences of the United States of America*, volume 102, 2005.

[16] J. E. Hirsch. An index to quantify an individual's scientific research output that takes into account the effect of multiple coauthorship. *Scientometrics*, 85(3), 2010.

[17] J. Kim, D. X. Le, and G. R. Thoma. Automated labeling in document images. In *Proc. SPIE: Document Recognition and Retrieval VIII*, pages 111–122, 2001.

[18] S. Klink, A. Dengel, and T. Kieninger. Document structure analysis based on layout and textual features. In *Proc. of International Workshop on Document Analysis Systems, DAS2000*, pages 99–111, 2000.

[19] J. Lafferty, A. McCallum, and F. Pereira. Conditional random fields: Probabilistic models for segmenting and labeling sequence data. In *Proceedings of the Eighteenth International Conference on Machine Learning*, pages 282–289, 2001.

[20] C. LaGuardia. Scopus vs. web of science. http://www.libraryjournal.com/article/CA491154.html.

[21] L. D. Lopez, J. Yu, C. N. Arighi, H. Huang, H. Shatkay, and C. H. Wu. An automatic system for extracting figures and captions in biomedical pdf documents. In *IEEE International Conference on Bioinformatics and Biomedicine*, pages 578–581, 2011.

[22] M.-T. Luong, T.-D. Nguyen, and M.-Y. Kan. Logical structure recovery in scholarly articles with rich document features. *International Journal of Digital Library Systems*, 1(4):1–23, 2010.

[23] T. Luukkonen, O. Persson, and G. Sivertsen. Understanding patterns of international scientific collaboration. *Science, Technology & Human Values*, 17(1):101–126, 1992.

[24] B. U. Stefan Wuchty, Benjamin F. Jones. The increasing dominance of teams in production of knowledge. *Science*, 316(1036), 2007.

[25] P. B. Teregowda, I. G. Councill, R. J. P. Fernández, M. Khabsa, S. Zheng, and C. L. Giles. Seersuite: developing a scalable and reliable application framework for building digital libraries by crawling the web. In *Proceedings of the 2010 USENIX conference on Web application development*, pages 14–14. USENIX Association, 2010.

[26] C. S. Wagner and L. Leydesdorff. Network structure, self-organization, and the growth of international collaboration in science. *Research Policy*, 34(10):1608 – 1618, 2005.

User-centered Approach in Creating a Metadata Schema for Video Games and Interactive Media

Jin Ha Lee, Hyerim Cho, Violet Fox
University of Washington
Mary Gates Hall, Suite 370
Seattle, WA 98195
+1 206.685.0153
{jinhalee, chohr113, vfox}@uw.edu

Andrew Perti
Seattle Interactive Media Museum
305 Harrison St
Seattle, WA 98109
+1 518.653.5864
andrew.perti@thesimm.org

ABSTRACT
Video games and interactive media are increasingly becoming important part of our culture and everyday life, and subsequently, of archival and digital library collections. However, existing organizational systems often use vague or inconsistent terms to describe video games or attempt to use schemas designed for textual bibliographic resources. Our research aims to create a standardized metadata schema and encoding scheme that provides an intelligent and comprehensive way to represent video games. We conducted interviews with 24 gamers, focusing on their video game-related information needs and seeking behaviors. We also performed a domain analysis of current organizational systems used in catalog records and popular game websites, evaluating metadata elements used to describe games. With these results in mind, we created a list of elements which form a metadata schema for describing video games, with both a core set of 16 elements and an extended set of 46 elements providing more flexibility in expressing the nature of a game.

Categories and Subject Descriptors
H.3.7 [**Information Storage and Retrieval**]: Digital Libraries – *Standards*, K.8.0 [**Personal Computing**]: Games

General Terms
Design, Standardization, Theory

Keywords
Video Games, Interactive Media, Cultural Artifacts, Metadata, Description, Seattle Interactive Media Museum

1. INTRODUCTION
Video games and interactive media have become an important artifact in our culture and everyday life in many aspects including entertainment, business, research, and so on. As video games, smartphone/tablet game apps, and other novel forms of interactive media become more popular with all types of users and communities, providing intelligent access also becomes increasingly important. Yet we still lack an organizational system that can effectively and thoroughly describe these video games in a standardized way. Current systems and standards fall short, whether originating from traditional library settings (e.g., FRBR [Functional Requirements for Bibliographic Records], RDA [Resource Description and Access], or LCSH [Library of Congress Subject Headings]) or from commercial settings such as game-related websites. They tend to focus only on providing basic descriptive information about games such as title, platform, publisher, etc.; their metadata elements and indexing terms are often not defined or explained at all [14], [22] (e.g., what does "genre" mean and what accounts for "strategy" games?) Moreover, it is often unclear where these organizational systems are sourcing their metadata from (i.e., is it the packaging such as the box or the manual? Or is it from playing the game itself or another secondary source?). In addition, it is not difficult to find examples of game representations that have misinformation or contradicting information as much of the metadata is unverified.

The objective of our research is to create a standardized metadata schema and encoding scheme (i.e., controlled vocabulary) that can be used to describe video games and interactive media across multiple organizations in different domains. This project started in 2011 as a joint effort between the University of Washington Information School and the Seattle Interactive Media Museum (SIMM). The objectives of the SIMM include aggregation, research, exhibition, and preservation of interactive media culture and the physical, digital, and abstract artifacts therein; thus robust and media-specific metadata is needed in order to serve a wide variety of use cases. Creating a metadata schema for the video game domain is a challenging task because it is almost impossible for anyone to have a thoroughly comprehensive understanding of games across multiple platforms, genres, and time periods. In order to ensure that we are reflecting as much domain expertise and knowledge as possible, we decided to conduct this research project in the form of a of graduate level course. A total of 21 people participated in Phase I of the project and 18 in Phase II of the project. In Phase I, we created the basic backbone of the schema, CORE16, which lists 16 core elements that should be included in any organizational systems describing video games and interactive media [15]. Phase II of our project focused on expanding this core list by developing a larger "recommended" set of metadata elements. In this paper, we report on our progress made in Phase II and introduce a list of recommended metadata elements in our schema. We will also describe how the schema was designed, followed by discussing some of the challenges we encountered throughout the process.

2. RELATED WORK
In the Library and Information Science (LIS) field, the description and organization of video games traditionally has not been given much consideration. Although interest in video games has grown

considerably in commercial, cultural, and academic domains, this deficiency still hampers the development of effective video game organization systems. Current library and archival collections focus mostly on books and similar text-based documents, often treating artifacts like video games as products of popular culture and therefore of less scholarly value [15].

In the field of knowledge organization, the problems of describing non-book artifacts have been frequently discussed. Lubetzky [17] was the first to seriously discuss integrating non-book items into the library catalog, offering the concept of the work [16]. Lubetzky recognized that a book is an edition of a particular work, which is closely related to other editions and translations of the work. The problems of applying book-based features to non-book items were noted by Hagler [6] and Leigh [16]. The lack of principles for describing non-book items resulted in description based on their physical form, rather than intellectual content [16]. We identified evidence of this issue for video games in LC subject headings used for WorldCat records (e.g., computer games, electronic games, mobile games, application software).

The limited applicability of traditional content description standards on video games has also been noted by McDonough et al. [18]. The authors attempted to apply the Functional Requirements for Bibliographic Records (FRBR) model [9] to classic computer games, but could not easily determine work, expression, manifestation, or item of video games. Moreover, the FRBR model is missing some potentially useful characteristics of multimedia objects including music or games; for example, mood or similarity to other objects which can be beneficial for users' discovery of new music or games [13].

As Winget [22] pointed out describing video games for preservation is a truly demanding task, as is illustrated by Massively Multiplayer Online Role-Playing Games (MMORPG). They are not only digital, but also consist of software systems that have significant hardware, peripheral, and network dependencies which are difficult to collect and formally represent. The more we understand the characteristics of video games, the harder it becomes to apply current organization standards and rules to describe them. In order to overcome these problems, several scholars have started exploring new ways to organize and preserve video game information (e.g., [18], [22]). However, these attempts tend to emphasize preservation rather than description of games and employ data-centric methods rather than considering the end user's point-of-view.

Currently, the only systematically designed descriptive framework for games can be found in Huth's master's thesis work [8] which was reviewed extensively in Anderson et al. [1]. Huth designed his framework by using existing elements from OCLC Metadata Elements and Dublin Core Metadata Set and adding some new elements [22]. However, in this study he focused on describing games for older platforms such as Commodore 64 and the Atari 2600 systems. With a limited focus on very early game systems, Huth's work does not take into account the current game environment, which includes experiences such as online real-time games involving multiple users, game mobile apps, etc.

In order to create a descriptive framework that can effectively describe games across multiple platforms and time periods, it is crucial to improve our general understanding of the video games themselves as well as users' information needs and behaviors related to video games. Our study aims, through a systematic domain analysis and user studies, to contribute to developing a theorized understanding of how people seek information related to games. This will inform our design of the metadata schema as it will help us select metadata elements that reflect the information needs of real users.

3. STUDY DESIGN

3.1 Methods

Metadata development processes are often relatively informal and draw upon professional experience rather than a more deliberate process [20]. However, as we developed our schema we strove for clarity, both in the process of creating the schema as well as presenting our result. Our methodological approach in designing the metadata schema can be described as a combination of domain analysis [7], in-depth interviews, and a user-centered design incorporating personas [3]. In approaching our metadata design from a user-centered perspective, we sought to address what we considered the missing component of many of the currently available organizational systems as pointed out in previous literature [23]. Figure 1 summarizes our whole design process (Phase I and II), following an iterative process.

In Phase I, we started by conducting an extensive domain analysis focusing on analyzing empirical data on how games are currently being described in the video game community as described in Hjørland [7]. Hjørland identified ways domains can be studied and understood in order to create metadata. We used the existing sources of information organization in order to understand how the domain was shaped, what was listed, and where there were gaps. We ended up collecting 61 existing metadata elements from a wide variety of video game-related websites as well as catalog records (Mobygames, Giantbomb, Allgame, Gamefaqs, Gamespot, IGN, Wikipedia, WorldCat, Amazon, to name a few). Afterwards, we developed 6 different personas epitomizing the most common types of people who would be interested in games: Player (Jeffrey, a junior high student), Parent (Marcia, a classroom assistant and a mother of 3), Collector (Sam, a copywriter for Amazon.com), Academic (Dr. Russell, an economics professor), Game Developer/Designer (Debra, a game designer), and Curator/Librarian (Nancy, an academic librarian). We found the use of personas (archetypes representing the needs, behaviors, and goals of a particular group of users [3]) useful for our goal-directed design of this system. Based on these personas and several use scenarios, we evaluated 61 elements and identified the core elements that were deemed to be most useful for the all the user groups. These elements were evaluated and further revised based on our cataloging activity of sample games. More detailed information on our research activity in Phase I can be found in Lee et al. [15].

For Phase II, we started by exploring a larger number of game-related websites to collect additional terms to add to our inherited master list of 61 elements from Phase I. At the same time, we also conducted a facet analysis [19] of video game genre terms in order to tease out the multiple dimensions represented in these terms and included some of these dimensions as new metadata elements (e.g., theme, style, setting). Duplicates were removed and some similar elements were merged (e.g., platform, console, and system; achievements, awards, and trophies). As a result, we ended up with a total of 135 metadata elements.

In order to understand which information is valued and sought by real users, we conducted in-depth interviews of 24 gamers. The interview data helped us improve our understanding of what video games mean to users, as well as how they obtain and organize their games, how they search and browse video games, and what kinds of information are useful for them for these tasks, etc. [Further discussion in Section 4.1].

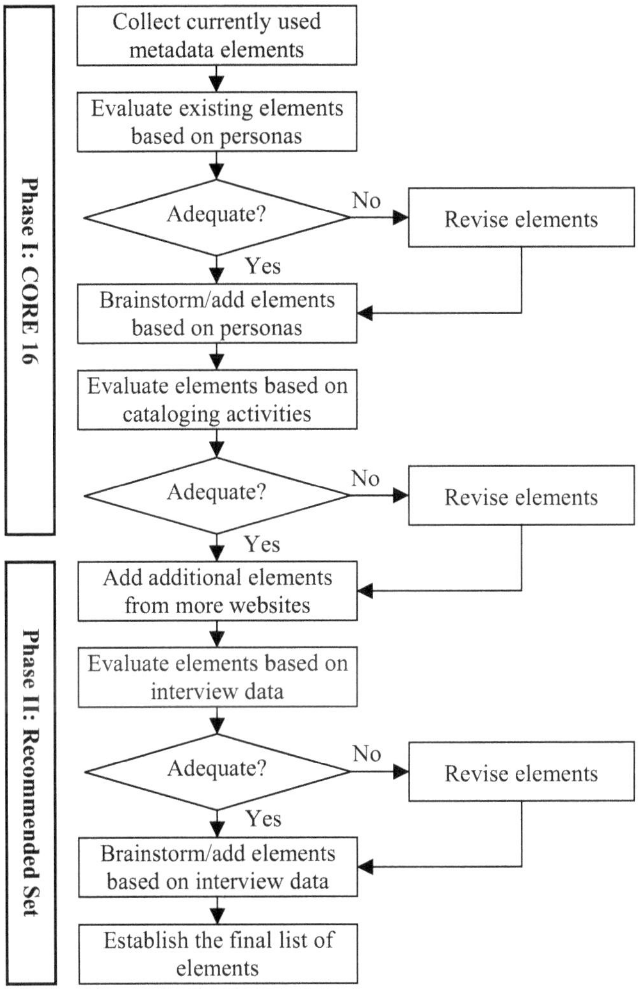

Figure 1. Metadata Design Process

Afterwards, each of the 135 metadata elements was evaluated based on our understanding of user needs as reflected in the interview data. We particularly focused on the elements that were mentioned as useful information by multiple interviewees. For the elements that were not specifically mentioned by interviewees, we tried to evaluate the value of the particular information from the users' perspectives based on what they told us about their needs and behaviors related to video games. We also considered the following factors to determine if we should include the element in the recommended set:

- Source of information: Can the metadata be obtained from the physical manifestation of the game (e.g., box, manual) or the game itself? Or does it need to be obtained from a secondary source (e.g., game websites)?
- Ease of acquisition: How easy it is to obtain this particular metadata? What is a reasonable estimation for the amount of time and effort necessary for capturing the data?
- Cost-benefit: Is it worth describing this data considering the cost needed and the value added?
- Objectivity: Is it possible to obtain relatively objective metadata or do we need to rely on subjective judgments or opinions?
- Stability: Is the information for the particular metadata element relatively stable over time? Or will it keep changing?

As a result, we ended up with a total of 46 metadata elements (including the CORE16) as a recommended set.

3.2 Limitation

The authors acknowledge that constructing a standard such as a metadata schema is not a trivial, nor a one-time task. It should be noted that our goal is not to attempt to construct a "complete" schema. Rather we seek to construct a comprehensive schema that reflects the needs of real users. We hope that this will serve as starting point for a discussion in the game research community on how to build a useful organizational system for these artifacts for multiple stakeholders involved, and a basic framework that the community can collaboratively build upon. We plan to continue working on this project through much iteration, maintaining a partnership with the Seattle Interactive Media Museum, in order to further revise and refine the schema. We also plan to conduct a more systematic evaluation of the schema by applying it to create metadata records of sample video game collections provided by SIMM, identifying potential problems and issues through that process.

4. DATA AND DISCUSSION

4.1 User Interviews

In order to obtain more information about users who play video games and seek games for their own use or for other people, we conducted in-depth interviews of 24 gamers, ranging from casual to hardcore. Some of these gamers also identified themselves as collectors, parents, and educators. Most of them were male (21 out of 24). 11 participants were in their 20s, another 11 in their 30s, and 2 in their 40s. In our interview, we asked a variety of questions with regards to video games including their experience with video games, their game collections, game organization, game-related information needs and seeking behaviors, and the meaning of games to them. Due to limited space, in this paper we focus on reporting our findings on their game-related information needs and seeking behaviors. Several themes emerged as user requirements for video game metadata and organizational systems from analyzing the interview data. In the following text, we use codes to refer to participants (e.g., P1, P2) in order to protect their privacy.

4.1.1 Need for Subject Access Points

A number of users wanted information about the content of the game that could help them make purchase decisions. Metadata such as genre was one of the primary access points that were being used for search and discovery (P4, P5, P11, P16). However, several participants also mentioned the need for more detailed description or categorization of genre information. This is because genre itself "*doesn't say a whole lot*" (P17) and "*genre alone can be somewhat misleading about how the game is actually designed to be played*" (P3) referring to the vastly different styles of games under the same genre. Users also recognize that genre is a significantly overloaded term and the multiple dimensions of genre need to be fleshed out. One participant (P17) said that there are two categories of genres: "structural" and "thematic." Structural categories are the common categories used by video game websites, and thematic categories cover plot and emotional content. Another participant (P6) used different terms to convey a similar idea: "elemental genre" for terms like "science fiction," "horror," "fantasy" that describe the details of the game universe, and "gameplay genres" such as RPG or FPS (first-person shooter). Other participants (P8, P13) used the term "setting" to refer to the same concept of the "elemental genre". The fact that users referred to the same idea using multiple terms illustrates the importance of establishing a standard way of describing game information. For gamers who preferred games that have a strong story component (such as RPGs), the plot/narrative was essential information:

> *"It had great plot twists ... betrayal, love, excitement, it had side stories which were great, character development. It really felt like a very complicated story, even more so than a book or a movie." (P3)*

> *"Storyline is really I think the most important to me. Like it's gotta have something that's gonna draw me in." (P11)*

> *"That's why I like the action-adventure, because there's usually a story to be told, it's not just "here's a gun, go kill that guy" kind of thing." (P22)*

In addition, information such as the theme was deemed useful by participants who said they wanted to seek (P6) or avoid (P4) particular types of themes such as sex or violence. One user (P17) felt that the ESRB tags provided with the rating are useful but are not comprehensive enough to describe the themes.

In our metadata schema, we incorporated a number of subject access points to meet the needs mentioned by our users such as genre/gameplay, style, plot/narrative, theme, setting, and mood/affect. These elements, when taken together, should provide much more detailed information about the content of the game compared to simple genre labels.

4.1.2 Divided Reaction on User Ratings and Reviews

Some users (P4, P7, P10) highly valued ratings and review information from other users and also from "professional reviewers" (P7). Information such as scores provided by websites such as Metacritic or user reviews/ratings seemed to have heavy impact in making the purchase decision for those users.

> *"I read the review (to find out) if it's worth to buy, worth to pay... since I would be a general user too, I would prefer to read general users' reviews first. Professional, they have their own point of view to the game or the way of playing and that's very biased. I believe the general user is right." (P4)*

Conversely, some users (P3, P5, P8) had negative opinions about this type of information, viewing it as too subjective, too crowded, and simply useless.

> *"I think allowing people to post videos all the time without restriction can get -- it just floods the market and overwhelms the senses. People creating like their own Top 10 lists and it just gets frustrating. Reposting the same videos and trying to compete with each other for certain amounts of views is also -- it's just a horrible idea for the consumer." (P3)*

> *"There are some games that get terrible ratings by other people that I absolutely love and some that get amazing ratings by other people that I'm not a big fan of." (P5)*

> *"As far as reviews go, I don't put any stock in them." (P8)*

Participants like P22 specified that balanced reviews (i.e., not all positive or negative) discussing different components of the game were helpful. P19 said he only goes to two specific sources (IGN, GameTrailers) he trusts for reviews and nothing else. After much discussion, in our metadata schema, we decided not to include elements that solely rely on user-generated content such as user ratings or reviews. This is due to the high subjectivity of information which does not align well with organizations such as SIMM's goal of providing highly authoritative and accurate information. Rather, we decided to provide a variety of different metadata that can help users more effectively determine the value of the game themselves such as box art, screenshots, trailers, and gameplay videos.

4.1.3 Visual Information on Games

Although most metadata standards tend to focus on providing textual description of the information objects, the interviews with our users revealed that visual information about the games was highly sought after. Artistic or visual style of the game seemed to heavily affect how users feel about games (P3, P5, P6, P13). It can determine how immersive the game is, and it was sometimes mentioned as the very reason for selecting certain games as their favorites.

> *"My favorite game is an old game for the Playstation 2, it's called Shadow of Colossus, very good game, very innovative. It's sort of -- it was really focused on artistic direction and wasn't really focused on making a huge commercial success. I thought it was more true to the experience of gaming than a lot of games at the time." (P3)*

> *"I can forgive the frustrating game mechanics in order to keep playing because the aesthetics are good, the storyline is good, the goal is compelling." (P6)*

A number of users (P3, P4, P5, P8, P11, P16) also said they highly value the images of the box, screenshots showing the characters and the environment, trailers, and gameplay videos because they immediately help them determine if they will enjoy the game or not. P4 said "*character is the most memorable thing for the video game's appearance*" and therefore he definitely wants pictures of the characters. P16 preferred games with Japanese RPG visual styles whereas P8 wanted games with realistic graphics and wanted to avoid "cartoon-y" graphics.

> *"Make it so it gives me enough detail on the box. If I see a game that looks good, I will occasionally go and look up a rating for it, see what other people are saying about it. More often I'll try to look at the box and generally I like to see that there's a lot of ways to customize my character." (P5)*

> *"Mainly watching game play video is the most important just because I've been playing games for so long, I have a very good idea about what I like and what I would enjoy. Watching a video is enough." (P3)*

In our schema, we decided to include an element visual style in order to describe the different styles of visual aesthetics which can hopefully be used in collocating similar games based on their appearance. Work by Järvinen [10] and Kyprianidis et al. [12] on artistic styles and techniques for images/videos provided the basis for creating a controlled vocabulary for this element.

4.1.4 Companies and Franchise

For video games, information on the companies involved in creating and distributing the games seemed to be highly valued by users, maybe more so than other media such as books. We conjecture that this may have to do with the unique nature of games which generally involves a large group of people in the creation process, making it difficult to attribute them to a single artist or creator. Therefore users tend to remember the publishers or developers of games more readily than the individual directors, designers, or composers. P16, for example, was generally positive towards any games published by Square Enix and even had a separate folder to organize their games on his iPhone. P10 said knowing who developed the game is extremely important to gauge the quality of the game. P5 showed strong loyalty to particular franchises as this information helped him discover new games similar to those he previously enjoyed. These major game franchises serve as recognizable brands associated with particular playing experiences and properties of a game and can serve as useful information for users who are seeking familiar games [11].

We added the distributor element to the recommended set in addition to publisher and developer in CORE16 since this information is becoming increasingly important, especially for digitally downloadable games. We also worked on creating a controlled vocabulary of game companies to be used for these elements [further discussion in Section 4.3.6].

4.1.5 Multiple Stages of Information Needs

P16 described his multiple stages in searching information about games as follows:

a) After announcement: When he receives advertisements about an upcoming game, he looks at the official description of the game as well as the images and videos to determine if the game interests him further.
b) Before purchase: He sets up email reminders to keep track of the release date and region information.
c) At the time of purchase: He looks at the screenshots and gameplay videos to make the final purchase decision.
d) Playing: For RPGs specifically, he avoids reading game cheats, walkthroughs or articles describing the game because of potential spoilers.
e) After the gameplay: If he is satisfied with the game, he will look for similar games by subscribing to email/RSS feeds.

P19 also mentioned that he tends to read reviews before purchasing a game and goes to wikis or walkthrough websites once he starts playing the game. Gamers' behavior of seeking different information as they proceed through the purchase path (e.g., publisher-released assets during pre-launch, advancement information during launch, and extension content during post-launch) was also noted in previous literature [4]. This implies that the organizational systems should provide options for hiding some of the detailed metadata elements (e.g., plot/narrative, theme, characters) in order to avoid revealing too much about the game content which may reducing the playability of the game.

4.1.6 Balance of Gameplay, Story, and Aesthetics

Multiple participants (P3, P6) mentioned that another important aspect is how a game balances the multiple components such as gameplay, story, and aesthetics. Depending on the user's taste, one of these components might be significantly more important than the others. For example, P8 said complicated storylines appeal to him and he searches for evidence of depth and developer's attention to the story. This also depends on the types of games as well. For example, puzzle or party games would typically focus on the gameplay whereas RPGs generally have a strong story component. It may be useful to employ a feature where the organizational system can calculate and display the ratio of how well these different components were represented in each game based on their metadata records and use such information for generating recommendations of games.

4.1.7 Background Information on Game

Multiple participants (P10, P11) wanted to know more about the background or context of the game. P11 said she greatly enjoys hearing about and sharing "behind-the-scene" stories from and about the creative teams behind the game. In order to satisfy those needs, organization and preservation efforts on video games will need to move beyond the object in hand and explore different ways of capturing and preserving the context of how the game was created and used. Although this is outside of the scope of this paper, the importance of this issue must be noted, especially if we are concerned about the future generation truly understanding how certain games were accepted by contemporary gamers and why they were perceived to be so significant at the time of release.

4.1.8 Other User Needs and Requirements

Character customization options were especially important for MMORPG users (P5, P7, P13). Narrative types such as "linear," "branching," or "open" were also mentioned as important information by P13 who likes MMORPGs and strategy games. Some participants (P5, P6) mentioned that their budget affects their video game purchasing and sharing behaviors, thus they put a high value on price information. Point-of-view was also mentioned as useful information as participants like P6 who strongly prefers the first-person, highly immersive point-of-view in his games. Some users (P4, P9) talked about wanting to know how long it takes to complete a game. Interviewees who were also parents or teachers (P1, P2, P9) discussed learning objectives and difficulty of the games. Somewhat contrary to what we initially expected, all the parents or teachers we interviewed seemed less determined to always try to find games that have certain educational values and were more willing to have their children or students play games to have fun (P1, P2, P9, P23, P24).

> *(Answering the question asking about the importance of a game having educational values) "Not so important. I believe that most games, the more involved games, whether or not the educational value is inherent or obvious, I think there's a lot of learning going on." (P23)*

> *"I think there's a value for just having fun. I think in today's world we have to kind of qualify everything. There is definitely some need for if it's being utilized in an educational sense, to have a goal. However, there's also importance placed on the fact that children just also need to play games." (P24)*

Some participants also talked about information overload, implying the importance of an organizational structure that is well thought out and displayed:

> *"I think the downfall of a lot of websites is actually having too much content and not organizing the content well enough that they have." (P3)*

> *"I don't want to get on a website and then have to feel like it's an 8-to-5 job trying to find information on one game. I want to be able to go in and within 2 or 3 clicks on the website, I want to be able to find what I'm looking for." (P8)*

4.2 Metadata Elements

The list of metadata elements we selected for the recommended set is provided in Table 1. The CORE16 elements are noted with asterisks next to the name of the element. We strove to adopt definitions of these elements from existing standards (e.g., FRBR, CIDOC CRM, Getty Art & Architecture Thesaurus) whenever possible, in order to maintain some degree of interoperability. However, due to the unique nature of the artifact, most definitions had to be newly created as it was impossible to identify reusable definitions from existing standards and vocabularies.

As part of our effort, we also created various encoding schemes (i.e., controlled vocabularies) for many of our elements. However, due to limited space, they will not be fully discussed in this paper. Another publication reporting the full encoding schemes is under preparation.

Table 1. Definitions of the Metadata Elements in the Recommended Set

Element	Definition
Title*	Proper names that are used to refer to a video game, assigned by the creator. (modified from CIDOC CRM, 2011, p.16)
Alternative title	Alternative titles of the video game, including the abbreviations.
Edition*	A word or phrase appearing in the manifestation of the game that normally indicates a difference in either content or form between the manifestation and a related manifestation previously issued by the same publisher/distributor (e.g., second edition, greatest hits), or simultaneously issued by either the same publisher/distributor or another publisher/distributor (e.g., collector's edition, limited edition). The edition designation pertains to all copies of the manifestation produced from substantially the same master and issued by the same publisher/distributor or group of publishers/distributors. (modified from FRBR, 2009, p. 41)
Format*	The distribution medium or method that provides the executable code of a video game.
Series *	The names referring to the creative universe from which the manifestation of the game derives.
Franchise/Universe	Proper names to refer to a cluster of video games that is characterized by the shared use of characters, or other component of games such as a similar gameplay or battle system.
Platform*	The hardware and firmware required to realize the game.
Developer*	An organization or group of individuals and/or organizations responsible for creation and/or realization of a game (i.e., writing the code of the game) (modified from FRBR, 2009, p.25)
Publisher*	An organization or group of individuals and/or organizations responsible for the manufacture, marketing, and distribution of a particular product manifestation.
Distributor	An organization or group of individuals and/or organizations responsible for distributing a game that has exclusive rights to market (within certain regions).
Special hardware*	A hardware that is required or recommended for playing the game in addition to the main platform/console.
Online capabilities*	The capabilities for playing the game online and/or downloading the game or additional features online.
System requirements	Software (or OS/firmware) requirements to realize the game in a particular platform.
Game credits	The intellectual contributors of the game and their roles as specified in the manual/end-game credits.
Official website	A URL and an archived copy or representation of the webpage as available from one of the officially associated companies on a specific date.
Price/MSRP	The suggested manufacturer's retail price (MSRP) at time of initial release in the region where the game was released.
Retail release date*	The date of the public/commercial release of the manifestation. (modified from FRBR, 2009, p.42)
Controls	The main default control buttons/keys and the corresponding main game actions.
Packaging	All items included in the original packaging of the game.
Number of players*	The number or range of the number of players the game can accommodate either separately or concurrently. Examples: 1, 1-2, 1-8, 1-Many (for massively multiplayer online games)
Rating*	The ratings designed to provide information about the content in video games for consumers' informed purchase decision by organizations such as the Entertainment Software Rating Board (ESRB). (modified from ESRB Game Ratings & Descriptor Guide) Examples: MA-13 Parental Discretion Advised. Mature Audiences; Everyone. E. (ESRB). Note that some older games do not have this rating information.
Purpose	The reason for why the game exists as intended by the game designer(s)/developer(s).
Customization options	The settings which can be modified by the player for personalized experience.
Difficulty levels	The options specifying the levels of challenge as defined internally in the game options (god mode, expert, etc.) and whether or not a user can freely change the difficulty setting during the game.
Achievements/ Awards/Trophies	Title, description, requirements, and emblems of all unlockable in-game notifications.
Region*	The names used to refer to a place, region or territory where a game is designated as playable.
Language*	The language in which the work is expressed. (from FRBR, 2009, p. 36)
Identifier*	An alphanumeric code uniquely assigned to a manifestation of the game. When available, use the Universal Product Code (UPC) which is a 12 digit number representing a barcode. For some games (e.g., downloadable game app), this information may not be available. Note: this element used to be UPC in an earlier version of CORE16.

Box art/cover	The image featured on the front of the box/packaging or the officially released image which virtually represents the downloadable games.
Screenshots	Still images taken from the video output during the main gameplay.
Trailers	Video footage released and/or endorsed by the developer/publisher of the game for promotional purposes.
Gameplay videos	Video footage of actual, in-game play (excluding introductions, cutscenes, or trailers).
Genre*/Gameplay	A category of games determined by the overall nature of the experience based on a pattern of interactions and game rules. Note: definition revised from an earlier version of CORE16.
Style	A particular distinctive characteristic, mode of action, or manner of a gameplay.
Plot/Narrative	A story or sequence of events, the central conflict, or other plot elements of the game. (modified from Getty Art & Architecture Thesaurus)
Theme	An underlying intent or meaning in the game; also a common thread, motif, subject, or idea that recur in the game. (modified from Getty Art & Architecture Thesaurus)
Setting	The surroundings or environment (spatial and temporal) in which the game takes place.
Mood/Affect	The pervading atmosphere or tone of the video game which evokes or recalls a certain emotion or state of mind.
Temporal aspect	The methods by which time passes in the game and/or manner in which events take place.
Presentation	The manner or style of game display.
Point of view	Perspective from which the player views the gameplay.
Character names	The given full name (if available) and role of the main game characters.
Character types	Classification of game character types based on physical or metaphysical embodiment.
Link to historical events	Event(s) from history that are the setting for (or play a significant role in) the game. This may be a named event, a historical period, or a time and geographic location. (e.g., U.S. Civil War or Ancient Rome).
Type of ending	The method by which the player is led to gameplay culmination.
Visual style	A cohesive and unifying visual aesthetic.

4.3 Problems and Challenges

4.3.1 Source of Information

One of the main challenges we encountered while developing this metadata schema was deciding which source should be used to obtain the game information. Many descriptive elements can be filled by observing and transcribing information from the physical object itself (e.g., title, edition, platform, number of players). However, a large number of elements require additional research on the game using secondary sources or by playing the game itself (e.g., price, release date, achievements/awards/trophies, theme, setting). This suggests that clearly specifying the chief source of information for each element is extremely important.

Moreover, the general trend of moving towards digital downloadable format of games aggravates this problem as many of the recent games are now published without any packages or manuals. The expectation is that the manuals are now embedded in the game itself or accessible from an associated company's website. While one can actually play the game or the website is still alive, it remains possible to obtain this information. However, in a long term, there is no guarantee that all the games today will be playable. New versions of video game consoles are rapidly being developed and released, often without backward compatibilities. We may come to a point in the future where we have a collection of old games that are simply not playable on any devices that are available at that time, which will mean the source for obtaining the most authentic metadata is also subsequently lost.

4.3.2 Level of Description

The recommended metadata elements presented in this paper serve to provide a set of descriptions which satisfy the requirements for a majority of users: consumers, academics, gamers, parents, and others. Based on the FRBR model of group 1 entities, most of the user requirements we identified fell within the manifestation level of description. This is not to say that item level of description (e.g., condition, provenance, location) will not be necessary, especially for organizations such as SIMM. In any kinds of organizations that deal with a video game collection, various administrative metadata elements will be necessary in order to manage the items in the collection (e.g., archivists need to describe the condition of a singular copy of a game, reference librarians need to know the exact location of a game in order to assist in retrieval of the item). Research for ascertaining the administrative metadata requirements will be conducted and explored in Phase III of this study as we work on establishing a larger "full" set of metadata for video games.

4.3.3 Background Knowledge of Games

In our metadata schema, we added several metadata elements that focus on describing the content or aboutness of the game rather than descriptive metadata (e.g., genre/gameplay, style, plot/narrative, theme). Many of these elements required establishing controlled vocabularies in order to ensure that catalogers can describe these elements in a consistent manner. However, the process of creating a controlled vocabulary for each subject metadata element not only takes a significant amount of time and effort, but also requires the creators to have extensive background knowledge of the video game domain. Consider "temporal aspect" as an example: without having played or researched numerous video games, it would be extremely difficult to understand and enumerate different ways that time passes and events take place in video games (e.g., real-time, turn-based, time manipulation, multiple game clocks, time travel, time action, calendar-based game clock).

4.3.4 Efficiency vs. Accuracy in Generating Metadata

Any controlled vocabularies we established for our metadata elements will inherently always be incomplete as there is a limitation on how many games can be considered as we establish these lists. Maintaining controlled vocabularies is particularly challenging in the video game domain because of its rapidly changing nature. Therefore it could be very helpful to involve users of the organizational system or other game enthusiasts to help generate and maintain these vocabularies. However, organizations such as SIMM may be reluctant to adopt this method for generating their data since the key objective of their organization is to provide and preserve the most accurate and authoritative information about video games. This conflict between efficiency versus accuracy in generating the metadata must be somehow resolved in the organizational system. We are currently discussing several possibilities including setting up an approval process for accepting user-generated content or distinguishing verified vs. non-verified information in the metadata records.

4.3.5 Subjectivity of Information

There were some elements that we initially determined useful but ended up not including because of the difficulty of obtaining objective data. One prime example is the "estimated time of completion" for games mentioned by multiple users (P4, P9, P22). This information was valued by users like P4 and P22 because they were often playing games on a bus ride and did not want games that take a long time to complete, and P9 who wanted to find games for his students to play during the class. However, depending on how the game is played, the time for completion can widely vary. This is especially the case for more complex games with a number of side quests. We discussed options of providing a range of hours or asking users' opinions and averaging the numbers. However, none of the options seem as a particularly satisfying solution as an individual's way of how to play a game is a very personal and subjective matter. User rating/review information is another example of metadata element that was excluded due to its inherently subjective nature.

4.3.6 Challenges for Particular Elements

There were also several challenges we encountered as we were defining and establishing controlled vocabularies for particular metadata elements.

- *Character Names*

Providing information about character names was judged to be a valuable way to collocate similar games, but quickly brought up questions about how we should define "character." What constitutes being designated a "main character" in a game? Does he/she/it have to be playable? Or can a game have a non-playable character that has a significant role in the narrative (such as the major villains/bosses)? Other games have very large character casts, such as the Pokémon series or games based on recruiting different party members (e.g., *Chrono Cross* with 45 possible members, *Radiata Stories* with 176 possible members). All these examples confirm that it is critical to provide very specific instruction on how to describe each of these elements in order to maintain the consistency in the granularity of data across all records.

- *Developer/Publisher/Distributor*

Compared to subject metadata elements such as genre or theme, developing a controlled vocabulary for video game companies used for developer, publisher, and distributor elements may be perceived as a tedious but relatively straightforward task. However, a closer investigation revealed the complexities of company evolution, the unpredictability of shifting markets, and the endless tangle of relationships involving numerous mergers, bankruptcies, and acquisitions. Sorting through all the different possible relationships is difficult: abbreviations and variations of names for equivalence relationship; acquisitions, subsidiaries, and regional branches for hierarchical relationship; and partial ownership, poly-hierarchical, and mergers are only a few examples of the many possible relationships that can exist among these companies. In addition, obtaining reliable information about the history of these companies is extremely challenging, especially for companies that are older or not US-based.

Even when a game has accompanying materials such as a box and/or manual, identifying this information is not a trivial issue. Many games simply show a logo representing a particular company on the packaging without specifying the specific role of the company [15]. Since one company can take multiple roles, it is often unclear how to accurately determine this information even with researching secondary source materials.

- *Plot/Narrative*

None of the game-related websites or organizational systems we reviewed had a standardized element encapsulating plot, even though a number of users we interviewed mentioned the importance of story or plot for selecting and enjoying a particular game and seeking similar games. Our exploratory attempt to create such an element uses a subject-verb-object structure to describe the most prominent storyline(s) in the game.

We began our work in this area by looking at different approaches in categorizing basic plots in literature including Foster-Harris (1959), Booker (2004), and Uther (2004). Compared to the plots of literature, the plots in video games seem less varied. This is perhaps due to the fact that games generally have to incorporate certain story elements, such as a major conflict between some entities or an extreme situation (e.g., the end of the world), in order to justify critical game components such as a battle system and character development. Our preliminary attempts at assigning plot confirmed the challenges of finding the most effective level of granularity in describing the plot. Describing a game's plot as the story of a hero saving the world would apply to an overly large number of games, rendering it useless; on the other hand, an extremely specific plot description such as "a tycoon builds roller coasters" (as in the *RollerCoaster Tycoon* series) would not allow for the ability to find similar games.

Separating the concept of gameplay from plot sometimes proved problematic. Certain features clearly describe gameplay without shedding light on the story (e.g., casting spells), but others are more ambiguous. For example, *Myst* is known for its clever puzzles which enable the player to explore the game's environment, but the plotline involves discovering the secrets behind mysterious books and their owners. In playing the game, the plot seems incidental to the compelling atmosphere and challenge of solving puzzles. In game such as *L.A. Noire*, the plot is complex and integral to the game's appeal. At the other end of the spectrum, some games have no plot (e.g., *Tetris*) or have a more or less irrelevant plot (e.g., *Mortal Kombat*). Another important consideration involves giving away too much of the plot; users have varying degrees of sensitivity to spoilers.

4.4 Application of the Schema

In order to demonstrate how this schema can be applied to capture the metadata of video games, the authors attempted to describe three sample games from different eras using our proposed schema [Table 2]. Some of the metadata elements (screenshots, trailers, gameplay videos) are not listed as it is impossible to embed the metadata in the paper, the content simply takes up too much space (controls, box art, game credits), or it is not applicable to all three examples (distributor, system requirements, achievements/awards/trophies, links to historical events).

Table 2. Application of the Metadata Schema for Sample Games

Metadata Element	Sample game 1	Sample game 2	Sample game 3
Title*	Super Mario Bros.	The Legend of Zelda: Ocarina of Time	Shin Megami Tensei: Persona 3 Portable
Alternative title	SMB; Super Mario Brothers; Mario	TLOZOOT; OOT	P3P; SMT P3P
Edition*	Retail	Retail	Persona 3 Portable; Enhanced remake of Shin Megami Tensei: Persona 3
Format*	Cartridge	Cartridge	UMD
Series *	Super Mario Bros.	The Legend of Zelda	Persona
Franchise/Universe	Mario	Zelda	Shin Megami Tensei
Platform*	Nintendo Entertainment System	Nintendo 64	PlayStation Portable
Developer*	Nintendo R&D4	Nintendo EAD	ATLUS
Publisher*	Nintendo of America, Inc.	Nintendo of America, Inc.	ATLUS USA
Official website	-	http://www.zelda64.com/	http://www.atlus.com/p3p/
Price/MSRP	Unknown	$69.95	$39.99
Retail release date*	1985	November 21, 1998	July 6, 2010
Packaging	Shrink Wrap, Box, Cartridge, Manual, Poster, Foam Block	Shrink Wrap, Box, Cartridge, Manual, Nintendo Power Catalog, Safety Information Guide	Shrink Wrap, Box, UMD, Manual
Number of players*	2 Alternating	1	1
Rating*	N/A	E	Mature 17+; Blood, Partial Nudity; Sexual Themes; Violence (ESRB)
Purpose	Entertainment	Entertainment	Entertainment
Customization options	N/A	N/A	Choice of male or female protagonist
Difficulty levels	Normal/Difficult; Difficult mode available after game ends	-	Beginner/Easy/Normal/Hard/Maniac; Cannot change once the game starts
Region*	North America	North America	North America
Language*	English	English	English
Identifier*	045496630140	045496870041	4984995900469
Genre*	Action	RPG	RPG
Style	Platformer	Action RPG	JRPG
Plot/Narrative	Protagonist-explores-world. Protagonist-defeats-bosses. Protagonist-rescues-princess.	Protagonist-explores-world. Protagonist-fights-evil. Protagonist-rescues-princess.	Protagonist-develop-friendship. Characters-confront-self. Characters-prevent-apocalypse.
Theme	Fantasy – Princess	Fantasy – Princess, Supernatural – Fairies	Supernatural – Demons
Setting	Spatial – Virtual Worlds, Nature	Spatial – Nature, Deserts, Tundra, Ocean	Spatial – Schools, Asian Temporal – Modern
Mood/Affect	Quirky	Humor, Dark, Mysterious, Adventurous	Dark
Character names	Mario (protagonist); Luigi (second player); Princess Toadstool; Bowser (main antagonist)	Link (protagonist); Zelda; Ganon (main antagonist)	Minato Arisato (protagonist); Female protagonist (name unknown); Junpei Iori; Ken Amada; Akihiko Sanada; Shinjiro Aragaki; Yukari Takeba; Mitsuru Kirijo; Fuuka Yamagishi; Aigis; Koromaru; Metis; Nyx (main antagonist)
Character types	Natural-Human; Supernatural-Other monster	Supernatural-Elf; Supernatural-Other monster	Natural-Human; Supernatural-Demon
Type of ending	Finite	Finite	Circuitous, Branching
Temporal aspect	Real-time	Real-time, Time manipulation, Time travel	Turn-based, Calendar-based
Presentation	2D, Side-scrolling	3D	2D, 3D
Point of view	Third person	Third person	Third person
Artistic style	Retro	Anime/Manga	Anime/Manga

5. CONCLUSION AND FUTURE WORK

In this paper, we provided an overview of our current schema for describing video games developed from a user-centered approach. As we developed a metadata schema and encoding schemes for video games and interactive media, a number of challenges and potential problems emerged. Although we do not currently have solutions for many of these challenges, we hope that our findings will serve as a catalyst for discussion in the digital libraries community. Many of the issues discussed here are also applicable to other artifacts from popular culture such as apps, video clips, comics, webtoons, etc. Without a standardized way for organizing and describing these artifacts, it will be impossible to search and discover that app you want, or the video clip you once watched and want to revisit.

In our future work, we plan to focus on revising the structure of this metadata schema: adopting attributes for particular elements (e.g., title, rating) and organizing certain elements (e.g., genre) in a hierarchical and faceted structure. We will also continue to work on detailed instructions for obtaining and transcribing metadata and providing examples to help catalogers understand how to apply the schema. Our work on establishing controlled vocabularies will be ongoing. In addition, we plan to conduct a large-scale user survey to test our current schema and achieve a deeper understanding of users' information needs to be reflected in later revisions of the schema. The authors hope that this work will augment existing standards in the LIS field (e.g., FRBR, CCO, LCSH) as well as assisting organizations such as SIMM by providing a more formal metadata schema and encoding schemes that can be used across academic and commercial domains.

6. ACKNOWLEDGMENTS

We thank Gregory Bem, Dr. Joseph Tennis, the SIMM, and all the participants of INFX 598 for their valuable contributions to the project. We also thank the University of Washington's Office of Research for their financial support for this research.

7. REFERENCES

[1] Anderson, D., Delve, J., and Pinchbeck, D. 2010. Toward a workable emulation-based preservation strategy: Rationale and technical metadata. *New Review of Information Networking* 15, 2, 110-131.

[2] Booker, C. 2004. *The seven basic plots: Why we tell stories.* Continuum, London.

[3] Cooper, A. 1999. *The inmates are running the asylum.* Sams, Indianapolis.

[4] Google. 2012. *Understanding the Modern Gamer: What Google search data says about gamer behavior.* Google Whitepaper.

[5] Foster-Harris, W. 1959. *The basic patterns of plot.* University of Oklahoma Press, Norman.

[6] Hagler, R. 1980. "Nonbook materials: Chapters 7-11." In *The Making of a Code: The Issues Underlying AACR2.* ALA, Chicago.

[7] Hjørland, B. 2002. Domain analysis in information science. Eleven approaches - traditional as well as innovative. *J Doc,* 58, 4, 422-462.

[8] Huth, K. 2004. *Probleme and Lösungsansätze zur archivierung von computer programmen—am beispeil der software des ATARI VCS 2600 und des C64.* Unpublished master's thesis, Humboldt Universitat.

[9] IFLA Study Group on the FRBR, IFLA Section on Cataloging, Standing Committee. 2009. *Functional requirements for bibliographic records: Final report.* K.G. Saur Verlag, München.

[10] Järvinen, A. 2002. Gran Stylissimo: The audiovisual elements and styles in computer and video games. In *Proceedings of Computer Games and Digital Cultures Conference.* Tampere University Press, Tampere, 113-128.

[11] King, D., Delfabbro, P. and Griffiths, M. 2010. Video game structural characteristics: A new psychological taxonomy. *International Journal of Mental Health and Addiction* 8, 1, (January 2010), 90-106.

[12] Kyprianidis, J., Collomosse, J., Wang, T., and Isenberg, T. 2012. State of the art: A taxonomy of artistic stylization techniques for images and video. *IEEE T Vis Comput GR*, 2012, 1-20.

[13] Lee, J. H. 2010. Analysis of user needs and information features in natural language queries seeking music information. *J Am Soc Inf Sci Tec,* 61, 5, 1025-1045.

[14] Lee, J. H., Tennis, J. T., and Clarke, R. I. 2012. Domain analysis for a video game metadata schema: Issues and challenges. *Theory and Practice of Digital Libraries, Lect Notes Comput SC*, 7489, 280-285.

[15] Lee J. H., Tennis, J. T., Clarke, R. I., Carpenter, M. 2013. Developing a video game metadata schema for the Seattle Interactive Media Museum. *International Journal on Digital Libraries*, 13, 2, 105-117.

[16] Leigh, A. 2002. Lucy is "Enceinte": The power of an action in defining a work. *Cataloging & Classification Quarterly,* 33, 3-4.

[17] Lubetzky, S., Connell, T. H., and Maxwell, R. L. 2000. *The future of cataloging: Insights from the Lubetzky symposium.* American Library Association, Chicago.

[18] McDonough, J., Kirschenbaum, M., Reside, D., Fraistat, N., Jerz, D. 2010. Twisty little passages almost all alike: Applying the FRBR model to a classic computer game. *Digital Humanities Quarterly,* 4, 2.

[19] Spiteri, L. 1998. A simplified model for facet analysis. *Can J Inform Lib Sci*, 23, 1-30.

[20] Tonkin, E. 2007. A user-centered approach to metadata design. In *Proceedings of the 11th European Conference on Digital Libraries (ECDL)*, Budapest, Hungary.

[21] Uther, H.-J. 2004. *The types of international folktales: A classification and bibliography based on the system of Antti Aarne and Stith Thompson.* Academia Scientiarum Fennica, Helsinki.

[22] Winget, M. A. 2011. Videogame preservation and massively multiplayer online role-playing games: A review of the literature. *J Am Soc Inf Sci Tec,* 62, 10, 1869-1883.

[23] Winget, M., Murray, C. 2008. State of the archive: A review of video game archives within the United States. In *Proceedings of the annual meeting of the American Society for Information Science & Technology.* ASIS&T, Columbus.

Automatic Tag Recommendation for Metadata Annotation Using Probabilistic Topic Modeling

Suppawong Tuarob
Computer Science and Engineering
Pennsylvania State University
University Park, Pennsylvania
suppawong@psu.edu

Line C. Pouchard
Scientific Data Group
Computer Sciences and Mathematics Division
Oak Ridge National Laboratory
Oak Ridge, Tennessee
pouchardlc@ornl.gov

C. Lee Giles
Information Sciences and Technology
Computer Science and Engineering
Pennsylvania State University
University Park, Pennsylvania
giles@ist.psu.edu

ABSTRACT

The increase of the complexity and advancement in ecological and environmental sciences encourages scientists across the world to collect data from multiple places, times, and thematic scales to verify their hypotheses. Accumulated over time, such data not only increases in amount, but also in the diversity of the data sources spread around the world. This poses a huge challenge for scientists who have to manually search for information. To alleviate such problems, ONEMercury has recently been implemented as part of the DataONE project to serve as a portal for accessing environmental and observational data across the globe. ONEMercury harvests metadata from the data hosted by multiple repositories and makes it searchable. However, harvested metadata records sometimes are poorly annotated or lacking meaningful keywords, which could affect effective retrieval. Here, we develop algorithms for automatic annotation of metadata. We transform the problem into a tag recommendation problem with a controlled tag library, and propose two variants of an algorithm for recommending tags. Our experiments on four datasets of environmental science metadata records not only show great promises on the performance of our method, but also shed light on the different natures of the datasets.

Categories and Subject Descriptors

H.3.3 [**Information Search and Retrieval**]

Keywords

Document Annotation, Tag Recommendation, Topic Model

1. INTRODUCTION

Environmental sciences have become both complex and data-intensive, needing access to heterogenous data collected from multiple places, times, and thematic scales. For example, research on bird migration would involve exploring and analyzing observational data such as the migration of animals and temperature shifts across the world, from time to time. While the needs to access such heterogenous data are apparent, the rapid expansion of observational data, in both quantity and heterogeneity, poses huge challenges for data seekers to obtain the right information for their research. Such problems behoove tools that automatically manage, discover, and link big data from diverse sources, and present the data in the forms that are easily accessible and comprehensible.

1.1 ONEMercury Search Service

Recently, DataONE, a federated data network built to facilitate accesses and preservation about environmental and ecological science data across the world, has come to exist and gain increasingly popularity[16]. DataONE harvests metadata from different environmental data providers and make it searchable via the search interface ONEMercury[1], built on Mercury[2], a distributed metadata management system. Figure 1 shows sample screen shots of the ONEMercury search interface (left) and the search result page with search query '`soil`'. ONEMercury offers a full text search on the metadata records. The user can also specify the boundary of locations in which the desired data is collected or published using the interactive graphic map. At the result page, the user can choose to further filter out the results by `Member Node`, `Author`, `Project`, and `Keywords`. The set of keywords used in the system are static-users cannot arbitrarily add new or remove the existing keywords- and managed by the administrator to avoid the emerging of spuriously new keywords. Such keywords are used for manually annotating metadata during the data curation process.

1.2 Challenge and Proposed Solution

Linking data from heterogenous sources always has a cost. One of the biggest problems that ONEMercury is facing is the different levels of annotation in the harvested metadata records. Poorly annotated metadata records tend to be missed during the search process as they lack meaningful keywords. Furthermore, such records would not be compatible with the advanced mode offered by ONEMercury as it

[1] https://cn.dataone.org/onemercury/
[2] http://mercury.ornl.gov/

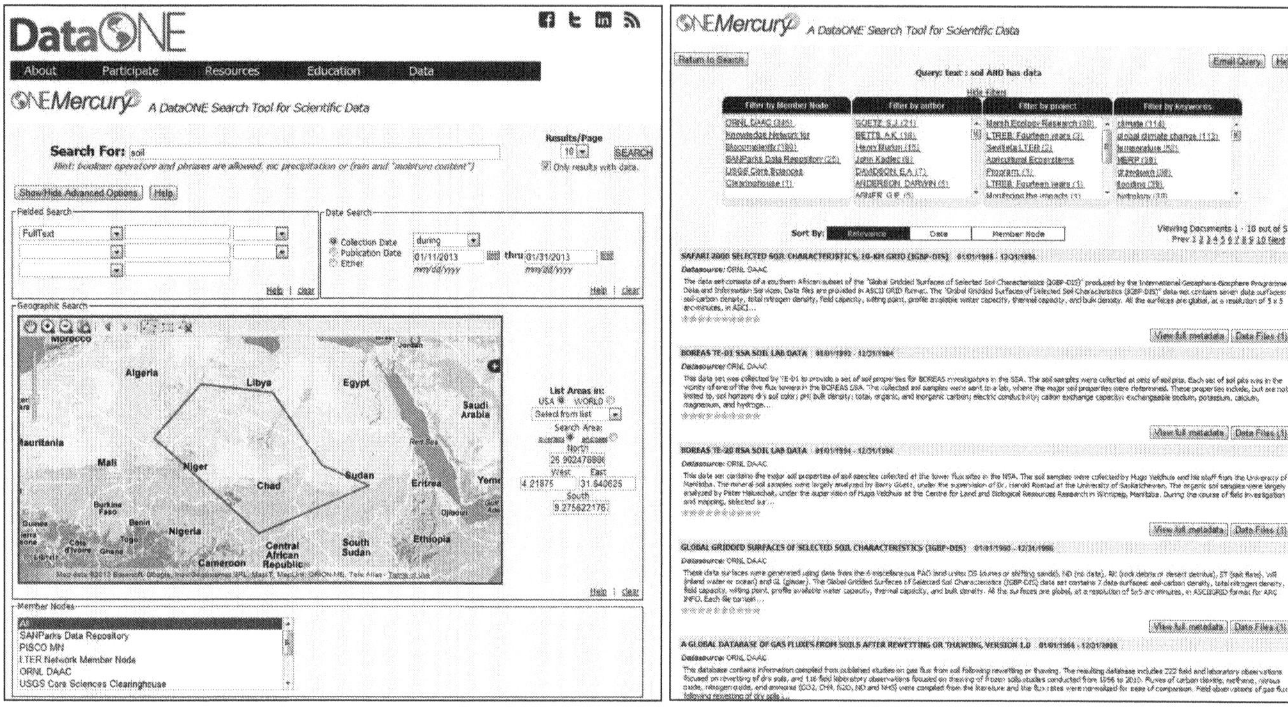

Figure 1: Screen shots of the ONEMercury search interface and result page using query '`soil`'.

requires the metadata records be annotated with keywords from the keyword library. The explosion of the amount of metadata records harvested from an increasing number of data repositories makes it even impossible to annotate them manually by hand, urging the need for a tool capable of automatically annotating these metadata records which are poorly annotated.

In this paper, we address the problem of automatic annotation of metadata records. Our goal is to build a fast and robust system that annotates a given metadata record with related keywords from a given keyword library. The idea is to annotate a poorly annotated record with keywords associated to the well annotated records that it is most similar with. We propose a solution to this problem by first transforming the problem into a tag recommendation problem with a controlled tag library, where the set of recommended tags is used to annotate the given metadata record, and then propose an algorithm that deals with the problem.

1.3 Problem Definition

We define a document as a tuple of textual content and a set of tags. That is `d = <c, e>`, where `c` is the textual content, represented by a sequence of terms, of the document `d` and `e` is a set of tags associated with the document. Given a tag library T, a set of annotated documents D, and a non-annotated query document q, our task is to recommend a ranked set of K tags taken from T to the query q. A document is said to be annotated if it has at least one tag; otherwise, it is non-annotated. The formal description of each variable is given below:

$$T = \{t_1, t_2, ..., t_M\}\, ; t_i \ is \ a \ tag.$$
$$D = \{d_1, d_2, ..., d_N\}\, ; d_i = \langle c_{di}, e_{di} \rangle\, , e_{di} \subseteq T, and \ e_{di} \neq \oslash$$
$$q = \langle c_q, \oslash \rangle$$

1.4 Contributions

This paper has four key contributions as follows:

1. We address a real word problem of linking data from multiple archives faced by ONEMercury. We transform the problem into the tag recommendation problem, and generalize the problem so that the proposed solution can further be applied to other domains.
2. We propose a novel technique for tag recommendation. Given a document query `q`, we first compute the distribution of tags. The top tags are then recommended. We propose two variants of our algorithms: term frequency-inverse document frequency (TF-IDF) based and topic model (TM) based.
3. We crawl environmental science metadata records from 4 different archives for our datasets: the Oak Ridge National Laboratory Distributed Active Archive Center (DAAC)[3], Dryad Digital Repository[4], the Knowledge Network for Biocomplexity (KNB)[5], and TreeBASE: a repository of phylogenetic information[6]. We select roughly 1,000 records from each archive for the experiments.
4. We validate our proposed method using aggressive empirical evaluations. We use document wise 10 fold cross validation to evaluate our methods with 5 evaluation metrics: Precision, Recall, F1, MRR (Mean Reciprocal Rank), and BPref (Binary Preference). These evaluation metrics are extensively used together to evaluate recommendation systems.

[3]http://daac.ornl.gov/
[4]http://datadryad.org/
[5]http://knb.ecoinformatics.org/index.jsp
[6]http://treebase.org/treebase-web/home.html

5. We make our datasets and source code available upon request for research purposes.

2. RELATED WORKS

Literature on document annotation is extensive. Hence we only present the work closely related to ours.

2.1 Automatic Document Annotation

Newman et al.[18] discuss approaches for enriching metadata records using probabilistic topic modeling. Their approach treats each metadata record as a bag of words, and consists of 2 main steps: i) generate topics based on a given corpus of metadata, ii) assign relevant topics to each metadata record. Hence a metadata record is annotated by the top terms representing the assigned topics. They propose 3 variations of their approaches. The first method, which they use as the baseline, uses full vocabulary (every word) from the corpus. The remaining two methods filter out the vocabulary by deleting useless words resulting in more meaningful topics. They compare the three approaches in 3 aspects: % of usable topics, % enhanced records, and average coverage by the top 4 chosen topics. They acquired the datasets from 700 repositories, hosted by OAISter Digital Library. The results show that, overall, the second method performs the best. However, such method requires manual modification of the vocabulary, hence would not scale well. The third method performs somewhere in between.

Bron et al.[4] address the problem of document annotation by linking a poorly annotated document to well annotated documents using TF-IDF cosine similarity. One corpus consists of textually rich documents (A_s) while the other contains sparse documents (A_t). In the paper, they address two research problems: document expansion and term selection. For the document expansion task, each targeted document (a document in sparse set) is mapped to one or more documents in the rich set, using simple cosine-similarity measure. Top N documents are chosen from the rich corpus, and the texts in these documents are added to the targeted documents as supplemental content. The term selection task was introduced because using the whole documents from the source corpus to enrich the targeted document might be too spurious and have a fair chance of topic drifts. This term selection task aims to select only meaningful words from each document in the source corpus to add to the targeted documents. Basically, top K% of the words in each document, ranked by TF-IDF scores, are selected as representative words of the document.

This work has a similar problem setting to ours, except that we aim to annotate a query document with keywords taken from the library, while their approaches extract keywords from the full content of documents.

Witten et al. propose *KEA*, a machine learning based key phrase extraction algorithm from documents [23]. The algorithm can also be applied to annotate documents with relevant keyphrases. Their algorithm first selects candidate keyphrases from the document. Two features are extracted from each candidate keyphrase: TF-IDF score and distance of the first occurrence of the keyphrase from the beginning of the document. A binary NaiveBayes classifier is trained with the extracted features to build a classification model, which is used for identifying important keyphrases. The algorithm is later enhanced by Medelyan et al. [15] to improve the performance and add more functionality such as document annotation and keyphrase recommendation from control vocabulary, where the list of keyphrases to be recommend are already defined in the vocabulary. We use keyphrase recommendation with control vocabulary feature of the *KEA* algorithm as our baseline.

2.2 Automatic Tag Recommendation

Since we have a tag recommendation problem, we briefly cover related literature. Tag recommendation has gained substantial amount of interest in recent years. Most work, however, focuses on personalized tag recommendation, suggesting tags to a user's object based on the user's preference and social connection. Mishne et al. [17] employ the social connection of the users to recommend tags for weblogs, based on similar weblogs tagged by the same users. Wu et al.[24] utilize the social network and the similarity between the contents of objects to learn a model for recommending tags. Their system aims towards recommending tags for Flickr photo objects. While such personalized schemes have been proven to be useful, some domains of data have limited information about authors (users) and their social connections. Liu et al. [12] propose a tag recommendation model using Machine Translation. Their algorithm basically trains the translation model to translate the textual description of a document in the training set into its tags. Krestel et al.[11] employ topic modeling for recommending tags. They use the Latent Dirichlet Allocation algorithm to mine topics in the training corpus, using tags to represent the textual content. They evaluate their method against the association rule based method proposed in [7].

3. DATASETS

We obtain 4 different datasets of environmental metadata records for the experiments: the Oak Ridge National Laboratory Distributed Active Archive Center (DAAC)[7], Dryad Digital Repository (DRYAD)[8], the Knowledge Network for Biocomplexity (KNB)[9], and TreeBASE: a repository of phylogenetic information (TreeBASE)[10]. The statistics of the datasets including the number of documents, total number of tags, average number of tags per document, number of unique tags (tag library size), tag utilization, number of all words (dataset size), and average number of word per document, are summarized in Table 1. Tag utilization is the average number of documents where a tag appears in, and is defined as $\frac{\#\ all\ tags}{\#\ unique\ tags}$. The tag utilization measure quantifies how often, on average, a tag is used for annotation.

The Oak Ridge National Laboratory Distributed Active Archive Center (ORNL DAAC) is one of the NASA Earth Observing System Data and Information System (EOSDIS) data centers managed by the Earth Science Data and Information System (ESDIS)[11] Project, which is responsible for providing scientific and other users access to data from NASA's Earth Science Missions. The biogeochemical and ecological data provided by ORNL DAAC can be categorized into four groups: Field Campaigns, Land Validation, Regional and Global Data, and Model Archive. After raw data is collected, the data collector describes the data and

[7]http://daac.ornl.gov/

[8]http://datadryad.org/

[9]http://knb.ecoinformatics.org/index.jsp

[10]http://treebase.org/treebase-web/home.html

[11]http://earthdata.nasa.gov/esdis

	# Docs	#All Tags	Avg Tags/Doc	#Uniq. Tags	Tag Util.	#All Words	Avg Words/Doc
DAAC	978	7,294	7.46	611	11.937	101968	104.261
DRYAD	1,729	8,266	4.78	3,122	2.647	224,643	129.926
KNB	24,249	254,525	10.49	7,375	34.511	1535560	63.324
TreeBASE	2635	1838	0.697	1321	1.391	30054	11.405

Table 1: Statistics of the 4 datasets.

annotates it using topic-represented keywords from the topic library.

Dryad is a nonprofit organization and an international repository of data underlying scientific and medical publications. The scientific, educational, and charitable mission of Dryad is to promote the availability of data underlying findings in the scientific literature for research and educational reuse. As of January 24, 2013, Dryad hosts 2570 data packages and 7012 data files, associated with articles in 186 journals. Metadata associated with each data package is annotated by the author with arbitrary choices of keywords.

The Knowledge Network for Biocomplexity (KNB) is a national network intended to facilitate ecological and environmental research on biocomplexity. For scientists, the KNB is an efficient way to discover, access, interpret, integrate and analyze complex ecological data from a highly-distributed set of field stations, laboratories, research sites, and individual researchers. Each data package hosted by KNB is described and annotate with keyword from the taxonomy by the data collector.

TreeBASE is a repository of phylogenetic information, specifically user-submitted phylogenetic trees and the data used to generate them. TreeBASE accepts all types of phylogenetic data (e.g., trees of species, trees of populations, trees of genes) representing all biotic taxa. Data in TreeBASE are exposed to the public if they are used in a publication that is in press or published in a peer-reviewed scientific journal, book, conference proceedings, or thesis. Data used in publications that are in preparation or in review can be submitted to TreeBASE but are only available to the authors, publication editors, or reviewers using a special access code. TreeBASE is produced and governed by the The Phyloinformatics Research Foundation, Inc[12].

In our setting, we assume that the documents are independently annotated, so that the tags in our training sets represent the gold-standard. However, some metadata records may not be independent since they may be originated from the same projects or authors, hence annotated with similar styles and sets of keywords. To mitigate such problem, we randomly select a subset of 1,000 annotated documents (except DAAC dataset, which only has 978 documents of land terrestrial ecology, hence we select them all.) from each archive for our experiments. We combine all the textual attributes (i.e. `Title`, `Abtract`, `Description`) together as the textual content for the document. We preprocess the textual content in each document by removing 664 common stop words and punctuation, and stemming the words using the Porter2's[13] stemming algorithm.

4. PRELIMINARIES

Our proposed solution is built upon the concepts of Cosine Similarity, Term Frequency-Inverse Document Frequency (TF-IDF), and Latent Dirichlet Allocation (LDA). We briefly introduce them here to fortify readers' background before going further.

4.1 Cosine Similarity

In general, cosine similarity is a measure of similarity between two vectors by measuring the cosine of the angle between them. Given two vectors A and B, the cosine similarity is defined using a dot product and magnitude as:

$$CosineSim(A, B) = \frac{A \cdot B}{\|A\| \, \|B\|} = \frac{\sum_{i=1}^{N} A_i \times B_i}{\sqrt{\sum_{i=1}^{N} (A_i)^2} \times \sqrt{\sum_{i=1}^{N} (B_i)^2}}$$

`CosineSim(A,B)` outputs `[0,1]`, with 0 indicating independence, and the value in between indicates the level of similarity. In information retrieval literature, the cosine similarity is heavily used to calculate the similarity between two vectorized documents.

4.2 Term Frequency-Inverse Document Frequency

TF-IDF is used extensively in the information retrieval area. It reflects how important a term is to a document in a corpus. TF-IDF has two components: the term frequency (TF) and the inverse document frequency (IDF). The TF is the frequency of a term appearing in a document. The IDF of a term measures how important the term is to the corpus, and is computed based on the document frequency, the number of documents in which the term appears. Formally, given a term t, a document d, and a corpus (document collection) D:

$$tf(t, d) = \sqrt{count(t, d)}$$

$$idf(t, D) = \sqrt{log\left(\frac{|D|}{|d \in D; t \in d|}\right)}$$

$$TFIDF(t, d, D) = TF(t, d) \cdot IDF(t, D)$$

We can then construct a TF-IDF vector for a document `d` given a corpus `D` as follows:

$$TFIDF(d, D) = \langle TFIDF(t_1, d, D), \cdots, TFIDF(t_n, d, D) \rangle$$

Consequently, if one wishes to compute the similarity score between two documents d_1 and d_2, the cosine similarity can be computed between the TF-IDF vectors representing the two documents:

$$DocSim_{TF-IDF}(d_1, d_2, D) = CosineSim\left(TFIDF(d_1, D), TFIDF(d_2, D)\right) \quad (1)$$

[12] http://www.phylofoundation.org/

[13] http://snowball.tartarus.org/algorithms/english/stemmer.html

4.3 Latent Dirichlet Allocation

In text mining, the Latent Dirichlet Allocation (LDA) [3] is a generative model that allows a document to be represented by a mixture of topics. Past literature such as [10, 20, 21] demonstrates successful usage of LDA to model topics from given corpora. The basic intuition of LDA for topic modeling is that an author has a set of topics in mind when writing a document. A topic is defined as a distribution of terms. The author then chooses a set of terms from the topics to compose the document. With such assumption, the whole document can be represented using a mixture of different topics. LDA serves as a means to trace back the topics in the author's mind before the document is written. Mathematically, the LDA model is described as follows:

$$P(t_i|d) = \sum_{j=1}^{|Z|} P(t_i|z_i = j) \cdot P(z_i = j|d)$$

$P(t_i|d)$ is the probability of term t_i being in document d. z_i is the latent (hidden) topic. $|Z|$ is the number of all topics. This number needs to be predefined. $P(t_i|z_i = j)$ is the probability of term t_i being in topic j. $P(z_i = j|d)$ is the probability of picking a term from topic j in the document d.

Essentially, the LDA model is used to find $P(z|d)$, the topic distribution of document d, with each topic is described by the distribution of term $P(t|z)$. After the topics are modeled, we can assign a distribution of topics to a given document using a technique called *inference*. A document then can be represented with a vector of numbers, each of which represents the probability of the document belonging to a topic.

$$Infer(d, Z) = \langle z_1, z_2, ..., z_Q \rangle; |Z| = Q$$

Where Z is a set of topics, d is a document, and z_i is a probability of the document d falling into topic i. Since a document can be represented using a vector of numbers, one can then compute the topic similarity between two documents d_1 and d_2 using cosine similarity as follows:

$$DocSim_{TM}(d_1, d_2, Z) = CosineSim\left(Infer(d_1, Z), Infer(d_2, Z)\right) \quad (2)$$

5. METHOD

The metadata annotation problem is transformed into the tag recommendation with a controlled tag library. A document is a tuple of textual information and a set of tags, i.e. $\langle text, tags \rangle$. A document query is a document without tags, $\langle text, \oslash \rangle$. Specifically, given a tag library $T = \langle t_1, t_2, ..., t_m \rangle$, a document corpus $D = \langle d_1, d_2, ..., d_n \rangle$, and a document query q, the algorithm outputs a ranked list $T_K^* = \langle t_1, t_2, ..., t_K \rangle$, where $t_i \in T$, of K tags relevant to the document query q.

Our proposed algorithm comprises 2 main steps:

STEP1 $P(t|q, T, D, M)$, the probability of tag t being relevant to q, is computed for each $t \in T$. M is the document similarity measure, which can be either *TF-IDF* or *TM*.

STEP2 Return top K tags ranked by the $P(t|q, T, D, M)$ probability.

$P(t|q, T, D, M)$ is the normalization of the relevance score of the tag t to the document query q, and is defined below:

$$P(t|q, T, D, M) = \frac{TagScore_M(t, q, D)}{\sum_{\tau \in T} TagScore_M(\tau, q, D)}$$

$$TagScore_M(t, q, D) = \sum_{d \in D} DocSim_M(q, d, D) \cdot isTag(t, d)$$

$TagScore_M(t, q, D)$ calculates the tag score determining how relevant the tag t is to document query q. This score can be any real non-negative number. $DocSim_M(q, d, D)$ measures the similarity between two documents, i.e. q and d, given a document corpus D and returns a similarity measure ranging between [0,1]. $isTag(t, d)$ is a binary function that returns 1 if $t \in d.tags$ and 0 otherwise. We propose two approaches to compute the document similarity: *Term Frequency-Document Inverse Frequency (TF-IDF)* based ($DocSim_{TF-IDF}(q, d, D)$) and *Topic Modeling (TM)* based ($DocSim_{TM}(q, d, D)$). These two approached are described in the next subsections.

5.1 TF-IDF based $DocSim_{TF-IDF}(q, d, D)$

The TF-IDF based document similarity measure relies on the term frequency-inverse document frequency principle discussed in Section 4.2. The function aims to quantify the content similarity based on term overlap between two documents. In order to compute the IDF part of the scheme, all the documents in D are first indexed. Hence the training phase (preprocess) involves indexing all the documents. We then compute the similarity between the query q and a source document d using $DocSim_{TF-IDF}(q, d, D)$ as defined in Equation 1.

5.2 TM based $DocSim_{TM}(q, d, D)$

The TM based document similarity measure utilizes topic distributions of the documents using the LDA algorithm as described in Section 4.3. The algorithm further extracts the semantic reposing within a document captured by its topic distribution. With this knowledge in mind, one can measure the semantic similarity between two documents by quantifying the similarity between their topic distributions. Indeed, our proposed TM based algorithm transforms the topic distribution of a document into a numerical vector, wherein Cosine similarity is used to compute the topic similarity between two documents using Equation 2.

6. EVALUATION AND DISCUSSION

We evaluate our methods using the tag prediction protocol. We artificially create a test query document by removing the tags from an annotated document. The task is to predict the removed tags. There are two reasons behind the choosing of this evaluation scheme:

1. The evaluation can be done fully automatically. Since our datasets are large, manual evaluation (i.e. having human identify whether a recommended tag is relevant or not) would be infeasible.

2. The evaluation can be done against the existing gold standard established (manually tagged) by expert annotators (i.e. data collectors, project principal investigators, etc.) who have good understanding about the

data, while manual evaluation could lead to evaluation biases.

We evaluate our TF-IDF and TM based algorithms against the baseline KEA document annotation algorithm with controlled vocabulary. In our setting, the tag library is used as the vocabulary in the KEA algorithm. The document-wise 10 fold cross validation is performed, where each dataset is first split into 10 equal subsets, and for each fold $i \in \{1, 2, 3, ..., 10\}$ the subset i is used for the testing set, and the other 9 subsets are combined and used as the source (training set). The results of each fold are summed up and the averages are reported.

For the TF-IDF based algorithm, we use LingPipe[14] to perform the indexing and calculating the TF-IDF based similarity. For the TM based algorithm, the training process involves modeling topics from the source using LDA algorithm as discussed in Section 4.3. We use the Stanford Topic Modeling Toolbox[15] with the collapsed variational Bayes approximation[2] to identify topics in the source documents. For each document we generate uni-grams, bi-grams, and trigrams, and combine them to represent the textual content of the document. The algorithm takes two input parameters: the number of topics to be identified and the maximum number of the training iterations. After some experiments on varying the two parameters, we fix them at 300 and 1,000 respectively. The inference method proposed by Asuncion et al. [2] is used to assign a topic distribution to a given document. The evaluation is done on a Windows 7 PC with Intel Core i7 2600 CPU 3.4 GHz and 16GB of ram.

6.1 Evaluation Metrics

This section presents the evaluation metrics used in our tasks, including precision, recall, F1, Mean Reciprocal Rank (MRR), and Binary Preference (Bpref). These metrics, when used in combination, have shown to be effective for evaluation of recommending systems[8, 13, 25].

6.1.1 Precision, Recall, F1

Precision, recall, and F1 (F-measure) are well-known evaluation metrics in information retrieval literature [14]. For each document query in the test set, we use the original set of tags as the ground truth T_g. Assume that the set of recommended tags are T_r , so that the correctly recommended tags are $T_g \bigcap T_r$. Precision, recall and F1 measures are defined as follows:

$$precision = \frac{|T_g \bigcap T_r|}{|T_r|}, recall = \frac{|T_g \bigcap T_r|}{|T_g|}, F1 = \frac{\cdot precision \cdot recall}{precision + recall}$$

In our experiments, the number of recommended tags ranges from 1 to 30. It is wise to note that better tag recommendation systems tend to rank correct tags higher than the incorrect ones. However, the precision, recall, and F1 measures do not take ranking into account. To evaluate the performance of the ranked results, we employ the following evaluation metrics.

6.1.2 Mean Reciprocal Rank (MRR)

MRR[22] measure takes ordering into account. It measures how well the first correctly recommended tag is ranked. The reciprocal rank of a query is the multiplicative inverse of the rank of the first correctly recommended tag. The mean reciprocal rank is the average of the reciprocal ranks of the results of the query set Q. Formally, given a testing set Q, let $rank_q$ be the rank of the first corrected answer of query $q \in Q$, then MRR of the query set Q is defined as follows:

$$MRR = \frac{1}{|Q|} \sum_{q \in Q} \frac{1}{rank_q}$$

If the set of recommended tags does not contain a correct tag at all, $\frac{1}{rank_q}$ is defined to be 0.

6.1.3 Binary Preference (Bpref)

Bpref measure considers the order of each correctly recommended tag [5]. Let S be the set of recommended tags by the system, R be the set of corrected tags , $r \in R$ be a correct recommendation, and $i \in S - R$ be an incorrect recommendation. The Bpref is defined as follows:

$$Bpref = \frac{1}{|R|} \sum_{r \in R} 1 - \frac{|i \ ranked \ higher \ than \ r|}{|S|}$$

Bpref can be thought of as the inverse of the fraction of irrelevant documents that are retrieved before relevant ones. Bpref and mean average precision (MAP) are similar when used with complete judgments. However, Bpref normally gives a better evaluation when used in a system with incomplete recommendations.

6.2 Results

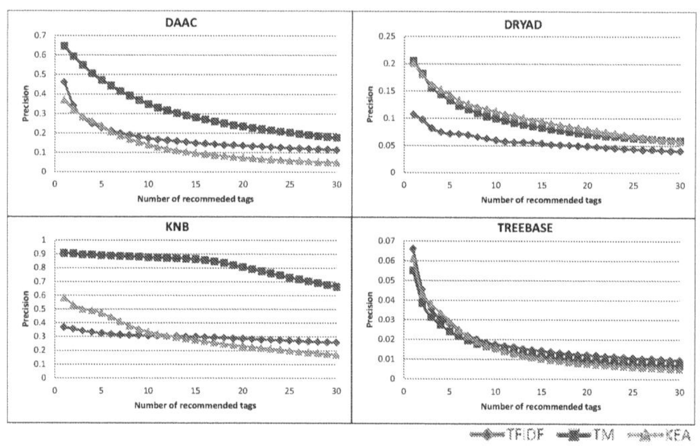

Figure 2: Precision of the TF-IDF, TM, KEA (baseline) algorithms on the 4 datasets.

Figures 2,3,4 plot the precision@K, recall@K, F1@K respectively evaluated at the top K recommended tags of the proposed TF-IDF and TM based algorithms against the baseline KEA algorithm on each dataset. Figure 5 summarizes the precision versus recall on each dataset.

According to the results, our proposed algorithms outperform the baseline KEA algorithm on the DAAC and KNB datasets (TM based approach outperforms at every K and TF-IDF based approach outperforms at larger K). This is because the tags used to annotate DAAC and KNB documents are drawn from the libraries of topics. Hence there is a high chance that a tag is reused for multiple times, resulting in high tag utilization. Since our algorithms tend to

[14]http://alias-i.com/lingpipe/
[15]http://nlp.stanford.edu/software/tmt/tmt-0.4/

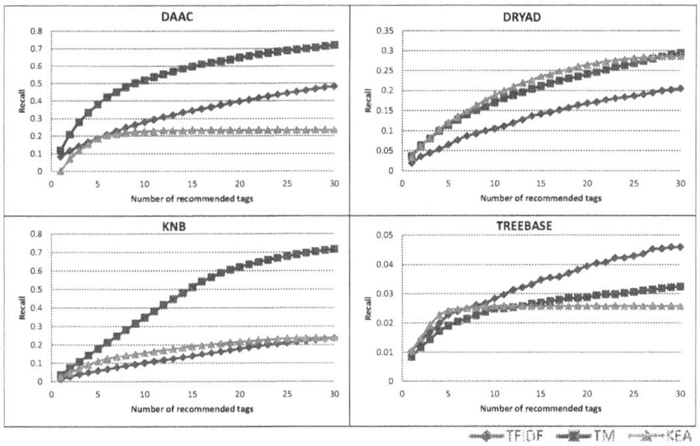

Figure 3: Recall of the TF-IDF, TM, KEA (baseline) algorithms on the 4 datasets.

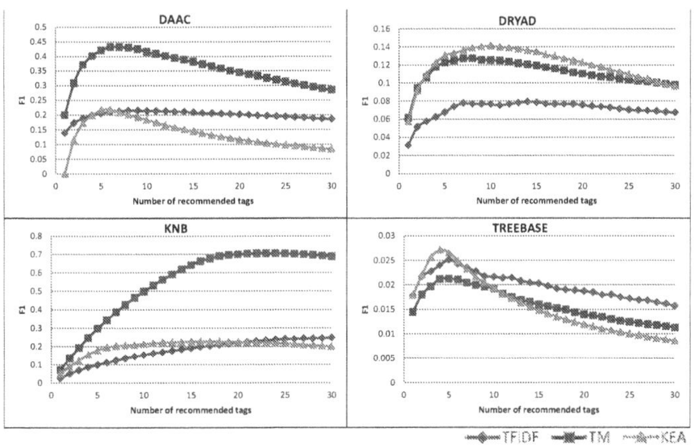

Figure 4: F1 of the TF-IDF, TM, KEA (baseline) algorithms on the 4 datasets.

give higher weight to tags that have been used frequently, datasets with high tag utilization (such as DAAC and KNB) tend to benefit from our algorithms.

However, our proposed algorithms tend to perform worse than the baseline on the DRYAD dataset. This is because, tags in each DRYAD document are manually made up at the curation process. Manually making up tags for each document results in a large size of tag library where each tag is used only a few times, leading to the low tag utilization. Datasets with low tag utilization do not tend to benefit from our proposed algorithms since the probability distribution given to the tags tends to be uniform and not very discriminative.

All the algorithms perform poorly on the TreeBASE dataset. This is because TreeBASE documents are very sparse (some do not even have textual content), and have very few tags. From the dataset statistics, each document on the TreeBASE dataset has only 11 words and only 0.7 tags on average. Such sparse texts lead to weak relationship when finding textually similar documents in the TF-IDF based approach, and the poor quality of the topic model used by the TM based approach. The small number of tags per document makes it even harder to predict the right tags.

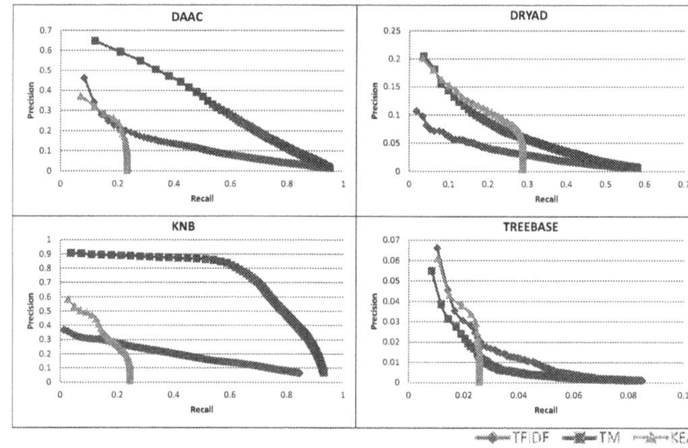

Figure 5: Precision vs Recall of the TF-IDF, TM, KEA (baseline) algorithms on the 4 datasets.

Dataset	Method	MRR	Bpref	ALT (s)	ATT (s)
DAAC	TFIDF	0.5649	0.8183	5.29	0.99
	TM	0.7546	0.9005	2430.82	49.63
	KEA	0.5109	0.2337	75.45	6.50
DRYAD	TFIDF	0.2022	0.4404	6.32	1.19
	TM	0.3264	0.4934	4486.09	83.76
	KEA	0.3423	0.2851	102.59	8.85
KNB	TFIDF	0.4944	0.6659	6.06	1.23
	TM	0.9226	0.9100	1159.81	49.60
	KEA	0.6823	0.2431	64.11	5.61
TREEBASE	TFIDF	0.0893	0.0695	6.15	1.08
	TM	0.0750	0.0636	401.50	16.99
	KEA	0.0745	0.0257	6.26	1.04

Figure 6: MRR, BPref, Average Learning Time (ALT) and Average Test Time (ATT) of TF-IDF, TM, KEA (baseline) algorithms on the 4 datasets.

Figure 6 lists the MRR, BPref, average learning time (in seconds) per fold, and average testing time (in seconds) per fold of the proposed TF-IDF and TM based algorithms against the baseline KEA algorithm on each dataset. MRR quantifies how the first correct recommendation is ranked. In terms of MRR, our TM based algorithm performs the best on the DAAC and KNB datasets, TF-IDF based algorithm performs the best in the TreeBASE dataset, and the KEA algorithm performs the best on the DRYAD dataset. The TM based algorithm achieves the notable MRR scores of 0.75 and 0.92 on the DAAC and KNB datasets receptively, and outperforming the baseline by 47.70% and 33.22% respectively.

Bpref measures the ranking of all the correctly recommended keywords. In terms of Bpref, our TM algorithm performs the best on the DAAC, DRYAD, and KNB datasets with the Bpref scores of 0.90, 0.49, and 0.91 respectively. The TF-IDF based algorithm performs the best on the TreeBASE dataset. Similar to the MRR results, notable BPref scores are achieved by the TM based algorithm on the DAAC and KNB datasets, outperforming the baseline by 285.32% and 274.33% respectively.

Figure 7 shows sample results of our proposed TF-IDF/TM based algorithms and the KEA algorithm against the 15 actual ground-truth tags associated to an DAAC metadata ti-

Actual Tags	TFIDF	TM	KEA(Baseline)
[1]albedo	[1]**field investig**	[1]**land cover**	[1]model
[2]land cover	[2]analysi	[2]**modi moder resolut imag spectroradiomet**	[2]geograph distribut
[3]veget cover	[3]**land cover**	[3]**terra morn equatori cross time satellit**	[3]classif
[4]veget index	[4]comput model	[4]**field investig**	[4]lba
[5]leaf area meter	[5]**reflect**	[5]**veget cover**	[5]amazonia
[6]terra morn equatori cross time satellit	[6]**veget cover**	[6]**reflect**	[6]area
[7]noaa nation ocean amp amp atmospher administr	[7]biomass	[7]**veget index**	[7]south america
[8]plant characterist	[8]primari product	[8]**leaf characterist**	[8]ecolog
[9]steel measur tape	[9]**steel measur tape**	[9]**canopi characterist**	[9]**reflect**
[10]canopi characterist	[10]weigh balanc	[10]**plant characterist**	[10]calibr
[11]modi moder resolut imag spectroradiomet	[11]precipit amount	[11]**albedo**	[11]field investig
[12]leaf characterist	[12]**canopi characterist**	[12]**steel measur tape**	[12]speci
[13]avhrr advanc high resolut radiomet	[13]**leaf characterist**	[13]**avhrr advanc high resolut radiomet**	[13]factor
[14]field investig	[14]water vapor	[14]**noaa nation ocean amp amp atmospher administr**	[14]sequenc
[15]reflect	[15]quadrat sampl frame	[15]**leaf area meter**	[15]hawaiian island
	[16]rain gaug	[16]analysi	[16]genera
	[17]surfac air temperatur	[17]comput model	[17]fern
	[18]air temperatur	[18]noaa	[18]systemat
	[19]meteorolog station	[19]avhrr	[19]**steel measur tape**
	[20]human observ	[20]popul distribut	[20]correl

Figure 7: Comparison of the recommended keywords by the TF-IDF, TM, and KEA (baseline) algorithms on a sample document "ISLSCP II IGBP DISCOVER AND SIB LAND COVER, 1992-1993". The first column lists the actual tags. The bold, underlined terms are correctly recommended items.

tled "*ISLSCP II IGBP DISCOVER AND SIB LAND COVER, 1992-1993*"[16]. Our TM based algorithm performs well on this particular example by capturing all the actual tags within the top 15 recommended tags.

6.3 TM vs TF-IDF Based Approaches

According to the results, our TM based approach performs better than TF-IDF based approach on DAAC, DRYAD, and KNB datasets, in terms of precision, recall, and F1 measure, while the TF-IDF based approach performs better on the TreeBASE dataset. Since the only difference between the two proposed methods is the document similarity function $DocSim(q, d, D)$, which computes the similarity score between the query document q and a source document $d \in D$, the analysis on the differences between the two document similarity measures could provide explanation about the performance difference.

The TF-IDF document similarity measures the cosine similarity between two TF-IDF vectors representing the two documents. Loosely speaking, the TF-IDF document similarity measures the quantity of term overlap, where each term has a different weight, in the two documents.

The TM based approach first derives a set of topics from the document source, each of which is represented by a distribution of terms. The ranked terms in each topic bare coherent semantic meanings. Figure 8 provides an example of the top 10 terms in sample 9 topics derived from the DAAC dataset using the LDA algorithm with 300 topics and 1,000 iterations. Once the set of topics has been determined, a document is assigned a distribution of topics using the inference algorithm mentioned in Section 4.3. The TM document similarity then measures the cosine similarity between the topic distribution vectors representing the two documents. Loosely speaking, the TM document similarity quantifies the topic similarity between the two documents.

The difference in performance of both the proposed methods could be impacted by the semantic representation of each document. It is evident from the experimental results on the DAAC, DRYAD, and KNB datasets, that representing a document with a mixture of topics lead to a more accurate semantic similarity interpretation, leading to better recommendation. However, the reason why the TM based approach performs worse than the TF-IDF based approach on the TreeBASE dataset could be because the documents in such dataset are very sparse (Each TreeBASE document has only 11 words on average). Such sparsity could lead to a poor set of topics, consisting of idiosyncratic word combinations.

Hence we recommend the TM based algorithm for datasets whose documents are rich in textual documents, and the TF-IDF based algorithm approach for those with textually sparse documents.

6.4 Limitations

Regardless of the promising performance, our proposed document annotation algorithms have the following limitations:

1. Our algorithms rely on the existence of a good document source (training set). The quality of the resulting annotation directly reflects the quality of the annotation of each document in the training data. Fortunately, the current ONEMercury system only retrieves the metadata from the archives wherein each metadata document is manually provided by Principal investigators and data managers. In the future, however, the system may expand to collect the metadata from the sources in which the data records may have poor or no annotation. Such problems urge the need for a

[16] *http://daac.ornl.gov/cgi-bin/dsviewer.pl?ds_id=930*

Topic1	Topic2	Topic3	Topic4	Topic5	Topic6	Topic7	Topic8	Topic 9
amazon	pine	aboveground	park	carbon dioxide	soil moisture	plant	bigfoot	environment
river	team	year	mongu	ssa	site average	water potential	modi product	radar
basin	black spruce	mortal	safari	energy	moisture bett	determin	evergreen	mosaic
ecology	chamber	woody biomass	zambia	exchange	neutron	leaf optic	land cover	geotiff format
floodplain	methane	hardwood	wet season	soil temperature	airborn	radiometer	bigfoot project	band
band	team collect	brown	photosynthetic	team	fife experiment	plant water	nasa	backscatter image
inundate	chamber flux	eastern	kalahari	tower flux	gamma	grass	flux tower	synthesize
meter	trace gas	softwood	botswana	vapor	gravimeter	leaf water	grassland	topograph
scale	plant	schroeder	store	water vapor	water content	leaf tissue	evergreen needleleaf	srtm
mosaic	spruce	commercial	activity	flux measure	gas flux	summer	ecology	develop

Figure 8: Top 10 terms in sample 9 topics derived using LDA algorithm from the DAAC dataset.

method that allows the automatic annotator trained with a high-quality training dataset to annotate the documents in different datasets. We plan to investigate into such cross-source recommendation in our future work.

2. Our TM based algorithm needs to model topics from scratch every time a significant amount of new documents are added to the training corpus, so that the modeled topics can reflect the new documents added. Since our TM based algorithm utilizes the traditional LDA algorithm to model topics, wherein incremental training is not a feature, we plan to explore into methods such as [1] and [9] which may enable our algorithm to adaptively model the topics from a dynamic corpus.

3. Regardless of the promising performance of our proposed TM based algorithm, the scalability can be an issue when it comes to mining topics from a larger corpus of documents. The scalability issues of our TM based algorithm is discussed in detail in the next sub section.

6.5 Scalability of the TM Approach

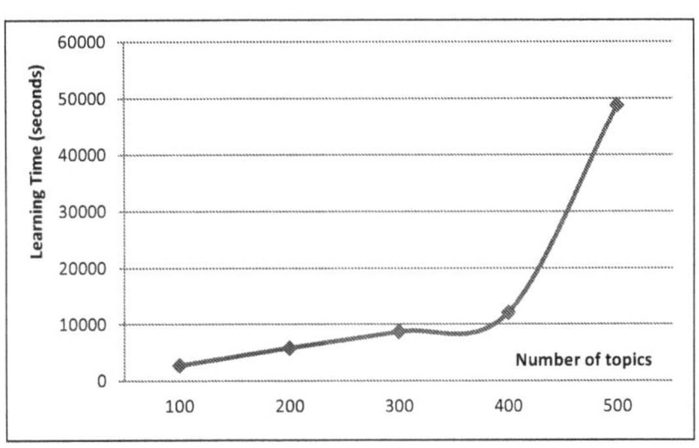

Figure 9: Learning time in seconds of the TM based algorithm as a function of numbers of topics.

Scalability issues should be taken into account since the algorithms will eventually be cooperated as part of the ONEMercury system, which currently hosts much larger datasets than the ones we use in the experiments. This section presents two scalability issues presented in the TM based algorithm: the increase in number of topics and the increase in size of the corpus.

We examine the scalability issues our TM based algorithm on the KNB dataset, using the Stanford Topic Modeling

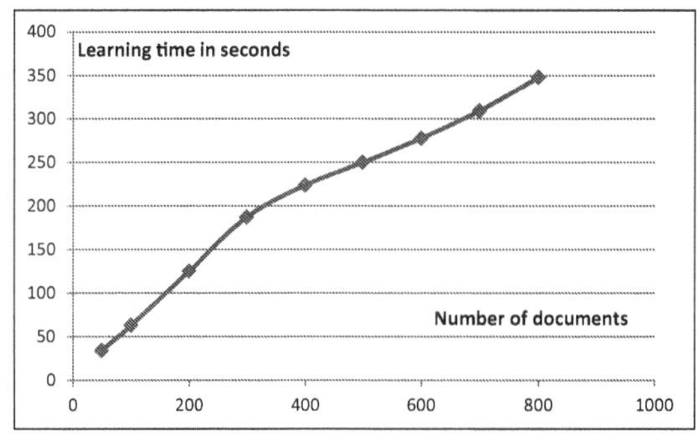

Figure 10: Learning time in seconds of the TM based algorithm as a function of numbers of training documents.

Toolbox with collapsed variational Bayes approximation and fixed 1,000 iterations, on the same machine we use for earlier experiments.

As the data grows larger, new topics emerge, urging the need for a new model that captures such increasing variety of topic. Figure 9 plots the training time (in seconds) as the function of number of topics. The training time grows approximately linearly with the number of topics up to 400 topics. The program runs out of physical memory, however, at 500 topics, leading to a dramatic increase in the training time. Hence, this study points out a more memory-efficient topic model algorithm should be explored.

Another scalability concern lies with the projected increase in the number of training documents. Figure 10 shows the training time of the TM based algorithm as the number of document increases. The results also show a linear scale with the number of training documents. Note that the experiment is only done with up to 1,000 documents, while there are roughly 47 thousands, and definitely increasing in the future, metadata records in the current system. Even with the current size of the ONEMercury repository, the algorithm would take approximately 5.3 hours to model topics, which is not feasible in practice. Hence a large-scale parallel algorithm such as MapReduce[6] should be investigated.

7. CONCLUSION AND FUTURE WORK

This paper presents a set of algorithms for automatic annotation of metadata. We are motivated by the real world problems faced by ONEMerucy, a search system for environmental science metadata harvested from multiple data archives. One of the important problems includes the different of levels of curation of metadata from different archives, which means that the system must automatically annotate poorly annotated metadata records. We treat each metadata record as a tagged document, and then transform the problem into the tag recommendation problem with a controlled tag library.

We propose two algorithms for tag recommendation, one based on term frequency-inverse document frequency (TF-IDF) and the other based on topic modeling (TM) using the Latent Dirichlet Allocation. The evaluation is done on 4 different datasets of environmental metdata using the tag prediction evaluation protocol, against the well known KEA document annotation algorithm. The results show that our TM based approach yields better results on datasets characterized to have high tag utilization and rich in textual content such as DAAC and KNB than those which do not (i.e. DRYAD abd TreeBASE), though with the cost of longer learning times. The scalability issues of the TM based algorithm necessitate investigation into more memory-efficient and scalable approaches. Finally, future steps could be implementing an automatic metadata annotation algorithm on the ONEMercury search service or explore online tagging[19].

8. ACKNOWLEDGMENTS

We gratefully acknowledge useful comments from Natasha Noy, Jeffery S. Horsburgh, and Giri Palanisamy. This work has been supported in part by the National Science Foundation (DataONE: Grant #OCI-0830944) and Contract No. De-AC05-00OR22725 of the U.S. Department of Energy.

9. REFERENCES

[1] L. AlSumait, D. Barbar, and C. Domeniconi. On-line lda: Adaptive topic models for mining text streams with applications to topic detection and tracking. In *ICDM*, pages 3–12. IEEE Computer Society, 2008.

[2] A. Asuncion, M. Welling, P. Smyth, and Y. W. Teh. On smoothing and inference for topic models. In *Proceedings of the Twenty-Fifth Conference on Uncertainty in Artificial Intelligence*, UAI '09, pages 27–34, Arlington, Virginia, United States, 2009. AUAI Press.

[3] D. M. Blei, A. Y. Ng, and M. I. Jordan. Latent dirichlet allocation. *J. Mach. Learn. Res.*, 3:993–1022, Mar. 2003.

[4] M. Bron, B. Huurnink, and M. de Rijke. Linking archives using document enrichment and term selection. In *Proceedings of the 15th international conference on Theory and practice of digital libraries: research and advanced technology for digital libraries*, TPDL'11, pages 360–371, 2011.

[5] C. Buckley and E. M. Voorhees. Retrieval evaluation with incomplete information. In *Proceedings of the 27th annual international ACM SIGIR conference on Research and development in information retrieval*, SIGIR '04, pages 25–32, New York, NY, USA, 2004. ACM.

[6] J. Dean and S. Ghemawat. Mapreduce: simplified data processing on large clusters. *Commun. ACM*, 51(1):107–113, Jan. 2008.

[7] P. Heymann, D. Ramage, and H. Garcia-Molina. Social tag prediction. In *Proceedings of the 31st annual international ACM SIGIR conference on Research and development in information retrieval*, SIGIR '08, pages 531–538, New York, NY, USA, 2008. ACM.

[8] W. Huang, S. Kataria, C. Caragea, P. Mitra, C. L. Giles, and L. Rokach. Recommending citations: translating papers into references. CIKM '12, pages 1910–1914, New York, NY, USA, 2012. ACM.

[9] T. Iwata, T. Yamada, Y. Sakurai, and N. Ueda. Online multiscale dynamic topic models. In *Proceedings of the 16th ACM SIGKDD international conference on Knowledge discovery and data mining*, KDD '10, pages 663–672, New York, NY, USA, 2010. ACM.

[10] S. Kataria, P. Mitra, and S. Bhatia. Utilizing context in generative bayesian models for linked corpus. In *AAAI'10*, pages –1–1, 2010.

[11] R. Krestel, P. Fankhauser, and W. Nejdl. Latent dirichlet allocation for tag recommendation. In *Proceedings of the third ACM conference on Recommender systems*, RecSys '09, pages 61–68, New York, NY, USA, 2009. ACM.

[12] Z. Liu, X. Chen, and M. Sun. A simple word trigger method for social tag suggestion. In *Proceedings of the Conference on Empirical Methods in Natural Language Processing*, EMNLP '11, pages 1577–1588, Stroudsburg, PA, USA, 2011. Association for Computational Linguistics.

[13] Z. Liu, W. Huang, Y. Zheng, and M. Sun. Automatic keyphrase extraction via topic decomposition. In *Proceedings of the 2010 Conference on Empirical Methods in Natural Language Processing*, EMNLP '10, pages 366–376, Stroudsburg, PA, USA, 2010. Association for Computational Linguistics.

[14] C. D. Manning, P. Raghavan, and H. Schtze. *Introduction to Information Retrieval.* Cambridge University Press, New York, NY, USA, 2008.

[15] O. Medelyan and I. H. Witten. Thesaurus based automatic keyphrase indexing. In *Proceedings of the 6th ACM/IEEE-CS joint conference on Digital libraries*, JCDL '06, pages 296–297, New York, NY, USA, 2006. ACM.

[16] W. Michener, D. Vieglais, T. Vision, J. Kunze, P. Cruse, and G. Janée. DataONE: Data Observation Network for Earth - Preserving Data and Enabling Innovation in the Biological and Environmental Sciences. *DLib Magazine*, 17(1/2):1–12, 2011.

[17] G. Mishne. Autotag: a collaborative approach to automated tag assignment for weblog posts. In *Proceedings of the 15th international conference on World Wide Web*, WWW '06, pages 953–954, New York, NY, USA, 2006. ACM.

[18] D. Newman, K. Hagedorn, C. Chemudugunta, and P. Smyth. Subject metadata enrichment using statistical topic models. In *Proceedings of the 7th ACM/IEEE-CS joint conference on Digital libraries*, JCDL '07, pages 366–375, New York, NY, USA, 2007. ACM.

[19] Y. Song, Z. Zhuang, H. Li, Q. Zhao, J. Li, W.-C. Lee, and C. L. Giles. Real-time automatic tag recommendation. In *Proceedings of the 31st annual international ACM SIGIR conference on Research and development in information retrieval*, SIGIR '08, pages 515–522, 2008.

[20] S. Tuarob, L. C. Pouchard, N. Noy, J. S. Horsburgh, and G. Palanisamy. Onemercury: Towards automatic annotation of environmental science metadata. In *Proceedings of the 2nd International Workshop on Linked Science*, LISC '12, 2012.

[21] S. Tuarob and C. S. Tucker. Fad or here to stay: Predicting product market adoption and longevity using large scale, social media data. In *Proc. ASME 2013 Int. Design Engineering Technical Conf. Computers and Information in Engineering Conf.*, IDETC/CIE '13, 2013.

[22] E. M. Voorhees. The trec-8 question answering track report. In *In Proceedings of TREC-8*, pages 77–82, 1999.

[23] I. H. Witten, G. W. Paynter, E. Frank, C. Gutwin, and C. G. Nevill-Manning. Kea: practical automatic keyphrase extraction. In *Proceedings of the fourth ACM conference on Digital libraries*, DL '99, pages 254–255, New York, NY, USA, 1999. ACM.

[24] L. Wu, L. Yang, N. Yu, and X.-S. Hua. Learning to tag. In *Proceedings of the 18th international conference on World wide web*, WWW '09, pages 361–370, 2009.

[25] T. Zhou, H. Ma, M. Lyu, and I. King. Userrec: A user recommendation framework in social tagging systems. In *Proceedings of AAAI*, pages 1486–1491, 2010.

The User-Centered Development and Testing of a Dublin Core Metadata Tool

Catherine Hall, Michael Khoo
College of Information Science & Technology, Drexel University
3141 Chestnut Street, Philadelphia PA 19104, USA
+1 215 895 5912
{ceh48, khoo}@drexel.edu

ABSTRACT
Digital libraries are supported by good quality metadata, and thus by the use of good quality metadata tools. The design of metadata tools can be supported by following user-centered design processes. In this paper we discuss the application and evaluation of several cognitively-based rules, derived from the work of Donald Norman, to the design of a metadata tool for administering Dublin Core metadata. One overall finding was that while the use of the rules supported users in their immediate interactions with the tool interface, they provided less support for the more cognitively intensive tasks associated with developing a wider conceptual understanding of the purpose of metadata. The findings have implications for the wider development of tools to support metadata work in digital libraries and allied contexts.

Categories and Subject Descriptors
H.3.7 [**Information Storage and retrieval**]: Digital Libraries – *collection, standards, user issues.*

General Terms
Management, standardization

Keywords
Metadata tools, metadata generation, Dublin Core

1. INTRODUCTION
Digital libraries are supported by good quality metadata. The creation of good quality metadata depends partly in turn on the use of good quality metadata tools.

Several inter-related factors impact the development and use of metadata tools. One is the complexity of metadata concepts and the cataloging tasks to be handled by the tool; another is the expertise of the tool users themselves; and a third is what has been referred to as the metadata 'gap' between the rapidly increasing numbers of resources that require metadata, and the limited number of trained metadata creators. Combined, these factors mean that there are increasing groups of users who do not have formal professional training in metadata work, but who also have an interest in creating metadata, who will be using metadata tools. Studies of metadata tools have shown that they can be difficult for non-professionals to use [5]. The findings of these DL studies echo those of a meta-study of bricks-and-mortar library usability studies of Web sites, OPACs, etc. which found that common library terminologies – such as *database*, *library catalog*, *e-journals*, *index*, *inter-library loan*, *periodical* and *serial*, *reference*, *resource*, and subject categories in general – were often little understood by users, and acted as cognitive barriers to use. [10]

Given the complex contexts of metadata creation, metadata tool development benefits from being user-centered, and following iterative design processes, in which designs are improved through iterative cycles of implementation and testing [1]. This paper reports an example of such a development process, an evaluation phase of the ongoing user-centered design and development *Erasmus*, a metadata tool being developed for use with ipl2 (http://www.ipl.org: formerly the Internet Public Library).

2. USER-CENTERED METADATA TOOLS
Researchers have outlined a variety of requirements for metadata tools. An analysis of metadata records contributed by resource creators found that while the subject domain metadata was generally good, there were often technical errors, especially related to formatting [12]. Recommendations include gaining a better understanding of contributors' thought processes, better guidelines, and improved interfaces, to "allow contributors to produce high-quality metadata records without having a great deal of organizational expertise." Despite the provision of a cataloging tool, online work and discussion spaces, face-to-face workshops, conference calls, etc., the cataloging activity of a group of K-12 teachers helping to build a digital library was slow, with the educators having difficulty understanding concepts such as *digital library*, *collection*, *catalog*, and *metadata* [6, 7]. A study of author-generated records in the National Institute of Environmental Health Sciences found that some users lacked understanding of the tool and metadata, despite having access to a tutorial [4]. "Succinctly explaining the fields of a standardized schema such as Dublin Core to metadata novices appears to be a key challenge for designers," and that "developing a conceptual understanding of metadata records and their use in retrieval was found to be challenging for users." [2]

Recommendations that have emerged from this research include that "For decentralized metadata creation to become a reality, better designs are needed to reduce users' cognitive load and lower barriers to efficient metadata entry" [1, c.f 10]. One approach to better design is to follow an iterative and user-centered approach to metadata tool development, by following the user-centered design approach of Donald Norman [11] who provides a suite of useful cognitive models that can be applied to

JCDL'13, July 22–26, 2013, Indianapolis, Indiana, USA.

ACM 978-1-4503-2077-1/13/07...$15.00.

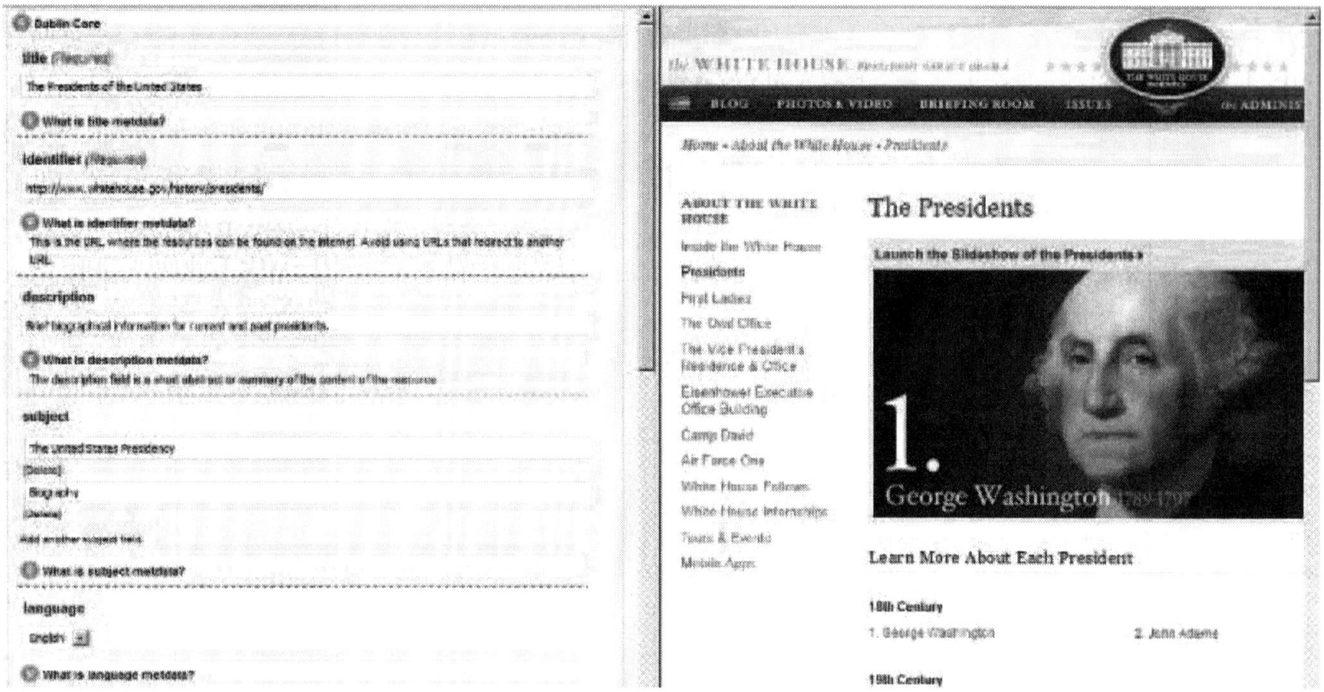

Figure 1. The 'split screen' Erasmus interface. Metadata fields in the left pane and resource in the right.

system design. Two inter-related concepts that are used in the current analysis are (a), knowledge in the head and knowledge in the world, and (b), designer images, user images, and system images [11].

Knowledge in the head is supported by processes such as short-term and long-term memory, and declarative and procedural memory. Short-term and declarative memory can be associated with explicitly engaging with an artifact, and also with learning. Long-term and procedural memory is often associated with skill, and with the application of expertise. In contrast to knowledge in the head, knowledge in the world is knowledge that is available to us in the environment. It can take the form of instructions, labels, affordances, and other perceptual cues that indicate how to use an artifact. We rely on knowledge in the world to use artifacts that are unfamiliar, complex, or which otherwise require knowledge apart from that in our heads.

A usable artifact strikes a balance between supporting these two different forms of knowledge, as well as between different forms of memory, and other cognitive processes. In the case of metadata tools, the knowledge in the head required to use the tool might consist of general knowledge of how to use an interface as well as any prior conceptual and technical understanding of metadata. Knowledge in the world, on the other hand, might include more specific information regarding schema requirements, controlled vocabularies, etc., that is required in order successfully to create good quality metadata.

In Norman's approach, the design of such forms of 'knowledge in the world' often takes place in what is called the 'system image.' His model of designer image, user image, and system image, states that the interface for a system (such as a metadata tool) should support user interaction with that system by clearly representing the tool's capabilities in ways that users will understand. The designer's image is 'the conceptualization that the designer has in mind,' and the user's image is 'the model … the user develops to explain the operation of the system.' The two images intersect in the system image, which represents the system components and their relationships to the user, in such a way that takes into account who the users are, and the type of tasks that they are trying to perform. When a system image accurately represents the underlying system model, then a system is easy to use, but when a system image is "incoherent or inappropriate … incomplete or contradictory" then usability problems can arise [c.f. 8].

Drawing on Norman's approach, user-centered metadata tool design should attend to issues such as knowledge in the head and knowledge in the world, and also the system image. An important general research question for metadata tool design therefore concerns the ways in which specialist metadata knowledge is represented to non-professionals in tool interfaces: How can we represent complex metadata concepts in ways that are not only easy for novices to understand, but which might also anticipate user misunderstandings?

3. APPROACH

In the rest of this paper, we discuss how this research question is being addressed in the ongoing design of a metadata tool for ipl2. ipl2 contains approximately 40,000 resources and receives 8 million visits and 22 million page views a year. In 2009, ipl2 began crosswalking its metadata to Dublin Core and added this metadata to a Fedora Commons database. To support the creation of metadata records by ipl2 staff, volunteers and graduate students, a new web-based tool, *Erasmus* (fig.1), was developed. Initial requirements gathering was undertaken by students in a graduate 'Introduction to HCI' class and a prototype was developed which doctoral students evaluated. Many of the usability problems found at this stage were related to how the tool represented the complex knowledge required for cataloging in an uncluttered and easily accessible form [9].

Following this round of expert usability testing and subsequent modifications, an assignment was designed for graduate students in an online Digital Libraries class to test the tool in a production-like environment. Students were provided with assignment instructions and a copy of the Erasmus "user manual". Each student was assigned 5 ipl2 links that had been reported as broken. Students were instructed to fix or replace these links where possible and edit and create new metadata as appropriate. Importantly, the student-generated metadata was reviewed by ipl2 staff and judged to be of acceptable quality. However, the focus for this paper is an analysis of student reports in which they summarized their activities, reflected on the process of creating metadata, and evaluated the tool. Over two terms, 46 student reports were collected and anonymized, after which the authors iteratively reviewed the reports and selected sections in which students commented on Erasmus, and also on metadata work in general. These selections were then sorted using an inductive card sort, in order to identify a number of overall themes.

3.1 Results

Four overall themes were identified: overall usability, conceptual difficulties, student suggestions, and educational/career value.

3.1.1 Overall usability

Erasmus was well liked by students. Many positive comments focused on its simplicity and ease of use, interface design, and support for metadata tasks. Importantly, the system was judged to be *"practical for a digital library that is maintained by people who are not necessarily all in the same area"*. *"The Erasmus tool has made this possible so that our inexperience does not jeopardize the integrity of the ipl2 library database"*.

The process of using the tool to create metadata was described as *"stress-free"* by one student and *"relatively effortless"* by another. One student remarked, *"considering the actual process of trying to recover records can be complicated, it was reassuring to find Erasmus so easy to use"*. Though this was the first experience with metadata creation for many students, others compared Erasmus favorably with data and content management tools they had used previously such as Archon, ContentDM, Solr and library cataloging tools.

The interface was described as *"user friendly"* and the metadata fields were judged to be *"well structured"* and *"clearly defined"*. Two features of Erasmus, in particular, received widespread praise. The first was the dual screen interface that presents the metadata form in the left pane and the resource (website) in the right. As one student noted, *"it makes adding correct information much easier than flipping between tabs or windows"*. The second feature was the incorporation of drop down 'tool tips' for each metadata field. *"I appreciated that the Erasmus interface showed brief descriptions of the Dublin Core fields beneath the text entry boxes making it easier to remember the distinct purpose of each metadata element"*, said one student. Tool tips also provided formatting instructions for elements as necessary. Although most students felt the provided descriptions and formatting examples were adequate, a few indicated they would have appreciated more guidance: *"I felt that the explanation of what was meant to go in each field was obtuse in certain cases"*.

Several students mentioned that they would have liked to see more controlled vocabularies in use. As one stated, *"I like to work from a set vocabulary because I feel more confident that the terms I am using to describe an object are the most semantically accurate"*. A small number of technical issues were also reported by students such as browser incompatibility, error messages when saving a new record (even though the record did save), and difficulty loading one metadata record while another was open in a different tab. These issues were not persistent and did not seem to affect completion of the task. Finally, the user manual was very well received by students who found it a helpful go-to resource.

3.1.2 Conceptual difficulties

Most of the difficulties reported with the tool and the assignment were of a conceptual nature. These reported difficulties are consistent with the findings of other studies suggesting that this is a general issue with metadata tools. Observations included the following:

- *One of the things I struggled with is deciding which metadata is appropriate for a record. Including as much metadata as possible is ideal, however, sometimes the requested metadata is not available and plugging a best guess into a field will not add value to a record.*
- *Throughout the assignment I had trouble deciding which Dublin Core fields were applicable and what to put in those fields.*
- *I had trouble determining whether fields like date and temporal coverage were referring to the website or the history of the paper.*

As noted earlier, despite these difficulties, all the metadata created was judged to be of a complete and accurate enough nature to be included in ipl2.

3.1.3 Student Suggestions

Students suggested a number of refinements and additional features they would like to see in future iterations of Erasmus. These included: enhanced search features and particularly the ability to retrieve a record by URL, spell checking tools, more embedded controlled vocabularies, and more examples within the tooltips to *"elucidate fields like coverage and temporal coverage that are fairly close in terminology"*. A small number of students explicitly asked for examples that helped not just with how to format metadata but where to find it in the source material. Other suggestions included *"A section where you can review the work you have completed"*, *"a log of changes made by one's account"*, and a *"live-consultation"* or *"issue, submission, triage tool"*.

3.1.4 Educational/Career value

Students found the "hands-on' process of metadata creation and editing to be very rewarding: *"I think this was a good exercise for students in this class to do because it got us to get in the trenches and actually do some metadata updating and editing instead of just writing about metadata schemes as a more theoretical manner"*. One student said they enjoyed the assignment as they *"got a real feel for metadata entry and the decisions that are involved in creating it correctly"* and another commented, *"working on the metadata database backend helped me to further understand how metadata can play a role in improving search features in a digital library"*

Looking beyond the classroom, some students also commented on the benefit the exercise had for their future career, *"I find the practical application very useful to my professional development and growing skill set as a librarian"* said one. Another said, *"I believe this brief encounter with Dublin Core will help me in the future to understand more complex details of other digital collections when I move on from my coursework*"

3.2 Discussion

Significant goals with the ongoing development work with Erasmus are both to develop a usable tool, and also to develop and report on a usability method that is appropriate for metadata tools. In this respect, the application of some of Norman's design principles (knowledge in the head and knowledge in the world, and designer images, user images, and system images) was found to positively support tool development, and also to produce a tool that users generally found to be usable. Many students commented positively on the educational and professional value of the exercise, in particular their increased understanding of metadata concepts and metadata application in a digital library environment. Though students had been introduced to Dublin Core and other metadata schemes earlier in course, for most this was their first time "*in the trenches*".

Within this overall result, there was a spectrum of outcomes and successes. More successful design strategies included those that were intended to find a balance between supporting easy use of Erasmus by not making it cluttered, and avoiding putting too much information in the interface so that it became unusable. For instance, the design affordance of the dropdown tooltips was an important one in this regard and between Norman's ideas of knowledge in the head and knowledge in the world. Tooltips use preserved the clean, uncluttered interface design that users found appealing, but also offered support for novice metadata creators. These design approaches also supported a relatively simple yet flexible system image that presented the underlying requirements of Dublin Core to the users in relatively simple ways. At the same time, conceptual difficulties with creating metadata remained a significant issue (although in many cases this was only a perceived difficulty; students created very good metadata but they were sometimes prone to doubt themselves). This latter finding confirms the findings of many of the previous studies of metadata tools cited in the Introduction, and the student suggestions provide inspiration as to how we might continue to address this issue. In cases where students struggled with either the structure or content of controlled vocabularies and data formats, in some case, solutions could be purely design-oriented (e.g. fixed format date fields), although there is scope for further and more complex solutions as well, such as providing an in-tool community forum and knowledge base where students and volunteers can discuss these issues.

4. CONCLUSION

This paper has offered reflection on the development and user evaluation of a digital library metadata tool for novice catalogers. It has shown that while some of the more immediate dimensions of metadata work are directly amenable to cognitively informed design solutions, in the case of other wider dimensions, such as overall understandings of the purposes of collections and metadata, well-designed tools are necessary but not sufficient components of metadata work, and this work should be supported through other means as well (tutorials, user manuals, etc.).

5. ACKNOWLEDGMENTS

Our thanks to the OCLC Library and Information Science Research Grant Program (LISGRP) for funding the initial development of Erasmus.

6. REFERENCES

[1] Crystal, A. (2003). Interface design for metadata creation. In: CHI '03 Extended Abstracts on Human Factors in Computing Systems, pp. 1038-1039. DOI = http://doi.acm.org/10.1145/765891.766136

[2] Crystal A., & Greenberg, J. (2005). Usability of a metadata creation application for resource authors. *Library and Information Science 27*(2005), 177-189.

[3] Greenberg, J. (2010). Metadata and digital information. In: M. J. Bates & M. N. Maack (Eds.), *Encyclopedia of Library and Information Sciences, Third* Edition, 3610-3623. New York, NY: Routledge.

[4] Greenberg, J., Crystal, A., Robertson, W. D., & Leadem, E. (2003). Iterative design of metadata creation tools for resource authors. Paper presented at the Dublin Core Conference 2003, September 28 - October 2, Seattle, WA, USA.

[5] Kastens, K.A., DeFelice, B., Devaul, H., DiLeonardo, C., Ginger, K., Larsen, S., Mogk, D., & Tahirkheli, A. (2005). Questions & challenges arising in building the collection of a digital library for education: Lessons from five years of DLESE. *D-Lib Magazine 11*(11). http://www.dlib.org/dlib/november05/kastens/11kastens.html

[6] Khoo, M. (2005). The Tacit Dimensions of User Behavior: The Case of the Digital Water Education Library. In: 5th ACM/IEEE Joint Conference on Digital Libraries (JCDL), Denver, CO, June 7-11, 2005, p. 213-222.

[7] Khoo, M., Devaul, H., & Sumner, T. 2002. Functional requirements for groupware to support community-led collections building. In *6th European Conference on Digital Libraries (ECDL)*, Rome, September 16-18, 2002, 190-203.

[8] Khoo, M., & Hall, C. 2012. What Would 'Google' Do? Users' Mental Models of a Digital Library Search Engine. In *Theory and Practice of Digital Libraries (TPDL) 2012*, Paphos, Cyprus, September 23-27, 2012, 1-12.

[9] Khoo, M., & MacDonald, C. (2012). Erasmus: A Flexible and Scalable Administrative Tool for Dublin Core Metadata. 2012 ALISE Annual Conference, Dallas, TX, January 17-20.

[10] Kupersmith, P. 2012. Library terms that users understand. UC Berkeley: UC Berkeley Library. Retrieved from: http://escholarship.org/uc/item/3qq499w7#page-2

[11] Norman, D. 1988. *The Design of Everyday Things*. Basic Books: New York.

[12] Wilson, A. (2007). Toward releasing the metadata bottleneck: a baseline evaluation of contributor-supplied metadata. *Library Resources and Technical Services, 51*(1), 16-28.

Identification of *Works* of Manga Using LOD Resources - An Experimental FRBRization of Bibliographic Data of Comic Books -

Wenling He
Graduate School of Library, Information and Media Studies, University of Tsukuba
1-2 Kasuga, Tsukuba, Ibaraki, 305-0821, Japan
benlin@slis.tsukuba.ac.jp

Tetsuya Mihara
Graduate School of Library, Information and Media Studies, University of Tsukuba
1-2 Kasuga, Tsukuba, Ibaraki, 305-0821, Japan
mihara@slis.tsukuba.ac.jp

Mitsuharu Nagamori
Faculty of Library, Information and Media Science, University of Tsukuba
1-2 Kasuga, Tsukuba, Ibaraki, 305-0821, Japan
nagamori@slis.tsukuba.ac.jp

Shigeo Sugimoto
Faculty of Library, Information and Media Science, University of Tsukuba
1-2 Kasuga, Tsukuba, Ibaraki, 305-0821, Japan
sugimoto@slis.tsukuba.ac.jp

ABSTRACT
Manga – a Japanese term meaning graphic novel or comic – has been globally accepted. In Japan, there are a huge number of monographs and magazines of manga published. The *work* entity defined in Functional Requirements of Bibliographic Records (FRBR) is useful to identify and find manga. This paper examines how to identify manga *works* in a set of bibliographic records maintained by Kyoto International Manga Museum. It is known that authority data is useful to identify *works* from the bibliographic records. However, the authority data of manga is not rich, because manga has been recognized as a sub-culture resource and is generally not included in library collections. In this study, we used DBpedia, which is a large Linked Open Data (LOD) resource created from Wikipedia, to identify FRBR manga entities in bibliographic records. The results of this study show that using LOD resources is a reasonable way to identify *works* from bibliographic records. It also shows the accuracy and efficiency of *work* identification depending on the quality of the LOD resources used.

ACM Classification: E.0 General

Keywords: Bibliographic Data of comic books, *Work* sets, FRBRization, Linked Open Data, DBpedia.

1. INTRODUCTION
Manga publishing has been a big market for long time, but libraries were not keen to collect manga until the 1990s because manga was recognized as being sub-culture content and was not included in primary collection items. Nowadays, there are large collections of manga not only in Japan but also in other countries, e.g., Kyoto International Manga Museum (KMM), Ohio State University Library and so on.

In the conventional business model of Japanese manga publishing, a manga is first published in a magazine, and then if the manga receives good feedback from the readers, it will be republished as a monograph or series of monographs. In general, readers of manga are likely to identify a manga not as an individual book or article in a magazine but as a distinct intellectual or artistic creation. In other words, they are likely to identify manga as a *work* but not as a *manifestation* or an *item* of FRBR [1].

However, there are no catalogues organized for *work*, and, in general, it is not straightforward to find a *work* using library bibliographic data. This paper presents a study to identify manga *works* from the bibliographic data of comic books maintained at KMM, and create relationships among *works*. Identification of a *work* means to create appropriate *work-expression* relationships. This study is aimed at creating appropriate relationships between a manga *work* and its several language *expressions*.

Hickey and Toves [2] showed that authority data has a key role in identification of fiction *works*. However, in the case of manga, authority data is not well developed yet because they are rather new to libraries. Fortunately, there are various information resources for manga on the Internet which could be used as a supplement to authority data to identify manga *works*, e.g., Wikipedia and manga portal sites provided by publishers and by hobbyists. The useful sites among them for automatically collecting information about manga are those that conform to the requirements of Linked Open Data (LOD) such as DBpedia [5].

2. *WORKS* OF MANGA
Morozumi et al. [4] defined a metadata framework for manga (MMF). MMF is defined based on two major standards – bibliographic description based on FRBR and structural description based on TV-Anytime. The structural description scheme of MMF defines a set of several general constructs of manga which include three major components – *title*, *story* and *episode*. A *title* represents a manga as a series of one or more *stories*, and a *story* is a series of one or more *episodes*. A typical manga monograph contains one or more *stories*. A typical manga contained in one issue of a magazine is an *episode* in a *story* or a *story* which fits to a page limit for publication. A single issue of a manga magazine contains several manga created by different creators. As a bibliographic record is generally created for each item held at a library, this structural definition does not correspond to cataloging conventions.

JCDL'13, July 22–26, 2013, Indianapolis, Indiana, USA.
ACM 978-1-4503-2077-1/13/07.

A single volume of a manga magazine is an aggregation of *stories*, and a series of *stories* of manga, i.e. a manga with a single title, is published in a series of magazines. On the other hand, a series of manga monographs covers the series of *stories* included in the *title*. Thus, both magazines and monographs are compilations of *stories*. We define the relationships among *stories*, *titles* and *compilations* as follows,

- A *story* of a manga is a part of a *title* of manga, and
- A *compilation* carries manga *titles*.

It is straightforward to apply the Group1 entity model of FRBR to the three components, *story*, *manga-title*, and *manga-compilation*. We then define the layered model of FRBRized entities and their relationships shown in Figure 1. The *manifestation/item* layer represents the bibliographic records in libraries. This study is aimed to identify the instances and their relationships in the layers from bibliographic data.

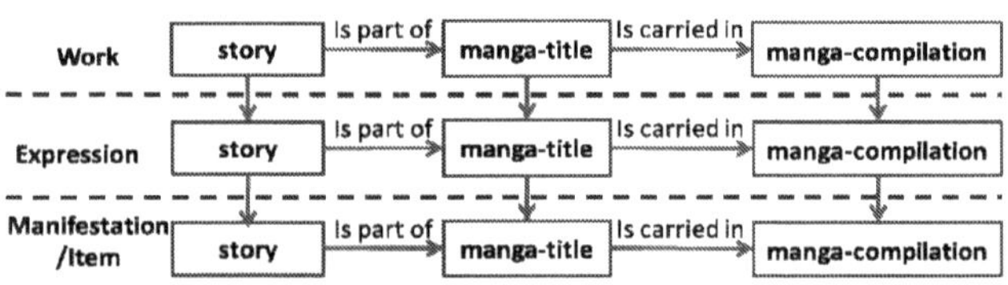

Figure 1. Manga entities and relationships between them

3. IDENTIFICATION OF MANGA *WORK*

3.1 Related Studies

Because of the high cost associated with the manual identification of FRBR entities, automated identification has been investigated. Preceding studies show that the combination of author and title, which are extracted from well-formed bibliographic records like MARC, is a useful identification key for automated identification. Hickey and Toves [2] found that an author combined with a title or a solitary uniform title is the key to uniquely and confidently identify a *work*-set from MARC records. Taniguchi [3] found that it is effective to identify works from JAPAN/MARC records to generate keys for every bibliographic hierarchical level, e.g., monograph-based level, aggregate level and component level, using data elements such as author headings, statements of responsibility, descriptive titles, and title headings.

Automated linking of the FRBRized data to LOD resources has been investigated to enrich FRBRied datasets. It has been shown that the attributes of *work*, e.g., author, title and type are useful mapping keys to link a *work* with LOD resources. Takhirov [6] presented a workflow to automatically link *works* identified in metadata to the corresponding entity in LOD resources. They found that *works* can be identified in the LOD cloud. Duchateau [7] presented a tool called *FRBRpedia*. As a part of its function, it links *works* to DBpedia, by matching title, creator and category of *works* with those of DBpedia resources. DBpedia Lookup Service is used in this approach.

3.2 Identification of Manga *Works* Using LOD Resources

As mentioned in section 1, since the authority data of comic books is not rich enough to identify manga *works*, we used LOD resources as an authority, i.e., a dictionary of manga. In this study, we used DBpedia as a LOD resource because of its rich manga information.

A *work* as an intellectual creation should be neutral to languages whereas its *expression* and *manifestation* are expressed in a language, e.g., Japanese, Chinese, English, etc. However, it is difficult to group bibliographic records for manifestation or items expressed in different languages as a single work instance without information about corresponding translated titles.

In order to solve this language issue in the identification of *works*, we propose to start from bibliographic records for manga in the same language, e.g., Japanese. We grouped bibliographic records by language, and we call each of them a *record-set*. In FRBR's definition, the *work-expression* relationship is a one-to-many relationship. Since a record-set is defined for a set of *manifestations* and/or *items* in a same language, a record-set represents an *expression* in the language, and then the record-set can be linked to a *work*. On the other hand, a *work* can be linked from one or more record-sets, i.e. *expression*. Thus, we create a temporary *work* instance for each *record-set*. A temporary *work* instance is an instance which represents a temporarily identified instance as a *work* of manga, from a record-set which represents a collection of bibliographic records that have the same title and author. Then, we use DBpedia resources of manga as a description of *works* for finding the name of a manga in a different language in DBpedia. We linked each of temporary *work* instances to its corresponding DBpedia resources for getting the name of a manga in a different language to generate a manga *work* instance and its relationships with its *expression* instances from bibliographic records. Similarly, since description about the relationships between *work* instances of story, *manga-title* and *manga-compilation* do not always appear in the bibliographic data of comic books, we also get the information from DBpedia to generate these relationships. The procedure is summarized into three steps as follows,

1. Create *Record-sets* from bibliographic records by matching title, author and language code. And temporarily create a *work* instance from each *record-set*.
2. Link each temporary *work* instance to an entry in DBpedia by matching author, title and type.
3. Integrate the instances in the two sub-steps, (1) Find the information needed for generating a manga *work* instance and its relationships with its *expression* instances and related *work* instances, (2) Create a *work* instance and relationships around it by integrating the bibliographic records.

There is an example shown by figure 2. In this example, we want to identify the *work* "Siki" (note) by grouping several bibliographic records, which expressed as both "Siki" in Japanese and "Shiji" in Chinese. However, there is no information showing that they represent the same *work*. (note: "Siki" is originally spelled as 史記 in Japanese characters. In this paper, non-English names are primarily transliterated in English for readability.)

In step 1 we create the *record-set* "Siki" by matching the title "Siki", the author "Yokoyama" and the language code "ja" from the records. We then create the temporary work instance "Siki" from the *record-set* "Siki". We then link the temporary *work* "Siki" to its corresponding resource "Siki" in DBpedia in step 2. From the resources "Siki" in DBpedia, we find that "Shiji" is the Chinese translation of "Siki" from DBpedia in step 3. By matching the language code "zh" and title "Shiji", we create the *record-set* "Shiji" from the bibliographic records. We can create a temporary *work* instance for "Shiji" as well. Then we create a *work* instance for "Siki" and "Shiji", which is a language neutral instance. Thus, we related the *work* "Siki" from bibliographic records of Japanese and Chinese items. If there is no record "Shiji" found in the bibliographic data, we create the instance of *work* for "Siki" and a one-to-one relationship between this *work* instance and the *record-set* "Siki".

The explanation above shows a case starting from Japanese bibliographic records and then link instances to those in difference languages. However, the model presented here allows starting from bibliographic records in any language.

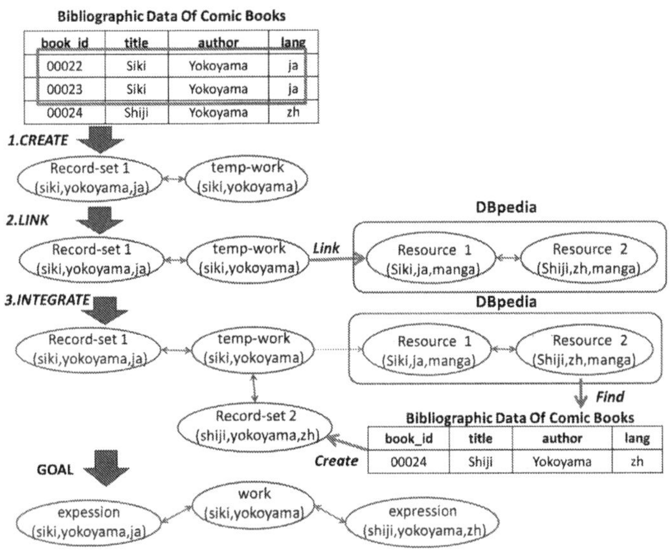

Figure 2. An example of procedure to identify manga *work*

4. EXPERIMENT

4.1 Sample Data Used for Experiment

We have applied the steps shown above to a set of bibliographic data extracted from the KMM OPAC database. 5000 bibliographic records in Japanese about monographs and corresponding translated records were used in the experiment. 1107 magazine titles and the authority control data relating to authors in Japanese extracted from the KMM database were also used.

The KMM bibliographic records are split into three groups – magazine, monograph and author records. The author information is recorded as structured authority data. It includes the pennames and notation variations for the names of each author, so that every author can be identified by an identifier in the KMM's database. Within magazine and monograph records, titles (and sub-titles) are recorded. This helps us identify the instances of *story*, *manga-title* and the relationship between them. The data about magazine volumes in KMM's records help us to identify the instances of *manga-compilation*. However, because there is no data showing the relationship between a manga and a magazine, we cannot create appropriate "is carried in" relationships. Furthermore, we cannot create appropriate "*is realized through*" relationships between *work* and *expression*, because there is no description showing the relationship between a single title and its translated titles.

Based on this observation, we found that DBpedia Japanese includes useful information to solve these problems. DBpedia Japanese has a property named "*dbpprop-ja:keisaishi*" which shows the relationship between a *work* and the magazine in which the *work* is published, and a property named "*dbpedia-owl:wikiPageInterLanguageLink*" which is used to link corresponding resources written in different languages. These properties are crucial for the identification of *work*s from KMM's bibliographic data. Thus, DBpedia Japanese is chosen as the LOD resource in our experiment.

4.2 Application of the Procedure

In step 1 of the identification procedure proposed in section 3.2, we normalized titles and sub-titles, and then combined them with author ID recorded in the authority data to create the identification keys. To group three kinds of *record-sets* (*manga-title, story* and *manga-compilation*) from KMM's record, 3 different identification keys are used. (See Table 1) After that, we created a temporary *work* instance for each *record-set*. The resulting datasets created throughout step 1 are stored in the RDF/XML format to create links with resources in DBpedia Japanese.

Table 1. Combination of identification keys

Record-set	identification key	Source Record
story	title + sub-title + author ID + language code "ja"	Monograph
manga-title	title + author ID + language code "ja"	Monograph
manga-compilation	title + publisher + language code "ja"	Magazine

In step 2, the temporary *work* instances are linked to a corresponding resource in DBpedia Japanese. In this study, links are created by matching title and type between the temporary *work* instances and the corresponding resources in DBpedia . Basing on the convention of URIs in Wikipedia, i.e., the encoding of title in a URI, we created a temporary DBpedia resource URI for each work instance from title, e.g., http://ja.dbpedia.org/resource/ONE_PIECE, and then ruled out temporary URIs not matching existing articles. DBpedia provided their resources with categories extracted from the Wikipedia. Manga resources in DBpedia are classified mostly in the "manga" category or its subcategories. According to this, we ruled out temporary URIs matching articles (resources) which are not about manga by judging whether the resources belong to these categories. *Work* instances are linked with the same resources in DBpedia Japanese by recording corrected URIs as the value of the property "rdfs:seeAlso".

In step 3 of the identification procedure, we refer to the information of the LOD resources linked throughout step 2. The "*is carried in*" relationships are created by referring "*dbpprop-ja:keisaishi*" directly as shown in Figure 3. The procedure to create the one-to-many *work-expression* relationships by using "*dbpedia-owl:wikiPageInterLanguageLink*" is similar to the example shown in the Section 3.2.

In this experiment, we identified 749 *work* instances and 3252 temporary *work* instances from 6107 KMM records. And also, we created both inter-layer and intra-layer relationships according to the model shown in Figure 1. 210 "*is part of*" relationships and 125 "*is carried in*" relationships are created as inter-layer relationships. For the inter-layer linking, we created 749 relationships between a *work and* its *expression*, all of which are one-to-one.

5. DISCUSSIONS

After having checked all of the result datasets manually, we came

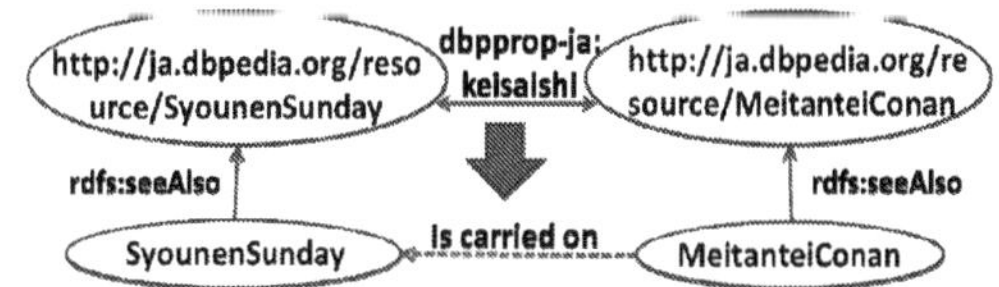

Figure 3. Creating a manga-title/manga-compilation relationship

to the conclusion that we can create the appropriate *work* instances and relationships from the bibliographic records using DBpedia. However, there are cases which failed in the identification process.

Within the 4001 record-sets grouped by step 1, we found 73 record-sets that were mismatched because of the notation variations of title in KMM's records. 2 record-sets were mismatched because of cataloging mistakes in the language code. These findings match Taniguchi's [3] conclusion that the quality of source records will influence the result. We created 3926 temporary work via this step.

In step 2, we linked 749 temporary *works* to their corresponding resources in DBpedia, while failing to create 3177 links. Table 2 shows the reasons for these failures. We found that 3095 cases (95.2%) were due to the fact that no similar resources existed in DBpedia. We were also concerned that there may be *works* linked to a wrong DBpedia resource at first, but we did not find any when we performed our manual check. There are 157 cases (4.8%) where the same resources existed in DBpedia but failed to link with *works*. These cases were caused by having different descriptions of the same manga resource in the KMM database and DBpedia. In this study, the combination of title and type is used as the mapping key to create links. We found that 131 *works* failed to link with the corresponding resources because of the difference in notation of titles between KMM and DBpedia. 26 links failed to be created because the corresponding resources in DBpedia were not under the category manga. We also tried using the combination of title and author as the mapping key to create links, however, only 210 links were created by using this method, because not every manga resource in DBpedia included the author information. We think the success rate of step 2 will be improved, if we use the redirect information in DBpedia to find the appropriate resources. However, use of the redirection information and a discussion of the reliability of redirect information in DBpedia are left as a future task.

Table 2. Reasons for failing to create links

Reasons		Amount	%
no same resources existed in DBpedia		3095	95.2
linking to a wrong DBpedia resource		0	0
different descriptions of the same resource	notation variations	131	4.8
	different categories	26	

In step 3, we found that not all of the 749 resources in DBpedia linked by step 2 contained the authority information we needed. There are 280 resources (37.4%) with the property "*dbpprop-ja:keisaishi*". All of the 749 DBpedia resources have the property "*dbpedia-owl:wikiPageInterLanguageLink*". However, we found none of the translation of the comics used in this experiment was included in the KMM database. In order to identify *work* instances independent of languages, we used bibliographic data available at Amazon, which covers a number of comic books currently available and commercially published in different languages. From the 749 DBpedia resources we obtained 272 English titles and 172 Chinese titles. Then, we manually checked if each of these titles represents an existing translation and found 83 English and 13 Chinese titles using the Amazon data. We found that there are variations of translations, notation differences between amazon and DBpedia. The difference of coverage between the KMM database and Amazon seems to be fundamental. Our important future work is to evaluate the proposed technology by a larger scale experiment using bibliographic data of manga collected from other institutions including non-Japanese libraries

Manga is a combination of graphic *expression* and textual *expression*. This study presents a procedure to create appropriate relationships between a manga *work* and its several language *expressions*. We have not yet created the relationships between a manga *work* and its graphic *expression*, because information about the graphic *expressions* in LOD resources is not straightforward enough to be used as the authority information.

This procedure is limited by the fact that the accuracy and efficiency depends on the quality of the LOD resources used. LOD resources are different from real authority data in its information, structure and resource quantity. So, we need to use the information from several LOD resources instead of only using DBpedia. And we also need to restructure this information into the authority dataset for identifying *work* from bibliographic data of manga.

6. CONCLUSIONS

This paper showed a procedure to identify *works* from a library catalog database for manga using DBpedia. Since, the authority data in the bibliographic data of comic books is not rich enough to identify manga *works*, DBpedia is used as a replacement for authority data. LOD resources like DBpedia include metadata that can be (semi-)automatically linked to bibliographic records, and these are useful to identify manga *works*. However, the accuracy and efficiency depends on the quality of the LOD resources that have been used. In future, we plan to develop a system to convert the LOD resources into authority datasets for manga.

7. ACKNOWLEDGEMENTS

The authors express our sincere thanks to Kyoto International Manga Museum for their support. We are grateful to Jan Askhoj and our colleagues involved in the manga research group for their help and contributions. This work is supported in part by JSPS Grants-in-aid for Scientific Research (#22240023, #25540153).

8. REFERENCES

[1] IFLA Study Group on the Functional Requirements for Bibliographic Records. 2009. Functional Requirements for Bibliographic Records F inal Report. http://www.ifla.org/files/assets/cataloguing/frbr/frbr_200 8.pdf

[2] Thomas B. Hickey, Jenny Toves. 2009. for OCLC Research FRBR *W ork*-Set Algorithm (Version 2.0) .http://www.oclc.org/content/dam/res earch/activities/frbralgorithm/2009-08.pdf

[3] Shoichi Taniguchi. 2009. Automatic identification of "*works*" toward construction of FRBRized OPACS: an experiment on JAPAN/MARC bibliographic records. Library and information science. 61. 119-151. (i n Japanese). http://lis.mslis.jp/pdf/LIS061119.pdf

[4] Ayako Morozumi, Satomi Nomura, Mitsuharu Nagamori, Shigeo Sug imoto.2009.Metadata Frame*work* for manga: A Multi-paradigm Metad ata Description Frame*work* for Digital Comics.http://dcpapers.dublinc ore.org/pubs/article/view/979/952

[5] DBpedia, http://dbpedia.org/

[6] Naimdjon Takhirov, Fabien Duchateau, Trond Aalberg. 2011.Linking FRBR Entities to LOD through Semantic Matching. Research and Ad vanced Technology for Digital Libraries Lecture Notes in Computer S cience. 6966. 284-295.http://liris.cnrs.fr/~fduchate/papers/duchateau-t pdl11-linking.pdf

[7] Fabien Duchateau, Naimdjon Takhirov,Trond Aalberg. 2011. FRBRP edia: a Tool for FRBRizing Web products and Linking FRBR Entities to DBpedia. In: Proc. of JCDL. http://dl.acm.org/citation.cfm?id=199 8183

Reading the Correct History? Modeling Temporal Intention in Resource Sharing

Hany M. SalahEldeen
Old Dominion University
Norfolk, VA, USA
hany@cs.odu.edu

Michael L. Nelson
Old Dominion University
Norfolk, VA, USA
mln@cs.odu.edu

ABSTRACT

The web is trapped in the "perpetual now", and when users traverse from page to page, they are seeing the state of the web resource (i.e., the page) as it exists at the time of the click and not necessarily at the time when the link was made. Thus, a temporal discrepancy can arise between the resource at the time the page author created a link to it and the time when a reader follows the link. This is especially important in the context of social media: the ease of sharing links in a tweet or Facebook post allows many people to author web content, but the space constraints combined with poor awareness by authors often prevents sufficient context from being generated to determine the intent of the post. If the links are clicked as soon as they are shared, the temporal distance between sharing and clicking is so small that there is little to no difference in content. However, not all clicks occur immediately, and a delay of days or even hours can result in reading something other than what the author intended. We introduce the concept of a user's temporal intention upon publishing a link in social media. We investigate the features that could be extracted from the post, the linked resource, and the patterns of social dissemination to model this user intention. Finally, we analyze the historical integrity of the shared resources in social media across time. In other words, how much is the knowledge of the author's intent beneficial in maintaining the consistency of the story being told through social posts and in enriching the archived content coverage and depth of vulnerable resources?

Categories and Subject Descriptors

H.3.5 [**Online Information Services**]: Data sharing

General Terms

Human Factors, Experimentation, Measurement

JCDL'13, July 22–26, 2013, Indianapolis, Indiana, USA.
Copyright 2013 ACM 978-1-4503-2077-1/13/07 ...$15.00.

Keywords

Social Media, Archiving, Temporal User Intention, Modeling, Memento

1. INTRODUCTION

The web is dynamic, and for most users, only the latest version of any particular resource is readily available. Although the web does not provide a direct mechanism for accessing prior states of a resource, these states can be accessed via web archives like the Internet Archive or in some cases (e.g., wikis) the web site software might implement a revision control system. However, the archival coverage is uneven and few people are aware of this archival existence. Thus, a temporal discrepancy can arise between the resource at the time the page's author created a link to it and the time when a reader follows that link. In other words, *did the author intend for you to see the web page as it existed when they shared it* (t_{tweet})*, or did they intend for you to see the version as it existed at the time the reader clicked on the link* (t_{click})*?*

If the period of time between the sharing and the clicking events is small, in most cases there will be no tangible difference. However, the more time that elapses between those two events, the greater the possibility of content change jeopardizing the consistency between the social post and the shared content.

If social media is supplanting journalism as the "first rough draft of history", then we cannot assume the time between sharing and clicking will be so small that the gap can be ignored. In preliminary research we have discovered after just one year, tweets about the Egyptian Revolution have lost (i.e., HTTP 404) approximately 11% of the resources they link to [32]. Furthermore, many of those that remained (i.e., HTTP 200) were no longer what the original author intended. If we consider such posts as part of the historical record (i.e., a library), then the pages that referenced in these posts are part of the historical record as well. If they are not preserved in the manner in which they were intended to be shared, then we are losing pieces of history. Many of the pieces needed to resolve this problem are in place: there is a growing infrastructure of web archives and the protocols to access them. Social media such as tweets provides uneditable creation dates to mark the sharing event, and often provides personalized, and unique URI aliases for the shared resource. All of these can be combined to create the proper context for determining the correct temporal intention.

2. PROBLEM DEFINITION

Every day, millions of pictures, videos, links, and tweets are shared between social media users all over the globe. Those social posts differ in purpose and expected audience. Some posts are made to convey mood, personal state or activity, opinion about a certain topic, humor, express anger, share useful information, or even pranking and spam. The author of a post is creating web content which may link to one or more other resources as well. These resources could be a web page, media file, another social post, or a document. While time passes, the content which the author created remains unchanged while the linked resources do not maintain the same stability as in most cases those resources are out of the author's control. In several cases, the shared resources go missing and we analyzed the percentages of missing shared resources as a function of time in earlier work [33]. However, in several other cases the linked resource is still on the live web but it has changed and no longer relevant to what the author intended to convey.

This change could be tolerated or have reduced effect if it was on an individual level. To elaborate, the effect of the change on a tweet depicting a family's cat is magnitudes lower than a change of a tweet showing a police officer pepper-spraying the faces of peaceful protesters (e.g., Occupy Wall Street). Losing the consistency of the former tweet affects only the individuals related to the family while losing the consistency of the latter more directly affects our cultural historical record.

To further explain the problem, let us examine the following scenario. On January the 14th, President Obama held his final news conference of his first term in the East Room of the White House. He discussed several issues among which was the third anniversary of the earthquake disaster in Haiti. On the same day, a user tweeted about it while watching the speech as shown in figure 1(a). Clicking on the link associated with the tweet, a page is rendered depicting a stream from the Mercedez-Benz superdome in New Orleans, Louisiana covering the Superbowl American football game of 2013 as shown in figure 1(b). This indicates a mismatch between the resource state at t_{tweet} and t_{click}. The text of the tweet makes it clear that the resource state at t_{click} was not the author's intention. Furthermore, using the new Twitter interface to expand the tweet and see the cached caption and embedded linked resource, we witness even a third mismatch. Figure 1(c) shows the cached caption pointing to a story about the attack on the American Embassy in Turkey on the 2nd of February 2013.

A possible solution would be to estimate the author's temporal intention (either the state of the resource at the time of the tweet t_{tweet} or the state of the resource at the time of reading) upon reading a tweet, and recommend to the user either an archived version of the resource at the closest time to the publishing timestamp, or the current version on the live web. Furthermore, we could preemptively push a copy of the resource at the time of the tweet into a web archive so that the intention is fully preserved.

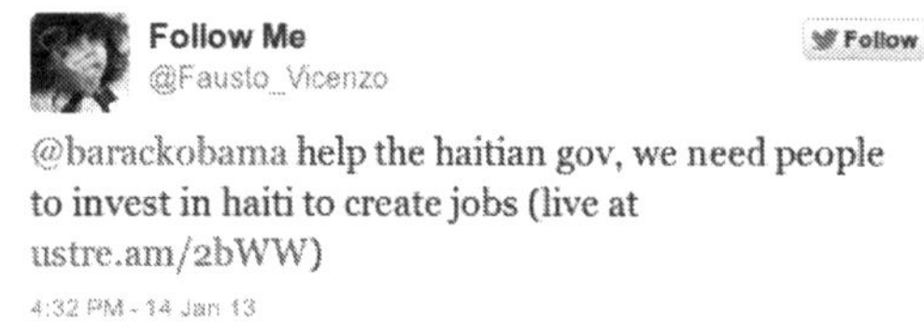

(a) A tweet depicting Obama's news conference and the topic of the Haitian Earthquake

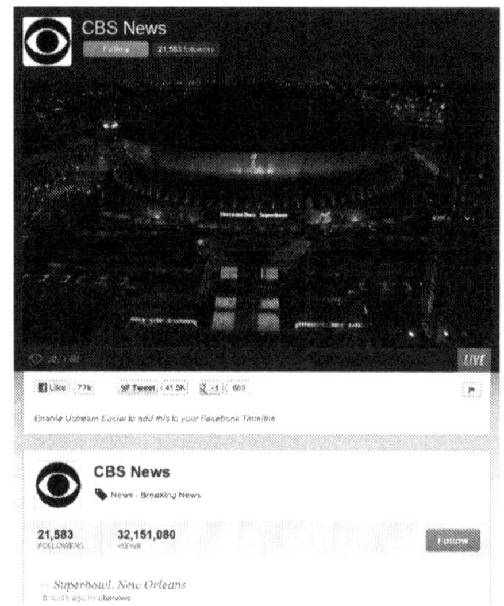

(b) The state of the embedded resource at the time of clicking depicting the 2013 Superbowl

(c) Using the twitter expanded interface showing a third state of the resource.

Figure 1: Different resource states at t_{tweet} and t_{click}.

3. RELATED WORK

Intention, mood, and sentiment have been analyzed in different contexts, but not with respect to time. Furthermore, this research builds on a large body of work involving detecting changes in web pages, archiving, and studying social media.

The web is ever-changing and what one might share or post today might change or disappear tomorrow. Losing web resources and finding them again has been the scope of several studies. For digital libraries, Nelson and Allen analyzed the persistence and availability of objects in a digital library [29]. From the aspect of web decay Bar-Yossef et al. [3] proposed a measure of decay and algorithms to compute it efficiently. Consequently, Klein and Nelson analyzed the loss and rediscovery of websites to pinpoint the reasons behind this behavior [20].

The problem of disappearing or changing resources has been well-studied. The changing aboutness of live web pages has been studied in the Walden's Path project [11] and the link vetting system [10]. For link rot, Kahle originally reported the expected lifetime of a web page is 44 days [17]. Loss of references and URIs appearing in the academic literature have been studied numerous times, with exact loss rates varying depending on the corpus [34]. In our "Just-in-time" preservation research we discovered new locations of web pages that are missing in the current web [19]. We investigated a variety of techniques, including using page titles [22], tags [21], and lexical signatures [23], all of which could be used as queries to search engines to find replacement copies of the missing web page.

Computing the change rates of web resources is a well-studied phenomena. Cho and garcia-Molina studied the change rate of web pages to determine the best policies for web crawlers [9], as well as studying how to handle late arrivers in a collection [31]. Other studies have been done about understanding the web content dynamics [1] and upon which to develop the crawl policies for enhancing archival coverage [4].

Due to the tremendous growth of the social media [13, 37] and the continuous expansion and addition of new social network-based applications on the web [30], a significant body of research has been created specifically to analyze social media networks from different angles. For example, the use of URI shorteners, especially with respect to their use in social media, was studied in [2]. There has been significant progress recently in sentiment analysis and gauges for public and individual mood, especially using Twitter feeds and blog content. Twitter, specifically, has been analyzed for collective sentiment thoroughly where mood transition observed in Twitter [28] has been utilized in politics [5], stock market [6] and others. Intention analysis and detection in web science have several flavors and can be found in different contexts. It was analyzed as an independent concept [16], in data mining [8], in query intent analysis [14], in user click models for search [26], in search result diversification [35], in cluster analysis [18], in spam and phishing attacks detection [39], and in microblogging [15]. To our knowledge, there is no published research describing temporal intention in the context of web navigation and social media dissemination.

In regards to data collection, we are in need of a large data set that captures human temporal intention. To collect this, prior and during the phases of experimental design, we examined several publications depicting crowd sourcing [36] and most specifically Amazon's Mechanical Turk [12] which has been used in generating ground truth data for a similar-scoped study in detecting music moods [25].

As for the archiving aspect of our study, the existence of Memento, TimeMaps, and multi-archive aggregators has greatly facilitated research with archives. The motivation for the Memento Framework [38] is achieving a tighter integration between the current web and remnants of the web of the past. Archival versions (or mementos) of web resources do exist, both in special-purpose web archives such as the Internet Archive and the on-demand WebCite archive, or in version-aware servers such as content management systems (CMS, e.g. Wikipedia) and version control systems.

4. CROWD SOURCING USER INTENTION

To have a better understanding of a user's temporal intention, we performed several experiments on Amazon's Mechanical Turk. Subsequently, we discovered that classifying temporal intention is difficult for Mechanical Turk workers. This, in turn, has influenced us to seek a transformation of the problem to another domain while maintaining the semantic consistency as shown in the next sections.

4.1 Preliminary Work

Initially, we attempted using Mechanical Turk directly in classifying intention. Our first set of experiments involved sampling 1000 tweets from the Stanford Network Analysis Project (SNAP[1]) Twitter data set. The first step was to prove that Mechanical Turk could be used in representing manually assigned classes of intention made by experts in the field. The classes targeted were as follows: did the author of the tweet intended the "Current State" of the resource for the reader at any time or the "Past State" of the resource at the time of the tweet? Or there not enough information?

To achieve this, from the set of 1000 tweets we constructed the ground truth responses for 100 tweets forming the gold standard dataset. The collection of the gold standard dataset was performed by polling via email the members of our Web Science and Digital Libraries (WSDL) research group and asking them to classify the intention of the intention of the author of a tweet as either the current version (t_{click}), the archived version (past) (t_{tweet}), or unknown by looking at the tweet. The reliability of agreement within our group of 12, all of whom are aware of web archiving, was surprisingly low (Fleiss' $\kappa = 0.14$). We ran the experiments in Mechanical Turk, acquiring five evaluations for each of the same 100 tweets from the gold standard dataset. Similarly, the inter rater between the Mechanical Turk workers was even lower (Fleiss' $\kappa = 0.07$).

$$Vote_{MT}(tweet) = \begin{cases} \text{Current}, & \text{if } \frac{\Sigma Vote_{current}}{N_{turkers}} > k \\ \text{Past}, & \text{otherwise} \end{cases} \quad (1)$$

The threshold k in equation 1 defines the vote cut off. In this case, $k = 0.5$ as we applied a simple majority vote in deciding the collective vote of the Mechanical Turk workers (i.e., whichever classification received three out of five voters), and similarly within the 12 WS-DL members. Treating each group as a single entity, the aggregated votes from each of the two datasets were used to calculate the inter rater agreement resulting in Cohen's $\kappa = 0.04$, indicating slight agreement. This slight agreement was yet not sufficient to proceed with our study. Examining the selection from the SNAP data set, we decided that too many of the tweets had vague contexts and were hard to classify.

Given the unclear contexts that were present in the first sample set, we then tried a richer set from which to sample. We used the tweets from the six historical events described in [33]. For 100 tweets, we built a web page with an image snap shot of the current version of the page, and a version of

[1] `http://snap.stanford.edu/`

		Tweet and resource are:	
		relevant	not relevant
Linked resource has:	changed	t_{click}	t_{tweet}
	not changed	t_{tweet}	either or undefined

Table 1: Temporal Intention Relevancy Model.

the page closest to t_{tweet} that could be found in a public web archive. We held a face to face meeting with our WSDL research group to determine the ground truth: for each tweet we went around the table and argued for whichever version we thought matched the author's temporal intent. We knew this data set would be biased toward t_{tweet} because most of the tweets described historic, cultural events from 2009-2011. After deliberation, we arrived at: 82% past, 9% current, and 9% undecided as our gold standard for this data set. When we submitted the jobs to Mechanical Turk, we defined levels of three, five, seven, and nine evaluations for each tweet. In the case where we had nine evaluations for each tweet, the Mechanical Turk workers would match our gold standard 58% of the time if we allowed 5-4 splits. If we were more discerning and counted agreement only in cases where workers agreed 6-3 or better, then the agreement with Mechanical Turk workers fell to 31% (and similarly for rating levels three, five, and seven).

In short, if we required clear agreement on the part of Mechanical Turk workers, then we did much worse than simply flipping a coin – in a data set with a clear bias toward t_{tweet} because of the focus on past events. It was at this point we decided our approach in guessing the author's temporal intent was simply too complicated for Mechanical Turk workers.

4.2 Temporal Intention Relevancy Model

To reach our goal of modeling users' temporal intentions, we need to collect a large dataset which is not, as discussed in the previous section, a trivial task. The difficulty in acquiring the data resides in generating the ground truth or gold standard for the temporal intention of the user who authored the original social media post. Initially, our intention was to generate a small set of gold standard data (e.g., links classified as representing the user's intention to be either "the resource at t_{tweet}" or "the resource at t_{click}"). We eventually decided that the notion of "temporal intention" was too nuanced to be adequately conveyed in the instructions for the workers of Mechanical Turk. Learning from our previous unsuccessful attempts, we chose to cast the problem of "temporal intention" to one of relevancy between the tweet and the resource as it exists now.

Table 1 presents the Temporal Intention Relevancy Model (TIRM) that we will use to inform our interaction with the workers at Mechanical Turk. To resonate with one of the common types of experiments in it, we designed our new experiment as a categorization of relevance problem which the workers are familiar with. In each Human Intelligence Task or HIT, the worker is presented with the full tweet, its publishing date, and in an embedded window, a snapshot of the page that the tweet links to in its current state. Instead of asking workers about temporal intention of the original author, and possibly confusing it with the temporal intention of them as a reader, we asked a simpler question "is this page still relevant to this tweet?". There is considerable precedence in the Mechanical Turk community for making relevance judgements as categorization problems are commonly available as HITs.

To explain this mapping from intention space to relevancy space, let us assume we have a resource R which has been tweeted by some author at time t_{tweet}. The state of the resource at t_{tweet} is R_{tweet}. Consequently, another user clicked on the resource to read it at a later time t_{click}. The state of the resource at t_{click} is R_{click}. The rationale for the model is:

Changed & Relevant: If the resource has changed (i.e., R_{tweet} is not similar to R_{click}) and it is still relevant to the tweet, then there is a strong indication that the temporal intention of the author must have been the resource as it exists at t_{click} (R_{click}). Figure 2(a) shows an author tweeting about the latest updates for a newsletter. The linked resource in the tweet continually changes while the tweet is always relevant to it. This indicates that the author's temporal intention is a *current* one.

Changed & Non-Relevant: If the resource has changed and it is not relevant to the tweet, we assume initial relevance and thus the original author must have meant to share the resource in the state as it existed at t_{tweet} which is R_{tweet} not R_{click}. Figure 2(b) shows an author tweeting about specific breaking news on CNN.com's first page, which by definition changes frequently. This indicates that the author's temporal intention to be the *past* version.

Not Changed & Relevant: If the resource has not changed and it is still relevant to the tweet, then we claim that the intention of the author was to share the resource as it existed at t_{tweet} (R_{tweet}), but it is just a fortunate coincidence that the resource has not changed and is thus still relevant. Figure 2(c) shows an author tweeting about an article which still exists. Surely, there is a possibility that the resource could change in the future and become non-relevant. This indicates that the author's intention was a *past* one.

Not Changed & Non-Relevant: If the resource has not changed and it is not relevant to the tweet, then we can not be sure of the intention and either t_{click} or t_{tweet} will suffice. This scenario can occur in spam, mistaken link sharing, or more likely that relevancy relies on out-of-band communication between the original author and the intended readers[2].

4.3 Gold Standard Dataset

After laying the basis of the intention-relevance mapping in TIRM, we must collect a large body of data to be utilized in the modeling and analysis phases. Since we are modeling human intention and mapping it to relevance judging, we will utilize Amazon's Mechanical Turk in collecting

[2]The Internet meme of "Rickrolling" http://en.wikipedia.org/wiki/Rickrolling is a humorous example of purposeful non-relevancy between the context of the link and the link which is to the 1987 pop song by Rick Astley; the point is to "trick" users into expecting one thing and the link delivers the song.

(a) Changed and Relevant

(b) Changed and no longer Relevant

(c) Not changed and Relevant

(d) Not Changed and not Relevant

Figure 2: Examples of the relevancy mapping of TIRM.

the training data. However, prior to collecting the training dataset we need to be confident in the ability of our data collection experiment in representing the real-life educated judgement. To achieve this goal we created a gold standard dataset by obtaining a small dataset and assigning it to members of our research group, whom we have confidence in their ability to perform the task accurately, and then assign the same dataset to workers in Mechanical Turk. We collect both sets of assignments and compare their similarity to ensure the ability of the workers to mimic the judgment of the experts. Mechanical Turk HITs are considerably cheaper, easier to manage, and faster to conclude than the expert assignments.

Engineering a relevance HIT for Mechanical Turk's workers was fairly straightforward. For the gold standard dataset we randomly picked 100 tweets from the SNAP dataset dating back to June 2009 and posted them to be classified as "still relevant" or "no longer relevant". As mentioned earlier, for each HIT we posted the tweet, the date, and a snapshot of the resource at t_{click} (R_{click}). The experiment requested five unique raters with high qualifications (more than 1000 accepted HITs and more than 95% acceptance rate). Each HIT cost two cents and a maximum time span of 20 minutes. The experiment was completed within the first hours from posting and the average completion time per hit was 61 seconds. We examined the data from the workers and dismissed all the HITs that took less than 10 seconds indicating a hastly decision. We also filtered out workers who exhibited low quality repetitive assignments and banned them. For the same 100 tweets, we invited our research group again to perform this same experiment of relevance. Their assignments have been collected along with the ones from the workers. The results are shown in table 2 showing an almost perfect agreement with Cohen's $\kappa = 0.854$.

Given this substantial agreement between the gold standard and the workers, we can claim that Mechanical Turk can be used in estimating the content's time relevance and in turn to gauge the author's temporal intention after utilizing TIRM. The next step is to expand our dataset and

Agreement in three or more votes	93%
Agreement in four or more votes	80%
Agreement with all five votes	60%

Table 2: Agreement between the research group and Mechanical Turk workers for 100 tweets.

collect a larger dataset, for training and testing, to utilize it in the modeling process.

From the SNAP dataset of tweets we extracted a large number of tweets starting from June of 2009 at random. For a social media post, in this case a tweet, we want to acquire as much data as possible about its existence such as content, age, dissemination, and size. Initially, we targeted the tweets which pass through these filters:

- Tweets in the English language.
- Each has an embedded URI pointing to an external resource.
- The embedded URI has been shortened using Bitly (bit.ly).
- The embedded URIs point to unique resources.

We chose the tweets which have links as the scope of the study is focused on detecting intention in sharing resources in social media. Also the shared resource provides extended context of the tweet making the social post more comprehensible. The reason behind choosing bitly shortened URIs is that their API provides invaluable information about the clicklog patterns, creation dates, rates of dissemination, and other information as will be described in the next section. Also bitly was fairly popular on Twitter at the time of the dataset collection (2009). To ensure our ability to collect information related to the embedded resource, we applied an extra filter ensuring that the linked resource is currently available on the live web (HTTP response 200 OK), at the time of the analysis, and that it is properly archived in the public archives with at least 10 mementos. Consequently, we extracted 5,937 unique instances to be utilized in the next stages.

To create the dataset that will be processed by Mechanical

5 Turkers Agreeing (5-0 cuts)	589	52.40%
4 Turkers Agreeing (4-1 cuts)	309	27.49%
3 Turkers Agreeing (3-2 close call cuts)	226	20.11%
Relevant Assignments	929	82.65%
Non-Relevant Assignments	195	17.35%

Table 3: The distribution of voting outcomes from turkers for the 1,124 assignments.

Turk workers, we selected 1,124 instances randomly from the previous dataset. This training dataset will be assigned to the workers in the same manner to the gold standard experiment. To have an insight of what the author was experiencing and reading upon the time of tweeting, we extracted the closest snapshot of the resource, to the time of the tweet, using the Memento framework. For each URI, the closest memento recorded ranged from 3.07 minutes to 56.04 hours from the time of the tweet, averaging 25.79 hours. Figure 3 shows the difference in hours between t_{tweet} and the closest memento in the public archives denoted by $R_{closestMemento}$. For the sake of simplicity we will consider the following approximation:

$$R_{closestMemento} \approx R_{tweet} \quad (2)$$

This shows that on average we can extract a snapshot of the

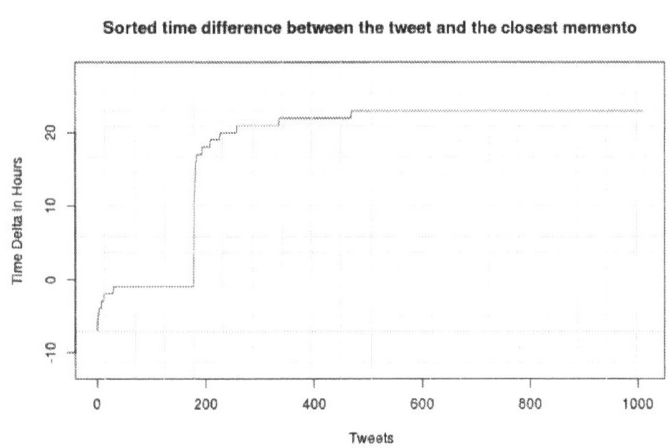

Figure 3: Sorted Time delta between tweeting time and the closest memento snapshot where the negative Y axis denotes existence prior to t_{tweet}.

state of the resource within a day from when the author saw it and tweeted about it. This time delta is in fact relative to the nature of the resource. In the case of continuously changing webpages such as CNN.com, one day will not capture everything. However, on the average, web pages are not expected to change as much within this time period.

Along with the downloaded closest memento snapshot $R_{closestMemento}$, we downloaded a snapshot of the current state of the resource $R_{current}$. For the sake of simplicity as well, we consider another approximation:

$$R_{current} \approx R_{click} \quad (3)$$

The agreement between Mechanical Turk workers in assigning relevancy to our training dataset of 1,124 tweets is shown in table 3.

5. INTENTION MODELING

In the previous section we collected the gold standard dataset using Mechanical Turk and tested its validity against expert opinions. Consequently, we were able to collect a larger dataset of tweets which have been deemed Relevant or Non-Relevant by Mechanical Turk workers as well. The dataset collected and classified contains tweets which have embedded shortened URIs or bitlys linking to a shared web resource. Each one of the resources is currently live and adequately covered in the public web archives at the time of this study (December 2012).

5.1 Feature Extraction

To complement the training dataset we collected in the previous section from Mechanical Turk we explore the different angles of sharing resources in social media beyond the tweet.

5.1.1 Link Analysis

As mentioned earlier, most of the tweets containing resources published in 2009 include a shortened URI. One of the reasons behind this use of shortners is due to the space constraints of a tweet (140 characters). We extracted the tweets containing URIs shortened by bitly shortner due to their abundance in the SNAP dataset tweet collection. Out of the 476 million tweets in the dataset, 87 million contain bitly shortened URIs. The bitly API provide several parameters that could be extracted as well. The total number of clicks, hourly clicklogs, creation dates, referring websites, referring countries, and other information could also be acquired.

The location of the resource in the domain is important. Surface web pages, as the main page or index, are different in nature from the deep web ones. Relying on the general notion that pages in the deep web are less likely to change as often as the root page, we need to calculate the estimated depth of the resource. Within each tweet, we expanded the resource's bitly to the original long URI and analyzed for hierarchy and depth in the web by counting the number of backslashes in the URI which correlates with the depth fairly well. Also we compare the lengths of the shortened URI and the original one to calculate the reduction rate. Hand in hand with these extracted data points, we proceed to examine the dissemination trends of that resource.

5.1.2 Social Media Mining

For each embedded resource in a tweet, we used Topsy.com's API[3] to extract the total number of tweets that have been recorded linking to this resource. We extract the number of tweets from influential users in the Twitter-sphere as well. Finally, we downloaded the other tweets posted by different users linking to the same resource. The API permits us to extract a maximum of 500 tweets per resource. This collection of tweets surrounding each resource can benefit us in many aspects: providing extended tweet-context for the resource, showing us the social media dissemination pattern by plotting the tweet timestamps against the timeline, and finally, to let us examine how many of those tweets still exist and how many have been deleted.

To complete the picture, Facebook was mined as well for

[3]http://code.google.com/p/otterapi/

each of the resources in the tweets to extract the total number of shares, posts, likes, and clicks.

5.1.3 Archival Existence

To investigate archival existence and coverage, we calculate how many total mementos, in the aggregated public archives, are available for the resource. We record as well how many archives hold at least a copy of the resource. As mentioned earlier, figure 3 shows the distribution of the delta time between closest archived memento and the tweet creation timestamp. Negative values on the Y-axis denote existence prior to t_{tweet}.

5.1.4 Sentiment Analysis

To go beyond the tweet text, we utilized the NLTK libraries [27] for natural language text processing to extract the most prominent sentiment in the text. For each tweet we extracted the positive, negative and neutral sentiment probabilities. These three probabilities give us an insight on the emotional state of the author at t_{tweet}.

5.1.5 Content Similarity

Finally, to measure the difference between the different snapshots of the resource downloaded earlier, we implemented similarity analysis functions. We transformed each of the resource's R_{tweet} and R_{click} to textual vectors and then calculated the cosine similarity between them. Furthermore, the collected tweets from Topsy.com's API associated to each resource have been accumulated in one document giving it a social context. This tweet document has been compared in similarity as well with R_{tweet} and R_{click} snapshots of the resource and the percentages were recorded. It is worth mentioning that to extract those similarities we downloaded the snapshots using the Lynx browser[4]. We used the *source* option which downloads the HTML. Subsequently, on the downloaded content, we used the boilerplate removal from HTML pages and full text extraction algorithms by Kohlschutter et al. [24]. Finally, we calculated the cosine similarity between the each of the pairs of documents.

5.1.6 Entity Identification

Analyzing hundreds of tweets from Twitter timeline we noticed some interesting points. Celebrities are mentioned in abundance and have the largest number of followers. In fan tweets, most celebrities are mentioned by their first and last name unless they are known by only one, and finally most tweets about celebrities are in reaction or as a description to contemporaneous events related to the celebrity. In the field of TV, cinema, performance arts, sports, and politics, millions of tweets are posted daily about celebrities as a huge demographic of users use twitter as a form of news feed. Given so, we wanted to analyze the effect of detecting celebrity-related tweets to intention and the possibility of using it as a feature. Wikipedia has published several lists of US, British, and Canadian actors, and singers. Also several lists of sports players and politicians in the English speaking world. We harvested those lists, parsed and indexed them. Finally, given an embedded resource and upon retrieving its tweet flock from Topsy.com's API we test for the existence of celebrity entities in the collective tweets and record celebrity-relevance feature as true.

[4]http://lynx.browser.org/

5.2 Modeling and Classification

In the features extraction phase we gathered several data points denoting context, dissemination, nature, archiving coverage, change, sentiment, and others. In this phase, we investigate which features have higher weights indicating importance in modeling and classifying temporal intention. We also investigate the several well known classifiers and their corresponding success rates.

In the first attempts to train the classifier and analyze the confusion matrix we noticed the instances which were classified by Mechanical Turk workers as close calls (3-2 split) highly populated the false positive/negative cells of the confusion matrix. These instances indicate a weak classification where one vote can deem the instance relevant or non-relevant. Thus, to reduce the confusion, we eliminated the training instances where this uncertainty of the workers reside. From the 1,124 instances, we kept 898 where the agreement on relevancy was 4 to 1, or 5 total agreement as shown in table 4. Thus, the cutoff threshold in equation 1 is increased $k >= 0.8$.

Relevant Assignments	807	89.87%
Non Relevant Assignments	91	10.13%

Table 4: The distribution of voting outcomes from turkers after removing close-calls.

Utilizing the sum of all the extracted features, we ran Weka's[5] different classifiers against the dataset. Subsequently, we train the model and test it using 10-fold cross validation. Table 5 and 6 show the corresponding precisions, recalls and F-measures of the Cost Sensitive classifier based on Random Forest, which outperformed the other classifiers yielding an 90.32% success in classification for our trained model.

The classifier processed 39 different features for each instance in the training dataset. The features were collected in the feature extraction phase explained earlier in section 5.1. Following the training phase we needed to understand the effect of each feature in the process of modeling intention. This knowledge will help us in reducing the number of required features, by the model, to estimate the intention behind a given social post. We applied an attribute evaluator supervised algorithm based on Ranker search method to rank the attributes or features accordingly. Analyzing the ranks, table 7 shows the strongest six features and the order of significance in ranking the features used in classifying user temporal intention along with each's information gain.

It is also worth mentioning that using the boilerplate removal algorithm along with cosine similarity gave more significance features than HTML similarity with SimHash [7].

5.3 Evaluation

The previous section indicates that modeling user intention via TIRM and using numerical, textual, and semantic features in a classifier is both feasible and accurate. In this section, we test the trained model against other tweet datasets.

[5]http://www.cs.waikato.ac.nz/ml/weka/

10-Fold Cross-Validation Testing					
Classifier	**Mean Absolute Error**	**Root Mean Squared Error**	**Kappa Statistic**	**Incorrectly Classified %**	**Correctly Classified %**
Cost Sensitive classifier based on Random Forest	0.15	0.27	0.39	9.68%	**90.32%**

Table 5: Results of 10-fold cross-validation against the best classifier along with the Precision, Recall and F-measure per class

Classifier	Precision	Recall	F-measure	Class
Cost Sensitive classifier	0.93	0.96	0.95	Relevant
based on Random Forest	0.53	0.37	0.44	Non-Relevant
Weighted Average	0.89	0.90	0.90	

Table 6: Precision, Recall and F-measure per class

Rank	Feature	Gain Ratio
1	Existence of celebrities in Tweets	0.149
2	Number of Mementos	0.090
3	Tweet similarity with current page	0.071
4	Similarity: Current & Past page	0.0527
5	Similarity: Tweet and Past page	0.04401
6	Original URI's depth	0.0324

Table 7: Classifier features ordered by significance resulting from Rank Search algorithm

5.3.1 *Extended Dataset*

In section 4.3 we extracted a dataset of 5,937 instances from which we extracted our training 1,124 instances training dataset. The remaining 4,813 instances formed a new testing dataset. For each instance in this dataset we extracted all the features analyzed in section 5.1. Finally, this dataset was evaluated by the trained model to test the performance and usability yielding the results in table 8.

5.3.2 *Historical Integrity of Tweet Collections*

As described in section 2, one of the main motives of our analysis of human intention is to maintain the historical integrity of social posts collections. Specifically in social posts related to historic events, preserving the consistency between the tweet and the linked resource is crucial. The link between the post and the resource is vulnerable to two kinds of threats: the loss of content itself (either the post or the linked resource) or the mismatch between the author's intention and what the reader is receiving (the resource is no longer intended by the author). In our prior work, we analyzed six datasets related to six different historic events and we evaluated how many of these resources are missing and how many are archived [33]. In this section, we utilize our trained model in predicting the temporal intention and in turn, in estimating the amount of mismatched resources where the reader is probably not reading the first draft of history intended by the tweet's author.

Due to the nature of the collections, we limit our analysis to the resources in the form of tweets. In this case, we use the tweet datasets from the 2009-2012 events related to: Michael Jackson's Death, H1N1 virus outbreak, Iranian Elections, President Obama's Nobel peace prize, and the Syrian uprising. Similarly to the extended testing dataset in section 5.3.1, we extract all the necessary features for each instance in the dataset. We test our model with the five datasets and report the results in table 8 as well. For each dataset we test the response headers once more to assess the percentage missing and alive, which we present in the same table. It is worth mentioning that when we started the experiments in September of 2012, the instances of the 3124 extended dataset were extracted to return a 200 OK response, but when we re-tested their existence 4 months later we noticed a loss of 3.23% confirming the results from our previous work.

5.3.3 *Evaluating TIRM*

After examining the relevancy of the datasets using our developed relevancy classifier, we now use our TIRM mapping scheme in transforming the results into the intention space. The classifier was trained to be conservative in handling the Non-Relevant categorization. Meaning, in classifying Non-Relevancy false negatives are more tolerated than false positives (i.e., the classifier only states a resource is non-relevant only if it was highly confident of this estimation). Another point worth mentioning is that for our training we used the resources that are currently available on the live web; and 404 resources were not included. Table 9 show the percentages in each of the six datasets per each class of the TIRM model after mapping relevancy to the similarity threshold of 70%. Taking the dataset of Michael Jackson's death for example, even though the resource is still accessible nearly 3% of the dataset is no longer reflecting the author's intention. It is worth noting that the results in the first quadrant of table 9 are over reported. Due to the sparsity of the archives, this over reporting is essential to avoid false negatives. As described in figure 3, the average time delta between sharing and the closest archived version is fairly large (26 hours), in some cases the resource will keep on changing then stops after a couple of hours and stay static. Tightening the bounds in the same figure by more frequent archiving will lead to a large improvement in our model.

6. CONCLUSIONS

In this work we investigate the problem of the temporal inconsistency in social media and how it is related to the author's intention. This intention proved to be non-trivial to capture and gauge. Our Temporal Intention Relevancy Model successfully translated the problem of user intention to a less complicated problem of relevancy. We used Me-

Dataset	Status 200	Status 404 or Other	Relevant %	Non-Relevant %
Extended 4,813 instances	96.77%	3.23%	96.74%	3.26%
MJ's Death	57.54%	42.46%	93.24%	6.76%
H1N1 Outbreak	8.96%	91.04%	97.48%	2.52%
Iran Elections	68.21%	31.79%	94.69%	5.31%
Obama's Nobel	62.86%	37.14%	93.89%	6.11%
Syrian Uprising	80.80%	19.20%	70.26%	29.75%

Table 8: Results of testing the extended dataset & the historic datasets in classifying relevancy along with the live percentage, and percentage missing of the resources.

	Relevant	Not Relevant
Changed	MJ:41%	MJ:3%
	Obama:42%	Obama:2%
	Syria:44%	Syria:25%
	Iran:49%	Iran:2%
	H1N1:6%	H1N1:0%
	Extended: 53%	Extended:2%
Not Changed	MJ:52%	MJ:4%
	Obama:51%	Obama:5%
	Syria:26%	Syria:5%
	Iran:46%	Iran:3%
	H1N1:91%	H1N1:3%
	Extended: 43%	Extended:2%

Table 9: TIRM Results

chanical Turk to collect a gold standard data of user temporal intention and we verified the results by comparing the Turkers' assignments to ones conducted by experts in the field and produced a near perfect agreement. After proving the validity of using Mechanical Turk in data gathering, we proceeded in collecting a dataset that was used in training the classifier. We extracted several numerical, textual, and semantic features and incorporated them in the training dataset. The trained model is then evaluated against an extended larger dataset and the datasets from our previous work regarding social posts from different five historical events in the period from 2009-2012. For the shared resources, we found temporal inconsistency to range from <1% to 25% depending on the dataset.

For our future work, we will expand the model further more by generalizing the resources and tweets utilized in the training process, and not just the currently available and well archived resources. Also, we will increase the size of the training dataset and investigate the effect of each of the features and the gain resulting from combining different permutations of them.

7. ACKNOWLEDGMENT

This work was supported in part by the Library of Congress and NSF IIS-1009392.

8. REFERENCES

[1] E. Adar, J. Teevan, S. T. Dumais, and J. L. Elsas. The web changes everything: understanding the dynamics of web content. In *WSDM '09: Proceedings of the Second ACM International Conference on Web Search and Data Mining*, pages 282–291, 2009.

[2] D. Antoniades, I. Polakis, G. Kontaxis, E. Athanasopoulos, S. Ioannidis, E. Markatos, and T. Karagiannis. we. b: The web of short urls. In *Proceedings of the 20th international conference on World Wide Web*, pages 715–724, 2011.

[3] Z. Bar-Yossef, A. Z. Broder, R. Kumar, and A. Tomkins. Sic transit gloria telae: towards an understanding of the web's decay. In *Proceedings of the 13th international conference on World Wide Web*, WWW '04, pages 328–337, New York, NY, USA, 2004. ACM.

[4] M. Ben Saad and S. Gançarski. Archiving the Web using Page Changes Pattern: A Case Study. In *JCDL '11: Proceedings of ACM/IEEE Joint Conference on Digital Libraries*, Ottawa, Canada, 2011.

[5] A. Bermingham and A. F. Smeaton. On using twitter to monitor political sentiment and predict election results.

[6] J. Bollen, H. Mao, and X.-J. Zeng. Twitter mood predicts the stock market. abs/1010.3003, 2010.

[7] M. S. Charikar. Similarity estimation techniques from rounding algorithms. In *Proceedings of the thiry-fourth annual ACM symposium on Theory of computing*, STOC '02, pages 380–388, New York, NY, USA, 2002. ACM.

[8] Z. Chen, F. Lin, H. Liu, Y. Liu, W.-Y. Ma, and L. Wenyin. User intention modeling in web applications using data mining. *World Wide Web*, 5(3):181–191, Nov. 2002.

[9] J. Cho and H. Garcia-Molina. Estimating frequency of change. *ACM Transactions on Internet Technology*, 3(3):256–290, 2003.

[10] N. Dai and B. D. Davison. Vetting the links of the web. In *Proceedings of the 18th ACM conference on Information and knowledge management*, CIKM '09, pages 1745–1748, New York, NY, USA, 2009. ACM.

[11] Z. Dalal, S. Dash, P. Dave, L. Francisco-Revilla, R. Furuta, U. Karadkar, and F. Shipman. Managing distributed collections: evaluating web page changes, movement, and replacement. In *JCDL '04: Proceedings of the 4th ACM/IEEE-CS Joint Conference on Digital Libraries*, pages 160–168, 2004.

[12] J. L. Elsas and S. T. Dumais. Leveraging temporal dynamics of document content in relevance ranking. In *Proceedings of the third ACM international conference on Web search and data mining*, WSDM '10, pages 1–10, New York, NY, USA, 2010. ACM.

[13] Facebook.com. Facebook official fact sheet. `http://newsroom.fb.com/content/default.aspx?NewsAreaId=22`, 2012. [Online; accessed 17-December-2012].

[14] B. J. Jansen, D. L. Booth, and A. Spink. Determining the user intent of web search engine queries. In *Proceedings of the 16th international conference on*

World Wide Web, WWW '07, pages 1149–1150, New York, NY, USA, 2007. ACM.

[15] A. Java, X. Song, T. Finin, and B. Tseng. Why we twitter: understanding microblogging usage and communities. In *Proceedings of the 9th WebKDD and 1st SNA-KDD 2007 workshop on Web mining and social network analysis*, WebKDD/SNA-KDD '07, pages 56–65, New York, NY, USA, 2007. ACM.

[16] V. Jethava, L. Calderón-Benavides, R. Baeza-Yates, C. Bhattacharyya, and D. Dubhashi. Scalable multi-dimensional user intent identification using tree structured distributions. In *Proceedings of the 34th international ACM SIGIR conference on Research and development in Information Retrieval*, SIGIR '11, pages 395–404, New York, NY, USA, 2011. ACM.

[17] B. Kahle. Preserving the Internet. *Scientific American*, 276(3):82–83, March 1997.

[18] A. Kathuria, B. J. Jansen, C. Hafernik, and A. Spink. Classifying the user intent of web queries using k-means clustering. *Internet Research*, 20(5):563–581, 2010.

[19] M. Klein. *Using the Web Infrastructure for Real Time Recovery of Missing Web Pages*. PhD thesis, Old Dominion University Department of Computer Science, 2011.

[20] M. Klein and M. L. Nelson. Revisiting lexical signatures to (re-)discover web pages. In *Proceedings of the 12th European conference on Research and Advanced Technology for Digital Libraries*, ECDL '08, pages 371–382, Berlin, Heidelberg, 2008. Springer-Verlag.

[21] M. Klein and M. L. Nelson. Find, new, copy, web, page - tagging for the (re-)discovery of web pages. In *Proceedings of TPDL*, pages 27–39, 2011.

[22] M. Klein, J. L. Shipman, and M. L. Nelson. Is This a Good Title? In *HT '10: Proceedings of the 21st ACM Conference on Hypertext and Hypermedia*, pages 3–12, 2010.

[23] M. Klein, J. Ware, and M. L. Nelson. Rediscovering missing web pages using link neighborhood lexical signatures. In *Proceedings of the 11th annual international ACM/IEEE joint conference on Digital libraries*, JCDL '11, pages 137–140, New York, NY, USA, 2011. ACM.

[24] C. Kohlschütter, P. Fankhauser, and W. Nejdl. Boilerplate detection using shallow text features. In *Proceedings of the third ACM international conference on Web search and data mining*, WSDM '10, pages 441–450, New York, NY, USA, 2010. ACM.

[25] J. H. Lee and X. Hu. Generating ground truth for music mood classification using mechanical turk. In *Proceedings of the 12th ACM/IEEE-CS joint conference on Digital Libraries*, JCDL '12, pages 129–138, New York, NY, USA, 2012. ACM.

[26] X. Li, Y.-Y. Wang, and A. Acero. Learning query intent from regularized click graphs. In *Proceedings of the 31st annual international ACM SIGIR conference on Research and development in information retrieval*, SIGIR '08, pages 339–346, New York, NY, USA, 2008. ACM.

[27] E. Loper and S. Bird. Nltk: the natural language toolkit. In *Proceedings of the ACL-02 Workshop on Effective tools and methodologies for teaching natural language processing and computational linguistics - Volume 1*, ETMTNLP '02, pages 63–70, Stroudsburg, PA, USA, 2002. Association for Computational Linguistics.

[28] A. Mogadala and V. Varma. Twitter user behavior understanding with mood transition prediction. In *Proceedings of the 2012 workshop on Data-driven user behavioral modelling and mining from social media*, DUBMMSM '12, pages 31–34, New York, NY, USA, 2012. ACM.

[29] M. L. Nelson and B. D. Allen. Object persistence and availability in digital libraries. *D-Lib Magazine*, 8(1), 2002.

[30] M. E. J. Newman and J. Park. Why social networks are different from other types of networks. *Physical Review E*, 68(3):036122+, sep 2003.

[31] A. Ntoulas, J. Cho, and C. Olston. What's new on the web?: the evolution of the web from a search engine perspective. In *WWW '04: Proceedings of the 13th international Conference on World Wide Web*, pages 1–12, 2004.

[32] H. M. SalahEldeen. Losing my revolution: A year after the egyptian revolution, 10% of the social media documentation is gone. http://ws-dl.blogspot.com/2012/02/2012-02-11-losing-my-revolution-year.html, 2012.

[33] H. M. SalahEldeen and M. L. Nelson. Losing my revolution: How much social media content has been lost? In *Proceedings of TPDL*, pages 125–137, 2012.

[34] R. Sanderson, M. Phillips, and H. Van de Sompel. Analyzing the persistence of referenced web resources with Memento. In *Proceedings of Open Repositories 2011*, 2011.

[35] R. L. Santos, C. Macdonald, and I. Ounis. Intent-aware search result diversification. In *Proceedings of the 34th international ACM SIGIR conference on Research and development in Information Retrieval*, SIGIR '11, pages 595–604, New York, NY, USA, 2011. ACM.

[36] Y. Tian and J. Zhu. Learning from crowds in the presence of schools of thought. In *Proceedings of the 18th ACM SIGKDD international conference on Knowledge discovery and data mining*, KDD '12, pages 226–234, New York, NY, USA, 2012. ACM.

[37] Twitter.com. Twitter numbers. `http://blog.Twitter.com/2011/03/numbers.html`, 2012. [Online; accessed 17-December-2012].

[38] H. Van de Sompel, M. L. Nelson, R. Sanderson, L. L. Balakireva, S. Ainsworth, and H. Shankar. Memento: Time Travel for the Web. Technical Report arXiv:0911.1112, 2009.

[39] M. Wu, R. C. Miller, and G. Little. Web wallet: preventing phishing attacks by revealing user intentions. In *Proceedings of the second symposium on Usable privacy and security*, SOUPS '06, pages 102–113, New York, NY, USA, 2006. ACM.

An Evaluation of Caching Policies for Memento TimeMaps

Justin F. Brunelle
Old Dominion University
Department of Computer Science
Norfolk, Virginia, 23508
jbrunelle@cs.odu.edu

Michael L. Nelson
Old Dominion University
Department of Computer Science
Norfolk, Virginia, 23508
mln@cs.odu.edu

ABSTRACT

As defined by the Memento Framework, TimeMaps are machine-readable lists of time-specific copies – called "mementos" – of an archived original resource. In theory, as an archive acquires additional mementos over time, a TimeMap should be monotonically increasing. However, there are reasons why the number of mementos in a TimeMap would decrease, for example: archival redaction of some or all of the mementos, archival restructuring, and transient errors on the part of one or more archives. We study TimeMaps for 4,000 original resources over a three month period, note their change patterns, and develop a caching algorithm for TimeMaps suitable for a reverse proxy in front of a Memento aggregator. We show that TimeMap cardinality is constant or monotonically increasing for 80.2% of all TimeMap downloads observed in the observation period. The goal of the caching algorithm is to exploit the ideally monotonically increasing nature of TimeMaps and not cache responses with fewer mementos than the already cached TimeMap. This new caching algorithm uses conditional cache replacement and a Time To Live (TTL) value to ensure the user has access to the most complete TimeMap available. Based on our empirical data, a TTL of 15 days will minimize the number of mementos missed by users, and minimize the load on archives contributing to TimeMaps.

Categories and Subject Descriptors

H.3.7 [**Online Information Services**]: Digital Libraries

General Terms

Design, Experimentation

Keywords

Web Architecture, HTTP, Web Archiving, Digital Preservation, Memento, TimeMaps

1. INTRODUCTION

The Memento Framework provides HTTP extensions for inter-archive communication and integrating the past and current Web [22, 21, 23]. Memento TimeMaps, part of the Memento Framework, provide an aggregate view of mementos of a URI-R existing in distributed archives as a single document called a TimeMap. These TimeMaps, identified by a URI-T, contain a set of URI-Ms that each have a datetime on which they were archived, or a Memento-Datetime [14]. For example, the TimeMap shown in Figure 1 gives a set of mementos aggregated from two repositories, the National Archives of UK and the Internet Archive's Wayback Machine.

It also spans from the first memento at Dec. 12, 2007 to the last memento at Dec. 14, 2011. Because TimeMaps can aggregate lists of URI-Ms from several sources, many factors can influence the cardinality of a TimeMap, including network downtime, availability of the archive, hardware malfunctions, routine maintenance, etc. Human-induced interruptions in memento availability can also occur. For example, the robots.txt protocol is a redaction method at the Internet Archive (IA) that has been well documented[1]. Copyright and content sensitivity can also cause mementos to be taken out of public access [2, 17]. These redaction requests are legitimate removals of mementos at the content owners' request, and not a failure on the part of the archives[2].

A related modification of archives' offerings is URI migration. For example, the migration of a URI such as `http://example.org/archives/http://thesite.com/` to a URI of `http://memento.example.org/archive/http://thesite.com/` would change all URI-Ms for the archive's contributions to the TimeMap of URI-R. Migrations of this nature assign new URIs to existing mementos.

1.1 Caching TimeMaps

Since TimeMaps do not always improve when they change (e.g., due to archive unavailability), caching policies become important – traditional caches could potentially cache a worse TimeMap than should be available. TimeMaps ideally follow a monotonically increasing growth pattern. That is, TimeMaps should never *lose* mementos (except in rare cases of redaction) – mementos should remain listed in a TimeMap after their first appearance. Since TimeMaps are

[1]`http://archive.org/post/778/exclusions-from-the-wayback-machine`
[2]`http://www2.sims.berkeley.edu/research/conferences/aps/removal-policy.html`

```
<http://http://mementoproxy.cs.odu.edu/aggr/Timemap/link/http://flare.prefuse.org/>;rel="self";
          type="application/link-format",
<http://mementoproxy.cs.odu.edu/aggr/timegate/http://flare.prefuse.org/>;rel="timegate",
<http://flare.prefuse.org/>;rel="original",
<http://api.wayback.archive.org/memento/20071213002102/http://flare.prefuse.org/>;rel="first memento";
          datetime="Thu, 13 Dec 2007 00:21:02 GMT",
<http://api.wayback.archive.org/memento/20080509125659/http://flare.prefuse.org/>;rel="memento";
          datetime="Fri, 09 May 2008 12:56:59 GMT",
<http://webarchive.nationalarchives.gov.uk/20080908074106/http://flare.prefuse.org/>;rel="memento";
          datetime="Mon, 08 Sep 2008 00:00:00 GMT",
...
<http://api.wayback.archive.org/memento/20100815085828/http://flare.prefuse.org/>;rel="memento";
          datetime="Sun, 15 Aug 2010 08:58:28 GMT",
<http://webarchive.nationalarchives.gov.uk/20100909131056/http://flare.prefuse.org/>;rel="memento";
          datetime="Thu, 09 Sep 2010 00:00:00 GMT",
<http://api.wayback.archive.org/memento/20101107020354/http://flare.prefuse.org/>;rel="memento";
          datetime="Sun, 07 Nov 2010 02:03:54 GMT",
```

Figure 1: Example Partial TimeMap for URI-R `http://flare.prefuse.org/`.

expensive to generate and change slowly, they are good candidates for caching.

1.2 Contributions

This paper studies a set of 4,000 URI-Rs; 1,000 URI-Rs each came from the Open Directory Project, Delicious, Bit.ly, and search engine caches [1]. We observed the TimeMaps of the 4,000 URI-Rs for a 3-month period (from May 1st to July 31st, 2012 for a total of 92 days) and we mapped and evaluated their evolution and change patterns. This paper shows that TimeMap cardinality is monotonically increasing (i.e., the same or increasing) for 80.2% of all TimeMap changes in the observation period.

We also proposes a new caching algorithm utilizing a TTL value for caching Memento TimeMaps. This caching algorithm exploits the knowledge that TimeMaps sometimes do not change "for the better" and therefore should not always be cached. The change patterns of the observed TimeMaps are used to empirically determine the optimal TTL value.

2. RELATED WORK

It is important to understand the behavior of TimeMaps and the associated availability of mementos. For example, the Warrick project [12] uses TimeMaps to recover mementos with the ultimate goal of recovering lost websites. Obviously, understanding how archives advertise their mementos and understanding how the availability changes is important for several aspects of Warrick. Caching TimeMaps is used to balance load on the archives vs. Warrick's need for the most recent mementos.

Due to the popularity of Memento, other services and tools have begun to consume and rely on TimeMaps to provide functionality. For example, the UK Web Archive is providing a visualization tool for TimeMaps [25]. Additionally, Android's Memento browser [18] and an iOS mobile memento browser [20] all rely on TimeMaps to provide time travel for the Web.

Observing and studying change on the Web is not new; several works have observed the changes that Web pages undergo over time, proving their ephemeral nature [6, 7, 4, 8, 16, 15]. In contrast to these studies, TimeMaps can be thought of as Web resources that cannot be evaluated as "fresh" solely on their age or change status.

Disk failures are one reason for changes in memento availability. A case study of failures at the Internet Archive (IA) is provided in Schwarz's 2006 work [19]. The organization of archives is also important; we must understand how an entire server failure affects the availability of mementos. Jaffe's work in 2004 describes the IA's architecture [11].

Caching is an important addition to the Web. It reduces latency, load, and user wait times. A set of caching methods commonly utilized on the Internet – including TTL values – are discussed in Wang's 1999 survey paper [24]. Other work has been done to benchmark the performance boosts achieved when implementing caching of dynamic contents [10]. Other works have studied best efforts for caching dynamically generated content, such as that generated on the server-side [5, 27].

Reverse proxies such as Squid [26] improve the efficiency of Web traffic by caching content. This caching is independent of the content server and requester, allowing both to operate without modification. The work we present can be implemented using a reverse proxy (e.g., Squid allows custom caching rules) or by modifying the Memento aggregator cache, and will reduce the load on the Memento proxies while increasing their reliability for users.

3. EXPERIMENT DESIGN

We observed TimeMap cardinality (number of mementos present in a TimeMap) daily for 4,000*92=386,400 total download attempts and the consistency of URI-Ms and the datetime values associated with a memento throughout the experiment. Once a day, a set of scripts downloaded the 4,000 TimeMaps so that we can analyze the daily changes of the mementos advertised in the TimeMaps, as well as how the contents of the TimeMaps differ between observations. To ensure the 4,000 TimeMaps could be retrieived in a 24 hour period, the scripts used a timeout for accessing the TimeMaps. A 45 second timeout was used because this is the upper limit that humans are willing to wait when accessing a resource [13]. The experiment also ran 11 parallel scripts to access different portions of the 4,000 URI dataset. With this concurrency and limited wait time, all 4,000 TimeMaps were accessed consistently within a 24 hour period.

3.1 Cache-less Memento Proxies

The first step in the experiment setup was to create and install a new set of Memento proxies separate from the production proxies at Los Alamos National Laboratory and Old Dominion University. The existing proxies are constantly being accessed by MementoFox, users, and other experiments. We installed a set of proxies on a separate, private experiment machine (`128.82.7.240`) to prevent any contamination from the public Memento uses. The proxies were installed just as they exist on the production Memento machines. However, the production proxies cache their responses in an infinitely-sized cache with a TTL=∞ to speed up the response time to the users, as well as to prevent unnecessary load on the archives. The caching software had to be removed from the experiment proxies to ensure fresh results of each observation. These memento proxies queried for, constructed, and served the TimeMaps throughout the experiment run.

3.2 TimeMaps as Web Resources

TimeMaps can change, evolve, and grow like traditional Web resources. However, TimeMaps differ from traditional Web resources in that they do not always change "for the better." Traditional Web resources can be maintained in a cache by monitoring any change to the resource content. TimeMaps can change in a detrimental way – they sometimes lose mementos due to intermittent contributions from archives, URI changes, or archival redactions. Archival redactions will results in a HTTP 404 response when dereferencing a URI-M but redactions are very rare. We are more concerned about transient errors. As such, TimeMaps cannot be cached in the same manner – only TimeMaps that have been changed in a positive way should be updated in a cache. Prior to this work, there was no method to designate a positive or negative change to a TimeMap.

The production Memento proxies utilize caching to limit the load on the archives and increase response time to users. The proxies are research prototypes, and as such, the caching algorithm for Memento was designed around one of two simple solutions. The two simplest caching algorithms are to cache everything or cache nothing. Caching nothing induces unneeded and unfair load on the archives contributing to the TimeMaps and increases the service time for users due to the latency between the Memento Proxies and archives. Therefore, the cache everything approach was taken. The proxies cache the first TimeMap observed in system and holds it until a cleansing of the cache is performed manually. If a *bad* TimeMap is cached, it persists in the cache until the cache is manually cleaned. TimeMaps that are entirely empty (i.e., receive an HTTP 404 response) are especially bad (the TimeMaps show that a URI-R is not archived, when in fact, it may have mementos that were not reported), and are discussed in more depth in Section 4.1.

3.3 Experiment Execution

During the experiment, three outages were observed as noted by the red circles in Figure 2. Annotation 1 in the figure indicates where the locally installed proxies were inoperable from May 16 – May 18 due to a system reset of the department machines. As indicated by 2 in the figure, the Internet Archive proxies were inoperable due to edits to the API occurring at the Internet Archive. As indicated by 3 in the figure, there was a massive power failure at at our university that caused the machines to automatically reboot, killing the experiment run. This failure went undetected for 6 days in June.

We took these time periods of low memento availability into consideration during the calculations of our results. The previous TimeMaps were substituted for the missing TimeMaps, effectively treating them as unchanged instead of nonexistent.

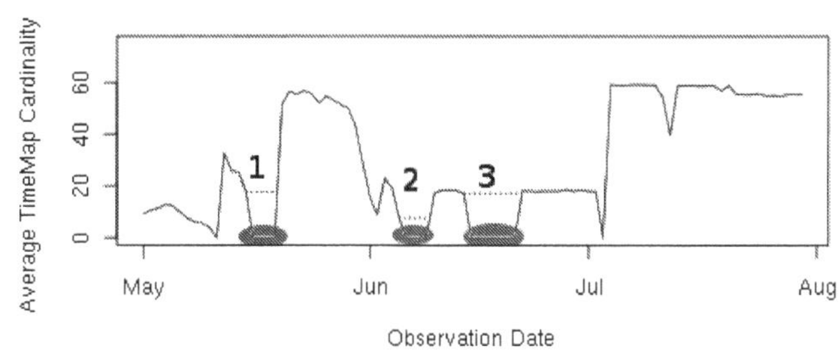

Figure 2: Average TimeMap Cardinality during experiment execution (2012).

4. EXPERIMENT RESULTS

It was immediately clear that TimeMaps were not monotonically increasing. That is, TimeMaps sometimes get smaller – or "worse" instead of staying the same or growing.

4.1 TimeMap Change Types

Utilizing the collected TimeMaps over the course of the observation period, we categorized the changes to the TimeMaps. We used the classifications in Table 1 to determine how changes affected the TimeMaps. The table uses a to denote the number of archives that contribute to a TimeMap at time t and a' to denote the number of archives that contribute to a TimeMap at time $t+1$. Similarly, the table uses m to denote the number of mementos in the TimeMap at time t and m' to denote the number of mementos in the TimeMap at time $t+1$.

TimeMaps can lose and gain mementos and contributing archives. This experiment utilizes the change patterns of TimeMaps to predetermine the change rates for the observed URI-Rs. The number observed changes are provided in Figure 3. Most TimeMaps changed 3 or 4 times over the course of the experiment.

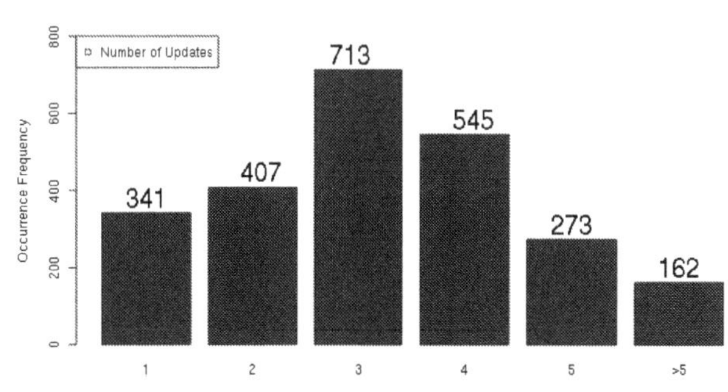

Figure 3: Number of changes to TimeMaps.

As shown in Figure 3, most TimeMaps underwent 3 changes throughout the observation period. Observing these change rates provides insight into the most appropriate TTL values for the TimeMaps. It also disregards TimeMaps that were always empty during the collection part of the experiment. On average, the TimeMaps observed in this experiment changed every 37.6 days, with the most frequently occurring change rate observed of every 30 days, which roughly equates to 3 changes throughout the observation period.

Mementos can be added by contributing archives, or mementos can be redacted by contributing archives. Contributing archives can also disappear from a TimeMap due to service interruption or other unavailability. New archives can begin contributing to a TimeMap if a new URI-R is added to the collection. Cases 6 and 7 are the most detrimental to a TimeMap – the overall cardinality of the TimeMap is reduced by the loss of mementos. Case 1 is the most observed case, and represents the TimeMap remaining consistent between two times. Cases 2, 3, 4, and 5 all result in additional mementos being added and are therefore improvements upon the TimeMap at the previous time. Case 4 is unique in that an archive is lost but there are still new mementos in the TimeMap; we lean toward updating the cache in Case 4. Given that Case 6 is the most frequently observed change to TimeMaps, we show that if a TimeMap changes, it is most often for the worse. The occurrence of cases throughout the experiment is provided in Table 1. These classifications of TimeMaps establish the notion of *better* and therefore how to handle cache replacement.

4.2 Definition of TimeMap Changes

The cardinality of a TimeMap at observation time t is shown as the red lines in Figures 5 - 6. The blue lines are the cumulative size of the set of all unique URI-Ms up to time t: $[0, t]$.

A memento is defined in Equation 1 as a version of a URI-R at time k.

$$m_{R,k} = (URI - R, k), \quad k \in \{\text{times in RFC 1123 format [9]}\} \tag{1}$$

The URI that identifies a memento is defined in Equation 2.

$$URI - M_{R,k} = \text{URI of } m_{R,k} \tag{2}$$

TimeMaps are composed of mementos of a URI-R, as defined in Equation 3.

$$TM_{R,t} = \bigcup_k URI - M_{R,k} \tag{3}$$

The cardinality of a TimeMap $TM_{R,t}$ is defined in Equation 4. Note that this refers to the number of unique URI-Ms that appeared in a URI-R's TimeMap as observed at time t.

$$|TM_{R,t}| \tag{4}$$

Thus, monotonically increasing TimeMaps would satisfy the condition in Equation 5.

$$|TM_{R,t_1}| \leq |TM_{R,t_2}|, \text{where } t_1 < t_2 \tag{5}$$

4.3 Strict versus Loose Policy

When comparing URI-Ms in a TimeMap to determine how TimeMaps grow over time, lexigraphically comparing URI-Ms is the intuitive method. We will refer to this method of matching as the *Strict Policy*.

The best possible set of URI-Ms is the cumulative set of all URI-Ms that have been observed in the TimeMaps until a time t. This represents the best possible TimeMap we would see if TimeMaps were monotonically increasing. This is represented by Equation 6.

$$M_{strict} = \bigcup_t TM_{R,t} \tag{6}$$

URIs are not expected to change [3], but, due to archives being restructured or changes in the URI-M structure, new URIs identifying existing mementos sometimes occur. The *Loose Policy* only matches the tuple of Memento-Datetime and archive ($archive(URI - M_{R,k})$, k) of a URI-M and the URI-R for which it is a memento. The archive is determined by the hostname and occasionally path of the URI-M. The *Loose Policy* is immune to URI changes and should recognize mementos identified by different URI-Ms across time, testing the theory that when mementos disappear from TimeMaps, they actually just change URI-Ms, and not Memento-Datetimes. Conditions under which this occurs include architecture modifications by the archives, URI scheme changes, or even errors with the URI-M listed.

TimeMap cardinality under the *Loose Policy* is measured in accordance with Equation 7.

$$M_{strict} = \bigcup_t TM_{R,t} \quad \forall \text{unique values of } archive(URI - M_{R,k}) \text{ and } k \tag{7}$$

For example, the TimeMap in Figure 4, the URI-Ms would *Loosely* match the other URI-Ms with the same Memento-Datetimes. Since they have the same archive (`web.archive.org`) and Memento-Datetime (`Mon, 01 Nov 2010 06:02:04 GMT`). All would be considered lexigraphically different and not match according to the *Strict Policy* because of the same Memento-Datetime but different URI-R (`http://aarp.org:80/Health/`).

Comparisons of cumulative mementos under the *Loose* and *Strict Policies* show that mementos receive new $URI - M_{r,k}$ but are still the same memento $m_{r,k}$. The *Loose Policy* graphs do not show an increase when this activity takes place, while the *Strict Policy* mistakes this new $URI - M_{r_k}$ as a new memento.

The two graphs of the yardsellr.com TimeMap, (Figures 5(a) and 5(c)) and whitehouse.gov TimeMap, (Figures 5(b) and 5(d)) both demonstrate well-behaved TimeMaps in which the *Loose* and *Strict Policy* graphs match one another. This shows that there is no difference between the TimeMap cardinalities according to the *Loose* and *Strict Policies*. However, these two TimeMaps change in different ways during the observation period. The yardsellr.com TimeMap incurs a spike of mementos in mid-May due to an influx of mementos from the Internet Archive. These mementos do not reappear in the TimeMap for the duration of the observation period, which results in a gap between the cumulative and observed mementos (observed as the gap between the blue and red lines, respectively). Alternatively, the whitehouse.gov TimeMap frequently has observed car-

Case #	|a|	|m|	Description	Action	Occurrence
1	a = a′	m = m′	Same TimeMap.	Do not update the cache.	77.4%
2	a < a′	m < m′	New archives and new mementos.	Update the cache.	2.4%
3	a = a′	m < m′	New mementos, same archives.	Update the cache.	0.4%
4	a > a′	m = m	Lost an archive, but an archive gained mementos.	Update the cache.	0.01%
5	a > a′	m < m′	Lost an archive, but gained more mementos.	Update the cache.	0.01%
6	a > a′	m > m′	Lost an archive and lost mementos.	Do not update the cache	19.7%
7	a < a′	m > m′	Gained archives, but lost mementos.	Do not update the cache.	0.1%

Table 1: Classifications of TimeMap Changes

```
<http://web.archive.org/web/20101101060204/http://aarp.org:80/Health/>;rel="memento";datetime="Mon, 01 Nov 2010 06:02:04 GMT",
<http://web.archive.org/web/20101101060204/http://www.aarp.org:80/Health/>;rel="memento";datetime="Mon, 01 Nov 2010 06:02:04 GMT",
<http://web.archive.org/web/20101101060204/http://www.aarp.org:80/health/>;rel="memento";datetime="Mon, 01 Nov 2010 06:02:04 GMT",
```

Figure 4: A subset of an example TimeMap for URI-R `http://aarp.org/Health/`.

dinality equal to the cumulative cardinality, thus showing that the maximum number of mementos frequently appears in the TimeMap. The consistent whitehouse.gov TimeMap demonstrates expected behavior from a TimeMap. There are some slight dips in TimeMap cardinality caused by an archive being temporarily unavailable. These dips are not permanent, as seen in the yardsellr.com TimeMap.

An additional scenario can occur when a memento, or subset of mementos, disappears from the TimeMap altogether. This is observed by the dip representing the loss of URI-Ms from the Google Code API TimeMap on May 22nd in Figures 6(b) and 6(d). This is noteworthy because there is a complete swapping of mementos that occurs. While the observed cardinality decreases, there is an increase in the cumulative number of mementos (the red line goes down while the blue line goes up). This is due to the swapping of an entire set of URI-Ms.

Google Translate has a TimeMap cardinality $|TM| =$ 5,800. These mementos are populated from several different archives, but the majority of URI-Ms come from the Internet Archive and from Archeif Web. The TimeMap size over time is provided in Figures 6(a) and 6(c) using the *Strict* and *Loose Policies*, respectively. These graphs differ greatly in their representation of the TimeMap sizes.

When using the *Strict Policy*, the TimeMap appears to be nearly consistently growing in cardinality (the blue line, and number of total unique URI-Ms observed over the observation period), while showing only slight (nearly static) growth in the cardinality of the TimeMaps observed on a given day. This is due to URI-Ms with the same Memento-Datetime appearing in a TimeMap for a short span of time and never returning.

The *Loose Policy* provides completely different results. As mentioned previously, the *Loose Policy* uses only the combination of URI-M's Memento-Datetime and the hosting archive as an identifier. The size of the daily observed URI-Ms rises above the total number of observed Memento-Datetimes. This is observed to be an error in the Archeif Web proxy – the proxy was providing `00:00:00` as the time portion of the Memento-Datetime for all mementos returned, causing a discrepancy between the *Strict* and *Loose Policies*.

Notice that some Memento-Datetime values are replicated, even though the URI-M is not. This is due to the simultaneous capture of resources by the archives. This produces a discrepancy between the *Strict* and *Loose Policies*.

5. EVALUATION

As observed in Section 4, Memento TimeMaps do not always change for the better. TimeMap cardinality can decrease due to various external influences. The Memento framework proxies currently have a cache with an *infinite* TTL – TimeMaps are cached on their first occurrence and never automatically replaced. This optimization was critical during the initial deployment of the research prototype Memento Aggregaters.

We tested a continuum of TTL values to find the best life span of an entity in the cache. A TTL=0 will maximize the freshness of the TimeMaps in the cache, but will also maximize the load on the archives and unnecessarily delay consumer applications. A TTL=∞ will minimize the load on the archives, but also minimize the freshness of the TimeMaps in the cache. Therefore, caching a bad TimeMap is especially bad if we are unfortunate enough to receive a TimeMap with a cardinality of 0, which will remain in the cache until the cache is cleared.

We tested TTL=n, where n={0...92} with 92 effectively equaling ∞. We assume the Aggregater can store an infinite number of TimeMaps and focus only on the possible invalidation of a single TimeMap when its TTL has expired.

5.1 Caching Policies

To determine the most effective cache policy, we tested the *current*, *unconditional*, and *conditional* policies. The *current* caching policy simulates the operation of the Memento Aggregater's current cache with a TTL=∞ to never replace TimeMaps. The *unconditional* policy employs TTL values of 0, ∞, and n. TTL values set a time limit for cache replacement – items in a cache are not replaced or removed until a set time limit expires. This policy is used as the baseline measurement since it does not exploit knowledge of the TimeMaps' contents. The *conditional* policy employs TTL values of 0, ∞, and n, but only replaces TimeMaps in the cache when they have improved according to the *Loose Policy*. The Cases 2-5 are cases that will update an entry in the cache because the TimeMap gains mementos (according to Table 1).

5.2 Evaluation Measures

To measure the impact and quality of the cache replacement policies, the MemDays penalty is defined in Equation

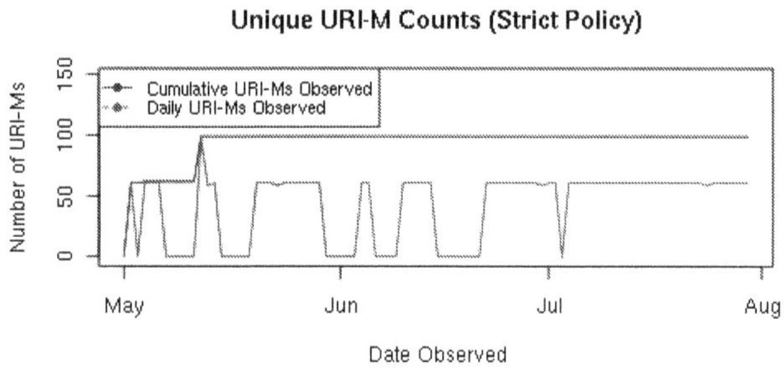

(a) *Strict Policy* for yardsellr.com

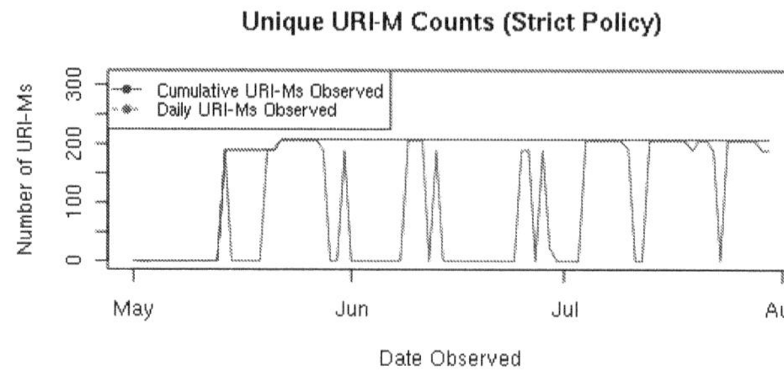

(b) *Strict Policy* for whitehouse.gov

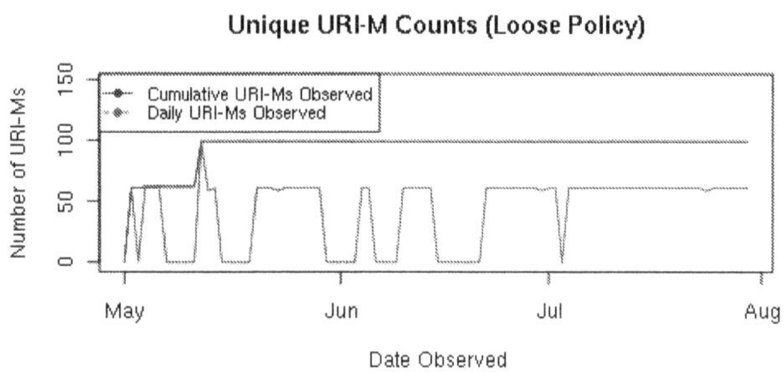

(c) *Loose Policy* for yardsellr.com

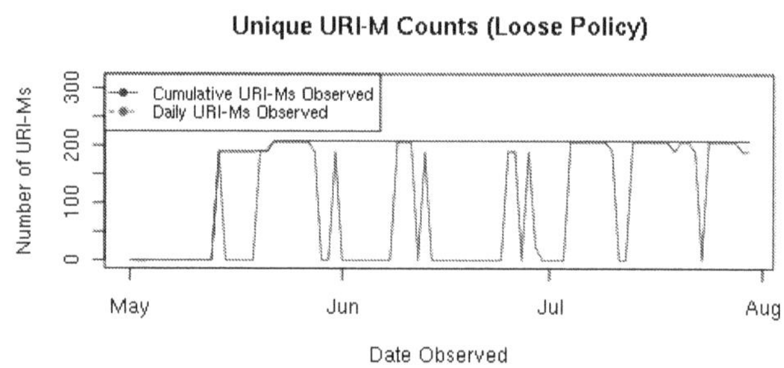

(d) *Loose Policy* for whitehouse.gov

Figure 5: The TimeMap of `http://yardsellr.com` shows identical graphs for *Strict* and *Loose Policies*, and demonstrates that mementos blink on and off in the TimeMap, but do not change the overall cumulative set of all observed mementos. The `http://www.whitehouse.gov/administration/eopcea/` TimeMap is well-behaved, with identical *Strict* and *Loose Policy* graphs.

8. The MemDays penalty is the sum of the number of mementos that are missed due to a cache hit when there is a better version of the TimeMap available over the time t of the experiment.

$$MemDays = \sum_{1}^{t} max((|\mathrm{TM}_{live}| - |\mathrm{TM}_{cache}|), 0) \tag{8}$$

MemDays provides a cumulative measure of the detrimental effects of the cache. This metric is the sum of fresh mementos missed for each day those mementos are not available in the cache. An example is provided in Figure 7. A TimeMap with $|TM| = 6$ is cached at time t=0. At t=1, $|TM|$=6. Since $|TM|$ remained consistent, the cumulative MemDay measure is 0. However, $|TM|$ increases to 8 at time t=2. Since the cached $|TM|$=6, the MemDay measure increases to 2 since 8-6=2. At time t=3, the difference between the cached and live $|TM|$ is still 2, increasing the cumulative MemDay to 4.

At time t=4, the live $|TM|$=8. The difference between the cached and live $|TM|$ is now 4, increasing the MemDay by 4 to 8. At t=5, the cache is updated with the new TimeMap $|TM|$=8, and therefore the cached and live $|TM|$ are equal, adding no additional MemDay penalty.

In this example, Q=2 because the archives contributed to the cached version twice at t=0 and t=5. The final accumulations of MemDay=8.

The complement to MemDays is the load on the repositories, or amount of queries Q (Equation 9). This is the sum of the number of times the cache requests a TimeMaps from the archives over the course of t days in the experiment, effectively measuring the cache misses due to expired TTL values. Notionally, this is inversely related to the MemDays measure in Equation 8. An optimal caching strategy can be determined by minimizing load on the Q and MemDays simultaneously.

$$Q = \sum_{1}^{t} \text{Cache Misses} \tag{9}$$

5.3 Results

At the conclusion of this experiment, we calculated the average number of TimeMap observations in which we observed a monotonically increasing trend. Only 80.2% of all observations either remained the same or provided an improvement to the existing TimeMap (Figure 3).

To recreate a series of TimeMaps, we used a three-month-long observation period to test the cache replacement policies. We ran a simulation to access the 4,000 TimeMaps with the three caching policies implemented with the *Loose Policy*. The cache size is unlimited for the purposes of this experiment; our goal was only to test the behavior of the replacement policies as they relate to TimeMap change patterns.

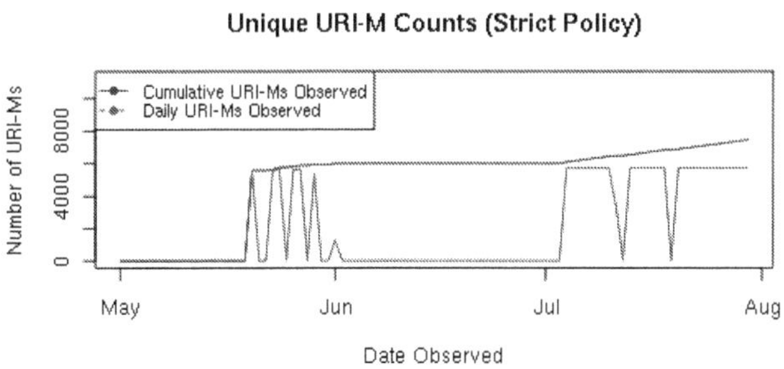

(a) *Strict Policy* for Google Translate

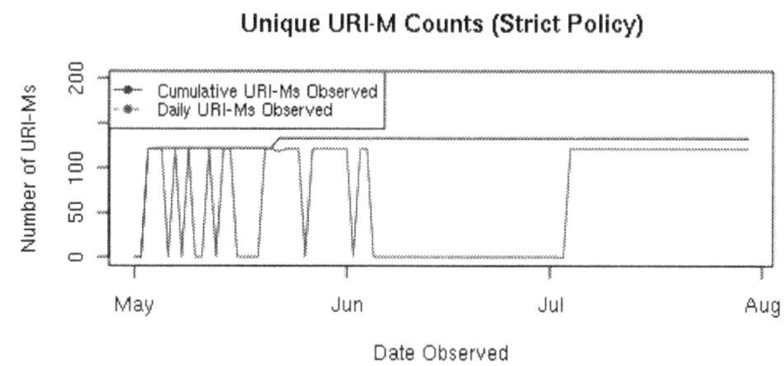

(b) *Strict Policy* for Google Code API

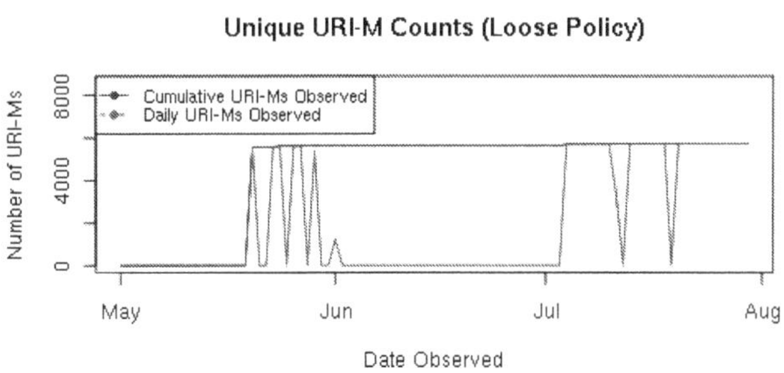

(c) *Loose Policy* for Google Translate

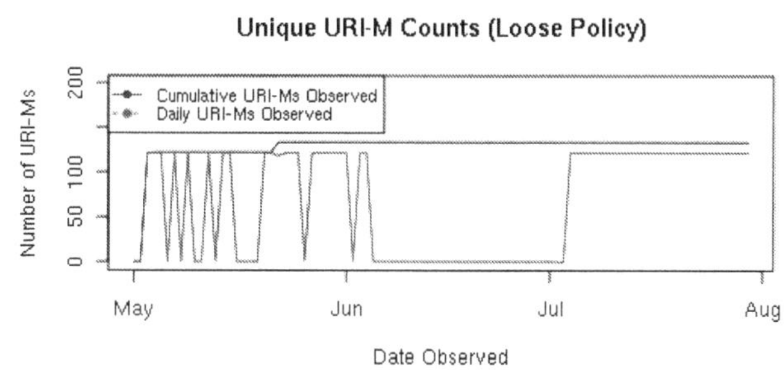

(d) *Loose Policy* for Google Code API

Figure 6: TimeMap with duplicate Memento-Datetime values as shown by the *Strict* and *Loose Policies* for `http://translate.google.com/`. Poorly formed Memento-Datetimes appear in the TimeMaps for `http://code.google.com/apis/g/data/client-cs.html`

5.3.1 Missed Mementos

As with any cache replacement policy, it is necessary to determine how many updates are missed by utilizing a cache. Since the concept of replacement in this unique cache replacement experiment is limited to those TimeMaps that are *better* (based on the cases in Table 1) than the currently cached version, this experiment counts only those replacements that would result in an improved TimeMap being placed in the cache. The results of this experiment are provided in Figure 8.

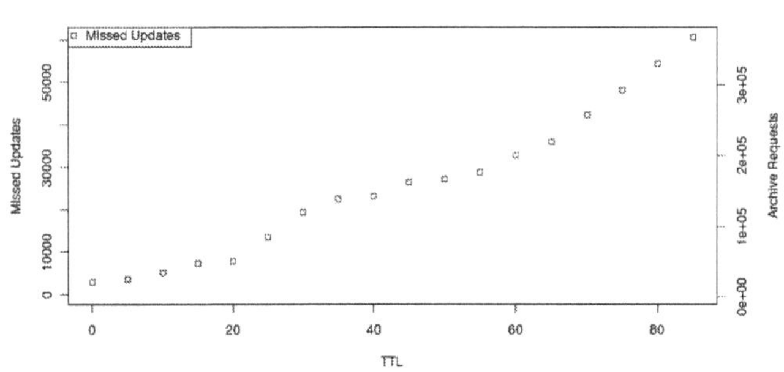

Figure 8: Number of missed cache replacements by TTL value.

A primary problem with the current caching algorithm is that TimeMaps with 0 mementos might be cached when TimeMaps with more than 0 mementos exist at another time. False 0-sized TimeMaps (i.e., a 404 response for a

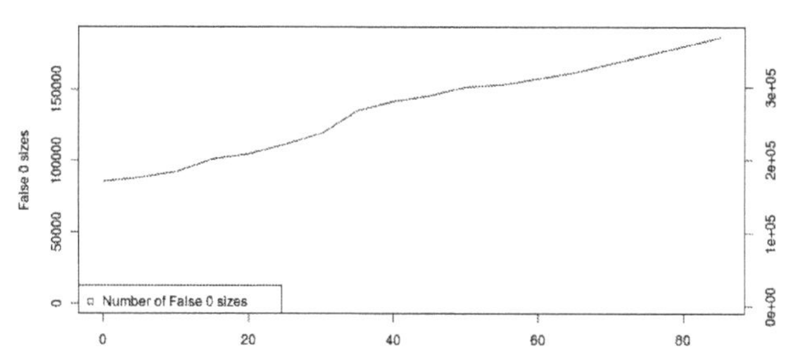

Figure 9: False 0-sized TimeMaps by TTL value for *conditional*.

TimeMap) are especially detrimental to consumers of TimeMaps since this suggests that a URI-R is not archived when, in fact, it has mementos. This experiment measures the occurrence of these false 0-sized TimeMaps. Additionally, given the rudimentary caching strategies available, a false 0-sized TimeMap should not replace a TimeMap that lists mementos. This is a particularly detrimental occurrence of Case 6 (Table 1 – lost an archive and lost mementos) to consumers of TimeMaps.

As shown in Figure 9, the best TTL value to minimize the false 0-sized TimeMaps is 0. However, this induces an unnecessarily large load on the archives. This shows that TimeMaps normally remain constant. However, when they do change, they tend to get worse, as shown in Figure 3.

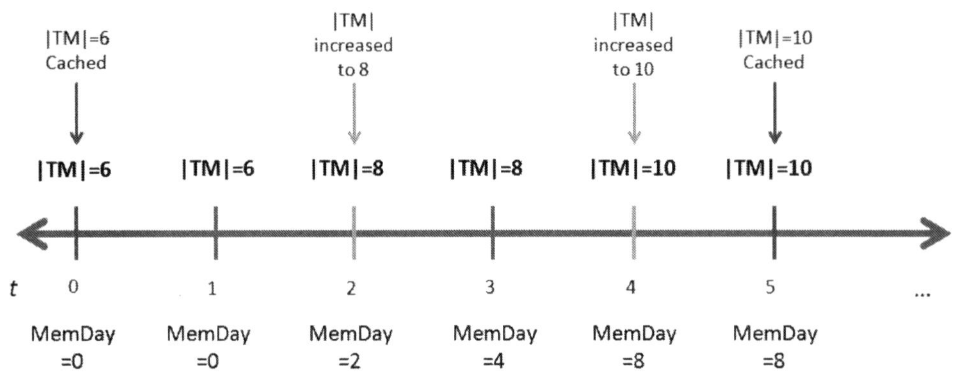

Figure 7: MemDay calculation example.

5.3.2 MemDays versus Q

The primary measure used in this experiment to determine how well the cache replacement policies are performing is the MemDay penalty (Section 5.1). Using *unconditional*, our experiment shows the MemDay penalty-saved trade-off in Figure 10(a). The MemDays for *conditional* are shown in Figure 10(b). Notice that *conditional* shows improvement over *unconditional* by accumulating fewer MemDays during the simulation. This is because *unconditional* has the potential to cache a TimeMap with $|TM|$ less than the one in the cache, while *conditional* ensures that the cached TimeMap has the highest $|TM|$.

As expected, lower TTL values result in fewer missed updates. However, lower TTL values lead to additional queries (Q) to the archives.

In *unconditional*, running a cache that updates TimeMaps at every transaction (TTL=0) results in MemDays=98,312, but Q=368,000 (368,000 requests made to the archives to update the cache). That is, 98,312 mementos are missed because the cache was updated with worse, lower-cardinality TimeMaps. When TTL=∞, MemDays=4,010,406 and Q=4,000. TTL=∞ is the *current* policy of the Memento Aggregater.

The optimal TTL value for *unconditional* can be found at the intersection of the Q line (red), and the MemDay line (blue) in Figure 10(a). At this point, MemDays=784,895 due to cache staleness, but Q=92,000. Subsequent data produces a worse trade off between requests to the archives and mementos missed by the users. The data shows that the best TTL value for a TimeMap cache, located at the intersection of the MemDay and Q lines, is 10 days.

In *conditional*, running a cache that updates TimeMaps at every transaction (TTL=0) results in MemDays=0 (or 0 mementos being missed), but Q=368,000 (368,000 requests made to the archives to update the cache). The *conditional* policy improves upon *unconditional* by 98,312 MemDays when TTL=0. Because *conditional* ensures the TimeMap with the highest cardinality remains in the cache, there are no MemDays incurred, as opposed to *unconditional* which blindly assumes improvement to TimeMaps when they change; this is an improper assumption as shown by the change patterns in Table 1. When TTL=∞, MemDays=4,010,406 and Q=4,000, identical to *unconditional*; in both policies, a TTL=∞ caches the first TimeMap available and never replaces it, accumulating MemDays for the duration of the experiment.

The optimal TTL value for *conditional* can be found at the intersection of the Q line (red), and the MemDay line (blue) in Figure 10(b). At this point, MemDays=588,368 due to cache staleness (only 7,207 missed TimeMap updates), but Q=23,000. Subsequent data produces a worse trade off between requests to the archives and mementos missed by the users. The data shows that the best TTL value for a TimeMap cache, located at the intersection of the MemDay and Q lines, is 15 days. The optimal TTL for *conditional* improves upon the optimal TTL for *unconditional* by reducing Q by 69,000 and MemDay by 196,527 due to the ability to only update the cache with *better* TimeMaps. This is also intuitively satisfying since TimeMaps change less frequently (every 30 days on average shown in Figure 3) than our optimal TTL of 15 days.

6. CONCLUSIONS

The study outlined in this paper observed 4,000 TimeMaps for URI-Rs over the course of three months and measured their consistency over time. We show that TimeMaps are monotonically increasing only 80.2% of the time. Due to this evidence, a new *conditional* caching algorithm must be implemented to ensure users have access to the best possible TimeMaps. The current Memento Aggregater operates with a TTL=∞, which produces MemDays=4,010,406 and Q=4,000; We have proposed a caching algorithm that implements a TTL value of 15 days and a *conditional* replacement policy in which responses that are smaller than previous responses are not cached. TTL=15 produces MemDays=588,368 and Q=23,000. This shows an improvement on the current Memento Aggregater operation by 3,422,038 MemDays while only making 19,000 more queries to the archives. It improves upon the *unconditional* policy by an observed Q=69,000 and MemDay=196,527.

7. ACKNOWLEDGMENTS

This work supported in part by the NSF (IIS 1009392) and the Library of Congress. We also thank Robert Sanderson

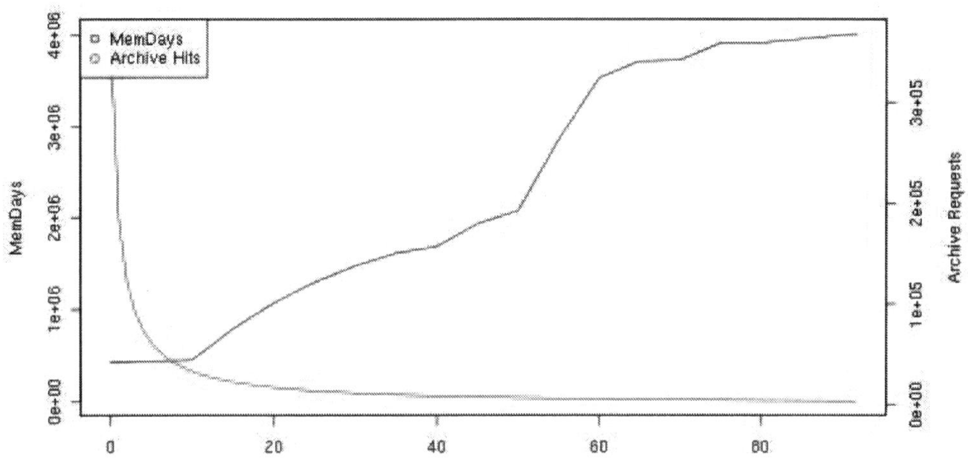

(a) MemDay Trade-off by TTL value for *unconditional*.

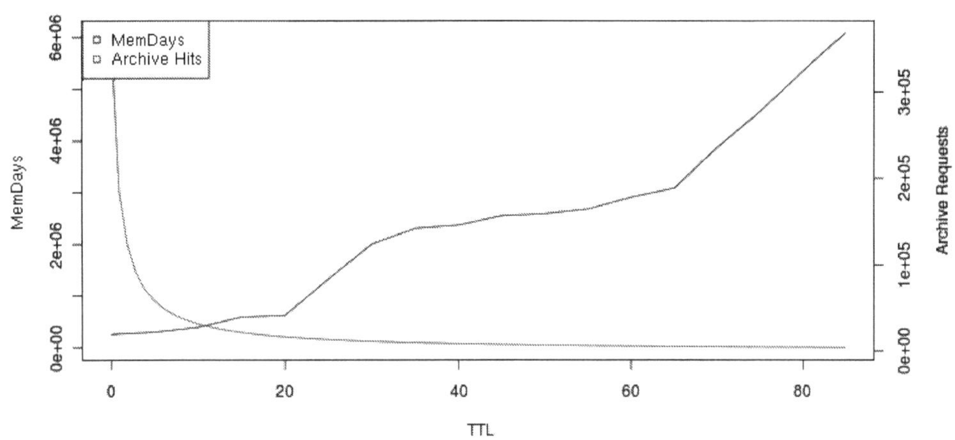

(b) MemDay Trade-off by TTL value for *conditional*.

Figure 10: Comparison of the *unconditional* and *conditional* policies. MemDays is shown as the blue line, and Q is shown as the red line.

(LANL) for the Memento Aggregater research prototype and Ahmed AlSum (ODU) for his assistance with the cache-less Memento Proxies. Memento is a joint project between the Los Alamos National Laboratory Research Library and Old Dominion University

8. REFERENCES

[1] S. Ainsworth, A. Alsum, H. SalahEldeen, M. C. Weigle, and M. L. Nelson. How much of the Web is archived? In *JCDL '11: Proceedings of the 11th annual international ACM/IEEE Joint Conference on Digital Libraries*, pages 133–136, 2011.

[2] Alyssa N. Knutson. Proceed With Caution: How Digital Archives Have Been Left in the Dark. http://www.btlj.org/data/review/24-437-473.pdf, 2009.

[3] T. Berners-Lee. Cool URIs don't change. http://www.w3.org/Provider/Style/URI, 1998.

[4] B. Brewington, G. Cybenko, D. Coll, and N. Hanover. Keeping up with the changing Web. *IEEE Computer*, 33(5):52–58, 2000.

[5] P. Cao, J. Zhang, and K. Beach. Active cache: caching dynamic contents on the web. In *Proceedings of the IFIP International Conference on Distributed Systems Platforms and Open Distributed Processing*, pages 373–388, 1998.

[6] J. Cho and H. Garcia-Molina. The evolution of the web and implications for an incremental crawler. In *Proceedings of the 26th international conference on very large data bases*, pages 200–209, 2000.

[7] F. Douglis, A. Feldmann, B. Krishnamurthy, and J. Mogul. Rate of change and other metrics: a live study of the World Wide Web. In *USITS'97: Proceedings of the USENIX Symposium on Internet Technologies and Systems on USENIX Symposium on Internet Technologies and Systems*, USITS'97, 1997.

[8] D. Fetterly, M. Manasse, M. Najork, and J. Wiener. A large-scale study of the evolution of web pages. *Software: Practice and Experience*, 34(2):213–237, 2004.

[9] Internet Engineering Task Force. Requirements for Internet Hosts – Application and Support, October 1989. http://www.ietf.org/rfc/rfc1123.txt.

[10] A. Iyengar and J. Challenger. Improving web server performance by caching dynamic data. In *USITS'97: Proceedings of the USENIX Symposium on Internet Technologies and Systems on USENIX Symposium on Internet Technologies and Systems*, USITS'97, 1997.

[11] E. Jaffe and S. Kirkpatrick. Architecture of the Internet Archive. In *Proceedings of SYSTOR 2009: The Israeli Experimental Systems Conference*, SYSTOR '09, 2009.

[12] F. McCown, J. A. Smith, M. L. Nelson, and J. Bollen. Lazy preservation: reconstructing websites by crawling the crawlers. In *WIDM '06: Proceedings of the 8th annual ACM international workshop on Web information and data management*, pages 67–74, 2006.

[13] F. F. Nah. A study on tolerable waiting time: how long are web users willing to wait? *Behaviour Information Technology*, (3):153–163.

[14] M. L. Nelson. Memento-Datetime is not Last-Modified. http://ws-dl.blogspot.com/2010/11/2010-11-05-memento-datetime-is-not-last.html, 2011.

[15] M. L. Nelson and B. D. Allen. Object persistence and availability in digital libraries. *D-Lib Magazine*, 8(1), January 2002.

[16] A. Ntoulas, J. Cho, and C. Olston. What's new on the web?: the evolution of the web from a search engine perspective. In *Proceedings of the 13th international conference on World Wide Web*, pages 1–12, 2004.

[17] Peter B. Hirtle. Digital Preservation and Copyright. http://fairuse.stanford.edu/commentary_and_analysis/2003_11_hirtle.html, 2012.

[18] R. Sanderson, H. Shankar, S. Ainsworth, F. McCown, and S. Adams. Implementing Time Travel for the Web. *Code4Lib Journal*, 13, 2011.

[19] T. Schwartz, M. Baker, S. Bassi, B. Baumgart, W. Flagg, C. van Ingen, K. Joste, M. Manasse, and M. Shah. Disk failure investigations at the Internet Archive. *14th NASA Goddard, 23rd IEEE Conference on Mass Storage Systems and Technologies*, May 2006.

[20] H. Tweedy, F. McCown, and M. L. Nelson. A Memento Web Browser for iOS. In *JCDL '13: Proceedings of the 13th ACM/IEEE-CS Joint Conference on Digital Libraries*.

[21] H. Van de Sompel, M. L. Nelson, and R. Sanderson. HTTP framework for time-based access to resource states – Memento draft-vandesompel-memento-05. https://datatracker.ietf.org/doc/draft-vandesompel-memento/, 2012.

[22] H. Van de Sompel, M. L. Nelson, R. Sanderson, L. L. Balakireva, S. Ainsworth, and H. Shankar. Memento: Time Travel for the Web. Technical Report arXiv:0911.1112, 2009.

[23] H. Van de Sompel, R. Sanderson, M. L. Nelson, L. L. Balakireva, H. Shankar, and S. Ainsworth. An HTTP-Based Versioning Mechanism for Linked Data. In *Proceedings of the Linked Data on the Web Workshop (LDOW 2010)*, 2010. (Also available as arXiv:1003.3661).

[24] J. Wang. A survey of web caching schemes for the Internet. *SIGCOMM Comput. Commun. Rev.*, 29(5):36–46, Oct. 1999.

[25] P. Webster. Surfing the web in time: Mementos. `http://britishlibrary.typepad.co.uk/webarchive/2013/01/surfing-the-web-in-time-mementos.html`, 2013.

[26] D. Wessels. *Squid: the definitive guide*. O'Reilly Media, Incorporated, 2004.

[27] H. Zhu and T. Yang. Class-based cache management for dynamic web content. In *IEEE INFOCOM*, pages 1215–1224, 2000.

Extending Sitemaps for ResourceSync

Martin Klein
Los Alamos National Laboratory
NM, USA
mklein@lanl.gov

Herbert Van de Sompel
Los Alamos National Laboratory
NM, USA
herbertv@lanl.gov

ABSTRACT

The documents used in the ResourceSync synchronization framework are based on the widely adopted document format defined by the Sitemap protocol. In order to address requirements of the framework, extensions to the Sitemap format were necessary. This short paper describes the concerns we had about introducing such extensions, the tests we did to evaluate their validity, and aspects of the framework to address them.

Categories and Subject Descriptors

H.3.5 [**Information Storage and Retrieval**]: Online Information Science—*Data Sharing*

Keywords

Sitemaps, Resource Synchronization, ResourceSync

1. INTRODUCTION

The ResourceSync collaboration between the National Information Standards Organization (NISO) and the Open Archives Initiative (OAI) focuses on designing an approach for the synchronization of web resources. As resources constantly change (being created, updated, deleted, and moved) [6, 7, 12] applications that leverage them would benefit from a standardized synchronization framework aligned with the Web Architecture [8]. The ResourceSync specification [10] (in beta phase at the time of writing) fulfills the needs of different communities and is, amongst others, targeted at cultural heritage portals such as Europeana[1], repositories of scientific articles such as arXiv[2], and linked data applications such as DBpedia Live[3]. In the framework we refer to a **Source** as a server that hosts resources subject to synchronization and to a **Destination** as a system that retrieves those resources to synchronize itself with the Source.

[1]`http://www.europeana.eu/`
[2]`http://arxiv.org`
[3]`http://live.dbpedia.org/`

JCDL'13, July 22–26, 2013, Indianapolis, Indiana, USA.
Copyright 2013 ACM 978-1-4503-2077-1/13/07 ...$15.00.

Different use cases imply distinct characteristics. From the Source's perspective the resource volume and the resource change frequency are most relevant, whereas synchronization latency and accuracy requirements are essential considerations for Destinations. The ResourceSync framework therefore offers multiple modular capabilities that a Source can selectively implement to address specific synchronization needs. For the purpose of this paper we discuss only two of the capabilities. An extensive discussion about the theoretical background of the framework can be found in Van de Sompel et al. [15] and we refer to the specification document [10] for a detailed description of all capabilities.

The here described capabilities are the **Resource List** and the **Change List**. The Resource List, as the name implies, is a list of resources and their descriptions that the Source makes available for synchronization. The Resource List presents a snapshot of the Source's resources at one particular point in time and a Source can publish a Resource List recurrently e.g., once a week or once a month. The Change List is a list that provides information about changes to the Source's resources. Depending on the publication and update frequency of the Change List, this capability can help decrease synchronization latency and reduce communication overhead. It is up to the Source to determine the publication frequency as well as the temporal interval that is covered by a Change List. It may, for example, describe all resource changes of one day, or one hour, or may simply contain a fixed number of changes, regardless of how long it takes to accumulate them. Both Resource List and Change List serve the following purposes:

- Synchronization: allow Destinations to obtain current resources; requires the resources' URI.
- Audit: allow Destinations to verify the accuracy of their synchronized content; requires the resources' last modification date and fixity information.
- Link: allow Sources to express alternate ways for Destinations to retrieve content; requires inclusion of links.

One example for the inclusion of such links is a Source providing a pointer to a mirror location. In this case the Source prefers Destinations to obtain the resource from that specified location and not from the original URI, with the intention to reduce the load on the Source. Another example is a Source providing a pointer to partial content, meaning only the part of the resource that has actually changed. A Destination can obtain this information and use it to patch its local copy of the resource.

1.1 Considering Sitemaps

For consistency and to minimize the barrier of adoption, it is desirable to implement all capabilities based on a single document format instead of using multiple formats within one framework. Sitemaps [3] serve the purpose of advertising a server's resources and support search engines in their discovery. In this sense a Sitemap is fairly similar to a Resource List, which motivated us to investigate the use of the Sitemap format for the ResourceSync framework.

A Sitemap is an XML document, which must contain three XML elements: the root element *<urlset>*, one *<url>* child element per resource, and exactly one *<loc>* element as a child of each *<url>* element that conveys the URI of the resource. The Sitemap schema [2], allows only the *<url>* element to be a child of the root element and none of the mandatory elements can have attributes. Listing 1 shows a simple Sitemap.

```
<?xml version="1.0" encoding="UTF-8"?>
<urlset xmlns="http://www.sitemaps.org/schemas/sitemap/0.9">
  <url>
    <loc>http://example.com/res1</loc>
    <lastmod>2013-02-01T13:00:00Z</lastmod>
  </url>
</urlset>
```

Listing 1: A Sitemap listing one resource

The *<loc>* element can be utilized in the ResourceSync framework to convey the URI of the resource that is subject to synchronization. Its last modification time can be provided with the Sitemap-native optional *<lastmod>* child element of the *<url>* element.

2. RESOURCESYNC SITEMAP EXTENSIONS

In order to use Sitemaps for all ResourceSync capabilities, extensions to the Sitemap format are required on two levels:

At the *resource level*, where child elements of an *<url>* element need to be included that provide:

- Audit: metadata about the resource such as the nature of the change, the resource's size, its content-based hash value, MIME-Type etc., and
- Link: links to related resources such as mirror locations or partial content.

At the *root level*, where child elements of the *<urlset>* element need to be included that provide:

- Audit: the document's last modification time,
- Link: links for navigational support for Destinations and to convey information about the Source, and
- an indication of the capability implemented by a specific Sitemap document since all capability documents have the same format.

In general, we wanted to avoid Google consuming ResourceSync documents in an unintended way because it does not understand the extensions, yet keep them valid from the perspective of the Sitemap XML schema and keep the door wide open for when Google understands and eventually consumes them. These intentions led to the following concerns:

Concern 1: It was unclear how Google would act upon the inclusion of additional child elements to the *<url>* element. Since the Sitemap schema allows for external child elements as long as they are properly declared in their namespace, we did not anticipate major issues but still had to convince ourselves that our extensions were compliant.

Concern 2: How Google responds to the inclusion of links, as children of the *<url>* element was unclear. If Google, for example, indexes both the URI provided in the *<loc>* element and the URI provided in the link to a mirror location, it would go against the Source's intention to reduce its load. Also, it is meaningless if Google indexes the URI of the partial content as it is not helpful without the full resource pointed to in the *<loc>* element. These would be unintended consequences of the inclusion of links.

Concern 3: Since the schema does not allow for child elements to the *<urlset>* root element other than *<url>*, the concern was that Google would reject the ResourceSync capability documents. The behavior towards included link elements on this level was unclear too.

3. TESTING SITEMAP EXTENSIONS

We conducted a series of informal experiments to determine how Google, as a major search engine, responds to ResourceSync enhanced Sitemaps. We submitted Sitemaps with varying degrees of modification to Google's Webmaster Tool [1], analyzed its immediately returned parsing report, and observed the effects of our Sitemaps to their index.

Metadata Additions at the Resource Level

The goal of this experiment was to test the addition of metadata elements to each *<url>* child element of the *<urlset>* root element. To convey the type of change the resource underwent, we tested the addition of an *rs:change* attribute to the *<lastmod>* element. For additional metadata, we tested new elements in the ResourceSync namespace such as *<rs:size>*, *<rs:fixity>*, and *<rs:mimetype>* to convey the resource's size, content-based hash value, and MIME-Type, respectively. Listing 2 shows a Sitemap-based Change List that we tested against Google.

```
<?xml version="1.0" encoding="UTF-8"?>
<urlset xmlns="http://www.sitemaps.org/schemas/sitemap/0.9"
        xmlns:rs="http://www.openarchives.org/rs/terms/">
  <url>
    <loc>http://example.com/res1</loc>
    <lastmod rs:change="updated">
      2013-01-02T13:00:00Z
    </lastmod>
    <rs:size>6230</rs:size>
    <rs:fixity type="md5">
      a2f94c567f9b370c43fb1188f1f46330
    </rs:fixity>
    <rs:mimetype>text/html</rs:mimetype>
  </url>
</urlset>
```

Listing 2: A Change List with added metadata

All tested child elements from the ResourceSync namespace were tolerated and the *rs:change* attribute, even though in violation to the Sitemap schema, was ignored.

However, even though this approach proved feasible, we decided against the addition of multiple child elements and in favor of just one additional child element with multiple attributes. We named the child element *<rs:md>* and the possible attributes to describe a resource in a Change List are *change*, *length*, *hash*, and *type* conveying the same metadata as above. This approach has two main advantages.

First, there is only one added child element that needs to be defined in the ResourceSync namespace and secondly, its attributes are defined in the Atom Syndication Format [11] and the Atom Link Extension Internet Draft [14]. Their semantics are inherited in the ResourceSync framework.

Link Additions at the Resource Level

To provide links to related resources we tested the *<rs:link>* element from the ResourceSync namespace with the URI being conveyed in its *href* attribute as seen in Listing 3. To provide a mirror location, the link has the relation type *duplicate* (defined in RFC6249 [5]) and for partial content (for example JSON patch [13]) a patch-specific relation type.

```
<?xml version="1.0" encoding="UTF-8"?>
<urlset xmlns="http://www.sitemaps.org/schemas/sitemap/0.9"
        xmlns:rs="http://www.openarchives.org/rs/terms/">
  <url>
    <loc rel="nofollow">http://example.com/res1</loc>
    <lastmod>2013-01-02T13:00:00Z</lastmod>
    <rs:link rel="duplicate"
             href="http://mirror.example.com/res1"/>
    <rs:link rel="http://www.openarchives.org/rs/terms/patch"
             href="http://example.com/res1-json-patch"
             type="application/json-patch"/>
  </url>
</urlset>
```

Listing 3: A Change List with related resource links

Google did not return an error but we did observe unintended consequences (concern 2) with this approach as we found both linked resources (`http://mirror.example.com/res1` and `http://example.com/res1-json-patch`) indexed. Our informal tests indicate that Google parses Sitemaps aggressively and indexes URIs it discovers. For a resource synchronization framework this can be a real detriment because resources in a Resource List or Change List are subject to synchronization but they may not be meant for indexing by search engines. To address this concern, we tested the *rel="nofollow"* attribute in the *<loc>* child element as well as in the *<rs:link>* child elements with the goal of preventing Google from indexing the referenced resource. However, the attribute was ignored in either child element. It did not cause any warnings or errors but it also did not prevent Google from indexing the resource. We were able to improve on this situation by renaming the child element to something different than *<link>* and include the URI as its content rather then the value of its *href* attribute. However, we adopted the former approach because expressing a link without using the *href* attribute is counterintuitive.

The resulting approach provides no guarantees that Google will not index the URIs provided in links. Therefore, we additionally introduced an approach that separates discovery of ResourceSync capability documents from discovery of regular Sitemaps. We define a **Capability List** as a document that lists links to all capability documents offered by a Source. Unlike a Sitemap, which is usually discovered via the *robots.txt* file, the Capability List is discovered via the well-known URI *./well-known/resourcesync*, as defined in the ResourceSync specification [10]. This distinct discovery is a best effort approach to implement a separation of concerns but there is no guarantee that Google does not discover the well-known URI and follow the links to the ResourceSync capability documents. We would be happy to see search engines such as Google adopting the ResourceSync format but as long as they do not understand how to interpret the content of the capability documents, the Source might be better off not to advertise them in the robots.txt.

An interesting aspect of the parsing of the Change List shown in Listing 3 was that Google returns a warning that it expects link elements (as well as "meta" elements) to be in the XHTML namespace. None of the above results changed when using the *<xhtml:link>* child element from the XHTML namespace and so, to remain within the ResourceSync namespace, we renamed the link element to *<rs:ln>*.

Capability Distinction and Last Modification at the Root Level

To help Destinations distinguish between capability documents and to convey the document's last modification time we tested the insertion of the *<rs:md>* child element to the *<urlset>* root element with two attributes. The attribute identifying the capability document is called *capability* (as defined in the ResourceSync specification [10]) and the document's last modification time is conveyed with the attribute *modified*. We included the child element into a Resource List (Listing 4) and submitted the document to Google.

```
<?xml version="1.0" encoding="UTF-8"?>
<urlset xmlns="http://www.sitemaps.org/schemas/sitemap/0.9"
        xmlns:rs="http://www.openarchives.org/rs/terms/">
  <rs:md capability="resourcelist"
         modified="2013-02-03T09:00:00Z"/>
  <url>
    <loc>http://example.com/res1</loc>
    <lastmod>2013-02-01T13:00:00Z</lastmod>
  </url>
</urlset>
```

Listing 4: Resource List with capability identifier and last modification date

Google did not reject the Sitemap, even tough it violated the XML schema. It merely returned a warning that the child element is not recognized. This supports our suspicion that the Google does not validate submitted Sitemaps against the schema but rather uses a different logic, which we can only speculate about, to evaluate its correctness.

Links at the Root Level

Two kinds of links at the root level of a ResourceSync document are featured in the framework. A navigational link pointing to the Capability List to support Destinations in discovering all offered capabilities and a link to a document that provides information about the Source.

```
<?xml version="1.0" encoding="UTF-8"?>
<urlset xmlns="http://www.sitemaps.org/schemas/sitemap/0.9"
        xmlns:rs="http://www.openarchives.org/rs/terms/">
  <rs:ln rel="resourcesync"
         href="http://example.com/capabilitylist.xml"/>
  <rs:ln rel="describedby"
         href="http://example.com/info-about-source.xml"/>
  <url>
    <loc>http://example.com/res1</loc>
    <lastmod>2013-02-01T13:00:00Z</lastmod>
  </url>
</urlset>
```

Listing 5: Sitemap with navigational and informational links

We tested this idea and included two *<rs:ln>* child elements from the ResourceSync namespace into the submitted Sitemap. The link to the Capability List has the relation type *resourcesync* (defined in [10]) and the informational link has the relation type *decribedby* (as defined in POWDER [4]). Listing 5 shows the structure of the Sitemap used for this experiment. Google did not reject the Sitemap, even though it contains child elements of the *<urlset>* element different than *<url>*. It did return a warning though that the child elements are not recognized. Unlike in our experiment with links in a *<url>* block, the URIs of these links were not indexed.

4. SUMMARY

The purpose of this series of experiments was to test our Sitemap format extensions and to see how Google would respond to them when submitted to their Webmaster Tool.
Concern 1 did not materialize. The Sitemap schema allows for external elements within the *<url>* block and hence these extensions are perfectly compliant.
Concern 2 did materialize as we saw unintended consequences in terms of indexed URIs that were provided with link elements. Our tests indicate that Google is rather aggressive in indexing URIs from link elements as they occur in *<url>* blocks. We approach this situation by isolating the discovery of ResourceSync capabilities (via the ResourceSync specific well-known URI) from regular Sitemaps (via robots.txt). The well-known URI refers to a Capability List containing pointers to all offered capability documents.
Concern 3 did not materialize. Even though the schema did not allow for child elements of the *<urlset>* root element, Google did not reject our syntax. We suspect that Google does not validate a submitted Sitemaps against the schema but rather uses some unknown logic to evaluate the correctness of the Sitemaps. In addition, our conversations with Microsoft and Google resulted in their adjustment of the Sitemap schema [2] to allow for child elements to the root element. This means that the ResourceSync enhancements to Sitemaps are now fully compliant. URIs provided in link elements on this level were not subject to be indexed. Listing 6 shows a Change List based on the Sitemap format as adopted in the specification.


```
<?xml version="1.0" encoding="UTF-8"?>
<urlset xmlns="http://www.sitemaps.org/schemas/sitemap/0.9"
        xmlns:rs="http://www.openarchives.org/rs/terms/">
  <rs:ln rel="resourcesync"
         href="http://example.com/capabilitylist.xml"/>
  <rs:ln rel="describedby"
         href="http://example.com/info-about-source.xml"/>
  <rs:md capability="changelist"
          modified="2013-02-03T09:00:00Z"/>
  <url>
    <loc>http://example.com/res1</loc>
    <lastmod>2013-01-02T13:00:00Z</lastmod>
    <rs:md change="updated"
             length="6230"
             type="text/html"
             hash="md5:a2f94c567f9b370c43fb1188f1f46330"/>
    <rs:ln rel="duplicate"
           href="http://mirror.example.com/res1"/>
    <rs:ln rel="http://www.openarchives.org/rs/terms/patch"
           href="http://example.com/res1-json-patch"
           type="application/json-patch"/>
  </url>
</urlset>
```


Listing 6: A ResourceSync Change List

We also tested the Atom Syndication Format and even introducing a ResourceSync-specific document format as alternatives to the Sitemap format. Our reasoning for the decision in favor of the Sitemap format is detailed in our previous work Klein et al. [9]. We did not run extensive tests with other search engines. While this is subject to future work, initial tests indicate that Microsoft's Bing, for example, is even more liberal in accepting our Sitemap extensions.

5. ACKNOWLEDGMENTS

The ResourceSync specification is the collaborative work of NISO and OAI. Funding is provided by the Alfred P. Sloan Foundation and UK participation is supported by Jisc.

6. REFERENCES

[1] Google Webmaster Tool. `https://www.google.com/webmasters/tools/`.

[2] Sitemaps XML schema. `http://www.sitemaps.org/schemas/sitemap/0.9/sitemap.xsd`.

[3] Sitemaps XML format, 2008. `http://www.sitemaps.org/protocol.html`.

[4] P. Archer, K. Smith, and A. Perego. Protocol for Web Description Resources (POWDER): Description Resources, September 2009. `http://www.w3.org/TR/powder-dr/`.

[5] A. Bryan, N. McNab, T. Tsujikawa, P. Poeml, and H. Nordstrom. Metalink/HTTP: Mirrors and Hashes, June 2011. `http://www.ietf.org/rfc/rfc6249.txt`.

[6] J. Cho and H. Garcia-Molina. Estimating Frequency of Change. *ACM Transactions on Internet Technology*, 3:256–290, August 2003.

[7] D. Fetterly, M. Manasse, M. Najork, and J. Wiener. A Large-Scale Study of the Evolution of Web Pages. In *Proceedings of WWW '03*, pages 669–678, 2003.

[8] I. Jacobs and N. Walsh. Architecture of the World Wide Web, December 2004. `http://www.w3.org/TR/webarch/`.

[9] M. Klein, R. Sanderson, H. Van de Sompel, S. Warner, B. Haslhofer, C. Lagoze, and M. L. Nelson. A Technical Framework for Resource Synchronization. *D-Lib Magazine*, 19(1/2), 2013.

[10] M. Klein, R. Sanderson, H. Van de Sompel, S. Warner, B. Haslhofer, M. L. Nelson, and C. Lagoze. ResourceSync Framework Specification. `http://www.openarchives.org/rs/resourcesync`.

[11] M. Nottingham and R. Sayre. The Atom Syndication Format, December 2005. `http://www.ietf.org/rfc/rfc4287.txt`.

[12] A. Ntoulas, J. Cho, and C. Olston. What's New on the Web?: The Evolution of the Web from a Search Engine Perspective. In *Proceedings of WWW '04*, pages 1–12, 2004.

[13] P.Bryan and M. Nottingham. JSON Patch, January 2013. `http://tools.ietf.org/html/draft-ietf-appsawg-json-patch`.

[14] J. Snell. Atom Link Extensions, June 2012. `http://tools.ietf.org/html/draft-snell-atompub-link-extensions-09`.

[15] H. Van de Sompel, R. Sanderson, M. Klein, M. L. Nelson, B. Haslhofer, S. Warner, and C. Lagoze. A Perspective on Resource Synchronization. *D-Lib Magazine*, 18(9/10), 2012.

Multimodal Alignment of Scholarly Documents and Their Presentations

Bamdad Bahrani
Department of Computer Science
National University of Singapore
bamdad.bahrani@nus.edu.sg

Min-Yen Kan[1,2]
[1]Department of Computer Science
[2]NUS Interactive and Digital Media Institute
National University of Singapore
kanmy@comp.nus.edu.sg

ABSTRACT

We present a multimodal system for aligning scholarly documents to corresponding presentations in a fine-grained manner (i.e., per presentation slide and per paper section). Our method improves upon a state-of-the-art baseline that employs only textual similarity. Based on an analysis of baseline errors, we propose a three-pronged alignment system that combines textual, image, and ordering information to establish alignment. Our results show a statistically significant improvement of 25%, confirming the importance of visual content in improving alignment accuracy.

Categories and Subject Descriptors

H.3.3 [**Information Storage and Retrieval**]: Information Search and Retrieval; H.3.7 [**Information Storage and Retrieval**]: Digital Libraries

Keywords

Digital library, fine-grained document alignment, slide presentation, slide image classification

1. INTRODUCTION

Scholars use publications to disseminate scientific results. In many fields, scholars also congregate at annual congresses to narrate their scientific discoveries through presentations. These two vehicles that document scientific findings are interesting in their complementarity; while they overlap in content, presentations are often aimed at an introductory level and may motivate one to take up the details in the more complete publication format.

As the presentation is often more visual and narrated by an expert, often it can be regarded as a summary of the salient points of a work, taken from the vantage point of the presenter. By itself, presentations may fufill information needs that do not require in-depth details or call for a non-technical perspective of the work (for laymen, as opposed to subject matter experts). In such cases, a useful function would be to link and present the vehicles in a fine-grained manner that would allow seamless navigation between both forms.

We follow the previous characterization of the *document-to-presentation alignment* problem [7]:

Given:	Presentation S: Slides $s_{1,\dots,n}$
	Document D: Text units $d_{1,\dots,m}$
Output:	Alignment $f(s) = (x, y)$

which maps each slide s_i to a contiguous set of document paragraphs d_x to d_y, or to *nil* (unaligned).

Previous work up to now has maintained a text matching approach to this task. However, some studies suggest that different methods for measuring the similarity between short segments of text (i.e search queries and tags) [9, 12]. However, our input data is neither as short as mentioned studies, nor long as usual text similarity studies. Therefore we use weighted TF*IDF for similarity measure as an baseline and then improve it from different aspect to gain better results. Hayama *et al.* first tackled this problem with Japanese technical papers and presentation sheets using a Hidden Markov Model [5]. In Kan's [7] SlideSeer digital library, the scope of the alignment work was enlarged to include the crawling of document-presentation pairs and the bi-modal (presentation- or document-centric) user interface. His work also recognized that certain slides should not be aligned – termed as *nil* alignment – when new material is introduced in the presentation that is not present in the document. More recently, Beamer and Girju [1] performed a detailed analysis of different similarity metrics' fitness for the alignment. All mentioned studies was not able not achieve high accuracy in their results. One thing that has always been missing in this task is taking advantage of visual content of the slides.

In related but separate vein of work, a few studies show the importance of proper slide structure identification: *i.e.*, differentiation between presentation body and title text, identification of graphical elements such as figures, charts and plots. Such structure is leveraged in downstream applications: slide reuse [6], retrieval [4, 8], and presentation generation from documents [10, 11]. In contrast, there has been minimal work to incorporate this information for document-presentation alignment.

We contribute to the state-of-the-art by addressing this weakness. Our system builds from existing text similarity baselines [7, 1], exploiting graphical information to specifically correct weaknesses of the text-only alignment when dealing with certain classes of presentation slides.

JCDL'13, July 22–26, 2013, Indianapolis, Indiana, USA.

Table 1: **Demographics from Ephraim's 20-pair dataset [3].**

Total # of slides	751
Average # of slides per presentation	37.5
Total # of sections	515
Average # of sections per document	25.75

2. CORPUS STUDY OF PRESENTATIONS

We take the publicly available document-presentation pair corpus from [3] as a starting point (Table 1). Their dataset consists of 20 pairs, drawn from papers in DBLP[1] (in .pdf) on databases and information retrieval, where an author-authored presentation in Microsoft Powerpoint format (.ppt) was found. The dataset is annotated with ground truth alignments, including non-alignable slides (*nil*).

To understand the weakness of previous work, we implemented a basic, text-only alignment system informed by the previous work. Employing standard textual similarity (cosine similarity with *tf.idf* weighting), we aligned the sections of the document to each slide to observe its performance.

Taking a slide-centric approach to analysis, we observe several classes of slides, detailed below. Interestingly, we also find that the performance of text-only alignment also varies per slide class.

- **Text** slides usually form the bulk of content in presentations. These are often bulleted points, distilling the content from the paper into a pithy form.
- *Nil*. These can be title, example, or ending slides (*i.e.*, Q&A, references) or any other content not directly extracted from the paper. The previous work reports that classifying such slides correctly may improve alignment performance anywhere from 3 to 25% [1, 7].
- **Outline**. These are an important sub-class of *nil* slides, that we have separated from the main class. These slides exist solely to present or recap the presentation structure, to help sync the audience to the material being presented.
- **Image** slides consist almost solely of image(s). These are challenging to align for the baseline, since there is little or no textual evidence for alignment.
- **Table** slides are self-explanatory. We note that text extraction often functions to extract the textual strings within the table, which when extracted verbatim from the document, constitute strong evidence for textual alignment.
- **Drawing.** These slides consist of drawing elements: simple shapes, arrows, graphs and text boxes, authored within the presentation software.
- **Continued.** These slides continue information from the previous slide, used when the content overflows from the previous slide. These slides sometimes have textual cues ("cont'd"), and slides identified as such should be aligned as a block with the initial slide.

[1]`http://www.informatik.uni-trier.de/~ley/db/`

Table 2 gives the distribution of these slide classes in terms of prevalence in the dataset by presence/absence in the presentations, and by raw number. We also indicate error rate (raw and percentage), in the last column. Note that we omit **Text** slides that are well-suited to alignment by textual similarity. We see that both *nil* and **Image** classes are found in the large majority of presentations, and also constitute a large number of errors in the baseline. These are the classes of errors we target to ameliorate by our multimodal technique.

Table 2: Analyses of the dataset. Frequency and baseline alignment performance shown by slide class.

Slide Type	Present in # of presentations (out of 20)	# of slides (out of 751)	# (%age) of incorrect alignments
nil	19 (95%)	128 (17%)	83 (64%)
Outline	8 (40%)	36 (4.8%)	13 (36%)
Image	19 (95%)	90 (12%)	73 (81%)
Table	5 (25%)	8 (1%)	4 (50%)
Drawing	12 (60%)	65 (8.7%)	35 (53%)
Continued	9 (45%)	61 (8.1%)	24 (39%)

3. METHOD

Our automated multimodal alignment system presupposes extracted text from both the document and the presentation. As text extraction from documents is a noisy process (even for those born digitally, as in our dataset), we spent a fair amount of work in creating a pipeline to engineer relatively clean output data. For documents, we leverage the PDFX package[2], which outputs an XML format that largely preserves the paper's title and text, recognizing sections, figure and table captions. For presentations, we used custom Visual Basic code to extract its title and body content.

Given this pre-processing, our system then exploits the textual content and slide images to perform the alignment, as in Figure 1. We architect our system to consider textual similarity evidence and natural, linear ordering as probabilistic preferences in the alignment process, building a separate module for each of these two analyses. Given a slide s_j, the two modules output a vector v_i of length $|D|$ that represents the probability of aligning the slide to the particular document section d_i. In the final fusion phase (marked as $\otimes$), we fuse these vectors into the final alignment through heuristic rules that consider the visual slide image. If no module yields strong evidence for alignment (*i.e.*, low probability), then the slide is deemed *nil*.

Text Similarity. This serves as the primary basis to align **Text** slides. We compute a cosine similarity between the two extracted texts (slide and section), using *tf.idf* weighting, as is recommended by the prior work [1, 7]. These similarity scores are summed to normalize the vector v_{Ti} to unity. We use this text similarity module alone as the baseline for comparison in our evaluation.

Linear Ordering. Studying our corpus, we find that most pairs' show that the ordering between slides and sections are monotonic. We thus output an alignment probability vector v_{Oi} that gives the linear mapping of M sections to N slides (i.e., for slide number i: $\lfloor \frac{i}{\lceil N/M \rceil} \rfloor$) the highest probability, and close neighbors a smaller probability. Doc-

[2]Available at `http://pdfx.cs.man.ac.uk/`

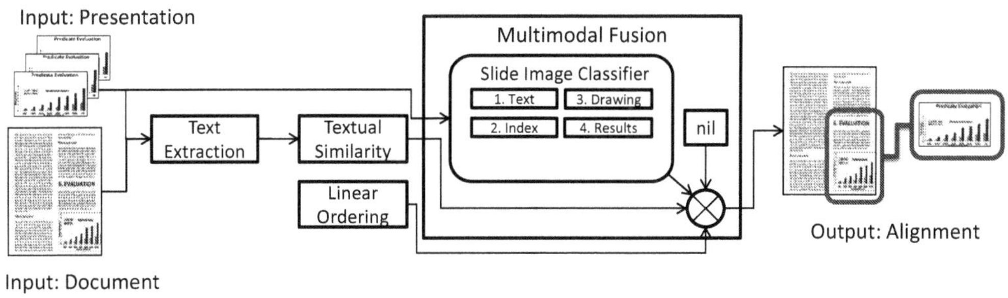

Figure 1: System Architecture.

ument sections not close to the natural alignment point are deemed to have zero probability.

3.1 Slide Image Classification-based Fusion

We observed that over 20% of our dataset are represented by visual cues, which attests to its importance in the alignment process. To enable a first attempt at using this information, we devised an slide image classification, aimed to distinguish four, easy-to-differentiate slide image classes. Note that this classification overlaps but is not identical to our earlier, baseline error-driven analysis.

The four classes covered by our classifier are: 1) *text*, 2) *outline*, 3) *drawing elements* and 4) *results*. *Results* slide images encompass charts, tables, and other visual objects that typically appear in the evaluation portion of a presentation.

Using 10-fold cross validation over a separate dataset of 750 manually annotated slides (by the first author), we trained a linear SVM using features representing the Histogram of Oriented Gradients (HOG) (as suggested in [2]) as computed over the slide image. HOGs are feature descriptors used in computer vision and image processing for the purpose of object detection [2]. The technique counts occurrences of gradient orientations in localized portions of an image. This method is similar to other vision techniques of edge orientation histograms, scale-invariant feature transform descriptors (SIFT) and shape contexts, but differs in that it is computed on a dense grid of uniformly spaced cells and uses overlapping local contrast normalization for improved accuracy. HOG relies on both the gradient and edges in an image and is more robust than its predecessor features. Also, it has been recently shown that HOG can be applied for text detection/extraction from images [13]. We used a patch size and bin size for HOG were 9 and [32 32], respectively, after appropriate manual tuning. Pre-processing was performed using blurring filters following by normalization (to enforce a mean of 0 and standard deviation of 1). Overall, the resulting image classifier returned an acceptable 87% average accuracy over our cross-validation runs (Table 3). Figure 2 gives sample classification probabilities on slides from two classes – *results* and *outline*: for each class the probability that classifier has assigned to some example slides is shown.

Table 3: 10-fold slide image classifier performance.

Slide Type	Text	Outline	Drawing	Results	Average
Accuracy	86%	95%	83%	84%	87.2%

The resultant slide image classification tells us what sources of evidence to trust for the final alignment: text, ordering, or the possible *nil* alignment. We find that the *results* class is

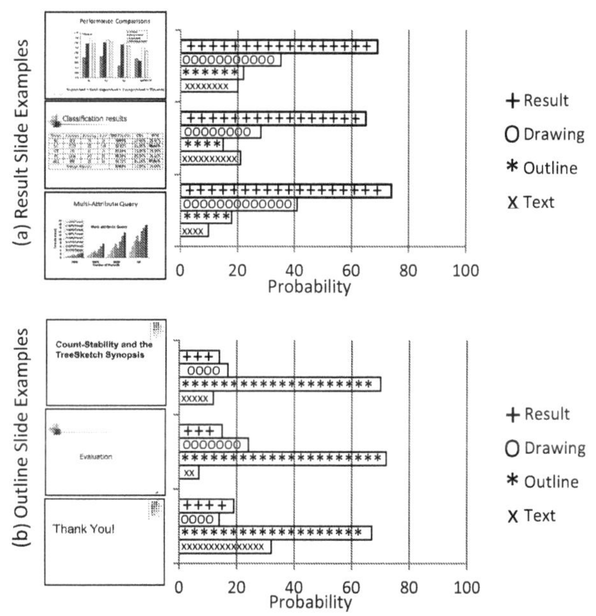

Figure 2: Image classification performance on two sets of example slides: (a) "Result" slide examples and (b) "Outline" slide examples.

accurate enough to use as an unconditional rule: if the image classifier deems a slide as a *result*, we attempt to locate the document section(s) marked by an appropriate header (*i.e.*, "Results", "Experiments", "Discussion"; actually determined by a regular expression over section headers); sample results are shown in Figure 3(a). For the other three classes, the text similarity, linear ordering alignment probability vectors are weighted and fused with a threshold for *nil* alignment to yield the final alignment.

— For *Text* slides, the system increases the weight for text alignment output by 2/3 of its current value, since text similarity measures are more accurate when sufficient amount of text is available in a slide.

— For *Outline* slides which are potentially *nil* slides, the system lowers both w_{Ti} and w_{Oi} to disfavor alignment, setting both as 1/3 of their current values. Figure 3(b) shows some examples of *Outline* slide thumbnails.

— For *Drawing* slides, no conclusion can be drawn from

the slide visual appearance. This kind of slides may relate to any section, thus our system gives uniform probability to all weights. Our system relies on the judgment of the other modalities for the alignment decision. We fuse the alignment vectors v_{Ti} and v_{Oi} and *nil*, re-weighting them with their coefficients as follows:

$$v_A i = argmax_i\{w_t(v_{Ti}) + w_o(v_{Oi}) + (1 - w_t - w_o)(nil)\} \quad (1)$$

The section i (or *nil*) that has the highest likelihood is thus deemed the correct alignment.

4. EXPERIMENTS AND RESULTS

We run through four experimental conditions to assess the performance of our methods.

Our first experiment starts with paragraph-to-slide alignment, as opposed to section-to-slide alignment, to make our evaluation comparable to Kan [7]. Here, we only used textual data to compute the probability vector. We achieve 52.1% accuracy, outperforming his results. We believe the main reasons for this improvement is due to 1) our preprocessing, which uses more accurate text extraction tools for both slides and papers, resulting in less noisy data; and 2) Kan's evaluation method uses a more complex weighted Jaccard accuracy, whereas in our proposed system, a slide is correctly aligned if the first suggested paragraph is correct. Thes best result achieved by Kan and our baseline system are shown in Table 4.

Aligning to coarser-grained sections instead of paragraphs will result in higher accuracy without any system chance. When we performed our bi-modal alignment to sections, accuracy improves by 8.6%. This simplifies the problem, but from a usability standpoint may be more useful, as a user interface is likely to show sections of a document rather than a single paragraph (the latter being too small a text unit to show individually).

Table 4: Alignment accuracy results for different experimental conditions.

Method	Accuracy
Kan (weighted Jaccard) [7]	41.2%
B&G (automated) [1]	50%
(1): Baseline	52.1%
(2): Section-to-slide	60.7%
(3): 2 + Ordering	66.8%
B&G (w/ manual *nil* removal) [1]	75%
(4): 3 + Image Classification	77.3%

A third condition adds in ordering alignment to the text-only baseline. In this multimodal alignment, we gave static, uniform weights to both probability vectors. We observe a real improvement of 6%, obtained by accounting for natural bias toward monotopic ordering.

Our final condition (Experiment 4) runs our entire system, adding in the proposed image classification system over the previous condition. Using the full functionality of multimodal method improves an additional 10.5%, for a aggregate accuracy of over 77%, a significant improvement over the baseline 52%. Our results also yield higher accuracies to that of Beamer and Girju's [1], even accounting for their manual removal of *nil* slides (a simplication of our problem).

5. CONCLUSION

We have shown that visual information constitutes an important source of evidence for document-presentation alignment. We design a simple, supervised image classifier that uses HOG features to distinguish slide images that are 1) primarily text, 2) outlines, 3) results, and consist of 4) drawing elements. This image classifier is used to properly weight image, text and ordering evidence in alignment. The results particularly help to identify non-alignable (*nil*) slides, improving accuracy substantially.

6. REFERENCES

[1] B. Beamer and R. Girju. Investigating automatic alignment methods for slide generation from academic papers. In *Proceedings of CoNLL*, page 111, 2009.

[2] N. Dalal and B. Triggs. Histograms of oriented gradients for human detection. In *Proceedings of CVPR*, volume 1, pages 886–893. IEEE, 2005.

[3] E. E. Ephraim. Presentation to document alignment. Undergraduate thesis, National University of Singapore, 2006.

[4] T. Hayama and S. Kunifuji. Relevant piece of information extraction from presentation slide page for slide information retrieval system. *Knowledge, Information, and Creativity Support Systems*, pages 22–31, 2011.

[5] T. Hayama, H. Nanba, and S. Kunifuji. Alignment between a technical paper and presentation sheets using a hidden markov model. In *Proceeding of Active Media Technology*, pages 102–106. IEEE, 2005.

[6] T. Hayama, H. Nanba, and S. Kunifuji. Structure extraction from presentation slide information. *Proceedings of PRICAI: Trends in Artificial Intelligence*, pages 678–687, 2008.

[7] M.-Y. Kan. Slideseer: A digital library of aligned document and presentation pairs. In *Proceedings of JCDL*, pages 81–90. ACM, 2007.

[8] G. Liew and M. Kan. Slide image retrieval: a preliminary study. In *Proceedings of JCDL*, pages 359–362. ACM, 2008.

[9] D. Metzler, S. Dumais, and C. Meek. Similarity measures for short segments of text. *Advances in Information Retrieval*, pages 16–27, 2007.

[10] M. Sravanthi, C. Chowdary, and P. Kumar. Slidesgen: Automatic generation of presentation slides for a technical paper using summarization. In *Proceeding of FLAIRS*, 2009.

[11] Y. Wang and K. Sumiya. Skeleton generation for presentation slides based on expression styles. *Intelligent Interactive Multimedia: Systems and Services*, pages 551–560, 2012.

[12] W. Yih and C. Meek. Improving similarity measures for short segments of text. In *Proceedings of Artificial Intelligence*, volume 22, page 1489. Menlo Park, CA; Cambridge, MA; London; AAAI Press; MIT Press; 1999, 2007.

[13] J. Zhang and R. Kasturi. Text detection using edge gradient and graph spectrum. In *Pattern Recognition (ICPR), 2010 20th International Conference on*, pages 3979–3982. IEEE, 2010.

Visual-Interactive Querying for Multivariate Research Data Repositories Using Bag-of-Words

Maximilian Scherer
TU Darmstadt
Interactive Graphics Systems Group
Fraunhoferstr. 5
64283 Darmstadt, Germany
maximilian.scherer@gris.tu-darmstadt.de

Tatiana von Landesberger
TU Darmstadt
Interactive Graphics Systems Group
Fraunhoferstr. 5
64283 Darmstadt, Germany
tatiana.von_landesberger@gris.tu-darmstadt.de

Tobias Schreck
University of Konstanz
Data Analysis and Visualization Group
Universitaetsstr. 10
78457 Konstanz, Germany
tobias.schreck@uni-konstanz.de

ABSTRACT

Large amounts of multivariate data are collected in different areas of scientific research and industrial production. These data are collected, archived and made publicly available by research data repositories. In addition to meta-data based access, content-based approaches are highly desirable to effectively retrieve, discover and analyze data sets of interest. Several such methods, that allow users to search for particular curve progressions, have been proposed. However, a major challenge when providing content-based access – interactive feedback during query formulation – has not received much attention yet. This is important because it can substantially improve the user's search effectiveness.

In this paper, we present a novel interactive feedback approach for content-based access to multivariate research data. Thereby, we enable query modalities that were not available for multivariate data before. We provide instant search results and highlight query patterns in the result set. Real-time search suggestions give an overview of important patterns to look for in the data repository. For this purpose, we develop a bag-of-words index for multivariate data as the back-end of our approach.

We apply our method to a large repository of multivariate data from the climate research domain. We describe a use-case for the discovery of interesting patterns in maritime climate research using our new visual-interactive query tools.

Categories and Subject Descriptors

H.3.7 [**Information Storage and Retrieval**]: Digital Libraries; H.3.1 [**Information Storage and Retrieval**]: Content Analysis and Indexing—*Indexing methods*

JCDL'13, July 22–26, 2013, Indianapolis, Indiana, USA.

ACM 978-1-4503-2077-1/13/07 ...$15.00.

Keywords

Research Data Repositories; Content-Based Retrieval; Bag-of-Words; Query Interfaces; Multivariate Data

1. INTRODUCTION

Multivariate data can be described as tabular data with dimensionality $m \times n$, where n is the number of variables (e.g., water density, water depth or pressure) and m is the number of observations (e.g., time of day or location). Such data arises in many areas of research, industrial production and other commercial applications. Due to increasing efforts in the digital library community over the last decade, such data, particularly that obtained for research purposes, is made publicly available in specialized research data repositories. For example, the PANGAEA repository [6] is a digital library for data-intensive environmental sciences. It hosts very large amounts of earth observation data of various kinds (e.g., time series, multivariate observations, image data, etc.), which are provided for public access. Similar to the search and access paradigms for multimedia databases, content-based access to such repositories has started to receive attention from the Digital Library community. Such access supports users to search and explore data patterns, in addition to annotated textual meta-data. Previous work has considered similarity functions and feature extraction techniques for relevant aspects of research data, including time series, functional, and bivariate data [14, 10, 7, 25], as well as their evaluation [13, 26]. Little research, however, focused on *interactive methods* which use these new similarity functions to help the user with the query formulation process based on data content. Such methods include highlighting of results to show why a document was retrieved, as well as search suggestions to provide the user with an overview of meaningful terms she can search for next. These functions are typically located on the front-end of a visual-interactive retrieval system, but require indexing structures in the back-end to be efficient.

In this work, we present a novel approach for providing the user with interactive search suggestions and result highlighting when querying multivariate data. Such visual-interactive tools are already successfully used in textual search engines and yield similar advantages to users querying non-textual research data documents. Search suggestions provide users with an overview of (often complex) data patterns and vari-

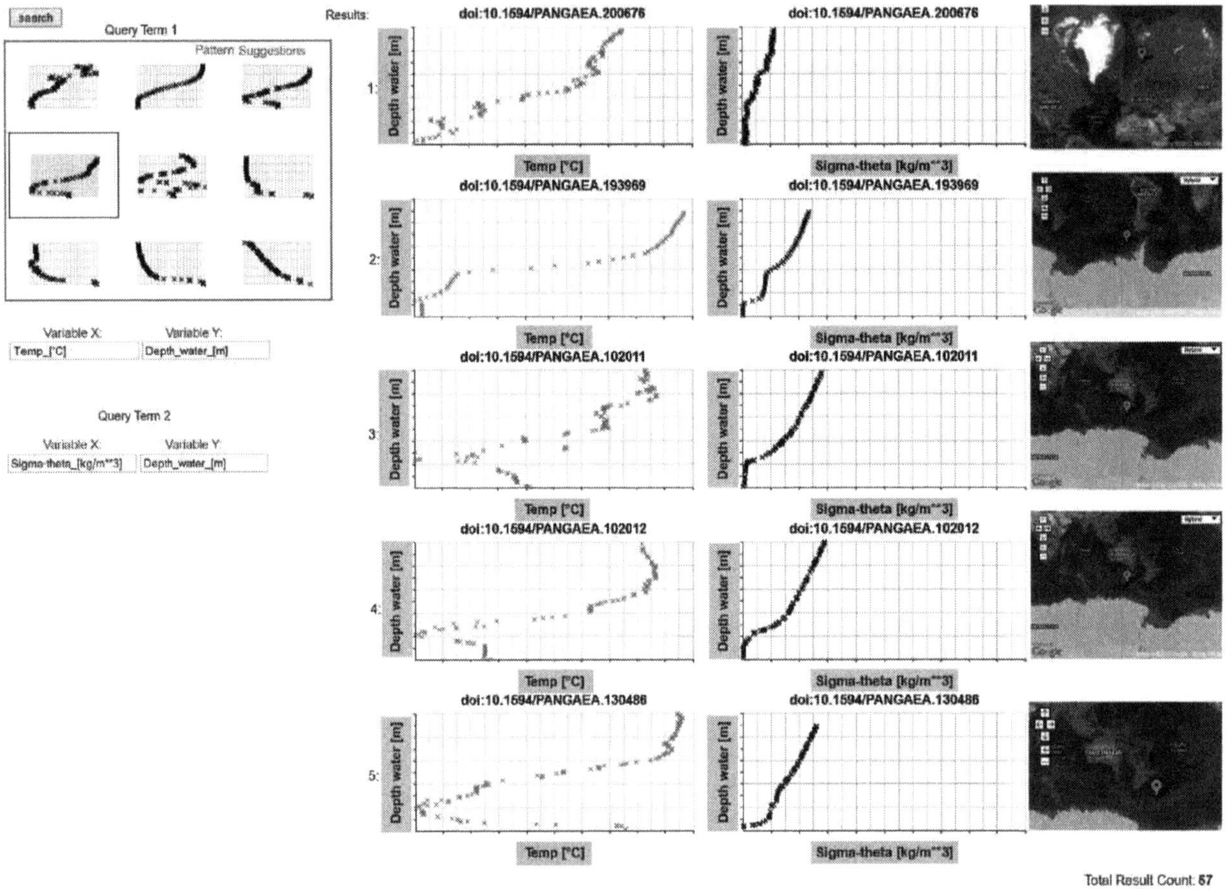

Figure 1: Case Study: We queried for a specific pattern between temperature and water depth to see whether the documents containing this pattern were measured at locations with a similar maritime climate.The first document is situated in the Norwegian sea, while documents 2 to 5 were obtained in the antarctic southern ocean. Both regions have a maritime subarctic climatic zone, explaining why the same pattern was found there. Map Data is attributed to Google Maps.

able names to search for or refine their search; result highlighting shows the user, which part of a document matched her query and thus explains *why* it was retrieved. Figure 1 shows a screenshot of the proposed system in action and illustrates these benefits for the users (the use-case is detailed in Section 4). By searching for a specific pattern of water depth versus temperature, we can find measurements that were obtained in areas with a similar maritime climate. Using only meta-data (the geo-location in this case) such a query would not have been possible.

Akin to search suggestions on popular web- or e-commerce search engines, we present the user with search suggestions and completions, based on her partial query as it is being entered. Figure 4 shows an example of this suggestion-approach. Furthermore we can provide the user with instant search results and also highlight those parts of a retrieved multivariate data-set, that corresponds to the user's query. Similar to paragraph highlighting in text retrieval, we propose to show those scatter-plots of a retrieved data-set, that contain parts of the query (e.g., a textual hit on the axis label or a particular scatter-plot pattern) and to highlight these parts. That way a user can see why a particular document was retrieved in the first place, and quickly skim through the results to find the data-sets she is most interested in. Another example in Figure 5 shows a result list and the highlighted scatter-plots.

To allow for this kind of visual-interactive querying in multivariate data, we develop a novel indexing method based on a bag-of-words approach. The bag-of-words approach has shown to yield state of the art retrieval performance in multimedia databases, e.g., for images, videos or music [12]. We propose to adapt it for retrieval in multivariate research data repositories. The basic idea is shown in Figure 2. By extracting bivariate features from each pair of variables in multivariate data, we obtain a set of local features for each document. We then quantize each feature vector, by assigning the id of the closest cluster centroid (obtained, e.g., via k-means clustering) to each feature vector. Thus we can represent a document with multivariate data by a set of content-based tokens obtained from this quantization. Such a representation allows us to leverage efficient indexing using inverted lists. The details of this indexing approach are described in Section 3.

We provide a case-study of our proposed approach in Sec-

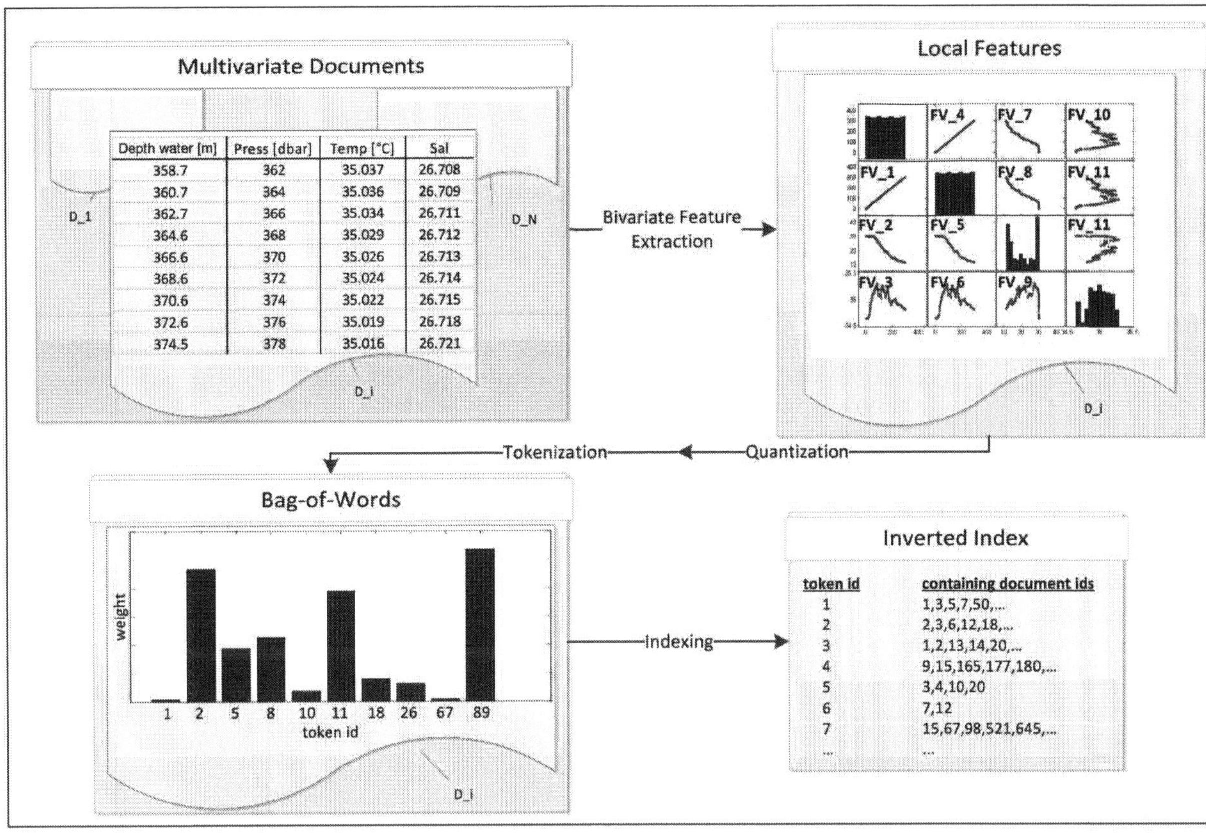

Figure 2: Overview of our bag-of-words approach for indexing multivariate research data.

tion 4. We index all publicly available research data documents of the data repository *PANGAEA* [6]. We show how our proposed indexing scheme and the newly enabled visual-interactive search tools can be used for this kind of research data documents.

2. RELATED WORK

This work is related to several aspects of digital libraries, multimedia information retrieval and data mining. In the following two subsections we outline recent work related to this paper.

2.1 Content-based and Visual Access Methods

Content-based analysis and indexing is an important research domain within digital libraries to provide additional access paradigms to documents besides access based on annotated meta-data [20].

Examples of recent digital library systems that provide different means of content-based access include systems for 3D models and classical music [3], images [23, 5], time-series data [1], climate data [25] and chemical data [16]. On top of access via annotated meta-data, these digital library systems extract domain-specific *descriptors* from the underlying data as a basis to implement distance functions in support of search and access functionality. Such access includes query-by-example, e.g., supplying an example image and retrieving similar images [23, 5]; query-by-sketch, e.g., drawing a shape and retrieving similar 3D models; or content-based layouts, e.g., clustering time-series by data similarity and presenting the user with an overview [1].

Visual access methods have shown to be highly successful for providing overview and search functionality for users in the Digital Library domain [9]. Effective interfaces can help to more effectively browse, search or analyze large data repositories [31]. The idea behind many approaches is based on Shneiderman's Visual Information Seeking Mantra to provide overview first and details on demand [27]. A recent example of such a system in the digital library context was presented in [2]. There, by analyzing meta-data and time-series based content at the same time, this system generates an interactive layout of research data to enable the discovery of interesting co-occurrences of meta-data based and time-series based patterns. Such approaches can combine traditional meta-data based and content-based methods and can extend the standard search support with elements of explorative search systems useful for hypothesis generation [30].

2.2 Bag-of-Words

The focus of this work is to provide the user with a set of interactive retrieval tools which can respond in real-time to user interaction. Our interactive approaches include instant display of search results, highlighting and search suggestions for querying multivariate research data. All of these functions require an efficient computation of similarities. A suitable, efficient content-based indexing method to this end is

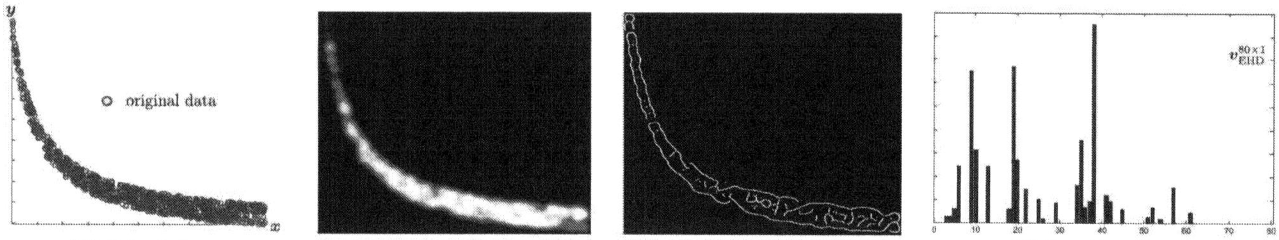

(a) Input data (b) Gaussian kernel density (c) Detected edges (d) Edge histogram

Figure 3: Bivariate feature extraction: Given bivariate input data (a), estimate Gaussian kernel density (b), apply canny edge detector (c) and compute edge histogram descriptor (d). This algorithm by Scherer et al. [26] has shown to yield state of the art performance for bivariate data retrieval.

the bag-of-words (BOW) approach that has become highly popular in multimedia information retrieval. It has been shown to yield state-of-the-art retrieval performance in different domains, including image and music retrieval [17, 22, 12]. In this paper we transfer it for the first time to the domain of multivariate research data. BOW approaches originate from text retrieval and natural language processing, where the inherent tokenization of textual documents was used for proposing efficient indexing and term weighting methods [24].

It was first applied to multimedia documents by Sivic and Zisserman for content-based image retrieval [28]. The basic approach is to extract local features, e.g., SIFT [19] or SURF features for images, quantizing these features via k-means or other suitable clustering methods [32], and finally indexing / weighting these tokens using techniques like tf-idf [24], (probabilistic) latent semantic indexing [11] or latent Dirichlet allocation [4]. This allows for similarity measurements between multimedia objects via their associated bag-of-words (usually the terms are encoded as a histogram), as well as querying or clustering the documents via specific terms (e.g., a predominant color in an image). Most recently, such a bag-of-words approach was also applied successfully to the retrieval of 3D models and 3D scenes [8] as well as to the retrieval of time-series data [18].

3. APPROACH

In our approach, we provide search suggestions and highlighting for querying multivariate data documents. To perform the required computations at interactive rates, we need efficient similarity functions for multivariate data. Therefore, we base our approach on constructing and utilizing a bag-of-words index.

In the following subsections, we first describe the construction of the index itself and then describe the interactive feedback functions for retrieval of multivariate data. We present several examples for retrieval, suggestions and highlighting using our proposed approach using data described in Section 4.

3.1 Bag-of-Words Indexing

As a basis of our approach we provide data indexing, whereby we adapt the bag-of-words approach to multivariate (tabular) data. The flow-chart in Figure 2 gives an overview of the required algorithmic steps. We describe how we adapted each of the these steps for indexing multivariate data.

1. Feature Extraction: extract a set of n local feature vectors $\vec{v}_i$ for each data object (scatter plot in our case)
2. Quantization: quantize each of the feature vectors $\vec{v}_i$ for all documents.(Offline Step: Training a quantizer model $q(\vec{v})$)
3. Tokenization: combine the quantized features with additional categorical information
4. Term Weighting: assign a suitable weight to each obtained term
5. Indexing: build inverted lists containing the relevance of a given token (quantized feature vector) for every document

Step 1: Feature Extraction.

We consider multivariate data documents that contain tabular data with dimensionality $m \times n$. In practice that means n different variables (like water density, water depth or pressure) where measured m times. To extract a set of feature vectors from such a document containing multivariate data, we propose to compute all bivariate variable combinations, and compute a feature vector from each of these two-dimensional point-clouds (scatter-plots). Much like the previously mentioned SIFT or SURF features for images, these feature vectors are also *local* in the sense that they represent a local pattern (bivariate) in the whole (multivariate) document.

Based on previous results on feature extraction and benchmarking for bivariate data [26], we will use the algorithm that yielded the best overall results in the benchmark: EDH. It is based on the MPEG-7 descriptor "edge histogram detector" used in shape retrieval. The basic idea of EDH is to render the actual scatter-plot of the bivariate data using Gaussian kernel-density estimation. During this process the scatter-plots is min-/max-normalized, resulting in translation and linear-trend invariance. Then an edge filter is applied to this rendered image and the orientation of the resulting edges are extracted as a histogram. Figure 3 shows an illustration of this extraction process.

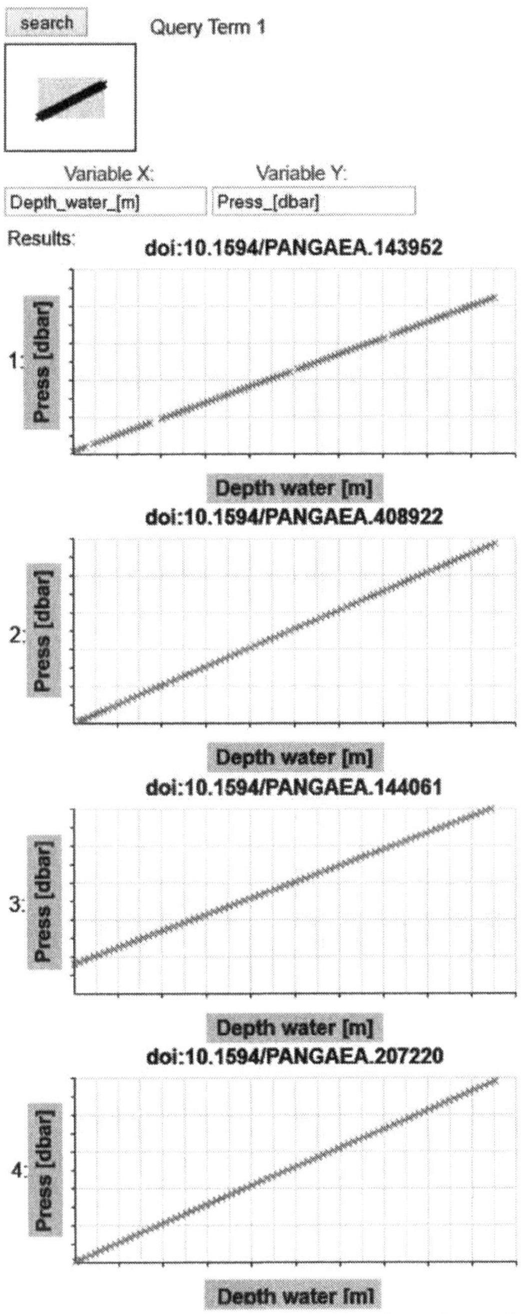

Figure 4: An example query using the *PANGAEA* data repository. We searched for a linear relationship between water depth and water pressure. This tri-gram (variable x, variable y, curve form) we searched for is highlighted in each retrieved dataset.

The result of this feature extraction step is a set of 80-dimensional feature vectors for each multivariate document. The number of feature vectors equals the number of possible scatter-plots, $n \cdot (n-1)$ for multivariate data with n dimensions.

Please note that the benchmark used for evaluation of bivariate descriptors [26] cannot be directly applied to our case, as we consider multivariate data retrieval.

Step 2: Quantization.

The result of the feature extraction is a set of feature vectors for each document. Since we need to obtain a set of tokens for each document, we train a quantization model that is suitable to project each input feature vector to a categorical integer value (the id of the codebook entry). There is a wealth of clustering algorithms suitable for this task [32]. We chose k-means clustering as this has shown good performance for image-retrieval tasks at reasonable computational costs. We choose a random subset of all feature vectors $\vec{v}_i$ and compute a k-means clustering on this subset. The number of clusters k was set to 5000 based on the literature for a compromise between discriminativeness and computational cost [33].

We can then represent an unlabeled feature vector by computing the nearest of the k centroids and assigning the ID of this centroid as the token for this feature vector.

Step 3: Tokenization.

Once we quantized the feature vectors of each document and obtained the categorical cluster ids, we tokenize the document. Since we are not only interested in bivariate data patterns (which are now encoded in the quantized features), but also in the variable combination that exhibits this pattern, we index the data tokens as all possible uni-, bi- and tri-gram terms. For example, if the feature vector of the scatter plot of variable a versus variable b was quantized to cluster id c, we would obtain the terms a, b, c, a_b, b_c, a_c, a_b_c.

Step 4: Term Weighting.

After obtaining a set of terms for each document, we have to choose a weighting scheme for these terms to allow for ranked retrieval (instead of just Boolean retrieval). A straight forward scheme to measure the relevance of a term to a given document is *term frequency* – the number of occurrences of a term in a document. This, however, is not suitable for our terms as the tri-grams – by construction – occur at most once in a given document. Hence, we propose to use the distance to the closest cluster centroid in feature space as the relevance of those terms respectively. As an alternative, we also experimented with introducing an inverse-document frequency (idf) weight, which had little to no effect on retrieval performance and was thus discarded.

Step 5: Indexing.

The final step is to index the set of weighted terms of each document. For each given, distinct term we build an inverted list. This means, that we save a hashed look-up from each term to each document that contains this term along with the associated weight. This allows for ranked retrieval by intersecting the inverted lists of each search term, aggregating the term weights and sorting them in descending order. This approach scales very well. The required main memory for this indexing structures increases linearly with the number of indexed documents. Retrieval time is constant with respect to the index look-up and is dominated by the time required to read the document data from the hard disks.

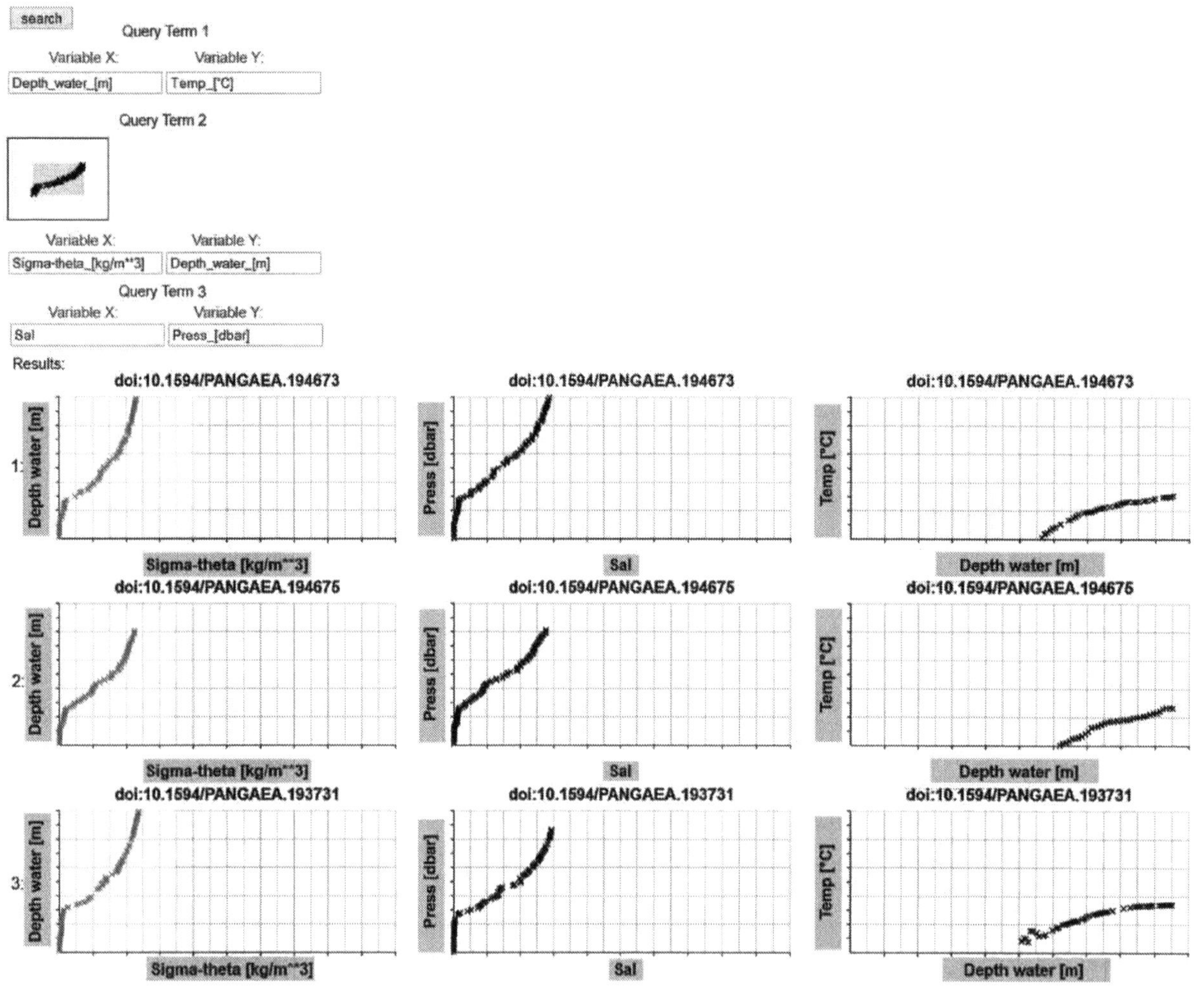

Figure 5: Search Result Highlighting on our front-end: For each of the retrieved multivariate documents, the scatter-plots that contain the search terms are highlighted by coloring the axis labels and/or the data points in yellow. We searched for multivariate documents that contain a sigmoid like relationship between water density (sigma-theta) and water depth, as well as an arbitrary relationship of water depth versus temperature and salinity versus pressure. Note that the retrieved documents contain all of these search terms; we highlight the results accordingly to show the user, why these documents were retrieved.

3.2 Retrieval

We use the bag-of-words index described in the previous subsection for content-based retrieval. A user can search for arbitrary meta-data, parameters, parameter combinations, data pattern id or a specific relationship of a versus b with pattern c. Figure 4 shows an example search query. In this example, we searched for a complete tri-gram by specifying both axis labels (water depth versus pressure) and a data pattern (a linear relationship between those two variables).

As with any full-text index that is based on inverted lists, we can efficiently combine several search terms by intersecting the associated lists. Thus, the default behavior of our approach is to look for all search terms, and only return those documents, that contain every search term and rank them according to their aggregated term weight as described above.

3.3 Instant Results

Due to the full-text-like indexing of our bag-of-words approach, we are able to perform search queries in less than 300 milliseconds, which is generally accepted as "instantaneous" in retrieval applications (see 4.1 for our test-setup). Thus, while the user is still formulating her query, we provide her with immediate results as this has been shown to speed up the retrieval process.

As long as the full-text-index and the primary key index of the database fully reside in the system's main memory, the look-up part of the query time is independent of the number of documents and is dominated by the time required to read the result data from the hard disk.

3.4 Result Highlighting

Highlighting of search results is very important to explain to the user, why a particular document is being returned.

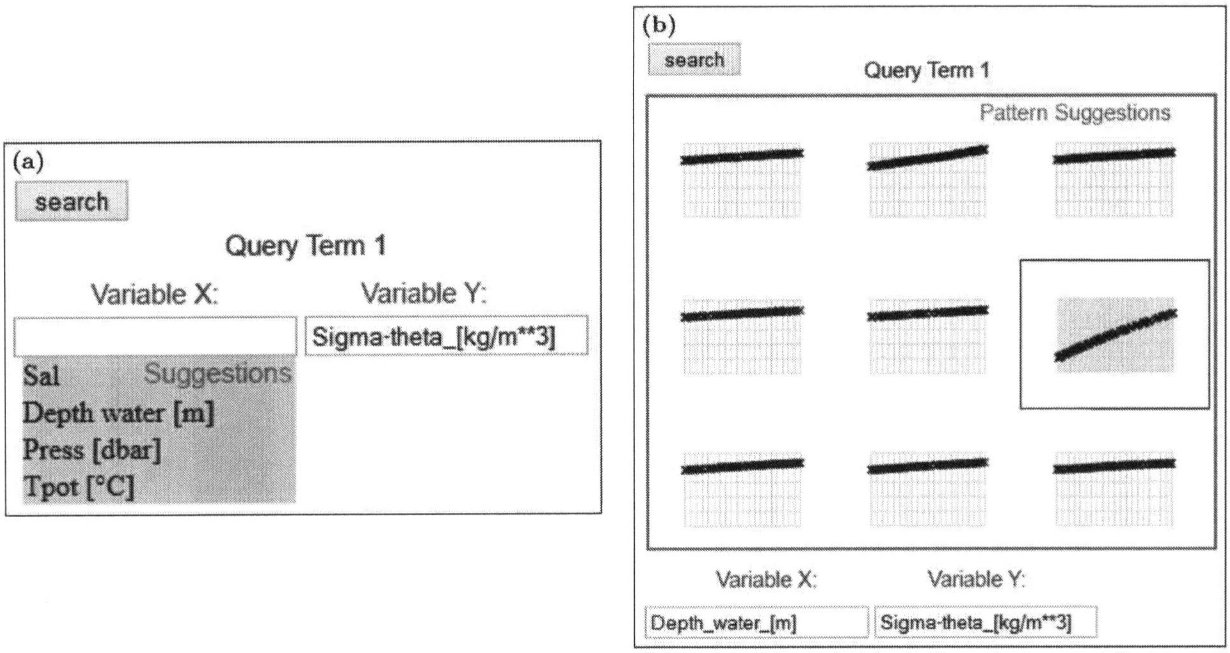

Figure 6: Search Suggestions on our front-end: (a) After specifying one axis label for our search term, the system presents search terms for the other axis. In this example we specified water density as the y axis. The system suggests to search for salinity, water depth, pressure or temperature – precisely those four variables that water density is functionally dependent of [29]. (b) After selecting one of the suggested x-axis labels, the system suggests search terms for the curve progression by visualizing small scatter-plots to the user.

For text retrieval, highlighting the search terms and showing a few surrounding sentences is a very suitable way to do so. We adapt this to our retrieval scenario. For each retrieved multivariate document, we show up to five plots of its scatter-plot-matrix. These scatter-plots visualize those bivariate patterns in each document that matched the user query. We further highlight those scatter-plots by coloring the axis labels and / or the data-points, depending on their match with the search term. Figure 5 shows an example query, where scatter-plots of each returned document highlight the user's query matches.

3.5 Search Suggestions

We provide users with search suggestions as they provide a major increase in useability for most retrieval systems. Search suggestions and auto-completions gained particular popularity due to their introduction into Google's and Amazon's search front-ends. Since then, search suggestions have also become central to the user's expectations (or mental model) how a search engine works [15]. As such, failure to provide the user with this functionality often leads to queries with no results due to the search for non-existent patters. In other cases, users do not have a precise pattern in mind to search for (or to continue / refine their search with). In these cases, search suggestions provide the user with a much needed overview of patterns she can search for next.

Our approach for search suggestions works as follows.

- retrieve d documents that contain all query terms the user searched for so far
- sum up the ranking scores for all tri-gram terms in the result set
- restrict possible tri-grams according to a partial search term (e.g., a partial axis label) the user supplied
- return the h tri-grams with the highest score as search suggestions and visualize them accordingly

The visualization shows a pop-up of potential x- and y-axis labels, as well as up to nine scatter-plots as small preview images the user can select from (see Figure 6).

The parameter d, the number of documents retrieved to select search suggestions from, influences the quality of the suggestions (higher d is better) but also the computational cost of the suggestions (lower d is better). We found d = 50 to be a good compromise between run-time and search suggestion accuracy.

4. APPLICATION

4.1 Data Source and Setup

We show the applicability and scalability our proposed approach to real-world data from *PANGAEA* Data Library [6, 21]. *PANGAEA* is a digital library for environmental sciences and it archives, publishes, and distributes georeferenced primary research data from scientists all over the world. It is operated by the Alfred-Wegener-Institute for Polar and Marine Research in Bremerhaven, and the Center for Marine Environmental Sciences in Bremen, Germany.

For this use-case, we considered every document that is currently available under the Creative Commons Attribution

License 3.0 and downloadable from http://www.pangaea.de. In total, we were able to obtain and index 98,416 such documents. The raw uncompressed data of these documents requires approximately 35 GB of disk space. Using our approach, we computed and indexed approximately 2.5 million terms. This requires about 2 GB of RAM to keep the index fully within the main memory of our test setup.

Each document is uniquely identified with a DOI (digital object identifier) and consists of a table of multivariate measurements, that include radiation levels, temperature progressions and ozone values, among many more. Each document available at *PANGAEA* is carefully annotated by the scientist who conducted the measurements. A data curator controls the quality of this annotation process. These meta-data annotations include standardized names along with base units for each measurement variable in the data table, which we use for tokenization as described in Section 3.

4.2 Case Study

We use this wealth of environmental data indexed with our approach for a case study. Assuming no prior knowledge of the contents of this data repository, we look for data sets that show similar measurement patterns as part of an explorative search process. It can be the basis to hypothesize about the reason for the observed similarities. First, we enter two intuitive variables, namely water temperature and water depth. Since we do not know what kind of pattern a measurement between these two variables should look like, we let the system provide us with an overview of important patterns (see upper left part of Figure 1). We initially assumed temperature to either drop or rise with water depth (depending on whether the environment is warm or cold). However, we were surprised the system suggested a pattern that indicates a temperature drop up until a certain water depth, and then an increase (see scatter-plot "'Suggestions"' in upper left of Figure 1). Thus, we searched for this pattern. Moreover, we wanted to highlight water density versus water depth in the result set, as we assumed this to be similar to each other as well. The result of this query can be seen in Figure 1.

The result set that was retrieved did exhibit the pattern we queried for and was highlighted accordingly. On top of that, the relationship of density versus depth was also similar. Looking at the locations where those measurements were taken, we were surprised to see such different locations as the Norwegian sea and the antarctic southern ocean. However, looking into some details about the Norwegian sea did reveal that it is a maritime subarctic climatic zone, explaining the similarity of the temperature patterns.

Further refinement of our search by selecting a specific pattern for the relationship between water density and water depth as well, did reduce the result set to a more homogeneous region as we expected at that point (see Figure 7). Using that query, all retrieved documents were measured in the antarctic southern ocean, approximately at the longitude of New Zealand (169°).

5. CONCLUSION AND FUTURE WORK

In this paper, we presented a novel approach for content-based indexing of multivariate data by using a bag-of-words approach. On this basis, we developed visual-interactive query modalities that were not available for this kind of document before. In particular, our approach provides the user with result highlighting and search suggestions. We showed the applicability and scalability of our approach by indexing the complete collection of multivariate research data that is publicly available from a data library for the environmental sciences. We provided an exemplary use-case on this repository by retrieving data documents measured in similar maritime climate zones, which would not have been possible using meta-data alone.

For future work, we plan to improve the similarity functions. One extension is to consider hierarchical relationships, which may exist between the observation variables. These could be included to provide approximate matches for variable queries in cases where queried variables do not match, but other related variables exist: An example, that has also been discussed in the application, is the variable of water pressure, which may be closely related to water depth. Another specific task for future work is to explore the parameter space for the algorithms used in this approach, such as the number of clusters for the k-means algorithm.

More generally, future work will include defining a suitable similarity measure between multivariate documents by using the bag-of-words index. Such a similarity measure will allow for query-by-example of complete multivariate data documents, as well as new interactive tools for exploratory search by layouting multivariate documents based on similar content. Finally, evaluation of the effectiveness of the expansion- and highlighting-based search proposed from a user perspective would be interesting. We note that ground-truth benchmarking is not directly applicable, as our approach supports explorative search. Ultimately, we need to measure the degree of insight or information increase, that is brought about by the approach, in a given domain problem.

Acknowledgments

We thank the Alfred-Wegener-Institute (AWI) in Bremerhaven, particularly Rainer Sieger, Hannes Grobe and Gert König-Langlo, and everyone involved with PANGAEA for supporting this research effort. We are especially grateful to the many scientists that contributed the data available through BSRN and other research projects.

6. REFERENCES

[1] J. Bernard, J. Brase, D. W. Fellner, O. Koepler, J. Kohlhammer, T. Ruppert, T. Schreck, and I. Sens. A visual digital library approach for time-oriented scientific primary data. *Int. J. on Digital Libraries*, 11(2):111–123, 2010.

[2] J. Bernard, T. Ruppert, M. Scherer, J. Kohlhammer, and T. Schreck. Content-based layouts for exploratory metadata search in scientific research data. In K. B. Boughida, B. Howard, M. L. Nelson, H. V. de Sompel, and I. Sølvberg, editors, *JCDL*, pages 139–148. ACM, 2012.

[3] R. Berndt, I. Blümel, M. Clausen, D. Damm, J. Diet, D. W. Fellner, C. Fremerey, R. Klein, F. Krahl, M. Scherer, T. Schreck, I. Sens, V. Thomas, and R. Wessel. The probado project - approach and lessons learned in building a digital library system for heterogeneous non-textual documents. In *ECDL*, pages 376–383, Sept. 2010.

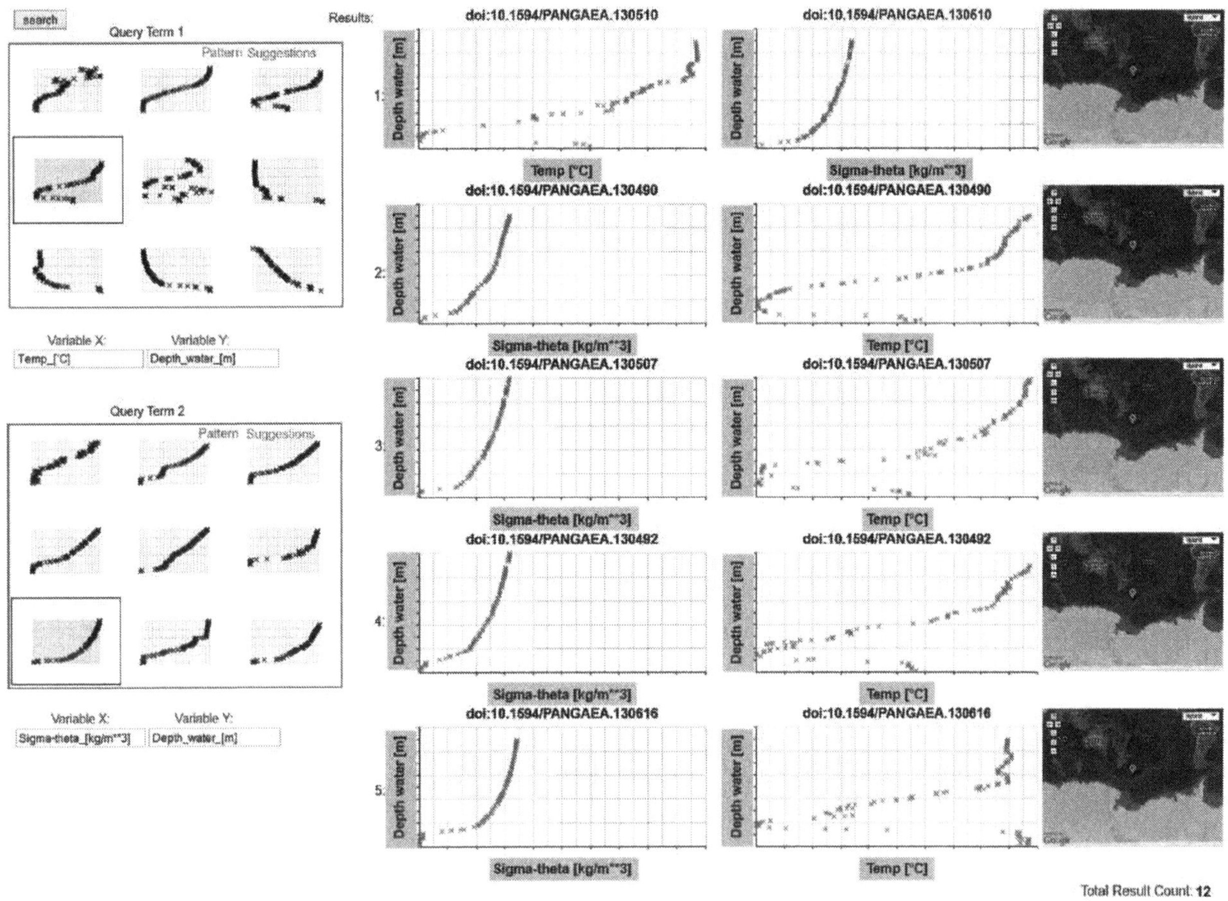

Figure 7: Case Study: We refined our original search query (see Figure 1) by also selecting a specific relationship between water density and water depth that was suggested by system. We see that this combination of patterns only occurs in documents that originate from the antarctic southern ocean at longitude 169°. Map Data is attributed to Google Maps.

[4] D. Blei, A. Ng, and M. Jordan. Latent dirichlet allocation. *the Journal of machine Learning research*, 3:993–1022, 2003.

[5] R. Datta, J. Li, and J. Z. Wang. Content-based image retrieval: approaches and trends of the new age. In *In Proceedings ACM International Workshop on Multimedia Information Retrieval*, pages 253–262. ACM Press, 2005.

[6] M. Diepenbroek, H. Grobe, M. Reinke, U. Schindler, R. Schlitzer, R. Sieger, and G. Wefer. Pangaea–an information system for environmental sciences. *Computers & Geosciences*, 28(10):1201–1210, 2002.

[7] H. Ding, G. Trajcevski, P. Scheuermann, X. Wang, and E. Keogh. Querying and mining of time series data: experimental comparison of representations and distance measures. *Proceedings of the VLDB Endowment*, 1(2):1542–1552, 2008.

[8] M. Eitz, R. Richter, T. Boubekeur, K. Hildebrand, and M. Alexa. Sketch-based shape retrieval. *ACM Trans. Graph. (Proc. SIGGRAPH)*, 31(4):31:1–31:10, 2012.

[9] M. A. Hearst. *Search User Interfaces*. Cambridge University Press, 1 edition, 2009.

[10] G. Hébrail, B. Hugueney, Y. Lechevallier, and F. Rossi. Exploratory analysis of functional data via clustering and optimal segmentation. *Neurocomput.*, 73(7-9):1125–1141, 2010.

[11] T. Hofmann. Probabilistic latent semantic indexing. In *Proceedings of the 22nd annual international ACM SIGIR conference on Research and development in information retrieval*, pages 50–57. ACM, 1999.

[12] H. Jégou, M. Douze, and C. Schmid. Improving bag-of-features for large scale image search. *International Journal of Computer Vision*, 87(3):316–336, 2010.

[13] E. Keogh and S. Kasetty. On the need for time series data mining benchmarks: A survey and empirical demonstration. *Data Mining and Knowledge Discovery*, 7(4):349–371, 2003.

[14] E. Keogh, J. Lin, and A. Fu. Hot sax: Efficiently finding the most unusual time series subsequence. In *IEEE International Conference on Data Mining*, pages 226–233, 2005.

[15] M. Khoo and C. Hall. What would 'google' do? users' mental models of a digital library search engine. In P. Zaphiris, G. Buchanan, E. Rasmussen, and

F. Loizides, editors, *Theory and Practice of Digital Libraries*, volume 7489 of *Lecture Notes in Computer Science*, pages 1–12. Springer, 2012.

[16] B. Köhncke, S. Tönnies, and W.-T. Balke. Catching the drift – indexing implicit knowledge in chemical digital libraries. In P. Zaphiris, G. Buchanan, E. Rasmussen, and F. Loizides, editors, *Theory and Practice of Digital Libraries*, volume 7489 of *Lecture Notes in Computer Science*, pages 383–395. Springer, 2012.

[17] M. Lew, N. Sebe, C. Djeraba, and R. Jain. Content-based multimedia information retrieval: State of the art and challenges. *ACM Transactions on Multimedia Computing, Communications, and Applications (TOMCCAP)*, 2(1):1–19, 2006.

[18] J. Lin, R. Khade, and Y. Li. Rotation-invariant similarity in time series using bag-of-patterns representation. *Journal of Intelligent Information Systems*, pages 1–29, 2011.

[19] D. G. Lowe. Distinctive image features from scale-invariant keypoints. *Int. J. Comput. Vision*, 60(2):91–110, Nov. 2004.

[20] C. A. Lynch. Jim gray's fourth paradigm and the construction of the scientific record. In T. Hey, S. Tansley, and K. M. Tolle, editors, *The Fourth Paradigm*, pages 177–183. Microsoft Research, 2009.

[21] PANGAEA Publishing Network for Geoscientific & Environmental Data. http://www.pangaea.de/.

[22] M. Riley, E. Heinen, and J. Ghosh. A text retrieval approach to content-based audio retrieval. In *Int. Symp. on Music Information Retrieval (ISMIR)*, pages 295–300, 2008.

[23] R. Rowley-Brooke, F. Pitié, and A. Kokaram. A ground truth bleed-through document image database. In P. Zaphiris, G. Buchanan, E. Rasmussen, and F. Loizides, editors, *Theory and Practice of Digital Libraries*, volume 7489 of *Lecture Notes in Computer Science*, pages 185–196. Springer, 2012.

[24] G. Salton and C. Buckley. Term-weighting approaches in automatic text retrieval. *Information processing & management*, 24(5):513–523, 1988.

[25] M. Scherer, J. Bernard, and T. Schreck. Retrieval and exploratory search in multivariate research data repositories using regressional features. In *Proceeding of the 11th annual international ACM/IEEE joint conference on Digital libraries*, JCDL '11, pages 363–372, New York, NY, USA, 2011. ACM.

[26] M. Scherer, T. von Landesberger, and T. Schreck. A benchmark for content-based retrieval in bivariate data collections. In *Proceedings of the Second international conference on Theory and Practice of Digital Libraries*, TPDL'12, pages 286–297, Berlin, Heidelberg, 2012. Springer-Verlag.

[27] B. Shneiderman. The eyes have it: A task by data type taxonomy for information visualizations. In *IEEE Visual Languages*, number UMCP-CSD CS-TR-3665, pages 336–343, College Park, Maryland 20742, U.S.A., 1996.

[28] J. Sivic and A. Zisserman. Video google: A text retrieval approach to object matching in videos. In *Computer Vision, 2003. Proceedings. Ninth IEEE International Conference on*, pages 1470–1477. IEEE, 2003.

[29] R. Stewart. *Introduction to physical oceanography.* Texas A & M University, 2004.

[30] R. W. White and R. A. Roth. *Exploratory Search: Beyond the Query-Response Paradigm.* Synthesis Lectures on Information Concepts, Retrieval, and Services. Morgan & Claypool Publishers, 2009.

[31] B. Wong, S. Choudhury, C. Rooney, R. Chen, and K. Xu. Invisque: technology and methodologies for interactive information visualization and analytics in large library collections. *Research and Advanced Technology for Digital Libraries*, pages 227–235, 2011.

[32] R. Xu, D. Wunsch, et al. Survey of clustering algorithms. *Neural Networks, IEEE Transactions on*, 16(3):645–678, 2005.

[33] J. Yang, Y. Jiang, A. Hauptmann, and C. Ngo. Evaluating bag-of-visual-words representations in scene classification. In *Proceedings of the international workshop on Workshop on multimedia information retrieval*, pages 197–206. ACM, 2007.

The Challenges of Digging Data: A Study of Context in Archaeological Data Reuse

Ixchel Faniel[1], Eric Kansa[2], Sarah Whitcher Kansa[3], Julianna Barrera-Gomez[1], and Elizabeth Yakel[4]
[1] OCLC Research
[2] University of California Berkeley, School of Information
[3] The Alexandria Archive Institute
[4] University of Michigan, School of Information
fanieli@oclc.org, ekansa@ischool.berkeley.edu, skansa@alexandriaarchive.org, barreraj@oclc.org, yakel@umich.edu

ABSTRACT

Field archaeology only recently developed centralized systems for data curation, management, and reuse. Data documentation guidelines, standards, and ontologies have yet to see wide adoption in this discipline. Moreover, repository practices have focused on supporting data collection, deposit, discovery, and access more than data reuse. In this paper we examine the needs of archaeological data reusers, particularly the context they need to understand, verify, and trust data others collect during field studies. We then apply our findings to the existing work on standards development. We find that archaeologists place the most importance on data collection procedures, but the reputation and scholarly affiliation of the archaeologists who conducted the original field studies, the wording and structure of the documentation created during field work, and the repository where the data are housed also inform reuse. While guidelines, standards, and ontologies address some aspects of the context data reusers need, they provide less guidance on others, especially those related to research design. We argue repositories need to address these missing dimensions of context to better support data reuse in archaeology.

Categories and Subject Descriptors

H.3.5[**Online Info Services**]: Data Sharing, Web-based Services; H.3.7[**Digital Libraries**]: Dissemination, Standards, User Issues

Keywords

Archaeology, Data management, Data reuse, Data standards

1 INTRODUCTION

Social and economic dynamics are pushing towards digital publication in archaeology. In the past, archaeologists primarily published books which included not only the interpretation but also selected data. Slowly the data has moved from formal monographs to site reports, which may now be on the web [18]. Publishers currently shy away from printing extensive datasets in paper form, especially since these data are increasingly digital. As a result, new publication venues are emerging in the form of digital repositories. It is in this environment that Open Context[1] was established as a data publisher. Open Context provides web-based data publication for cultural heritage and field research. Consequently, when the U.S. National Science Foundation (NSF) began requiring data management plans with all grant proposals, it named Open Context as a venue for data deposit in the archaeology program. Initially focused on building data supply, more recently Open Context has increased attention on satisfying the demand for data with a major objective to improve standards to support data reuse over the long term. There are two types of standards needed to support data reuse over time: standards focused on the actual research process; and repository standards to support discovery, data manipulation, and integration. Unfortunately no robust set of standards for field archaeology exists and those that do exist are not widely followed. For field archaeology specifically, standards development has been limited, since centralized data curation, management, and reuse is still a fairly new phenomenon.

The existing literature on data reuse informs standards development, but it has shortcomings. Although the data reuse literature suggests providing access to a dataset's context of production improves the data reuse experience, much of the work has been done in the science and engineering fields. Moreover, there have been no attempts to systematically consider the implications data reuse findings have on the development of standards. Therefore we pose two research questions in this study. 1) How does contextual information serve to preserve the meaning of and trust in archaeological field research over time? 2) How can existing cultural heritage standards be extended to incorporate these contextual elements? More specifically, we will examine archaeologists' current data reuse practices to consider how existing metadata standards might be extended to preserve the meaning of cultural heritage materials related to archaeological field studies.

2 BACKGROUND

We begin this section with a discussion of modern archaeological practice and how this influences data collection and management issues related to reuse. We then discuss guidelines and standards attempting to facilitate reuse and end with a discussion of what we know about data reuse in archaeology.

2.1 Archaeological Practice and Data Management Challenges

Archaeology represents an informative domain to explore issues in data management, curation and reuse because of the large amount of documentation generated in carrying out archaeological

JCDL'13, July 22–26, 2013, Indianapolis, Indiana, USA.

ACM 978-1-4503-2077-1/13/07...$15.00.

[1] http://www.opencontext.org

research as well as the divergence in data practices among different specialties in the discipline. Archaeologists attempt to understand ancient societies and social processes primarily through the documentation and analysis of the material remains of past societies. Investigation of these remains typically requires cross-disciplinary teams where members have different areas of expertise. For example, soil scientists investigate excavation deposits, zooarchaeologists (a sub-discipline with close ties to zoology and the biological sciences) identify and analyze animal remains from archaeological sites, and material scientists analyze the chemical composition of artifacts to identify raw-material sources or to investigate ancient production technologies. Coordinating the efforts of these diverse team members is a tremendous challenge involving complex data management skills.

Effective data management and preservation are particularly pressing for archaeology, because archaeologists often rely upon destructive data collection methods, destroying the very sites they seek to understand [1]. These ancient sites and other critical sources of evidence are limited and non-renewable resources, also damaged or destroyed through development, vandalism, and looting [7]. Archaeologists must carefully document the associations and stratigraphic relationships between finds, architectural remains, soil deposits, and other features as such associations are disrupted and destroyed through excavation. Archaeologists use the term "context" when they refer to such associations, and contextual information is critical to documentation and interpretation [19].

The legal and regulatory regimes governing archaeology are also changing in ways that impact data management issues. Many nations now prohibit the export of artifacts and other finds, even for research purposes. This puts added pressure on researchers to document objects as comprehensively as possible, since they may have difficulty in securing access to collections in the future. At the same time, public agencies and private granting foundations have adopted "Data Management Policies[2]". While these policies do not explicitly mandate data dissemination or archiving, they make the disposition of data part of the peer-review evaluation of grant proposals.

Research design and documentation are more critical for archaeological research since not only the destroyed sites must be documented but also the artifacts left behind must be analyzed in their countries of origin [28]. Thus, the only records available to archaeologists for future analysis are digital documentation about sites and artifacts now destroyed or inaccessible. Archaeologists describing the documentation process demonstrate that it is anything but straightforward. Many interpretative decisions which affect later reuse are made during the excavation and documentation processes [19, 20]. This represents an important issue for standards and ontology development, since researchers may need to rely upon legacy datasets, often described according to obsolete recording systems.

Finally, archaeology is not a cohesive discipline with universally adopted methods, concepts, or theoretical perspectives [11, 14]. Archaeologists work across the world in many research settings to investigate past societies in all of their diversity. The methods and research questions used by an archaeologist working at a Roman urban site will be very different from those used by an archaeologist working at a Paleolithic cave site. Moreover, research circumstances vary. Some teams will have the time and expertise available to develop more thorough and varied documentation, while other teams must work very rapidly, especially in the context of "salvage archaeology" where development or construction projects impact archaeological sites. This diversity, coupled with the need to reference and adapt legacy data to new research questions, represents a great challenge in developing information standards for the field. The difficulties are only multiplied as archaeologists have transitioned from analog to digital recordkeeping, including sophisticated CAD and GIS modeling techniques which require significant context to communicate meaning:

> *Once the question of format has been dealt with, the archivist must confront questions relating to the use of the model by others. For instance, my model has more than 200 different data segments. In-situ stones of cut marble, with specific date span, and lying in the stair of the entrance structure are in one data segment; the nearby tripod base, also of cut marble and with the same dates, is in another. The particulars of these data segments are not important for this discussion, but the model cannot be used effectively without an understanding of the segments and the way they have been named. That information is not implicit in the model; it must be supplied in a set of documentation that I must have prepared* [14, p. 23].

As we will discuss, an important dimension of context that needs to be captured to inform data reuse centers on the methods, people, and research conditions surrounding data creation.

2.2 The Use of Guidelines, Standards, and Ontologies

Data reuse is more complicated due to the emergent and diffuse nature of guidelines, standards, and ontologies in archaeology. We discuss two categories of these: guidelines and standards aimed at data producers which address data collection, documentation, and deposit; and standards and ontologies aimed at data repositories to facilitate long-term data management, discovery and reuse.

2.2.1 Guidelines and Standards for Data Producers

Various national and professional bodies have developed guidelines for data documentation in archaeology [31, 1, 5, 6, 21]. These guidelines provide information about the types of documentation expected, preferred file formats, and data points desired. However, they often do not accommodate the realities of field work or the interpretation that occurs in the field. More recently, guidelines for data deposit have emerged in the UK and the Netherlands [1, 6, 10, 30]. In other countries, such as Canada, archaeologists are legally expected to deposit research records in repositories, but guidelines for deposit are lacking [28, 31, 38].

2.2.2 Standards and Ontologies for Repositories

Leading archaeologists have promoted data integration as a key motivating factor in data sharing and archiving [27]. However, ontology development in archaeology is in early stages. Most archaeologists have no exposure to formal ontologies or their use. The Digital Archaeological Record[3] (tDAR) is developing tools for researchers to apply ontologies to the datasets it archives. In contrast, Open Context editors increasingly apply ontologies as part of their "data publication" workflow [24]. In the case of Open Context, the technical and conceptual challenges of applying ontologies are taken on by dedicated "data editors," rather than by users or data contributors. As more archaeologists deposit their

[2]http://www.nsf.gov/news/news_summ.jsp?cntn_id=116928

[3]http://www.tdar.org

datasets in repositories, the research rewards and opportunities for computational methods, including development and application of ontologies, will expand. For the time being, the expertise and motivation to use formal ontologies remains rare in archaeology. Furthermore, the standards for data collection, documentation and deposit speak more to the ability to preserve and communicate context while repository metadata and ontologies address access and discovery. In spite of early claims that "metadata also provides a means of reflecting changes in the intellectual and social context in which information exists. Therefore it can enable data collected within one theoretical framework to be reused within another by providing the potential re-user with information about previous recording systems and methods which would allow them to take the original interests and biases of the recorder into account" [32, p. 1059], metadata has not fulfilled this promise in archaeological repositories. Experiments in creating a more "reflexive" repository system to accommodate changing interpretations of data are still largely untested [15].

2.3 Data Reuse Challenges in Archaeology

Much of the data reuse literature, which focuses on the sciences and quantitative social sciences, has found that data reusers need to know the context in which data were produced in order to evaluate the data [e.g. 16, 37, 36]. For instance, information about how data were defined and measured helped quantitative social scientists understand the data, decide whether it met their needs, and trust the data [16]. Knowing how colleagues selected and calibrated data collection instruments allowed habitat ecologists to trust resulting data [37]. Earthquake engineering researchers, who knew both that problems occurred during a laboratory experiment and how they were resolved, were less likely to misinterpret data during reuse [17]. We know much less about the context qualitative social scientists and humanists need to support data reuse.

Archaeologists use other's research data through a variety of venues: person to person sharing, museum archives, and more recently digital repositories. Archaeologists reuse data directly from other archaeologists created in the course of an excavation or survey (e.g., field notes, spreadsheets of finds, photographs) as well as museum collections (for example, comparing a complete figurine in a museum to multiple figurine fragments found in an excavation). In person-to-person sharing, "data sharing (particularly the open dissemination of data not presented in archival publication) is constrained by a variety of factors, including stakeholder interests, the sensitivity of archaeological sites, fear of poaching, concerns about the 'messiness' of data, and the lack of common data standards" [18, p. 70; see also 24 for more discussion of data sharing incentives].

We know little about archaeologists' use of museum collections. In fact, Merriman and Swain concluded that "even within the archaeological profession, archives remain largely unused as reference collections, as support to sites and monuments records or as resources for contractors, even though they represent the prime evidence for the archaeology of an area" [29, p. 259]. More recent evidence suggests that museum metadata is rarely enough for scholarly researchers and that associated documentation on provenance, acquisition, etc. is needed [26]. In her survey of users of archaeological collections in museums, Czyrnyj found that archaeologists were interested in different types of information and less satisfied with that information than other categories of respondents. Overall respondents identified "visual representations of the artefacts and contextual information" as the two major issues for improvement [9, p. 103].

Condrun et al.'s [8] user report for the Archaeological Data Service in the UK is the earliest evidence we have of repository reuse in archaeology. They found that many of the barriers to using digital archaeological data were technological. Still, their recommendations focused on the need for data creation and data archiving standards. More than a decade later, the need for standards remains. Detailed examples of data reuse by archaeologists are scarce. In one example, three zooarchaeologists analyzed 30,000 animal bone specimens in an "orphaned dataset" from excavations during the 1960s at Chogha Mish, Iran. University of Chicago archaeologists transferred the data from punch cards to Excel spreadsheets and made the spreadsheet publicly available, as the only record of the fauna from the site. Each zooarchaeologist analyzed and interpreted the data independently and arrived at different conclusions based on objective measures of the bones as well as conjectures about the original data collection. "They lamented that certain data were not present, specifically contextual and methodological information" [2, p. 5]. In another example of archaeological data reuse, Brody [4] reexamined household artifacts originally excavated between 1926 and 1935 northwest of Jerusalem. He did not dwell on the difficulties of reuse but noted that only certain methodological approaches worked with the data given the original "excavation methods, collection strategies, and records" [4, p. 252]. The consistent themes concerning reuse here are the need for information about the methodological and interpretative contexts in which the original research took place.

3 METHODOLOGY

In this paper, we focus on archaeologists to examine the reuse of research data, particularly digital data. We selected archaeology to study data reuse for two reasons. First, archaeology has an emergent data sharing culture, so data reuse is a relatively new phenomenon and repositories for archaeological data are young. Second, archaeologists use heterogeneous data often triangulating data from multiple sources created using local practices and a variety of de facto standards. Given our interest in exploring a field less experienced in data sharing and reuse, we partnered with Open Context, an open access venue which reviews, documents, standardizes, and publishes archaeological research data, and offers tools and services for archaeologists using that data. Open Context makes use of many available standards and ontologies, such as ArchaeoML [25] and the Encyclopedia of Life[4] respectively, to create a robust platform for data publication. As such, Open Context has gone far to address the need for "consistent standards for data" within archaeology [18].

Between September 2011 and April 2012, we conducted 22 semi-structured, hour-long interviews during which we asked archaeologists about their data reuse experiences. We used both snowball and convenience sampling to recruit participants. Beginning with individuals associated with our collaborators, we moved on to recruit additional participants through workshops, conferences, and by asking interviewees to nominate colleagues. Through our selection process, we recruited a range of archaeologists in terms of research questions, methodology, the centrality of data reuse to their work, and level of expertise. Interviewees were paid $25 US dollars for their participation.

We audio recorded and transcribed the interviews and used NVivo, a qualitative data analysis software tool, for coding and analysis. We based our codes on the topics addressed in our interviews. As a result, the high level categories included context,

[4]http://www.eol.org

data reuse, data sharing, and repository codes. We were also open to emergent codes arising from the transcripts. Two project team members coded the interview transcripts and achieved an interrater reliability percentage of 0.73 using Scott's Pi.

4 RESULTS

Most striking about the findings was respondents' reuse of data despite the persistent lack of context. The respondents either found ways to make do with the context they did receive or took action to obtain more. Given the nature of context in field archaeology, data collection procedures and research design were in greatest demand during data reuse. For some respondents, the presentation of documents created in the field also had bearing on data reuse as well as the archaeologists' reputations and scholarly affiliations and the repository where the data were housed. Each of these will be discussed in the paragraphs that follow.

4.1 Lack of Context Was a Persistent Problem during Data Reuse

The lack of context was a persistent problem encountered during the reuse of archaeological data. At issue were the data collection and recording procedures. The lack of context associated with museum collections resulted from the way the objects were collected, whereas some of the early field studies suffered from insufficient recording of context. The lack of context continued for contemporary field studies, given the transition from capturing context on paper to capturing it digitally and archaeologists' protection of the context that they did record.

4.1.1 Museum Collections

Respondents cited distinct issues when reusing data from museum collections versus data from fellow archaeologists. Respondents explained that there was often less concern and ability to record context for the museum objects. For instance, CCU20 acknowledged that although the museum field was changing, "...There was less concern about provenance information or context information. So objects are treated as objects and not as objects within their contextual world..." (CCU20). CCU01 explained why even the most basic context was hard to come by with museum objects he accessed from a major university's on-line collection. When asked whether cataloging information about where the objects were found and who found them was provided, he replied, "If that was known, yes. This was again the old days when they were just kind of ... They would buy things on the market and not wonder where they came from" (CCU01). Given the way museum collections were acquired in the past, it made sense that context was limited. However, respondents had higher expectations for field archaeology because archaeologists recorded context during data collection. They expected not only cataloging information about who found what objects at which site, but also more detailed information about the objects themselves (e.g. at what strata were the objects found and what was found with them).

4.1.2 Field Archaeology

Even though artifacts were not merely treated as objects in field archaeology, the availability of context was still uneven. For older studies, lack of context was attributed to evolving recording procedures that ranged from meticulous to sloppy. In contrast, contemporary studies were challenged with the transition from paper-based to digital recording procedures and archaeologists' protection of context that was recorded.

4.1.2.1 The Good Old Days

Some respondents discussed the thoroughness of some of the early archaeologists' recording procedures. CCU05 discussed the meticulousness of one excavator's data recording procedures over four decades of research. "[He] ... was far ahead of his time in real scientific archaeology and documentation methods. And because of that, we just have so much in the way of material, there are 21,000 glass plate negatives just for [Site Location] alone ... There are 45,000 plates all together. And then thousands of pages of register books of logging in the finds and diary pages, noting with daily activities and manuscripts and note cards and all kinds of things" (CCU05). In contrast, others thought early archaeologists were careless recorders of their field work. CCU09 described excavators from the 1950s as the "sloppiest", because they did not include critical context. She recalled her reuse of a series of maps. "...they never put North on their map. They never actually gave me the grid locus of where they were. So I had a really hard time using those maps ... I could scan them, but I didn't know where to put them" (CCU09). During CCU16's reuse of a dataset from the 1960s, he recalled missing context as "...one of the most severe problems. So we did not have access to critical information, such as archaeological contexts, excavation methods, sampling methods, even identification methods. We didn't know if the analysts actually used comparative collections or just published manuals to identify specimens or how did she sample... She didn't mention or detail those things." (CCU16). However, the data from these older field studies were valuable and respondents found ways to make it work. Several respondents, including CCU09 and CCU16 described various channels used to search for additional context to enable data reuse, including publications, field reports, accession books, field notes, and visits to museums to talk with staff and the original excavators. In one case, it took CCU09 years to track down the context needed to reuse data, but she did it because she thought it was "...critical to incorporate the data and work with it to the extent that you can. You can't do everything with it, but you can do a lot..." (CCU09).

Although CCU09 blamed archaeologists for the lack of context associated with some of the older field studies, several others attributed archaeologists' shortfall to the era. In explaining why notes from an excavation during World War II were spotty, CCU15 explained "the metadata recording of archaeology has evolved over the last 120 years of its discipline in the [Region Name]. And so the kinds of issues that people were paying attention to and actually 'recording' are very different than today". As the discipline evolved, so did the way archaeologists collected data and recorded context. "... the way things were excavated and the rapidity in which things were excavated, and then just sort of the amount of notes that were taken ... as opposed to the amount of stuff that was excavated is almost the inverse today. So we dig a lot less and record a lot more in current times. And back in the good old days, they dug a lot more and recorded a lot less" (CCU20). Likewise others thought "... the general standard and awareness among [today's] archaeologists [vs. those from 20 years ago] is rising, so that they would tend to include more information" (CCU19).

4.1.2.2 Contemporary Field Work

Whether it was an evolution of the discipline or an increased awareness, data collection improved and, over time, archaeologists recorded more contextual information. Yet, respondents still experienced difficulty reusing data from their contemporaries, in part because of limited access. CCU02 actually described this as a "permanent problem", where "the metadata you need is, a lot of the contextual data that you need is not provided". He believed the lack of access stemmed from using paper-based rather than digital data collection and recording procedures in the field. In contrast, CCU21 worried about the move from paper to digital. He thought context would get lost in the absence of more robust recording procedures, especially for terminology, which varied across archaeologists and over time. In order to understand what the data meant he explained needing to know whose vocabulary was being used. "...okay, I've got this table, or these tables, and I can see how they're related, but gee whiz, I don't know what set of vocabulary they're using. I don't know whether this is Scholar Q's version of Greek geometric pottery, or Scholar Z's version of Greek geometric pottery in terms of the terminology. Where they keep saying Late Bronze I, what did that mean then" (CCU21)? Respondents also discussed challenges around creating data interoperability. In a study of cultural groups across state lines CCU12 needed to combine data from multiple field studies held by different State Historic Preservation Offices. He noted, "You need to do a lot of cleaning and translating to make things work. But the concepts in the archaeological ontologies that are being used to describe are still professionally the same, but they're recorded in various scales. They may use different terminologies, different data types" (CCU12).

For other respondents, the worry was archaeologists who were not providing access to all context that they may have recorded. For instance, CCU08 thought the laboratories she worked with to get metallurgical data were less than transparent. Oftentimes, she had to request information about how samples from the ore bodies were retrieved and received it only occasionally. "They would sometimes just say it was an ore sample, but other times they would say it was taken from an artifact found near an ore. I had to specifically request the latter. It should be given transparently" (CCU08). Many respondents mentioned accessing the documents archaeologists created in the field to understand the interpretations and decisions archaeologists made in situ. Unfortunately, the documents were difficult to access, because they were not being shared or not available online. For instance, CCU10 noted, "A lot of times you don't have access to the notes of another site and it seems... It seems like its relatively territorial that's kind of sensitive information, so lots of times excavators aren't so willing to share their primary notes. Sometimes you have to wait until things come out in print." However, even after print publications came out, critical context was still missing or unclear. Although CCU02 primarily used journal articles to locate data for reuse, he often ended up contacting archaeologists directly to learn details about the field studies. "...it always, always ends up with me contacting the researcher and asking them, 'Well, how did you collect the data? What were your excavation technologies? And then, how did you analyze the data after all this? How did you analyze these animal bones? So, what research question or reference question did you use'" (CCU02).

4.2 The Role of Data Collection Procedures during Data Reuse

Despite challenges, respondents still managed to reuse others' data, often seeking additional context in the process. Given the nature of the field archaeology research, data collection procedures were highly sought during data reuse. Not only did archaeologists make interpretations of the context during data collection, context was also destroyed as a result of excavation. In addition, the way archaeologists conducted and recorded their research varied. Having access to data collection procedures helped respondents understand and verify the data against the archaeologists' research objectives and interpretations. Respondents also relied on archaeologists' presentation of documents created during field work, the reputations of the archaeologists, their scholarly affiliation, and the institutions where the data were housed for additional insight into the data.

4.2.1 Accounting for Interpretations of Context Made in the Field

Archaeologists' interpretations of data unfolded in the field during data collection and provided supporting evidence for the conclusions drawn about the data. For instance, the chronology of a site was determined through a series of assumptions an archaeologist made based on the artifacts unearthed. CCU18 described how he might determine the nature and date of a site given the excavation of a floor. "In a perfect world when I excavate the floor and there's a piece of pottery underneath that, and the floor can't have been laid down before that piece of pottery exists ..., [and] it's a piece of pottery from a second century AD pot that means the floor was in the second AD or later. ... We make a sort of series of interlocking assumptions about the certificate of a finding and the material that I'm processing ..." (CCU18). Our findings indicated respondents needed access to these interpretations as well and looked to access them via documents created in the field. Interested in how landscapes changed over time from 1500-1650 AD, CCU06 wanted to reuse animal remains data and data from zooarchaeological collections. She needed the data to have a certain level of chronological control and looked for stratigraphic information in archaeologists' field reports. "So, I need to be able to say, 'Okay, this particular part of the collection dates from 1490 to 1550. This part dates from 1550 to '60', or that sort of thing. ... I can ... tell by looking at the [archaeological] report whether there is stratigraphic information so, I can tell whether the site is stratified, and whether it looks like if there's going to be that kind of fine scale of chronological control or not". Archaeologists collected and interpreted stratigraphic information in the field as they excavated and distinguished different strata (i.e. layer of sedimentary rock or soil) to identify time periods. CCU06 looked for stratigraphic drawings that clearly labeled each excavated strata.

4.2.2 Accounting for Context Destroyed in the Field

Archaeologists also thought it was critical to know how the archaeological data were collected, because the context was destroyed as a result of excavation. As CCU12 discussed, recognizing the veracity of data depends on the context captured. "... if you dig the majority of an archaeological site and put those materials in boxes, no one can ever go back to that exact site and say, 'Wait a minute, these materials weren't organized that way', because the context is completely lost. They're all put in boxes. ... The verification of whether or not the data are real is something that, ... it's frequently measured on the metadata about how everything was recovered and whether or not it ultimately corresponds with similar works that have been done and are done later" (CCU12). Data collection procedures were the only means respondents had of understanding how archaeologists obtained evidence that supported the data gathered during field work. Data reuse cannot happen without context: "Every object needs a context; otherwise, it's almost meaningless. I mean, that's the bottom line ... Just knowing an object is there is nothing. You have to know all about it. You need to know where it comes from, how it was acquired, how it was excavated. Everything we know has to be tied to that object, otherwise, it's useless" (CCU11).

4.2.3 *Accounting for Different Approaches in the Field*

The variety of approaches archaeologists employed in the field was another reason respondents needed to access data collection procedures. In some cases, the variability was a response to a particular research setting, in others it had to do with archaeologists' research interests and objectives. Regardless of the case, being aware of and accounting for the differences helped respondents understand archaeologists' research objectives and intentions and evaluate the data accordingly.

For instance, CCU16 acknowledged that characteristics of a research setting, such as the time period under study and the nature of a site, impacted his research design, data collection procedures, and strategies. Given his field work in caves and urban sites, he described three aspects of context that were important to know as he worked with data. "... I would say the first most important aspect would be the archaeological context, where my data is coming from. The second would be recovery, that is, how we are recovering, actually, data from the grounds. And the third would be sampling ... I mean if [it's] complete recovery or whole recovery" (CCU16). Findings indicated that respondents needed similar context during data reuse, given variance in archaeologists' excavation methods. As CCU02 explained, "You can only sort of reconstruct that [the research design] from the field notes and sort of the nature of their observation and there's sort of no standardized features for archaeology. Everybody excavates in a slightly different way..." (CCU02).

Contextual details, such as site location, recovery procedures, and sampling, helped respondents not only understand archaeologists' research design, but also their rationale behind collecting and interpreting the data. Knowledge about archaeologists' rationale was useful in understanding their research objectives and intentions regarding the breadth versus depth of their studies. CCU07's analogy for breadth versus depth was excavating with bulldozers versus tooth picks. "So some people started digging with bulldozers and that's a different kind of resolution than digging with dental picks. And instead of saying that the bulldozer data is bad data, I think you just have to say that's bulldozer data, that's broad data". Similarly, CCU01 was not interested in downgrading broad data collection strategies; rather he wanted to be able to connect the strategies with archaeologists' research intentions and the resulting data. Simply declaring interest in the breadth of a site was not enough for CCU01. He needed to know how the archaeologists conducted their field surveys. "We have to look at their field methods and that's, for example, did they walk with spacing close enough so that they were picking up ... [in] a survey that went on in Paphlagonia in northern Turkey where they spread out their survey walkers maybe a 100 yards apart. So, they're walking huge tracts of land, but they're only hitting big things. They'll hit a site, but they'll walk by little tiny sherd scattered things. So you kind of need to know that. I've heard of things like shoulder surveys, where they literally walk side by side and pick those little things, but then, again, you've only, you're doing a very narrow tract. So there are procedures" (CCU01). The data collected in field surveys depended on the density of archaeologists' searches. Knowing more about the methods and research objectives when accessing the data helped CCU01 determine how and why archaeologists restricted their field work.

Archaeologists cited the type of tools used in the field as another aspect of context related to data collection that impacted reuse. For instance, archaeologists often used mesh screens to sift dirt when collecting objects. The screen size was an important element of context, because it determined the size of objects archaeologists found. "...when we excavate sites, we put things... We toss what's called the back dirt, the dirt through a screen. And because I'm so interested in small fauna, the size of the screen that was used is a critical piece of information that is very often left out of reports ... To me, whether it's screened or what level of screen it is, it really impacts what I can say from that collection" (CCU06). Archaeologists noted that location information, another aspect of context, was also impacted by the tools used in the field, which meant respondents needed clear specifications. "I have to know what the parameters are in which they gathered those coordinates. So I have to know the type of GPS, [or if] they collected it from a map, the map systems, et cetera. So for example, not just the difference between differential GPS and like a recreation grade GPS but like if you're using a recreation grade GPS, did you average your points? ... did you use [coordinates from an existing] dataset, or did you use the WGS 84 data? Those are the pieces of information that have to be entered ..." (CCU03).

4.3 The Role Additional Context Plays in Data Reuse

Since data were interpreted in the field and the context was then destroyed, archaeologists had the additional burden of recording their thoughts and actions in situ. Respondents relied heavily on this kind of information to account for and to link archaeologists' actions and interpretations that occurred in the field. However, respondents also mentioned using other aspects of context to determine the extent to which data could be trusted, including the documents created in the field, the archaeologists' reputations and scholarly affiliations, and the reputation of the data repository.

4.3.1 *Data Recording Procedures*

Respondents often relied on documents created in the field not only to access context, but also to assess how diligently archaeologists carried out their field studies and in turn the extent to which the data could be trusted. In looking for data from 1500-1650 AD, CCU06 believed clearly labeled stratigraphic drawings were a sign of an archaeologist's carefulness in capturing context important for chronological control. "And so, if they had labeled stratigraphy, let's say, A, B, C, D, E, and if they're comparing the fauna from E to A, that tells me that when they excavated, they were really careful about preserving that information" (CCU06). Another respondent evaluated sections (stratigraphic drawings) and top plans (horizontal maps of excavated areas). "And if those were done pretty meticulously and if they adhere to a standard, then I was more trusting of other data, the data that was less standardized" (CCU10). She also paid attention to the narratives archaeologists wrote to describe their excavations. "If somebody was writing about, say, a loci that they were digging and they were talking about some of the major finds before they were talking about the dirt, the matrix, and kind of its relationship to the other squares around it, I was more wary than if it was someone that was talking about kind of following a more standardized pattern, but also talking about the soil itself, the matrix, its relationship to the squares around it, and then the find spots" (CCU10). Similarly, CCU21 believed that archaeologists' organization of data told him a lot about their organization of associated excavations. "... and I got both tables [from the data repository], the one that has the description of the material, and the actual item-by-item lists of the things they found. And one of the things I discovered was that there are several entries in material that don't exist in the material table. So, maybe it wasn't really a relational database, it really was just two databases that...

I mean, I don't know. But from my point of view as a user, I need to know that. I need to be able to have that overall context. In addition to which, it tells you a great deal about how somebody approaches a site if you see that kind of data organization because it tells you about their excavation organization" (CCU21). Respondents used recording procedures, particularly the supporting documents archaeologists created in the field that provided evidence of their actions and interpretations, as clues into how carefully archaeologists paid attention to and captured the context during data collection.

4.3.2 Reputation and Scholarly Affiliation of the Archaeologist

The reputation and scholarly affiliation of archaeologists also impacted respondents' decisions to reuse data. Scholarly affiliation was a frequent indicator of quality for respondents. They often linked it to assumptions about archaeologists' training and the overarching reputation for quality and reliability of their field work. As CCU06 commented "there are individuals that I have a lot of respect for, and I really respect their training. If it's somebody whose training I don't know about, I'm going to be less likely to use their dataset because I'm not sure how reliable it is" (CCU06). Affiliation and training were also seen as a type of legacy that gave archaeologists an aura of reliability as well. As CCU13 pointed out, "You gravitate towards the people you trust and you trust the people you trust because they come from, sort of, they have a history of a lineage...so, those senior scholars [and] their students are the ones that you trust." This lineage was important for establishing precursory trust in data, because as CCU13 said, "if I don't know their advisor or the program they come from, I would be much more hesitant to put as much weight on, well particularly on their interpretations, but I'd be much more questioning of their data" (CCU13). Therefore, when considering reputation and scholarly affiliation, respondents were much more interested in where and with whom archaeologists trained, not their current institutional affiliation.

4.3.3 Reputation of the Data Repository

Interestingly, knowledge about a data repository's processes, including selection or submission requirements and transparency in repository processes, were reported as important factors in trusting the data housed within them. As CCU02 explained, a repository's metadata requirements signaled higher quality data, because it made it easier to check the data. "They're very keen on producing the comprehensive metadata. And it's not that I trust each research [study]... but I trust that the metadata is there for me to go back and check out each file on my own. I don't give [the repository] a sort of blanket trust that all the data in there is correct, but...I sort of trust going there because I know that I can find the information I need to validate it" (CCU02). A data repository's reputation was also linked to the transparency of the collection and curation methods. As CCU04 pointed out, working with a "famous museum that has a reputation, it does make the source more reliable…knowing that they developed the work and that they were backing up the information" were important indicators of data validity. In addition to validating the content, documenting repository actions was also important for establishing trust through transparency. "They are explicit about everything that they did. They tell you all the methods that they use. They tell you every single person who wrote down anything. They tell you all the updates that they did with the material" (CCU04).

In sum, respondents took cues from other aspects of context beyond archaeologists' collection and interpretation of the data when deciding whether to trust the data. In some cases, how context was recorded was as important as what context was recorded, in terms of the diagrams archaeologists created and the wording and ordering of their narratives. In addition, archaeologists' training, particularly their doctoral degree granting institution and advisor, were weighed during reuse. Lastly, the repository where data were stored was considered, with particular emphasis placed on its metadata criteria and the degree of transparency in its processes.

5 DISCUSSION

The results illustrate a number of interrelated challenges for data reuse. With the recent establishment of data repositories in archaeology, the need to consider researcher needs with respect to data reuse becomes all the more pressing.

Some of the results indicate needs already addressed by existing archeological data documentation standards. These include:

- The basic provenance of objects – when and where they were found, and by whom

- The chronology of a site, including stratigraphic information for all objects and relationships between strata

Digital repositories, such as tDAR and the UK Archaeological Data Service (ADS) document basic provenance and chronology information as metadata to describe datasets. Existing archaeological data repositories document data creators, so conceivably, researchers can make their own inferences about data reliability based on their knowledge of the reliability and professionalism of data creators. Open Context recently adopted ORCID to identify individual researchers.[5] By using the ORCID web API to display current biographical and publication information about data contributors, Open Context provides up-to-date information relating to the expertise and credentials of data creators.

While existing repositories document data creators, archaeology faces some surprising challenges for other basic forms of metadata. For instance, there is no universally agreed upon chronology for archaeology. Archaeology lacks an analog to the Global Standard Stratigraphic Age used in geology[6]. The lack of disciplinary-wide consensus on chronological designation reflects common concerns researchers identified in data-reuse:

- Differences or changes in terminology/vocabulary – whose terminology is being used, what do certain phrases mean at the time of a field study (e.g. Late Bronze I)?

Addressing the challenges inherent in comparing datasets described according to different vocabularies represents a common research priority for many informatics initiatives in archaeology [27].

5.1 Emerging Data Standards

Research efforts in archaeological data integration often center on the development and application of ontologies. Nevertheless, such efforts are typically small in scale and experimental [22]. Only a few large-scale applications, such as the ADS's "ArchaeoTools" project [23, 33] currently use formal ontologies in archaeology.

[5]http://www.orcid.org

[6]http://www.stratigraphy.org/GSSP/index.html

Thus far, the most successful attempt to integrate multiple collections of archaeological (and related historical) data uses less formalized (and less complicated) approaches. The UK-based (JISC-funded) Pelagios[7] project uses a Linked Data approach to integrate several archaeological, museum, and ancient history collections. These collections are aggregated and indexed according to references to place concepts in the Pleiades Gazetteer[8], but semantics of place references have little formal semantic modeling.

The most widely used and recognized formal ontology relating to archaeology is the CIDOC-CRM[9] [12, 13]. However, its main focus and area of application is in the context of museums and museum collections, not directly with field archaeology. The CIDOC-CRM's complexity and orientation toward enabling inferences on data as developed by museum curators makes it somewhat difficult to apply directly to field archaeology. The landscape is rapidly evolving however. A research group at English Heritage recently extended the CIDOC-CRM to include more concepts specific to field archaeology[10] [3].

In addition, some groups have developed machine-readable (and open) controlled vocabularies that supplement the abstract classes and properties defined by the CIDOC-CRM. Whereas the CIDOC-CRM focuses on abstracted concepts defining cultural heritage events, such as the discovery of an object, or transfers in its custody [e.g. 35], archaeologists often focus their attention on the classification and description of objects and archaeological contexts. The controlled vocabularies recently released by the British Museum as Linked Open Data (accessible via a Web API and SPARQL endpoint) may facilitate large-scale alignment of artifact typologies and classification systems. The British Museum has a vast collection of objects from across the globe, making its controlled vocabulary potentially valuable for many chronological and regional specializations in archaeology. The recent Open Context data publication of Murlo[11] (an Etruscan site) used the British Museum's controlled vocabulary for annotation of the project's internal classification system.

In addition to the development of ontologies and controlled vocabularies specific to archaeology, data integration efforts in archaeology can borrow from ontology developments in related disciplines. This is especially the case for zooarchaeology. Zooarchaeology already has many common (informal) conventions in recording, especially with regard to biological taxa, bone element, and to a lesser extent measurements and characteristics related to age determinations [2]. In both the tDAR digital repository and the Open Context data publishing system, efforts to align datasets to formal ontologies focus on zooarchaeology. However, application of ontologies in zooarchaeology varies in these two systems:

- tDAR is developing features to enable zooarchaeologists to select and apply ontologies on collections held in tDAR [34]. It currently has about 34 "ontologies" (many of which can be better defined as controlled vocabularies) relating to zooarchaeology.
- For zooarchaeological data, Open Context mainly uses ontologies / vocabularies developed outside archaeology by other bioinformatics research communities. These include the Encyclopedia of Life for annotation of biological taxa and now UBERON[12] for annotation of anatomical entities.

Besides having more widely used recording conventions, zooarchaeologists sense more clear and immediate research applications and uses for using shared ontologies. Ontology enabled data integration can facilitate larger scale analysis of data exploring regional and chronological variation across many zooarchaeological bone assemblages.

5.2 Gaps in Archaeological Data Standards

The previous discussion reviews recent developments in archaeological data standards. The recent introduction of increasingly comprehensive and open (in an intellectual property and interoperability sense) controlled vocabularies may help to address frustrations about terminologies identified in our study. Nevertheless, we note that archaeology's emerging ontologies address only part of the data reuse challenges identified in our study. Besides vocabulary and terminology alignment, our results show researcher interest in the following issues:

- Methodological procedures for excavation and/or survey, including specifications of field tools e.g. maps and map systems, type of GPS used, including hardware and software specifications and how data were collected (i.e. were points averaged, is it WGS 84), excavation strategy, including mesh screen size if contexts were sieved. Well-documented procedures for sampling, recording, and analysis, including use of comparative collections for identifications, use of standards, data validation techniques, and carefully-written narratives.
- Information about the archaeologist who conducted the work: The training and previous work of this person (i.e. their reputation) are important in assessing data quality.
- Information about the repository holding the data: The overall reputation of the repository, the amount of metadata it provides, and transparency in its collection and curation procedures, all help increase the perceived quality of a dataset.

These points indicate researcher interest in the entire data lifecycle, from excavation to deposit in a repository. Details of the methods and participants involved in excavation and analysis of the material increases researcher trust in the quality of datasets. However, most of ontology development in archaeology centers on classification (e.g. British Museum thesaurus) and semantic inference (CIDOC-CRM). Existing archaeological ontologies provide less guidance for modeling the methods and research conditions at the point of data creation. As noted by our interviews however, researchers expressed concern that methodological differences may make certain datasets incompatible. Our results show that the conditions and methods that shaped data creation therefore needs much greater elaboration in archaeological ontologies so that archaeologists can make more

[7]http://pelagios-project.blogspot.com/

[8]http://pleiades.stoa.org/

[9]http://www.cidoc-crm.org/

[10]http://crmeh.files.wordpress.com/2011/10/arch_ontological_modellingv4.pdf

[11] http://opencontext.org/projects/DF043419-F23B-41DA-7E4D-EE52AF22F92F

[12]http://www.uberon.org

informed judgments about the suitability of datasets for different forms of reuse.

Finally, archaeological ontologies, even if more fully developed to describe the conditions of data creation can only address part of archaeology's data management challenges. Our results illustrated complex records management and inventory control needs, as artifacts and samples move through several steps from the ground to museum storage facilities. Each step introduces new chances for mishaps that may alienate the artifacts from or garble key contextual information. As archaeologists increasingly come to use shared datasets, there will be increasing need for better managed and reliable data creation processes throughout the entire research cycle.

6 CONCLUSION

A major objective of Open Context is to improve standards to support data reuse over the long term. An examination of data reuse practices in field archaeology showed that context surrounding the research methods, people, and repository processes were particularly important, but often not readily available. For instance, the methodological procedures for field studies, such as specifications of field tools, excavation strategies, and sampling, recording, and analysis procedures were used to understand, verify, and trust the data. In addition, the reputation and scholarly affiliation of the archaeologists, the phrasing and structure of the narratives created during field work, and information about the repository where the data were held were used to assess data quality. However, examination of current data documentation guidelines, standards and ontologies showed much of the context needed for reuse was not being incorporated into practice. For instance, basic forms of context, such as chronology, lack disciplinary consensus on chronological designation. CIDOC-CRM, a well-established formal ontology, is oriented to meet the needs of museum curators, not producers and reusers of archaeological field data. On a positive note, there are several small scale, experimental data integration projects developing and applying formal ontologies. In addition, data repositories and data publishing systems have stepped in to implement tools and recruit data editors to align datasets with formal ontologies and controlled vocabularies in the meantime. As experimental projects, data repositories, and data publishing systems continue work in the area, our examination of data reuse practices has highlighted critical aspects of context that must be considered to facilitate long term data reuse.

7 ACKNOWLEDGMENTS

This research was funded by a National Leadership Grant from the Institute of Museum and Library Services, LG-06-10-0140-10, "Dissemination Information Packages for Information Reuse".

8 REFERENCES

[1] Aitchison, K. 2009. Standards and Guidance in Archaeological Archiving: The Work of the Archaeological Archives Forum and the Institute for Archaeologists. *The Grey Journal,* 5 (2), 67–71.

[2] Atici, L, Kansa, S., Lev-Tov, J., and Kansa, E. 2012. Other People's Data: A Demonstration of the Imperative of Publishing Primary Data. *J ARCHAEOL METHOD TH* (April 11), 1–19.

[3] Binding, C. May, K. and Tudhope, D. 2008. Semantic Interoperability in Archaeological Datasets: Data Mapping and Extraction Via the CIDOC CRM. In *Proceedings of the 12th European conference on Research and Advanced Technology for Digital Libraries* (ECDL '08), B. Christensen-Dalsgaard, D. Castelli, B. Ammitzbøll Jurik, and J. Lippincott, Eds. Springer-Verlag, Berlin, Heidelberg, 280-290.

[4] Brody, A. 2011. The Archaeology of the Extended Family. In *Household Archaeology in Ancient Israel and Beyond,* A. Yasur-Landau, J. R. Ebeling, and L. B. Mazow, Eds. Boston, MA.

[5] Brown, A, and Perrin, K. 2000. *A Model for the Description of Archaeological Archives*. English Heritage Centre for Archaeology, Fort Cumberland. http://www.eng-h.gov.uk/archives/archdesc.pdf.

[6] Brown, A. 2007. *Archaeological Archives: A Guide to Best Practice in Creation, Compilation, Transfer and Curation.* Archaeological Archives Forum. http://www.archaeologyuk.org/archives/

[7] Childs, C. 2010. *Finders Keepers: A Tale of Archaeological Plunder and Obsession*. Little, Brown and Co., New York.

[8] Condron, F., Richards, J., Robinson, D. and Wise, A. 1999. *Strategies for Digital Data - A Survey of User Needs. Archaeology Data Service.* York, UK. http://ads.ahds.ac.uk/project/strategies/

[9] Czyrnyj, A. 2011. *Presenting the University of Manitoba's Archaeo-logical Collections Online: Implementation and User Feedback.* Doctoral Thesis. University of Manitoba, Winnipeg, Manitoba.

[10] Data Archiving and Networked Services (DANS). 2011. *Instructions for Depositing Archaeological Data in EASY.* http://www.dans.knaw.nl/sites/default/files/file/archief/Instructies0deponeren/Instructions_for_depositing_archaeological_data_DEF%281%29.pdf

[11] Dibble, H. L., and McPherron, S.P. 1988. On the Computerization of Archaeological Projects. *J FIELD ARCHAEOL,* 15 (4), 431–440.

[12] Doerr, M. 2003. The CIDOC Conceptual Reference Module: An Ontological Approach to Semantic Interoperability of Metadata. *AI MAG,* 24 (3) (September 2003), 75-92.

[13] Doerr, M. and Iorizzo, D. 2008. The Dream of a Global Knowledge Network- A New Approach" *J COMPUT CULT HERIT,* 1 (1), 1–23.

[14] Eiteljorg, II, H. 1998. Archiving Archeological Data in the Next Millennium. *ONE WORLD ARCHAEOL,* 21 (6), 21–23.

[15] Esteva, M., Trelogan, J., Rabinowitz, A., Walling, D. and Pipkin, S. 2010. From the Site to Long-term Preservation: A Reflexive System to Manage and Archive Digital Archaeological Data. In *Proceedings of the Society for Imaging Science and Technology*, Den Haag, the Netherlands, May 2010, 1-6.

[16] Faniel, I. M., Kriesberg, A. and Yakel, E. 2012. Data Reuse and Sensemaking Among Novice Social Scientists. In *Proceedings of the American Society for Information Science and Technology*, Baltimore, MD, October 2012.

[17] Faniel, I.M., and Jacobsen, T.E. 2010. Reusing Scientific Data: How Earthquake Engineering Researchers Assess the Reusability of Colleagues' Data. *COMP SUPPORT COMP WORK* 19 (3-4) (August), 355–375.

[18] Harley, D., Acord, S.K., Earl-Novell, S., Lawrence, .S and King, *C.J. 2010. Assessing the Future Landscape of Scholarly* ***Communication□: An Exploration of Faculty Values and Needs*** *in Seven Disciplines. University Of California Press, Berkeley, CA.*

[19] Hodder, I, and Hutson, S. 2003. *Reading the Past: Current Approaches to Interpretation in Archaeology.* Cambridge University Press, Cambridge, UK.

[20] Holtorf, C. 2002. Notes on the Life History of a Pot Sherd. *J MAT CULT,* 7 (1), 49–71.

[21] Institute for Archaeologists. 2009. *Standard and Guidance for the Creation, Compilation, Transfer and Deposition of Archaeological Archives.*

http://www.archaeologists.net/sites/default/files/node-files/Archives2009.pdf.

[22] Isaksen, L. 2011. *Archaeology and the Semantic Web*. Doctoral Thesis. University of Southampton, Southampton, UK.

[23] Jeffrey, S., Richards, J., Ciravegna, F., Waller, S., Chapman, S. and Zhang, Z. 2009. The Archaeotools Project: Faceted Classification and Natural Language Processing in an Archaeological Context. *PHILOS T ROY SOC,* 367 (1897) (June), 2507–2519.

[24] Kansa, E. 2012. Openness and Archaeology's Information Ecosystem. *WORLD ARCHAEOL,* 44 (4): 498–520.

[25] Kansa, S.W., Kansa, E.C., and Schultz, J.M. 2007. An Open Context for Near Eastern Archaeology. *NEAR EAST ARCHAEOL* 70 (4) (December), 188–194.

[26] Keene, S. 2005. *Fragments of the World: Uses of Museum Collections*. Elsevier, Boston, MA.

[27] Kintigh, K.W. 2006. The Promise and Challenge of Archaeological Data Integration. *AM ANTIQUITY* 71(3):567-578.

[28] McManus, E. 2012. *Unearthing Archives: An Examination of Documents Generated in the Course of Archaeological Fieldwork in Canada.* Doctoral Thesis. The University of British Columbia Vancouver, Canada.

[29] Merriman, N. and Swain, H. 1999. Archaeological Archives: Serving the Public Interest? *EUR J ARCHAEOL* 2 (2), 249–267.

[30] Niven, K. 2008. *Guidelines for Depositors Version 1.3*. Archaeology Data Service. http://ads.ahds.ac.uk/project/userinfo/deposit.cfm

[31] Parks Canada. 2005. *Archaeological Recording Manual: Excavations and Surveys*. http://www.pc.gc.ca/eng/docs/pc/guide/fp-es/titre-title.aspx.

[32] Richards, J. 1997. Preservation and Re-use of Digital Data: The Role of the Archaeology Data Services. *ANTIQUITY,* 71 (274) (December), 1057–1059.

[33] Richards, J., Jeffrey, S., Waller, S., Ciravegna, F., Chapman, S and Zhang, Z. 2011. The Archaeology Data Service and the Archaeotools Project: Faceted Classification and Natural Language Processing. In *Archaeology 2.0: New Approaches to Communication and Collaboration,* E.C. Kansa, S.W. Kansa and E. Watrall, Eds. Cotsen Institute of Archaeology, Los Angeles, CA, 31-56.

[34] Spielmann, K., and Kintigh, K. 2011. "The Digital Archaeological Record: The Potentials of Archaeozoological Data Integration Through tDAR" *The SAA Archaeological Record* (January), 22–25.

[35] Tudhope, D., Binding, C. and May, K. (2008), Semantic Interoperability Issues from a Case Study in Archaeology. In *Semantic Interoperability in the European Digital Library,* Proceedings of the 1st International Workshop (SIEDL 2008), associated with 5th European Semantic Web Conference, S. Kollias and J. Cousins, Eds. Tenerife, Spain, 88-99.

[36] Van House, N. 2002. Digital Libraries and Practices of Trust: Networked Biodiversity Information. *Social Epistemology: A Journal of Knowledge, Culture and Policy* 16 (1): 99.

[37] Wallis, J.C., Borgman, C.L., Mayernik, M.S., Pepe, A., Ramanathan, N., and Hansen, M. 2007. Know Thy Sensor: Trust, Data Quality, and Data Integrity in Scientific Digital Libraries. In *European Conference on Research and Advanced Technology for Digital Libraries* 4675, 380–391. Budapest, Hungary.

[38] Winter, B.J. 1996. *Out of Sight, Out of Mind: The Reposition of Archaeological Collections in Canada.* Doctoral Thesis. Simon Fraser University, British Columbia, Canada.

Constructing an Anonymous Dataset From the Personal Digital Photo Libraries of Mac App Store Users

Jesse Prabawa Gozali[1,2*] Min-Yen Kan[1,2] Hari Sundaram[3]
[1]Department of Computer Science, National University of Singapore, Singapore
[2]NUS Interactive and Digital Media Institute, Singapore
[3]Arts Media & Engineering, Arizona State University, USA
{jprabawa, kanmy}@comp.nus.edu.sg hari.sundaram@asu.edu

ABSTRACT

Personal digital photo libraries embody a large amount of information useful for research into photo organization, photo layout, and development of novel photo browser features. Even when anonymity can be ensured, amassing a sizable dataset from these libraries is still difficult due to the visibility and cost that would be required from such a study.

We explore using the Mac App Store to reach more users to collect data from such personal digital photo libraries. More specifically, we compare and discuss how it differs from common data collection methods, *e.g.* Amazon Mechanical Turk, in terms of time, cost, quantity, and design of the data collection application.

We have collected a large, openly available photo feature dataset using this manner. We illustrate the types of data that can be collected. In 60 days, we collected data from 20,778 photo sets (473,772 photos). Our study with the Mac App Store suggests that popular application distribution channels is a viable means to acquire massive data collections for researchers.

Categories and Subject Descriptors

H.5.2 [**Information Interfaces and Presentation**]: User Interfaces

General Terms

Measurement, Human Factors

Keywords

Personal digital library, Photography, Data collection, Ground truth, Crowd-sourcing

*This research is supported by the Singapore National Research Foundation under its International Research Centre @ Singapore Funding Initiative and administered by the IDM Programme Office.

1. INTRODUCTION

Researchers in personal digital photo libraries (DLs) require access to such DLs to conduct their studies. For example, works on photo summarization [10], photo stream alignment [11], automatic albuming [9], and event photo stream segmentation [3] require various features and ground truth annotations from DLs. Acquiring such personal data, however, tends to be a challenging process – especially when sizable data is desired. Common methods to obtain photos, such as from volunteers or from study participants, do not scale well to thousands of photo sets due to the remuneration costs and the limited reach that study advertisement has in gathering interested participants.

To collect ground truth annotations on such collected photos, even more human effort is required. For example, in automatic albuming, the ground truth is the true grouping of photos into separate events. In some works, the authors themselves produced the ground truth [9] or external annotators were employed [8], which may be problematic due to unfamiliarity, bias, or ignorance of events that transpired in the photos. The semantics associated with personal photos render these tasks difficult to annotate by parties not privy with the context of the photos. In our own experience with event photo stream segmentation [3], we find that the average agreement of external annotators to be unsatisfactory.

For such reasons, studies often require that the photo owners themselves produce the ground truth [7]. Data collection thus involves both 1) accessing the DLs, and 2) acquiring the efforts of the photo owners themselves to produce the ground truth annotations. These two issues exacerbate the difficulty in scaling up the data collection process. We encountered this exact problem in building upon our previous work on event photo stream segmentation.

We propose using a popular application distribution channel, the Mac App Store (hereafter, MAS), to alleviate issues with cost and reaching potential study participants. We use our own research needs as a case study to explore using the MAS as a platform to acquire the needed data. To the best of our knowledge, this is the first study to explore collecting anonymous data from personal digital photo libraries at a large scale, *i.e.* our data collection application was downloaded by over 2,500 users in 60 days.

The contributions of our study is two-fold. First, we report and discuss our experiences with the design of the data collection application, timeline, visibility, and cost in using the MAS in Section 2. Secondly, we present the large collected data to the research community in Section 3, providing an in-depth analysis of a few pertinent features.

2. DATA COLLECTION

The goal of our study is to explore the MAS for data collection in personal digital photo libraries. Primarily, we were motivated by its large user base: on Jan 7th, 2011, after only 24 hours of being available, the MAS had received over one million downloads[1]. We hypothesize that with its large user base in multiple countries, using the MAS will increase the visibility of our study and thus yield more collected data.

To facilitate the study, we used our own data collection needs. In our previous work[3], we developed an event photo stream segmentation method that relied on a dataset of photo features to compute smoothing weights and parameters. We also collected the ground truth segmentation from these sets to evaluate against baselines: between each pair of consecutive photos, we need to know if a segment boundary exists. To obtain better smoothing weights and parameters, we need to collect features from a larger dataset. Additional ground truth segmentations would also expand our evaluation and strengthen the validity of the results.

Design. With any data collection method, a means for the collection needs to be designed and created. Even when the data to collect is small in scale, researchers still need to create a way to collect the data (*e.g.* from the volunteers) and a way for annotators to provide ground truth (*e.g.* for parameter tuning, supervised learning, or evaluation). When large-scale data collection is necessary, other scaling issues arise. For example, with crowd-sourcing platforms like Amazon Mechanical Turk (MTurk), recent works [6] have noted that verification questions or qualification task is necessary to ascertain if the annotators are suited for the task. Results also often have to be filtered to remove fake data from cheating crowd-sourcing users [1].

For the MAS, its review guidelines outline very specific *functionality requirements* for any application it distributes. One of the requirements states that applications *"that are not very useful"* may be rejected. As such, in the design of our application, we needed to relegate the data collection to a secondary function. While this seems counter-intuitive, we argue that generally, the data is collected to ultimately serve some practical purpose for the users; this purpose is a natural fit as the primary function of the application.

In our case, we need the data to improve our event photo stream segmentation algorithm. In our previous study on chapter-based photo organization [4], we developed CHAPTRS, a photo browser that utilizes the algorithm to automatically group users' event photos into chapters. Thus for the MAS, we improved upon CHAPTRS from the feedback and results of our previous study. At the same time, we can use CHAPTRS for data collection, *i.e.* as a secondary function.

When CHAPTRS is launched for the first time, a window appears and explains how the automatic segmentation works and then appeals to the user to participate in the study to help improve the algorithm (Figure 1). Participation is voluntary and opt-in, but we entice users by stating that a future improved algorithm would be provided exclusively to participants. We also explained that the data is anonymized and the 60-day study was approved by our Institutional Review Board, as described in detail in a provided link[2].

[1]http://apple.com/pr/library/2011/01/07macappstore.html

[2]http://www.chaptrs.com/research

Figure 1: Window (sheet) inviting users to participate in a study to help improve our algorithm

Cost. Currently, there is no mechanism in the Mac Software Development Kit (SDK) to allow MAS developers to send money to their users, and thus we opted not to remunerate participants monetarily. This reduces the overall cost of the study as it no longer grows with the number of participants. At the same time, the participants are more likely to be users who are genuinely interested in helping to improve the algorithm so they can benefit from the future algorithm, unlike many crowd-sourced users who may cheat.

We made CHAPTRS a free application to maximize number of downloads. All the cost in the study is then attributed to the Mac Developer Program annual fee of 99 USD. Past works with MTurk [6] have reported paying about 0.02 USD per annotationm on top of the 60.50 USD Amazon fee, while others paid 0.10 USD per translation (Urdu into English) [1]. For data collections that involve no human judgement or annotation, *e.g.* collecting Short Message Service (SMS) messages, recent work [2] reported paying at most 0.01 USD per message.

In our case, we collected features from 20,778 photo sets, comprising of 473,772 photos, of which 60 sets have ground truth segmentations, comprising of 8,107 photos. This translates to 0.0002 USD per photo, or if we attribute all the cost to the collected annotations, 0.012 USD per annotation[3].

When we consider the first 19 days of the study — the time taken by [6] to collect 2,500 annotations from MTurk — we collected 5,787 photo sets, comprising of 227,969 photos, of which 23 sets have ground truth segmentations, comprising of 4,559 photos. This translates to a similar cost of 0.02 USD per annotation, but without any other additional fees.

This illustrates another difference between our study and existing data collection methods. Because the cost of our study does not scale with the amount of data collected, the cost per collected data (*e.g.* photo or annotation) decreases with the duration of the study and with the number of concurrent studies.

Visibility. We define visibility as the exposure obtained by CHAPTRS to MAS users. This includes both MAS users who downloaded CHAPTRS and those who did not. While visibility is difficult to ascertain, we can produce a lower bound by determining the number of MAS users who downloaded CHAPTRS. The daily number of downloads for the study can be seen in Figure 2, where the best-matching

[3]*i.e.* whether there are segment boundaries in the pairs of consecutive photos in a photo set

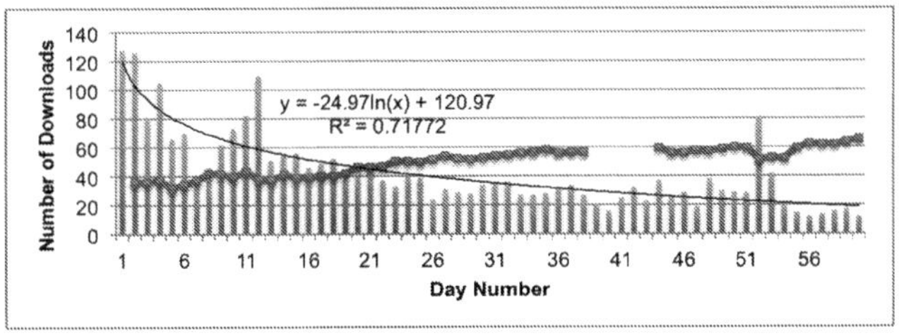

Figure 2: Daily number of downloads (columns) with trendline and average rankings (line) for Chaptrs in the 60 days of study

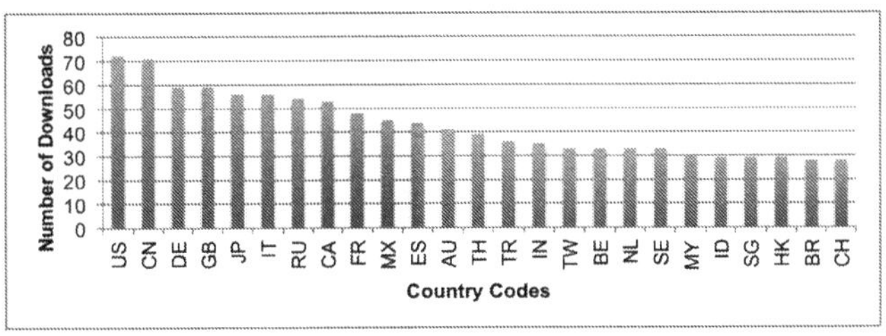

Figure 3: Top 25 Countries with Highest Number of Downloads

trendline is logarithmic: $y = -24.97ln(x) + 120.97$ with a coefficient of determination, $R^2 = 0.71$, where y and x correspond to the number of downloads and the day number respectively.

We note that there are two anomalous spikes in the number of downloads on Days 12 and 52. Both spikes are attributed to the unusually high number of downloads in the Japan MAS on those days (47 and 38). These high number of downloads are caused by a snowballing effect from CHAPTRS taking the number 2 and 4 positions in the top photography category in the Japan MAS. The line graph in Figure 2 plots the average photography category ranking for Chaptrs among various MAS stores. We can observe that the ranking decays linearly with time. Figure 3 shows a time series plot of the top 25 countries with the highest number of downloads. This ranking shows relative market sizes that would be useful for planning pilot studies.

As CHAPTRS is a free application, one tendency is for users to download and delete the application after only a brief experience. This is undesirable especially if the data collection is meant to contribute to a longitudinal study. To estimate the percentage of deletions, we submitted an update to the MAS. As the MAS only notifies updates to users with the application still installed, this gives us a good estimate. The update was released on Day 50 (see Figure 4). Comparing the number of downloads in the first 49 days (2,261) and the number of updates in the last 11 days (2,226), we can estimate that there is only at most a 1.5% deletion rate.

Timeline. It took 19 days to collect 23 photo sets with ground truth annotations, comprising of 4,559 photos. In the same amount of time, [6] collected 2,500 music mood annotations using MTurk. The work on SMS collection [2], which was considerably simpler as it involved no annotations from contributors, reported less success with 43 submissions (over 200 SMS per submission on average) over 40+ days.

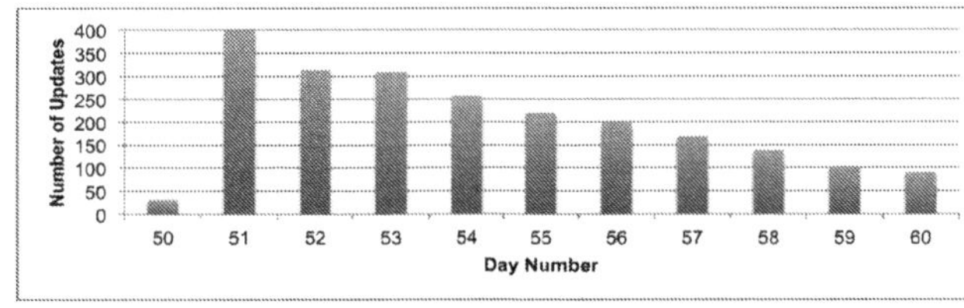

Figure 4: Number of updates from Day 50 to 60

We note that there is some temporal overhead with using MAS as a distribution channel. This is because applications need to undergo a review process before it becomes available for download. The review time fluctuates over time and usually takes 1-2 weeks[4]. Additional time is required for resubmission if the application is rejected.

3. DATA SET

While there are publicly available datasets (*e.g.* Corel), there are none that are event photos from personal photo libraries. We have previously noted that researchers have so far made use of their own collections to conduct studies. This poses a hurdle for new researchers. In practice, producing a public dataset of personal photos is challenging due to the private nature of the photos and their semantics.

We believe that a compromise is possible. The data we collected is a "blind" dataset of personal photos because the photos themselves are not in the dataset. Instead, only anonymized photo features and annotations are contained[5].

The dataset currently contains features that we use for our own work on event photo stream segmentation: time gap, focal length, aperture diameter, logLight, and an 8-bin color histogram, but can be easily extended to collect others. Here we provide some brief analysis of the data set, details of which are packaged with the dataset[6].

Using k-means, we clustered the color distributions and searched for an optimal value for k, $k < 9$, which was found to be 6. Figure 5 shows the color distributions of the cluster centroids. We observe that there is a large percentage of black in all clusters due to the binning of dark colors to the nearest color, black. We also observe that Cluster 2 represents the blue/cyan photos while the red/yellow photos are represented by Cluster 3. These two clusters thus show the color distribution of the "blue/cyan" photos and "red/yellow" photos in the dataset. The other three clusters seem to represent different ratios of white to black while the ratios of the remaining 6 colors remain fairly constant.

We also analyzed for bursts of photo taking activity [5], *i.e.* a sequence of photos (> 2) taken in succession with a certain average time gap. In our analysis, we looked for 15 kinds of bursts, each with a different average time gap[7]. Figure 6 shows the number of bursts found and the average number of photos for each kind of burst. We observe that the most frequent burst has an average time gap of 9s. Also, the

[4]Trend is reported at reviewtimes.shinydevelopment.com

[5]An externally-hosted web application was used to collect the data. As the incoming traffic was rerouted through its servers, the origin IP address is unknown.

[6]`http://wing.comp.nus.edu.sg/~jeprab/chaptrs_dataset/`

[7]While photos taken > 1 min apart can hardly be considered a burst, we analyze such "bursts" for completeness

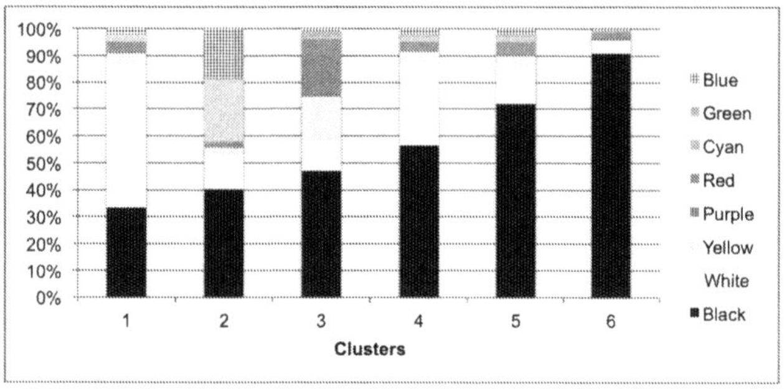

Figure 5: Color distributions of the six cluster centroids in the dataset

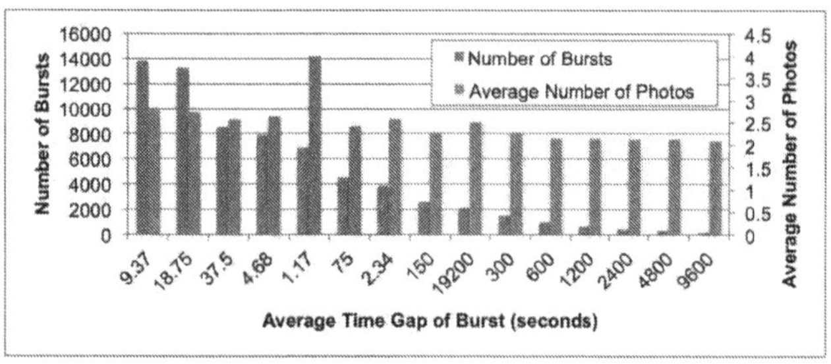

Figure 6: Dataset statistics of photo taking bursts

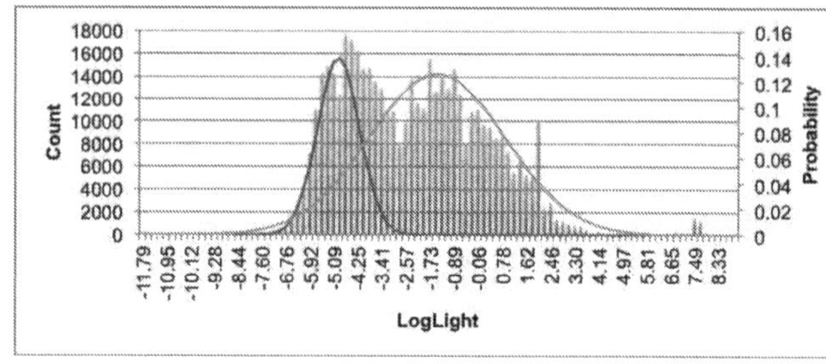

Figure 7: Histogram of LogLight values and the estimated Gaussian mixtures. The probabilities of the mixtures have been multiplied by their mixture ratios (0.26, 0.74) to aid with the visualization.

burst with the lowest average time gap in our analysis has the highest average number of photos. This suggests that when people take photos in quick succession (~1s), they do so with 4 photos on average.

Figure 7 shows a histogram of LogLight values. Fitting a two-mixture Gaussian to the histogram ($\mu = \{-4.91, -1.47\}$, $\sigma = \{0.74, 2.35\}$, $\lambda = \{0.26, 0.74\}$) yields results that suggest that the LogLight values correspond to two normal distributions, that plausibly represent day (left mixture) and night (right mixture). LogLight values are small (large) for high (low) levels of ambient light, respectively.

4. CONCLUSION

There is a lack of publicly available datasets for personal photos. We believe that the challenge lies is in the issue of privacy and in the difficulty in collecting sizable data. In this paper, we have demonstrated how such a dataset can be constructed by collecting anonymous photo features and ground truth annotations using an application distributed through the Mac App Store.

Aside from the review time overhead and conceptual overhead of designing the data collection application, we have demonstrated that the MAS with its large user base allows CHAPTRS to achieve high number of downloads, collects data at a faster rate and with lower cost than the data collection experiences from some recent works.

Ultimately, there is a self-filtering process because only genuinely interested users would volunteer to participate in the studies. This is in contrast with other data collection means, *e.g.* crowd-sourcing platforms where some users may only be interested in the monetary remunerations.

We note that in the works that we have reviewed, the types of data and annotations collected are very different and thus we should not discount the possibility of confounding variables affecting our comparisons. Nonetheless, our experiences with CHAPTRS shows that the MAS provides a fruitful and viable alternative for data collection especially in reaching out to personal digital photo libraries. In future work, we can adjust CHAPTRS to collect a different set of anonymous features from the photos to expand on the dataset and its analysis.

5. REFERENCES

[1] M. Bloodgood and C. Callison-Burch. Using Mechanical Turk to build machine translation evaluation sets. In *Proc. NAACL 2010 Workshop on AMT*, 2010.

[2] T. Chen and M.-Y. Kan. Creating a live, public short message service corpus: The NUS SMS Corpus. *Language Resources and Evaluation*, pages 1–37, Aug. 2012.

[3] J. P. Gozali, M.-Y. Kan, and H. Sundaram. Hidden Markov Model for event photo stream segmentation. In *Proc. ICME 2012 Workshop on HFC3D*, 2012.

[4] J. P. Gozali, M.-Y. Kan, and H. Sundaram. How do people organize their photos in each event and how does it affect storytelling, searching and interpretation tasks? In *Proc. JCDL*, pages 315–324, 2012.

[5] J. Kleinberg. Bursty and hierarchical structure in streams. In *Proc. KDD*, pages 91–101, 2002.

[6] J. H. Lee and X. Hu. Generating ground truth for music mood classification using Mechanical Turk. In *Proc. JCDL*, pages 129–138, 2012.

[7] A. C. Loui and A. E. Savakis. Automated event clustering and quality screening of consumer pictures for digital albuming. *IEEE Trans. Multimedia*, 5(3):390–402, September 2003.

[8] A. Pigeau and M. Gelgon. Spatial-temporal organization of one's personal image collection with model-based ICL clustering. In *Proc. CBMI*, 2003.

[9] J. C. Platt. AutoAlbum: Clustering digital photographs using probabilistic model merging. In *Proc. CAIV*, pages 96–100, 2000.

[10] P. Sinha, S. Mehrotra, and R. Jain. Summarization of personal photologs using multidimensional content and context. In *Proc. ICMR*, 2012.

[11] J. Yang, J. Luo, J. Yu, and T. Huang. Photo stream alignment and summarization for collaborative photo collection and sharing. *IEEE Trans. Multimedia*, 14(6):1642–1651, Dec. 2012.

Modeling Heterogeneous Data Resources for Social-Ecological Research: A Data-Centric Perspective

Miao Chen, Umashanthi Pavalanathan, Scott Jensen, Beth Plale
School of Informatics and Computing
Indiana University
Bloomington, Indiana U.S.A
{miaochen, umapaval, scjensen, plale}@indiana.edu

ABSTRACT

Digital repositories are grappling with an influx of scientific data brought about by the well publicized "data deluge" in science, business, and society. One particularly perplexing problem is the long-term archival and reuse of complex data sets. This paper presents an integrated approach to data discovery over heterogeneous data resources in social-ecological systems research. Social-ecological systems data is complex because the research draws from both social and natural sciences. Using a sample set of data resources from the domain, we explore an approach to discovery and representation of this data. Specifically, we develop an ontology-based process of organization and visualization from a data-centric perspective. We define data resources broadly and identify six key categories of resources that include data collected from site visits to shared ecological resources, the structure of research instruments, domain concepts, research designs, publications, theories and models. We identify the underlying relationships and construct an ontology that captures these relationships using semantic web languages. The ontology and a NoSQL data store at the back end store the data resource instances. These are integrated into a portal architecture we refer to as the Integrated Visualization of Social-Ecological Resources (IViSER) that allows users to both browse the relationships captured in the ontology and easily visualize the granular details of data resources.

Categories and Subject Descriptors

H.3.5 [**Information Storage and Retrieval**]: Online Information Services – *data sharing.*

Keywords

Scientific Data, Ontology, Semantic Web, NoSQL Data Store.

1. INTRODUCTION

The explosive growth that scientific domains have experienced in both the volume and velocity of data generation has led to the Big Data era, which presents new challenges in data representation, management, archival, and other data operations. Big Data is characterized by a high degree of heterogeneity [15], resulting in a variety of data formats and representations (e.g., XML files, microdata, tables, databases) that have led to issues in the interoperability and discoverability of relevant data. One particularly perplexing problem is the long-term archival and access to complex data sets.

A field that exhibits many of the challenges of Big Data is sustainability science since it is inherently cross-domain. In this paper we present a data-centric approach to representing the relationships between data resources in social-ecological systems (SES). Researchers in SES study the complex interactions in human-natural systems such as forests, fisheries, and irrigation systems that contain subsystems composed of multiple layers [12], so data for such systems exhibit a high degree of complexity. This type of research produces a large number of small-scale heterogeneous data sets and presents an excellent test case for relating resources using a Semantic Web approach since it merges two scientific domains, and as noted by Ostrom in [12], "the ecological and social sciences have developed independently and do not combine easily".

Field data is often collected through significant effort in remote locations and can be time-consuming due to a need to gain the trust of participants. The data consist of both measurements of natural resources (e.g., biodiversity of a forest) and surveys and interviews with those using and governing the use of a resource system. Due to the social science aspects of these projects, the studies involved are often bound to research frameworks that are conceptually well structured, but the research designs are expressed as text instead of using a structured semantic language. This lack of structure can inhibit the reuse and wider dissemination of irreproducible field data. In addition, other related research materials such as theories, models, and survey instruments, may not always be directly associated with the collected data. In this paper we consider the varied materials of SES research to all be data resources that need to be managed together with the collected data sets in a structured approach. Some of the resources are individual granules specific to a single project while other resources relate to multiple projects.

Many social-ecological resources are implicitly interconnected, however without a model that makes these connections explicit, data discovery is difficult. Our model uses semantic web languages (e.g., RDF and OWL), to make these linkages explicit so they can be used for data discovery. We identify important classes of resources such as domain concepts, collected research data, research instruments, research theories and models, publications, and research designs. This model has implications for digital libraries as they tackle the organization of and access to heterogeneous scientific data sets.

JCDL'13, July 22–26, 2013, Indianapolis, Indiana, USA.
Copyright © ACM 978-1-4503-2077-1/13/07...$15.00.

To illustrate how the model works, we have chosen some exemplar social-ecological data resources: the International Forestry Resources and Institutions (IFRI) database (as a research data set), the Social-Ecological System (SES) Framework (as a research theory), the research design from a paper published using IFRI data (as a research design), and a collection of SES concepts from a semantic wiki (as a set of domain concepts). After constructing an abstract ontology, we analyze the relationships between data resources and concretize the ontology with these real-world instances. Some data resources are composed of smaller data objects which we store in MongoDB [10] at different levels of granularity. We extend WebProtégé [18] to provide an interface that allows users to explore the relationships between objects and view the data.

In the remainder of this paper we review relevant work, introduce the major data resources categories we model in social-ecological science, address the methodology used to model the domain and visualize the data and relationships, and conclude with a discussion of future work.

2. RELATED WORK

The ecological and social sciences have respectively developed the Ecological Metadata Language (EML) [5] and the Data Documentation Initiative (DDI) [16] XML metadata standards that provide a structured approach to describe complex data sets. We see these as complementary to IViSER in that such metadata would be linked to the dataset it describes and to domain concepts captured as keywords in the metadata. Semantic Web languages have been used less frequently to describe data sets, although there is an RDF implementation of the Dublin Core metadata standard and an RDF implementation of DDI was proposed in [3]. A Vocabulary of Interlinked Data (VoID) was proposed in [1] as a generalized approach to describing RDF data sets, but differs from our research in that it only applies to data already represented in RDF and does not address the research lifecycle.

Another means to facilitate scientific discovery is through a Resource Map as defined in the OAI-ORE standard which uses linked data principles to describe an aggregation of resources [17]. OAI-ORE has been implemented in varied contexts such as Australian literature [6] and life cycle of sensor applications [13] to describe compound objects. The Research Object (RO) proposed in [2] builds on the idea of the aggregation in OAI-ORE to further define the relationships between resources in a scientific investigation; such as data, model, and people. IViSER addresses some key features of an RO and can be viewed as the first iteration of a RO architecture for capturing and aggregating social-ecological research. Our approach shares similarities with stereotypical ROs in other domains.

3. SOCIAL-ECOLOGICAL RESEARCH AND DATA RESOURCES

As the first step in building an ontology of social-ecological data we analyzed the data resources used and generated during the lifecycle of research projects in this domain. This analysis identified the following six key categories of data resources that form the backbone of the ontology:

1) ***Research data collected through field studies and experiments***. Researchers collect both quantitative and qualitative data based on research designs and instruments. In this paper we use data collected by IFRI through hundreds of site visits to forest systems on a global basis for the past 18 years [8]. Detailed field data is collected manually, entered into a relational database, and then federated and shared between 13 Coordinating Research Centers (CRCs) worldwide.

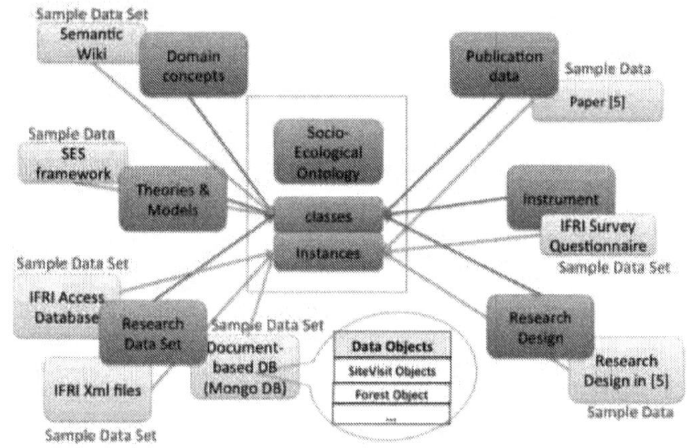

Figure 1. Data-centric view of data resources in the social-ecological domain.

2) ***Domain concept definitions***. Researchers have defined important concepts and variables used in social-ecological research. We have extracted the definitions compiled by social-ecological researchers in the Social Ecological System Semantic Wiki [14].

3) ***Research instruments***. These include data resources such as surveys and questionnaires. Such instruments provide a rationale for the data collection and usually correspond to a research framework.

4) ***Theories and models***. These are conceptual frameworks that explain important aspects of the domain and the relationships between variables. A theoretical framework that has seen increasing uptake in social-ecological research is the Social-Ecological System (SES) Framework [11]. In this paper we integrate the SES Framework using the OWL Semantic Web language.

5) ***Publication data***. This class of research data represents articles published in journals and conferences. The ontology could be linked to article repositories, but as an example of how such data is represented in the ontology, we have included a publication based on the IFRI data as an example.

6) ***Study design***. Research projects are often guided by a study design which outlines the relevant variables (concepts) and their associations. For some studies, the design is not explicitly stated in research output such as publications, but can be extracted by understanding the content. As an example, we include the design used in [4], which has variables for carbon storage, livelihoods, and three factors related to forest commons and their interaction.

Some of these categories represent data collections, whereas others more frequently represent individual data resources (e.g., theories, models, and research instruments). Each resource category and the corresponding example instances discussed above is shown in Fig. 1. In section 4 we discuss how the ontology builds on these generalized categories and show how the dependencies between these resources are captured in the ontology. For example, "research instruments" pose questions related to "domain concepts" and link to instances in the "research data" captured using the instrument.

4. METHODOLOGY: ONTOLOGY AND VISUALIZATION

In this section, we introduce our approach to modeling the social-ecological domain as an ontology and visualizing that ontology via a portal interface.

4.1 Constructing the Social-Ecological Ontology

The ontology is composed of two layers: classes and instances. The class layer contains abstract entities that represent generalized concepts about scientific data resources and the semantic relationships between such classes. The instance layer contains concrete entities that represent data resource instances, descriptions of the instances, and application of the generalized classes to these instances. The class layer is specified using the OWL language and instances are represented using RDF.

The ontology serves as a registry for the actual research data instead of duplicating existing data. The data resources themselves are not converted to RDF, but instead the ontology includes references to the original data resource or as stored in MongoDB for faster access (see Section 4.2). The ontology provides information about social-ecological data resources instead of capturing the content per se. If users want to access the data resources, the ontology provides a description and pointer to the resources.

Classes

The classes included in the ontology include both general high-level classes that are applicable across scientific domains, and domain-specific concepts from within social-ecological research. The highest level of the ontology consists of the six categories of data resources discussed in Section 3, and their subclasses and related classes that capture domain-independent characteristics of data resources. Such additional domain-independent classes include: (1) "Author", which identifies the author(s) of a "publication" data resource, and (2) "SurveyQuestion" which are the individual questions within a "ResearchInstrument" data resource.

Specific classes from the IFRI research instrument are also incorporated into the ontology as concepts. The instrument is composed of several forms, each of which reflects important concepts in the researcher's mental model. Therefore, broad data collection categories in the IFRI instrument such as site visit, forest, and forest plot are added to the ontology as classes. "DomainConcept" is a special type of class about variables, factors, and constructs in the domain, (e.g. "ResourceSystem" and "Biodiversity"). They are important components for research design and theories.

Relations and Properties

The relationships between classes are defined as OWL properties. As an example, the classes "Theory" and "DomainConcept" are related through the "contains" property in that "Theory" contains one or more "DomainConcept" instances. To link semantic resources that independently define the same class, the "owl:sameAs" property is used to indicate equivalent classes in the ontology. This allows us to link social-ecological resources defined by different sources. For instance, the SES Semantic Wiki [14] defines domain concepts, so we use the "owl:sameAs" property to link between the "Concept" class in the wiki and the "DomainConcept" class in the ontology. As additional such resources are identified, they can be linked to the ontology's "DomainConcept" class through the "owl:sameAs" property to form a linked web of social-ecological concepts.

The flexible semantics of OWL and RDF are also used in the ontology to describe the hierarchy of concepts used in a theory. Starting with the SES Framework [11], which has 8 first tier variables and 44 second tier variables, each variable in the theory is first mapped to concepts in the SES Semantic Wiki, and then the hierarchical relationships between variables in the Framework are added to the ontology as OWL properties.

Instances

Using the concepts defined as OWL classes, each of the example data resources listed in section 3 are added to the ontology as instances based on their corresponding class. Some instances can be directly imported into the ontology such as the concepts defined in the SES Semantic Wiki which are linked to the "DomainConcept" class through the equivalence property. For some instances the process can be at automated such as instances of the "Forest" class from the IFRI research instrument. For some instances, such as the SES Framework as an instance of "Theory", the instances in the ontology need to be created manually because they require human interpretation.

4.2 Object-based Representation

The classes, instances, and relations between them in the ontology allow users to explore the relationships both between and within data resources. In addition, by registering data resources as instances of classes, scientists can explore the data at a more granular level as described in Section 4.3.

Some resources, such as the IFRI data which is stored in a relational database, are not easily registered as instances in the ontology. For this reason, we build on an XML archive representation of each IFRI site visit as described in [9]. The IFRI instrument is applied at the level of a site visit, and that is the level at which the XML representation is generated. The ontology captures key components of the IFRI instrument such as "site visit" and "forest" as classes since they represent the mental model of the researcher. To make the granular data for these instances easy to register in the ontology and visualize, we extract the XML data for each site visit and instances of classes contained in each site visit (such as forests) and represent them in a JSON-style document format that is then stored in the MongoDB [10] document-oriented NoSQL data store.

MongoDB was selected because of three benefits it provides to the system: 1) its object based architecture maps well to the class instances used in research instruments such as IFRI, 2) it enables linking the instances registered in the ontology to objects in MongoDB to provide researchers fast access to the granular details of a data resource, and 3) since some research data is sensitive in nature, it provides a mechanism for restricting access to the details of a data resource that would not be possible if the content were made directly accessible in a semantic web language.

4.3 Visualization: the IViSER System

The IViSER (Integrated Visualization of Social-Ecological Resources) system leverages WebProtégé [18], the Google Web Toolkit (GWT) [7], and MongoDB [10] to provide domain scientists and policy makers with an easy-to-use web portal for exploring the relationships represented in the ontology and examining details of data resource instances. We leverage its plug-in architecture to extend the functionality of the portal through a new *portlet* that can quickly access the details of a data

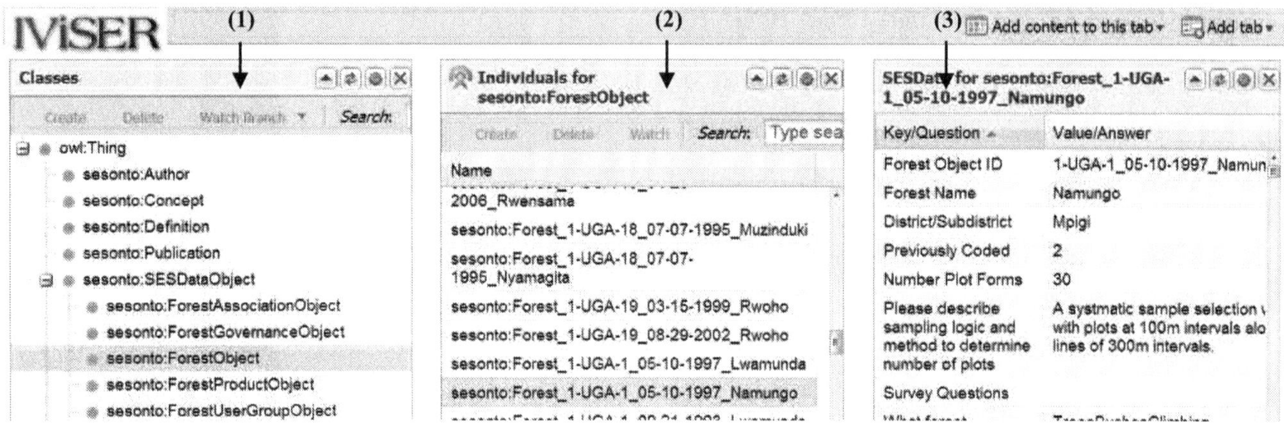

Figure 2. IViSER interface (1) – Classes of the ontology, (2) – ForestObject instances, (3) – Data and metadata retrieved from MongoDB for a ForestObject instance.

resource stored in MongoDB. The ontology is imported into WebProtégé and each instance of a class in the ontology that is stored in MongoDB is assigned an rdf:about URI that identifies the instance. This URI is also used as the identifier for the corresponding document object in MongoDB to enable the retrieval and visualization of details regarding a data resource in a tabular format as shown in Fig. 2.

5. DISCUSSION AND FUTURE WORK

In this paper we show how social-ecological data resources can be modeled using a data-centric approach that links distributed heterogeneous resources via semantic web languages. An ontology is constructed that starts at a high level with 6 key resource types we have identified and links data resource instances through both general and domain-specific classes. Scientists and policy makers can easily examine data resources at a granular level using the ontology through our WebProtege-based portlet coupled with the MongoDB backend data store. One challenge lies in how we can incent scientists to describe their data resources and establishing linkages between the resources in the IViSER system.

In future work we plan to: 1) identify additional social-ecological data resources to add as instances and expand the classes captured in the ontology, 2) enhance the ontology through additional feedback and from domain experts, and 3) evaluate the ontology by using another set of data sets as testing data.

6. REFERENCES

[1] Alexander, K., and Hausenblas, M. 2009. Describing linked datasets-on the design and usage of void, the vocabulary of interlinked datasets. In *Proceedings of LDOW2009*.

[2] Bechhofer, S., De Roure, D., Gamble, M., Goble, C., and Buchan, I. 2010. Research Objects: Towards Exchange and Reuse of Digital Knowledge. In *1st Int'l Workshop on The Future of The Web for Collaborative Science* (Raleigh, North Carolina).

[3] Bosch, T., Cyganiak, R., Wackerow, J., and Zapilko, B. 2012. Leveraging the DDI model for linked statistical data in the social, behavioral, and economic sciences. In *Proceedings of the Int'l Conference on Dublin Core and Metadata Applications*.

[4] Chhatre, A., and Agrawal, A. 2009. Trade-offs and synergies between carbon storage and livelihood benefits from forest commons. *P NATL ACAD SCI USA,* 106, 42, 17667-17670.

[5] Fegraus, E. H., Andelman, S., Jones, M. B., and Schildhauer, M. 2005. Maximizing the value of ecological data with structured metadata: an introduction to ecological metadata language (EML) and principles for metadata creation. *Bulletin of the Ecological Society of America*, 86,3, 158-168.

[6] Gerber, A., and Hunter, J. 2008. LORE: A Compound Object Authoring and Publishing Tool for the Australian Literature Studies Community. In *Proceedings of 11th Int'l Conference on Asia-Pacific Digital Libraries (ICADL) 2008.*

[7] Google Web Toolkit. Last accessed May19, 2013 at https://developers.google.com/web-toolkit/

[8] IFRI (International Forestry Resources and Institutions). Last accessed May 19, 2013 at http://www.ifriresearch.net/

[9] Jensen, S., Plale, B., Liu, X., Chen, M., Leake, D., and England, J. 2012. Generalized representation and mapping for social-ecological data: Freeing data from the database. In P*roceedings of* IEEE *eScience Conference 2012.*

[10] MongoDB. Last accessed May 19, 2013 at http://www.mongodb.org/

[11] Ostrom, E. 2007. A diagnostic approach for going beyond panaceas. *P NATL ACAD SCI USA*, 104, 9, 15181-15187.

[12] Ostrom, E. 2009. A general framework for analyzing sustainability of social-ecological systems. *Science*, 325, 5939, 419-422.

[13] Pepe, A., Mayernik, M., Borgman, C., and Van de Sompel, H. 2010. From Artifacts to Aggregations: Modeling Scientific Life Cycles on the Semantic Web. *Journal of the American Society for Information Science and Technology*, 61(3), 567-582. DOI http://dx.doi.org/10.1002/asi.21263.

[14] Social-Ecological Systems Semantic Wiki. Last accessed May 19, 2013 at http://socialecologicalsystems.referata.com

[15] TechAmerica Foundation's Big Data Commission. 2012. *Demystifying big data: A practical guide to transforming the business of government.*

[16] Vardigan, M., Heus, P., and Thomas, W. 2008. Data Documentation Initiative: Toward a Standard for the Social Sciences. *Int'l Journal of Digital Curation*, 3,1, 107-113.

[17] Van de Sompel, H., Lagoze, C., Nelson, M. L., Warner, S., Sanderson, R., & Johnston, P. 2009. Adding eScience assets to the data web. In *Proceedings of LDOW 2009.*

[18] WebProtege. Last accessed May 19, 2013 at http://protegewiki.stanford.edu/wiki/WebProtege

Non-Linear Book Manifolds: Learning from Associations the Dynamic Geometry of Digital Libraries

Richard Nock
CEREGMIA — Univ. Antilles-Guyane
97259 Schoelcher, France
rnock@martinique.univ-ag.fr

Frank Nielsen
Sony Computer Science Laboratories, Inc.
Tokyo 141-0022, Japan
nielsen@csl.sony.co.jp

Eric Briys
CEREGMIA — Univ. Antilles-Guyane
97259 Schoelcher, France
eric.b@cyberlibris.com

ABSTRACT

Mainstream approaches in the design of virtual libraries basically exploit the same ambient space as their physical twins. Our paper is an attempt to rather capture automatically the actual space on which the books live, and *learn* the virtual library as a non-linear book manifold. This tackles tantalizing questions, chief among which whether modeling should be static and book focused (*e.g.* using bag of words encoding) or dynamic and user focused (*e.g.* relying on what we define as a *bag of readers* encoding). Experiments on a real-world digital library display that the latter encoding is a serious challenger to the former. Our results also show that the geometric layers of the manifold learned bring sizeable advantages for retrieval and visualization purposes. For example, the topological layer of the manifold allows to craft *Manifold* association rules; experiments display that they bring dramatic improvements over conventional association rules built from the discrete topology of book sets. Improvements embrace *each* of the following major standpoints on association rule mining: computational, support, confidence, lift, and leverage standpoint.

Categories and Subject Descriptors

H.3.3 [**Information Storage and Retrieval**]: Information Search and Retrieval—*retrieval models*

Keywords

Non-linear manifold learning; Pattern mining; Visualization

1. INTRODUCTION

Digital libraries are on the brink of Big Data for the man in the street [9]. Scientific analyses at this size level are recent [15], but another challenge is being faced for digital libraries, that will necessitate a leap forward on tools to crunch information, to find and visualize its useful core for the end readers. Ideally, a working digital library should stimulate serendipitous browsing: one finds some book at some place in the digital library, and an even more interesting book is sitting right next to it. In the physical library, centuries of optimization of arrangements have led to *Classifications* like the Library of Congress and Dewey Decimal Classifications (resp. LCC and DCC). These are finely-tuned ways to cope with the discrete topology on a set of books $\mathbb{B}$, and find the right partition of $\mathbb{B}$ that fits a set of physical shelves. This is a common-point physical libraries share with their digital twins: digital libraries also adopt a direct standpoint on their content's *ambient space* [3, 7, 18, 19].

In this paper, we claim that perhaps this approach is not optimal when it comes to fit to one's palm — or tablet — a complete digital library. We tackle the question of whether the digital library's organization can be *learned* as a nonlinear *submanifold* of its books contents, or as a *submanifold* of the traces that leave readers wandering round the virtual shelves. Our answer, obtained over a real-world experiment for a major international actor of digital libraries, is clear-cut affirmative. It brings new materials to the table of manifold learning algorithms, and a new application of these algorithm to craft association rules. *Manifold association rules* exploit the topological layer of the learned manifold. From both the computational and accuracy standpoints, they are found to dramatically improve upon techniques relying on the first layer of data, the discrete topology of $\mathbb{B}$, that are mainstream in association rule mining [12]. Our contributions also include (i) the design and test of an encoding for books, *bag of readers* (BoR), which is shown to be a serious challenger to the popular bag of words encoding (BoW) to capture the library's content; (ii) an improvement of a manifold learning algorithm [24] (iii) the design of information-geometric interfaces to browse through the library's content. We end up with a seamless and scalable integration of manifold-based techniques to digital libraries. Other approaches, pioneered in Latent Semantic Indexing [4], also use a similar algebraic toolbox as ours — singular value decomposition — to come up with a reduced representation of data, and many of them have been used in document or text related works [13]. A crucial difference with our work, however, is that such approaches rely on linear manifolds, like *e.g.* PCA in statistics, and thus fit projections of the ambient space and fall short of the discriminative power of (arbitrary) non-linear manifolds, that are important to capture fine grained structures in the data [22].

The following section defines and explain how to craft book manifolds and manifold association rules. Two experimental sections follows, and a last section concludes with perspectives on non-linear book manifolds.

JCDL'13, July 22–26, 2013, Indianapolis, Indiana, USA.

Algorithm 1: `learn-`$f(\mathbb{B}, d')$

Input: $\mathbb{B} = \{\boldsymbol{b}_i, i = 0, 1, ..., m-1\}$, $d' \in \mathbb{N}_*$;

Output: Classification function $f : \mathbb{B} \rightarrow \mathbb{R}^{d'}$;

1. Compute $\mathbf{W} \in \mathbb{R}_+^{m \times m}$ with $w_{ij} \doteq s(\boldsymbol{b}_i, \boldsymbol{b}_j) = w_{ji}$;
2. Normalize $\mathbf{W}$ to obtain matrix $\mathbf{N}$ with spec $(\mathbf{N}) \subset \mathbb{R}$;
3. Diagonalize: $\mathbf{N} = \mathbf{P}^{-1}\mathbf{D}\mathbf{P}$, where $d_{ii} \geq d_{jj}, \forall i \leq j$;
4. Finish-up: $f(\boldsymbol{b}_i) \doteq (p_{i1}, p_{i2}, ..., p_{id'}), \forall \boldsymbol{b}_i \in \mathbb{B}$;

2. NON-LINEAR BOOK MANIFOLDS

Capitalized bold letters like $\mathbf{M}$ denote matrices, and italicized bold letters like $\boldsymbol{v}$ denote vectors. m_{ij} and v_i respectively denote coordinate (i, j) of $\mathbf{M}$, and coordinate i of $\boldsymbol{v}$ (coordinates start from zero). Blackboard notations like $\mathbb{S}$ denote subsets of (tuples of, matrices of) reals, and $|\mathbb{S}|$ their cardinal. The identity matrix is denoted $\mathbf{I}$, and the all-1 vector is denoted $\mathbf{1}$. Matrix $\mathbf{M}$ is (row) stochastic iff $m_{ij} \geq 0, \forall i, j$ and $\mathbf{M1} = \mathbf{1}$. $\mathbf{M}$ is doubly stochastic iff both $\mathbf{M}$ and $\mathbf{M}^\top$ are stochastic, where "$\top$" denotes transpose. The spectrum of $\mathbf{M}$ is denoted spec $(\mathbf{M})$.

2.1 Learning the digital library

We let $\mathbb{B} \subset \mathbb{R}^d$ denote a set of books, $\mathbb{B} = \{\boldsymbol{b}_i, i = 0, 1, ..., m-1\}$, for some respective dimension and size $d, m \in \mathbb{N}_*$. Without additional assumption, the *ambient* space of books is a d-dimensional real-valued *feature space.* Prior to defining this space, we first focus on the way we use it to *learn* the actual geometry of the library. Assume that the library we seek lives on a *non-linear low-dimensional manifold* of $\mathbb{R}^d$. We chose to rely mainly on three prominent historical approaches to learn this manifold [14, 24]. We also crafted a novel variant of [24] for the task at hand, which makes overall four tested approaches to learn the library's geometry. Assume we have a symmetric similarity function between books, $s : \mathbb{B} \times \mathbb{B} \rightarrow \mathbb{R}_+$. From this, we can *learn* from book similarities the *classification* function[1] $f : \mathbb{B} \rightarrow \mathbb{R}^{d'}$ which places the books on the $d' \ll d$ dimensional manifold we seek. Algorithm 1 (`learn-`f) presents the four main steps used to learn f. Its basic ingredient is a *similarity matrix* $\mathbf{W}$ whose coordinates are the similarities between books.

The four approaches we use to learn the geometry of the library differ on the way the normalization is performed in step **2.** of `learn-`f. The two main normalizations are the normalized Laplacian and the Markov chain normalization, respectively denoted [14]:

$$\mathbf{N} \doteq \mathbf{D'}^{-\frac{1}{2}}\mathbf{W}\mathbf{D'}^{-\frac{1}{2}} , \quad (1)$$

$$\mathbf{N} \doteq \mathbf{D'}^{-1}\mathbf{W} , \quad (2)$$

where $\mathbf{D'}$ is diagonal, with $d'_{jj} \doteq \sum_k w_{jk} = \sum_k w_{kj}$. The probabilistic interpretation of (2) in terms of percolation between states of Markov chains is particularly interesting for our task [14]. Assume $s(\boldsymbol{b}_i, \boldsymbol{b}_j)$ is roughly proportional to the probability of being jointly interested by books $\boldsymbol{b}_i$ and $\boldsymbol{b}_j$. In this case, books that are brought close by function f tend to maximize this joint interest, acting somehow in favor of serendipitous browsing (See Section 1).

One can also remark that both (1) and (2) are each the first step — of different algorithms — which iteratively approximate $\mathbf{W}$ by a doubly stochastic matrix. It was remarked by by [20] for (2) and much later for (1) [24]. Since $\mathbf{W}$ is symmetric, [24] propose to explicitly seek the symmetric doubly stochastic matrix $\mathbf{N}$ which best approximates $\mathbf{W}$, according to the minimization of the Frobenius norm, or the entropy. We abstract this problem as find:

$$\arg \min_{\mathbf{N} \in \mathbb{R}_+^{m \times m}} d_r(\mathbf{N}||\mathbf{W}), \quad \text{s.t. } \mathbf{N} = \mathbf{N}^\top, \mathbf{N1} = \mathbf{1} , \quad (3)$$

where $d_r(\mathbf{N}||\mathbf{W}) \doteq \sum_{ij} d_r(n_{ij}||w_{ij})$ and $d_r(x||y) \doteq r(x) - r(y) - (x-y)r'(y)$ is a Bregman divergence with generator r, a strictly convex differentiable function [2] with dom$r \supseteq [0, 1]$, and r' is the derivative of r. Frobenius norm and the entropy used in [24] are particular cases of Bregman divergences [2]. The third algorithm we have used to find $\mathbf{N}$ is the iterative procedure for the Frobenius norm of [24] to solve (3).

Compared with this approach, (1) and (2) achieve a compromise between improving the doubly stochastic approximation of $\mathbf{N}$ with respect to $\mathbf{W}$ *while* limiting the drift between the eigensystems of $\mathbf{N}$ and $\mathbf{W}$, since a single step of the algorithm is performed. To what extent do these two concurrent objectives play in the accuracy of the final manifold is an interesting question. Our fourth approach adds a preprocessing *scaling* step to (3) in which we replace $\mathbf{W}$ by a matrix which is the closest to a doubly stochastic matrix under the constraint that its eigenvectors are the *same* as $\mathbf{W}$. If the closedness is evaluated using the same divergence as (3), then this amounts to finding $\mathbf{W}' = u\mathbf{W}$ with:

$$u \quad = \quad \arg \min_{v \in \mathbb{R}_+} D_r(v\mathbf{W1}||\mathbf{1}) . \quad (4)$$

Through closed-forms solutions to (4) are not always available, their fast approximation is trivial, as explained below.

Lemma 1. *$u \in [(\max_i \mathbf{1}_i^\top \boldsymbol{W}\mathbf{1})^{-1}, (\min_i \mathbf{1}_i^\top \boldsymbol{W}\mathbf{1})^{-1}]$, with $\mathbf{1}_i$ the all-0 vector with a 1 in coordinate i.*

(proof omitted) Hence, a fast dichotomic search is enough to approximate u. In the case where we consider the Frobenius norm ($r(x) = x^2$), the solution to (4) is explicit as we have $u = \mathbf{1}^\top\mathbf{W1}/\mathbf{1}^\top\mathbf{W}^2\mathbf{1}$. Let us summarize the four different normalizations performed in step **2.** of `learn-`f: (`NL`) normalized Laplacian (1); (`MC`) Markov chain normalization (2); (`DS`) doubly-stochastic approximation (3) with Frobenius norm; (`SDS`) doubly stochastic approximation preceded by scaling. We have also tested, for each of these normalizations, an additional preprocessing step to step **2.** which consists in replacing $\mathbf{W}$ by a sparse symmetric matrix, as follows (for some $k \in \mathbb{N}_*$): $w_{ij} = 1$ iff $\boldsymbol{b}_i \in k$-SNN$(\boldsymbol{b}_j)$ and 0 otherwise. k-SNN$(\boldsymbol{b}_j)$ is the set of k *symmetric* nearest neighbors of book $\boldsymbol{b}_j$ [17]. The sparsified matrix is a truncated version of the geodesic distance matrix of ISOMAP [22], but in which k-NNs are replaced by k-SNNs, guaranteeing to keep the symmetry.

2.2 Books and similarities

2.2.1 Books: bag of words vs bag of readers

The first solution to code the ambient space of books is to consider the books' content, and more precisely treat books as *bag of words* (BoW) [10]. Experimentally, rather than parsing words from the books' contents — which would make a very large d —, we use the books' XML descriptions of their titles and abstracts. Vectors are post-processed in the usual way [10], with TF-IDF weighting and normalization to

[1] We can think of it as a virtual equivalent of DDC or LCC.

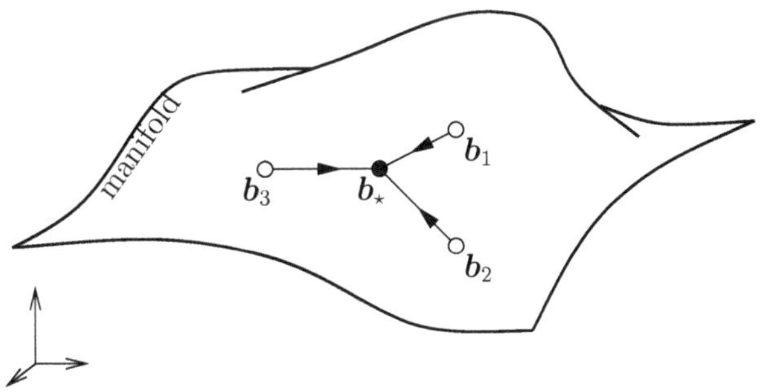

Figure 1: A bookshelf $\{b_\star, b_1, b_2, b_3\}$ obtained after affinity propagation. The star shows that book $b_\star$ is the exemplar of the bookshelf: it may be thought as its most accurate representative (see text).

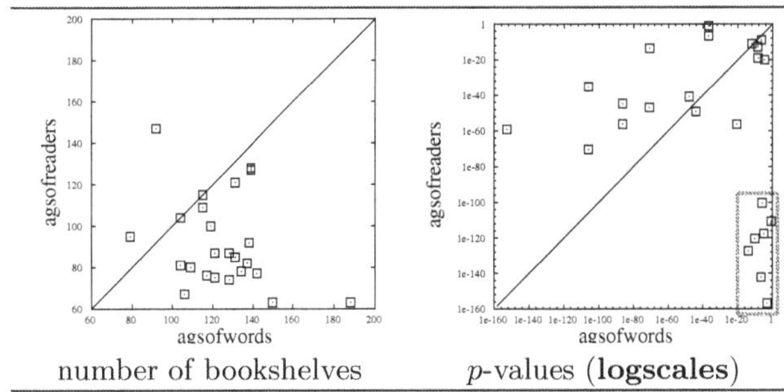

Figure 2: Scatterplot comparing BoW encoding versus BoR encoding, according to the number of bookshelves (left) and χ^2 p-values (right, see text for details about the implementation). On both plots, the diagonal is the $y = x$ line. Points *below* the $y = x$ line represent smaller numbers of bookshelves for BoR (left) and smaller (hence, better) p-values for BoR (right). The green thick dashed rectangle (right plot) on the lower-right distinguishes a region for which (i) $\log(p_{\mathrm{BoW}}/p_{\mathrm{BoR}}) \in [80, 140]$ — *i.e.* BoR is much more accurate than BoW, and (ii) p-values for BoW are "close" to 1 relatively to the other p-values.

unit norm. There is however another way to represent books, which consists in taking the binary Users×Books matrix that would be used to describe the users as a function of the books with which they have interacted[2], and then transpose it to reveal a description of books as a simple function of the users who have interacted with the books, considering that similar books should be the subject of joint interactions for many readers. This is what we call a *bag of readers* (BoR) encoding. Though this encoding is accessible only once a sufficiently large number of interactions have occurred, it is perhaps more appealing than BoW, as it is dynamic and evolves with the readers' habits, and it makes also possible to reveal associations between books that would have been missed from the books' contents alone.

2.2.2 *Book similarities*

We have considered three kinds of similarities, each of which falls in $[0, 1]$, "1" being the maximal similarity always achieved for $s(\boldsymbol{b}_i, \boldsymbol{b}_i)$. The first one, derived from the Heat kernel, belongs to the most popular in manifold learning [1]:

$$s_{\mathrm{hea}}(\boldsymbol{b}_i, \boldsymbol{b}_j) \quad = \quad \exp(-\|\boldsymbol{b}_i - \boldsymbol{b}_j\|_2^2/T) \ , T > 0 \ . \qquad (5)$$

The second one is built from the cosine similarity:

$$s_{\cos}(\boldsymbol{b}_i, \boldsymbol{b}_j) \quad = \quad \frac{1}{2}\left(1 + \frac{\boldsymbol{b}_i^\top \boldsymbol{b}_j}{\|\boldsymbol{b}_i\|_2 \|\boldsymbol{b}_j\|_2}\right) \ . \qquad (6)$$

The last one is the Jaccard index, that we note by a minor abuse of notation as:

$$s_{\mathrm{jac}}(\boldsymbol{b}_i, \boldsymbol{b}_j) \quad = \quad \frac{\hbar(\boldsymbol{b}_i)^\top \hbar(\boldsymbol{b}_j)}{\|\hbar(\boldsymbol{b}_i + \boldsymbol{b}_j)\|_2^2} \ . \qquad (7)$$

Here, $\hbar : \mathbb{R}^d \to \{0, 1\}^d$ denotes the Heaviside function which replaces > 0 coordinates by 1.

2.3 Bookshelves

So far, we have described the way we shape the digital library as a submanifold of $\mathbb{R}^d$. The next step is the building of virtual *bookshelves*, that is, clusters of books. There exists an important literature on clustering in the context of digital libraries [11]. A natural approach to crafting bookshelves consists in performing a (hard) clustering of the manifold, under the constraint that the number of bookshelves is sufficiently (but not too) large. Because of this constraint, algorithms that are known to be subject to trapping in local minima — like k-means — gave poor results. Even improvements that guarantee on average to approach global minima [16] gave better but still unsatisfactory results, and were outperformed by an algorithm which comes in the nick of time for such an application: affinity propagation [6]. Affinity propagation is a message passing algorithm which ends with a hard clustering solution whose number of clusters is not fixed in advance; it depends on a user-fixed preference parameter P. Affinity propagation brings, from its ancestry in median-based clustering methods a rare plus: each bookshelf contains an *exemplar* [6], that is, a book which is supposed to embody the best all books in the bookshelf. Figure 1 provides a schematic view of what are exemplars and bookshelves. One can provide a high-level description of the algorithm as a process alternating between exchanges of two types of messages between books until convergence. In a first round, each book $\boldsymbol{b}_i$ sends a real-valued *responsibility* message to each book $\boldsymbol{b}_k$, telling to which extent $\boldsymbol{b}_k$ may serve as an exemplar for $\boldsymbol{b}_i$. Then, Each $\boldsymbol{b}_k$ sends a real-valued *availability* message to each $\boldsymbol{b}_i$, telling to which extent $\boldsymbol{b}_i$ may choose $\boldsymbol{b}_k$ as exemplar. Before a new round of message exchanges begins, each book elects its exemplar on the basis of the current availabilities and responsibilities [6]. Each bookshelf is thus a set of books having chosen the same exemplar.

[2]In our experiments, users may not just read the books online: they can also place them on public or private bookshelves, or buy physical copies. Hence, "interacted" is more suited than simply "read".

2.4 MARs: Manifold association rules

Most of the theoretical works on association rule mining work on the discrete topology on $\mathbb{B}$. This is natural: itemsets are the basic building blocks of association rules, and they are also the open sets of the discrete topology. This is, however, everything but efficient from the computational standpoint, and finding the best rules resembles finding a needle in a haystack as $\mathbb{B}$ gets larger [8, 23]. The library's

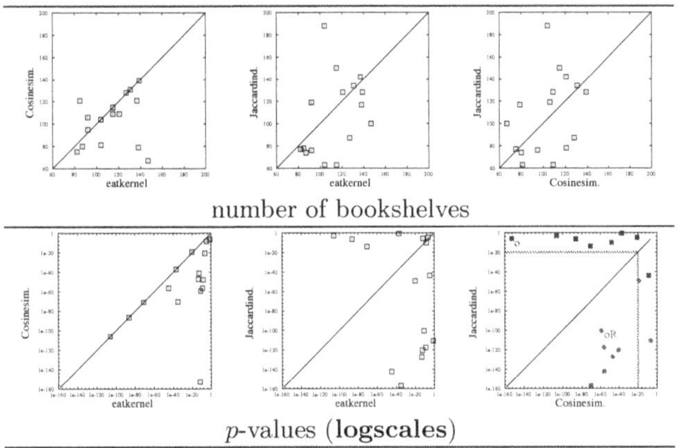

Figure 3: Scatterplots comparing the results of the three similarities tested in (5), (6) and (7). The top row displays the number of bookshelves, and the bottom row the p-values. Conventions follow Figure 2. On the lower right plot, the green thick dashed lines delineate a region in which at least one of the p-values is "large" ($\geq 10^{-20}$); this scatterplot also depicts the results of BoW encoding (blue squares) and BoR encoding (red circles, see text for details).

manifold provides us with a topological layer which comes in handy to reduce the number of candidates.

An *association rule* is a logical rule over the discrete topology of $\mathbb{B}$, which can be written $\mathbb{B}_l \Rightarrow \mathbb{B}_r$, where $\mathbb{B}_l \cup \mathbb{B}_r \subseteq \mathbb{B}, \mathbb{B}_l \cap \mathbb{B}_r = \emptyset$ [21]. In the context of the digital library, it can be interpreted as: if a reader has interacted with the books of $\mathbb{B}_l$, then he has also interacted — or will likely interact — with the books from $\mathbb{B}_r$. Set $\mathbb{B}_l \cup \mathbb{B}_r$ is called the *itemset* of the association rule. We have chosen to rely on four of the most popular criteria to evaluate association rules: the *support* of the rule $\mathbb{B}_l \Rightarrow \mathbb{B}_r$ is the support of its itemset, noted $\textsc{Supp}(\mathbb{B}_l \cup \mathbb{B}_r)$, equal to the proportion of readers having interacted with all the corresponding books. The *confidence* of the association rule is:

$$\textsc{Conf}(\mathbb{B}_l \Rightarrow \mathbb{B}_r) \doteq \frac{\textsc{Supp}(\mathbb{B}_l \cup \mathbb{B}_r)}{\textsc{Supp}(\mathbb{B}_l)} . \quad (8)$$

The *lift* of the association rule is:

$$\textsc{Lift}(\mathbb{B}_l \Rightarrow \mathbb{B}_r) \doteq \frac{\textsc{Supp}(\mathbb{B}_l \cup \mathbb{B}_r)}{\textsc{Supp}(\mathbb{B}_l)\textsc{Supp}(\mathbb{B}_r)} . \quad (9)$$

Finally, the *leverage* is defined as:

$$\textsc{Leve}(\mathbb{B}_l \Rightarrow \mathbb{B}_r) \doteq \textsc{Supp}(\mathbb{B}_l \cup \mathbb{B}_r) - \textsc{Supp}(\mathbb{B}_l)\textsc{Supp}(\mathbb{B}_r) . \quad (10)$$

Remark that the support, lift and leverage are invariant to the permutation of the left-hand sides and right-hand sides of an association rule.

We let *Manifold association rules* (MARs) denote association rules built from the topological layer of the book manifold itself, and not directly from the discrete topology of $\mathbb{B}$. Typically, this means building itemsets out of the geometric proximities between books on the manifold. We give a simple and efficient example of MARs: the candidate itemsets are restricted to be subsets of the bookshelves, and thus subsets of the clusters found by affinity propagation. In Figure 1, bookshelf $\{\boldsymbol{b}_\star, \boldsymbol{b}_1, \boldsymbol{b}_2, \boldsymbol{b}_3\}$ would thus generate 6 candidate itemsets of size 2. To save space, we shall work in this paper only, but extensively, on association rules of size two, with a single book on the left- and right-hand sides.

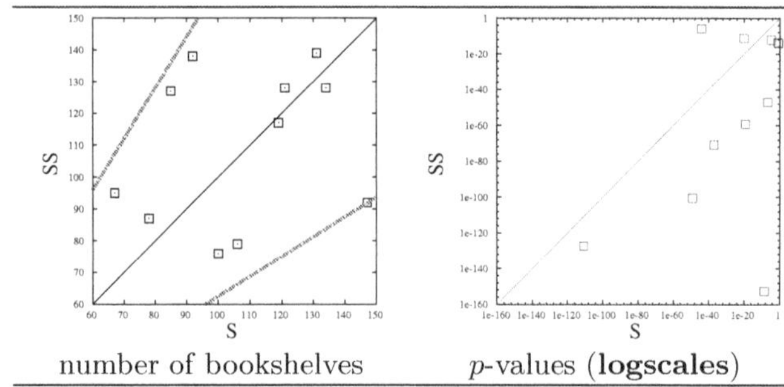

Figure 4: Scatterplots comparing the results of DS and our scaled modification SDS, according to the number of bookshelves (left) and the χ^2 p-values (right). Conventions follow Figure 2; on the left plot, the green thick dashed lines are lines of equation $y = (147/92)x, y = (92/147)x$ (see text for details).

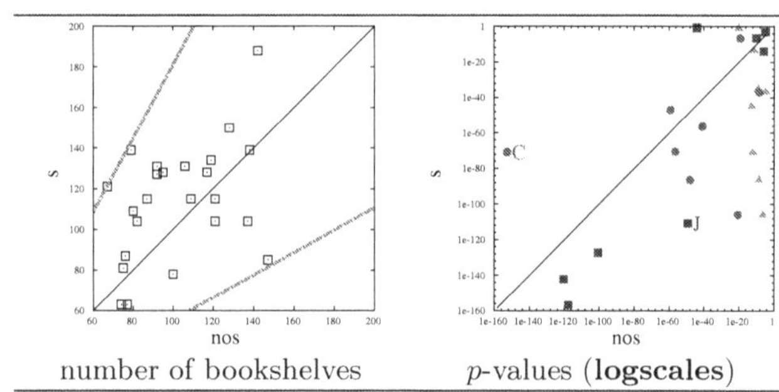

Figure 6: Scatterplots evaluating the influence of sparsifying W with symmetric nearest neighbors, according to the number of bookshelves (left) and p-values (right). Conventions follow Figure 2; on the left plot, the green thick dashed lines are the lines of equation $y = (121/67)x, y = (67/121)x$; the right plot distinguishes the results of the different similarity functions: green triangles are the (H)eat kernel (5), red circles are the (C)osine similarity (6) and blue squares are (J)accard index (7) (see text).

This size constraint leaves us space to study a very interesting particular case of MARs. Because affinity propagation makes a clearcut distinction between the exemplar of a bookshelf and its other books, it is interesting to define MARs in which either the left- or the right-hand side of the association rule is an exemplar. For example, $\boldsymbol{b}_\star \Rightarrow \boldsymbol{b}_1$ is an example of such a rule from Figure 1; $\boldsymbol{b}_2 \Rightarrow \boldsymbol{b}_\star$ is another example. We denote the subset of MARs in which $\boldsymbol{b}_\star$ is in the left-hand side as F-MARs, for centri*F*uge-MARs, while those in which $\boldsymbol{b}_\star$ is in the right-hand side shall be denoted P-MARs, for centri*P*ete-MARs. For example, the bookshelf of Figure 1 would yield 12 MARs, 3 F-MARs and 3 P-MARs.

3. EXPERIMENTS

Domain: Experiments related in this Section have been pursued during the deployment of a digital library, built for individual readers by Europe's leader on digital books

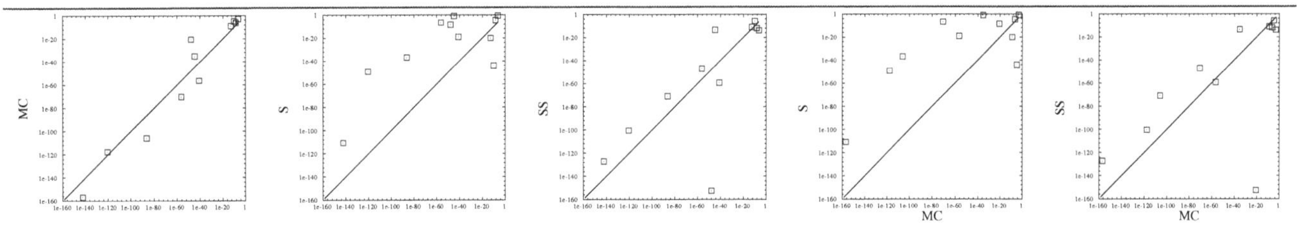

Figure 5: Logscale scatterplots comparing p-values for the four different types of normalizations (Subsection 2.1). Conventions follow Figure 2 (see text for details).

rental[3] over a year in 2010-2011. We recorded the complete behavior of the first seven thousands readers of the digital library during the first year of their membership. Any such user can perform three types of actions on books: (i) read books online, (ii) place books of his/her choice on a virtual bookshelf which can be shown to other users, (iii) buy physical copies of the books of his/her choice. We filtered out the books on which no user had interacted, to ensure that BoR encoding was meaningful; the resulting set of books (more than eight thousands) was also used for BoW encoding for the purpose of manifold comparisons.

The remaining parameters still not fixed in Section 2 have been chosen as follows: $k = 5$ in k-SNN, $T = 1000$ in (5), P in affinity propagation was fixed to be the 90th percentile of similarities, and finally $d' = 3$ for visualization purposes.

Evaluation metrics to rank manifolds: We have computed and visualized all manifolds for every possible choice of parameters described in Section 2. This represents 4 (normalization) $\times$ 2 (sparsification with -SNN) $\times$ 2 (books encoding) $\times$ 3 (similarities) = 48 manifolds, and as many different digital libraries. This task is unsupervised, yet there is a possibility to compare between each others the manifolds obtained, *via* the bookshelves computed. Intuitively the set of bookshelves should be sufficiently correlated with the high-leveled topics of the books, and it turns out that each book of the digital library is classified according to one of six primary topics (cooking, home, family, money, leisure, health) — obviously, informations about topics are not used to learn whichever of the manifolds. Out of the set of b bookshelves obtained, we compute a $6 \times b$ contingency table and compute the p-value of a $\chi^2_{5(b-1)}$ independence test for the observed contingency. The primary goal of p-values is not to make inference, but rather rank manifolds: manifolds are indeed compared on the basis of the log-ratio of their associated p-values. Still, inference would be possible on each manifold with the χ^2 test of independence, the minute p-values obtained in general and the small number of bookshelves observed (given the number of books used) raising little possibilities of type II errors.

3.1 Books encoding: BoR challenges BoW

Figure 2 summarizes the p-values that were obtained for the two different encodings of books. Since primary topics are heavily correlated to the books' titles and abstracts, one would expect BoW encoding to beat hands down BoR encoding. Figure 2 displays that it is not the case, and it is even the opposite which happens sometimes, as witnessed by the green dashed rectangle of dots, for which BoW performs quite "poorly" ($p \approx .2$ for the rightest point), while p-values of BoR are all of minute order ($\leq 10^{-100}$). Thus, choosing the dynamic information contained in the user's traces in lieu of the static information of the books contents yields in some cases dramatic improvements in the library's manifold. The number of bookshelves is also significantly smaller for BoR encoding (sign test p-value $\approx 10^{-12}$), but the ratio with BoW encoding is almost always in the interval $[.5, 2]$, which denotes a remarkable stability in the results of affinity propagation.

3.2 Books similarity: Cosine and Jaccard similarities perform the best

Comparing the three similarities in terms of number of bookshelves gives no clear-cut pattern as to whether one similarity would bring different results than the others, as evidenced by the top row of Figure 3. When it comes to comparing p-values, the observations are much different. Indeed, the heat kernel similarity performs extremely poorly compared with the cosine similarity — a single point is (slightly) above the $y = x$ line —, and quite poorly, even when it is less noticeable, compared with Jaccard index. It is important to emphasize the fact that these poor results should not stem from a bad choice of parameter T of the heat kernel, as it was tuned to get the best results. We believe that there is a technical rationale to this phenomenon — which represents good news for manifold association rules. Both BoW and BoR encoding, with TF-IDF weighting and normalization, approximate maximum likelihood fitting, incorporating knowledge about all books into the modeling of each of them [5]. The normalizations of $\mathbf{W}$ are also related to a probabilistic modeling of transitions between books. It turns out that (6) and (7) still follow this probabilistic modeling, while (5) does not. It is quite obvious for Jaccard index (7), which, in the BoR encoding, estimates the probability that a user interacts with two books:

$$s_{\mathrm{jac}}(\boldsymbol{b}_i, \boldsymbol{b}_j) \doteq \hat{\Pr}[\boldsymbol{b}_i \cap \boldsymbol{b}_j] \ . \quad (11)$$

The cosine similarity (6), on the other hand, relies on a Laplacian normalization of joint marginals. Whenever $\boldsymbol{b}_i, \boldsymbol{b}_j \in \{0,1\}^d$, it is indeed not hard to see that up to an additive constant,

$$s_{\cos}(\boldsymbol{b}_i, \boldsymbol{b}_j) \propto \hat{\Pr}[\boldsymbol{b}_i \cap \boldsymbol{b}_j] \left(\hat{\Pr}[\boldsymbol{b}_i]\hat{\Pr}[\boldsymbol{b}_j]\right)^{-\frac{1}{2}} \ .$$

Figure 3 (lower right plot) also displays that the accuracy of these two similarities heavily relies on book encodings: while cosine similarity works better with BoW encoding, Jaccard index favors BoR encoding.

[3] `http://www.cyberlibris.com`

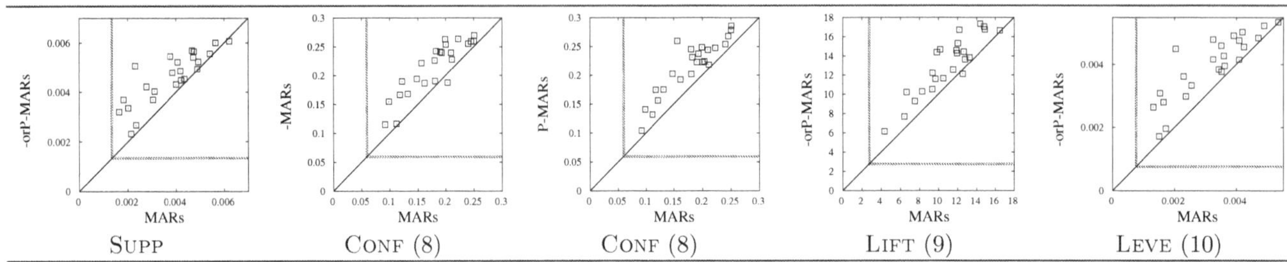

Figure 7: Scatterplots comparing the resuls of MARs vs P- and/or F-MARs, from the support, confidence, lift and leverage standpoints (from left to right). Each point is the average (over all manifolds) of the parameters computed over *all* manifold association rules obtained. General conventions follow Figure 2. On each scatterplot, the green thick dashed lines represents the average performances of size-two association rules (See text for details); in the squares delineated by these green lines, any point denotes manifold association rules performing on average *better* than the whole set of association rules.

3.3 Doubly stochastic approximation: SDS > DS

Recall that DS may be understood as a generalization of the Laplacian and Markov chain normalizations, in which rather than making a single iteration towards doubly stochastic approximation, one performs all necessary iterations [20, 24]. SDS is a variant of DS in which DS is given a similarity matrix already "close" to a doubly stochastic matrix *while* keeping the same eigenvectors as the initial similarity matrix **W**. DS and SDS were compared on our domain, and the results obtained, both in terms of the number of bookshelves and p-values, are displayed in Figure 4. Conclusions from both scatterplots are quite easy to draw: first, none of the algorithms yields a significant increase (or decrease) in the number of bookshelves: ratios do not exceed $147/92 \approx 1.6$ (Figure 4). Second, p-values tend to display that SDS performs better than DS: all but two point are below the $y = x$ line (sign test p-value ≈ 0.016), with log ratios that can be very large: $\log(p_{\text{DS}}/p_{\text{SDS}}) \approx 144$ for the lower right point.

3.4 Manifold normalization: SDS is competitive against NL and MC

We have compared the four different techniques to normalize **W** in learn-f. Figure 5 presents the scatterplots obtained. The first conclusion that can be drawn is that DS performs poorly with respect to all other approaches. MC, SDS and NL produce results that are quite equivalent. The slight advantage for NL and MC observed from the points that are slightly above the $y = x$ line (on scatterplots 3 and 5, starting from the left) is dampened by the significant outlier on which SDS clearly beats the two other approaches, with $\log(p_{\text{NL}}/p_{\text{SDS}}) > 100$ and even $\log(p_{\text{MC}}/p_{\text{SDS}}) > 130$. This outlier is however important as it corresponds to mixing popular settings to learn the manifold: BoW encoding, cosine similarity (6) and no sparsification of **W**. This might indicate that SDS may be a valuable candidate to compete again standard normalization techniques on other domains as well. This may also indicate that the normalization step in manifold learning has to achieve a compromise between finding a doubly stochastic approximation of **W**, while staying close to the original **W** from the spectral standpoint.

3.5 Sparsifying W may improve the results

An important question in the context of the digital library is the way sparsifying **W** works in manifold learning, and whether it allows to keep or improve the results. This question is important from two standpoints, the first of which being the computational complexity standpoint: a sparse **W** opens possibilities of faster algorithms to diagonalize **N**; the second standpoint is robustness: if sparsification works, it indicates that the digital library's organization does not degrade with local information loss. We have thus compared the manifolds obtained with and without sparsification by k-SNN. Fixing $k = 5$ results in a harsh sparsification: in our case, since $2kn$ coordinates of **W** remain non-zero, we end up with less than 1% non-zero values on the sparsified **W**. Figure 6 displays the way sparsification influences manifold learning. Sparsification has a small, but significant, qualitative influence, as it tends to increase the number of bookshelves (sign test p-value ≈ 0.02). From the quantitative standpoint, the increase is in fact quite small as seen from the two lines in between which the data is sandwiched (See Figure 6), and from the barycenter of data, accounting for only roughly 10% increase in average. p-values display that sparsification tends to improve the results (sign test p-value≈ 0.02), but its positive influence is the most dramatic when **W** is the least sparse: using the heat kernel as similarity (5) brings a similarity matrix with no zero coordinate. Without sparsification, p-values are always $\geq 10^{-20}$. Sparsification helps to decrease p to minute values $< 10^{-100}$. The impact of sparsification may explain that DS performs poorly in part because it tends to de-sparsify **W**. Among all runs,

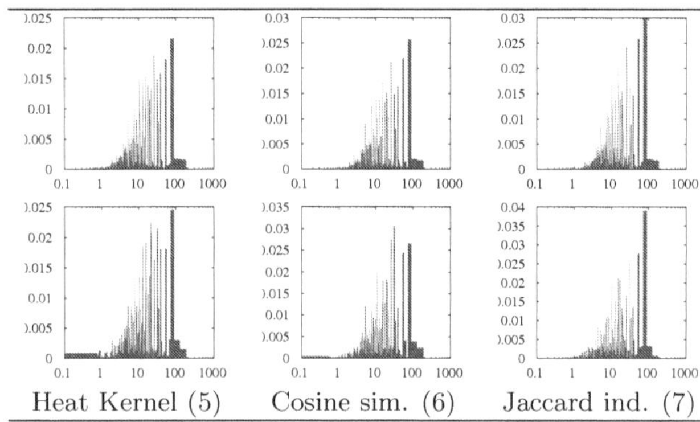

Figure 9: Truncated distributions of non-zero lifts for MARs (upper row) and F- or P-MARs (bottom row), as a function of the similarity $s(.,.)$ (Subsection 2.2). x-scales are *logscales* (see text for details).

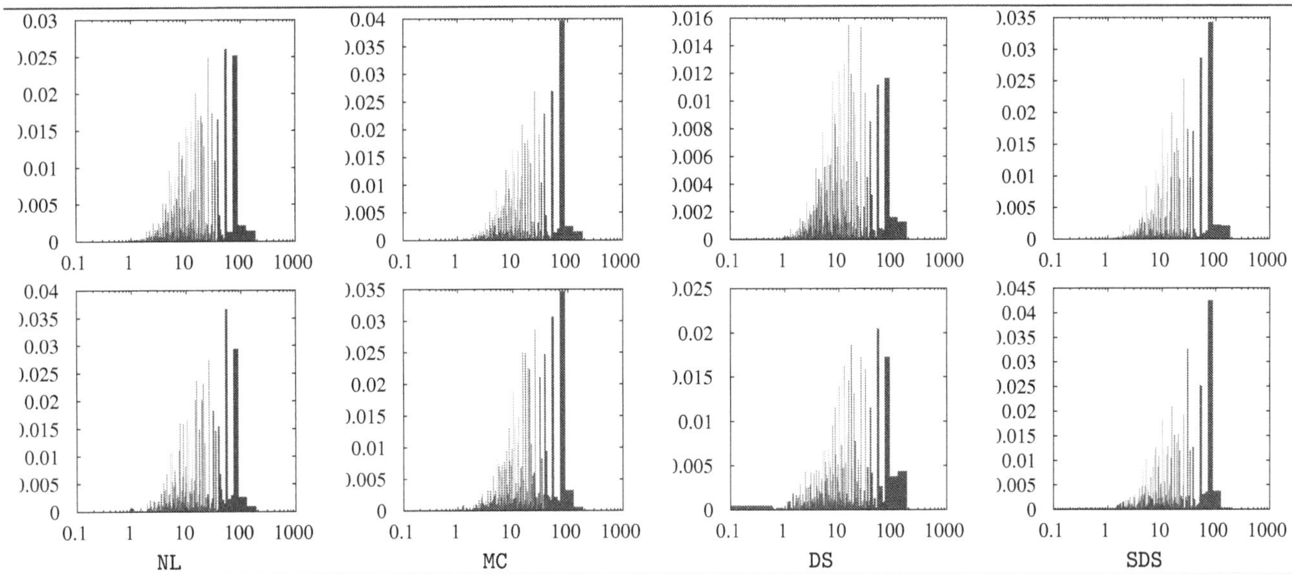

Figure 8: Truncated distributions of non-zero lifts for MARs (upper row) and F- or P-MARs (bottom row), as a function of the normalization of W (Subsection 2.1). x**-scales are** ***logscales*** **(see text for details).**

the two poorest results (p-values $= 0.09, 0.19$) are obtained when running DS after having sparsified $\mathbf{W}$. In these particular cases, *a single* iteration of DS yields a matrix already without zeroes, as this matrix is $\mathbf{W} + (1/n)\mathbf{1}\mathbf{1}^\top$ [24].

3.6 Manifold association rules always improve upon association rules

General patterns on MARs, F- and P-MARs.

We have first compared the average parameters (support, confidence, lift, leverage) of the sets of MARs for each possible way of building the manifold with BoR encoding. This represents 24 ways of building the manifold, on each of which we computed the averages of the four parameters — support, confidence, lift, leverage — for the three different types of MARs: general MARs, F-MARs and P-MARs. For each type of MARs, we generated *every* association rule following the setting of Subsection 2.4, thus without minimal support requirement. We compared the results obtained with Apriori generating *all* association rules with two books — thus, still without minimal support constraint. Manifold association rules obtained are thus a subset of the association rules output by Apriori, and our first objective is to assess the quality of the subsets with respect to the whole set.

The results are displayed on Figure 7. All comparisons are clear-cut: regardless of the combination of parameters to build the manifold, regardless of the criterion used to compare the sets of association rules obtained (average support, confidence, lift or leverage), manifold association rules *systematically* improve upon the whole set of association rules on average, and most of the times by orders of magnitude. This implies that the manifold geometrically captures the most prominent associations between books. This is not surprising: learning the manifold relies on basic building blocks that call to a probabilistic modeling of data: book similarities (Subsection 2.2), normalization of $\mathbf{W}$ (Subsection 2.1), etc. . Since the criteria used to evaluate association rules have probabilistic backgrounds (8—10), it is not surprising that the best association rules "pop out" on the manifold.

Improvements on F- and P-MARs.

There is more: drilling down into MARs displays that affinity propagation succeeds in pinpointing important books as exemplars. For example, the average support of F- or P-MARs is greater than MARs' for all but one manifolds (Figure 7, left plot). Both F-MARs and P-MARs also improve confidences compared to MARs, but there is no difference on average between F-MARs and P-MARs from the confidence standpoint (scatterplot not shown to save space). Results from the lift and leverage criteria confirm the conclusion that MARs select very accurate subsets of association rules, an improvement which is even better for F- and P-MARs.

These conclusions are to be read in the light of the number of association rules selected: the number of MARs ranged from 4.8% of the total association rules to 12.9% of the total, and the numbers of F- or P-MARs were remarkably stable, ranging from 0.22% to 0.26% of the total association rules *regardless of the manifold*. Once again, this stability of affinity propagation is remarkable.

Criteria at a glance: the case of the lifts.

We have also drilled down into the influences of the manifold construction's parameters on association rules, to see to what extent the choices made upstream on the manifold construction also impact downstream, on the association rules built from the manifold itself. We focus on the lifts of the association rules, and first consider the influence of the normalizations of $\mathbf{W}$, as displayed in Figure 8 for the lifts' distributions obtained. To keep the best viewing of plots, we filtered out MARs whose left- or right-hand side has zero support, showing only the truncated part of distributions for MARs with non zero lift. Notice that for more than 95% of the curves, the remaining truncated part still represented a mass $> .5$, sometimes even exceeding $.75$. Three notable facts emerge: (i) DS performs the worst among all four nor-

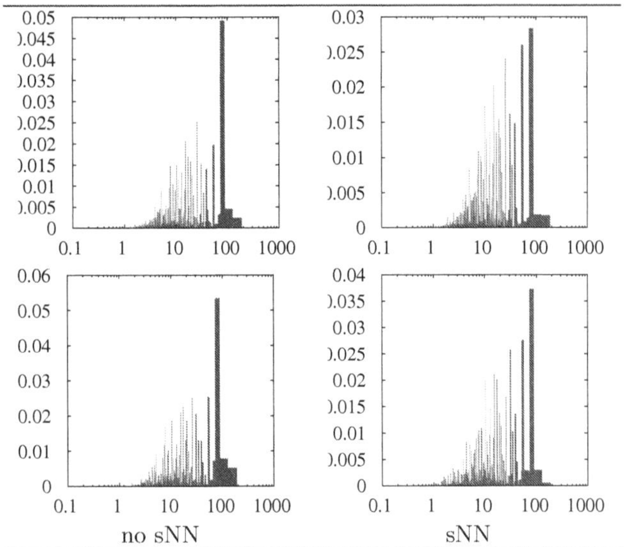

Figure 10: Truncated distributions of non-zero lifts for MARs (upper row) and F- or P-MARs (bottom row), as a function of the sparsification of W (Subsection 2.1). x-scales are *logscales* (see text).

malizations; (ii) the strictly positive lifts for MC (MARs, F- or P-MARs) and SDS (MARs) are, for more than 99.9% of the association rules, *strictly greater than one* — once again, this accounts for the fact that the manifold is built around the most prominent dependences between books; (iii) MC and SDS peak on MARs with very large lifts (≥ 100), and seem to be the best normalizations from this standpoint. To summarize, the choice of the normalization of $\mathbf{W}$ impacts quite similarly on the quality of the association rules (from the lift standpoint), and on the quality of the book manifold.

Drilling down into the global influence of the similarity function on the lift of the association rules somehow confirms an intuition, namely that the choice of Jaccard index provides the best lifts on whichever of MARs, F-MARs or P-MARs, as displayed in Figure 9 (right column). In Subsection 3.2, we emphasized the quality of the manifold associating BoR encoding and Jaccard index. Figure 9 somehow confirms the positive impact downstream of this combination, but the intuition also suggests that the positive impact may be boosted by the fact that Jaccard index already encodes in $\mathbf{W}$ a quality (support) of association rules with two books (11). We also remark that Cosine similarity still wins — but this time by a whisker — over the Heat kernel. This, again, goes hand in hand with remarks in Subsection 3.2 according to which the Cosine similarity is seemingly a better associate to BoW encoding.

Last, but not least, Figure 10 depicts the influence of sparsification on the lifts obtained for MARs, F- and P-MARs. While all curves peak on association rules with large lifts, the plots clearly display that the peaks are more pronounced when $\mathbf{W}$ is not sparsified. The plots display that the difference is much more pronounced for MARs: lifts ≈ 100 peak round 5% without sparsification, while they peak approximately at 2.8% with sparsification. This general picture hides in fact significant discrepancies appearing as one drills down into the influences of the choice of the similarity function and the normalization of $\mathbf{W}$. Figure 11 reveals the most significant differences between this "reference peak" (lift ≈ 100) for MARs taken without and with sparsification of $\mathbf{W}$. The first pattern is that DS normalization is in fact the worst setting for sparsifying $\mathbf{W}$. This parallels the results of Subsection 3.5, according to which sparsification before using DS already produces the worst manifolds, and should thus reasonably produce association rules of lower quality as well. We also remark that the normalized Laplacian NL provides pattern which is similar in all but one aspect: sparsifying $\mathbf{W}$ still produces good results according to the reference peak. Hence, the lost of information due to sparsification does not prevent to obtain good association rules. When we look at the best results obtained, including results not shown to save space, the most dramatic density is the one shown in Figure 11 for Jaccard index, SDS normalization and no sparsification of $\mathbf{W}$. The peak of lifts ≈ 100 is the tallest (it peaks at $\approx 7\%$) of all experiments, by far. Once again, this sounds like a confirmation that selecting good parameters to build the manifold also impact positively on the selection of manifold association rules: in particular, recall that Jaccard index favors BoR encoding (Subsection 3.2). We also think that this result may be interpreted as the matrix $\mathbf{W}$ should be sparsified, but not too much to produce good results from the manifold association rules standpoint. Indeed, Jaccard index already produces a sparse matrix $\mathbf{W}$ given that few users had more than a dozen books in their traces, from which it comes that roughly 3% of the matrix $\mathbf{W}$ is potentially non-zero. Finally, we notice from the rightmost column of Figure 11 that in some cases, sparsifying $\mathbf{W}$ improves the results as witnessed by MC's normalization with Cosine similarity.

Other criteria: summary.

We lack space to provide results as detailed for the support, confidence and leverage parameters, but we can sketch general patterns: results of MARs, F- and P-MARs follow similar trends. Without sparsification, the best results are obtained in general for MC, while they are obtained in general for SDS with sparsification. The poorest normalization is always, and sometimes by far, DS. Hence, we see once again that the best parameters to build the manifold also yield the most accurate manifold association rules.

3.7 Manifold visualization

A very important perspective on manifold-based learning is the way we map the manifold on end-user devices. From the geometrical standpoint, conventional Euclidean embeddings become suboptimal with respect to more sophisticated embeddings: for example, making all data fit into the display may reduce the readability of data (Figure 12, (a)). This problem does not hold for the Poincaré and Beltrami-Klein disks (resp. (b) and (c) in Figure 12; manifold computed using Jaccard index (7), and SDS normalization of $\mathbf{W}$ without sparsification). These mappings keep invariant the Voronoi diagram, and hence the wings of the digital library observed in (b), from the organization of colors, actually exist in the manifold. Here, the east green part of the picture is a wing of cooking; it is noticeable that a lot of health books (deep blue) are attached to cooking books (green), and two of the health books that are the closest to cooking's turn out to be diet books. Such topics did not belong to the data used: they have been brought together and define clear-cut wings in the digital library only because manifold learning was

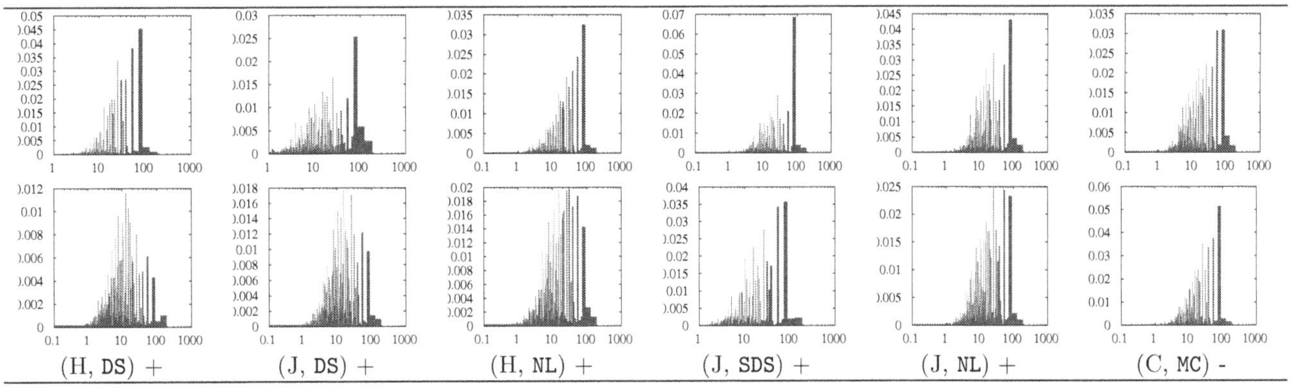

Figure 11: Truncated distributions of non-zero lifts for MARs without (top row) and with (bottom row) sparsification of W. Plots displayed are those for which we observe the most significant differences between the situation with and without sparsification. This difference is taken as the ratio between the proportion of very large lifts ($\approx$ 100). The bottom line gives the indication of the similarity function ((H)eat kernel, (C)osine similarity, (J)accard index) and the normalization of W, along with a symbol indicating whether the proportion of large lifts is larger without (+) or with (-) sparsification. x-scales are *logscales* (see text).

successful in capturing, from the local behaviours of users, a global contextual structure meaningful for the librarian or the expert. This map is a concrete example of the power a careful application of non-linear manifold learning techniques. In (c), lines denote itemsets that belong to the same association rules. Remark that this geometric visualization of association rules offers, on a single picture, a general view which carries out more informations than the equivalently long lists of association rules that would be displayed in a more conventional way.

4. SCALING UP TO A GROWING LIBRARY

Armed with the best set of parameters from Section 3, the digital library is currently being scaled up to its real size since the end of 2011. Figure 12 (d, e) presents 2D and 3D focus+context visualizations that were specifically developed from hyperbolic geometric visualizations (Subsection 3.7), to fit rectangle displays like TVs or tablets. The dataset now contains 60 000+ readers (mainly scholars, students and library patrons, mostly from Europe and Maghreb countries) and containing 9 980 books dealing with science, travel, business and cooking[4]. In the same way as was remarked the correlation between the manifold learned and the book topics — not included in data — in subsection 3.7, we can remark, from (e), the strong correlation between Dewey classification subjects — not included in data — and the organization of the manifold on this larger domain.

5. CONCLUSION AND PERSPECTIVES

When it comes to digital libraries, the Big Data phenomenon reminds the magical realistic tale of the (huge) Library of Babel of J.-L. Borges, and in particular the metaphor that the library's random content is so big that any book ever written must be hidden somewhere, but the human population roaming the library — including the librarians — is left in a state of complete despair. Digital libraries face the challenge of lifting their tools towards an always improved meaningful handling of their content for the end-user. Our paper is a step towards a roadmap to handle this problem with non-linear manifold learning algorithms. Its solution is not straightforward, yet experimental clues provide us with sets of working parameters that seem to perform well, among which the emphasis on a "bag of users" encoding allowing to learn the dynamics of users wandering around virtual bookshelves. The current scaling up to a whole digital library, and the feedback being received from readers comfort us in this opinion. From a research standpoint, the topological layer of the manifold provides us with a material to build association rules with striking results. More than just our application to the digital library, computational complexity is perhaps the strongest advocate for the application of manifold association rules to other domains [23].

[4]`http://www.scholarvox.com/?sitelang=en`

6. ACKNOWLEDGMENTS

The authors wish to thank the reviewers for constructive comments that helped to improve the paper.

7. REFERENCES

[1] M. Belkhin and P. Niyogi. Laplacian eigenmaps and spectral techniques for embedding and clustering. In T. G. Dietterich, S. Becker, and Z. Ghahramani, editors, *NIPS*14*. MIT Press, 2001.

[2] J.-D. Boissonnat, F. Nielsen, and R. Nock. Bregman voronoi diagrams. *DCG*, 44(2):281–307, 2010.

[3] J. Chim, R.-W.-H. Lau, H.-V. Leong, and A. Si. CyberWalk: a web-based distributed virtual walkthrough environment. *IEEE T. Mult.*, 5:503–515, 2003.

[4] S. Deerwester, S.-T. Dumais, T.-K. Landauer, G.-W. Furnas, and L. Beck. Improving information retrieval with latent semantic indexing. In *51st Ann. Meeting of the Am. Society for Inf. Science*, pages 36–40, 1988.

[5] C. Elkan. Deriving TF-IDF as a Fisher kernel. In *String Processing and Information Retrieval*, volume 3772 of *LNCS*, pages 295–300. Springer Verlag, 2005.

[6] B.-J. Frey and D. Dueck. Clustering by passing messages between data points. *Science*, 315:972–976, 2007.

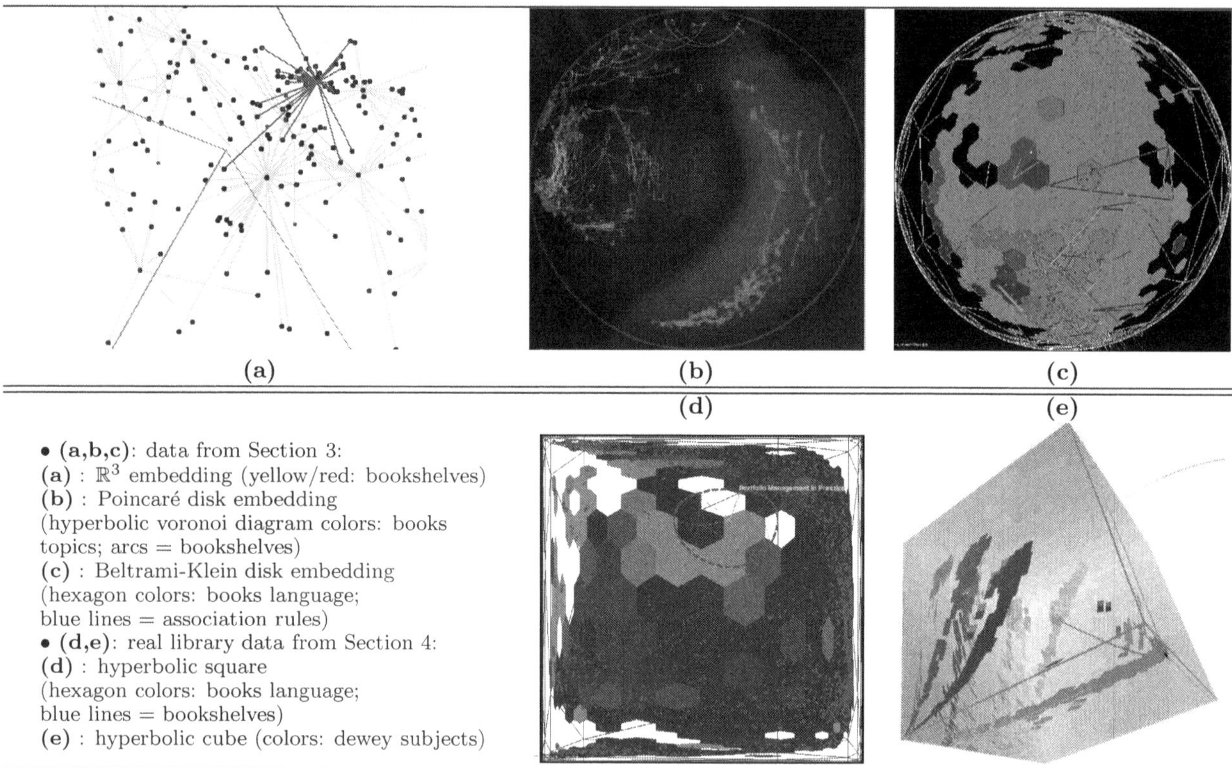

Figure 12: Different kinds of viewing for the digital library (see Subection 3.7 and Section 4 for details).

[7] K. Grønbæk, A. Rohde, B. Sundararajah, and S. Bech-Petersen. Infogallery: informative art services for physical library spaces. In 6th *JCDL*, pages 21–30, 2006.

[8] J. Han, J. Pei, Y. Yin, and R. Mao. Mining frequent patterns without candidate generation. *Data Mining and Knowledge Discovery*, 8:53–87, 2004.

[9] Q. Hardy. Harvard Releases Big Data for Books, 2012. http://bits.blogs.nytimes.com/2012/04/24/harvard-releases-big-data-for-books/.

[10] T. Joachims. Text categorization with suport vector machines: Learning with many relevant features. In *Proc. of the* 10th *ECML*, pages 137–142, 1998.

[11] W. Ke. Information-theoretic term weighting schemes for document clustering. In 13th *JCDL*, 2013.

[12] Y. Ke, J. Cheng, and W. Ng. Mining quantitative correlated patterns using an information-theoretic approach. In 12th *KDD*, pages 227–236, 2006.

[13] T.-K. Landauer, D.-S. McNamara, S. Dennis, and W. Kintsch. *Handbook of Latent Semantic Analysis.* University of Colorado Institute of Cognitive Science Series, 2007.

[14] M. Meilă and J. Shi. Learning segmentation by random walks. In T. G. Dietterich, S. Becker, and Z. Ghahramani, editors, *NIPS*14*. MIT Press, 2001.

[15] J.-B. Michel, Y.-K. Shen, A.-P. Aiden, A. Veres, M.-K. Gray, The Google Books Team, J.-P. Pickett, D. Hoiberg, D. Clancy, P. Norvig, J. Orwant, S. Pinker, M.-A. Nowak, and E.-L. Aiden. Quantitative analysis of culture using millions of digitized books. *Science*, 331:176–182, 2010.

[16] R. Nock, P. Luosto, and J. Kivinen. Mixed Bregman clustering with approximation guarantees. In 19th *ECML*, pages 154–169, 2008.

[17] R. Nock, M. Sebban, and D. Bernard. A simple locally adaptive nearest neighbor rule with application to pollution forecasting. *IJPRAI*, 17:1–14, 2003.

[18] P. Serdyukov, V. Murdock, and R. van Zwol. Placing flickr photos on a map. In 33rd *ACM SIGIR*, pages 484–491, 2009.

[19] H.-Y. Shiaw, R.-J.-K. Jacob, and G.-R. Crane. The 3D vase museum: a new approach to context in a digital library. In 4th *JCDL*, pages 125–134, 2004.

[20] R. Sinkhorn. A relationship between arbitrary positive matrices and doubly stochastic matrices. *Annals of Mathematical Statistics*, 35:876–879, 1964.

[21] R. Srikant and R. Agrawal. Mining generalized association rules. In 21th *VLDB*, pages 407–419, 1995.

[22] J. B. Tenenbaum, V. de Silva, and J. C. Langford. A global geometric framework for nonlinear dimensionality reduction. *Science*, 290:2319–2323, 2000.

[23] G. Yang. The complexity of mining maximal frequent itemsets and maximal frequent patterns. In 10th *KDD*, pages 344–353, 2004.

[24] R. Zass and A. Shashua. Doubly-stochastic normalization for spectral clustering. In *NIPS*19*, 2006.

LSH-Based Large Scale Chinese Calligraphic Character Recognition

Yuan Lin
College of Computer Science
Zhejiang University
Hangzhou, China
lin_yuan@zju.edu.cn

Jiangqin Wu*
College of Computer Science
Zhejiang University
Hangzhou, China
wujq@zju.edu.cn

Pengcheng Gao
College of Computer Science
Zhejiang University
Hangzhou, China
gaopengcheng@zju.edu.cn

Yang Xia
College of Computer Science
Zhejiang University
Hangzhou, China
21121255@zju.edu.cn

Tianjiao Mao
College of Computer Science
Zhejiang University
Hangzhou, China
21121260@zju.edu.cn

ABSTRACT

Chinese calligraphy is the art of handwriting and is an important part of Chinese traditional culture. But due to the complexity of shape and styles of calligraphic characters, it is difficult for common people to recognize them. So it would be great if a tool is provided to help users to recognize the unknown calligraphic characters. But the well-known OCR (Optical Character Recognition) technology can hardly help people to recognize the unknown characters because of their deformation and complexity. Numerous collections of historical Chinese calligraphic works are digitized and stored in CADAL (China Academic Digital Associate Library) calligraphic system [1], and a huge database CCD (Calligraphic Character Dictionary) is built, which contains character images labeled with semantic meaning. In this paper, a LSH-based large scale Chinese calligraphic character recognition method is proposed basing on CCD. In our method, GIST descriptor is used to represent the global features of the calligraphic character images, LSH (Locality-sensitive hashing) is used to search CCD to find the similar character images to the recognized calligraphic character image. The recognition is based on the semantic probability which is computed according to the ranks of retrieved images and their distances to the recognized image in the Gist feature space. Our experiments show that our method is effective and efficient for recognizing Chinese calligraphic character image.

Categories and Subject Descriptors

J.5 [**Computer Application**]: Arts and Humanities – *Arts and Humanities*

General Terms: Algorithms, Experimentation, Performance

Keywords

Calligraphy, LSH-based Search, Character Recognition

1. INTRODUCTION

Chinese calligraphy is one of the finest Chinese art forms and the most important and inseparable part of Chinese history. Its delicate aesthetic effects are generally considered to be unique among all calligraphic arts. Nowadays more and more calligraphic works are digitized, preserved and exhibited in digital libraries. But as shown in Figure 1, for common users sometimes recognizing some of the calligraphic characters is somewhat difficult. So technologies which can help users to recognize the unknown calligraphic characters are urgently required.

(a) (b) (c) (d)

Figure 1. Calligraphic character images and their semantic meaning. (a) 风; (b) 有; (c) 颜; (d) 长.

Unfortunately, though Optical Character Recognition (OCR) technology performs well on machine printed characters against clean backgrounds, it does not work well on Chinese calligraphic character recognition. We used commercial software Hanvon (Http://www.hanvon.com/en/) to recognize 100 binary character images randomly selected from the Internet, only seven of these characters were correctly recognized. The OCR results of characters in Figure 3 and Figure 4 are shown in Figure 2.

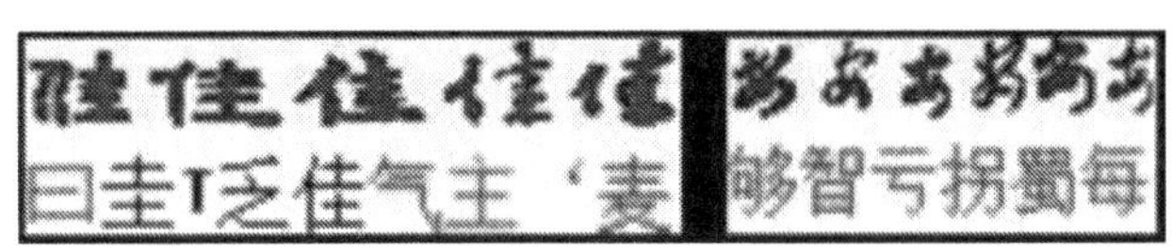

Figure 2. OCR results of Figure 3 and Figure 4 through commercial software Hanvon.

So OCR technology is not suitable for Chinese calligraphic recognition. This is mainly due to:

1).Complexity: Different writing styles exist in Chinese calligraphy, such as *seal script*, *clerical script*, *standard script*, *semi-cursive script*, and *cursive script* (Figure 3). Moreover, *XingKai* and *XingCao* mix different styles together, which makes recognition more difficult. In addition, authors tend to write the same character in different shapes even for the same style (Figure 4).

2). Deformation: Strokes are not regular in callgraphic characters, in that some strokes are connected with each other and some are broken. Taking Figure 3 as an example, the first stroke in the first character is broken, but it is connected with the second stroke in the fifth character.

3). Degradation: Calligraphic works tend to be degraded by natural changes, which makes characters more noisy.

JCDL'13, July 22–26, 2013, Indianapolis, Indiana, USA.

Figure3 Five main styles of one character. From left to right: *seal script, clerical script, standard script, semi-cursive script,* and *cursive script.*

Figure 4. Characters written by *Xi-zhi WANG*. Although written by the same author and with the same style, they are quite different.

For Chinese calligraphic character recognition, Yu *et al.* [2] ever proposed a skeleton-based calligraphic character recognition method. The method depends on the skeleton of the character image, which usually can't be appropriately extracted because of the different styles and shape complexity of calligraphic characters. Furthermore, with the increase of the database, the skeleton-based method is very time-consuming because it requires calculation of the similarities between the input calligraphic character and all the candidates in database. So it is not suitable for large scale calligraphic character recognition.

Numerous collections of historical Chinese calligraphic works are digitized and stored in CADAL (China Academic Digital Associate Library) calligraphic system [1], and a huge database CCD (Calligraphic Character Dictionary) is built, which contains character images labeled with semantic meaning by calligraphic experts. In this paper, we propose a novel method, called LSH-based large scale Chinese calligraphic character recognition on CCD. As we know, most calligraphic characters in CCD were written in ancient times, most common people can't recognize them without the help of experts, so we invited experts to help us build CCD. Therefore, CCD can be used to check the semantic meaning of the shape matched calligraphic character images to the user's unknown calligraphic character. The idea is common to many approaches in the content based image retrieval (CBIR). The key issues of the large scale calligraphic character recognition are the efficient and effective representation of the calligraphic character image as a collection of feature vectors and the quick similarity searching method for huge CCD.

Unlike CBIR, we seek to recognize the given calligraphic character image, not just retrieve the similar calligraphic character images from the CCD. In our paper, we use the GIST descriptor [3], which represents orientation energy at different scales and orientations, to represent the given calligraphic character image and the calligraphic character images of CCD. In addition, LSH (Locality-sensitive hashing) [4] is used to search CCD to find the similar character images to the given calligraphic character image. The recognition is based on the semantic probability which is computed according to the ranks of retrieved images and their distances to the given image on Gist feature space.

The remainder of this paper is organized as follows: related work is briefly reviewed in section 2. Section 3 gives the recognition steps of a calligraphic character image. In section 4, experimental results are presented and section 5 gives our conclusion and future work.

2. RELATED WORK

Numerous promising research works have been done on handwriting recognition, such as, [5] uses word matching technology to recognize George Washington's manuscripts, and [6] identifies ancient Hebrew manuscripts. In [7] an offline Chinese character recognition method was proposed, which depends on the radical decomposition. OCR (Optical Character Recognition) technology is frequently used to recognize machine printed characters against clean background. But all these methods are not suitable for recognizing calligraphic character because calligraphic characters are usually complex and deformed. The same writer under different moods can generate different styles of the same characters. Furthermore, a character is sometimes deformed consciously to get a better artistic effect, such as the dry stroke.

Another way to recognize calligraphic character is retrieval based. This is quite common in CBIR. In [8] Doermann *et al.* proposed an approach dealing with logo recognition. Yu *et al.* [2] proposed a skeleton-based method to recognize the Chinese calligraphic character. Many other works relying on a description of image objects and a subsequent matching step can be found. But all these methods are not suitable for retrieving a large scale database because of the huge cost of time.

The GIST descriptor was initially proposed in [3] and has recently shown good results for image search. The idea is to develop a low dimensional representation of the scene, which does not require any form of segmentation. In [9], GIST feature is used for image completion. The algorithm proposed patches up holes in images by finding similar image regions in the database based on the GIST descriptor. M. Douze *et al.* [10] give the evaluation of GIST descriptors for web-scale image search.

Locality-sensitive hashing was originally introduced by Indyk and Motwani [11] for the purpose of devising main memory algorithms for approximate nearest neighbor search. The key idea is to hash the points using several hash functions so as to ensure that, for each function, the probability of collision is much higher for objects which are close to each other than for those which are far apart. Then, one can determine near neighbors by hashing the query point and retrieving elements stored in buckets containing that point. In [11, 12] the authors provided such locality-sensitive hash functions for the case when the points live in binary Hamming space $\{0,1\}^d$. They showed experimentally that the data structure achieves large speedup over several tree-based structures. The LSH algorithm has been since used in numerous applied settings, e.g., see [13-21].

In this paper we will use the GIST descriptor to represent a calligraphic character image. Then the LSH-based method will be used to have a quick similarity search. Finally, we give the recognition result based on the searching results.

3. LSH-BASED CHINESE CALLIGRAPHIC CHARACTER RECOGNITION

3.1 Overview

Let m be the number of calligraphic character images in CCD, C_i $(i = 1,2,\dots,m)$ be calligraphic character images in CCD, C_q be the calligraphic character image to be recognized. The LSH-based large scale Chinese calligraphic character recognition on CCD is described as following:

Preparation:

1) Binaryzation: Binarize all the calligraphic character images

C_i $(i = 1,2,\dots,m)$ in CCD into binary images B_i $(i = 1,2,\dots,m)$.

2) Representation: Extract B_i's GIST feature, represented as a point p_i $(i = 1,2,\dots,m)$ in $\mathbb{R}^d$,where d is the dimension of GIST feature vector.
3) Storage: Store each p_i $(i = 1,2,\dots,m)$ in the bucket $g_j(p_i)$ $(j = 1,\dots,L)$. (The detail is described in section 3.3 and 4.1)

Recognition:

1) Binaryzation: Binarize C_q into binary image B_q.
2) Representation: The GIST feature of B_q is generated and represented as a point q in $\mathbb{R}^d$.
3) LSH-based Similarity Searching: For the query point q, search all buckets $g_1(q),\dots,g_L(q)$. For each of the retrieved point p_i $(1 \le i \le m)$, compute the distance from q to it, and report the point p_i and the distance $Dist(q,p_i)$ if it is a $(R, 1-\delta)$ neighbor . (The detail is described in section 3.3 and 4.1)
4) Recognition: The probability of each candidate annotations of C_q is computed.
5) Output: The annotation with maximum probability is returned as the recognition result of C_q, i.e., the semantic meaning.

3.2 Calligraphic Character Image Representation

The GIST descriptor, which has recently shown good results for image search, was initially proposed in [3]. In this paper, we use the GIST descriptor to represent the calligraphic character image.

Before the computation, we need to normalize the character images to the same size. In this paper we choose a size of 60×60 pixles. This is sufficient due to the low dimensionality of the GIST descriptor, i.e., it does not need representing the details of an image. The image is then decomposed by a bank of multiscale oriented filters. Here in this paper, we use 8 orientations and 3 scales. Next, the output magnitude of each filter is averaged over 9 non-overlapping windows arranged on a 3×3 grid. So the final character image representation is a $3 \times 8 \times 9 = 216$ dimensional vector, which can be seen as a point p in $\mathbb{R}^d$ $(d = 216)$. Figure 5 shows two binary calligraphic character images and their corresponding GIST descriptors.

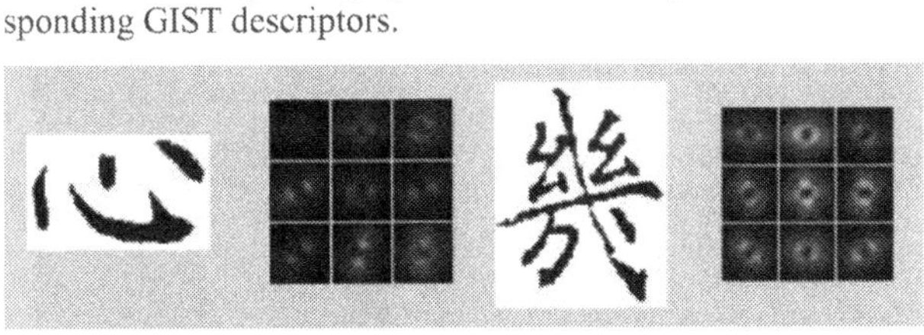

Figure 5. Calligraphic character images and their corresponding GIST descriptors.

3.3 LSH-based Similarity Searching

We were inspired by the work in [4] and proposed our LSH-based similarity searching method, where we turn the similarity search problem on the whole CCD into a $(R, 1-\delta)$-near neighbor problem under some distance function.

The $(R, 1-\delta)$-near neighbor problem is defined as follows. Given a radius $R > 0$, construct a data structure that answers the following queries: for the query point q, each point p_i $(1 \le i \le m)$ satisfying $Dist(q,p_i) \le R$ has to be reported with a probability at least $1-\delta$ (thus, δ is the probability that a near neighbor p is not reported). $Dist(q,p_i)$ denotes the distance between q and p_i in $\mathbb{R}^d$. In this paper, we will use the Euclidean distance as the distance function, which is defined as:

$$Dist(q,p_i) = \left(\sum_{j=1}^{d}(p_i[j] - q[j])^2\right)^{1/2}$$

$p_i[j]$ denotes the jth coordinate of p_i, for $j = 1 \dots d$.

To solve the $(R, 1-\delta)$-near neighbor problem, we use the technique of LSH (Locality Sensitive Hashing). We will briefly describe how we use the LSH to solve the $(R, 1-\delta)$-near neighbor problem.

Inspired by the work in [22], we chose our LSH function as:

$$h_{a,b}(p) = \left\lfloor \frac{a \cdot p + b}{r} \right\rfloor$$

where a is a random vector in $\mathbb{R}^d$, whose each entry is chosen independently from the Gaussian (normal) distribution. r is the size of segments width, so we can assign hash value to vector p based on which segment it project onto. b is a real number chosen uniformly from the range $[0, r]$. Formally, each hash function $h_{a,b}(p)$: $\mathbb{R}^d \to \mathbb{I}$ maps p onto the set of integers. Therefore, we can collect a hash family $\mathcal{H} = \{h : \mathbb{R}^d \to \mathbb{I}\}$ by randomly choosing different a and b. Next, we define a function family: $\mathcal{G} = \{g: \mathbb{R}^d \to \mathbb{I}^k\}$ such that $g(p) = (h_1(p),\dots,h_k(p))$, where $h_i \in \mathcal{H}$. For an integer L, we chooses L functions $g_1,\dots,g_L$ from $\mathcal{G}$, independently and uniformly at random. During preparation, we store each p_i $(i = 1,2,\dots,m)$ in the bucket $g_j(p_i)$, for $j = 1,\dots,L$. To process a query q, we search all buckets $g_1(q),\dots,g_L(q)$. For each point p_i $(1 \le i \le m)$ found in a bucket, we compute the distance from q to p_i, and reports the point p_i and the distance if $Dist(q,p_i) \le R$.

In order to ensure that we report the R-near neighbor point with a probability at least $1-\delta$, we need to specify the parameters R, r, k and L. R is an empirical parameter which decides whether a point p_i is a near neighbor. In our method, we set $R = 0.5$, which is sufficient to find certain amount of neighbors for our further recognition. As it was suggested in [22] that $r = 4$ provides good results, therefore, we use the value $r = 4$ in our implementation. Let τ denotes the probability that the query q collides with p at distance R. So the value of τ is $\int_0^r \frac{1}{R} f(\frac{t}{R})(1 - \frac{t}{r})dt$, where function f denotes the probability density function of the absolute value of the Gaussian (normal) distribution. It follows (see [4] Strategy 2 for details) that if we set $L = \left\lceil \frac{\log \delta}{\log(1-\tau^k)} \right\rceil$ then we can ensure the R-near neighbor point be reported with a probability at least $1-\delta$. As the left parameter k determines the running time of a query, then we only need to choose a proper value of k, which we will discuss in our experiment section.

So given a query image represented by its GIST descriptor q, using LSH to find the $(R, 1-\delta)$-near neighbor in CCD, we return the similar character image points p_i and the distance $Dist(q,p_i)$ with a probability at least $1-\delta$.

3.4 Recognition

We sort the result given in section 3.3 by distance $Dist(q,p_i)$ in ascending order and only take the first fifteen similar character images as the candidate character images if the number of similarities is beyond this. Suppose the first $N(N \le 15)$ candidate character images in the sorted list are $C_1, C_2, \dots, C_N$, the weight $w_i(i = 1,2,\dots,N)$ of each candidate character image can be defined as:

$$w_i = \frac{1}{i^2} + \frac{1}{Dist(C_q, C_i)}$$

,where $Dist(C_q, C_i)$ is the distance from character image C_i to the query image C_q, which equals to the GIST distance $Dist(q, p_i)$ returned from section 3.3.

Suppose there are X annotated characters $A_1, A_2, \dots, A_X$ for the N candidate character images. And n_i images $C_{i_1}, C_{i_2}, \dots, C_{i_{ni}}$ are the calligraphic character images whose annotated character is A_i. Thus, the probability that C_q's meaning is A_i is

$$prob_i = \frac{\sum_{k=1}^{n_i} w_{i_k}}{\sum_{j=1}^{X}\sum_{k=1}^{n_j} w_{j_k}}$$

Finally the X annotated characters are sorted again by the probability and we return the annotation with the maximum probability as the recognition result of C_q.

4. EXPERIMENTS

Chinese calligraphy has five different styles, named as *seal script*, *clerical script*, *standard script*, *semi-cursive script*, and *cursive script*. The CCD has 110,737 labeled calligraphic character images, with 49,481 *standard script*, 30,915 *semi-cursive script*, 8,035 *seal script*, 12,193 *clerical script* and 10,113 *cursive script*. 200 calligraphic character image samples in each style were chosen randomly from Internet as the character images to be recognized in experiment 4.1 and 4.2, which were not included in the CCD.

4.1 Optimal Parameter Learning For Similarity Searching

Parameter δ denotes the probability that a near neighbor is not reported. With a fixed δ, k determines the running time of a query. For a fixed value of k and $L = L(k)$, we can decompose the query time into two terms. The first term is $T_g = O(dkL)$ for computing the L functions g_i for the query point q as well as retrieving the buckets $g_i(q)$ from hash tables. The second term is $T_c = O(d \cdot \#collisions)$ for computing the distance to all points encountered in the retrieved buckets. $\#collisions$ is the number of points encountered in the buckets $g_1(q), \dots, g_L(q)$; the expected value of $\#collision$ is $E[\#collisions] = L \cdot \sum_{p_i \in CCD}[p(Dist(q,p_i))]^k$, where $p(Dist(q,p_i))$ denotes the probability that the query q collides with p_i whose value is $\int_0^r \frac{1}{Dist(q,p_i)} f(\frac{t}{Dist(q,p_i)})(1-\frac{t}{r})dt$. Intuitively, T_g increases as the increase of k, while T_c decreases as the increase of k. Thus there exists an optimal value of k that minimizes the sum of $T_g + T_c$ (for a given query point q). Note that there might be different optimal k for different query points, therefore 200 calligraphic character image samples in each style were chosen as the query points and the goal would be to optimize the mean query time for these query points.

We calculated the mean query time with different δ and k (see Figure 6). Figure 7 shows some examples of the similarity searching results with different δ (We only list the first five similarity character images of the searching results).

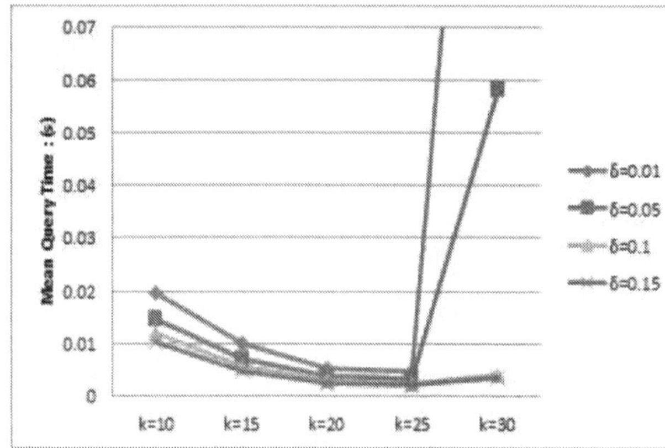

Figure 6. Mean query time with different δ and k.

Query Image	δ	Similarity Searched Results (Ordered By Distance)
	0.01	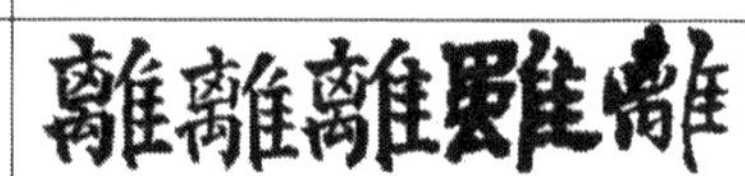
	0.15	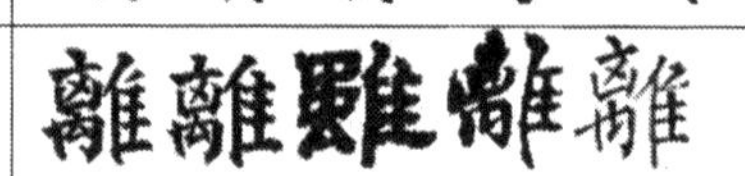
	0.01	
	0.15	
	0.01	
	0.15	
	0.01	
	0.15	
	0.01	
	0.15	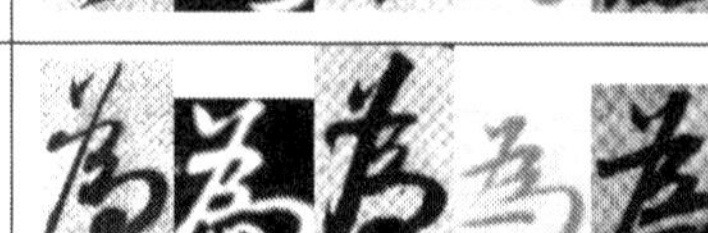

Figure 7. Examples of the similarity searching results.

From Figure 6, we see that the similarity searching scheme reached the best performance when k was about 25 and the searching speed was surprisingly fast. As it is, it cost more time with the decrease of δ. As δ denotes the probability that a near neighbor is not reported, the smaller the δ is, the higher accuracy the recognition can reach. And we see from Figure 6 that, when $k = 25$, the mean query time with different δ was very close. Therefore, we set $\delta = 0.01$ and $k = 25$ in our LSH-based method.

4.2 Recognition Performance

We compared our method with Yu's in both recognition rate and time. Table 1 shows the experimental result. For these two methods of recognizing a calligraphic character, we can decompose the whole recognition time into three terms. The first term T_1 is for binarizing the image. The second term T_2 is for similarity searching and the third term T_3 is for recognition. We see from Table 1 that our method was particularly fast. This is because that using the LSH-based method for similarity searching greatly reduced the time of T_2 (T_2 was about 0.004 second in our experiment), which is very time-consuming in Yu's because it calculate the skeleton similarity between the input calligraphic character and all the candidates in the huge CCD.

Also, our method performs well in recognition rate and show robustness in different calligraphic styles. We see that despite the simplicity of the GIST descriptor and the fact that it represents the full calligraphic images rather than each local region separately, the GIST descriptor performed surprisingly well in representing the calligraphic images. As Yu's method is based on skeleton, which usually can't be appropriately extracted especially when the character is scratchy or complex, the recognition rate will be pretty low in *clerical script* and *cursive script*.

Figure 8 shows some recognition results of five different calligraphic styles using our LSH-based method. If the recognition was right, we marked a "√" in recognition result row; otherwise we marked a "X" and gave the correct result in brackets. We see that the wrong recognition result in *clerical script* and *cursive script* were visually very similar to their correct one. The reason why the recognition of the fifth calligraphic character of *semi-cursive script* failed was that the background of the character image was too noisy, so the corresponding binary character image lost its identity (see Figure 9). As to the failure of the sixth character image of *seal script*, whose recognition result was "null", the reason was that we couldn't find similar images when we set $R = 0.5$. This could be modified by setting a higher value of R.

Table 1. Performance comparison between our method and Yu's

	Recognition Rate: (%)		Time: (s)	
	Ours	*Yu's*	*Ours*	*Yu's*
Standard script	89	86.5	2.14	111.05
Semi-cursive script	84.5	82	2.25	151.75
Seal script	87.5	87.5	1.79	114.50
Clerical script	66.5	41.5	2.04	145.04
Cursive script	65	31.5	1.83	107.06

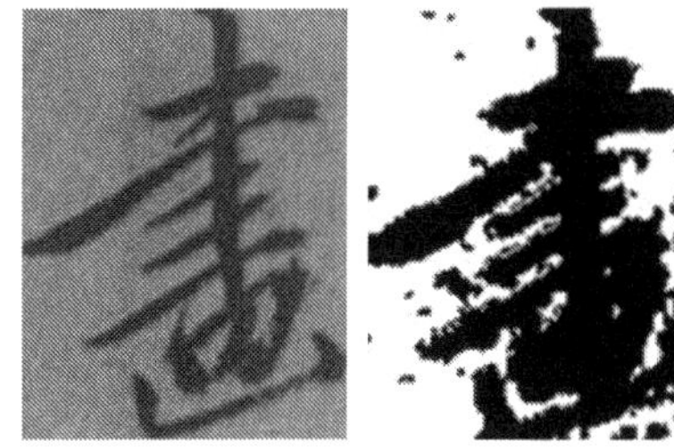

Figure 9. The failed recognition of *semi-cursive script* and its corresponding binary image.

5. CONCLUSIONS AND FUTURE WORK

This paper proposed a novel approach to recognize Chinese calligraphic characters by making full use of CCD and using a $(R, 1-\delta)$-near neighbor LSH method to have a quick search of the similar images represented in GIST descriptor. Our experiments show that the LSH-based method is effective and efficient for recognizing Chinese calligraphic character and show robustness in different calligraphic styles.

In future we plan to make more comparison of our image representation and other descriptors, such as SIFT and HOG. And furthermore, we plan to extend our approach by developing more calligraphic feature related descriptor (e.g. shape related) and combine it with the GIST descriptor as the representation of calligraphic character image.

6. ACKNOWLEDGMENTS

This work is supported by National Natural Science Foundation of China (No. 61070066), the CADAL Project and Research Center, Zhejiang University. We sincerely thank Xiafen Zhang for her advices and help during the work.

7. REFERENCES

[1] CADAL calligraphic system web site: http://www.cadal.zju.edu.cn/Calligraphy/.

[2] K. Yu, J. Wu, and Y. Zhuang. Skeleton-Based Recognition of Chinese Calligraphic Character Image. In *Proceedings of the 9th Pacific Rim Conference on Multimedia: Advances in Multimedia Information Processing*, page 228-237. Springer, 2008.

[3] A. Oliva and A. Torralba. Modeling the shape of the scene: a holistic representation of the spatial envelope. *International Journal in Computer Vision*, 42:145-175, 2001.

[4] Andoni and P. Indyk. Near-optimal hashing algorithms for approximate nearest neighbor in high dimensions. In *FOCS*, pages 459–468, 2006.

[5] T.M. Rath, S. Kane, A. Lehman, E. Partridge and R. Manmatha, Indexing for a Digital Library of George Washington's Manuscripts: A Study of Word Matching Techniques. CIIR Technical Report, 2002.

[6] Itay Bar Yosef, Klara Kedem, Its' hak Dinstein, Malachi Beit-Arie, Edna Engel: Classifi-cation of Hebrew Calligraphic Handwriting Styles: Preliminary Results. In *Proceedings of the First International Workshop on Document Image Analysis for Libraries* (DIAL' 04), pages 299-305, 2004.

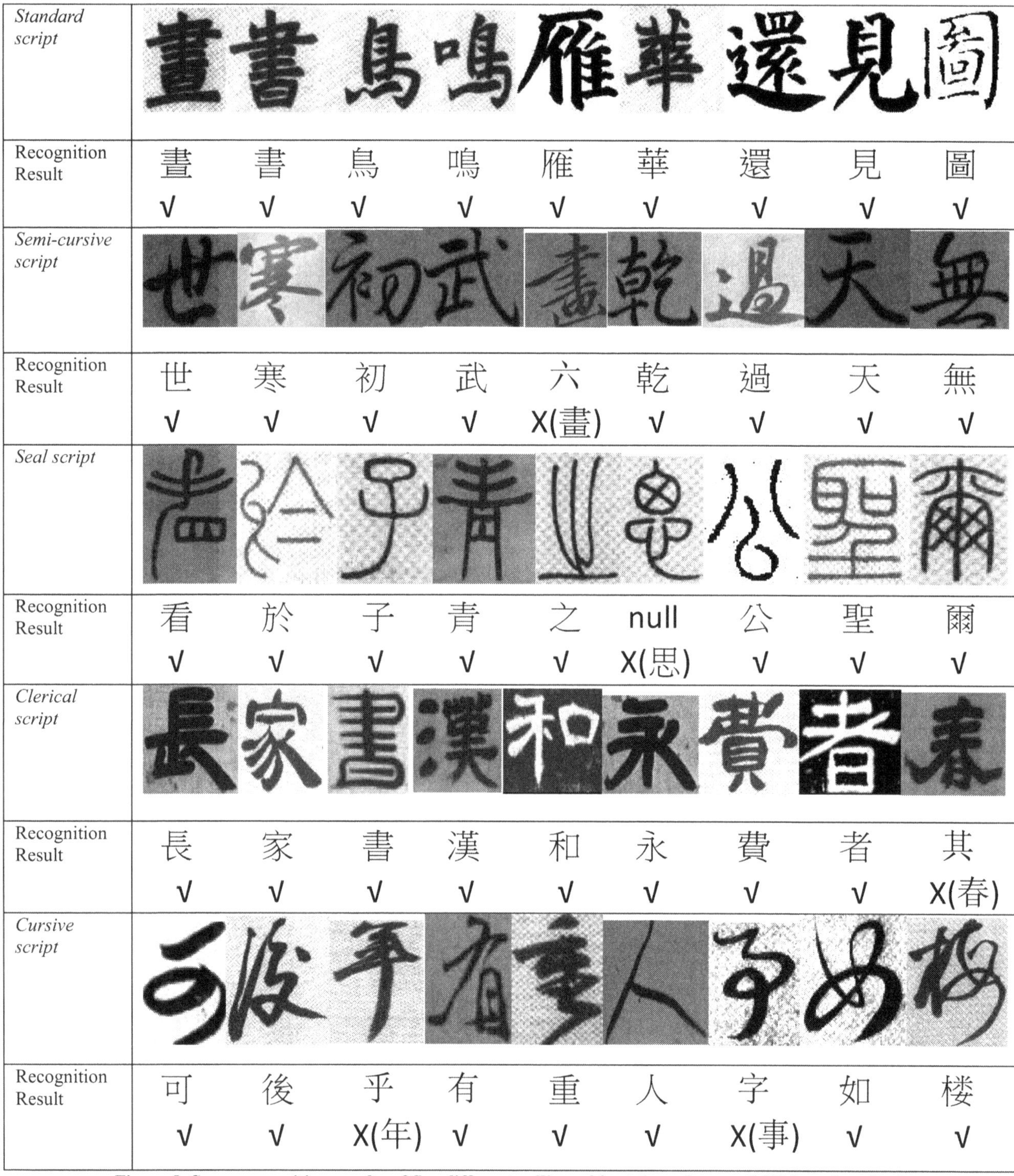

Figure 8. Some recognition results of five different calligraphic styles using our LSH-based method.

[7] Daming Shi, Robert I. Damper, Steve R. Gunn. Offline handwritten Chinese character recognition by radical decomposition. *ACM Transactions on Asian Language Information Processing* (TALIP), pages 27-48, 2003

[8] D. Doermann, E. Rivlin, and I. Weiss. Applying algebraic and differential invariants for logo recognition. *Machine Vision and Applications*, pages 73 – 86, 1996.

[9] J. Hayes and A. Efros. Scene completion using millions of photographs. In *SIGGRAPH*, 2007

[10] M. Douze, H. Jégou, H. sandhawalia, L. Amsaleg and C. Schmid, Evaluation of Gist descriptors for web-scale image search. In *Proceedings of the ACM International Conference on Image and Video Retrieval*, 2009.

[11] P. Indyk and R. Motwani. Approximate nearest neighbor: towards removing the curse of dimensionality. In *Proceedings of the Symposium on Theory of Computing*, 1998.

[12] A. Gionis, P. Indyk, and R. Motwani. Similarity search in high dimensions via hashing. In *Proceedings of the 25th In-*

ternational Conference on Very Large Data Bases, pages 518 - 529. Morgan Kaufmann, 1999.

[13] J. Buhler. Efficient large-scale sequence comparison by locality-sensitive hashing. *Bioinformatics*, 17:419-428, 2001.

[14] J. Buhler. Provably sensitive indexing strategies for biosequence similarity search. In *Proceedings of the Annual International Conference on Computational Molecular Biology* (RECOMB02), 2002.

[15] J. Buhler and M. Tompa. Finding motifs using random projections. In *Proceedings of the Annual International Conference on Computational Molecular Biology* (RECOMB01), 2001

[16] E. Cohen, M. Datar, S. Fujiwara, A. Gionis, P. Indyk, R. Motwani, J. Ullman, and C. Yang. Finding interesting associations without support pruning. In *Proceedings of the 16th International Conference on Data Engineering* (ICDE), 2000.

[17] B. Georgescu, I. Shimshoni, and P. Meer. Mean shift based clustering in high dimensions: A texture classification example. In *Proceedings of the 9th International Conference on Computer Vision*, 2003.

[18] T. Haveliwala, A. Gionis, and P. Indyk. Scalable techniques for clustering the web. *WebDB Workshop*, 2000.

[19] Z. Ouyang, N. Memon, T. Suel, and D. Trendafilov. Cluster-based delta compression of collections of files. In *Proceedings of the International Conference on Web Information Systems Engineering* (WISE), 2002.

[20] N. Shivakumar. Detecting digital copyright violations on the Internet (Ph.D. thesis). *Department of Computer Science*, Stanford University, 2000.

[21] C. Yang. Macs: Music audio characteristic sequence indexing for similarity retrieval. In *Proceedings of the Workshop on Applications of Signal Processing to Audio and Acoustics*, 2001.

[22] M. Datar, N. Immorlica, P. Indyk, and V. Mirrokni, Locality-sensitive hashing scheme based on p-stable distributions. In *Proceedings of the twentieth annual Symposium on Computational Geometry*, pages 253–262, 2004.

Automatic Performance Evaluation of Dewarping Methods in Large Scale Digitization of Historical Documents

Maryam Rahnemoonfar, Beth Plale
School of Informatics and Computing, Indiana University
maryrahn@indiana.edu

ABSTRACT

Geometric distortions are among the major challenging issues in the analysis of historical document images. Such distortions appear as arbitrary warping, folds and page curl, and have detrimental effects upon recognition (OCR) and readability. While there are many dewarping techniques discussed in the literature, there exists no standard method by which their performance can be evaluated against each other. In particular, there is not any satisfactory method capable of comparing the results of existing dewarping techniques on arbitrary wrapped documents. The existing methods either rely on the visual comparison of the output and input images or depend on the recognition rate of an OCR system. In the case of historical documents, OCR either is not available or does not generate an acceptable result. In this paper, an objective and automatic evaluation methodology for document image dewarping technique is presented. In the first step, all the baselines in the original distorted image as well as dewarped image are modelled precisely and automatically. Then based on the mathematical function of each line, a comprehensive metric which calculates the performance of a dewarping technique is introduced. The presented method does not require user interference in any stage of evaluation and therefore is quite objective. Experimental results, applied to two state-of-the art dewarping methods and an industry-standard commercial system, demonstrate the effectiveness of the proposed dewarping evaluation method.

Categories and Subject Descriptors

H.3.4 [**Systems and Software**]: Performance evaluation (efficiency and effectiveness); I.4.1 [**Digitization and Image Capture**]: *Imaging geometry*; I.4.3 [**Enhancement**]: *Geometric correction*

Keywords

Performance Evaluation, Arbitrary Warping, Large Scale Digitization

1. INTRODUCTION

Commercial OCRs are tailored for flat pages with straight text lines. Even moderate warping can cause most current OCR systems to fail. For modern documents, the importance of geometric distortion correction is placed on extracting the printed text and making it recognizable by the commercial OCR. However, for historical manuscripts the goal of digitization is to produce digital facsimiles that represent the original printed content as faithfully as possible. Here "the correction procedure" aims at producing the original flat document; that is, a document image which resembles the original page as much as possible.

While there are many dewarping techniques in the literature [2; 4; 6; 7; 9; 13; 14] there exists no standard methodology for the comparison of their performance. Most of the evaluations done so far concentrate on subjective and qualitative visual comparison of the output and the input image[3; 7]. In some cases, the recognition rate of an OCR system is used for the evaluation of dewarping techniques [10]. According to this approach, the increase of the recognition rate which OCR achieves between the original image and the dewarped image indicates the improvement of the dewarping method. Therefore the improvement of OCR as a performance evaluation metric is highly dependent upon the performance of the OCR itself. In the case of historical documents, however, often OCR does not generate acceptable results or no OCR system exists. In recent years, some quantitative dewarping evaluation methodologies [5; 11; 12] have been proposed in the literature. The proposed evaluation methodology in [5] uses the original camera-captured image previous to any distortion. In most cases and especially in historical documents, we do not have access to the perfect original image of any document that belongs to previous centuries. In the evaluation methodologies proposed in [11; 12], in the first stage, the user is supposed to mark several points on a number of text lines of the original warped image. The points should be selected on the long text lines which are considered to be most representative of the image. The rest of the method essentially involves matching a polynomial curve fitting and an area approximation by integration. The advantage of this method is that it does not depend on OCR for evaluation. However this approach is strongly dependent upon the user. Therefore, the evaluation is inevitably very subjective. Moreover in many historical documents, arbitrary warping is common, which is to say that each line has its own distortion. In such a case, selecting a few lines (for example, 3 or 6 lines) in a page with approximately 30 arbitrary text lines cannot guarantee a comprehensive evaluation. In addition, if a dewarping method fails to work properly and ends up distorting shorter lines, its performance cannot be evaluated by this evaluation methodology. It also has to be noted that polynomial curve fitting is not suitable in the arbitrary page situation, as it is capable of modelling only very smooth page curls.

In this paper a flexible, accurate, quantitative and objective performance evaluation methodology which is independent of OCR or human interference is presented. In the first step, the precise baselines are modelled with a robust mathematical formula presented in [9] both on the original image and on the dewarped one. The proposed baseline detection method avoids using any curve fitting or energy minimization concept such as the snake method and therefore is both more accurate and more

JCDL'13, July 22–26, 2013, Indianapolis, Indiana, USA.

ACM 978-1-4503-2077-1/13/07...$15.00.

flexible and can be applied on a wide range of curves. In methods which use curve fitting algorithms such as spline or polynomials [8], the types of distortion (smooth curl, cylindrical, fold, etc.) have to be known to be able to fit the best curve to the baseline. Given the fact that arbitrary baselines can take any form, it is thus impossible to model them with polynomials or splines. Moreover, spline and polynomial curve fitting or energy minimization techniques such as active contours and snake [4] fail to give precise baselines and there is always an inclination towards descenders in the above methods. In the second step of our evaluation methodology, based on the mathematical function of each line, a comprehensive metric which calculates the performance of a dewarping technique is introduced.

The proposed evaluation methodology has several advantages in comparison to existing evaluation methodologies. Firstly, it does not depend on OCR or the perfect original image such as the method in [5]. Secondly, it evaluates and examines all the lines in the image and not only a selected number of lines such as the method in [12]. Thirdly, it models all kinds of lines including curl and arbitrary warping and not only smooth curves in a document with known distortions. Fourthly, it is the first evaluation methodology which works successfully on historical document images and it is completely automatic.

The remainder of this paper is structured as follows: in Section 2, the proposed technique is described in detail. In Section 3, experimental results are presented and discussed. Finally, in Section 4, conclusions are drawn.

2. Performance Evaluation Methodology

The main purpose of a dewarping method is to have consistent, horizontal, straight lines in the final dewarped image. Therefore any deviation from the straight line in the dewarped image is considered an error and reflects some degree of failure of the dewarping technique. To define a metric for the automatic evaluation and to measure the deviation of each line from the straight line, it is necessary to detect precise baselines.

The precise baselines were detected using our proposed text line methodology in [9]. The integral I of the final parametric equation of each line after having been updated with new coordinate points when t varies between 0 and 1 indicates the area under the curve:

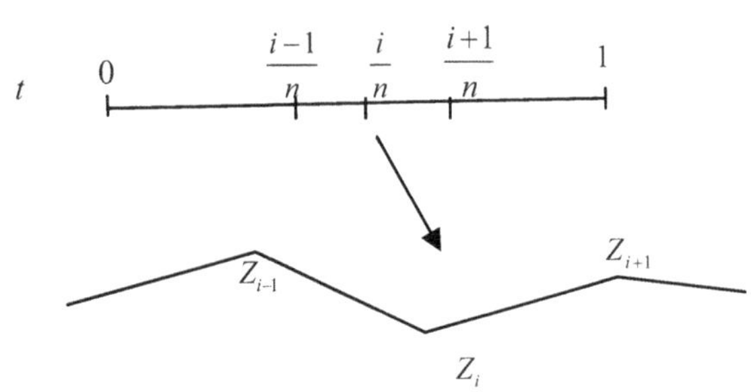

$$I = \int_0^1 \left|(1 - \{nt\}Z_{[nt]} + \{nt\}Z_{[nt+1]}\right| dt \qquad (1)$$

where n is the number of partitions in the line, [] represents the *floor* function, and {} represents the *fractional part* function. The area under the curve which is a potential metric for evaluating a dewarping technique indicates the deviation of each line from the horizontal straight line. The closer the line is to the horizontal straight line, the less is the value of the integral. According to this approach, the integral or the area under a horizontal straight line is 0.

The integral of a curve calculates the area between the curve and the horizontal axis (x-axis). In the image, the origin of all coordinate points is calculated from the top-left corner of the image. Obviously the area between each text line and the upper boundary of the image is not a good metric for dewarping evaluation because with this approach, even the integral of a straight horizontal line is not zero but rather is the area enclosed by the line and the upper boundary. Therefore, for each text line a different coordinate system would have to be defined. The y-axis of the coordinate system would remain the same for all text lines, which is the left border of the image. However the origin and x-axis would change for each text line.

To determine the best level, where the deviation of the curve from the straight line is minimized, different levels including *minimum, maximum, average and modal level* were examined. The minimum level means the horizontal line equal to the minimum value of points in each curve; we can have something similar for the maximum and average levels. In some cases, the area between the curve and the *minimum level* can produce extra shift and therefore extra error. For example in Figure 1a, there is a minimum point on the curve which is the valley of the curve; therefore the integral of the curve in regard to the *minimum level* produces error at both sides of the valley. The average height of the curve can also create extra shift and extra error for the same reason.

The level which is finally selected as the x-axis for calculating the integral is the level where the most points of the curve are located; the rationale behind this choice is that in this case the vertical distance between the most points on the curve and the horizontal level would be zero and thus the error would be minimal. This level is the level on which the curve sits, or in other words it is the most horizontal part of the curve. We call this level the *modal level*.

Figure 1b shows the case where the integral of the curve is calculated in regard to the *modal level*. It can be seen both from the Figure and as confirmed by numerical values that in this case the integral of the curve will decrease and it does not include any constant shift in the integral.

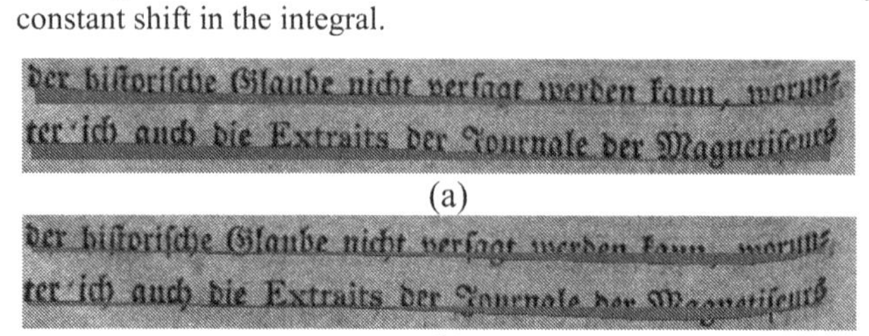

Figure 1. Integral of the baseline curve in regard to (a) *minimum level* and (b) *modal level*

Although, for integral computation, the modal level is the best one which gives the minimum error, the relation between *maximum level*, *minimum level* and *modal level* can be used for interpreting the shape of a curve. For instance, when the integral in regard to the minimum *level* is equal to that of the *modal level*, the curve has a concave shape; on the other hand when the integral in regard to the *maximum level* is equal to that of the modal level, the curve has a convex shape. When the *modal level* integral is between the *minimum level* and *maximum level* integral, the baseline has a wavy shape. The same interpretation is applicable to the integral value of the function and its absolute value. These measurements can help in determining the type of distortion which exists in each line and whether a dewarping technique has removed the whole distortion, removed a part of it, or has created a new type of distortion.

Two metrics can be defined for dewarping evaluation. The first metric indicates the deviation of each line from the horizontal straight line. Thus each line can have a metric indicating its straightness. Error metric EM_j indicates the deviation of each line from the straight line and is defined independently for each line in the image as follows:

$$EM_j = L_j^{-1}\int_0^1 \left|(1-\{nt\})Z^{\mathrm{mod}}_{[nt]} + \{nt\}Z^{\mathrm{mod}}_{[nt+1]}\right| dt \qquad (2)$$

In this equation, Z^{mod} are the updated coordinate points calculated in regard to the modal level and L_j is the length of the jth line. Dividing the integral by its length normalized the metric. This is especially necessary for images which do not have text lines with the same length. The lower the value of the EM_j, the less is the deviation of the line from the straight line. This metric can even be defined for the original image, showing how far it is from the straight line.

The second evaluation metric is the accuracy metric (*AM*) and is defined according to the following equation.It shows the accuracy of each line AM_j or the overall accuracy AM in a dewarped image.

$$AM_j = 100\left(1-\frac{EM_j}{EM_j^0}\right)$$
$$AM = \frac{1}{N}\sum_{j=1}^{N} AM_j \qquad (3)$$

In this equation, EM_j, is the deviation of line j from the straight line, EM^0_j is the corresponding metric in the original image and N is the number of lines in the image. The higher the value of AM_j, the more superior is the accuracy of the dewarped line. A complete horizontal straight line has the accuracy of 100% while a line which has the same distortion as the original image has the accuracy of 0%.

3. Experimental Results

The proposed evaluation methodology was examined on a dataset of 30 representative historical document images with geometric distortions using two state of the art dewarping methods for Arbitrary Warped Historical document images (AWH) [9] and for Camera Based Document images (CBD) [13] and the Book Restorer commercially available software [1]. The first method [9] uses a novel segmentation and precise baseline model to detect the exact shape of distortion and then using a flow line approach to rectify the image. The second method [13] uses a two step approach, namely coarse and fine dewarping to rectify the image.

Figure 2 shows a sample image from the dataset with an arbitrary warping. One of the advantages of the presented dewarping evaluation method is that the error metric--which measures the deviation of each line from the horizontal line--can be calculated for each line in every image and even in the original image. In this way, the most distorted lines both in the original distorted image and in the dewarped images can be detected. Figure 3 shows the error metric (EM_j) for each line and each image. As can be observed from figure 3, for most of the lines the dewarped methods show less error than the original distorted image. But for some lines the error measure is equal to the distorted image or even is worse. For example, figure 3 shows that the CBD [13] method and Book-restorer [1] in lines 22, 23, 24 have more distortion than the original image. Figure 4 shows the qualitative measurements in lines 22-24 for all four images in figure 2. The red regions show the deviation of each line from the horizontal line. The qualitative results in figure 4 confirm the quantitative measurements in figure 3.

The presented dewarping evaluation technique measures the error in each single line and not only in some represetative lines, such as the evaluation method in [12]. Our evaluation technique thus gives more accurate and comprehensive evaluation metrics while also detecting the all the errors in the whole page and not only on selected lines. The accuracy metric (*AM*) for the above image for the AWH method [9] is 92%%. The Book-Restorer [1] and CBD method [13] reach the average accuracy of 41% and 25%, respectively. Table 1 illustrates the average *AM* of all dewarping techniques on all images in the dataset.

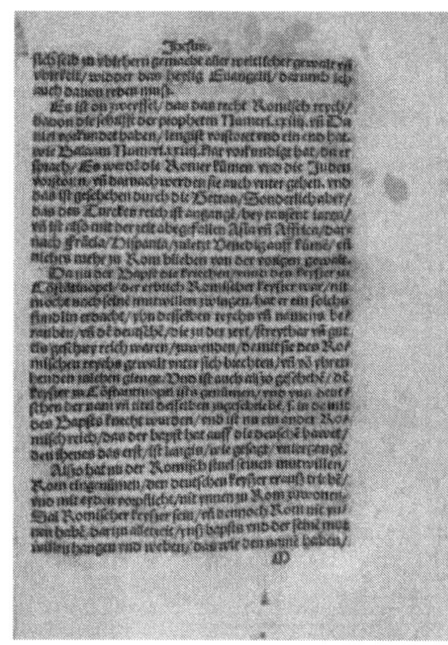

Figure 2. Image with Arbitrary Warping (Copyright: Bavarian State Library)

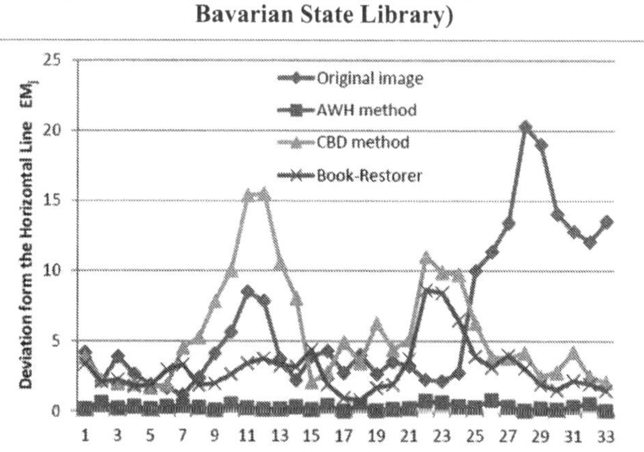

Figure 3. The error metric for each line in original image and dewarped images: AWH [9], CBD [13], Book Restorer [1]

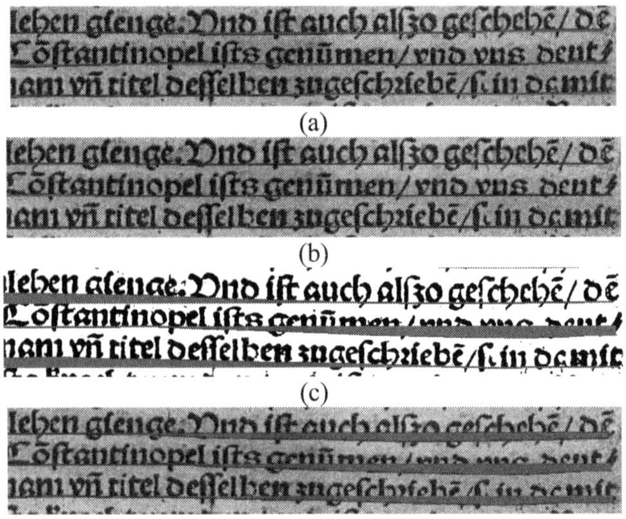

Figure 4. Deviation from the horizontal line for lines 22-24 in figure 2 for (a) original image (b) AWH method [9] (c) CBD method [13] (d) Book-Restorer[1]

Table 1. Comparative results using the proposed evaluation methodology

Dewarping Technique	Accuracy Metric (*AM*)
BookRestorer [1]	66.57%
CBD dewarping method [13]	57.61%
AWH dewarping method method [9]	**94.33%**

4. Conclusion

In this paper a flexible, unsupervised and objective method for the evaluation of document image dewarping is presented. First, the precise baselines are modelled with a robust mathematical formula both on the original image and on the dewarped one. Then based on the mathematical function of each line, a comprehensive metric which calculates the performance of a dewarping technique is introduced. Supervised evaluation methods need a perfect image to evaluate the output image based on the ground-truth one, while unsupervised or fully automatic methods can evaluate the performance independent of the perfect image, based on the simple idea that the final text lines should be straight. Although the process of ground-truthing can produce the possible perfect image, it is a very time-consuming procedure and it can take several hours to make a ground-truth, while for the proposed method the evaluation is quite fast and using the precise baseline detection and a comprehensive metric it gives exact measurement. Another advantage of the proposed method is that it is independent of OCR, which often is not available for historical documents. Experimental results, applied to two leading dewarping methods and an industry-standard commercial system, demonstrate the effectiveness and superiority of the proposed dewarping evaluation method.

5. References

[1] Book-Restorer image restoration software. In *http://www.i2s-bookscanner.com.*

[2] Brown, M., Sun, M., Yang, R., Yun, L.and Seales, W. 2007. Restoring 2D Content from Distorted Documents. *IEEE Transactions on Pattern Analysis and Machine Intelligence 29*, 1904-1916.

[3] Brown, M.and Tsoi, Y. 2006. Geometric and shading correction for images of printed materials using boundary. *IEEE Transactions on Image Processing 15*, 1544-1554.

[4] Bukhari, S., Shafait, F.and Breuel, T. 2009. Dewarping of Document Images using Coupled-Snakes. In *Proceedings of Third International Workshop on Camera-Based Document Analysis and Recognition*, Barcelona, Spain.

[5] Bukhari, S., Shafait, F.and Breuel, T. 2011. An image based performance evaluation method for page dewarping algorithms using SIFT features. In *Camera-Based Document Analysis and Recognition*, 138-149.

[6] Cao, H., Ding, X.and Liu, C. 2003. Rectifying the Bound Document Image Captured by the Camera: A Model Based Approach. In *Proceedings of the Seventh International Conference on Document Analysis and Recognition (ICDAR).*

[7] Gatos, B., Pratikakis, I.and Ntirogiannis, K. 2007. Segmentation based recovery of arbitrarily warped document images. In *International Conference on Document Analysis and Recognition (ICDAR)*, 989-993.

[8] Lu, S.and Tan, C.L. 2006. Document flattening through grid modeling and regularization. In *Proceedings of the Internationa Conference on Pattern Recognition*2006, 971–974.

[9] Rahnemoonfar, M.and Antonacopoulos, A. 2011. Restoration of Arbitrarily Warped Historical Document Images Using Flow Lines. In *Proceedings of the Eleventh International Conference on Document Analysis and Recognition (ICDAR)*, 905-909.

[10] Shafait, F.and Breuel, T.M. 2007. Document image dewarping contest. In *Proceedings of the 2nd Int. Workshop on Camera-Based Document Analysis and Recognition*2007, 181–188.

[11] Stamatopoulos, N., Gatos, B.and Pratikakis, I. 2009. A Methodology for Document Image Dewarping Techniques Performance Evaluation. In *ICDAR* 956-960.

[12] Stamatopoulos, N., Gatos, B.and Pratikakis, I. 2012. Performance evaluation methodology for document image dewarping techniques. *IET Image Processing.*

[13] Stamatopoulos, N., Gatos, B., Pratikakis, I.and Perantonis, S.J. 2011. Goal-oriented rectification of camera-based document images. *IEEE Transactions on Image Processing 20*, 910-920.

[14] Zhang, Y., Liu, C., Ding, X.and Zou, Y. 2008. Arbitrary Warped Document Image Restoration Based on Segmentation and Thin-Plate Splines. In *ICPR 2008*, 1-4.

Semiautomatic Recognition and Georeferencing of Places in Early Maps

Winfried Höhn
Dept. of Computer Science
University of Würzburg, Germany
winfried.hoehn@informatik.uni-wuerzburg.de

Dr. Hans-Günter Schmidt
Dept. of Manuscripts and Early Printed Collections
University Library of Würzburg, Germany
hans-guenter.schmidt@bibliothek.uni-wuerzburg.de

Hendrik Schöneberg
Dept. of Computer Science
University of Würzburg, Germany
schoeneberg@informatik.uni-wuerzburg.de

ABSTRACT

Early maps are a valuable resource for historical research, this is why digital libraries for early maps become a necessary tool for research support in the age of information. In this article we introduce the Referencing and Annotation Tool (RAT), designed to extract information about all places displayed in a map and link them to a place on a modern map. RAT automatically recognizes place markers in an early map according to a template specified by the user and estimates the position of the annotated place in the modern map, thus making georeferencing easier. After a brief summary on related projects, we describe the functionality of the system. We discuss the most important implementation details and factors influencing recognition accuracy and performance. The advantages of our semiautomatic approach are high accuracy and a significant decrease of the user's cognitive load.

Categories and Subject Descriptors

H.3.7 [**Information Storage and Retrieval**]: Digital Libraries; H.3.1 [**Information Storage and Retrieval**]: Content Analysis and Indexing; I.4.6 [**Image Processing and Computer Vision**]: Segmentation; I.7.5 [**Image Processing and Computer Vision**]: Document Capture—*Document analysis*

Keywords

Annotation; early maps; georeferencing; linked data

1. INTRODUCTION

Early maps are a rich source of information for historical research, therefore digital libraries for early maps become a necessary tool for research support in the digital age. Annotation and georeferencing make the information contained in early maps accessible for information retrieval systems and allow to create a link among different sources of information about places, for example early maps and a modern map of the same region or dictionaries of historical topography.

The digitization process usually solely generates image data, which leaves the source semantics uncovered. Enriching the source with structural metadata is a key requirement to enable search engines to link to a document, provide related articles and cross-reference to other resources. A digitization process does therefore not end with the production of a digital representation for a document. It is necessary to cover the retrieval of semantics and metadata as well, which calls for a specialized workflow.

Georeferencing and annotation of early maps is a topic of intensive research. Recent contributions in this domain are for example MapAnalyst [3], Georeferencer [1], and the YUMA Map Annotation Tool [7]. The main development goal of MapAnalyst is the evaluation and visualization of the planimetric and geometric accuracy. The focus of Georeferencer is to determine the spatial extent of a map, which helps for example to find maps which display a certain area. The YUMA Map Annotation Tool allows collaborative annotation of historic maps where the annotations can be augmented with structured information.

Since early maps (and maps in general) do not always display all places in the depicted area, it is sometimes not satisfactory to capture only the spatial extent of a map. In addition, certain types of information are encoded in place markers, for example special symbols for villages, towns, villages with a church or glass factories. This information can be made accessible for automated retrieval through annotation. Moreover, place names changed over time and are spelled differently on different maps from the same age, therefore place names annotations offer valuable information about these changes. Furthermore new locations arise, disappear again or merge with neighboring places over time. All this makes georeferencing a challenging but crucial task when it comes to digitizing early maps. Above all, most maps contain many thousands of place markers, thus georeferencing without proper tool support would be a cumbersome task. However, detailed georeferencing and annotation within early maps is not well supported by the tools mentioned previously in this section.

The purpose of this paper is to present the Referencing and Annotation Tool (RAT), designed to gather information about all places displayed in a map and link them to a place on a modern map, if possible. In Section 2 we describe the

JCDL'13, July 22–26, 2013, Indianapolis, Indiana, USA.
Copyright 2013 ACM 978-1-4503-2077-1/13/07 ...$15.00.

digitization workflow and the methods implemented to support the user in the task of finding, annotating and georeferencing the place markers in a map. Thereafter, in Section 3 we discuss the implementation details and the performance. In Section 4 we conclude, give an outline on system functions, which are in an early prototyping stage, and share several ideas for further user support.

2. SYSTEM DESCRIPTION

The Digitization Center of the University Library of Würzburg specializes in creating and publishing high-quality reproductions of ancient manuscripts, prints and maps. The used custom workflow-system [6] supports the creation of digital copies of a given source and provides means to augment digital representations for a source with automatically extracted metadata. The modules responsible for this task work independently and can be chained arbitrarily. This provides a flexible approach to adapt to a source's unique requirements.

RAT can be integrated into the workflow-software as an additional information retrieval module. It is well-suited to enrich syntactically challenging documents with valuable structural metadata. Many examples of navigable documents digitized and augmented with such metadata can be found on Franconica-Online[1].

RAT offers automatic identification for place markers and also supports the georeferencing task. For each place on an early map the user can assign four types of information: the original place name, place type (for instance village, town or monastery), a link to the same place in a modern map, and a free text comment. We explain these steps in the following subsections in detail.

2.1 Place Marker Detection

In early maps different symbols have been used as place markers for different place types. In addition place markers in different maps are not standardized, therefore symbols used for the same place type in different maps can be different. This can be seen in Figure 1, which shows the symbols for monastery, village, hamlet, and town occurring in two different maps. Moreover place markers within a single map also vary, since the maps have been created manually. An example for this variance in map symbols is given in Figure 3 and explained in section 3.1.

To initiate an automatic detection of place markers, the user needs to specify a template for the place marker by selecting a rectangular area, and name the type of the place marker. The system then uses a template matching algorithm to find positions with similar symbols in the map. Scores are assigned to possible positions of further occurrences of the template, based on their similarity. The user then has to specify a threshold up to which RAT should mark these positions as places of the previously specified type.

Due to the very heterogeneous character of an early map's symbols, it is not trivial to reach a required high accuracy in automatic recognition of place markers, this is why manual post-processing is necessary. Therefore, the automatically detected place markers and their assigned types can be changed manually. Missed place markers can also be added

[1]http://franconica.uni-wuerzburg.de/

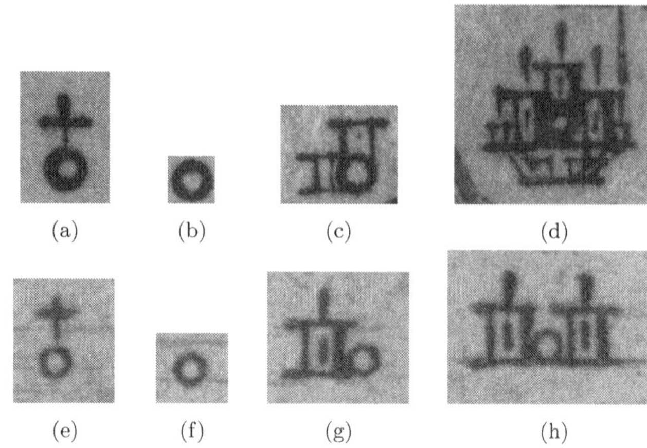

Figure 1: Place markers from two different maps. Each row shows the symbols for monastery, village, hamlet, and town from left to right.

manually and a suggestion for their place type is generated by comparison with the already specified templates.

This detection can be used with symbols selected directly from the map or from the map legend. If a map has a legend, it is a straightforward task to collect all templates and their meanings from the legend. Otherwise the symbols have to be collected directly from the map and their meaning needs to be inferred. However, it is a nontrivial task to find all symbols used in a map, especially rarely used ones. If a legend is given, not all symbols have to be present in the map, since maps and legends may have been created separately and been reused for similar or corrected maps. The detection feature can be used to verify the actual use of certain symbols listed in the legend and find the occurrences of a symbol.

2.2 Georeferencing Support

To support the georeferencing of place markers, a database with place names and their geocoordinates is used. The system maps pixel coordinates in the early map and modern geocoordinates according to an estimation function. After selecting a place in the early map, the system provides suggestions for a mapping to a modern place based on places nearby the estimated geocoordinates. These suggestions can also be refined by an instant search, which can execute an exact search or list phonetically similar names. If the user annotated a place with the original spelling of the place name as specified in the early map without using the instant search for the annotation, then a phonetic search with the original spelling of the place name is automatically executed.

Search results are displayed as a list of place names and by markers at their geoposition on a modern map. These two representations are linked, so that a selection in one representation also highlights the corresponding place in the other representation. Also both representations indicate by a marker when there already is an assignment of a place in the current map to its modern equivalent. However there is no mechanism to prevent the assignment of multiple places in an early map to the same place in a modern map, since it is possible for two places to merge.

The assigned places are displayed in the early map and the modern map. The linking is visualized by highlighting

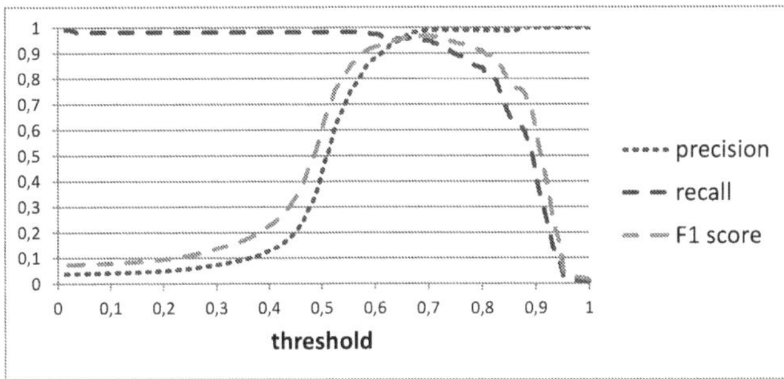

Figure 2: Precision, recall, and F1 score of the template matching for the template in Figure 1b.

the counterpart of the selected place on the other map. If a modern place with multiple assigned places is selected, a popup with a list of the assigned places in the early map is displayed and the desired mapping can be selected. This also helps in correcting wrong multiple assignments.

3. IMPLEMENTATION AND DISCUSSION

RAT is implemented as an AJAX Web App, developed with the Google Web Toolkit (GWT)[2]. This implementation as a web application allows collaborative annotation, and parts of the system can also be reused for presenting the annotated maps online.

3.1 Template Matching

The template matching introduced in subsection 2.1 uses the normalized cross-correlation [4] (NCC) to find symbols similar to a template. Figure 4b shows an example of the NCC for a map fragment displayed in Figure 4a with the template shown in Figure 1b. The correlation image contains values in the range from -1.0 to 1.0, with 1.0 (white) for a perfect match and -1.0 (black) for an inverted match. All local maxima in the correlation image that lie above a threshold are selected as positions of place markers. The threshold is selected empirically for each template and map separately to optimize the precision and recall values. An example is shown in Figure 2 containing the results of a matching of the template from Figure 1b against a fragment of the historic Seutter map (1731)[3] with 120 occurrences of this type of place marker. Figure 2 displays precision, recall and F1 score depending on the selected threshold for the NCC. In this case, the best F1 score of 0.97 is reached for 0.67 as threshold with a recall of 0.96 and a precision of 0.98. In this case, 115 from the total of 120 place markers where found with 2 false positive matches.

The recognition accuracy is influenced by various factors. The NCC is resistant to linear changes in brightness and contrast. However, it is not resistant to other distortions, for instance scaling and rotation. In addition, early maps contain symbols which have some substructures in common, see for example the place markers in Figures 1a and 1b. In this case, the recognition accuracy depends on the order in which different symbols are detected. If first a search with the template from Figure 1b is carried out and then for Figure 1a, the first template will block subsequent matches of further templates at the same position. Thus, the matching should be started with the biggest templates in size.

Since early maps are handcrafted, complex symbols often show a high variance, see for instance the symbols used for glass factories in a single map shown in Figure 3. The symbol used in the map legend is depicted in Figure 3a and various symbols actually used throughout the map can be found in Figures 3b to 3f. If the symbol from the legend is used as a template for the automatic detection, the symbols in Figures 3b and 3c can be found with only one false positive match. To find the remaining three symbols (3d-3f), the threshold needs to be decreased. In this case the automatic recognition would also produce more than 300 false positive matches.

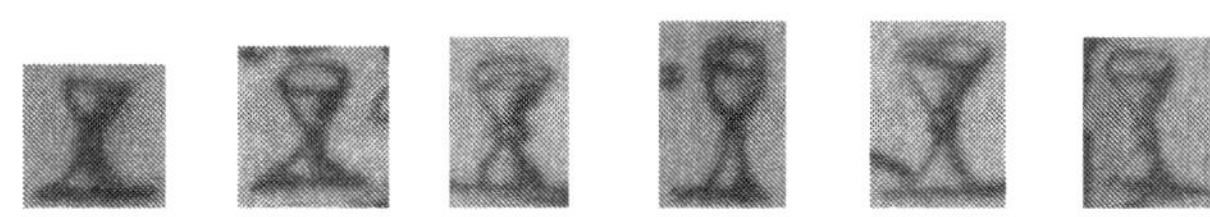

(a) (b) (c) (d) (e) (f)

Figure 3: Different symbols for a glass factory from a single map.

3.2 Geoposition Estimation and Linking

To estimate the geoposition for the new places, RAT calculates a transformation matrix, which is a projective transformation, between the points on the map and the geographic coordinates. This transformation matrix is calculated with the least squares method based on the previous georeferences. The maps contain inaccuracies and distortions, see for example Figure 5. The projective transformation can only map straight lines to straight lines, thus, even after the estimation there remain inaccuracies in the geoposition prediction. However, combined with the phonetic search, the efforts the user needs to invest in the place search can be considerably reduced.

Since the maps in Franconica-Online mostly cover German speaking regions, it is reasonable to take into account German language resources for suggestion generation, specifically phonetic algorithms and compound analysis. The Cologne Phonetics (orig. German "Kölner Phonetik") is a phonetic algorithm, similar to the Soundex or Metaphone algorithm but optimized for German pronunciation [5], and is used by RAT to find phonetically similar matches.

The instant search is implemented as prefix search. Prefixes that may have been added to the place name over time are subsequently stripped and multiple variants of the name are used for phonetic matching. Thus, a new substring is generated at each non-letter character in a modern place name. For example, "Bad Rippoldsau-Schapbach" results in "Bad Rippoldsau-Schapbach", "Rippoldsau-Schapbach", and "Schapbach" which are used for the phonetic search. In this way, the former names "Rippoldsau" and "Schapbach" are prefixes or matches of a generated string. In addition typical prefixes which were added over time are also stripped from place names, for example Markt-, Burg-, Münch-, and

[2] https://developers.google.com/web-toolkit/

[3] Circulus Franconicus : in quo continentur Episcopat(us) Würtzburgens(is), Bambergensis, et Aichstadiensis. Status Equitum Teutonicorum, Ducat(us) Coburgensis, Marchionat(us) Culmbac. Baruth. Et Onoldinus, Principatus Schwarzenberg, Comitat(us) Henneberg, Wertheim, Holach, Reineck, Pappenheim, Erpach, Hanau, Castell, Baronatus Sensheim, Territor(ium) Noribergense /accurate delineatus per Matthaeum Seutter. - Augsburg, (1731) - coloured etching, 55,3 x 47,4 cm - scale approximately 1:450 000.

(a) Map section of the Seutter map (b) normalized cross-correlation

Figure 4: Figure 4b shows the normalized cross-correlation of the template in Figure 1b with Figure 4a.

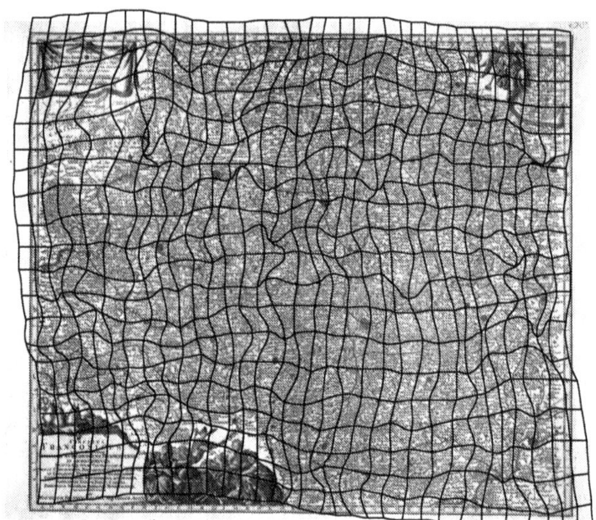

Figure 5: Distortion grid with an cell size of 0.1°, calculated with MapAnalyst[3] from about 3,200 georeferenced places exported from RAT.

Mönch-. Similar language-specific resources can be used for maps covering different regions and languages.

4. CONCLUSION AND FUTURE WORK

The presented approach provides structural and semantic metadata for early maps. The functionality of RAT partially overlaps with a georeferencing and annotation tool for dictionaries of historical topography, which is also part of Franconica-Online. Cross-linking between these modules allows the user to easily navigate within heterogeneous resources.

The user support during the annotation can be improved by adding negative templates for other symbols which are ambiguous with place markers, as for instance a circular place marker and the letter "g" of "Hamelburg" in Figure 4. Negative templates will help to reduce false positive matches. Template matching algorithms invariant to changes in scale and rotation are also of interest.

Automatic recognition of place names in early maps remains extremely challenging, however we have already made efforts in this direction, specifically text/graphics separation and finding text parts in early maps [2]. We also consider automatic detection of different topographic features like for instance mountains, rivers, and borders. Finally, a transfer of annotations between maps could drastically reduce the amount of work required to georeference certain maps.

5. REFERENCES

[1] C. Fleet, K. Kowal, and P. Pridal. Georeferencer: Crowdsourced georeferencing for map library collections. *D-Lib Magazine*, 18(11):5, 2012.

[2] W. Höhn. Detecting arbitrarily oriented text labels in early maps. In *6th Iberian Conference on Pattern Recognition and Image Analysis*, 2013.

[3] B. Jenny and L. Hurni. Cultural heritage: Studying cartographic heritage: Analysis and visualization of geometric distortions. *Computers & Graphics*, 35:402–411, April 2011.

[4] J. Lewis. Fast template matching. In *Vision Interface*, volume 95, pages 15–19, 1995.

[5] H. J. Postel. Die Kölner Phonetik–Ein Verfahren zur Identifizierung von Personennamen auf der Grundlage der Gestaltanalyse. *IBM-Nachrichten*, 19:925–931, 1969.

[6] H. Schöneberg, H.-G. Schmidt, and W. Höhn. A scalable, distributed and dynamic workflow system for digitization processes. In *JCDL*, 2013. accepted for publication.

[7] R. Simon, B. Haslhofer, W. Robitza, and E. Momeni. Semantically augmented annotations in digitized map collections. In *Proceedings of the 11th annual international ACM/IEEE joint conference on Digital libraries*, JCDL '11, pages 199–202, New York, NY, USA, 2011. ACM.

Access Patterns for Robots and Humans in Web Archives

Yasmin AlNoamany, Michele C. Weigle, Michael L. Nelson
Old Dominion University
Norfolk, VA, USA
{yasmin, mweigle, mln}@cs.odu.edu

ABSTRACT

Although user access patterns on the live web are well-understood, there has been no corresponding study of how users, both humans and robots, access web archives. Based on samples from the Internet Archive's public Wayback Machine, we propose a set of basic usage patterns: Dip (a single access), Slide (the same page at different archive times), Dive (different pages at approximately the same archive time), and Skim (lists of what pages are archived, i.e., TimeMaps). Robots are limited almost exclusively to Dips and Skims, but human accesses are more varied between all four types. Robots outnumber humans 10:1 in terms of sessions, 5:4 in terms of raw HTTP accesses, and 4:1 in terms of megabytes transferred. Robots almost always access TimeMaps (95% of accesses), but humans predominately access the archived web pages themselves (82% of accesses). In terms of unique archived web pages, there is no overall preference for a particular time, but the recent past (within the last year) shows significant repeat accesses.

Categories and Subject Descriptors

H.3.7 [**Digital Libraries**]: Web Archives—*Retrieval models*

Keywords

Web Archiving, Web Server Logs, Web Usage Mining, User Access Patterns, Web Robot Detection

1. INTRODUCTION

The web has become an integral part of our lives, shaping how we get news, shop, and communicate. In turn, web archives have become a significant repository of our recent history and cultural heritage. The Internet Archive [19] is the largest and oldest of the various web archives, holding over 240 billion web pages with archives as far back as 1996 [13]. Access to this vast archive is available through the Wayback Machine [30], which sees about 82 million requests per day, based on our dataset.

JCDL'13, July 22–26, 2013, Indianapolis, Indiana, USA.

Previous work has studied how users access the live web [31] and search engines [12], but few studies have investigated how users access web archives. Understanding the current demand for access to web archives can provide insights into how to make the best use of limited archiving and access resources.

In this paper, we provide an analysis of user accesses to a large web archive. We examine a set of anonymized Wayback Machine server access logs from February 2012. We investigate the differences between human and robot accesses of the Wayback Machine, identify four major web archive access patterns, and uncover the temporal preference for web archive access. In particular, we find that robots (such as crawlers and spiders) account for 91% of all sessions and 93% of all page requests. Yet, robots only outnumber humans 5:4 in terms of raw, unfiltered requests and 4:1 in terms of megabytes transferred. Humans download more information per session, as they typically download embedded resources (e.g., images and stylesheets), which robots ignore.

We introduce four basic user access patterns of web archives: Dip, Slide, Dive, and Skim. Dip is requesting for a single URI. Slide is browsing different archived copies of the same URI. Dive is following the hyperlinks of a page, but staying near the same datetime. Skim is requesting only the TimeMaps (list of all archived copies for a specific original resource). Robots exhibit the Dip and Skim patterns equally, both about 49% of their sessions, and almost exclusively request TimeMaps. Humans exhibit the Dip (39%) and Dive (30%) patterns the most and access archived pages significantly more than TimeMaps.

This paper is organized as follows. Definitions of important terms and a review of related work on web usage mining and web archive studies are presented in Section 2. Section 3 contains the patterns for accessing web archives along with an explanation and example for each pattern. A description of the Wayback Machine's web server logs, the dataset we used in the analysis, and the methodology of this study are presented in Section 4. Section 5 contains the results from analyzing the Wayback Machine access logs. Future work and conclusions are presented in Section 6.

2. RELATED WORK

Despite the significance of web archives in preserving web heritage, the aspect of web archive usage has been overlooked. The only previous related work is a study of the search behavior characterization for web archives [7]. We highlight this work, but first we define the terms for our discussion.

2.1 Memento Terminology

Memento [33] is an HTTP protocol extension which enables time travel on the web by interlinking the current resources with their prior state. Memento introduces content negotiation in the datetime dimension using a special HTTP header, Accept-Datetime [32]. Memento defines the following terms:

- URI-R denotes the original resource. It is the resource as it used to appear on the live web; it may have 0 or more mementos (URI-Ms).
- URI-M is an archived snapshot for the URI-R at a specific datetime, which is called Memento-Datetime. e.g., URI-M_i= URI-R@t_i.
- URI-T denotes a TimeMap, a resource that provides a list of mementos (URI-Ms) for a URI-R with their Memento-Datetimes, e.g., $URI-T(URI-R) = \{URI-M_1, URI-M_2, ..., URI-M_n\}$. (We will also refer to a TimeMap as TM URI-R, to emphasize the URI-R in later examples)

Although we use Memento terminology, the logs we analyze are from the public access Wayback Machine and not the Memento API.

2.2 Web Usage Mining

The breadth and depth of research in the area of web usage mining is massive and increasing [3, 14, 23, 5]. Web usage mining involves discovering usage patterns from web data using data mining [25]. The results obtained from web usage mining can be used in different applications, such as web traffic analysis, site modification, system improvement, personalization, business intelligence, and usage characterization. Our study provides traffic analysis and usage characterization by providing abstract models for accessing web archives.

Adams et al. explored the usage patterns of scientific and historical data repositories [1]. However, their study focused on a variety of archive types (e.g., public vs. private, digital but non-web resources) and does not directly address the issue of archiving the web. The only web usage mining research that has been conducted on the usage of web archives is the study of search behavior characterization of web archives based on a quantitative analysis of the Portuguese Web Archive (PWA) search logs [7]. The authors introduced a comparison between search patterns of web archives and web search engines. Despite the different information needs for web archives and web search engine users, the search patterns for web archives had shown adoption of web search engine technologies. They found that most web archive users conducted short sessions. In our study, the sessions that are composed of one request contribute the most to the number of sessions. One important finding from analyzing the search interactions of the PWA logs is that the users prefer older documents. This is in contrast to what we found, that web archive users have significant repetitions for requests in 2011 (the year prior to our sample).

The challenge that faces web usage mining is detecting the robots who camouflage their identity and pretend to be humans. The robot detection problem has been examined in several studies [27, 9, 15, 11]. Doran et al. characterized robot detection techniques into four categories: syntactical log analysis, traffic pattern analysis, analytical learning techniques, and Turing test systems [10]. We used syntactical log analysis (simple processing by finding the self-identified robots) and traffic pattern analysis (specifying features for contrasting robots with humans).

3. ABSTRACT MODELS FOR ACCESSING WEB ARCHIVES

Through our analysis, we discovered four major patterns for web archive access. We present the model for each pattern along with an example from the logs in Figures 1-4. Each example consists of three columns: the client IP, the access time, and the requested URI. The times annotating the transition arrows in Figure 2-4 represent the inter-request time in the given examples. Note that we use TM URI-R to denote a TimeMap in the figures. We use Memento terminology (URI-T, URI-M, and URI-R) in the definitions. We refer to the original resource for URI-T and URI-M with URI-R(URI-T) and URI-R(URI-M), respectively.

3.1 Pattern 1: Dip

Dip is the pattern where a user accesses only one URI. The request can be for a URI-T (Figure 1(a) and the first example) or a URI-M (Figure 1(b) and the second example).

$$Dip = \{\text{URI-X}_i |\, i = 1 \text{ and URI-X} \in \{\text{URI-T, URI-M}\}\}$$

3.2 Pattern 2: Slide

Slide is the pattern in which a user accesses the same URI-R at different Memento-Datetimes. In this pattern, the user requests a URI-R and walks through time browsing its different copies (Figure 2).

$$\begin{aligned} Slide &= \{\text{URI-X}_i |\, i > 1, \text{URI-X} \in \{\text{URI-T, URI-M}\} \\ &\quad \text{and URI-R(URI-X}_i) = \text{URI-R(URI-X}_{i-1})\} \end{aligned}$$

Navigation between different URI-Ms can be done in many ways, e.g., directly from URI-M_1 to URI-M_2 (URI-R@t_1 $\Rightarrow$ URI-R@t_2) or from URI-M_1 to URI-M_2, but in the middle the user returns to the TM URI-R to choose between the available datetimes (URI-R@t_1 $\Rightarrow$ URI-T $\Rightarrow$ URI-R@t_2).

3.3 Pattern 3: Dive

Dive is when a user accesses different URI-Rs at nearly the same datetime. In this pattern, the user accesses one URI-R at a specific time, URI-R_1@t_0, then navigates to different hyperlink(s) of URI-R_1's page (e.g., URI-R_2@t_0) and so on (Figure 3).

$$\begin{aligned} Dive &= \{\text{URI-X}_i |\, i > 1, \text{URI-X} \in \{\text{URI-T, URI-M}\} \\ &\quad \text{and URI-R(URI-M}_i) <> \text{URI-R(URI-M}_{i-1})\} \end{aligned}$$

3.4 Pattern 4: Skim

Skim is when a user accesses a number of different TimeMaps for different URI-Rs (Figure 4). Skim does not include any access for mementos.

$$Skim = \{\text{URI-X}_i |\, i > 1 \text{ and URI-X} \in \{\text{URI-T}\}\}$$

4. METHODOLOGY

In this study, we introduce an analysis of the user access patterns of web archives. The analysis was conducted on

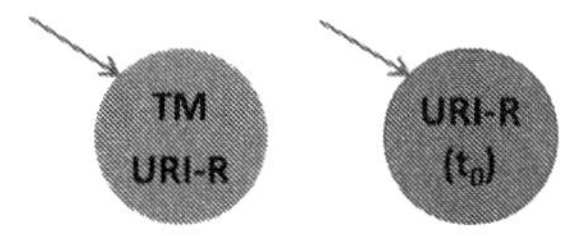

(a) URI-T (b) URI-M

0.100.61.20	02/Feb/2012:06:48:24	http://wayback.archive.org/web/*/http://iyasizuku.com
0.1.134.90	02/Feb/2012:07:08:28	http://web.archive.org/web/19961022174810/http://altavista.com

Figure 1: Dip: A simple access to either a TimeMap or a memento.

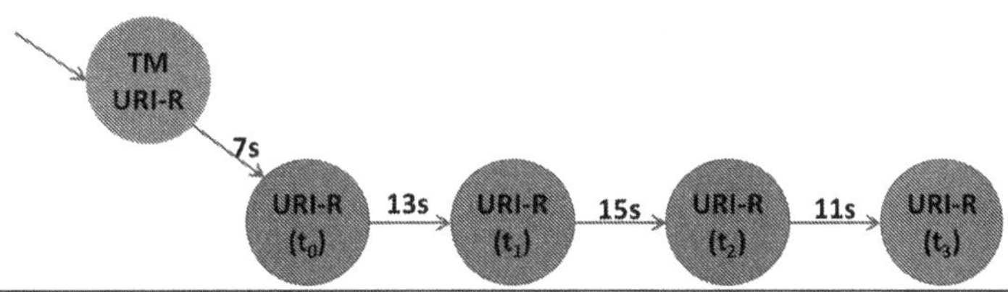

0.248.211.54	02/Feb/2012:07:04:52	http://wayback.archive.org/web/20000715000000*/http://google.com
0.248.211.54	02/Feb/2012:07:04:59	http://web.archive.org/web/20000301105534/http://google.com/
0.248.211.54	02/Feb/2012:07:05:12	http://web.archive.org/web/20051101145803/http://www.google.com
0.248.211.54	02/Feb/2012:07:05:27	http://web.archive.org/web/20080730200402/http://www.google.com/
0.248.211.54	02/Feb/2012:07:05:38	http://web.archive.org/web/20110215024256/http://www.google.com/

Figure 2: Slide: Accessing the same URI-R at different Memento-Datetimes.

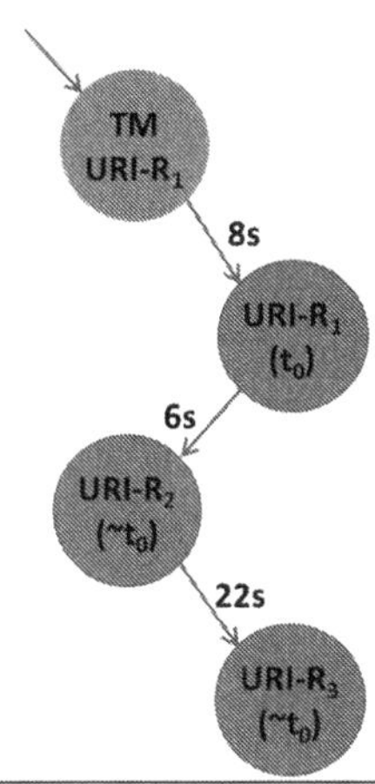

0.106.160.155	02/Feb/2012:07:07:10	http://wayback.archive.org/web/*/http://my-ru.net
0.106.160.155	02/Feb/2012:07:07:18	http://web.archive.org/web/20100709124643/http://my-ru.net/
0.106.160.155	02/Feb/2012:07:07:24	http://web.archive.org/web/20100709124643/http://my-ru.net/home.php
0.106.160.155	02/Feb/2012:07:07:46	http://web.archive.org/web/20100706170736/http://my-ru.net/carousel.php

Figure 3: Dive: Browsing different URI-Rs at (approximately) the same Memento-Datetime.

0.10.212.177	02/Feb/2012:06:45:24	http://wayback.archive.org/web/*/laquadrature.net
0.10.212.177	02/Feb/2012:06:46:10	http://wayback.archive.org/web/*/parti-du-plaisir.com
0.10.212.177	02/Feb/2012:06:46:22	http://wayback.archive.org/web/*/humanite.fr

Figure 4: Skim: Traversing only TimeMaps for different URI-Rs.

```
0.247.222.86 - - [02/Feb/2012:07:03:46 +0000] "GET http://wayback.archive.org/web/*/http://www.aura.vu
HTTP/1.1" 200 96433 "http://www.archive.org/web/web.php" "Mozilla/5.0 (Macintosh; Intel Mac OS X 10_6_8)
AppleWebKit/535.7 (KHTML, like Gecko) Chrome/16.0.912.77 Safari/535.7"

0.247.222.86 - - [02/Feb/2012:07:03:55 +0000]
"GET http://web.archive.org/web/20020404020224/http://www.aura.vu/ HTTP/1.1" 200 18875
"http://wayback.archive.org/web/*/http://www.aura.vu" "Mozilla/5.0 (Macintosh; Intel Mac OS X 10_6_8)
AppleWebKit/535.7 (KHTML, like Gecko) Chrome/16.0.912.77 Safari/535.7"}
```

Figure 5: Sample of the Wayback Machine access log.

the Internet Archive's Wayback Machine access logs. The first step in preparing the Wayback access logs for usage mining was transforming the raw log file into server sessions through web-log preprocessing, which included data cleaning, user identification, and session identification [6]. Then, we performed feature extraction, robot detection, and user access pattern detection.

4.1 Wayback Machine Access Logs

A Web server log file is a plain text file that records the activity information of the submitted requests from the users on the web server. The Wayback Machine access logs contain the following fields: client IP, access time, HTTP request method (GET or HEAD), URI, protocol (HTTP), HTTP status code (200, 404, etc.), bytes sent, referring URI, and User-Agent. For privacy purposes, the Internet Archive anonymized the client IP address. A segment from the Wayback Machine server logs, which we will call Wayback access logs, is shown in Figure 5. The first line shows a request for a URI-T. The second line shows a request for a URI-M.

4.2 Dataset

The Wayback Machine allows users to browse archived copies of web pages across time. The Wayback access logs were sampled using two probability techniques [29]: cluster sampling, which is choosing a cluster of data randomly, and random sampling, where each sampling unit has an equal chance of being included. We performed cluster sampling by choosing a week (Feb. 2-8, 2012) and random sampling by taking a random slice from each day of the week. Each sample comprised a slice of 2M requests to the Wayback Machine web server. Table 1 shows the characteristics of each dataset. It contains the following features for each sample:

- **Duration:** the difference between the last request time and the first request time of each sample in HH:MM:SS format.
- **GET:** the percentage of requests that used the GET method.
- **Embedded:** the percentage of requests that were for embedded resources of web pages (such as images and CSS files, etc.).
- **SI Robots:** the percentage of requests by self-identified robots based on the User-Agent field.
- **NullRef:** the percentage of requests that had an empty referral field.
- **s2xx:** the percentage of successful requests (2xx status code).
- **s3xx:** the percentage of redirections (3xx status code).
- **s4xx:** the percentage of client errors (4xx status code).
- **s5xx:**: the percentage of server errors (5xx status code).
- **Cleaned:** the percentage of requests remaining after removing requests for embedded resources, HEAD requests, and requests that resulted in status codes other than 200, 404, or 503.
- **Sessions:** the number of sessions.

The last three columns of the table show the mean, standard deviation, and corresponding standard error between the samples. We use the Feb. 2, 2012 sample in our analysis because as we see from Table 1, it is a representative sample.

In the Feb. 2 sample, we note that HTTP 3xx accounts for 52% of the total number of requests. This is related to the default Wayback Machine behavior. First, the Wayback Machine rewrites all of the hyperlinks of a memento's embedded resources with the mementos's timestamp. Second, in the resolution of these URIs, the Wayback Machine will redirect the request of the embedded resources and hyperlinks to the nearest (timestamp) available memento. Furthermore, the Wayback Machine responds with a 302 status first when the requested URI-R is not available on the Wayback Machine, and then responds with a 404 status.

4.3 Data Cleaning

The first step in preprocessing our dataset was data cleaning, i.e., removing log entries that were not needed for the mining process [17, 28]. In similar studies for log analysis, robots that identify themselves in the User-Agent field were removed. Because robots crawl web archives intentionally, we did not exclude their requests in the cleaning step. We eliminated the following items which were irrelevant in terms of user behavior:

- Requests that were generated automatically by the web browser for embedded resources of the requested web page (such as graphic files, page style files, etc.).
- Entries with an HTTP status code other than HTTP 200, 404, or 503. We kept only these because we considered them to be requests executed by the user.
- Requests using the HEAD request method (as suggested by [16]).
- Static resources of the Internet Archive web site and the URIs of the liveweb service, which the Internet Archive introduces to redirect the user to the live web when the copy is not found on the Wayback Machine.
- Invalid requests from web sites which included a link for malformed URI-Rs (for example, about:blank) among their embedded resources, so that each request on their web sites caused automatic requests to the Wayback Machine server. Similar behavior had been detected by Omodei [21].

Days	Feb 2	Feb 3	Feb 4	Feb 5	Feb 6	Feb 7	Feb 8	Mean	SD	SE
Duration	0:33:12	0:31:15	0:40:34	0:42:57	0:29:35	0:25:45	0:24:33	0:32:33	0:06:29	0:02:27
GET	98.4%	99.3%	97.7%	97.9%	99.4%	99.7%	99.8%	99%	0.8%	0.3%
Embedded	47.4%	34.8%	43.7%	42.7%	41.9%	44.7%	46.8%	43.1%	3.9%	1.5%
SI Robots	6.2%	12.0%	7.7%	7.7%	2.9%	3.5%	3.8%	6.3%	3.0%	1.1%
NullRef	42.6%	56.6%	47.5%	47.0%	49.4%	42.6%	43.9%	47.1%	4.6%	1.7%
s2xx	33.7%	32.4%	34.2%	33.2%	34.1%	33.4%	33.6%	33.5%	0.6%	0.2%
s3xx	51.8%	52.3%	50.8%	52.2%	51.7%	51.9%	53.2%	52.0%	0.7%	0.3%
s4xx	11.7%	13.1%	12.0%	11.6%	11.2%	10.3%	10.1%	11.4%	0.9%	0.4%
s5xx	2.8%	2.3%	3.0%	2.9%	3.0%	4.4%	3.1%	3.1%	0.6%	0.2%
Cleaned	21.3%	23.0%	17.6%	17.7%	20.7%	18.1%	16.9%	19.3%	2.2%	0.8%
Sessions	37,634	31,731	32,159	28,750	36,087	35,848	32,117	33,475	2,896	1,094

Table 1: Features for each sample of 2M records, Feb. 2-8, 2012.

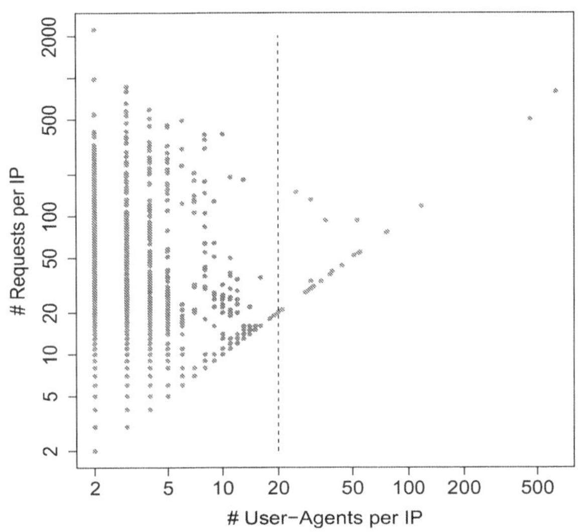

Figure 6: The number of user requests per IP against the number of User-Agents per IP.

4.4 User Identification

To identify the users, the log files were first sorted by the IP, then by the request time. At first, we identified users by the 2-tuple (IP, User-Agent), but we found instances of malicious robots who not only did not self-identify, but who also changed their User-Agent with every request. There are some legitimate cases for humans to have different User-Agents and the same IP, for instance, two simultaneous users coming from behind a firewall. So, we needed to determine a reasonable threshold for the number of User-Agents per IP to detect malicious robots.

Figure 6 shows the relationship between the number of User-Agents per IP and the number of requests per IP (for those IPs with more than one User-Agent). We excluded self-identified robots from the graph to avoid biasing the results. We found only 24 users who had changed their User-Agent field more than 20 times. The median value for the number of User-Agents per IP for the dataset is 3 (excluding users who had one User-Agent only). We concluded that 20 different User-Agents per IP is a good threshold for this dataset. For IPs with at most 20 different User-Agents, we used the 2-tuple (IP, User-Agent) to identify individual users. The 24 IPs with more than 20 different User-Agents were classified as 24 separate robots.

4.5 Session Identification

A session is the set of web pages that are requested by particular user [17]. Session identification is performed by dividing a web server log file into web server sessions. First, we group all the requests based on the IP and User-Agent (as described in Section 4.4). Second, we apply a threshold timeout, so that if the time elapsed between two consecutive requests is longer than this threshold, the second request is considered to be the first request of the new session. There have been several suggested timeout thresholds including 25.5 minutes [5], 30 minutes [27, 14], and 60 minutes [2]. Others proposed 10 minutes as a conservative threshold to capture the time for staying on one page [16, 24]. In our study, we divided the requests of each user into individual sessions based on a 10 minute timeout threshold. Future research is required to verify that searching and browsing models for the current web are valid for browsing the past web (i.e., web archives).

After identifying the sessions, we extracted features for each session to be used further in the analysis. A session, S, is 7-tuple.

$$S = \langle URI, S_l, S_d, BS, \bar{S}_{rt}, stdev(S_{rt}), IH \rangle$$

The following is the description of each item:

- URI is the set of URIs that the user visited in the session. The set of URIs are defined as:

$$URI = \{\text{URI}_i \mid i \text{ is an integer}, 1 \le i \le S_l \text{ and URI} \in \{\text{URI-T, URI-M}\}\}$$

- S_l, session length, is the number of webpages the user requested during the session.
- S_d, session duration, is calculated by subtracting the timestamp of the first request of the session from the timestamp of the last request of the session.
- BS is the browsing speed of each session in requests/second. $BS = S_l/S_d$.
- $\bar{S}_{rt}$ is the mean inter-request time of the session.
- $stdev(S_{rt})$ is the standard deviation of the inter-request time of the session.
- IH, image-to-HTML, is the ratio between the number of image files and the number of HTML files per session.

4.6 Robot Detection

Because of the increasing numbers of web crawlers that are engaged in web harvesting, many studies have been con-

Heuristics	# Detected Robots out of 37,634 sessions	out of 426,317 requests
SI Robots	1,410	68,967
#UA per IP	24	2,747
Robots.txt	55	90
Browsing Speed	1,601	47,320
Image-to-HTML	33,244	326,019
Total Robots	**34,203 (90.9%)**	**396,627 (93.9%)**

Table 2: The number of detected robots from applying each heuristic independently and the number of the records after applying all the filters together.

Filters	% Excluded Requests (out of 2M)
Status Code	51.8%
Embedded Resources	47.4%
Static and Liveweb	10.0%
Invalid Requests	3.7%
HEAD	1.6%
All Filters	**78.7%**

Table 3: The characteristics of data cleaning filters. Some of requests fell into multiple categories, so the percentages add up to more than 100%.

ducted for investigating the robot detection problem [27, 15]. In this study, we used different types of robot detection techniques [10]. First, we applied syntactical log analysis by checking the User-Agent field to identify the self-identified robots. Second, we applied traffic pattern analysis techniques to distinguish humans from robots based on their navigational behavior. In this section, we describe heuristics we used for distinguishing robots from humans.

4.6.1 User-Agent Check

The User-Agent check is applied for requests from crawlers and robots which declared their identity to the web server through the User-Agent field (SI robots). We excluded these robots by applying this heuristic before the calculations of the session features to avoid biasing the results.

4.6.2 Number of User-Agent per IP

As explained earlier (Section 4.4), we used 20 as a threshold for the maximum number of different User-Agents for each IP. Users with more than 20 different User-Agents were classified as robots.

4.6.3 Robots.txt file

Web site administrators put a list of access restrictions to specify which parts of their web site are not allowed to be visited by robots. We labeled the sessions in which users downloaded the robots.txt file for the Wayback Machine (http://web.archive.org/robots.txt) as robots.

4.6.4 Browsing Speed (BS)

The importance and the effect of BS has been discussed and used for detecting robots many times [20, 28, 22]. We use $BS \leq 0.5$ (i.e., no faster than one request every two seconds) as a threshold for human browsing speed [4]. We observed that this threshold is appropriate for our dataset, so we classify the sessions with $BS > 0.5$ as robots.

4.6.5 Image-to-HTML Ratio (IH)

Human sessions should have more images than robot sessions because of the embedded images present in most HTML pages. Robots tend to retrieve only HTML pages, while ignoring image formats. We used the IH metric calculated previously for each session to detect robots. In [26], 1:10 IH had been suggested as a good threshold for distinguishing robots from humans. We label a session with less than one image file for every 10 HTML files as a robot. IH is the only heuristic that does not require a session have at least two requests. This heuristic is the best predictor for robots [27, 26], and it has a strong effect on our dataset.

5. RESULTS AND ANALYSIS

In this section, we explain the results of preprocessing the dataset (described in Sections 4.3-4.5) and of applying the heuristics for robot detection (described in Section 4.6). We analyze the resulting data and contrast the behavior and access patterns of humans and robots. We conclude with an analysis of the temporal preference of human users.

5.1 Traffic Analysis

To extract the user access patterns for web archives from the Wayback access logs, we first applied data preprocessing techniques (data cleaning, user identification, session identification) to convert the log file into web server sessions. The raw log file contains 2M requests from which we determined 21,932 unique IPs. Because of the stateless nature of the log files, we identified the users based on the IP and User-Agent to identify 33,841 users who created 37,634 different sessions.

The characteristics of each filter (3xx status code, embedded resources, static resources and liveweb, invalid requests, HEAD) and the total number of excluded requests after applying all the filters together are shown in Table 3. The number of records in the Feb. 2 sample was decreased from 2M to 426,317 (21.3% of the requests in the raw file).

5.2 Robots vs Humans

Table 2 contains the results of applying the heuristics for detecting robots. The rules are not mutually exclusive, but we calculated the number of requests which had been labeled as robots from each filter separately. IH had the largest effect on detecting robots. We used a 1:10 IH as a threshold for distinguishing robots from humans. We found that 99.93% of the sessions which were detected by this heuristic had 0 images. BS is also important, because it classified a significant number of robots who had a BS (more than 0.5 requests/second) impossible for humans.

Users	# Requests (Filtered)	# Requests (Raw)	# Sessions	# Transferred MB	# URI-Ts	# URI-Ms
Robots	396,627 (93.0%)	1,002,573 (50.1%)	34,203 (90.9%)	20,010	378,201 (95.4%)	18,426 (4.6%)
Humans	29,690 (7.0%)	810,049 (40.5%)	3,431 (9.1%)	4,459	5,505 (18.5%)	24,185 (81.5%)

Table 4: HTTP activity of robots and humans.

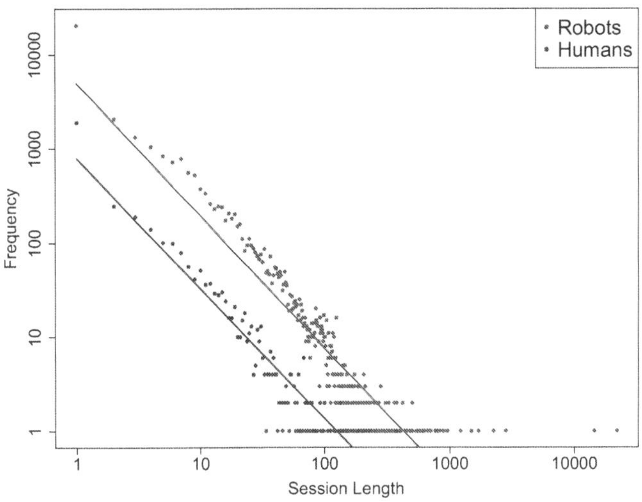

Figure 7: The frequency of session lengths (# of requests) for humans and robots.

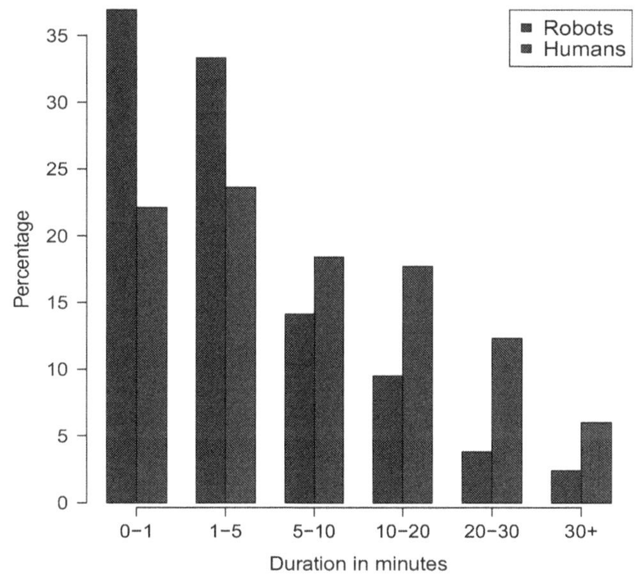

Figure 8: The percentage of sessions for each interval. The number of humans and robots sessions are 2024 and 17019 (excluding the sessions with one request), respectively.

Table 4 contains the summary of the activity of humans and robots. From the table, we notice that the sum of the percentage of raw requests from humans and robots did not equal 2M requests. The reason is that there are many accesses that were created by invalid requests to the web server. Furthermore, there are many requests to embedded resources only, which were filtered. The percentage of human requests after cleaning and separating robot requests is only 1.5% of the 2M requests.

The significant discovery here is the 10:1 ratio of robot sessions to human sessions. This ratio is a strong motivation for building an API interface that serves robot accesses in order to decrease the load of robots on the Wayback Machine. A typical human session costs more than a robot session as humans average 1.30 MB/session and robots average 0.58 MB/session. Human requests include automatic downloads of the embedded resources of the web pages they access, and robots usually ignore downloading these embedded resources.

We discovered that most of the robots had a breadth search strategy in downloading the web pages from the Wayback Machine; more than 95% of the robots downloaded TimeMaps only, as shown in Table 4. On the other hand, of all human requests, only 18.5% were for TimeMaps.

5.2.1 *Session Length* (S_l)

After detecting the robots, we separated them from humans and analyzed their behaviors individually. Figure 7 shows the session length frequency for robots in red and for humans in blue. We notice from the figure that many more robots have longer sessions than humans. The $\bar{S_l}$ for robots is 10 requests/session, while humans have an $\bar{S_l}$ of 9 requests/session.

5.2.2 *Session Duration* (S_d)

We computed session duration by subtracting the time of the first request from the time of the last request for each session. Session duration requires at least two requests. Figure 8 shows the percentage of sessions with different session durations for robots and humans. We can see that the majority of the sessions were short, taking into consideration that we did not count the time spent on the last requested web page. The $\bar{S_d}$ is 10 minutes for robots and 5 minutes for humans.

5.2.3 *Inter-Request Time*

We also calculated $\bar{S_{rt}}$ and $stdev(S_{rt})$ for each session. We found that the median values of $\bar{S_{rt}}$ for human and robot sessions are 19 seconds and 40 seconds, respectively. The median of $stdev(S_{rt})$ values is 37 seconds for robots and 11 seconds for humans. This indicates that robots tend to have more irregular periods between HTML requests than humans, and this matches the finding by Tan et al. [27].

5.3 Web Archive User Access Patterns

How do users go through web archives? Do they go in deeply from URI-R$_1$ to URI-R$_2$, do they browse broadly from URI-M$_1$ to URI-M$_2$ for the same URI-R, or do they use a combination of these two patterns? Are robot accesses similar to human accesses?

In this section, we answer the previous questions by extracting the user access patterns for web archives from our

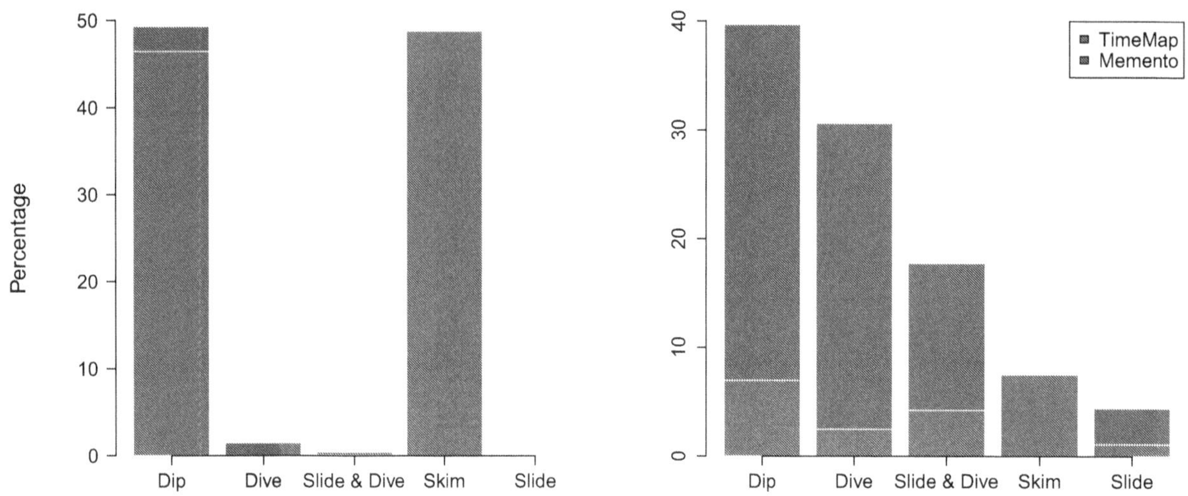

(a) Robots (34203 sessions)

(b) Humans (3431 sessions)

Figure 9: Robots and humans exhibit different access patterns.

filtered dataset. The requested URIs for each session were extracted and then identified based on their type, URI-M or URI-T. We also extracted the URI-R of each requested URI to compare it with the other URI-Rs from the same session. Because of the existence of different forms of URIs which refer to the same website [18], we applied URI canonicalization for the URI-Rs to normalize them under one host [8].

We discovered four basic building blocks (Dip, Slide, Dive, Skim) of the user access patterns for web archives. Figures 1-4 show the models along with examples of the four patterns. The percentages of each pattern exhibited in robot and human sessions are shown in Figures 9(a) and 9(b) along with the percentages of requests to TimeMaps and mementos for each pattern.

Dip

Dip is the pattern where the user requests a single URI. This URI can be a URI-M or a URI-T. It represents the most repeated pattern for humans (33% of all sessions) and robots (49% of all sessions). URI-Ms contribute to 83% of human sessions that exhibit the Dip pattern, although 94% of the robot Dips are requests for URI-Ts.

Slide

The user who is interested in travelling through time, browsing different copies of the same URI-R, creates the Slide pattern. There are only a few humans who access the web archives broadly then navigate away (4.2% of all sessions). Robot sessions do not have this pattern with a noticeable percentage (0.1% of all sessions).

Dive

Dive represents the second highest percentage of human sessions, 29.7%. In this pattern, the user goes deeply for browsing hyperlinks of URI-Ms. The robot sessions which were composed of this pattern crawl the web sites deeply, but they are not a significant number of sessions.

Skim

Skim is the pattern for which the users access different numbers of TimeMaps. Robot sessions exhibit this pattern 48.7% of the time. Investigating the relationship between the topics of the URI-Rs of the requested TimeMaps during a single session is one of our goals for upcoming research.

User	Pattern	Median	Mean	SD
Robots	Slide	3	3	1.4
	Dive	3	15	53.2
	Skim	3	21	267.0
Humans	Slide	3	4	3.4
	Dive	4	8	14.3
	Skim	3	6	7.2

Table 5: Statistics for the length of all Slides, Dives, and Skims

Slide and Dive

A large number of human sessions consist of at least two occurrences of the Dive and Slide patterns. In these sessions, the users request URI-R_1 and browse its different copies at different times (URI-$R_1@t_1 \Rightarrow$ URI-$R_1@t_2 \Rightarrow$ URI-$R_1@t_3$), then dive through a hyperlink (URI-$R_2@t_3$) from URI-$R_1@t_3$, then repeat Dive or Slide. In contrast, users may start by going deeply through different mementos for different URI-Rs (Dive pattern), then go broadly through one of these mementos to browse other captures at different times (Slide pattern) (e.g., URI-$R_1@t_1 \Rightarrow$ URI-$R_2@t_1 \Rightarrow$ URI-$R_3@t_1 \Rightarrow$ URI-$R_3@t_2$, etc.). The percentage of human sessions that were composed of a combination of these two patterns is 17.2%. We calculated the number of Slides

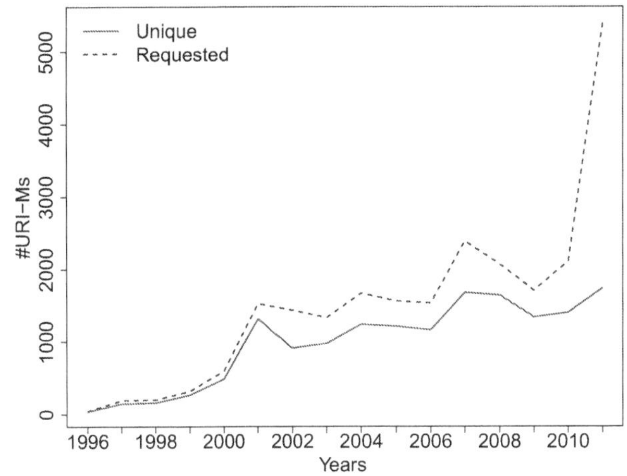

Figure 10: Distributions of the years for the unique and requested mementos by humans.

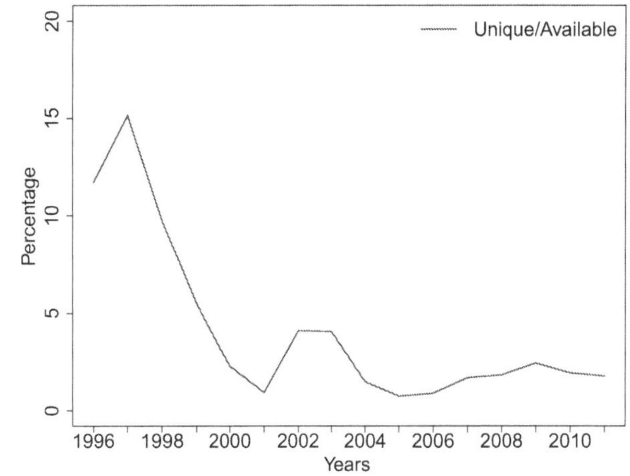

Figure 11: The proportion of unique URI-Ms requested out of the potential requested for each year.

and Dives for these sessions and found 1167 Slides and 1942 Dives. For robot sessions that were composed of Slide and Dive, we found 328 Slides and 571 Dives.

Pattern Length

Each pattern is made up of a number of requests, which we call the pattern length. We calculated the pattern length for all sessions. The median, mean, and standard deviation of the lengths of each pattern for robots and humans are summarized in Table 5. For humans, the longest mean pattern length is an 8-request Dive, while for robots the longest mean pattern length is 21 requests in a Skim.

5.4 Temporal Analysis

Figure 10 shows both the unique and total number of mementos referenced grouped by the year of their Memento-Datetime. Although there is no clear temporal preference for any one year of the unique mementos, there were a significant number of repeated requests for mementos from 2011. This locality of reference suggests that there is an important benefit to be gained by caching the mementos from the recent past. Figure 11 shows that the total number of mementos available for 2011 was similar to previous years. In both Figures 11 and 10, pre-2001 data is included although in those years the archives are too sparse for meaningful comparison with later years.

6. CONCLUSIONS AND FUTURE WORK

We introduced the basic building blocks (Dip, Slide, Dive, and Skim) for user access patterns for web archives through an analysis of the Internet Archive's Wayback Machine access logs. We applied heuristics for detecting robots and found that robot sessions outnumber human sessions 10:1. This suggests that there is utility in building an API interface that serves robot accesses. Robots account for 91% of sessions and 93% of requests to the Wayback Machine, yet robots outnumber humans 5:4 only in terms of raw, unfiltered requests and 4:1 in terms of megabytes transferred. We found that humans download more information per session due to embedded resources, which robots ignore. We also analyzed human and robot access patterns to emphasize the similarities and the differences between them. We found that robots mainly exhibit the Dip and Skim patterns, with about 49% of their sessions for each pattern, and that they access TimeMaps almost exclusively. Humans exhibit the Dip and Dive patterns the most with 39% and 30% of their sessions, respectively. Unlike robots, humans mainly access archived pages rather than TimeMaps. Finally, we provide an analysis for the temporal preferences of humans based on the Memento-Datetime (by year) of their requests and discovered significant repetitions for requests in 2011. This suggests that there is a benefit to be gained by caching mementos from the recent past.

Web server logs are a rich source for information about web archives. We are planning to extend our analysis to serve other applications of web usage mining, such as personalization for making dynamic recommendations to web archive users based on their navigational behavior patterns by using data mining techniques. Further, we will study the validity of applying searching and browsing models for the current web to web archives. We also expect that Slides and Dives that users create on web archives may create stories around a particular event. We plan to extend our study on a large data set to detect stories that humans might create from their access patterns, which will be integrated into the live web to produce automatic stories about specific event for the users.

7. ACKNOWLEDGMENTS

This work was supported in part by the NSF (IIS 1009392) and the Library of Congress. We thank Kris Carpenter Negulescu (Internet Archive) for access to the anonymized Wayback Machine logs.

8. REFERENCES

[1] I. Adams, E. L. Miller, and M. W. Storer. Analysis of workload behavior in scientific and historical long-term data repositories. Technical Report UCSC-SSRC-11-01, University of California, Santa Cruz, Mar. 2011.

[2] P. Anick. Using terminological feedback for web search refinement: a log-based study. In *Proceedings of the 26th annual international ACM SIGIR conference on*

Research and development in informaion retrieval, SIGIR '03, pages 88–95. ACM, 2003.

[3] T. T. Aye. Web log cleaning for mining of web usage patterns. In *3rd International Conference on Computer Research and Development*, ICCRD, pages 490–494. IEEE, Mar. 2011.

[4] G. Castellano, A. M. Fanelli, and M. A. Torsello. LODAP: a log data preprocessor for mining web browsing patterns. In *Proceedings of the 6th WSEAS International Conference on Artificial Intelligence, Knowledge Engineering and Data Bases*, volume 6 of *AIKED '07*, pages 12–17, Feb. 2007.

[5] L. D. Catledge and J. E. Pitkow. Characterizing browsing strategies in the World-Wide web. *Computer Networks and ISDN Systems*, 27(6):1065–1073, Apr. 1995.

[6] R. Cooley and B. Mobasher. Data Preparation for Mining World Wide Web Browsing Patterns. *Knowledge and Information Systems*, 1:5–32, 1999.

[7] M. Costa and M. J. Silva. Characterizing Search Behavior in Web Archives. In *Proceedings of Temporal Web Analytics Workshop*, TWAW, 2011.

[8] M. Cutts. SEO advice: URL canonicalization. `http://www.mattcutts.com/blog/seo-advice-url-canonicalization/`, Jan. 2006.

[9] M. D. Dikaiakos, A. Stassopoulou, and L. Papageorgiou. An investigation of web crawler behavior: characterization and metrics. *Computer Communications*, 28(8):880–897, May 2005.

[10] D. Doran and S. S. Gokhale. Web robot detection techniques: overview and limitations. *Data Mining and Knowledge Discovery*, 22(1-2):183–210, June 2010.

[11] W. Guo, Y. Zhong, and J. Xie. A Web Crawler Detection Algorithm Based on Web Page Member List. In *Proceedings of 4th International Conference on Intelligent Human-Machine Systems and Cybernetics*, pages 189–192, Aug. 2012.

[12] B. J. Jansen and A. Spink. How are we searching the World Wide Web? A comparison of nine search engine transaction logs. *Information Processing & Management*, 42(1):248–263, Jan 2006.

[13] B. Kahle. Wayback Machine: Now with 240,000,000,000 URLs. `http://blog.archive.org/2013/01/09/updated-wayback/`, Jan. 2013.

[14] R. Kumar and A. Tomkins. A characterization of online browsing behavior. In *Proceedings of the 19th international World Wide Web conference*, WWW '10, pages 561–570. ACM, 2010.

[15] S. Kwon, M. Oh, D. Kim, J. Lee, Y.-G. Kim, and S. Cha. Web Robot Detection based on Monotonous Behavior. In *Proceedings of the Information Science and Industrial Applications*, volume 4, 2012.

[16] H. Liu and V. Kešelj. Combined mining of web server logs and web contents for classifying user navigation patterns and predicting users' future requests. *Data Knowledge Engineer*, 61(2):304–330, May 2007.

[17] Z. Markov and D. T. Larose. *Data Mining the Web: Uncovering Patterns in Web Content, Structure, and Usage*. John Wiley & Sons, Inc., 2007.

[18] F. McCown and M. L. Nelson. Evaluation of crawling policies for a web-repository crawler. In *Proceedings of the 17th conference on Hypertext and hypermedia*, HT '06, pages 157–168, Aug. 2006.

[19] K. C. Negulescu. Web Archiving @ the Internet Archive. Presentation at the 2010 Digital Preservation Partners Meeting, `http://1.usa.gov/XSjDG8`, 2010.

[20] P. Nithya and P. Sumathi. Novel Pre-Processing Technique for Web Log Mining by Removing Global Noise, Cookies and Web Robots. *International Journal of Computer Applications*, 53(17):1–6, 2012.

[21] M. Omodei. Trends in Use of Pandora Archive. International Internet Preservation Consortium, `http://bit.ly/11jtwi2`, 2012.

[22] K. S. Reddy, G. P. S. Varma, and I. R. Babu. Preprocessing the web server logs: an illustrative approach for effective usage mining. *ACM SIGSOFT Software Engineering Notes*, 37(3):1–5, May 2012.

[23] D. S. Sisodia and S. Verma. Web usage pattern analysis through web logs: A review. In *Proceedings of 9th International Conference on Computer Science and Software Engineering*, JCSSE, pages 49–53, May 2012.

[24] M. Spiliopoulou, B. Mobasher, B. Berendt, and M. Nakagawa. A Framework for the Evaluation of Session Reconstruction Heuristics in Web-Usage Analysis. *INFORMS Journal on Computing*, 15(2):171–190, Apr. 2003.

[25] J. Srivastava, R. Cooley, M. Deshpande, and P.-N. Tan. Web usage mining: discovery and applications of usage patterns from Web data. *ACM SIGKDD Explorations Newsletter*, 1(2):12, Jan. 2000.

[26] A. Stassopoulou and M. D. Dikaiakos. Web robot detection: A probabilistic reasoning approach. *Computer Networks*, 53(3):265–278, Feb. 2009.

[27] P.-N. Tan and V. Kumar. Discovery of Web Robot Sessions Based on their Navigational Patterns. *Data Mining and Knowledge Discovery*, 6(1):9–35, Jan. 2002.

[28] D. Tanasa and B. Trousse. Advanced data preprocessing for intersites Web usage mining. *IEEE Intelligent Systems*, 19(2):59–65, Mar. 2004.

[29] C. Teddlie and F. Yu. Mixed Methods Sampling: A Typology With Examples. *Journal of Mixed Methods Research*, 1(1):77–100, Jan. 2007.

[30] B. Tofel. Wayback for Accessing Web Archives. In *Proceedings of International Web Archiving Workshop*, IWAW, 2007.

[31] M. Tsagkias and R. Blanco. Language intent models for inferring user browsing behavior. In *Proceedings of the 35th international ACM SIGIR conference on Research and development in information retrieval*, SIGIR '12, pages 335–344. ACM, 2012.

[32] H. Van de Sompel, M. L. Nelson, and R. Sanderson. HTTP framework for time-based access to resource states – Memento. `https://datatracker.ietf.org/doc/draft-vandesompel-memento/`, 2012.

[33] H. Van de Sompel, M. L. Nelson, R. Sanderson, L. L. Balakireva, S. Ainsworth, and H. Shankar. Memento: Time Travel for the Web. Technical Report arXiv:0911.1112, 2009.

Free Benchmark Corpora for Preservation Experiments: Using Model-Driven Engineering to Generate Data Sets

Christoph Becker
Vienna University of Technology
Vienna, Austria
www.ifs.tuwien.ac.at/~becker

Kresimir Duretec
Vienna University of Technology
Vienna, Austria
www.ifs.tuwien.ac.at/~duretec

ABSTRACT

Digital preservation is an active area of research, and recent years have brought forward an increasing number of characterisation tools for the object-level analysis of digital content. However, there is a profound lack of objective, standardised and comparable metrics and benchmark collections to enable experimentation and validation of these tools. While fields such as Information Retrieval have for decades been able to rely on benchmark collections annotated with ground truth to enable systematic improvement of algorithms and systems along objective metrics, the digital preservation field is yet unable to provide the necessary ground truth for such benchmarks. Objective indicators, however, are the key enabler for quantitative experimentation and innovation.

This paper presents a systematic model-driven benchmark generation framework that aims to provide realistic approximations of real-world digital information collections with fully known ground truth that enables systematic quantitative experimentation, measurement and improvement against objective indicators. We describe the key motivation and idea behind the framework, outline the technological building blocks, and discuss results of the generation of page-based and hierarchical documents from a ground truth model. Based on a discussion of the benefits and challenges of the approach, we outline future work.

Categories and Subject Descriptors

H.3 [**Information Storage and Retrieval**]: H.3.7 Digital Libraries

Keywords

Repositories; Digital Preservation; Characterisation; Benchmark; Data Set; Ground Truth; Corpora; Model Driven Engineering

JCDL'13, July 22-26, 2013, Indianapolis, Indiana, USA.
Copyright 2013 ACM 978-1-4503-2077-1/13/07 ...$15.00.

General Terms

Algorithms, Experimentation, Measurement, Performance

1. INTRODUCTION

The field of Digital Preservation is concerned with keeping digital information authentic, understandable, and usable, through time and across changing socio-technological environments to achieve digital longevity [19]. Essentially, the fundamental problem addressed is a misalignment of technology: To render information usable to any human, an algorithm needs to produce an interpretation that can be perceived by the human. Digital preservation (DP) is in this sense often seen as a case of interoperability through time. Taking a Shannon communication channel [22] as a metaphor, the core problem is that transmission is asynchronous and may last an indefinite time. At the time of receiving the message, the recipient may not possess an appropriate decoder, the sender may not exist anymore, and the recipient may not be the original addressee. The communication channel thus will often need to convert the message so that the original message intention is preserved. Theoretically, any type converter function carrying out such a transcoding should respect the type of the original message [31]. However, the complexity and change rate of common environments and information representations today have the effect that this is rarely the case.

From its origin in the areas of cultural heritage and eScience, DP has emerged as a key challenge for information systems in almost any domain from eCommerce and eGovernment to manufacturing, finance, health, and private lifestyle. However, the field of DP is approaching a phase in which several key areas of research are hitting a glass ceiling. This applies in particular to the time-intensive area of object- and collection level analysis of existing content, which is an active area of research and development [6, 7, 10, 13, 25, 26, 27].

Authenticity as key requirement for digital preservation requires the converter to prove that the type conversion was respectful. Alternatively, the communication environment needs to provide an appropriate decoder at the time of rendering the message to the receiver. Similar verification is necessary to assure the authentic message is communicated successfully. Unfortunately, current verification methods are often insufficient for this purpose, independent on whether the primary action taken is object migration or environment emulation [2, 5, 13].

There is a profound lack of objective, standardised and comparable metrics and benchmark collections for experimentation. While fields such as Information Retrieval have for decades been able to rely on benchmark collections annotated with ground truth to enable systematic improvement of algorithms and systems along objective metrics, DP is yet unable to provide the necessary ground truth for such benchmarks. These alone, however, are the key enabler for systematic quantitative experimentation, measurement and improvement against objective indicators.

The current approach to creating benchmarking collections relies on an ex-post analysis of existing content collections with existing tools. However, they produce interpretations with unknown reliability, since prior to exposure to such a computational interpretation, the properties of any digital object are entirely unknown.

This causes a fundamental problem: There is no ground truth that can be used safely to evaluate approaches and system parameters on a large scale [2]. This 'black box phenomenon' differentiates the design problem from scenarios with known ground truth, where key experiment parameters can be explored systematically in large-scale experiments.

In this article, we present a novel approach to the problem of benchmark data sets in preservation. Our hypothesis is that we can turn around the approach towards the construction of such a benchmark from previous ex-post analysis of real-world data to a theory-based, fundamentally model-driven and statistically solid generative approach. To this end, we outline a conceptual framework that combines in-depth statistical profiling of real-world collections with a generative approach based on model-driven engineering. We demonstrate the feasibility of the approach on the example domain of page-based documents. We present results that demonstrate the feasibility of successfully generating of data with fully-known ground truth, and discuss future steps of research and development.

The article is structured as follows. The next section will outline the state of art in characterisation for digital preservation and summarise the challenges that the field is currently facing. Section 3 motivates and outlines the framework of our approach. Section 4 provides a discussion of the technology stack in use and presents the results that can be obtained using the current early prototype of the dataset generation framework. Section 5 summarises and evaluates the key contributions and outlines next steps ahead.

2. CHARACTERISATION AND BENCHMARKING IN DP

Given how central the notion of data format has been to much of DP research and development, it is not surprising that characterisation has received much attention. A distinction is generally made between *identification* of the format of an object, *validation* of the conformance of the object to the format specification, and *feature extraction* of the object's properties, which is sometimes just called *characterisation*.

The National Archives' DROID tool and siblings such as fido[1], but also the well-known Unix command *file* are typical examples of tools for identification, while tools such as the eXtensible Characterisation Languages XCL [25] and the JSTOR/Harvard Object Validation Environment JHove[2] are probably the most widely cited examples for feature extraction. The File Information Tool Set (FITS)[3] wraps several other tools and combines their output. Following up on the widely used JHove, the JHove2 framework promises to be much improved [1]. However, the improvements are described as "performance improvements and significant new features, most notably, a flexible rules-based assessment capability" [1], and it is unclear whether objective indicators for functionality and functional correctness are used.

While it is clear to the community that in practice, better tools are needed[4], there is much less clarity as to how the quality of these tools is to be tested systematically.

Recent reports from Australia and Europe describe attempts to systematic experimentation. The SCAPE project[5] evaluated the performance and stability aspects of identification tools, touching briefly on aspects such as accuracy and format coverage, using a private data set and manual testing of tools [27]. Aiming at larger scales, the project then ran a number of identification tools against the publicly available Govdocs1 corpus[6]. The 'ground truth' used to evaluate identification accuracy was generated by a forensics tool provided by Forensic Innovations[7] [26]. However, the veridicality of this ground truth is unclear, and the experiment was restricted to identification only.

Others have explored large-scale analysis and aggregation of tool results, as well as visualisation. Tarrant [24] presented a platform for experiment data publication including some visualisation; Jackson discusses longitudinal analysis of format identification results from the UK web [12], and Petrov demonstrated large-scale aggregation of in-depth characterisation results [17]. However, no objective, trustworthy validation of functional correctness of any of the underlying characterisation tools has been published. Hutchins [10] did include feature extraction in their testing process, but did not attempt to systematically verify the correctness of extracted features. Where indications are found that the results may be incorrect, the conclusion is to not recommend usage of the tool in question.

Arguably, the *functional correctness* of such tools is their most important, crucial quality [3]. It refers to the "degree to which a product or system provides the correct results with the needed degree of precision" [11]. Achieving functional correctness within certain time and resource constraint is a key development challenge, and only by providing solid evidence can we assure full trust in the accuracy of tools. However, little solid evidence exists that describes the functional correctness of any of these tools with objective indicators.

In order to make this critical quality attribute measurable, we need to define meaningful metrics that can be compared objectively, i.e. external measures with unambiguously specified semantics. Consider a set of objects $O = \{o_1, o_2, ...o_n\}$ and a set of properties $P = \{p_1, p_2, ...p_m\}$. This might simply be a set of images and the property set $\{imageWidth, imageHeight, RGBpixelArray, creatingApplication\}$, to use an oversimplified example. The task of feature extraction involves computing the values of each property for each object, which may involve complex transformations. We can

[1] https://github.com/openplanets/fido
[2] http://jhove.sourceforge.net/
[3] http://code.google.com/p/fits/
[4] http://www.openplanetsfoundation.org/blogs/2012-10-19-practitioners-have-spoken-we-need-better-characterisation
[5] http://http://scape-project.eu/
[6] http://digitalcorpora.org/corpora/files
[7] http://www.forensicinnovations.com/

express the metrics for measuring correctness directly as the well-known metrics of precision and recall, where

- *Precision* is the fraction of measures obtained that are relevant and within a certain error margin, and
- *Recall* is the fraction of requested measures that are obtained correctly, i.e. within a certain error margin.

Note that we are not concerned with the relevance of each property, which is a contextual decision to be made by the curator, depending on the goals and intents of an organisation [30, 3]. Hence, this specific retrieval problem is independent of the much disputed relevance question asking in which context these properties are deemed significant (cf. [4],[30], and others) and of the applicability of precision and recall to other real-world Information Retrieval problems.

The need for testbed corpora has been a subject of discussion for years [15]. It is clear that annotated benchmark data are needed to support the objective comparison of new approaches and quantify the improvements over existing techniques. However, publicly available data sets are devoid of useful annotations to validate feature extraction, and only limited information is available to provide solid verification for identification. A combination of barriers still prevent the community from actually having these building blocks:

- There are legal constraints on sharing existing data.
- It is technically challenging to develop robust benchmark data.
- There are economic resource constraints on data collection, annotation, sharing, and developing systematic and coherent approaches.
- There is no central reference point or body to coordinate such benchmarking

The technical challenge in this case lies in the well-known, but often forgotten duality of data and computation: In contrast to analog artifacts, any digital artifact is per se a black box, inaccessible to any user. Instead, a computing environment will parse the file, convert it to an internally transformed model and initiate a performance that enables a consumer to conceptualise the *object* (or not, if the performance is inadequate for this goal) [9]. The fundamental issue is one of representation, model equivalency, and interaction: How can information properties be assured across changing environments? Projects such as SCAPE are developing Quality Assurance tools to compare renderings in different environments to produce quantitative measures of equivalence. However, these developments do not address the fundamental obstacle that opposes any such endeavour: The lack of a ground truth that can be used for objective, quantitative evaluation. However, such benchmarking is the irreplaceable milestone that alone enables quantitative improvement and baseline comparison.

Generating ground truth semi-manually is very effort intensive even for tasks such as document image understanding, where the rendering is assumed to be perfect [23]. In areas such as document analysis and recognition, small-scale datasets exist that are created and annotated semi-manually [29, 28]. For page segmentation, a system has been presented that generates images and the corresponding ground truth automatically [8].

To be useful for validating characterisation processes, however, we would need an annotation that maps the conceptual content of objects to their symbol structures used for encoding the digital artifact. This is computationally complex and almost impossible for human experts even for simple file formats. Consequently, it has not been attempted for the problem at hand. However, Hartle demonstrated the principal feasibility of representing the information content of files, and the projection of the content onto the encoded symbol structures, in formal models that enable formal reasoning [6, 7]. This could be combined beneficially with approaches such as the typed object model proposed earlier [31].

How have been comparable problems addressed in other disciplines?

The problem of quality-assuring products in industrial production uses an exact specification, calibrated measurement routines and devices, and approved model products that new products are compared with. In astronomy, a common problem is presented by turbulences in the atmosphere that distort light and thus blur the picture received on our planet's surface. To address this, adaptive optics use a reference light source to objectively measure distortions generated by the atmosphere and correct these distortions using a deformable mirror. Using a real star as a light source has severe limitations on the scope of applying the technique, since the ground truth is essentially unknown. Instead, a reference light source is generated, e.g. by a laser illuminating sodium gas in the mesosphere in about 15-25km height. By comparing the obtained distorted result with the known ground truth of the actual light source, the distortion function can be calculated. Using this reference source to correct atmospheric distortions yields astonishing improvements [18].

In information theory, Shannon introduced approximations of English language with the goal of creating a message source that has the same statistical properties, on various orders of approximation, as a message from a "real" source [22]. He thus created a model capable of producing messages that correspond closely enough to "real" messages so that the communication problem essentially becomes equivalent to transmitting "real" messages. Corresponding to this, what is ultimately necessary is a mathematical model of digital objects that is capable of producing objects that correspond closely to "actual" objects, closely enough so that the problem of "understanding" (accessing, preserving) them becomes essentially equivalent to understanding, accessing and preserving "actual" objects.

In current information management and preservation, however, the approach so far has been to apply algorithmic extraction in the form of static analysis on real-world objects with essentially unknown characteristics. This creates a circular dependency, since the algorithms have not been verified in large-scale experiments on real content. Moreover, the few systematic experimentation initiatives that try to establish a baseline of measures are not publicly available, since the content they are based on cannot be shared by the respective organisations [15].

The fundamental problem is one of angle: We need to approach the analysis of digital content from a different side and construct baseline benchmarks with known ground truth from bottom-up. This can then be complemented by a perceptual validation from the user side that is correlated to objectively obtained measures.

Instead of characterising objects taken from real collections, the solid bootstrapping approach presented in this article relies on generating test data from a fact base, from

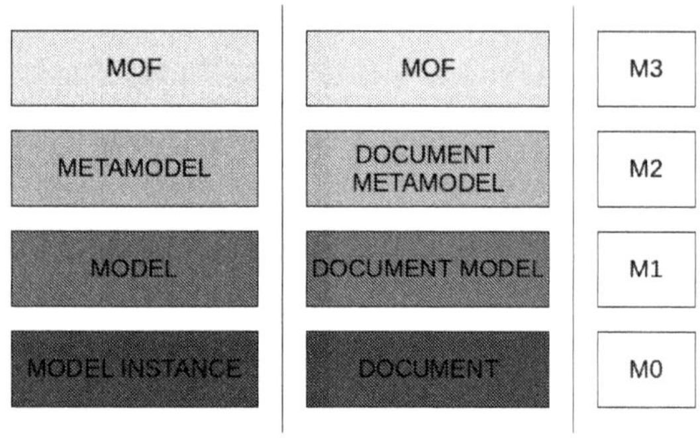

Figure 1: Meta-Object Facility layers

a content model with specified properties. This is supported by a novel application of model-driven engineering. To this end, the next section will introduce the basic background of model-driven engineering and how it can be applied to the design problem at hand.

3. MODEL-DRIVEN BENCHMARK DATA SETS GENERATION

Model driven engineering (MDE) addresses software complexity by shifting the focus of the engineer from algorithmic computing aspects to abstract representations of the knowledge and activities in relevant domains [21]. To this end, a *model* describes the level of reality which is needed for a certain purpose. This work uses model-driven engineering in a novel way where it adapts its methods and concepts so the final result is not an executable software product, but a test artefact.

3.1 Model Driven Engineering

The history of MDE starts with Computer Aided Software Engineering (CASE) but has evolved rapidly over the years. A leading approach in MDE is Model Driven Architecture (MDA)[8]. The key goals of MDA are to increase portability, interoperability and reusability through architectural separation of concerns, achieved by introducing three types of models: (1) The *Computation Independent Model (CIM)* focuses on the conceptual perspective of a system's requirements in a certain context. (2) The *Platform Independent Model (PIM)* focuses on the analytical specification perspective and describes the system and its operation independent of a specific target platform. (3) The *Platform Specific Model (PSM)*, finally, focuses on the design and operation of a system specific to a particular platform.

The main value proposition lies in an increased ability to re-generate platform-specific artefacts based on the platform-independent model that can be managed and evolved.

MDA is based on standards such as UML and the Meta-Object Facility (MOF). MOF defines a 4-layer architecture for building metamodels and supporting core capabilities for model management, shown in Figure 1. The top level M3 provides support for defining metamodels at level M2. A *metamodel* is an abstraction of a domain in which concepts, relations among concepts and constraints that apply to those concepts and relations are defined. By creating a *metamodel*, a user defines a modelling language for building *models* which are defined at level M1. A prominent example of the relation between metamodels and models is UML, whose metamodel is specified in MOF. Once a model is defined, a running instance can be created on level 0. MOF provides a standardized platform for working with metamodels and models. Through *model transformations*, automatic translations of models based on one metamodel to another model based on the same or a different metamodel are enabled. A *model transformation* is a set of mappings which translate one model into another. In MDA, this enables an automatic translation from PIM to PSM.

This work relies on concepts defined by MDA and the 4-layer architecture defined by MOF. The right side of Figure 1 shows how the layered architecture is used in the case of generating documents. A key difference to mainstream MDA in this case is that the artefacts to be created are not necessarily software components and systems that should be maintained over time, but digital artefacts such as documents, images, databases and web pages. The intermediate artifacts used to create them can include software code, but the focus is not on improving interoperability and reusability *of that code*, but instead on gaining fine-grained control over the generation process of information objects to generate test data. In this case, the test data should ideally correspond closely enough to "actual" objects so that the problem of preserving it becomes essentially equivalent to preserving "actual" objects. This is of course an approximation problem, and it will be difficult to prove the exact degree of approximation, just as it was with English language [22].

[8]`http://www.omg.org/mda/`

3.2 Conceptual framework

Figure 2 shows the main high-level framework of this work. There are four main aspects: Analysis of real-world content, generation of fully annotated data sets that approximate real content, systematic automated evaluation, and open publication of the annotated data sets, artifacts, and experiment results.

Large-scale real-world content profiles of massive data collections are used to populate feature distribution models and domain-level as well as technical statistics and thus control the distribution of features and introduce fine-grained control over the feature space desired. This will be described in Section 3.3.

The resulting feature distributions inform the creation of PIMs for representing information objects in an application-independent way. These can be automatically varied and diversified using predefined vocabulary elements in model mutation processes. Model transformation can project such model instances onto the space of platform-specific model representations (PSMs), from which specific artefacts can be generated. Section 3.4 presents examples of model transformations towards generating content.

Automated evaluation and the question of experimentation and measurement is discussed in Section 3.5. Section 4 will provide concrete example models and generated artefacts.

A key feature of this framework is the possibility to re-generate different representations of the same original information model with additional platforms when they become available, and to compare the direct transformation with representations created by conversion processes. This addresses some of the critical problems noted in the discussions of quality assurance [13].

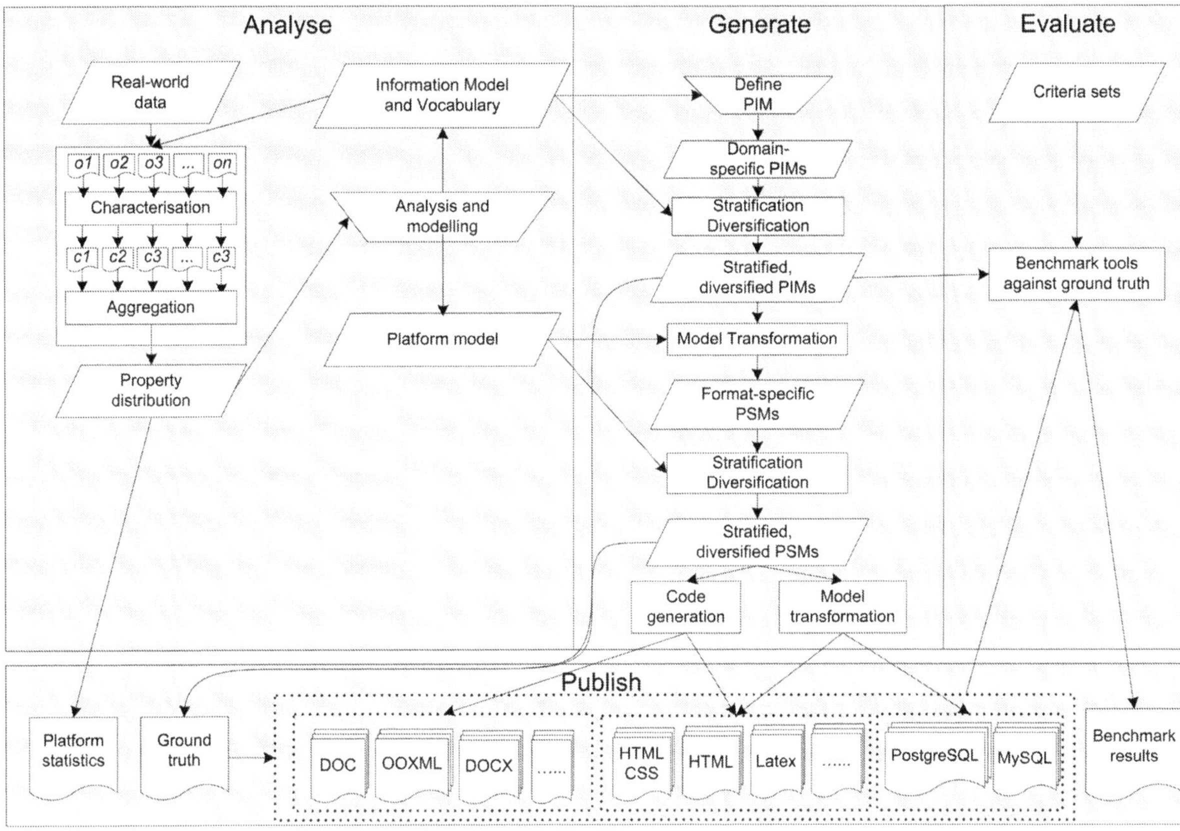

Figure 2: Model-driven benchmark generation framework

3.3 Analyse

The step of large-scale analysis is supported by the content profiling system c3po[9], first presented in [17]. As shown in the left part of Figure 2, digital objects (*o1...on*) are first characterised, producing technical and descriptive metadata (*c1...cn*, each of which consists of a set of measures). These are then aggregated into a content profile, which can be analysed systematically.

The system analyses and aggregates the technical metadata generated by FITS on a scale-out map-reduce based platform (MongoDB)[10] with currently about 100.000 objects per minute per node. It supports multiple heuristics for selecting representative sample objects. This means it can be feasibly employed on a cluster to analyse very large collections. It is currently being tested on analysing almost half a billion web resources harvested over a ten year period[11] in a single profile.

Aggregated statistics can be produced on any of the (potentially sparse) measures collected. Figure 3 shows exemplary property distributions for the number of documents with varying page counts (top) and the log-scaled number of web pages for occurrence frequencies of the `<table>` tag.

It is beyond the scope of this paper to discuss the features themselves in detail. The key observation, however, is that we can measure aggregate statistical feature distributions on the content level (such as page counts) as well as on the technical level (such as tags and combinations of tags frequently used on web pages), and hence model the aggregate target distribution appropriately. The hypothesis is that the complex interplay of such features is what leads to issues of understanding, rendering and hence preservation. Varying these feature sets in a controlled way, combined with automated testing, should hence be a powerful tool for systematic assessment and improvement.

[9] `http://http://ifs.tuwien.ac.at/imp/c3po`

[10] `http://www.mongodb.org/`

[11] `http://www.openplanetsfoundation.org/blogs/2013-01-09-year-fits`

3.4 Generate: Models and transformations

3.4.1 Platform Independent Models

The starting point of generating annotated sets of content artefacts lies with a domain-specific PIM. This will typically correspond to a class such as *page-based documents* or *vector shapes*. Such PIMs are currently defined manually, but could in the future be derived from genre models. While the discussion here focuses on the coverage of the current prototype, it is worth noting that any content type can in principle be modelled. To give but one example, audio can be generated through MIDI representations and sound generation.

A crucial question is the platform-independent representation of features that occur across different environments. Consider a grid structure of elements found on a page, such as items in a typical bill sent via email to an eCommerce customer. This grid structure can be represented in a platform-independent model, but in any specific instance, it can be represented by a number of different constructs – a Word table, an Excel table embedded in a Word document as an

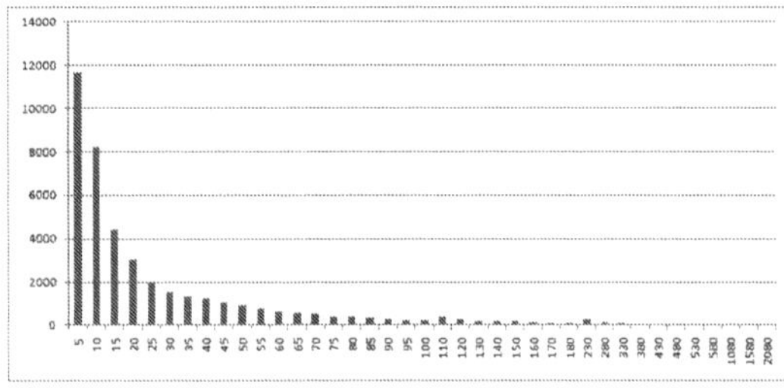

(a) Page count distribution on 45.000 PDF documents

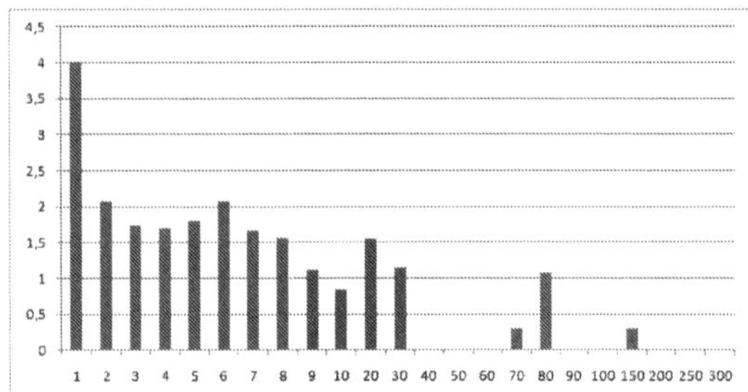

(b) Log-scaled <table> tag occurrence in 82.000 web pages

Figure 3: Sample property distributions

OLE object (with or without formulas to calculate sums), tabbed text elements directly included in Word, a picture generated by an e-billing application, an HTML table construct, or an HTML/CSS construct for creating table structures, to name a few.

Within each of these feature spaces, there are a number of ways that elements can be grouped differently to achieve the same overall result. For example, the width of columns in a grid can be determined in a number of different ways such as percentage, automated layout, and fixed width settings. Real-world grids vary in dimensions such as size that are largely (but not fully) representation-invariant. They also exhibit representation-specific variation across the feature space of the continuously evolving platforms that are used to create and transmit them.

The independent representation can be projected onto specific instantiations using different symbol structures that cause the same *performance* to be created. This can be fine-tuned to represent the variety that is encountered in real-world collections, but it can also be tuned to represent boundary conditions for testing the behaviour of analysis and rendering environments.

3.4.2 Metamodels and transformation steps

The idea behind the Platform Independent Meta-Model is to model building blocks and their relationships without a concern about platform specific implementation features. Figure 4 shows part of a platform independent metamodel for web pages. The model can contain several *Document* elements, each of which consists of zero or more *AbstractElements*. Apart from *ContainerElements*, the diagram shows three types of concrete *ContentElements*: *Media*, *Text*, and a *Grid*. A *Text* is described as a composition of *SequenceOfCharacters*, including simple formatting options. A *Grid* element contains an array of *Cells* with coordinates. On the right side, media elements include images and video. While

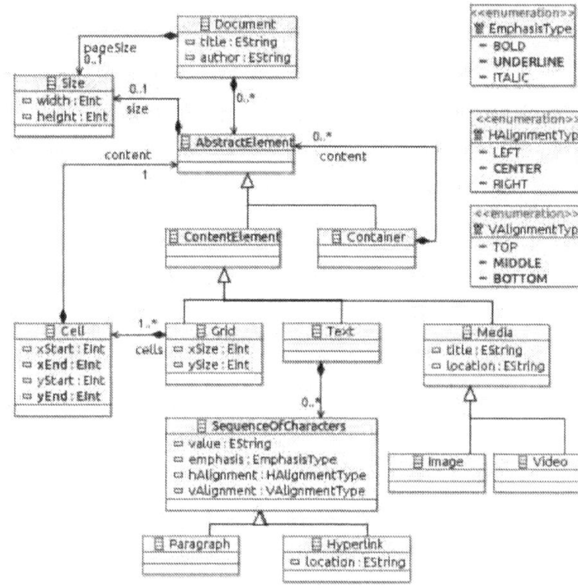

Figure 4: PIM metamodel for web documents

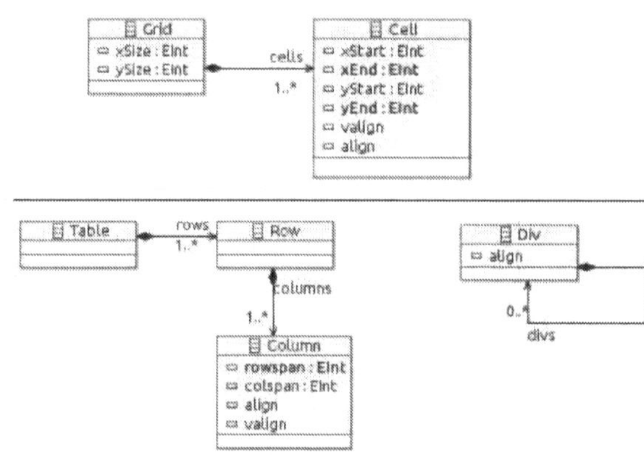

Figure 5: Multiple PSM variants of `Grid`

this simple model will hardly suffice to approximate real-world content, it serves to demonstrate the projection from PIM to platform-specific representations.

Figure 5 shows a fragment of Figure 4 above and two corresponding PSM fragments below. In this example of the *Grid*, possible representations include the html construct `<table>` and a set of `<div>` tags with appropriate hierarchical groupings. Both of these representations occur in real web pages with varying probability, and each needs to be decoded and rendered appropriately by a viewing application such as a browser.

Further model transformation and code generation elements allow the construction of born-digital information objects created directly within their native environments. Generation of content from the platform-specific models can employ two principal means: For certain well-defined content types, objects can directly be created from the PSM. This requires a descriptive specification of the projection which can be formally expressed and verified. For content types with more particular variety, where the semantics are often shared between the objects and the creation environment, code generation will be employed that automates the native environments to create the objects directly within these environments. For example, Office automation languages can be used to control applications such as Microsoft Word® in writing, formatting, and exporting page-based and web documents in much the same way that human editors do. This effectively creates a simulation of a typical content production and editing process, and it allows the framework to include code that observes the state of the application at the time of creating the artefact and documents it to create additional traceability between the representations.

3.4.3 Diversificatio

Diversification processes can be used to create multiple instances with controlled variation of properties on both the intellectual domain and the technical implementation level. An example of the first level is diversifying platform independent features like number of tables or images in the document. The second level focuses on platform specific features like representing a table in a Word document as a normal Word table or an embedded Excel table. This diversification is informed by the statistics obtained from real-world data analysis.

3.4.4 Ground truth annotation

At each level of transformation, a set of properties can be documented to feed into the ground truth specification. While the ground truth of the PIM can connect models such as the one shown in Figure 4 to significant property specifications defined by domain experts [2], the PSM-specific documentation should also include the description of the features used to represent the PIM elements. Finally, if active code is used to automate content creation environments, this code can actively observe the state *inside* the application to document the original performance of creating the document. Similar concepts apply with other content types and environments.

3.5 Evaluate

Experimentation and automated measures have been a topic of intense research and development in DP. To evaluate precision and recall of characterisation tools, we need to define the property sets that describe the measures to be taken. This can be derived from decision criteria collected in preservation planning [2]. Current work is developing an ontology to represent these criteria and enable characterisation tools to declare which properties they measure[12]. This enables direct integration through experimentation platforms such as the experimentation environment *Taverna*[13] and the workflow sharing platforms *myExperiment*[14].

To evaluate the data set generation process itself on a technical level, the expressiveness of the model-driven benchmark generation approach can be quantified with respect to relevant properties and features of specific content types as described in [2]. The coverage of these significant features of various content types can be calculated in a straightforward way. Similarly, the coverage of the content generation framework in terms of recreating the diversity of large-scale real-world content profiles can be assessed and quantified.

[12]`http://purl.org/DP/quality/measures`

[13]`http://taverna.org.uk/`

[14]`http://myexperiment.org/`

```
mapping PIM::Cell :: Cell2Cell() : PIM::Cell
{var horizontalAlignmentAsString :=
  GetValueFromDistribution("HorizontalAligmentTableCell",
        GetCellScenario(self)).repr();
 switch
 {
  case(horizontalAlignmentAsString = "Left") {
        horizontalAlignment := HorizontalAlignment::Left };
  case(horizontalAlignmentAsString = "Center") {
        horizontalAlignment := HorizontalAlignment::Center };
  case(horizontalAlignmentAsString = "Right") {
        horizontalAlignment := HorizontalAlignment::Right };
 };
  content += self.content.CellContent2CellContent();
}   ...
```

Figure 6: Example projection using QVT

4. RESULTS AND DISCUSSION

4.1 Proof-of-concept domains and platforms

In order to evaluate the proposed approach, we have developed several proof-of-concept workflows for generating documents and databases. We will focus the discussion on two document-oriented experiments: One generated page-based documents and uses Macro-code generation and a runtime Office® environment to create Word files, while the other relies on XML and XSLT technologies to produce a variety of web pages. The purpose of the experiments was to validate the feasibility of the proposed framework, evaluate the applicability of different modelling and transformation technologies to the dataset generation problem, and analyse in more depth the challenges and key questions arising in the model transformation workflow.

4.1.1 Page-based documents

The creation of page-based documents relied on the Eclipse Modelling Framework (EMF)[15]. Transformation from PIM to PSM as well as diversification to a given property distribution is implemented using the standard Query/View/-Transformation [16]. Figure 6 shows a QVT fragment which diversifies the *alignment* property of a cell in a grid structure according to a stochastic property distribution similar to the one shown in Figure 3.

We used the statically typed template language Xpand[16] for generating VisualBasic macro code. The resulting macros were executed in Office 2007 and 2003. The features covered include tables, embedded OLE documents, embedded images, standard layout and fonts features, as well as page breaks, headers and footers. Figure 7 shows a code fragment from a generated artefact that creates a document, writes *Hello world*, and adds an embedded Excel sheet with a few cells containing numbers. The bottom lines of code query the state of the original application at the time of generating the artefact.

4.1.2 Hierarchical documents: web pages

For the creation of hierarchical documents, XML technologies were chosen for reasons of simplicity. An XML schema was defined for the PIM, and a set of transformation rules covered transformations to HTML 3.2, HTML 4.02, HTML 4 + CSS, and HTML 5. Features covered included tables, hyperlinks, sizes and alignment, font properties, colors, but also codecs and plugins. While this approach only relies on the availability of an XSLT processor, it does not directly

[15]`http://www.eclipse.org/emf/`

[16]`http://wiki.eclipse.org/Xpand`

```
Function Out_9_Word07(outputPath As String) As String()
    Documents.Add Template:="Normal", NewTemplate:=False,
        DocumentType:=0
    ...
                Selection.Font.Size = 16.0
                Selection.TypeText Text:="Hello"
                Selection.Font.Size = 9.0
                Selection.TypeText Text:="World"
        Selection.InlineShapes.AddOLEObject
                ClassType:="Excel.Sheet.12",
                LinkToFile:=False, DisplayAsIcon:=False
        Dim xlApp As Object
        Set xlApp = GetObject(, "Excel.Application")
        With xlApp.Application
          .Cells(1, 1).Select
          .ActiveCell.Font.Size = 10.0
          .ActiveCell.FormulaR1C1 = "Foo"
          .Cells(1, 2).Select
          .ActiveCell.Font.Size = 20.0
          .ActiveCell.FormulaR1C1 = "Bar"
          .ActiveCell.HorizontalAlignment = xlRight
        End With
        Set xlApp = Nothing
                Selection.Font.Size = 15.0
                Selection.TypeText Text:="Goodbye."
...
        ActiveDocument.Repaginate
        numberOfPages = ActiveDocument.
          BuiltInDocumentProperties(wdPropertyPages)
        numberOfWords = ActiveDocument.Range.
          ComputeStatistics(wdStatisticWords)
        numberOfCharacters = ActiveDocument.Range.
          ComputeStatistics(wdStatisticCharacters)
...
```

Figure 7: Generated macro code fragment

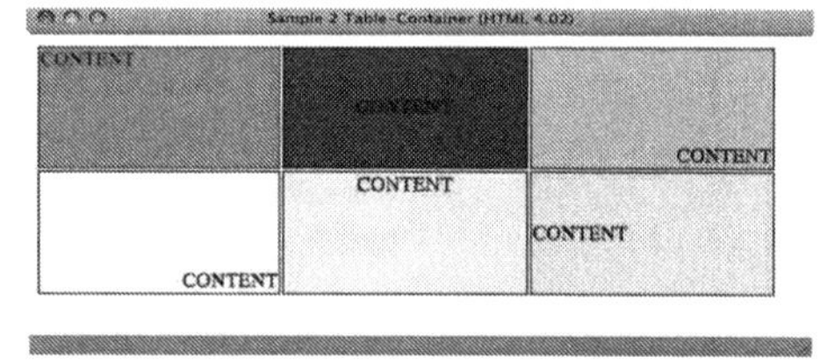

(a) Grid represented using `<table>`

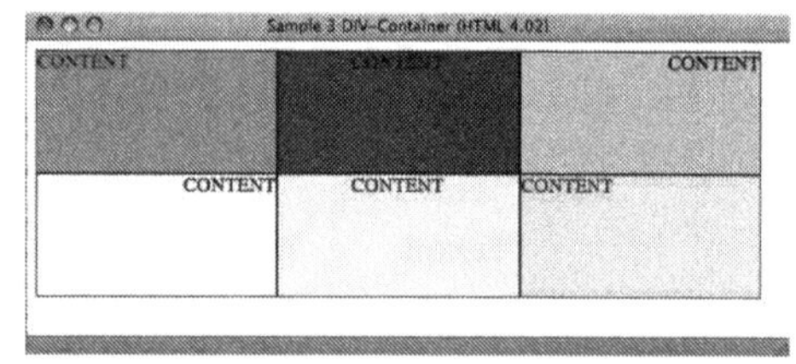

(b) Grid represented using `<div>`

Figure 8: Partial mapping of PIM features in a PSM

support the expressive model transformation and code generation features delivered by EMF.

As an alternative test that relied directly on a visual inspection of test results, we rendered the generated set of documents automatically using the cloud service *browsershots*[17]. This creates a visual snapshot of the artefacts using an entire array of environment configurations. Figure 8 shows an example of the above-mentioned *Grid* structure, projected to different HTML representations and rendered in a browser. The visual shows that the vertical alignment (a feature of the PIM) is not present in the rendering that uses `<div>` tags. The reason is that `<div>` tags cannot represent the vertical alignment feature, which leads to a partial mapping from PIM to PSM. This also points to a limitation of the simple XML/XSLT approach, which does not directly provide the sophisticated model verification facilities of EMF. However, the approach facilitated fast comparison of multiple renderings across browsers and has low technical requirements.

4.2 Discussion

While the scope of this paper prevents an in-depth discussion of the feature sets, technical intricacies of mappings, and detailed discussion of model transformation, it becomes clear that the basic approach of generating annotated test data is viable and enables the fine-grained control of test data. Combining this with large-scale data analysis creates a powerful framework to support the experimental evaluation of characterisation tools. This implies a number of clear benefits.

- **Open datasets.** All of the data sets generated by this framework can be freely published and redistributed without requiring careful verification of copyright, as is often the case with collected data [14].
- **Re-generation of content models across content platforms** is readily supported, which provides for a powerful extension mechanism to cover additional technology platforms and feature sets and can enable customized data set generation.
- **Full annotation of data sets with detailed ground truth.** The degree of detail that is provided as annotation with the data set can be fine-tuned to the degree desired. It should in all cases comprise the key attributes of PIM and PSM. In the case of automating a content creation environment to simulate a real creation process, even the actual state of the application can be observed and documented.
- **Extensible, reusable framework.** All structured knowledge produced in activities is passed on in fully specified models. All these models passed between activities can eventually be entry points interfacing with external systems.
- **Standard metrics** can be applied in a straightforward way to quantify the quality of tools, similar to established fields such as Information Retrieval. This can be a powerful market mechanism for both research and innovative practice, as can be seen on public competitions in IR such as TREC[18] [20].

Hence, the approach enables quantitative experimentation as a key instrument for scientific rigor and practical improvement in digital preservation. Baseline benchmark data sets will be created and used to validate existing methods and tools for content analysis against decision criteria sets in digital preservation. The results discussed above demonstrate the technical feasibility of the approach. However, before these benefits can be realised, several obstacles of the technical kind have to be overcome:

- The notion of *platform* as describing a technical platform such as *Mirosoft Word 2007* falls short of capturing the complex features that can be freely combined and mixed, even within a single (composite) object. Instead, we need to view the platform level as describing a *feature set.* This increases the complexity of the workflow generation.
- Much richer models will be required to achieve real-world approximation of documents, appeal to practi-

[17] `http://browsershots.org/`

[18] `http://trec.nist.gov/`

tioners, and demonstrate that boundary conditions of automated tools can be explored in a realistic, but controlled way.

- An experimentation platform for measures, including an ontology for metrics, is needed to systematically publish datasets and experiment results. This can build on existing Linked Data platforms such as LDS3 [24].

While the initial statistical analysis is relying on characterisation tools itself, it only relies on aggregate-level statistics, not individual object-level precision. Even if the errors are not evenly distributed and hence the distribution of features in fact incorrectly reported with a systemic bias, this does only affect the approximation accuracy of the feature distribution, not the precision of individually created items. Furthermore, as soon as these items are created, the systemic bias can be discovered and corrected. It is only through such a bootstrapping approach that the 'black box conundrum' can be tackled.

5. CONCLUSION AND OUTLOOK

It is clear that the DP field direly misses proper frameworks for benchmarking of the key information processing components, most importantly content characterisation. Going back to the dictionary, we find "*1: usually bench mark: a mark on a permanent object indicating elevation and serving as a reference in topographic surveys and tidal observations. 2 a: a point of reference from which measurements may be made. b: something that serves as a standard by which others may be measured or judged. c: a standardized problem or test that serves as a basis for evaluation or comparison (as of computer system performance)*"[19]. Key building blocks for benchmarking hence need to include

- A clear, unambiguous understanding of the processes that we want to measure,
- a clear set of attributes and indicators for taking measures,
- a well-defined value system for judging and assessing measures,
- solid hypotheses that can be tested and falsified,
- public, openly available data sets that can be shared and referenced,
- ground truth that annotates these data sets with useful and trusted measures corresponding to the attributes above, where trusted at least means that we know how reliable they are (something which is almost entirely absent in the data sets currently available), and
- a means for publication of benchmark results and all of the above elements.

This article discussed the state of art in such benchmarks in Digital Preservation and showed that a new approach is needed to successfully move research and development on content analysis and characterisation to a systematic, fundamentally solid approach. We outlined a conceptual framework for generating test data sets using Model Driven Engineering and demonstrated the technical feasibility of the approach.

[19]`http://www.merriam-webster.com/dictionary/benchmark`

Possessing a benchmark suite for information objects opens up new lines of R&D in digital preservation. It also enables commercial vendors, which have been reluctant to provide components specifically for digital preservation purposes, to leverage Return on Investment as a quantified benefit of improvement over existing solutions, something which currently is profoundly absent in digital preservation and which presents a fundamental inhibitor for innovation. As such, it can spur investment into specific products. Moreover, it will enable research to be much more focussed on essential key performance indicators. The principles of the framework can be extended easily for different content types. Quantitative experimentation will enable a deep understanding of the causal relationships of loss of authenticity, degrading, and digital decay. By empirically analysing which feature sets have which effects in which processes, we can enable simulation of digital decay over time. At the same time, establishing objective, quantitative performance indicators such as Precision and Recall for Digital Preservation will enable us to integrate on a systematic basis hitherto separated and isolated subdisciplines such as Information Retrieval and Digital Preservation.

One limitation that needs to be further explored is the question of malformed object artefacts. To investigate the behaviour of characterisation tools on objects that are *outside* of the technical specifications, i.e. the format constraints, we require data sets of objects that are carefully designed, and thoroughly annotated, to violate specific constraints and produce specific expected behaviour. These would represent meaningful test data sets that can be used to benchmark the robustness of existing preservation tools and processes and uncover the causes of typical errors. While this can in principle be supported by model-driven generation, it requires a model of these errors to be explicitly represented and addressed. This has not yet been attempted.

The medium-term objective is to showcase the generation of realistic approximations of common real-world information objects for at least page-based documents, web pages and databases, where the variation and combination of features can be controlled on a fine-grained basis and full ground truth is documented with the benchmark data. The expected benefits can be validated on a number of levels, starting with the achieved distribution of significant features over generated collections and the amount of errors in preservation processes that can be uncovered using the resulting benchmarks. Finally, we will use the benchmark collection to create baseline benchmark assessments of characterisation tools such as JHOVE2 and those delivered by projects such as SCAPE to measure precision and recall of relevant features for different formats. The generated benchmark data sets and their associated ground truth will be published with a royalty-free license, alongside evaluation results of tools common in the DP community.

The next steps correspondingly are the setup of a platform for experimentation and benchmark data set publication; the creation of large-scale platform statistics and longitudinal analysis based on 400 million web archive objects [20]; implementation of in-depth diversification and feature distributions; and the systematic testing of the functional correctness of commonly used tools.

[20]`http://www.openplanetsfoundation.org/blogs/2013-01-09-year-fits`

Acknowledgements

Part of this work was supported by the Vienna Science and Technology Fund (WWTF) through the project *BenchmarkDP* (ICT12-046), and by the European Union in the 7th Framework Program, IST, through the *SCAPE* project, Contract 270137. The authors wish to thank Harald Mezensky, Clemens Sauerwein and Florian Stäuble for carrying out some of the work that led to this article.

6. REFERENCES

[1] S. Abrams, S. Morrissey, and T. Cramer. 'What? So What?' The Next-Generation JHOVE2 Architecture for Format-Aware Characterization. In *Proc. IPRES*, 2008.

[2] C. Becker and A. Rauber. Decision criteria in digital preservation: What to measure and how. *JASIST*, 62(6):1009–1028, June 2011.

[3] C. Becker and A. Rauber. Preservation decisions: Terms and Conditions Apply. Challenges, Misperceptions and Lessons Learned in Preservation Planning. In *Proc. JCDL 2011*, June 2011.

[4] A. Dappert and A. Farquhar. Significance is in the eye of the. stakeholder. In M. Agosti, J. Borbinha, S. Kapidakis, C. Papatheodorou, and G. Tsakonas, editors, *Proc. ECDL*, volume 5714 of *LNCS*, pages 39–50. Springer, September 2009.

[5] M. Guttenbrunner and A. Rauber. A measurement framework for evaluating emulators for digital preservation. *ACM Transactions on Information Systems (TOIS)*, 30(2), 3 2012.

[6] M. Hartle, A. Botchak, D. Schumann, and M. Mühlhäuser. A Logic-based Approach to the Formal Description of Data Formats. In *Proc. IPRES*, pages 292–299, London, United Kingdom, September 2008. The British Library.

[7] M. Hartle, F.-D. Möller, S. Travar, B. Kröger, and M. Mühlhäuser. Using Bitstream Segment Graphs for Complete Data Format Instance Description. In *Proc. ICSOFT*, pages 198–205, Porto, Portugal, 2008.

[8] P. Heroux, E. Barbu, S. Adam, and E. Trupin. Automatic ground-truth generation for document image analysis and understanding. In *Proc. ICDAR*, ICDAR '07, pages 476–480, Washington, DC, USA, 2007. IEEE Computer Society.

[9] H. Heslop, S. Davis, and A. Wilson. An approach to the preservation of digital records. Green paper, National Archives of Australia, 2002.

[10] M. Hutchins. Testing software tools of potential interest for digital preservation activities at the national library of australia. Technical report, National Library of Australia, 2012.

[11] ISO/IEC. *Systems and software engineering – Systems and software Quality Requirements and Evaluation (SQuaRE) – System and software quality models (ISO/IEC 25010)*. International Standards Organisation, 2011.

[12] A. N. Jackson. Formats over time: Exploring UK web history. In *Proc. IPRES*, 2012.

[13] N. Milic-Frayling. Digital object characterization: Document conversion and quality assurance. In *Automation in Digital Preservation: Dagstuhl Seminar Proceedings 10291*, Germany, 2010. `http://drops.dagstuhl.de/opus/volltexte/2010/2901`.

[14] R. Neumayer, C. Becker, T. Lidy, A. Rauber, E. Nicchiarelli, M. Thaller, M. Day, H. Hofman, and S. Ross. Development of an open testbed digital object corpus. DELOS Digital Preservation Cluster, Task 6.9, March 2007.

[15] R. Neumayer, H. Kulovits, M. Thaller, E. Nicchiarelli, M. Day, H. Hofmann, and S. Ross. On the need for benchmark corpora in digital preservation. In *Proc. of the 2nd DELOS Conference on Digital Libraries*, 2007.

[16] Object Management Group. Meta Object Facility (MOF) 2.0 Query/View/Transformation Specification, 2008. `http://www.omg.org/spec/QVT/1.0/PDF`.

[17] P. Petrov and C. Becker. Large-scale content profiling for preservation analysis. In *Proc. IPRES*, 2012.

[18] F. Roddier. *Adaptive Optics in Astronomy*. Cambridge University Press, 1999.

[19] J. Rothenberg. Ensuring the longevity of digital documents. *Scientific American*, 272, 1995.

[20] B. R. Rowe, D. W. Wood, A. N. Link, and D. A. Simoni. Economic Impact Assessment of NIST's Text REtrieval Conference (TREC) Program. RTI International, July 2010.

[21] D. Schmidt. Model-driven engineering. *IEEE Computer*, 39(2):25, 2006.

[22] C. Shannon. A mathematical theory of communication. *The Bell System Technical Journal*, 27:379–423 and and 623–656, July and October 1948.

[23] T. Strecker, J. v. Beusekom, S. Albayrak, and T. M. Breuel. Automated ground truth data generation for newspaper document images. In *Proc. ICDAR*, ICDAR '09, pages 1275–1279, Washington, DC, USA, 2009. IEEE Computer Society.

[24] D. Tarrant and L. Carr. LDS3: Applying digital preservation principals to linked data systems. In *Proc. IPRES*, 2012.

[25] M. Thaller, editor. *The eXtensible Characterisation Languages – XCL*. Verlag Dr Kovac, 2009.

[26] The SCAPE project. D9.1 characterisation technology, release 1 and release report. Technical report, SCAPE, 2012.

[27] The SCAPE project. Evaluation of characterisation tools. Technical report, SCAPE, 2012.

[28] D. Tkaczyk, A. Czeczko, K. Rusek, L. Bolikowski, and R. Bogacewicz. Grotoap: ground truth for open access publications. In *Proc. JCDL*, JCDL '12, pages 381–382, New York, NY, USA, 2012. ACM.

[29] L. Todoran, M. Worring, and M. Smeulders. The uva color document dataset. *Int. J. Doc. Anal. Recognit.*, 7(4):228–240, Sept. 2005.

[30] C. Webb, D. Pearson, and P. Koerbin. 'Oh, you wanted us to preserve that?!' Statements of Preservation Intent for the National Library of Australia's Digital Collections. *D-Lib Magazine*, 19(1/2), January/February 2013.

[31] J. M. Wing and J. Ockerbloom. Respectful type converters. *IEEE TSE*, 26(7):579–593, 2000.

A Scalable, Distributed and Dynamic Workflow System for Digitization Processes

Hendrik Schöneberg
Dept. of Computer Science
University of Würzburg, Germany
schoeneberg@informatik.uni-wuerzburg.de

Dr. Hans-Günter Schmidt
Department of Manuscripts and Early Printed Collections
University Library of Würzburg, Germany
hans-guenter.schmidt@bibliothek.uni-wuerzburg.de

Winfried Höhn
Dept. of Computer Science
University of Würzburg, Germany
winfried.hoehn@informatik.uni-wuerzburg.de

ABSTRACT

Creating digital representations of ancient manuscripts, prints and maps is a challenging task due to the sources' fragile and heterogeneous natures. Digitization requires a very specialized set of scanning hardware in order to cover the sources' diversity. The central task is obtaining the maximum reproduction quality while minimizing the error rate, which is difficult to achieve due to the large amounts of image data resulting from digitization, putting huge computational loads on image processing modules, error-detection and information retrieval heuristics.

As digital copies initially do not contain any information about their sources' semantics, additional efforts have to be made to extract semantic metadata. This is an error-prone, time-consuming manual process, which calls for automated mechanisms to support the user.

This paper introduces a decentralized, event-driven workflow system designed to overcome the above mentioned challenges. It leverages dynamic routing between workflow components, thus being able to quickly adapt to the sources' unique requirements. It provides a scalable approach to soften out high computational loads on single units by using distributed computing and provides modules for automated image pre- / post-processing, error-detection heuristics, data mining, semantic analysis, metadata augmentation, quality assurance and an export functionality to established publishing platforms or long-term storage facilites.

Categories and Subject Descriptors

H.4.1 [**Information Systems Applications**]: Office Automation—*workflow management*; H.3.7 [**Information Storage and Retrieval**]: Digital Libraries—*collection, dissemination, standards*; H.3.1 [**Information Storage and Retrieval**]: Context Analysis and Indexing—*linguistic processing*; H.3.4 [**Information Storage and Retrieval**]: Systems and Software—*distributed systems*; D.1.3 [**Programming Techniques**]: Concurrent Programming—*distributed programming, parallel programming*

JCDL'13, July 22–26, 2013, Indianapolis, Indiana, USA.

Keywords

Akka; data mining; digitization; digital library; distributed; dynamic computing; event-driven design; fault-tolerance; information retrieval; metadata extraction; workflow

1. INTRODUCTION

Digitization projects have massively grown in scale within the last years and are of central interest to libraries, archives and initiatives like Google Books[1], which seek to make documents accessible to a wide audience. As of today around 40 established departments for digitization exist in Germany, globally the numbers might go up to a few thousands.

Due to complex requirements regarding digitization quality, metadata extraction and compliance to established publishing standards, the usage of workflow-supporting software becomes mandatory for digitization centers when exceeding a certain production volume.

The digitization center of the University Library of Würzburg specializes in creating and publishing high-quality reproductions of ancient manuscripts, prints and maps. As the digitization process usually solely generates image data, a source's semantics and structural metadata is left uncovered. Obviously though this information is of high value, as it is a key requirement to enable search engines to link to a document, provide related articles, cross-reference to other sources, etc. Especially in ancient documents retrieving the semantics and structural metadata is a tedious and error-prone manual task. While many automated information-retrieval approaches exist for well-defined, well-conserved documents, the ancient sources' syntactically loosely defined language and (often poor) conservation state pose special challenges that need to be overcome. A digitization process does therefore not end with the production of a source's digital representation, it should cover the retrieval of semantics and metadata as well, which calls for a specialized workflow-system.

[1] http://books.google.de/

1.1 Related Work

There already are a few workflow systems for digitization processes: *Goobi*[2], for instance, is a platform-independent workflow-system, which is split into self-contained modules, each being responsible for a different aspect of the digitization workflow. Goobi concentrates on the production part of the digitization process by providing a project management tool, that aides with task-scheduling and resource management. Our presented workflow-system on the other hand goes beyond pure project-management and provides means to obtain the highest possible reproduction quality by leveraging a wide array of automated analysis and information retrieval modules (compare Section 2). Another example workflow tool for digitization projects is ZEND[3]. While it too supports a manual augmentation of project-related metadata with several specialized modules, it lacks the multitude of the information retrieval modules, which are part of our semi-supervised feedback-cycle (see Figure 1) and go great lengths to provide the user with automatically extracted metadata. Generally said, many workflow systems (*Itemright+*[4], *LIMB*[5]) focus on the project management subtask and provide little or no means to support the user with automated error detection and metadata augmentation, which our product aims to do.

2. WORKFLOW

The workflow system leverages a message-routing framework to create dynamic workflow paths, ensuring a loose coupling of the application's integral parts while focusing on modularity and extensibility. The following sections illustrate this concept.

2.1 Concept

The workflow-system is entirely written in Java and comprises a client- and a server-application. The client is deployed via Java WebStart[6], which makes it easily accessible for a wide range of devices. Client and Server communicate in a solely event-driven, asynchronous fashion. Events are passed using a simple text-message format, which complies to the *JMS*[7] standard. Apache Camel[8], a framework which supports most of the *Enterprise Integration Patterns*[9] (EIPs), is then used to abstract from the message layer and create complex, dynamic message routing between different parts of the application. This architecture guarantees application responsiveness, stability and a loose coupling of all integral parts.

Central to a digitization project's completion is that it successfully passes a semi-supervised analysis feedback loop. Automated quality assurance modules, error heuristics and information retrieval modules analyze the image data and present the result to a supervisor. Once all quality requirements are met, a project can be deployed to long term storage. From this point users may edit existing or add new metadata with specialized instruments like a metadata editor. The workflow system features a template-based export engine, which allows an export of scans and their metadata to well-established container-formats for digital libraries, e.g. *TEI: P5*[10] or *METS / MODS*[11] and online publication platforms like *Libri Sancti Kiliani*[12]. Figure 1 demonstrates the basic idea behind a project's lifecycle.

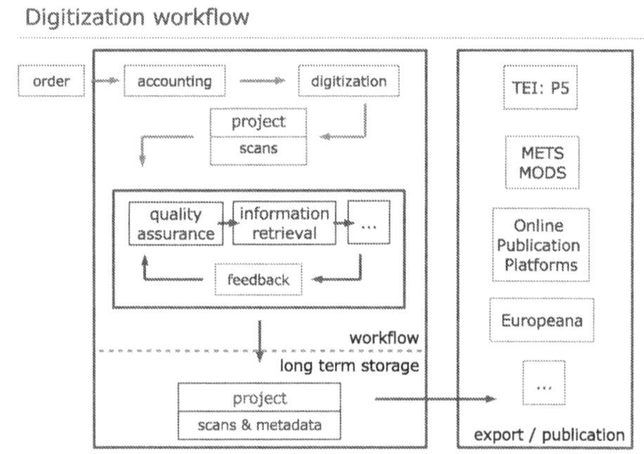

Figure 1: Digitization project workflow including supervised feedback-cycle.

2.2 Dynamic Workflow Pathways

Depending on the document, the imaging hardware and the designated application of its digitized copy the workflow comprises different pre- and post-processing steps. The workflow system features a variety of analysis modules, capable of checking the digitization project for errors, extracting / augmenting information or processing the image data (see Chapter 3). Each module is a valid endpoint for the message-based communication within the workflow, which essentially allows us to create dynamic processing chains involving a specific subset of analysis modules routes on-the-fly (compare *EIP: Pipes and Filters*[13]). With this method a source's unique processing requirements can be met dynamically. Figure 2 shows an exemplary analysis- and export-process within the workflow system.

3. AUTOMATED ANALYSIS MODULES

Some noteworthy image processing and information retrieval modules will be introduced in the subsequent paragraphs.

3.1 Quality Assurance and Image Processing Modules

A digitized image has to pass several automated quality assurance modules before being presented to a supervisor. There are modules checking for **slanted** images, **erroneous image margins** or even **blurry pictures**. Figure 3 illustrates how the analysis module uses the *Sobel operator* to

[2]http://www.goobi.org/
[3]http://www.digitale-sammlungen.de/index.html?-c=digitalisierung-zend&l=en
[4]http://www.academicimaging.com/specs/itemright-plus.html
[5]http://www.i2s-digibook.com
[6]http://docs.oracle.com/javase/6/docs/technotes/guides-/javaws/
[7]http://www.jcp.org/en/jsr/detail?id=914
[8]http://camel.apache.org/
[9]http://www.eaipatterns.com/eaipatterns.html
[10]http://www.tei-c.org/release/doc/tei-p5-doc/en/html/
[11]http://www.loc.gov/standards/mets
[12]http://www.libri-kiliani.eu
[13]http://www.eaipatterns.com/PipesAndFilters.html

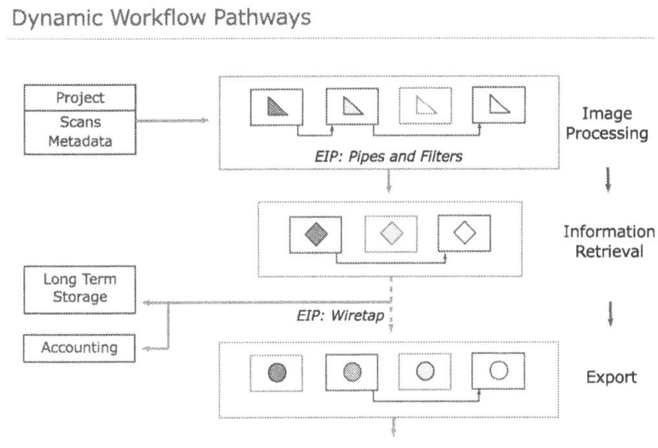

Figure 2: The workflow chain is determined by the source's unique requirements.

detect blurry parts within an image. If an image fails to pass an analysis, it will be marked accordingly and presented to the supervisor. All this happens according to the analysis-feedback-cycle as described in Figure 1. Unless all issues are resolved, a digitization project cannot advance. Post-processing modules can for instance create web-optimized images for the presentation in online publication platforms.

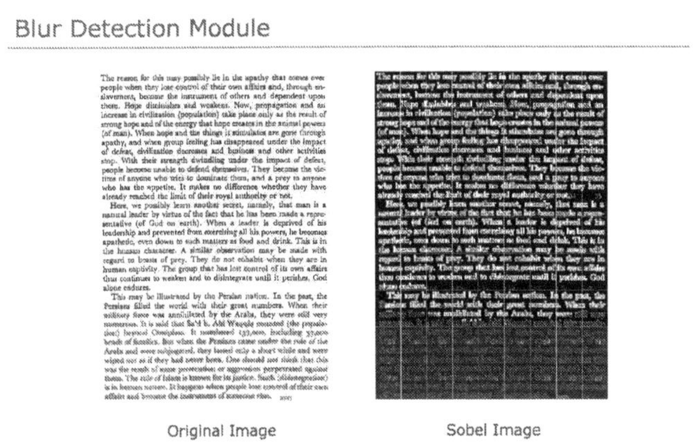

Figure 3: Automated check for blurred images.

3.2 Information Retrieval Modules

As the workflow-software specializes in the digitization of ancient documents, information retrieval analysis modules will have to face the challenges that occur with this class of documents.

3.2.1 Contextual Classification of Terms

In ancient documents orthography was not nearly as restrictively defined as today, resulting in many valid spelling variants for terms. Many ancient documents tend to have a poor conservation state, which of course adds to the complexity of the problem, as damaged regions within the document can only be reconstructed heuristically (if at all). For further information see [2]. The above mentioned points result in a syntactically challenging environment with small, brittle domains in which information retrieval modules have to operate. In order to compensate for those problems, statistical evaluation and domain-specific knowledge can be applied. In [3] and [2] this approach is addressed and evaluated. Within the workflow system a contextual classification module can overcome the source's challenging syntax and extract or augment metadata by identifying terms like **places**, **persons** or **dates**. Those terms are of high interest, as they can be cross-referenced to other documents and are valuable targets for search-engine queries.

3.2.2 Semantic Analysis of Early Maps

Early maps are a rich source of information for historic research: You can derive the linguistic development of place-names or see places appear, disappear or merge with each other over time. Moreover you can extract geo-spatial relations between places from the information encoded within a map's markers for villages, towns or monasteries. For this type of research it is mandatory to know a map's extent and which places are contained within. It is also a prerequisite to be able to retrieve metadata about a place from multiple maps. Therefore the workflow contains a module which supports the user in semi-automated annotation of all places within a map. The module supports finding places and identifying the meaning of the used place marker through template matching. Additional support is given to identify a corresponding modern place for a historic place. Annotations for the actual used historic place name and a free text comment are furthermore available. These annotations enable a search for information contained in a map and linking between multiple maps and annotated places in books (see Section 3.2.1) and maps.

3.2.3 Table of Content Extraction

Another noteable information retrieval module allows the automated extraction of table of contents (ToC) from digitized documents. It operates on a textual representation of the document (either provided by the user or obtained via Optical Character Recognition approaches). The algorithm uses domain-specific heuristics and statistic evaluation to overcome the challenges mentioned in Section 3.2.1.
The generated ToC can then be used to provide an intuitive navigation within the newly digitized source. Many examples of navigable documents digitized by the digitization center of the University Library of Würzburg can be found at *Franconica-Online*[14].

3.3 Export Modules

The workflow system features a template-based export- and publishing-engine, enabling exports to long-term storage facilities, as well as an extensible list of well-established container-formats (TEI: P5, METS/MODS, ...) for digital documents and collections, which simplifies exchange with other digital libraries. Furthermore exports to online presentation platforms are supported, allowing a wide audience easy access to the digitized document with few clicks. See *Libri Sancti Kiliani*[15] for many examples of published digitization projects.

[14]http://franconica.uni-wuerzburg.de/
[15]http://libri-kiliani.eu

4. DISTRIBUTED COMPUTING

The server part of the workflow-system does all the heavy lifting when it comes to image processing and information retrieval tasks on the digitized projects. Depending on the source and digitalization conditions the size of single images can exceed 0.5 gigabytes within a project of several hundreds of images. Processing these large amounts of data creates a huge computational load on the server application. In order to soften out these peak loads, a scalable, distributed, actor-based approach is currently being evaluated (compare [4]).

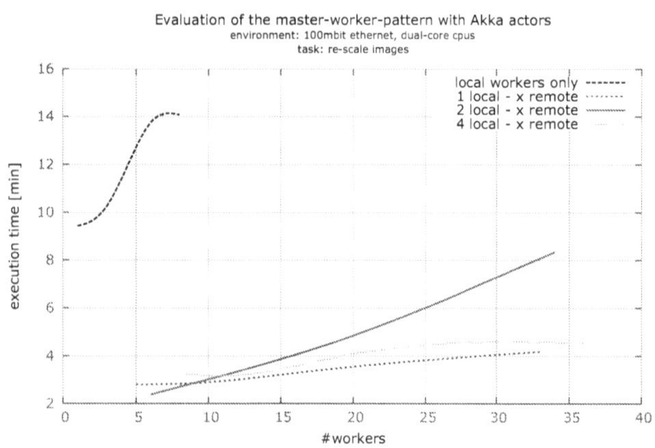

Figure 4: Evaluation of distributed actor configurations.

The core concept behind distributing the server's computational load is using all clients that are currently connected to the server as workers for small computational tasks. This concept was implemented using Akka[16] and the *master-worker-pattern*[17]. A central benefit of Akka and this pattern is, that the occurrence of errors is anticipated and embraced by arranging workers in supervision-hierarchies: If a (remote) worker fails to perform a task, its supervisor can react accordingly by redistributing workloads to another worker, restart the failed worker or report to the tasks initiator. This results in a very robust distributed architecture. For more information compare [1]. Figure 4 shows a large reduction of computation time for a image-rescaling task when adding remote clients as workers.

5. RESULTS

The staff of the digitization center estimates the effect of the workflow system on the production speed to be a speedup of at least factor two. The quality assurance modules greatly reduce the amount of iterations needed to comply to quality requirements. Errors are detected at earlier stages and with higher reliability, saving time and preserving the sensitive documents, as they are less likely to be re-digitized. As the workflow system takes care of moving the digitization project's data, the amount of defensive copies is reduced to a minimum, saving storage space and cleanup-time. Furthermore, manpower requirements are reduced significantly, as many processing steps are performed by the workflow system in an automated manner.

6. CONCLUSIONS

This paper introduced a dynamic workflow system, which stands out from other workflow management tools owing to the (extensible) list of automated image processing and information retrieval modules, which enable the user to recognize flaws in reproduction quality as early as possible and augment the digitization project with metadata. The processing modules can be chained together on-demand, creating dynamic pathways that meet the source's unique requirements. Computational peak loads are distributed among clients that are part of the workflow system, decreasing the time needed for computation and relieving the server, effectively increasing its stability and responsiveness. The workflow system provides means to maintain a digitized project's metadata, publish it to online platforms and export it to storage destinations or interchange container-formats.

7. FUTURE WORK

The presented workflow system offers an extensible lists of analysis modules. One goal for the future is covering more digitization error types with analysis modules and providing a more specialized image pre- and postprocessing. Right now an object-recognition module is under development, which is able to cut the digitized document from the image, removing the background and possibly visible fixtures. The approach of distributing computational loads between remote clients of the workflow system has proven to be very efficient. The most important task for the future is to identify parallelizable computational problems and adapt the existing analysis modules accordingly. Furthermore a strong integration with existing digital libraries, publishing platforms and long-term storage facilities is strived for. The template-based export of digitized projects and their metadata already provides a multitude of export-targets, but modules for several well-established platforms (like World Digital Library[18], Europeana[19], Rosetta[20]) need to be developed.

8. REFERENCES

[1] J. Armstrong and T. Helen. Making reliable distributed systems in the presence of software errors, 2003.

[2] H. Schöneberg. Context vector classification - term classification with context evaluation. In A. L. N. Fred and J. Filipe, editors, *KDIR*, pages 387–391. SciTePress, 2010.

[3] H. Schöneberg and F. Müller. Contextual approaches for identification of toponyms in ancient documents. In A. L. N. Fred, J. Filipe, A. L. N. Fred, and J. Filipe, editors, *KDIR*, pages 163–168. SciTePress, 2012.

[4] E. D. Tiona. Efficency and Fault-Tolerance in Workflows for Early Documents (in German). Master's thesis, University of Würzburg, to appear 2013.

[16] http://akka.io

[17] http://letitcrash.com/post/29044669086/balancing-workload-across-nodes-with-akka-2

[18] http://www.wdl.org/en/

[19] http://www.europeana.eu/

[20] http://www.exlibrisgroup.com/de/category/Rosetta

Domain-specific Image Geocoding: a Case Study on Virginia Tech Building Photos

Lin Tzy Li[1,2], Otávio A. B. Penatti[1], Edward A. Fox[3] and Ricardo da S. Torres[1]
[1]RECOD Lab, Institute of Computing, University of Campinas (UNICAMP), Campinas, SP – Brazil, 13083-852
[2]Telecommunications Res. & Dev. Center, CPqD Foundation, Campinas, SP – Brazil, 13086-902
[3]Digital Library Research Laboratory, Department of Computer Science, Virginia Tech, Blacksburg, VA 24061
{lintzyli, penatti, rtorres}@ic.unicamp.br, fox@vt.edu

ABSTRACT

The use of map-based browser services is of great relevance in numerous digital libraries. The implementation of such services, however, demands the use of geocoded data collections. This paper investigates the use of image content local representations in geocoding tasks. Performed experiments demonstrate that some of the evaluated descriptors yield effective results in the task of geocoding VT building photos. This study is the first step to geocode multimedia material related to the VT April 16, 2007 school shooting tragedy.

Categories and Subject Descriptors

H.3.1 [**Information Storage and Retrieval**]: Content Analysis and Indexing; I.2.10 [**Artificial Intelligence**]: Vision and Scene Understanding

Keywords

geocoding; map-based browsing; content-based video retrieval

1. INTRODUCTION

Since geographic information is involved in people's daily lives, there is a great amount of data about geographical entities on the Web. This information is often found in digital objects (e.g., documents, images, and videos) of several digital libraries. The process of associating a geographic location with photos, videos, and documents is called *geocoding* by the Geographic Information Retrieval (GIR) community, but it is also known as *geotagging* or *georeferencing* [9]. When a digital object is geocoded, it is related to some place on Earth, and therefore it can be browsed on a map. That opens new opportunities for establishing new relations based on geographic location.

In this work, we are interested in geocoding documents about the Virginia Tech (VT) April 16, 2007 school shooting tragedy, where 32 people were murdered before the shooter killed himself. A collection of documents about this event was archived by CTRnet (Crisis, Tragedy and Recovery Network)[1], a digital library network for providing a range of services relating to different kinds of tragic events [3]. The aim of our present work is to support the creation of map-based browsing services based on photo content. The first step towards that is to be able to geocode images. This work describes preliminary experiments related to the evaluation of image descriptors in image geocoding tasks.

2. RELATED WORK

From 1995 to 2004, a project led by the University of California (UC Santa Barbara) called ADEPT - Alexandria Digital Earth ProtoType [4] focused on geocoding digital library objects by taking into account textual metadata.

Geocoding approaches based on visual clues are proposed in the context of landmark recognition, as well as for non-landmark images [9]. Usually, those approaches are modeled as image classification or content-based image retrieval (CBIR) problems. Those approaches often take advantage of a huge collection of geotagged images that is used as a knowledge base [6].

In our previous work [10], we explored a strategy based on global descriptors to tackle the challenge of geocoding videos based only on visual features. In more recent studies [7, 8], we combined visual and textual features for video geocoding.

Previous initiatives, such as [12], perform matching of local descriptors to find similar regions within images of a dataset of buildings. Therefore, although they are not explicitly geocoding images, their approaches could be used for that purpose. The approach presented in [12] works with buildings from the University of Oxford[2]. After describing images with a scheme based on a visual vocabulary (quantized local features), a matching strategy is performed between a given query image and images from the dataset. They compare the performance of different vocabulary sizes, as well as vocabularies generated by different methods. In this work, we employ a similar strategy. Our work aims at evaluating the performance of local image description approaches in the task of geocoding building photos.

3. EXPERIMENT

This section presents experiments aiming at evaluating the effectiveness of visual-dictionary-based descriptors in the task of assigning locations to building photos.

[1]http://www.ctrnet.net/ (as of May 13, 2013).
[2]http://www.robots.ox.ac.uk/~vgg/data/oxbuildings/ (as of May 13, 2013).

3.1 Image collections

We use two datasets in our experiments. One is used as our visual knowledge base and will be referred to as training data. The other is the test data images whose locations will be predicted by the proposed geocoding system.

Training dataset

The training data is a subset of 4,852 photos from VT's University Relations (UniRel) Photo Library. Each photo has some metadata associated, such as keywords, caption describing the scene, date, camera model, and photographer's name. For our purpose, we filtered the photos by the content of keywords and caption fields. As we were interested in the university buildings, we searched for photos whose metadata (keywords or caption) contains building and place names (e.g., Duck Pond). The building/place names list was built up from both the VT site[3] and the campus building database maintained by GIS staff for campus facilities. The resulting training set contains photos of buildings or places with their location. Figure 1a shows the spatial distribution of buildings whose photos are in the training set.

Test dataset

The test dataset[4] contains 565 photos of VT buildings. Most of them were obtained from personal collections while some others were downloaded from the VT Web site[3]. The photos were obtained under different angle and light conditions. The locations of these photos are shown in Figure 1b. Note that the test set covers a smaller area (near to the Drillfield in the campus center) when compared to the training set.

(a) Training set. (b) Test set.

Figure 1: Spatial distribution of photos used as (a) training and (b) test set. Generated using http://www.sethoscope.net/heatmap/ (as of May 2013). Map tiles by Stamen Design, under CC BY 3.0. Data by OpenStreetMap, under CC BY SA.

Ground truth

The ground truth for the images in training and test data sets, that is, the "correct" location for each of them, was inferred from the corresponding building/place name associated with the photo. For the training photos, we used the place/building name that appears in their metadata. For the test photos, we use the name that we manually labeled each photo. The ground truth for these photos is based on the lat/long from the VT site[3], as well as on building names geocoded by Google's geocoding service (via the geopy toolbox[5], a Python wrapper). However, if no matches were found by the geocoding service or if disambiguations were needed, the place/building was manually located and confirmed in the Google Map using its name. Additionally, some photos and some of the resulting geocoding locations were visually and manually inspected to decide their final location and/or coordinates.

3.2 Geocoding Process

The geocoding scheme adopted is based on performing K-nearest neighbor (KNN) searches. In this exploratory study, the location of a test photo is defined based on the geographic coordinates of the most similar image in the training set, i.e., is defined in terms of the location of the 1-nearest neighbor (i.e., $K = 1$) of the test photo. The visual distances between an input test image and all training images are computed. Training images are then ranked in ascending order of their visual distance to the input test image, and the latitude and longitude coordinates of the top-ranked training photo is assigned to the test image.

3.3 Evaluation criteria

The evaluation criterion used here is inspired by the evaluation procedure adopted in the Placing Task at MediaEval [13]. The effectiveness of a method is based on the geographic distance (great-circle distance) of the estimated geo-coordinates of a digital object to its corresponding ground truth location, in a series of widening circles of radius. An estimated point is counted as correct if it is within a particular circle size, that is, a radius value or precision level.

In our case, we are interested in determining as accurately as possible the location for a photo image. Furthermore, our area of interest is restricted to the Virginia Tech campus, so our precision level should be in meters. Taking into account that the two farthest points of the town of Blacksburg (where VT is located) are about 10 km apart, we can accept that two points on the VT campus should not be further apart than 5 km. The precision levels adopted are 1, 50, 100, 150, 200, 250, 300, 350, 400, 450, 500, 550, 600, 650, 700, 750, 800, 850, 900, 950, 1000, 1100, 1200, 1300, 1400, 1500, 1600, 1700, 1800, 1900, 2000, 3000, 4000, and 5000 meters.

3.4 Setup

First, the visual content properties of each provided image are encoded into feature vectors, considering all evaluated descriptors. Then, the visual distances between the photos in the test set and all photos in the training set are computed. Finally, for each test photo, a ranked list of training photos is produced.

To represent each image, we used the bag-of-visual-word model [14]. In that model, after extracting low-level features with local descriptors, we quantize the feature space in order to obtain a visual dictionary (codebook) and then we represent each local description according to the dictionary. For low-level feature extraction, we used: dense SIFT

[3]http://www.vt.edu/about/buildings/ (as of May 13, 2013).

[4]http://www.recod.ic.unicamp.br/VTBuildings/ (as of May 13, 2013)

[5]https://github.com/geopy (as of May 13, 2013).

(6 pixels) [15], sparse SIFT (Harris-Laplace detector) [15], and sparse SURF (Fast-Hessian detector) [1]. We randomly quantized the feature space [17], generating two dictionary sizes: 1,000 and 10,000 visual words.

To compute the bag-of-word representation, we used soft assignment (σ=60 for SIFT and σ=0.08 for SURF) [16] and two pooling methods: max pooling [2] and Word Spatial Arrangement (WSA) [11]. WSA was used only over the sparse SIFT, while max pooling was used for all low-level features. Table 1 lists the evaluated methods.

Table 1: Image representations evaluated.

Acronym	Method
D.SIFT.1k	dense SIFT, 1,000 words, soft assignment (σ=60), max pooling
D.SIFT.10k	dense SIFT, 10,000 words, soft assignment (σ=60), max pooling
S.SIFT.1k	sparse SIFT, 1,000 words, soft assignment (σ=60), max pooling
S.SIFT.10k	sparse SIFT, 10,000 words, soft assignment (σ=60), max pooling
S.SURF.1k	sparse SURF, 1,000 words, soft assignment (σ=0.08), max pooling
S.SURF.10k	sparse SURF, 10,000 words, soft assignment (σ=0.08), max pooling
WSA.1k	sparse SIFT, 1,000 words, soft assignment (σ=60), WSA
WSA.10k	sparse SIFT, 10,000 words, soft assignment (σ=60), WSA

4. RESULTS

Figure 2 presents the geocoding results for evaluated methods, considering different precision levels. Observe that the S.SURF.10k descriptor yields better results starting from the 150 m precision level on, followed by the D.SIFT.1k descriptor. Given that there are neighboring buildings in VT that are apart from each other (measured from their centroid) about 100 to 200 meters, it is reasonable to tolerate a maximum estimation error around 200 m. The S.SURF.10k method geocoded correctly 20% of the photos within 150 m precision radius and almost 80% within 600 m. For the precision level of 1 m, WSA.10k geocoded more images.

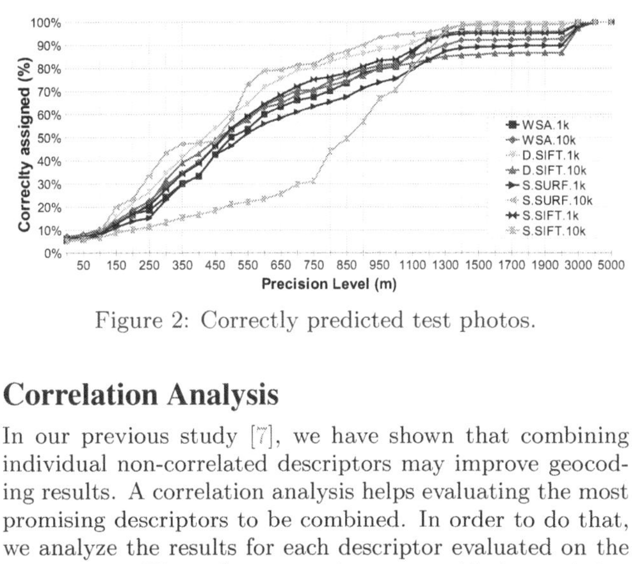

Figure 2: Correctly predicted test photos.

Correlation Analysis

In our previous study [7], we have shown that combining individual non-correlated descriptors may improve geocoding results. A correlation analysis helps evaluating the most promising descriptors to be combined. In order to do that, we analyze the results for each descriptor evaluated on the training set. We perform experiments considering each image of the training set as a query photo. In this case, given that the query photo always is the best match to itself (thus it will be the first in this list), we use the second photo of available ranked lists to define the final location.

Figure 3 shows the correlation graph (*corrgrams* R package) for the results of the training set. In this case, for each method and query image, its geocoding result is the geographic distances between a predicted point and its ground truth. Thus, we studied the correlation of these results for the evaluated methods.

This kind of plot is presented in [5] and shows the correlation values for each pair of methods as a square matrix. A darker color indicates higher correlation value. In the lower triangle, the correlation values are encoded by the intensity of the cell color. In the upper triangle, the same values are represented by the painted area in the circles and its color intensity. The diagonal of this matrix holds the name of the descriptor corresponding to each row and column. In this case, the lowest correlations are between S.SIFT.1k and the others, as shown by the lightest colors in the first column and the smallest painted area in circles in the first line.

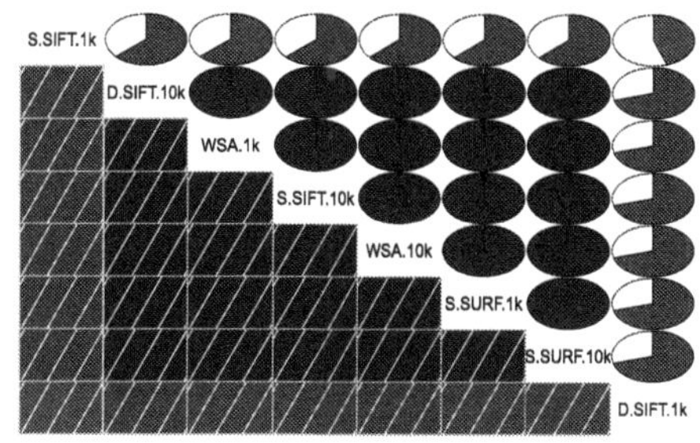

Figure 3: Correlation among evaluated descriptors.

Figure 4 shows the geocoding results of evaluated descriptors on the training set. We can observe that WSA.10k and S.SIFT.1k yield the best performance, followed by WSA.1k and D.SIFT.10k. On the other hand, S.SIFT.1k is less correlated with other descriptors (see Figure 3), which suggests that its combination with other descriptors may improve the geocoding results.

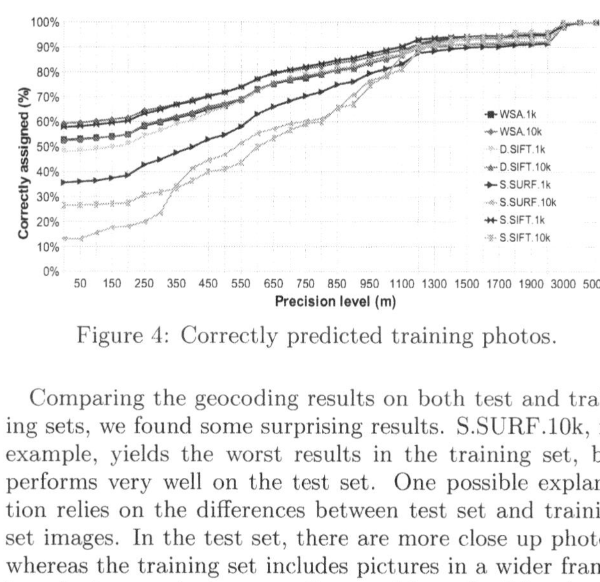

Figure 4: Correctly predicted training photos.

Comparing the geocoding results on both test and training sets, we found some surprising results. S.SURF.10k, for example, yields the worst results in the training set, but performs very well on the test set. One possible explanation relies on the differences between test set and training set images. In the test set, there are more close up photos, whereas the training set includes pictures in a wider frame, i.e., the images depict more distant objects (buildings).

Examples of geocoding results

Table 2 shows two examples of query photos of the test set and its corresponding top-similar images in the training set for each visual descriptor. Each table cell also presents the geographic distance between the top-ranked training image and the query photo's ground truth.

Consider, for example, the top-ranked image in the case of query P1080710 (picture of Torgersen Bridge). The S.SURF

Table 2: The best visual match for each query image and its geocoding result. Values below the photo thumbnail refer to the geographic distance (in meters) to the ground-truth location of the query image.

Query	Building Name	D.SIFT.1k	D.SIFT.10k	S.SIFT.1k	S.SIFT.10k	S.SURF.1k	S.SURF.10k	WSA.1k	WSA.10k
 P1080012	Lane Hall	 424.08	 86.87	 349.62	 161.13	 217.67	 1231.06	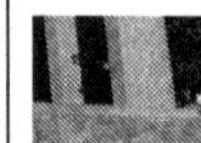 238.44	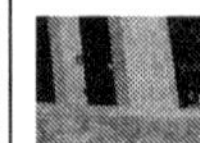 238.44
 P1080710	Torgersen Bridge	 906.41	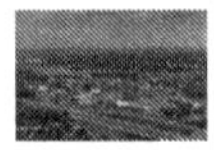 2801.90	 74.33	 1070.43	 0.00	 0.00	 275.15	 74.33

(1k and 10k) descriptor is able to match it to a photo that only pictures a detail of that building, whereas WSA.10k and S.SIFT.1k match that to a photo from the same building but under a different light (darker) condition. However, as this photo was labeled as Torgersen Hall instead of Torgersen Bridge, its geographic distance was not zero. The query P1080012 (Lane Hall) shows an example where S.SURF.10k performed very badly. D.SIFT.10k, in turn, matched it to a photo of a building (Shanks Hall) that is close (86.87 m) to the Lane Hall, while S.SIFT.10k found the query similar to a picture of Torgersen Bridge (161.13 m from there) at night. In summary, each descriptor provides different, but potentially complementary information that could be combined to improve geocoding results.

5. CONCLUSIONS

This paper presented an evaluation of several image content local descriptors in the context of geocoding building photos. Our objective is to determine appropriate image content description approaches to be used to geocode images related to the Virginia Tech April 16, 2007 school shooting tragedy. Geocoded photos can be used later in the construction of map-based browsing services in the context of the CTRnet (Crisis, Tragedy and Recovery Network) project. Performed experiments show that some of the evaluated descriptors (e.g., S.SURF.10k, WSA.10k, D.SIFT.1k) yield effective results in geocoding tasks. Future work will focus on the use of data fusion techniques to combine non-correlated descriptors. We also plan to consider available textual descriptions in geocoding tasks and new geocoding schemes.

Acknowledgements

The authors are grateful to CAPES, FAPESP (grant number 2009/10554-8), and CNPq, as well as the CPqD Foundation for their support. We also thank VT University Relations for providing access to some of the photographs used in this work. Additionally, we would like to thank the Center for Geospatial Information Technology (CGIT) and the GIS Manager for VT campus facilities for providing access to the campus building database. Finally, we thank the National Science Foundation (IIS-0916733) for supporting our 'Crisis, Tragedy and Recovery Network' research[1].

6. REFERENCES

[1] H. Bay, T. Tuytelaars, and L. Van Gool. Surf: Speeded up robust features. In *ECCV*, pages 404–417, 2006.

[2] Y.-L. Boureau, F. Bach, Y. LeCun, and J. Ponce. Learning mid-level features for recognition. In *CVPR*, pages 2559–2566, 2010.

[3] E. A. Fox, C. Andrews, W. Fan, J. Jiao, A. Kassahun, S. C. Lu, Y. Ma, C. North, N. Ramakrishnan, A. Scarpa, and Others. A Digital Library for Recovery, Research, and Learning From April 16, 2007, at Virginia Tech. *Traumatology*, 14(1), 2008.

[4] M. Freeston. The Alexandria Digital Library and the Alexandria Digital Earth Prototype. In *JCDL*, page 410, 2004.

[5] M. Friendly. Corrgrams: Exploratory displays for correlation matrices. *The American Statistician*, 56(4):316–324, 2002.

[6] J. Hays and A. A. Efros. IM2GPS: estimating geographic information from a single image. In *CVPR*, 2008.

[7] L. T. Li, J. Almeida, D. C. G. Pedronette, O. A. B. Penatti, and R. da Silva Torres. A multimodal approach for video geocoding. In *Working Notes Proc. MediaEval Workshop*. CEUR-WS.org, 2012.

[8] L. T. Li, D. C. G. Pedronette, J. Almeida, O. A. B. Penatti, R. T. Calumby, and R. da Silva Torres. Multimedia Multimodal Geocoding. In *ACM SIGSPATIAL GIS*, pages 474–477, 2012.

[9] J. Luo, D. Joshi, J. Yu, and A. Gallagher. Geotagging in multimedia and computer vision–a survey. *MTA*, 51:187–211, 2011.

[10] O. A. B. Penatti, L. T. Li, J. Almeida, and R. da S. Torres. A Visual Approach for Video Geocoding using Bag-of-Scenes. In *ACM ICMR*, 2012.

[11] O. A. B. Penatti, E. Valle, and R. da S. Torres. Encoding spatial arrangement of visual words. In *CIARP*, volume 7042, pages 240–247, 2011.

[12] J. Philbin, O. Chum, M. Isard, J. Sivic, and A. Zisserman. Object retrieval with large vocabularies and fast spatial matching. In *CVPR*, pages 1–8, 2007.

[13] A. Rae and P. Kelm. Working Notes for the Placing Task at MediaEval 2012. In *MediaEval*, 2012.

[14] J. Sivic and A. Zisserman. Video Google: a text retrieval approach to object matching in videos. In *ICCV*, volume 2, pages 1470–1477, 2003.

[15] K. E. A. van de Sande, T. Gevers, and C. G. M. Snoek. Evaluating color descriptors for object and scene recognition. *TPAMI*, 32(9):1582–1596, 2010.

[16] J. C. van Gemert, C. J. Veenman, A. W. M. Smeulders, and J.-M. Geusebroek. Visual word ambiguity. *TPAMI*, 32(7):1271–1283, 2010.

[17] V. Viitaniemi and J. Laaksonen. Experiments on selection of codebooks for local image feature histograms. In *VISUAL*, pages 126–137, 2008.

A Classification Scheme for Algorithm Citation Function in Scholarly Works

Suppawong Tuarob[†], Prasenjit Mitra[†‡] and C. Lee Giles[†‡]
[†] Computer Science and Engineering, [‡] Information Sciences and Technology
The Pennsylvania State University
University Park, PA 16802
suppawong@psu.edu, {pmitra, giles}@ist.psu.edu

ABSTRACT

Algorithms are ubiquitous in the computer science literature. A search engine for algorithms has been tested as part of the Citeseer^X suite; however, it only retrieves algorithms whose metadata is textually matched with the search query. Such a limitation occurs because a traditional search engine does not have the ability to understand what algorithms are and how they work. Here, we present an initial effort in understanding the semantics of algorithms. Specifically, we identify how an existing algorithm can be *used* in scholarly works and propose a classification scheme for algorithm function.

Categories and Subject Descriptors

H.3.3 [**Information Search and Retrieval**]

Keywords

Algorithm Citation, Algorithm Function, Classification

1. INTRODUCTION

An algorithm search engine has been tested as a part of Citeseer^X [1, 7, 6]. However, the search is only a text based matching of user queries to algorithm metadata and the results are ranked based on full text TF-IDF. The limitations of the traditional text-based search emphasizes the need for a more semantic understanding of algorithms in scholarly works, such as knowing how researchers utilize the existing algorithms in their work. For example, Walker et al. [9] ***extended*** the PageRank algorithm [4] to create a CiteRank algorithm which utilizes the characteristics of citation networks to rank academic publications. Tuarob and Tucker [8] ***directly used*** the LDA algorithm [2] to mine product features from tweets.

Here we propose a classification scheme for algorithm citation function in scholarly works. We make an assumption that authors indicate how a previous algorithm is utilized in the context of where the algorithm is cited, which we denote as *algorithm citation context*. We propose a classification scheme with 9 classes of an algorithm citation function, divided into 3 groups based on the authors' attitudes. We then manually classify a set of 300 algorithm citation contexts randomly selected from 2,000 papers from Citeseer^X[1] and describe the statistics. Discovering the functionality of a cited algorithm could provide an insight into how and where the algorithm is used and could give insight into interesting applications such as algorithm trend discovery and algorithm impact.

JCDL'13, July 22–26, 2013, Indianapolis, IN, USA.
ACM 978-1-4503-1154-0/12/06.

2. PROPOSED CLASSIFICATION SCHEME FOR ALGORITHM CITATION FUNCTION

2.1 Classification Scheme

Figure 1 illustrates our proposed scheme for classification of algorithm citation function in scholarly works, along with descriptions. The scheme consists of 9 classes representing possible ways in which an algorithm can be used. The 9 classes can be divided into 3 groups based on the authors' attitude towards the cited algorithms: favorable, neutral, and critical. We hypothesize that authors are 'favorable' towards algorithms that they choose to incorporate or build upon in their work; whereas they feel 'critical' about algorithms they use as baselines or those that cannot solve the problems they address. Such criticism is often reflected in discussion about the disadvantages of the cited algorithms.

2.2 Methodology

```
... What we are planning to do in this paper, we show that
this formula (1) can indeed be theoretically justified. Our
justification for this formula will use methods motivated
by the neural network approach (see, e.g., [10]). We must
choose a family of functions, not a single function A. ...
```

Table 1: Example of algorithm citation context, consisting an algorithm citation sentence (in italic) and the sentences surrounding it.

Our work can be considered an extension of Teufel et al. on citation function analysis [5]. However, we focus on algorithm citations only. An algorithm citation context is a tuple of an algorithm citation sentence (a sentence in which one or more algorithms are cited) and the sentences that immediately precede and follow it. Table 1 shows an example

[1]http://citeseer.ist.psu.edu

Attitude	Category	Description
Favorable	**Extension**	The cited algorithm is extended or modified by the citing work.
	Direct-use	Part or whole of the cited algorithm is used as part of the citing work. (No modifications to the cited algorithm)
Neutral	**Suggestion**	The authors suggest a potential improvement using the cited algorithm.
	Similarity	The authors point out the similarity between the cited algorithm and their work.
	Difference	The authors point out the difference(s) between the cited algorithm and their work.
	Analysis	The citing work performs further study (usually proofs) on the cited algorithm.
	Mention	The context just mentions the cited algorithm exists, usually along with some related description.
Critical	**Baseline**	The authors compare the performance of their algorithms with the cited algorithm.
	Argument	The authors bring up disadvantages or flaws in the cited algorithm, usually to emphasize the advantages of the citing work.

Figure 1: Proposed algorithm function classification scheme consisting of 9 categories, divided into 3 groups based on the authors' attitudes: Favorable, Neutral, Critical.

of an algorithm citation context taken from [3]. We manually label 300 algorithm citation contexts randomly selected from Citeseer^X, using the scheme in Figure 1.

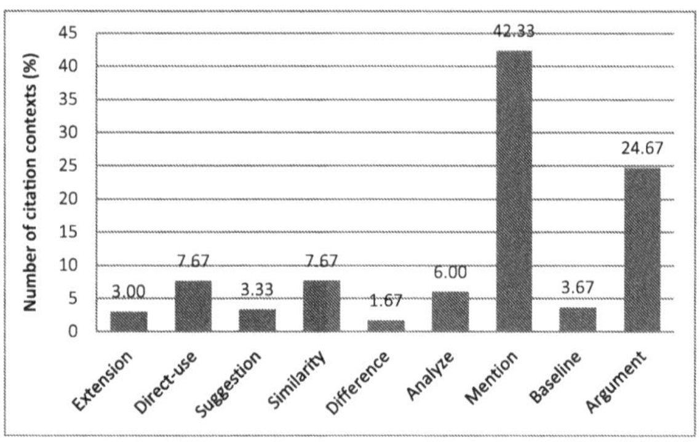

Figure 2: Distribution of different algorithm citation functions found in 300 randomly selected algorithm citation contexts.

Figure 2 represents the distribution of algorithm citation functions over different classes. Based on the results, most cited algorithms belong to the 'Mention' and 'Argument' classes. This supports the intuition that authors usually only mention and/or discuss the disadvantages of the existing algorithms to make the readers aware of the motivation and the completeness of their proposed work. We find that authors are mostly respectively 60.99% of the time neutral, 28.34% critical, and 10.67% favorable towards other algorithms. We interpret this to mean that most of the time few algorithms are actually used for further algorithm development.

2.3 Algorithm Citation Function in Different Sections

In this section, we analyze the distribution of the algorithm citation functions as seen in different sections in scholarly documents. The same set of 300 manually labeled algorithm citation contexts are further classified into 6 groups based on the sections in which they appear, including *Abstract* (*ABS*), *Introduction* (*INT*), *Background and Related Works* (*BCK*), *Methodology/ Experiment/ Results and Discussions* (*RAD*), *Conclusion* (*CON*), and *Other sections* (*OTHER*). Figure 3 illustrates the percentage distribution of each algorithm citation function over different sections.

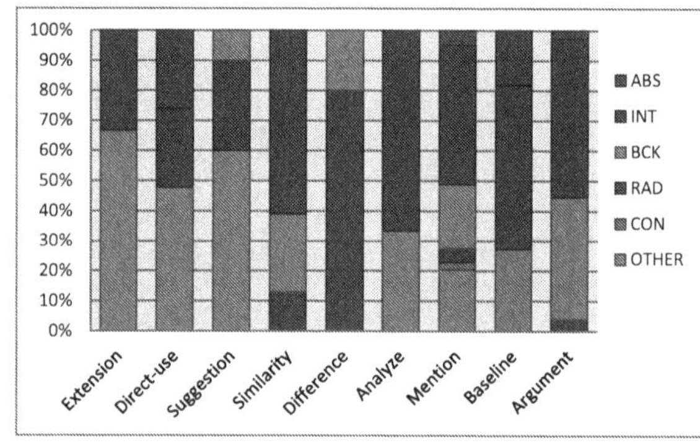

Figure 3: Distribution of algorithm citation functions over different sections.

3. ACKNOWLEDGMENTS

We gratefully acknowledge partial support from the National Science Foundation (NSF).

4. REFERENCES

[1] S. Bhatia, S. Tuarob, P. Mitra, and C. L. Giles. An algorithm search engine for software developers. In *Proceedings of the 3rd International Workshop on Search-Driven Development: Users, Infrastructure, Tools, and Evaluation*, SUITE '11, pages 13–16, 2011.

[2] D. M. Blei, A. Y. Ng, and M. I. Jordan. Latent dirichlet allocation. *the Journal of machine Learning research*, 3:993–1022, 2003.

[3] Y. Mendoza and R. Osegueda. Theoretical explanation for the empirical probability of detection (pod) curve: a neural network-motivated approach. In *Circuits and Systems, 1999. 42nd Midwest Symposium on*, pages 435–438, 1999.

[4] L. Page, S. Brin, R. Motwani, and T. Winograd. The pagerank citation ranking: bringing order to the web. 1999.

[5] S. Teufel, A. Siddharthan, and D. Tidhar. Automatic classification of citation function. In *Proceedings of the 2006 Conference on Empirical Methods in Natural Language Processing*, EMNLP '06, pages 103–110, 2006.

[6] S. Tuarob, S. Bhatia, P. Mitra, and C. L. Giles. Automatic detection of pseudo-codes in scholarly documents using machine learning. In *ICDAR' 2013*, 2013.

[7] S. Tuarob, P. Mitra, and C. L. Giles. Improving algorithm search using the algorithm co-citation network. In *Proceedings of the 12th ACM/IEEE-CS joint conference on Digital Libraries*, JCDL '12, pages 277–280, 2012.

[8] S. Tuarob and C. S. Tucker. Fad or here to stay: Predicting product market adoption and longevity using large scale, social media data. In *Proc. ASME 2013 Int. Design Engineering Technical Conf. Computers and Information in Engineering Conf. (IDETC/CIE2013)*, 2013.

[9] D. Walker, H. Xie, K. Yan, and S. Maslov. Ranking scientific publications using a model of network traffic. *Journal of Statistical Mechanics: Theory and Experiment*, 2007(06):P06010, 2007.

A Figure Search Engine Architecture for a Chemistry Digital Library

Sagnik Ray Choudhury†, Suppawong Tuarob‡, Prasenjit Mitra†‡, Lior Rokach*, Andi Kirk*, Silvia Szep*, Donald Pellegrino*, Sue Jones*, C. Lee. Giles†‡
†Information Sciences and Technology, ‡Computer Science and Engineering, The Pennsylvania State University, University Park, PA 16802 USA
*Information Systems Engineering, Ben-Gurion University of the Negev, Beer Sheva, Israel 84105
*The Dow Chemical Company, Spring House, PA 19477 USA
{sagnik, suppawong}@psu.edu, pmitra@ist.psu.edu, liorrk@bgu.ac.il, {andikirk,sszep,dapellegrino,susanjones}@dow.com,giles@ist.psu.edu

ABSTRACT

Academic papers contain multiple figures representing important findings and experimental results; we present a search engine specifically focused on figures in academic documents. This search engine allows users to search on figures in approximately 150,000 chemistry journal articles though the method is easily extendable to other domains. Our system indexes figure caption and mentions extracted from the PDF in documents using a custom built extractor. Recall and precision performance of extracted figures is in the 80 to 90 % range. We give the frame work for the extraction algorithm, architecture and ranking function.

Categories and Subject Descriptors

H.4 [**Information Extraction and Retrieval**]

Keywords

Information Extraction, Figure Search

1. INTRODUCTION

In general, figures are considered to be an important part of any document; [1] showed that the text in a document was not able to convey the message in 61% of the figures. This motivates search engines specifically focused on indexing and ranking figures in PDF documents. Currently, only three digital library search engines (Yale Image Finder [1], BioText [2], and askHermes[3]) exist with this functionality, all in the biosciences. In most cases academic document repositories have only the document PDF files, from which figures and metadata will have to be extracted. However, with these systems, there has been no discussion of the process of figure and metadata extraction.

Our contributions are: 1. an automatic extractor for figures and their associated metadata (caption, mentions) from documents and 2. a scalable Solr/Lucene[4] based figure metadata search engine with a modified generic Lucene ranking function to improve the quality of search results.

2. RELATED WORK

Recent work [4] describes a methodology for extraction of images and captions from PDF files, whereby images are extracted from PDF using Xpdf[5] and captions are extracted using regular expressions and heuristics. We use regular expressions and document layout information for the same task (section 4). Previously, similar techniques were used in identifying, extracting and indexing tables[3], algorithms and acknowledged entities [2]. Our system is an continuation of this line of work and, more importantly, can be readily integrated with other search features.

3. SYSTEM DESCRIPTION

Given a PDF document, our system automatically finds and extracts related text content, figures, and figure metadata from the document using a custom built extractor, using PDFBox library[6]. For each extracted figure, a metadata file is created, which contains figure caption, figure mention and other information. Figure caption and mention are indexed as separate fields using Lucene[7]. Users can search on both caption and mention fields separately. The SERP provides a ranked list of all figures found.

4. EXTRACTION AND RANKING

Extraction: The extraction process is summarized in algorithm 1. First, a figure and corresponding text identifier (such as, "Fig. 1") is extracted together. In most cases the caption of the extracted figure starts with the identifier. As such, a paragraph starting with the figure id f_i is a probable caption for the figure f_i. However, all such paragraphs are not the actual caption and need to be filtered out. Also,

[1]`http://krauthammerlab.med.yale.edu/imagefinder/`
[2]`http://biosearch.berkeley.edu/`
[3]`http://figuresearch.askhermes.org`

[4]`http://lucene.apache.org/solr`
[5]`http://www.foolabs.com/xpdf/`
[6]`http://pdfbox.apache.org/`
[7]`http://lucene.apache.org/`

JCDL'13, July 22–26, 2013, Indianapolis, Indiana, USA.
ACM 978-1-4503-2077-1/13/07.

determining the paragraph boundary in PDF documents is a non trivial task. Therefore, we reduce the problem to two subproblems - identifying the beginning and ending line of a caption. A set of document layout information based filters are used for these tasks: 1. **Line_length(i,j)**: Returns **true** if length of line i > length of line j by a threshold, else returns **false**. 2. **FontSize_change(i,j)**: Returns **true** if average font sizes of line i and j are different, else returns **false** and 3. **Bold_font(i)**: Returns **true** if a character in the line i is written in bold font, else returns **false**. These filters are defined based on a set of simple observations: 1. font size changes take place in the caption boundary; 2. the starting line of a caption usually has a bold font character (such as **Fig. 1**); and 3. the ending line of a caption is usually shorter than the next line.

```
Data: A PDF file of a document.
Result: Figures and associated captions and mentions
        extracted from the PDF.
From a document d, extract all text lines that contain the
term "figure" or "fig" in a list L_rv;
for Each line in the whole text of the document do
  | Store length of the line, font size, font weight in a list) ;
end
for Each figure f_i in the document d do
    Extract figure f_i using PDFBox ;
    Extract the text in a rectangle below the figure f_i ;
    From the extracted text, find out the id fid_i ;
    if no id is extracted then
        Output the image file of the figure ;
        break;
    end
    else
        Caption=Extract_Caption(id);
        Mention=Extract_Mention(id);
        if caption is null then
          | caption=Mention[1]
        end
        Output image file for the figure, metadata file for the
        caption and mention ;
    end
end
```

Algorithm 1: Algorithm for extracting figures, associated caption and mentions from an article.

Ranking: As figures in documents have rich textual metadata, we used textual features such as term frequency and inverse document frequency for ranking. Instead of the whole text of a document, only caption and mentions of a figure are indexed in our system. This way, less weight is assigned to the terms which are common in the whole document, but uncommon in the figure description. The caption field is given an index time boost of five times.

5. EXPERIMENTS AND RESULTS

Extraction: The evaluation parameters for the extraction process were defined as: 1. **Figure-caption recall**: { Number of (figure, caption) pairs extracted } / { Total number of (figure, caption) pairs present in the dataset}. 2. **Caption precision** : Ratio of retrieved captions that were correct. and 3. **Hard accuracy test**: Whether the percentage of match between the extracted and original caption was $\geq 95\%$.

For scalability we ran our extractor on 150,000 chemistry documents to extract more than 90,000 figures. The accuracy evaluation of the system was done on a sample of 150 non scanned documents, containing 883 figures. We extracted figures and associated metadata using two systems: 1. Our PDFBox based extractor (E_{pdbx}) and 2. Xpdf based extractor (E_{xpdf}) reported in [4]. Results in table 1 shows that our system performs well in precision and recall.

Comparison parameter	E_{pdbx}	E_{xpdf} [4]
Figure-caption recall	0.84	0.82
Caption precision	0.95	0.90
CE hard accuracy	0.91	0.92

Table 1: Comparative results of extraction efficiency of our system (E_{pdbx}) with [4] (E_{xpdf}).

Ranking: Three chemistry graduates evaluated the quality of the search results. Average precision at 10, 20 and 30 was found to be 0.7, 0.6 and 0.4, respectively, over a range of nine queries.

6. CONCLUSION AND FUTURE WORK

We report an extraction process of figure and associated metadata from chemistry PDF documents and a novel figure search engine on the extracted metadata. Currently, very few digital libraries allow this functionality. Future work would be to improve the extraction algorithm using linguistic features and to evaluate the scalability of the extraction process on millions of documents. Effective ranking of figures in documents remains an open question, which demands further investigation.

7. ACKNOWLEDGEMENTS

We gratefully acknowledge partial support from the National Science Foundation and suggestions by Madian Khabsa and Hung-Hsuan Chen.

8. REFERENCES

[1] S. Carberry, S. Elzer, and S. Demir. Information graphics: an untapped resource for digital libraries. In *Proceedings of the 29th annual international ACM SIGIR conference on Research and development in information retrieval*, SIGIR '06, pages 581–588, New York, NY, USA, 2006. ACM.

[2] M. Khabsa, P. Treeratpituk, and C. L. Giles. Ackseer: a repository and search engine for automatically extracted acknowledgments from digital libraries. In *Proceedings of the 12th ACM/IEEE-CS joint conference on Digital Libraries*, JCDL '12, pages 185–194, New York, NY, USA, 2012. ACM.

[3] Y. Liu, K. Bai, P. Mitra, and C. L. Giles. Tableseer: automatic table metadata extraction and searching in digital libraries. In *Proceedings of the 7th ACM/IEEE-CS joint conference on Digital libraries*, pages 91–100. ACM, 2007.

[4] L. Lopez, J. Yu, C. Arighi, H. Huang, H. Shatkay, and C. Wu. An automatic system for extracting figures and captions in biomedical pdf documents. In *Bioinformatics and Biomedicine (BIBM), 2011 IEEE International Conference on*, pages 578–581. IEEE, 2011.

A Memento Web Browser for iOS

Heather Tweedy
Harding University
Computer Science Dept
Searcy, Arkansas, USA 72149
htweedy@harding.edu

Frank McCown
Harding University
Computer Science Dept
Searcy, Arkansas, USA 72149
fmccown@harding.edu

Michael L. Nelson
Old Dominion University
Computer Science Dept
Norfolk, Virginia, USA 23529
mln@cs.odu.edu

ABSTRACT

The Memento framework allows web browsers to request and view archived web pages in a transparent fashion. However, Memento is still in the early stages of adoption, and browser-plugins are often required to enable Memento support. We report on a new iOS app called the Memento Browser, a web browser that supports Memento and gives iPhone and iPad users transparent access to the world's largest web archives.

Categories and Subject Descriptors

H.3.7 [**Information Storage and Retrieval**]: Digital Libraries – *Collection*

Keywords

Mobile web, web archiving, web browser, Memento

1. INTRODUCTION

The Memento framework provides transparent client access to archived web resources [7]. It introduces a modification to the HTTP protocol that allows a client to request a particular time version of web resource without the user having to navigate through various archives in search of the resource. The archived resources discovered with Memento are called *mementos*. A number of web archives have implemented Memento, including the open-source Wayback Machine software [8], but client support has mainly been limited to the Firefox browser running the MementoFox add-on [3][4].

We introduce a new iOS app called Memento Browser [2]. As pictured in Figure 1, the Memento Browser looks like the stock iOS browser except that it introduces a toolbar that allows the user to 1) view all the mementos available for a particular URL, 2) navigate to previous and next mementos, and 3) view the web page as it looks right now. The mementos are discovered using a Memento TimeGate running at Los Alamos National Laboratory (LANL) which aggregates archived URLs from Internet Archive, WebCite, UK Web Archive, and others. Figure 1 shows the Memento Browser displaying an archived web page from the Internet Archive. Memento Browser has also been implemented for Android; both browsers implement Memento's "simple" mode which we introduce in this poster. We also discuss some of the challenges viewing the Past Web on a mobile device.

JCDL'13, July 22–26, 2013, Indianapolis, Indiana, USA.
ACM 978-1-4503-2077-1/13/07.

Figure 1. Memento Browser showing a cnn.com archived page from Internet Archive

2. MEMENTO CLIENT MODES

Web pages are normally composed of an HTML file and other supporting files: style sheets, JavaScript, images, etc. Most web archives do their best to archive all these resources at the same time, but this is technically challenging because web crawlers must be "polite" when crawling the web, meaning they must delay a few seconds between requests. Archiving a website can thus take hours, days, or weeks depending on its size. During this time resources might be modified, be moved to new URLs, or even disappear. Therefore, most archived websites experience various degrees of temporal incoherence [6].

When a client is using Memento to discover and display a web page from an earlier datetime *T*, it will request a Memento-enabled web server for the web page as it existed at time *T*. There are three HTTP requests involved in this request, and the details of this process can be found in [4]. The end result of these requests is that the client will have a URI where the archived resource closest to datetime *T* can be found. The resource may be on the web server or in some web archive. When the HTML for the page is retrieved, the client should make subsequent requests for the images, style sheets, etc. using the same process (three HTTP requests) for each of the resources. In other words, datetime content negotiation should be performed for *all* components making up the web page. This strict application of Memento across all requests is what we call **thorough mode**.

To speed up the process of rendering a memento web page, a client may use **faster mode**. In this mode, the client uses Memento to discover the HTML for the web page, but it does not make Memento requests for all the embedded resources. Instead, it takes advantage of the fact that many web archives rewrite the URLs of the embedded resources so they point back to the archive. So the embedded resources are fetched as-is, and the returned resources are checked to ensure they are also mementos (by checking the link rel HTTP response headers or checking against a white list of archive URL patterns). If the archive does not rewrite the embedded URLs, they will point to the "live" web, and they will not be used to display the memento web page.

Although thorough mode requires three HTTP requests per resource, it is more likely to produce better approximations of historical web pages because the web page will be composed potentially from resources from multiple archives that are closest to the desired historical datetime. Faster mode requires fewer HTTP requests, but it may produce poorer approximations of historical web pages because the entire page is composed of resources coming from only one archive. It also requires the web archives producing the HTML to rewrite all embedded URLs. MementoFox supports both thorough and faster modes.

When developing Memento Browser for iOS and an earlier version for Android, we were forced to support a new mode that is somewhat like faster. We used the stock controls provided on both these platforms for rendering web pages. The iOS version uses the `UIWebView` control, and the Android version uses the `WebView` control. Neither of these controls support Memento, and they do not allow the programmer to trap the outgoing HTTP requests and incoming responses for embedded resources. The iOS app will therefore get a TimeMap using the LANL proxy server (discussed below) in order to discover all the available mementos for the web page's URL that is currently being viewed. It will then display the memento matching the datetime chosen by the user.

So Memento Browser only uses Memento for discovering web page mementos, but it does not use Memento for making the requests for all embedded resources. We call this new mode of Memento support **simple mode**. Simple mode is just like fast mode except that the embedded resources are not checked to see if they are mementos. It is easy to implement but problematic when a web archive does not rewrite the URLs of embedded resources that point to the "live" web.

Memento is not yet widely implemented in web browsers and web servers, so it is not uncommon for Memento-enabled clients to use a proxy server which speaks Memento. Both MementoFox and Memento Browser use a proxy server at LANL which aggregates archived URLs from Internet Archive, WebCite, UK Web Archive, and others. If the proxy were asked for a web page as it existed at datetime T, it will reply back with a TimeMap listing the archived URLs that are closest to T from the list of supported archives. Because of the temporal coherence issue mentioned earlier, the web page's images and style sheets closest to T might be found in different archives. In other words, a web page from datetime T could be composed of HTML from Internet Archive, an image from WebCite, and a style sheet from UK Web Archive.

The value of having access to resources from a variety of archives can be demonstrated by a simple example [1]. Querying the LANL proxy for http://www.cnn.com/ mementos on January 30, 2013, reveals 17,188 archived copies. A large majority of these pages (98.5%) come from the Internet Archive, but there are only 77 total archived copies from 2012; they come from the UK National Archives (58.4%), Archiefweb (33.8%), and Archive-It! (7.8%).

3. PAST WEB ON A MOBILE DEVICE

Many websites will redirect a mobile browser like Memento Browser to a mobile-friendly website that uses a different URL. These mobile sites are usually much newer than their stationary counterparts, and they are less likely to be archived [5]. For example, there are only 185 total copies of http://m.cnn.com/ in the Internet Archive compared to 17K for http://www.cnn.com/. Therefore the Memento Browser will sometimes discover far fewer mementos than MementoFox running on a desktop would. We are interested in allowing Memento Browser to see historical mobile pages and traditional web pages.

4. ACKNOWLEDGMENTS

We would like to thank Steve Baber for writing the initial version of Memento Browser for iOS. We also thank members of the Prototyping Team at the Research Library of the Los Alamos National Laboratory for their feedback on Memento Browser. This research was supported by the National Science Foundation (IIS 1008492 and 1009392) and the Library of Congress.

5. REFERENCES

[1] Ainsworth, S., AlSum, A., SalahEldeen, H., Weigle, M., Nelson, M. L. 2012. How much of the Web is archived? In *Proceedings of the 11th annual international ACM/IEEE Joint Conference on Digital Libraries* (JCDL '11). ACM, New York, NY, USA, 133-136.

[2] Memento Browser for iOS and Android. http://code.google.com/p/memento-browser/

[3] MementoFox Add-on. https://addons.mozilla.org/en-US/firefox/addon/mementofox/

[4] Sanderson, R., Shankar, H., Ainsworth, S., McCown, F., Adams, S. 2011. Implementing time travel for the Web. *Code4Lib Journal*, Issue 13 (Apr S2011). http://journal.code4lib.org/articles/4979

[5] Schneider, R., McCown, F. 2013. First steps in archiving the mobile web: automated discovery of mobile websites. *Proceedings of the 13th annual international ACM/IEEE Joint Conference on Digital Libraries* (JCDL '13). ACM, New York, NY, USA.

[6] Spaniol, M., Denev, D., Mazeika, A., Weikum, G., Senellart, P. 2009. Data quality in web archiving. In *Proceedings of the 3rd Workshop on Information Credibility on the Web* (WICOW '09). ACM, New York, NY, USA, 19-26.

[7] Van de Sompel, H., Nelson, M. L., Sanderson, R., Balakireva, L., Ainsworth, S., Shankar, H. 2009. Memento: Time Travel for the Web. Technical Report (Nov 2009). http://arxiv.org/abs/0911.1112

[8] Web Archive Access Utilities. Wayback. http://sourceforge.net/projects/archive-access/files/wayback

A Retrospective Review on a Decade of Building a National Science Digital Library to Transform STEM Education

Sarah Giersch
Broad-based Knowledge, LLC
206 West 99th St.
New York, NY 10025
+011 919-614-6424
sholsted@gmail.com

Dr. Flora McMartin
Broad-based Knowledge, LLC
5935 Orchard Ave
Richmond, CA 94804
+011 515-237-4795
flora.mcmartin@gmail.com

ABSTRACT
Since 2000, the National Science Foundation's NSDL program has made many direct contributions to digital library research and STEM education. Originally called the National STEM Digital Library (and now National STEM Distributed Learning), the program catalyzed significant technology developments and served to advance state-of-the-art teaching and learning practices during a period of dramatic technological change. This poster describes the results of a three-day writing workshop, convened in April 2012, which generated a retrospective report and a series of interviews on the NSDL library-building process.

Categories and Subject Descriptors
K.3.0 [**Computing Milieux**]: Computers and Education – *General*

Keywords
Digital Libraries; STEM Education; Program History

INTRODUCTION
The term "NSDL" has come to represent many things:

- The *NSF program*—the NSDL program was envisioned in the mid-1990s and ran from 2000-2012;
- The *website*—NSDL.org, a digital library of high-quality, online, educational STEM resources that continues to support teaching and learning for K-16 and informal audiences;
- The *projects*—more than 200 projects were funded through NSF's NSDL program;
- The *community*—initially, anyone who worked on an NSDL-funded project; eventually, the network of teachers, learners, and partners who used or contributed NSDL resources or attended NSDL events.

As several of the workshop participants noted, the vision for NSDL, established in the original NSF program solicitation [2], has not changed. In fact, this vision has been the glue that held together a diverse, interdisciplinary group of people who dedicated large portions of their careers to creating a National Science Digital Library. What has changed is participants' understanding of what it means to realize and sustain the vision for NSDL within the context of a rapidly changing technology environment and evolving priorities for STEM education.

JCDL'13, July 22–26, 2013, Indianapolis, Indiana, USA.
ACM 978-1-4503-2077-1/13/07.

METHODOLOGY
The four workshop organizers and 22 attendees, drawn from the NSDL community, represented a cross cutting sample of roles that were integral in the various stages of developing NSDL, including writing the vision document for NSDL in 2001 [1]. Workshop participants addressed the following research questions in group meetings and writing sessions of small teams:

- How has the vision for the NSDL been realized?
- How has NSDL developed over time?
- What new knowledge has been generated as a result?
- Where are / were successes and challenges for NSDL?
- How could the NSDL inform cyber-learning programs?

The resulting workshop report [3] is structured as a series of essays and highlights a number of the significant lessons learned and contributions made by the hundreds of individuals who worked to advance digital library research and STEM education. To complement the report, 17 participants completed interviews about the professional, and sometimes personal, impact that their projects and the NSDL program had on their careers.

LESSONS LEARNED

1.1 Transforming Teaching & Learning
NSDL's promise or potential was (and still is) in its ability to: engage learners with authentic scientific practices; identify quality educational resources; and, empower content consumers to become content creators. *Lessons learned* include: 1) The *context* of the where, how, and why of learning is important. 2) First provide quality resources; then design complementary services to help users discover them. 3) Fostering user communities is essential to sustainability and growth.

1.2 Scaling Digital Library Technology
The NSDL technology imperative was to move from a research project into a production system. Despite many challenges, NSDL made progress in the areas of metadata creation, automatic extraction, and the alignment between educational standards and curriculum resources. *Lessons learned* include: 1) Technology development processes and solutions do not scale easily, especially within the context of a distributed project. 2) Assumptions about the ease of integrating new technology (i.e., that plug-and- play code was a solution for all projects) were not substantiated. 3) Each NSDL project had different requirements,

which made communication and technology integration difficult, time consuming, and resource intensive.

1.3 Organization Evolution & Effectiveness

The NSDL community was guided by two organizational structures over its lifespan: grassroots committees, comprised of volunteer representatives from NSDL-funded projects; and, a Core Integration (CI) team, funded by the NSDL program to develop the library technical infrastructure and to support the NSDL community library-building efforts. *Lessons learned* include: 1) The NSF funding model poses challenges for creating organizational structures that support development of a coherent and comprehensive whole. Long-term, collaborative NSF projects require a funding model that supports strategic growth and sustainability. 2) Organizational structures need dedicated funding, time, and flexibility to develop. 3) Effective communication across large, collaborative organizations must be open, adaptive, and inclusive. 4) Evaluation activities require careful planning, systematic application, and integration into an organization's management.

1.4 Library as Metaphor

NSDL was conceived at a time when both the promise and the shortcomings of the World Wide Web for education were apparent. NSDL was rooted in the notion that values added by libraries were critically important to realizing the potential of the Web and addressing its shortcomings. *Lessons learned*: The library metaphor allowed the NSDL community to achieve a level of agreement that helped catalyze the NSDL collaborative initiative. However, the term "library" is overloaded with meanings that have become both assets and liabilities. Comparison to a library, with its traditional role as selector and purveyor of published information, can perpetuate the view of library as distribution channel, perhaps overlooking or underestimating its place and potential in supporting users in the creation of new resources.

1.5 Developing & Sustaining Communities

NSDL created and sustained several, diverse communities around library-building activities, and they are primarily linked by Internet technologies. Each community brought their own strengths and mores, but the vision of an interdisciplinary effort blurred the boundaries between previously disparate groups. For example, digital library developers brought the traditions and research cultures of scientific and educational associations. But NSDL also attracted a large population of users whose focus was engaging in STEM teaching and learning activities. *Lessons learned* include: 1) Large projects need to anticipate and provide support to multiple communities organized around their functional needs. 2) Communities in large projects are most likely to be self-organizing and will emerge at different stages of the project's life cycle. 3) Even in projects that are primarily based on electronic resources and communication, face-to-face meetings and other forms of personal communication are critical to support work across disparate, and distributed, communities.

CONCLUSION

Three central messages emerged from the workshop and were supported in interviews with participants. Summarized here, they are explained more fully in the workshop report [3]:

1. **Large, collaborative, interdisciplinary projects require organizational structures to support the efforts of the whole.** As such, grant-funded projects need organizational models that balance centralized *and* distributed management structures. Finding the "right" organizational structure requires time and testing.
2. **An organization's vision and goals must actively guide management and planning.** Choose the words used to describe vision and goals carefully. Use goals as guideposts to ensure alignment of project activities in a distributed organization. For effective collaboration, value the success of individual parts as highly as the whole.
3. **Keeping collaborative projects collaborative requires strong communication networks.** In distributed contexts, communication needs to be both rich and nurtured. Projects should not underestimate the amount of communication management or the cost (i.e., fiscal and time) that a distributed program requires.

What made NSDL unique among many other initiatives was its interdisciplinary approach to developing a STEM education digital library. In its many manifestations (program, website, projects, community), "NSDL" developed high-quality collections and innovative tools and created and sustained a broad and lively intellectual community, all in a distributed setting. NSDL's vision served as a catalyst for interdisciplinary research (1) on digital libraries; (2) on the transformative role of technology in the classroom; and (3) on the pedagogies and information literacy skills used by STEM teachers and learners.

The NSDL program and its component projects have demonstrated the power of digital libraries to improve the quality of STEM education and to widen the reach of the very best resources. At the same time, NSDL has been a grand socio-technical experiment. As with any experiment, negative results can be as valuable as positive ones. Viewed through that lens, NSDL has been successful at the program, project, and personal levels, although the divergent perspectives on the definition and scope of NSDL may mask the achievements at each level.

However, almost every workshop participant noted that one of the reasons they valued participating in NSDL was the opportunity to exchange ideas and collaborate with colleagues from other disciplines. Working to realize the vision of NSDL has had a lasting impact on the direction of their work, and indeed, their lives.

2. ACKNOWLEDGMENTS

This research is supported by the National Science Foundation, DUE #0937784. The authors are extremely grateful for the efforts of workshop participants and the NSDL community.

3. REFERENCES

[1] Manduca, C., McMartin, F. & Mogk, D. (2001). Pathways to Progress: Vision and Plans for Developing the NSDL. Retrieved 3 May 13: http://serc.carleton.edu/resources/37429.html.

[2] National Science Foundation. (2000). National Science, Mathematics, Engineering, and Technology Education Digital Library (NSDL) Program Solicitation – NSF 00-44. Retrieved 3 May 13: http://www.nsf.gov/pubs/2000/nsf0044/nsf0044.htm.

[3] Retrospective Essays on a Decade of Building a National Science Digital Library to Transform STEM Education. (2012). NSDL Writing Workshop, Carleton College Northfield, Minnesota. Retrieved 3 May 13: http://serc.carleton.edu/p2p_redux/index.html.

A Roadmap for Data Services

Inna Kouper
Indiana University
Data to Insight Center
inkouper@indiana.edu

Katherine G. Akers
Emory University
Woodruff Library
katherine.g.akers@emory.edu

Natsuko H. Nicholls
University of Michigan
Clark Library
hayashin@umich.edu

Fe C. Sferdean
University of Michigan
Clark Library
sferdean@umich.edu

ABSTRACT
This poster describes our experiences as four CLIR/DLF postdoctoral fellows in developing data services at our respective universities. We report on our particular activities and achievements, which we synthesize into a common framework that can guide the development of data services at other academic institutions. The analysis of our experiences suggests the necessity of stronger cooperation of units within universities as well as increased and more diverse collaborations among universities.

Categories and Subject Descriptors
A.1 INTRODUCTORY AND SURVEY; H.3.5 Online Information Services - *Data sharing;* H.3.7 Digital Libraries - *User issues*

General Terms
Management, Human Factors, Standardization.

Keywords
Data services, data preservation, libraries.

1. INTRODUCTION
Data services are increasingly being recognized as a crucial component of library services. While researchers are grappling with a deluge of data, libraries are trying to find ways to improve data storage, management, sharing, and preservation. How can researchers and libraries work together toward the common goals of facilitating innovative, reproducible research and increasing opportunities for data sharing and re-use? Can or should libraries take the lead in encouraging best practices in data exchange?

Here, we approach these questions from a practical standpoint. We contrast and compare our recent work as CLIR/DLF postdoctoral fellows placed in three different institutions [2]. The goals of our fellowship are to raise awareness of the need for proper data management and preservation as well as to promote data curation as a professional activity. Each fellow has a different set of responsibilities, creating challenges for the establishment and achievement of common goals. We propose the metaphor of a roadmap to capture and chart the variety of aims and activities undertaken in different universities with regard to the development of data services.

2. A ROADMAP AND ITS MILESTONES
A roadmap for data services can be viewed as a strategic plan guiding the development of services that support the creation, storage, sharing, and preservation of research data. It identifies the final destination – the provision of data services that address researchers' needs and that facilitate preservation and innovation in research. It also helps to a) match goals (i.e., destinations) with actions and solutions (i.e., paths or milestones); b) navigate toward reaching a consensus and coordinating developments; and c) connect with other "travelers" (i.e., establish partnerships within and across institutions that help to promote individual and collective goals).

The roadmap can be depicted as follows:

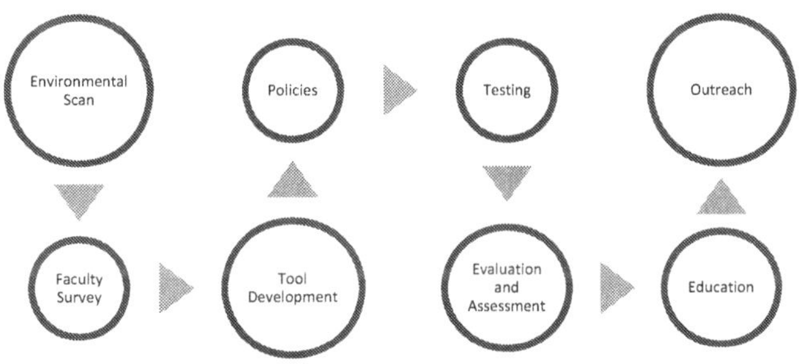

Figure 1. A roadmap for data services.

Our experiences cover the first three milestones of this journey: environmental scan, faculty survey, and tool development. Our poster will provide a detailed description of each of these milestones followed by a summary of the differences and similarities among our institutions' paths.

3. UNIVERSITY OF MICHIGAN: ENVIRONMENTAL SCAN
The University of Michigan Libraries offers a range of services for researchers at various stages of their research, from planning studies to the dissemination of their results. At the same time, a comprehensive set of services that support the full lifecycle of research data for faculty and students is at an early stage of development.

To develop strategies toward establishing data services, the University of Michigan Libraries tasked two new staff members—both CLIR/DLF fellows—to conduct an environmental scan of existing data services at other institutions.

The fellows selected institutions at various stages of data service development. They compiled questions in the light of four crucial components of data services: consultation, infrastructure, policy, and education/awareness. In general, their interviews focused on different ways of establishing data services, the scope of available services, and the distinctive features of various data services.

JCDL '13, July 22–26, 2013, Indianapolis, Indiana, USA.
ACM 978-1-4503-2077-1/13/07.

They contacted key players in data services at the following institutions: Emory University, Indiana University, Purdue University, Cornell University, California Digital Library, Johns Hopkins University, University of Virginia, Penn State University, University of Illinois at Urbana-Champaign, and University of Wisconsin-Madison

The detailed results of the environmental scan will be available later for public viewing. The main findings of their analysis are:

- Data services should be developed around research and data lifecycles [1]. To efficiently accomplish this goal, campus resources and services at each stage of the lifecycle should be identified.
- There is a need for active "agents of change" (i.e., those who can support, engage, and promote data services among faculty and students). We view such people as "data champions", whom our primary goal is to find.
- Cooperation and collaboration are crucial for the successful establishment of data services.

4. EMORY UNIVERSITY: FACULTY SURVEY

The Emory University Libraries have long supported data acquisition and analysis but are beginning to expand this support to encompass data sharing and preservation. Led by two new staff members—a Data Management Specialist and a CLIR fellow/e-Science Librarian—the research data management team is figuring out how they can best support the data management needs of campus researchers.

Over the past several months, they have started to reach out to faculty, students, and staff to communicate the importance of good data management. So far, they have created a library webpage, met with campus partners, held library workshops, given guest lectures in graduate courses, and begun collaborating with data management librarians at the neighboring Georgia Institute of Technology. These actions represent the first steps toward their goal of creating a suite of data services.

To identify the greatest needs of campus researchers, they recently conducted an online survey of faculty practices and perspectives on research data management. One question specifically solicited interest in several data services. They found that the two most desired services are workshops on general data management practices (52% of respondents) and assistance with preparing data management plans required by federal funding agencies (51%). Other services that garnered interest were consultation on data-related confidentiality/legal issues (40%), personalized consultation on best practices in data management (39%), having an institutional repository to store and/or preserve data (38%), and assistance with data documentation and metadata creation (37%). These findings will help guide the Emory University Libraries in developing services that will effectively support the creation, preservation, and dissemination of research data.

5. INDIANA UNIVERSITY: TOOL DEVELOPMENT

The development of data services at Indiana University is approached as an opportunity to engage multiple units within the university, particularly the libraries, IT services, and computational centers. While the libraries are focusing on the customization of existing tools, such as the DMPTool or Dspace software for institutional repositories (IRs), the Data to Insight (D2I) Center—a collaboration between the School of Informatics and Computing, Indiana University Libraries, and University Information Technology Services (UITS)—is taking the lead in developing innovative tools that cross the boundaries between digital libraries, data management, and computer science.

The CLIR/DLF fellow at Indiana University has been placed within the D2I Center as a liaison to the libraries. One of the projects that build upon the library-D2I partnership is the NSF-funded DataNet project, called Sustainable Environment-Actionable Data (SEAD). This project focuses on the development of tools and services for the curation and long-term preservation of scientific data while also engaging researchers through social networking tools. D2I activities focus on building a federation of institutional repositories in sustainability science. Such a federation (SEAD Virtual Archive) will serve as a thin layer that offers the community of sustainability scientists a coherent view of their collective data. It will enhance the functionality of institutional repositories, ease the burden of data submission to IRs, help to handle the heterogeneity of data in sustainability science, and increase data discovery for researchers working on related problems.

6. DISCUSSION AND CONCLUSION

Even a brief look at the activities that postdoctoral fellows take on in their jobs reveals that there is no straight path toward a single destination in the development of data services. Data services are intended to address specific needs within each university, while at the same time creating opportunities for sharing and collaboration. This requires extensive effort toward not only identifying needs but also establishing partnerships, negotiating boundaries, developing tools and infrastructure, and re-evaluating outcomes. The success of data services depends on good vision, leadership, collaboration, proper funding, and hard work.

As we will demonstrate in this poster, working individually while sharing results among ourselves and others helps to improve our work, coordinate actions across institutions, and work toward establishing globalized data services. We invite all librarians, IT staff, researchers, and others into a shared conversation about possible milestones in establishing data services in academic institutions, and we hope that our roadmap for data services can stimulate and facilitate such conversation.

7. REFERENCES

[1] The Digital Curation Centre. DCC Curation Lifecycle Model. Retrieved from http://www.dcc.ac.uk/resources/curation-lifecycle-model.

[2] Fellowships in Data Curation for the Sciences and Social Sciences. Retrieved from http://www.clir.org/fellowships/postdoctoral-fellowship-in-academic-libraries-new/program-information/clir-dlf-data-curation-sciences.

ArcLink: Optimization Techniques to Build and Retrieve the Temporal Web Graph

Ahmed AlSum
Department of Computer Science
Old Dominion University
Norfolk VA, USA
aalsum@cs.odu.edu

Michael L. Nelson
Department of Computer Science
Old Dominion University
Norfolk VA, USA
mln@cs.odu.edu

ABSTRACT

We present ArcLink, a proof-of-concept system that complements open source Wayback Machine installations by optimizing the construction, storage, and access to the temporal web graph. We divide the web graph construction into four stages (filtering, extraction, storage, and access) and explore optimization for each stage. ArcLink extends the current web archive interfaces to return content and structural metadata for each URI.

Categories and Subject Descriptors

H.3.4 [**Information Storage and Retrieval**]: Systems and Software; H.3.7 [**Information Storage and Retrieval**]: Digital Libraries

General Terms

Design, Experimentation

1. INTRODUCTION

The web graph is a directed graph where each vertex represents a URI and the edges represent a hyperlink between them. Web archives preserve web pages before they change or disappear forever. Each page, identified by a URI, may have one or more snapshots (called mementos) with different timestamps from which we can construct a Temporal Web Graph. The temporal web graph may have more than one memento for each URI. So the graph structure is changing through the time.

We used the collaborative IIPC Olympics 2010 collection[1], a collection of websites about the 2010 Winter Olympics for experimental use. The collection was crawled between 11/2009 and 03/2010 during the 2010 winter Olympics, the corpus size was 700GB+.

Various research motivated the implementation of ArcLink. The International Internet Preservation Consortium (IIPC) proposed a set of use cases for accessing web archives [3]; the report highlighted the importance of the linking information (the outgoing and the incoming links) of the archived web for analysis purposes. AlNoamany et al. [1] found that more than 90% of the sessions and 50% of the requests to the IA's Wayback Machine came from robots. This high percentage of robots in the archives suggests that there is significant demand for content and link structure metdata about mementos and a significant portion of the current load on the IA's Wayback Machine could be offloaded to an API. We used Memento protocol notation [4]. Memento is an extension for HTTP protocol to allow the user to browse the past web as the current web. More details about ArcLink can be found in [2].

2. ARCLINK STAGES

ArcLink is a distributed processing system to pre-process the link structure information from the archived web collections and create a temporal web graph. ArcLink has four main stages: filtering, extraction, storage, and access.

2.1 Filtering Optimization

The goal of the filtering optimization is to reduce the size of the input corpus to focus on the snapshots that carry link structure information. The input for the ArcLink system is a list of the URIs within a collection. For Heritirix[2]-based web crawlers, the URI list could be found in the crawler log entitled "CDX file"[3]. ArcLink uses this log to create a unique list of mementos that will contribute to the web graph. Reducing the input size will improve the extraction time and the required storage space. The following set of filtering rules could be used: HTTP Status, Content Mimetype, Resource extension, and Content checksum. Filtering rules are written with PigLatin script that is capable of loading the CDX file fields, then applying INCLUDE/EXCLUDE filters.

The experimental results showed that 75% of the mementos had HTTP status 200; 33% were for embedded resources, (e.g., images, stylesheets); 61% were duplicates. Finally, applying all rules showed that the efficiency was so significant to reduce the input records to 29% of the original size.

2.2 Extraction Optimization

Optimizing the extraction stage focused on two things: the creation of the URI-ID, and extraction mechanism (data source and tools).

[1]http://olympics.us.archive.org/

[2]http://crawler.archive.org/index.html

[3]http://archive.org/web/researcher/cdx_file_format.php

JCDL'13, July 22–26, 2013, Indianapolis, Indiana, USA.
ACM 978-1-4503-2077-1/13/07.

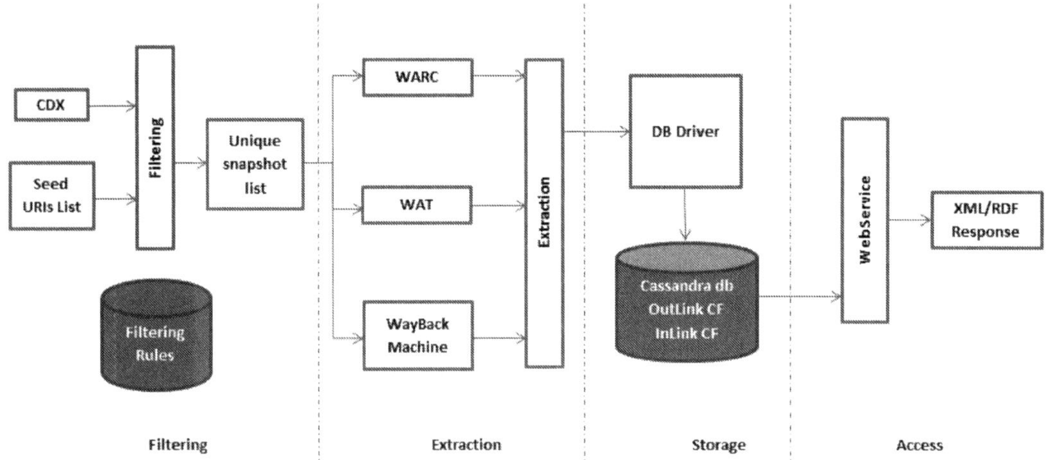

Figure 1: ArcLink Architecture

ArcLink generates a unique ID for each URI as the following: first, canonicalized the URI into SURT format[4]; second, ArcLink encodes this canonicalized SURT string using SimHash with a length of 128 bits. Using this 1-1 mapping between the URI and the ID gives the ability to incremental and distributed processing for the same URI on different cycles or different machines because the ID generation depends on the URI only.

ArcLink can extract the link structure from three sources based on the availability of the input: Web ARChive file (*WARC*), Web Archive Metadata file (*WAT*), and Web Archive UI. The experimental results showed that using WARC as data source took 61% of the time required for page scraping the Wayback Machine HTML interface.

ArcLink uses a partition technique to avoid simultaneous multi-access to the same file that affects the performance of the extraction. ArcLink uses unix commands (sort and split) to partition the input files to ensure single access to the WARC file per task.

2.3 Storage Optimization

ArcLink preserves the structure of the extracted links for future access using a database which will be the repository of the link structure information for any further experiments. We built *Content-centric temporal web graph*. In this schema, we replaced the $URI-R$ with the checksum for the content for this memento. The duplicate mementos have the same content (with same checksum) which evolve to the same vertex. This schema focused on the content and will avoid having duplicate nodes. This schema was easily implemented using Cassandra db "*Super Column Family*" feature.

The content-centric schema focused on the content more than the URI. The same checksum may belong to one URI in one timestamp (unique memento), one URI in different timestamps (duplicate mementos), or different URIs in different timestamps (duplicate content). We found duplicate content was common, for example, the Olympics collection has 23K+ mementos that have custom "Page not found" responses that return 200 instead of 404. In the regular web graph, each one of these snapshot will have one vertex that has the same outlinks.

2.4 Access

ArcLink provides APIs to enable the applications to access the link structure information. ArcLink delivery method depends on REST web services. ArcLink response is annotating the $URI-R$ with the outlinks and inlinks predicates through the time.

ArcLink APIs interface is in RDF/XML format that could be aggregated with other ArcLink instances that carry information about the requested $URI-R$. The aggregation could be done on the response level to give each ArcLink implementer the freedom to adjust the implementation details based on the requirements and capabilities.

3. CONCLUSIONS

We presented ArcLink, a distributed system to construct, preserve, and deliver the temporal web graph for large-scale web archives. ArcLink extends the current Wayback Machine with APIs interface to access the link structure metadata on fine-grained level. ArcLink optimization techniques reduced the input corpus to 29%, extracted efficiently from the WARC files with 61% of the regular page scraping, and deliver the link structure in RDF/XML format.

4. REFERENCES

[1] Y. AlNoamany, M. C. Weigle, and M. L. Nelson. Access Patterns for Robots and Humans in Web Archives. In *Proceedings of the 13th ACM/IEEE-CS joint conference on Digital Libraries*, JCDL '13, 2013.

[2] A. AlSum and M. L. Nelson. ArcLink: Optimization Techniques to Build and Retrieve the Temporal Web Graph. Technical Report arXiv:1305.5959, 2013.

[3] IIPC Access Working Group. Use cases for Access to Internet Archives. Technical report, International Internet Preservation Consortium Publications, 2006.

[4] H. Van de Sompel, M. L. Nelson, and R. Sanderson. HTTP framework for time-based access to resource states – Memento. `https://datatracker.ietf.org/doc/draft-vandesompel-memento/`, 2011.

[4] `http://crawler.archive.org/articles/user_manual/glossary.html#surt`

Checking Out: Customizing and Downloading Complex and Compound Digital Library Resources

Scott Britell
Computer Science Department
Portland State University
Portland, OR
britell@cs.pdx.edu

Lois Delcambre
Computer Science Department
Portland State University
Portland, OR
lmd@cs.pdx.edu

Categories and Subject Descriptors
H.3.7 [**Digital Libraries**]: Systems issues; Standards

General Terms
Management; Standardization.

Keywords
Complex Resources; Offline Usage; Data models.

1. INTRODUCTION

As the idea of a digital library resource evolves from the notion of a single resource potentially "consisting of multiple datastreams" [6] to complex resources composed of possibly many other distinct resources, our traditional notions of digital library usage and "check-out" should also evolve. Consider for example, a school curriculum composed of instructional materials and assessments. The individual resources in the complex resource may exist on their own, outside of the context of the compound resource, as first-class objects. Each resource may also be used in multiple compound resources—for example, an instructional material may appear in any number of curricula.

If an end user would like to check out a curriculum for use in their classroom or for reading on a mobile device, they are currently limited to a basic form of checkout where they may take out a single resource or perhaps a list of resources. We believe that the complex structure and context of the compound resource is valuable and, to that end, we present a new approach to complex check-out within a digital library. We provide users with a drag-and-drop interface, mimicking the navigational structures in the digital library, which allows users to customize which resources, in which structure, they would like to check out. Users then receive an archived package of their resources that can be used offline or installed as a web-accessible mini-repository.

We demonstrate this capability in the STEMRobotics [9] repository of middle and high school robotics curriculum. This repository is built using the Drupal [4] content management system and is part of the Ensemble [5] digital library portal for computing education resources. The capabilities demonstrated here can be applied to any repository built using Drupal.

2. THE COMPLEX DIGITAL LIBRARY

STEMRobotics was designed with the goal of creating a digital library of robotics educational resources where content authors can create complexly structured resources with a focus on collaboration and reuse. We encourage educators to author content in the repository with the structure that they use in their classrooms and are familiar with. This has led to a large amount of heterogeneity in structure within the site where one educator has a deeply nested course—with units, lessons, differentiated instructional materials and assessments—while others have courses consisting of a list of challenges or videos (e.g., like Khan Academy [7]) and yet others may be complex structures of all of those resources.

We leverage Drupal's ability to create arbitrary content types and relationships between them to create the structures our authors desire. In our previous work we demonstrated how to use *canonical structures* (domain-specific data model fragments) to enable generic navigational features in a repository [3] as well as how to transmit complex structure between digital libraries [1, 2]. Here we build upon that work to enable a generic mechanism for complex resource check-out.

3. CHECKING OUT

Figure 1 shows the interface for checking out complex resources in the STEMRobotics repository. The user is given a set of instructions on how to use the download interface and is asked to name their download. The user is then presented with a navigational structure from the repository, modified with check boxes, so they may choose which resources to download. The interface also allows the user to drag-and-drop resources within the navigational structure to customize their course structure. Once a user has arranged the resource to their liking, they can generate their customized check-out by clicking the *Download* button. The navigational structure may be a simple hierarchical tree as shown in this example or may be a more complex structure like a graph. The download functionality embeds the customized structure in the checked out resource.

The system then dynamically generates a zip archive of the customized resources and presents this archive to the user. A static HTML page of each resource and any associated documents or videos are placed in a directory for each resource. Metadata is also stored in an XML file with the OAI-PMH [8] record information for each resource. While any resource may be used multiple times in the complex resource, the download only creates a single directory for each resource. Since the complex structure is embedded in the navigational structure with links to the individual resource there is no need to store multiple copies of each resource.

Figure 2a shows the content of the downloadable archive. Two HTML files are generated at the root level of the archive—an index file and a download-at-a-glance file—as well as directories containing style and javascript files—to enhance the user

JCDL '13, July 22–26, 2013, Indianapolis, Indiana, USA.
ACM 978-1-4503-2077-1/13/07.

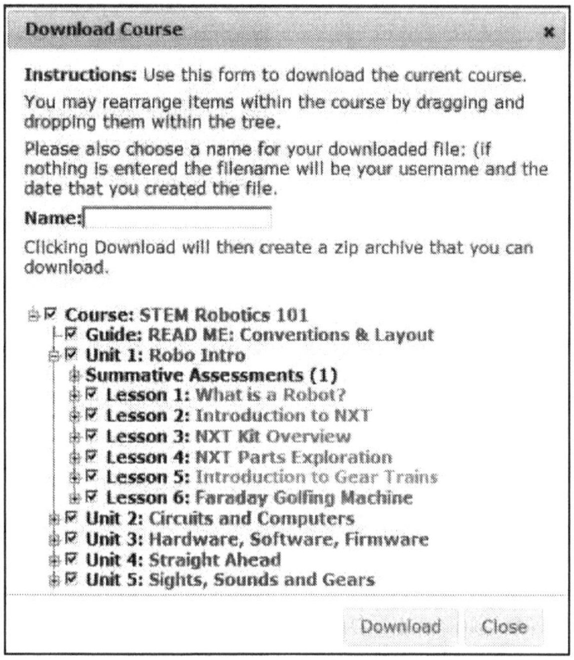

Figure 1 The content download interface in the STEMRobotics repository.

experience—and the *node* directory containing the individual resources that constitute the complex resource. Figure 2b shows the content of a specific resource directory. The index file contains the customized navigational structure generated by the user as well as a frame that displays each individual resource of the check-out when browsed through the navigational structure (shown in Figure 3). The download-at-a-glance file contains a serialized, brief overview of the entire downloaded resource.

The download is self-contained so that it may be used in an offline context—e.g., in a school where students are not allowed to access the Internet—or the download may be extracted to a webserver and act as small repository without requiring Drupal or any other supporting software. This allows an educator to take a master curriculum from the digital library and then customize it for each offering of their course and place the customized curriculum in their local website for their students each term.

4. CONCLUSION

Leveraging our previous work on complexly structured digital libraries we have developed a generic check-out capability for digital libraries supports and maintains complex resource

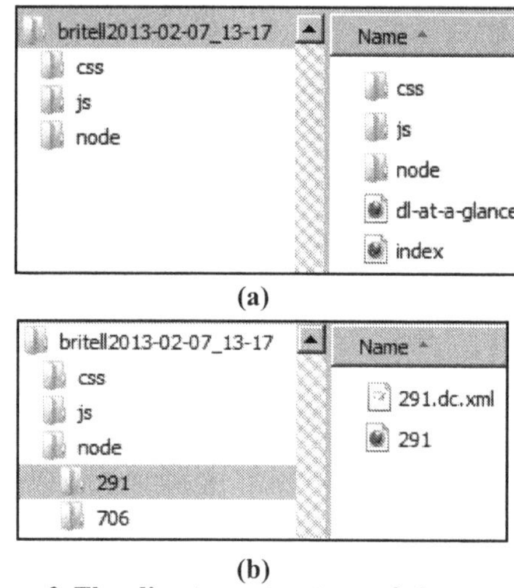

Figure 2 The directory structure of the complex check-

customization in an out of library context. By expanding the use of heterogeneous structures in digital libraries we hope to further increase their adoption. We hope to encourage these users by letting them create the structures that best represent their content and then use that content in any form they see fit.

5. ACKNOWLEDGEMENTS

This work has been funded in part by NSF Grants 0840668 and 1250340.

6. REFERENCES

[1] Britell, S. et al. 2012. Enhancing Digital Libraries and Portals with Canonical Structures for Complex Objects. *TPDL '12.*

[2] Britell, S. et al. 2012. Exploiting canonical structures to transmit complex objects from a digital library to a portal. *JCDL '12.*

[3] Britell, S. and Delcambre, L.M.L. 2012. Mapping Semantic Widgets to Web-based, Domain-specific Collections. *Conceptual Modelling ER '12.*

[4] Drupal: *http://drupal.org..*

[5] Ensemble: *http://www.computingportal.org/.*

[6] Herbert, M. Resource Harvesting within the OAI-PMH Framework. *D-Lib Magazine.* 10, 12.

[7] Khan Academy: *http://www.khanacademy.org/.*

[8] Lagoze, C. et al. 2008. Open Archives Initiative - Protocol for Metadata Harvesting - v.2.0. (Dec. 2008).

[9] STEMRobotics: *http://stemrobotics.cs.pdx.edu.*

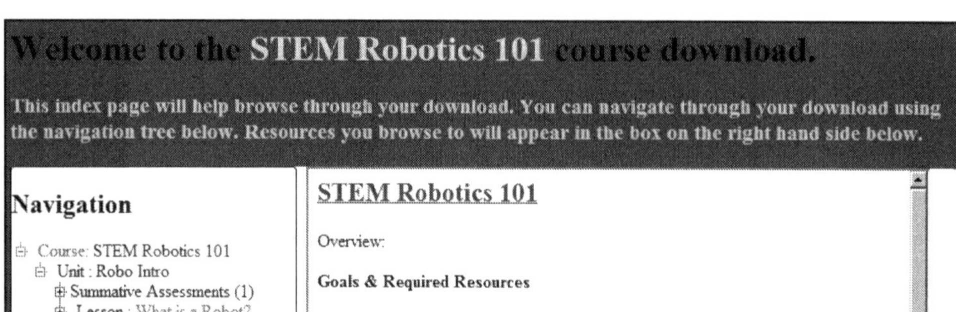

Figure 3 The customized download index page.

CSSeer: an Expert Recommendation System based on CiteSeerX

Hung-Hsuan Chen[†], Pucktada Treeratpituk[‡], Prasenjit Mitra[†‡], C. Lee Giles[†‡]
[†]Computer Science and Engineering, [‡]Information Sciences and Technology
The Pennsylvania State University, University Park, PA 16802, USA
hhchen@psu.edu, pxt162@ist.psu.edu, pmitra@ist.psu.edu, giles@ist.psu.edu

ABSTRACT

We propose CSSeer[1], a free and publicly available keyphrase based recommendation system for expert discovery based on the CiteSeerX digital library and Wikipedia as an auxiliary resource. CSSeer generates keyphrases from the title and the abstract of each document in CiteSeerX. These keyphrases are then utilized to infer the authors' expertise. We compared CSSeer with the other two state-of-the-art expert recommenders and found that the three systems have moderately divergent recommendations on 20 benchmark queries. Thus, we recommend users to browse through several different recommenders to obtain a more complete expert list.

Categories and Subject Descriptors

H.4 [**Information Systems Applications**]: Miscellaneous; H.3.7 [**Information Storage and Retrieval**]: Digital Library—*Collections, Dissemination*; H.3.3 [**Information Storage and Retrieval**]: Information Search and Retrieval—*relevance feedbacks, retrieval models, selection process*

Keywords

Expert Recommendation, CSSeer, CiteSeerX, Information Extraction, Text Mining, Keyphrase Extraction

1. INTRODUCTION

We introduce the data analysis flow of CSSeer framework. The keyphrases of each document and an expert's list of phrases are analyzed and indexed offline. When a user inputs a term for which an expert is sought, the query processor communicates with the indexed expert list and related keyphrases online.

From CiteSeerX corpus, the field analyzer extracts the title, abstract, published venue name, reference list, author names, author emails, and author affiliations for each document using ParsCit [1]. A Support Vector Machine based header parser is utilized to extract other metadata. The author names are disambiguated by Random Forests [2].

CSSeer harvests the titles and the hyperlink texts from the introduction paragraphs of Wikipedia pages related to computer science, statistics, and mathematics. These phrases are used to compile keyphrase candidates. To increase recall, CSSeer extracts bigrams, trigrams, and quadgrams appearing at least 3 times in titles of papers in CiteSeerX as keyphrase candidates. Since the titles and hyperlink texts in Wikipedia are edited by users, they are typically high quality phrases with meaningful semantics. To identify keyphrases for each CiteSeerX document, CSSeer compares the title and abstract of each document with all the Wikipedia keyphrase candidates and uses the matched terms as keyphrases.

CSSeer discovers experts of a given term by considering both textual relevance and quality (inferred by citation counts) of the authors' published papers. The expert score of an author a to a query term q is defined as follows.

$$p(a,q) := \sum_{\forall d \in pub(a)} \log(c(d)) \left(tf(q) / \sum_{\forall q' \in d} tf(q') \right), \quad (1)$$

where $pub(a)$ returns a set of publications of author a, $c(d)$ returns the citation counts of the document d, and $tf(q)$ returns the term frequency of q in d.

2. COMPARISON OF DIFFERENT EXPERT RECOMMENDERS

Manually evaluating an expert recommendation system requires the evaluators to have sufficient domain knowledge to judge the quality of the recommended expert list. Recruiting knowledgable evaluators is not easy, and asking the evaluators to label the recommended list is time consuming. Instead, we compared the expert list returned by CSSeer with the other two state-of-the art expert recommenders. We define consensus score $S@n$ of one expert recommendation system e_i to the other systems $e_1, \ldots, e_{i-1}, e_{i+1}, \ldots e_n$ in Equation 2.

$$S@n := \left| \bigcup_{\forall k \neq i} \left(r_i^{(n)} \cap r_k^{(n)} \right) \right|, \quad (2)$$

where $r_i^{(n)}$ is the set of the top n returns of the recommendation system e_i, and the $|\cdot|$ function returns the set length.

The consensus score involves no user evaluation and as such could be automated for a large number of queries. However, different expert recommendation systems record

[1]`http://csseer.ist.psu.edu/`

JCDL'13, July 22–26, 2013, Indianapolis, Indiana, USA.
ACM 978-1-4503-2077-1/13/07.

Table 1: The consensus score@10 and consensus score@20 of 20 benchmark queries among the returns of CSSeer, ArnetMiner, and Microsoft Academic Search (MAS).

	$n = 10$			$n = 20$		
Query	CSSeer	ArnetMiner	MAS	CSSeer	ArnetMiner	MAS
algorithm	1	2	1	5	4	3
security	3	4	1	12	10	9
software engineering	3	3	4	11	9	11
information retrieval	6	7	5	14	15	12
machine learning	2	3	1	8	8	9
database	4	6	6	9	10	14
programming language	4	3	5	9	7	10
data structure	6	4	5	12	8	13
world wide web	4	5	6	9	11	14
social network	2	2	3	5	5	6
compiler	4	4	3	12	12	13
vlsi	1	1	1	2	2	1
computer network	1	1	0	2	4	2
support vector machine	1	4	4	9	12	8
semantic web	7	7	7	11	13	14
nonparametric statistics	2	2	0	2	4	2
markov chain monte carlo	4	0	4	9	2	9
quality of service	5	2	5	8	6	6
virtual machine	4	3	1	6	6	4
intelligent agent	5	8	6	9	12	10
Average Consensus Score	3.45	3.5	3.5	8.2	8.0	8.5
Standard Deviation of Consensus Score	1.82	2.09	2.28	3.53	3.83	4.35

the same expert with different name variations. For example, W. Bruce Croft at the University of Massachusetts is recorded as "W. Bruce Croft" in both CSSeer and MAS but is "Bruce Croft" in ArnetMiner; ChengXiang Zhai at UIUC is stored as "ChengXiang Zhai" in both CSSeer and ArnetMiner but is "Cheng-xiang Zhai" in MAS. Therefore, naïvely regarding names as strings and performing string matching could generate misleading results.

As a result, we intentionally selected 20 benchmark diverse queries that contain both broad and narrow topics, including hardware ("vlsi"), low level machine concepts ("compiler" and "virtual machine"), software development ("programming language", "data structure", and "software engineering"), statistical techniques ("nonparametric statistics" and "markov chain monte carlo"), data mining techniques ("information retrieval", "support vector machine", etc.), and so on. We did not use the relevant judgements provided by ArnetMiner directly[2] [3], because there these terms are mostly limited to the artificial intelligence domain.

We compared $S@10$ and $S@20$ for the three systems for 20 benchmark queries. The results were manually examined and reported in Table 1. Note that in the table the name variations for different systems were unified for better representation. As can be seen, the average consensus scores $S@10$ and $S@20$ are low for all three systems. Specifically, on average only 3.45 to 3.5 names out of the top 10 returned by one system overlapped with at least one of the other two systems. For the top 20 returns, the numbers of overlapping names are still small, on average ranging from 8.0 to 8.5. This suggests that the current state-of-the-art expert recommendation systems have divergent opinions. Relying on only one expert recommendation system may produce a biased expert list.

Although we try to select benchmark queries that cover several different domains in Computer Science, the number of queries is still small. A large scale experiment is limited by the evaluation process which requires users with domain knowledge. Although it is possible to automatically compare the overlap of top-n returns across different systems, the name variations can still be an issue in practice. For future work, we are planning to use regular expression and edit distance to compare the same names in different systems. Such a system could automatically compare the consensus of different expert recommendation systems. Currently, the expert scores are calculated offline on a fixed keyphrase list. However, users might submit a valid term which is not included in the pre-defined keyphrase list. For this one could integrate the search tool Solr/Lucene for fast document lookup and online expert score approximation.

Acknowledgments

We gratefully acknowledge partial support by the National Science Foundation and Dow Chemical.

3. REFERENCES

[1] I. Councill, C. Giles, and M. Kan. Parscit: An open-source crf reference string parsing package. In *Proceedings of LREC*, volume 2008, pages 661–667. European Language Resources Association (ELRA), 2008.

[2] P. Treeratpituk and C. Giles. Disambiguating authors in academic publications using random forests. In *Proceedings of the 9th ACM/IEEE Joint Conference on Digital Libraries*, pages 39–48. ACM, 2009.

[3] Z. Yang, J. Tang, B. Wang, J. Guo, J. Li, and S. Chen. Expert2bole: From expert finding to bole search. In *Proceedings of the ACM SIGKDD International Conference on Knowledge Discovery and Data Mining,(KDD'09)*, pages 1–4, 2009.

[2] `http://arnetminer.org/lab-datasets/expertfinding/`

Environmental Studies Faculty Attitudes Towards Sharing of Research Data

Nathan Hall
Virginia Tech
P.O. Box 90001
Blacksburg, VA 24062-9001
1-540-231-1751
nfhall@vt.edu

ABSTRACT

This research explores the attitudes of Environmental Studies faculty towards sharing research data. The findings are drawn from a broader unpublished study in progress on information behavior of Environmental Studies faculty in e-science and scholarly communications. The author conducted fourteen semi-structured interviews with tenure-track and tenured faculty in various environmental studies and earth science disciplines at two large state universities. Early findings and areas for further analysis are described.

Categories and Subject Descriptors

J.4 [**Social and Behavioral Sciences**]: *Economics, psychology, sociology.*

General Terms

Economics, Human Factors

Keywords

1. Data sharing, User behavior and modeling, Scientific data curation, Social-technical perspectives

INTRODUCTION

In the current fiscal and economic climate, academic libraries have greater budgetary constraints, yet technological advances give libraries opportunities to remain relevant through new services around data management and open access dissemination. This is an especially pertinent area due to recent mandates from federal and private funding agencies requiring that principal investigators account for and, in many cases, provide access to their research data.

In order to improve research data management services, academic libraries need to better understand faculty attitudes, concerns, and behaviors towards their research data. A recent study by Scaramozzino, Ramirez, and McGaughey (2012) explores faculty attitudes and behaviors about data curation, including a component about the importance of data sharing. They found that "while the majority of researchers believe that colleagues should share their data, only a minority of respondents actually share their own data with individuals who did not help in gathering the data" (361). Researchers are increasingly expected to manage and share research data, especially for federally sponsored research, but reasons for why few researchers share scientific data are poorly understood.

JCDL '13, July 22–26, 2013, Indianapolis, Indiana, USA.
ACM 978-1-4503-2077-1/13/07.

METHODOLOGY

The methodology described here comes from a broader unpublished study in progress. The researcher uses a phenomenological approach in fourteen semi-structured interviews at Virginia Tech and University of North Texas. Due to the exploratory nature of this study, the scope was limited to teaching and research faculty only, as opposed to graduate students or other populations. Environmental Studies was identified as an appropriate scope for the study, since as an interdisciplinary field it includes researchers with backgrounds physical sciences, social sciences, and humanities, which provides a diverse sample in how research participants conduct research and organize data. An initial convenience sample of participants in relevant departments was selected, and further participants were recruited through snowball sampling. Interviews were conducted face-to-face or via the voice over IP software, Skype. The researcher transcribed the interviews and will analyze the transcripts using an iterative process of identifying and labeling common themes in the interviews. Validation occurs through member-checking, triangulation, and clarification of bias.

RESULTS

The interviews explore reasons that some researchers hesitate to share their research data. Early analysis indicates a number of overlapping, and at times conflicting views about providing free global access to research data.

Nearly all participants see value in sharing research data. The faculty members who saw little value in sharing their data believed that their data was too narrow to be useful in a different study.

Other reasons for hesitating to share research data included concern about IRB compliance and the protection of research subjects. Another common reason some participants did not want to share their data was the amount of work required to organize the data to make it useful to someone else.

While many researchers in the sample felt that sharing data was necessary for transparency of the scientific process, some were concerned that their data could be taken out of context and politicized. These participants were all senior faculty.

Faculty who already have tenure were more likely to speak favorably about data sharing to improve the transparency of the scientific process and some indicated they would appreciate having any impact at all (on environmental policy, for example). Many junior faculty members expressed concern about their ability to publish the findings on their own data before someone else could.

CONCLUSIONS

Interview transcription is ongoing and has not undergone any formal clustering or post-collection validation, however, from the interviews completed and transcribed to this point, many participants' concerns would be addressed to some extent if datasets were legitimized as a research output and given weight in the promotion and tenure process. This is unlikely without significant development in data management standards and practices by institutions, funders, and research disciplines.

The conclusions drawn in this preliminary reading are still undergoing member-checking but will inform future research design in order to gather data from a larger sample and produce generalizable findings.

Some areas for further exploration include expanding the sample to include a more diverse sample of participants, such as graduate students and postdoctoral research associates, as well as researchers from more student-centered institutions, which could have different cultures of data sharing than research universities.

Further study in this area will improve library and administrative awareness of the needs and concerns of investigators as stakeholders in data management and dissemination projects. This will in turn lead to more informed development of systems and services, and a more efficient use of project resources.

2. REFERENCES

[1] Scaramozzino, J. M., Ramirez, M. L., and McGaughey, K. J. 2012. A study of faculty data curation behaviors and attitudes at a teaching-centered university. *College and Research Libraries*. 73, 4 (2012), 349-365. URL= http://crl.acrl.org/content/73/4/349.full.pdf+html

Evaluation of Header Metadata Extraction Approaches and Tools for Scientific PDF Documents

Mario Lipinski, Kevin Yao, Corinna Breitinger, Joeran Beel, Bela Gipp
University of California, Berkeley, CA, USA
mario@lipinski.tk, {kzyao, breitinger, jbeel, gipp}@berkeley.edu

ABSTRACT

This paper evaluates the performance of tools for the extraction of metadata from scientific articles. Accurate metadata extraction is an important task for automating the management of digital libraries. This comparative study is a guide for developers looking to integrate the most suitable and effective metadata extraction tool into their software. We shed light on the strengths and weaknesses of seven tools in common use. In our evaluation using papers from the arXiv collection, GROBID delivered the best results, followed by Mendeley Desktop. SciPlore Xtract, PDFMeat, and SVMHeaderParse also delivered good results depending on the metadata type to be extracted.

Categories and Subject Descriptors

H.3.4 [**Information Storage and Retrieval**]: Systems and Software – *performance evaluation (efficiency and effectiveness).*

General Terms

Algorithms, Measurement, Performance, Experimentation.

Keywords

Information Retrieval; Metadata Extraction; Evaluation; PDF

1. INTRODUCTION

Obtaining structured metadata from documents, including title, authors, and publication date, is important to support retrieval tasks, e.g., in digital libraries [2]. Various tools exist to automatically extract this information from PDF documents. However, the extraction is error prone given that no standards specify how metadata should be structured or formatted. Different style guides imposed by various publishers and venues, as well as the scope of metadata information provided by individual authors, increase the difficulty of automatic metadata extraction. In this paper we evaluate tools for metadata extraction from scientific articles.

A recent publication compared the metadata extraction capabilities of Mendeley and ParsCit, concluding that Mendeley's two-staged SVM solved the problem of metadata extraction for crowdsourced bibliographic metadata management [5]. Several approaches for extracting metadata have been proposed and independently examined. Since studies used different methods and data sources for their evaluation, a direct comparison is not possible. Currently, no comprehensive evaluation of tools for metadata extraction exists.

Fundamental methods used for metadata extraction are stylistic analysis, machine learning, and the use of knowledge bases. Metadata extraction tools using stylistic analysis extract titles using heuristics, e.g., font sizes and position information of examined elements. Machine learning techniques for metadata extraction use support vector machines (SVM), hidden Markov models (HMM), or conditional random fields (CRF). These approaches rely on previous training and natural language processing. Knowledge base approaches make use of databases, such as Google Scholar, or pronoun repositories, e.g., lists of common names, to act as a cross-reference to extracted entities. Software systems for metadata extraction combine these methods.

The JISC ConnectedWorks project published an overview of available software for processing PDF documents [6]. For our study, we focus on tools that are freely available and do not require user interaction so that the tools can be integrated into custom projects. Although Mendeley Desktop cannot be included in custom software, we include it in the evaluation as a widely used software with metadata extraction capabilities. We did not include Zotero, since its 25-document limit makes it unsuitable for bulk processing. Also the recently developed Docear's PDF Inspector [4] was not included since it was not yet available at the time of evaluation. Table 1 gives an overview of tools for extracting header information from PDF documents.

Table 1. Tools for Metadata Extraction from PDF Documents

Name of Tool Link	Approach used
Docear's PDF Inspector* http://docear.org	Style information analysis
GROBID https://github.com/kermitt2/grobid	CRF
Mendeley Desktop http://www.mendeley.com/	SVM, web-based look-up
ParsCit http://aye.comp.nus.edu.sg/parsCit/	CRF
PDFMeat http://code.google.com/p/pdfmeat/	Queries Google Scholar, pdftotext
PDFSSA4MET http://code.google.com/p/pdfssa4met/	Structure/Syntax analysis of XML
SciPlore Xtract http://sciplore.org/	Style information analysis of XML
SVMHeaderParse http://citeseerx.sourceforge.net/	SVM
Zotero* http://zotero.org	Queries Google Scholar

* not evaluated

2. METHODOLOGY

To meet the suitability requirement, extraction tools must fulfill three requirements. First, the tools had to provide an interface that allowed the integration into custom projects. They either had to provide a library for integration into other programs, or a stand-alone program that either accepted plain text or PDF as input. Second, they were not allowed to require user interaction to allow bulk processing. Third, the examined tools had to output machine-readable data, for example in XML format.

JCDL'13, July 22–26, 2013, Indianapolis, Indiana, USA.
ACM 978-1-4503-2077-1/13/07.

Table 2. Results (A_{100}: First evaluation setup with 100 articles, B_{100}: Second evaluation setup with 100 articles, B_{1153}: Second evaluation setup with 1,153 articles)

	Title			Authors			Authors' last names		Abstract			Year	
	A_{100}	B_{100}	B_{1153}	A_{100}	B_{100}	B_{1153}	B_{100}	B_{1153}	A_{100}	B_{100}	B_{1153}	B_{100}	B_{1153}
GROBID	N/A	0.92	0.92	N/A	0.83	0.83	0.90	0.91	N/A	0.75	0.74	0.64	0.69
Mendeley Desktop	N/A	0.84	0.82	N/A	0.72	0.70	0.78	0.77	N/A	N/A	N/A	0.23	0.26
ParsCit	0.59	0.52	0.54	0.47	0.29	0.31	0.36	0.37	0.49	0.31	0.26	0.06	0.07
PDFSSA4MET	0.13	0.21	0.18	0.05	0.02	0.01	0.20	0.18	N/A	N/A	N/A	N/A	N/A
PDFMeat	0.60	N/A	N/A	0.6	N/A	N/A	N/A	N/A	0.14	N/A	N/A	N/A	N/A
SciPlore Xtract	0.76	0.81	0.78	N/A	N/A	N/A	N/A	N/A	N/A	N/A	N/A	N/A	N/A
SVMHeaderParse	0.50	0.57	0.61	0.64	0.70	0.73	0.74	0.76	0.37	0.64	0.64	0.21	0.20

Since the tools are written in different languages and have different output formats, we created a Java framework to provide a uniform interface for the variety of tools. The framework requires a PDF file as input and converts it, if required by the tool, to plain text using pdftotext. The output is wrapped into a unified Java data structure that stores the extracted fields.

To evaluate the tools, we compiled a test collection from arXiv.org, a scientific publication archive, which contains articles from various disciplines with various document formatting. Given the diverse document styles in the arXiv collection, it provides a good data source to test the performance of metadata extraction tools on articles in Physics, Mathematics, Computer Science, Quantitative Biology, Quantitative Finance and Statistics. In examining publications only from these fields, the results might not apply to other fields. By using arXiv's API, we obtained 1,153 random PDF articles including their metadata, dated from 2006 to 2010.

We performed three evaluations with two independent test setups. For the first setup, we randomly chose 100 articles from the test collection and the metadata extracted from the PDF documents was manually compared against the metadata from arXiv. We created a scoring scheme to assess the performance of the individual tools on the following metadata types: title, authors, and abstract. Each field was scored individually. For every field a score of 1 was given if the extracted metadata matched the reference data. A score of 0 was assigned if the field was extracted incorrectly. For title, authors, and abstracts a reduced score of 0.5 was allotted if the data was retrieved, but some characters, such as accents or ligatures produced problems. If only a fraction of the correct data was detected, a score of 0.25 was allotted.

For the second test setup, we performed two evaluations. First, we used the 100 documents from the first setup and second we used all 1,153 documents. In this setup, we developed a program to automatically determine the scores for extraction of title, author full names, author last names, abstract, and publication year. The program used the Levenshtein distance and normalized it using the length of the reference value. The resulting score approximately fits the percent match. The scores for all documents from the test collection were averaged.

3. RESULTS

Table 2 shows the results of the evaluations. In the following, we point out noteworthy results and give their accuracy scores. GROBID performs best; 0.92 for titles, 0.83 for authors, 0.91 for authors' last names, 0.74 for abstracts, and 0.69 for publication date. We believe that by working directly with PDF files without losing information in preprocessing, and by accurately engineered models, GROBID has an advantage over other methods. Mendeley Desktop ranks second for all extracted metadata types (0.82 for titles, 0.70 for author first names, and 0.77 for author last names). Mendeley leverages its extensive online database to enrich the extracted metadata. While the authors in [5] claim that Mendeley's two-stage SVM performs best, our results show that GROBID's CRF implementation can deliver better metadata extraction without consulting external resources.

SciPlore Xtract shows a good accuracy of 0.78 in extraction of the title. By taking into account the article's style information (font sizes and layout information), SciPlore Xtract can gain an advantage over other tools that ignore this information [3]. Nevertheless, the low score of 0.18 for PDFSSA4MET demonstrates that relying solely on font size is insufficient. Looking at the data revealed that PDFSSA4MET often extracted arXiv's document ID banner in the left margin as the title, so the tool may be at a disadvantage for the chosen test collection.

SVMHeaderParse delivered good results for extracting author names (0.73) and abstracts (0.64). The results for SVMHeaderParse and ParsCit for extracting titles and abstracts slightly differed between our two test setups. We believe that different versions of the tool for transforming PDFs into plain text can affect the performance of these tools. PDFMeat delivered relatively good results of 0.60 on title and author extraction. The relative good quality of the extracted data may result from incorporating results from Google Scholar [1].

The evaluation framework, including test collection, the ground truth and the test-software, is available from the authors by request.

4. ACKNOWLEDGEMENTS

We greatly acknowledge support by the VIGRE Program to work on this project at the Department of Statistics at the University of California, Berkeley.

5. REFERENCES

[1] Aumueller, D. 2009. Retrieving metadata for your local scholarly papers.

[2] Beel, J., Gipp, B., Langer, S., Genzmehr, M., Wilde, E., Nürnberger, A. and Pitman, J. 2011. Introducing Mr. DLib, a Machine-readable Digital Library. *JCDL'11*.

[3] Beel, J., Gipp, B., Shaker, A. and Friedrich, N. 2010. SciPlore Xtract: Extracting Titles from Scientific PDF Documents by Analyzing Style Information (Font Size). *ECDL'10*.

[4] Beel, J., Langer, S., Genzmehr, M. and Müller, C. 2013. Docears PDF Inspector: Title Extraction from PDF files. *JCDL'13*.

[5] Granitzer, M., Hristakeva, M., Knight, R. and Jack, K. 2012. A Comparison of Metadata Extraction Techniques for Crowdsourced Bibliographic Metadata Management. *SAC'12*.

[6] JISC ConnectedWorks Project 2010. *Research on existing PDF processors*. University of Cambridge.

Exploring the Usability of Folksonomies in the Online Art Museum Community

Crystal Boston-Clay
School of Informatics, IUPUI
719 Indiana Avenue
Indianapolis, IN 46202
bostonc@iupui.edu

Malika Mahoui
Polis Center, IUPUI
1200 Waterway Blvd,
Indianapolis, IN 46202
mmahoui@iupui.edu

Kyle Jaebker
Indianapolis Museum of Art
4000 N. Michigan Rd,
Indianapolis, IN 46208
kjaebker@imamuseum.org

ABSTRACT

This paper presents a usability evaluation of the Indianapolis Museum of Art website - as a typical art museum website supporting both tag-based search and user tagging of artwork - in an effort to explore how users access artwork while interacting with the museum online search and retrieval system. The usability study examined the extent of usage of Steve Tagger capabilities (annotation and use of tags in the process of searching/accessing artwork resources) deployed on the website. The usability test results showed that 55% of the users were able to successfully locate information on the website using both traditional searching techniques and folksonomies. However, only 34% of the users were able to successfully locate artwork using tags only. On the other hand, 95% of the participants were able to annotate an object by adding a term or tag to describe the artwork.

Categories and Subject Descriptors

H.3.7 [Digital Libraries]: Collection; H.5.4 [Hypertext/Hypermedia]: Navigation; H.1.2 [User/Machine Systems]: Human Factors

Keywords

Folksonomy, usability study, tagging, annotation, digital library

1. INTRODUCTION

Researchers found that there are more efficient ways to enhance indexing and cataloging of online art collections beyond the use of metadata [1]. As a result of this innovative idea, the Steve Tagger Project (http://tagger.steve.museum/) was launched in 2005 with the aim to promote user tagging of art museum web sites. Tagging is commonly referred to as "social tagging" whereby typical users describe and classify resources in a shared environment, while the term "folksonomy" is a concatenation of the words folk and taxonomy, meaning that taxonomies on the internet are created by average people [1, 2]. There have been several research studies including [3-5] that evaluated the usefulness of user tags in supporting the search of artwork collections. However, the adoption of tag-based searching in online art collections has been underexplored. This study seeks to examine the relationship between folksonomies and search and retrieval capabilities. We chose the Indianapolis Museum of Art (IMA) website (www.imamuseum.org/) as a typical art museum website supporting both tag-based search and user tagging of artwork. An empirical study was conducted to explore the usage of IMA's website resources including user tags, metadata, and a combination of the two resources to search for different works of art within the online collection. A usability test was conducted to evaluate the effectiveness, efficiency, and satisfaction of users' interaction with folksonomies. This study investigated the following questions:

1. Are users able to successfully search for artwork using folksonomies?
2. Does a combination of tags and metadata improve users' ability to retrieve artwork?
3. Are users able to annotate artwork and do they realize the value of adding tags to searched resources?

JCDL'13, July 22–26, 2013, Indianapolis, Indiana, USA.
ACM 978-1-4503-2077-1/13/07.

2. METHODOLOGY

2.1 Website evaluated

Indianapolis Museum of Art website was evaluated because it is one of the 11 museums that have collaborated with the Steve Tagger Project. The tagging environment on IMA's website is enabled by a tagging tool that is available on the Internet (*http://tagger.steve.museum*) where tags are managed in a structured environment through steve.museum. Two primary Steve Tagger features were evaluated which were searching (using tags) and annotating (adding tags to label artwork).

2.2 Participants

The participants consisted of 20 student volunteers from a mid-western university in the United States. 55% of the participants were females and 45% were males. 50% of the participants were familiar with IMA's website of which 80% of those familiar had also visited the website prior to the usability test.

2.3 Tasks evaluated

Participants were asked to attempt six tasks that allowed the observers to evaluate the tagging features on IMA's website. In tasks one and three, the participants were allowed to use whatever search technique that was familiar to them, thus including the traditional search box and the browser's "Find" option (used to locate specific words on the screen); while in the tasks two and four through six, the participants were restricted to only using tags or tags with metadata (e.g. title, author) provided in the advance search option on the website. Each task required the participants to locate specific artwork.

2.4 Evaluation procedure

Several dimensions of both qualitative and quantitative *data were collected.* Data collection techniques included: (1) a pre-test demographic survey to gather general participant information; (2) a usability test, where tasks were administered and evaluated for efficiency (time on task) and effectiveness (success rate); (3) a post-task questionnaire after performing tasks on IMA website, and (4) an open-ended interview to get feedback on the participant's IMA experience using the Steve Tagger features.

3. RESULTS

3.1 Effectiveness and efficiency

Effectiveness and efficiency were measured by determining whether or not the participants were able to successfully complete each task and by evaluating the amount of time required to complete each task. The average completion time across all six tasks was 188 seconds or 3.33 minutes. The time on task (the unit of measurement for efficiency) was negatively correlated with the success rate per task (effectiveness). As shown in task one, were the participants were not restrained by the search technique that they could use to find the artwork; therefore, users opt to use the search box which yielded an effectiveness of 100% and required the least amount of time to complete, 69 seconds on average.

The efficiency rate declined when the participants were limited to searching via tags as indicated by task two. Task two required participants to search by mapping several tags together. Only 40% of the participants used tags before to search for information on the Internet, which was disclosed in the effectiveness and efficiency of task two. Participants that had never used a tag cloud before were not aware that the words in the cloud were actually links and were clickable (60%); consequently those participants took more time perusing the page looking for the correct link. The participants who were familiar with tag clouds tended to be confused about how to pair tags correctly to locate the correct image (40%).

The efficiency and effectiveness of the tagging and annotation features were further analyzed based upon the user groups that emerged from the sample population. 40% of the participants had used tags to search and half of those also annotated information on websites prior to the study. The data was split to evaluate how participants with prior experience (referred to as taggers) perform compared to those without prior experience (referred to as non-taggers). Although the participants with prior experience with tagging did complete the task with higher efficiency and effectiveness than those participants without prior experience, there was not a significant difference between the two groups with a confidence interval of 95% ($p < .05$). The average success rate for taggers was 50% and 41% for non-taggers. The average time on task for taggers was 200 seconds and 219 seconds for non-taggers.

3.2 User satisfaction

To analyze the open-ended questions - especially in terms of analyzing users' sentiments - we chose to do it manually as using automatic sentiments extraction tools did not perform well. This is mainly due to the highly mixed content of the responses. The open-ended interview responses revealed that 45% of the participants felt that searching the website was easy while 35% of the participants felt that searching using the tags was difficult, confusing and complicated. 20% of the participants thought that the interface was crowded and pertinent information was hidden and not easily accessible.

4. DISCUSSION

This section highlights the findings that address the answers to the previously explained research questions. ***Searching with Tags**:* The tagging features on the website were not presented to the users in an easily accessible manner. As a way to improve the accessibility and usage of the tag search and browsing feature, it is recommended that the web designers place the collection tag search option in a more visible location of the website, such as in the top level navigation.

***Combining Metadata with Folksonomies**:* Coupling metadata with tags would improve the search and retrieval experience; however, the current interface structuring negatively affect the intended search enhancement because the metadata advance search option is often hidden within the content on the search page.

***Adding Tags to Artwork**:* The participants favored the activity of adding terms or keywords to describe artwork, which aids the search process. The website supported the users' ability to contribute to the annotation. The users were not able to see the tags that were added to the artwork immediately after, however, they were confident that their tags would appear at some point.

5. CONCLUSION

Improving access to online art museum collections is an ongoing commitment of researchers in the museum informatics discipline. Implementing folksonomies has the potential to enhance users' access to art collections online. Although the techniques offer great potential, the way the techniques are deployed in the interface can have an impact on the usability of those features. This study offered a baseline for future research on how to improve the usability and accessibility of folksonomies in the online art museum collection.

6. ACKNOWLEDGMENTS

This study is supported by the Office of the Vice President for Research at Indiana University with the grant title: New Frontiers in the Arts & Humanities.

7. REFERENCES

[1] Trant, J. Tagging, Folksonomy and Art Museums: Results of steve.museum's research. Available: *http://conference.archimuse.com/files/trantSteveResearchReport2008.pdf*, 2009.

[2] Golder, S.A., Huberman, B.A.: Usage patterns of collaborative tagging systems. J. Inf. Sci. 32(2), 198–208 (2006)

[3] Smith, M. K. Viewer Tagging in Art Museums: Comparisons to Concepts and Vocabularies of Art Museum Visitors. 17th ASIS SIG/CR Classification Research workshop, 2006.

[4] Mahoui, M., Boston-Clay, C., Stein, R., Tirupattur, N. Collaborative Tagging of Art digital Libraries: Who Should be tagging, Theory and Practice of Digital Libraries (TPDL), 2012.

[5] Arend, M, Weingartner, M., Froschauer, J., Goldfarb, D., Merkl, D. Learning about Art History by Exploratory Search, Contextual View and Social Tags. 12th IEEE International Conference on Advanced Learning Technologies, 2012.

Flickr Feedback Framework: A Service Model for Leveraging User Interactions

Jacob Jett
Center for Informatics Research in Science and Scholarship, Graduate School of Library and Information Science, University of Illinois at Urbana-Champaign
501 E. Daniel St, MC-493, Champaign, IL 61820-6211
+1-217-244-2164
jjett2@illinois.edu

Megan Senseney
Center for Informatics Research in Science and Scholarship, Graduate School of Library and Information Science, University of Illinois at Urbana-Champaign
501 E. Daniel St, MC-493, Champaign, IL 61820-6211
+1-217-244-5574
mfsense2@illinois.edu

Carole L. Palmer
Center for Informatics Research in Science and Scholarship, Graduate School of Library and Information Science, University of Illinois at Urbana-Champaign
501 E. Daniel St, MC-493, Champaign, IL 61820-6211
+1-217-244-0653
clpalmer@illinois.edu

ABSTRACT

It has been well documented that cultural heritage institutions can enhance their metadata by sharing content through popular web services such as Flickr. Through the Flickr Feasibility Study, the IMLS Digital Collections and Content project examined how an aggregation service can facilitate participation of cultural heritage institutions in popular web services. This poster presents a proposed feedback framework through which an aggregation service can facilitate and increase the impact of Web user interactions with shared cultural heritage collections through direct metadata enhancement and user analysis.

Categories and Subject Descriptors

K.6.4 [**Management of Computing and Information Systems**]: System Management – *centralization/decentralization, quality assurance.*

General Terms

Management, Measurement, Documentation, Performance, Design, Human Factors.

Keywords

Cultural heritage institutions, digital collections, feedback framework, Flickr, IMLS DCC, Web 2.0, digital aggregation, user-generated content, tags.

1. BACKGROUND

The Flickr Feasibility Study (FFS) is an experimental service developed by the IMLS Digital Collections and Content (DCC) project to facilitate participation by cultural heritage institutions in Web 2.0 spaces such as Flickr. The project team worked with five contributors to the IMLS DCC aggregation, diverse cultural heritage institutions ranging from large academic archives to small public libraries, to create the IMLS DCC Flickr photostream. The photostream, containing 8 distinct collections with a total of 4,471 images, offered institutions a viable approach to sharing their content outside of the limitations associated with participation in the Commons on Flickr [1]. We have previously reported on the FFS metadata scheme; methods and workflows developed for uploading images; engagement with the library and museum data providers; and user interactions with the collection [1], [2]. In this poster we report on a framework to facilitate both the analyses of the accelerating use of the photostream and interactions with contributing institutions to examine trends, benefits, roadblocks, and services for cultural heritage institutions that wish to participate in Web 2.0 sharing.

JCDL '13, July 22–26, 2013, Indianapolis, Indiana, USA.
ACM 978-1-4503-2077-1/13/07.

2. FFS OUTCOMES & OBSERVATIONS

There are ample reasons for cultural heritage institutions to share their content in Web 2.0 social spaces, such as Flickr [3], [4], [5]. The outcomes of the FFS have given us a deeper understanding of how an aggregation service can help cultural heritage institutions benefit from greater levels of exposure and interaction, as well as the communal expertise of Web 2.0 users. During the course of the FFS over 300 photos in the IMLS DCC Photostream were enhanced in some way by Flickr users through the use of tags, notes, and substantive user comments. In addition to the contributions that Flickr's users make to image descriptions, which are well documented [3], [4], [5], [6], [7], [8]. Users of the FFS photostream were also observed using the photostream in more novel ways such as through retrospective photography, curating the images into new collections via Flickr's galleries and groups features, and linking the images to other web resources, (e.g., Flickr user *nohomeontherange* linked a photograph of David Denny's log cabin,[1] circa 1889, to a 100 pp. report on the restoration of Mr. Denny's log cabin).[2]

3. A FEEDBACK FRAMEWORK

From the onset of the FFS, the IMLS DCC project team gathered data on the daily usage of the photostream and both the quantity and the kinds of social interactions taking place around the photos in the stream. The aim was to feed the quantitative and qualitative information gathered back to the contributing institutions for them

[1] http://www.flickr.com/photos/imlsdcc/4712197024/

[2] http://www.federalwayhistory.org/powercms/files/DavidTDennyCabinJuly272011.pdf

to benefit from the results of the experiment while also gaining exposure for their digital materials. The framework, illustrated in Figure 1 and described below, formalizes the process for an aggregator to provide systematic feedback as part of the intermediary services offered by FFS.

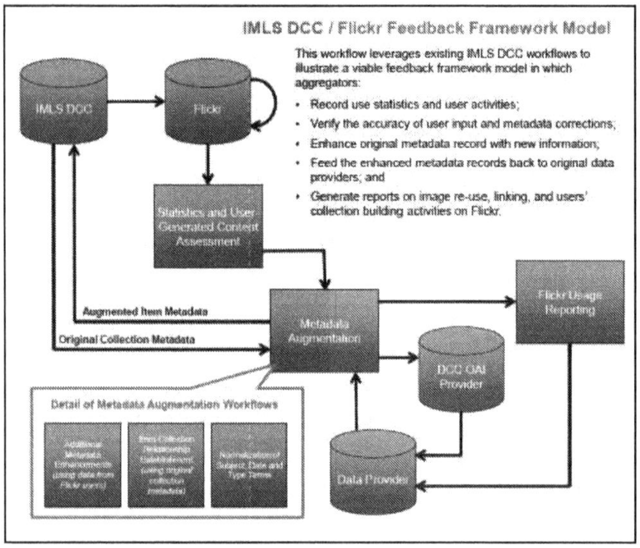

Figure 1: IMLS DCC / Flickr Feedback Framework Model

The parent project, the IMLS DCC, is deeply rooted in the architectural requirements of OAI-PMH, therefore the feedback framework also relies heavily on the OAI architecture. The process depicted above consists of five primary activities:

1. Record use statistics and user activities.
2. Analyze user comments, tags, notes, and linking for information that can be leveraged for metadata enhancements and collection development strategies.
3. Enhance original metadata records with new information.
4. Feed enhanced metadata records to original data providers via OAI-PMH.
5. Report usage trends and comparison data back to initial data provider institutions.

With the feedback provided, participating data providers can easily review and ingest the enhanced metadata records.

This allows cultural heritage institutions participating in state, regional, or national-scale aggregations to avoid duplication of effort by consolidating collection and analysis of user interactions with a single service provider. For example, in addition to providing metadata enhancement services, aggregations like the IMLS DCC are well positioned to quantify and systematically describe user interactions with cultural heritage content for institutions but also across institutions and more globally across types of content. To date, we have been able to identify and report on niche user groups and hidden collection strengths. Participating cultural heritage institutions can then exploit the range of information provided to inform collection evaluation, development, and outreach activities.

4. CONCLUSION

The FFS has proven to be a highly valuable experiment and demonstration for the IMLS DCC project. It clarified the roles, workflows, and specific data and analyses that aggregators can provide to support cultural heritage institutions that wish to pursue participation in Web 2.0 spaces such as Flickr. Interactions with end users are not only useful for enhancing existing metadata but, by revealing hidden strengths within collections and connecting cultural heritage content to niche and long tail interest communities, can also help shape an institution's collection development policies.

While the DCC Feedback Framework has not yet been implemented, we believe it offers a viable service model for digital content aggregators. By connecting cultural heritage institutions to the large knowledge base of Web users and instituting comprehensive feedback workflows, service providers can help institutions fully benefit from the range of social interactions emerging as users interact with shared cultural heritage content.

5. ACKNOWLEDGMENTS

This work was supported in part by Institute of Museum and Library Services, LG-06-07-0020. All expressed opinions are those of the authors, not the funding agency.

6. REFERENCES

[1] Jett, J., Palmer, C.L., Fenlon, K., & Chao, Z. (2010), Extending the reach of our collective cultural heritage: The IMLS DCC Flickr Feasibility Study. Proc. Am. Soc. Info. Sci. Tech., 47: 1–2.

[2] Palmer, C. L. (2010). Aggregating collections to advance our collective cultural heritage. WebWise Conference, March 4, 2010, Denver CO.

[3] Affleck, J. (2007). Memory capsules: discursive interpretation of cultural heritage through digital media. (Doctoral dissertation). University of Hong Kong.

[4] Burgess, J. (2007). Vernacular creativity and new media. (Doctoral dissertation). Creative Industries Faculty, Queensland University of Technology.

[5] Zarro, M.A. & Allen, R.B. (2010). User-Contributed Descriptive Metadata for Libraries and Cultural Institutions. *Lecture Notes in Computer Science, 6273*, 46-54.

[6] Springer, M., Dulabahn, B., Michel, P., Natanson, B., Reser, D., Woodward, D., & Zinkham, H. (2008). *For the Common Good: The Library of Congress Flickr Pilot Project.* Retrieved May 21, 2012, from http://www.loc.gov/rr/print/flickr_report_final.pdf

[7] Terras, M. (2011). The Digital Wunderkammer: Flickr as a Platform for Amateur Cultural and Heritage Content. *Library Trends*, *59*(4), 686-706.

[8] Library of Congress. (2008). On the record: Report of the Library of Congress Working Group on the Future of Bibliographic Control. Retrieved May 21, 2012, from www.loc.gov/bibliographic-future/news/lcwg-ontherecord-jan08-final.pdf

Formal Foundations for Systematic Digital Library Generation

Jonathan P. Leidig
School of Computing and Information Systems
Grand Valley State University
Allendale, MI
jonathan.leidig@gvsu.edu

Edward A. Fox
Department of Computer Science
Virginia Tech
Blacksburg, VA
fox@vt.edu

ABSTRACT

Many digital library design, development, and deployment processes are not based on systematic generation activities. The utilization of generation processes enables the precise definition of digital libraries, identification of existing software components, co-generation of multiple digital libraries, and evaluation of a digital library's coverage and completeness. The foundation of a digital library generation process is in the formal framework in which it is described. Two notable formal frameworks have previously been proposed for describing digital libraries and their content, architecture, functionality, and related societies. These two frameworks are merged in this effort to provide the foundation for a generation framework in support of an emerging class of scientific digital libraries.

Categories and Subject Descriptors

H.3.7 [**Info. Storage and Retrieval**]: Digital Libraries

Keywords

Collaboration, Collections, Domain Ontology, Simulations

1. INTRODUCTION

Digital libraries (DLs) have historically had success in providing information management and satisfaction. DLs have been deployed in support of many domains, including fields within the humanities, sciences, and education. However, DLs are becoming more complex as they are given new features in support of emerging content and scientific domains. The lack of collaboration between digital library designers and developers has prevented the reuse and dissemination of DL software and services apart from several widely used, open-source DL software. There is an increasing likelihood of failing to properly describe available systems and services, failing to identify existing solutions, and repeating similar development efforts. Digital library research and practice has generally not yet made use of standard underlying foundational frameworks to mitigate these issues.

While one-off unique DLs will continue to be developed, DL generation frameworks provide the ability to systematically describe, develop, and deploy custom DLs based on an underlying formal foundation. The formal foundation must provide a descriptive language to properly encode a DL's content, services, architecture, functionality, and user society. A systematic DL generation framework must utilize one or more formal foundations to semi-automate at least some of the functions required to maintain, compare, and evaluate formalisms; maintain a software component pool or toolkit; select from existing software components; produce software for a complete DL; and deploy the software to provide a running DL instance for a particular organization.

2. FORMAL FRAMEWORKS

Within a formal framework, formal definitions provide a concise method of conveying precise specifications of terms, artifacts, relationships, concepts, and approaches. The formal framework provides a grammar and structure for producing and reasoning with formal definitions. The 5S Formal Framework [2, 3] and the DELOS Reference Model [1] have previously been used to formally define topics related to digital libraries.

These frameworks have been successfully utilized to define a wide range of representative DLs. The formal definitions produced in previous work have provided a rigorous, mathematics-based understanding of concepts that is often lacking in the reporting and understanding of projects. As examples, formal definitions were used to describe the content, users, and services of digital libraries in the fields of archeology [8], fisheries and wildlife management [6], and education [7].

3. MERGING OF FRAMEWORKS

In developing a series of DLs to support scientific and medical research communities, the need emerged for a generation framework that could produce DLs with the ability to support highly numeric content and experimental workflows. A simulation-supporting DL framework, SimDL, was produced to generate DL instances for the domains of computational epidemiology and network science [4]. The formalisms for this domain were encoded in 5S notation [5]. To produce formalisms for this context, functionality provided by both the 5S formal framework and DELOS Reference Model was required.

JCDL'13, July 22–26, 2013, Indianapolis, Indiana, USA.
ACM 978-1-4503-2077-1/13/07.

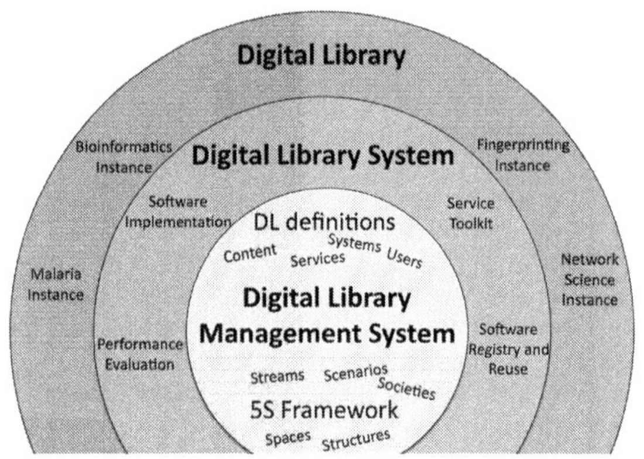

Figure 1: SimDL generation framework based on the inclusion of the 5S Formal Framework within the organization of the DELOS Reference Model, as described in [4].

The DELOS Reference Model provides a guiding multi-layer view of the DL universe. This view splits design and development into three separate layers. The first layer is the production of a digital library management system (DLMS). The DLMS consists of a formal description of the required features of a proposed class of digital libraries. The second layer consists of the digital library system (DLS). The DLS is a software toolkit that fully implements the features described in the DLMS and may be used to produce numerous DL instances. The third layer is the digital library (DL) instance. The DL is produced from the software components available in the DLS toolkit and deployed within an organization. This view provides the basis for SimDL's workflow of formalizing a class of DLs, matching formalisms with a toolkit, producing a set of available software components, and developing DL instances from the toolkit. See Figure 1 for a detailing of the generation process.

The SimDL framework requires the ability to precisely define specific types of scientific content, simulation software, analysis software, experimental workflows, and scientific services. The 5S Formal Framework provided the ability to mathematically define each of these entities within a DLMS. This framework also allowed the SimDL generation framework to evaluate a proposed software toolkit in order to prove whether it proposes to provide fully implemented coverage of the DLMS formalisms. A complete description of this process and generation framework is required in order to educate developers and practitioners in the best practices of utilizing formal frameworks.

4. DISCUSSION AND FUTURE WORK

The SimDL framework was produced to utilize the 5S formal framework as the mechanism of completing each stage of the DELOS view of the DL Universe. SimDL has been utilized to formalize (as a DLMS) and produce (as DLs) a class of public health related digital libraries. The 5S formalisms proved useful in evaluating the completeness and performance of each layer [4].

Continued work in the area of a merged 5S formal framework and DELOS Reference Model will lead to improvements in the DL development process based on formal proofs. Formal proofs may be produced regarding the nature of existing components in a toolkit or software component registry, interoperability of existing components given certain content, identification of reusable components, identification of missing software components or scripting wrappers, evaluation of the completeness of DL designs, performance of components, and overall performance of a DL instance. This work lays the groundwork for a future toolkit registry, systematic software reuse, and semi-automated DL generation and evaluation.

Aknowledgement

We thank members of the 5S formal framework and DELOS Reference Model communities for their collaboration and contributions to the foundations of this effort and field.

5. REFERENCES

[1] D. Castelli, Y. Ioannidis, S. Ross, H.-J. Schek, and H. Schuldt. Reference Model for DLMS. *DELOS Network of Excellence on Digital Libraries*, 2006.

[2] E. A. Fox, M. A. Gonçalves, and R. Shen. *Theoretical Foundations for Digital Libraries: The 5S (Societies, Scenarios, Spaces, Structures, Streams) Approach.* Morgan and Claypool Publishers, San Francisco, 2012.

[3] M. A. Gonçalves, E. A. Fox, L. T. Watson, and N. A. Kipp. Streams, structures, spaces, scenarios, societies (5S): A formal model for digital libraries. *ACM Trans Inf Syst*, 22(2):270–312, 2004.

[4] J. P. Leidig. *Epidemiology Experimentation and Simulation Management through Scientific Digital Libraries.* PhD thesis, Virginia Tech, Blacksburg, VA, USA, 2012.

[5] J. P. Leidig, E. Fox, M. Marathe, and H. Mortveit. Epidemiology experiment and simulation management through schema-based digital libraries. In *Proceedings of the 2nd DL.org Workshop at ECDL*, pages 57–66, 2010.

[6] U. Murthy, E. A. Fox, Y. Chen, E. Hallerman, R. Da Silva Torres, E. J. Ramos, and T. R. C. Falco. Superimposed image description and retrieval for fish species identification. In *Proceedings of the 13th European conference on Research and advanced technology for digital libraries*, ECDL'09, pages 285–296, Berlin, Heidelberg, 2009. Springer-Verlag.

[7] C. A. Shaffer, M. Akbar, A. J. D. Alon, M. Stewart, and S. H. Edwards. Getting algorithm visualizations into the classroom. In *Proceedings of the 42nd ACM technical symposium on Computer Science Education*, SIGCSE '11, pages 129–134, New York, NY, USA, 2011. ACM.

[8] R. Shen, N. S. Vemuri, W. Fan, and E. A. Fox. Integration of complex archeology digital libraries: An ETANA-DL experience. *Information Systems*, 33(7-8):699 – 723, 2008.

Full-text and Topic Based AuthorRank and Enhanced Publication Ranking

Jinsong Zhang
College of Transportation Management
Dalian Maritime University
Dalian, China, 116026
zhangjinsong85@163.com

Xiaozhong Liu
School of Library and Information Science
Indiana University
Bloomington, IN, USA, 47405
liu237@indiana.edu

ABSTRACT

The idea behind AuthorRank is that a content created by more popular authors should rank higher than the content created by less popular authors. This paper brings this idea into scientific publications analysis to test whether the optimized topical AuthorRank can replace or enhance topical PageRank for publication ranking. First, the PageRank with Priors (PRP) algorithm was employed to rank topic-based publications and authors. Second, the first author's reputation was used for generating an AuthorRank score. Additionally, linear combination method of topical AuthorRank and PageRank were compared with several baselines. Finally, as shown in our evaluation results, the performance of topical AuthorRank combined with topic-based PageRank is better than other baselines for publication ranking.

Categories and Subject Descriptors

H.3.7 [**Digital Libraries**]: Digital Libraries

Keywords

AuthorRank, Paper Ranking, Full-text, Labeled-LDA, PageRank with Priors, Citation Analysis.

1. INTRODUCTION

AuthorRank was first proposed in 2005 in a Google Agent Rank patent considering that the author or creator of content is significant for ranking. While it has not yet been implemented, cause of the challenging task for determining an author's (creator's) relative reputation or contribution. Fortunately, in the scientific literature domain, author metadata is a common element in publications, simple and easy to extract.

In this paper, we first used an optimized topic-sensitive PageRank algorithm, PageRank with Priors (PRP), to determine the scientific publications and authors topical ranking score. PRP algorithm was proposed in our previous work [6], which combined PageRank and a supervised topic modeling algorithm (Labeled-LDA) [8] via full-text extraction with two priors: a publication topic probability and a citation transition probability. We then used AuthorRank [1] to enhance the performance of publication ranking based on the assumption that a paper from a reputable author on a given topic (the publication topical prior) is more important than other papers for this topic.

The contributions of this paper is that, 1) the authors ranking scores calculated by PRP algorithms, and then topical AuthorRank generated by the first author's reputation; 2) the publication ranking results by linear combination method to validate whether AuthorRank can either replace or enhance classical PageRank.

JCDL '13, July 22–26, 2013, Indianapolis, Indiana, USA.
ACM 978-1-4503-2077-1/13/07.

2. PREVIOUS RESEARCH

Different from the traditional method of citation analysis (citation counts[4]), PageRank algorithm [7] is a significant method for evaluating node importance via complex graphs analysis. Haveliwala [5] proposed a topic-sensitive PageRank algorithm in 2003, computing a set of PageRank vectors biased using a set of representative topics. Rodriguez and Bollen [9] then described implementation of a particle-swarm that could simulate performance of PageRank in both its global- and relative-rank incarnations.

On the other hand, AuthorRank differs from author ranking in that the former determines how the ranking of content is affected by the creator (author). Thus, AuthorRank does so based upon author ranking. In fact, there are many studies on author ranking. The most popular approaches are Generative Probabilistic Models, Discriminative Probabilistic Models, Voting Models, and Graph-based Models [3]. Dom et al. [2] studied various graph-based ranking measures, including HITS and PageRank. The results showed that PageRank performed noticeably better whereas HITS was slightly worse than the other methods.

3. RESEARCH METHODS

3.1 PRP Algorithm

In bibliometrics, most previous studies on citation network analysis are based on the links between publications. Hence, citation graphs for scientific literature are usually defined as $G = (V, E)$, where V means the publication and E is the citing relationship between two publications.

In this paper, we represent two kinds of prior knowledge in a citation graph by LLDA: publication topic probability and citation transition probability. $W=\{w_1, w_2, \cdots, w_n\}$ is a set of words, chosen from a document d in the training text. $\mathrm{P}_{key_m}(p_d) = \frac{P(key_m|p_d)}{\sum_{x=1}^{|V|} P(key_m|p_x)}$, representing the co-occurrence probability of paper (p_d) and label (key_m).

For each vertex $v_i \in V$, the publication topic probability is $p_{z_{key_m}}(v) = \mathrm{P}_{key_m}(p_d)$, the prior probability of vertex v for topic z_{key_m}. Each edge, $e_i \in E$, on the graph represents a citation connecting v_i and v_j (v_i cites v_j). The citation topic transitioning probability is $p_{z_{key_m}}(v_i|v_j)$ is the probability of transitioning from vertex v_i to v_j for topic z_{key_m}. So, the PRP algorithm takes into account these two kinds of priors, $p_{z_{key_m}}(v)$ and $p_{z_{key_m}}(v_i|v_j)$, to calculate the relative importance of vertices in the citation graph. So the vertex's (topic relative) importance can be calculated by

$I_{key_m}(p_i|PR) = \pi_{key_m}(v),$

$\pi_{key_m}(v)^{i+1} = (1-\beta_b)\left(\sum_{u=1}^{d_{in}(v)} p_{z_{key_m}}(v|u)\,\pi_{key_m}{}^{i+1}(u)\right) + \beta_b p_{z_{key_m}}(v)$

3.2 Author Ranking and AuthorRank

In most cases, one author has multi-publications, so v_i', the vertex for a given author, is a set of papers, i.e., $v_i' = \{p_1, p_2, p_3, \cdots, p_s\}$. Similarly, the number of edges between two vertices $\langle v_i', v_j' \rangle$ is always more than one, each edge $e_i'$is expressed as$\langle v_i', v_j' \rangle = \{\langle p_1, p_2\rangle, \langle p_1, p_3\rangle, \cdots, \langle p_l, p_k\rangle\}$, only when $p_l \in v_i'$ and $p_k \in v_j'$. Therefore, $I_{key_m}(v'|R) = \pi_{key_m}(v')$.

The following defines the relationship between paper and author. $p_i = \{a_1, a_2, a_3, \cdots, a_s\}$, where p_i is the paper, always created by at least one author a_i. How the author affects the publication ranking score, $I_{key_m}(p_i|\text{AR})$, can calculate by First Author.

First Author: The ranking score of a publication (AuthorRank) depends only on the first author's ranking. The publication's topical importance, $I_{key_m}(p_i)$, is based on the score of only the first author ($\pi_{key_m}(a_1)$). $I_{key_m}(p_i|\text{AR}) = \pi_{key_m}(a_1)$

3.3 AuthorRank Combined with PRP

We have introduced two methods for publication ranking, PRP and AuthorRank. Ideally, we would like recommended publications to have both high AuthorRank and high PageRank, meaning that they are really important for the topic. In contrast, papers with low AuthorRank and low PageRank have little importance for the topic.

In this part, we would like use a method to combine the results of PRP and AuthorRank. **Linear Combination:** $I_{key_t}(p_i) = \alpha * I_{key_t}(p_i|PR) + (1-\alpha) * I_{key_t}(p_i|AR)$, where α is a parameter between 0 and 1, which controls the weight of $I_{key_t}(p_i|PR)$ and $I_{key_t}(p_i|AR)$. $I_{key_t}(p_i|PR)$ is the relative importance score for $paper_i$ on $topic_t$ calculated by the PRP algorithm, whereas $I_{key_t}(p_i|AR)$ is the importance ranking score for $paper_i$ on $topic_t$ generated by the AuthorRank algorithm.

3.4 Evaluation Method

We tried to use review or survey papers to find the most important publications for a specific scientific keyword. In order to achieve this goal, a list of review or survey papers along with their cited papers was collected. Collected review papers were screened so that they only focused on one topic (keyword). We assumed that if a publication was cited by a review paper, and if this review paper concentrated on keyword, key_i, then this publication was important for key_i.

4. EXPERIMENTS

The experimental data for this paper were derived mainly from the ACM digital library. We used 41,370 publications and 223,810 citations. In these publications, there are 63,323 authors. In this graph, we extracted 28,013 publications' text, including titles, abstracts, and full text. We then wrote a regular expression rules to extract all possible citations from paper's full text. A text window surrounding the target citation, [*–150* words, *+150* words], was used to infer the citation topic distribution via LLDA.

In order to compare the different methods for publication ranking results, we compared several baselines, **PageRank** is the original PageRank algorithm, **PRP** mentioned in 3.1, **First Author** was proposed in section 3.2 for calculating AuthorRank. **Linear Combination** described in 3.3.

Table 1: Methods based on PageRank and AuthorRank (MAP)

	PageRank	PRP	First Author	Linear Combination
MAP@10	0.0168	0.2238	0.1314	0.2271
MAP@100	0.0182	0.1619	0.0957	0.1623
MAP@1000	0.011	0.1199	0.0519	0.1172
MAP@all	0.0037	0.0996	0.0382	0.1002

Table 2: Methods based on PageRank and AuthorRank (nDCG)

	PageRank	PRP	First Author	Linear Combination
nDCG@10	0.0093	0.1229	0.0509	0.1254
nDCG@100	0.0107	0.1847	0.0963	0.1868
nDCG@1000	0.0392	0.2738	0.1816	0.2743
nDCG@all	0.1904	0.3445	0.2761	0.3456

5. CONCLUSION

From the results of our experiment, we can conclude that: 1) PRP with two priors outperforms significantly the original topic-insensitive algorithm of PageRank. 2) AuthorRank cannot replace topic-based PageRank, although it is better than the traditional PageRank algorithm. 3) AuthorRank can improve publication ranking. We also found that AuthorRank is effective for assessing the importance of publications where content or citation metadata is missing or partially missing. When we don't have publication content information, we cannot use topic modeling to infer the topic distribution, but AuthorRank can still help us to estimate the prior probability of these papers.

6. REFERENCES

[1] AuthorRank. http://www.blindfiveyearold.com/author-rank.

[2] Dom, B., Eiron, I., Cozzi, A., and Zhang, Y., 2003. Graph-based ranking algorithms for e-mail expertise analysis. In *Proceedings of the ACM SIGMOD Workshop on Research Issues in Data Mining and Knowledge Discovery*, 42–48.

[3] Fang, H. and Zhai, C. 2007. Probabilistic models for expert finding. *Lecture notes in computer science*. 4425, 418–430.

[4] Garfield, E. 1972. Citation analysis as a tool in journal evaluation. *Science*, 178, 471–479.

[5] Haveliwala, T.H. 2003. Topic-sensitive pagerank: A context-sensitive ranking algorithm for web search. *Knowledge and Data Engineering, IEEE Transactions on*. 15, 4 (Aug.), 784–796.

[6] Liu, X., Zhang, J., and Guo, C. 2012. Full-text citation analysis: enhancing bibliometric and scientific publication ranking. In Proceedings of the 21st ACM international conference on information and knowledge management, 1975–1979.

[7] Page, L., Brin, S., Motwani, R. and Winograd, T. 1999. *The PageRank citation ranking: Bringing order to the web*. Technical Report. Stanford InfoLab.

[8] Ramage, D., Hall, D., Nallapati, R. and Manning, C.D. 2009. Labeled LDA: A supervised topic model for credit attribution in multi-labeled corpora. In *Proceedings of the Conference on Empirical Methods in Natural Language Processing*. (Suntec, Singapore, Aug. 6–7, 2009), 248–256.

[9] Rodriguez, M.A. and Bollen, J. 2006. Simulating network influence algorithms using particle-swarms: PageRank and PageRank-priors.

HathiTrust Research Center: Computational Access for Digital Humanities and Beyond

Beth Plale
Robert McDonald
Yiming Sun
Inna Kouper
Ryan Cobine
Indiana University
Bloomington, IN 47405
{plale, rhmcdona, yimsun, inkouper, rcobine}@indiana.edu

J. Stephen Downie
University of Illinois
Champaign, IL 61820
jdownie@illinois.edu

Beth Sandore Namachchivaya
University of Illinois
Urbana, IL 61801
sandore@illinois.edu

John Unsworth
Brandeis University
Waltham, MA 02453
unsworth@brandeis.edu

ABSTRACT
Academic libraries are increasingly looking to provide services that allow their users to work with digital collections in innovative ways, for example, to analyze large volumes of digitized collections. The HathiTrust Research Center (HTRC) is a large collaborative that provides an innovative research infrastructure for dealing with massive amounts of digital texts. In this poster, we report on the technical progress of the HTRC as well as on the efforts to build a user community around our cyberinfrastructure.

Categories and Subject Descriptors
C.0 Computer Systems Organization: GENERAL - *System architectures;* H.2.8 Database Applications - *Data mining;* H.3.6 Library Automation - *Large text archives*; J.5 Computer Applications: ARTS AND HUMANITIES

General Terms
Algorithms, Management, Design

Keywords
Digital library, cyberinfrastructure, text analytics, HathiTrust

1. INTRODUCTION
The ongoing changes in academic institutions and in the nature of scholarship prompt academic libraries to advocate for new services that go beyond traditional collection development and preservation. Academic libraries are increasingly looking to provide services that allow their users to work with digital collections in innovative ways, for example, to analyze large volumes of digitized collections. Such innovative types of research require access to massive digital data as well as robust cyberinfrastructure that can support fast and distributed computations.

JCDL'13, July 22–26, 2013, Indianapolis, Indiana, USA.
ACM 978-1-4503-2077-1/13/07

In this poster, we report on the progress of the HathiTrust Research Center (HTRC), a large collaborative that provides an innovative research infrastructure for dealing with massive amounts of digital texts. Leveraging data storage and computational infrastructure at Indiana University and the University of Illinois at Urbana-Champaign, the HTRC offers a secure environment for scholars to perform research using public domain works from the HathiTrust Digital Library. The center has successfully developed and released the core cyberinfrastructure and a set of analytical tools [1, 4]. Beyond its technical contribution of the Phase I, the HTRC identifies building user communities as its next main focus of the Phase II. We expect to learn from users and their needs in order to enhance the HTRC tools and services.

2. HTRC DATA
The HTRC collections contain public domain materials from the HathiTrust digital library. The overall number of volumes is about 2.6 million, which amounts to about 30% of the HathiTrust collections (about 10.6 million total volumes). The collections are text-based, i.e., the HTRC provides access to machine-encoded text rather than scanned images.

The public domain corpus ranges across different times (from the 16th to the 20th century), countries, languages, and topics. It can be valuable to researchers from a variety of disciplines, including digital humanities, information and computer sciences, education, and so on.

A significant percentage of the materials (51%) has been published in the United States and in the United Kingdom. At the same time, a good proportion (the remaining 49%) of materials represent other countries and languages. The subject areas of the HTRC corpus can be characterized based on the distribution of call numbers according to the main classes of the Library of Congress Classification. A large fraction of the HTRC corpus (30%) belongs to the social sciences group, which consists of history (letters C, D), social sciences (H), political sciences (J) as well as geography and anthropology (G). The second largest segment belongs to sciences, technology and agriculture (letters Q, R, S and T in the LC classification), covering 11% of the works. The third largest segment is works in the domain of education, which comprised 9% of the corpus. The rest of the knowledge domains are represented by smaller numbers of works.

3. ARCHITECTURAL INFRASTRUCTURE & COMPUTATIONAL TOOLS

The initial architectural design of the HTRC environment was constructed during Phase I of the project in 2011-2012. A simplified diagram of the HTRC architecture is provided below:

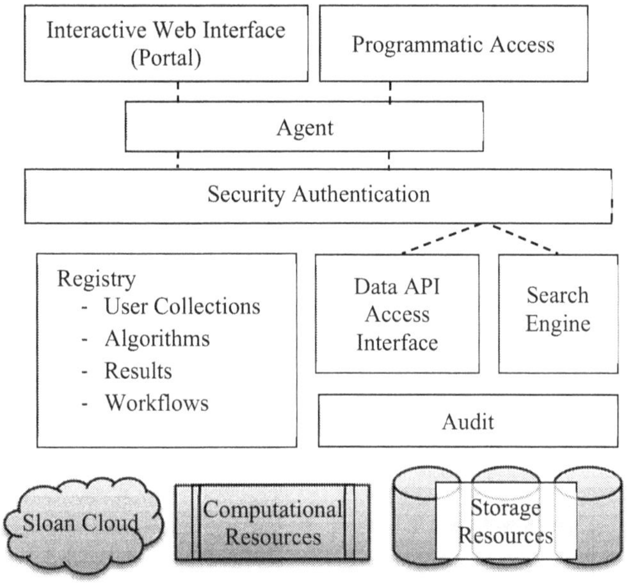

Figure 1. Key Architectural Components

The interactive web interface (the Portal) is a java application that provides the primary access point to the HTRC infrastructure. Computations and collection building tasks are performed via the HTRC Agent. The Registry is a middleware component that serves as a structured repository for keeping track of collections that have been built by users as well as algorithms, result sets and workflows. The Data API allows users to retrieve works by providing volume IDs or page IDs. The search capabilities in the HTRC environment are powered by the Apache Solr search engine server.

To analyze large digitized collections from the HathiTrust corpus, the HTRC environment offers several analytical tools. We use the Software Environment for Advancement of Scholarly Research (SEASR) suite of algorithms and Meandre dataflow execution environment for text analytics services [2, 3]. Each algorithm performs a standardized set of tasks before and after the main procedure: load the selected collection, clean it, identify necessary entities to work with (e.g., words or part of speech) and display the results on the screen. Currently, the following algorithms have been tested and implemented: topic modeling, MARC downloader, simple word count, spellcheck report, tag cloud, entity list, and text distribution statistics.

4. USER COMMUNITY

In Phase II, we rolled out an infrastructure with three components: the *development* component for tests and ongoing improvements, the *production* component for hosting the corpus and stable up-to-date software, and the *sandbox* component for small trials by users.

We interact with users and build a community through all three components of the HTRC infrastructure. We have three general categories of users: librarians, informatics users, and digital humanities (DH) users. Each user group has a unique perspective and we work towards creating multiple channels to solicit user feedback from these groups. We visit universities that are interested in digital humanities, organize informal hands-on events, such as the UnCamp [1] and online sessions with actual and potential users, present our work at conferences such as the JCDL, and maintain discussions via mailing lists.

Even though our user community work is still in its early stage, we have already received a large number of constructive comments. The HTRC team compiles a list of suggestions, evaluates them and makes implementation decisions that ensure the balance between user requirements and development resources. Currently, we are looking at ways of enhancing bibliographic metadata by adding such information as book length, word frequencies, gender of the author, genre types and some others.

5. CHALLENGES AND FUTURE WORK

This research is a work in progress, and we invite discussions and feedback from the JCDL audience in the following areas: 1) enhanced optical character recognition, 2) enriched metadata that expands beyond full-text and MARC bibliographic metadata, 3) community engagement, 4) auditing and ensuring non-consumptive research methodologies to use the entire HTRC corpus, 5) detection of additional characteristics of materials, such as genre, gender, or style, 6) interoperability and collaborations with other similar projects.

6. ACKNOWLEDGMENTS

The HTRC is a collaborative effort and the authors acknowledge the contributions of all members of the project, particularly Stacy Kowalczyk, Aaron Todd, Jiaan Zeng, Guangchen Ruan, Zong Peng, Milinda Pathirage, Samitha Liyanage and Miao Chen from Indiana University and Loretta Auvil, Boris Capitanu, Craig Willis and Kirk Hess from the University of Illinois at Urbana-Champaign.

This research was partially funded by the Alfred P. Sloan Foundation program in Digital Information Technology.

7. REFERENCES

[1] The HathiTrust Research Center UnCamp. September 10-11, 2012, Indiana University, Bloomington, IN. http://d2i.indiana.edu/htrc/uncamp2012/

[2] Meandre. Retrieved from http://seasr.org/meandre/

[3] The Software Environment for the Advancement of Scholarly Research (SEASR). Retrieved from http://seasr.org

[4] New tools available to mine world's largest digital repository of books. Retrieved from http://ovpitnews.iu.edu/news/page/normal/24146.html

How Do Users' Search Tactic Selections Influence Search Outputs in Exploratory Search Tasks?

[Extended Abstract]

Soohyung Joo
University of Wisconsin-Milwaukee
P.O. Box 413, Milwaukee, WI 53211
sjoo@uwm.edu

Iris Xie
University of Wisconsin-Milwaukee
P.O. Box 413, Milwaukee, WI 53211
hiris@uwm.edu

ABSTRACT
This study investigates the relationships between users' search tactic selections and search outputs while conducting exploratory searches in digital libraries. Frequencies of different types of search tactics applied in an exploratory search task were counted. Based on correlation analysis and multiple regression analysis, we identified types of search tactics that are associated with aspectual recall. Preliminary results indicate that browsing and evaluating item tactics affect aspectual recall in exploratory search tasks.

Categories and Subject Descriptors
H5.m Information interfaces and presentation; H3.3 Information search and retrieval

Keywords
Search tactics, exploratory search, aspectual recall, digital libraries

1. INTRODUCTION
Users engage in search processes by applying different types of search tactics. Users select different types of search tactics sequentially to obtain information that is needed to resolve search tasks. Selection of search tactics is fundamental activities in search processes, and can influence IR effectiveness.

Previous interactive information retrieval studies have mostly focused on system features, specific interfaces or query behaviors in exploratory searches [2,3]. Less research has attempted to examine the relationships between search tactic selection and search outputs. This study investigated how users' search tactic selection influence search outputs in exploratory search tasks.

2. TYPES OF SEARCH TACTICS
This study is based on the assumption that users' search behaviors are represented by a series of search tactics that users apply during search processes. Search tactics refer to user intention or actions to achieve specific objectives during the search process [4]. Research on search tactics has been conducted in relation to the identification of types of search tactics and analysis of search tactic patterns [1,4,5]. In this study, we adopted Xie and Joo's [5] identification of search tactics summarized in Table 1.

JCDL '13, July 22–26, 2013, Indianapolis, Indiana, USA.
ACM 978-1-4503-2077-1/13/07.

Table 1. A coding scheme of search tactic types

Code	Search tactic	Objective
Create	Creating search statement	Come up with a search statement for searching.
Mod	Modifying search statement	Change a previous search statement to specify or broaden search results.
EvalI	Evaluating individual item(s)	Assess relevance/usefulness of an item, or authority of an item.
EvalR	Evaluating search results	Quickly assess the relevance of search results.
AccF	Accessing forward	Go to a specific item or web page that has not been accessed in the search by using direct location, tracking meta-information, or hyperlinks.
AccB	Accessing backward	Go back to a previous page by using direct location, tracking meta-information, or hyperlinks
Xplor	Exploring	Browse information/items in a specific site.
Obt	Obtaining	Use retrieved information to satisfy information needs or obtain information in physical or electronic formats
Others	Minor tactics	Infrequently observed tactics, such as organizing search results or items (Org), learning how to use the system (Lrn), etc.

3. METHODOLOGY
To investigate the relationship between users' search tactic selection and search outputs, a user study was conducted with sixty subjects from a state university in the United States. When recruiting subjects, we considered their major and academic status (Table 2). Each subject was paid $30 as an incentive for his/her participation in the project. The subjects consists of 34 female (56.7%) and 26 male (43.3%).

Table 2. Major and status of sixty subjects

	Arts/ Humanities	Social Sciences	Science/ Engineering
Undergraduate	10 (16.7%)	10 (16.7%)	10 (16.7%)
Graduate	10 (16.7%)	10 (16.7%)	10 (16.7%)

Subjects were asked to conduct an exploratory task that requested them to find as many aspects as possible on a specific topic within eight minutes using the Library of Congress Digital Collections (http://www.loc.gov/library/libarch-digital.html). Using Morae usability testing software, researchers recorded subjects' search activities and think-aloud protocols.

User search sessions were coded using the coding scheme identified in Table 1. Frequencies of search tactics were tallied for each session. Aspectual recall rate was used to indicate search outputs, which refers to the percent of aspects saved by a searcher divided by the total number of aspects in the collections [6]. Correlation analysis and multiple regression analysis were used to examine the relationships between search tactic selection and search outputs.

4. PRELIMINARY RESULTS

On average, 58.24 tactics were observed in a single session. EvalI tactics were most frequently selected during the search process, which makes up 24.4%. Accessing forward and backward were also frequently observed as searchers needed to move around pages during the search process. Xplor tactics were slightly more frequently chosen than EvalR tactics. Query formulation (Creat) and reformulation (Mod) were less frequently used, 2.3% and 2.8% respectively.

Table 3. Search tactic occurrences in a single session

Tactic	Frequency per session (%)	STD
Creat	1.33 (2.3%)	0.91
Mod	1.63 (2.8%)	2.02
Xplor	7.45 (12.8%)	4.65
AccF	13.12 (22.5%)	5.02
AccB	7.97 (13.7%)	3.78
EvalR	6.38 (11.0%)	4.67
EvalI	14.2 (24.4%)	5.97
Obt	5.6 (9.6%)	3.25
Others	0.56 (1.0%)	-

Table 4 presents correlation coefficients between the frequencies of search tactics and aspectual recall. The results indicated that aspectual recall rate is positively associated with AccF, EvalI, Xplor, and Obt at the alpha level of 0.01. It is not surprising that the frequency of Obt tactics is closely correlated to aspectual recall rate (r=0.687) because obtaining activities could directly increase the aspectual recall rate. Also, AccF and EvalI turn out to be positively related to aspectual recalls as searchers need to access to items and evaluate the relevance or usefulness of the accessed items before using them to fulfill their search tasks. Xplor was moderately correlated with aspectual recall (r=0.352) while query related tactics (Creat, Mod, EvalR) were not. This implies that users would obtain more useful items from Xplor tactics rather than query related tactics in exploratory search tasks.

Multiple regression analysis was conducted to examine the causal relationship between the frequencies of search tactics and aspectual recall. A stepwise method was selected since collinearity existed among different tactics. Obt tactic was excluded in the regression model, as it was an obvious predictor to explain aspectual recall rate. Five independent variables were eliminated from the stepwise method. EvalI and Xplor were identified as predictors that account for aspectual recall rate. As shown in Table 5, the result presents an aspectual recall estimation model that can be explained by frequencies of EvalI and Xplor tactics (R^2 = 0.404).

Table 4. Correlation analysis between frequency of search tactic application and aspectual recall (Pearson r)

Tactic	Aspectual recall
Freq. of Creat	-0.237
Freq. of Mod	0.226
Freq. of EvalR	-0.237
Freq. of AccF	0.479^{**}
Freq. of EvalI	0.580^{**}
Freq. of AccB	0.191
Freq. of Xplor	0.352^{**}
Freq. of Obt	0.687^{**}

$^{*}p<0.05$; $^{**}p<0.01$

Table 5: Multiple regression: Effects of search tactic selection on aspectual recall (stepwise method)

Predictor	B	Std. Error	β	t	Sig.
(Constant)	0.074	0.023		3.165	0.002
Freq. of EvalI	0.007	0.001	0.537	5.222	0.000
Freq. of Xplor	0.005	0.002	0.263	2.562	0.013

Dependent variable: aspectual recall

5. CONCLUSION

This study investigates which tactics are more influential in producing higher aspectual recall rate in exploratory searches of digital libraries. In exploratory tasks, frequencies of browsing (Xplor) and item evaluation (EvalI) are closely associated with search outputs measured by aspectual recall. Qualitative analysis reveals that the browsing structure of the digital library well supported searchers' browsing tactics to identify different aspects of information to complete the exploratory search task. Also, in exploratory search tasks, searchers benefited from iterative loops of browsing and item evaluation as this type of task requires users to find a variety of items in different aspects with similar characteristics.

REFERENCES

[1] Bates, M. J. (1979). Information search tactics. *Journal of the American Society for Information Science*, 30(4), 205–214

[2] Kules, B., Capra, R., Banta, M. and Sierra, T. (2009). What do exploratory searchers look at in a faceted search interface? In *Proceedings of the 9th ACM/IEEE-CS Joint Conference on Digital Libraries*, Austin, TX, USA, June 15-19, 2009: JCDL '09 (pp. 313-322). New York, NY: ACM Press.

[3] White, R W., Kules, B., Drucker, S.M., & Schraefel, M.C. (2006). Supporting exploratory search. *Communications of the ACM*, 49(4), 36–39.

[4] Xie, I. & Joo. S. (2010). Transitions in Search Tactics during the Web-based Search Process. *Journal of American Society for Information and Science Technology*, 61(11): 2188-2205.

[5] Xie, I. & Joo, S. (2012) Factors Affecting the Selection of Search Tactics during the Web-based Searching Process. *Information Processing and Management*, 48(2):254-270.

[6] Kelly, D. (2009). Methods for evaluating interactive information retrieval systems with users. *Foundations and Trends in Information Retrieval*, 3(1-2), 1-224.

Information Visualization of Nuclear Decay Chain Libraries

Electra Sutton
Inst. for the Study of Societal Issues
UC Berkeley
electra@berkeley.edu

Charles Wang
School of Information
UC Berkeley
charleswang@berkeley.edu

David Weisz
Dept. of Nuclear Engineering
UC Berkeley
weiszdg@berkeley.edu

Fredric Gey
Inst. for the Study of Societal Issues
UC Berkeley
gey@berkeley.edu

Ray R. Larson
School of Information
UC Berkeley
ray@ischool.berkeley.edu

ABSTRACT

This poster presents multiple information visualization techniques for scientific visualization of the nuclear isotope decay process, including (but not limited to) circle packing and directed graphs. The practical goal of this visualization process is to support nuclear forensics, the identification of the origin of intercepted smuggled nuclear materials.

Categories and Subject Descriptors

I.6.8 [**Simulation and Modeling**]: Types of Simulation—*Visual*; D.1.7 [**Programming Techniques**]: Visual Programming

Keywords

nuclear forensics; nuclear decay; visualization; circle packing; directed graph

1. INTRODUCTION

In the "Recasting Nuclear Forensics Discovery as a Digital Library Problem" project, we are applying a variety of Digital Library (DL) methods to support the identification, localization and detection of illicit nuclear materials. One issue that has arisen is how to present scientific measurements and findings in a clear and cogent manner. Information visualization gives us a method to present this complicated information when it is designed with techniques that optimize understanding of the analysis and support the requirement that it be defensible in a courtroom. Visualization is complementary to underlying DL information structures which support implementation of nuclear forensics discovery[3].

Nuclear material data is a digitized record of assays for component isotopes[1] and elements. Search of this data is complicated by the fact that radioactive atoms decay or morph constantly into atoms of different isotopes as the material decays. This morphing activity creates a new component for the same material. Therefore matching the original record is impossible against itself or any other nuclear material data unless the decay activity is built into the search algorithm. A nuclear material is composed of multiple radioactive isotopes. Therefore the decay visualization design must handle multiple events which can be confusing and difficult to comprehend unless the information is presented for optimal understanding.

JCDL'13, July 22–26, 2013, Indianapolis, Indiana, USA.
ACM 978-1-4503-2077-1/13/07.

2. VISUALIZATION DESIGN MODES

Our poster presents multiple approaches to the visualization of the nuclear decay process and its application to nuclear materials matching. We will also describe the entire digital library structure that we are developing for nuclear forensics discovery.

2.1 Circle Packing

Nuclear material isotope composition can be visualized using circle packing, a geometry where enclosure diagrams use containment to represent the hierarchy. In a Euclidean plane, the circle packing mechanism configures circles with a prescribed pattern of tangencies, yielding no two overlap circles in a contained boundary with most of the circles mutually tangent. The circle packing theorem is founded upon a rich body of classical geometries and we draw inspiration from Wang[5] and Heer[2] where circle packing was used to illustrate large datasets with hierarchies.

We visualize isotope composition of measured nuclear material assay taken from the Los Alamos National Laboratory (LANL)[1], which undertakes classified work towards the design of nuclear weapons and together with Lawrence Livermore National Laboratory (LLNL) are the two major laboratories doing such security nuclear forensics work to enhance the nation's defense. The nuclear material sample is analyzed by dividing it into aliquots which are subjected to isotopic specific tests. In the example, three samples measured on different dates are presented with unit circles. Within

[1]The data demonstration items are unclassified weapons grade nuclear material samples from the Plutonium Metal Standards Exchange Program at the Laboratory Chemistry and Materials Science Division, Los Alamos National Laboratory.

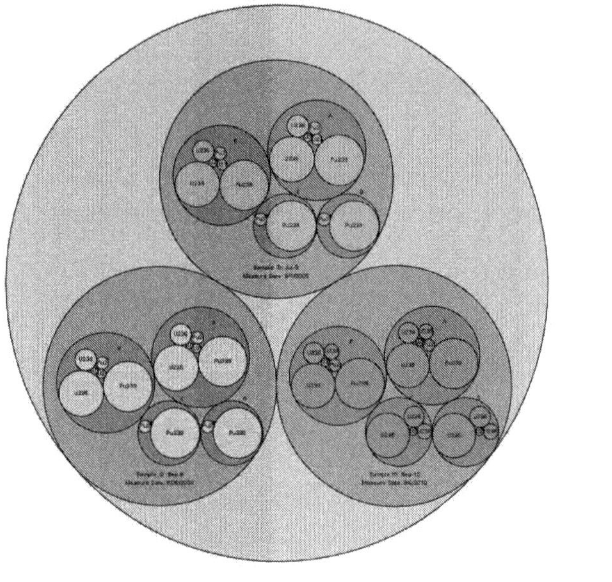

Figure 1: Example of circle packing visualization of three samples measured in LANL with their isotope composition.

each circle are the sample's aliquots and various isotopes observed are displayed inside the aliquot circles. The area of the isotope circle is determined by the numerical value of weight percentage of that isotope within its element. For instance, aliquot A from sample ID Sep-10 consists of U-234 (2.5% U), U-235 (73% U), U-236 (16% U), U-238 (8.7% U), Pu-239 (94% Pu) and Pu-240 (5.8% Pu). The area of the corresponding circles is proportional to the element percentages. Accordingly, isotope circle with larger area suggests that the isotope is more abundant within the element.

2.2 Directed Graph

The decay events of a nuclear material can also be modeled as a directed graph where isotopes are represented by nodes and decay events from parent to daughter are represented by directed arcs. Modeling the decay activity as a directed graph allows for visualization of the process but also produces new information possible with graph analysis methods.

The following directed-graph visualization example shows the result of decay-chain generation using data from the Nuclear Wallet Cards database[4], which catalogues properties for ground and isomeric states of all known nuclides. The graph displays a composite of nuclear decay chains with root parents being the various isotopic assays recorded in the sample nuclear material. Those isotopes are Pu-238, Pu-239, Pu-240, Pu-241, Pu-242, U-234, U-235, U-236, and U-238. Types of radioactive decay and isotope half-lives are highlighted on the graph. The directed-graph of networked decaying isotopes is built to illustrate the decay network until the isotopes reach a stable state at which they stop decaying.

3. ACKNOWLEDGMENTS

We thank Lav Tandon and Kevin Kuhn from LANL for their support. We also thank Richard B. Firestone, group leader of the Isotopes Project from LNL Nuclear Science Division. The work described in this paper is supported by the grant "ARI-MA: Recasting Nuclear Forensics Discovery as a Digital Library Search Problem" funded by the U.S. National Science Foundation and Department of Homeland Security (award #ECCS-1140073).

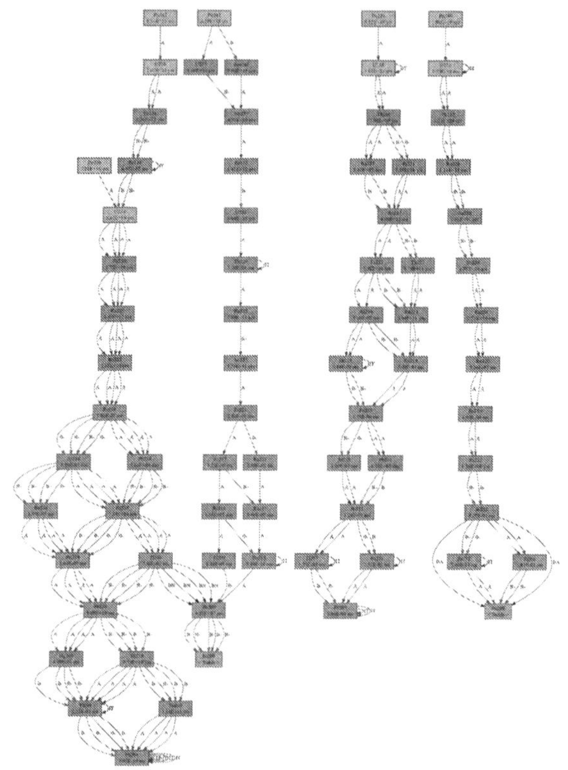

Figure 2: Example of directed-graph visualization of isotope assays of LANL measured nuclear material (Aliquot A, Sample ID: Sep-10).

4. REFERENCES

[1] R. Firestone, V. Shirley, C. Baglin, S. Chu, and J. Zipkin. *Table of Isotopes*, volume 8th Edition. John Wiley & Sons, Inc., New York, 1999.

[2] J. Heer, M. Bostock, and V. Ogievetsky. A tour through the visualization zoo. *Communications of the ACM*, 53:59–67, June 2010.

[3] E. Sutton, C. Reynolds, F. C. Gey, and R. R. Larson. Applying digital library technologies to nuclear forensics. In *TPDL*, pages 144–149, 2012.

[4] J. K. Tuli. *Nuclear Wallet Cards*. National Nuclear Data Center, Brookhaven National Laboratory, October 2011.

[5] W. Wang, H. Wang, G. Dai, and H. Wang. Visualization of large hierarchical data by circle packing. *Proceedings of ACM CHI '06*, pages 517–520, April 2006.

Institutional Structures for Research Data and Metadata Curation

Matthew S. Mayernik
National Center for Atmospheric Research (NCAR)
University Corporation for Atmospheric Research (UCAR)
P.O. Box 3000, Boulder, CO, USA
mayernik@ucar.edu

Categories and Subject Descriptors
E.0 [**Data**]: General

Keywords
Data curation, research data management, metadata, institutions.

1. EXTENDED ABSTRACT

Institutions can be conceptualized as “regulative, normative and cultural-cognitive elements that, together with associated activities and resources, provide stability and meaning to social life” [14]. These regulative, normative, and cultural-cognitive elements provide the institutional structures in which organizations or individuals are embedded. By providing particular courses of action, institutions serve as patterns that constrain and empower individuals [13].

Information organizations that develop research data and metadata curation systems and services sit at the nexus of multiple types of institutions. Digital libraries based within universities must articulate with funding organizations and regulations, library standards and standards organizations, the scholarly publication system, governments and their higher education policies, and professional societies. In addition, many of the issues that digital library systems face in relation to research data and metadata cross academic disciplinary boundaries [11, 15].

The processes for creating, documenting, sharing, and managing research data and metadata are institutionalized within a number of social systems, including 1) formal organizations (such as universities and research centers), 2) codified rules and sanctions (such as funding agency requirements and professional society guidelines), and 3) the norms of modern Western science [9, 12]. Researchers encounter and become embedded within these institutions through their formal education, as well as their informal personal activities [10].

Digital library systems for research data and metadata management face tremendous variation in the kinds of projects, data, and metadata that they must support. In this poster, I outline four categories of institutional carriers that are central to understanding scientific data and metadata practices: 1) norms and symbols, 2) intermediaries, 3) routines, scripts, and standards, and 4) material objects. The approach described here provides a way to reduce heterogeneity at the conceptual level by identifying institutional structures that surround data and metadata:

- Norms and Symbols – scientific research institutions are rife with normative expectations for how scientific work should be conducted, shared, and evaluated. These norms serve as carriers of institutional priorities and expectations. Symbols, on the other hand, serve as carriers of institutional myths and ceremonies through which social activities are categorized and infused with meaning [7].
- Intermediaries – Institutional relationships function through intermediaries. Intermediaries can be individuals or organizations. Libraries and librarians, for example, have long served as intermediaries between people and documents, specifically in selecting, organizing, displaying, and finding documents in ways that both enable and constrain library users. As institutional changes occur in relation to internet and digital library technologies, “re-intermediation” is also occurring [8]. New organizations and interest groups spring up, and professional groups re-defined themselves. Librarians, for example, have not disappeared as library services have gone digital. Instead they have changed roles and developed new skills to meet changing institutional needs [6].
- Routines, Scripts, and Standards – Institutions, as typified patterns of social activities and relations, manifest most clearly in habitualized behaviors and routines. As Agre describes, much of everyday human behavior takes the form of routines, including eating breakfast, going shopping, interacting with colleagues, taking care of children, etc [1]. When examined more broadly, routines can be generalized as habitualized and patterned forms of human action, which Barley and Tolbert term "scripts" [3]. Standards are highly codified forms of institutionalized scripts. The vast majority of the effort in institutionalizing standards, however, is in building adoption [5]. In order to succeed, standards must become part of the scripts and routines within the institutional settings in which people live and work.
- Material Objects – Institutions are constituted by material things as well as humans and social patterns. Changes to material objects can cause changes and re-negotiations of institutional boundaries [2,4]. Technologies can change work practices and professional roles. While technological revolutions may occur frequently, institutional changes related to those technologies are typical evolutionary in nature.

JCDL'13, July 22–26, 2013, Indianapolis, Indiana, USA.
ACM 978-1-4503-2077-1/13/07.

I apply these four categories of carriers to two institutional settings: 1) the Center for Embedded Networked Sensing (CENS), and 2) the National Center for Atmospheric Research (NCAR). From 2002-2012, CENS was a National Science Foundation (NSF) Science and Technology Center based at UCLA with four partnering institutions in southern and central California. CENS supported the research and development of sensing systems for real-world scientific and social applications through interdisciplinary collaborations between engineers and scientists. NCAR is a NSF Federally Funded Research and Development Center that conducts research in the atmospheric and related sciences. NCAR also provides tools and services, including data management and archiving capabilities, for internal and external scientific communities.

Through ethnographic study and participant observation methods, I outline how these four categories of institutional carriers can be used to illustrate how the institutional support for data and metadata management are not uniform within a single organization or academic discipline. Instead, a broad spectrum of institutional structures exist across CENS and NCAR, with many different configurations of norms, routines, intermediaries, and material objects in place for managing data and metadata from different projects and research communities.

CENS, for example, provided significant material support for data management through computational services, but was slow to develop norms related to data and metadata management. In addition, few projects had well defined responsibility for data and metadata management, meaning there were few established routines, few relevant intermediaries, and few researchers who had expertise with, or were even aware or, data and metadata standards that might be applicable for their projects. Looking across CENS projects, different configurations of these four carrier types were in place, leading to different levels of success with regards to data and metadata management and preservation.

NCAR projects and labs show similar wide-ranging levels of institutional support for data and metadata management. The technical infrastructure for data storage is very comprehensive and widely used. In addition, a number of data management groups exist around the organization, and provide a high level of technical support and standards expertise for archiving data and metadata of particular kinds, or for particular projects. Many projects, however, do not have the same level of institutional support because of their smaller scale or topic scope that falls outside of these data management groups. The organization as a whole is investigating whether/how to create norms and routines for data management through the creation of formal data policy.

Together, the four categories outlined above provide a way to identify the interconnections and interdependencies of particular institutional structures. Researchers' data and metadata practices vary across disciplines (one type of institutional structure), but vary just as much within disciplines due to the variability of norms, routines, and intermediaries across organizations.

2. REFERENCES

[1] Agre, P.E. 1997. Computation and Human Experience. New York: Cambridge University Press.

[2] Agre, P.E. 2003. Information and institutional change: The case of digital libraries, in A.P. Bishop, N.A. Van House, & B.P. Buttenfield (Eds.) Digital Library Use: Social Practice in Design and Evaluation, Cambridge, MA: MIT Press (pp. 219-240).

[3] Barley, S.R. & Tolbert, P.S. 1997. Institutionalization and structuration: Studying the links between action and institution. Organization Studies, 18(1): 93-117. http://dx.doi.org/10.1177/017084069701800106

[4] Blanchette, J.F. 2012. Burdens of Proof: Cryptographic Culture and Evidence Law in the Age of Electronic Documents. Cambridge, MA; MIT Press.

[5] Carpenter, T. 2012. Standards and data citations. In P.E. Uhlir (Rapporteur) For Attribution -- Developing Data Attribution and Citation Practices and Standards: Summary of an International Workshop. Board on Research Data and Information, National Research Council of the National Academies. Washington, D.C.: National Academies Press (pp. 173-176). http://www.nap.edu/catalog.php?record_id=13564

[6] Fourie, I. 2004. Librarians and the claiming of new roles: How can we try to make a difference? Aslib Proceedings, 56(1): 62-74. http://dx.doi.org/10.1108/00012530410516877

[7] Friedland, R. & Alford, R.R. 1991. Bringing society back in: Symbols, practices, and institutional contradictions. In W.W. Powell & P.J. DiMaggio (Eds.) The New Institutionalism in Organizational Analysis. University of Chicago Press, Chicago, IL, 232-263.

[8] Hawkins, R., Mansell, R., & Steinmueller, W.E. 1999. Toward digital intermediation in the information society, *Journal of Economic Issues,* 33(2): 383-391. http://www.jstor.org/stable/4227450

[9] Jepperson, R.L. 1991. Institutions, institutional effects, and institutionalism. In W.W. Powell & P.J. DiMaggio (Eds.) The New Institutionalism in Organizational Analysis. University of Chicago Press, Chicago, IL, 143-163.

[10] Lave, J. & Wenger, E. 1991. Situated Learning: Legitimate Peripheral Participation. New York: Cambridge University Press.

[11] Marcial, L.H. & Hemminger, B.M. 2010. Scientific data repositories on the web: An initial survey. Journal of the American Society for Information Science and Technology, 61(10): 2029–2048. http://dx.doi.org/10.1002/asi.21339

[12] Mayernik, M.S., Batcheller, A.L., & Borgman, C.L. 2011. How institutional factors influence the creation of scientific metadata. In Proceedings of the 2011 iConference (iConference '11). New York, NY: ACM (pg. 417-425). http://doi.acm.org/10.1145/1940761.1940818

[13] Meyer, J.W. 2010. World society, institutional theories, and the actor. Annual Review of Sociology, 36: 1–20. http://dx.doi.org/10.1146/annurev.soc.012809.102506

[14] Scott, W.R. 2008. Institutions and Organizations: Ideas and Interests. Third Edition. Los Angeles, CA: Sage, pg. 48.

[15] Willis, C., Greenberg, J., & White, H. 2012. Analysis and synthesis of metadata goals for scientific data. Journal of the American Society for Information Science & Technology, 63(8): 1505-1520. http://dx.doi.org/10.1002/asi.22683

Investigating Influential Factors Influencing Users to Share News in Social Media: A Diffusion of Innovations Perspective

Long Ma
Wee Kim Wee School of Communication and Information
Nanyang Technological University
malo0001@ntu.edu.sg

Chei Sian Lee
Wee Kim Wee School of Communication and Information
Nanyang Technological University
leecs@ntu.edu.sg

Dion Hoe-Lian Goh
Wee Kim Wee School of Communication and Information
Nanyang Technological University
ashlgoh@ntu.edu.sg

ABSTRACT
This study aims to investigate the factors influencing news sharing in social media. Drawing from the diffusion of innovations theory (DOI), the influential factors identified are opinion leadership, homophily, tie strength, and news attributes. By incorporating social network analysis with multiple regression analysis, our results indicate that opinion leadership was the strongest factor predicting users' news sharing, followed by news attribute and tie strength. Unexpectedly, we also found that homophily hampered news sharing in social media. Implications are discussed

Categories and Subject Descriptors
J.4 [Computer Applications]: Social and Behavioral Sciences;
H.3.5 [Online Information Services]: Data sharing.

General Terms
Human Factors, Theory, Measurement,

Keywords
Social media, news sharing, diffusion of innovations theory, social network analysis

1. INTRODUCTION
Social media has changed the way people consume and share news stories. In particular, the social environmental factors such as the people, the connections as well as the new stories play important roles in information sharing and discovery in social media. However, past research on news sharing mainly focused on traditional media contexts (e.g., newspaper). Except for a few studies (e.g. [1], [2]) that focus on individuals' perceptions and motivations, research examining the social network environmental effects on news sharing in social media is limited.

To fill this gap, we draw from the diffusion of innovations theory (DOI) which explains how an innovation diffuses via communicational channels over time. The DOI has a strong focus on the social environment surrounding the communication channels and hence is appropriate in this study as our objective is to examine the influence of social environmental factors on news sharing behavior in social media.

JCDL'13, July 22–26, 2013, Indianapolis, Indiana, USA.
ACM 978-1-4503-2077-1/13/07.

2. LITERATURE RIVIEW
DOI explains how innovation is communicated through the social environment where individuals are interconnected [3]. News is considered as a social commodity characterized to be timely and novel, which is consistent with the criteria of innovation. According to the theory, there are important factors in the social environment which may influence the diffusion process. First, opinion leaders within the social network are found to play a crucial role in the diffusion process of informational content [4]. In particular, opinion leaders tend to exhibit more exploratory and innovative behavior. Second, characteristics of diffusion networks such as homophily (i.e. similarities with others in the network) and tie strength (i.e. strong tie versus weak tie) have been found to be influential. Third, attributes of the innovation have effects on the diffusion process. Thus, news attributes in terms of hard and soft news are important consideration in this study [5]. Collectively, from the lens of DOI, factors such as opinion leadership, homophily, tie strength, as well as the news attributes are identified as influential factors in the diffusion process. Hence, this study aims to answer the following research question: *How opinion leaders, homophily, tie strength and news attributes influence news sharing behavior in social media?*

3. METHODOLOGY
Our network data was collected from Digg (http://digg.com), a social media website on news sharing. A program based on the Digg API was developed to automatically crawl the network data. We applied the snowball sampling technique to collect the sample consisting of 5430 users (i.e. 713 active and 4717 inactive users). From these users, we collected a total of 70292 news stories.

We applied a hybrid approach combining social network analysis with multiple regression analysis to analyze our data. The metrics to measure opinion leadership, tie strength, and homophily were derived from the social network analysis using the software, Pajek. Figure 1 illustrates the whole network of our sample and figure 2 illustrates a homophily subgroup. Then, we applied multiple regression analysis to test the effects of the identified independent variables on news sharing in social media. The software used was SPSS.

4. RESULTS
The results of the regression analysis (shown in Table 1) indicate that all the social network variables and news attributes were significant. The entire model was significant (Adjusted R^2= .515, F=963.3, p<0.001).

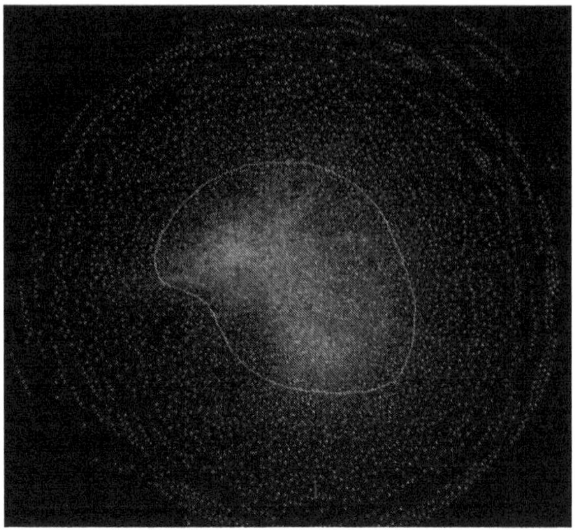

Figure 1. The whole network with a "core" subgroup

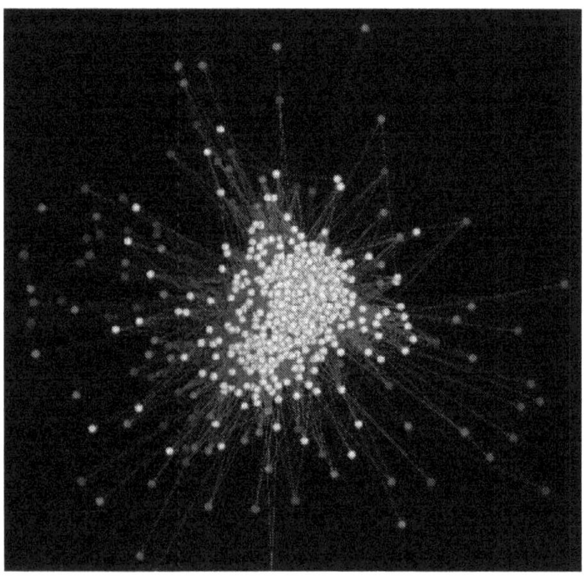

Figure 2. The structure of the subgroup

Table 1. Regression Analysis (N=5430)

Independent Variables	Standardized Beta	t-values
Opinion leader (Degree)	.703	36.523***
Homophily	-.032	-2.879**
Tie Strength	.037	2.269*
News Attributes	.040	4.249***
F(6, 5423)	963.3***	
Adjusted R2	.515	

5. DISCUSSION AND CONCLUSION

Our results indicate that the factors derived from DOI have significant influences on news sharing in social media. Specifically, opinion leadership is regarded as the strongest factor that motivates users to share news in social media. Here, we show that individuals strive to share news to establish their influential positions as opinion leaders. Next, news attributes was also found to be positively associated with news sharing behavior. Our results suggest that users who prefer hard news are more likely to share them in social media. Our study also revealed that stronger ties, indicated by reciprocal connections in the network, could significantly motivate users to share news. Here, we show that news sharing can be regarded as a way for users to accumulate online social capital by exchanging new information with other users in the network. Surprisingly, homophily has negative effects on news sharing. This indicates that when individuals were embedded in homophilious networks, they would be less likely to share news. However, we also found that these networks were densely connected indicating that even though users might not be actively sharing new news stories they could be actively connected in other ways such as discussing or commenting about the news stories contributed.

In conclusion, our study has both theoretical and practical contributions. First, we identified factors based on the DOI which suggests that the social network environment exert significant influence on news sharing in social media. It will be interesting to examine how these factors influence other forms of content sharing (e.g. multi-media, reviews) in different social media platforms (e.g. YouTube, Facebook). Next, the hybrid approach combining social network analysis with regression analysis in our study provides an innovative way to investigate the influence of social network variables on the content sharing process in social media. As for practical contributions, our study indicates the importance of social environmental factors in the diffusion of news stories in social media. In particular, identifying the appropriate opinion leaders is crucial in the delivery and promotion of news stories. In terms of homophily, our results highlight that social media may lead to a narrowing of the scope of news and views when one is embedded in a homopilious network.

6. ACKNOWLEDGMENTS

This work was supported by Nanyang Technological University Academic Research Fund Program (Tier 1), Grant No. 59/09.

7. REFERENCES

[1] Lee, C.S. and L. Ma, *News sharing in social media: The effect of gratifications and prior experience.* Computers in Human Behavior, 2012. **28**(2): p. 331–339.

[2] Hanson, G. and P. Haridakis, *YouTube users watching and sharing the news: A uses and gratifications approach.* Journal of Electronic Publishing, 2008. **11**(3): p. http://dx.doi.org/10.3998/3336451.0011.305

[3] Rogers, E.M., *Diffusion of innovations.* 5 ed. 2003, New York, NY: Free Press.

[4] Lyons, B. and K. Henderson, *Opinion leadership in a computer mediated environment.* Journal of Consumer Behaviour, 2005. **4**(5): p. 319-329.

[5] Nguyen, A., *The contribution of online news attributes to its diffusion: An empirical exploration based on a proposed theoretical model for the micro-process of online news adoption/use.* First Monday, 2008. **13**: p. 4-7.

Mapping the Intersection of Science & Philosophy

[Extended Abstract — Poster]

Jaimie Murdock
Indiana University
School of Informatics & Computing
jammurdo@indiana.edu

Robert Light
Indiana University
School of Library & Information Science
lightr@indiana.edu

Colin Allen
Indiana University
College of Arts & Sciences
colallen@indiana.edu

Katy Börner
Indiana University
School of Library & Information Science
katy@indiana.edu

ABSTRACT

This poster presents what we believe to be the first attempt to empirically measure and visualize the cross-pollination of science and philosophy through citation patterns. Using the Stanford Encyclopedia of Philosophy as a proxy for the philosophical literature, we plot SEP citations onto the UCSD Map of Science to highlight areas of science which overlap with philosophical discussion. An outline of further studies is also discussed.

Categories and Subject Descriptors

I [**Applied Computing**]: Arts and Humanities; II [**Human-centered Computing**]: Scientific Visualization

Keywords

Visualization; digital humanities; science of science

1. INTRODUCTION

Despite C.P. Snow's infamously pessimistic (and controversial) assessment of the gulf between the two cultures of science and the humanities [4], there is, in fact, a long history of cross-pollination. Philosophy provides a particular nexus of such interactions, with philosophers seeking to understand and often exploit the knowledge produced by science while scientists sometimes turn to philosophers for ideas or analysis. But where in particular have philosophers turned their attention to science, or scientists to philosophy? One way to answer these questions is to look at the citation practices of each community, identifying references to the scientific literature in works by philosophers, and references to the philosophical literature in works by scientists.

JCDL'13, July 22–26, 2013, Indianapolis, Indiana, USA.
ACM 978-1-4503-2077-1/13/07.

Here we provide an example of the first of these approaches, mapping papers cited in the Stanford Encyclopedia of Philosophy (SEP)[1] onto the UCSD map of science [1]. The SEP serves as a proxy for philosophy as a whole by virtue of its comprehensive treatment (over 1400 articles comprising almost 15 million words) of the discipline of philosophy.

The USCD map is built from article level data from Thompson Reuters' Web of Science and Elsevier's Scopus. Scientific journals, classified by subject area, are considered more similar to each other in proportion to the number of citations they contain to each other. For any set of journals represented in the UCSD map, one can compute the number of SEP citations to those journals. Thus we can measure the influence of various science areas in the SEP. By overlaying a representation of the number of "citation hits" from the SEP bibliographies into the various regions of the UCSD map, it is possible to visualize which areas of science have received relatively more or relatively less attention from philosophers.

Do philosophers pay more attention to biology or physics? Geology or anthropology? Initial answers to these questions can only be provided by the analysis of large data sets. However, this represents only a starting point for the Digging by Debating project. To realize our goal of exploiting large datasets in support of traditional humanities research, we need to develop computational methods that will assist scholars in the humanities more directly. Scientometric and text mining methods can suggest hypotheses, but unless these are linked to more powerful tools for semantically rich textual analysis and critical work, the role of these methods is limited to early stages of an investigation. The Digging by Debating project aims to fill this niche. High-level maps of the interaction between science and philosophy suggest places to look for more details about those interactions. How exactly, for instance, do scientific studies get used to support philosophical arguments? Identifying the places where those interactions are happening is the first step towards more detailed work on the exact nature of the interactions.

[1]http://plato.stanford.edu/

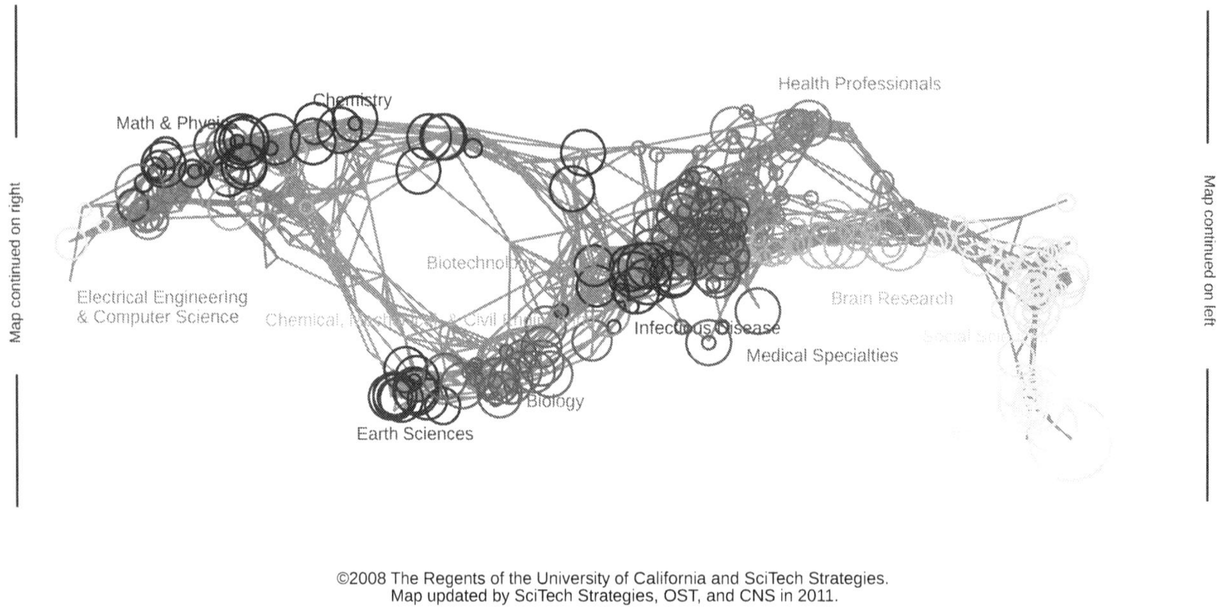

Figure 1: Philosophical content on the UCSD Map of Science. The size of each circle corresponds to the number of SEP editorial areas citing material from the UCSD Map of Science subdiscipline (minimum: 0, maximum: 43). The color of each circle corresponds to one of 13 disciplines identified by the map of science.

2. METHODS

To generate this representation of philosophical content on the map of science, we took a dataset of 36,129 citations from the SEP parsed into BibTeX citation format. Using the Sci^2 Tool [3], citations with the type "article" were then matched to UCSD Map of Science subdisciplines using the "journal" field. However, as some areas of philosophy cite the sciences more heavily than others (e.g., bioethics), plotting the number of journals cited by the SEP for each subdiscipline results in a skewed map that does not reflect the reach of a science across the whole philosophical literature.

To control for this effect, we examined how many of the 43 SEP editorial areas reference a journal, rather than how many journals are referenced across the whole SEP. This is a measure of how ubiquitous the topic is in philosophy. For example, scientific studies in the area of *speech recognition* are discussed in the philosophical areas of *philosophy of cognitive science, philosophy of language, and philosophy of mind.* Of the 554 subdisciplines, 275 contained a publication cited by at least one SEP article. The UCSD subdiscipline of *psychology & philosophy* was cited by at least one article in all 43 SEP editorial areas. This relationship between subdisciplines and SEP editorial areas on the UCSD Map of Science is shown in Figure 1. An interactive version of the map with continually updated data can be found at `https://inpho.cogs.indiana.edu/scimap/`.

3. FUTURE WORK

Further studies investigating the intersection of philosophy and the sciences will map three additional spaces: 1) Philosophical content on the map of science, as seen by science; 2) Scientific content on the map of philosophy, as seen by philosophy; 3) Scientific content on the map of philosophy, as seen by science.

To create a map of philosophical content as seen by science (1), we will take the papers from the Scholarly Database[2] and align them with papers in the PhilPapers index[3]. Areas with high numbers of publications appearing in the PhilPapers index will have higher philosophical relevance.

For the latter two maps, we will create a base map of philosophy using similar methods, drawing on expertise from the InPhO project in computational representations of philosophy [2]. For scientific content as seen by philosophy and scientific content as seen by science, we would use the same datasets, but instead plotted on the different topography.

4. ACKNOWLEDGMENTS

This work has been funded by the National Endowment for the Humanities, award HJ-50092-12: "Digging by Debating: Linking massive datasets to specific arguments".

5. REFERENCES

[1] K. Börner, R. Klavans, M. Patek, A. M. Zoss, J. R. Biberstine, R. P. Light, V. Larivière, and K. W. Boyack. Design and Update of a Classification System: The UCSD Map of Science. *PLoS ONE*, 7(7):e39464, 2012.

[2] C. Buckner, M. Niepert, and C. Allen. From Encyclopedia to Ontology: Toward a Dynamic Representation of the Discipline of Philosophy. *Synthese*, 182:205–233, 2011.

[3] Sci^2 Team. Science of Science (Sci^2) Tool, 2009. Indiana University and SciTech Strategies. http://sci2.cns.iu.edu.

[4] C. P. Snow. *The Two Cultures*. Cambridge University Press, 1998/1959.

[2]http://sdb.cns.iu.edu/

[3]http://philpapers.org/

Modeling Search Assistance Mechanisms within Web-Scale Discovery Systems

William H. Mischo
Grainger Engineering Library Information Center
University of Illinois at Urbana-Champaign
01-217-333-7497
w-mischo@illinois.edu

Mary C. Schlembach
Grainger Engineering Library Information Center
University of Illinois at Urbana-Champaign
01-217-333-3158
schlemba@illinois.edu

Michael A. Norman
Library Content Access and Management/Database Management
University of Illinois at Urbana-Champaign
01-217-333-8350
manorman@illinois.edu

ABSTRACT
The University of Illinois Library has been conducting transaction log analyses to model user search behaviors within our Library gateway. These analyses have informed the development and implementation of various search assistance mechanisms designed to facilitate search strategy modification and enhance user search navigation methods. This paper discusses the efforts to effectively overlay search assistance mechanisms into the web-scale discovery system environment. These search assistance mechanisms seek to meet user search needs and to address known issues with web-scale systems. This paper describes an evolving search assistance model being deployed in a web-scale environment and reports our findings from transaction log studies and user surveys.

Categories and Subject Descriptors
H.3.3 [**Information Search and Retrieval**]: Search Process, Query formulation. H 3.7 [**Digital Libraries**]: User Issues.

Keywords
Search Assistance, Web-Scale Discovery Systems, Transaction Log Analysis, Library Gateways.

INTRODUCTION
Academic libraries are transitioning from access systems based on federated or broadcast search technologies to web-scale discovery systems with centralized, aggregated indexes, web 2.0 technologies, faceted limit features, and blended displays of journal articles, books, newspaper articles, reviews, and local digital content [1, 2].

The early use studies on web-scale systems have identified a number of issues. User studies have revealed problems with confusion over blended results displays, concerns about the large number of hits returned in searches, uneven use of facets, an ignoring of advanced search features, and questions about the scope and purpose of web-scale systems [3. 4, 5]. In particular studies have shown that users have difficulty distinguishing between material formats and interpreting the blended result displays.

JCDL'13, July 22–26, 2013, Indianapolis, Indiana, USA.
ACM 978-1-4503-2077-1/13/07.

As we transition to this new paradigm, it is important to more clearly understand user search behaviors and practices. There is a clear need for an evidence-based analysis of user search behaviors in retrieval environments characterized by access to distributed information resources, such as those offered by web-scale discovery systems [6]. The Illinois Library has been gathering and recording information in custom transaction logs on user search behaviors within our main interface gateway The gateway was built over a locally developed federated search system, called Easy Search, which provides access to the journal literature, online catalog records, publisher e-book result matches, web search engines, e-resource A-to-Z lists, and other targets.

The primary focus of the Illinois gateway transaction log project has been to identify and characterize user search behaviors within an academic library portal or discovery system.

Using the data gathered from transaction logs, the Easy Search team has introduced and tested a number of key search assistance functions designed to guide users in search strategy modification and reformulation and in the selection of relevant information resources. These Search assistance mechanisms offer users suggestive prompts, guided and adaptive help, reformulation suggestions, and added links and facets all within the context of their specific search.

A detailed analysis of Easy Search transaction logs from the Fall 2010 through the Spring 2011 semesters - covering 1.3 million searches and 1.5 million clickthroughs - was conducted [8].

IMPLICATIONS FOR WEB-SCALE
The University of Illinois at Urbana-Champaign Library has licensed the Primo Central system from Ex Libris. We have been working closely with Ex Libris on the deployment of a custom tile that appears above the Primo search results display and contains adaptive and contextual search assistance suggestions and prompts - similar to the suggestions pane in Easy Search results. The transaction log findings show the great importance of supporting known-item searching and journal, book, and article title searches. It is clear that users possess a mental model of search and discovery system performance that expects sophisticated parsing of their search arguments. Users expect the system to understand searches comprised of a combination of author names, title words, and journal title abbreviations. This makes system mechanisms to properly understand user expectations and to assist in query modification and reformulation critically important.

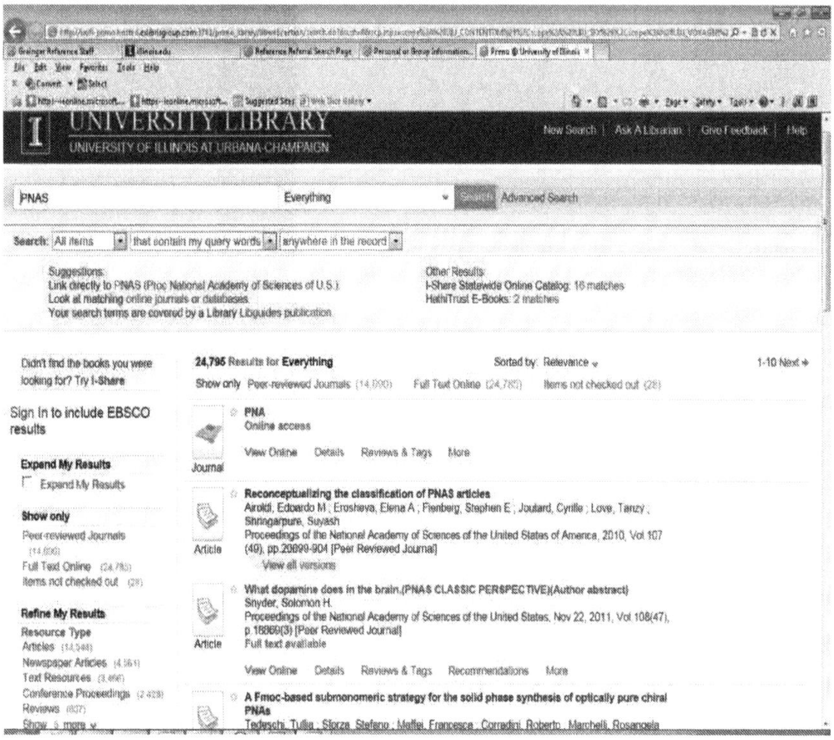

Figure 1: Primo custom tile suggestions

Unfortunately, performing journal article title, book title, or journal name searches in a web-scale system involves a confusing combination of limiting to the "journals", "book", or "articles" facet in combination with changing the default search to title only in a pull down search type menu.

In addition, because the web-scale aggregated indexes contain heterogeneous metadata from various publishers, A & I Services, and OAI provider sites, author name formats and punctuation will vary greatly. To offset these issues, we have currently implemented within the custom tile the following search assistance functions:

Information from a preliminary look-up table that contains links to frequently searched journal titles (e.g. Nature, PNAS, Science, Web of Science) and other frequently redirected sites (Facebook, Library names, campus departments);

A "do you mean" spelling suggestion prompt and link when appropriate;

A pre-constructed link back into Primo for search arguments that match journal titles using the SFX A-to-Z list;

A link into our Libguides system when the search term is contained in any Library Libguide;

A link to the doi.org site with a user entered DOI;

When the system feels that the user is interested in performing an author search, a pre-constructed link back into Primo that constructs an expanded custom author search formatted in the optimum manner (e.g. a search for *william h mischo* or *mischo, william h* will perform the search: *"mischo, william h" OR "mischo, w h" OR "mischo, wh"* in Primo to maximize results.;

A user search argument of more than 4 words will produce a prompt for the user to re-do the search in Primo as a title search.

In addition, supplementary searches in the statewide online catalog and HathiTrust are performed and result links are displayed when Primo search results are below a threshold value.

Further analysis is being performed and additional search assistance functionality will be added. Figure 1 shows a Primo custom tile result that demonstrates the functionality described above.

ACKNOWLEDGMENTS

This work is supported by IMLS grant LG-06-07-0023-07 and NSF NSDL grant DUE 07-34992.

REFERENCES

[1] Fagan, J. C. (2011). Federated search is dead -- and good riddance. *Journal of Web Librarianship, 5*(2), 77-79.

[2] Vaughn, J. (2012). Investigations into library web-scale discovery systems. *Information Technology and Libraries,* 31(1), 32-82.

[3] Comeaux, D. J. (2012). Usability testing of a web-scale discovery system at an academic library. College & Undergraduate Libraries, 19(2-4), 189-206.

[4] Fagan, J. C., Mandernach, M., Nelson, C. S., Paulom J. R., & Saunders, G. (2012). Usability test results for a discovery tool in an academic library. *Information Technology and Libraries,* 31(1), 83-112.

[5] Gross, J. & Sheridan, L. (2011). Web scale discovery: the user experience. *New Library World,* 112(5/6), 236-247.

[6] Markey, K. (2007b). Twenty-five years of end-user searching, part 2: Future research directions. *Journal of the American Society for Information Science and Technology, 58*(8), 1123-1130.

[7] Markey, K. (2007a). Twenty-five years of end-user searching, part 1: Research findings. *Journal of the American Society for Information Science and Technology, 58*(8), 1071-1081.

[8] Mischo, W. H., Schlembach, M. C., Bishoff, J., & German, E. M. (2012). User Search Activities within an Academic Library Gateway: Implications for Webscale Discovery Systems. In M. Popp and D. Dallis (ed.), *Planning and Implementing Resource Discovery Tools in Academic Libraries,* IGI Global, 153-173.

MOOD-lighting: Massive Open Online Discovery Using Solr and Blacklight

Juliet L. Hardesty
Indiana University Libraries
1320 East 10th Street
Bloomington, Indiana
1-812-855-3710
jlhardes@iu.edu

Courtney Greene
Indiana University Libraries
1320 East 10th Street
Bloomington, Indiana
1-812-855-4217
crgreene@indiana.edu

ABSTRACT
In this poster, we present findings from the user experience and metadata perspectives of using Blacklight and Solr to combine large and distinct resource sets. We also share results of a survey of academic and educational institutions on their approaches to Solr indexing and end-user options and identify next steps toward articulating best practices for user experience around discovery in the context of metadata.

Categories and Subject Descriptors
H.3.1 [**Information Storage and Retrieval**]: Content Analysis and Indexing – *indexing methods.*

General Terms
Performance, Design, Experimentation, Standardization.

Keywords
Solr, Blacklight, discovery, access

1. INTRODUCTION
Many have watched with interest recently as developments in open online education have led to a surge in popularity for MOOCs (Massive Open Online Courses). Similarly, libraries and librarians have long been interested in providing better and more comprehensive access to physical and digital collections, both institutionally and collectively. The challenges are many, including but not limited to issues related to access and licensing, the multiplicity of classification and metadata schemas, the intricacies of, first, indexing the diversity of formats represented, and then, returning meaningful, relevant results sets, and the sheer scope of the data itself.

2. CONCEPT OF MOODs
Indiana University (IU) is improving its discovery tools with multiple projects in active development, using Blacklight as a primary interface for IUCAT, the online public catalog [1], and as an interface for a cross-collection search of digital objects from the library's digital repository [2]. Blacklight, with its Solr indexing capabilities for different types of collections, represents a potential means of achieving the overall goal of Massive Open Online Discovery systems (MOODs): enabling more seamless discovery and access across the aforementioned resources and others, including the IU Libraries' website and library digital collections outside of the repository, and moving towards open collections of this size and scope that can combine with other institutional datasets to further scholarly discovery on the general web.

JCDL '13, July 22–26, 2013, Indianapolis, Indiana, USA.
ACM 978-1-4503-2077-1/13/07.

3. OUTCOMES
This poster presents outcomes of the following investigations.

3.1 Experimentation Results
Findings and practical considerations will be reported from user experience and metadata/indexing perspectives for combining large and distinct resource sets using Blacklight and Solr drawn from the process of undertaking such a project at IU.

3.2 Survey Results
Results of a survey of academic and educational institutions will report on discovery/access projects using applications relying on Solr (e.g. Blacklight, VuFind, etc.) investigating approaches to indexing and user interface choices in the community.

3.3 Next Steps
Next steps will be outlined for capitalizing on the data collected via the survey to further explore best practices in user experience specific to discovery in the context of metadata.

4. REFERENCES
[1] Moore, K.B. and Greene, C. 2012. The Search for a New OPAC: Selecting an Open Source Discovery Layer. *Serials Rev.* 38, 1 (Mar. 2012), 24–30. DOI = http://dx.doi.org/10.1016/j.serrev.2011.12.005.

[2] Zhang, H. and Dunn, J. 2011. *Overview of IU Digital Collections Search.* Digital Library Brown Bag Presentation. Indiana University. http://www.dlib.indiana.edu/education/brownbags/fall2011/search/search.pdf.

OmniMea: An Approach to Improved Content Recruitment for Institutional Repositories

James C. French
Corporation for National Research Initiatives
301 E. High Street
Charlottesville, VA 22911
1-703-620-8990
jfrench@cnri.reston.va.us

Allison L. Powell
Corporation for National Research Initiatives
1895 Preston White Drive
Reston, VA 20191
1-703-620-8990
apowell@cnri.reston.va.us

ABSTRACT
A common complaint of providers of institutional repository services is that they have low utilization by their intended user base. The reasons are varied, but two are germane to our project: lack of individual incentives among potentially participating faculty; and a perceived high barrier to entry. The *OmniMea* project adopts a user-centric focus by advocating for *personal* repositories as a more appealing concept and by directing relevant intellectual output placed in these personal repositories to the institutional repository for long-term curation. While our approach was explicitly aimed and capturing long-tail data, it has turned out to be more generally applicable.

Categories and Subject Descriptors
H.3.7 [**Digital Libraries**]: Collection; Dissemination

Keywords
Institutional repository, personal repository, data collection.

1. INTRODUCTION
Data acquisition and archiving is a necessary step in the preservation of data for subsequent access and analysis by current researchers, as well as new generations of researchers. The *OmniMea™ (http://omnimea.org)* project is aimed at data acquisition and curation strategies in support of single principal investigator or small group research projects at academic institutions – data in the so-called "long tail." Long-term data management in these projects is problematic and particularly acute. Smaller research projects are often strapped for funds to conduct the research that generates the data; management of the data was in the past often an afterthought.

With the advent of "data management plans" now being required by funding agencies, data management issues must be considered as part of a proposal, but the funding available for data management is still frequently small and resources available to researchers still need to be cultivated. The obvious resource available in academic institutions is academic research libraries, and these units have embraced the challenges at many institutions. In recent years, many academic research libraries have adopted the concept of *institutional repositories,* "digital collections capturing and preserving the intellectual output of a single or multi-university community" [3] as a means of harnessing technology to improve scholarly communication. Initially the institutional repository was seen as a means of disseminating scholarly publications but early on the value of including data in an institutional repository was recognized. The institutional repository concept has been widely adopted with projects building out such repositories at universities world-wide.

JCDL'13, July 22–26, 2013, Indianapolis, Indiana, USA.
ACM 978-1-4503-2077-1/13/07.

2. PROBLEM
Institutional repositories have a broad intuitive appeal to all the stakeholders involved with science and engineering data management. They have, however, met with very limited acceptance in practice [1][2]. The reasons are varied but there are some common threads providing barriers to adoption:

1. Lack of individual incentives among potentially participating faculty; and
2. A perceived high barrier to entry.

In an effort to improve "content recruitment" for institutional repositories, Foster and Gibbons have identified some key issues preventing broad acceptance of the institutional repository operated at their institution (University of Rochester), noting that "without content an [institutional repository] is just a set of empty shelves." [2] Figure 1 of their article is especially illustrative. It shows a complete misalignment of faculty perceptions when it comes to the notions of institutional repository, metadata and open-source software. However, faculty fully understand and appreciate who should *control* the content – them.

Nevertheless, it is clear that institutional repositories are a logical way to proceed provided the barriers to their broad acceptance are overcome. We attack that problem by seeking solutions to the two barriers to adoption cited above.

3. APPROACH
3.1 General
The work reported here is aimed at eliminating two key barriers to the routine inclusion of research data into the institutional repositories being operated at research institutions today. Our approach is to create personal repositories and federate their content into the institutional repository of a university. Our approach involves a marketing change from "institutional" to "personal" repositories together with an evolutionary approach aimed at gradually increasing participation by researchers. The key elements of our approach follow.

- Provide individual researchers or research groups or both with personal repositories as a service.
- Provide each data set a digital object identifier – a unique, persistent identifier.[5]

- Provide each participating individual with a unique, persistent, portable identifier and assure access to the "owning" individual in perpetuity.
- Provide a persistent archive for research artifacts.

3.2 A Concrete Example: CV as UI

Early in the project it became obvious that before we could adequately address the capture and submission of research data to the institutional repository it would be necessary to address the issue of providing an appropriate user interface to personal research materials. This would be key to acquiring all research artifacts, not just research data.

Our position is that content recruitment for institutional repositories begins with faculty and student recruitment to personal repositories. We have chosen to model the initial UI on the academic CV to provide a familiar interface that fits naturally into the daily life of an academic. Our approach is to provide extremely low barrier tools for importing information, and sufficient value to the transition, that one would elect to undertake a small amount of manual work for the subsequent benefits.

OmniMea utilizes CNRI's Handle System *(http://www.handle.net)* and Digital Object Repository *(http://dorepository.org)* technologies. The power of our approach is that the imported CV is not treated as a monolithic entity. Each item imported into the *OmniMea* personal repository, be it a journal article, a data set, or a professional activity, is represented as a digital object. This representation allows a great deal of flexibility and allows us to support a number of key benefits, including flexible display options, data visualization, and customizable export.

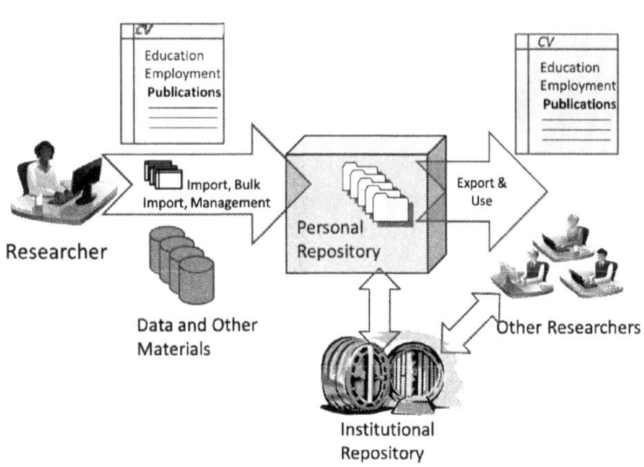

Figure 1: The *OmniMea* Workflow and Key Features

Having chosen the CV as our initial UI, it remains to describe how we will capture research artifacts for submission to the institutional repository when appropriate. The opportunity to capture items for inclusion in the personal repository occurs naturally when one updates a CV. When the citation for a publication is added to a CV, the interface asks for the location of the publication and uploads into the personal repository. The service can also ask if the associated publication should be placed in the institutional repository and facilitate that upload if requested.

Data is handled analogously. We have the potential to support multiple ways to reference data. Our CV currently supports a section for *data papers* as proposed by the California Digital Library (CDL) [4]. While the format of a data paper has not been standardized, we believe the CDL specification provides appropriate guidelines including metadata such as title, creator, abstract and URL(s) to the actual datasets. When a data paper is added to a CV we have the opportunity to acquire the associated data as well.

4. PROJECT STATUS

We have made excellent progress on the development of a low barrier user interface, the ordinary CV, as one form of personal repository UI. This provides the means for academic users, our initial target audience, to manage and access some of their personal repository using their CVs, something they need to maintain anyway. The deployment of our personal repository prototype, *OmniMea*, is key to gauging the effectiveness of personal repositories to support content recruitment for institutional repositories – the central thesis of the project. The key to a successful deployment is a robust service with low barrier to entry and significant value to motivate entry. To lower the barrier to entry we need to provide some supporting services such as the following.

- Provide cut/paste entry of publications from a traditional CV.
- Provide for ingest of publication metadata from other resources, e.g., ACM DL and IEEE DL.
- To the maximum extent possible provide access to digital representations of publications and data by looking up and adding persistent identifiers such as DOIs for published articles and providing persistent IDs for other content.
- Provide on demand "hardcopy," i.e., pdf file, for disseminating or printing.

Our present prototype provides all these services and we continue to look for ways to increase value while lowering barriers to usage. Our prototype CV service is currently available for demo.

5. ACKNOWLEDGMENTS

This material is based upon work supported by the National Science Foundation under Grant no. 1152481. Any opinions, findings, and conclusions or recommendations expressed in this material are those of the author(s) and do not necessarily reflect the views of the NSF. We would also like to acknowledge Ben Hadden, the project team leader, and undergraduate interns Sarah Elder, Emily Tran, Kelly Croswell and Claire Kannapell, who produced much of the code under Ben's guidance.

6. REFERENCES

[1] Davis, P. M. and M. J. L. Connolly, "Institutional Repositories: Evaluating the Reasons for Non-use of Cornell University's Installation of DSpace," D-Lib Magazine, 13(3/4), March/April 2007.

[2] Foster, N. F. and S. Gibbons, "Understanding Faculty to Improve Content Recruitment for Institutional Repositories," D-Lib Magazine, 11(1), January 2005.

[3] Johnson, R. K., "Institutional Repositories: Partnering with Faculty to Enhance Scholarly Communication," D-Lib Magazine, 8(11), November 2002.

[4] Kunze, John. "New Metaphors: Data Papers and Data Citations," Presentation at National Federation of Advanced Information Services, Philadelphia, February 27-28, 2012.

[5] Paskin, N., "Digital Object Identifiers for Scientific Data," Data Science Journal, 4, 28 April 2005: 12-20.

Pretty as a Pixel: Issues and Challenges in Developing a Controlled Vocabulary for Video Game Visual Styles

Andy Donovan, Hyerim Cho, Chris Magnifico, Jin Ha Lee
University of Washington
Mary Gates Hall, Suite 370
Seattle, WA 98195
+1 206.685.0153
idonovan@uw.edu; chohr113@uw.edu; magnific@uw.edu; jinhalee@uw.edu

ABSTRACT

Despite the increase in interest in video games across commercial and academic areas, organizational systems for classifying them remain inadequate, particularly in describing the visual styles of video games. Because video games are by and large a visual medium, the ability to describe their visual "look" coherently and consistently greatly contributes to their discovery through classification. A set of controlled terms would be instrumental in complementing game recommendation engines and search applications in digital libraries to meet users' content-related information needs. In our study we examine the academic and user-generated content about video games' visual styles in order to extract potentially useful controlled vocabulary terms. These terms are then organized into facets and arranged into a classified schedule. In this poster, we discuss the challenges in our controlled vocabulary term definitions and their application.

Categories and Subject Descriptors

H.3.1 [**Information Storage and Retrieval**]: Content Analysis and Indexing – *Thesauruses*

General Terms

Design, Standardization

Keywords

Video game, Interactive media, Aesthetics, Artistic style, Visual style, Thesaurus, Taxonomy, Controlled vocabulary

1. INTRODUCTION

Recent years demonstrate a huge growth of interest in video games. As interest in video games increases, so does the need for intelligent access to them. Organizational systems for video games that are currently available, however, are severely lacking due to several reasons such as the unique nature of video games as cultural artifacts, and the lack of efforts for standardization [2]. McDonough et al. [3] have examined the difficulty of applying FRBR and explored how to utilize existing metadata schemas, respectively, to collections of video games with varying results and many caveats. Other organizational systems provide only minimal information about each game. For example, most of the metadata provided in WorldCat or commercial game-related websites tend to be basic descriptive information such as title, platform, publisher, release date, and so on [2]. Catalogers turning to the Library of Congress Subject Headings, moreover, will find little help in achieving specificity in their classifications. In order to improve the search and discovery of video games, it is necessary to explore different kinds of metadata elements that can provide useful information about the content of the game itself.

JCDL '13, July 22–26, 2013, Indianapolis, Indiana, USA.
ACM 978-1-4503-2077-1/13/07.

In addition to the genre, one possible subject metadata that can potentially assist users' access to video games is the artistic or visual style of the game. Visual style categories already richly augment "traditional" artistic objects like paintings and sculpture by providing descriptive information about their shared visual elements, thereby allowing users to better understand, and make connections about, the artistic concept. For video games, the importance of identifying and categorizing this information is increasing as the tools and techniques for creating the visuals of the games evolve and the styles become widely diversified. However, there is currently no known standardized controlled vocabulary that can effectively describe video game artistic styles and be used in organization systems and recommendation engines.

The objective of our research is to create a controlled vocabulary for describing video game visual styles. This is a challenging task for two main reasons: 1) a significant lack of previous scholarship on the subject, and 2) the very nature of classifying "art." In this paper, we adopt a definition of *visual style* as "a cohesive and unifying visual aesthetic," a simple but prickly notion. As one can see, there are potential issues from the start, for what actually makes an aesthetic *cohesive* can be quite subjective. Here, we are not trying to argue why certain video games belong together per se, but rather provide a framework and terminology for such aesthetic justifications in the future. We have attempted to create a way in which video game visual styles can be defined and described from the various facets of their aesthetic "look", such that gamers, librarians, curators, historians, and researchers can make useful and consistent determinations about video games.

In addition to aiding resource description, we foresee many other benefits of having a controlled vocabulary for visual styles. Such a vocabulary would enhance the performance of information retrieval and organizational systems of video games by providing semantic information and linguistic structure [1]. Similarly, these terms may improve online video game recommendation engines or in-person reader's advisory services. Moreover, since a number of other media employ similar types of artistic or visual styles, this vocabulary may also be useful for describing not only video games, but also other popular cultural artifacts such as animations, comics, etc. that are important parts of digital library collections.

2. DESIGN METHOD

We started our term search with a review of the existing scholarly literature. This was difficult endeavor as very few papers exist that share our particular intent. One notable exception was the work of the Digital Games Research Association and, in particular, by Järvinen [1], which we drew on heavily for informing our own top-level artistic style distinctions. We also examined amateur and professional resources for terms-of-art, including such sources as blogs, gamer and industry websites, designer forums, and video game art appreciation websites. Due to their common use of technique and technology, we broadened our scope to include other forms of digital and computer-based art. These communities were helpful for advancing terms that describe artistic techniques. With our initial set of collected terms, we developed a preliminary taxonomy for describing a game's visual style. These terms were assigned preferred or non-preferred status, with the preferred terms collected into a classified schedule.

3. FINDINGS

During the discovery process we determined that a "visual style" might best be captured by describing the different aesthetic *facets*, or ways in which a visual look could be perceived. We decided to group our set of terms according to three facets: 1) the artistic style facet, 2) the artistic technique facet, and 3) the artistic dimension facet. The artistic style facet includes terms that describe the intentional aesthetic organization of the game's artistic elements. These terms help users understand, through visual reference, how artistic elements like color, composition, and line weight might be used. Examples of the artistic style facet include *photorealism*, *caricature*, and *engraving*. The artistic techniques, on the other hand, are the tools by which that particular style is realized, typically the modeling and rendering methods used to create the "look" of the game. *Rotoscoped* and *rasterized* are examples of artistic techniques. Finally, the artistic dimension facet simply describes the "dimensionality" of the art (but not the player's perspective). This facet is limited to three values—*2D*, *3D*, and *multiple* (a combination of 2D & 3D).

Our encoding scheme uses the term-combination mechanism known as a "triplet" to capture the information from each of these facets. The term combination offers a multifaceted understanding of the game's artistic style. For example, a game like *Okami* could be described "*sumi-e / cel-shaded / 3D*. This triplet combines *sumi-e* from the artistic styles facet, *cel-shaded* from the artistic techniques facet, and *3D* from the artistic dimension facet (Fig.1).

Figure 1. Screenshot from Okami (2010)

We defined a total of 38 preferred terms to be used when describing video game artistic styles. In addition, we developed several rules for using the terms and the classified schedule, in order to aid applications of the controlled vocabulary.

4. DISCUSSION

As previously mentioned, one of the greatest challenges was the lack of coherent and consistent terms used in this domain. Both styles and techniques tended to be described by academics, practitioners, and gamers alike in highly variable ways. Further, terms such as "ray tracing," while indeed describing a technique, are not necessarily obvious to the cataloger as being readily apparent in the game's visuals. Additional complications arise in the application of style terms like "photorealism" to games that may have intended that look but achieved it differently through different techniques perhaps not available to older games Additional complications and issues are described below.

- Characters and objects in video games are often stylistically distinct from the background environment or worlds in which they inhabit, complicating the application of terms.
- Video game art might intentionally replicate the visual style of a past art movement (e.g. Impressionism or De Stijl), causing some terms to be added or modified.
- Technology used to limit the art style possible, but now this is not so. Some games today, however, intentionally replicate the older *look* of a game, challenging the proper usage and meaning of some terms.

5. CONCLUSION AND FUTURE WORK

Our controlled vocabulary attempts to define visual styles as "universally" as possible, limiting the subjective and inconsistent use of terms by providing a framework for interpretation. Due to the paucity of literary warrant and critical authority, much remains to be debated about the usage and placement of our indexing terms. The authors acknowledge this limitation and look forward to starting a discussion in the digital library community to further develop and refine our vocabulary to be more useful and comprehensive. This is our first attempt in creating a controlled vocabulary for this type of metadata, and is naturally incomplete. However, because it is faceted and hierarchically structured, the scheme is flexible and easily extendable. Catalogers can add terms under the facet trees when they need to in the future, according to future uses and needs. In future works, we hope to expand our controlled vocabulary by revising definitions and adding new terms for different artistic styles or techniques.

6. REFERENCES

[1] Järvinen, A. 2002. Gran stylissimo: The audiovisual elements and styles in computer and video games. In *Proceedings of Computer Games and Digital Cultures Conference*, 113-128.

[2] Lee, J. H., Tennis, J. T., Clarke, R. I., and Carpenter M. 2013. Developing a video game metadata schema for the Seattle Interactive Media Museum. *International Journal on Digital Libraries*, 13, 2, 105-117.

[3] McDonough, J., Kirschenbaum, M., Reside, D., Fraistat, N., Jerz, D. 2010. Twisty little passages almost all alike: Applying the FRBR model to a classic computer game. *Digital Humanities Quarterly*, 4, 2.

[3] Milstead, J. L. 1997. Thesaurus in a full-text world. In *Visualizing subject access for 21st century information resources*. UIUC, GSLIS, Urbana-Champaign, IL, 28-38.

Providing Context for Digital Library Content

Pamela Campbell
Federal Reserve Bank of St. Louis
P.O. Box 442
St. Louis, MO 63166
1-314-444-8907
pamela.d.campbell@stls.frb.org

Katrina Stierholz
Federal Reserve Bank of St. Louis
P.O. Box 442
St. Louis, MO 63166
1-314-444-8552
katrina.l.stierholz@stls.frb.org

ABSTRACT

In 2004, the Federal Reserve Bank of St. Louis created FRASER (Federal Reserve Archival System for Economic Research, http://fraser.stlouisfed.org), a digital library of economic, financial, and banking data and policy documents. The history of American economic policy is documented in these publications, records, and archival materials. It has become evident that FRASER's growing user base needs additional context to improve users' ability to navigate, select, and understand the continually growing content. We have taken three approaches to improve the accessibility of our content: changes to the database, integration with other web databases, and addition of material to support teaching activities. We hope that these changes will broaden our audience and increase site traffic.

Categories and Subject Descriptors

H.3.7 [**Information Storage and Retrieval**]: Digital Libraries – *collections, user issues,* H.1.2 [**Models and Principles**]: User/Machine Systems – *human information processing.*

General Terms

Design, Experimentation, Human Factors.

Keywords

Digital library, metadata, organization, content, context, understanding, common core.

1. INTRODUCTION

The centennial of the Federal Reserve System begins on December 23, 2013. We plan to leverage the significance and publicity surrounding this historic event to promote broader use of FRASER (Federal Reserve Archival System for Economic Research, http://fraser.stlouisfed.org), a digital library of economic, financial, and banking data and policy documents. The publications, records, and archival materials in FRASER document the history of the American economy and economic policy.

FRASER, which started in 2004 with fewer than 10 publication titles, now provides access to over 700 publication titles containing over 28,000 issues, as well as 5 archival collections containing nearly 13,000 documents. Collections from the Records of the Federal Reserve System held at the National Archives and Records Administration and a collection of over 300,000 historical bank call reports will soon be added to FRASER in response to centennial projects and interest. FRASER offers full-text search, powered by a Google Search Appliance, as well as searching and browsing by basic metadata including title (publication title or archival document title) and author.

Currently, economic historians and other historians plumb the depths of FRASER—they dig deeply into the archival and historical material for their research. We believe that the materials in FRASER are also useful to many other audiences. We desire to expand our audience to educators and members of the general public. However, this audience is unfamiliar with key historical events in Federal Reserve history or the key concepts that might be found in those documents. Educators and members of the general public require more information and context to understand the materials that are presented in our quickly growing digital library.

2. METHODOLOGY

2.1 Overview of Methods

We have identified three methods to improve the accessibility of our content: changes to the database, integration with other web databases, and addition of material to support teaching activities.

2.2 Database and Website Changes

For our first method, we have identified several changes to our website and database to improve the experience for a naïve user:

- Improving search results by
  - Sorting results by date or by relevance
  - Related search terms
  - Filters for date, author, publication title, archival collection, and other tags
  - Additional link options in PDF results, including links to the file's parent publication, special collection, and author
  - Preview images
- Identifying documents by type (data publication, speech, congressional hearings, and so on) and using icons to visually convey the document type. Users can browse and filter by these facets.
- Creating a timeline with layers that can be displayed on the timeline to help users identify the time period they

JCDL '13, July 22–26, 2013, Indianapolis, Indiana, USA.
ACM 978-1-4503-2077-1/13/07.

are interested in and the associated documents available on FRASER.

- Grouping librarian-selected documents into topical categories to scaffold users in identifying the most important or most relevant documents relating to a topic.
- Adding descriptive images and explanatory text to topic pages, author pages, and so on.
- Adding biographical information to authors, including birth date, death date, and office held and dates of office for key figures in economic history.
- Attributing authors to publication issues and extracted articles from publication issues, in addition to their publications.
- Importing additional metadata from OCLC records, including publisher, LC subject headings, and SuDoc identifiers.
- Expanding metadata for archival collections to include the provenance. This has involved adding institution, collection, series, box, and folder information to each record, and making all archival documents browsable by these metadata.

To implement these changes, we have added new fields to the relational database around which the FRASER website is built and modified the public web interface to make this new information usable. A combination of manual and automated tagging has been done to add the new metadata needed.

2.3 Integration with Other Web Databases

For our second method, we have sought opportunities to integrate FRASER content into other web databases. By making FRASER available via these external access points, we place FRASER materials in the context of information sources used by our new target audiences who may have not yet discovered FRASER, and thus draw in new users.

- Standardizing metadata and developing an XML feed to get FRASER into DPLA (http://dp.la/) and improve availability in various bibliographic databases.
- Extracting journal articles from publication issues and loading article title, author, and date/issue information, along with links to the files, into these economic bibliographic databases: RePEc (http://repec.org/) and Fed in Print (http://www.fedinprint.org/).
- Identifying and linking between data series in FRED (Federal Reserve Economic Data; http://research.stlouisfed.org/fred2/), an aggregated database of economic time series, and the scanned publications on FRASER that contain those data.
- Linking to FRASER content in a historical web gateway being created for the Federal Reserve's centennial anniversary that features brief essays on significant people and time periods in the Federal Reserve's history.
- Starting a Twitter account for FRASER (@FedFRASER), which will highlight new additions, along with notable documents from this day in history (#TDiH).

2.4 Classroom Integration

For our third method, we collaborated with the Federal Reserve Bank of St. Louis's economic education professionals to identify and digitize materials that support common classroom topics and current curriculum practices. Our economic education staff created a lesson plan using FRASER resources to provide teachers with a structured way to teach their students primary source material and economic concepts, and we hope to create more lesson plans featuring FRASER content in the future. This lesson plan aligns to the Common Core State Standards adopted by 45 of the 50 states.

In our first lesson plan, students explore the changes in women's participation in the labor force as well as changes in women's occupations over the past 100 years by looking at data publications on FRASER identifying trends in the data and making projections about women's labor force participation. As part of their study of women's occupations, students attempt to place pictures of Barbie dolls since 1959 on a timeline according to when students believe each career Barbie was released and explain the reasoning behind their date choices. They choose which career Barbie might represent next year and explain that choice in a one-page essay.

3. CONCLUSION

These improvements help us tell the story of the Federal Reserve and its purposes, functions, and history. Adding context to our historical content allows us to expand intellectual access to our collection and encourage a greater understanding of the Federal Reserve while increasing the transparency of the institution. While not one of our primary purposes, an additional benefit is that we anticipate these changes will improve search engine rankings and greatly increase site traffic to a broader audience.

As the centennial progresses, we expect to find other tools to provide information to educators and the public about the materials in our digital library and archives and to scaffold the users' understanding of the Federal Reserve and economic history with information about the context of the documents.

Publishing Earthquake Engineering Research Data

Stanislav Pejša
Network for Earthquake Engineering Simulation (NEES)
207 S. Martin Jischke Drive
West Lafayette, IN 47907
001-765- 496-3736
spejsa@purdue.edu

Cheng Song
Network for Earthquake Engineering Simulation (NEES)
207 S. Martin Jischke Drive
West Lafayette, IN 47907
001-765- 496-3736
song74@purdue.edu

ABSTRACT
Earthquake engineering brings together researchers from seismology, structural, mechanical, and geotechnical engineering whose research results in saving lives and protecting property during earthquakes and tsunamis. Such diversity poses unique challenges for data management, data archiving, preservation, and data publication. The poster demonstrates new innovative approaches to curation, visualization, and publishing of earthquake engineering research data in the NEEShub, a collaborative platform that provides a combined virtual research environment and data repository to researchers participating in the Network for Earthquake Engineering Simulations (NEES) and to the earthquake engineering community in general.

The poster provides graphical depictions demonstrating the curation workflows established in NEES, the progression of data from unprocessed sensor measurements to datasets that can be analyzed by a variety of analytical and visualization tools, and finally their transformation into a citable published product. It documents ways in which NEEShub exposes research data and facilitates collaboration and sharing, as well as re-use and repurposing of the datasets.

Furthermore, the poster illustrates some of the successes of the NEEShub in its four years of existence including continuous growth in uploaded files, users, number of downloaded files, curated projects, and published datasets.

Categories and Subject Descriptors
H.3.7 [Information Systems]: Digital Libraries – *collection, standards, dissemination.*

Keywords
Data publishing, Data curation, Data reuse, Data management.

1. INTRODUCTION
The network is funded through the National Science Foundation (NSF) and consists of 14 engineering laboratories located at major research institutions across the United States that specialize in several types of experimental work: geotechnical centrifuge research, shake table tests, large-scale structural testing, tsunami wave basin experiments, and field site research. Earthquake engineering brings together researchers from seismology, tsunami, structural, mechanical, and geotechnical engineering that create an interdisciplinary environment that fosters innovative and cutting-edge research. The NEES Data Repository is open to all researchers in earthquake engineering who are encouraged to deposit their data in the repository, but its primary mission is to preserve and provide access to data that result from research funded by the NSF through its NEES Research program.

2. CURATION AND QUALITY CONTROL
Curation at the NEEShub focuses primarily on research data and relevant documentation and metadata uploaded to the Project Warehouse. It is a service to the research teams to help them archive their data so that their data can be preserved and accessible in the long-term. The NEEScomm Requirements for Curation and Archiving of Research Data [7] identify the metadata and documentation required, so that research project can be accepted into the NEES Data Repository where NEES provides data management and preservation services following the OAIS reference model [1].

A digital preservation self-audit based on TRAC [11] was conducted in January 2012 to assess readiness of the NEES data repository to provide preservation services to accommodate the needs of the earthquake engineering community for long-term access to research data. This self-audit resulted in a thorough upgrade of curation documentation, especially the Data Sharing and Archiving Policies (DSAP) [5] and the NEEScomm Requirements for Curation and Archiving of Research Data. The self-audit also led to re-structuring of the curation workflows to better accommodate some of the TRAC requirements regarding inventory of formats and preservation planning. The self-audit results keep guiding further hardware and software development in the repository in the area of preservation on both the collection and file level.

Quality assurance in the NEES data repository is part of the curation process and focuses on two key areas: the technical quality of data, documentation and provided metadata, and its content and completeness. The latter is closely entwined with the timeliness of archiving as researchers are expected to make their data available one year after the data are collected. The key function of curation is to ensure that data are archived with all necessary documentation and metadata, so that an experiment or simulation can be correctly understood and interpreted at present and in the future without the need to ask the original research teams.

JCDL'13, July 22–26, 2013, Indianapolis, Indiana, USA.
ACM 978-1-4503-2077-1/13/07

3. REUSE

Facilitating technology transfer through sharing data and their reuse is one of the primary NEES data goals [4]. All data that are curated are made public within 12 months after an experiment is completed at the lab. During the embargo period researchers should analyze their data and work on publication of their findings. During the same period they also work on archiving their data, so that the data can be reviewed before their release to the community provided they meet curation requirements. For successful and purposeful reuse, the data not only must be accessible, but they need to be available in a format the community can use. The users also need to know that they can freely reuse the data. The NEES Data Repository is using Open Data license with attribution (ODC-BY 1.0) [10] which allows researchers to copy, distribute and use the repository, to produce works from it, and build upon the data in the repository as long as they attribute any public use of the repository and the datasets. A credit to the authors of the data set should naturally also be given. NEEEScomm provides both a preferred citation for the dataset and wording for the attribution of the NEES Data Repository in the Data Sharing and Archiving Policies and in a file that is appended to the data downloaded from the repository. All publically accessible datasets are clearly identified with the Open Data license button.

4. TOOLS AND VISUALIZATION

NEEShub also hosts a number of tools that enable analysis of data, telepresence, simulation, and visualization of data in variety of earthquake engineering disciplines. [8] Among the most successful are OpenSEES Lab, a tool that provides access to the Grid infrastructure to run computationally demanding operations and the educational version of the SAP2000, a tool that can be launched directly in the NEEShub. Most of the tools are, however, developed by the researchers themselves, e.g. SLAMMER that enables sliding block displacement analyses for seismic slope stability, or PocketStatics, a structural analysis program. Another important tool is inDEED (**in**teractive **D**isplay for **E**arthquake **E**ngineering **D**ata) that enables researchers to process, visualize, analyze, and compare their experimental and numerical earthquake simulation data

Simulation and visualization tools are intensively developed areas that are particularly suitable to utilize the strength of the NEEShub collaborative platform and the opportunities offered by the Internet2 connection and access to grid infrastructure. There is an effort to provide each curated project with some kind of visualization and at the same time to educate users about the visualization tools and their benefits. Many publically available datasets are equipped with at least one inDEED visualization file.

An aggregation of testing results from a variety of experiments that focus on a particular problem is another example of NEEScomm efforts to produce instruments that can quickly transition the earthquake engineering research to the practice. NEEShub databases are resources that re-use previous results, further enhanced by appending a visualization component. [2]

5. PUBLICATION

As a part of the NEES effort to encourage re-use of and improve access to research data, NEES started to provide datasets on the experiment level with a DOI (permanent identifiers). A citable published dataset should also incentivize younger researchers at the beginning of their research career to get more actively involved in the NEEShub community and consider archiving in the NEES repository even after their NEES-funded research comes to its closure or they complete their studies. The fact that the NSF allows to list datasets or software among other accessible and citable information products in researchers' bio sketches and resumes [9] may make this opportunity even more appealing.

6. CONCLUSION

NEEShub, now in its fourth year of its existence, has grown considerably in all respects since its initial implementation in July 2010. The number of users has more than quadrupled; all significant metrics measuring success of the network such as the number of uploaded files, number of curated projects and experiments, have also significantly increased.

NEES aspires to lead the earthquake engineering community to embracing the potential that cyberinfrastructure has to offer. It cannot afford to lag behind the needs of its community of service. [3] The current developments implemented by the NEEScomm IT team in computational simulation, experimentation with hybrid simulation, as well as new efforts to encourage reuse of research data and energize the field with new publication opportunities, such as published datasets with DOIs attest to its commitment to keep up with the newest trends in e-Research and e-Science.

7. ACKNOWLEDGEMENTS

George E. Brown, Jr. Network for Earthquake Engineering Simulation (NEES) is funded through the National Science Foundation (NSF) under Award Number CMMI-0927178.

8. REFERENCES

[1] CCSDS (2012). Reference Model for an Open Archival Information System (OAIS), http://public.ccsds.org/publications/archive/650x0m2.pdf

[2] J. Browning et al. (2013). NEEShub Databases. Quick Access to Concrete Data. Concrete International, vol. 35, no. 4, pp. 55-58, April 2013, http://nees.org/resources/5768

[3] S. Dyke et al. (2010), "2020 Vision for Earthquake Engineering Research: Report on an OpenSpace Technology Workshop on the Future of Earthquake Engineering," https://nees.org/resources/1636

[4] T. J. Hacker et al, "The NEEShub Cyberinfrastructure for Earthquake Engineering," Computing in Science and Engineering, Vol. 13, no. 4, pp. 67-78, July-Aug. 2011, doi:10.1109/MCSE.2011.70

[5] NEEScomm Data Sharing and Archiving Policy (2011), https://nees.org/resources/2811

[6] NEEScomm Guidelines for Data Upload (2012), https://nees.org/resources/4757

[7] NEEScomm Requirements for Curation and Archiving of Research Data (2012), https://nees.org/resources/4401.

[8] NEEShub Tools, http://nees.org/resources/tools

[9] NSF (2013). Proposal and Award Policies Procedures Guide. http://www.nsf.govpubs/policydocs/pappguide/nsf13001/gpg_2.jsp

[10] ODC Attribution Summary. http://opendatacommons.org/licenses/by/summary/

[11] Trustworthy Repositories Audit & Certification CC (2007). http://www.crl.edu/sites/default/files/attachments/pages/trac_0.pdf

Recovering Missing Citations in a Scholarly Network

A 2-Step Citation Analysis to Estimate Publication Importance

Zhuoren Jiang
College of Transportation Management
Dalian Maritime University
Dalian, China, 116026
jzr_dlmu@hotmail.com

Xiaozhong Liu
School of Library and Information Science
Indiana University
Bloomington, IN, USA, 47405
liu237@indiana.edu

ABSTRACT

Citation relationships between publications are important for assessing the importance of scholarly components (e.g., authors, publications, and venues) within a network. Missing citation metadata in scholarly databases, however, creates problems for classical citation-based ranking algorithms. In the ACM database, for example, 18.5% of publications don't have citation metadata. In this research we propose an innovative, 2-step method of citation analysis, to investigate the importance of publications for which citation data is missing. Preliminary evaluation results show that this method can effectively uncover the importance of publications without using citation metadata.

Categories and Subject Descriptors

H.3.3 [Information Storage and Retrieval]: Information Search and Retrieval

Keywords

Metadata Quality, Information Retrieval, Reference Metadata, Scientific Publication, PageRank, Prior, Ranking

1. INTRODUCTION AND MOTIVATION

While rapid access to digital publications via scientific information retrieval and recommendations can accelerate research, some challenges remain to be addressed. In particular, citation metadata, which is key for determining relationships between publications, is not always available in repositories. In the ACM digital library, for example, 18.5% of publications do not have any citing information, while 55.6% of publications do not have any cited information.

Low quality scientific metadata [1, 5] threatens citation-based ranking algorithms like PageRank and HITs. For instance, two papers might both have zero citations, and hence receive the same ranking score, but if citation information quality is low, then we can't know whether this is due to low importance or to missing citations.

In this paper, we propose a 2-step citation analysis method. The first step uses publication information. Author and co-author information is then used to enhance ranking performance. Preliminary evaluation shows that this method can improve ranking performance when citation metadata quality is low.

JCDL '13, July 22–26, 2013, Indianapolis, Indiana, USA.
ACM 978-1-4503-2077-1/13/07.

2. 2-STEP CITATION ANALYSIS

To solve the metadata quality problem to improve publication ranking, we propose a 2-step solution. First, we create a citation network based on available citation relations between papers, and between papers and authors. Second, using author and co-author data we create another network using authority scores from first step as prior knowledge. This 2-step process is illustrated in Figure 1.

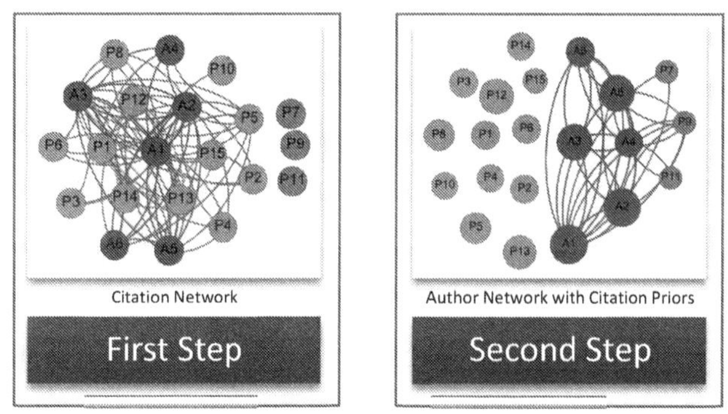

Figure 1: Two-step network analysis diagrammatic sketch

As shown in Figure 1, we first create a classical citation network with missing citations. $G_{first} = (V, E_C)$, where G is the directed graph of the citation network, V is the set of vertices, and E is the set of edges.

There are two kinds of vertices in this graph, $V = V_p \cup V_a$. Each vertex $v \in V_p$ represents a publication. Each vertex $v \in V_a$ represents an author. There are also four kinds of edges in this graph: $E_C = E_{C_{pp}} \cup E_{C_{pa}} \cup E_{C_{ap}} \cup E_{C_{aa}}$. Each edge $e \in E_{C_{pp}}$ represents a publication-citing-publication connecting v_i between v_j (v_i cites v_j ; $v_i, v_j \in V_p$). Each edge $e \in E_{C_{pa}}$ represents a publication-citing-author connecting v_i between v_j (v_i cites v_j; $v_i \in V_p, v_j \in V_a$). Each edge $e \in E_{C_{ap}}$ represents an author-citing-publication connecting v_i between v_j (v_i cites v_j; $v_i \in V_a, v_j \in V_p$). Each edge $e \in E_{C_{aa}}$ represents an author-citing-author connecting v_i between v_j (v_i cites v_j ; $v_i, v_j \in V_a$).

Using the classical PageRank algorithm [2] to calculate the PageRank authority score for the vertices, each vertex (author or paper) receives a scholarly impact score. In this step, vertices that have no incoming links (citations) receive a small value.

In second step, we create an author and co-author relation network with citation authority priors, $G_{second} = (V, E_A)$. Publication and author citation priors for this graph are calculated in the first step.

Using the PageRank with Priors algorithm [3], we update the vertex importance $\pi(v)$ by using vertex prior knowledge $P_{prior}(v)$.

$$\pi(v)^{i+1} = (1-\beta)\left(\sum_{u=1}^{d_{in}(v)} \pi^{i+1}(u)\right) + \beta P_{prior}(v)$$

Please note that for this step we use author and co-author relationships for PageRank. This assumes that 1. Authors co-authoring with an important author are important, and 2. Papers written by an important author are important. These hypotheses works *only if* we know which author is "more important" than another, and this is exactly the prior knowledge $P_{prior}(v)$ from the first step. Author authority, from the first step, is highly likely to be more accurate than the paper authority score in that most authors in our database have more than one publication and accumulated citation information can enhance author authority accuracy. Paper authority scores, when citation information is missing or partially missing, can be biased or misleading.

3. EXPERIMENT AND EVALUATION

In order to evaluate this method, we compared 2-step citation ranking results with 'ground truth' ranking results based purely on citation relations. We constructed three ranking lists:

(1) PageRank of Author Citation (PAC) based ranking list (author ground truth). (2) PageRank of Paper Citation (PPC) based ranking list (paper ground truth). (3) 2-Step Citation Analysis of publication-author network with different percentage citation information randomly removed. For instance, for 15% missing citations, we randomly selected 15% of publications in the corpus and removed their citation (citing and cited) information.

We used the Kendall rank correlation coefficient [4] between 2-Step ranking and ground truth rankings to evaluate algorithm performance. It is a measure of rank correlation; specifically, it can measure the similarity of the orderings of the data when ranked by each of the quantities. In our case the quantity is the scholarly impact score. The Kendall coefficient must be in the range [−1, 1]. If the agreement between the two rankings is perfect, the coefficient has value 1; otherwise, it will have value -1. It will have value 0 if the rankings are completely independent.

We selected 41,370 publications with 63,323 authors from 111 journals and 1,442 conference proceedings or workshops on computer science for the experiment (mainly from the ACM digital library), which were published between 1951 and 2011.

In order to validate the 2-step algorithm's performance, we simulated different citation missing scenarios, from 5% of citations missing to 90% of citations missing. For each group, we randomly removed a fixed percentage of citing and cited relations. The experiment was repeated 50 times.

The average Kendall coefficient for paper and author ranking is presented in the following table and visualized in Figure 2.

	5%	10%	15%	18.50%	20%	30%
Paper coefficient	0.6637	0.6084	0.5563	0.5203	0.5044	0.4224
Author coefficient	0.7348	0.6805	0.6306	0.5964	0.5821	0.5040
	40%	50%	60%	70%	80%	90%
Paper coefficient	0.3491	0.2743	0.1971	0.1194	0.0422	0.0282
Author coefficient	0.4343	0.3667	0.2980	0.2281	0.1598	0.0922

Table 1: 2-step analysis for paper and author ranking

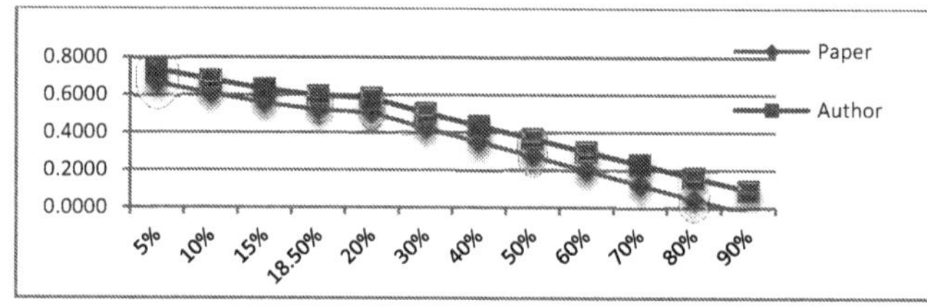

Figure 2: 2-step analysis for paper and author ranking

In order to compare with other baselines, we also tested the other relationships between publications by using PageRank.

	Author	Has-author	Co-author	Author+Co-author	All citations
Publication	-0.1128	-	-	-0.1128	0.7042
Author	-	0.2675	0.2675	0.2675	0.7691

Table 2: Other base lines for paper and author ranking

In Table 2, we compare simple Author, Has-author, Co-author, Author + Co-Author, and all citations (between papers and authors). It is clear that, except for all citations, all other indicators cannot effectively measure author and publication importance. When we used both citation relationships between authors and papers, the ranking performance can reach to 0.7042, and 0.7691, where all citation information is available.

For 2-step analysis, when less than 20% of citation information is missing, both paper and author ranking coefficients are larger than 0.5, which means that 2-step analysis can effectively cope with h-the missing citation problem.

When citation information is missing for 60% of publications in the repository, the paper ranking coefficient drops to 0.1917, whereas the author ranking coefficient is 0.2980. It is clear that author ranking is more robust than paper ranking when using the 2-step ranking method.

4. CONCLUSION

In this paper, we proposed a 2-step citation analysis method for paper and author ranking. First, we used low quality citation metadata to find important authors. We then employed those authority scores as prior to enhance ranking results with author and co-author relationships. Preliminary results show that 2-step citation analysis is a promising method for improving ranking when citation quality is low.

REFERENCES

[1] Guo, C., Zhang, J. & Liu, X. (2013) Scientific Metadata Quality Enhancement for Scholarly Publications. iConference

[2] Page, Lawrence and Brin, Sergey and Motwani, Rajeev and Winograd, Terry, 1999. The PageRank Citation Ranking: Bringing Order to the Web. Technical Report. Stanford InfoLab.

[3] White, S. and Smyth, P., 2003. Algorithms for estimating relative importance in networks. In Proceedings of the ninth ACM SIGKDD international conference on Knowledge discovery and data mining. ACM, 266- 275.

[4] Kendall, M. 1938. A New Measure of Rank Correlation. Biometrika. 30: 81-93.

[5] Zeng, M.L. & Qin, J. (2008). Metadata, Chapter 9 Metadata Research Landscape. New York: Neal-Schuman.

Semi-Automated Rediscovery of Lost YouTube Music Videos

Daniel Sebastian
Harding University
Computer Science Dept
Searcy, Arkansas, USA 72149
dsebasti@harding.edu

Frank McCown
Harding University
Computer Science Dept
Searcy, Arkansas, USA 72149
fmccown@harding.edu

Michael L. Nelson
Old Dominion University
Computer Science Dept
Norfolk, Virginia, USA 23529
mln@cs.odu.edu

ABSTRACT

Users frequently post popular material to YouTube, and in response, others link to these videos from social media, blogs, forums, and email. However, this content may be removed for numerous reasons, only to resurface again at another URL. This continuous movement and breaking of the web graph makes it difficult for users to relocate content that has moved in YouTube. We present Volitrax, an add-on for FireFox which redirects users to YouTube music videos that have moved to a different URL within YouTube. Volitrax acts as an intermediary that corrects the web graph transparently so YouTube links continue to work even after the content has changed locations.

Categories and Subject Descriptors

H.3.7 [**Information Storage and Retrieval**]: Digital Libraries – *Systems Issues.*

General Terms

Design, Experimentation.

Keywords

Music video, web graph, linkrot, web browser add-on.

1. INTRODUCTION

YouTube is one of the world's largest and most popular video digital libraries, and it is home to millions of music videos. Many of the videos posted to YouTube garner a great number of links by music fans in social media, blogs, forums, and email. However, many of the music videos are subsequently inaccessible from YouTube for a number of reasons: users delete videos or close their accounts, or copyright owners petition for the removal of copyrighted work. Copies of the removed music videos can often be found at other URLs or resurface later as music lovers and copyright owners engage in a game of cat-and-mouse. This continuous movement and breaking of the web graph requires users to manually relocate content that has moved in YouTube.

In order to extend the life of links to YouTube music videos, we have created Volitrax, a FireFox add-on that redirects users to YouTube music videos that have moved locations within YouTube. (Volitrax is a combination of "volatile" and "tracks", as in music tracks.) Volitrax acts as an intermediary that corrects the web graph transparently so YouTube links continue to work even after the content has changed locations.

JCDL'13, July 22–26, 2013, Indianapolis, Indiana, USA.
ACM 978-1-4503-2077-1/13/07.

2. BACKGROUND & RELATED WORK

YouTube has been the source of study in a number of contexts including characterization [2], video sharing [1], video discovery [3], and preservation [5][8]. In previous work [7], we have shown that the half-life for a music video in YouTube ranges from 9 to 18 months, depending on the publication date of the video, and there are frequently hundreds if not thousands of copies of the same music video within YouTube at any one time. This work is an extension of [7] where we make use of the fact that multiple copies of music videos are available at other URLs, and we have built a tool to aid in the discovery of these new URLs. This work fits into a larger framework of rediscovering lost web resources [4] and correcting broken links in the web graph [6].

3. FINDMOBILE TOOL

3.1 Overview

Volitrax works in a client-server environment where clients (those with the Firefox add-on installed) make use of central server which stores music metadata locally and pushes the data out to the Web Infrastructure where it may outlive the lifetime of the service. Figure 1 shows the Volitrax server interfacing with the Volitrax add-ons and various services like Blogger, tumblr, and delicious. These services all offer APIs which make pushing and pulling information straightforward. Data is supplied to Volitrax from volunteer user input and from the last.fm API.

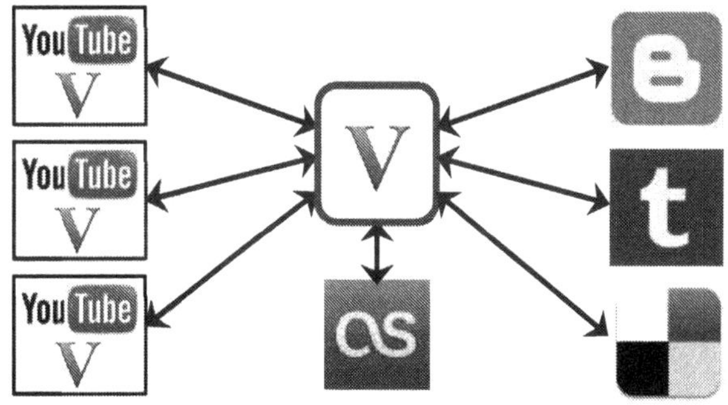

'hich
licious

The Volitrax add-on examines the HTTP traffic when the user is visiting URLs on youtube.com. The add-on uses the YouTube API to obtain information about the video being viewed, and when it suspects the user is viewing a music video (by examining the categorization and video title), it will use the last.fm service to find additional metadata about the song and perform spell corrections. The user may also be asked to verify the metadata (see Figure 2) although this option can be turned off easily.

Metadata about the music video is stored on the server and is pushed to long-term data storage (the Web Infrastructure).

Figure 2. Volitrax Asking the user for metadata about the music video

When the user accesses a YouTube music video that has been removed (as shown in Figure 3), the YouTube API will return a 40x http status code. When this happens, Volitrax will look for an alternate location in its database of music videos so it can automatically redirect the user to another copy. If this is the first time the URL has been seen by Volitrax, it will prompt the user for information about the missing video. The user is able to provide the title and artist if they know it and a new URL if they can discover a copy themselves.

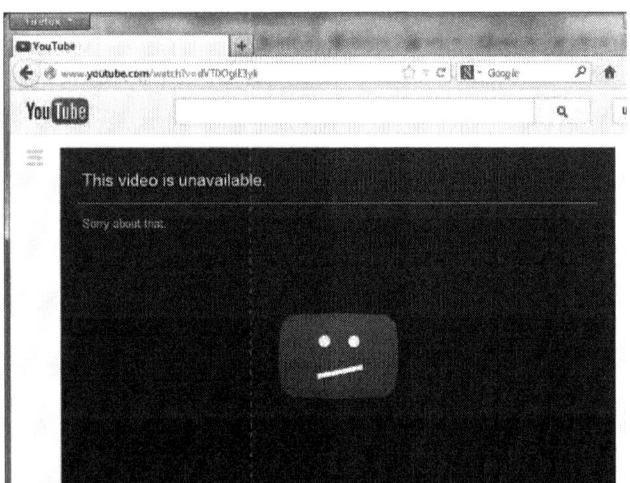

Figure 3. Music video has been removed from YouTube with no hint where to find a replacement

3.2 Voting on User Input

Volitrax makes use of information supplied by users to improve the redirection experience for all users. Any system that relies on the collective anonymous input of the public will ultimately require separating out good input from bad input. Volitrax uses a voting system to determine which inputs are better than others. For example, if more users agree that a song's title is *A* instead of *B*, then *A* will be the selected title. Users are also given the chance to confirm if an automated redirect is resulting in a "good enough" copy of the requested video. Of course this voting method is not full-proof, but it is an adequate light-weight solution that does not require user authentication. In the future, other trust metrics could be employed such as giving new users less weight when issuing votes.

3.3 Long-term Storage

As mentioned earlier, Volitrax stores data in a number of commercial services that are not originally designed for such purposes. However, storing music video information in these services will significantly increase the chance of such information surviving well past the lifetime of the Volitrax application. Because these services were not intended to be used as a database, their APIs are throttled to at best one request per second. This makes starting a new server with no local information very slow.

4. ACKNOWLEDGMENTS

Thank you to Vivens Ndatinya who laid some of the groundwork for the Volitrax add-on. This research was supported by the National Science Foundation (IIS 1008492 and 1009392).

5. REFERENCES

[1] Cheng, X., Dale, C., Liu, J. 2007. Understanding the characteristics of internet short video sharing: YouTube as a case study. Technical Report arXiv preprint arXiv:0707.3670.

[2] Cheng, X., Dale, C., Liu, J. 2008. Statistics and social network of YouTube videos. In *2008 16th International Workshop on Quality of Service*, 229-238.

[3] Cunningham, S.J., Nichols, D.M. 2008. How people find videos. In *Proceedings of the 8th ACM/IEEE-CS Joint Conference on Digital Libraries* (JCDL '08), ACM, New York, NY, USA, 201–210.

[4] Klein, M., Nelson, M. L. 2010. Evaluating methods to rediscover missing web pages from the web infrastructure. In *Proceedings of the 10th annual international ACM/IEEE Joint Conference on Digital Libraries* (JCDL '10). ACM, New York, NY, USA, 59-68.

[5] Marchionini, G., Shah, C., Lee, C.A., Capra, R. 2009. Query parameters for harvesting digital video and associated contextual information. In *Proceedings of the 9th ACM/IEEE-CS Joint Conference on Digital Libraries* (JCDL '09). ACM, New York, NY, USA, 77-86.

[6] Popitsch, N., Haslhofer, B. 2011. DSNotify – A solution for event detection and link maintenance in dynamic datasets. *Web Semantics: Science, Services and Agents on the World Wide Web*, 9(3):266-283, September 2011.

[7] Prellwitz, M., Nelson, M. L. 2011. Music video redundancy and half-life in YouTube. In *Proceedings of the 15th international conference on Theory and Practice of Digital Libraries: research and advanced technology for digital libraries* (TPDL '11). Springer-Verlag, Berlin, Heidelberg, 143-150.

[8] Shah, C. Tubekit: a query-based YouTube crawling toolkit. 2008. In *Proceedings of the 8th ACM/IEEE-CS Joint Conference on Digital Libraries* (JCDL '08). ACM, New York, NY, USA, 433.

Streamlining User Interaction in Tag-Based Conversational Navigation of Knowledge Resource Libraries

Jinyue Xia
Department of Software & Information Systems
University of North Carolina at Charlotte, NC
jxia3@uncc.edu

David C. Wilson
Department of Software & Information Systems
University of North Carolina at Charlotte, NC
davils@uncc.edu

ABSTRACT

This paper presents an approach for helping users more quickly discover relevant information resources in a tag based system, where each resource is associated with a number of descriptive meta-data tags. Our approach builds an adaptive conversational decision-tree structure to minimize the number of interactive cues required to help a user navigate to resources of interest. Initial experiments demonstrate the potential of the approach, with shallower decision trees supporting better overall interaction performance.

Categories and Subject Descriptors

H.3.3 [**Information Systems**]: Information storage and Retrieval —*Digital Libraries*

Keywords

Knowledge navigation, Recommender systems, Decision tree, User interaction

1. INTRODUCTION & RELATED WORK

In order to find relevant resources within digital libraries, two main avenues are available to users: searching by content (e.g., words in a document) and by meta-data (e.g., category keywords or tags). Particularly when users are not very familiar with a domain, it can be difficult to formulate content-based queries, and presenting relevant meta-data categories, such as tags, can help to facilitate knowledge navigation. Such knowledge navigation can be viewed as a conversational zooming process, where a system prompts the user with potentially applicable tags, the user makes some choices, the system presents a refined set (possibly with some example resources), and so on until a reasonable set of resources is identified. Our approach successively splits the pool of library resources by calculating the entropy across remaining tags and resources at each level of a decision tree. Complementary to the technique, we have also developed an interactive visualization tool for digital library maintainers to explore different parametrizations.

The purpose of traditional decision tree induction, such as ID3 [5], C4.5 [6], and CART [2], is predominately for classification tasks. More recently, techniques have been developed to deal with data instances that are associated with multiple labels or categories [7]. For example, Clare and King [3] modified the C4.5 algorithm for multi-label phenotype data by modifying the formula of entropy calculation. There are other ways to reduce user interaction times between users and the system including query refinement and case-based reasoning. For example, Doyle and Cunningham [4] presented an incremental case-based reasoning (I-CBR) based technique to reduce dialogue in on-line decision guide and they also took the advantage of information gain [5]. Aha et al. [1] developed a case-based approach to interact with users by retrieving cases (items) from a case library.

2. CONVERSATIONAL NAVIGATION

In our approach, each resource is labelled by zero or more meta-data tags. This can be represented as a binary matrix across resources and tags, where the v_{ij} value indicates whether resource i is associated ("1") or not ("0") with the corresponding tag j. The primary issue at each conversation step is to select the tag that best splits the remaining resources, in order to minimize conversation length for a majority of resources overall. For this, we use entropy to measure "impurity" at each step, where $p(i)$ denotes the

$$\text{Entropy(t)} = -\sum_{i=0}^{n-1} p(i)log_2p(i)$$

fraction of resources belonging to tag i at given node t, and n is the number of classes. A skeleton decision tree induction called **Generate_Tree** is shown in Algorithm 1.

3. EVALUATION

As an initial evaluation of the approach, we consider movies from the 1M MovieLens dataset[1] as digital library resources with 19 genres as tags. Users' ratings are separated by timestamp into an approximate 80/20 split of training and testing data. The conversation length for each point is computed as the length from the root to the node that contains the resource, with results shown in Figure 1. Tags not associated with any resource can be filtered as a parameter for results.

[1]http://www.grouplens.org/node/12

JCDL'13, July 22–26, 2013, Indianapolis, Indiana, USA.
ACM 978-1-4503-2077-1/13/07.

Algorithm 1 Generate_Tree(D, *taglist*, *tag_selection*)

```
create a node current
create a tag tag ← tag_selection(D, taglist)
if tag is not NULL then
    current.tag ← tag, current.resources ← D, taglist ←
    taglist − tag, root ← current
else {tag is NULL}
    current = NULL
end if
while D is not empty do
    create a node parent, set parent ← current
    for each outcome i of split tag tag do
        let D_i be the set of outcome resources satisfying outcome
        i, i could be "0" or "1"
        a new tag tag ← tag_selection(D_i, taglist)
        if i == 0 then
            current ← parent.leftchild
        else {i == 1}
            current ← parent.rightchild
        end if
        if tag is not NULL then
            current.tag ← tag, current.resources ← D_i, taglist ←
            taglist − tag
        else {tag is NULL}
            attach a leaf with D_i to current and current has no
            tag
        end if
        D ← D − D_i
    end for
end while
return root
```

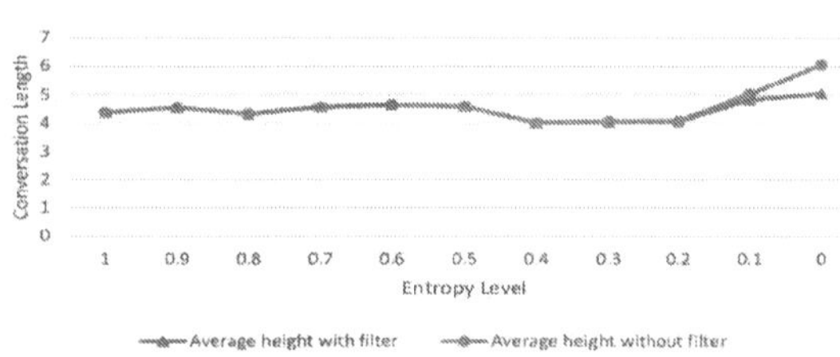

Figure 1: Average Conversation Times

In addition to average conversational length, we expect that shallower overall conversational trees should provide better interaction performance across all users. We examined the average height of resulting conversational decision trees across three conditions: a dataset with 25 movies, 50 movies and 200 movies respectively. Two main results are shown in Figure 2. First, as expected the overall tree height tends to increase as the entropy level decreases. Second, as the number of movies grows, the difference between the largest and smallest conversational height decreases.

4. DISCUSSION AND CONCLUSION

While our initial experiments are primarily illustrative, they show the potential for our approach to support both end users (streamlining conversational navigation) and library maintainers (designing for streamlined navigation). To operationalize the technique, we have developed a browser-based interactive visualization tool to explore conversational structures, as illustrated in Figure 3. In this example, the system might begin by asking whether the user is interested in "Drama"; if "yes" then following the left branch to prompt about the "Action" genre, otherwise the "Comedy" genre on the right branch. The system continues to prompt until movies of interest are reached. In addition, a basic interface (not shown) is provided for library maintainers to explore different starting tags (known initial context) and entropy levels (shaping conversational style). Given the tag context and entropy level, a tree is displayed to the maintainer and it can help understand the structure of the resource library and the potential for different kinds of conversational pathways through the resources from different starting points.

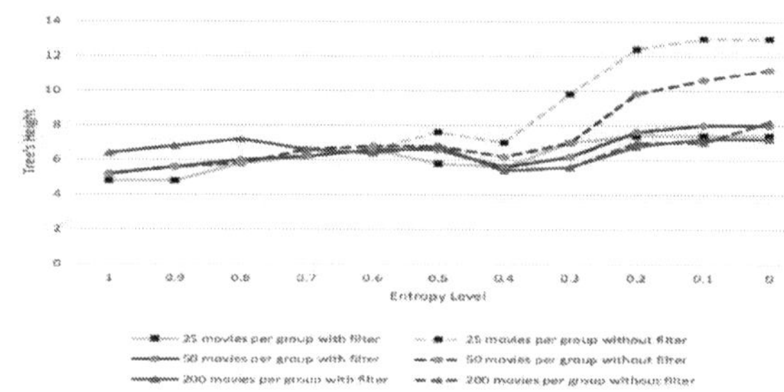

Figure 2: Comparison of Trees heights

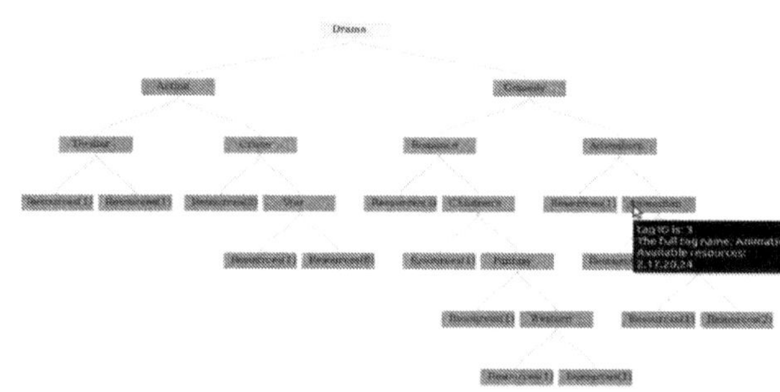

Figure 3: Example Conversation Tree

Overall, initial experiments show that our approach can support design and deployment of streamlined conversational interaction for digital library navigation, and illustrate the importance of support tools to explore different conversational structures for resource navigation.

5. REFERENCES

[1] D. W. Aha, L. A. Breslow, and H. Muñoz Avila. Conversational case-based reasoning. *Applied Intelligence*, 14:9–32, 2001.

[2] L. Breiman, J. H. Friedman, R. A. Olshen, and C. J. Stone. *Classification and Regression Trees*. 1984.

[3] A. Clare and R. D. King. Knowledge discovery in multi-label phenotype data. In *Proc. of PKDD'01*, 2001.

[4] M. Doyle and P. Cunningham. A dynamic approach to reducing dialog in on-line decision guides. In *Proc. of EWCBR'00*, 2000.

[5] J. R. Quinlan. Induction of decision trees. *Machine Learning*, 1:81–106, 1986.

[6] J. R. Quinlan. *C4.5: programs for machine learning*. Morgan Kaufmann Publishers Inc., 1993.

[7] G. Tsoumakas and I. Katakis. Multi-label classification: An overview. *IJDWM*, 3(3):1–13, 2007.

Studying the Data Practices of a Scientific Community

Besiki Stvilia
bstvilia@fsu.edu

Charles C. Hinnant
chinnant@fsu.edu

Shuheng Wu
sw09f@my.fsu.edu

Adam Worrall
apw06@my.fsu.edu

Dong Joon Lee
dl10e@my.fsu.edu

Kathleen Burnett
kburnett@fsu.edu

Gary Burnett
gburnett@fsu.edu

Michelle M. Kazmer
mkazmer@fsu.edu

Paul F. Marty
marty@fsu.edu

College of Communication and Information, Florida State University, PO Box 3062100, Tallahassee, FL 32306

ABSTRACT
To be effective and at the same time sustainable, a community data curation model has to be aligned with the community's current work organization: practices and activities; divisions of labor; data and collaborative relationships; and the community's value structure, norms, and conventions for data, quality assessment, and data sharing. This poster discusses a framework for developing a community data curation model, using a case of the scientific community gathered around the National High Magnetic Field Laboratory, a large national lab. The poster also reports findings of preliminary research based on semi-structured interviews with a sample of the main stakeholder groups of the community.

Categories and Subject Descriptors
H.1.0 [**Models and Principles**]: General

General Terms
Documentation, Management, Measurement.

Keywords
Data curation, data management, condensed matter physics, data quality, activity theory.

1. INTRODUCTION
Scientific communities have long established, culturally justified and sustainable models of sharing scholarly publications. As science becomes increasingly data driven, the need for building similar shared, sustainable, community models for data curation and for integrating them with publication models becomes of greater interest and concern for funding agencies, scientific institutions and communities [1].

Data curation is "the activity of, managing and promoting the use of data from its point of creation, to ensure it is fit for contemporary purpose, and available for discovery and re-use" [2]. Many general models of research data and related curation activities, processes, architecture components, and risks have been proposed in the literature (e.g., DCC Curation Lifecycle Model, OAIS, DRAMBORA). However, data curation work is context specific. General models and tools are valuable knowledge sources to plan data curation activities, but they do not define context specific models or incorporate perceptions and value structures for data, metadata, and data quality problems. These general models do not address the social aspects of scientific work that may enable or alternatively hinder data curation activities. Furthermore, these models and toolkits provide little guidance and insight into data practices at the team level and how those practices interact with the data curation norms, policies, and infrastructure at the organization and community levels.

2. FRAMEWORK
To study data practices at the community level one needs a theoretical framework, which can not only provide high-level conceptualizations of different data intensive activities of the community, but also mechanisms for integration, learning, and harmonization of the community's data practice conceptualizations by different stakeholder groups. Activity Theory [3] and an information quality assessment framework and value based quality assessment model developed by one of the authors in earlier research [4,5] were selected to guide this research. According to Activity Theory, context can be viewed as an interplay between general cultural and community structures (language, norms, conventions, social networks, and relationships) and the structure of a particular activity or an activity system (goal oriented actions, tools, roles, rules, strategies, etc.). This activity theoretic framework helps conceptualize the typified activities of creation and use of particular data types: their structures, values, the types of quality problems that each data type may be prone to, and the criticality of these problems to the activity's success or failure. This conceptualization of the activity system can be used to guide an empirical analysis of data objects and other documents (e.g. lab notebooks), development of interview protocols and survey questionnaires, and iterative participatory design of metadata and knowledge organization tools and templates.

The framework was developed to study data work of a condensed matter physics (CMP) community gathered around the National High Magnetic Field Laboratory (NHMFL). The NHMFL is a unique interdisciplinary scientific center, one of the largest of its kind, collaboratively operated by Florida State University, the University of Florida, and Los Alamos National Laboratory. It provides scientists with free access for research involving magnetic fields, superconducting magnetometry, magnetic resonance imaging, and magnetic spectroscopy. In preliminary research, the activity theoretic framework was used to bootstrap the interview protocol and coding schema for semi-structured interviews. Twelve interviews were conducted. The interviewees

JCDL'13, July 22–26, 2013, Indianapolis, Indiana, USA.
ACM 978-1-4503-2077-1/13/07.

represented different stakeholder groups and roles at the NHMFL, including sample material growers, experimentalists, theorists, visiting scientists, local scientists, administrators, senior scientists, junior scientists, postdoctoral researchers, and students. The preliminary research was limited to exploring the following fundamental questions: *(1) What are the data-related activities present in the community? (2) What is data quality in the community? (3) What is the value of data quality and how it can be evaluated?*

3. FINDINGS OF PRELIMINARY RESEARCH

3.1 Data, Activities

CMP scientists study the properties, including the structure and state dynamics, of condensed matter. At the NHMFL, scientists measure and interpret the effects and dynamics of interaction of different stimuli, such as magnetic fields, on matter. Research processes at the NHMFL consist of multiple activities and are usually performed by small teams of scientists, often with complementary skills and knowledge, who play different roles. In addition to general project activities such as experimentation, computation, and recordkeeping, scientists also spend significant time in planning and preparing for a research project (e.g., writing research proposals, building instruments) and building and maintaining their social networks in the community.

The literature and our preliminary work suggests that, depending on their specialization and research task, scientists even within the same discipline may have different perceptions of what constitutes data. A scientist growing a new material may consider the chemical formula or an actual physical sample of the material as data. For another scientist measuring the properties of the same material, data could be readings of the instruments or sensors attached to that sample. To a theorist, additional types of data could be obtained from simulations and/or analytical calculations. Finally, to a reader or reviewer of a manuscript submitted to a scholarly journal, data could be the graphs and analytical calculations included in the manuscript. This study did not differentiate among the different types of data (e.g., physical samples, measurement data, metadata, publications) and referred all of them as data. Figure 1 presents an initial, preliminary model of the data curation activities of the CMP community associated with the NHMFL.

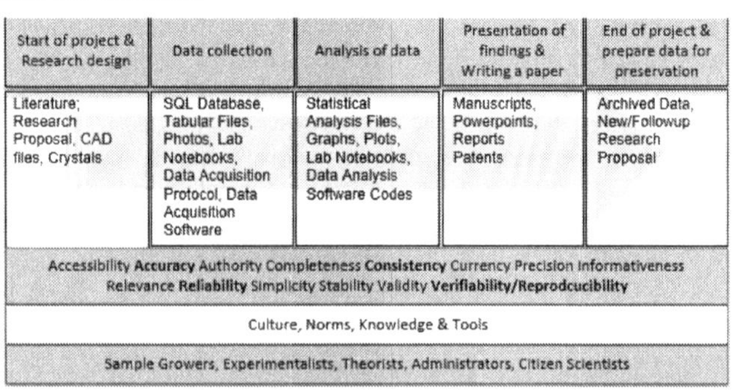

Figure 1. Model of data curation activities of the CMP community

3.2 Quality

Quality is usually defined as "fitness for use." Data quality problems may arise in any of the activities constituting the complex process of CMP research and scholarly communication. These activities may include manufacturing material samples, designing an experiment, manufacturing instruments and parts for the experiment, measuring and/or simulating the characteristics of the sample under different treatments and conditions, interpreting the results of the measurements, theorizing possible characteristics or relationships, and communicating findings to the community. Perception of quality may also change indirectly due to changes in the community's culture, knowledge and research technology. The interview data showed that scientists particularly cared about the *reproducibility*, *accuracy*, and *consistency* of data (see Fig. 1).

3.3 Value

The study found instances of all five categories of data quality value change from [4] (see Table 2).

Table 2. Measures of data quality value

Measures	Explanation
A function of the activity success or failure	Success or failure of an activity
A function of the cost and rework	Cost of equipment use and the time spent by scientists to generate and/or massage data
A function of the amount of use	Amount of data use, or the use of derived data products such as publications
A function of the activity cost	Change in the cost of an activity in which data is used
A combination of the above factors	Some combination of the above factors

4. CONCLUSIONS

This poster reported on a conceptual framework for studying the data work of a large scientific community. Future research will collect additional data and develop a more detailed community level data curation model through participatory design involving all major stakeholder groups within and having impact on the CMP community.

5. REFERENCES

[1] Atkins, D. E., Droegemeier, K. K., Feldman, S. I., Garcia-Monlina, H., Klein, M. L., Messerchmitt, D. G., Messina, P., & Wright, M. H. (2003). *Revolutionizing science and engineering through cyberinfrastructure: Report of the National Science Foundation Blue-Ribbon Advisory Panel on Cyberinfrastructure.* Arlington, VA: NSF.

[2] Lord, P., & Macdonald, A. (2003). *E-Science curation report: Data curation for e-Science in the UK: An audit to establish requirements for future curation and provision.* Bristol, UK: The JISC.

[3] Engeström, Y. (1990). Learning, working and imagining: Twelve studies in activity theory. Helsinki: Orienta-Konsultit Oy.

[4] Stvilia, B., & Gasser, L. (2008). Value based metadata quality assessment. *Library & Information Science Research, 30*, 67-74.

[5] Stvilia, B., Gasser, L., Twidale, M. B., & Smith, L. C. (2007). A framework for information quality assessment. *Journal of the American Society for Information Science and Technology, 58*, 1720-1733.

The New ACM CCS and a Computing Ontology

Lillian N Cassel
Villanova University
Dept of Computing Sciences
Villanova PA 19085 USA
1 610 519 7341
cassel@acm.org

Sudhamsha Palivela
Villanova University
Dept of Computing Sciences
Villanova PA 19085 USA
1 610 519 7310
spalivel@villanova.edu

Srikanth Marepalli
Villanova University
Dept of Computing Sciences
Villanova PA 19085 USA
1 610 519 7310
srikmarepally@gmail.com

AhiMahidhara Padyala
Villanova University
Dept of Computing Sciences
Villanova PA 19085 USA
1 610 519 7310
apadyala@villanova.edu

Rahul Deep
Villanova University
Dept of Computing Sciences
Villanova PA 19085 USA
1 610 519 7310
rdeep@villanova.edu

Siddhartha Terala
Villanova University
Dept of Computing Sciences
Villanova PA 19085 USA
1 610 519 7310
sterala@villanova.edu

ABSTRACT
This poster presents an overview of the new ACM Computing Classification system and compares it with work done in creating an ontology of all computing-related topics. There are similarities and differences and the differences lead to conclusions about both approaches.

Categories and Subject Descriptors
H.1.0 Information Models and Systems, General

Keywords
Ontology, computing classification

1. INTRODUCTION
The ACM Computing Classification System (CCS) [1] serves a critical role in organizing and categorizing publications in the computing domain. It is a necessary component of the ACM Digital Library and has served as the de facto labeling system for computing research for four decades. The first version appeared in 1964 with major revisions released in 1991 and 1998. Intermediate revisions served to reflect changes in the disciplines. In 2012, ACM undertook a major revision, not only of the content, but also of the structure. The letter and number hierarchy levels are replaced by a semantic vocabulary.

The Computing Ontology [2-5] project developed with support from NSF and the ACM Education Board. The motivation was to produce a comprehensive representation of all of the computing disciplines, with equal attention to use in curriculum development and research classification. The project proceeded in fits and

JCDL'13, July 22–26, 2013, Indianapolis, Indiana, USA.
ACM 978-1-4503-2077-1/13/07.

2. RELATED WORK
Approaches to constructing an ontology vary. With an available digital library of resources known to be relevant in a given domain, text extraction offers an opportunity to capture relevant concepts without the complication of differing views of subject experts. [11, 12] However, extracting terms only begins the work. Matching terms that have the same meaning and noting when the same term conveys different meanings in different contexts complicates the effort.

3. TWO CLASSIFICATION SYSTEMS
3.1 The ACM CCS
The new ACM CCS consists of 14 top level categories: General and Reference, Hardware, Computer systems and organization, Networks, Software and its engineering, Theory of computation, Mathematics of computing, Information systems, Security and privacy, Human-centered computing, Computing methodologies, Applied computing, Social and professional topics and Proper nouns: People, technologies and companies. Each of the top-level categories is refined

General and reference as a heading reflects the need for this scheme to categorize published work, and serves the purpose of categorization for library resources. The area is subdivided into Document types and Cross-computing tools and techniques. Document types include surveys, reference works, general literature, etc. This provides a way to label works that are not about a specific computing topic. Cross-computing tools and techniques include subcategories of reliability, empirical studies, evaluation, performance and others that apply across a computing topic area.

Physical elements appear in the Hardware category, but also in Computer Organization and in Networks. Network security and security protocols appear in network properties. Validation and verification appear in the Hardware category, but there are no explicit mentions of security there. Similarly, Computer organization includes aspects of reliability and availability, but no explicit mention of security. Software and its engineering is a large topic, encompassing all of programming languages (Software notations and tools) as well as software engineering**..**

3.2 The Computing Ontology

Compilation of the terms included in the Computing Ontology began with mining lists of computing related terms from a variety of sources. These included the curriculum documents [6-8, 10] as well as the 1998 ACM CCS. Documents from other organizations and other countries provided terms and arrangements of terms to consider. Peter Denning's Great Principles of computing [9] provided some ideas as well. A grant from NSF supported meetings in the U.S. and in Europe with individuals representing all of the high level domains of computing. Most, but not all of the individuals involved had at least some interest in computing education.

After a failed attempt to classify everything as one or more of Hardware, Software, Information, or People-related topics, the work proceeded to develop a taxonomy with 17 top level categories. Eventually, revisiting the number of categories led to an organization with seven top level categories, as seen in Figure 1. The figure reflects the top levels and also an initial idea for the relationships among the top levels. An ontology is much more than a taxonomy and developing the attributes and relationships associated with each of the concepts is a necessary component.

Some of the ACM CCS topic areas have no equivalent in the Computing Ontology. The *General and Reference* area does not match a computing-specific topic area and so does not appear in the computing ontology. The category *Proper nouns: People, technologies and companies* corresponds to instances of topics rather than topic areas and so also is not included in the ontology.

4. ACKNOWLEDGMENTS

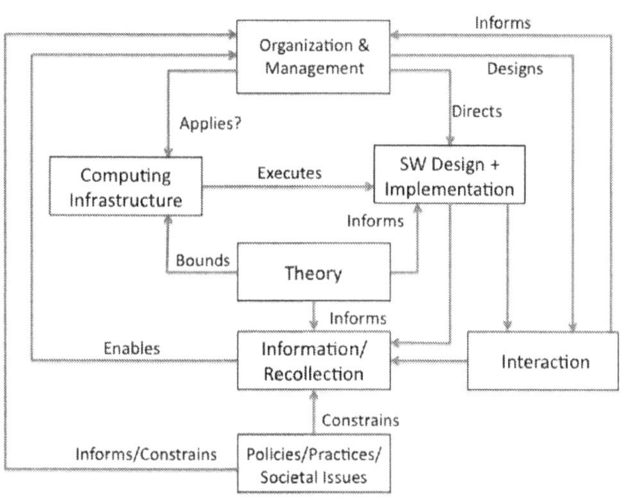

Figure 1 A Computing Ontology

This work is funded in part by NSF CISE CNS 0338546.

Many people have worked on aspects of the computing ontology for nearly 10 years. There are too many to mention, but Gordon Davies, Heikki Topi, and Richard LeBlanc deserve special notice. Michael Wrinn, with support from Intel, helped to develop materials related to parallelism.

The poster will illustrate the common features and distinctive elements of the two schemes.

5. REFERENCES

[1] The 2012 ACM Computing Classification System http://www.acm.org/about/class/2012

[2] Computing Ontology http://www.distributedexpertise.org/computingontology

[3] Cassel, L., LeBlanc, R., McGettrick, A. and Wrinn, M. Concurrency and parallelism in the computing ontology. In *Proceedings of the Proceedings of the 14th annual ACM SIGCSE conference on Innovation and technology in computer science education*, 2009). ACM

[4] Cassel, L., Shackelford, R. and Sloan, R. H. A synthesis and ontology of all of computing. In *Proceedings of the Proceedings of the 36th SIGCSE technical symposium on Computer science education*, 2005). ACM

[5] Cassel, L. N., Inguva, S. K. and Buzydlowski, J. An ontology of all of computing: an update on challenges and approaches. In *Proceedings of the Proceedings of the 14th international conference on Artificial intelligence: methodology, systems, and applications*, 2010). Springer-Verlag

[6] Computing curricula 2001. *J. Educ. Resour. Comput.*, 1, 3es (2001), 1.

[7] *Curriculum Guidelines for Undergraduate*

Degree Programs in Software Engineering ACM and IEEE-CS, 2004, http://sites.computer.org/ccse/SE2004Volume.pdf.

[8] *Curriculum Guidelines for Undergraduate Degree Programs in Computer Engineering*. ACM and IEEE-CS, 2004, http://www.acm.org/education/education/curric_vols/CE-Final-Report.pdf.

[9] Denning, P. J. Great principles of computing. *Commun. ACM*, 46, 11 (2003), 15-20.

[10] Gorgone, J., Davis, G. B., Valacich, J. S., Topi, H., Feinstein, D. L. and Longenecker, H. E. *Model Curriculum and Guidelines for Undergraduate Degree Programs in Information Systems* ACM, AIS, AITP, 2002.

[11] Niles, I. and Pease, A. Towards a standard upper ontology. In *Proceedings of the Proceedings of the international conference on Formal Ontology in Information Systems - Volume 2001*, 2001). ACM

[12] Velardi, P., Fabriani, P. and Missikoff, M. Using text processing techniques to automatically enrich a domain ontology. In *Proceedings of the Proceedings of the international conference on Formal Ontology in Information Systems - Volume 2001*, 2001). ACM

The Nuestra Iowa Project – Creating a Digital Collection as a Tool for History Education

Audrey Altman, Kelly Thompson, and Haowei Hsieh
School of Library and Information Science
The University of Iowa, Iowa City, Iowa, USA
1-319-335-5713
{audrey-altman, haowei-hsieh}@uiowa.edu

ABSTRACT
This poster describes the progress of a research project exploring how public digital publishing affects undergraduate research and learning. Participants are students in "Latina/o Immigration", an undergraduate-level history course at the University of Iowa. Students use a custom web interface to create a digital exhibit about the history of Latino/as in Iowa, using multimedia primary-source materials from the Iowa Women's Archives (IWA). Students also use the tool to learn the concepts related to metadata and digital libraries.

Categories and Subject Descriptors
K.3.1 **[Computers and Education]**: Computer Uses in Education – *collaborative learning*; K.3.m **[Computers and Education]**: Miscellaneous – *computer literacy*; H.3.7 **[Information Storage and Retrieval]**: Digital Libraries – *Collection*

General Terms
Design, Experimentation, Human Factors

Keywords
Digital humanities, archival research, digital libraries, education

1. INTRODUCTION
Nuestra Iowa is a digital exhibit of Iowa Latino history. It features items from the Mujeres Latinas and other collections housed at the Iowa Women's Archives (IWA). The IWA at the University of Iowa library maintains hundreds of personal papers and organizational records of Iowa women. We hope to promote public access to explore these specialized regional collections by creating location-aware digital exhibits for users to access items and their descriptions through an interactive map interface. During the process of creating the digital exhibit, we saw the opportunity to motivate undergraduate history students to conduct primary research using the IWA special collections. In this way, students became contributors to the creation of the digital collection.

The digital age offers new opportunities and challenges for undergraduate humanities educators. Cathy N. Davidson and David Theo Goldberg use the term "open source education" to describe a collaborative learning process in which students actively participate in the creation of culture, and share these cultural products with the public through digital technologies [1].

The Nuestra Iowa project implements a working model of "open source education" and measures its impact on undergraduate literacies. In the age of Web 2.0, undergraduates are expected, and often desire to produce rather than merely consume culture. James Elmborg defines literacy as "the ability to read, interpret, and produce "texts" appropriate and valued within a given community" [2]. Traditionally, undergraduate humanities students are asked by their professors to produce written coursework. In other words, they must produce texts that are valued within academia, using the appropriate forms, styles, and themes. Writing for a public audience requires a different set of literacy skills. In the Nuestra Iowa project, we expect that students will develop these skills by selecting culturally significant materials and presenting them in a way that is both interesting and accessible to the general public. They will also learn to explain complex historical themes to non-academic audiences.

The project team includes faculty, archivists, and graduate and undergraduate students at the University of Iowa. The exhibit features undergraduate essays about the history of Latino/as in Iowa, along with multimedia primary-source materials from the Iowa Women's Archives.

2. THE PROJECT
The implementation of the Nuestra Iowa project includes the following phases: (1) system implementation, (2) the undergraduate lesson plan and content creation and (3) the study of the students.

2.1 System Design and Implementation
The current Nuestra Iowa includes a web-based digital exhibit supported by a database, a web-based review interface for administrators, and a web-based data-upload interface for students (Figure 1). The goal of the class is to have the digital exhibit feature student-written essays about the history of Latino/as in Iowa with accompanying multimedia materials from the Iowa Women's Archives. The exhibit utilizes the Google Map API with pins indicating the location of significant historical events and document origins. When a user clicks on a pin, a bubble appears with a link to corresponding essay(s) and historical documents. A mobile-optimized version of the digital exhibit is also implemented to better take advantage of the location service capabilities on mobile devices. Student essays, multimedia materials, and corresponding metadata are stored in the database and a web-based data-upload interface allows students to upload and edit this content.

JCDL'13, July 22–26, 2013, Indianapolis, Indiana, USA.
ACM 978-1-4503-2077-1/13/07.

The Google Maps API was used not only for the exhibit but also in the data-upload interface. Students use the Google Maps API to geolocate their essays (Figure 1). The API allows for multiple entry methods, including street address, dragging and dropping a pin, or choosing a location already entered in the system (keeping authority control of place names somewhat consistent). An additional benefit of using Google Maps is that most students will have had significant experience using Google Maps or similar digital tools to consume geospatial information prior to participating in the Nuestra Iowa project. This familiarity with Google Maps affords researchers the opportunity to measure how students' ability to critically analyze Google Maps changes when they use it to produce rather than consume information.

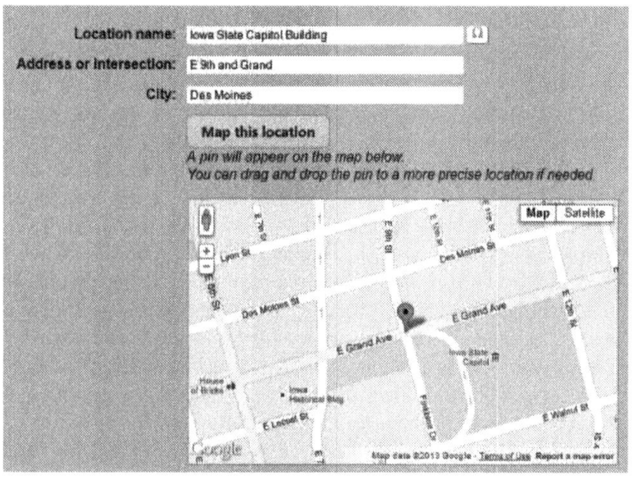

Figure 1: Web-based interface for data entry and update. This shows the part where Google Maps API is used to help students create geolocation metadata for their essays.

2.2 The Lesson Plan, Content and Metadata

Undergraduate students in "Latina/o Immigration", a history course at the University of Iowa, produced content for Nuestra Iowa. Students conducted archival research at the Iowa Women's Archives and selected multi-media materials to analyze and display in the digital exhibit. A set of mappable (i.e., related to specific places) documents was selected by the researchers for students to choose from. Students evaluate and conduct research on the material using IWA and online sources. Students have to practice the curatorial role of selecting and presenting documents for a public exhibit, which demonstrates acquisition of an important information literacy skill. Applying themes from their history course, each student composed an essay to accompany their selected materials in the exhibit.

Understanding how information is organized is a crucial component of information literacy, because it informs the way that information is accessed, retrieved, and presented. In digital environments, organization of information often includes the creation of metadata. In the Nuestra Iowa project, students are required to produce a small amount of metadata to organize their essay, including geolocation and date metadata.

Some class time was devoted to literacy education relevant to the project, such as analyzing primary documents, writing for public audiences, and understanding metadata. Additional class time was allocated for collaborative workshopping of essays. At the end of the content creation phase, students uploaded their essays to the database, along with appropriate metadata, such as geolocations and dates. Student submissions were reviewed by their history professor and by archivists prior to being made public.

2.3 EVALUATION AND EXPECTATION

The pilot-study described in this poster will be followed by a voluntary survey given to students after they have completed content creation. The survey will include both quantitative questions, measured on a five-point Likert scale, and open-ended questions to provide qualitative feedback. In addition to student surveys, researchers will conduct interviews with the professor of the course and the archivists involved the project. In these interviews, the professor and archivists will be asked to compare the students' performance on this project compared with similar projects with traditional assignments.

At present, the class has come to completion we are now in the data collection phase. We hope to have analyzed the results of the survey and interviews by the summer.

The survey and interviews will explore the impact of the Nuestra Iowa project on student literacies. In particular, it will measure how students' research and learning processes are impacted by writing for a public audience, using a common digital tool to produce information, and creating metadata.

We expect that using Google Maps as a tool for cultural production will improve students' digital literacy with Google Maps and similar digital platforms. We also expect that targeted digital literacy lessons in the classroom will facilitate more substantial improvement in research skills.

This requirement of generating metadata will help students to understand what metadata is and how it functions within unique digital environments. We hope students will improve their ability to evaluate and analyze existing metadata in other research contexts.

3. FUTURE WORK

The presented pilot study will collect feedback from participants regarding the data entry interface for the digital library, lesson plans associated with the project, and the interface of the digital exhibit. This information will be used in the following ways:

1. To improve subsequent studies by aiding researchers in developing methods to investigate the pedagogical benefits of implementing multimedia technology in humanities classrooms, providing a framework for future support of digital educational projects.
2. To streamline the process of digital content creation and incentivize the training of undergraduate scholars to contribute to digital libraries.

4. ACKNOWLEDGMENTS

Our thanks to Kären Mason, Janet Weaver, Omar Valerio-Jiménez, the Iowa Women's Archives, and the University of Iowa History Department.

5. REFERENCES

[1] Davidson, Cathy N. and Goldberg, David Theo. *The Future of Learning Institutions in a Digital Age*. The MIT Press, Cambridge, MA, 2009.

[2] Elmborg, James. Critical Information Literacy: Implications for Instructional Practice. *The Journal of Academic Librarianship* 32(2):192-199, 2006.

The Open Parks Network

Yongyang Yu
Dept. of Computer Science,
Purdue University
305 N. University Street
West Lafayette, Indiana 47907
USA
765-494-6010
yu163@cs.purdue.edu

Michael Witt
Purdue University Libraries
504 W. State Street
West Lafayette, Indiana 47907
USA
765-494-8703
mwitt@purdue.edu

Mohamed S. Abdelfattah
Dept. of Computer Science,
Purdue University
305 N. University Street
West Lafayette, Indiana 47907
USA
765-494-6010
msaberab@cs.purdue.edu

Christopher Vinson
Clemson University Libraries
116 Sigma Dr
Clemson, South Carolina
29634 USA
864-656-3622
vinsonc@clemson.edu

Scott Hammel
Clemson University Libraries
116 Sigma Dr
Clemson, South Carolina
29634 USA
864-656-8118
prov356@clemson.edu

ABSTRACT

The goal of the Open Parks Network (OPN) is to create a portal that connects park managers, researchers, policy makers, and citizens to each other and to valuable cultural resources related. Led by Clemson University in collaboration with the National Parks Service and Purdue University, OPN is designed to provide a virtual community of professionals in parks and protected areas with the tools, resources, and knowledge base they need to conduct intensive research, perform their jobs duties effectively, and share information with colleagues and users on an international scale. To date, 80,000 of 200,000 archival images and 500,000 out of 2 million bound pages have been digitized from various parks, and a beta version of the platform will be available for demonstration in March 2013. The project includes the integration of a Fedora repository with the Joomla! content management system with extensions to enable GIS functionality, expose metadata as Linked Data and for harvest using OAI-PMH, and enable users to create their own custom collections.

Categories and Subject Descriptors

H.3.7 [**Information Storage and Retrieval**]: Digital Libraries.

General Terms

Experimentation, Standardization

JCDL'13, July 22–26, 2013, Indianapolis, Indiana, USA.
ACM 978-1-4503-2077-1/13/07.

Keywords

Open Parks Network, Virtual Research Environments, Mass Digitization.

1. INTRODUCTION

Parks and protected areas are important for the overall health and quality of life for people and the environment, in-situ conservation of biological diversity, protection of ecosystem services, protection of threatened cultural and historic sites, centers for education, opportunities for recreation, economic engines, and as places for enhancing community cohesion and building social capital. Because of the diversity of goals parks and protected areas serve, the professions linked to these areas, and the field in general, are vast. The Open Parks Network (OPN) seeks to "connect all the dots" and foster a virtual community of parks researchers, managers, policy makers, educators, advocates and users. Its purpose is to:

- unite the highly distributed parks community;
- gather and disseminate the best available science;
- assemble key data on climate change, species loss, ecosystems change, and other macro-level concerns that can be accessed by scientists world-wide;
- monitor and project visitation data at multiple scales to analyze visitation patterns spatially and temporally (regional visitation models do not exist);
- and virtually open the door to our parks to a vast number of citizens who do not have the opportunity to visit, thus increasing awareness and the educational value of the world's most treasured resources.

2. ASSEMBLING A DIGITAL LIBRARY FOR PARKS

2.1 Digitized Materials

Archival and bound materials were identified, cataloged, and scanned from an initial group of parks in the United States including Yellowstone, Kings Mountain, Congaree, and Great Smoky Mountains Nationals Parks, Fort Sumter National Monument, Cowpens National Battlefield, and North and South Carolina State Parks as well as from organizations such as the Fort Collins Water Resources Division, Intermountain Region, Clemson and Winthrop Universities, and the Universities of South Carolina and Georgia. Materials digitized included photographs and negatives, maps, blueprints, 3-dimensional objects, books, newspapers, and manuscripts. Equipment included Epson, Kodak, and Betterlight scanners, an Atiz book scanner, and an Internet Archive Scribe unit. To date, 80,000 of 200,000 archival images and 500,000 out of 2 million bound pages have been digitized in a dedicated facility at Clemson University. Although the project originated in the southeastern United States, the OPN is in the process of expanding to a global scope by identifying new material for digitization and accepting digitized or born-digital content that is submitted by users. Figure. 1 shows a photo about the past and present of the Grand Canyon national park. OPN provides a standard search-and-browse interface for users to discovery and interact with content.

2.2 Incorporating Geospatial Information Systems (GIS)

OPN also includes a GIS tool that supports data sharing, geoprocessing and access to secondary data sources including real-time and historic GIS data. A tool called MapIT allows a user to display geographic data from different time periods in the same map, which provides an ideal comparing function for various datasets about the same area. The visualization can be shared not only in OPN community but also in other social communities, such as Facebook and Twitter. For instance, the current as well as the historical tigers' geo locations can be visualized through the world map[1]. The snapshots of the visualization from MapIT can be saved and contributed to OPN as image resources.

2.3 Enabling Users to Create Their Own, Custom Collections

The collection tool is an extension for Joomla! and HUBzero [1, 2]. It is implemented as a Joomla! module that provides a convenient way of reorganizing resources already existing in OPN as well as incorporating resources outside OPN. For example, a researcher of ecology, working on the climate changes in the Great Smoky Mountains, is able to create a collection of technical reports, historic manuscripts, and photos of the area, which can only be accessed via OPN in digital formats, along with external resources on the Web together for his study. Without OPN, he will have to collect all these materials in their print-only format, which is time consuming. In addition to creating a useful collection that can be viewed in OPN, the tool also provides options to share the collections (e.g., all the users have access to the collection by default and accesses can be restricted to private groups). Even though the collection tool is tailor-made for OPN, it is applicable to any other platform based on Joomla! with little modification as well. The tool is configurable for system administrators to apply customized changes for different applications.

To create a collection, a user has two options. After one has logged in to his account, he can navigate to the profile page and access the creation page to generate a new collection by selecting from a whole list of resources in OPN and binding them together. Another option is browsing each individual resource and adding it to a new collection on the fly. When a user finds some interesting resource, he can save it and continue to browse other materials. Once satisfied with all the contents of a new collection, one can create it by providing a unique title.

When the compilation of a new collection is complete, the whole collection is stored in the back-end MySQL database. Besides resources in OPN, the collection tool allows a user to include external URLs, as well as citations information for publications. By default, the new created collection can be publicly accessed by registered users. Moreover one can control the access by only allowing a private group of members to view his own collections. In the meanwhile, the structural semantic of a collection is modeled by OAI-ORE Aggregations. The whole user's collection can be viewed as an Aggregation consisting of individual collections in terms of Nested Aggregations of internal and external resources. The OAI-ORE Resource Maps are serialized in RDFa+XHTML format, which can be leveraged by both human users and machine agents [3].

[1] `https://maps.clemson.edu/opn/index.html`

3. ACKNOWLEDGMENTS

This work was sponsored by a National Leadership Grant (LG-05-10-0117-10) from the Institute of Museum and Library Services in collaboration with Clemson University and the National Parks Service.

4. REFERENCES

[1] G. Klimeck, M. McLennan, S.P. Brophy, G.B. Adams, and M.S. Lundstrom. Nanohub.org: advancing education and research in nanotechnology, *Computing in Science & Engineering* 10(5): 17–23, October 2008.

[2] M. McLennan, and R. Kennell. HUBzero: a platform for dissemination and collaboration in computational science and engineering, *Computing in Science & Engineering* 12(2): 48–53, March 2010.

[3] M. Witt, and Y. Yu. Refactoring HUBzero for Linked Data, *Proceedings of the 12th ACM/IEEE-CS Joint Conference on Digital Libraries*, pages 149–152, June 2012.

Figure 1: A photo about the Grand Canyon in OPN

TheAdvisor: A Webservice for Academic Recommendation

Onur Küçüktunç[1,2], Erik Saule[1], Kamer Kaya[1], and Ümit V. Çatalyürek[1,3]
[1]Dept. of Biomedical Informatics, The Ohio State University
[2]Dept. of Computer Science and Engineering, The Ohio State University
[3]Dept. of Electrical and Computer Engineering, The Ohio State University
kucuktunc.1@osu.edu, {esaule,kamer,umit}@bmi.osu.edu

ABSTRACT

The academic community has published millions of research papers to date, and the number of new papers has been increasing with time. To discover new research, researchers typically rely on manual methods such as keyword-based search, reading proceedings of conferences, browsing publication lists of known experts, or checking the references of the papers they are interested. Existing tools for the literature search are suitable for a first-level bibliographic search. However, they do not allow complex second-level searches. In this paper, we present a web service called the**advisor** (`http://theadvisor.osu.edu`) which helps the users to build a strong bibliography by extending the document set obtained after a first-level search. The service makes use of the citation graph for recommendation. It also features diversification, relevance feedback, graphical visualization, venue and reviewer recommendation. In this work, we explain the design criteria and rationale we employed to make the the**advisor** a useful and scalable web service along with a thorough experimental evaluation.

Categories and Subject Descriptors

H.3.5 [**Information Search and Retrieval**]: On-line Information Services

Keywords

Literature search; citation graph; random walk; paper recommendation; relevance feedback; visualization; result diversification

1. RECOMMENDATION FRAMEWORK

Here we describe the components of the service, and present our design choices. Figure 1 gives an overview of the**advisor**'s framework and the relationship between its components.

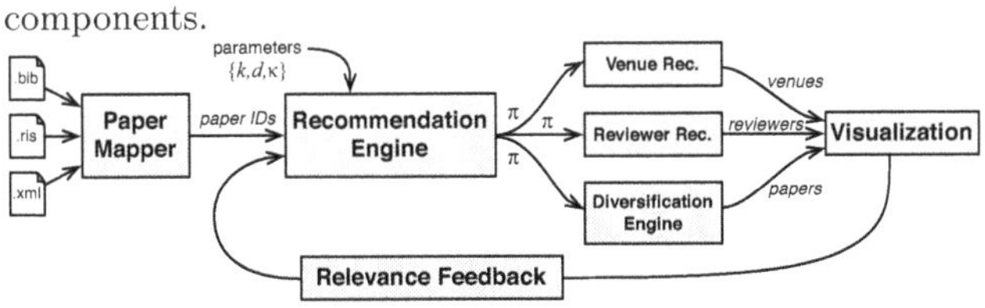

Figure 1: Overview of the theadvisor framework.

JCDL'13, July 22–26, 2013, Indianapolis, Indiana, USA.
ACM 978-1-4503-2077-1/13/07.

The framework has four main components [6]:
Paper mapper. The recommendation process starts with uploading the user's bibliography file to the website in BibTeX, RIS, or EndNote XML format. While mapping the papers given in different file formats, we extract the alphanumeric characters from each title, split them into words, and use an inverted index on title words to find the matched papers in our database. Since there can be very similar titles and/or a conference version of an extended journal paper, or vice versa, we also employ the publication date and Levenshtein distance to find the exact match. This process makes the paper matching step more accurate and efficient.
Recommendation engine highlights a diversified set of papers/citations, venues, and experts to the user.
Visualization uses graph drawing techniques on the recommended paper set to visualize the relations between them.
Relevance feedback gets the comments from the user on the recommendations and refines the search accordingly.

1.1 Recommendation engine

Direction-aware Random Walk with Restart. We define a *direction awareness* parameter $\kappa \in [0,1]$ to obtain either more recent or more traditional results in the top-k documents [3]. Given a query with inputs k, a *seed* paper set $\mathcal{Q}$, a damping factor d, and a direction awareness parameter κ, Direction-aware Random Walk with Restart (DaRWR) computes the steady-state probability vector π. The rank vector at iteration t is computed with the following linear equation $\mathbf{p}_{t+1} = p^* + \mathbf{A}\mathbf{p}_t$, where p^* is an $n \times 1$ restart probability vector, and $\mathbf{A}$ is a structurally-symmetric $n \times n$ transition matrix of edge weights, such that $a_{ij} = \frac{d(1-\kappa)}{\delta^+(i)}$ if $(i,j) \in E$, and $a_{ij} = \frac{d\kappa}{\delta^-(i)}$ if $(j,i) \in E$, and $a_{ij} = 0$, otherwise.

Venue and reviewer recommendation. Since we target the manuscript preparation and submission process, venue recommendation queries are useful while deciding the conference or journal for submission, and reviewer recommendation queries are useful while submitting a manuscript to some journals which require a set of names of potential reviewers or the editor of a journal looking for reviewer for a particular paper.

Improving the efficiency of the ranking. As described above, each iteration of the ranking algorithm DaRWR contains a sparse-matrix dense-vector multiplication (SpMV). This sparse linear algebra kernel is the building block of the**advisor**'s recommendation engine. We observed that the nonzero pattern of the citation matrix is highly irregular and the computation suffers from this irregularity due to the high number of cache misses. Since there will be a penalty for each cache miss, we apply preprocessing steps, partitioning and ordering, to reduce the number of cache misses and make the ranking algorithm faster. Using a hypergraph partitioning model and Approximate Minimum Degree (AMD) ordering technique, we obtained 3× speedup [1, 2].

Result diversification. Methods such as DaRWR tend to naturally return many recommendations from the same area of the graph, which leads to a poor coverage of the potential interests of the users. Diversifying the recommendations refers to the methods that increase the amount of distinct information one can reach via an automatized search. We argue that finding the vertices which are locally maximum in the graph w.r.t. their ranks and returning the k most relevant ones will diversify the results and increase the coverage of citation graph. In order to keep the results within a reasonable relevancy threshold and to diversify them at the same time, we incrementally compute the local maximas only within the top-γk ranked results and remove the selected vertices from the subgraph for the next iteration until k results are obtained. We refer to this algorithm as parameterized relaxed local maxima (γ-RLM) [4, 5].

1.2 Relevance feedback

Users of the**advisor** are given the option of providing explicit relevance feedback to the set of recommended papers. The feedbacks can be either positive or negative, making a recommendation relevant or irrelevant for the query. When the user refines the query with the relevance feedback, the relevant results are added to $\mathcal{Q}$, and the irrelevant results are removed from the citation graph with all of their incident edges. Relevance feedback can also be incorporated with the diversification feature explained in [4]. As the diversified set of results may represent different sets of papers from different areas of interest, the user of the service can easily guide the recommendation process towards the fields that she is interested in.

1.3 Data visualization

Representation of the recommendations in a web service is crucial for user experience. Aside from displaying the full bibliographic entries for the list of suggested papers, we also visualize the results and their relationships to the references and papers that are given positive feedback before. The sample graph (see Fig. 2) consist of the seed papers $\mathcal{Q}$ (*blue*), recommendations (*green*), and top-100 relevant papers (*white*). The subgraph is extracted from those vertices and all the edges within this subset. We then apply a force-directed layout algorithm to improve the representation as well as expose the paper clusters.

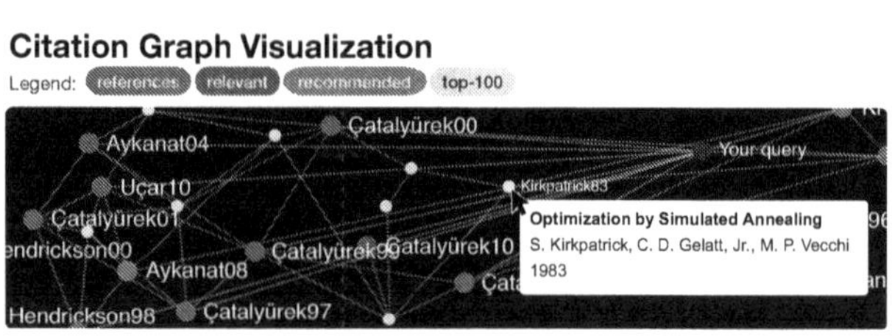

Figure 2: Visualization of a sample query.

1.4 API

For the users and third-party application developers, we provide an interface to query our citation database with an API (`http://theadvisor.osu.edu/apireference.php`) similar to RESTful. The API enables users to query the**advisor** database with a bibliography file, obtain metadata for a given list of papers (as internal IDs), and run the recommendation algorithm with various settings (e.g., specify the direction awareness parameter, ask for a diverse set of results, provide positive and negative feedback, etc.). The complete the**advisor** service, in fact, can be externally implemented using only the provided actions. This API allows to interconnect external applications and web services with the**advisor**. For instance, websites that let users create and group papers of interest (e.g., Mendeley, CiteULike, etc.) could perform recommendation using the**advisor**.

2. CONCLUSIONS

Bibliographic search has become a herculean task due to the vast literature published every year by researchers. Web services have appeared to help researchers in this task. Yet, we felt that these methods only provided a first insight in the existing literature. To further help the researchers, we developed the**advisor**, a publicly available web service which extends a set of given documents via recommendation based on the citation analysis. It provides multiple features such as direction awareness, relevance feedback, graphical visualization, venue recommendation, and reviewer recommendation. It can also be used automatically thanks to a well defined API. All the features of the system are based on sound algorithmic decisions and are shown to be very beneficial in practice. We believe that the**advisor** will find its place in the ecosystem of academic web services.

Acknowledgments

This work was partially supported by the U.S. Department of Energy SciDAC Grant DE-FC02-06ER2775 and NSF grants CNS-0643969, OCI-0904809 and OCI-0904802. The authors would like to thank DBLP and CiteSeer^X for making their datasets available.

3. REFERENCES

[1] O. Kucuktunc, K. Kaya, E. Saule, and U. V. Catalyurek. Fast recommendation on bibliographic networks. In *Proc. IEEE/ACM Int'l Conf. Advances in Social Networks Analysis and Mining (ASONAM)*, 2012.

[2] O. Kucuktunc, K. Kaya, E. Saule, and U. V. Catalyurek. Fast recommendation on bibliographic networks with sparse-matrix ordering and partitioning. *Social Network Analysis and Mining (SNAM)*, 2013. (to appear).

[3] O. Kucuktunc, E. Saule, K. Kaya, and U. V. Catalyurek. Direction awareness in citation recommendation. In *Proc. Int'l Workshop on Ranking in Databases (DBRank'12) in conjunction with VLDB'12*, 2012.

[4] O. Kucuktunc, E. Saule, K. Kaya, and U. V. Catalyurek. Diversifying citation recommendation. Technical Report arXiv:1209.5809, ArXiv, Sep 2012.

[5] O. Kucuktunc, E. Saule, K. Kaya, and U. V. Catalyurek. Diversified recommendation on graphs: Pitfalls, measures, and algorithms. In *Proc. Int'l Conf. World Wide Web (WWW)*, 2013.

[6] O. Kucuktunc, E. Saule, K. Kaya, and U. V. Catalyurek. Towards a personalized, scalable, and exploratory academic recommendation service. In *Proc. IEEE/ACM Int'l Conf. Advances in Social Networks Analysis and Mining (ASONAM)*, 2013.

User Interface Evaluation of Meta-Indexes for Search

Michael Huggett and Edie Rasmussen
University of British Columbia
470 – 1961 East Mall
Vancouver, Canada
1-604-822-2404
{m.huggett, edie.rasmussen}@ubc.ca

ABSTRACT

In the Indexer's Legacy Project, we have created meta-indexes for domain-oriented collections of digital books in order to promote searching, navigation and browsing in digital collections. Because the meta-index is a new knowledge structure, we have used focus groups and sample tasks to collect information on user's perception and use of meta-indexes. User's responses were positive and their suggestions led to improvements in our online Meta-Dex User Interface (MUI) tool, which will be tested in subsequent user studies.

Categories and Subject Descriptors

H.3.7 [**Information Systems**]: Information Storage and Retrieval – *Digital libraries*

Keywords

Digital libraries, digital books, digital collections, indexes.

1. INTRODUCTION

Scholarly books are increasingly available in digital form, due to local and large-scale digitization projects such as the Gutenberg Project, the Million Books Project, the Open Content Alliance, and Google Books [1]. Traditionally, scholars have used back-of-book indexes (BoBI) to access the content of monographs in print form [2]. These indexes, each a careful distillation of book content by a professional indexer, are a concentrated representation of knowledge in the field of study. A book's index offers a valuable alternative to keyword search for locating relevant information [3, 4, 5]. In the Indexer's Legacy project, we aggregate multiple BoBIs in a subject domain into a monolithic *meta-index* that typifies and defines a controlled vocabulary in a topic area. We have built a test collection comprising books in seven digital domains (such as anatomy, geology, etc.)

In evaluating use of the meta-index to improve search, we have run two preliminary user studies on our prototype, using focus groups to obtain feedback on assigned tasks. We find that the Meta-Dex (MUI) tool appears to allow users to fulfill their assigned tasks in a timely manner. We also find that user training, motivation, and background knowledge are important for the understanding and efficient use of the interface.

2. METHODOLGY

Users access the meta-index through the MUI [6,7], a Web-based user interface that allows users to search and navigate domains in various ways (Figure 1). By searching for a term or concept in the Search View, the user discovers which books give it the greatest coverage, and sees a view of the meta-index for that topic in the Entry View. The Entry View links to books that cover the topic (green numbers), and to the relevant pages within those books (blue numbers). The user can navigate to a page of interest in the Book View, see the terms highlighted, and read and page through the relevant text. This mode of searching allows the user to quickly find the most representative books for the search terms, review the relevant entries, and drill down to the terms' occurrence on the book pages.

In the user study, participants are given a series of tasks that require them to search for and evaluate relevance of information in the meta-index across several domains. For example, one question was "You are considering writing a paper on the Renaissance. How well is this topic covered in the collection? What sub-topics would you select?" Users wrote their responses as they worked through the questions.

Following completion of the tasks, users participated in a group discussion that asked them to comment on the choice of tasks, their use of digital collections, what they liked or disliked about the interface, and their information-seeking habits.

3. RESULTS AND DISCUSSION

The six participants in two focus sessions were all graduate students in library, archival, and information studies. They reported considerable previous experience in information searching in sources such as the Hathi Trust, Internet Archive, Project Gutenberg, and Google Books, often using keyword searches, tables of contents, and indexes to find sections within book chapters that met their needs. When doing their own research, in some cases users changed the target terms of their search when they found related words in the book's index. Although they often started with a TOC, they used indexes as final arbiter of whether a book touched upon a topic of interest.

Specific habits depended to some extent on the subject area: participants in the classics claimed to start with broad subject matter searches, only later narrowing down to the level of domain vocabulary (such as found in indexes).

User comments on the use of meta-indexes were positive. Users enjoyed the comprehensiveness of the meta-index, noting that they would typically search only one resource at a time, often using keyword search. They liked that (in the Entry View) they could see all the different ways that a topic was described in one place, and could see how many references each book provided on a given topic, which made cross-referencing easier and helped them better decide which books to investigate first.

They also acknowledged greater faith in indexes as a source for search keywords, since a human indexer (and often more than one) had selected these terms to describe the topic area. Users liked the exposure to the variations in vocabulary describing a domain's sub-topics, which suggested alternative keywords and context that they could use in future research.

JCDL'13, July 22–26, 2013, Indianapolis, Indiana, USA.
ACM 978-1-4503-2077-1/13/07.

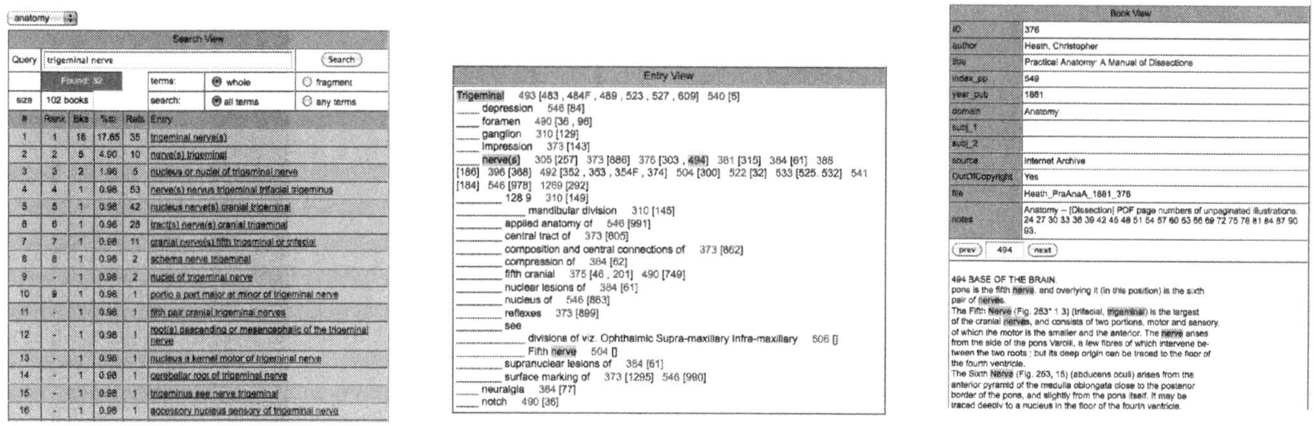

Figure 1: The Meta-Dex User Interface: Search View, Entry View, and Book View

Their impression of relevance of results was very strong. Some suggested that meta-index search is a powerful way to review the content of a large number of books to narrow down to one or two that they would be willing to retrieve from the library to use in depth. Comments on the interface were generally positive. Comments were also plentiful, as all users have extensive experience with interfaces of all sorts, and have their own strong preferences on interface design and affordances.

Above all, users liked that the MUI was fast, useful, and had good coverage of a range of domains. They liked the ranking of related entries (by frequency in the domain) as suggestions of good places to start their searches. They liked the use of colour to disambiguate the functionality of different elements. They liked the MUI's cleaner, more organized, more hierarchical style better than the information overload of Google Books. They also appreciated the fact that once directed by a search result to a page in the Book View, they could scroll through previous and next pages to gain understanding of the context. In particular, contrasted with how they would usually do online research of this type, they greatly appreciated working through a common interface instead of having dozens of tabs open in a browser, each displaying a different book.

Negative comments dealt primarily with appearance and incomplete functionality. The over-all impressions of the tool's aesthetics were that it is basic, unattractive, and 'clunky'. Users missed seeing actual book covers, and the related library-like shelf-browsing experience that displays neighbouring related books. They identified the need for legends that would indicate the meaning and functionality of interface items. Indentation is used in the Entry View to indicate sub-entries, but some sub-entries are 5 levels deep, which makes it difficult to remember which entries are under which. Although search terms are highlighted in the Entry View (see Figure 1), users found that very large entries were overwhelming and required a great deal of scrolling to find keywords: sometimes they skipped over them accidentally. Users were also distracted by some of the content displayed in the Book View that included random characters and miss-spellings, due to the sometimes poor quality of the OCR text (as downloaded from Internet Archive). Since our project focuses on textual meta-indexes, users sometimes wondered why images were not displayed where expected in the Book View text.

4. CONCLUSIONS AND FUTURE WORK

The general consensus of the users was that if the tool were available to them in the performance of actual work, they would definitely use it. The most common rejoinder was that although there were some negative aspects to the system, the most important thing for them was simply familiarization---once they understood how the MUI worked, it was fairly easy to use.

We have already made some changes to the user interface in response to participants' suggestions. A simple mouse-over of an entry in the Entry View shows the entry path all the way up to the main entry in a pop-up, which obviates the need for scrolling. Clicking on highlighted terms in the entry view hides all the sub-entries that follow, up to the next term in the query. The Book View now appears next to the page link that is clicked, instead of appearing at the top of the page. Users commented on the lack of agreement between different books on how they named or spelled the same entities (people and places) in the subject area; we have implemented a *synonyms* mechanism that specifies a canonical representation of an entity and any variations; the meta-index can then be rebuilt to better aggregate term variants that may otherwise be too widely spaced in the meta-index to be found.

With these changes in place, we are undertaking a formal user study to measure searcher's success in using the meta-index for a series of tasks. Our preliminary results are encouraging, and suggest that the meta-index has a role to play as a new knowledge structure for searching and navigating digital collections.

5. ACKNOWLEDGMENTS

Funding from the UBC Hampton Fund and the Social Science and Humanities Research Council is gratefully acknowledged. We also thank the many Graduate Research Assistants who acquired and preprocessed books for the test collection.

6. REFERENCES

[1] Coyle, K. 2006. Mass digitization of books. *Journal of Academic Librarianship* 32,6, 641-645.

[2] Jörgensen, C. and Liddy, E.D. 1996. Information access or information anxiety?—an exploratory evaluation of book index features. *The Indexer* 20, 64-68.

[3] Abdullah, N. and Gibb, F. 2008. Using a task-based approach in evaluating the usability of BoBIs in an E-book environment. *ECDL 2008, LNCS* 4956, 246-257.

[4] Egan, D.E., Remde, J.R., Gomez, L.M., Landauer, T.K., Eberhardt, J. and Lochbaum, C.C. 1989. Formative design evaluation of Superbook. *ACM Transactions on Information Systems* 7(1), 30-57.

[5] Liesaputra, V., Witten, I.H., and Bainbridge, D. 2009. Searching in a book. *ECDL 2009, LNCS* 5714, 442-446.

[6] Huggett, M., and Rasmussen, E. 2012a. Dynamic online views of meta-Indexes. *Proceedings of JCDL 2012.* 233-236.

[7] Huggett, M. and Rasmussen, E. 2012b. Integrative online research-data management. *Proceedings of SIGIR 2012*, 1007.

Using Google Analytics to Explore ETDs Use

Midge Coates
Auburn University Libraries
231 Mell Street
Auburn, AL 36849-5606
+1.334.844.8716
coatemi@auburn.edu

ABSTRACT

This poster presents preliminary Google Analytics usage data for a collection of electronic theses and dissertations (ETDs). Correlation of page views with page type, user location, and source (referring link) shows that, during the study period, most in-state users found the collection via internal sources (University links) and viewed mostly home and navigation pages, while most out-of-state users found the collection via external sources (search engines, databases) and viewed mostly bibliographic information pages. Nearly all of those who viewed actual ETDs were out-of-state "direct" users who may have bookmarked the collection during a previous visit.

Categories and Subject Descriptors

H.3.7 [**Information Storage and Retrieval**]: Digital Libraries – *dissemination, user issues*

General Terms

Management, Measurement, Human Factors

Keywords

ETDs; evaluation; Google Analytics; usage; web analytics; web metrics.

1. INTRODUCTION

There has been little published research on usage patterns for theses and dissertations. In 1995, surveys done at Oregon State University indicated that graduate students were the primary user of theses and dissertations held locally and that they were using these for general research and for research for their own theses and dissertations [3]. The transition to electronic versions should make these documents more accessible to a wider audience [1].

One of the few usage studies available for an ETDs collection is from the Korea Institute of Science and Technology Information, where researchers examined transaction logs and found that 20% of their users were located outside of Korea [4]. Web metrics tools may make it easier for librarians to analyze usage patterns for these collections [2]. This poster presents preliminary Google Analytics usage data for Auburn University's ETDs collection.

JCDL'13, July 22–26, 2013, Indianapolis, Indiana, USA.
ACM 978-1-4503-2077-1/13/07.

2. METHODOLOGY

2.1 Description of AUETDs Collection

The Auburn University Electronic Theses and Dissertations (AUETDs) collection is a collaboration between the Graduate School at Auburn University (GSAU) and the Auburn University Libraries (AUL). All GSAU students are required to deposit their approved theses or dissertations into the dSpace repository (replacing the earlier requirement for two bound copies). As of January 31, 2013, AUETDs contained over 3,400 theses and dissertations in pdf format. Although students are allowed to place an access embargo on their documents for a period of up to five years, the system default is public access.

There are many avenues of access both to the AUETDs repository itself and to the individual documents in it. GSAU and AUL provide multiple links to the repository from their respective Web sites, as do some individual Colleges and departments within Auburn University. Some of the latter also provide direct links to their own students' individual theses and dissertations. The University Web site's search function can also be used to locate the repository and its contents. All theses and dissertations are included in AUL's Voyager and VuFind catalogs. Documents in the AUETD repository are also indexed by commercial search engines, by some scholarly databases, and by the Networked Digital Library of Theses and Dissertations (NDLTD) and Open Access Theses and Dissertations (OATD).

2.2 Data Collection

The structure of dSpace and its public interface results in different types of URLs for different page types (home page, search and advanced search pages, browse pages, bibliographic pages for individual items, pdf viewing pages, etc.). Google Analytics tracking code has been inserted into the AUETDs page template, and page views for each type can be counted.

Data were collected for a period of one year (13 January 2012 – 12 January 2013). Variables included page URL, user location, and source (referring link). Data were exported as comma-separated values text files which were opened in Excel for processing.

3. RESULTS AND DISCUSSION

3.1 AUETDs User Location vs. Page Type

Table 1. Page views for AUETDs: user location correlated with page type (13 January 2012 – 12 January 2013).

User location	Home page	Nav. pages	Bib. pages	PDF views
Local	8,610	42,833	27,954	4
Ala. (non-local)	1,443	8,391	3,934	1
US (non- Ala.)	3,569	18,764	38,337	48
World (non-US)	2,293	19,540	46,488	97

Local: Users with City = Auburn (Ala.) or Opelika (Ala.); Ala. (non-local): Users with Region = Alabama minus Local users; US (non-Ala.): Users with Country = United States minus Alabama users; World (non-US) = All users minus United States users. Nav. pages: Navigation pages (browse, search, and advanced search); Bib. pages: Bibliographic information pages for individual items (brief and full metadata); PDF views: Views in the browser window only (right-click downloads could not be counted at this time). Navigation pages constituted well over half of the pages viewed by in-state users, while bibliographic information pages for individual ETDs were only about a third of the pages viewed. These proportions were reversed for out-of-state users. Over 95% of the PDF views were from out-of-state users.

3.2 AUETDs User Location vs. Source

Table 2. Page views for AUETDs: user location correlated with source (referring link) (13 January 2012 – 12 January 2013).

User location	Direct	AU sources	Data-bases	Search engines	Other
Local	17,627	65,909	79	15,510	196
Ala. (non-local)	1,957	8,421	47	5,030	264
US (non-Ala.)	7,244	12,884	2,799	40,994	1,752
World (non-US)	12,870	4,063	4,834	46,211	3,111

User location designations are the same as for Table 1. Direct: users who access the repository via a bookmark or by typing the URL directly into a browser; AU sources: all GSAU and AUL links and links from AU Colleges and departments; Databases: Google Scholar, ETD directories such as NDLTD, WorldCat, etc.; Search engines: commercial search engines including Google, Yahoo!, Bing, etc. Auburn University sources were the referring links for the majority of pages viewed by in-state users but significantly fewer for out-of-state users. The proportions were reversed for search engines and scholarly databases.

3.3 AUETDs Page Type vs. Source

Table 3. Page views for AUETDs: page type correlated with source (referring link) (13 January 2012 – 12 January 2013).

Page type	Direct	AU sources	Data-bases	Search engines	Other
Home page	3,316	8,102	91	3,972	434
Nav. pages	13,841	45,628	732	27,300	2,027
Bib. info. pages	11,248	26,078	6,856	70,073	2,458
PDF view pages	130	0	1	15	3

Page type designations are the same as those for Table 1, while source designations are the same as those for Table 2. Users who came to the repository via University links viewed home and navigation pages more than bibliographic information pages. The proportions are reversed for users who came via databases and search engines. Over 85% of users viewing ETD pdfs were "direct" users, that is, they came via a bookmark or by typing or pasting the URL into their browsers. Presumably some or all of these found the collection earlier and bookmarked it for future use.

4. CONCLUSIONS

During the study period, most in-state users found the collection via internal sources (University links) and viewed mostly home and navigation pages, while most out-of-state users found the collection via external sources (search engines, databases) and viewed mostly bibliographic information pages. Nearly all of those who viewed actual ETDs were out-of-state "direct" users who may have bookmarked the collection during a previous visit.

5. REFERENCES

[1] Eaton, J. L. 2004. Enhancing graduate education through electronic theses and dissertations. In *Electronic Theses and Dissertations: A Sourcebook for Educators, Students, and Librarians*, E. A. Fox, S. Feizabadi, J. M. Moxley, and C. R. Weisser, Eds. Marcel Dekker, Inc., New York, NY, 1-7.

[2] Khoo, M., Paganom J., Washington, A. L., Recker, M., Palmer, B, and Donahue, R. A. 2008. Using web metrics to analyze digital libraries. In *JCDL '08* (Pittsburgh, Pennsylvania, USA, June 16 - 20, 2008). JCDL '08. ACM, New York, NY, 375-384. DOI= http://doi.acm.org/10.1145/1378889.1378956.

[3] Lee-Smeltzer, J., and Hackleman, D. 1995. Access to OSU theses and dissertations in Kerr Library: how are they used ... or are they? *Technical Services Quarterly* 12, 4 (1995), 25-37.

[4] Zhang, Y., Lee, K., and You, B.-J. 2001. Usage patterns of an electronic theses and dissertations system. *Online Inform. Rev.* 25, 6 (2001), 370-377.

The SEAD DataNet Prototype: Data Preservation Services for Sustainability Science

Beth Plale, Robert H. McDonald, Kavitha Chandrasekar, Inna Kouper, Robert Light, Stacy R. Konkiel
Indiana University
Bloomington, IN 47408
{plale, rhmcdona, kavchand, inkouper, lightr, skonkiel} @indiana.edu

Margaret Hedstrom
James Myers
University of Michigan
Ann Arbor, MI 48109
{hedstrom, myersjd}@umich.edu

Praveen Kumar
University of Illinois
Urbana-Champaign, IL 61801
kumar1@illinois.edu

ABSTRACT
In this poster we will present the SEAD project [1] and its prototype software and describe how SEAD approaches long-term data preservation and access through multiple partnerships and how it supports sustainability science researchers in their data management, analysis and archival needs. SEAD's initial prototype system currently is being tested by ingesting datasets from the National Center for Earth Surface Dynamics (1.6 terabyte of data containing over 450,000 files) [2] and packaging them for transmission to long-term archival storage.

Categories and Subject Descriptors
H.3.5 [**Online Information Services**]: Data Sharing, H.3.7 [**Information Storage and Retrieval**]: Digital Libraries – system issues, user issues

Keywords
Cyberinfrastructure, Digital Preservation, Sustainability Science, Data Management, SEAD, DataNet

1. INTRODUCTION
Sustainability science is a data-intensive area that focuses on the complex interactions between nature and human activities. Scientific work in the area of sustainability science requires heterogeneous data from across the earth, physical and social sciences disciplines. These data are often difficult to find, use and archive because different disciplines collect, describe and store their data in different ways.

We are addressing the challenges of sustainability science data in a recently funded National Science Foundation DataNet project, the Sustainable Environments – Actionable Data (SEAD) [1,3].

2. SEAD GOALS
The SEAD project addresses the needs of sustainability researchers in terms of discovery, aggregation, and data management along with supporting long-term data reuse scenarios. We are integrating and extending existing tools and services to create a generalizable framework of services that provide a rich curation infrastructure along with a robust archiving infrastructure that can provide long-term access to preserved datasets via a network of institutional and disciplinary repositories.

The SEAD strategy addresses the goals of improving quality, relevance, and usefulness of data and reducing cost of data management and preservation in the following ways:

- Moving data curation tasks earlier in the data life cycle, toward the beginning of research projects.
- Involving domain scientists in setting priorities for evolution of data and services.
- Developing mechanisms for facilitating and improving data discoverability, such as automatic metadata capture in diverse forms and community annotation of data.
- Re-engineering long term curation processes to leverage rich metadata and volunteered efforts in data curation.

3. SEAD PROTOTYPE
We realize our strategy by implementing the three component architecture, presented in Figure 1 below.

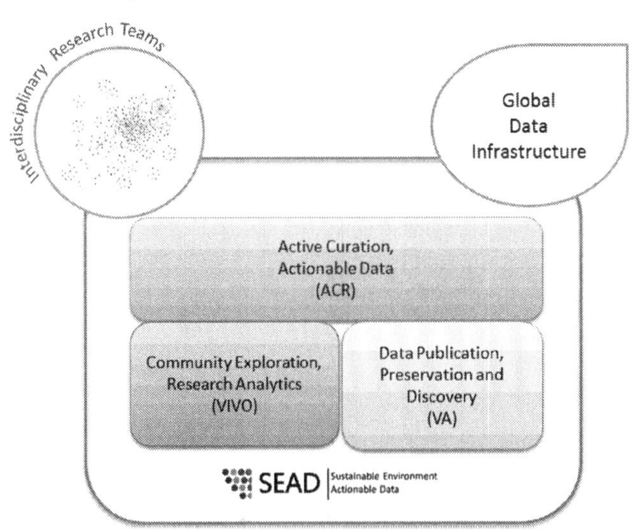

Figure 1. SEAD End-to-End Prototype components.

The three interacting components of the SEAD architecture are the active curation services in the Active Content Repository

(ACR), which provide interfaces to upload, store, organize, and annotate data; community social curation services, SEAD-VIVO, which connect researchers profiles to data and research products with rich network exploration and visualization capabilities; and the SEAD Virtual Archive (VA), which allows researchers to easily store data long-term and search for data across multiple institutional repositories.

The SEAD prototype represents the efforts of a large collective of software developers, data curators, scientists and librarians, who contribute their diverse expertise to define and enable new practices related to active curation, research social networks, and long-term preservation. SEAD leverages existing open source software including the Tupelo and VIVO semantic web technologies, Medici data repository software, MySQL database, Data Conservancy software, and other components.

Currently, SEAD has implemented core functionality for uploading, annotating, and viewing data, linking data to researcher profiles, and mechanisms to package this information and transfer it to institutional repositories or archival cloud storage. The curation pipeline to institutional repositories via the VA supports both long-term preservation and search and discovery workflows.

The SEAD prototype is currently being tested by ingesting, annotating, and preserving datasets from the National Center for Earth Surface Dynamics (1.6 terabytes of data containing over 450,000 files) [2] which involves transfer of data and metadata between SEAD ACR, VIVO and VA components.

4. SEAD USE CASES

SEAD aims to support the following use cases:

1.) Ingestion for heterogeneous data types (images, geo-spatial data, sensor data) in an Active Content Repository (ACR) that allows for semantic relationships among the research data collections as well as semantic annotation and tagging.

2.) Support data discovery through the use of best practices in interoperability, social networking and data publishing.

3.) Add value to existing data through automated scientific metadata extraction and data visualization plugins.

4.) Ingestion of new data sets directly from bench-science work tools.

5.) Community curation of data via the SEAD Virtual Archive and its repository matchmaker for help in identifying appropriate institutional and disciplinary repositories for use in long-term data publishing.

5. ACKNOWLEDGMENTS

SEAD is funded by the National Science Foundation under Cooperative Agreement #OCI0940824. SEAD gratefully acknowledges all of our partner participants who have been involved in developing our services framework for Active Content Repository, Social Curation Services, and Virtual Archive. This includes the following research teams: Margaret Hedstrom, George Alter, Bryan Beecher, James Myers, Marietta Van Buhler, Karen Woollams and Ann Zimmerman from the University of Michigan, Beth Plale, Katy Börner, Robert Light, Inna Kouper, Kavitha Chandrasekar, Ryan Cobine and Robert Ping from Indiana University, Ram Prassana, Robin Liu, and Yudong Zhang from Rensselaer Polytechnic Institute, Praveen Kumar from the University of Illinois, and Rob Kooper, Jong Lee, and Luigi Marini from the National Center for Supercomputing Applications at the University of Illinois at Urbana-Champaign.

We would also like to thank our collaborators at NCED [2] and the Johns Hopkins University Data Conservancy project [4].

6. REFERENCES

[1] Sustainable Environment Actionable Data (SEAD) project. Retrieved from http://sead-data.net

[2] The National Center for Earth Surface Dynamics (NCED). Retrieved from http://www.nced.umn.edu

[3] McDonald, R. H., Kumar, P., Plale, B., Myers, J. & Hedstrom, M. 2012. Active and Social Data Curation: Reinventing the Business of Community-scale Lifecycle Data Management. *The American Geophysical Union Fall meeting*, San Francisco, CA.

[4] The Data Conservancy (DC) project. Retrieved from http://dataconservancy.org

CORE: Aggregation Use Cases for Open Access

Petr Knoth
Knowledge Media institute
The Open University
Milton Keynes, United Kingdom
petr.knoth@open.ac.uk

Zdenek Zdrahal
Knowledge Media institute
The Open University
Milton Keynes, United Kingdom
zdenek.zdrahal@open.ac.uk

ABSTRACT

The push for free online availability of research outputs promoted by the Open Access (OA) movement is undoubtedly transforming the publishing industry. However, the mere availability of research outputs is insufficient. To exploit the full potential of OA, it must be possible to search, discover, mine, analyse, etc. this content. To achieve this, it is essential to improve the existing OA technical infrastructure to effectively support these functionalities. Many of the vital benefits of OA are expected to come with the ability to reuse OA content in unanticipated ways. Access to the OA content must therefore be flexible, yet practical, content-based and not just metadata based. In this demonstration, we present the CORE system, which aggregates millions of OA resources from hundreds of OA repositories and journals. We discuss the use cases aggregations should support and demonstrate how the CORE system addresses them, including searching, discovering, mining and analyzing content. We also show how aggregated OA content can be reused to build new applications on top of CORE's functionality.

Categories and Subject Descriptors

H.3.7 Digital Libraries, H.3.6 Library Automation

Keywords

digital libraries, cyberinfrastructure architectures, open access, content harvesting

1. INTRODUCTION

In the context of digital libraries, we understand *aggregations* as systems or cyberinfrastructures supporting the acquisition, storage, management, integration, enrichment and other types of information processing of digital resources, distributed beyond the scope of a single institution. In our previous paper [1], we have analysed the role of aggregations in supporting the Open Access movement. We have discussed the functionalities aggregations should provide and articulated the need for an OA technical infrastructure providing seamless access at three levels: *raw data access, transaction access* and *analytical access* (see Table I). We also showed that there is currently no aggregation of all OA materials that would provide harmonised, unrestricted, transparent and convenient access to OA metadata and content, on top of which it would be possible to build services forming the necessary infrastructure. The CORE system aims to fill this gap.

In this paper, we provide a set of use cases for each of these access levels, building on the experience gathered during talks with stakeholders while building the CORE service and during aggregation requirements gathering carried out for the UK RepositoryNet+ project.

JCDL'13, July 22–26, 2013, Indianapolis, Indiana, USA.
ACM 978-1-4503-2077-1/13/07.

2. THE CORE AGGREGATOR

The main goal of the CORE system[1] is to deliver a system aggregating research papers from multiple sources and providing a wide range of value-added services on top of this data. The purpose of CORE is to use this platform to establish the technical infrastructure for Open Access content taking into account the different needs of users participating in the OA ecosystem. CORE has been built to support a wide range of users [1] including those who need programmable access to metadata and content to build new applications (e.g. for the purposes of text-mining or bibliometrics), general users who need to search and explore content, repository administrators who need to manage collections and increase their visibility or Open Access analysts and advocates.

2.1 Raw data[2] access

Raw data access is needed to enable passing the aggregated information to programs for further processing. It is a flexible type of access allowing others to extend existing infrastructures. It can be considered as the foundational access type, since all other functionalities can be built on this access level. Quite surprisingly, the existing aggregation systems in most cases do not provide this functionality or provide it in a very incomprehensive way [1], which might be in some cases intentional (protecting their own market, not wanting 3rd parties to easily build new services, etc.).

Aggregations should provide a free API allowing access to the aggregated metadata and content. Others should be able to use this API to build new services and software applications, for example making use of text-mining, semantic web or other technologies. The aggregation APIs should provide value-added services, i.e. services that are not or cannot be offered by the individual data providers, but can be useful to users.

CORE offers a free API, which provides functions for searching, downloading and finding similar (and duplicate) resources across the metadata and content aggregated from many sources. Additionally, CORE allows downloading content directly in plain text, accessing citation and reference information and offers also experimental services for content classification, URL extraction and data source benchmarking and analysis. The list of functions offered by the CORE API is growing to allow more convenient access to this large dataset. At the moment, we are also working towards releasing downloadable datasets complemented by a software library to provide flexible access for those who might have specific application or hardware requirements.

[1] http://core.kmi.open.ac.uk

[2] In this paper, the concept of raw data refers to structured or unstructured publication manuscript data provided by repositories, or resulting from processing at the level of aggregation, to be used for further machine processing. Our concept of raw data is different from the more frequently discussed concept of research data which typically refers to data in the form of facts, observations, images, computer program results, recordings, measurements or experiences, on which an argument, test or hypothesis, or another research output, is based.

Access level	What it provides	Users group
Raw data access	Access to the raw metadata and content as downloadable files or through an API. The content and metadata might be cleaned, harmonised, pre-processed and enriched.	Developers, digital libraries, eResearchers, companies developing software, ...
Transaction information access	Access to information primarily with the goal to find and explore content of interest typically realised through the use of a web portal and its search and exploratory tools.	Researchers, students, life-long learners, general public, ...
Analytical information access	Access to statistical information at the collection or sub-collection level often realised through the use of tables or charts.	Funders/government, business intelligence, repository/library managers, ...

Table I: The three access levels defined [1].

2.2 Transaction access

This type of access is perhaps the area mostly associated with the role of aggregations. It refers to the ability of aggregations to help users searching, exploring and discovering the aggregated information typically at the granularity of individual documents or small sets of documents. Yet, in the era of Google Scholar, Microsoft Academic Search and other academic search engines, the role aggregations should play in this domain is often misunderstood and not sufficiently appreciated.

First of all, OA aggregations should provide (fulltext-based and not just metadata-based) cross-search facilities exclusively for OA content. Current commercial search engines do not distinguish between subscription based and Open Access content, which often leads to users' frustration (when they only discover content they cannot download). Second, aggregations should work hand in hand with search engines to ensure that OA content is indexed thoroughly by exposing content and metadata according to the search engine recommendations (this is often not the case and OA content is paradoxically difficult to find). Third, aggregations should offer alternative cross-search interfaces for those users who require some specialist search functionality not important to the general users. For example, it has been reported that many users require faceted browsing (e.g. when looking into content provenance) or various exploratory and visual interfaces. The strength of aggregations should also be in the ability to utilize their raw data access layer, allowing the implementation of novel search and exploration interfaces. The right to deploy these interfaces at a web scale should no longer be reserved to a few powerful companies.

The CORE system offers a faceted cross-search interface tailored to Open Access content. The offered facets are currently the repositories (content providers), language of the content, full-text availability and publication date. The system exposes metadata tags according to Google Scholar recommendations, helping to increase the visibility of the aggregated content. CORE also offers content recommendation and visualization tools. There is even a native interface for mobile devices (Apple and Android) and a recommendation plugin that can be embedded to 3rd party systems. Furthermore, the CORE API allows building new search interfaces on top of the aggregation, such as an exploratory search interface discussed in [2].

2.3 Analytical access

The ability to generate transparent and justifiable content statistics is without doubts one of the main reasons why we need OA aggregations. Today, we are unable to accurately answer even the simplest questions, such as how many full-texts are available as Open Access. Aggregations have the potential to change this. Apart from providing various types of metadata and content statistics, aggregations should provide information about growth of content in different disciplines, research trends, subject clusters, funder statistics, source and collection citation statistics, etc. across repositories. These statistics are already needed and should be monitored on an ongoing basis. Furthermore, the characteristic sign of these statistics should be transparency (it is clear which data sources are used to generate these statistics) and extensibility (it is possible to generate new statistics from the data available on the raw data access level). Apart from statistical information, aggregations should also serve the community as a tool that encourages standardization. Aggregations can detect data inconstancies across sources and inform about them thereby helping to speed up adoption of standards and improving interoperability.

The CORE system offers an experimental tool called Repository Analytics. Repository Analytics report content statistics from the different content sources. The tool also indicates the ability or inability to perform content harvesting and shows the log of the harvests. The statistics are available through a dashboard as well as an API. There is lot of potential for providing more sophisticated analytical services in CORE, which is a direction we are following.

3. CONCLUSIONS

In this demonstration paper, we introduced some of the main use cases in which (Open Access) aggregation systems should assist different types of users and described how this functionality is currently implemented in the CORE system. More details will be provided during the demonstration.

4. ACKNOWLEDGMENTS

Our work has been supported by JISC. The use cases have been discussed with and provided to UK RepositoriesNet+ as part of the requirements-gathering for UK aggregation services.

5. REFERENCES

[1] Knoth, P. and Zdrahal, Z. (2012) CORE: Three Access Levels to Underpin Open Access, D-Lib Magazine, 18, 11/12, Corporation for National Research Initiatives. DOI= http://dx.doi.org/10.1045/november2012-knoth

[2] Herrmannova, D. and Knoth, P. (2012) Visual Search for Supporting Content Exploration in Large Document Collections, D-Lib Magazine, 18, 7/8, Corporation for National Research Initiatives. DOI= http://dx.doi.org/10.1045/july2012-herrmannova

Docear's PDF Inspector: Title Extraction from PDF Files

Joeran Beel
OvGU, Magdeburg
Germany
beel@ovgu.de

Stefan Langer
Docear, Magdeburg
Germany
langer@docear.org

Marcel Genzmehr
Docear, Magdeburg
Germany
genzmehr@docear.org

Christoph Müller
Docear, Magdeburg
Germany
mueller@docear.org

ABSTRACT

In this demo-paper we present *Docear's PDF Inspector* (DPI). DPI extracts titles from academic PDF files by applying a simple heuristic: the largest text on the first page of a PDF is assumed to be the title. This simple heuristic achieves accuracies around 70% and outperforms the tools ParsCit and SciPlore Xtract in both run-time and accuracy. In addition, DPI is released under the free open source license GPL 2+ at http://www.docear.org, written in JAVA, and runs on any major operating system.

Categories and Subject Descriptors

H.3.1 [Information Storage and Retrieval]: Content Analysis and Indexing – *Indexing methods.*

General Terms

Management, Documentation

Keywords

title extraction; pdf processing; style information; heuristic

1. INTRODUCTION

Several applications in the field of Academia require extracting titles from PDF files. For instance, academic search engines identify PDFs found on the Web, and reference managers such as Mendeley and Zotero extract titles (and other metadata) from PDFs to help users creating bibliographies. In the ideal case, a PDF's title is stored in the PDF's metadata and can easily be retrieved with standard PDF libraries (e.g. PDFBox, jPod, or iText). However, often a title is not available via the PDF's metadata. To retrieve a title anyway, the full-text of a PDF must be analyzed.

In the past years, several tools used machine learning to identify titles from PDFs [3–5, 7], some of them being open source. However, the recently developed "SciPlore Xtract" [2] showed that a simple heuristic outperformed machine learning approaches. SciPlore Xtract extracted the largest font from the first page of a PDF and assumed this to be the title. Although researchers often claim accuracies of around 90% for title extraction [4, 5, 7], we recently showed that under "real-life" conditions, accuracies are rather between 50% to 70% [2].

All solutions have some shortcomings. Either they are proprietary solutions being not freely available (Mendeley), have problems in processing PDF files that do not comply 100% to the PDF standard (SciPlore Xtract), don't process PDFs at all and require third party tools (ParsCit), are rather slow and achieve low accuracies (ParsCit), are not available for all operating systems, or are available only as stand-alone tools which cannot be easily integrated into other applications.

JCDL'13, July 22–26, 2013, Indianapolis, Indiana, USA.
ACM 978-1-4503-2077-1/13/07.

2. DOCEAR'S PDF INSPECTOR

We developed "*Docear's PDF Inspector*" which identifies titles from (academic) PDF files and does not suffer from the aforementioned shortcomings. Namely, Docear's PDF Inspector (a) achieves good accuracies with excellent run times (see next section for details) (b) can be used as library by other JAVA applications which means other tools can easily integrate Docear's PDF Inspector (c) can be used as a stand-alone application that returns a PDF's title on the command line or stores the data into a CSV file (Figure 1) (d) can process several PDFs in a batch (e) can process all PDF files of all PDF versions, including those with minor deviations from the PDF standard. In the rare cases that a PDF cannot be parsed the title from a PDFs metadata is returned (if available) (f) is written 100% in JAVA 1.6 which means Docear's PDF Inspector runs on any major operating system, including Windows, Linux, and MacOS, without any other tools required (besides the JAVA runtime environment, of course) (g) is released under the GNU General Public License (GPL) 2 or later, which means it is completely free to use and its source code can be downloaded and modified by anyone. Both source code and compiled library can be found at *http://www.docear.org.*

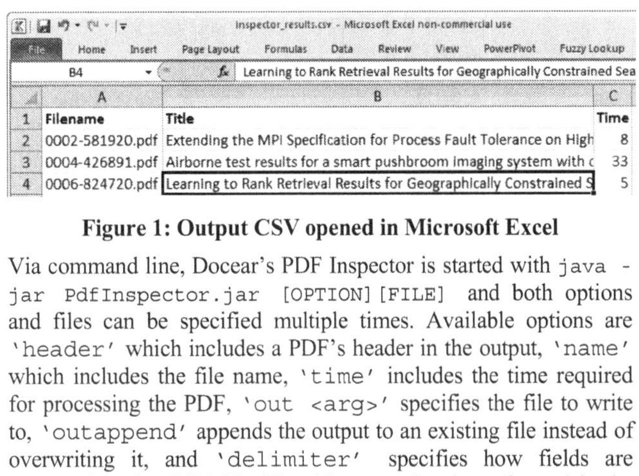

Figure 1: Output CSV opened in Microsoft Excel

Via command line, Docear's PDF Inspector is started with `java -jar PdfInspector.jar [OPTION][FILE]` and both options and files can be specified multiple times. Available options are `'header'` which includes a PDF's header in the output, `'name'` which includes the file name, `'time'` includes the time required for processing the PDF, `'out <arg>'` specifies the file to write to, `'outappend'` appends the output to an existing file instead of overwriting it, and `'delimiter'` specifies how fields are separated in the CSV file. The title extraction is performed in the same way as *SciPlore Xtract* does [2]: the largest font on the first page that is not exceeding eight lines is assumed to be the title. For processing PDF files the PDF library *jPod* is used.

3. METHODOLOGY

To evaluate the performance of Docear's PDF Inspector we created a test collection of 500 PDF files. To have a PDF collection that contains various formats of academic articles we sent 500 search queries to Google Scholar and from the result pages (each with 100 entries) we randomly downloaded one paper. 57 PDFs were removed from the collection because they had no title or were no academic articles at all, i.e. 443 articles remained for the evaluation. The search queries were randomly generated from words contained in the mind maps of the users of our literature management software Docear [1]. We did not conduct a detailed analysis of the downloaded papers but it appeared to us that most papers were written in English, and some in German, French and Spanish. Papers were from various disciplines (computer science, psychology, biology, social sciences, business, etc.) and there was a very high variety of different formats of the articles. The collection of 500 PDFs is available upon request, so other researchers can use this PDF collection for their research and making their results comparable to ours. We also publish our research data, i.e. the extracted titles and charts we created, on http://labs.docear.org.

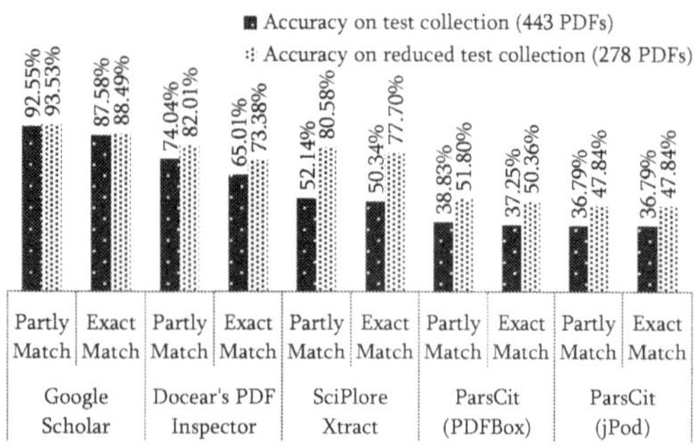

Figure 2: Accuracies of the tools on the two test collections

We evaluated Docear's PDF Inspector against SciPlore Xtract and ParsCit to have a comparison of how good the achieved results are. Because ParsCit cannot process PDF files by its own, we converted PDFs to plain text with PDFBox and jPod and run ParsCit on both text sets. If an extracted title was identical to the actual title, we classified the result as "exact match". If the extracted title was a substring of the actual title we classified the result as "partly match". Such a partly match occurred, for instance, when a tool failed to extract a PDF's sub-title. For both, exact and partly match comparisons, we ignored spaces and special characters.

Some PDFs caused parsing errors probably because they did not comply 100% with the PDF standard. For SciPlore Xtract and PDFBox (and hence ParsCit) this problem was most apparent: 35.21% (SciPlore) and 20.77% (PDFBox) of the 443 PDFs could not be parsed at all, for jPod the error was only 5.19%. While we consider the original test collection to be representative for a real-life scenario that applications such as academic search engines or reference managers face, we also wanted to have a test collection that could be processed by all tools, to evaluate the effectiveness of the title extraction algorithms (ignoring any PDF parsing problems). Therefore, we inferred a 'reduced test collection' by removing all PDFs from the original test collection which couldn't be processed by at least one of the tools. This resulted in a subset of 278 PDFs.

4. RESULTS

The results we present in this section also show how often titles from Google Scholar were accurate. We need to emphasize that accuracies from Google Scholar are not comparable with results from the other tools evaluated because Google Scholar often receives metadata directly from the publishers. That means, Google Scholar does not always extract metadata from PDFs. We provided these results only to show that even Google Scholar seems to have problems with extracting titles in some cases.

Docear's achieves the highest accuracies (Figure 2). For our standard test collection Docear's PDF Inspector outperforms the second best tool (SciPlore Xtract) notably. Docear extracts 65.01% of the titles exactly, i.e. without any errors, while SciPlore Xtract extracts only 50.34% accurately. ParsCit performs worst with an accuracy of 37.25% (PDFBox) and 36.79% (jPod). Docear also performs best measured by 'partly matches' with an accuracy of 74.04% (SciPlore 52.14%; ParsCit 38.83% and 36.79%).

Looking at the reduced test collection the picture slightly changes. Now, Docear and SciPlore perform about the same. Docear extracts 73.38% of the titles flawlessly, SciPlore 77.70%. Based on 'partly matches' Docear extracts 82.01% of the titles correctly, SciPlore 80.58% (differences are statistically not significant). ParsCit still performs far worse with accuracies around 50%.

Docear's PDF Inspector also performs best in terms of runtime. On average (mean), Docear's PDF Inspector needs 50ms to extract a title from a PDF while SciPlore Xtract needs 428ms and ParsCit 2965ms with the PDFBox library and 1786ms with jPod (Table 1). The comparison is not completely fair because ParsCit does not only extract the title (as Docear does) but also other metadata such as authors. However, for those users being only interested in the title, Docear's PDF Inspector identifies a title definitely fastest.

Table 1: Runtimes (in milliseconds) per PDF

	Docear	SciPlore	ParsCit (PDFBox)	ParsCit (jPod)
Mean	50	428	2965	1786
Std. Dev.	61	611	1383	1332
Median	23	352	2706	1394
Max	475	17667	15131	17585

Summarized, from a user perspective, Docear's PDF Inspector is the most effective tool. It is about 50% more effective than SciPlore Xtract and almost twice as effective as ParsCit for a PDF collection we consider representative for real-life scenarios. In addition, Docear's PDF Inspector is around 40 to 100 times faster than ParsCit and eight times as fast as SciPlore Xtract which uses basically the same heuristic. From a research perspective (i.e. on the reduced data set), the simple heuristic applied by Docear and SciPlore is around 50% more effective than the machine learning approach applied by ParsCit.

Final note: A recent study showed very good results for some tools which we were not aware of at the time of our evaluation [6]. Otherwise, we would have tested them against Docear's PDF Inspector.

5. REFERENCES

[1] Beel, J., Gipp, B., Langer, S. and Genzmehr, M. 2011. Docear: An Academic Literature Suite for Searching, Organizing and Creating Academic Literature. *Proceedings of the 11th annual international ACM/IEEE joint conference on Digital libraries* (2011), 465–466.

[2] Beel, J., Gipp, B., Shaker, A. and Friedrich, N. 2010. SciPlore Xtract: Extracting Titles from Scientific PDF Documents by Analyzing Style Information (Font Size). *Research and Advanced Technology for Digital Libraries, Proceedings of the 14th European Conference on Digital Libraries (ECDL'10)* (Glasgow (UK), Sep. 2010), 413–416.

[3] Councill, I.G., Giles, C.L. and Kan, M.Y. 2008. ParsCit: An open-source CRF reference string parsing package. *Proceedings of LREC*.

[4] Han, H., Giles, C.L., Manavoglu, E., Zha, H., Zhang, Z. and Fox, E.A. 2003. Automatic document metadata extraction using support vector machines. *Proceedings of the 3rd ACM/IEEE-CS Joint Conference on Digital libraries* (2003), 37–48.

[5] Hu, Y., Li, H., Cao, Y., Teng, L., Meyerzon, D. and Zheng, Q. 2006. Automatic extraction of titles from general documents using machine learning. *Information Processing and Management*. 42, (2006).

[6] Lipinski, M., Yao, K., Beel, J. and Gipp, B. 2013. Evaluation of Header Metadata Extraction Approaches and Tools for Scientific PDF Documents. *Proceedings of the JCDL* (2013).

[7] Peng, F. and McCallum, A. 2004. Accurate information extraction from research papers using conditional random fields. *HLT-NAACL04* (2004), 329–336.

Docear4Word: Reference Management for Microsoft Word based on BibTeX and the Citation Style Language (CSL)

Joeran Beel
Docear, Magdeburg
Germany
beel@docear.org

Marcel Genzmehr
Docear, Magdeburg
Germany
genzmehr@docear.org

Stefan Langer
Docear, Magdeburg
Germany
langer@docear.org

ABSTRACT
In this demo-paper we introduce Docear4Word which enables researchers to insert and format their references and bibliographies in Microsoft Word. Docear4Word is based on BibTeX and the Citation Style Language (CSL), features over 1,700 citation styles (Harvard, IEEE, ACM, etc.), is published as open source tool on http://docear.org, and runs with Microsoft Word 2002 (and later) on Windows XP (and later). Docear4Word is similar to the MS-Word add-ons that reference managers like Endnote, Zotero, or Citavi offer with the difference that it is being developed to work with the de-facto standard BibTeX and hence to work with almost any reference manager.

Categories and Subject Descriptors
H.4.1 [**Information Systems Applications**]: Office Automation – *word processing, workflow management.*

Keywords
bibtex; citation style language; CSL; microsoft word; reference management; reference manager

1. INTRODUCTION
Reference management probably is the most tiring task for students and researchers. They have to re-type and format bibliographic information over and over, for each paper, assignment or thesis. This is particularly frustrating if they need to change citation styles in a document. This might become necessary, for instance, because a supervisor changes his mind on his favorite citation style, or a paper is submitted to another journal which requires a different citation style than the previous journal.

In the past decades many software tools evolved to facilitate this workflow. Commercial tools such as Endnote and Citavi enable researchers to maintain a database with all the bibliographic data of their references. These so called 'reference managers' usually offer add-ons for Microsoft Word allowing users to insert and format references and bibliographies in a convenient way. Also some open source tools offer such add-ons, for instance Zotero. However, all these tools use proprietary data formats. Accordingly, a Microsoft Word add-on from one of these tools (e.g. Endnote) works only with corresponding data format of that particular tool.

There is one alternative to the proprietary formats, namely BibTeX. BibTeX was created by Oren Patashnik in 1988 [4] and is the de-facto standard to store references. There are many reference mangers directly supporting BibTeX, for instance JabRef, BibDesk and our own reference manager Docear [1]. Even proprietary tools such as Endnote usually allow exporting their database to BibTeX. There is a Microsoft Word add-on for BibTeX-based databases named BibTeX4Word[1]. However, BibTeX4Word requires the installation of additional tools and is difficult to setup and use. For instance, in the Blog MedicalNerds more than 250 comments were made on BibTeX4Word, mostly questioning about the usage – especially installing new citation styles is complicated [3].

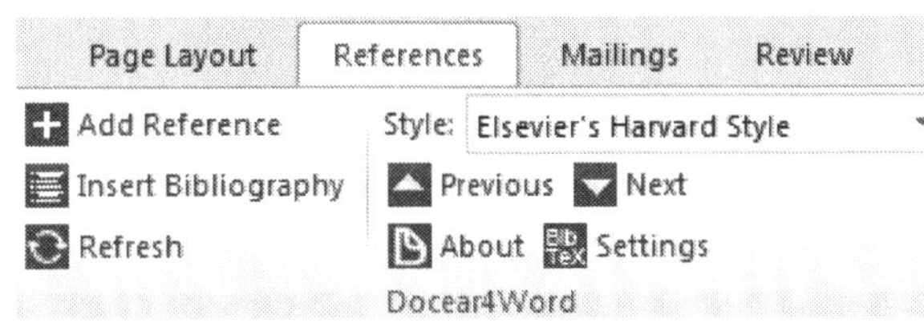

Fig. 1. Docear4Word ribbon in Microsoft Word 2010

We developed Docear4Word[2], a Microsoft Word add-on to insert and format references directly in MS-Word, based on BibTeX. Docear4Word is open source and runs with Microsoft Word 2002 (and later) on Windows XP (and later). After the installation, Docear4Word is accessible in the "Reference" ribbon when Microsoft Word 2007 or later is used (Fig. 1). In Word 2002 and 2003 a separate toolbar is installed. Docear4Word was primarily intended for users of our literature management tool Docear [1], but it can be used with any BibTeX file from any reference manager. In contrast to BibTeX4Word, Docear4Word is more user-friendly and uses the citation style language (more details in the following section).

The remainder of this paper provides a detailed overview of Docear4Word.

2. DOCEAR4WORD
2.1 Maintaining a BibTeX database
BibTeX is a text-based format. Accordingly, a BibTeX file can be created and edited with any text editor. However, there are several tools offering a graphical user interface to create BibTeX files, for instance JabRef and our own reference manager Docear. Fig. 2 shows a screenshot of Docear. Docear provides a graphical user interface for specifying title, authors, and other bibliographic data of academic literature. Based on this data Docear automatically creates a BibTeX entry. Instead of Docear, or a text editor, any reference management tool can be used that uses the BibTeX format or that may export its proprietary format to BibTeX.

JCDL'13, July 22–26, 2013, Indianapolis, Indiana, USA.
ACM 978-1-4503-2077-1/13/07.

[1] http://www.ee.ic.ac.uk/hp/staff/dmb/perl/index.html
[2] http://www.docear.org/software/add-ons/docear4word/overview/

2.2 Inserting references in Microsoft Word

Fig. 3 shows the dialog to search and insert references. The dialog allows selecting several references at once and specifying individual page numbers. Once, the references are selected and the "Add References" button is clicked, references are added in the document and formatted accordingly to the selected citation style (Fig. 5).

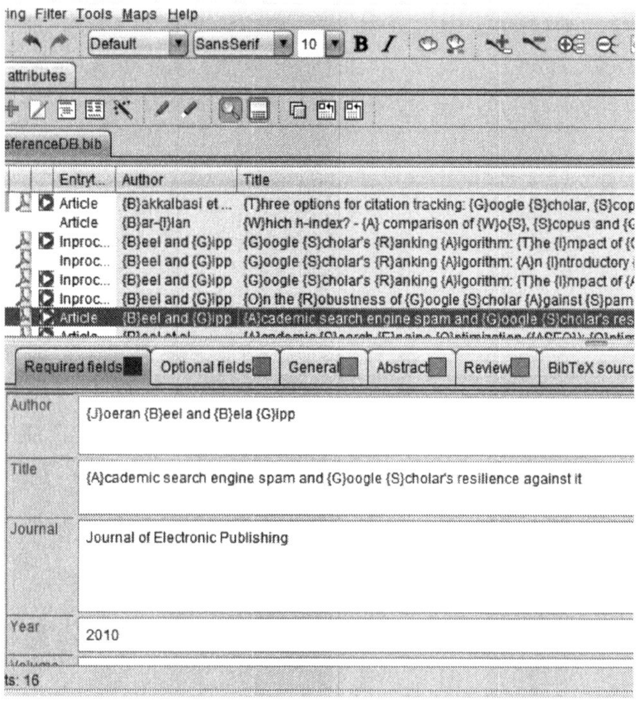

Fig. 2. Maintaining the BibTeX database with an external reference manager (e.g. Docear)

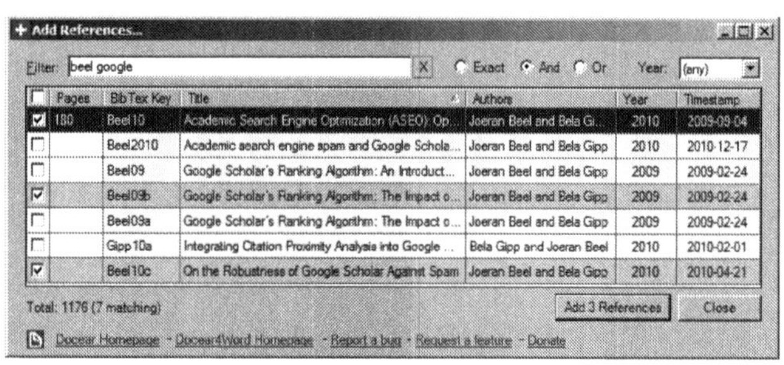

Fig. 3. Selecting and inserting a reference

2.3 Changing the Citation Style

Docear4Word uses the citation style language [5] and citeproc-js citation processor [2] to format references. The citation style language supports more than 1,700 citation styles such as IEEE, Harvard, MLA and ACM in several variations. Docear4Word users can select a style in the style box (Fig. 4) and install new styles from the style repository. When a new style is selected all references are formatted accordingly.

2.4 Insert a Bibliography

Docear4Word automatically creates a bibliography based on the references in the body of the document (Fig. 5). The user can choose where to insert the bibliography and the bibliography is automatically updated when new references are inserted.

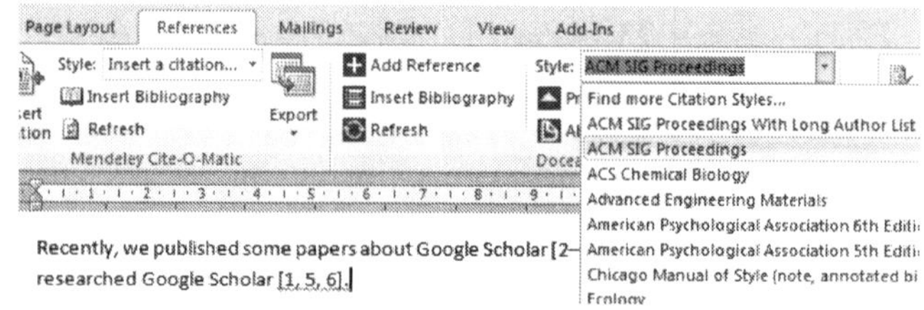

Fig. 4. Style chooser

3. OUTLOOK

Docear4Word was released as final and stable version 1.0 on http://docear.org. However, we will continue to improve Docear4Word. Among others, it is planned to offer a version for Microsoft Word on MacOS; implement support for footnotes; enable suppressing author and/or year in a reference; implement an installer for new citation styles; and allow using multiple BibTeX files at the same time. As Docear4Word is available as open source, we sincerely invite other researchers to join the development.

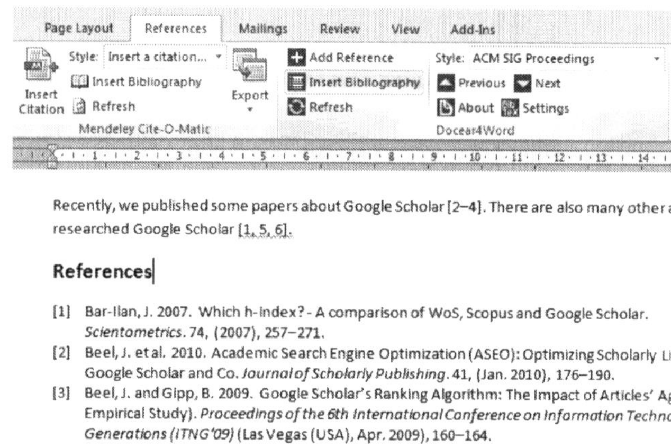

Fig. 5. Automatically created bibliography

4. ACKNOWLEDGEMENTS

We are very grateful for the Citation Style Language and CiteProc-JS by Bruce D'Arcus, Frank G. Bennett, Jr. Rintze M. Zelle, and many others. In addition, we are glad for all the support we received from Simon Hewitt.

5. REFERENCES

[1] Beel, J., Gipp, B., Langer, S. and Genzmehr, M. 2011. Docear: An Academic Literature Suite for Searching, Organizing and Creating Academic Literature. *Proceedings of the 11th JCDL* (2011), 465–466.

[2] Frank G. Bennett, J. 2011. The citeproc-js Citation Processor. http://gsl-nagoya-u.net/http/pub/citeproc-doc.html

[3] Medicalnerds 2007. How to use JabRef (BibTeX) with Microsoft Word 2003. http://www.medicalnerds.com/how-to-use-jabrefbibtex-with-microsoft-word-2003/

[4] Patashnik, O. 1988. BibTexing. http://bibtexml.sourceforge.net/btxdoc.pdf

[5] Zelle, R.M. 2010. Citation Style Language 1.0. http://citationstyles.org/2010/03/22/citation-style-language-1-0/

FishTraits Version 2: Integrating Ecological, Biogeographic and Bibliographic Information

Zhiwu Xie
University Libraries
Virginia Tech
Blacksburg, VA 24061
zhiwuxie@vt.edu

Emmanual A. Frimpong
Department of Fish and Wildlife Conservation
Virginia Tech
Blacksburg, VA 24061
frimp@vt.edu

Sunshin Lee
Department of Computer Science
Virginia Tech
Blacksburg, VA 24061
sslee777@vt.edu

ABSTRACT
In this paper we describe the new development of FishTraits. Originating from an ecological database that documents and consolidates more than 100 traits for 809 fish species, the new version focuses on the integration of these traits data with the bibliographic and biogeographic information. We explain the overall design as well as the implementation details.

Categories and Subject Descriptors
H.3.7 [**Information Storage and Retrieval**]: Digital Libraries

Keywords
Digital library; architecture; specie traits.

1. INTRODUCTION
Species traits offer instructive lenses through which to view spatial and temporal variation in the distribution and abundance of species. Ecologists have a long history of using traits to study patterns of species distribution, abundance, and responses to anthropogenic impacts. Partially funded by the U.S. Geological Survey Aquatic Gap Analysis program, FishTraits version 1 compiled and consolidated more than 100 traits for 809 (731 native and 78 nonnative) fish species found in freshwaters of the conterminous United States, including 37 native families and 145 native genera [1, 2]. It contains information on four major categories of traits:

- trophic ecology
- body size, reproductive ecology, and life history
- habitat preferences
- salinity and temperature tolerances

Information on geographic distribution and conservation status was also compiled. The first version of the database [1] was released as a web application in 2009 and soon became the most cited web resource in the area.

The limitations of the original web development also started to surface soon after its public release. Due to technical difficulties, the website was briefly taken offline in 2011 and was later resumed. Starting from 2012, a redesign and rebuild of both the frontend web interface and the backend database was underway. This paper briefly describes the architectural design as well as the implementation details of FishTraits Version 2.

JCDL'13, July 22–26, 2013, Indianapolis, Indiana, USA.
ACM 978-1-4503-2077-1/13/07.

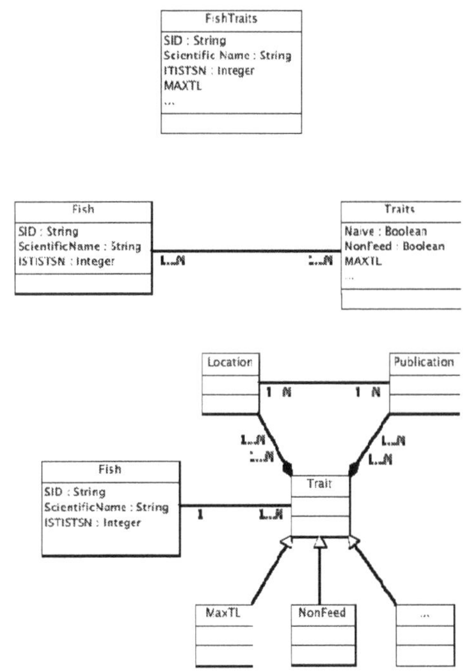

Figure 1. Evolving FishTraits Data Model.

2. INFORMATION INTEGRATION
The first version of FishTraits reports the consolidated data from various sources. These sources include the state and regional fish accounts, three general texts, and numerous specialized texts, peer-reviewed articles, technical reports such as species recovery plans, online catalogs, and state and federal agency websites. In version 1 design, a "NOTES" field was included to document the original sources and how these sources were consolidated to reach the resulting data values. This field, however, was not populated in version 1 and was left for future work.

During the version 2 development multiple limitations of the original design were exposed through the use-case analysis: First, a combined "NOTES" field cannot clearly differentiate the original sources from the consolidation process. Second, the per-species granularity is too restrictive for the much more complicated referencing and interlinking relations between the traits and the resources.

We started by separating the bibliographic information from the NOTES field, and designate a N-to-N relation between the Species and the Publication objects. Further use case analysis exposed more complicated scenarios. In particular, since the state and regional fish accounts are organized by political boundaries whereas species traits transcend political and biogeographic boundaries, multiple resources may report different trait values on the same species but in different locations. This calls for the data model to further evolve. Figure 1 illustrates some of the data model changes during the development.

Bibliographic information is an important part of the Version 2 development. Although we need many functionalities from a bibliographic information management system, such as cross-referencing, it would be overkill to build a full-fledged system just to manage the publications. We decided to leverage the existing developments in the field and build an interface with Zotero to import bibliographic information through the standard BibTeX format.

As illustrated above, biogeographic information can easily complicate the architectural and the model design. We therefore need not only a flexible data model, but also sufficient geographic information support at the database level. This puts restrictions on our technology options. Furthermore, we expect the data model to continue evolving when more complicated relations are discovered between traits, their referencing publications and geographic locations. Such evolution usually put pressures on technology development because most frontend code and backend queries may need to be fully rewritten if data model changes.

FishTraits Version 1 was a simple ASP application built on Access database and IIS. It lacks many crucial web components and cannot handle heavy query load. When the original hosting server was upgraded, many old technologies became obsolete and the support was eventually dropped. Learning from the past experience, we decided to rebuild the system with mature, stable, and well-adopted open source technologies. We picked Python/Django as our web framework due to its excellent capabilities to evolve code with the data model. Its Object-Relation Model allows the development to be much more agile and flexible. As for the geospatial database, we chose the open source PostGIS, which adds spatially-explicit biogeographic information support to PostgreSQL database and allows many routine geospatial operations. Figure 2 shows the query interfaces of the new version. Compared with its predecessor, the new version also supports autocomplete that allows the users to easily retrieve data values including the species names.

FishTraits Version 2 will eventually export all its data to be merged into USGS's computing infrastructure, but the frontend functionalities will not be replicated. It will continue to run as a standalone web application. FishTraits Version 2 also adds support to easily backup and restore from VTechWorks, Virginia Tech's institutional repository via the SWORD protocol [3]. Through VTechWorks planned interfacing with DataOne, FishTraits data may be further disseminated.

Figure 2. FishTraits Version 2 Screenshots.

3. CONCLUSION

In this paper we describe the new development of FishTraits. Our emphasis is on its architectural design and implementation details that integrate ecological information with biogeological and bibliographic information.

4. ACKNOWLEDGEMENTS

FishTraits is funded by the US Geological Survey, Aquatic Gap Analysis Program

5. REFERENCES

[1] FishTraits. http://ww.fishtraits.info

[2] Frimpong, E. A. and Angermeier, P. L. 2009. Fish Traits: A Database of Ecological and Life-history Traits of Freshwater Fishes of the United States. *Fisheries*, vol. 34, no. 10, 2009, 487–495.

[3] Allinson, J., François, S. and Lewis, S. 2008. SWORD: Simple Web-service Offering Repository Deposit. *Ariadne*, Jan, 2008.

Greenbug: A Hybrid Web-inspector, Debugger and Design Editor for Greenstone

David Bainbridge Sam J. McIntosh David M. Nichols
University of Waikato
Hamilton, New Zealand
{davidb,sjmc,dmn}@cs.waikato.ac.nz

ABSTRACT

In this paper we present Greenbug: a hybrid web inspector, debugger and design editor developed for use with the open source digital library software Greenstone 3. Inspired by the web development tool Firebug, Greenbug is more tightly coupled with the underlying (digital library) server than that provided by Firebug; for example, Greenbug has a fine-grained knowledge of the connection between the underlying file system and the rendered web content, and also provides the ability to commit any changes made through the web interface back to the underlying file system. Moreover, because web page production in Greenstone 3 is the result of an XSLT processing pipeline, the necessarily well-formed hierarchical XML content can be manipulated into a graphical representation, which can then be manipulated directly through a visual interface supplied by Greenbug. We showcase the interface in use, provide a brief overview of implementation details, and conclude with a discussion on how the approach can be adapted to other XSLT transformation-based content management systems, such as DSpace.

Categories and Subject Descriptors

H.3.7 [**Information storage & retrieval**]: Digital Libraries

Keywords

General Purpose Digital libraries, Web Inspector, Graphical Debugger, Design Editor

1. INTRODUCTION

Striking a balance between expressive capability and ease of use is a challenging aspect to Digital Library (DL) software design. Interface issues, in particular, are a significant source of problems for those learning about digital libraries [2]. Here we present a new level of abstraction to digital library design, fashioned after the web development tool Firebug,[1] but specifically designed for DL software. We start the paper with a demonstration of its features in the context of Greenstone 3 [4] before giving an overview of the implementation and conclude with a discussion of the wider applicability of the developed technique.

[1] https://getfirebug.com/

JCDL'13, July 22–26, 2013, Indianapolis, Indiana, USA.
ACM 978-1-4503-2077-1/13/07.

2. WALKTHROUGH

Figure 1 shows a snapshot of Greenbug—the name we have given to our developed prototype—in use. Like its namesake, Firebug, initially the software is not active. The digital librarian navigates around the constructed digital library (viewing the home page, query results, preferences information, *etc.*) looking for any imperfections that need to be corrected—or else refinements they wish to make—in the presentation and structure of the DL. When they encounter a page they wish to change, they switch Greenbug on. Unlike Firebug, this is done by logging into the digital library since changes are saved back to the server, thus affecting all users who subsequently access the DL. Figure 1 shows the situation where the digital librarian has logged in because in browsing by titles, they have noticed a rather glaring error present in every title surrogate where it starts with "Aaabbbccc" (artificially introduced for the purposes of demonstration). At the bottom of the browser window the following buttons appear:

Enable debugging; Select new element; Close editor;
Save changes; and Use XML Editor,

where only "Enable debugging" is initially active. Clicking this button shifts the user to a mode where, as they move their mouse cursor over the HTML elements on the page, a red highlighting box snaps to the individual element. Clicking on an HTML element of interest calls up internal details from the digital library as to how the page was formed. The nested sequence of XSLT template rules that have been fired to produce the selected element are shown along the bottom of Figure 1. In the figure the digital librarian has chosen to click on the right-most rule: *documentNode*, which in turn displays a visual representation of the XSLT template that produced the selected HTML element.

From here the user can interact with this visual representation, altering the attribute values they contain and rearranging the nested boxes through direct manipulation. The left-hand side offers new elements that can be dragged into the visual representation. New elements are grouped into three categories: HTML, XSL, and GSF (the latter providing DL-based elements, such as access to metadata). Furthermore, the user can interactively select inner-boxes in the visual view to help focus their attention, and the dis-

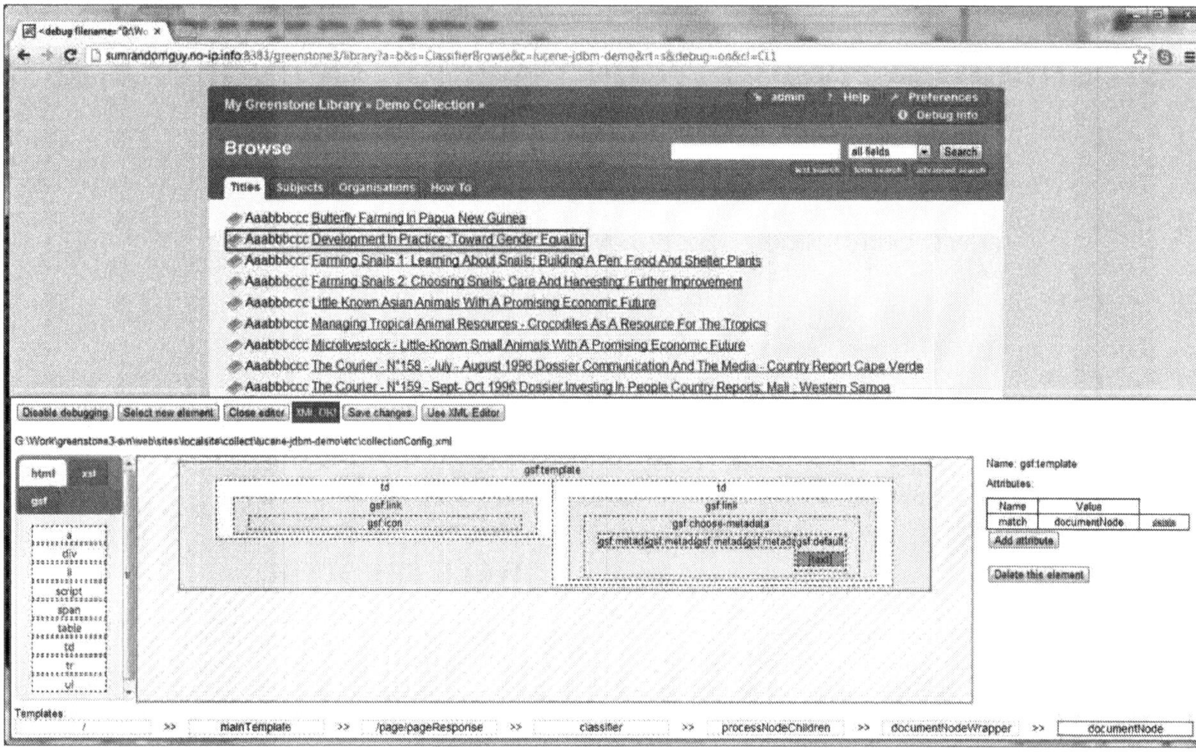

Figure 1: The Design View to Greenbug.

play responds by enlarging the area of interest in an animated fashion. Clicking on the outermost-most rectangle reverses the operation. Attributes to the selected element are shown on the right-hand side of the visual display; values can be edited, and new attributes added. In our example, the digital librarian has located the erroneous string "Aaabbbccc", deleted it, and then pressed "Save changes". Greenbug also provides a raw XSLT display mode (not shown) where the user can directly edit XML content in a syntax colour-highlighted editor window.

3. DISCUSSION

In terms of implementation, the XSLT processing pipeline to Greenstone 3 [1] was altered to keep track of where the various template rules are located on the file system, factoring in the effect of the inheritance mechanism provided by the *<xsl:import>* element. This information is spliced into the generated HTML as custom *<debug>* elements, relying on the HTML convention that elements that are not understood by the browser are ignored when rendering the page. These debug elements mark the various points within the page where XSLT rules have been applied in generating the page, and attributes within the element record both the name of the template used and its underlying file location.

The second modification we made to the server code was to add an additional (authenticated) service for receiving XML content and saving it to disk. The Greenstone 3 software architecture already has services for saving edited metadata and reconfiguring the server, and the new ability was added to this service group. With these two modifications in place, the end-user interface has been implemented using JavaScript, DOM manipulation, and AJAX calls.

In terms of the general applicability of the approach, there are a variety of XSLT pipeline-based content management systems that would be amenable to being augmented with this form of interactive debugging support, such as DSpace [3] which is based on the Apache Cocoon[2] rendering pipeline. The base functionality required is: user authentication, an instrumented XSLT pipeline, and a URL-based "write file back" and reconfigure service. With these elements in place, the debugging interface (*i.e.*, the JavaScript and AJAX calls) could then be layered on top. In the specific case of DSpace there would be benefit in applying the Greenbug approach to both the Aspects and Themes components of the software design.

4. REFERENCES

[1] D. Bainbridge, K. J. Don, G. R. Buchanan, I. H. Witten, S. Jones, M. Jones, and M. I. Barr. Dynamic digital library construction and configuration. *Research and Advanced Technology for Digital Libraries*, pages 1–13, 2004.

[2] D. M. Nichols, D. Bainbridge, and M. B. Twidale. Constructing digital library interfaces. In *Proceedings of the 7th ACM/IEEE-CS joint conference on Digital libraries*, JCDL '07, pages 331–332, New York, NY, USA, 2007. ACM.

[3] S. Phillips, C. Green, A. Maslov, A. Mikeal, and J. Leggett. Manakin: A new face for DSpace. *D-Lib Magazine*, 13(11/12), November/December 2007.

[4] I. H. Witten and D. Bainbridge. The Greenstone digital library software. *Handbook of Research on Digital Libraries*, pages 61–72, 2009.

[2]http://cocoon.apache.org/

IssueLab: The Social Sector's Digital Library

Lisa Brooks
Director of Knowledge Management Systems,
Foundation Center
79 Fifth Avenue
New York, NY 10003
1-773-649-1790
lisa@issuelab.org

Gabriela Fitz
Director of Knowledge Management Initiatives,
Foundation Center
79 Fifth Avenue
New York, NY 10003
1-773-882-8250
gabi@issuleab.org

ABSTRACT
In this paper, we describe IssueLab, a digital library and distribution network for social sector publications and resources.

Categories and Subject Descriptors
H.3.5 [**Information Storage and Retrieval**]: Online Information Services – *data sharing, web-based services.* H.3.7 [**Digital Libraries**]: Digital Libraries – *collection, dissemination.*

Keywords
Collaboration, copyright, Creative Commons, crowdsourcing, cyberinfrastructure, digital libraries, distributed networks, open access, open licensing, orphan works.

1. INTRODUCTION
IssueLab (http://www.issuelab.org) is a digital library and distribution network that provides free and open access to resources that analyze the world's most pressing social, economic, and environmental challenges and their potential solutions. It contains more than 13,000 documents from over 2,500 social sector organizations including family, community, public, and private foundations, direct service providers, non-governmental organizations (NGOs), advocacy groups, policy think tanks and watchdog organizations, and academic research centers. It represents one of the largest collections of social sector knowledge, spanning 40 issues areas, from agriculture to immigration to welfare.

IssueLab is a service of the Foundation Center, a nonprofit organization established in 1956 that is a leading source of information about philanthropy worldwide. The Center maintains a comprehensive database on U.S. and global grantmakers and their grants. It also operates five regional library/learning centers and has a network of 470 funding information centers located in public libraries, community foundations, and educational institutions nationwide and around the world.

The resources collected in IssueLab include white papers, reports, case studies, program and project evaluations, official testimony, polls and survey results, and policy briefs that are almost entirely shared in Portable Document Format (PDF). Our work includes ingesting, storing, and distributing these files, generating metadata, indexing fulltext, and developing useful assessment and access tools for end users. What we collect is essentially grey literature as there is no commercial publishing activity pertaining to these resources. We run into a number of thorny issues when it comes to preservation and distribution, including: social sector organizations release publications through their websites without any long term plan to archive and preserve these documents; publications and datasets released in PDF format make content reuse difficult if not impossible to work with; and, not many social sector organizations are aware of alternatives to "all rights reserved" copyright notification creating one more barrier to easy sharing and reuse.

JCDL'13, July 22–26, 2013, Indianapolis, Indiana, USA.
ACM 978-1-4503-2077-1/13/07.

2. A UNIQUE APPROACH TO COLLECTING AND SHARING SOCIAL SECTOR RESOURCES
Given the nature of the resources we collect, and the problems inherent in collecting and sharing them, our approach to ingestion, distribution, and preservation is multifaceted and unique. The following areas of our work will be of great interest to those interested in creating and maintaining a digital library, and getting a glimpse of the systems and processes underpinning a distributed network meant to mainstream social sector resources: creating a collaborative and participatory information environment; developing a cyberinfrastructure for the social sector; fostering a distributed information network; managing and informing social sector copyright practices; the long-term archiving and preservation of orphaned resources; and, future tool development.

2.1 Creating a Collaborative and Participatory Information Environment
Anyone who is or has been affiliated with a social sector organization – a current or past employee, intern, volunteer, board member, vendor/consultant, etc. – can, on behalf of that organization, create a free IssueLab account, upload files to our system, and describe the resources they share using a mix of constrained and unconstrained metadata points. Our system enables users to affiliate themselves with multiple organizations through a single account. We actively cultivate our user base through webinars, presentations, social media, and other ongoing communications efforts. Currently, we have approximately 825 unique user accounts and collect a steady stream of resources through their participation.

2.2 Developing a Cyberinfrastructure for the Social Sector
The IssueLab platform was built with open source technologies including Linux, Apache, PHP, MySQL, CodeIgniter (PHP-based Model-View-Controller framework), jQuery (javascript

framework), HTML, and CSS. It includes an Open Archives Initiative-compliant data provider service that is regularly harvested by OAI-compliant data harvesters.

IssueLab shares its metadata with any individual or group that would like to use it. The metadata we share includes: title, abstract, publication date, publishing organization(s), author(s), funder(s), geographic coverage, issue area, keywords, document type (eg., report/whitepaper, case study, evaluation, annual report, etc.), copyright, language, publication cover graphic file location, Scribd.com document identifier (for embed purposes), and file format, and permalink. We provide metadata in XML format through our OAI data service which uses Dublin Core descriptors. We are developing an application programming interface (API) for data consumers who are not familiar or do not use OAI. Plans for our API include providing data in XML and JSON formats.

Our system interfaces with other Web-based services such as Scribd.com's API to convert files into dynamic scrollable documents that we embed into document description pages alongside the metadata we generate. Visitors can glance at a file or use Scribd's full-screen mode to conduct an in-depth review of a file before downloading it. Our system also interfaces with Creative Commons's license-chooser API to enable users adding resources to IssueLab to apply an open license to their work. We also embed social media tools into the IssueLab user interface via the ShareThis API.

2.3 Fostering a Distributed Information Network

We apply a Creative Commons Attribution-NonCommercial-ShareAlike (CC BY-NC-SA) license to our metadata and freely share it with others for use within their own websites and online services. For example, Wiserearth.org, an online community with approximately 70,000 members concerned with environmental issues, ingests our metadata and embeds it in their site pages to provide it to their members.

Another distribution method is IssueLab's Custom Knowledge Center Service where a version of IssueLab's search and browse tools is embedded within customer websites, creating an easily maintained "plug-and-play" eLibrary. Customers can include their own resources, any resource from IssueLab's collection, or resources from around the Web. Adding a resource to a Knowledge Center also adds it to the larger IssueLab platform where it is made available to IssueLab's global audience, to data harvesters and partners, and to other Foundation Center web properties. IssueLab's platform connects these resources into a single system that catalogues, indexes, and shares these works through a distributed network, bringing them to thousands more users where they are already gathering online.

2.4 Managing and Informing Social Sector Copyright Practices

In order to distribute the resources collected in IssueLab, most of which are shared by individuals on behalf of social sector organizations, our system has had to accommodate and manage existing copyrights. Many of the resources we hold carry an "all rights reserved" rights notice; others have detailed and lengthy descriptions regarding how the resource can be used; some have no obvious copyright notice at all. We have devised an elaborate "opt-out" system that is part technical, part consistent communications methods to manage this. We also conduct a persistent open licensing education campaign to help the social sector understand alternative licensing options.

2.5 Long-term Archiving and Preservation of Orphaned Resources

In 2012, the Foundation Center was contacted by two nonprofit organizations, Public/Private Ventures (P/PV) and Public Education Network (PEN). Each was closing its doors forever after decades of operation. The Foundation Center became the stewards of P/PV and PEN's publication archives, and their resources continue to be available through special collections hosted at IssueLab. One aspect of this preservation work focused on copyright. Both P/PV and PEN had previously applied "all rights reserved" copyright notification to their resources. Both organizations agreed to apply an Attribution, Noncommerical Creative Commons License (CC BY-NC) to all of their works, allowing for limited use of the material provided it is properly credited to the appropriate organization and the Foundation Center, and is for noncommercial purposes. Users do not need to secure permission from P/PV, PEN, or the Foundation Center before using, copying, or sharing this material, or developing derivative works based on it.

In addition to P/PV and PEN, IssueLab houses the works of several other nonprofit organizations that are no longer in operation.

2.6 Future Tool Development

In addition to collecting, disseminating, and preserving social sector resources, and maintaining and growing a distributed network, IssueLab develops tools and technologies meant to assist end users – nonprofit practitioners, grantmakers, policy professionals, program and project evaluators, legislators and legislative aids, advocates, direct service providers, and researchers – with discovering, assessing, and obtaining information that is helpful to them. We have a number of tools under development to aid these people with their work.

2.6.1 Key Findings Tool

The key findings tool will extract and index the findings and recommendations embedded in electronic files in order to mobilize this information for use in searching and browsing.

2.6.2 Text and Sentiment Analysis Tools

Text and sentiment analysis tools will extract and summarize primary ideas and patterns within documents.

2.6.3 Annotation Tools

Annotation tools will enable end users to collaboratively read, mark-up, and understand resources in the IssueLab collection.

2.6.4 Chunked Content Tools

Chunked content tools will provide easy-to-navigate portions of documents – citations, table of contents, charts and graphs.

The Apollo Archive Explorer

Douglas W. Oard
College of Information Studies/UMIACS
University of Maryland, College Park, MD USA
oard@umd.edu

Joseph Malionek
Eleanor Roosevelt High School
Greenbelt, MD USA
jmalionek@gmail.com

ABSTRACT

A system for exploring the rich recorded legacy of the Apollo missions to the Moon, using the event structure of each mission as an organizing principle, will be demonstrated. A scalable implementation is achieved by automating temporal, spatial, and topical content alignment across diverse media. Multiple access points are supported, including event-based access through the flight plan, time-based access using event timelines, and content-based access using information retrieval techniques.

Categories and Subject Descriptors

H.3.7 [Information Systems]: Information Storage and Retrieval – digital libraries.

General Terms

Design, Human Factors.

Keywords

Information integration, streaming media, archival sources.

1. INTRODUCTION

In a four-year period between December 1968 and December 1972, Twenty-four Americans traveled to Earth's Moon; twelve of them landed. It is one of the most extensively documented events in human history. Paradoxically, no one knows what happened. Many people know a little and some people know a lot, but nobody knows the whole story. Of course, that's the case for any complex undertaking, and it is why making sense of the historical record requires consultation of multiple sources. As more primary source materials come online, new opportunities emerge to support analysis and synthesis of the historical record. The Apollo missions offer an outstanding testbed for applying time-synchronized event reconstruction to archival materials because several large collections of primary source materials from the Apollo program are online, a substantial subset of that record includes sufficiently precise timing information for automatic alignment, and individual records (documents, audio recordings, and still and moving images) tell only a part of the story. This paper describes our work to date with some of those materials.

2. THE LEGACY OF APOLLO

At the dawn of the Web in the early 1990's, Eric Jones created the Apollo Lunar Surface Journals (ALSJ), a set of annotated radio transcripts for the lunar surface period of each mission. He (and many others) scanned the typewritten originals, performed OCR, manually corrected the resulting errors, formatted the result using HTML, and then interviewed ten of the twelve moonwalkers to obtain commentary and clarification [1]. The idea caught on, and Apollo Flight Journals (AFJ) are now being created to provide a similar presentation for the other parts of the Apollo missions.

In addition to the transcribed radio communications in the Apollo Lunar Surface Journals, transcripts of onboard recordings are also available. The Apollo program used two crewed spacecraft, one of which (the Lunar Module or LM) was designed to land on the moon; the second spacecraft (the Command Module or CM) remained in lunar orbit awaiting the LM's return from the surface. Each contained a combined voice and data recorder which were later transcribed. The idea for the Apollo Archive Explorer started with the release of a complete set of Apollo mission transcripts in 2001 [4].

Video from the Apollo missions is available from three sources: Earth-based cameras (for launch and splashdown), television signals transmitted to earth during the mission, and video filmed during the mission and developed upon return to Earth. Along with recording video, the Apollo astronauts also took about 6,000 still photographs using Hasselblad cameras which were usually mounted on the astronaut's chest, yielding an unmatched sequence of first person views of lunar surface operations.

Oral history interviews are a useful source that can help fill gaps in the documentary record of the Apollo program. The Johnson Space Center oral history project has interviewed a multitude of people from the Apollo missions, and transcripts from almost all of those interviews are available online in PDF format. Audio from those interviews can also be ordered (for a modest fee, in CD format) from the University of Houston, Clear Lake.

3. THE APOLLO ARCHIVE EXPLORER

The design goal of the Apollo Archive Explorer is to provide rich experiential access to the records of what actually happened during the Apollo missions to the Moon. By "experiential" access, we mean that we seek to provide a richer experience than could be achieved with individual sources. Our focus on "what actually happened" places a primacy on the events <u>during</u> a mission, rather than on design issues, mission planning, or training. "Rich access" has a second meaning here as well—users of the system should be able to get to the reconstruction of an event in ways that best suit their thought process.

Figure 1 depicts the user interface of the Apollo Archive Explorer, which is implemented as a Java application. The screen is divided into four regions: control (upper left), images (upper right), and two tab-selectable document display zones (lower left and lower right). The top row of the control region displays the Ground Elapsed Time (GET) since launch from Earth for the present point in the replay along with a "Pause" button, selection of the mission to be displayed (presently Apollo 11, 14, 15, 16, or

JCDL '13, July 22–26, 2013, Indianapolis, Indiana, USA.
ACM 978-1-4503-2077-1/13/07.

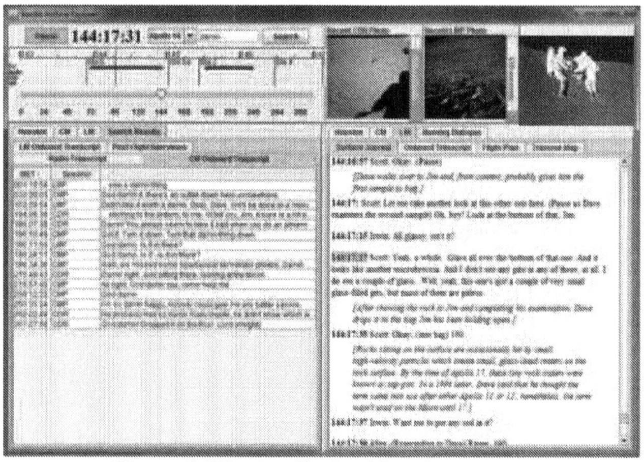

Figure 1. The Apollo Archive Explorer.

17), and a term-based search capability. Below these, a major-event timeline is displayed on which availability is indicated for television (TV), audio, the transcript from the CM recorder, and the transcript from the LM recorder. In the depicted major event timeline, television is shown as available from shortly after the beginning of the second Extra-Vehicular Activity (EVA) until shortly before arrival at Station A (one of several pre-planned locations on the lunar surface where geological activities were conducted). The long red vertical bar graphically indicates the same replay GET as is shown as digits above. Clicking in the major event timeline resets the ground elapsed time to the selected point. The slider bar at the bottom of the control region allows the user to reset the replay to any time (in one-hour increments).

The image area in the upper right shows (from left to right) the most recent photograph taken by the Commander (CDR, one of the astronauts), the most recent photograph taken by the other astronaut (the Lunar Module Pilot, or LMP), and (when available) television video. The vertical progress strips to the right of the CDR and LMP photographs indicate the time elapsed since the photograph was taken; when the progress bar fills after two minutes, the image is removed. Two levels of tabs are used to control the selection of content for display. The top set of tabs controls the broad perspective (Houston, the CM, or the LM), and selecting one of those broad perspectives then makes a set of specific documents available for selection using the lower set of tabs. For the LM perspective the available documents are: Surface Journal (the ALSJ, which appears on the right in Figure 1), Onboard Transcript, Flight Plan and Traverse Map.

Each type of document has some document-specific functions. For the Surface Journal, the ground elapsed time of the most recent utterance is highlighted. For scanned transcripts (LM recorder, CM recorder, and radio), a bounding box is drawn around the most recent utterance and labeled with the ground elapsed time. Selection of the traverse map results in display of a depiction of the route taken by the astronauts, overlaid with a moving bulls-eye symbol representing the approximate location of the astronauts at the currently displayed ground elapsed time.

The results of conducting a text-based search of the scanned transcripts are illustrated on the left in Figure 1. Here, the user has entered a term in the query box at the top right of the control region of the display and then clicked on the "Search" button. That action automatically replaces the lower left document display area with the search results. Results from any one of the scanned transcripts (CM recorder, LM recorder, radio) or the oral history interviews can then be examined by selecting the appropriate tab. Selecting any line in a search result from a scanned transcript will reset the ground elapsed time to the time associated with that result. The search function is implemented using the Lucene text retrieval system. The text of each utterance in each scanned transcript is indexed in advance, thus yielding rapid response to queries at run time. The most significant innovation required to build the Apollo Archive Explorer was the ability to represent structural elements of scanned transcripts in ways that allowed effective time synchronization and content-based search. We modified the Bilingual Resource Inference and Dictionary Generation Environment (BRIDGE) system, which had originally been developed to extract translation lexicons from bilingual dictionaries, to perform this structural analysis [4].

4. CONCLUSION

The policy of the U.S. National Archives for appraisal of records for retention states, in part: "The future research potential of records is the most difficult variable to determine. What is of relatively low research use today may become of great research use in the future. Perhaps even more important and difficult to predict are the issues and topics that will be considered of significance in the future. Nevertheless, it is important to consider this question in making appraisal decisions. It is necessary to consider the kinds and extent of current research use and to try to make inferences about anticipated use both by the public and by the Government." [3]

Envisioning the kinds of richly textured event alignment that the Apollo Archive Explorer demonstrates would have been challenging forty years ago in an era when even the simple computers that flew to the Moon cost $46 million to design and build. As a result, some sources that we could now productively integrate simply are not available today in any known location. By building systems such as the Apollo Archive Explorer, we can help to inform tomorrow's records retention decisions (e.g., from the extensive records generated by the 135 Space Shuttle missions).

ACKNOWLEDGMENTS

This material is based upon work supported by NSF under Grant 1218159. Opinions, findings and conclusions or recommendations expressed in this material are those of the authors and do not necessarily reflect the views of the National Science Foundation.

REFERENCES

[1] Heiken, G. & Jones, E. (2007). *On the Moon: The Apollo Journals*, Springer Praxis.

[2] Ma, H., Doermann, D., Karagol-Ayan, B., Oard, D. & Wang, J. (2004). "Parsing and Tagging Bilingual Dictionaries," *Traitement Automatique des Languages*, 44(2)125-150.

[3] National Archives and Records Administration (2007). *Appraisal Policy of the National Archives and Records Administration*, NARA Directive 1441, September.

[4] Swanson, G. (2001). "We Have Liftoff!: The Story behind the Mercury, Gemini and Apollo Air to Ground Transmissions," *Spaceflight*, vol. 43, Feb.

The Avalon Media System: A Platform for Access-Controlled Delivery of Time-Based Media

Jon W. Dunn
Indiana University Libraries
1320 E. 10th St.
Bloomington, IN 47405, USA
jwd@iu.edu

Stuart L. Baker
Northwestern University Library
1970 Campus Drive
Evanston, IL 60208, USA
stubaker@northwestern.edu

ABSTRACT
This demonstration will show version 1.0 of the Avalon Media System, an open source system being developed by Indiana University and Northwestern University to allow libraries and archives to provide online access to audio and video collections.

Categories and Subject Descriptors
H.3.7 [**Information Storage and Retrieval**]: Digital Libraries – *collection, dissemination, systems issues*. H.5.1 [**Information Interfaces and Presentation**]: Multimedia Information Systems – video.

Keywords
Audio; video; digital libraries; repositories; authorization.

1. INTRODUCTION
The Avalon Media System (http://avalonmediasystem.org/) is a robust, fully open source solution for curating and providing online access to digital audio and video collections in libraries and archives. The system is being developed collaboratively by the libraries at Indiana University and Northwestern University, in partnership with ten additional institutions that have committed resources for testing, evaluation, and feedback.

2. DEMONSTRATION
In this demonstration, we will show the capabilities of Version 1.0 of Avalon, released in May 2013. This first release provides: 1) an audio and video player that works in desktop and mobile web browsers; 2) integration with multiple authentication systems and management of group-based authorization of access to media content; 3) both manual and automated batch ingest capabilities; 4) a search interface for MODS descriptive metadata based on the Blacklight (http://projectblacklight.org/) discovery tool; and 5) ingest and management functionality built using the Ruby on Rails-based Hydra (http://projecthydra.org/) framework.

JCDL'13, July 22–26, 2013, Indianapolis, Indiana, USA.
ACM 978-1-4503-2077-1/13/07.

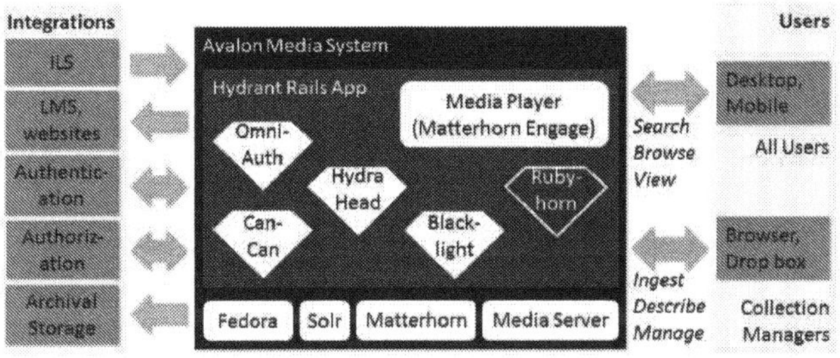

Figure 1. Avalon Architecture

The system also leverages a number of other open source tools. In addition to the use of Hydra and Blacklight, audio and video processing and playback capabilities are based on technology from the Opencast Matterhorn (http://opencast.org/) project, and metadata persistence is provided by the Fedora digital repository system (http://fedora-commons.org/).

The architecture of Avalon is designed to be modular and extensible in order to support integration into and with other academic systems, including integrated library systems, learning management systems, and eventually, scholarly annotation and research tools.

Future versions will add support for more granular access control and authorization, structural metadata for navigation of content, capabilities for bookmarking and playlists, and transcripts.

3. ACKNOWLEDGMENTS
We would like to acknowledge the contributions of the many Avalon project team members at Indiana and Northwestern. The Avalon Media System project is supported by a National Leadership Grant from the Institute of Museum and Library Services and is based in part on previous work on the open source Variations digital music library system [1] supported by the National Science Foundation, grant IIS-9909068, and by IMLS.

4. REFERENCE
[1] Dunn, J.W., Byrd, D., Notess, M., Riley, J., Scherle, R. Variations2: retrieving and using music in an academic setting. *Communications of the ACM* 49, 8 (Aug. 2006), 53-58. DOI= http://dx.doi.org/10.1145/1145287.1145314.

The Digital Atlas of American Religion

Sharon M. Kandris
The Polis Center at IUPUI
Indianapolis, IN
skandris@iupui.edu

Neil Devadasan
The Polis Center at IUPUI
Indianapolis, IN
ndevadas@iupui.edu

Malika Mahoui
The Polis Center at IUPUI
Indianapolis, IN
mmahoui@iupui.edu

David J. Bodenhamer
The Polis Center at IUPUI
Indianapolis, IN
intu100@iupui.edu

ABSTRACT
In this demonstration-paper we introduce DAAR, the Digital Atlas of American Religion (www.religionatlas.org). The DAAR is a web-based research platform with innovative data exploration and visualization tools to support research in the humanities. Using a user-centered design approach, we incorporated historic religion data on adherence, membership, and congregations with historic census data and new religion typologies as the test-bed for the tools that we developed to establish the technology infrastructure and framework that can be used for other humanities data.

Categories and Subject Descriptors
H.2.8 [Database Applications]: *Spatial databases and GIS.* H.3.7 [Digital Libraries]: Collection, Dissemination, Standards, System Issues, User Issues. H.5.2 [User Interfaces]: Interaction style, Screen design, User-centered design

General Terms
Management, Design

Keywords
Digital humanities, digital Atlas, spatial temporal visualization, data exploration, typologies, information visualization, GIS

1. INTRODUCTION
Time and location are essential components of humanities exploratory research. Indeed, the vast majority of the data manipulated by humanists come with a spatial component. It originates from, or describes, some place, and we can use its location to relate it to all other data about this location either directly or within some nested hierarchy. For instance, by using location we can relate a diary from a neighborhood to an image or to census data describing the same place, as well as link it to similar data from a city, county, or a state, etc., and we can portray these relationships on a map or in some other spatially referenced visualization. A similar argument can be built with respect to the importance of the temporal dimension when studying humanities data. Humanities scholars have begun to use these data, but even GIS technology, especially in its web form, does not support easy exploration and visualization of the complex spatial-temporal data manipulated by humanists nor does it allow them to display diversity within geographies [1]. The Digital Atlas of American Religion (DAAR) is an effort to bring researchers in humanities innovative approaches to explore complex data with the support of an integrated solution stemming from several fields including GIS, visualization, and classification theory. DAAR originated from an existing and well-used interactive web mapping site on twentieth-century US religious adherence, the North American Religion Atlas, or NARA. While DAAR's main goal is to incorporate new ways to visualize complex spatially-referenced data using NARA as a test-bed, an equally important goal was to provide on-the-fly categorization and aggregation of data to permit easier, more flexible data exploration.

In this demonstration-paper we will focus on the data exploration and visualization features of DAAR.

2. HUMANITIES DATA: DIVERSITY AND COMPLEXITY
DAAR encompasses two main types of data to support exploration and visualization.

2.1 Religion Data
DAAR contains religion census data from the Association of Religion Data Archives (ARDA). The data available from the ARDA include raw counts of members, adherents, and congregations for nearly 600 denominations at 12 different points in time between 1890 and 2010. In order to present the data meaningfully and succinctly to scholars, we imposed a *religion classification structure*, or typology, whereby the denominations are grouped into families and families into religions based on similar doctrines. For each denomination and each family, we tabulate the number and percent of members, adherents, and congregations (*religion statistics*) for each year by county, state, and region. Scholars can visualize those data in various tools in DAAR to get an understanding of the religious landscape across the US or within a particular state or county. *Religion dominance by rank order* (1890 to 2010) provides researchers with the ability to see what is the most dominant religious denomination for every county and state in the US, then the 2nd most dominant, and so forth to the 9th most dominant denomination in each geography. Drill-down tools allow researchers to explore the diversity of religion within a geography as well. There are two significant challenges in the religion data: 1) the data are not consistently available across all years for all denominations, and 2) denominations have shifted over time, including splits and mergers, which complicates time series analysis.

Finally, using the source data, researchers contributing to the DAAR project developed five new data characteristics (also referred to as religion characteristics) including: *Central Authority* - the degree to which each denomination is characterized by the consolidation of authority in a broad hierarchy, *Giving* - the degree to which each denomination tithed, *High Education Support* - the degree to which a denomination is formally invested in higher education, and two others.

2.2 Census Data
This category includes information on socio-economic factors such as race, ethnicity, urban vs. rural, foreign born vs. native born,

JCDL'13, July 22–26, 2013, Indianapolis, Indiana, USA.
ACM 978-1-4503-2077-1/13/07.

educational attainment, and income (including numbers and percentages) for the years 1890 – 2010. Here also, data availability varies by census year, which in turn has an impact on data exploration and visualization.

3. DATA CATEGORIZATION

Two objectives of DAAR are to provide researchers with the capability to perform data exploration using multiple facets or categorization schemes and the ability to combine these different categories to refine the data exploration process [2]. To meet these objectives we created the following categorization schemes:

1. *Religion dominance ranking scheme* to rank denominations and denominational families.
2. *Religion characteristics* such as Central Authority, Giving, and Higher Education Support.
3. *Socio-economic classification scheme* (race, education level, income level, etc.).
4. *Religion statistics scheme* that describes for each denomination default characteristics such as counts of congregations, adherents and members.
5. *Religion classification hierarchy* that assigns each denomination to a family and religion.
6. *Geospatial classification* providing spatial granularity by county, state, region, and nation.
7. *Temporal category* describing year.

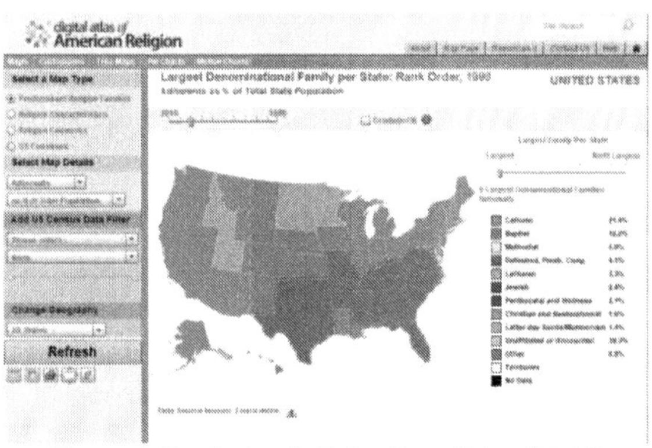

Figure 1: Exploring Religion Data Using DAAR

Note that *religion statistics* are used to instantiate the religion dominance classification scheme and the religion characteristics typology. For example, we can explore religion dominance based on the percentage of adherents or the number of congregations. The last three schemes are used to provide the religion, space, and time granularity to the data exploration process. In addition, users can filter the geographies using US census data parameters.

The combination of these categorization schemes within the DAAR project and how it is visualized is based on continuous feedback received by researchers in humanities.

4. DATA EXPLORATION AND VISUALIZATION

Researchers using DAAR are provided with the following exploration/visualization tool: maps, cartograms, tree maps, pie charts, animated bar charts, and animated bubble charts. We adopted an iterative user-centered approach to the interface design, including both the functionalities to be supported and their layout.

The interface includes two main parts: the data exploration panel and the results visualization panel. The visualization panel displays the results in a geospatial map, tree map, charts, or cartogram. A time slider allows users choose from years 1890 to 2010. An additional slider-based filter is used to visualize data by level of dominance. Figure 1 shows the results of exploring the data using the *Religion dominance ranking scheme* where the dominant religion family for each state based on adherents as a percent of the population are shown in the map. The dominance slider will allow the exploration of the data from the most dominant family to the 9th largest family. Clicking on a state reveals a pie chart of all religion families represented in that state.

The data exploration panel uses a multi-category approach instead of a standard categorical data browsing panel. Figure 2 shows the exploration panel. Using maps as an example, the top sub-panel labeled "Map Type" allows selection from the categorization schemes 1-4 described in section 3. The middle sub-panel labeled "Map Details" provides the filtering options available for each type of map. For example, the "map details" for *Religion characteristics* allow the user to specify the characteristic, (e.g., higher education support) and the supporting statistic (e.g., adherents). The next panel allows the overlaying of socio-economic census data, while the last option specifies the geospatial granularity to be explored.

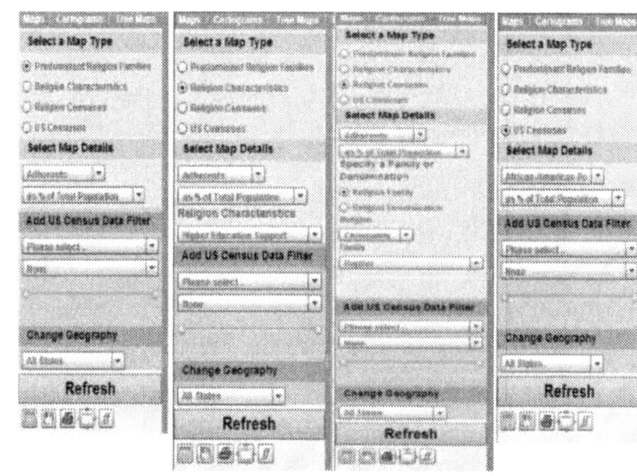

Figure 2: Data Exploration Features of DAAR

DAAR allows researchers to explore patterns, trends, and relationships in the data that otherwise are not apparent with traditional GIS or statistical software. It allows researchers to understand the multiple dimensions and diversity of religion across geographies, or within geographies. Paired with census data, it allows them to explore relationships to give better context and meaning to the patterns and trends. Maps provide the spatial patterns and relationships, tree maps show relative strength and relationships, charts show trends, and cartograms show relative numbers of adherence.

5. ACKNOWLEDGMENTS

The DAAR project is supported by a grant from the National Endowment for the Humanities and was developed in partnership with John Corrigan (Florida State University) and Trevor Harris (West Virginia University).

6. REFERENCES

[1] Bodenhamer, D. J., Corrigan, J.C., and Harris, T.M., eds., *The Spatial Humanities: GIS and the Future of Humanities Scholarship* (Indiana University Press, 2010).

[2] Hearst, M.A. UIs for faceted navigation: Recent advances and remaining open problems. In HCIR 2008 Second Workshop on Human-Computer Interaction and Information Retrieval, 2008.

Introducing Docear's Research Paper Recommender System

Joeran Beel
Docear
Magdeburg, Germany
beel@docear.org

Stefan Langer
Docear
Magdeburg, Germany
langer@docear.org

Marcel Genzmehr
Docear
Magdeburg, Germany
genzmehr@docear.org

Andreas Nürnberger
OvGU, FIN, DKE Group
Magdeburg, Germany
andreas.nuernberger@ovgu.de

ABSTRACT

In this demo paper we present Docear's research paper recommender system. Docear is an academic literature suite to search, organize, and create research articles. The users' data (papers, references, annotations, etc.) is managed in mind maps and these mind maps are utilized for the recommendations. Using content-based filtering methods, Docear's recommender achieves click-through rates around 6%, in some scenarios even over 10%.

Categories and Subject Descriptors

H.3.3 [**Information Storage and Retrieval**]: Information Search and Retrieval – *information filtering*

General Terms

Management, Design

Keywords

recommender systems; user model; mind map; mind mapping; research paper recommender system; content-based filtering

1. INTRODUCTION

Literature management, i.e. searching, organizing and creating literature, is important for researchers and students. The search for relevant literature is especially challenging due to the millions of articles and books being published every year and the fact that most search services such as the *ACM Digital Library* focus only on publications of selected publishers (e.g. *ACM*). Additionally, full-text articles can incur a fee if your library does not hold a subscription to the article database or publisher.

Our open source tool *Docear* (www.docear.org) supports researchers with literature management by bundling several applications that help in searching, organizing, and creating academic literature [2]. Docear has the unique feature of utilizing mind maps for information management. That means users organize their data in a tree-like data structure and not in a table or with social tags. Figure 1 shows an example of a mind map we created as draft for this paper. The mind map we created outlines the skeleton of this paper and the nodes (i.e. the "entities" with the words) link to articles in which the information was originally found. More information on Docear can be found in [2].

In this paper we present the research paper recommender system which we developed for Docear.

JCDL'13, July 22–26, 2013, Indianapolis, Indiana, USA.
ACM 978-1-4503-2077-1/13/07.

2. RELATED WORK

One of the earliest research paper recommender systems was TechLens [8]. TechLens used the two most popular recommendation approaches – content-based filtering (CBF) and collaborative filtering (CF). In CBF, words of a user's documents are taken to build a user model, and documents containing the same words as the user model are recommended. In CF, similar users are determined by comparing how they rated items and items one user liked are recommended to the other user(s).

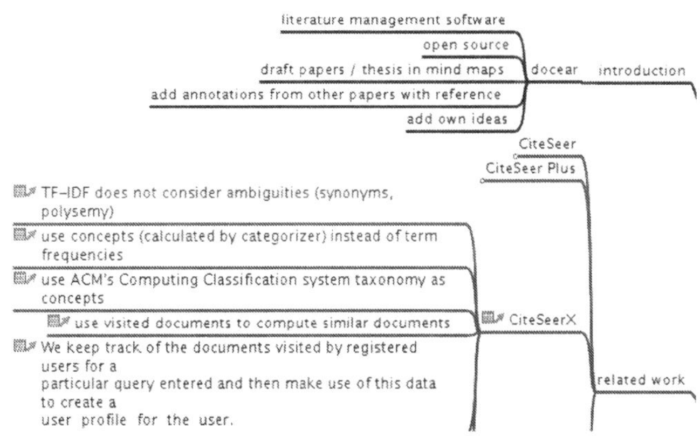

Figure 1: Draft of this paper as mind map

For the academic search engine CiteSeer there have been several different recommender systems proposed – some from the CiteSeer developers [4] and some from third parties [5]. Among others, they used citations instead of words to find similar scientific articles. Other research paper recommender systems include CiteULike's recommender system [3], Claper [9], and SCuBA [1].

All these recommender systems suffer from one problem: They have rather limited information about their users. For instance, if a recommender system analyses the papers a researcher has published [5], there may be a few dozen papers to analyze. In contrast, recommender systems in other domains often have access to much more information about their users. For instance, on *Last.fm* user typically listens to dozens of songs – on a single day.

3. DOCEAR'S RECOMMENDER SYSTEM

Docear has access to a large amount of information about its users that is quite diverse. With Docear, users search for literature, they organize their literature, and they draft their own literature. That means Docear knows what a researcher is currently looking for, which articles a researcher already knows, which ones he is currently reading and on which new papers he is currently working. In addition, Docear allows its users to make annotations in PDF files, i.e. adding comments or highlighting passages they consider important. Consequently, Docear does not only know which papers a researcher currently is reading but also which parts of an article he considers particularly important. This allows highly personalized recommendations.

We are experimenting with different variations of content-based filtering for Docear. All of the content-based variations under consideration have a common thread whereby from a user's mind map collection a model is built. This model is matched with Docear's Digital Library containing around 1.8 million research articles from various disciplines (Figure 2). The Docear desktop software synchronizes all mind maps of a user every couple of minutes with Docear's server. When a user requests recommendations, Docear sends the request to Docear's Digital Library. This creates a user model and returns ten recommendations which are all accessible in full-text. Some users have reservations against having their mind maps transferred to Docear's server and having them analyzed. Therefore, Docear allows users to turn recommendation off which about 2/3 of users do (when users turn recommendations off, they still can use Docear to manage their literature).

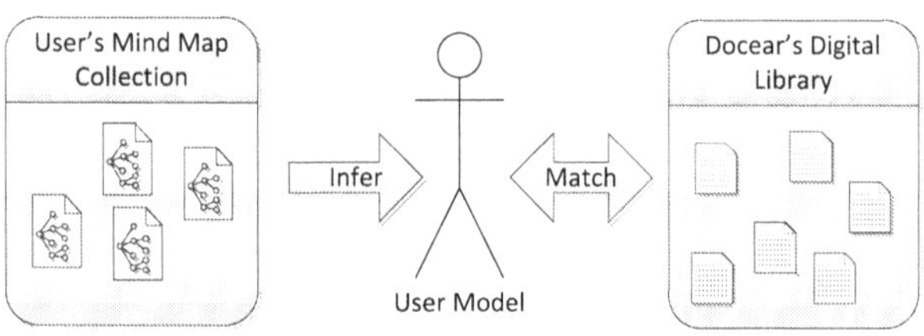

Figure 2: Basic recommendation model

Currently, we are experimenting with different variations of content-based filtering. For instance, we are varying the number of mind maps and nodes that are analyzed for creating a user model (e.g. all mind maps the user created vs. only the last edited mind map), the user model size and the type of TF-IDF being used. Based on an evaluation with 938 users and 32,790 delivered recommendations, the average click-through rate (CTR) is 6.03%. However, for specific variations such as when stop-words are removed, TF-IDF is applied instead of term frequency only, *and* only user requested recommendations are analyzed, click-through rates increase to 10.31% (Figure 4), and in some specific scenarios even more. In comparison, a typical click-through rate in advertisement is 0.5% [6]. Research paper recommender systems typically achieve CTRs of around 8% [7]. Further details on the recommendation algorithms will be published in a forthcoming paper.

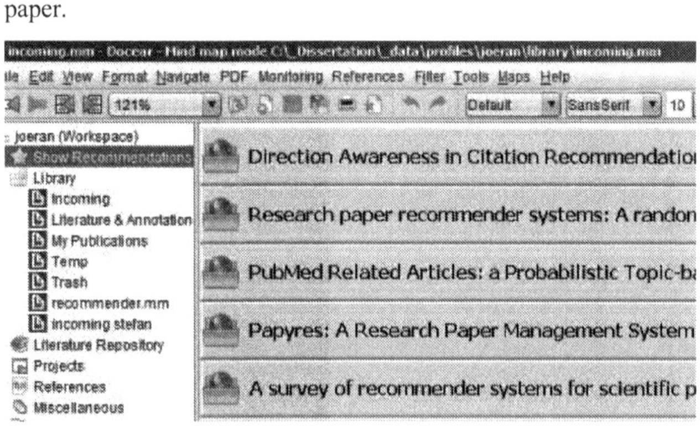

Figure 3: Recommendations in Docear (screenshot)

4. OUTLOOK

Although Docear's recommender system is in a rather early development stage, it already performs quite well. We are confident that the performance can still be improved. For instance, as soon as the number of Docear users increases, collaborative filtering might become an interesting addition to content-based filtering (right now, there are too few similar users to perform CF). An extension of Docear's digital library should also improve the recommender's performance. With 1.8 million articles available, there are only few relevant articles to choose from for many researchers. When more papers are added to the digital library, there will be more potentially relevant recommendations. Finally, we plan on extending the recommender to not only recommend research papers but other items relevant to researchers. For instance, journals and conferences, research grants, and for students we would like to recommend university programs.

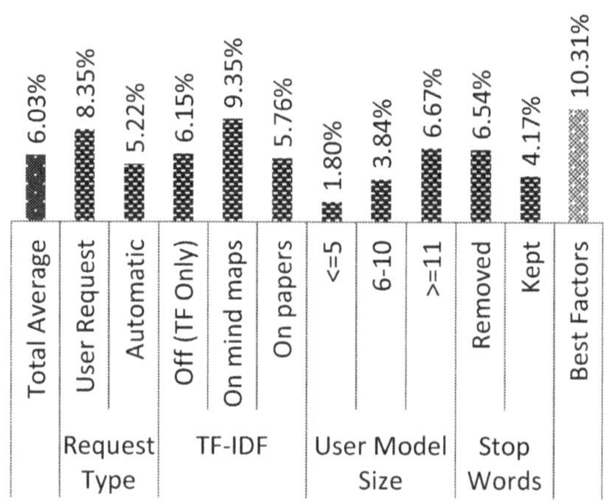

Figure 4: Results of content-based filtering variations

5. REFERENCES

[1] Agarwal, N., Haque, E., Liu, H. and Parsons, L. 2006. A subspace clustering framework for research group collaboration. *International Journal of Information Technology and Web Engineering*. 1, (2006), 35–58.

[2] Beel, J., Gipp, B., Langer, S. and Genzmehr, M. 2011. Docear: An Academic Literature Suite for Searching, Organizing and Creating Academic Literature. *Proceedings of the 11th annual international ACM/IEEE joint conference on Digital libraries* (2011), 465–466.

[3] Bogers, T. and Bosch, A. van den 2008. Recommending scientific articles using citeulike. *Proceedings of the 2008 ACM conference on Recommender systems* (2008), 287–290.

[4] Bollacker, K.D., Lawrence, S. and Giles, C.L. 1998. CiteSeer: An autonomous web agent for automatic retrieval and identification of interesting publications. *Proceedings of the 2nd international conference on Autonomous agents* (1998).

[5] Chandrasekaran, K., Gauch, S., Lakkaraju, P. and Luong, H. 2008. Concept-based document recommendations for citeseer authors. *Adaptive Hypermedia and Adaptive Web-Based Systems* (2008), 83–92.

[6] Manchanda, P., Dubé, J.P., Goh, K.Y. and Chintagunta, P.K. 2006. The effect of banner advertising on internet purchasing. *Journal of Marketing Research*. 43, (2006), 98–108.

[7] Pohl, S., Radlinski, F. and Joachims, T. 2007. Recommending Related Papers Based on Digital Library Access Records. *Proceedings of the 7th ACM/IEEE-CS Joint Conference on Digital Libraries* (Vancouver, BC, Canada, 2007), 417–418.

[8] Torres, R., McNee, S.M., Abel, M., Konstan, J.A. and Riedl, J. 2004. Enhancing Digital Libraries with Techlens+. *Proceedings of the 4th ACM/IEEE-CS Joint Conference on Digital Libraries* (Tuscon, AZ, USA, 2004), 228–236.

[9] Wang, Y., Zhai, E., Hu, J. and Chen, Z. 2010. Claper: Recommend classical papers to beginners. *Seventh International Conference on Fuzzy Systems and Knowledge Discovery* (2010), 2777–2781.

Author Index

www.ingramcontent.com/pod-product-compliance
Ingram Content Group UK Ltd.
Pitfield, Milton Keynes, MK11 3LW, UK
UKHW051413290926
15471UKWH00009B/1587

9 781450 325189